# LET'S GO

# EUROPE

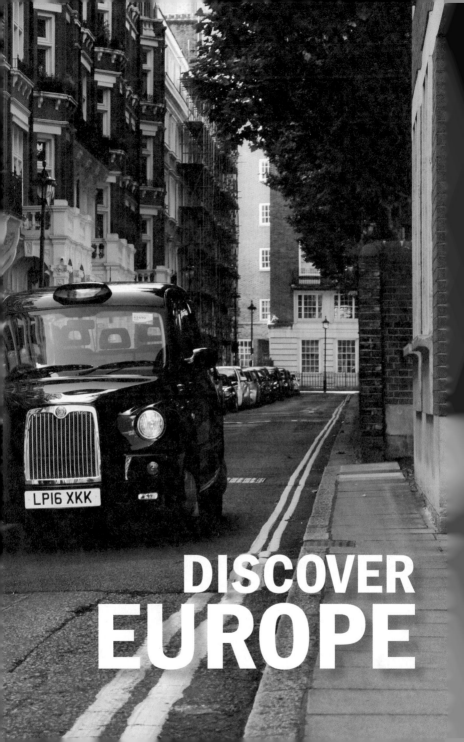

# DISCOVER
# EUROPE

**So, you want to go to Europe?** But how could you not? There's something awfully romantic about spending midnight in Paris, watching the lights glisten on the famed La Seine. There's something special about hearing the growls and grunts of cars on and around the vias and piazzas of Rome. There's something magical about walking on the streets of London in front of Buckingham Palace as the roads close down for the iconic Changing of the Guard.

Europe—rich with history, culture, art, and adventure—is the ultimate destination for any backpacker from any background. For all the hullabaloo around this small continent, the fairy-tale-like legends that you hear from old men in parks, friends, and parents are, for the most part, true stories. Well, maybe all except Uncle Marty's story claiming he found an old manuscript of *Ulysses* on a Dublin bar crawl..

Pub crawls and pretentious reading material aside, Europe awaits you. Paraglide above the Swiss Alps, shimmy your way into Berlin's most exclusive clubs, or scuba dive between two tectonic plates in Iceland. When in Dubrovnik, find love on Lokrum Island and, in Athens, find your Adonis or Aphrodite. Get blown away by the beat of Pamplona's Running of the Bulls and cheer on European sports teams in Munich's beer gardens. Europe has been, and will likely continue to be, the starting point for the adventures of students all around the world. Join the company of your fellow wanderlust-stricken adventure seekers and set your trip apart from the rest. Ready, set, *Let's Go*!

# CONTENTS

# MEET THE TEAM

## MASTHEAD

### Kathleen Cronin, Publishing Director

Katie is a junior in Mather House studying English and Economics. In addition to working at Let's Go, Kathleen is a member of Harvard Women in Business, an executive board member of *The Harvard Crimson's Fifteen Minute Magazine,* and Director of Finance for Cambridge Alpha Phi. In her free time, she enjoys spending time and traveling with her crazy family, watching nature documentaries with her blockmates, loitering in Starbucks until she can snag a free refill, and reading celebrity autobiographies.

### Kristine Guillaume, Editor in Chief

Apart from pointing out comma faults and comma splices (read: two entirely different sins against humanity), Kristine spends her time experiencing some serious wanderlust while reading accounts of her Researcher-Writers' adventures. Her own adventures, however, consist of fast-talking and fast-walking her way through New York City and pretending to be Miranda Priestley, even though she more often resembles a soft mother duck who gushes over puns and clever allusions to *Gatsby, Ulysses,* and *Gossip Girl* (they're all the same thing, really, aren't they?). While she's not fixing misplaced colons, lamenting the ugliness of passive voice, or adding more punch to a joke that didn't quite come across, Kristine indulges in the idea that she can someday write the Next Great American Novel — Hemingway style. Jury's out on if she can truly pull off the whole tip-of-the-iceberg technique (*Let's Go* isn't like that at all, now is it?), but here's to trying. In the meantime, though, she spends her time writing unfinished short-stories that no one will ever read, reporting for the News Board of *The Harvard Crimson,* and watching Sitcoms such as *The Office, 30 Rock,* and *Parks and Recreation.* And when she's not reading or watching anything, there's a 60% chance she's on her way to pick up some coffee and a 40% chance she's pranking one of her friends. Mariah, your mattress is across the hall.

### Austin Eder, Creative Director and Associate Editor

California native and traveler at heart, Austin spent most of her summer doing something characteristically against her nature—sitting. Though frequently tempted to snag a last-minute deal on Norwegian Air and join her Researcher-Writers across the pond, she managed to remain seated long enough to help make the 672 pages you've currently got locked between your fingers come to life. This entailed spearheading a redesign of both the cover and the internal layout, editing hundreds of pages of copy, and, most importantly, making sure the creative geniuses behind that copy remained alive (read: sober) long enough to write it. Equipped with an impressive knowledge of Europe and unparalleled navigational skills, Austin is ready to jet off on her own adventure. Next year, she'll be island-hopping. Now, which archipelago she intends to play hopscotch with has yet to be announced—maybe Greece, maybe the Faroes, maybe New Zealand, maybe Japan. No matter the locale, she'll be more in her element exploring and experiencing the world for herself than interpreting it through words. In the meantime, catch her discussing domestic and international affairs at Harvard's

Institute of Politics, designing the daily newspaper for *The Harvard Crimson,* cultivating her pranayama in one of Cambridge's yoga studios, meandering through art museums, jamming to Young the Giant's newest album, or studying—because, well, apparently that's what you're supposed to do in college.

## Nicholas Nava, Marketing Director

Nick is a junior in Mather House studying economics. Aside from *Let's Go,* Nick teaches a fifth-grade civics and government class through the IOP's CIVICS program, is on the Mather House Committee, and works as a senior staffer for Harvard Model Congress. As a Miami native, Nick spends much of his free time watching his beloved Miami Heat, Marlins, and Dolphins play even though they thoroughly disappoint him every season. In his free time, he enjoys FaceTiming his parents, siblings, and nephews and nieces, all while consuming medically concerning amounts of pizza. Sometimes, he stays up until the wee hours of the night playing John Mayer songs with his roommate and watching Planet Earth documentaries while getting far too emotionally attached to the smaller animals in peril. He occasionally annoys the entire office by blasting The 1975 through his speakers and screaming about Kevin Durant being soft. He also loves his mom and dad a lot.

## Lev Asimow, Editorial Assistant

Lev is a senior in Mather House concentrating in Social Studies. He appears intermittently in the *Let's Go* office to correct everyone's grammar and spelling. His other summer pursuits include thesis research—that is, reading a variety of dead European philosophers—and making tacos every Tuesday. He's served as Captain of the Harvard Debate Council and an Editor for the *Harvard Review of Philosophy.* Given his role at *Let's Go,* it would be particularly embarrassing if there were typos in this bio.

# RESEARCHER-WRITERS

## Julia Bunte-Mein

Brace yourselves for an intense gastronomical experience featuring wine, cheese, and tapas in Eastern Spain and Southern France, courtesy of world nomad extraordinaire: Julia. A proud foodie, linguaphile, art-lover, and fitness aficionada, catch Julia doing early-morning yoga in the most obscure of places, scouring cities for little-known art galleries, and going to the most extreme lengths to sample the local cuisine. When she's not getting lost in European countries, Julia studies Government and Environmental Sustainability at Harvard.

## Eric Chin

Warm Mediterranean sun on the back of his neck, the feeling of sand between his toes on an Italian beach, champagne on a tiled French portico… Wait—Eric's going where? Iceland and Scandinavia? *Shit.* He may have to trade in sandals for hiking boots and survive on a diet of sheep's head and "putrescent" shark meat (seriously, look it up), but at least he'll get to take advantage of the free education, right? Oh, it's summer? Well what about the free healthcare? Hopefully not? Okay, fine. He'll just have to settle for climbing behind waterfalls, kayaking through fjords, hiking on glaciers, and fulfilling his mission of finding as much IKEA furniture as he possibly can.

## Emily Corrigan

Emily prepared for her travels in France, Belgium, and the Netherlands this summer in a *Rocky*-esque training montage: speed-eating croissants, running up hills wearing comfortable walking sandals, and bench pressing her 30-liter Osprey travel backpack. However, she realized the intense training may have been getting to her when she drop-kicked a box of macaroons off the Eiffel Tower, injuring three. For the rest of the summer, she recovered by playing chess with nice Flemish people. She ate *frites*. She took a silly yet endearing picture intentionally missing the point of the Louvre pyramid with her finger. She is now fully rehabilitated.

## Nick Grundlingh

Nick Grundlingh is going to spend the summer traveling through Germany, Poland, and the Czech Republic. He's looking forward to—*Sorry, what was that? What's Nick wearing?* That's his fanny pack. Anyway, Nick is looking forward to meeting—*Look, Nick really doesn't see what's so funny about it, unless you think keeping your valuables safe is some sort of joke. Now, where was he?* Oh yeah. Nick can't wait to meet new people and—*Seriously, guys. Knock it off. You know, in Europe, people make fun of you if you don't wear one.* At least Nick assumes they do. He hasn't actually been yet. But it's probably very similar to how he just described it.

## Adrian Horton

Hailing from Cincinnati, Ohio, Adrian will be honing her bakery-finding skills in Greece and southern Italy this summer. Prior work experience: ranch-hand, gardener, fruit bat cage cleaner, one-time contributor to her hometown's Wikipedia page. Her current interests include distance running, 90s music, and convincing people she has seen *Game of Thrones* Seasons 1-5 (she hasn't, but oh my god wasn't the Red Wedding in Season 3 BANANAS?!). When she isn't watching movie trailers on YouTube, she studies History and Literature at Harvard and sometimes writes about pop culture.

## Mia Karr

Mia is packing up her set of all seven *Harry Potter* books and the collected James Joyce before heading off to the U.K., and then getting realistic and replacing them with a flashlight and extra underwear. She plans to find out exactly how much beer is in a pint while gallivanting around Ireland and aspires to show her parents that she is putting her (forthcoming) English degree to use by communing with Shakespeare's homeland. When she's not making plans to get the royal family to adopt her, she enjoys drinking coffee and talking about the severity of her coffee addiction.

## Alejandro Lampell

Continuing with a desire to explore new places that stems from his time living in six different countries, Alejandro has set off on a new adventure in France and Switzerland, in which he will try to discover how much solitude he can handle while carrying all the clothes he needs for eight weeks in one hiking backpack. Not one to shy away from a challenge, Alejandro will explore the mountains of Switzerland and the beaches of Southern France, and indulge in the exquisite cuisine both countries have to offer. While not daydreaming about studying abroad, Alejandro likes to spend his time trying to learn to play the guitar or in the library, nestled between towers of books.

## Gavin Moulton

On a quest to commune with his Slavic heritage, Gavin will surely encounter an ungodly number of Yugoslav bunkers, empty bottles of *rakija*, and communist carbonated beverages as he roams Croatia this summer. Always equipped with his trusty headlamp and Adidas tracksuit, he hopes to gain firsthand experience for a future dissertation on the evolution of Slavic memes. Expect rants about the Venetians, nostalgic poems about glories of pan-Slavism, and a thorough investigation of Croatia's greatest contribution to the world: the necktie. When he's not exploring the Balkans, you can find Gavin schlepping his way across Boston to find the best Polish deli, dragging his friends to art museums, and avoiding checked baggage like the plague.

## Emma Scornavvachi

Emma's 11th-grade Spanish teacher told her the most beautiful men in the world live in the South of Spain; she's spending the summer fact-checking that statement. Before her main priorities were sangria, *chorizo,* and the coolest sunsets on the Iberian Peninsula, Emma was at Harvard studying History and Literature and attending to a non-stop, color-coded Google Calendar. She's trading all this in for a summer of spontaneous stumbling around Spain and Portugal—follow along while she gets really lost, really sweaty, and probably laughed at a little?

## Antonia Washington

Antonia is spending her summer pretending she knows a lot about wine and collecting tourist keychains she has no use for throughout Austria, Hungary, Slovakia, and Germany. Originally from Portland, Oregon, she spends much of her time schlepping through the wilderness and enjoys backpacking, kayaking, and low-pressure longboarding (because she's just not good enough to brake efficiently so crowds make her nervous). Catch Antonia eating carbs, looking fly in white Crocs (Crocs is the most innovative company in the world), and pleading for her mom's REI dividend. Her interests include running a very dedicated Instagram for her dog @lily_the_alpine_pup. Stay tuned to watch her adventure unfold.

## Joseph Winters

Joseph immersed himself in the culture of Northern Italy, a major departure from his small-town, Washington State roots. Clad in thrift-store shorts, a pair of sneakers, and a T-shirt from the clearance section at REI, Joseph mispronounced his way through Versace, Gucci, and Gianfranco Lotti stores. "Dolce and Bananas?" He sputtered in Milan. "Giorgio Armonkey?" He stammered in Florence. By the time he got to Venice, he decided to get onto a gondola and keep his mouth shut about fashion. Interestingly, though, he had no problem saying "gelato," "gnocchi," or "biscotti" when placing his order in an Italian "ristorante." Apart from his linguistic misadventures, Joseph toiled through the extensive *Let's Go* "requirements" like seeing Michelangelo's *David* or da Vinci's *The Last Supper,* making it through the month mostly in one piece.

# WHEN TO GO

**Summer is the most popular time to travel to Europe, meaning that if you take a trip during high season, thousands of backpackers will be right there with you.** It's the perfect opportunity to meet students from around the world in hostels of varying social degrees, restaurants with communal tables, and in the long lines for incredible churches and monuments (small talk is a real thing, especially if you're alone). While it is very possible to complete a budget trip in the summertime, it's important to note that the season's many festivals can jack up prices for accommodations, restaurants, and general sightseeing. Keep an eye out for huge summertime events such as Pamplona's Running of the Bulls, Dublin's Bloomsday, Lisbon's Festas de Lisboa, and Edinburgh's Fringe. You'll need to plan ahead—like way ahead—if you intend to travel while these world-renowned events take place. They're definitely worth the extra effort (and perhaps even extra cash).

If you're not into the summer backpacking experience, late spring and early autumn attract fewer tourists, meaning that you can save a bit on airfare and bookings, but it can be difficult to take time off during these seasons. Unfortunately, spring break isn't quite long enough to do a full tour.

For those looking to celebrate the holidays in Venice or shred the slopes of the Italian Alps, winter travel is also a viable option. However, this isn't the best time to hit the clubs of Ibiza or take a walking tour of Prague. You'll also find that some hotels, restaurants, and sights have reduced hours or are on vacation…from you.

# WHAT TO DO

**As cliché as it sounds, Europe does indeed have something for everyone.** We've broken the continent down so you can design your trip exactly what you're looking for. Check out these highlights.

*For the Art Lover:* (the circle-glasses-wearing hipster who looks at a Picasso painting from the Blue Period and hums softly, expressing satisfaction with this feat of human creativity…or just someone who loves art):

- **THE LOUVRE** (Paris, France): Start your trip off with the big kahuna and swing by to say, "Hi!" to our homegirl, Mona. We just can't get enough of her smile. **(see p. 199)**
- **THE NATIONAL GALLERY** (London, UK): Classic mythology, portraits of rich people, rooms and rooms filled with images of Jesus and Jesus' mom, and Van Gogh's *Sunflowers* await you all for the cost of…well, nothing! Free art! **(see p. 301)**
- **UFFIZI GALLERY** (Florence, Italy): A U-shaped gallery filled with quintessential European Renaissance art, including Botticelli's *Birth of Venus* and works by our main man, Leonardo. **(see p. 418)**
- **FUNDACIÓ MIRÓ** (Barcelona, Spain): Twentieth-century artistic genius awaits you in Joan Miró's exquisite collection of abstract and contemporary art in Lego-like buildings. **(see p. 566)**
- **DOX** (Prague, Czech Republic): You. A 42-inch blimp. Contemporary art. Now. Be prepared to ponder questions you never thought would cross your mind. **(see p.116)**
- **VAN GOGH MUSEUM** (Amsterdam, The Netherlands): You didn't think we were going to forget about Vinny, did you? This museum is dedicated to our favorite earless painter and you need to see it. **(see p. 480)**

For the History Buff: (the textbook-carrying nerd who passed Advanced Placement US History by acing all the DBQs #documentbasedquestions):

- **THE ACROPOLIS** (Athens, Greece): The epicenter of cultural diffusion once housing pagan idolatry, safeguarding National Treasures, and serving as a mosque. Perhaps the most iconic landmark in Greece. **(see p. 322)**
- **THE CABINET WAR ROOMS** (London, UK): Think the Situation Room, but instead during World War II, featuring Winston Churchill working in an underground bunker. Relive the story of courage in dire circumstances. **(see p. 298)**
- **POMPEII AND HERCULANEUM** (Pompeii, Italy): Mt. Etna is powerful and takes no prisoners. Check out the ruins of one of the most mysterious and devastating natural disasters of all time in what's left of these preserved Roman ruins. **(see p. 434)**
- **AUSCHWITZ** (Kraków, Poland): Europe has seen many tragedies throughout the ages and Auschwitz represents one of its most harrowing. This former concentration camp will be a somber stop on your tour. **(see p. 511)**
- **PALAIS DES NATIONS** (Geneva, Switzerland): Remember that time Woodrow Wilson had that idea in 1914 to start a League of Nations? It didn't work, but eventually, after WWII, the United Nations took shape. The action happened and still happens here. **(see p. 636)**

- **COLOSSEUM** (Rome, Italy): Gladiator flights were a thing…like, a really big thing. Envision these epic battles in the amphitheater and, when you're done, head to Palatine Hill to see where the Roman patricians lived. (see p. 451)

FOR THE GOURMAND: (the person who posts pictures of food and solely food, captured in exactly the right light every single time, on their Instagram):

- **RESTAURANT KOPUN** (Dubrovnik, Croatia): Their specialty is none other than castrated rooster. Don't tell your significant other you ate here or they might not want to kiss you… (see p. 81)
- **CAFÉ LOKI** (Reykjavík, Iceland): Time for some *hákarl*, the signature Icelandic dish of fermented shark, which is cut into strips and hung out to dry several weeks before landing on the plate in front of you. It's actually delicious. (see p. 366)
- **L'AUBERGE DES CANUTS** (Lyon, France): Registered as one of the "Authentiques Bouchons Lyonnais" (if you're a real foodie, you know what this means), L'auberge des Canuts provides the perfect setting for you to gorge on the gastronomic phenomenon that is *bouchons, bouchons, bouchons* (*hon hon hon*). (see p. 176)
- **BONNIE** (Budapest, Hungary): If you're missing home on the road, this is the place to get a home-style meal of traditional Hungarian *goulash* (stew), guaranteed to make your stomach happy. (see p. 348)
- **CHOCOLATERIA SAN GINÉS** (Madrid, Spain): Don't think we forgot about your sweet tooth. This churro/chocolate joint has been open 24 hours a day since 1894 and there's no stopping this chocolately goodness now or ever. (see p. 596)
- **DA MICHELE PIZZA** (Naples, Italy): The birthplace of pizza… it was so good we ate it on a street corner by ourselves surrounded by cat pee and garbage, but we didn't care because it was SO GOOD. (see p. 437)

FOR THE SPORTS FANATIC: (that one person in the bar who screams at the television as if the players can actually hear them):

- **FIFA WORLD MUSEUM** (Zurich, Switzerland): FIFA is the force behind all the world's soccer tournaments from the World Cup to the UEFA Champions League. Pelé, Maradona, the Hand of God—the greats are all here. (see p. 660)
- **SAN BERNABEU STADIUM** (Madrid, Spain): This is the home turf of Real Madrid, one of Europe's top football clubs. Breathe the same air as Portuguese star Cristano Ronaldo and feel greatness wash over you. (see p. 590)
- **NATIONAL FOOTBALL MUSEUM** (Manchester, UK): England is home to the world-renowned clubs of the English Premier League. Whether you're an Arsenal, Manchester United, or Chelsea fan, this museum pulls out all of the stops to give you a crash course in football history. (see p. 314)

For the Avid Reader: (the horn-rimmed-glasses-clad geek who has read *Gatsby* twice, is not afraid of Virginia Woolf, and speaks like Hemingway writes):

- **JAMES JOYCE STATUE** (Dublin, Ireland): Joyce put Dublin on the map by creating an encyclopedic map. Enter *Ulysses*. Also the famous milieu of Joyce's short story collection, *Dubliners*. (see p. 385)
- **RUNNING OF THE BULLS FESTIVAL** (Pamplona, Spain): Channel Jake Barnes and

Lady Ashley as you head down for the ultimate Hemingway event. Drink like a champ. Run like a bull. (**see p. 599**)

- **LIVRARIA LELLO** (Porto, Portugal): If you love *Harry Potter*, you'll be glad to know that this little bookshop inspired none other than the Queen herself, J.K. Rowling, for the scenes in the series (Flourish and Blotts, anyone?). (**see p. 540**)
- **BASTILLE** (Paris, France): You didn't think we were going to do this without a Dickens reference, did you? Sidney Carton broke our heart, too. (**see p. 187**)

*For the Wild Child:* (the person who thinks camping is a romantic date opportunity, hikes 100 miles instead of taking transportation, and is dangerously unafraid of hitchhiking):

- **PARAGLIDING** (Gimmelwald, Switzerland): Get ready for a wild ride while you paraglide in the Alps. Move side to side, up and down, and turn around for an unparalleled view of nature's majesty. (**see p. 639**)
- **THE RING ROAD** (Iceland): We call this the ultimate challenge. Scuba dive between tectonic plates, walk around the Golden Circle, and hike between glaciers all while traversing dirt roads (hopefully in a car). (**see p. 369**)
- **LAKE COMO** (Milan, Italy): Shaped like a pair of pants, this is your chance to hike to the crotch of something—sadly, it's a body of water. (**see p. 428**)
- **LOW TATRAS NATIONAL PARK** (Slovakia): We're talking a skier's haven with mountain views and the Demänovská Ice Cave. Intrigued? (**see p. 552**)
- **SZÉCHENYI THERMAL BATH** (Budapest, Hungary): Twenty indoor pools, three large outdoor pools, all in different temperature ranges so you can pick and choose whether you want to be hot or cold. Paradise? We think so. (**see p. 347**)

For the Other Wild Child: (the person who sleeps all day and parties all night so much that their friends are afraid they're becoming nocturnal):

- **BERGHAIN** (Berlin, Germany): The most exclusive club in Berlin and we know exactly how to get you in. (**see p. 231**)
- **PACHA** (Ibiza, Spain): Time for Flower Power throwbacks on Mondays, house music with Martin Solveig on Wednesdays, and "Fuck Me, I'm Famous" Thursdays with David Guetta. (**see p. 585**)
- **CARPE DIEM** (Hvar, Croatia): Roll out the red carpet and throw down with the lux yachters of the Dalmatian coast… straight floatin' on a boat on the deep blue sea. (**see p.89**)
- **PARADISE BEACH** (Mykonos, Greece): Shirtless bartenders, bikini-clad women, dancing on the bar, and beats reverberating through the club; beach-goers galore know this is where the party happens. (**see p. 327**)
- **ICE BAR** (Stockholm, Sweden): The dress code here is pretty strict: a furry poncho with attached gloves, drinking from a glass made of ice while surrounded by ice. A little gimmicky, but nonetheless an experience you won't forget. (**see p. 631**)
- **TRAVEL SHACK** (Vienna, Austria): You'll consume the wildest drinks you ever dreamed of at Travel Shack—picture concoctions called "Cum Shot" and "Tequila Suicide," designed to create moments you might regret. (**see p. 53**)
- **DUBLIN PUB CRAWL** (Dublin, Ireland): We couldn't choose just one Irish pub, so our RW in Ireland, Mia Karr, curated a special pub crawl for you to enjoy pint upon pint of Guinness. (**see p. 393**)

# SUGGESTED ITINERARIES

## THE GRAND TOUR (40 DAYS)

For the travel-hungry soul who wants to see the most famous highlights of Europe—buckle up, you're in for a wild ride. We highly recommend tackling this bad boy with the trusty help of budget airlines or a rail pass.

- **LONDON** (4 days)—God save the Queen. Your first stop on your full-fledged adventure begins in an English-speaking country (baby steps). Make London your cup of tea by delving into its music culture and royal history. Here's hoping you'll catch a glimpse of the Queen (no, no, no not Elizabeth, J.K. Rowling). **(see p. 284)**
- **COPENHAGEN** (2 days)—It's time to venture north, as in Nordic. Blond people, Viking history, a whole soap opera of feuds with Sweden, and, of course, insane taxes await you in Denmark. Time to immerse yourself in Copenhagen's *hygge*. **(see p. 131)**
- **AMSTERDAM** (3 days)—Amsterdam has it all: imperial history, artistic pedigree, and killer music. Burn some calories in one of the most bike-friendly cities in the world and see some classic Dutch windmills. Let's not forget crossing over to the dark side either; if you so choose, the coffeeshop scene is out there—just keep this part of the trip to yourself (Mom doesn't want to know). **(see p. 476)**
- **PARIS** (4 days)—Go ahead, be romantic. This is the quintessential European destination for artists, lovers, tourists, foodies, and romantics alike. If you don't go here on your Grand Tour, you didn't go to Europe. Paris, *enchanté*. **(see p. 187)**
- **BARCELONA** (3 days)—Get your Gaudí on in one of the hottest (and we mean searing hot) parts of Europe. Architecture geeks will be awestruck by the beauty of La Sagrada Familia, foodies will triumph in the exquisite Catalan cuisine, and soccer fans will rejoice in the buzz of one of the world's most beloved teams at the Camp Nou. Let's get Messi. **(see p. 558)**
- **LISBON** (2 days)—Part of the beauty of Lisbon is that it's largely undiscovered. This hidden gem is bound to blow your mind with its seafood delights and geographic wonders. It's time for leg day, so gear up to hike as you soak up the sun and culture in Lisboa. **(see p. 532)**
- **MADRID** (2 days)—The Spanish capital reigns with the promise of pitchers of sangria, one of the most poppin' nightlife scenes on the globe, and countless opportunities to explore Spanish history from the Age of Exploration to present day. Madrid loves you already and you will fall for it even harder. **(see p. 586)**
- **ROME** (4 days)—Hop on that vespa, baby. It's time to talk fast, move your hands fast, and drive even faster. Get the best of the old Roman Empire and the new Roman paradise in the Eternal City. Gelato will cool you down as you climb Palatine Hill and pretend to be a gladiator in The Roman Colosseum. **(see p. 444)**
- **FLORENCE** (3 days)—Travel back in time to the Renaissance and get #cultured in this epicenter of art. This is Michelangelo's hometown, but today it is a

modern hotspot for art, music, shopping, and gelato-mongering. (see p. 409)

- **PRAGUE** (3 days)—Prague's Old Town looks like a fairytale and it's time to make your dreams come true. This often-overlooked gem boasts must-sees like the Charles Bridge and castle, but the young and grungy bars, beer gardens, and galleries are more eager to see you. (see p. 109)
- **MUNICH** (2 days)— Munich is the quintessential German city, layered in tradition. Munich is a little quieter than other cities, but you can still appreciate its Bavarian roots as you tour its high-quality beer gardens. (see p. 250)
- **BERLIN** (3 days)— Pick up the pace and head to a city that never sleeps. Riddled with the history of a war-torn city and trendy, exclusive club scenes, Berlin is a true cosmopolitan center. Make sure you say, "Hallo!" to Merkel for us. (see p. 218)
- **ATHENS** (3 days)— Make your way back down south and turn up the temperature. Climb Mount Olympus, walk around the ruins of the Acropolis, and find your Adonis or Aphrodite under the sweet, Greek sun. Apollo, is that you? (see p. 320)
- **SPLIT** (2 days)—Top it all off in the Balkans. Split is the place to cool down, relax, and enjoy the beach as you dance the night away. (see p. 89)

## ISLAND HOPPING (14 DAYS)

Does Europe even have any islands, you ask? That's preposterous. Tons of lively ones eagerly await you on your European adventure. We're talking palm trees, sand, pebbly beaches, bumping party beats, and master DJs. Tell Corona we've found our beach.

- **IBIZA, SPAIN** (2 days)—Kick it off with superstar DJs like David Guetta and show Mike Posner you can handle a rager better than he can in the nightclubs of this iconic Spanish island. (see p. 582)
- **MALTA** (3 days)—Combine cliff-jumping with clubbing in this 122-mile archipelago. The best part? You can mix the history of repeated conquest by the Phoenicians and Romans and the colonial rule of the British into your island vacation by visiting limestone temples, ancient ruins, and monumental forts. (see p. 414)
- **MYKONOS, GREECE** (3 days)—Party animals all around the world hear the word "Mykonos" and know it's the holy grail of fun. Skip the architectural wonders of Ancient Greece and head straight here for nights to remember. (see p. 326)
- **HVAR TOWN, CROATIA** (3 days)—Hvar are you doing today? Not good? Swing by this Croatian island on the iconic Riva of Hvar. You've got nothing but clubbing, beach parties, and cheap alcohol ahead of you. (see p. 83)
- **VENICE, ITALY** (3 days)—Okay, well Venice isn't exactly one island. Think more like 118. Venice is connected by a series of foot bridges that cross over the city's 170 boat canals. Close out your trip with a little culture on the glass-making island of Murano and with the lace-specialists in Burano. (see p. 462)

## STOP AND SMELL THE ROSES (23 DAYS)

If you've got a green thumb, then you'll be glad to know Europe has much for you to see in the form of extravagance. The Romans, for example, were fixated with controlling nature and, as a result, created beautiful gardens with immaculately manicured plants in the strangest of shapes. We're not quite sure of the origins of the other gardens around the continent, but these are feats of man and nature that would make even the most talented gardener jealous. What do *you* have? Tomato vines? Growing upside down? Amateur.

- **FLORENCE, ITALY** (3 days)—The Boboli Gardens at Florence's Palazzo Pitti are truly a sight to behold. Climb lots (and we mean lots) of stairs as you walk through what feels like the gardens of Sleeping Beauty's castle—without Maleficent trying to keep the prince out. (see p. 409)
- **VIENNA, AUSTRIA** (4 days)—The gardens of Schönnbrunn Palace await your royal highness. And, if that doesn't entertain you, the Hapsburgs also have gardens at the Belvedere for your pleasure. (see p. 43)
- **PARIS, FRANCE** (5 days)—The Jardin des Plantes lies in the fifth arrondissement and is the main botanical garden in France. (see p. 187)
- **BARCELONA, SPAIN** (4 days)—Parc Güell. Garden? Outdoor space? Architectural wonder of Antoni Gaudí? All of the above. (see p. 558)
- **MALMÖ, SWEDEN** (2 days)—*Aah* Slottsträdgården, complete with orderly, manicured hedges and multiple plots including a Steppe Garden and Japanese Garden that will make your jaw drop. (see p. 616)
- **LONDON, UK** (5 days)—The Royal Parks are undoubtedly majestic. Hyde Park and Regent's Park are full of green spaces in an urban setting while the famed Kensington Gardens serves as the front yard for a king, situated right in front of the stunning palace. (see p. 284)

# CALL OF THE WILD (14 DAYS)

We get it—you're Wilderness First-Aid Certified, you've spent every summer as a camp counselor in the middle of the forest, and you've hiked 111 miles solo. You're coming to Europe for the outdoor adventures—to get in touch with nature, if you will. In that case, we've got you covered. Lace up your hiking boots.

- **REYKJAVIK, ICELAND** (3 days)—Reykjavik is an excellent place to set up camp to do outdoorsy day trips in Iceland. Some of our favorites include the Blue Lagoon and Golden Circle. (see p. 362)
- **OSLO, NORWAY** (2 days)—Oslo Sommerpark is guaranteed to put the overeager kid spirit back in you, featuring a wicked obstacle course that allows you to climb 20 meters into the trees. Tarzan who? (see p. 497)
- **GIMMELWALD, SWITZERLAND** (3 days)—This secluded mountain town in the Alps is a hidden gem: paraglide in the mountains, watch glaciers collide, and hike difficult, pristine trails. (see p. 639)
- **SPLIT, CROATIA** (2 days)—Get a drink on the rocks and then cliff jump off the rocks (into the Mediterranean). Note: *Let's Go* does not endorse drinking and jumping. (see p. 89)
- **TIHANY, HUNGARY** (2 days)—The Lake Balaton Bike Paths span 130 miles, wrapping around the beautiful Lake Balaton. If you're not up for this challenge, then biking in the fairytale-esque town is also a scenic way to burn some kcals. (see p. 355)
- **LAGOS, PORTUGAL** (2 days)—If outdoor adventures at the beach are what you seek, opt for a change of pace in southern Portugal, kayaking off the coast in the Iberian Peninsula. (see p. 528)

# HOW TO USE THIS BOOK

## CHAPTERS

*Let's Go Europe 2018* covers 24 countries in its 22 chapters. Each chapter contains comprehensive content that is designed to make your trip easy to plan. Chapters are organized in alphabetical order by country, so the book kicks off with Austria and culminates with Switzerland. The countries covered in this book are Austria, Belgium, Croatia, the Czech Republic, Denmark, France, Germany, Great Britain, Greece, Hungary, Iceland, Ireland, Luxembourg, Malta, Montenegro, The Netherlands, Norway, Poland, Portugal, Slovakia, Spain, Sweden, and Switzerland.

Each chapter has been written by at least one *Let's Go* **Researcher-Writer.** Researcher-Writers (RWs) are students at Harvard College who spend a maximum of eight weeks of their summer covering a pre-planned route of cities for publication in *Let's Go Europe.* Credits are given after the name of each city.

Within a chapter, cities are arranged in alphabetical order, so don't be alarmed when you see the France chapter begins with Avignon instead of Paris. We promise we did not forget Paris; we did our due diligence.

### Structure of a Chapter

Each chapter begins with a country introduction and, from there, it is divided into city sections. The first section in a city always consists of an **introduction** followed by an **orientation** and **city essentials,** which includes all of the important information you should know—the location of tourist offices, police stations, hospitals, a list of BGLTQ+ resources, and numbers to call in the event of an emergency—before traveling to a given place. Although Google Maps is a fantastic resource that can be downloaded on your phone and accessed offline, it is important to pick up a paper map from a tourist office in case of emergency.

On to the fun stuff: city chapters include several sections, each of which will help you plan your days. These sections are also in alphabetical order, with our *Let's Go* Thumbpicked™ establishments listed first and followed by all of the other wonderful things we've covered:

> **Accommodations:** *Let's Go's* accommodation listings consist of budget options, which are often hostels. In smaller cities, accommodation options are often limited, so we have included some B&Bs and budget hotels to ensure you have a comfortable stay without breaking the bank.
>
> **Sights:** Our "Sights" section is further broken down into four categories— Culture, Landmarks, Museums, and Outdoors.
>
>> **Culture:** These listings cover everything from churches to theaters to markets to interesting bookstores.
>>
>> **Landmarks:** These are your Eiffel Towers, Colosseums, and Buckingham Palaces. All of the biggest sights and attractions are listed here.
>>
>> **Museums:** Fairly self-explanatory, but here's where you'll find Prague's Dox, Paris' Louvre, and Zagreb's Museum of Broken Relationships.
>>
>> **Outdoors:** Here's where you'll find listings of a city's green spaces, beaches, and outdoor activities.
>
> **Food:** You need to eat when you're abroad, right? For your convenience, we have included restaurants that cater to a backpacker's budget with a few splurge options interspersed. Treat yo' self.
>
> **Nightlife:** Sleep all day, party all night, sightsee all day, party all night—

whatever your travel lifestyle is, we've got the right bars, clubs, and cafés to ensure your evenings are well spent.

**Listings**—a.k.a. reviews of individual establishments—constitute the majority of *Let's Go's* content, and consist of essential information (address, phone number, website, and hours), a review of a given establishment, followed by any miscellaneous information that may be useful.

---

### ESTABLISHMENT NAME ($-$$$)
Address; phone number; website; hours
Review goes here.
*Miscellaneous information such as prices, cash/card, dietary restrictions, whether or not an establishment is certified BGLTQ+ friendly, wheelchair accessibility, etc.*

---

Every piece of content in *Let's Go Europe 2018*—the introductions, the orientations, the essentials, the listings, and the features—was researched and updated during the summer of 2017.

The end of each country chapter contains a **country essentials** page in which we detail information that is applicable to the entire country. This includes the country code, regulations and laws surrounding drug and alcohol use, and country-wide safety and health information. This also contains information about attitudes toward BGLTQ+ travelers and minorities.

### The *Let's Go* Thumbpick™

is an icon you will see a lot in this book. Whenever a listing has a Thumbpick™ next to the establishment name, it indicates that it was a favorite of the Researcher-Writer who visited that city. These are, in other words, our top-choice accommodations, sights, and food and nightlife establishments.

### Price Diversity

Another set of icons in the book corresponds to what we call our "price diversity" scale, which approximates how much money you can expect to spend at a given establishment. We have noted price diversity in our Accommodations and Food listings only. For accommodations, we base our range on the cheapest price for which a single traveler can stay for one night. For food, we estimate the average amount one traveler will spend in one sitting. Keep in mind that no scale can allow for the quirks of all individual establishments.

# BEFORE YOU GO

**Planning a good trip takes a lot more effort than you think it will.** The worst thing you can do is get off the plane in Warsaw, for example, and not know what you want to do or what resources are available to you. Each chapter of this book includes a list of country-specific resources that will help you out in a pinch, but this chapter contains overarching information for all of Europe. We've condensed the knowledge we've acquired over 58 years of travel to ensure you have a safe, enjoyable experience in Europe. Planning your trip? Check. How to get around? Check. Safety and health resources? Check. There is also a phrasebook at the back of the book for your convenience.

## PLANNING YOUR TRIP

### DOCUMENTS AND FORMALITIES

There's a lot of country-specific information when it comes to visas and work permits, but don't forget the most important piece of documentation: your passport.

#### Passport

You cannot board a plane to another country without a passport. If you do not have a passport, you should apply for one several months in advance, as the process can take a long time. US citizens can apply for a passport online at www.travel.state.gov or at a local United States Post Office. Adult passports are valid for 10 years while children's passports are valid for five. If you already have a passport, check the expiration date of your document before booking any flights or accommodations. **Your passport must be valid for at least six months after you return from your trip in order to travel to Europe. Your passport should also have at least two blank pages, depending on your destination.**

#### Visas

Those lucky enough to be EU citizens will not need a visa to travel throughout the continent. Being an EU citizen has other perks too, such as shorter security lines. However, citizens of Australia, Canada, New Zealand, United States, and various other non-EU countries do not need a visa for a stay of up to 90 days. This three-month period begins upon entry to any of the EU's **freedom-of-movement zones.** Those staying longer than 90 days may apply for a longer-term visa; consult an embassy or consulate for more information.

Double check entry requirements at the nearest embassy or consulate for up-to-date information, as political situations can make it easier or more difficult to move between countries. US citizens can also consult www.travel.state.gov. Keep in mind that admittance to a country as a traveler does not include the right to work, which is authorized only by a work permit. You should check online for the process of obtaining a work permit for the country in which you are planning to work.

## THE EUROPEAN UNION: HOW IT WORKS

The European Union is a union of 28 countries within the continent of Europe based in Brussels, Belgium. This number includes the United Kingdom. The countries covered in this book that are not part of the European Union are Iceland, Norway, Montenegro, and Monaco.

The European Union's policy of freedom of movement means that most border controls have been abolished and visa policies harmonized. This treaty, formerly known as the Schengen Agreement, means you still have to carry a passport (or government-issued ID card for EU citizens) when crossing an internal border, but, once you've been admitted to one country, you're free to travel to other participating states. Iceland and Norway are members of the Schengen Agreement, meaning that the rule extends to those countries as well.

It is important, however, to note that recent fears over immigration have led to calls for suspension of this freedom-of-movement and strengthening of borders. One of the most covered situations is **Brexit,** the vote by the citizens of the United Kingdom to leave the European Union. Lawmakers from the United Kingdom and the European Union, as of August 2017, are still in conversation about the new border restrictions and rules between the United Kingdom and European Union, so it is important to inform yourself about the situation before planning travel to the UK.

## TIME DIFFERENCES

Most of Europe is on Central European Time, which is 1hr. ahead of Greenwich Mean Time (GMT) and observes Daylight Savings Time in the summer. This means that, in summer, it is 6hr. ahead of New York City, 9hr. ahead of Los Angeles, 1hr. ahead of the British Isles, 8hr. behind Sydney, and 10hr. behind New Zealand. In winter, it is 10hr. behind Sydney and 12hr. behind New Zealand. However, the UK, Ireland, and Portugal are on GMT, also known as Western European Time, which means they are 1hr. behind the Central European Time countries. In addition, Greece and some parts of Eastern Europe are on Eastern European Time, which means they are 1hr. ahead of Central European Time countries.

## MONEY MATTERS

### BEFORE YOU GO

Call your bank. The first thing you should do is alert your bank that you will be abroad for a period of time. You should be prepared to give the bank representative the exact dates of your travel and where you will be if you plan to use your debit card in that country. Keep in mind that there may be a foreign transaction charge from your bank whenever you use your card. If your bank is a local US bank that does not have branches outside of a given city, you may want to consider changing your bank or opening a new account to one that is more widespread so that you can access customer service lines with larger networks in case of emergency.

Before you go, you should decide which credit cards to use before packing. It is advisable to pack credit cards that are widely accepted in Europe to avoid being caught in a pinch where you do not have any form of payment. Call your credit card company before going to alert them you will be abroad. As with banks, be prepared to give the representative the exact dates of your travel. Some credit card companies have online systems in which you can input the dates of your travel to skip the step of calling ahead.

### CURRENCY BREAKDOWN

Nineteen countries in Europe use the euro, which is the currency of the European Union, meaning you will not have to worry about changing currencies when you hop from country to country. However, if you are traveling outside of the eurozone, you should be aware that you will need to convert once you leave. Countries outside the eurozone in the European Union are Croatia, Czech

Republic, Denmark, Hungary, Sweden, and the United Kingdom. For an up-to-date list, check a currency converter (such as www.xe.com).

## GETTING MONEY FROM HOME
Things happen and, if they do, you might need money. The easiest and cheapest solution to get you out of a pinch is to have someone back home make a deposit to your bank account directly. If this isn't possible, consider one of the following options:

### Wiring Money
Arranging a **bank money transfer** means asking a bank back home to wire money to a bank wherever you are. This is the cheapest way to transfer cash, but it's also a slow process, taking several days. Note that some banks may only release your funds in local currency, potentially sticking you with a poor exchange rate; you should inquire about this in advance.

Money transfer services like **Western Union** are faster and more convenient than bank transfers—but also much pricier. Western Union has many locations worldwide. To find one, visit www.westernunion.com or call the appropriate number:
- Australia: 1800 173 833
- Canada: 800 235 0000
- UK: 0808 234 9168
- US: 800 325 6000
- France: 08 00 90 01 91

Money transfer services are also available to American Express cardholders and at selected Thomas Cook offices.

### US State Department (US Citizens Only)
In serious emergencies only, the US State Department will help your family or friends forward money within hours to the nearest consular office, which will then disburse it according to instructions for a $30 fee. If you wish to use this service, you must contact the Overseas Citizens Services division of the US State Department (+1 202 501 444 or, from the US, 888 407 4747)

## WITHDRAWING MONEY WHILE ABROAD
ATMs are readily available throughout Europe, excluding some rural areas, so you should also check ahead of time if you will be able to withdraw money in a given country. To use a debit or credit card to withdraw money from a cash machine (ATM) in Europe, you must have a four-digit Personal Identification Number (PIN). If your PIN is longer than four digits, ask your bank whether you can just use the first four digits or whether you'll need a new one. If your PIN includes a 0, you may need to make a new PIN, as some ATM machines in Europe do not have that key.

Travelers with alphabetical rather than numerical PINs may also be thrown off by the absence of letters on European cash machines. Here are the corresponding numbers to use:
- QZ = 1
- ABC = 2
- DEF = 3
- GHI = 4
- JKL = 5
- MNO = 6
- PRS = 7
- TUV = 8
- WXY = 9

It is also important to note that if you mistakenly punch the wrong code into the machine multiple (often three) times, it can swallow up your card for good.

Credit cards do not usually come with PINs, so if you intend to use ATMs in Europe with a credit card to get cash advances, call your credit card company before leaving to request one.

## DEBIT AND CREDIT CARD FRAUD

If you check your account and notice that money has been stolen or is missing, you should call your bank immediately to remedy the situation and file a claim for the missing money. Many credit card companies have similar help lines and some online applications will allow you to automatically freeze your account. For this reason, we recommend that you always have some form of hard cash on you at all times.

## TIPPING

Unlike in the United States, Europe does not have some unwritten universal tipping code of conduct. No one in the world tips like Americans, so tipping might just be a giveaway that you are a tourist. Although you are not required to tip, you can still leave one; even just 10% will seem quite generous.

## TAXES

Members of the EU have a value-added tax (VAT) of varying percentages. It is most often between 19-21%. Non-EU citizens have the opportunity to be refunded this tax if you are taking these goods home. When shopping, make sure to ask for a VAT refund form that you can present with the goods and receipts at customs upon departure. Note: you must have the goods with you in order to be refunded.

# GETTING AROUND

## BY PLANE

### Commercial Airlines

For small-scale travel on the continent, *Let's Go* suggests budget airlines for budget travelers, but more traditional carriers have begun to offer competitive deals. We recommend searching on www.cheapflights.com for the most affordable flights to Europe. You should look to book flights months in advance.

### Budget Airlines

No-frills airlines make hopscotching around Europe by air remarkably affordable, as long as you avoid their rip-off fees. The following airlines will be useful for traveling across the pond and hopping from country to country:
- EasyJet: www.easyjet.com
- Eurowings: www.eurowings.com
- Iceland Air: www.icelandair.com
- Norwegian: www.norwegian.com
- Ryanair: www.ryanair.com
- Pegasus: www.flypgs.com
- Transavia: www.transavia.com
- Wizz Air: www.wizzair.com

## BY TRAIN

European trains are generally comfortable, convenient, and reasonably swift. You should always make sure you are in the correct car, **as sometimes trains split**

**midway through route to dock at different destinations.** Towns in parentheses on European train schedules require a train switch at the town listed immediately before the parentheses.

You can either buy a **railpass,** which, for a high price, allows you unlimited, flexible travel within a particular region for a given period of time, or buy individual **point-to-point** tickets as you go. Almost all countries give students and youths (under 26, usually) direct discounts on regular domestic rail tickets and many also sell a student or youth card that provides 20-50% off all fares for up to a year. Tickets can be bought at stations, but most Western European countries offer big discounts to travelers booking online in advance.

Check out the following sites to get discounts on train tickets and book trips in advance:

- www.raileurope.com
- www.railsaver.com
- www.rome2rio.com

## BY BUS

Although train travel is much more comfortable, it may be cheaper to travel via bus from city to city. There are numerous operators across the continent, but Eurolines is the largest company running international coach services (www. eurolines.com). Inquire about 15- or 30-day passes when you book. For a higher price tag, Busabout offers numerous hop-on-hop-off bus circuits covering 29 of Europe's best bus hubs (www.busabout.com).

With that in mind, it is highly advised that you avoid travel at night via bus at all costs. It is much safer to book an early morning trip than it is to leave in the dead of the night, as drivers can be exhausted and many roads are narrow and unsafe to navigate in the dark. *Let's Go* has a policy with our Researcher-Writers in which we do not allow them to travel via bus at night.

# PLACES TO STAY

For the budget traveler, accommodations options are limited, as expensive hotels are out of price range. That means hostels will be your best friend. All of the hostels in *Let's Go Europe 2018* have been visited by a Researcher-Writer and are therefore verified by this guide.

You should, at least for the first few nights of your stay, book a hostel before departing, that way you do not land without a place to stay. We recommend using HostelWorld (www.hostelworld.com), Homestay (www.homestay.com), or Booking.com (www.booking.com) to make reservations.

There are a few red flags to look out for before deciding to stay at a hostel, even if you have already made a reservation online. We advise looking at the area or neighborhood surrounding the hostel to see if it feels and looks safe. If it does not, we recommend finding another hostel in a more suitable area. Many a time there are hostels with little lighting in front of the establishment, which is a signal that it is not completely safe. Many hostels have 24hr. security and lockout times, which can be reassuring. In addition, you should avoid hostels where you see pests, bedbugs, or signs of rampant uncleanliness. If you feel uncomfortable talking to staff members or if staff members make sexual advances, this is also a concern and you should find another place to spend the night.

# SAFETY AND HEALTH

In any crisis, the most important thing to do is **keep calm.** In every chapter, we have included the address of the nearest US embassy or consulate so that you can seek help in an emergency; your country's embassy is your best resource in precarious situations. The following government offices can also provide travel information and advisories.

- Australia: Department of Foreign Affairs and Trade (+61 2 6261 3305; www.smartraveller.gov.au)
- Canada: Global Affairs of Canada (+1 800 267 8376; www.international.gc.ca)
- New Zealand: Ministry of Foreign Affairs and Trade (+64 4 439 8000; www.safetravel.govt.nz)
- UK: Foreign and Commonwealth Office (+44 20 7008 1500; www.fco.gov.uk)
- US: Department of State (+1 888 407 4747 from the US, +1 202 501 4444 from abroad; www.travel.state.gov)

## PRE-DEPARTURE HEALTH

Matching a prescription to a foreign drug equivalent is not always safe, easy, or even possible. Remember to take **prescription drugs** with you and carry up-to-date prescriptions or a statement from your doctor stating the medication's trade names, manufacturers, chemical names, and dosages. Be sure to keep all your medication in your carry-on luggage.

### Immunizations and Precautions

Travelers over two years of age should make sure that the following vaccinations are up to date:

- MMR (for measles, mumps, and rubella)
- DTaP or Td (for diphtheria, tetanus, and pertussis)
- IPV (for polio)
- Hib (for Hemophilus influenzae B)
- HepB (for Hepatitis B)

For recommendations on other immunizations and prophylaxis, check with a doctor and consult the **Centers for Disease Control and Prevention (CDC)** in the US (800 232 4636; www.cdc.gov/travel) or the equivalent in your home country.

# KEEPING IN TOUCH

## BY EMAIL AND INTERNET

**Wireless hot spots** (Wi-Fi) make internet access possible in public and remote places. Unfortunately, they can also pose security risks. Hot spots are public, open networks that use unencrypted, unsecured connections. They are susceptible to hacks and "packet sniffing"—the theft of passwords and other private information. To prevent problems, disable "ad hoc" mode, turn off file sharing and network discover, encrypt your email, turn on your firewall, beware of phony networks, and watch for over-the-shoulder creeps.

    **Data roaming** lets you use mobile data abroad, but it can be pricey. If you refuse to "later 'gram" and hyperventilate at the idea of losing access to Google, first consider that you are many hours ahead of the United States and can post when you return to your hostel and remember that Google Maps is available offline. If that doesn't placate you, though, you should get an international travel plan with your carrier or consider getting a local phone.

## BY TELEPHONE

If you have internet access, your best (i.e. cheapest, most convenient, and most tech-savvy) means of calling home are probably Skype, FaceTime, or whatever calling app you prefer. **Prepaid phone cards** are common and a relatively inexpensive means of calling abroad. Each one comes with a Personal

Identification Number (PIN) and a toll-free access number. Call the access number and follow the subsequent directions for dialing your PIN. To purchase prepaid phone cards, check online for the best rates (www.callingcard.com).

Another option is a **calling card,** linked to a major national telecommunications service in your home country. Calls are billed collect or to your account. Cards generally come with instructions for dialing both domestically and internationally. Placing a collect call through an international operator can be expensive but may be necessary in case of an emergency. You can frequently call collect without even possessing a company's calling card just by calling its access number and following the instructions.

## How to Make a Call

1. Dial the international dialing prefix,
   - Australia: 0011
   - Canada or the US: 011
   - Ireland, New Zealand, and most of Europe: 00
2. Then the country code of the country you want to call,
   - Australia: 61
   - Austria: 43
   - Belgium: 32
   - Canada: 1
   - Croatia: 385
   - Czech Republic: 420
   - Denmark: 45
   - France: 33
   - Germany: 49
   - Greece: 30
   - Hungary: 36
   - Ireland: 353
   - Italy: 39
   - The Netherlands: 31
   - Norway: 47
   - New Zealand: 64
   - Poland: 48
   - Portugal: 351
   - Slovenia: 386
   - Spain: 34
   - Sweden: 46
   - Switzerland: 41
   - UK: 44
   - US: 1
3. Followed by the city/area code,
4. And finally the local number.

## Cellular Phones

The international standard for cellular phones is the **Global System for Mobile Communication (GSM).** To make and receive calls in Europe, you will need a GSM-compatible phone and a **SIM (Subscriber Identity Module) card,** a country-specific, thumbnail-sized chip that gives you a local phone number and plugs you into the local network. Most modern SIM cards will work in any country, but the charges for this can vary wildly, so check with your carrier and decide whether it might be cheaper to get a new SIM at your destination. Many European SIM cards are prepaid, and incoming calls are frequently free. You can buy additional cards or vouchers (usually available at convenience stores) to "top up" your phone. For more information on GSM phones, check out www.telestial.com. Companies like Cellular Abroad (www.cellularabroad.com) and **OneSimCard** (www.onesimcard.com) rent cell phones and SIM cards that work in a variety of destinations around the world.

## BY SNAIL MAIL

### Sending Mail Home

**Airmail** is the best way to send mail home from Europe. Write "airmail," "par avion," or the equivalent in the local language on the front. For simple letters or postcards, airmail tends to be surprisingly cheap, but the price will go up sharply for weighty packages. Surface mail is by far the cheapest, slowest, and most antiquated way to send mail. It takes one or two months to cross the Atlantic, which may be ideal for heavy items you won't need for a while, like souvenirs you've acquired along the way and the dresser you bought from that antique store that deep down, you know you don't need.

### Receiving Mail in Europe

There are several ways to arrange pickup of letters sent to you while you are abroad, even if you do not have an address of your own. Mail can be sent via **Post Restante** (General Delivery). Address Poste Restante letters like so:

First and Last Name
**Poste Restante**
City, Country

The mail will go to a special desk in the city's central post office, unless you specify a local post office by a street address or postal code. It's best to use the largest post office, since mail may be sent there regardless. Bring your passport (or other photo ID) for pickup; there may be a small fee. If the clerk insists there is nothing for you, ask them to check under your first name as well. *Let's Go* lists post offices in the **Essentials** section for each city we cover. It's usually safer and quicker, though more expensive, to send mail express or registered. If you don't want to deal with Poste Restante, consider asking your hostel or accommodation if you can have things mailed to you there. Of course, if you have your own mailing address or a reliable friend, that is the easiest method.

# CLIMATE

Europe may be the smallest continent in the world, but it has a surprisingly diverse climate. Some of its countries border the seas while others are landlocked. Some have mountains and glaciers, others have valleys and sandy ruins. Here's how it works: Southern Europe is known for warm weather surrounding the Mediterranean Sea. This area has mild, wet winters and hot, dry summers. Northern and Eastern areas are marked by temperate forests, where cold Arctic air contrasts with hot, warm summers and rain whenever the universe feels like mocking you. In between sits the exception: the mile-high Alps, where things are generally colder and wetter.

# MEASUREMENTS

Like the rest of the rational world, Europe uses the metric system. The basic unit of length is the meter (m), which is divided into 100 centimeters (cm) or 10000 millimeters (mm). One thousand meters make up one kilometer (km). Fluids are measured in liters (L), each divided into 1000 (mL). A liter of pure water weighs one kilogram (kg), the unit of mass that is divided into 1000 grams (g). One metric ton is 1000kg. Gallons in the US and in Britain are not identical: one US gallon equals 0.83 Imperial gallons. Pub aficionados will note that an Imperial pint (20 oz.) is larger than its US counterpart (16 oz.)—we'll drink to that!

# AUSTRIA

**Arguably the world's capital of classical music, Austria is home to many of history's greatest musical minds.** Mozart is, of course, the country's favorite son, and visitors on pilgrimages inspired by the prodigal musician will find windows into Mozart's life in the house where he was born and his later residencies in Salzburg and Vienna, but the musical landmarks don't stop there. The Vienna State Opera is world famous, the Haus der Musik demonstrates the creation of music down to the scientific mechanisms of sound reverberation, and Salzburg's ball season offers dancing until the early morning in the birthplace of the waltz.

This music scene comes into the modern age with a visit to the country, where melodies old and new seem to hang in the air like electricity. You may find public outdoor symphony concerts in Vienna that draw attendees of all ages to stand, sway, chat with neighbors, and pop open bottles of wine. Classical music has never felt more casual and enveloping. In Salzburg, side effects of The Sound of Music settings may include running, skipping, and spinning with arms outstretched. Here, the city does seem to be alive with the sound of music, and visitors may find the voice of Queen Julie Andrews (this title is legitimate, just ask the people of Genovia) rattling around their heads, seemingly with no end.

Meanwhile, Austria is a sight to behold, a stunning vision of mountains and man-made edifices wishing they could be mountains, too. Cities boast architectural works that reach for the skies, from the towering Gothic spires of the Rathaus and St. Stephen's Cathedral in Vienna to the clunky hilltop fortress of Salzburg that cradles the clouds in its own right. In Hallstatt, hillside churches and sharp, elongated steeples sit alongside a glistening lake, nestled between mountains. Home to its own corner of the Alps, the road through Austria winds among jagged peaks and sparkling bodies of water. Here, you'll find the air fresh, the language German, and the living easy.

# SALZBURG

Coverage by **Antonia Washington**

The name Salzburg translates to "mountain of salt," and it was this very resource—known colloquially as "white gold"—that made this city great (and the archbishops that reigned here incredibly rich). With the spoils from mining, the members of the ruling class built opulent state rooms and concert halls. The city took shape within just a few decades, and is now considered one of the most exemplary showcases of Baroque architecture in the world. Salzburg's city center is arguably the best preserved in Central Europe with tall domes peeking over the rooftops of Old Town and hillside fortresses looming overhead. Additionally, Salzburg is notable for its exquisite cultural composition. Once the social and governmental seat of its region, Salzburg was an independent state for nearly 300 years, after breaking from Bavaria and before becoming part of Austria in the early 1800s. It is also the birthplace of Wolfgang Amadeus Mozart (and the von Trapp family—can't forget about them), whose work is emblematic of the region's musical legacy.

## ORIENTATION

Salzburg is a relatively small city built up on either side of the Salzach River, a right tributary of the **Inn River** and your number-one tool for orienting yourself. The city center spans both sides of the river. To the east you will find the **Mirabell palace and gardens**, the main train station, and Mozart's residence. Areas to note include **Linzer Gasse**, a major pedestrian street, and **Mirabellplatz**, a major square just in front of Mirabell palace and a frequent rendezvous site for tour groups and open-air markets. To the west lies Salzburg's **Old Town**. Here, pedestrian streets bustle with people from all walks of life, and most of the city sights, including Mozart's birthplace and the **Salzburg Cathedral** in the DomQuartier, stand in all of their former glory. Areas to note on this side of the river include **Judengasse**, Linzer Gasse's western counterpart, **Residenzplatz**, a main square in the middle of the **Residenz Palace**, the Salzburg Cathedral and the **Salzburg Museum**.

## ESSENTIALS

### GETTING THERE

The Salzburg airport, named for Wolfgang Amadeus Mozart, can be reached on flights from most major cities in Europe and many major cities around the world, though the latter requires a connecting flight. If you are coming from elsewhere in Europe, travel via train is often the most convenient, as the Salzburg Hauptbahnhof train station is situated just on the northeast corner of the city center, easily within a bus ride or walking distance of many sights and accommodations.

### GETTING AROUND

Salzburg does not have an underground metro, but buses run just about anywhere you may wish to go, and 1hr. tickets cost just over €2. Once in the city center, Salzburg is very walkable, and, in fact, you will often be forced to walk, as much of Old Town consists of pedestrian streets. Bikes are also a popular method of transportation. Rental stores can be found throughout the city.

### PRACTICAL INFORMATION

**Tourist Offices:** Located in Old Town in Mozartplatz, a smaller square right off of Residenzplatz (Mozartplatz 5; 66288 98 70; www.salzburg.info/en; open daily 9am-6pm).

**Banks/ATMs/Currency Exchange:** Most establishments in Salzburg only accept cash, but banks and ATMs are widely available to withdraw money.

**Post Offices:** There are many post offices throughout the city, one central location is listed (Residenzplatz 9; 0800 010 100; open M-F 8am-6pm).

**Internet:** Internet access is fairly standard at most accommodations in Salzburg, but worth checking ahead on.

**BGLTQ+ Resources:** The brochure "Austria Gay Guide" includes information about gay resources and establishments in cities including Salzburg. Find more information online at www.gayguide.me.

## EMERGENCY INFORMATION

**Emergency Number:** 112

**Police:** Police stations are located throughout the city. Listed below is the information for the station located in Salzburg's town hall (Rudolfskai 2; 059 133 55 88100).

**US Embassy:** Austria's US Embassy is located in Vienna (Boltzmanngasse 16; (+43-1) 31339-0; open M-F 8am-4:30pm). In case of emergencies, the US consulate in Munich, Germany may be easier to access (Königinstraße 5; 8928880).

**Hospitals:** Unfallkrankenhaus (Doktor-Franz-Rehrl-Platz 5; 059 3934 4000; open daily 24hr).

**Pharmacies:** Pharmacies in Salzburg are widespread and easy to find. Pharmacies are called "apotheke," and are marked with a red symbol that looks like a cursive "L" or the number four. Engel-Apotheke (0662 87 32 21) is the most central pharmacy.

## ACCOMMODATIONS

### NATURFREUNDEHAUS STADTALM ($)

Mönchsberg 19c; 0662 84 17 29; www.stadtalm.at; reception open daily Sep-Apr 10am-6pm, May-Aug 10am-11pm

You'll find this hostel on the second floor of a restaurant, housed inside a castle, and sitting on top of a mountain. Amid a combination of stone and wooden décor, you'll feel like fairytale royalty, though in real life you'll probably be a lot dirtier and sweatier, especially because getting up to the hostel on foot means hiking up the hill. Once you make it to the top, however, the recently renovated rooms and bathrooms will welcome you warmly. Another perk: the price of the room includes breakfast.

*i* Dorms €24.50; reservation required; no wheelchair accessibility; breakfast included

### YOHO INTERNATIONAL YOUTH HOSTEL ($)

Paracelsusstrasse 9; 0662 87 96 49; www.yoho.at; reception open 24hr

Yoho International Youth Hostel is one of the youngest, most centrally located, and cheapest options in Salzburg. The rooms are clean, simple, and spacious, and communal areas like a bar and a lounge with daily *Sound of Music* screenings make Yoho a fun place to hang out with your new hostel friends. Plus, as a family-run establishment, staying here can mean sticking it to the man. Our only complaint is the name, which reminds us of Yoo-hoo chocolate milk (which we are missing dearly while abroad).

*i* Dorms €20-26; reservation required; max stay one week; Wi-Fi; limited wheelchair accessibility; towels €0.50; laundry €2.50 per wash/dry; breakfast buffet €4, dinner €3.50-7

## SIGHTS

### CULTURE

### ⬛SALZBURG CATHEDRAL

Domplatz 1a; 662 80477950; www.salzburger-dom.at; open May-Sept M-Sa 8am-7pm (subject to change for worship)

The Salzburg Cathedral is a massive seventeenth-century Baroque edifice where **Mozart** once served as the church organist. If the exterior looks large, the interior feels even larger, with a nave that seems impossibly vaulted and a series of orange frescoes that heighten the intensity of the white walls. The decorative moulding inside is accented by un-painted groove-work, creating a stark aesthetic contrast and severity that may make you feel meek in comparison. It's exactly the kind of self-esteem booster you were looking for.

*i* Cathedral free, museum admission €12, €10 student; limited wheelchair accessibility

### NONNBERG ABBEY

Nonnberggasse 2; 662 841607; www.benediktinerinnen.de/index.php/adressen/2-uncategorised/26-nonnberg; open daily 7am-dusk (7pm in summer), visits not permitted during worship

The Nonnberg Abbey in Salzburg, established during the beginning of the eighth century, is one of the oldest continuously active nunneries in the world. Created in the late gothic style, the abbey is also known for its smaller works of art and murals. Its true claim

# KEHLSTEINHAUS (EAGLE'S NEST)

Now the location of an upscale restaurant, the Eagle's Nest was once a mountain getaway for Nazi officials, including Adolf Hitler himself. Getting to the Nest involves a winding bus ride up the tree-lined Kehlstein Road, a walk through a long, damp tunnel, and a 124-meter elevator lift straight up through the heart of the Kehlstein mountain. Built in the late 1930s, the house has served a variety of purposes—retreat, symbol of political power, and meeting place, among others. The building itself, however, is relatively unassuming. All of the furnishings, save the stone fireplace, have been removed to avoid glorifying its history.

One thing that hasn't changed over the years is the view from the top of the Kehlstein. On hazy days, you can experience the same panoramas of the Bavarian Alps that the Nest's initial tennants experienced some 90 years before, and on clear days, you can gaze out upon the vast expanses of the Austrian and German countrysides. With walking paths leading to several viewpoints along the rocky summit, it seems that around every corner, beyond every crag, and up every scramble, there is an outlook to rival the last.

If you intend to arrive via public transport, prepare to spend a lot of time on buses. A round-trip ticket to the Eagle's Nest costs about €26.10 and requires two transfers: the first (€10) from bus #840 (which leaves from Mirabellplatz) to bus #838 at the Schießstättbrücke stop in Berchtesgaden, and the second (€16.10) from bus #838 to the Eagle's Nest shuttle at Dokumentation Obersalzberg. Once you've reached the end of Kehlstein Road, you will be asked to register your return time before exiting the bus. Allow yourself an hour, minimum, to explore the grounds, as the line for the lift will take about 20 minutes. Also, remember to pack layers, as the top is often several degrees cooler than the base of the mountain.

to fame, however, may be its role as the abbey of Maria soon-to-be-von-Trapp, whose story was brought to the global stage in the smash-1965-hit, *The Sound of Music*. When the von Trapps married in 1927, they wed at the church of Nonnberg Abbey, though the movie filmed the scene elsewhere. Today, there are 21 nuns living at the abbey.

*i* Free; limited wheelchair accessibility

## ST. PETER'S ABBEY

St. Peter Bezirk ½; 662 8445760; www. erzabtei.at; church open daily Apr-Oct 8am-9pm, Nov-Mar 8am-7pm; cemetery open daily Apr-Sept 6:30am-8pm, Oct-Mar open daily 6:30am-6pm; catacombs open daily May-Sept 10am-6pm, Oct-Apr 10am-5pm

One of the oldest continuously-employed monasteries in German-speaking Europe, St. Peter's Abbey was founded in the seventh century, more than a millennium before its female counterpart, the Nonnberg Abbey. Long connected to the likes of musical geniuses such as **Johann Michael Haydn** and the **Mozart**

family, St. Peter's possesses some 100 autographs of the former and two dozen manuscripts of the latter. Haydn and the sister of W. A. Mozart are also buried in St. Peter's cemetery. The monastery is a large complex with much to see, but the cemetery—famous for its beautiful gravesites—is certainly a highlight.

*i* Catacombs €2, €1.50 student; limited wheelchair accessibility

## LANDMARKS

### ◪RESIDENZ PALACE

Residenzplatz 1; 662 80422109; www. domquartier.at; open M 10am-5pm, W 10am-8pm, Th-Su 10am-5pm

Touring through the Residenz Palace will give you an insight into the Salzburg line of Prince-Archbishops, who dominated both political and religious life in the region until the early nineteenth century. Because of the region's hugely successful salt mining industry, the prince-archbishops had no shortage of funds and were constantly renovating and redecorating the residence, creating lavish series of rooms that are now open for visitors to explore. Come see ceiling frescoes featuring images of Alexander the Great (even supreme rulers need role models), intricately woven tapestries with interpretations of the months of the year—a trending topic at the time—, and works of stucco that will make you say stucc-no you didn't!

*i* Admission €12, €10 student; wheelchair accessible

### FESTUNGSBERG FORTRESS

Hohensalzburg Fortress Mönchsberg 34; 662 84243011; www.festung-salzburg. at; open daily May-Sep 9am-7pm, Oct-Apr 9am-5pm

This mountainside fortress is one of the most important sights in Salzburg and the largest fully-preserved castle in Central Europe. Today, it consists of expansive castle grounds, a restaurant, and walkways along the outer walls with incredible views of the city. The central building has been converted to a museum, where visitors can learn about the fortress' military history as well as what life was like in the Middle Ages. It also includes an exhibit on the use of torture on prisoners during the same era. There is a funicular that shuttles visitors from the base of Festungsberg hill to the entrance of the fortress, but expect the commotion of tourists in line for this option to be downright insanity. We recommend choosing to hike the hill, so long as you're okay spending the rest of the day dripping with sweat.

*i* Basic tickets €12, standard tickets €15.20, discount €2-3 (without lift); guided tours available; last entry 30 minutes before close; limited wheelchair accessibility

### MIRABELL PALACE AND GARDENS

Mirabellplatz; open daily 8am-6pm

The Mirabell Palace and Gardens are, we think, the most significant sight in Salzburg east of the **Salzach River.** The palace itself does not factor significantly into this because, though the Marble Hall is open to the public, the rest of the building is used for office space. The gardens, on the other hand, are a sight to behold. Covered in roses, trees, fountains, and tourists, the gardens include the site upon which The Sound of Music's iconic "Do-Re-Mi" scene was filmed and provide the perfect opportunity to run down a tunnel of vines with your arms outstretched skipping and weaving about wildly.

*i* Free; wheelchair accessible

## MUSEUMS

### ▨MOZART'S GEBURTSHAUS (MOZART'S BIRTHPLACE)

Getreidegasse 9; 662 844313; www. mozarteum.at; open daily 9am-5:30pm

The museum at Mozart's Birthplace is more personal than many accounts you'll find of the great musician's life. Of course, plenty of attention is paid to his career and compositional genius, and the exhibits paint a clear enough picture of his early life as a child prodigy for you to feel inadequate. But, we truly appreciated the displays dedicated to the people who formed the man. See where Mozart spent the first 17 years of his life, learn about his family's involvement in his musical upbringing, and speculate on whether his ex-wife's marriage to his biographer was awkward because they were both in love with the guy. If you're into fetish history, you may also like the several locks of Mozart's hair the museum has managed to preserve.

*i* Admission €11, €9 student; no wheelchair accessibility

### SALZBURG MUSEUM

Mozartplatz 1; 662 620808700; www. salzburgmuseum.at; open Tu-Su 9am-5pm

Voted Europe's best museum in 2009—a title that seems incredibly relevant and we keep falling for even though it was awarded almost a decade ago—the Salzburg Museum houses exhibitions celebrating Salzburg itself. Many of the exhibitions focus on the artistic development of the city itself through a variety of media, including literature, science, craftsmanship, and archeology, among others. The museum is housed in the **Neue Residenz,** across from the **Residenz**

# HALLSTATT

**Describing Hallstatt as "a picturesque lakeside town" as we, admittedly, were about to do, would be a huge understatement.** Compared to the reality of the scene, the adjective "lakeside" is about as lackluster as it gets. Standing on the shore of Hallstätter See, surrounded by stone cliffs and beautiful wooden structures that somehow, despite enduring centuries of harsh weather, are just as vibrant as they were when they were first constructed, is an experience that no image, no matter how enhanced, can truly capture. Hallstatt's nested configuration is accented by the towers of the Lutheran Protestant and Catholic Parish Churches, which draw the eye upward along the steep slopes of the Alps to the sky above. The town is indeed closely linked to the mountains themselves, as its history was shaped by the salt mining industry. Check out the history of saltmining at the Hallstatt Museumor or take a cable car up to see the salt mines themselves.

Hallstatt sits on the southwestern bank of **Hallstätter See**, which itself is located in the southwestern part of Austria. The small town hugs the lake pretty closely, with the city center and promenade—the most tourist-dense region— literally sitting on its shore. For this reason, the water is the simplest way to orient yourself in town. It is almost always visible between buildings, above buildings, or right in front of you. Hallstatt's main street, **Seestraße**, intersects with major thoroughfare **Hallstättersee Landesstraße** (and by major we mean you'll maybe pass a dozen other cars while following it) near **Marktplatz**, the town's main square.

## GETTING THERE

Getting to Hallstatt is easiest by train. Trains stop at many towns surrounding the lake; Hallstatt's station is across the lake from the town itself. A ferry runs back and forth between the station and the center of town, and is both a convenient and fun way to start your visit (€2.50 one-way). Buses also loop from Hallstatt back and forth between Obertraun and Bad Goisern.

## GETTING AROUND

Walk! Apart from bus and ferry services to get in and out of town, walking is your best option, and it's half the fun of visiting the town. Bicycles are a hassle to navigate in the city center, but can be great options for exploring the promenade, nearby beaches (the best are on the southernmost tip of Hallstätter See), or surrounding region.

## Swing by...

### LUTHERAN PROTESTANT CHURCH OF CHRIST IN HALLSTATT
Oberer Marktplatz 167; 6134 82 54; hours vary

A place of worship since 1863, the Lutheran Protestant Church is an interesting cultural sight, sure. Upon entering, you'll be greeted by an understated interior and a note written by the church's pastor encouraging visitors to take whatever words of encouragement they may need from bible verses on display and to have a pleasant visit to the region. But the real reason we love this sight (and the reason we think of it as a crucial landmark) is because of its tall steeple, which reaches far above all but the highest hillside buildings in town and defines the Hallstatt skyline.

*i* Free; limited wheelchair accessibility

## Check out...

### MUSEUM OF HALLSTATT

Seestraße 56A; 6134 8280 15; www.museum-hallstatt.at; open daily 10am-6pm

The Museum of Hallstatt tells the history of the region, beginning in 7000 BCE and reaching the current day, through exhibits of archaeological artifacts uncovered at excavation sites in the region (some of the findings can also be seen at the **Natural History Museum in Vienna**). The most important part of the region's history is its relationship with salt mining, which the museum explains in detail. In our opinion, the highlights of the museum were the interactive videos that accompany each exhibition, some of which are even 3D.

*i* Admission €10, €8 student; last entry 5pm; no wheelchair accessibility

## Grab a bite at...

### CAFÉ ZUM MÜHLBACH ($$)

Oberer Marktplatz 53; 0676 534 85 19; open Tu-Su 10am-7pm

Just slightly off **Seestraße**, Café zum Mühlbach offers a handful of quick-seller menu items—burgers, pizza, pastries, and beer—alongside fish, caught fresh from the lake daily. The patio seating spans the width of multiple buildings, creating its own de facto square on the small, quiet street. As for the pizza, the crust is fluffy and delicious, but for a cheese pizza, the amount of cheese is admittedly borderline paltry, not the gooey cheese-laden dairy swamp we prefer.

*i* Entrées €5.50-13.30, fresh fish €18-20; cash only; vegetarian options available; limited wheelchair accessibility

## Don't miss...

### HALLSTÄTTER SEE

Boat rental hours in season 6am-8pm

The best part about visiting Hallstatt is the Hallstätter See, so use it! Of all of the outdoor activities available, we recommend hitting the beach or renting a boat. Beaches can be found on the south rim of the lake, between Hallstatt and Obertraun, and are free to use. Signs for boat rentals are visible all over Seestraße. If you're traveling in a small group, we recommend the paddle boats, an age-old tourist classic, but small motor boats are also available.

*i* Boat rentals €10-20, depending on boat type and time

41

**Palace,** which once belonged to the prince-archbishops of the city.

*i* *Admission €8.50, €4 student; wheelchair accessible*

# FOOD

### CAFÉ LATINI ($$)

Judengasse 17; 662 842338; cafelatini.at; open summer M-Sa 9am-10pm, Su 10am-10pm; winter M-Sa 9am-7pm, Su 10am-6pm

Drawn by the promise of a Latini Panini (they don't call them this, but they should), we gravitated to this café after a tiring stint in the **DomQuartier museums.** The café name may have "Latin" in it, but Café Latini still offers Austrian foods at an affordable price, like goulash and a pastry (€5.70) or sausages with mustard and horseradish (€4.80). Often, the specials board includes an offering of paninis (€6.80), piled high with salami, bacon, tomato, and mozzarella.

*i* *Entrées €4-13; vegetarian options available; limited wheelchair accessibility*

### CAFÉ TOMASELLI ($$)

Alter Markt 9; 662 8444880; www.tomaselli.at; open M-Sa 7am-7pm, Su 8am-7pm; summer open M-Sa 7am-9pm, Su 8am-9pm; summer kiosk open M-F 11am-6pm, Sa 10am-6pm

Established in 1705 as Café Staiger, this charming establishment was once frequented by members of the Mozart family and is now one of Salzburg's most famous cafés. It takes great pride in the tradition of Austrian coffee houses and serves a food menu of Austrian breakfast classics: eggs, ham, and toast with jam. Though many of the options are admittedly out of the backpacker price range, some egg dishes won't break the bank, and you can enjoy one on a second-floor balcony overlooking a courtyard next to the **Residenz Palace.** Café Tomaselli is worth a visit for its history alone, so if you're hungry but not willing to splurge, grab a bite at nearby Kiosk Tomaselli.

*i* *Entrées €5-17; vegetarian options available; wheelchair accessible*

### FUCHSHOFER BAKERY ($$)

Linzergasse 13; 6769 352551; open M-Sa 9am-7pm, Su 11am-6pm

A quaint café on a main pedestrian street on the east side of the river, Fuchshofer serves light breakfasts, smoothies, and refreshments. Its true draw, however, lies in the pile of fresh-made pastries sitting in the storefront. When we visited, the display case was literally overflowing with sweet, breaded treats. Walking past it takes an inconceivable amount of will-power. Better to just give in, we'd say, and opt for a **plate-sized sticky bun.** Though it won't last long in your hands, it'll last long in your stomach, giving you the kick in the ass (more like sticking to your ass, are we right?) needed to get up off your chair and on your way.

*i* *Breakfast €4-20, cakes and pastries €2-3; vegetarian options available; limited wheelchair accessibility*

### GASTHAUS WILDER MANN ($$)

Getreidegasse 20; 662 841787; www.wildermann.co.at; open M-Sa 11am-9pm

Nestled in an alleyway that took us way too long to find (seriously, we walked right past it five times–turns out it's the

alley next to Café Mozart), Gasthaus Wilder Mann is a local favorite for regional cuisine. As such, you should be aware that "Salzburg's calf's lights" refers to calf lung and heart, which we found out when we tried to order it and the waiter was like, "Um, I don't think you have any idea what that is. You're getting your advice from experts here," and that salad refers to a small bowl of sauerkraut topped with shredded carrots and a few leaves of lettuce. A menu section of light fare items also provides options at a lower price.

*i* *Entrées €9-15; limited wheelchair accessibility*

# NIGHTLIFE
## AUGUSTINE BREWERY AND BEER HALL
Lindhofstraße 7; 662 431246; www. augustinerbier.at; open M-F 3pm-11pm, Sa-Su 2:30pm-11pm

If you are a human visiting Salzburg, we recommend a trip to the Augustinian Brewery. The beer hall includes a range of food vendors covering all five food groups: ham, sausage, salami, pretzels, and strudel. Beer is sold only by the liter (€6.20) or half liter (€3.10). Where the beer is always flowing, there is little time to fret about the timid naïveté of novice travelers, so when you get to the taproom entrance, fall in line and do what the person in front of you is doing. Soon you'll have a cold beer thrust #unfabulously into your hands by a grumpy bar-keep in a rush to fill the next pint. Take your bounty to one of the cafeteria halls or hang out in the massive beer garden, packed with people drinking their weight in the liquid gold.

*i* *No cover, half-liter €3.10, liter €6.20*

## CITY BEATS
Griesgasse 23; 0664 149 10 00; www. citybeats.at; open Th-Sa 9pm-5am

One of Salzburg's only real nightclubs, City Beats doesn't get busy until around 1am, making it the perfect last stop for a night full of cocktails and dance battles. Depending on the night, you may be greeted at the door by glittering shirtless gladiators or women on stilts—a ploy, we're convinced, to distract you from the three bouncers lumbering at the door. A big part of getting into City Beats is making sure you look the part. If you arrive dressed head to toe in workout clothes, regardless of the fact that you made the conscious decision to wear all black in hopes that your travel-wear could pass for club-wear, you will not make the cut.

*i* *Cover up to €10, drink prices vary; cash only; upscale club attire recommended*

## MENTOR'S BAR KULTURE
Gstättengasse 3; 6649133810; open M-W 4pm-1am, Th-Sa 4pm-2am

"Trendy" is the word that first comes to mind when describing Mentor's Bar. There's so much hip shoved into such a small space that it's easy to feel suffocated by it, but it'll also make you feel way cooler than you normally are. Clad in skinny jeans, suspenders, facial hair, and manicured button-downs that scream Los-Angeles hipster, the bartenders serve up a variety of drinks, including originals concocted on the spot. If you like gin, you'll get a kick out of the **Cranberry Cobbler** and **Torino Smash,** mixed with homemade cranberry syrup and mint, respectively. Mentor's serves some damn good cocktails, so go ahead, sip yours slowly and experience some Urban-Outfitters-circa-2013-euphoria.

*i* *No cover, cocktails €9-15; BGLTQ+ friendly; limited wheelchair accessibility*

# VIENNA

Coverage by **Antonia Washington**

With a look and feel something between the likes of Paris and Manhattan, Vienna is a dream in the heart of Central Europe. One of the most open and fun-loving cities in the area, Vienna is also one of the music capitals of the world and boasts a proud history of operatic and orchestral music. Its claim to fame is arguably its ties to great composers from Mozart to Beethoven to the guy who was super jealous of Mozart (what was his name again? Oh yeah, Salieri). Sit endlessly in cafés sipping cappuccinos and eating strudel, stroll major shopping streets, or relax in one of Vienna's many parks to soak in the city's spirit. A haven of chic, fashion-forward sun-seekers (who are perhaps less stuffy than those of Paris), Vienna is the place to take a risk. Break out those mustard yellow trousers, wear beige from head to toe like a Kardashian, or try to bring back flare jeans. We still, however, recommend against wearing a fedora, as with anytime and anywhere in the world. (Possibly the only exception is if you are in Cuba, under very specific circumstances. We think you should be Cuban, wearing white and/or linen pants, and your name should not be Pitbull because something about that guy just pisses us off. If you're racially ambiguous and playing someone Cuban for a movie like Vin Diesel in *The Fate of the Furious,* that's probably fine. You didn't even wear a fedora in that movie, but you're eternally off the hook, Vin.) With that digression, enter Vienna, land of culture, land of fashion, land of modern European living. Think New York City, if it were sunnier and more pedestrian-friendly.

## ORIENTATION

Vienna rests on the **Danube River** (known as *Donau* in German), but because the river used to flood the city in the rainy-season, the city center makes less use of the river and it isn't as useful as rivers typically are in Central Europe. Damn the floods. Instead, orient yourself in relation to the **Ring Boulevard** (the name of this street changes in its different segments, but "Ring" is always in the name, and it is easy to identify on a map because of its circular shape). This street encircles the inner city, running the approximate route of the former city walls. Within the ring is the historic city center, including the **Hofburg Imperial Palace** and **St. Stephen's Cathedral**. Rimming the ring to its southern and western edges are many important public buildings like **City Hall**, the **Vienna State Opera**, and **Maria-Theresien-Platz**, which ties the city center to the **Museums Quartier**. Within the city center, major streets include **Kärntnerstraße** and **Herrengaße**. Another important neighborhood in the city is **Neubaugasse**, situated southwest of the city center in the seventh district. The neighborhood centers around **Neubaugasse** and **Mariahilfer Straße**, especially to the northeast of their intersection.

## ESSENTIALS
### GETTING THERE

Vienna is accessible by plane or train from just about anywhere. Trains come right into the city at Wien Mitte (city center), Wien Westbanhof, or Vienna Central Station. Planes fly into the Vienna International Airport ("Flughafen Wien"). Be aware that the airport is not actually that close to the city. From the airport, the fastest public transport to the city is the C.A.T. train to Wien Mitte (€12). The S7 train (€4) also runs from the airport to Wien Mitte, although it makes several stops. Wien Mitte is a metro transfer station to metro lines U3 and U4. Taxis are expensive, but may cost less than the C.A.T. if you are traveling in a group.

### GETTING AROUND

Public transport in Vienna is easily navigable. If you need to go a significant distance within the city, the metro is often the simplest way to travel. Metro stops are demarcated by a "U" and each line is associated with a number and a color. For example, the first metro line is called "U1" and is always marked in red. Single ride tickets for the metro are €2.20. Within the historic city center, most destinations tend to be reachable on foot. Bicycles are also extremely popular in Vienna. City Bike in Vienna is free for the first hour and then the cost doubles in each of the three following hours.

## PRACTICAL INFORMATION

**Tourist Offices:** There is one main tourist office in the city center called Tourist-Info Wien (Albertinaplatz S; www.wien.info/en; open daily 9am-7pm).

**Banks/ATMs/Currency Exchange:** Even in this large city, do not expect every business to accept cards. Cafés, especially, often only take cash. ATMs, however, are widely available; if at all possible, though, avoid using ATMs in major tourist areas such as St. Stephen's Cathedral because there have been increasing reports of ATM fraud.

**Post Offices:** There are post offices throughout the city. The post office website, with a branch locator, can be found at www.post.at. We have listed a central location (Fleischmarkt 19; open M-F 7am-10pm, Sa-Su 9am-10pm).

**Internet:** Many major attractions, plazas, and public transport stations have free Wi-Fi (look for networks like Freeware or Free Austrian Internet), though network connection and strength are often unpredictable. Free Wi-Fi access is also available at the tourist office.

**BGLTQ+ Resources:** The tourist information office of Vienna produces a pamphlet called the Gay & Lesbian Guide (and stocks others) with information on BGLTQ+-specific events, sights, bars, and more. Pick up a pamphlet in person or go to www.vienna.info/gay to learn more.

## EMERGENCY INFORMATION

**Emergency Number:** 112

**Police:** There are police stations available all over Vienna, and most of them are marked on tourist maps. We have listed one central location (Brandstätte 4; open M-F 8am-6pm).

**US Embassy:** The US Embassy in Vienna is located on the north side of the city center (Boltzmanngasse 16; 1 31339 0; open M-F 8am-4:30pm)

**Rape Crisis Center:** If you have been a victim of sexual assault, you can reach out to Weisser Ring. They are not a sexual assault-specific crisis center, but they specialize in victim advocacy and their services are free (Nußdorfer Straß, 67, 1090 Wien; 01 712 14 05; open M-Th 9am-4pm, F 9am-3pm).

**Hospitals:** There are two main hospitals in Vienna. The first is Allgemeines Krankenhaus (AKH), which typically treats sickness and disease; if you contract Ebola, you should go here. The second is Unfallkrankenhaus (UKH), which typically treats traumatic injuries; if you're hit by a car, you should go here. In case of a life-threatening emergency, an ambulance will transport you to the nearest one; they are both well equipped to deal with a range of medical issues.
- AKH (Währinger Gürtel 18-20; 1 40400 0; open daily 24hr).
- UKH (Kundratstraße 37; 5 93 934 50 00; open daily 24hr).

**Pharmacies:** Pharmacies typically will say "Apotheke." They are marked with a red symbol that looks like a cursive "L" connected to a pillar, making a shape that looks sort of like a "4."
- Internationale Apotheke (01 512 28 25).
- Apotheke am Naschmarkt (01 586 51 59).

# ACCOMMODATIONS

### HAPPY HOSTEL ($$)

Kurzgasse 2; 1 208 26 18; www.happyhostel.at; reception open 24hr

Happy Hostel offers a quiet, sleepy stay on the western edge of the **Naschmarkt district,** with small but homey rooms and facilities. All rooms are equipped with access to a kitchenette, but the hostel also provides breakfast. The hostel donates the tips from breakfast to their partner NGO Happy Africa, which works building schoolhouses and medical facilities in the Democratic Republic of the Congo. Unfortunately, the existence of dorms at the Happy Hostel is on the fritz because of noise considerations for the building's other tenants, but apartment prices are generally still affordable.

*i* Apartments with shared facilities single €35-36, double €24-26, triple €22-24, quad €21-22, private facilities; other dorms €20-50; reservation recommended; BGLTQ+ friendly; limited wheelchair accessibility; Wi-Fi; laundry facilities €2 per wash or dry; breakfast served for tips

### A&O WIEN HAUPBAHNHOF ($$)

Sonnwendgasse 11; 1602 0617 3800; www.aohostels.com; reception open 24hr

A&O Wien Hauptbahnhof feels more like a hotel than a hostel, with wide tiled corridors and a lobby where kids run around or cling to their parents' legs waiting to check-in. Between the tile and the blue and orange color scheme, it somehow seems like a public pool doing its best to seem sterile. Large common areas provide opportunities to meet other solo travelers, but it may take a little extra effort. Our greatest critique is that A&O will nickel and dime you. Here, you'll pay for everything from using the foosball table (€5/hr.) to renting sheets (€3.50).

*i* Dorms from €20-30; reservation recommended; 14 nights max stay; wheelchair accessible; Wi-Fi; €2.95 fee if paying with card; towels and linens not included

### HOSTEL RUTHSTEINER ($$)

Robert Hamerlinggasse 24; 1 89 34 202; www.hostelruthensteiner.com; reception open 24hr

Hostel Ruthensteiner sometimes feels like a commercial. Sitting in the common areas or sipping a beer in the garden, you will find groups of travelers planning their activities, meeting other backpackers for the first time, or breaking out a deck of Uno playing cards. Ambiguous rock music plays in the background and occasionally, someone pulls down a guitar or a ukulele from the wall and starts strumming out a familiar melody. With spacious, usually well-populated common areas and helpful staff, Ruthensteiner is a great place to meet other travelers.

*i* Dorms €10-30, singles €36-50; reservation recommended; BGLTQ+ friendly; no wheelchair accessibility; Wi-Fi; 3% charge if paying with card; laundry facilities €2 per wash or dry; breakfast buffet €4.50

### MENINGER HOSTEL CENTRAL STATION ($$)

Columbusgasse 16; 0720 88 14 53; www. meininger-hotels.com; reception open 24hr

Part hostel and part hotel, Meininger Central Station (Hauptbahnhof) has a clean, modern aesthetic. A huge but basic breakfast room dominates the main floor, and the common rooms next to it are comfortable areas for hanging out. Meininger sometimes hosts large groups and, in our few days there, we overlapped with a lacrosse team, a boys' choir, and a bunch of other people rubbing it in our face that they travel with friends. The group dynamic of travelers here can make it hard to meet people, so we recommend the hostel to groups more than solo travelers. It is a convenient ride on the **U1** from the city center, which is ideal because the walk is not particularly exciting.

*i* Dorms €20-30; reservation recommended; min stay 2 nights on peak weekends; wheelchair accessible; Wi-Fi; towels not included; breakfast €6.90; packed lunch €4.50

### SEVEN HOSTEL ($)

Lindengasse 4A; 1070; 06908 012 813; www.bestlocation.at; reception open daily 9am-11:30am, 1:30pm-7pm, and 9-11pm

Seven Hostel Vienna will not be the cleanest hostel you have ever stayed in, and you won't stay too long to hang out there. But if all you need is a bed, it does the trick. The hostel isn't insurmountably dirty, but most of the time it smells just a little bit like sweat and urine, reminiscent of that one kid we all had in our high school PE class. The shower-stall floors are always wet and, on summer nights, when everyone gets in bed, it can become extremely humid. The perks of the hostel are few, but significant: the showers are hot and well pressured, the location is very central, and the beds are some of the cheapest in the city.

*i* Dorms €10-20; reservation recommended; BGLTQ+ friendly; wheelchair accessible; Wi-Fi

# SIGHTS

## CULTURE

### KARLS KIRCHE (ST. CHARLES CHURCH)

Karlsplatz; 1 505 62 94; www.karlskirche. at; open M-Sa 9am-6pm, Su noon-7pm

You'll find St. Charles Church looming over the plaza at **Karlsplatz,** where dogs splash nearby in the fountain and the sun beats down on the church's high, green dome. Inside, incense burns steadily, making the air as thick as a Young Thug music video. Behind the haze, a huge altar shows off an opulent work of gold and stone meant to depict God's light. The dome of the church is 74m. high and guests can visit the top, where there is a view of the city, though unfortunately it hides behind windows and fencing. The walk to the top will take you through a monstrous collection of scaffolding, giving you a rare personal look at the ceiling frescos, but if you drop your phone, you're so screwed.

*i* *Admission €8, €4 student; no wheelchair accessibility*

## MUSIK MÜLLER

Krugerstraße 4A; 01512 28 75; www.mayrische.at; open M-F 10am-1pm and 2-7pm

In the heart of Vienna lies a small storefront that reads "Musik Müller." Musik Müller is a sheet music store where you will find a selection ranging from orchestral classics to the score of *La La Land*. Our favorites are titles that claim to offer "The 14 Most Passionate Latin Songs," and "Love Songs from the Movies," with music from *Pretty Woman, Dirty Dancing,* and *Footloose,* among others. Maybe one day, they'll have sheet music written by you. Because in a city of music, the true magic is to play your own. The highest form of being is artistry; isn't that why Kanye claimed to be a god?

*i* *Free entry; no wheelchair accessibility*

## NASCHMARKT

Naschmarkt; www.naschmarkt-vienna.com

Open air markets are often where cities show off their best selves. The Naschmarkt, at the confluence of Vienna's first, fifth, and sixth districts, pulls out all the stops. Picture this: aisles lined with colorful assortments of food from ripe red tomatoes to fresh baklava to Turkish delight to dried fruit. Booths are stacked high with hundreds of bags of curry powder. Restaurants range from fish counters to bakeries. On Saturdays, a flea market sets up shop. Beware: excessive flirting with the young vendors along the walk may get you swindled into buying an absurd amount of candied nuts. Then again, who doesn't love candied nuts?

*i* *Prices vary by stand; wheelchair accessible; flea market Sa 6:30am-6pm*

## OPERA HOUSE

Opernring 2; 1514 442 250; www.wiener-staatsoper.at

Built in the mid-nineteenth century, the Vienna State Opera is a central feature in the music history of a city whose enormous contributions have been confirmed again and again. Though only the front portions of the opera house remain in their original form because much of it was destroyed during WWII, it still feels like one of Europe's great opera houses (take that, Paris). Standing room tickets sell for a handful of euros, allowing you to explore the building and experience the opera for cheaper than a guided tour, though you may miss tidbits about the emperor drinking in his tea room instead of watching the show or figures on how much people spend for a table at the Opera Ball (let's just say it's a lot).

*i* *Tours €7.50, €3.50 student, standing room at performances vary by show as low as €3-5; tours daily in English 2pm and 3pm (may vary by season); wheelchair accessible*

## STEPHANSDOM (ST. STEPHEN'S CATHEDRAL)

Stephansplatz; 1 51552 3054; www.stephanskirche.at; open M-Sa 6am-10pm, Su 7am-10pm

This massive work of medieval Gothic style and home of the **Roman Catholic Archdiocese** is one of the most visited sights in all Vienna. At its highest point, the south tower of St. Stephen's Cathedral stands 137m. tall, making it one of the tallest built in the Middle Ages. The church's cavernous interior features an assortment of altars and ornamental characteristics of note, but our favorite part is perhaps the simple stained glass windows reflecting light off the massive stone-carved pilasters, making the ceiling of the nave look submerged in water. Visiting the cathedral's towers is also essential, as they offer visitors expansive views of the city, though a view devoid of the cathedral itself, a characteristic piece of the skyline.

*i* *Free admission, towers and catacombs €4-6; wheelchair accessible; tour times and prices vary by sight at St. Stephen's, check the website for more information*

# LANDMARKS

## 🏛BELVEDERE PALACE

Prinz Eugen-Straße 27; 1 795 57 134;
www.belvedere.at; palace open daily 9am-
6pm (21er Haus opens 11am), lower Belvedere and 21er Haus open W until 9pm,
palace stables open daily 10am-noon

The Belvedere Palace, once home to
nobility of the **Habsburg dynasty,**
now houses the world's largest single
collection of works by celebrated
Viennese painter **Gustav Klimt.**
Klimt's famous masterpiece, *The Kiss,*
is the Belvedere's prized possession.
Not only can you stand in front of the
original, but you can visit the "selfie
room" right next door where a poster
board of the painting lets visitors
pucker up and snap a picture alongside
the lovebirds. Pick your favorite pose,
but we like standing next to the couple
and giving the classic "I knew I was
going to be the third wheel" eye-roll.
Make sure to experience the palace
itself, which is said to be one of the
most important Baroque structures
in Austria, with gardens that you can
peruse for free.

*i* Upper Belvedere €15, €12.50 student,
Lower Belvedere €13, €10 student, both
Upper and Lower Belvedere €20, student
€17; both Upper and Lower Belvedere with
Winter Palace €26, €22 student; include
21er Haus museum of contemporary art
€23, €19.50 student, audio guides €3-4;
gardens free; wheelchair accessible

## HOFBURG

Michaelerkuppel; www.hofburg-wien.
at; open daily Sept-June 9am-5:30pm,
July-Aug 9am-6pm

Hofburg Imperial Palace is an elegant
monstrosity of Baroque architecture
where you could spend all day getting
lost in the museum and then even
more lost on the palace grounds. The
complex is so big that you may find
yourself asking, "Why do rich people
do this? They couldn't have just had a
normal sized palace with one building
and common sense hallways?" One
of the most celebrated sights at the
palace is the **Sisi Museum,** where
you can view famous portraits of
legend-inspiring **Empress Elisabeth.**
The museum is by no means the only
attraction on the grounds, though:
check out the state hall of the **Austrian**

**National Library,** the largest Baroque
library in Europe.

*i* Prices vary by attraction; tours of Sisi
Museum and Imperial Apartments €16.90,
€15.90 students; tours of Sisi Museum
and Imperial Apartments daily 2pm; last
entry 30min. before closing; wheelchair
accessible

## PRATER

Prater 7/3; 1 729 20 00; www.praterwien.
com; open daily Mar 15-Oct 31 noon-midnight

The Prater is an amusement park on
the north end of the city where you
will find Vienna's **Giant Ferris Wheel.**
Built in the nineteenth century, it was
one of the largest ferris wheels in the
world during its heyday and it still
offers incredible views of the city. A
staple of Vienna and a symbol of the
city's fun-loving character, it was one
of the first major constructions to be
restored after WWII. Call it old-age,
since it moves at a glacial pace. But
that's not a big deal since you don't
want to miss the perfect shot of
Vienna, rollercoasters, and children
driven to the edge of madness by the
ecstasy of sugar and adrenaline.

*i* Free entry to park, rides have individual
prices, Giant Ferris Wheel €10; wheelchair
accessible

## RATHAUS (VIENNA CITY HALL)

Friedrich-Schmidt-Platz 1; 1 525 50; www.
wien.gv.at/english/cityhall

Vienna City Hall is a display of Gothic
showmanship that will make you think
of the city hall in your hometown and
be grateful your tax dollars only pay
for the bare necessities. The building's
high gothic towers are reminiscent of
the spires built on cathedrals, and we've
heard of multiple people mistaking city
hall for **St. Stephen's Cathedral** upon
first glance. We don't think taking a
tour of this landmark is necessary, but
it's definitely worth checking out. The
park out front is lined with benches
squeezed tightly shoulder to shoulder if
you need to rest in the shade.

*i* Free; wheelchair accessible

## SCHÖNBRUNN PALACE

Schloß Schönbrunn; 181 11 30; www.
schoenbrunn.at; open daily Apr-June 8am-
5:30pm, July-Aug 8am-6:30pm, Sept-Oct

8am-5:30pm, Nov-Mar 8am-5pm; main gardens open daily 6:30am, closing times vary by season

Schönbrunn Palace, the summer residence of the **Habsburg monarchs,** is the largest and most ostentatious of the palaces in Vienna, expanded in size because of the industrious procreation of the Habsburg family (Empress Maria Theresa had 16 children, which we think sounds excruciatingly awful, but to each their own). Visitors can tour the palace rooms, visit the **Schönbrunn Zoo,** or spend time meandering the gardens. Built on more than 400 acres of land, the gardens are expansive, with extremely varied designs. Think, grass areas, rose gardens, an enormous fountain, and tunnels and mazes of vines. Bring a picnic or a book and spend some time enjoying what the Habsburgs once thought of casually as their backyard—probably procreation.

*i* *Palace tickets €14.20-17.50, main gardens free, other garden attractions €3.80-5.50 each, all-attraction pass €24; wheelchair accessible*

## MUSEUMS

### LEOPOLD MUSEUM

MuseumsQuartier, Museumsplatz 1; 1 52 57 00; www.leopoldmuseum.org; open daily M-W 10am-6pm, Th 10am-9pm, F-Su 10am-6pm

The Leopold Museum, one of the major institutions within Vienna's **MuseumsQuartier,** is known especially for its collection of works by painter Egon Schiele, who was inspired and advised by (guess who?) **Gustav Klimt.** The founder of the Leopold Museum, Rudolf Leopold, spent more than a half century compiling the collection of Schiele's work. Can anyone say, um, stalker? Though Schiele is particularly well-known for his self portraits, one of our favorite pieces is **House Wall on the River** (1915), which depicts a patchworked house. But in front of the cracked and graying concrete façade, a clothesline is strung with colorful shirts and fabrics. The oil paint is raised from the canvas especially on these fabrics, so that they seem to float in the foreground of the scene.

*i* *Admission €13, €9 student, audio guide €4-7; wheelchair accessible*

### MUMOK

MuseumsQuartier, Museumsplatz 1; 1 52 50 00; www.mumok.at; open M 2pm-7pm, Tu-W 10am-7pm, Th 10am-9pm, F-Su 10am-7pm

We can never guess what's showing at mumok, the museum of modern arts, on any given day – though it's sure to be something that piques your curiosity. With exhibitions curated by both the artists themselves and guest curators, the museum provides an uninhibited space for the curator's vision, allowing it to be completely transformed with the intention of display in mind: in effect, the museum itself becomes part of the exhibition. This is all very vague, we know, but mumok holds the true surprise in its MuseumsQuartier location.

*i* Admission €11, €7.50 student; tours in English Sa 4pm; wheelchair accessible

### VIENNA MUSEUM KARLSPLATZ
Karlsplatz 8; 1040; 01 505 87 47; www. wienmuseum.at; open Tu-Su 10am-6pm

The Vienna Museum focuses on the history of the city itself. Though it displays many exhibitions from Viennese artists and features installments tracing the history of the city's nobility, our favorite pieces are those dedicated to the city's physical form. These include several large, wood-carved models of Vienna over time; they are attempts to define the whole of Vienna, but their image of the whole will never be objective or complete. It's all very "existential teen realizing there are no universal truths," but we're into it.

*i* Admission €10, €7 student, free first Su of the month; free tours Su 11am; wheelchair accessible

## OUTDOORS

### THE CANAL
In the summer months, the canal is the perfect place to see the city and the river come together. Wide walkways give lots of room for foot traffic, biking, and roller blading. Friends and couples out for a stroll often sit on the edge of the canal wall and dangle their feet into the water. Check out the canal area next to **Schwedenplatz square.** Here, you'll find beverage and snack stands with sand areas and lounge chairs for reclining in the sun (somebody call Corona because it may be artificial, but we found our beach). Nearby, the **Badeschiff Wien** offers a pool above the river, a restaurant, and a sun deck. Be aware that more forested parts of the canal may be unsettling areas to walk alone at night.

*i* Pool day-pass at Badeschiff €5; most of the access points are stairs, but there are occasional cars down there so there has to be a ramp somewhere

# FOOD

### AMERLINGBEISL ($)
Stiftgasse 8; 1070; 15261660; www. amerlingbeisl.at; open summer daily 9am-2am, winter M-Sa noon-midnight, Su 9am-midnight

The outdoor seating is a major key when it comes to Amerlingbeisl restaurant. With garden and patio space, outdoor seating is extensive but still often nearly full. Tendrils of hanging vines dot the garden, nearly tickling the heads of guests walking through to find their seats. Eat amid soft yellow light from wall lamps that sit in vinyl records molded into lampshades. The food is mostly standard Austrian fare, and we recommend the beef goulash with bread dumplings, though this may be personal bias because we are suckers for bread dumplings.

*i* Dishes €6-12; vegetarian options available; limited wheelchair accessibility

### CAFÉ TIROLERHOF ($)
Führichgasse 8; 1010; 01 512 78 33; open M-Sa 7am-10pm, Su 9:30am-8pm

A café house that feels a bit like a *Sherlock Holmes* movie, Café Tirolerhof features those old tea room style booths that nobody knows the name of but we find delightful and intriguing. Take a seat at a velvety booth rounded inward to hang out with friends, or at one rounded outward to sit with your back to your arch nemesis Moriarty and inconspicuously whisper threats to each other without ever seeing the other's face. Serving Viennese breakfast until 11am, it also has all-day menu consisting mostly of egg dishes.

*i* Dishes €4-8; vegetarian options available; limited wheelchair accessibility

### MOZART'S ($$)
Haidmannsgasse 8; 1150; 1892 08 78; www.mozartsvienna.com; open daily M-Th 6pm-2am, F-Sa 6pm-6am, Su 6pm-2am

Mozart's is a dinner and late-night restaurant serving delicious Austrian cuisine. Grab a booth, hang your hat on the coat rack at every table, and take a seat on a sheepskin rug covering the restaurant's smooth wood benches. We recommend the pan-fried dumplings and scrambled eggs (€6.90), a savory scramble of potato, egg, and onion that is comfort food at its finest. For dessert, go for the apple strudel (€4.20) or try the pulled fluffy pancakes with rum-soaked raisins and stewed plums (€6.80), which come as bite sized poppers that are easy to share between friends. If that wasn't enough, put in an order online and they'll deliver.

*i* *Entrées €6-16; vegetarian options available; no wheelchair accessibility*

### 🗝VOLLPENSION ($)

Schleifmühlgasse 16; 1585 04 64; www.vollpension.wien; open Tu-Th 9am-10pm, F-Sa 9am-midnight, Su 9am-8pm

In a brick basement, amid a soundtrack of tunes from the golden oldies, Vollpension has created an antique living room café. You might recognize it from *I Love Lucy* reruns, all the time you spent obsessing over mid-century aesthetics on Tumblr, or your actual grandma's house. With offerings made by a group of grandparents, watch an 80-year-old man bake cake after cake right at the counter while you sip a cappuccino or a wine spritzer. Live a *Pink Lady* fantasy when you order **Gerti's Breakfast,** a bun with butter and homemade jam served with a glass of prosecco, a tabloid magazine, and pink nail polish (€4.80). Or treat yourself to a tart (€3.90). Pastry selections vary by chef, dictated by which of their own family recipes they'd like to share with the world.

*i* *Cake €3.20, tart €3.90, breakfast €4.80-8.90, other light dishes €4-8.90; vegetarian, vegan, or gluten-free options available; no wheelchair accessibility*

### CENTIMETER II RESTAURANT ($$)

Stiftgasse 4; 1070; 1 470060 642; www.centimeter.at; open M-Th 8:30am-midnight, F-Sa 8:30am-1am, Su 8:30am-midnight

For those of you leaving the United States out of devotion to the metric system (probably the reason for most of our expats, don't you think?), and for the rest of you with a little metric pride, this is the restaurant for you. Centimeter Restaurant takes its name seriously, with measuring tape decor, "science experiment" beaker shots by a ruler stand, and even measurement based foods! Try one of their specialty bread pastries ordered by the centimeter (€0.20-0.25/cm

depending on warm or cold). Treat yourself to two meters of sausage (€9.20), or if you're with a group, get one Meter of Austria, a meter-long box with six different servings of traditional Austrian cuisine (€28).

*i* *Entrées €6-15; vegetarian options available; limited wheelchair accessibility*

### FIGLMÜLLER ($$)

Wollzeile 5; 1512 61 77; www.figlmuller.at; open daily 11am-10:30pm

A popular restaurant in Vienna's central city, Figlmüller claims to be the home of the **schnitzel,** a massive, flat, breaded pork dish, which, from afar, looks something like a cross between fried chicken and an elephant ear dessert. The reality is a larger than life meat pancake. You can give it a go (€14.90), but it's large enough to split if you're not up for the commitment. This is usually paired with potato field salad (€4.70), but be warned that the dressing has a flavor we can only describe as a combination of mayonnaise and balsamic. If you plan to eat here for dinner you will need reservations, but you might be able to wiggle in for lunch.

*i* *Entrées €9-15; no wheelchair accessibility*

### WIENERWALD RESTAURANT ($$)

Annagasse 3; 1010 Wien; 15123766; www.wienerwald.at; open daily 11am-11pm

Our eyes see Wienerwald, but our brains see Wiener World. Think of the comedic potential; all the thinly veiled references to museums in Iceland. We were so ready to write, "Sorry, you'll have to go to Reykjavík for that." Sadly, the menu is surprisingly devoid of sausage; we only counted four schnitzel dishes. Mostly, there is a wide variety of breaded and fried meats. Pro-tip: skip the fried stuff (your cardiologist will thank you) and order the grilled chicken in garlic butter with a baked potato and sour cream (€11.90). With a portion size of one half chicken, once you get around the bones the meat is tender and the garlic butter gives it a soft, melt-in-your-mouth taste.

*i* *Main dishes €8-15; vegetarian options available; limited wheelchair accessibility*

# NIGHTLIFE

## 1516 BREWING COMPANY

Schwarzenbergstraße 2; 1961 15 16; open M-Su 10am-2am

If you're in the market for a killer local beer, look no further than Vienna's own 1516 Brewing Company. Offering an array of unfiltered beers (mostly ales and lagers), it's hard to go wrong. Try one of their summery selections like an IPA spiced with earl grey tea, a lager and lemonade shandy, or an elderflower gose. We recommend coming with friends, ordering a round of different styles to pass around, and getting a big plate of bar snacks to split. One of our favorite bar snacks was the potato wedges with aioli and cheddar cheese melted on top, a slippery and cheesy delight that, similar to Totino's Pizza Rolls, will scald your mouth in all the right ways.

*i* No cover, drinks €2.10-4.50, food €4-12; BGLTQ+ friendly

## DANZÓN

Johannesgasse 3; 676 5505 840; www. danzon.club; open daily Tu 6pm-2am, W-Th 6pm-4am, F-Sa 6pm-6am

If you need some Latin flavor in your Central European adventure (don't we all?), Danzón is a lounge where you can expect to see some serious dancing with couples twirling around the dance floor to salsa, bachata, and rumba. Frankly, we need those couples to lower the barrier to entry for the rest of us. The club lends itself to stylized dancing more than downright clubbing, but the mood is light and receptive to veterans and beginners alike. Spanish-speakers may find a bartender dressed head to toe in white chatting them up about those family members who salsa way too aggressively.

*i* Cocktails €8-12; cash preferred, card accepted

## GRELLE FORELLE

Spittelauer Lände 12; www.grelleforelle. com; www.grelleforelle.com; open daily F-Sa 11pm-6am

If you're looking for a place to dance all night to live DJs and performances of mostly electronic music, Grelle Forelle is a dark nightclub on the canal where people go to rage into the morning hours. With rules explicitly banning

photo and video, the club hopes to promote an atmosphere where people are free to dance however feels right without fear of it being preserved or judged. Though dancing here can take any form, people really go for it, and we have seen people stop to stretch out between songs. As one of our friends told us, "You just have to close your eyes for like five minutes, and then when you open them, you're dancing way better."

*i* Cover €7, extra charge for live shows; card minimum €30

## RED CARPET BAR

Magdalenstraße 2; 676 7822966; www. redcarpet.co.at; bar hours M-Th 9pm-4am, F-Sa 9pm-6am; club hours F-Sa 11pm-6am

A small bar on weekdays and a dance club on weekends, casually black-lit even when the lights aren't fully down, Red Carpet is a hangout catering mostly to gay and lesbian patrons. Amid the neon lighting, the DJ plays the hits of 2000s pop icons like The Pussycat Dolls and Pink! (quick pause for us all to wonder, where did Pink! go?). A great place to bring a group of friends and meet new people, you can also come here to check up on community news, as a TV in the corner cycles through local BGLTQ+ news and events, a counter in the back lounge offers pamphlets with BGLTQ+ resources.

*i* No cover; BGLTQ+ friendly

## THE SIGN

Liechtensteinstraße 104-106; 66496 432 76; www.thesignlounge.at; open daily 6pm-2am

If you're looking for fancy cocktails whose cost might make you cry in the US but might just make you cringe momentarily here, The Sign offers a menu full of creative combinations served in unexpected presentations. Here, we sipped fruity vodka drinks topped with fortune cookies, and espresso and rum concoctions served in ceramic, cigar-smoking chimp mugs. If you're looking for something simple, we recommend the **Special Pimm's Cup** (€9.50), a gin and tonic with blackberry and elderflower. Feeling extravagant? Get the **Lei Lani Volcano** (€11), a pineapple and Malibu combination served in a bird-shaped watering can with a burning cinnamon stick for incense.

*i* *No cover, most cocktails €9-15; BGLTQ+ friendly*

### TRAVEL SHACK VIENNA

Mariahilfergürtel 21; 0196 101 31; www. travelshackvienna.com; open daily 4pm-4am

Travel Shack Vienna is a popular destination for college students looking to make mistakes on their spring break trip to Europe. If you want to take your top off and smoke out of every orifice of your body, do that here. Go wild under the disco ball or add your bra to the rack hanging along the bar. Try their specialty interactive drinks where the theme is self-humiliation: the evidence is Snapchat and the consequences are your friends never letting you live it down. One of these is called the "Cum Shot," which involves liquor being poured into your mouth from a dildo. Another is the "Tequila Suicide," which involves snorting the salt, tossing back the tequila, and squirting lemon into your eye. Planning to make it out with your dignity intact? Good luck.

*i* *No cover, specialty shots €2-4; BGLTQ+ friendly*

# AUSTRIA ESSENTIALS

## MONEY

**Tipping:** Tipping in Austria is common in interactions with most service workers. Generally, tip by simply rounding up to the next convenient number. Tipping about 5% is standard and a tip should not surpass 10%. It is common for a service charge to be included in the bill, so look on menus and bills to find out whether the tip has already been included.

**Taxes:** Many goods in Austria are subject to a value added tax (VAT) of 20%, included in the purchase price of goods. The VAT is a standard rate, though it fluctuates based on the goods purchased, so you should ask the retailer for exact rates. Non-EU visitors taking these goods home unused can apply for a VAT refund for goods exceeding €75 at one retailer. To apply for this refund, ask the store for a VAT refund form and carry your passport with you as retailers may ask to see it. Present the refund form and be prepared to show the unused goods you are exporting at the customs office at your point of departure from the EU. Refunds usually must be claimed within 90 days of the original purchase.

## SAFETY AND HEALTH

**Local Laws and Police:** Police in Austria are reliable if you need assistance, but always have your passport with you when interacting with police officers, as they may ask to see it. Under Austrian law, you must either have your passport with you, or be able to produce it within one hour.

**Tobacco, Drugs, and Alcohol:** The drinking age in Austria is 16 for beer and wine and 18 for distilled alcohols. Penalties for driving under the influence of alcohol tend to be stricter than in the United States. The legal blood alcohol limit for driving in Austria is 0.05%. Use or possession of illegal drugs in Austria can come with long prison sentences and harsh fines. Tobacco stores are the place for purchasing tobacco products in Austria and are marked with a sign depicting a cigarette. It is also common to purchase tobacco products in grocery stores and even occasionally restaurants. It is illegal to sell tobacco to persons under the age of 18.

**Prescription Drugs:** Austrian medical centers will not accept American medical insurance, so you will have to pay out of pocket for services and then seek a reimbursement from your insurer independently. Carry any prescription medications in their original packaging.

# BELGIUM

**Belgium tends to fall victim to mis-understanding: "Don't they all speak Dutch?" "Brussels is boring," and the dreaded "I thought (fill in the blank) was French." But this multi-faceted nation is worth being understood.**

With its northern Flemish and southern Walloon influences, there may be some tension between cultures and governing bodies, but its people are primarily, and proudly, Belgian. Charming small cities and the natural beauty of the Ardennes provide stunning scenery, while Brussels is not only the nation's capital but the home of the most important institutions of Europe. As the seat of the European Union and the NATO, it holds tons of international professionals (who you can find looking to blow off steam after work). That being said, its relaxed culture means that the country was also able to go 589 days in 2010 and 2011 without an elected government.

As far as Belgian specialties, it's not all chocolate, waffles, Belgian (not French) fries, and admittedly excellent beer. Moules-frites, jenever, carbonade flamande, and waterzooi provide more fodder for the imagination and the stomach. As far as art, the Dutch masters have nothing on the Flemish Primitives like Jan van Eyck and Breughels, or surrealists like Magritte. And as far as cities, Belgium is home to some undiscovered gems; they're underrated as hipper, cheaper, and less touristy alternatives to the typical Eurotrip itinerary.

# BRUSSELS

Coverage by **Emily Corrigan**

When you first arrive in Brussels, you may be confused to find that the streets have multiple names: one in Dutch and the other in French. Even the city itself has two different names to its residents (Brussel and Bruxelles). This lingual and cultural mélange speaks to the city's character as a true melting pot. Brusseleirs tend to be laid-back and welcoming, especially since Brussels isn't as much of a tourist madhouse as many other major cities. Outside the city center, it has an authentic feel that finds its roots in cafés where little old ladies sip from giant goblets of beer and in the many parks frequented by couples making out and joggers working off the delicious, so-worth-the-calories fries. Even the parts that feel like tourist traps turn out to be satisfying; popping into a chocolate shop or buying a waffle from a cart is actually something that a lot of locals do. Public murals and the ever-present comic book stores frequented even by adults are reminders of the city's artistic passions. Brussels is full of wonderful restaurants, old breweries, and lively squares. You'll find yourself wondering how everyone seems to have so much time for just hanging out and drinking beer. Relax, you're in Brussels.

## ORIENTATION

The Brussels city center is where you'll find the photo ops. **The Grand Place** dominates the tourist attractions while small streets and tall, narrow buildings give it a characteristic Belgian feel. The two **Sablon churches** (Grand and Petit) are the centerpieces of the historic **Salon** neighborhood just southeast of the center. Further southeast is **Ixelles,** bordered by the upscale **Avenue Louise,** which leads down to the forest of **Bois de la Cambre.** Attractive townhouses, European institutions, and the lovely **Parc du Cinquantenaire** define **Etterbeek** to the east. **Schaerbeek** to the north features wide avenues, lovely architecture, and a vibrant mix of international residents. Even with buses, trams, and metro lines connecting the various neighborhoods it's easy to get around on foot to explore Brussels' various neighborhoods.

## ESSENTIALS

### GETTING THERE

Brussels Airport lies northeast of the city center. The easiest way to get into the city is by bus, using the bus station a level below the arrivals. The bus costs €4 at the station, but €6 if you buy it on the bus. Brussels also has a number of train stations throughout the city, making it easy to arrive by train fairly close to where you need to go

### GETTING AROUND

Bus, tram, and metro lines run across the city and are fairly easy to use. It's possible to use the same type of ticket for all three. Tickets cost €2.10 and are valid for one hour. The Villo! public bike service is free for the first half hour and has stations throughout the city. The basic rate for a day is €1.60.

### PRACTICAL INFORMATION

**Tourist Offices:** Flanders and Brussels Information Office (Rue du Marché aux Herbes 61; 02 504 03 00; open M-F 8am-6pm, Sa-Su 10am-5pm).
**Banks/ATMs/Currency Exchange:** Bank of Baroda (Rue de la Loi 28; 2 285 00 40).
**Post Offices:** 5, Bd. Anspach 1; 02 201 23 45; open M-F 8:30am-6pm, Sa 10am-4pm.
**Internet:** The city of Brussels offers free public Wi-Fi in many points around the city. It will prompt you to register with your name and email.
**BGLTQ+ Resources:** Rainbowhouse (Rue du Marché au Charbon 42; 02 503 59 90).

### EMERGENCY INFORMATION

**Emergency Number:** 112
**Police:** Brussels Police Station (Rue du

Marché au Charbon 30; 02 279 79 79).
**U.S. Embassy:** There is a US Embassy in Brussels (Bd. du Régent 27; 02 811 40 00; open M-F 7:30am-5:30pm).
Rape Crisis Center: US State Department Rape and Incest National Network; 1-800-656-HOPE (4673).
**Hospitals:** Institut Jules Bordet (Bd. de Waterloo 121; 02 541 31 11).
**Pharmacies:** De Brouckere (02 218 05 75).

# ACCOMMODATIONS

### 2G04 HOSTEL CITY CENTER ($)
Bd. Emile Jacqmain 99; 022 19 30 19; www.2go4.be/qualityhostel; reception open 7:30am-1pm and 4pm-11pm

This hostel's lounge looks more like a vintage motorcycle shop owned by an eclectic and reclusive old man who wears horn-rimmed glasses than a hostel lounge. Old go-carts hang from the walls alongside punching bags, a piano, and tiny chairs topped with potted plants. Confusing new treasures reside in every nook and cranny of the open space. The surrounding area is equally busy, perhaps even cluttered. The hostel is close to the shopping street **Rue Neuve** and the hustle and bustle of the **Grand Place.** After you've burned all your extra cash shopping, you can still save money in this popular area by cooking at the hostel's fully stocked kitchen and grabbing coffee for free every morning. So GO4 it!

*i* *Dorm rooms from €21; reservation required; no wheelchair accessibility ; Wi-Fi; luggage storage; towels for rent*

### BRXXL 5 CITY CENTRE HOSTEL ($)
Rue de Woeringen 5; 02 5 02 37 10; www.brxxl5.com; reception open 24hr

A lively lounge area complete with pool table sets the tone at this social hostel, located within walking distance of the city center and train station **Gare du Midi.** People congregate downstairs and in the outdoor courtyard to hang out, watch music videos, and use the Wi-Fi. It doesn't hurt that there are cute kitties living here, too. The services are top-notch, with free hot drinks, vending machines, and an attentive staff. The one fallback is the microscopic-sized beds, but we doubt you'll be spending much time in bed

anyway when there's fun to be had and kittens to pet, amirite?

*i* *Dorms from €23; reservation required; wheelchair accessible; Wi-Fi; linen included; towels for rent; luggage storage; lockers provided*

### HOSTEL BRUEGEL ($)
Rue du Saint-Esprit 2; 25 11 04 36; www.jeugdherbergen.be/en/youth-hostels/city-hostels/brussel-bruegel; reception open 7am-1:30pm and 2pm-1am

Walking out of Hostel Bruegel, you'll have to avoid running headfirst into the beautiful **Église Notre-Dame de la Chapelle** about six feet away. The church isn't all this hostel is close to; it's within easy walking distance of many of Brussels' best sights and nightlife, too. If you're taking advantage of the latter, just make sure to put a deposit down for a late-night key, or else you'll get locked out when reception closes at 1am. Rooms with only a handful of beds as well as en suite bathrooms certainly trump the dozen-bed barracks of other hostels, and a free breakfast rounds out this comfortable and affordable place to stay.

*i* *Dorm rooms from €23; reservation required; wheelchair accessible; Wi-Fi; luggage storage; free breakfast*

# SIGHTS
## CULTURE

### AVENUE LOUISE/BOIS DE LA CAMBRE
Southeast from Place Louise to Bois de la Cambre; open daily 24hr

When window shopping is on the itinerary, Avenue Louise is there to make you regret following your dreams instead of taking a soul-sucking job that gets you tons of money. Miles of beautiful and expensive shops make up this wide avenue. On one end, near the **Louise tram stop,** is a ledge overlooking the entire city of Brussels (spot the **Atomium!**) and on the other end is Bois de la Cambre, a beautiful forest with a large pond. Walk along the road until you get tired of not being able to buy every designer backpack or expensive chocolate assortment that you see, and then take the #93 or #94 tram straight to Bois de la Cambre to reassure yourself that

# ANTWERP

**The people of Antwerp may be known for their big talk (especially in neighboring Ghent) but they certainly have the city to back it up.** From a train station widely considered the world's most beautiful to picturesque vine-covered buildings, a castle on the river, and a main square with gold-covered guildhalls, Antwerp is certainly attractive. It also boasts a dialect that many used to consider the first language to emerge on earth (however inaccurately) and the largest diamond district in the world. Antwerp is closer in culture and language to the south of the Netherlands than many of its fellow Belgian cities, yet a strong international community lends it a worldly vibe. Antwerp won't disappoint as a place to spend the day strolling (or biking) around, visiting its many museums, or just enjoying its relaxed Flemish lifestyle.

Arriving at the stunning **Antwerpen-Centraal train station** will find you on the eastern side of the city. The station is right near the zoo, Flemish painter **Peter Paul Ruben's house**, the **diamond district**, and the **Jewish quarter**, with a small **Chinatown** directly across from it. To the west, bordered by the scenic **Scheldt river**, you'll find the **Oude Stad**, or "old city" district, where the **Grote Markt** dominates as the main square and the lovely churches define the skyline. Many streets here are reserved for pedestrians.

## GETTING THERE

Antwerp has a small international airport. Antwerpen-Berchem train station is near the airport and provides national connections. Buses 51, 52, and 53 stop right in front of the airport and can take you to Antwerpen-Berchem in about 10 minutes, where more bus lines are available. International trains and many national trains arrive at Antwerpen-Centraal, a beautiful train station on the eastern side of the city with easy connections to the bus and metro. Most buses also arrive at Antwerpen-Centraal.

## GETTING AROUND

Bus and tram tickets can be purchased at newsstands, supermarkets, and machines at many stops. An individual ticket costs €3, while a day pass costs €6. Antwerp's public bike rental service, Velo, has stations all around the city. Just look for the rows of red bikes. The first half hour is free, the second half hour is €0.50, the next is €1, and after that it's €5 per hour. A day pass costs €4.

## Swing by...

### GROTE MARKT
Old City Quarter; open daily 24hr

Without a doubt the most photogenic guildhall-lined square featuring a fountain in the old medieval part of town (there are so many competitors for this title), the Grote Markt is a must-see. This gorgeous spot is close to the castle and the **Scheldt River**, and the spire of the **Cathedral of Our Lady** towers over it. The land was originally donated to the city by **Duke Henry I of Brabant** way back in 1220, meaning you're hardly the first to have a beer in the surrounding cafés or scoff at the at least seven different places advertising the best mussels in the city. In the winter, you'll find a Christmas market, the rest of the year the tourist office, the beautiful city hall, and even the **Antwerp Jazz Club**.

*i* Free entry; wheelchair accessible

## ANTWERP ZOO

Koningin Astridplein 20-26; 03 224 89 10; www.zooantwerpen.be/en; open daily 10am-7pm

The efficacy with which some of the snakes in Antwerp's zoo hide, even in an enclosure, will certainly make you look over your shoulder more often in the forest. But these elusive creatures are far from the only ones to be seen. We're talking kangaroos. We're talking large cats. We're talking primates, zebras, giraffes, and a butterfly garden. This place has all the animals you know and love and plenty you never knew existed. Catch the sea lion shows, walk through the large aquarium, and marvel at koalas sleeping and monkeys grooming each other. The zoo is massive and the animals are allowed ample space to roam. It may be expensive, but it's a koala-ty zoo, we're not lion.

*i* *Admission €26, €24.50 if booked online, €24 student; times for sea lion shows and feedings can be found at the museum entrance; wheelchair accessible*

## Grab a bite at...

### BENI FALAFEL ($)

Lange Leemstraat 188; 03 218 82 11; www.benifalafel.be/en; open M-Th 11:30am-10pm, F 11:30am-2:30pm, Su noon-10pm

In the historic Jewish Quarter, this Israeli falafel restaurant boasts some of the most delicious and moist falafel in Belgium. See? We think it's even tasty enough to justify the use of the horrible word moist! For a cheap and quick lunch, grab a thick piece of pita full of vegetarian and kosher delights, even to-go if you so please. Spicy sauces come alongside your meal, making it a flavorful and sometimes steam-out-the-ear inducing lunch. Soup, sides, and dessert are also on the menu if you decide your falafel needs a friend.

*i* *Soup €3-5, falafel dishes €3-7; kosher and vegetarian options available; limited wheelchair accessibility*

## Don't miss...

### MUSEUM PLANTIN MORETUS

Vrijdagmarkt 22-23; 03 221 14 50; www.museumplantinmoretus.be/nl

Located in the gorgeous and historic former home of sixteenth-century printer **Cristophe Plantin**, this museum holds objects from his famous nine-generation printing business, the **Officina Plantiniana**. Aside from the home itself, with its artwork and its courtyard that drew queens and princes, the house holds Plantin's finest handiwork, libraries of books, and the printing room with the original printing presses (including the two oldest surviving presses in the world). Books are ubiquitious, from a manual of Arabic proverbs to a Hebrew grammar book, to collections of delicate illustrations and colorful maps. Countless interesting objects await your discovery, like the old type cases holding over 90 fonts. Plantin would be rolling over in his grave to know that today some people use Comic Sans. TL;DR: every bibliophile needs to see this.

*i* *Admission €8, €6 student; wheelchair accessible on the ground floor, no wheelchair accessibility on the top floor; keep your wrist band because you can leave and return throughout the day* the simple pleasures of life are the most important.

### PARC DE BRUXELLES AND THÉÂTRE ROYAL DU PARC ($$)

Rue de la Loi 3; 25 05 30 30; www.the-atreduparc.be; open Tu-F noon-7pm

A few minutes in the Parc de Bruxelles will have you wondering why Belgium doesn't continually win all the Olympic medals in track and field. There are certainly enough joggers training in the park to warrant them. Other than moving out of the way of stampeding runners, you can enjoy looking at ducklings bob around an enormous fountain, recline in the shade under a canopy of vines, and day dream about the more attractive marble statues coming to life. The cultural experience, however, comes from enjoying a stage performance at the Théâtre Royal du Parc, a beautiful theater on the edge of the park.

*i* Show prices vary, free entry to the park; Check online schedule for show times; wheelchair accessible

## LANDMARKS

### GRAND PLACE

Grand Place; www.brussels.be/grand-place-brussels; open daily 24hr

Known in Dutch as the *Grote Markt,* this large square is Brussels' main tourist attraction, like the **Colosseum** is to Rome or the one

inhabitable place on the continent is to Antarctica. Skip the unnecessarily expensive restaurants and chocolate shops in its immediate vicinity, but don't skip gawking at the incredible buildings. It's dominated by the town hall with its 96-meter-high tower, as well as the **Museum of the City of Brussels** and a number of ornate guildhalls. The square began as an outdoor market in the eleventh century, but much of the architecture dates from the seventeenth, rebuilt after French bombardment in 1695. If you're lucky, you may be able to see the spectacular flower carpet that fills the square every other year in August.

*i* Free; wheelchair accessible

### ROYAL PALACE

Rue Brederode 16, B; 25 51 20 20; www.monarchie.be/en/heritage/royal-palace-of-brussels; open July 21-Sept 1 Tu-Su 10:30am-3:45pm

Across from the **Parc de Bruxelles** and just around the corner from the **Royal Palace of Fine Arts,** this impressive palace is a necessary and convenient stop on your sight-seeing tour of Brussels. It's the official home of the King and Queen of the Belgians. Even though visitors aren't allowed inside except from July 21st to the beginning of September, the palace is impressive enough from the outside to warrant a quick visit. Trimmed shrubs in every imaginable shape line the courtyard and regal golden gates frame the front. Plus, you may be lucky enough to witness the changing of the solemn-faced guards or catch a glimpse of an important-looking person walking through a hallway. Riveting!

*i* Free

### ÉGLISE NOTRE-DAME DU SABLON

Rue de la Régence 3; 320 25 11 57 41; www.upbxlcentre.be/eglises/notre-dame-du-sablon/; open M-F 9am-6:30pm, Sa-Su 9am-7pm

The construction of the Notre-Dame au Sablon church began in 1400 and lasted for over a century. However, its history goes back much farther, to when a group of crossbowmen

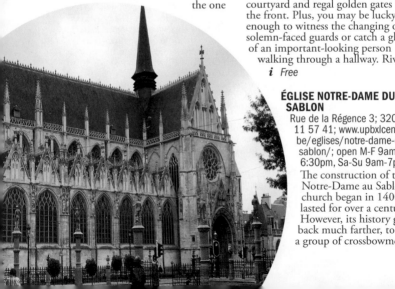

obtained the land in order to build a chapel honoring the Virgin Mary. On the inside, high stained glass windows are decorated with coats of arms of families who lost members to **World War II**. There's also a statue of the Virgin Mary, but not the one that was originally brought to Brussels in 1348. The earlier statue used to be carried in a procession around the church annually, probably the most exciting day of the year for a statue that spent the other 364 days listening to organ music and staring into space.

*i* Free; No wheelchair accessibility; must cover shoulders and knees to enter; must observe silence in building

## MUSEUMS

### CENTRE BELGE DE LA BANDE DESSINÉE (BELGIAN COMIC STRIP CENTER)
Rue des Sables 20; 22 19 19 80; www. comicscenter.net/en/home; open daily 10am-6pm

"Bande dessinée," or comic strips, are a big part of Belgian culture. Humorous characters like **Tintin** and **Asterix** are household names. The medium casts a wide net, including everything from serious and painstakingly drawn dramas to wordless collections of short scenes. The Centre Belge de la Bande Dessinée (CBBD) is a tribute to this Belgian art form and proof of how serious the national obsession is. The museum starts way back at the beginning of drawing before showcasing the drawing, script-writing, and production processes and finally displaying countless examples of artists' funny and beautiful work. In addition to the museum, visitors can page through comic books in the library and bookstore. Any fan of the form shouldn't miss it.

*i* Admission €8, student €7; no wheelchair accessibility

### MUSEUM OF MUSICAL INSTRUMENTS
Rue Montagne de la Cour 2; 25 45 01 30; www.mim.be; open Tu-F 9:30am-5pm, Sa-Su 10am-5pm

This might be painful to get through for the pun averse, but bEAR with us. We're not trying to harp on you, but

the Musical Instrument Museum is certainly a can't miss. After receiving headphones at the ticket counter, guests should take note of the floor plan featuring four levels of musical instruments. The earphones are no treble to use; numbers on the floor indicate what to punch in to hear songs from each instrument. Even though it may seem strange to stand around a room full of silent people looking at everything from pianos to Ukrainian *banduras* to wind-up music boxes, you'll be trumpeting your praises of this museum from the rooftops. Plus, the €6 youth price will be music to your ears.

*i* Admission €8, €6 student; wheelchair accessible

### MAGRITTE MUSEUM
Rue de la Régence 3; 25 08 32 11; www. fine-arts-museum.be/en; open Tu-F 10am-5pm, Sa-Su 11am-6pm

René Magritte was either a brilliant artist who redefined what it means to paint or just a guy with the imagination of a six-year-old on psychedelics, we're not sure which. Either way, looking at the largest collection of his works in the world will leave you dazed and confused in the best way possible. In Magritte's world, a bird morphs into a leaf. Candles produce dark instead of light. And a painting of a carrot turning into a bottle can be titled "The Explanation" despite explaining nothing. Remember the *Mona Lisa*? Yeah, Magritte has one of those too, but instead of a half smiling woman, it's two red curtains suspended from thin air, a chunk of blue sky, and a strange white ball. This Belgian surrealist truly got away with a lot.

*i* Admission €8, €2 student and child; audio guide €4; wheelchair accessible

### MUSEUM OF COCOA AND CHOCOLATE
Rue de la Tête d'Or 9; 25 14 20 48; www. choco-story-brussels.be; open daily 10am-5pm

A museum of chocolate isn't exactly a hard thing to sell. There are free samples. Yet, even after you gorge yourself on them, it's worth sticking around. You'll learn about cocoa production and its history (like how Aztecs used cocoa beans as currency

# BRUGES

**There's much to see in this small city, whose old architecture (some of it fake-old but who's checking?), fine art, and picturesque small streets and canals make it a popular place for a day trip from the area's larger cities.**
Once an important harbor city, and then one of the most significant early stock exchanges in Europe, Bruges is as historic and medieval as it is a modern-day tourist attraction. Its skyline is defined by the old tower of the Church of Our Lady, the belfry, and the spire of the St Salvatore Cathedral. While tourists may flock to the square by the belfry and the more well-known landmarks, dipping down lesser-known side streets can yield surprising discoveries like second-hand book shops, a park that's home to dozens of swans, or a scenic place for a picnic. It would be hard to have an unpleasant day in Bruges.

There's not much orienting to be done in this town that's more or less the size of an American Super Walmart. The belfry borders the busy, wide square right in the center of the city, with the **Sr Salvatore Cathedral** and the **Church of Our Lady** slightly to its south. A trip around the edges of the city will reveal parks and other small green spaces along the canals. Outside the city center are twisting medieval streets and more affordable restaurants and bars, and a bike trip farther north to **Zeebrugge** will take you to the beach. To get back to Brussels or Ghent, just find the train station to the southwest.

## GETTING THERE

Getting to Bruges for the day from surrounding cities is simple. Just take a quick train ride to the city's only station. They run fairly often since it's a popular destination. On the southwest side of the city, the station is within walking distance of the city center and main sights.

## GETTING AROUND

Public transport in Bruges is largely unnecessary because of its small size. Getting around by foot is easy, but bike rental is fairly cheap and may give you a better picture of the city outside of the main squares and tourist spots.

## Swing by...

### BELFRY OF BRUGES
Markt 7; 05 044 87 43; www.visitbruges.be/nl/belfort; open daily 9:30am-6pm
Belfries were celebrated as symbols of municipal autonomy in the Middle Ages, common in Flanders and Northern France. The one in Bruges is stunning, even if getting to the top of the tall tower means €8, a potentially long wait, and 366 steps. At least the wooden structure that used to rest on top of the existing belfry in the Middle Ages is no longer there, finally abandoned after a couple rounds of being struck by lightning and burned. Live and learn, as they say. If you make it to the top of this seven-century old building you'll be rewarded with gorgeous panoramic city views and an elevated heart rate that will let you delude yourself into thinking you did enough cardio for the day.
*i* Admission €10, €8 student; no wheelchair accessibility

## Check out...

### GROENINGEMUSEUM (MUSEUM)

Dijver 12; 05 044 87 11; www.visitbruges.be/nl/groeningemuseum; open
Tu-Su 9:30am-5pm

You may have seen Bruge's statues of **Jan van Eyck** and **Hans Memling**, but to see the artists' finest work you'll have to head to the Groeningemuseum. This museum features the largest collection of "Flemish Primitives" in the world ("primitive" as in the fifteenth and sixteenth century, not learning how to make fire and doing cave paintings). Don't miss the Jan van Eyck masterpiece "Madonna and Child with Canon Joris van der Paele." A few things to keep in mind: you can access the museum until 4:30pm but you'll certainly want to have more than just half an hour here. In addition, if you try to go on Monday you'll be out of luck. Guess you'll just have to resort to the priceless Michelangelo masterpiece in the **Church of Our Lady.** Sigh, life is hard.

*i* Admission €8, €6 student; last entry 4:30pm; wheelchair accessible

## Grab a bite at...

### SOUP ($)

Hallestraat 4; open daily 11am-3:30pm

The owner of this adorable little lunch spot must have a cat named "Cat" and a child named "Mistake" because the place's nomenclature really leaves no question about its nature. For some warm and filling comfort food on a budget, grab one of this restaurant's five soups with fruit—and not just those lackluster melon cups restaurants always seem to have—and bread for €6 or pair it with half a panini for €8.50. A mural of rolling hills and some red-checked trays will make it feel like an indoor picnic, but to-go options are also available if you feel like riding off on your rental bike for a real one.

*i* Soup with bread and fruit for €6 or add half panini for €8.50; cash only; gluten-free, vegan, and vegetarian options available; limited wheelchair accessibility

## Don't miss...

### 🚲RENT A BIKE!

Bruges is small enough that you can see most of it in just a day. However, having a bike for the day can lead you to small and off-the-beaten-path gems you probably wouldn't make it to on foot. For example: ride by the water at the city's edge and spot the handful of windmills to the north. Stop in at an abandoned house now full of potted plants on **Bottenmakkerstraat** (at your own risk since the house is always on the verge of collapse). Pay a visit to some friendly sheep at **Hof de Jonge**. You can ride north to **Zeebrugge**'s beach. And finally, get lost! In Bruges, it's always scenic and you're never really lost. There are bike rentals all around the city (for one hour, four hours, or the whole day), but make sure you ask for the student discount.

*i* Rentals typically run €6-15 for a day, with places further outside the city center having better deals and regarded it as the food of the gods). Posters with chocolate facts cover the walls, as well as decorated tins and special hot chocolate pourers. The museum traces chocolate's appearance in Europe, too, from its status as a symbol of wealth to its widespread popularity when Napoleon III abolished the chocolate tax. Don't miss the machine where you can dip cookies into this liquid gold, or the chocolate making demonstrations where you'll be able to see how this famous Belgian treat is crafted (with more free samples of course).

*i* *Admission €5.50, €4.50 student; Last entry 4:30pm; No wheelchair accessibility*

### OLD MASTERS MUSEUM

Rue de la Régence 3; 25 08 32 11; www. fine-arts-museum.be/en/museums/ musee-oldmasters-museum; open Tu-F 10am-5pm, Sa-Su 11am-6pm

The **Royal Museums of Fine Arts** in Belgium are dominated by the Old Masters Museum, which takes up the upper section of the museum's great hall. Many of the works shown here are truly regarded as masterpieces, and special interactive screens allow you to flip through slides that detail the composition and meaning behind them. Particularly of note are the works of the sixteenth century Belgian painter **Pieter Bruegel I,** as well as those of his son **Pieter the Younger.** It was quite a family business. Here, you can see some of the works that have changed the course of Western art at a super cheap student price. Now you have no excuse to not get cultured.

*i* *Admission €8, €2 student, €6 senior, free on every first Wednesday of the month after 1pm; last entry 30min. before closing; wheelchair accessible*

## OUTDOORS

### PARC DU CINQUANTENAIRE

Av. de la Joyeuse Entrée; www.brussels. info/parc-du-cinquantenaire/
Sure, Paris has that big triumphant arch. Brussels, on the other hand, has a monument consisting of not one, not two, but *three* arches, dedicated to glorifying Belgium's independence. This massive structure, from which a huge Belgian flag

flutters, is the centerpiece of the Parc du Cinquantenaire. Behind it are a number of museums on subjects from art to autos to the army. In front are dogs playing, a treehouse nestled into the shade, and Brussels' corporate titans picnicking on their lunch breaks. Just watch out around the impeccably gardened and manicured sections: you could knock a tooth out on the corner of a perfectly square hedge.

*i* *Free entry; wheelchair accessible*

# FOOD

### ⓘDE NOORDZEE ($)

Rue Sainte-Catherine 45; 25 13 11 92; www.vishandelnoordzee.be; open Tu-Sa 8am-6pm, Su 11am-8pm

The only way to get fish soup fresher than that of Nordzee would be to drink your goldfish out of its bowl. However, we can guarantee that Noordzee's option will be a lot tastier than poor little Goldie. This lunch spot in **Place Saint-Catherine** doubles as a fish market, so you know exactly where your delicious grilled fish or fried calamari come from. Eat at high standing tables in the square with a view of **Saint-Catherine Church** to one side and the bustling activities of the fish sellers on the other. A filling bowl of fish soup goes for only €5, and you can pair it with a glass of wine for €2.75.

*i* *Fish soup €5, other entrées €6-10; gluten-free options available; wheelchair accessible*

### ⓘFANNY THAI ($$)

Rue Jules Van Praet 36; 25 02 64 22; www.fannythai.com; open M-F noon-3pm, 6pm-11:30pm, Sa-Su noon-11:30pm

The smell that greets you upon entering Fanny Thai is essentially the equivalent of tantalizing aromatic spices having a *ménage à trois* in your nose. We're convinced this is some of the best Thai food you can get outside Thailand, beating out the numerous other Thai restaurants at the fun and bustling **Place Saint-Gery.** The curries are warm and wonderful and the soup is full of complex flavors that will render you incapable of enjoying a can of Campbell's ever again. Try an entree

for €12-13, or upgrade to a three-course fixed menu at around €18.

*i* *Three-course menus €18, curries and other entrées €12-13; vegetarian, vegan, or gluten-free options available; wheelchair accessible*

### BIA MARA ($$)

Rue du Marché aux Poulets 41; 25 02 00 61; www.biamara.com; open M-Th noon-2:30pm, 5:30pm-10:30pm, F-Su noon-10:30pm

When you think of fish and chips you may think of greasy hunks of battered cod or British people in a sports pub. Yet, Bia Mara does fish and chips its own way. First choose a batter, like the delicious lemon basil tempura. Next, pick from out-of-the-box sauces such as garlic truffle sauce or thyme (or the classic tartar, they're not entirely insane). Finally, add sides like hot ink squid or popcorn mussels and a rhubarb ginger lemonade. The fresh and flavorful fish comes with thick seaweed salted potatoes, too.

*i* *Fish and chips €12-13; limited wheelchair accessibility*

### LE CORBEAU ($)

Rue Saint-Michel 18; 22 19 52 46; www.lecorbeau.be; open M-Th 10am-midnight, F-Sa 10am-4am

Le Corbeau strikes us as the kind of place that has a lot of regulars: a large screen broadcasts sports in the back of the restaurant, the drinks are cheap, and there's a sign on the wall that says "free beer tomorrow." Old movie and beer posters decorate the establishment and give it a vintage feel. The real draw, however, is the daily lunch special. For only €9.50, guests can have the "plat du jour," which is anything from a

hearty helping of steak and fries to a delicious pasta, as well as their choice of either the daily soup or the daily dessert.

*i* *Lunch special €9.50; vegetarian, or vegan options available*

## NIGHTLIFE

### CAFÉ BELGA

Pl. Eugène Flagey 18; 26 40 35 08; open M-Th 7:30am-2am, F 7:30am-3am, Sa 8am-4am, Su 8am-midnight

You know that friend that never seems stressed out and owns a bunch of bean bags? That person probably comes to Café Belga. This laid-back bar is always packed, inside and out, with beer-drinking students and young professionals reclining on low chairs as if they don't have work tomorrow. The wide square of **Place Flagey** sprawls out next to the bar while a fountain surrounded by weeping willows and a tall church border its other sides. By night, the indoor tables are removed and the bar turns into a packed nightclub. Luckily, the free entry and €4 beers on tap are there to stay.

*i* *Beers €3-5*

### DELIRIUM CAFÉ

Impasse de la Fidélité 4; 25 14 44 34; www.deliriumcafe.be; open M-Sa 10am-4am, Su 10am-2am

They say it takes a village. Délirium Café certainly took this adage to heart when they created a multi-bar complex practically large enough to possess its own zip code. Because of its **Guinness World Record** fame for serving the largest menu of beers in the world (over 2000), this spot is especially popular among tourists, but still worth a visit. Its international crowd also means that it's packed even on a Monday night. (They're tourists, the only thing they have to worry about doing tomorrow is going chocolate shopping). From the "slippery slope" absinthe bar to the "bottom of the slope" basement, this place is large enough that people of all preferences will be able to find a place to party, quite deliriously.

*i* Prices vary by bar; wheelchair accessible

### PLACE DU LUXEMBOURG
European Quarter; hours vary by venue

This square, known affectionately as "Place Lux" or even "Plux" by its dedicated fans, completely transforms on Thursday nights. The police even block it off for some government-sanctioned tomfoolery. That's because hundreds of young professionals from the surrounding European institutions, including the European parliament, spill into it right after work to blow off steam. Some are even still wearing suits. Bars and clubs line the square, but if you really want to live like a local, buy some cheap beers from the convenience store down the street and claim a place in the grass. You'll find plenty of English-speaking friends, since much of the European Quarter's international crowd uses English at work.

*i* Prices vary by venue; limited wheelchair accessibility

# GHENT

Coverage by **Emily Corrigan**

Since people settled the area at the confluence of the Lys and Scheldt rivers, a long and fascinating history has unfolded. From being a major European city and important center for cloth trade during the Middle Ages to being the home of influential Flemish painters to playing a hand in ending the War of 1812, this city has a story along with modern-day appeal. Now a mid-sized northern Belgian city with scenic inland waterways, old guild houses with stepped gables, a castle, and a skyline defined by the towering spires of a cathedral, a bell tower, and a church, it's a charming place to visit, but seems like an even more charming place to live. Local life buzzes around you, on bikes and in waterside cafés surrounded by flowers. Toss in some niche bars, historic squares, and fascinating museums and this city has the whole package.

## ORIENTATION

The waterways that first drew people to the area curve through the city, acting as a guide throughout and drawing you to many of the city's cafés and restaurants. On the northern side of the city center, you'll find the castle, **Gravensteen,** right on the water. Just south are the three buildings making up Ghent's distinct skyline in a line from west to east: **St. Nicholas's Church,** the **bell tower,** and **St. Bavo's Cathedral.** Heading northeast from there will take you past the graffiti street and **St. Jacob's Church,** just past which is the historic **Vridagmarkt Square.** Finally, outside the city center to the south is **Citadelpark,** the home of the city's noteworthy art museums.

## ESSENTIALS
### GETTING THERE

If traveling from an international destination, Ghent is located 45min. away from the international airport, Zavantem (Brussels Airport). From there, you can take a train to Ghent.

The Brussels South/Charleroi airport is located 70min. from Ghent; you can connect to Ghent via train. There are nine shuttles from Brussels South airport to Ghent's main train station. Ghent is perhaps easiest to reach via train, as it has two main stations: the Gent-Sint-Pieters Station and Dampoort Station. Take the tram #1 from the former to reach the city center and, from the latter, hop on buses #3, 17, 18, 38, or 39.

## GETTING AROUND

Buses and trams are the methods of public transportation in Ghent, although you can easily walk to everything you want to see. Purchase tickets from Linjwinkels at main bus terminals and railway stations.

## PRACTICAL INFORMATION

**Tourist Offices:** Sint-Veerleplein 5; 09 266 56 60; open daily 10am-6pm
**Banks/ATMs/Currency Exchange:** Steendam 108 (09 269 17 20; open M-F 8:30am-5:45pm, Sa 9:30am-4:30pm).
**Post Offices:** Bpost (Franklin Rooseveltlaan 2; 02 201 23 45).
**BGLTQ+ Resources:** This website is a good link for members of the BGLTQ+ community traveling in Ghent: www.stad.gent/over-gent-en-het-stadsbestuur/stadsbestuur/wat-doet-het-bestuur/uitvoering-van-het-beleid/welzijn-gezondheid/holebis-en-transgenders.

## EMERGENCY INFORMATION

**Emergency:** 100 for ambulance; 101 for police
**Police:** Politie Commissariaat Gent Centrum (Belfortstraat 4; 09 226 61 11; www.lokalepolitie.be/5415)
**US Embassy:** The nearest US Embassy is located in Brussels (Bd. Du Régent 27, 1000 Bruxelles; 02 811 40 00; open M-F 7:30am-5:30pm).
**Rape Crisis Center:** RAINN (800 646 4673) and National Coalition Against Domestic Violence (303 839 1852).
**Hospitals:** Ghent University Hospital (De Pintelaan 185; 09 332 21 11).
**Pharmacies:** Small green crosses mark pharmacies. Pharmacy Denys (Kasteellan 74; 09 225 20 69; open M-F 8am-12:30pm and 2pm-6:30pm).

## ACCOMMODATIONS

### 🏚HOSTEL UPPELINK ($)

Sint-Michielsplein 21; 92 79 44 77; www.hosteluppelink.com; reception open 7:30am-11pm

The location of Hostel Uppelink really couldn't be better (speaking about Ghent, so excluding an imaginary, enchanted puppy forest). A sitting area and bar overlook the city's inland waterways right across from St

Christopher's Church, and countless bars and restaurants lie within a small radius. In addition to offering Belgian beer tastings every Tuesday and Thursday (they know what the people want) the hostel also conducts free walking tours and assists with convenient kayak rentals. A word of advice: beer tasting and kayak rental do not mix well.

*i* Dorms from €19; reservation required; max stay 7 nights ; limited wheelchair accessibility; Wi-Fi; linens included; towels for rent; laundry facilities €5; free breakfast

### HOSTEL DE DRAECKE ($$)

Sint-Widostraat 11; 92 33 70 50; www.jeugdherbergen.be/en/youth-hostels/city-hostels/gent-de-draecke; reception open 7am-11pm

Hostel de Draecke offers the small perks that every traveler rejoices to see after a long time on the road. En suite bathrooms along with an included breakfast (no stale-and-hurriedly-eaten-on-the-way-to-a-landmark muffins here) and a free walking tour make you appreciate the little things in life, like not wearing flip flops in the shower. The neighborhood, right across the water from the castle, is surprisingly secluded and quiet, although all the main sights and activities of the city center are still just a stone's throw away.

*i* Dorms from €23; reservation required; wheelchair accessible; Wi-Fi; lockers available; free breakfast

## SIGHTS
## CULTURE

### GRAFFITI STREET

Werregarenstraat; open daily 24hr

Even if your only experience with graffiti was writing "Fill in the blank was here" on some wet cement or drawing penises in your friends' notebooks when they weren't looking (don't deny it, we've all done it), you'll appreciate this colorful alleyway. On this small street, it's legal for artists to paint as much as they want, and the result is a vibrant and constantly evolving public work of art. It has everything from ultra-realistic whales and giant heads to complicated signatures and messages on the floor.

## TREATY OF GHENT

Hearing the words "the Treaty of Ghent" may bring you straight back to high school United States History. Although this is a student travel guide and not a dreaded "document based question" we're still here to educate, and no, there won't be a quiz at the end. So, what does a treaty signed in a town then in the Southern Netherlands in 1814 have to do with the United States, you ask?

In 1812, the United States had declared war against Great Britain. The War Hawks in the legislative body had been pushing for war for some time, since Great Britain was struggling against France and declaring war at this time could potentially result in territorial gains for the Americans. Way to kick 'em while they're down, guys. In addition, the British had been blockading France which was detrimental to the American economy. This supported certain Native American tribes who were (perhaps rightfully so) hostile to the newer inhabitants, and had been poaching American seamen for their navy.

After Napoleon Bonaparte ceased to pose a threat from France, the British gained ground and took Washington D.C. in mid-1814. President James Madison was clearly not pleased, especially since they burned down the White House and even ate his dinner. The British were not as successful at bombarding Fort McHenry, the event that inspired the American National Anthem, the "Star-Spangled Banner." After the naval battle of Plattsburg, the British retreated, ending the peace negotiations that had been going on since August in Ghent, which had been chosen as a neutral city.

The Treaty of Ghent was at last signed on Christmas Eve in 1814, and it would have been a great Christmas gift had news of it traveled faster. Instead, it took almost two months for British forces in the United States to learn of the end of the war, too late to avoid the Battle of New Orleans that caused devastating British losses. Nowadays, a simple "war's over" text would suffice.

So, in addition to having its own fascinating history complete with Vikings, Flemish artists, and medieval castles, Ghent played an important role in British and American history, too. Are you ready for the quiz?

If you're feeling bold, grab some spray paint and give it a go. We just hope you've matured past phallic symbols.
*i* *Free; wheelchair accessible*

### VRIDAGMARKT
Vridagmarkt; open F 7:30am-1pm, Sa 11am-6:30pm
The Vridagmarkt is a square surrounded by eighteenth-century guildhalls that houses cafés, bars, and restaurants. However, it's also the site of one of Ghent's old traditions; since 1199, the square has transformed into a market on Fridays (hence its name, meaning "Friday market"). Now, there's a market on Saturday too, but "Vridagenzaterdagmarkt" doesn't have the same ring to it. After perusing the market stalls, check out the statue of **Jacob van Artevelde,** who was murdered at the market, and grab one

of 250 Belgian beers from the menu at **Tavern Dulle Griet.**
*i* *Prices vary by stand; wheelchair accessible*

## LANDMARKS
....................................

### ◙BELFRY OF GHENT
Sint-Baafsplein; 92 33 39 54; www.belfort-gent.be; open daily 10am-6pm
The construction of Ghent's belfry began around 1313. A visit to the bell tower today will take you through the cloth halls (from the Middle Ages when Ghent was an important center for wool and cloth) and even through the hidden "secrecy room," where a German command center was concealed with a false floor during World War II. Taking the stairs or elevator up the tower will reveal the enormous drum and bells still used to mark the hour, as well

as panoramic views of the city. This **UNESCO World Heritage** site also displays various dragon vanes that have decorated the summit of the tower since 1380. Try to go around the hour, when you can watch the drum rotate and ring the bells like a giant city-sized music box.

*i* *Admission €2.70; guided tours at 3:30pm for €3; no wheelchair accessibility*

### GRAVENSTEEN

Sint-Veerleplein 11; 92 25 93 06; www. gravensteen.stad.gent; open daily 10am-6pm

Across from the old fish market with its statue of Neptune, this castle from the Middle Ages has been a count's residence, a cotton spinning mill, and the seat of the Council of Flanders. Now, in addition, to walking on the ramparts for a stunning view of the city, visitors can explore the dungeons and peruse the torture museum inside. English explanation cards offer cheery titles like "Case 5: Stabbing." Rows of bludgeons, spiky collars, and even a guillotine will have you flinching. Nevertheless, this giant castle emerging out of the middle of a modern city is sure to impress.

*i* *Admission €10, €6 student; no wheel-chair accessibility*

## MUSEUMS

### MUSEUM VOOR SCHONE KUNSTEN (MUSEUM OF FINE ARTS)

Fernand Scribedreef 1; 92 40 07 00; www.mskgent.be; open Tu-F 9:30am-5:30pm, Sa-Su 10am-6pm

Needless to say, the Museum of Fine Arts has some really fine arts. Yet it's really impressive to realize that much of the finest arts in the world actually come from this very region. The museum's centerpiece is the **Ghent Altarpiece** (also

known as the Adoration of the Mystic Lamb) from the **Van Eyck brothers,** described by the museum as the "highlight of fifteenth-century Flemish panel painting." Cards with English explanations are scattered throughout, detailing everything from the composition of religious paintings from the Middle Ages to the symbolism behind a tapestry collection from Brussels. Don't miss the massive modern art installation in the center either, a piece that takes up the entire room with water beds on which to relax and immerse yourself in the artwork.

*i* *Admission €8, €2 student; wheelchair accessible*

### STAM (GHENT CITY MUSEUM)

Godshuizenlaan 2; 92 67 14 00; www. stamgent.be; open daily 10am-6pm

Not many museums ask you to put on shoe covers to enter. It's not because it's actually a model home or the staff is made up of insane neat freaks; it's because the highlight of the museum is an enormous satellite map of the city spread across a huge floor. In the center is an astonishingly large and detailed scale model of the city center, and, throughout the museum, there are computers where visitors can click through tons of interactive

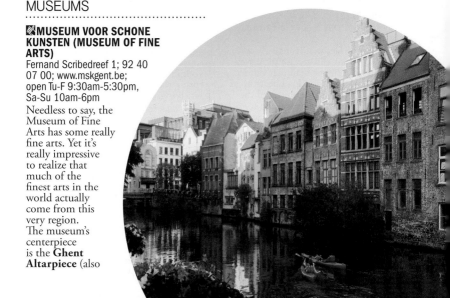

exhibits about the city's history. The museum goes all the way back to Ghent's beginnings, showing why people first settled at this relatively high point at the confluence of the **Lys** and **Scheldt rivers.**

*i* *Admission €8, €2 19-25 years old, free for under 19; wheelchair accessible*

## OUTDOORS

### CITADELPARK
Citadelpark; open daily 24hr

Citadel Park has historically been a site of great military defenses in Ghent. It takes its name from the citadel built here (although eventually demolished) by **King William** of the UK in 1819. Now instead of heavy fortifications, you'll find a small waterfall, hills and caves, and even a playground (although you may be too young for children of your own and too old to play on it without getting at least a few glances from concerned parents). It's also the home of city's modern and fine art museums, so the park is a great place to relax and reflect on the life changing Flemish masterpiece you just saw.

*i* *Free admission; limited wheelchair accessibility*

## FOOD

### ⬛SOUP'R ($)
Sint-Niklaasstraat 9; open Tu-Sa 11am-5pm

Despite the fact that its name is a total dad joke, this restaurant serves up soups far better than that canned chicken noodle soup Dad heats up at home. A crowd clusters around the door before lunchtime waiting for the place to open up, and it's clear why. The soups, ranging from Belgian classics to Thai and Vietnamese curries, are both soup'r delicious and soup'r affordable. Three sizes of soups with bread and butter can be garnished with your choice of free toppings or paired with a sandwich or salad. You may have some trouble deciphering the Dutch menu, but even with pointing blindly, you're sure to end up with some piping

hot and flavorful soup on the table eventually.

*i* *Soups €4.50-9.50; vegetarian, vegan, and gluten-free options available; limited wheelchair accessibility*

### GREENWAY ($$)
Nederkouter 42; 92 69 07 69; www.greenway.be; open M-Sa 11am-10pm

The name is not only indicative of the green plants covering seemingly every surface of this healthy "fast food" spot's interior; the vegetarian and vegan menu will satisfy those seeking a quick green meal, even on the go. With everything from veggie burgers to salads to wraps to lasagnas, the menu is sure to accommodate diverse diets in a way that's satisfying and flavorful. Be sure to check the specials and soups of the day for the freshest additions.

*i* *Salads €12-13, burgers €8.90, wraps, lasagna, curry €12-14; vegetarian, vegan, and gluten-free options available; limited wheelchair accessibility*

### SELI'S NOODLE BAR ($$)
Limburgstraat 28; 92 23 58 88; www.selinoodlebar.be; open daily noon-9:30pm

There are some things you just don't want to see being made: sausage, cigarettes, and your brother. However, if you've never seen noodles being made you need to sit inside at Seli's and watch as their own house-made noodles are stretched, cut, and prepared. Next, you need to get these very same noodles in your belly. Order a big bowl of salty and delicious noodle soup, full of plenty of vegetables and your choice of meat. Sides like fresh spring rolls and gyoza are equally satisfying.

*i* *Noodle soup €10.50-13.50; vegetarian and gluten-free options available; limited wheelchair accessibility*

## NIGHTLIFE

### ⬛'T VERLOOTJE
4, Kalversteeg 2; 92 23 28 34; open daily noon-3am

Trying to describe the strange and wonderful experience of having a beer at 't Verlootje is like Alice trying to describe Wonderland to your average Joe. You'll be greeted on the tiny street by Lieven, the owner, whose short shorts and fuzzy beard will identify him immediately. An eccentric man with a welcoming spirit, he'll be happy to show you his bar/house, where bikes hang from the walls and ceiling and cover just about every actual surface in sight. He even claims to have a bike from **Napoleon III.** Everyone at the place is encouraged to chat, get to know one another, and sign the thick guest book. It's not uncommon for everyone to hug their new friends before they leave. So, go ahead, fall down this amazing rabbit-hole! You'll be mad for it.

*i* *Beers €6; cash only; limited wheelchair accessibility*

### HOT CLUB GENT ($$)

Schuddevisstraatje 2; 92 56 71 99; www. hotclub.gent; open daily 3pm-3am

At a place with a name like Hot Club, you would expect to find a slightly stuffy, dark nightclub where the only thing keeping you there is the fact that you already paid a cover to get in. Yet the actual Hot Club is a classy affair, not a nightclub at all, but rather a small jazz bar with live music five nights a week named after **Hot Club de France,** a jazz club in Paris founded in the 30s. After dipping down a tiny unassuming alleyway, you'll find a charming courtyard and a small stage with piano and drum set at the ready. Hot Club isn't meant for a party; the neighborhood quiet hours begin at 10pm, and guests are asked to b e silent during the concerts. Grab your 1920s-looking hat like the jazz cat you are and spend another night drinking, except this time, *culturally.*

*i* *Long drinks €7, beers €3-4.50; cash only; limited wheelchair accessibility; silence required during performances*

# BELGIUM ESSENTIALS

## VISAS

Belgium is a member of the EU, meaning that citizens of Australia, New Zealand, the US, and other European countries do not need a visa for a stay up to 90 days.

## MONEY

**Tipping:** In Belgium, service charges are included in the bill at restaurants, so there is no need to leave a tip, as waiters are paid fully for their service. If you do receive excellent service though, leaving a 5-10% tip would be appreciated. Tips in bars are uncommon and cab drivers are typically tipped 10%.

**Taxes:** The marked price of goods in Belgium includes a value-added tax (VAT). This tax on goods is generally levied at 21% in Belgium, although some good are subject to higher rates. Non-EU citizens who are taking these goods home unused may be refunded this tax. When making purchases, be sure to ask and fill out a VAT form and present it at a Tax-Free Shopping Office, found at most airports, borders, or ferry stations. Refunds must be claimed within six months.

## SAFETY AND HEALTH

**Drugs and Alcohol:** Belgium has fairly liberal attitudes regarding alcohol with no legal drinking age. You must be 16 to buy your own alcohol (18 for spirits), but it's perfect legal for someone else to buy alcohol for someone under 16. Public drunkenness, however, is frowned upon. Belgium's attitude toward even soft drugs is traditional and conservative. Marijuana is illegal and not tolerated.

# CROATIA

**This is the country that gave the world both the necktie and parachute, so unsurprisingly it's a bit like James Bond—sexy, elegant, but not afraid to down *rakija* shots at 2am before going hiking, sailing, and cliff jumping the next morning.** Plus, a location smack dab in the middle of Europe means that Croatia combines everything we like about the western and eastern halves of the continent, not to mention easy access to major European cities. It's a place where you can go out with friends for pizza before belting out Croatian pop hits at a locals-only club or lounge on one of its many islands like you're ballin' at St. Tropez, but instead on a Balkan budget.

Don't be fooled by the country's communist past, while less than 30 years ago Croatia was a key part of Yugoslavia, the scars of communism and the subsequent wars of independence have been almost totally repaired. Traveling across Croatia you'll see that the country's L-shape creates two distinct sides: the coast and the hinterland. Zagreb falls in the latter category, showing strong influence from Austria in both its architecture and cuisine. Here you'll be able to see churches with onion domes and try gastronomic specialties such as štrukli, a savory version of baked strudel with cheese. The coast, however, historically had stronger connections with Italy, so brace yourself for Roman ruins, seafood, and risotto galore. And the best part: though Croatia is well-established as a tourist destination, its location in the Balkans translates to ideal prices. Oh, and did we mention the islands? Croatia's got over 1000 of 'em. So take your pick: Hvar-ever you like it, there's an island for that. Welcome to budget-traveler heaven. Cliff jump in Split, appreciate the art of Ivan Meštrović in galleries across the country, and sip ridiculously good coffee in one of Zagreb's ubiquitous cafés. And remember, you can't spell formerly part of Yugoslavia without U, so make sure you catch yourself along those Instagram jealousy inducing, pristine, and party-filled coastlines. *Živjeli*, my friends.

# DUBROVNIK

Coverage by **Gavin Moulton**

Your grandma loves Dubrovnik. Your second cousin twice-removed won't shut up about his trip here. Your ex-girlfriend's uncle's stepfather's in-laws are still posting photos on Facebook from their time in the city. So, what's the hype? Dubrovnik is drop dead gorgeous. Even if you're just here for a day, you'll start looking up study abroad options in Croatia and attempt to get a job here. There are beaches, bars, Baroque architecture, and those are the only b's we need besides beautiful babes. Prices in the city are more expensive, but cheap supermarkets, ice cream shops, and bakeries make budget life bearable. Outside of the old town there are plenty of outdoor activities: climbing Mt. Srd is a definite favorite. But, let's be real, you came here for the coast—so pack your suntan lotion, it's Croatian Riviera time.

## ORIENTATION

Dubrovnik is located on a peninsula jutting into the Adriatic Sea. It's surrounded by massive medieval walls, so the only entrances to the **Old Town** are through the city gates. The main ones are the **Pile** (west side) and **Ploče** (east side) gates. The bus station and port are located a 20-minute bus ride to the west of the city and the airport is 30 minutes to the south. The main street is the Stradun, but the rest of the city is dominated by narrow alleyways and stairs, punctuated with the occasional piazza. The city center is walkable, and public transit is only needed for daytrips or rides to the airport. The airport shuttle shop is next to the cable car station, and tickets are 30-40 kn.

## ESSENTIALS

### GETTING THERE

Both international and domestic airlines land at Dubrovnik Airport. For budget prices, look at flights carriers such as Norwegian, Croatia Airlines, and Easyjet. You can also get to Dubrovnik by ferries from Bari, Italy or from neighboring Croatian islands.

### GETTING AROUND

Dubrovnik's Old Town is small and easily navigable by foot. You will most likely not be staying in the Old Town, but 99% of what's interesting in Dubrovnik is located there. Buses regularly connect the various parts of Dubrovnik to the Old Town; if you exit the Pile Gate, you'll find a major hub for buses. Pro tip: if you're staying outside the city, walk to the Old Town and take a bus home (otherwise, you'll likely be walking uphill)

### PRACTICAL INFORMATION

**Tourist Offices:** Turistička Zajedica Grada Dubrovnika (Brsalje ul. 5; 20 323 887).

**Banks/ATMs/Currency Exchange:** Addiko Bank-Poslovnica Dubrovnik (Vukovarska ul. 15; 1 603 000).

**Post Offices:** Hravatska pošta (Široka ul. 8; 20 362 842; open daily 24hr).

**Internet:** There are a lot of cafés, but few public spots, with Wi-Fi available in Dubrovnik.

**BGLTQ+ Resources:** A good resource for members of the BGLTQ+ community is http://www.gaywelcome.com/gay-dubrovnik.php.

### EMERGENCY INFORMATION

**Emergency Number:** 112

**Police:** Dubrovnik Police Department (Ul. Dr. Ante Starčevića 13; 20 443 777).

**US Embassy:** The US Embassy in Croatia is located in Zagreb (Ul. Thomasa Jeffersona 2; 1 661 2200; open M-F 8:30am-4:30pm).

**Hospitals:** Opća bolnica Dubrovnik (Dr. Roka Mišetića 2; 20 431 777; open daily 24hr).

**Pharmacies:** Ljekarn (Ul. Mata Vodopića 30).

# ACCOMMODATIONS

## OLD TOWN HOSTEL ($$$)

Ul. od Sigurate 7; 20 322 007; www.
dubrovnikoldtownhostel.com; reception
open 8am-11pm

Sometimes you splurge unnecessarily.
Sometimes you splurge on basic
necessities. Old Town Hostel fits into
the latter category. This place is kind
of like paying extra for organic milk
when it tastes exactly the same as the
pumped-full-of-artificial-hormones
full-fat store brand. But at least the
Old Town location is ideal and the
exposed stone walls and wooden floors
are a nice touch. Console yourself for
overpaying while gorging yourself on
the free breakfast.

*i* *Dorms from 300 kn; reservation recommended; Wi-Fi; reception open 8am-11pm;
free breakfast*

## HOSTEL AND ROOMS ANA ($)

Kovačka Ul. 4; 098 674 188; reception
open 8am-1am

"Communal" can only begin to
describe the vibe at Hostel and Rooms
Ana. An inordinate number of people
squeeze into what essentially amounts
to the attic that Ana inhabits with
her son. But don't judge a book by
its cover: the close quarters build
community. Or, on second thought,
it might be the free alcohol that Ana
provides. Regardless, a night spent
around the wooden table drinking
homemade *rakija* with newfound
friends is reason enough to stay here.

*i* *Dorms 185 kn; reservation recommended; Wi-Fi; kitchen*

## HOSTEL CITY WALLS ($$)

Svetog Simuna 15; 917 992 086; www.
citywallshostel.com; reception open 8am-
10pm

Bright blue walls await you at this
hostel located high up next to the
old city walls. A far walk from the
attractions of downtown as well as
the **Ploče** and **Pile gates,** the hostel
is typical of Dubrovnik options. The
rooms are overpriced, but we all need
a place to crash, we guess—probably
a better plan than sleeping in a public
park to the west of town to save money.

For all it's worth, though, the lobby is a
nice space to hang out.

*i* *Dorms from 245 kn; reservation recommended; Wi-Fi*

# SIGHTS
## CULTURE

### LAZARETI
Ul. Frana Supila 1

Forget hostels, if you came to
Dubrovnik five centuries ago, you'd
have even worse accommodations...
and that's saying something. In order
to prevent the spread of disease, the
Lazareti was established as a quarantine
for foreigners and goods passing
through the city. Today, the complex
has been converted into a restaurant,
shops, and a nightclub. Pro tip: for one
of the best (read: most romantic) views
of the city, head down the staircase in
the middle to the rocks by the water.

*i* *Prices vary; limited wheelchair accessibility*

### STRADUN
Stradun; open daily 24hr

This is *the* street in Dubrovnik. See
and be seen on this most expensive and
tourist-infested stretch of stone-paved
glory that crosses town to connect
the **Ploče** and **Pile gates.** On the Pile
side is **Onofrio's Fountain,** one of the
city's most important landmarks (with
potable water!). The street is flanked
on the other end by the **City Hall Bell
Tower,** which is home to two sculpted
copper boys who strike the bells every
hour.

*i* *Free; wheelchair accessible*

## LANDMARKS

### CITY WALLS
Gundulićeva Poljana 2; 020 324 641;
open daily Jan 1-Feb 28 10am-3pm, Mar
1-Mar 31 9am-3pm, Apr 1-May 31 9am-
6:30pm, June 1-July 31 8am-7:30pm,
Aug 1-Sept 15 8am-7pm, Sept 15-Oct 31
9am-6pm, Nov 1-Dec 31 9am-3pm

From the window to the two-kilometer
walls, there is plenty of walking—a.k.a.
pretending to majestically defend the
city—to do here. Forget swashbuckling
pirates or armies though, these days the

walls only protect Dubrovnik against thousands of cruise-ship tourists. There's really nowhere else in Europe like this. The city walls are still almost entirely intact and encircle the city. With the number of steps, if you don't bring water you'll surely die—if not from dehydration, then from the absurd prices that the bars in the walls charge.

*i* *Admission 20 kn; no wheelchair accessibility*

## CATHEDRAL OF DUBROVNIK

Ul. kneza Damjana Jude 1; open Apr 4-Nov 1 M-F 9am-5pm, Sa 11am-5pm, closed in winter M-Sa noon-3pm

While you won't see Sean Connery or Robin Hood, the Cathedral of Dubrovnik was founded by **Richard the Lionheart** himself, according to legend. Whether or not you believe in the legend, however, the since-renovated cathedral is a must-see sight in Dubrovnik due to the **Titian polyptych** located above the main altar. The church was constructed in Baroque style and occupies a prominent place with *piazzas* on three sides. At night, the illuminated dome of the church is particularly beautiful.

*i* *Free admission*

## CHURCH OF ST. IGNATIUS

Poljana Rudera Boškovića 7; 020 323 500; open daily 8am-7pm

As any Georgetown student will tell you, the Jesuits don't mess around. So, it's not really a surprise that their church occupies one of the most prominent vantage points in the Old City. The church is based on earlier Jesuit churches in Rome, but we can forgive the plagiarism for the innovative Lourdes Grotto. To us heathens, that basically means there's a manmade cave with a statue of the Virgin Mary that was built in the late seventeenth century.

*i* *Free admission*

## FORT LOVRIJENAC

Ul. od Tabakarije 29; open daily 8am-7pm

This is the sans-CGI Red Keep from *Game of Thrones,* and it might be a bit less impressive than the show. But it's also less expensive than the **City Walls,** and the views are not to be missed. There is a small internal courtyard with three stories worth of steps, cannons, and ramparts. Beware that if you stay past closing time, you will get locked inside (we speak from experience). After closing time, the steps outside make a nice spot for a BYO drink.

*i* *Admission 50 kn; no wheelchair accessibility*

# MUSEUMS

## ■DOMINICAN MUSEUM

Ul. Svetog Dominika 4; open daily summer 9am-6pm, winter 9am-5pm

Slightly more off the beaten path than the **Franciscan Pharmacy** is the Dominican Monastery, home to the best religious art collection in Dubrovnik. The church is currently closed to the public, as it is undergoing renovations, but the small museum with a Titian painting of St. Mary Magdalene makes

# MISTER MESTROVIC

If you've seen one too many kissing couples by Rodin, think Calder is overrated, and that Brancusi is too complex to understand, the sculptures of **Ivan Meštrović** will be more than a welcome sight for your sculpturally aware eyes. Born in the boondocks of rural Croatia, Meštrović later joined the influential Vienna Secession group (of Gustav Klimt and *The Kiss* fame). His sculptures are semi-realistic, but show elements of stylization. Since he grew up in a Catholic country, Meštrović's sculptures are heavily influenced by Biblical themes. Put your hours in Sunday school to use as you admire statues of Jesus and Mary, juxtaposed with classically influenced sculptures such as his *Vestal Virgin*. The artistically inclined will be more than happy to know that there are plenty of works by Meštrović in Croatia. Here are our top picks:

**1. Galerija Meštrović**—"Villa" is an inaccurate description of Meštrović's palatial summer house, located outside of Split. Designed by the architect himself and later donated to the state, this museum has the most important works of the artist anywhere. There are no frauds in the sublime white marble sculptures displayed back to back in his carefully planned villa. And with views of the Adriatic Sea to boot, it's a classic example of killing two birds with one stone.

**2. Račić Mausoleum**—Started from the bottom now we're here: that is at the top of a hill just outside the old center of Cavtat, an easy ferry or bus trip to the south of Dubrovnik. The Račić Mausoleum was one of Meštrović's first architectural works, and made headlines when it won an architectural prize in Paris in the 1920s. The building is unlike any architectural style you've seen with its incredible dome. Surrounding the mausoleum is a small cemetery with great views of the peninsula and surrounding water.

**3. Statue of St. Greogry of Nin**—We are hype for this over nine-foot statue outside the historic center of Split. It basically looks like a giant statue of Santa Claus, except it's not. It's Gregory of Nin, a Croatian that no one we met has ever heard of. But hey, you learn something new every day.

up for the church's closing. Smack dab in the center of it all is the **cloister,** objectively the most beautiful in the city.

*i* Admission 30 kn, 20 kn student

## AQUARIUM
Kneza Damjana Jude 12; 020 0323 978; open daily 9am-8pm

Sure, you've been to aquariums before. Sure, you've been to medieval towers before. Sure, you've been to modern art museums before. But have you been to a combination of all three? That's right, you haven't. Painfully fork over that 60 kn and saunter through this pretty piscatorial place. What the museum lacks in size, it makes up for in ambiance. The stone walls are impressive, especially with the projections and reflections of the water. Be sure to say "hi" to the dancing octopus and sea turtles for us. We miss them already.

*i* Admission 60 kn

## FRANCISCAN MONASTERY AND PHARMACY
Placa 2; open daily summer 9am-6pm, winter 9am-5pm

This is the seventeenth-century version of CVS. Forget endless aisles and industrial fluorescent lighting, and instead think of painted *majolica* jars and homemade remedies. But this isn't your average old pharmacy. If that's what you're looking for, you can stop next door at the functioning pharmacy that the Franciscans continue to run. The main attraction of the complex, however, is the cloister. Columns topped with gothic quatrefoils stand in the picturesque setting. Rooms leading

# KOTOR

**Thought Europe's only fjords were located in Norway? Think again. Montenegro is home to one of 'em.** And boy, it is pretty grand. Kotor is located on the eastern part of the fjord's interior. For centuries, this was an important port town in the conflict between the Venetians and Ottomans. Although not caught between those empires anymore, Montenegro is at the crossroads of Russia and Europe. You'll quickly notice the many Russian tourists who leave their miserable sunless country for the near constant sunshine and beaches in the summer months. Aside from gawking at the worst sunburns this side of Vladivostok, there are walls to climb, orthodox icon screens to admire, and plenty of places to take a dip in the clear waters. Welcome to the Russian Riviera.

Kotor is a triangle shaped town hypotenuse-d against Sveti Ivan (St. John's) mountain, smack dab on top of which is the town's fortress. To the north of the historic center is the **Škurda River,** which feels like a moat due to Kotor's massive walls. Continuing north is a small beach and large modern shopping center. Southwards is a small inlet of the **Bay of Kotor.** The cruise ship terminal where many tourists arrive is located due west from downtown. The historic center is quite small with minimal streets and piazzas, you can get lost but it is easy to reorient yourself based on the tall cathedral towers, mountain, and city walls.

## GETTING THERE

Getting to Kotor from Dubrovnik is fairly easy. Buses run the approximately two hour ride from just €15. Book a bus after looking at the schedule at Dubrovnik Bus Station.

## GETTING AROUND

Kotor itself is small and best navigated on foot. Cars cannot get into the old town regions, although some golfcarts are used as taxis or city tour transportation devices. Renting a bike is also a viable option for navigating your way around the city.

## Swing by...

### CATHEDRAL OF ST. TRYPHON
Pjaca Sv. Tripuna

Romanesque to the bone (or baptistery rather) this is the largest church in the city. Historically, Kotor has had a mostly Catholic population, and this is still an operational Catholic church. Due to the large influx of Orthodox Christians in the city, however, several of the city's other churches have since converted. Immediately after entering the cathedral, take note of the remaining frescoes on the soffit of the arches. Admission to the cathedral museum located beyond the left side aisle is included in admission to the church. Climb the steps to the small reliquary chapel, the most evocative spot in the cathedral.

*i* *Admission €2.50; limited wheelchair accessibility*

## Check out...

### FORTIFICATIONS
Put do Svetog Ivana; open daily 24hr

"City walls" fails to describe the straight-up-the-face-of-a-mountain fortifications that protected the city of Kotor for centuries. We're not quite sure how horses and soldiers made their way up the steep grades of the mountain, because it's nearly impossible to walk straight up the switchbacks without using the steps on the side. Should you survive, halfway up the mountain lies a small chapel dedicated to the Virgin Mary. You'll need divine help to hike all the way up to the fortress at the top where there are even better views of the surrounding mountains. Be sure to bring water as during midday it can get quite hot in the summer.

*i* Admission €3; no wheelchair accessibility

## Grab a bite at...

### BOKUN ($)
Ul. 1; 69 290 019; open daily winter 8am-11pm, summer 8am-1am

Many people come here for the live music, the exposed stone walls, or the wine. We come here for the sandwiches. Hold the jazz, please, we want the arugula and prosciutto goodness served on a wooden platter. Prices are reasonable and there is plenty of seating both outside and in the trendy interior. The sandwiches themselves are not only delicious, but also made for Instagram. Make all your followers jealous and add a splash of food from Bokun to your feed.

*i* Sandwiches €4.50

## Don't miss...

### MARITIME MUSEUM
Trg Bokeljske Mornarice 391; 32 304 720; www.museummaritimum.com; open Apr 15-July 1 M-F 8am-6pm, Su 9am-1pm, open July 1-Sept 1 M-F 8am-11pm, Su 10am-4pm, open Sept 1-Oct 15 M-F 8am-6pm, Su 9am-1pm, open Oct 15-Apr 15 M-F 9am-5pm, Su 9am-noon

This ain't Seaworld, we're at the Maritime Museum, that's as real as it gets. While T-Pain might not agree with our evaluation of the museums of Kotor, this is the place to go for model ships (or model boats rather). There are old naval uniforms, trade documents from Venetian times, and maps on maps on maps. Many of the written documents seen here would commonly be housed in archives in other cities, and it's neat to be able to look at them up close. For the landlubbers out there, the nineteenth-century rooms of a noble family may be easier to appreciate.

*i* Adult admission €4, student €1, child €1.50

off the cloister feature religious art from the history of the complex.

*i* *Admission 30 kn, 15 kn reduced*

### MUSEUM OF MODERN ART DUBROVNIK

Put Frana Supila 23; 020 426 590; open Tu-Su 9am-8pm

Take me to the beach beach let's go get away way, to the Museum of Modern Art which is conveniently located above **Banje Beach.** Situated in an old palace, the museum is dedicated to nineteenth-century and contemporary art from the Dubrovnik area, which means you won't know anyone or anything here. Jury's still out on whether English language descriptions would help with understanding the abstract art that dominates the museum. Regardless, the terrace is easier to appreciate with its stunning views of **Old Town** and a few sculptures by our homeboy, **Ivan Meštrović.**

*i* *Admission 20 kn*

## OUTDOORS

### MT. SRĐ

Ul. kralja Petra Krešimira IV; 020 414 355; www.dubrovnikcablecar.com; open daily Jan 9am-4pm, Feb-Mar 9am-5pm, Apr 9am-8pm, May 9am-9pm, June-Aug 9am-midnight, Sept 9am-10pm, Oct 9am-8pm, Nov 9am-5pm, Dec 9am-4pm

Beached out? Hike Mt. Srđ, the giant hunk of rock located just behind the city. There is a cable car that goes to the top, but we recommend buying a one-way ticket and hiking the way down. In full knowledge that more people hiking down would decrease their revenue, the cable car company has graciously not sign-posted the route, ensuring the path is hidden—the path behind the concrete fort is located just to the west of the top cable car station. The view from the top of the mountain does not disappoint. On a clear day, you can see **Montenegro**, **Bosnia**, and **Herzegovina**. You might not be able to check them off your bucket list, but at least you saw them.

*i* *Round-trip 130 kn, one-way 80 kn, children up to age 4 free; limited wheelchair accessibility*

### BANJE BEACH

Ul. Frana Supila 10

Go east, young man! Fulfill your Dubrovnik version of Manifest Destiny by claiming a spot at Banje Beach. For the real homesteaders out there, the eastern part of the beach is free, but, if an easier settlement is what you seek, stake your claim by putting down 100 kn for a **beach chair rental** from the Banje Beach Club. The beach has great views of Dubrovnik, but then again, where doesn't? The beach is an easy five-minute walk to the east of the city.

*i* *Free admission; beach chair rental 100 kn*

### LOKRUM ISLAND

Lokrum Island

Lokrum Island seems like an ideal romantic getaway with its heart shaped gardens and azure waters. That is, until middle-aged tourists start mimicking the peacocks that roam freely on the island. If you can overcome those terrifying, soul crushing sounds, trek over from the small harbor to the old **Benedictine Monastery.** Legend has it that when the monks were kicked off the island, they left a curse on all those who come to Lokrum to seek pleasure. So instead, come as a *Game of Thrones* pilgrim to see an exact copy of the **Iron Throne** located in the visitors' center. On the top of the island is an **old fort** with panoramic views.

*i* *Ferry 120 kn round trip, island entrance 90 kn with self-provided transportation; last ferry departs at 7pm; limited wheelchair accessibility*

# FOOD

### ◪TRATTORIA CAPRICCIO ($$$)
Ul. Kneza Damjana Jude; 020 454 433; open daily 11am-midnight

Should you happen to be in Dubrovnik with your girlfriend's grandparents and want to pull off that sophisticated-man-of-the-world charm, look no further than Trattoria Capriccio. Run by a husband and wife team, the trattoria specializes in Italian food sourced entirely from local merchants and made fresh in the kitchen. The results do not disappoint. This place will impress your future in-laws enough for them to love you more even than your girlfriend. The prices are a bargain for the quality of food you'll eat, but considerably more than standard backpacker fare.

*i* *Entrées 100 kn*

### DOLCE VITA ($)
Nalješkovićeva 1a; 989 449 951; open daily 9am-midnight

While you can't live the suite life in your hostel dorms, enjoy the sweet life at this combo crepe and ice cream parlor. The 10 kn prices are lower than the Dubrovnik average for a scoop and trust us, there was a thorough investigation (we may or may not have spent the equivalent of $100 on various ice cream retailers in the area). While we cannot but condone consumption of the crepes (which are typical of the overly sweet varieties usually served in trendy places in eastern Europe), if you're into that kind of thing, you can find it here, too.

*i* *Scoops 10 kn*

### RESTAURANT KOPUN ($$$)
Poljana Rudera Boskovica 7; 020 323 969; www.restaurantkopun.com; open daily 11am-midnight

We're not joking, **castrated rooster** is quite literally the specialty of this place. How do we feel about it? Tastes like chicken. After a trip to Europe, you can out gastronome all your friends when you tell them you ate castrated rooster, and, for good measure, tell them you castrated the rooster yourself. Travel is all about new experiences; this one is for the brave. If you need to convince a friend to come with you, they can order other milder local specialties such as risotto or various seafood options.

*i* *Entrées 100 kn*

### TAJ MAHAL ($$)
Nikole Gučetića 2; 020 323 221; www.tajmahal-dubrovnik.com; open daily 9am-1am

Forget India and instead take a gastronomic trip to neighboring Bosnia, the kind of cuisine that Taj Mahal actually specializes in. After all the fish options that are typical of the Croatian coast, the massive meat platters the restaurant serves up are a welcome relief for carnivorous backpackers. While the prices are average, the portion sizes are not. Bowls of fresh-out-of-the-oven bread accompany dishes with plenty of hearty sides such as *knmpir,* traditional stuffed potatoes. Other options include shish kebabs and *pljeskavica,* which is essentially a hamburger without the bun that's large enough to satisfy all of your homesickness for America.

*i* *Entrées 90 kn, soups 45 kn, beer 35 kn; reservation recommended*

# NIGHTLIFE

### ◪DODO BEACH BAR
Od Kolorine; 914 432 826

Don't try this at home kids: Dodo replaces bar stools with swings. Although alcohol and swings make for an unsettling combination, what really puts this place over the edge is its cliffside location above a beach. The views are drop-dead gorgeous: just don't fall over the edge or you might actually drop dead. For those late nights, Dodo has toast sandwiches, perfect for attempting to stop a hangover before it starts. And in the Balkans, that's probably a good idea.

*i* *Cocktails 60 kn, shots 30 kn, sandwiches 35 kn; no wheelchair accessibility*

## BUZZ BAR

Prijeko 21; 020 321 025; open daily 8am-2am

No bees here, the buzz at this bar is fueled by alcohol. And why not? With quotes on the wall from Ernest Hemingway convincing you to drink, there's no reason not to imbibe (not that we really needed one in the first place). After all the tourist places on the **Stradun,** the lowkey vibes and soccer matches on the TV give this bar a homier feel. While no place in Dubrovnik is truly a local joint, this is about as close as it gets.

*i* *Cocktails 55 kn*

## CULTURE CLUB REVELIN

Svetog Dominika 3; 020 436 010; www.clubrevelin.com; open daily 11pm-6am

There's nothing cultured in this club: even its location in a medieval tower in the city walls can't make up for the stripper poles and dancing cages. That said, not too many fortifications get lit like the Revelin does. Expect giant glowing balls hanging from the ceiling, roaming photographers, and working your way through massive drunk crowds on the smoky dance floor—that is, if you can afford the hefty cover fee or sneak your way in through the glitzy VIP entrance.

*i* *Cover 130 kn, beer 35 kn*

## SKYBAR NIGHTCLUB

Ul. Marojice Kaboge 1; 914 202 094; open daily 10pm-6pm

Walking the stairs down into Skybar Nightclub is a bit like descending through Dante's layers of hell. The levels gradually shift from semi-chill hang-out spaces to the final floor where you'll physically feel the bass speaker

## SO MANY DAMN LIONS

You're walking along a picture-perfect Adriatic town, meandering your way through narrow alleys, between red tile roofs, and in and out of quaint *piazzas,* all totally minding your business—when there it is, staring you down from the church portal. The fearsome **Lion of St. Mark**, symbol of Venice. *How can this be?,* you think. Every town you've been to so far has had one. Ailurophobiacs beware, not only are there countless street cats to contend with, but, the influence of Venice is still prevalent along the Croatian coast. Most of the northern coast, with the notable exception of Dubrovnik and surrounding lands, was under the control of the **Doge** for hundreds of years before being conquered by the Austrians or Ottomans.

What does that all mean? Venice was a republic and its symbol was the winged lion of St. Mark. The proud Venetian rulers had no qualms about visibly displaying their control. Churches built from this era surely have a stone relief carving with Venetian symbols. Many are dedicated, or at least have altars dedicated, to St. Mark, patron of Venice.

As a maritime empire, the connection with the sea is obvious in most Venetian monuments. In the **Cathedral of Korčula**, the wooden beams of the roof are inspired by local ship design, and, in **Split**, the **Prokurative**, built long after the rule of Venice ended, is composed of Neo-Venetian architecture that resembles the *palazzi* of **St. Mark's Square**.

The cultural influence of Venice is prominent as well. **Tintoretto**, perhaps the most famous Venetian artist, has paintings scattered throughout islands along the Adriatic coast. In Korčula's cathedral, you can find his recently restored St. Mark altarpiece. In the town of **Stari Grad** on **Hvar** lies his Lamentation of Christ, housed in the museum of the **Dominican Monastery**.

five feet over your head send shock waves pulsing your body. Drinks are expensive, but the location outside the Pile gate is easily accessible. Best to drink before coming to this place, not just to save money, but also to forget about the night the next day.

*i* *Cover 30 kn, prices may vary by night ; no wheelchair accessibility*

# HVAR

Coverage by **Gavin Moulton**

Hvar are you doing today? Let's be real, you'd probably be better off in Hvar. At least that is the mentality of the celebrities, bohemian backpackers, and jet-set elites who vacation here. All that money and energy means that Hvar has the wildest nightlife anywhere on the Adriatic coast. For those rare moments when you're sober, there's plenty of other stuff to do, though, with all Hvar's beaches and sea caves. And even if you're not the adventurous type, the Venetian architecture and year-round sun make this a nice place to just relax. Hvar is the holiday destination of Croatia.

## ORIENTATION

Hvar Town is the largest tourist destination on the island of Hvar, which consists of other cities such as **Stari Grad.** The central point of the city is the **Pjaca,** the main square. The square marks the location of the eighteenth-century **St. Stephen's Cathedral of Hvar.** This is pretty hard to miss and, if you don't see it, you're really not looking. The **Riva** area, which is near the coast and the location of much of the nightlife in Hvar, can be found west of the Pjaca. If you're looking to do more sightseeing, the **Franciscan Monastery** is south of the Pjaca and the **Fortica Spanjola** is north.

## ESSENTIALS

### GETTING THERE

If traveling internationally, the closest international airports are in Split and Dubrovnik. From there, you'll need to take additional transportation to Hvar via ferry. You can take a ferry from Split or a cross-island ferry from Korčula, Vis, or Brac to get to Hvar. There is also an international ferry line that runs from Italy that stops in Hvar. Most ferries will dock at Stari Grad from which you'll have to take a 20min. bus to Hvar Town.

### GETTING AROUND

Hvar Town is pretty small and easily walkable, so you won't need to worry about using public transportation or taxis. To get to other cities on the island, there are buses to connect you. The bus to Stari Grad is a 20min. ride.

## PRACTICAL INFORMATION

**Tourist Offices:** Main tourist office (Trg. Svetog Stepana 42; 021 741 059; www.tzhvar.hr; open July-Aug daily 8am-2pm and 3pm-9pm).
**Banks/ATMs/Currency Exchange:** Privredna Banka (Fabrikia b.b.; 021 421 413; open M-F 9am-2pm, Sa 9am-noon).
**Post Offices:** Hrvatska pošta (Riva b.b.; 021 742 588).
**Internet:** The tourist office offers free Wi-Fi in Hvar, but otherwise, your best bet is accommodations.

## EMERGENCY INFORMATION

**Emergency Number:** 112
**Police:** Police headquarters (Ive Milicica 5; 021 504 239; www.splitsko-dalmatinska.policija.hr.).
**US Embassy:** The nearest US Embassy is located in Croatia's capital, Zagreb (Ul. Thomassa Jeffersona 2; 016 612 200; open M-F 8am-4:30pm).
**Hospitals:** Health Center Hvar (Ul. biskupa Jurja Dubokovića 3).

# STARI GRAD

If your WWII history is a little mixed up, let us set the record straight for you. Stari Grad is not Stalingrad. The only battles waged here are wealthy French tourists competing over a bill at a restaurant. This is the type of town where wine is served by the liter over dinners that last long into the night. It's where the lowkey yachters and upper middle class Western European tourists come to get away from the hubbub of their real lives. They're attracted like moths to a light to the historic architecture, relaxed nightlife, and plentiful vineyards, but in numbers much less than neighboring Hvar. So don your striped sailor shirt and do as the yachters do; visit the many breathtaking churches, bike through Ancient Greek vineyards, and stroll along the stone corniche.

## GETTING THERE

Stari Grad is on the island of Hvar, which is commonly reached by boats. The Port of Stari Grad is the largest island port on Hvar and is not far from Stari Grad itself. It receives frequent ferries from Split. If you are traveling to Stari Grad from Hvar, you can also take a 20-minute bus.

## GETTING AROUND

Stari Grad is best explored by foot and you can easily walk to all of the town's sites on foot. The town is situated at the end of an inlet and has characteristically narrow streets.

## Swing by...

### DOMINICAN MONASTERY OF ST. PETER THE MARTYR
Ul. kod Svetog Petra 1P; open daily 9:30am-12:30pm, 4pm-6:30pm
Art history nerds should know two things about Tintoretto: he was Venetian and he's famous. How did one of his paintings end up in this obscure Dominican monastery on a remote Croatian island? Well, a few centuries back this part of the world used to be controlled by Venice under the rule of the Doge (and most definitely not by a doggo or pupper). Beyond Tintoretto's Pietà, the church and courtyard of the monastery are beautiful, complete with flower covered columns and arches. The museum, included with admission, lacks significant English descriptions, but displays important Greek and Roman artifacts from the nearby UNESCO world heritage site, Stari Grad Plain.
*i* Admission to church and museum 20 kn

## Check out...

### TVRDALI CASTLE
Priko b.b.; 922 252 391 daily 10am-7pm
Tvrdalj Castle is an innovative take on the cliché rich-people-building-whimsical-castles theme. We expected lots of Renaissance faire kitsch, but were instead rewarded with the melodious poetry of Petar Hektorović and an ethereal fish pond. Without a doubt, ten minutes in this fifteenth-century palace will turn you into a true Andrea Bocelli loving

troubadour ready to sing longingly about your days in this most beautiful of Croatian villas. But we're warning you: inspired locals and travelers alike have written many a poem about this place, so the bar is pretty high.

*i* *Admission 15 kn*

## Grab a bite at...

### CAFÉ BAR ANTIKA ($)
Donja Kola 34; 021 765 479; Feb-Oct open daily 12pm-3pm, 6pm-1am
Tucked in a side street near the main square, Antika is everything you'd expect from a restaurant in a town called "Old Town." Vintage pepper mills, traditional foods, and plenty of wine are exactly what you'll get here. Grab a wooden menu and squeeze into the dining room or sit outside and enjoy the company of smokers on wooden benches. The offerings are similar to most restaurants in Dalmatia with fish, meat and pasta.

*i* *Starters 25 kn, entrées 80 kn*

## Don't miss...

### STARI GRAD PLAIN
Open daily 24hr
It's all Greek to me, at least at Stari Grad Plain that is. After creating the first settlement at Stari Grad (Pharos), the Greeks divided up the nearby fields into small family plots that have been used continuously for 24 centuries. Within the fields, there is a grid system of roads and dirt trails that connect chapels and ancient ruins that makes hiking or biking easy. Alternatively, you could check out the village of Doland the Church of St. Michael Archangel, for a view of the entire plain. Bike rentals start at 60 kn for half a day and a detailed guide to the ruins and sights of the plain is available from the tourist office.

*i* *Free; limited wheelchair accessibility; bike rentals from 60 kn*

## Top it off at...

### EREMITAŽ ($)
Obala hrvatskih branitelja 2; open daily noon-3pm and 6pm-midnight
With the best waterfront views in town and a location in a 16th century hermitage, we're unsure how Eremitaž stays in business with entrees starting at 80 kn. But when something's good, don't question it. Eremitaž is across from the main part of town and a relaxing walk (or dare we suggest, Vespa ride) will get you there in ten minutes (or less…we didn't actually take a Vespa).

*i* *Starters 25 kn, entrées 80 kn*

**Pharmacies:** Ljakarna Lakoš-Marušic (Trg. Sv. Stjepana 18; 021 741 002).

# ACCOMMODATIONS

### EARTHERS HOSTEL ($)
11 Martina Vučetića; 099 267 9889; reception open 24hr

Earthers Hostel is what happens when a location 15min. outside of town forces its guests to bond with each other. The result borders on a cult: Earthers has a strong community vibe and a stunning garden terrace, with a view to boot. Oh, and did we mention the hammocks? Kick back after a long day of sightseeing in one of these babies. For your more practical needs, unlike the other hostels in Hvar, Earther's has in-house washing and a drying rack.

*i* *Dorms 100 kn, private rooms 350 kn; reservation recommended; Wi-Fi; luggage storage; linens included; towels included; laundry facilities*

### HOSTEL MARINERO ($)
Sveti Marak 9; 091 410 2751; reception open 9am-1am

This place may not be better than marinara sauce on mozzarella sticks, but you also can't stay in a hostel made of tomato sauce...at least that we've seen. The rooms are new and clean; some even have in-suite bathrooms (gasp). The dark secret of Hostel Marinero, though, is that the only common space is the stairs that they put pillows on. Be warned, if you come here with a big backpack you may accidentally knock out a fellow traveler who is j-chilling on the steps.

*i* *Dorms from 100 kn; reservation recommended; Wi-Fi; luggage storage*

### WHITE RABBIT HOSTEL ($)
Stjepana Papafave 6; 021 717 365; reception open 24hr

You don't need a rabbit foot to be lucky at White Rabbit Hostel. Wacky names aside, the rooms are clean and showers have good water pressure, and that's about all we ask for. The rooftop bar is a nice gathering space for "interaction with fellow travelers" (i.e. drinking games), except the roof closes at 11pm due to the hostel's location in **central Hvar's** residential area. It's not

a terrible tradeoff for White Rabbit's proximity to all Hvar has to offer.

*i* *Dorms from 100 kn; reservation recommended; Wi-Fi; luggage storage; meals available*

# SIGHTS
## CULTURE

### ARSENAL
Trg Sv. Stjepana; hours vary by show times

Located on the main square of Hvar, there's not much one can do here besides take a selfie. In its heyday, Hvar's Arsenal was used to service the Venetian navy before being converted into a theater. Times have changed, though, and now the building itself is under renovation. But its location on the terrace right by the water makes this a nice place to chill with gelato and enjoy views of Hvar.

*i* *Ticket prices vary by show; wheelchair accessible*

### RUINS OF ST. MARK'S CHURCH
Trg Sv. Stjepana

Although it's apparently too dangerous to enter the church itself, the guardian may be kind enough to let you into the courtyard outside the church, which houses old graves. Not your typical graveyard, the space feels ethereal with palm trees, marble tombstones, and old stone pavement. If you don't catch such a stroke of luck and nothing is open, hop on up the steps to the concrete walkway with stellar views of the church bell tower and Hvar Town.

*i* *Free; no wheelchair accessibility*

## LANDMARKS

### FORTICA ŠPANJOLA
Ul. Higijeničkog Društva; 021 741 816; open daily 8am-9pm

Forget romantic sunset pictures on the beach: Fortica Španjola is the place to go. This fortress protected Hvar over the centuries of rule by the Byzantines, Venetians, and French, just to name a few. While it's a bit of hike to get up here (read: stairs galore), the views make it all worth it and your legs will thank you for the unintended workout later. If you don't feel like paying for the fortress itself, you can always walk around below, where the views are still stunning. We recommend visiting the fortress right at sunset, so you can watch Hvar glow when the pink rays hit the tan stone.

*i* *Admission 40kn; no wheelchair accessibility*

### ST. STEPHEN'S CATHEDRAL OF HVAR

Trg Sv. Stjepana; 099 576 3019; open 9am-noon, 4pm-6pm

It's impossible to miss the Cathedral of Hvar, as it lies on the main piazza and dominates the city's skyline. The white stone façade is typical of Dalmatian churches and dates from the late Renaissance. The church is dedicated to **St. Stephen,** who is unsurprisingly the patron saint of Hvar. Expect to see artwork inside penned by Venetian artists who worked on the cathedral when Hvar was part of the Republic.

*i* *Admission 10 kn; wheelchair accessible*

## MUSEUMS

### BENEDICTINE CONVENT AND HANIAL LUCIC MUSEUM

Kroz Grodu bb; 021 741 052; open M-Sa 10am-midnight

Your vegan friends know agave syrup as a healthy alternative to sugar. Our cloistered Benedictine nun friends know agave as a plant out of which to make lace, and they've been doing it for hundreds of years. This method of lace production is unique to Hvar. In a small part of the nun's convent is a museum that displays examples of agave lace as well as artwork and artifacts from the history of the convent itself.

*i* *Admission 10 kn*

### FRANCISCAN CHURCH AND MONASTERY MUSEUM

Šetalište put 13; 021 741 193; church open daily 24hr, museum open M-Sa 9am-3pm, 5pm-9pm

The world's most famous Last Supper may be in Milan, but Hvar's own rendition in the old refectory of the Franciscan Monastery is nothing to

scoff at.

Located a five-minute walk from the main piazza, the Franciscan church has a perfect position overlooking a small bay. Inside, there is a small cloister with the church entrance on the right. The church is an agglomeration of different styles with both Baroque and Gothic influences. For more artwork and Roman artifacts, the museum has a medium-sized collection. Don't miss the massive Last Supper painting and the works by none other than **Ivan Meštrović.**

*i* *Free church admission, museum admission 35 kn; limited wheelchair accessibility*

## OUTDOORS

### HVAR'S BEACHES

Open daily 24hr

Walking to the east of the **Riva,** past the ferry landing and next to the Franciscan Monastery is a small pebble beach. If you continue to walk east, there are plenty of rocks and ladders that make swimming and sun-tanning effortless. Another option is to take the 40 kn water taxi to one of the beaches on the **Pakleni Islands.** But why pay, when the water is just as crystal clear in Hvar.

*i* *Beach entry free; water taxi 40 kn; limited wheelchair accessibility*

# FOOD

### ⬛MIZAROLA ($)
Vinka Pribojevica 2; 098 799 978; open daily 11am-11pm

Eating on a budget in Hvar is hard. Eating good food on a budget is damn near impossible. Fortunately, Mizarola is here to help with 55 kn pizzas and 80 kn pastas, which makes it as friendly to the wallet as it is to the stomach. But don't get us wrong: we'd come here even if the prices were the same as the rest of Hvar. The terrace is next to the red-tiled roof of an old chapel and the food is blissfully well-seasoned. Plus, the servers are genuinely nice human beings.

*i* *Pizza 55 kn, pasta 80 kn, other entrées 90 kn; vegetarian options available*

### ALVIŽ ($)
Dolac 2; 021 742 797; www.hvar-alviz.com; open M-F 6pm-midnight, Sa-Su 6pm-1am

Is the secret to Alviž's pizzas in the tomato garden on the terrace? Years of experience? The local water? We'll never know, but we do know that they quickly churn out pies straight from the oven. Plus, at low prices, it's a sweet relief from the higher priced seafood and meat that most Hvar town digs serve. If you're not feeling pizza tonight, there are plenty of savory entrées at similar prices, such as vegetable risotto and mussels alla Buzara.

*i* *Entrées 70 kn, pizza 50 kn; vegetarian options available*

### GURME TAPAS BAR ($$$)
Ul. Marije Maričić br. 9 predio Groda; 098 192 4150; open daily 6pm-midnight

Traditional yet cool and trendy, Gurme is kind of like the Justin Trudeau of Croatian tapas bars. Sleek bar lights hang next to legs of ham next to antique horseshoes. But just like politics, you might not get everything you want here: portion sizes are small, although the tapas are relatively inexpensive. There are, however, tasting menus with a glass of wine and multiple tapas that make a better value.

*i* *Tapas 20-50 kn, tapas tasting with wine 70 kn, wine 30 kn*

### RESTAURANT "ROOFTOP LUVIJI" ($$)
Jurja Novaka 6; 091 519 8444; open daily 6pm-1am

Since you'll be paying for overpriced food in Hvar, might as well do it with a view and polka dotted table cloths. Rooftop Luviji is located in an alleyway behind the cathedral, which is convenient, but also off the beaten path from the easily spotted restaurants on the **Riva** and **Pijaca.** The food is typical and not outstanding, but the real reason to come here is the picturesque view of the fortress and cathedral.

*i* *Entrées 100 kn*

# NIGHTLIFE

### ⬛KIVA BAR
Fabrika b.b.; 091 512 2343; open daily summer 9pm-2:30pm, winter F-Sa 9am-2:30pm

We're pretty sure Croatia is in the EU and even surer that the EU bans smoking inside buildings, but Bar Kiva doesn't give a shit. Wild stuff happens here. People are packed into small spaces where strangers will grind on you—not out of attraction, but instead by being pushed by other strangers trying to get a drink from the bar. Don't be surprised to see fiery sparklers, girls dancing on the bar, and spilled alcohol. If you're looking for an experience akin to fighting your way through a mosh pit, though, look no further than Bar Kiva.

*i* *No cover, cocktails 50 kn*

### CAFÉ BAR ALOHA
Fabrika 15; 91 514 27 66; bar open 5pm-2am

Café by day, bar and wannabe club by night, Café Aloha is typical of the nightlife on the **Riva.** It's overpriced, there are gimmicky cocktails, and, if you can afford it, you can order literal fishbowls of alcohol. While the bar is acceptable, do not come for the coffee, as they're the only café in Croatia that didn't give us water with our cappuccino. We have standards.

*i* *No cover, cocktails 50 kn*

## CARPE DIEM

Riva 32; 021 742 369; www.carpe-diem-hvar.com; open daily 9am-2am

Rain drop, drop top, where that Dom Perignon pop pop? That would be at Carpe Diem, where the lux yachters come to walk on the literal red carpet and pretend that Hvar is the French Riviera. Drinks are priced accordingly, and are thus some of the most expensive in town. In high season, the club goes until late in the morning. Outside there is a nice lounge with ridiculously comfy wicker sofas for those who would like a more relaxed party.

*i* *No cover, drinks from 50 kn; may need reservations in high season*

## KONOBA KATARINA

Kroz Grodu 22; 095 547 5438; open daily 10am-11pm

This is the Croatian family wine cellar you never had. We're talking stone floors and ceilings, demijohns, and homemade wooden seating. There are even family photos. The place has old-world vibes, which happens to be our kind of vibes. Though the appetizers are limited and expensive, the glasses of wine are some of the cheapest in Hvar. Enjoy a glass on the steps or inside as you turn back time and savor a quiet, laid-back night on the island.

*i* *Wine from 8 kn, appetizers 50 kn*

# SPLIT

Coverage by **Gavin Moulton**

Thoughts about Balkan cities don't typically conjure images of palm trees, but then again Split is far from your average Balkan city. There are plenty of Roman monuments to gawk at, cliffs to jump off, and works of art to admire. But, in reality, you don't need to make much of an effort to enjoy Split. This is a place to do one of two things: relax and party. Split is where everyone goes to pregame for their individual island vacations. That said, let's be real. If your idea of a good time happens to be dancing at the Ultra music festival or partying on the beach until 6am, Split has much in store for you.

## ORIENTATION

Split is easily walkable and therefore not really divided into separate regions. If we were to Split it though, we'd say there are two main parts: **Old Town** and the waterfront **Riva.** To be frank though, the entire city could fit inside **Diocletian's Palace,** which is front and center in Old Town. Weave through the tiny, compact streets of Old Town Split to uncover all its nooks and crannies, including but not limited to shops, restaurants, and museums. Just south of Old Town lies the renowned **Riva,** best known for its breathtaking views of the Dalmatian coast and lively nightlife scene. If you're looking to escape, the neighborhoods flanking Old Town, **Veli Varos** and **Manus** offer a quaint reprieve.

## ESSENTIALS

### GETTING THERE

If flying, you'll have to get transport to Split from either Zagreb Airport or Dubrovnik Airport. There are daily flights by Croatia Airlines between these cities and Split. We highly recommend flying from Dubrovnik (or taking a 14hr. bus… the choice is yours). From Zagreb, Split is approximately a 7hr. bus or train ride. Bus schedules and tickets can be booked at Zagreb Bus Terminal. The best way to book a train is to look up schedules for Croatia Railways. Split also has a massive ferry port that connects to several Croatian islands; the only international connection is, however, to Italy.

### GETTING AROUND

The attractions in Split's Old Town are easily walkable; the streets are so narrow that car or rail travel is impossible and illogical. Public buses connect the Split city center with the suburbs, as well as neighboring cities like Omis (Bus #60) and Trogir (Bus #37). Tickets can be purchased at Tisak kiosks or on the bus.

## PRACTICAL INFORMATION

**Tourist Offices:** Main tourist office (Peristil; 02 134 80 74; open M-Sa 8am-9pm, Su 8am-8pm).

**Banks/ATMs/Currency Exchange:** ATMs are located throughout the town. There are plenty located on the Riva such as Splitsha Banks ATMs. ATMs in Croatia typically dispense cash in 100 and 200 kn bills, which can get annoying.

**Post Offices:** Papandopulova Ul. 1; 02 134 80 74; open M-F 7am-8pm, Sa 7am-1pm.

**Internet:** There are several cafés with free Wi-Fi in Split. There are other public hotspots like the Riva and Fish Market.

**BGLTQ+ Resources:** LGBT Center Split (Ul. kralja Tomislava 8; 91 620 8990).

## EMERGENCY INFORMATION

**Emergency Number:** 112
**Police:** Mike Tripala br.6; 192
**U.S. Embassy:** The US Embassy is located in Zagreb at Ul. Thomassa Jeffersona 2; 1 6612 200; open M-F 8am-4:30pm
**Hospitals:** Hospital Firule (Spinčićeva 1; 21 556 111).
**Pharmacies:** Bačvice Kralja Zvonimira 2; 21 482 830.

# ACCOMMODATIONS

### 🏯SPLIT WINE GARDEN HOSTEL ($)
Poljana Tina Ujevića 3/3; 098 480 855; reception open 24hr

Sweet, sweet air conditioning. If you've been missing this American staple, Split Wine Garden Hostel will hook you up. Their recently renovated rooms and relaxed wine terrace vibe are a nice break from the ubiquitous Split party hostel. Located on the **Marjan** side of Split, it's a longer haul from the train/ferry/bus station and not ideal for a late arrival. Regardless, the staff is friendly and the vine-covered terrace is a perfect space to get to know fellow travelers.
*i* Dorms from 160 kn; reservation rec-

ommended; Wi-Fi; linens included; towels included; luggage storage

### DESIGN HOSTEL GOLI+BOSI ($$)
Morpurgova Poljana; 021 510 999; www.golibosi.com; reception open 24hr

What is a design hostel? We sure don't know and we doubt that Goli+Bosi knows either. But it's got futuristic lockers that open with a keypad, optical-illusion-style hallways lathered in yellow, and a swanky restaurant/bar combo. The hostel is ultra clean and the ensuite bathroom and shower are a definite plus. The downside is that Goli+Bosi feels more like a hotel than a hostel with hella impersonal staff and a lack of community bonding spaces.
*i* Dorms from 200 kn; reservation rec-ommended; Wi-Fi; linens included; towels included

### HOSTEL KISS ($)
Stari Pazar 2; 095 838 4437; reception open 9am-1pm and 3pm-9pm

That moment when you run out of money but your plane doesn't leave until next week is the kind of desperation that should lead you to Split's budget king: Hostel Kiss. The general mustiness may worsen any allergies, colds, or stuffy noses you arrived with and you'll have to hold the shower head yourself, but it's survivable as long as you don't forget your keys after 9pm. If that happens you'll be stuck with a locked door and forced to sleep on the streets of Split until the police make you move—all hypothetically speaking of course. But granted, it's half the price of every other hostel in town and has a helpful staff.
*i* Dorms from 140 kn in the summer, 100 kn during the off-season; Wi-Fi; linens included; towels included

# SIGHTS
## CULTURE

### 🏯CROATIAN NATIONAL THEATER
Trg Gaje Bulata 1; 021 306 908; www.hnk-split.hr

The performances at the Croatian National Theater are truly straight out of *Amadeus*. The 1893 theater itself was constructed in **neoclassical style** and

its interior is reminiscent of the great opera houses of Europe, down to the red velvet chairs and gilded box seating. Throughout the year, the theater puts on operas, ballets, and concerts—all at dirt cheap prices. So don your cleanest, least wrinkled shirt and try not to be intimidated by the elegantly-dressed and music-loving locals as you take a break from the sun and soak up some culture.

*i* *Tickets from 25 kn; wheelchair accessible; dress code semi-forma*

## LANDMARKS

### CATHEDRAL OF ST. DOMINUS
Ul. Kraj Svetog Duje 5; open M-Sa 8am-7pm, Su 12:30pm-6:30pm

Split's center fits entirely within the former **Palace of Diocletian,** and, within what was Diocletian's mausoleum, is the Cathedral of Split. This must-see is one of the most important monuments remaining from the Roman Empire and a **UNESCO World Heritage Site** (casual, we know). From the many parts of the complex, we recommend seeing the cathedral itself and the bell tower. Not for the faint of mind, body, or spirit, prepare yourself for the hike up remarkably small steps and be rewarded with stunning city views. The main building of the cathedral dates back to the time of Diocletian, but has undergone extensive renovation, with architectural elements from the Romanesque and Baroque periods.

*i* *Admission 45 kn; limited wheelchair accessibility*

### PROKURATIVE (TRG REPUBLIKA)
Trg Republika; open daily 24hr

The Prokurative is St. Mark's Square minus all the pigeons. The Republic Square, built in the 1880s, is heavily inspired (read: plagiarized) from Venetian sources. Located just outside the confines of **Diocletian's Palace,** the reddish-pink buildings frame the ocean in a three-sided piazza filled with cafés. During the summer season, be on the look-out for concerts and other public events frequently held here.

*i* *Free; wheelchair accessible*

## MUSEUMS

### ⬛GALERIJA MEŠTROVIĆ
Šetalište Ivana Meštrovića 46; 021 340 800; www.mestrovic.hr; open Tu-Sa 9am-4pm, Su 10am-3pm

**Ivan Meštrović** is the one Croatian artist you've never heard of, but really should have. He's essentially Rodin, minus most of the fame. The little celebrity status that Meštrović enjoyed, however, was enough to afford a giant villa and, once you're that rich, does fame truly matter? Ponder this philosophical question while gazing at Meštrović's mesmerizing secessionist sculptures located inside the villa, out in the surrounding garden, and in a chapel 200m down the street. The artist's works were influenced heavily by religious and classical themes, so you can finally put those years of high school Latin (and Sunday school) to use.

*i* *Admission 15 kn student*

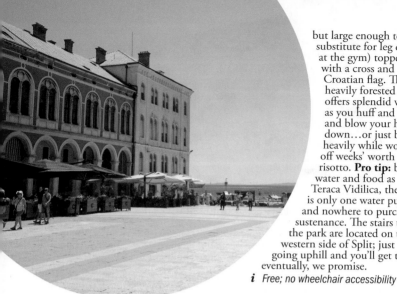

but large enough to substitute for leg day at the gym) topped with a cross and the Croatian flag. The heavily forested area offers splendid views as you huff and puff and blow your house down…or just breath heavily while working off weeks' worth of risotto. **Pro tip:** bring water and food as after Teraca Vidilica, there is only one water pump and nowhere to purchase sustenance. The stairs to the park are located on the western side of Split; just keep going uphill and you'll get there eventually, we promise.

*i* Free; no wheelchair accessibility

### MUZEJ GRADA SPLITA (SPLIT CITY MUSEUM)
Papalićeva 1; 021 360 171; www.mgst.net; open M-Su 8:30am-9pm

The Split City Museum is a giant guide to all the history you'll experience but fail to fully understand in downtown Split. Something we learned, for example: locals used to fear the **Egyptian sphinxes** brought by our homie, **Emperor Diocletian,** because they thought the sphinxes cast bad luck. The museum's collection covers Split's history from start to present and the building is an attraction in itself. The second floor's Gothic ceiling, for example, is one of the few remaining pieces of **Gothic architecture** in the city.

*i* Admission 20 kn, 10 kn student

## OUTDOORS

### PARK MARJAN
Obala Hrvatskog narodnog preporoda 25; open daily 24hr

While you can't have stacks on stacks on stacks because Split will drain your wallet, you can have stairs on stairs on stairs at Park Marjan. Overlooking Split, Park Marjan is the giant mountain (okay maybe not giant,

### BAČVICE BEACH
Šetalište Petra Preradovića 5; open daily 24hr

This is the most popular beach in Split due to its convenient location and over 20 feet of clear knee-deep water. More importantly, it's also the home of *picigin,* a game of group hacky sack played with a racquetball that will put your family beach volleyball tournaments to shame. The falls of players here are more dramatic than an Italian soccer player trying to get his opponent a red card. The beach is also **blue flag certified,** meaning it's one of the cleanest in Europe. At night, the many bars and restaurants on the beach come to life with parties in the high season lasting until the wee hours of the morning.

*i* Free; wheelchair accessible

## FOOD

### KONOBA GREGO LEVANTE ($$$)
Radovanova 2; 021 488 488; www.pizzeri-abakra.com; open daily 9am-11pm

Grego Levante should really make their own rendition of the classic "What Would I Do For A Klondike Bar" jingle, because we would seriously do some crazy shit for anything on the menu here. This is the food you will dream about, Instagram about, and then dream about again. What's not to like with an emphasis on fresh and local ingredients, the friendliest servers in Split, and prices better than competitors. The menu focuses on specialties of the region such as *pastičada,* a typical meat dish with gnocchi.

*i* Entrées 60-120 kn

### ARTIČOK ($$)
Bana Josipa Jelačića 19; 095 670 0004; open M-Th 9am-11pm, F-Sa 9am-midnight
Artichoke puns aside, there are art puns. The interior walls of this restaurant are covered in murals that would fit perfectly in a modern art museum. Adding to the cultured theme is the jazz music that's as smooth as the tomato sauce they put on their oh-so-good homemade gnocchi. Prices are slightly lower compared to the bland tourist trap restaurants in **Diocletian's Palace,** but what makes Artičok a gem is a more authentic gastronomic experience that includes dishes outside of traditional Dalmatian cuisine.

*i* Entrées 60-100 kn

### LUKA ICE CREAM & CAKES ($)
Ul. kralja petra svačića 2; 091 908 0678; open daily 9am-midnight
With the exception of **Gelateria Spalato,** the quality of ice cream in the rest of Split pales in comparison to Luka. Luka, however, undoubtedly takes the cake for the best value with their massive (and we mean *massive*) scoops. Its charming café vibe and seasonal flavors are also major game changers. If you're lucky enough to summer in Split, enjoy your ice cream at an outdoor shop around the corner from the main café under the guise of a giant mural of a Roman emperor. I scream for Luka's ice cream; *et tu, Brute?*

*i* Scoops 8 kn

### RESTORAN ŠPERUN ($$)
Šperun ul.; 021 346 999; open daily 9am-11pm
The Croatia of yesteryear may not survive in the straight-off-the-cruise ship swamped **Riva,** but it does at Restaurant Sperun, located in the less touristy Varoš neighborhood. The vibe is pure *Roman Holiday:* checkered tablecloths, old prints, and model ships. Only the *bocca della verità* hasn't come out to play. Soups and pastas are well within even the most constrained backpacker's budget, while splurge options include grilled meats and fish. If Audrey Hepburn doesn't show up, you can console yourself with the highly recommended *zuppa inglese* dessert. Either way, you're #blessed.

*i* Soups 30 kn, pasta 60 kn, meat and fish entrées 100 kn

# NIGHTLIFE

### ◪BAČVICE
5 Šetalište Petra Preradovića; 091 883 3710; www.zyhdi-munisi.com/zbirac; open M-Th, Su 7am-1am, F-Sa 7am-2am
If you go where the night takes you in Split, you're bound to end up at Bačvice. When all else fails and the downtown bars shut down, Bačvice will be faithfully waiting for you with its clubs and alcohol flowing and going late into the morning. Yes, it's a bit of a walk from downtown. Yes, the clubs could be a little bit nicer. And yes, it's easy to fall into the water because the sidewalks don't have guardrails. But that might not be the worst thing—after a long night of drunken debauchery, there's nothing like a sunrise swim to cure a hangover.

*i* Cocktails 30 kn

### ACADEMIA GHETTO CLUB
Dosud 10; 091 197 7790; Tu-Th, Su 4pm-midnight, F-Sa 5pm-1am
People come here to rage, but not in the all-you-can-drink-pub-crawl kind of way. It's more like the: "Let's have stimulating intellectual conversation while dancing and drinking gin" kind of way. Thus, it's not super surprising that this is one of the few places in Split well-stocked with absinthe. Never fear: should absinthe not suit your taste, but another niche alcohol would, go for the specials on Armenian brandy and drink talk like Hemingway in Academia's spacious courtyard.

*i* Beer 20 kn, cocktails 50 kn

## CAFFE BAR SKALINA

Obala Hrv. Nardnog preporoda 20; 021 344 079; open daily 9am-11pm

Lying on the **Riva,** Split's landscaped limestone path that rings the harbor, is a series of bars with overpriced drinks and overeager tourists. One of those bars is Caffe Bar Skalina. Typical of the variety on the Riva—bars that are slightly less classy than their bougier cousins in France—most drinks are in the 60 kuna range. It wouldn't be our first choice, but, for the Riva, it does the trick.

*i* Drinks 60 kn, gelato 30 kn

## PARADOX WINE & CHEESE BAR

Bana Josipa Jelačića 3; 021 787 778; open daily 8am-midnight

With a selection of wines that range from the affordable (26 kn) to the ungodly priced (120 kn) per glass, Paradox Wine Bar is a great place to test out if you can actually fake your way through a wine tasting. Take this as an opportunity to learn about the rich varieties of Croatian wine, as Paradox's offerings are arranged by type on the extensive menu. While we're not whining about the wine selection, the cheese and bread sides can be a bit pricey. Pro tip: this isn't the place to end your night, but rather a spot to kick it off.

*i* Wine 26 kn, starters 50 kn

# ZAGREB

Coverage by **Gavin Moulton**

Ever wondered what it would be like to live somewhere where everyone was just Zen? Look no further than Croatia's capital: Zagreb, otherwise known as the epicenter of chill. What do the one million inhabitants of Zagreb do for fun? Banter in cafés or hang at bars. We recommend you follow their lead—take part in the laid-back lifestyle as you let your taste buds savor melted cheese, let your eyes take in both contemporary and ancient art, and let the night take you to some of the most interesting bars Europe has to offer. Zagreb is the perfect antidote to the high prices of Vienna and an oasis after the party scene of Berlin. With the world's shortest funicular, good craft coffee, and brewery startups, we're not complaining.

## ORIENTATION

Zagreb is Croatia's capital, located in the northwestern region of the country. If you count the surrounding Zagreb country, Zagreb is the only Croatian city with a population of over one million people, but, that said, it doesn't feel that large. The city center, known as **Upper Town,** is famous for landmarks such as the **Zagreb Cathedral** and the very photogenic **St. Mark's Church.** In Upper Town lies **Trg bana Jelačića** (Governor Jelačić Square), the home of crowds and the largest tram stop in Zagreb. Many tourist destinations are concentrated in this area, which is also characterized by Austro-Hungarian architecture that lends it a charming old timey feel. On the northern end of Upper Town is Gradec, the oldest region of Zagreb that is easily accessible via the funicular (4 kn). Just south of **Upper Town** (and perhaps a bit obviously) lies **Donji grad** (Lower Town). This area has a more modern feel than its northern neighbor with more urban spaces and office buildings.

## ESSENTIALS

### GETTING THERE

The best way to get into Zagreb is by plane. Franjo Tuđman Airport, more commonly known as Zagreb Airport, is the largest airport in Croatia and serves many airlines, both domestic and international. From within Europe, travel to Zagreb by train, docking at Zagreb Central Station (Trg kralja Tomislava 12). Like the airport, the train station is the largest and busiest in all of Croatia, making it the main hub of the Croatian Railways network. Traveling in and out of Zagreb is also possible via bus at the station located at Avenija Marina Držića 4.

## GETTING AROUND

Zagreb has a functioning tram system with major hubs at Ban Jelačić Square and by the Zagreb Central Station. Tickets (10 kn during the day) are valid for 90min. If you don't want to walk to Upper Town, you can take the funicular (4 kn); Zagreb's funicular is the shortest inclined railway in the world. At the city outskirts, you must make the switch to Zagreb's buses.

## PRACTICAL INFORMATION

**Tourist Offices:** Tourist Information Centre (Trg Bana J. Jealčića 11; 01 481 40 51; open M-F 8:30am-9pm, Sa 9am-6pm, Su and holidays 10am-4pm).
**Banks/ATMs/Currency Exchange:** ATMs are located throughout the city, but most ATMs will dispense money in 200 and 100 kn bills. An exchange office is located at the bus station.
**Post Offices:** Hrvatska pošta (Jurišićeva ul. 13; open M-F 7am-8pm, Sa 7am-2pm).
**Internet:** The many coffee shops and cafés of Zagreb serve as Wi-Fi hotspots. Trg bana Jelačića also offers free public Wi-Fi.
**BGLTQ+ Resources:** Iskora (Petrinjska ul. 27; 091 244 4666).

## EMERGENCY INFORMATION

**Emergency Number:** 112. The American Embassy in Croatia also maintains an emergency number for American citizens: 01 661 2400.
**Police:** Petrinjska ul. 30; 192
**US Embassy:** There is a US Embassy in Zagreb (Ul. Thomassa Jeffersona 2; 1 6612 200; open M-F 8am-4:30pm).
**Rape Crisis Center:** Centre for Women War Victims - ROSA (Kralja Drzislava 2; 1 4551 142; open daily 10am-6pm).
**Hospitals:** Clinical Hospital Center Zagreb (Šalata 2; 1 49 20 019).
**Pharmacies:** Gradska Ljekarna Zagreb (Trg Petra Svačića 17; 01 485 65 45).

# ACCOMMODATIONS

## ◪SUBSPACE HOSTEL ($)

Ul. Nikole Tesle 12; 1 481 9993; www.subspacehostel.com; reception open 24hr

Subspace is not subpar, unless you're claustrophobic that is. Instead of bunks, this newly opened hostel has space capsules stacked on top of each other. Each one is soundproof and comes equipped with a mirror, blue mood lighting, and a TV. The space theme extends to the bathrooms where you shower inside a "regeneration unit" that, in reality, is a large repurposed industrial pipe. The ceiling glows with a mural of the stars and the whole hostel is covered with sci-fi themed art. While we're still trying to figure out why the bathroom doors are so damn hard to close and why you have to unlock the hostel door before you exit (rookie errors we suppose), we hope that these kinks will be ironed out in the first year of this baby hostel's existence.

*i* *Dorms from 170 kn; reservation recommended; Wi-Fi*

## HOSTEL CHIC ($$)

Pavla Hatza 10; 1 779 3760; www.hostel-chic.com; reception open 2pm-11pm

Chic is a word that describes a Parisian fashion show, not a budget hostel with purple and green walls. If you can overlook this poor usage of the French language, Hostel Chic is a comeback kid, as it's a solid, centrally-located budget option. Many of the rooms have balconies, which is a definite plus considering the hostel's social spaces are relatively small. Unlike the other comeback kid, Joe Montana, however, "The Catch" to Hostel Chic is not positive: namely, the small kitchenette (emphasis on the -ette) is *très petite* indeed.

*i* *Dorms from 85 kn, private rooms 260 kn; reservation recommended; Wi-Fi; kitchen*

## HOSTEL SWANKY MINT ($$$)

Ilica Ul. 50; 1 400 4248; www.swanky-hostel.com; reception open 24hr

You shouldn't need any encourage-mint to stay at this establish-mint, but, in the rare case that the "Best Hostel in Croatia" commend-mint isn't convincing, let the free towels, locks, and welcome shot of rakija do the job. While we wish there were more bathrooms, the proximity to Zagreb's center makes it worth the stay. Swanky, boasting an added cool factor of being converted from an old laundry factory, has a bar-pool complex frequented both by locals and tourists. Although that disrupts the traditional hostel community vibe, if it turns out you're mint to be with someone, you can always upgrade to a private room, no judge-mint.

*i* Dorms from 150 kn, private rooms from 520 kn; reservation recommended; Wi-Fi

# SIGHTS
## CULTURE

### DOLAĆ MARKET
Tržnica Dolać; open daily 7am-1pm
In the center of Zagreb lies the Dolać Market. Think of your typical farmer's market, then multiply it to fill a city square and add in some souvenir stands. You can always grab materials for a picnic and then head behind the cathedral to **Ribnjak Park** to enjoy your fresh acquisitions. While there, don't miss out on seeing the Roman monument in the park's center.

*i* Prices vary; wheelchair accessible

### FUNICULAR
Uspinjača; open daily 6:30am-9:50pm
When you have an opportunity to ride the world's shortest funicular for 75 cents, go for it. Although built in the late nineteenth-century to practically connect the **Upper** and **Lower Towns,** today it's used more by tourists than locals. Like all of Zagreb's public transit, the funicular is blue and easily spotted on the hillside. But if you're not one to roll out those 4 kuna, there are steps located parallel to the funicular.

*i* Ride 4 kn; funicular runs every ten minutes; wheelchair accessible

### KAMENITA VRATA (STONE GATE)
Kamenita ul; open daily 24hr
The Stone Gate is the only surviving gate from Zagreb's medieval heyday when walls defended the Upper Town against attack. Today, the gate is most

notable for the small chapel dedicated to an icon of Mary. Although a street runs through the gate, there are pews on one side and a small shop sells candles to the faithful. At almost any hour of the day, several members of the faithful can be found praying at the shrine.

*i* Free; wheelchair accessible

### ST. MARKS CHURCH
Trg Sv. Marka 5
The colorful tiles on the roof of the thirteenth-century St. Marks church depicting the coat of arms of Zagreb and Croatia make the perfect photo op to show everyone back home that you are indeed in Croatia. St. Mark's, located across from the **Croatian parliament building,** has played an important role in the history of government in Zagreb, as one of the oldest churches in the city. Its south entrance is particularly notable for its impressive **Gothic portal,** complete with sculptures.

*i* Often closed, but the portal may be open to peek into the interior; wheelchair accessible

## LANDMARKS

### TUNEL GRIČ
Tomićeva ul; open daily 9am-11:30pm
Need to update your Instagram with some James Bond style dramatic photos of yourself? We've got you covered. Tunel Grič is Zagreb's very own air raid shelter turned subterranean pedestrian passageway. Translation: a long tunnel with surprisingly good lighting and dramatic cavernous spaces. If we haven't convinced you yet, where else in the world can you go and walk in a tunnel for fun? (Put your hand down, Montreal. We're in Europe.) There are multiple entrances to the tunnel, but the best is just to the west of the **funicular,** as there is an art exhibition before the entrance.

*i* Free; wheelchair accessible

### ZAGREB CATHEDRAL
Kaptol ul. 5; 1 481 4727; www.zg-nadbi-skupija.hr
This Cathedral is to Zagreb what St. Stephen's is to Vienna, albeit a smaller,

less impressive version, kind of like the city in general. But don't worry, a visit to this tallest building in Croatia is rewarded with gothic architecture and cultural insights. Take, for example, the Glagolitic script on the back wall immediately to its right entrance. And, if you didn't know what that was, **Glagolitic script** is an alphabet that was used for centuries in Croatian religious texts after being introduced by St. Cyril in the ninth century before he teamed up with his brother, St. Methodius, to create the more widely used Cyrillic.

*i* Free; wheelchair accessible

### ZAKMARDIJEVE STUBE (ZAKMARDI STAIRS)

Zakmardijeve Stube; open daily 24hr
Paris has the Pont des Arts and Rome the Ponte Milvio, and Zagreb the Zakmardijeve Stairs to express their affection through a lovelock. Why stairs, you may ask? These boast the most breathtaking and most romantic view of the city. More than just a set of stairs, they connect the lower town to the upper town and lead to the **Gradec Plateau,** next to **St. Catherine's church,** which is also a highly-recommended viewpoint. So, if the **Museum of Broken Relationships** isn't working with your significant (or soon-to-be significant) other, maybe this will do the trick.

*i* Free; no wheelchair accessibility

## MUSEUMS

### ▧MUSEUM OF CONTEMPORARY ART

Av. Dubrovnik 17; 1 605 2700; www.msu.hr; open Tu-Su 11am-6pm, Sa 11am-8pm
Maybe it's the violins hanging from the ceiling or the museum's brutalist concrete architecture, but the Museum of Contemporary Art feels like a scene from a dystopian nightmare. The wacky exhibits waiting inside don't help either. We're talking naked women laying on trees, optical illusions,

and giant piles of coconuts. But the real reason to take the 15-minute tram out to **Novi Zagreb** is the **three-story slide.** It does not disappoint. Should you want to see Croatian modern art but don't want to make the trek out south, check out the **Moderna Galerija** for similarly mind-bending pieces.

*i* Admission 30 kn, 15 kn student, seniors, disabled, groups; wheelchair accessible

### ARCHAEOLOGICAL MUSEUM

19 Nikola Šubića Zrinskog; 1 487 3100; www.amz.hr; open Tu-W 10am-6pm, Th 10am-8pm, F-Sa 10am-6pm, Su 10am-1pm
The world's longest text written in Etruscan? Cremated human remains sitting in the open with no glass? An American sports bar in the middle of a courtyard with Roman sculptures? No, this is not just a natural history museum, funeral home, or restaurant—it's the Zagreb Archaeological Museum. For an entrance fee of a mere 15 kuna, gain access to the best collection of **Egyptian** and **Roman artifacts** in Croatia. The renovated first and second floors feature stellar English descriptions, while the **Stone and Bronze Age** content on the third floor is translated in                orange

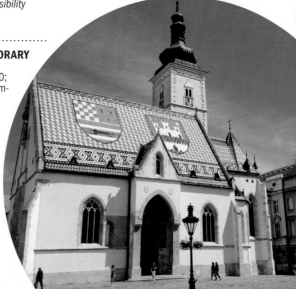

## ZAGREB'S COFFEE CULTURE

Given the ungodly amount of time people in this city spend at cafés, we figured Zagreb must have some quality coffee. Turns out, it does. Check out these three joints and the aforementioned Cogito Coffee, for the best Cups of Joe in northern Croatia.

**42 Coffee Co.** — *Vlaška ul. 42.; open M-Sa 7am-10am*
With its communal seating, industrial gear tables, and arched brick ceilings, 42 Coffee Co. scores high in the cool category. Single source roasts and a top-of-the-line La Marzocco espresso machine ensure that people come here for more than just the ambiance.

**Eliscaffe** — *Ilica 63; open M-F 8am-7pm*
While its logo is alarmingly similar to that of the Entertainment TV (read: Hollywood gossip) channel, the crowd at the Eliscaffe is decidedly laidback. The entirety of the interior is painted black, but that doesn't seem to bother the newspaper readers and laptop warriors who like to pass time here. A unique offering is the triestino, a cross between a cappuccino and a macchiato from the Italian city of Trieste.

**Pithos** — *Jurja Žerjavica ul. 7; open M-F 9am-5pm*
A café-brunch combo spot, Pithos wins for their use of fresh ingredients and offerings in addition to coffee. While Eliscaffe and 42 Coffee Co. have little in the way of food, Pithos offers a delicious array that runs the gamut from baklava to goulash.

notebooks found throughout the exhibits. And, if reading all these historical facts stresses you out, relax with a beer in the courtyard restaurant while sitting next to a Roman sarcophagus.

*i* *Admission 30 kn, 15 kn student, 50 kn family; wheelchair accessible*

### MUSEUM OF NAÏVE ART
Sv. Ćirila i Metoda 3; 1 485 1911; www.hmnu.hr; open M-Sa 10am-6pm, Su 10am-1pm
Ever looked at a piece of art and thought "I could paint that"? That's the entire idea behind **naïvism,** the most important movement in twentieth-century Croatian art. Not quite as bizarre as the **Museum of Contemporary Art,** the Museum of Naïve Art keeps it real with a small, but interesting collection. What is naïvism, you ask? It's when artists without formal training or experience create works of art. The results may reinforce the value of art school, but they also make for a treasured experience. Expect giant roosters and multicolor cathedrals.

*i* *Admisson 25 kn, 15 kn student*

### MUZEJ MIMARA
Rooseveltov trg 5; 1 482 8100; www.mimara.hr; open Oct 1-June 30 Tu-W, F-Sa 10am-5pm, Th 10am-7pm, Su 10am-2pm, July 1-Sept 30 Tu-F 10am-7pm, Sa 10am-5pm, Su 10am-2pm
The Mimara Museum is Zagreb's response to New York's Frick Collection, as it is entirely composed of works from the collections of **Ante Topić Mimara,** Croatia's most famous art collector. It's also where we go for the best non-contemporary art in Zagreb. **Renoir?** Got two of 'em. **Rubens?** You betcha. Strong holdings in impressionist painting and medieval sculpture round out the collection. English descriptions are lacking, but there is a free Wi-Fi guide that works in some galleries.

*i* *Admission 40 kn, 30 kn reduced; wheelchair accessible*

## FOOD
### ◪LA ŠTRUK ($$)
Skalinska 5; 1 483 7701; open daily 11am-10pm
We're never okay with missing an opportunity to eat melted cheese. And

if you're like us and didn't grow up with a Croatian grandma, *štrukli* will be a game changer. It is a specialty of the Zagreb region and the only item on the menu at La Štruk. Think cheese strudel baked like lasagna with cheese on top. While the most typical version is baked, the restaurant also has variations such as in soup or boiled. La Štruk gets major bonus points for the picturesque garden terrace hidden around the corner where you can dine under the warm Croatian sun.

*i* *Strudel 30-40 kn*

### ◪STARI FIJAKER ($)
Mesnička 6; 1 483 3829; starifijaker.hr; M-Sa 11am-10pm, Su 11am-9pm

If Zagreb were Pawnee and restaurants were people, Stari Fijaker would be Ron Swanson: unapologetically traditional, meat loving, and a little over-the-top—but we aren't complaining. Stari Fijaker will care for your physical, emotional, and spiritual (yes spiritual) needs, with its large portions of hearty Balkan food, comfortable chairs, and large crucifix. (Who doesn't need a bit more Jesus in their life after a week of partying on the Croatian coast?) The menu, with English subtitles, consists of traditional dishes such as shepherds stew: think goulash with gnocchi that clearly shows the historical influences on local gastronomy due to its location between Hungary and Italy.

*i* *Entrées 80-100 kn*

### ...NISHTA ($)
Masarykova 11; 1 889 7444; www.nishtar-estaurant.com; open Tu-Su noon-7pm

If you or a loved one is a big fan of gluten free, vegan, vegetarian, pescatarian, or Sagittarian food, … Nishta may be for you. Located in the homey second story of a small building in the center of a courtyard off the main street, …Nishta is not your mom's Croatian restaurant. Expect menus written on plates, unusual punctuation, and lots and lots of seasonal vegetables. While the upside down pots with vegetables painted beneath are somewhat endearing, the gold sharpie-esque writing on the purple walls is less so. But, when it comes to quality diet conscious food, we can overlook the occasional oddity.

*i* *Entrées 50-60 kn; vegan and vegetarian options available*

### BISTROTEKA ($$)
Nikole Tesle 14; 1 483 7711; www.bistroteka.hr; open M-Th 8:30am-midnight, F-Sa 8:30am-1am

Bistroteka is the incarnation of the word "aesthetic." We're talking exposed brick, faux majolica floors, and chalkboard walls. Even better than the aesthetic are the reasonably priced starters (30 kuna). Perhaps more impressive than that is the multi-functionality of the place. Brunch spot? Check. Café? Check. Bar? Dinners, lunches, birthday cakes? Check, check, check, and check. If only we could multitask as efficiently, and deliciously, as Bistroteka.

*i* *Starters and sandwiches 30-40 kn, meat entrées 100 kn*

### COGITO COFFEE SHOP ($)
Varšavska 11; www.cogitocoffee.com; open M-F 8am-10pm, Sa 9am-7pm

Ditch the ubiquitous street cafés of central Zagreb in exchange for the holy grail of coffee. Welcome to Cogito, the pilgrimage destination of in-the-know Zagrabian hipsters, yuppies, and the otherwise cool. This coffee bar is the brainchild of Cogito Coffee Roasters, a 2014 startup dedicated to bringing quality, in-house roasted coffee to the Croatian capital. As you enjoy your artisanal flat white, elderflower juice, or homemade iced tea, don't be jarred by the seemingly eclectic décor: modern art, a vintage map of Africa, and a potted plant. We admit this is a bit over-the-top, but there is additional seating in a non-decorated exterior courtyard.

*i* *Coffee 10-20 kn, cappuccino 14 kn*

# NIGHTLIFE

### ◪A MOST UNUSUAL GARDEN ($)
Horćanska 3; 091 464 6900; open daily 8am-midnight

A sculpture of an octopus with a giant cucumber in a bathtub is the first thing you'll see at A Most Unusual Garden. This bar is truly unlike anything else in Zagreb, or the world for that matter.

Part-gin bar, part-treehouse, part-wall murals, this joint, frequented by locals, will make you feel like you're a character in *Alice in Wonderland*. Aside from the steampunk décor, there is a large outdoor seating area with steps, tables, and you guessed it, a treehouse—all underneath string lights and empty bottles of gin with candles. Although you'll have to take a tram to get here (#14/17), it's a straight shot from downtown.

*i* No cover, drinks 20-40 kn

### CLUB ROKO
Jarunska 5; 097 659 2000; open daily 8pm-3am

"You can go there, but they play trashy Croatian pop from the 90's," said the university students. "If you want to get lit on a Wednesday, it's the only place," said our bartender. "It's the sole club in the area," confirmed a stranger on the street. And they were all right. Club Roko, a locals-only joint south of the city center, gets going around 1am on weekday nights. No worries if you don't speak Croatian, with live music and the entire club belting out the chorus, you'll learn fast. If not, there's always the special on a handle of whiskey, which is sure to help. Those brave enough to survive the smoke-filled interior will be rewarded with an authentic Zagreb experience and clothes that smell like a chain smoker's.

*i* No cover, drinks 25 kn

### RAKHIA BAR
Tkalčićeva 45; 098 964 0587; open daily 8am-midnight

The first word you'll learn in Croatia is probably *rakija*. Found throughout the Balkans, it's the national drink of Croatia. And Rakhia Bar has every type of this brandy imaginable. The plum flavor is the strongest, but our favorite was the walnut. But, with over fifty options, why not find your personal pick? Just not too many, otherwise the steampunk interior might make your stomach turn. If all fails and Rakhia Bar is full, try out **Bar 45** or the many other options on Tkalčićeva Street.

*i* No cover, shots 11 kn

### TOLKIEN'S HOUSE
Opatovina 49; 1 485 2050; open daily 8am-midnight

A pub with walls covered in swords, maps of Middle Earth, and maces? Now that's what we're Tolkien about. Note: do not confuse Tolkien's House with a hobbit house. For those, you'll have to go to New Zealand. But, if a small pub with lots of *Lord of the Rings* paraphernalia and a solid selection of beers sounds like a good alternative, check it out on Opatovina ul., the cooler and more local cousin of the main bar drag, Tkalčićeva ul.

*i* No cover, beers 20 kn

# CROATIA ESSENTIALS

## VISAS

Croatia is a member of the European Union. Citizens of Australia, Canada, New Zealand, the US, and many other non-EU countries do not need a visa for stays of up to 90 days. Citizens of other EU countries may enter Croatia with only their national identity cards. Passports are required for everyone else. Despite being part of the EU, Croatia is not in the Schengen area, however holders of a Schengen visa are allowed to visit Croatia for up to 90 days without the need of an additional visa.

## MONEY

Despite being a member of the EU, Croatia is not in the Eurozone and uses the Croatian kuna (HRK or kn) as its currency.

**Tipping:** Tipping is not always expected, but often appreciated in Croatia. For bars and cafés, tips are not compulsory, but it is common to round up the bill. So, if the bill comes to 18 kn, leave 20 kn. Tipping in restaurants is much more common, and you should tip your server about 10% and 15% for really exceptional service. Taxi drivers also do not expect tips, but customers generally round up the bill.

## SAFETY AND HEALTH

**Drugs and Alcohol:** The minimum age to purchase alcohol in Croatia is 18, though technically there is no minimum age to drink alcohol (cheers!). Remember to drink responsibly and to never drink and drive. The legal blood alcohol content (BAC) for driving in Croatia is under 0.05%, significantly lower than the US limit of 0.08%.

**Travelers with Disabilities:** Croatia is largely not wheelchair accessible, as many of the sights require climbing stairs to reach the main attraction and elevators are not often provided. Streets themselves in Croatia often do not lend themselves to wheelchair travel, as they are not evenly paved ground and cobbled roads.

**BGLTQ+ Travelers:** Homosexuality has been legal in Croatia since 1977. It is also illegal to discriminate on the basis of sexuality and production of homophobic material can result in up to one year of imprisonment. However, there is still controversy and homosexuality is still not widely accepted. Public displays of affection between same-sex couples may be met with hostility.

# CZECH REPUBLIC

**Whether it's called Bohemia, Czechoslovakia, the Czech Republic, or now, as of a 2016 government initiative, Czechia, the Czech Republic (sorry, government—stop trying to make "Czechia" happen) is the golden child of Eastern Europe.** But, on the surface, the country's history follows the same old Eastern European sob story: it was part of big, fancy imperial powers (the Holy Roman Empire and the Austro-Hungarian one) from the Middle Ages until the First World War, independent until the Germans crashed the party in 1939, Nazi-occupied until the USSR said otherwise in 1945, Soviet-occupied despite Czech attempts to say otherwise, and otherwise enjoying this whole democracy thing since 1989. But dig a little deeper and some idiosyncrasies begin to pop up. From 1335 until 1437, the Kingdom of Bohemia wasn't just part of the Holy Roman Empire; Prague was the home of its imperial court. During the Second World War, it wasn't just any Nazi-occupied territory, but the only one to successfully assassinate a senior Nazi. When communism fell, it wasn't the result of any old revolution, but the Velvet Revolution, which implemented democracy without the loss of a single life.

Walking through the fairytale streets of Prague, the kaleidoscopic valley of Karlovy Vary, the rolling mountains of Bohemian Paradise Nature Park, or the skull and bone-laden chapel of Kutna Hora, you, like a person looking through movies filed under "Children's Fantasy" on Netflix, will find yourself enchanted. Spawning the likes of Franz Kafka, Antonin Dvořak, Sigmund Freud, and Ivana Trump, the Czech Republic is a collection of many pretty faces, and over the years, it's attracted a formidable number of backpackers, beer-drinkers, outdoor enthusiasts, elderly tour groups, and bachelor parties.

# KARLOVY VARY

Coverage by **Nicholas Grundlingh**

Unless you're a connoisseur of the world's hot springs, you've probably never heard of Karlovy Vary. But if you're a James Bond fan, you've probably already seen it. The home of the titular casino in *Casino Royale*, Karlovy Vary, with its thermal springs, architectural beauty, and walking trails, is the ideal place for a secret agent to kick back and relax while simultaneously thwarting evil in a high-stakes poker game. Although just two-hours west of Prague, this quaint spa town feels a million miles away from the city's bachelor parties. But the spa isn't the only place where you'll find some peace and quiet. A sense of serenity unspools itself as you walk amongst the gorgeous neo-this and art-that buildings that line the Tepla River, the grandest and largest of which is the 132-meter-long Mill Colonnade, while the most out of place of which is the brutalist Soviet-era Hotel Thermal. When you're in need of a pick-me-up, take a hike or funicular ride up Friendship Hill and meet someone new. Karlovy Vary prides itself as the birthplace of Becherovka liqueur and Moser luxury glassworks, and you can tour both of these factories during your stay. It would be too generous to say the town has a young, trendy feel. It really only comes to life during the first week of July, when Eastern Europe's biggest film festival draws over 10,000 hipsters, cinephiles, and celebrities to Karlovy Vary for a week-long party. If you have even the smallest cinematic bone in your body, you would be wise to join them. After visiting one tourist-overrun European capital after another, a couple of days in Karlovy Vary is the perfect way to rejuvenate.

## ORIENTATION

The **Ohře River** divides the greater region of Karlovy Vary into two parts, and the majority of the town's action (see: spas, colonnades, accommodations, restaurants, bars, museums) takes place south of it. This small southern area is itself split into two sections—north and south of the **Mill Colonnade.** If you're traveling from Prague via the more convenient bus option, you'll arrive north of the Mill Colonnade, either at the Tržnice bus terminal just north of the town's center or **Dolní nádraží,** the main bus station located a few minutes to the west. The former station serves most of the local bus lines, which travel to Moser glassworks factory, **Loket Castle,** and other surrounding areas. Following **T. G. Masaryka** street to the east will lead you to the **Tepla River.** Walking south along the river, you'll pass the best examples of the town's stunning architecture, the **Metropolitan Theater,** the **Karlovy Vary Museum,** as well as many historic landmarks, such as the **Hotel Thermal,** and the **Mill and Spring Colonnades.**

## ESSENTIALS

### GETTING THERE

The most convenient way to get to Karlovy Vary from Prague is via bus, which will disembark at either the Tržnice bus terminal or Dolní nádraží, the main bus station, which is a 5min. walk from the center. A map of the bus stops in Karlovy Vary can be found at www.dpkv.cz/cz/mapa-zastavek-mhd. Alternatively, if you're arriving via train, you will arrive at Horni Nadrazi, located north of the city center across the Ohře River. It's a 10min. walk from the station to the city center, but it's much more convenient to wait for bus #1 or 13, both of which are one stop away from Tržnice bus terminal.

### GETTING AROUND

Karlovy Vary is very walkable, and it takes around 25min. to walk along the Tepla from the bottom of the town to the Grandhotel Pupp at the top. A bus system (a map of the stops can be found at www.dpkv.cz/cz/mapa-zastavek-mhd) can take you around the main town as well as to places in the greater Karlovy Vary region (bus #1, 16, 22, and 23). Ticket options include: single trip (18Kč), 24hr

(80Kč), 7-days (220Kč). Two night bus lines run from 10:30pm into the early hours of the morning. Intercity buses that run across the Czech Republic can be taken to the Loket Castle, 30min. journey.

## PRACTICAL INFORMATION

**Tourist Offices:** T.G. Masaryka street Tourist Office (T.G. Masaryka 53; 355 321 171; open M-F 8am-1pm, 1:30-6pm, Sa-Su 9am-1pm, 1:30-5pm).

**Banks/ATMs/Currency Exchange:** Many ATMs are found on or nearby T.G. Masaryka street. South of Dvořákovy sady (Dvořák Park), ATMs can be found along the east bank of the Tepla. UniCredit Bank (Zeyerova 892/7; 955 959 823; open M, Tu, Th 9am-5pm, W 9am-6pm, F 9am-4pm). Chequepoint currency exchanges should be avoided; we recommend withdrawing cash from ATMs.

**Post Offices:** Czech Post (T. G. Masaryka 559/1; 954 330 304; open M-F 7:30am-7pm, Sa 8am-1pm, Su 8am-noon).

**Internet:** Free Wi-Fi can be found in most cafés in Karlovy Vary.

**BGLTQ+ Resources:** The Czech Republic is generally considered one of the most liberal Central European nations in terms of BGLTQ+ rights, legalizing same-sex partnerships in 2006. However, while Czech society is accepting and tolerant, BGLTQ+ individuals do not yet have full legal equality. Counseling for BGLTQ+ individuals in Karlovy Vary (Palackého 8; 731 549 171; www.ss-po.cz; Rp.cheb@ss-po.cz).

## EMERGENCY INFORMATION

**Emergency Number:** 112

**Police:** 158; The City Police station (Moskevská 913/34, 353 118 911).

**US Embassy:** The nearest US Embassy is in Prague (Tržiště 365/15; 257 022 000; open M-F 8:15am-11:30pm).

**Rape Crisis Center:** There is no Rape Crisis Center in Karlovy Vary, but there is one located in Prague.
- Elektra (Chomutovická 1444/2; 603 812 361; www.centrumelektra. cz, poradna@centrumelektra.cz; open W, F 9am-4pm).

**Hospitals:** The general emergency number is 353 115 640.

- Karlovarská krajská nemocnice (Bezručova 19; 353 115 111; open daily 24hr).
- Policlinics (náměstí Dr. M. Horákové 1313/8; 353 112 213; open M-F 6:30am-6pm).

**Pharmacies:** Dr. Max (Horova 1223/1; 353 233 900; open M-F 7am-7pm, Sa-Su 8am-8pm).

# ACCOMMODATIONS

### ◪HOTEL KAVALERIE ($$)

T. G. Masaryka 53/43; 353 229 613; www. kavalerie.cz; reception open daily 7:15am-6pm

If Karlovy Vary is indeed Coolio's fabled "Gangsta's Paradise," it's no wonder the song never mentions any hostels, seeing as the town has none. Thankfully, Karlovy Vary is home to a few, very affordable three-star hotels, of which Hotel Kavalerie is among the cheapest. Its location along **T. G. Masaryka** positions it smack dab in the middle of the town's nightlife hubs, and only a five-minute walk from the **collonades.** For a hotel, the amenities are pretty basic—a clean and comfortable room and a free breakfast, but that's about it. That said, after you've spent your whole day walking through what Coolie describes as "the valley of the shadow of death," it will feel like the Ritz.

*i* Twin from 703Kč; reservation recommended; BGLTQ+ friendly; no wheelchair accessibility; linens included; free breakfast

### A. DALIA ($$)

5.Kvetna 1; 222 539 539; www.adalia. hotels-karlovy-vary.com; no reception, check-in from 2pm

With its homey rooms, manicured garden, and friendly owners, A. Dalia is one of the best back-up options you could ask for. Yet, while nowhere in Karlovy Vary is ever more than a ten-minute walk away, this B&B, peacefully secluded atop a hill overlooking **Hotel Thermal,** will probably be one of the more strenuous 600-second walks you'll take. Luckily, a nearby bus, which runs to the town center every five minutes, will save you the trouble.

*i* Single from 750Kč, twin from 1000Kč; reservation recommended; BGLTQ+ friendly; no wheelchair accessibility

# SIGHTS
## CULTURE
. . . . . . . . . . . . . . . . . . . . . . . . . . . . . . . . . . .

### ◼KARLOVY VARY INTERNATIONAL FILM FESTIVAL
Ivana Petroviče Pavlova 2001/11; 221 411 011; www.kviff.com

If you had told us that one of Central Europe's biggest and most prestigious film festivals was situated in a small, Czech spa town where drinking hot, blood-tasting water was considered a treat, we would've called you a fat, stinking liar! But look who's got egg on their face now! The Karlovy Vary International Film Festival is as real as it gets. Held in the first week of July, the KVIFF screens over 200 films from nearly 50 countries and attracts around 15,000 visitors. It's by the far the most exciting time to visit the town—clubs, bars, and restaurants pop up everywhere (keep a look out for something called Aeroport), while the area surrounding Hotel Thermal—a brutalist structure built specially for the festival—is full of things to do and drink.

*i* Festival pass 1200Kč, reduced 900Kč; one day pass 250Kč, reduced 200Kč; limited wheelchair accessibility

### ◼MUNICIPAL THEATRE
Divadelní náměstí 21; 353 225 621; www.karlovarske-divadlo.cz; hours and show times vary

If there's one place in Karlovy Vary that we can't stand, it's the Municipal Theatre. This is partly because it's full of seats, but also because we can't bear its stunning Neo-Baroque beauty. Built in 1884 along the **Vltava River,** the theater is considered one of the country's most magnificent with its interiors painted by a couple of goofy Austrian twenty-somethings named **Gustav and Ernst Klimt.** Their greatest contribution is the incredibly intricate, hand-painted curtain that hangs in front the stage. As far as we can tell, the theater doesn't put on any

English-language productions, but it often hosts orchestras, ballets, and operas.

*i* Ticket prices vary; wheelchair accessible

### SPRING COLONNADE
Divadelní nám. 2036/2; 353 362 100; open daily 6am-6pm

Karlovy Vary's spring water is probably what a vegetarian vampire would drink, because even though it's 100% natural, it still retains that lovely blood taste. But where would this vampire go to get his fix? The Spring Colonnade, of course! The Colonnade's three natural geysers pump out water at 30°C, 50°C, and 70°C, and hordes of tourists stomach the water's bloody tang in exchange for its abundance of nutrients and minerals. Bring your own water bottle or purchase the traditional spa cups (120-190Kč), which also serve as a thoughtful souvenir to give to your favorite bloodsucker back home. The floor above functions as a gallery of locally-produced glassworks, while the area below is home to the thermal springs that you can tour every half hour.

*i* Free; wheelchair accessible

## LANDMARKS
. . . . . . . . . . . . . . . . . . . . . . . . . . . . . . . . . . .

### MILL COLONNADE
Mlýnské nábř.; open daily 24hr.

If you walk along the **Tepla River,** you will inevitably come across the Mill Colonnade. It's the de facto symbol of Karlovy Vary and one of the most beloved structures in town. In 1871, **Josef Zitek,** the architect behind Prague's National Theatre and Rudolfinum, designed this Neo-Renaissance colonnade, which let spa guests enjoy the spring waters come rain, shine, or one of those pesky nineteenth-century plagues. Pretty cool, right? This next one's even cooler. The structure is 132-meters long and it features 123 columns and an impressive five mineral springs.

*i* Free; wheelchair accessible

# SPAS IN KARLOVY VARY

Traveling to Karlovy Vary without checking out a spa is like going to San Francisco and not committing a bank robbery, getting locked up in Alcatraz, and then pulling off a daring escape. You'd be missing out on a one-in-a-lifetime experience that you simply can't find anywhere else! But if you're a traveler on a budget, it might seem as if bank robbery is the only way you could afford an afternoon in a spa. Luckily, Alžbětiny Lázně, or Elisabeth's Spa, is not only one of the most affordable spas in town, but also one of the most picaresque.

The pseudo-baroque spa complex was built in 1906 in honor of the Austro-Hungarian Emperor's murdered wife. Luckily, the spa's setting emanates a mood diametrically opposite to that of its origin story. Alžbětiny Lázně is the centerpiece of Smetanovy sady park, which sits next to the Teplá River. If this doesn't put your mind at ease, then the spa's prices certainly will. Whereas most spas charge upwards of 1000Kč for an hour-long classic massage, a 50-minute massage at Alžbětiny lázně a relative bargain of 790Kč, and most treatments embody the same price philosophy.

However, traveling to Karlovy Vary only to get a run of the mill massage is sort of like getting arrested in San Francisco and asking to be kept in a prison that's much less iconic than Alcatraz. If we were you, we'd pay special attention to the spa's list of "Special Treatments." These include: Oxygen therapy (290Kč), where you're strapped to an oxygen mask for an hour with the aim of strengthening your immune system and injecting some energy into your tired and unproductive soul; an hour in an infra-red sauna (340Kč), which is a little less suffocatingly-hot than a regular sauna and uses infra-red rays to detoxify your body of God knows what it's ingested while you've been in Prague; and 45 minutes sitting in a plush armchair inside of a chamber entirely constructed from natural salts (120Kč) which is the equivalent to a couple of days at sea and will supposedly boost your health and your mood. If these treatments sound a little too far out, why don't we reach a compromise? 15 minutes. 1 Massage. Your body = lathered in honey (440Kč). Deal?

## MUSEUMS

### ⬛MOSER FACTORY AND MUSEUM
Kpt. Jaroše 46/19; 353 416 132; www.moser-glass.com/en/pages/factory-tour; museum open daily 9am-5pm, factory tours 9:30am-2:30pm

Moser makes glassware like Mercedes Benz makes cars. Yes, in a factory—but also to an insanely high standard. Founded in 1857, this factory has produced some of the most celebrated luxury glassware in Europe, used by everyone from the saint-like Whoopi Goldberg to the hilarious Pope Pius. The museum documents the factory's history through a series of video exhibits. Most exhibits follow the same basic structure of "Moser did 'x' collection in 'y' year, and it was interesting because [insert uninteresting reason] and owned by 'z' dynasty/celebrity." The museum isn't

an essential visit. That said, we highly recommend a 30min. tour of the factory, during which you'll see 1200°C furnaces and sweat-drenched men blowing bubbles of glass.

*i* Museum and factory tour 180Kč, 100Kč reduced; factory tour 120Kč, 70Kč reduced; museum 80Kč, 50Kč reduced; wheelchair accessible

### KARLOVY VARY MUSEUM
Nová louka 23; 736 650 047; www.en.kvmuz.cz; open May-Sept W-Su 10am-6pm, Oct-Apr 10am-5pm

What's the deal with all the spas? Why are there so many colonnades? Did **Goethe's** love affair with a girl 55 years his junior have anything to do with his frequent visits? Did melting butter have anything to do with 97% of the town burning down in 1604? A visit to the Karlovy Vary Museum, which covers the town's modern and prehistoric past, will answer all these burning questions. The highlights include a large model of the town, parts of which you can illuminate to learn more, and an interactive screen with anecdotes about the town's famous visitors, including **Sebastian Bach, Karl Marx,** as well as **Sigmund Freud** and his mother.

*i Regular 100Kč, 60Kč reduced; wheelchair accessible*

## OUTDOORS

### 🏛DVOŘÁK PARK
360 01 Karlovy Vary; open daily 24hr

Nowadays, when someone does something cool, the mayor will give them the key to the city. But back in the day, cool people had a park named in their honor, and the notoriously cool Czech composer **Antonin Dvořák** was no exception. Given that Dvořák was one of the most celebrated late-romantic composers of the nineteenth century, it's no coincidence that the park is one of the most romantic spots in the city. The ornate Neo-Renaissance Park Colonnade forms the southern perimeter, inside which are lush lawns, vibrant flowerbeds, cherry blossoms, and perhaps most romantically of all, a statue of Dvořák himself. The colonnade often hosts concerts during the summer, but you really don't need an excuse to sprawl yourself in the shade of these 200-year-old trees.

*i Free; wheelchair accessible*

## FOOD

### 🏛DOBRA CAJOVNA TEA HOUSE
Bulharská 2; 608 822 827; www.tea.cz/obsah/27_dc-karlovy-vary; open daily 2-11pm

Whether it's an actor-singer-dancer like Gene Kelly or a talking animal-comedian-corporate spokesperson like the Geico Gecko, we love a triple threat. That's why this vegetarian restaurant-tea house-hookah bar is near the top of our list for places to eat in Karlovy Vary. Inconspicuously located in a basement on Zeyerova street, Dobra Cajovna is conspicuously adorned in Middle Eastern and Himalayan décor, with Nepalese prayer flags draped along the ceiling, Islamic geometric patterns covering the walls, and rugs and cushions on the floor. The food menu dabbles in hummus, falafel, and cheese and the drinks menu makes it possible to go around the world in 80 teas.

*i Entrées 98-108Kč; vegetarian options available; no wheelchair accessibility*

### PANOPTIKUM ($)
Bělehradská 1004/3; 728 520 822; open M-Th 11am-2am, F-Sa 11am-3am, Su 11am-midnight

If you're near the bottom of town and desperate for some authentic Czech goulash/soup/schnitzel/whatever, you better tie yourself to the mast of your ship and resist the siren song of the touristy, restaurant-lined Zeyerova street as you make your way to Panoptikum. Just a three minute-walk away from the city center, this pub has portions fit for a future Weight Watcher and drafts on tap fit for a beer connoisseur/current alcoholic. The wooden walls are decorated with old-timey photos that document Czech history, and although there's no outdoor seating, for those of the nicotine-persuasion, there's a smoking area where you can indulge yourself as well as a non-smoking area where you can irritate the nerds who won't shut up about their precious lungs.

*i Food 93-245Kč; vegetarian options available; limited wheelchair accessibility*

### REPUBLICA COFFEE
T. G. Masaryka 894/28; 720 347 166; www.e-restaurace.cz/u-krizovniku; open M-F 7am-7pm, Sa-Su 8am-7pm

Republica Coffee is a contender for the best café in town, especially if this accolade went to the café with the most tables covered in comic book panels or the comfiest leather armchairs. The coffee is drip, both in the brewing sense and in the-shaking-the-cup-above-your-mouth-to-make-sure-every-last-delicious-drop-drips-into-your-mouth-sense, and the hot chocolate is just the right mixture of creamy and thick. Once you collect your drink, sandwich, or pastry, chillax in the courtyard, or head upstairs and luxuriate in the aforementioned leather chairs.

*i Coffee 45-70Kč; vegetarian options available; wheelchair accessible*

### RESTAURACE U KRIZOVNIKU ($)

Moravská 2093/2a; 353 169 500; www.e-restaurace.cz/u-krizovniku; open daily 11am-11pm

Flannery O'Connor might've thought that a good man is hard to find, but finding a tasty, well-priced restaurant south of the colonnades might be even harder. While most places aren't bad per se, they'll leave your wallet at least 250-300Kč lighter. Luckily, this traditional Czech cuisine pub serves as good a meal as you'll eat in Karlovy Vary, and save you some money. Its paintings on the walls and medieval torches hanging from the ceilings give it an authentic feel, and its location—just to the east of the Spring Colonnade—means it's nearby tourist spots but not crawling with them.

*i* *Food 105-240Kč; vegetarian options available; limited wheelchair accessibility*

# NIGHTLIFE

### BARRACUDA CARIBBEAN COCKTAIL BAR

Jaltská 7; 608 100 640; www.barracuda-bar.cz; open M-Th 7pm-1am, F-Sa 7pm-3am

After waiting half an hour for the friends you met at the sauna earlier in the day to return from the bathroom downstairs, you might assume you've been abandoned—a feeling that you're all too accustomed to. Seeing as things can't get any worse, you might use the five straws sticking out of the Cuba Libre bucket (450Kč) in front of you to make a giant straw and finish the whole drink in one giant slurp. But don't do that! Your friends haven't (purposely) abandoned you. They've just discovered the small club hidden downstairs, which, replete with tiki masks and fish nets, echoes the above bar's beachy aesthetic. It's a cozy and slightly cheesy space that can be a ton of fun. But if you're less of a dancer and more of a drinker, the bar's 14pg. cocktail menu will make you forget all about your abandonment issues.

*i* *Cocktails from 80Kč, beer from 25Kč; cash only*

### KLUB PEKLO

Ivana Petroviče Pavlova 2001/11; 728 496 978; open M-Sa 9pm-6am

Occupying the basement of the monument to Soviet brutalism that is **Hotel Thermal,** Klub Peklo is a kind of a monument to Western garishness—a tourist-filled, EDM-blasting space where your level of enjoyment is directly proportional to the number of shots consumed. The club is one large, low-ceilinged room. The bar "bananas" around a third of the club's perimeter while the center is cluttered with sleek rolling leather chairs and glowing green prisms. A multigenerational melting pot of land dads, and their female equivalents, populate the dance floor, which is presided over by a DJ backlit by an LED screen of someone doing the worm. It's fun and stupid, and you should approach it with the same mindset, lest your communist sympathies prevent you from having a good time.

*i* *Cover up to 50Kč; cash only*

# PRAGUE

Coverage by **Nicholas Grundlingh**

So you want to experience the beauty of Paris, but don't think buying a cappuccino should require taking out a bank loan? You love the edginess of Berlin, but wish that—by virtue of you being a tourist—you weren't immediately excluded from it? You dream of a city that rivals those descriptions and is basically a "Now That's What I Call Music!"-esque compilation of the best architecture from the last thousand years where culture and history flood every street, bridge, fortress, and castle, yet despite this, never takes itself too seriously, while also being one of the best places to party in Europe? Why, that sounds an awful lot like Prague! Of course, if you're planning on traveling to Prague, you already know this. You know that the Old Town looks like an illustration from a fairytale, but you'll soon find out that it's one of those fairytales full of tourists. You know that the Charles Bridge and the Prague Castle are indisputable must-sees, but you'll soon find out, with everything else the city has to offer, they certainly won't be your highlights. Get lost amongst the bars, beer gardens, and galleries of the young and grungy Holesovice and Zizkov areas, bask in the unmatched tranquility of the Vysehrad fortress and park, and discover hidden gems in the heart of the city like the underworld bar Vzorkovna, the majestic Wallenstein Gardens, or the magical Karel Zeman Museum.

## ORIENTATION

Just like the skull of some punk who got into a fight with the star of Stand by Me, Prague is split by a river, which, in this case, is the Vltava River rather than the late River Phoenix. **Josefov** (Jewish Quarter), **Stare Mesto** (Old Town), and **Nove Mesto** (New Town) line the east bank of the river, and **Mala Strana** (Lesser Town) and **Hradcany** (Castle District), line the West Bank. Numerous bridges connect the two banks, the most famous of which is the Charles. These areas are often populated by hordes of tourists, but you can escape them by heading further inland east to the more local and residential **Zizkov** and **Vinohrady** neighborhoods, or crossing the Vltava north of Stare Mesto, where you'll find the grungy and artsy **Holesovice** district. What these less-touristy areas lack in sights, they make up for in cafés and dangerously chill vibes. The central bus and train stations are located just east of Stare Mesto in the **Florenc District,** while the Vaclav Havel Airport is found about an hour to the west.

## ESSENTIALS

### GETTING THERE

No direct train or bus lines run from the airport to the city center, but there are buses that connect to metro lines, which will take you into the city. Bus #119 runs from the airport to Veleslavín metro station on the green Line A. Bus #100 runs from the airport to Zličín metro station on the yellow line B. Both these lines will take you into the city center. The total journey is around 40min. Purchase tickets from Public Transport counters in Terminals 1 and 2 from 7am-10pm. Alternatively, use the coin-operated vending machines at the bus stop. Note that drivers usually accept small notes and change. You may need to purchase a half-price ticket (10Kč) for large pieces of luggage. Remember to validate tickets in the yellow machines before boarding any public transport. If you're arriving by train, you'll most likely disembark at Praha Hlavní Nádraží, the main railway station, located between Nove Mesto and Zizkov. The railway station is connected to the metro system (red line C). One stop north will connect you to the yellow line B, and one stop south to the green Line C; both will take you to the city center. Trains along the Berlin-Prague-Vienna/

Bratislava route may disembark at the Praha Holešovice station, which is located in the north region of Prague. This station also connects to the metro via red line C. Most international buses disembark at Florenc Bus Station, which is just east of the Old Town.

### GETTING AROUND

The public transport system is convenient and consists of three metro lines (green line A, yellow line B, red line C), trams, and buses. The same ticket is used for all forms of public transportation. Ticket options include: 30min. (for tram rides only, or metro journeys up to five stops, 24Kč), 90min. (32Kč), 24hr (110Kč), and 72hr (310Kč). Be sure to validate your ticket in the yellow machines on buses and trams or at the base of escalators in metro stations. Plainclothes police officers will often inspect tickets. They are notoriously strict and will fine you up to 1000Kč if you have not validated your ticket. The metro runs from 5am-midnight, and buses and trams operate from 4:30am-12:15am. Night buses and trams operate less frequently from 12:15am-4:30am. The central point of nighttime transfers is Lazarska in Nove Mesto. Be wary of potential pickpockets on crowded trains, trams, and buses, especially on trams #22 and

23. The minimum taxi fare is 28Kč/km. It is recommended that you order a taxi though a dispatch office where you can get information on fares in advance. Dispatch services that speak English include AAA radiotaxi (222 333 222; aaataxi.cz), Citytaxi Praha (257 257 257; www.citytaxi.cz) and Modry andel (737 222 333; www.modryandel.cz).

## PRACTICAL INFORMATION

**Tourist Offices:** Old Town Hall Tourist and Information Center (Staroměstské náměstí 1; open daily 9am-7pm).

**Banks/ATMs/Currency Exchange:** ATMs can be found in the city center and tourist areas, belonging to local and international banks. Many are located in or around Wenceslas Square and can generally be found in shopping centers and metro stations. In the city, beware of currency exchanges that charge high commission fees. Exchange (Kaprova 14/13; 800 22 55 88; open M-F 9am-10pm, Sa-Su 9am-8pm) is found in Josefov and known as one of the most reliable currency exchanges.

**Post Offices:** Czech Post (Jindřišská 909/14; 221 131 445; open daily 2am-midnight).

**Internet:** Free Wi-Fi can be found at nearly every café, hostel, and most restaurants also provide free Wi-Fi.

**BGLTQ+ Resources:** The Czech Republic is generally considered one of the most liberal Central European nations in terms of BGLTQ+ rights, legalizing same-sex partnerships in 2006. However, while Czech society is accepting and tolerant, BGLTQ+ individuals do not yet have full legal equality. Here are some resources, if needed:
• Gay Iniciativa (gay.iniciativa.cz/www/index) offers a 24hr hotline (476 701 444).
• GLBTI Counseling Center (Cílkova 639/24; 775 264 545; glbtiporadna.unas.cz, martina.habrova@gmail.com).

## EMERGENCY INFORMATION

**Emergency Number:** 112
**Police:** 156; the police headquarters are located directly at the bottom of Wenceslas Square (Jungmannovo nám. 771/9; 974 851 750, 24hr hotline).

**US Embassy:** The US Embassy (Tržiště 365/15; 257 022 000; open M-F 8:15am-11:30pm) is located in Mala Strana, near Malostranské náměstí).

**Rape Crisis Center:** There are two rape crisis centers located in Prague, which provide national crisis helplines.
• Elektra (Chomutovická 1444/2; 603 812 361; www.centrumelektra.cz, poradna@centrumelektra.cz; open W, F 9am-4pm).
• proFem o.p.s (Plzeňská 846/66; 608 222 277; www.profem.cz, poradna@profem.cz; open Tu 9am-noon, W 5:30-8:30pm).

**Hospitals:**
• The University Hospital in Motol (V Úvalu 84; 224 431 111).
• Nemocnice Na Momolce (Roentgenova 37/2; 257 271 111).

**Pharmacies:** Pharmacies in Prague are known as "Lékárnas."
• Lékárna Palackého (Palackého 720/5; 224 946 982; open daily 24hr).
• Lékárna U Svaté Ludmily (Belgicka 37; 222 513 396).

# ACCOMMODATIONS

## ART HOLE HOSTEL ($$$)
Soukenická 1756/34, Staré Město; 222 314 028; www.artholehostel.com; reception open 24hr

Art Hole feels more like a communal living area than a hostel. The reception and kitchen areas function as social spaces and the staff prepare nightly dinners that'll make you realize the true meaning of *ohana* (meaning "family"). Like many hostels in Prague, Art Hole only allows 18-to-35-year-olds to stay in its dorms, which injects the place with a youthful energy and rids it of old people smell. The wall murals are a hodgepodge of twentieth-century art, and you'll find the minimalism of De Stijl, the maximalism of Warhol, or the mickeyism of Walt Disney in nearly every room you enter. Even though the bathroom space is a little cramped, Art Hole's positives, such as its 5-minute walking distance from the **Old Town Square**, outshine such negatives.

*i* *Dorms from 450Kč during summer; reservation recommended; linens included; towels included; laundry facilities; free breakfast*

## ◼SIR TOBY'S HOSTEL ($)

Dělnická 1155/24, Holešovice; 246 032 610; www.sirtobys.com; reception open 24hr

If you're interested in staying in the hip part of Prague, making friends with fellow travelers, and sleeping in spacious rooms with debunked beds, then Sir Toby's hostel is your knight in shining armor. Found near the bottom of **Holešovice,** Sir Toby's is a short walk away from fantastic cafés, galleries, clubs, and bars, the nearest of which is found in their brick cellar basement. Whether you're participating in a nightly event (game night, beer tasting, BBQ, etc.) or enjoying the 25Kč per beer happy hour, you're guaranteed to meet fellow guests. The **Prague Castle** and **Old Town** are just 10 to 15 minutes away by tram.

*i* Dorms from 250Kč, single and twin from 768Kč; reservation recommended; BGLTQ+ friendly; wheelchair accessible; lockers provided; linens included; laundry facilities

## ADAM AND EVA ($$)

Zborovská 497/50, Mala Strana; 733 286 804; www.adamevahostelprague.com; reception open 8am-10pm

We have two theories about how this hostel got its name. 1) It possesses the peace and tranquility of the Garden of Eden. 2) It was built using a man's ribs. But then again, these are just theories—why don't we look at the facts? Composed of just two floors, Adam and Eva is as cozy as a cloth you drape over your nether regions. Each floor has a small balcony area that overlooks a courtyard, the reception has a map that points out all the best things to do in the area, and each bottom bunk bed is fitted with a curtain, which gives a sense of professionalism to any puppet shows you might want to put on for fellow guests.

*i* Dorms from 312Kč, twins from 390Kč; reservation recommended; no wheelchair accessibility; Wi-Fi; linens included; laundry facilities

## AHOY HOSTEL ($$$)

Na Perštýně 10, Stare Mesto; 773 00 4003; www.ahoyhostel.com; reception open 24hr

Everyone always talks about how "size matters," but we think location matters too. After all, a penis on an elbow is not sexy. Ahoy Hostel understands this, with its location in the swankier region of **Stare Mesto. Wenceslas Square** is a five-minute walk away. **Charles Bridge** is only double that. The proximity is prime, and while there aren't too many landmarks in the immediate vicinity, tram and metro stations are practically on the hostel's doorstep. Although the hostel's dorms are scarce on charging outlets, its rooms are big on cleanliness and comfort.

*i* Dorms from 492Kč, twin from 1378Kč; reservation recommended; no wheelchair accessibility; linens included; laundry facilities

## CZECH INN ($)

Francouzská 240/76, Vinohrady; 267 267 612; www.czech-inn.com; reception open 24hr

Check in at the Czech Inn and you'll be overwhelmed with things to check out! The only Prague member of the prestigious Europe's Famous Hostels group, Czech Inn boasts 36-bed dorms (a budget traveler's dream), a large and vibrant bar downstairs, as well as a series of nightly events. Every week, the basement bar hosts live music performances as well as one of the few English-language comedy nights in Prague, the latter of which is worth checking out even if you aren't staying at the hostel. While Vinohrady is a 15min. tram ride away from the city's main attractions, the hip and trendy area is littered with less-touristy restaurants and cafés.

*i* Dorms from 125Kč, twins from 975Kč; reservation recommended; BGLTQ+ friendly; no wheelchair accessibility; no Wi-Fi; linens included; laundry facilities; breakfast 150Kč

## MOSAIC HOUSE ($$$)

Odborů 278/4, Nove Mesto; 221 595 350; www.mosaichouse.com; reception open 24hr

"Mosaic House" doesn't just refer to the assortment of sculptures and installations that adorn its façade and entrance, but also its myriad purposes. A hostel, a hotel, a restaurant, a trendy bar-lounge, and a zero-carbon emissions establishment, this place is truly the Harry Styles of accommodations (by the time this is published, we assume *Dunkirk* will have launched Harry's acting career and he'll be recognized for versatility). Mosiac House has the feel of a chic hotel, and as such, prices higher than those of your average hostel. While there's a common area in the main building for hotel and hostel guests alike, you have to exit the building to access the kitchen/common room specific to the hostel, which remains open until 9pm.

*i* *Dorms from 416Kč, twins from 3126Kč; reservation recommended; wheelchair accessible; Wi-Fi; linens included; laundry facilities; breakfast buffet 40Kč*

### SOPHIE'S HOSTEL ($)
Melounova 2, Nové Město; 246 032 621; www.sophieshostel.com; reception open 24hr.

Although the name may indicate otherwise, this place is really a hostel of the people. With nightly events, a 24hr. bar and a 25Kč per beer happy hour, it's almost impossible not to befriend fellow guests, which makes it perfect for solo travelers and a nightmare for misanthropes. The rooms, like the rest of the hostel, have a modern and chic feel. They come mercifully equipped with a fan, making hot summer nights bearable. Located in the center of Nové Město and thus in the center of Prague, the hostel is very nearby to tram and metro stations.

*i* *Dorms from 250Kč, double from 1200Kč; reservation recommended; BGLTQ+ friendly; no wheelchair accessibility; linens included; laundry facilities*

# SIGHTS
## CULTURE

### BIO OKO
Františka Křížka 460/15, Holešovice; 233 382 606; www.biooko.net; show times vary

People get homesick in different ways. While some tend to miss their mother's home-cooked meals, others long for their country's independent cinema.

Bio Oko primarily caters to the latter, but its café might just have something to offer the former as well. Screening three films a day during the week and five a day on weekends, the movie theatre showcases local, international, and American art-house films. When we visited, Bio Oko was holding a **Christopher Nolan** retrospective (or maybe we just dreamt that it was?) as well as outdoor summer screenings at the **Prague Exhibition Grounds.** Even by Czech standards, the tickets are extremely affordable, and your options for reclining are leather chairs, beach loungers or giant bean bags.

*i* *Tickets 100-140Kč; wheelchair accessible*

### JATKA78
Jatecní 1530, Holešovice; 773 217 127; www.jatka78.cz; open M-F 10am-midnight, Sa 9am-midnight, Su 6pm-midnight

A circus in a slaughterhouse. While it could be the name of some angsty emo band you liked as a teen, it's actually a pretty accurate description of Jatka78. In 2015, a group of performers successfully crowdfunded the conversion of an abandoned slaughterhouse into two theatre halls and a gallery/café space. Throughout the year and more intermittently during the summer, Jatka78 puts on performances as often as once a day. But even if you can't make it to a show, the space alone is worth a visit, with its large snakelike wooden structure that twists and coils itself around the inside of the building.

*i* *Tickets 250-490Kč; wheelchair accessible*

### MEETFACTORY
Ke Sklárně 3213/15, Smíchov; 251 551 796; www.meetfactory.cz; open daily 1-8pm, evening programs run later

A night at MeetFactory will drive you up the wall. Not just because of the two red cars vertically hanging above its entrance, but also due to the frustration you'll feel that your middle-of-nowhere hometown doesn't have a concert venue/art gallery/theater space/outdoor cinema as cool as this. The brainchild of "the Czech Banksy" David Cerny, MeetFactory is an industrial space that consistently attracts the biggest names in indie and

electronic music, hosts a week-long summer film program, and curates three art galleries.

*i Tickets vary by event; wheelchair accessible*

## SHAKESPEARE AND SONS

U Lužického semináře 91/10, Malá Strana; 257 531 894; www.shakes.cz; open daily 11am-8pm

Normally, even the best English-language bookstores in non-English-speaking countries pale in comparison to your average Barnes and Noble back home. However, Shakespeare and Sons, which is unaffiliated with but of a similar quality to the famous Shakespeare and Co. in Paris, breaks this trend. The store's selection, while not as large as a Barnes and Noble, is incredibly well curated, meaning that you're just as likely to find the debut novel of the latest literary sensation as you are works by every big name in the western canon. The poetry, philosophy, and second-hand collections are particularly impressive, and the Czech section is impressively particular, containing almost the entire bibliographies of national sweethearts, **Kafka** and **Kundera.**

*i Books 200-400Kč; limited wheelchair accessibility*

## LANDMARKS

### ◾SS. CYRIL AND METHODIUS CATHEDRAL

Resslova 9a, Nove Mesto; 224 920 686; open Tu-S 9am-5pm

Quentin Tarantino would have you believe that Brad Pitt was the most notorious Nazi killer of the Second World War, but in truth, it was a group of Czech paratroopers, who, in May 1942, assassinated the architect of the Holocaust, Reinhard Heydrich. Unfortunately, the Czechs didn't have much time to celebrate. Three weeks later, the Germans, who had launched a vicious retaliatory attack on the Czechs, found the assassins hiding out in the crypt of the Ss. Cyril and Methodius Cathedral, and after a heated battle, the remaining paratroopers, in order to avoid capture, took their own lives. Today, the bullet-hole ridden crypt serves as an exhibition and memorial dedicated to the heroes of the assassination. The cathedral represents a part of Czech history that tourists often overlook.

*i Admission 75Kč, 35Kč reduced; no wheelchair accessibility*

### ◾VYSEHRAD

V Pevnosti 159/5b, Vinohrady; 241 410 348; www.praha-vysehrad.cz; open daily Nov-Mar 9:30am-5pm, Apr-Oct 9:30am-6pm

Recommended by nearly every local we met, Vysehrad, a tenth-century fortress, sits atop a rocky promontory overlooking the **Vltava River,** and is the most idyllic spot in the city. Vysehrad served as the royal seat of Bohemia for a glorious 40 years before its role was usurped by **Prague Castle.** Today, the castle building itself no longer exists, but the infinitely tranquil parks and what, in our opinion, is the most stunning church in Prague still do. The fortress walls also contain the eleventh-century **Rotunda of St. Marti,** which is one of the city's oldest surviving buildings, the underground Casements, which store six of the original Charles Bridge statues, and a cemetery, home to the graves of **Antonin Dvořak** and **Alfons Mucha,** and the **Slavin tomb.**

*i* *Free entry to Vysehrad fortress; Church of St. Peter and St Paul 50Kč, 30Kč reduced; The Brick Gate, Casemates, Gorlice Hall and Permanent Exhibition 60Kč, 30Kč reduced; last entry 30min. before closing; limited wheelchair accessibility*

## CHARLES BRIDGE

Karlův most, Staré Město; www.prague.cz/charles-bridge; open daily 24hr

A walk across the Charles Bridge is a rite of passage, although during the high season, it's not so much a walk as it is a swim through a sea of bodies, which is why the perfect time to visit is early in the morning after a big night out. At 5:31am on July 9, 1357, the Czechs' beloved King Charles IV laid the first stone of the bridge, doing so at that exact time because it formed an auspicious "numerical bridge" (1357 9/7 5:31). The bridge once served as the royal passageway from the **Old Town** to the **Prague Castle,** but nowadays it's occupied by street vendors and caricature artists. Impressive Baroque statues line the sides of the bridges but—just between us—these statues are actually replicas and the originals can be found at the Vysehrad fortress. Oh, we forget to mention that the bridge is allegedly the pickpocket capital of Europe, so if you're looking for a good place to pickpocket, you should probably choose somewhere less mainstream.

*i* *Free; wheelchair accessible*

## JEWISH QUARTER

Josefov, Stare Mesto; 222 317 191; www.jewishmuseum.cz; open summer Tu-S 9am-6pm, winter 9am-4:30pm

Found just north of **Old Town Square,** the Jewish Quarter is one of the most historic sites in the city, home to five synagogues and the Old Jewish cemetery. A standard ticket (Ticket B, 330Kč) will give you access to most of the sights, including the cemetery as well as the **Pinkas and Spanish synagogues,** but access to the **Old-New Synagogue**—the oldest synagogue in Europe—can only be

secured through the purchase of Ticket A+B (500Kč). Beyond its historical significance, the Old-New Synagogue isn't much to look at, and thus, if you're on a budget, Ticket B will suit you just fine. The Pinkas Synagogue's walls are covered in the names of the 78,000 Czech-Jews who died in the Holocaust, and the exhibits upstairs showcase drawings created by children from the Theresienstadt concentration camp.

*i* *With Old-New Synagogue 500Kč, 340Kč reduced; without Old-New Synagogue 330Kč, 220Kč reduced; limited wheelchair accessibility*

## JOHN LENNON WALL

Velkopřevorské náměstí, Malá Strana; open daily 24hr

A visit to the John Lennon Wall is obligatory. Created in the late 1980s as a rebuke to the country's communist regime, which had banned western music, the wall symbolized the desire amongst Czech youth for "Lennonism, Not Leninism." However, following the fall of communism, the wall transformed from a counterculture icon to a fun spot for tourists and locals to spraypaint messages of peace and love, the most memorable of which is a mural of an Ewok doing the black power salute, captioned "Fuck Wars." It's just a minute from Charles Bridge, which means you really have no excuse for not checking it out, unless, of course, you are virulently pro-war.

*i* *Free; wheelchair accessible*

## OLD TOWN SQUARE AND ASTRONOMI-CAL CLOCK

Staroměstská náměstí, Staré Město; 236 002 629; www.staremestskaradnicepraha.cz; clock tower open M 11am-10pm, Tu-Su 9am-10pm

Old Town Square is effectively the heart of Prague, and the area's history and architectural beauty make it a compulsory visit. In the middle of the square sits a memorial dedicated to the Czech hero **Jan Hus,** who was one of the first people to do the now unthinkable act of giving the Catholic Church a hard time. You'll also find the double-towered, Gothic Church of Our Lady before Týn, as well as the one and only Astronomical Clock, in front of which hundreds of people gather outside to watch puppets representing Death, Vanity, Greed, and Pleasure jump out of the clock face and stiffly move a few limbs for a couple of minutes each hour. It's not worth the hype, but something you might as well see if you're in the square.

*i* *Clock tower 120Kč, 70Kč reduced; wheelchair accessible*

## PRAGUE CASTLE

119 08 Prague 1, Hradcany; 224 373 368; www.hrad.cz; castle complex open daily Tu-S 6am-10pm, historical buildings 9am-5pm

Castle, castle on the hill, do you provide visitors with a thrill? Visitor, visitor down below, the answer is yes and no. Yes, because Prague Castle—which isn't so much a castle as a collection of palaces, churches, and towers—contains **St. Vitus Cathedral,** whose stained-glass windows make it one of the most stunning structures in Prague. No, because from an aesthetic perspective the other buildings in the castle don't offer much, which given that regular tickets cost at least 250Kč (we recommend the Circuit B option) and a half hour of queuing, leaves us on the fence.

*i* *Circuit A (350Kč, 175Kč reduced), Circuit B (250Kč, 125Kc reduced), Circuit C (350Kč, 175Kč reduced); last entry at 4:40pm; limited wheelchair accessibility*

## MUSEUMS

### DOX CENTRE FOR CONTEMPORARY ART

Poupětova 1, Holešovice; 295 568 123; www.dox.cz; open M 10am-6pm, W 11am-7pm, Th 11am-9pm, F 11am-7pm, Sa-Su 10am-6pm

With a façade that functions as a work of art, a 42-meter-long blimp suspended in the courtyard, and a giant crucifix made out of sneakers hanging from a wall below it, DOX is arguably just as interesting a space as it is a gallery. But that argument would be shut down quickly given the quality of the center's exhibits. Aiming to provide a "critical reflection on current social topics," DOX's constantly changing exhibition spaces deal with topics such as big data, capitalism, "the cage of one's own mind," and many other

cheerful things, none of which, at least when we visited, featured a single painted canvas, but one of which contained three VR headsets. The regular tickets are pretty reasonably priced.

*i* *Admission 180Kč, 90Kč reduced; last entry 1hr. before closing; wheelchair accessible*

### KAFKA MUSEUM

Cihelná 635/2b, Malá Strana; 257 535 373; www.kafkamuseum.cz; open daily 10am-6pm

Kafka, perhaps more than any other writer, explored what it meant to be a cockroach, and this museum, certainly more than any other museum, explores what it meant to be Kafka. The museum is filled with Kafka's own letters, manuscripts, sketches, and diary entries, as well as critical commentaries that help make sense of his life and work. What's more, the dimly lit rooms, eerie background music, and unsettling exhibit layouts work together to produce an atmosphere that can only be described by the term named after the writer himself: Kafkaesque. The museum is worthwhile, as it provides the perfect starting point for learning about a writer that everyone should know how to pretentiously reference.

*i* *Admission 200Kč, 120Kč reduced; wheelchair accessible*

### KAREL ZEMAN MUSEUM

Saská 80/1, Malá Strana; 724 341 091; www.muzeumkarlazemana.cz; open daily 10am-7pm

Karel Zeman is one of the most celebrated animators and Czech filmmakers of the twentieth century, having inspired everyone from *Monty Python* to Wes Anderson. But, unless you grew up in the Czech Republic during the Cold War, you've probably never seen his work. Zeman's films embody a rare combination of artistic brilliance and childlike innocence, and walking through the museum—where you'll encounter props, costumes, puppets, and most prominently, video clips from his films—you'll likely be overcome with the same wonder and awe that you'd get from Pixar movies, which—surprise, surprise—owe a great debt to Zeman.

*i* *Admission 200Kč, 140Kč reduced; last entry 1hr. before closing; wheelchair accessible*

## NATIONAL GALLERY
Sternberg Palace (Hradčanské náměstí 15), Trade Fair Palace (Dukelských hrdinů 47), Kinsky Palace (Old Town Square 12); 224 301 122; www.ngprague.cz; open Tu-Su 10am-6pm

Prague's National Gallery comprises many individual galleries scattered throughout the city. The most popular galleries include the **Sternberg Palace** in Hradcany, which showcases European art from the fourteenth to eighteenth century, and the **Trade Fair Palace** in Holesovice, which is the largest exhibition and focuses on contemporary works. Skip the Alfons Mucha museum and head to the Trade Fair Palace, if you're content with seeing just a few works by Prague's prodigal Art-Nouveau son. In Old Town Square, Kinsky Palace houses an interesting, but inessential Asian art exhibition.

*i* *Admission 150Kč, 80Kč reduced, free student; wheelchair accessible*

## OUTDOORS

### BOAT RENTAL ALONG VLTAVA RIVER
Janáčkovo nábř, Staré Město; 10am-sundown (varies)

Whether you're pedaling a car-shaped boat or rowing a boat-shaped boat, an hour on the Vltava River is one of the best ways to spend an afternoon in Prague. Boat rental companies are scattered along the Staré Město bank between the Charles and Legií bridges, with many found on Slovansky ostrov island. Once you've paid 200-300Kč (depending on the kind of boat), you are free to roam anywhere between the Charles and the Jiráskůvmost bridges. While most kiosks remain open until sundown, some offer the option of renting an oil lamp-lit boat at night, which makes for a great date idea. What's more, if the date goes badly, you can just push the other person into the river.

*i* *Boat rental 200-300Kč; limited wheelchair accessibility*

### LETNÁ PARK AND METRONOME
Badeniho; www.prahazelena.cz/letenske-sady.html; open daily 24hr.

Why spend ten bucks on the latest Drake album when you could get #views like this for free? That's a question we asked ourselves many times as we sat in Letná Park overlooking the entire city, feeling like fools as we stared at Drake's stupid face on the cover of the CD we bought. The optimum viewing point is, without a doubt, on a ledge under the giant **Prague Metronome,** which occupies the former spot of the reviled Stalin monument and serves as a reminder of the city's past. When the sun's about to set, there's no better place to be. But there's more to this park than just breathtaking vistas and historically-significant landmarks. Walk west and you'll encounter one of the most idyllic beer gardens in Prague.

*i* *Free; limited wheelchair accessibility*

## NAPLAVKA RIVERBANK
Rašínovo nábřeží, Vinohrady; open daily 8am-3am

It would be trippy if we told you that the best beer garden in Prague wasn't a garden, wouldn't it? Well, we hope you don't suffer from vertigo, because the best garden in Prague isn't a garden, or even park, but a riverbank. Woah! Every summer evening, locals and in-the-know tourists swarm the stretch of the Vltava riverbank between Palackého most (Palacký Bridge) and Železniční most (Railway Bridge). The area is lined with beer-serving barges, hole-in-the-wall cocktail bars, food stalls, as well as a Captain Morgan-sponsored club in the hull of a pirate ship. Hunt down a 25Kč pilsner and find a spot on the edge of the river, or hunt down a few and you might just fall in.

*i*  *Free; limited wheelchair accessibility*

## PETRIN HILL AND TOWER
Petřínské sady, Mala Strana; 257 320 112; www.muzeumprahy.cz/198-petrinska-rozhledna; Funicular open daily 9am-11:20pm, Tower open daily Nov-Feb 10am-6pm, Mar, Oct 10am-8pm, Apr-Sept 10am-10pm

France's best-kept secret for over a hundred years, the Eiffel Tower first received international exposure in the 2000 box-office smash *Rugrats in Paris*. However, Prague, undoubtedly anticipating the tower's future popularity, decided to build its own in 1891. The Petrin Tower is a 60-meter-tall structure that, when you take into account the hill it sits atop, is nearly as tall as the 324-meter original. Take a 30min. walk from the base of the hill to its peak, a 299-step hike to the tower's viewing platform, and reward your hard work with stunning panoramic views of the city. Alternatively, use your public transport ticket for a ride up in a funicular and double down on your laziness by paying 60Kč to take an elevator the rest of the way.

*i*  *Funicular free with public transport ticket, tower 150Kč, 80Kč reduced; wheelchair accessible*

## KUTNA HORA'S BONE CHAPEL

Kutna Hora is an old silver mining town, but more than that, it's one of the Czech Republic's twelve **UNESCO World Heritage Sites,** but more than that, it's home to the stunningly eerie and eerily stunning Sedlec Ossuary, otherwise known as the Bone Chapel, and the pretty enormous and enormously pretty gothic church of St. Barbara. Just an hour's train ride outside of Prague, the town makes for the perfect daytrip.

Following a bout of the Black Death in the fourteenth century and a war between the proto-Protestant Hussites and the Holy Roman Empire 50-odd years later, the Sedlec Abbey found itself faced with the classic serial killer conundrum: too many bodies and not enough space to bury them. The problem was made worse by the fact that, a few hundred years earlier, the Abbey had been sprinkled with "holy soil" from the Grave of the Lord in Jerusalem, which meant everyone and their plague-ridden dog wanted to be buried here. In 1511, the surplus bones were moved to the chapel underneath the Abbey, but it wasn't until the early nineteenth century that the House of Schwarzenberg, one of the most prominent families in Europe, employed a local woodcarver to create various decorations and artistic arrangements out of the chapel's collection of over 40,000 bones. The woodcarver made magnificent bone chandeliers, bone pyramids, bone chalices and even a bone version of the Schwarzenberg coat of arms, which features a raven skeleton pecking at the skull-ified severed head of a Turk. If you're looking for a reminder of life's impermanence and the inevitability of death, or just want to see one of the coolest sights in the Czech Republic (or both!), the Sedlec Ossuary will not disappoint.

# FOOD

## ▨CAFÉ LOUVRE ($$)

Národní 22, Nove Mesto; 224 930 949;
www.cafelouvre.cz; open daily 8am-
11:30pm

Café Louvre is fantastic, but don't just take our word for it—take Albert Einstein's and Franz Kafka's. Back in the day, this café was a favorite amongst Prague's intellectual community, and when these geeks and nerds weren't discussing nuclear physics and the futility of man, they were most likely chomping on some very reasonably priced traditional Czech food. Enter under the "Café Louvre" marquee, follow a long hallway and head upstairs, where you'll encounter a scene straight out of your *Gatsby* nightmares. The ceilings are high, the tablecloths white, the lighting fixtures unusual, and the walls covered in a mix of old-school advertisements and black-and-white photos.

*i* *Entrées 139-349Kč; vegetarian options available; no wheelchair accessibility*

## ▨PARALLEL POLIS ($)

Dělnická 475/43, Holešovice; 702 193 936; www.paralelnipolis.cz; open M-F 8am-8pm, Sa-Su noon-9pm

Parallel Polis is the world's first bitcoin café, which means you can only pay with, you guessed it, bitcoin. If you're some kind of luddite who doesn't have a healthy stash of bitcoins already saved in the cloud, don't worry. There's a bitcoin ATM inside the café that'll sort you out. What's with this café's obsession with bitcoin anyway? Is it, like, run by some sort of crypto-anarchist hacking collective? Yes. Yes, it is. Above the café is the **Institute of Cryptoanarchy,** which aims to promote personal privacy, liberty, and all those other things that make people enemies of the state. But don't let all this cyber mumbo-jumbo distract you from that fact that the café, equipped with fancy V60 and aeropressfilters, knows how to make a damn good cup of joe.

*i* *Coffee 40-60Kč, cash and credit cards accepted for bitcoin exchange; vegetarian options available; wheelchair accessible*

## CHOCO CAFE ($)

Red Chair, Liliová 250/4, Staré Město; 222 222 519; www.choco-cafe.cz; open daily 10am-8pm

If you gave this hot chocolate its own Instagram account, you'd be guaranteed to have at least one hundred dudes commenting "thicc af (peach emoji)" on every single post. But when a drink's this creamy, rich, and, yes, thick, what else would you expect? Even calling it a drink is a bit of a stretch. It has much more in common with a chocolate bar left in your pocket on a summer's day. If this is your first rodeo at Choco, stick to the most basic options, lest you risk a cardiac arrest of the senses. But if you think a trip to your sensory cardiologist is long overdue, then go for one of the chili, ginger, or alcoholic varietals.

*i* *Hot chocolate 59-99Kč; wheelchair accessible*

## CRÊPERIE "U SLEPE KOCICKY" ($$)

M. Horákové 600/38, Holešovice; 233 371 855; www.slepakocicka.cz; open daily 11am-11pm

While any restaurant with the word "crêpe" in the title will inevitably catch our eye—which, in the past, has led to heartbreak and stomachache—these crêpes are a cause to celebrate. With a comprehensive range of both sweet and savory pancakes and crêpes at very affordable prices, you can order everything from salmon, sour cream, and chicken to banana, chocolate, nuts, and eggnog. Beyond the food, the restaurant looks like it's straight out of a fairytale about a nice, old woman who's obsessed with cats. The wood-paneled interiors are decked out with feline-themed paintings, statues, and lampshade decorations. Luckily, the flowerpots dangling from the ceiling provide a merciful counterbalance to the cat-holism.

*i* *Savory crêpes 139-176Kč, sweet crêpes 69-142Kč; wheelchair accessible*

## FERDINANDA ($)

Karmelitská 379/18, Mala Strana; 257 534 015; www.ferdinanda.cz; open M-Sa 11am-11pm, Su 11am-5pm

If your money's about as tight as a nun's budget to buy school supplies for the poor orphans she looks after, look no further than Ferdinanda.

The restaurant's underground setting deprives it of the street-side seating common to most **Mala Strana** eateries, but when a bowl of goulash and a half pint of beer cost a mere 148Kč, we couldn't care less. The locals and tourists that regularly pack the place don't either. The menu also includes a vegetarian section, which isn't always guaranteed in most Czech cuisine places. Seeing as most of the nearby restaurants in Malostranske Nam. charge 200Kč or more per main, it's best to remember the unofficial Trump motto of "When they go high, we go low" and seek out the budget-friendly underworld of Ferdinanda.

*i* *Entrées 85-249Kč; vegetarian options available; no wheelchair accessibility*

### FOOD OF LOVE ($$)
Nerudova 219/32, Mala Strana; 736 633 098; www.foodoflove.cz; open daily 11am-10pm

With the overabundance of meat-heavy Czech cuisine restaurants, being a vegetarian in Prague can sometimes make you feel like the only free-range chicken in an industrial slaughterhouse. Thankfully for everyone who found that simile in poor taste, there's Food of Love, a quaint vegetarian restaurant situated in a courtyard just below **Prague Castle.** Beyond the vegetarian options, the menu is loaded with raw vegan and gluten-free meals. It also offers vegetarian goulash and over 20 varieties of tea. To find the restaurant, walk up Nerudova street, and about 20-meters before a more obnoxiously signposted vegan restaurant, turn into a small art gallery to the right and continue into the courtyard.

*i* *Entrées 165-240Kč; vegetarian, vegan, and gluten-free options available; wheelchair accessible*

### LOKAL DLOUHÁÁÁ ($$)
Dlouhá 33, Staré Město; 222 316 265; www.lokal-dlouha.ambi.cz; open Su-F 11am-1am, Sa 11am-midnight

While most people are rightfully suspicious of **Old Town** restaurants that make a big deal about their local cuisine, you can let your guard down at Lokal. A huge beer hall populated by locals and tourists alike, this restaurant serves a wide array of traditional Czech cuisine that's as tasty

as it is filling. After one plate of fried cheese and a helping of sausages, we felt simultaneously at one with the universe and practically comatose. The Old Town location is just one of many scattered across Prague, but thankfully the fact that it's a chain doesn't detract from the quality of the food or the restaurant's authentic feel, the latter of which is bolstered by the 40Kč mugs of beer.

*i* *Entrées 115-269Kč, starters 85-119Kč; wheelchair accessible*

### MR. HOT DOG ($)
Kamenická 24; Holešovice; 732 732 404; www.mrhotdog.cz; open daily 11:30am-10pm

"Is there a Mrs. Hot Dog?" we ask breathlessly after guzzling down a deliciously messy chili-cheese dog. "Uh, no," the waiter replies, which we take as a signal to get down on one knee and propose on the spot. Because, folks, these hot dogs are marriage material, but more than that, they're one of the best value-for-money meals we found. Sure, it's an obnoxious tourist move to go to the American hot dog joint when you're here, but if you're on-the-go and in need of a quick mouthwatering meal, cut yourself some slack and be an obnoxious tourist. And while you're at it, why don't you go the whole nine yards and order a margarita—they're great!

*i* *Hot dogs 49-139Kč; wheelchair accessible*

### THE CRAFT ($)
Náměstí Míru 1221/4, Vinohrady; 306 577 4230; www.thecraft.cz; open Su-F noon-midnight, F-Sa noon-2am

When your beers are microbrewed and you treat burgers as an artisanal practice, there's no better name for your restaurant than The Craft, which, just off **Namesti Miru** (Peace Square), is a go-to-place for the young **Vinohrady** crowd. Although you have eight burger options to choose from, you can feel safe with the knowledge that each will be served with a juicy and tender patty between a warm and toasty bun, both of which are impaled with a giant steak knife instead of a measly toothpick. We found the tiger-prawn-topped Surf and Turf burger to be a revelation. The restaurant is decked out in rustic-chic decor and the bathrooms are stocked with cotton wool and Q-tips, which may or may not come in handy for a less-than-clean backpacker such as yourself.

*i  Burgers 209-249Kč; wheelchair accessible*

# NIGHTLIFE

## ⛎NEONE
Bubenská 1477/1, Holešovice; 723 063 209; open F-Sa 10pm-6am

Devoid of drunken tourists and trashy music, Neone is an electronic music lover's dream and a British bachelor party's worst nightmare. Originally created as a temporary venue, Neone was so popular amongst the more artsy and hip locals that it became a permanent fixture of Prague's nightlife scene. Found at the bottom of **Holešovice,** the club occupies an unsuspecting, office-like building, identifiable by the façade's green neon "N." It draws the most cutting-edge electronic DJs and producers from across Europe, and mesmerizing visual art projections usually accompany their sets. With its DIY-attitude and communal feel, Neone is possibly the closest thing you'll find to a Berlin-esque club in Prague.

*i  Cover 130Kč; cash only*

## CLUB ROXY
Dlouhá 33, Stare Mesto; 608 060 745; www.roxy.cz; open daily 11pm-5am

Karlovy Lazne, the five-story club next to **Charles Bridge,** is the symbol of the trashy side of Prague's nightlife, and, unless you're the kind of person who likes doing things "for the experience," should be avoided. However, for those wanting to experience Prague's mainstream clubbing scene without a tourist trap reputation and a 200Kč entrance fee, Club Roxy is a worthy alternative. Near the north of **Stare Mesto,** the club boasts a massive, techno/house-heavy dance floor and a crowd of tourists and locals alike. People of all ages flock here as if it's Macy's Thanksgiving Day Parade. If you like minimal entry fees and, by

club standards, cheap drinks, you'll have a lot to be thankful for.

*i  Cover up to 250Kč, beer from 50Kč, wine 45Kč, shots 65-80Kč, cocktails 95-200Kč; cash only*

## CROSS CLUB
Plynární 1096/23, Holešovice; 736 535 053; www.crossclub.cz; open daily 2pm-5am

To put it simply, Cross Club evokes Optimus Prime deciding to go steampunk and, due to violating the sleek Autobot aesthetic, being subsequently broken down into his constituent parts, which were then sold to the villain from *Mad Max* and used to furnish a local resto-bar-club. So now that we've broadly described the Cross Club aesthetic, what do we make of the place itself? Well, once you've figured out how to navigate the multiple floors of this labyrinthine complex, you'll find it full of punks, hippies, locals, and tourists, all of whom are looking for something more alternative than Prague's mainstream nightlife offerings. The music spans several genres—electro, drum and bass, techno, house, you name it—and is blasted out of one of the best sound systems in the city.

*i  Beer 22-62Kč, cocktails 66-114Kč; cash only; BGLTQ+ friendly*

## KLUB UJEZD
Újezd 422/18, Mala Strana; 251 510 873; www.klubujezd.cz; open daily 2pm-4am

Klub Ujezd must be on a sea monster diet, because as soon as you step inside this bar, you see monsters. And not just any monsters, sea monsters. The Loch Ness monster protrudes from the yellow walls, while other mythical creatures hang from the ceiling and coil around the light bulbs. Hang out upstairs, play some foosball, and shout your drink order across the steampunk-y barrier that separates you from the bartender, or venture down into the stone-cobbled basement where things get a little grungier. Regularly hosting live music, DJs, and art exhibitions, Klub Ujezd is one of the most beloved spots west of the Vltava River.

*i  Beer and spirits from 30Kč, shots 49-59Kč; cash only*

### VLKOVA 26

Vlkova 699/26, Zizkov; open Tu-Sa 8pm-3am

The cool kids of Prague wouldn't touch a lot of the bars and pubs in **Old Town** with a ten-foot pole. So where are the bars they touch? Well, of course, there's Holešovice, but there's also the even more local and residential neighborhood of Žižkov, in the heart of which you'll find Vlkova 26. A minimal and candle-lit space, replete with concrete walls and leather couches, you'll find an indie/hip hop/electronic-spinning DJ. During the weekdays, the bar is vibrant, but not crowded. But when the weekend comes around, Vlkova 26's bar is full and the dance floor is FULL (Fun, Underground, Lively, Life-affirming).

*i* *Cocktails 100-150Kč; cash only*

### VZORKOVNA

Národní 339/11, Nové Město; open M-F 5pm-3am, Sa-Su 6pm-3am

In both the below street level-sense and the shabby and cool-sense, Vzorkovna is an underground playground. After descending the stairs, you'll pass a circle of swings suspended from the ceiling, walk through a brightly-lit room with three back-to-back foosball tables and leather seats nailed to the wall, eventually stumbling on a series of grimy rooms plastered in graffiti and strewn with antiques with the only source of light coming from the string of fairy lights snaking around the exposed pipes overhead. You'll encounter shirtless punks, 20-something hipsters, bachelorette parties, and a comically large dog. The drinks aren't half bad either. One bar specializes in craft beers served in mason jars while another brews tea.

*i* *Beer from 30Kč*

# CZECH REPUBLIC ESSENTIALS

## VISAS

The Czech Republic is a member of the EU and the Schengen area. Citizens from Australia, Canada, New Zealand, the US, and many other non-EU countries do not require a visa for stays up to 90 days. However, if you plan to spend time in other Schengen countries, note that the 90-day period applies cumulatively to all of them.

## MONEY

**Currency:** Although the Czech Republic is a member of the EU, it is not in the Eurozone and uses the Czech Koruna (Kč or CZK) as its currency. ATMs can be found in shopping malls, banks, and most public spaces. Avoid currency exchanges at airports and use ATMs instead. The best currency exchanges are those that advertise the "buy" and "sell" rates, which allow you to calculate exactly how much you will receive and don't charge a commission fee. To find out what out-of-network or international fees your credit or debit cards may be subjected to, call your bank.

**Tipping and Bargaining:** In restaurants, tips are usually not included in the bill, so it's customary to tip 10-15% for good service. Another way to tip is to round your bill to the nearest 10Kč and then add 10% of the total. When you pay the bill, include the tip. A 10% tip for taxis is acceptable. It is not customary to leave tips on the table before you leave. Bargaining is only done in open-air markets or antique shops.

# SAFETY AND HEALTH

**Local Laws and Police:** The Czech police have a reliable reputation and you should not hesitate to contact them if needed. Be sure to carry your passport with you, as police have the right to ask for identification. However, police can sometimes be unhelpful if you're the victim of a currency exchange scam, in which case it's best to seek advice from your embassy or consulate.

**Drugs and Alcohol:** If you carry insulin, syringes, or any prescription drugs on your person, you must also carry a copy of the prescription and a doctor's note. The drinking age is 18. There is a zero-tolerance policy for people who drive under the influence, meaning that the legal blood alcohol content (BAC) is zero. The possession of small quantities of marijuana (less than 15g), 40 pieces of magic mushrooms, 5 grams of hashish, five LCD-laced papers or other materials with LSD, 1.5 grams of heroin, 1 gram of cocaine, and 2 grams of methamphetamine were decriminalized in 2009. However, carrying any of these drugs is still a misdemeanor, which could result in a fine up to 15,000Kč. Carrying drugs across an international border—drug trafficking—is a serious criminal offence.

**Petty Crime and Scams:** These types of crime are common in the Czech Republic. A common scam in bars and nightclubs involves a local woman inviting a traveler to buy her drinks, which end up costing exorbitant prices. The proprietors of the establishment may then use force to ensure the bill is paid. In bars and nightclubs, never open a tab and instead pay for each drink as you order it, as the tab bill may include drinks you never ordered, and once again, the proprietors will force you to pay. One should also always check the prices of drinks before ordering. Con artists may also pose as police officers in metro stations and tell you your ticket is invalid, demanding that you pay large fines. To avoid this, make sure you buy a ticket and validate it, in which case you know you are in the right. Another scam involves one person approaching you in Old Town Square and asking if you'd like to hear a riddle, such as "Why are there no mirrors in the Old Town Hall?" While you're distracted, an accomplice may try to steal your personal belongings.

**Credit Card Fraud:** Credit card fraud is also common. If you think you've been a victim of this, contact your credit card company immediately. Children may also approach you asking to sign a petition and provide a donation. These petition sheets are often fake, and the children are in cahoots with con artists.

**Pickpockets:** Pickpockets are common in crowded tourist areas such as Old Town Square, Prague Castle, and the Charles Bridge, as well as on public transport. Avoid trains, buses, and trams that are too crowded and always keep an eye on your personal belongings. If there's ever been a city where a fanny pack is appropriate, it's Prague.

# DENMARK

**The Scandinavian countries are Rand Paul's worst nightmare.** They're the ultimate "nanny states"— overly taxing their people (most of whom are pretty okay with it), and giving back something more akin to a safety king-sized bed than a net. Denmark has characteristically high taxes and significant benefits for its people, but compared to Sweden and Norway, Denmark really plays it fast and loose. The Danes love to drink all day (and all night), still allow smoking indoors in some places, and, best of all, don't have a ridiculous government monopoly on alcohol (looking at you, Sweden and Norway). Whatever's going on over there seems to be working, though. The Danes are routinely ranked the happiest people in the world, thanks largely to a cultural mindset that is equal parts bemusing and unpronounceable (see: *hygge*). Long story short, the Danes just think happy, and it works. For the whole country. Incredible.

Denmark straddles the border between Scandinavia and the rest of Europe. Like its northern neighbors, it is still obsessed with Vikings and you'll find at least one museum exhibition dedicated entirely to furniture, but Denmark also contains the Renaissance castles of France, the picturesque canal-side waterfronts of Italy, and the bike-friendliness of Amsterdam. Don't worry, though: with typical Scandinavian prices, you won't mistake Denmark for Germany any time soon. Your dollar won't take you as far here as, well, pretty much anywhere else, but, as Socrates once said, "you get what you pay for." In Denmark, that means "hostels" that are more like four-star hotels and "street food" markets reminiscent of premium food courts. But, if you're okay setting a budget, trying to stick to it, and quickly realizing that your bank account is emptying faster than Copenhagen during the summer vacation season (seriously, it's so damn long), experiencing Denmark is worth every krone.

125

# AARHUS

Coverage by **Eric Chin**

Aarhus has come a long way since it was founded in the eighth century as a Viking settlement. Over the centuries, buildings rose, buildings burned, Christianity and the plague arrived with mixed results, and people came—so many people that Aarhus is now Denmark's second largest city. Today, Aarhus is trying out a bold new look—one with apartment buildings designed to look like icebergs and libraries and playgrounds under the same roof – but it hasn't forgotten its origins. The oldest part of the city, Latinerkvarteret, remains a cultural center for shops and restaurants, and despite several new high-rise buildings, the towering spire of Aarhus Cathedral remains still stands as the tallest point in the city. Despite this rich history, Aarhus is Denmark's youngest city demographically, thanks to a large student population. Combine that with a bustling tourism industry, and the result is everything from budget hostels to grand hotels, burgers and Vietnamese to Michelin-starred restaurants, and Irish pubs to Bond-style cocktail bars. Copenhagen may be the city to visit in Denmark, but you'd be remiss not to give Jutland a try, and there's no better place than Aarhus.

## ORIENTATION

While Aarhus doesn't have neighborhoods that are as distinct as in, say, **Copenhagen**, there are certainly distinct areas. The area known as **Aarhus C** is sometimes also called **Midtbyen**, and stretches north from **Aarhus H** to several streets past **Aarhus Cathedral**. Here you'll find almost all the major sights in the city, including restaurants, museums, and the busy nightlife streets **Åboulevarden**, **Skolegade**, and **Frederiksgade**. The area between Aarhus Cathedral and the **Ring 1 Road** to the north is known as **Latinerkvarteret** (The Latin Quarter), and is the oldest part of the city. To the west of the city center is **Vesterbro**, a largely-residential neighborhood that includes cultural attractions like the **Botanical Garden** and **Den Gamle By**.

## ESSENTIALS

### GETTING THERE

Aarhus Airport (AAR) is a tiny airport located about 35mi. northeast of the city. There are only a few departures each day, mostly to Copenhagen. There is an airport bus between Aarhus Central Station and Aarhus Airport scheduled for each flight. Tickets can be purchased on the bus for DKK 115. The easiest way to get to Aarhus is by train via Copenhagen, a journey of 3-4hr. Aarhus's main train station is Aarhus Central Station (Aarhus H), and there are many trains between Aarhus H and Copenhagen Central Station (København H) each day, often more than one per hour. Train service in Denmark is operated by DSB. Tickets can be purchased at either station, and normally cost around DKK 400.

## GETTING AROUND

Aarhus has a compact city center, and most attractions are within walking distance. To go beyond the city center (to the Moesgaard Museum, for example), Aarhus has a system of buses run by Midttrafik with several ticket options. Single tickets can be purchased with cash at a kiosk on the bus for DKK 20 for two zones, which covers the city center and immediate suburbs. Tickets can also be purchased for 24hr (DKK 80), 48hr (DKK 120), or 72hr (DKK 160) at the Aarhus bus station (Aarhus Rutebilstation, Fredensgade 45). The Danes are famous for loving their bicycles, and Aarhus is no exception. The city has a free city bike system for use October-April: that's right— free! There are a few important rules, though. Lights must be used at night, and you have to provide your own. You also need a 20 DDK coin to unlock a bike, which is returned to you when you return the bike. There are bike stands near many important cultural and recreational sites, and can only be used in the city center (check out a map online).

## PRACTICAL INFORMATION

**Tourist Offices:** Dokk1 (Hack Kamp-manns Plads 2; 87 31 50 10; open M-Sa 10am-4pm, Su 11am-2pm).
**Banks/ATMs/Currency Exchange:** Credit and debit cards are widely accepted in Aarhus, though you may have to pay a small fee to use an international card. Currency exchange and ATMs (sometimes called "pengeautomat") can be found at Aarhus Central Station or on main streets Sønder Allé and Store Torv.
**Post Offices:** The Danish postal service is run by PostNord (Posthus Superbrugsen; Vesterbro Torv 1; 70 70 70 30; open M-F 1pm-5pm).
**Internet:** Free internet is widely available in Aarhus, and can be found in hostels, museums, and most cafés and coffee shops. Many shops and restaurants will advertise free Wi-Fi with window stickers.
**BGLTQ+ Resources:** LGBT Aarhus is available on Thursdays 6pm-8pm at Café Sappho (Mejlgade 71; 86 13 19 48; lgbt. dk; Facebook @LGBTAarhus).

## EMERGENCY INFORMATION

**Emergency Number:** 112. The police can be reached at 114 in non-emergency situations.
**Police:** The police headquarters in Aarhus can be found near Dokk1 (Ridderstræde 1; 87 31 14 48; open daily 9:30am-9:30pm and 24hr for emergencies).
**Rape Crisis Center:** The Center for Rape Victims can be found in the emergency department of Aarhus University Hospital (Nørrebrogade 44; 78 46 35 43; open daily 24hr).
**Hospitals:** The main hospital in Aarhus is Aarhus University Hospital. In an emergency, call 112. In urgent, non-emergency situations, call the emergency doctor service at 70 11 31 31. Emergency Department (Nørrebrogade 44; open daily 24hr).
**Pharmacies:** Pharmacies (called apotek in Denmark), can be found on main streets. Løve Apoteket is located near Aarhus Cathedral and is open 24hr (Store Torv 5; 86 12 00 22).

# ACCOMMODATIONS

## CITY SLEEP-IN ($)
Havnegade 20; 86 19 20 55; www.citysleep-in.dk/en; reception open M-F 8am-11am, 4pm-10pm, Sa-Su 8am-11am, 4pm-11pm

This place is truly a budget hostel; you get exactly what you pay for. The dorm rooms are cramped, top-bunk ladders are a bit rickety, and, much like your grandfather's old house, there's sometimes a subtle hint of stale cigarettes. Bottom line: it's not the Ritz, but you knew that already, you seasoned traveler, you. On the bright side, the kitchen and dining area are clean and well-equipped. There's an outdoor courtyard with ample seating, and the lobby and hallways are covered with charming, if a bit faded, murals to add a homey touch. Expect to encounter some families and more than a few random old hostel guys (you know the type), but it's a small price to pay for... well, a small price to pay.
*i* Dorms DKK 190, doubles DKK 460; reservation recommended; BGLTQ+ friendly; wheelchair accessible; Wi-Fi; linens DKK 50; laundry facilities DKK 40; breakfast DKK 70

## SIMPLEBED HOSTEL ($$)
Åboulevarden 86; 53 23 21 89; www.simplebedhostel.com; reception open 24hr

The name pretty much says it all. This is a very basic, small hostel with a great location right on **Åboulevarden,** one of Aarhus's main restaurant and nightlife streets. The entire hostel is an apartment with just a few rooms: one six-bed dorm, a small kitchen, a common room, and a single bathroom. There's also a double with a private bathroom, but don't expect to see much of whoever is staying there. The bunk beds are huge (near to queen-size), and are fitted with mattress toppers and included linen, which guarantees you the best night's sleep of your trip. Booking is through the website or Facebook page, and payment is cash only.
*i* Dorms DKK 250, private double DKK 550; reservation required; BGLTQ+ friendly; no wheelchair accessibility; Wi-Fi; linens included; towel included

# SIGHTS
## CULTURE

### ÅBOULEVARDEN

Åboulevarden; hours vary by venue

Åboulevarden, named for the **Aarhus River** (*Aarhus Å* in Danish) that it follows, is one of the busiest streets in the city, all day and all night. The pedestrian-only street is lined with establishments from shawarma shops, to dawn-to-dusk café-bars and full-on, weekend-only nightclubs. Tables line the buildings and waterfront, equipped with enough heat lamps when the sun goes down to make up for the savings of that sustainable Danish energy sector. Meals on Åboulevarden can be somewhat pricey and the nightlife a bit more exclusive, but even if you don't want to dress up or pay out, it's still a great place to people watch and remind yourself that you really don't need to spend half a day's paycheck on brunch.

*i* Prices vary by venue

### MUSIKHUSET

Thomas Jensens Allé; 89 40 40 40; www. musikhusetaarhus.dk/en; foyer open daily 11am-6pm, box office open M-Sa noon-5pm

Musikhuset Aarhus is the largest concert hall in Scandinavia, with over 1600 seats in its largest hall. It's home to the Danish National Opera, the Aarhus Symphony Orchestra, and Comedy Zoo Aarhus, an organization for Danish stand-up which, despite the promising name, is sorely lacking in squirrels, monkeys, cats, and other, similarly funny, animals. There are events every week, including concerts, operas, theater performances, and comedy shows, and, while most will be out of reach on a backpacker's budget, Musikhuset also puts on several free performances (mostly concerts) each month.

*i* Prices vary by show; wheelchair accessible

## LANDMARKS

### AARHUS CATHEDRAL

Store Torv; 86 20 54 00; www.aarhusdom-kirke.dk/english; open M 9:30am-4pm, Tu 10:30am-4pm, W-Sa 9:30am-4pm

Aarhus Cathedral has changed its look more often over the years than Brittany Spears has changed. Since construction began in the twelfth century, the cathedral has been built up, burned down, expanded, restyled between Romanesque, Gothic, and Baroque numerous times, always adding to its collection of tombs of old white men. The vast interior is packed with everything you've come to expect out of an old cathedral: paintings, statues, gravestones, gold leaf, and pipe organs (yes, plural). Tall windows provide natural light to illuminate the vaulted Gothic arches, decorated with white-based murals that can only be described as minimalist when compared to other great cathedrals of Europe.

*i Tower admission DKK 20; wheelchair accessible*

## DOKK1

Hack Kampmanns Plads 2; 89 40 92 00; www.dokk1.dk/english; open M-F 8am-10pm, Sa-Su 10am-4pm

Dokk1 is something of a cultural hub in Aarhus—a place where art, architecture, and of course, blond children, come together in an incredibly Danish place. This modern behemoth of a building sits right on the harbor, clad in steel, glass, and concrete. Inside, Dokk1 serves many purposes: it's home to the city's public library and tourist information center. It also houses a café and small performance hall. Outside, it's practically a playground, with slides and climbing walls that resemble sculptures more than toys. All these attractions draw all kinds of people, from coffee-chugging students working in private study rooms to stroller-pushing soccer moms to children running everywhere. Stop for a drink, grab a book, or watch somebody's dad make a fool of himself on the playground. Seriously, whose man is that?

*i Free; wheelchair accessible*

## MUSEUMS

### ⬛AROS AARHUS KUNSTMUSEUM

Aros Allé 2; 87 30 66 00; www.en.aros.dk; open Tu 10am-5pm, W 10am-10pm, Th-Su 10am-5pm

Start in the basement with a gallery called *The 9 Spaces* (an allusion to Dante's *Inferno*), containing works from a seemingly-infinite room composed of mirrors to a simulation of a whole day compressed into eight minutes. From there, ARoS stretches high with ten floors of concrete, steel, and glass, culminating in *Your rainbow panorama,* a circular rooftop skywalk with rainbow-tinted walls that affords vast, if a little green, view of the city. Exhibitions range from *Human Nature,* which asks the viewer to consider the difference between nature and landscape to *No Man is an Island,* which has a 4.5 meter-tall, hyper-realistic statue of a crouching boy to another statue simply titled, *Fucked.* You don't even need to own a turtleneck; there's something here to interest even the casual art critic.

*i Admission DKK 130, DKK 100 student and under 28, free under 18; wheelchair accessible*

### MOESGAARD MUSEUM

Moesgård Allé 15; 87 39 40 00; www.moesgaardmuseum.dk/en; open Tu 10am-5pm, W 10am-9pm, Th-Su 10am-5pm

This museum of archaeology and ethnography is built into a grassy hillside in a suburb of Aarhus like some sort of concrete and glass *Little House on the Prairie.* The collection is vast, including everything from Viking swords to Roman pottery to Egyptian gold jewelry. There are also a slightly disturbing number of human remains on display, including a 2000-year-old corpse, incredibly preserved after spending two millennia buried in a peat bog. Looking at rusty farm tools and dead bodies doesn't sound like the most exciting way to spend a day, but the entire museum is modern and interactive, with video presentations mixed in, and a "laboratory" where you can pretend to be an archaeologist and actually do something with your life, for once.

*i Admission Apr 8-Oct 22 DKK 140, DKK 110 student, Oct 23-Apr 7 DKK 120, DKK 90 student; wheelchair accessible*

## OUTDOORS

### MOESGAARD STRAND

Strandskovvej 2; 8270

Moesgaard Strand is a large stretch of sandy beach along the coast, just south of Aarhus itself. It has earned **Blue Flag** status for having exceptional water quality, meaning it's especially clean and safe. How Danish. The beach is a bit far from the city center, but it is easily accessible via city bus #31. It's also just a short walk from the **Moesgaard Museum,** so you can go relax in the sun after a long morning of getting #cultured while looking at skeletons.

*i* *Free; wheelchair accessible*

## SURF AGENCY
Fiskerivej 2; 60 89 05 15; www.surfagency.dk; open Tu-Th 10am-6pm, F 10am-8pm, Sa 9am-8pm

SUP. No, not the favored salutation of ninth graders who wear baggy jeans. We're talking stand-up paddle boarding, the watersports craze that's sweeping Instagrams worldwide. This conceptually silly but aesthetically pleasing activity has spread from sunny California to stormy New England to Aarhus. Surf Agency is a watersports hub located right on the harbor specializing in SUP classes and rentals. If you're a newbie on the water, you can sign up for a somewhat expensive introductory course or you can just throw yourself right off the deep end with an hourly rental. For the health nuts out there, Surf Agency also offers SUP yoga classes led by an instructor. Unfortunately, artsy photos are not included.

*i* *No wheelchair accessibility*

# FOOD

## 🍜PHO C&P ($)
Sønder Allé 14; 86 16 16 42; www.pho-cp.dk; open M-Th noon-8:30pm, F-Sa noon-9:30pm, Su noon-8:30pm

Good morning, Vietnam! Well, maybe not, since Pho C&P doesn't serve breakfast, but this popular spot will definitely serve up a good lunch or dinner. The menu is inspired by Vietnamese street food, (arguably the best in the world), and Pho C&P does it justice, from traditional *bánh mì* sandwiches to *pho,* the world's most mispronounced soup. And though the authenticity doesn't quite translate into Ho Chi Minh City prices, the place is definitely a bargain in Aarhus. Located just off of one of the city's main shopping streets, Pho C&P is no secret, so try to eat during off-peak hours, or order takeout.

*i* *Bánh mì from DKK 45, pho and other entrées from DKK 75, beer from DKK 25; vegetarian and vegan options available; no wheelchair accessibility*

## AARHUS STREET FOOD ($$)
Ny Banegårdsgade 46; www.aarhusstreet-food.com; open M-Th 11:30am-9pm, F-Sa 11:30am-10pm, Su 11:30am-9pm

Imagine if a huge fleet of food trucks all simultaneously got flat tires and jacked up their prices to pay for new ones, and you pretty much have Aarhus Street Food. Located in an old warehouse, food stands are designed to look like anything from corrugated metal shipping containers to plywood, cartoon-lemonade-stand-style shops. There's even greater variety in the cuisine, so you'll find everything from Afro-Caribbean jerk chicken and fries cooked in duck fat to Danish classics like *rugbrød* and *flæskesteg.* Smaller entrées like sandwiches go from DKK 50, but the price for a more substantial meal with a side and drink can quickly top DKK 100.

*i* *Entrées from SEK 50; vegetarian, vegan, and gluten-free options available; wheelchair accessible*

## BILL'S COFFEE ($$)
Vestergade 58; 20 74 71 96; open M-F 7:30am-6pm, Sa 9am-6pm, Su 9am-5pm

Try to hop on the Wi-Fi at Bill's and you'll be greeted with a locked network called "BILLS is NOT an office," which is a not-so-subtle request for you to get your millennial head out of the sand (and more specifically, off your phone) and into a book or mug of Bill's coffee. So, have a seat at the counter, on a bench outside, or at a table underneath one of the strange, corrugated cardboard-esque lamps with a cappuccino poured by a denim-apron-clad barista, and take a minute to appreciate the eclectic reggae-jazz mix playing in the background. Or wonder how Bill's manages to make a needlepoint pillow look modern. Your phone battery will appreciate it.

*i* *Coffee/espresso drinks DKK 25-40, pastries/cakes DKK 15-25; wheelchair accessible*

# NIGHTLIFE

## 🎵FATTER ESKIL

Skolegade 25; 21 35 44 11; www.
fattereskil.dk; open W 8pm-midnight, Th
8pm-2am, F 4pm-5am, Sa 8pm-5am

Fatter Eskil is one of Aarhus's top
live music venues with concerts most
Wednesday through Saturday nights.
Performances range from rock and
metal, to R&B and dance music,
and even after the concert is over, a
DJ often comes on to keep the party
going. Admission to **Thursday Jam
Nights** is free, where you can show up
and hop on stage for a song or two, or
just sit and enjoy the cheap beer and
live music. If you're not feeling the
vibe, or if the place dies down after
the show is over, Fatter Eskil is located
on Skolegade, which is also home to a
number of other bars and nightclubs
that are popular with the kids.

*i* *Cover DDK 40-80 depending on night,
drinks from DKK 25; BGLTQ+ friendly;
limited wheelchair accessibility*

## THE TAP ROOM

Frederiksgade 40; 86 19 19 10; www.
tirnanog.dk; open M-Th noon-3am, F-Sa
noon-5am, Su 1pm-3pm

If you want the perfect pint of
Guinness or glass of whiskey on the
rocks, look no further. There are several
Irish pubs in Aarhus (turns out
the Irish know a thing or two about
drinking), but The Tap Room is one
of the best. The bartenders are Irish
(or British or Australian), the whiskey
is Irish, and the music is… American?
The crowd is a great mix of young, not
so young, Danish, Irish, American,
and more, and the playlist contains
everything from Arctic Monkeys to
the Strokes. Thursday at 9pm is **quiz
night,** but you can expect rugby
or football (sorry, "soccer") on the
televisions during the week, and live
music late into weekend nights.

*i* *Draft beer from DKK 50, cocktails
from DKK 70, shots from DKK 30; BGLTQ+
friendly; wheelchair accessible*

# COPENHAGEN

Coverage by **Eric Chin**

There are a few things that generally hold true of Scandinavian cities: they're
small (Stockholm, Scandinavia's largest, tops the list with just under one million
people living in the city proper), they're expensive (can't argue there), and they're
obsessed with Vikings. In short, they're great places to travel, but get a bit sleepy
after a few days. Copenhagen is different. It's not just the capital city of Denmark;
it feels like the cultural capital of all of Scandinavia. Between the city itself
and the many towns within reach via commuter rail, Copenhagen boasts truly
impressive Renaissance castles, Baroque gardens that would make Louis XIV
raise an eyebrow, and one of the best food and microbrewery scenes in the north.
You'll feel right at home in Copenhagen's vibrant young population, filled with
starving art majors and wingtip-clad start-up founders alike. There's something
for everyone here, from the casual nightclubs of the Meatpacking District and
the smoky bars of Nørrebro, to the bohemian paradise of Christiania with its
alternative architecture and open marijuana trade. The discerning diner will love
Copenhagen's massive food halls and local delicacies. Don't miss the *smørrebrød*
or the greasy, crunchy goodness of *flæskesteg*. The casual cyclist will be amazed
both by the sophistication of the city's bike lanes, and by how uncharacteristically
aggressive a Dane on a bicycle can be. It won't be cheap (nothing in the Nordics
ever is), but Copenhagen is one of the only Scandinavian cities where you could
spend a week and still not have scratched the surface. It's small but busy, modern
but timeless, and of course, it's very, very *hygge*.

## ORIENTATION

The city center of **Copenhagen** (also known as **Indre By** or **København K**),
extends from **Copenhagen Central Station** all the way to the northern end of
the city. Like city centers everywhere, it's touristy, crowded, and expensive. It's

also where you'll find many of Copenhagen's main attractions, including **Strøget** (one of Europe's longest pedestrianized shopping streets), a number of museums and palaces, and the people-watching meccas of **Kongens Nytorv** and **Nyhavn.** Just to the east is **Christianshavn,** a network of islands and canals constructed by **Christian IV** in the style of **Amsterdam.** Within Christianshavn is the offbeat community (and favorite of twenty-somethings from all over the world) of **Christiania,** famous for its open marijuana trade. North of the city center is **Østerbro,** an upscale residential neighborhood with plentiful parks and high prices. Just west is a funkier alternative: **Nørrebro,** a classic example of a once-heavily-immigrant neighborhood overtaken by broke hipsters and art students. Directly west of the city center is **Frederiksberg,** another wealthy neighborhood filled with parks and baby strollers (**Frederiksberg Have** and the **Cisterns** are worth a visit). South of Frederiksberg is **Vesterbro,** home to the **Meatpacking District** and old **Carlsberg Brewery.** Copenhagen is also a great hub for exploring other cities on the island of **Zealand,** Denmark's largest (except Greenland). To the west is **Roskilde,** one of Denmark's foremost Viking cities, and to the north are **Helsingør** and **Hillerød,** home to famous Renaissance castles.

# ESSENTIALS

## GETTING THERE

Copenhagen Airport, Kastrup (CPH), known as Københavns Lufthavn in Danish, is Scandinavia's busiest airport. The metro is the easiest way to get to the airport; Copenhagen's main train station is Copenhagen Central Station (København H), which connects to the rest of Scandinavia and other major European cities.

## GETTING AROUND

Copenhagen's public transportation system includes buses, a metro, and trains, which are all covered under the same ticket. The capital region is divided into zones, with ticket prices varying accordingly. A two-zone single ticket (covering most of the city center) costs DKK 24, and a three-zone ticket (necessary for travel to the airport) costs DKK 36. Tickets can be purchased at metro stations and at 7-Elevens, but you can also buy them on buses (with cash only). A 24hr pass is DKK 80, and a 72hr pass is DKK 200. Copenhagen has a city bike program, but they're expensive (DKK 30 per hour) and bulky since they're equipped with unnecessary electric motors. Renting from a shop or company like Donkey Republic is a better option. With so many bikes on the road, there are a few things you should know. Danes bike with a purpose and don't tolerate slow cyclists or pedestrians clogging up the bike lane, so make sure to stay clear. Additionally, city bus stops are often set up so that dismounting passengers step right into the bike lane, so look both ways before you get off the bus.

## PRACTICAL INFORMATION

**Tourist Offices:** Copenhagen Visitor Service (Vesterbrogade 4; 70 22 24 42; check www.visitcopenhagen.com for monthly hours, but generally 9am-5pm or later during high season).

**Banks/ATMs/Currency Exchange:** Credit and debit cards are widely accepted in Copenhagen, though some places may charge a small fee for using an international card. ATMs (often called *pengeautomat,* or some variation thereof) can be found on the street and outside most banks. A branch of Forex Bank can be found inside Copenhagen Central Station (33 11 22 20; open daily 8am-9pm).

**Post Offices:** There is a centrally located post office on Pilestræde (Pilestræde 58; 70 70 70 30; open M-F 8:30am-7pm, Sa 8:30am-2pm).

**Internet:** Internet is widely available in Copenhagen. Most cafés and many museums provide free Wi-Fi, as do Copenhagen Central Station and the visitor center.

**BGLTQ+ Resources:** Denmark is one of the most gay-friendly cities in the world and in Scandinavia, and that's saying a lot. It's home to Denmark's oldest gay bar, Centralhjørnet, and a number of guides, and even an app (GAY CPH) is dedicated to BGLTQ+ travel. LGBT Denmark is the Danish national organization for BGLTQ+ advocacy (Nygade 7; 33 13 19 48).

## EMERGENCY INFORMATION

**Emergency Number:** 112. In non-emergency situations, call 1813 for a nurse or doctor, or 114 for police.

**Police:** Politigården, the Copenhagen Police Headquarters, is located near Copenhagen Central Station (open M-F 8am-9pm, Sa-Su 10am-5pm).

**US Embassy:** There is a US Embassy in Copenhagen (Dag Hammarskjölds Allé 24; 33 41 71 00; telephone open M-F 8:30am-5pm, appointments from M-Th 9am-noon).

**Rape Crisis Center:** The Centre for Victims of Sexual Assault at Rigshospitalet in Østerbro has a 24-hour crisis center and hotline (Blegdamsvej 9; 35 45 50 32).

**Hospitals:** Always call 1813 before visiting an emergency room, or you may not be admitted. The doctor or nurse you talk to will also help you find the nearest hospital.
* Bispebjerg Hospital (Bispebjerg Bakke 23; 35 31 35 31).

**Pharmacies:** Pharmacies (called *apotek* in Danish) are common on the street. Steno Apotek near Copenhagen Central Station is open 24hr (Vesterbrogade 6C; 33 14 82 66).

# ACCOMMODATIONS

### ⚑GENERATOR HOSTEL ($$)
Adelgade 5-7; 78 77 54 00; www.generatorhostels.com/copenhagen; reception open 24hr

Generator has built arguably the most successful hostel franchise in Europe, and its Copenhagen location doesn't disappoint. It feels like the kind of place a Saudi prince might stay—you know, if Saudi princes stayed in hostels and not five-star hotels. Most dorms have en suite bathrooms, the bar has two happy hours each night, and the lounge area has arcade games, pool tables, and plenty of plush couches for lounging. Its location near Copenhagen's largest square is close to the lively nightlife along **Gothersgade,** and provides easy access to **Nørrebro.** The one downside: there's no guest kitchen. But Saudi princes don't cook for themselves anyway.

*i* Dorms from DKK 250, privates from DKK 600; reservation recommended; BGLTQ+ friendly; wheelchair accessible; Wi-Fi; linens included; storage lockers provided; laundry facilities DKK 50; breakfast DKK 75

### COPENHAGEN DOWNTOWN HOSTEL ($)
Vandkunsten 5; 1467; 70 23 21 10; www.copenhagendowntown.com; reception open 24hr

Copenhagen Downtown is a bustling, loud, whirlwind of a hostel smack in the middle of the city center. It's a place for the weekend and weekday warrior alike with a lobby bar always filled with booming music covering everything from "Macarena" to "Africa," and an outdoor seating area packed with people enjoying an afternoon beer or four. Live music twice a week, cheap beer (especially during happy hour from 8pm-9pm), and events like quiz nights and pong tournaments make this the best choice if you're the kind of person who wonders why people limit themselves to just two nights of partying a week.

*i* Dorms from DKK 200, privates from DKK 400; reservation recommended; BGLTQ+ friendly; wheelchair accessible; Wi-Fi; storage lockers provided; linens included; laundry facilities DKK 40; breakfast buffet DKK 70

### URBAN HOUSE ($)
Colbjørnsensgade 11; 33 23 29 29; www.urbanhouse.me; reception open 24hr

Urban House is massive, loud, and just as raucous as you'd expect a hostel next to a strip club to be. This hostel/hotel hybrid has every type of room from singles to family rooms and ten-bed dorms, drawing a varied crowd accordingly. Though it can often be difficult to meet people in such a large setting, Urban House gives you plenty of opportunities. There's a large guest kitchen and lounge area, and the restaurant and bar in the lobby are busy every night of the week. There are even events like walking tours and salsa dance nights, all free for guests. Each room has a private bathroom, but don't worry if it's occupied in the morning—there are extra showers on the third floor.

*i* Dorms from DKK 190, singles from DKK 650; ; reservation recommended; BGLTQ+ friendly; wheelchair accessible; Wi-Fi; linens included; towels included; breakfast DKK 75

# SIGHTS
## CULTURE

### ⌖ROSENBORG CASTLE

Øster Voldgade 4A; 33 15 32 86; www.kongernessamling.dk/en/rosenborg; open Jan 2-Feb 11 Tu-Su 10am-2pm, Feb 11-Feb 26 daily 10am-3pm, Feb 26-Apr 10 Tu-Su 10am-2pm, Apr 11-Apr 17 daily 10am-4pm, Apr 18-June 15 daily 10am-4pm, June 16-Sept 15 daily 9am-5pm, Sept 16-Oct 31 daily 10am-4pm, Nov 1-Dec 22 Tu-Su 10am-2pm, Dec 26-Dec 30 daily 10am-4pm, Dec 31 10am-2pm, closed Jan 1, Apr 24

If Bernie Sanders thinks the 1% have it good now, don't let him to come to Rosenborg and see what wealth inequality looked like in the Middle Ages. He'd probably have a heart attack! Rosenborg was built in the early 1600s by **King Christian IV** and became a place to showcase the Danish royal family's wealth, mostly in the form of lavishly-decorated rooms and excessively ornate artifacts. See chess sets made of amber, Christian IV's porcelain-paneled privy, and an entire model ship made of ivory. Downstairs in the windowless, concrete vault sit the most important artifacts from Danish royal history, from **Christian III's Sword of State,** to **Christian IV's** crown and the **Danish Crown Jewels.** The **King's Garden** outside is a wonderful park in which to relax, after frantically googling how you can marry into the royal family.

*i* Admission DKK 110, DKK 70 student; guided tour DKK 45; guided tours daily at 2:10pm in summer season (check website for dates); no wheelchair accessibility in castle

### CHRISTIANSBORG PALACE

Prins Jørgens Gård 1; 33 13 44 11; www.kongeligeslotte.dk/en; Royal Reception Rooms May-Sept

This is actually the third Christiansborg Palace erected here and there were two castles even before that. Today, it's the seat of the Danish government, and, while the royal family no longer lives here (not since 1794, when the first Christiansborg burned down),

---

## HYGGE

Denmark is consistently rated one of the happiest countries in the world, whatever that's supposed to mean. How can you even measure happiness? The question stumped all the great philosophers, from Confucius and Plato to Thomas Aquinas. Not to worry, though, the United Nations thinks it has figured it all out.

Each year, after rigorously collecting scores of data in six categories from GDP per capita to the somewhat subjective "generosity," the UN publishes the World Happiness Report. While the Nordic countries generally outperform most of the rest of the world, Denmark is almost always at or near the top. Fun fact: the US was fourteenth in the 2017 report. These results aren't that surprising; after all, the Danes are almost as famous for being happy as they are for being blonde. But why?

Sure, free healthcare and weeks of paid vacation time each year don't hurt, but it's a cultural phenomenon as well. At the center of it all is the concept of hygge (pronounced—albeit poorly—HUE-ge).

*Hygge* doesn't have a direct equivalent in English, and each Dane has a slightly different way of explaining the idea. Some would say that it's the act of hanging out and having a good time, while others might liken it to a state of being happy, comfortable, and unhurried. In a word, "cozy" is often cited as the best translation.

*Hygge* has caught fire around the western world, especially with yogis, granola-eaters, and similar types. Everyone wants to know how to live with a little bit more *hygge*. Unfortunately, it's not as simple as just doing yoga or drinking a nice cup of tea in the morning; it's more nuanced than that. You can light as many candles as you want and stop for multiple coffee breaks each day, but the best way to get started is to come straight to the source and find out for yourself.

one wing holds the **Royal Reception Rooms,** which are still used for official business. This area is open to the public, where you can see lavish marble-floored and velvet-curtained rooms in which **Queen Margrethe II** greets her guests. Blue, surgeon-style shoe covers are provided to protect the floors from the filth on your commoner shoes. Underneath the palace, visit the ruins of the first two buildings that existed here, **Absalon's Castle** (which was knocked down for fun by the Germans) and **Copenhagen Castle** (which simply went out of style).

*i* Combination ticket, including Royal Reception Rooms, Royal Kitchen, Ruins, Royal Stables DKK 150, DKK 125 students; tour of Royal Reception Rooms daily at 3pm, Royal Kitchen Sa 4pm, Ruins Sa noon; wheelchair accessible

## NYHAVN
Open daily 24hr

Nyvavn is Copenhagen's prime people-watching area. Its name literally means "new harbor" in English, but there's nothing new about this place. It's one of the most historic areas of the city with ancient wooden sailboats moored along the docks and steep-gabled, brightly-colored buildings on both sides of the canal. The streets are lined with cafés, ice cream shops, and even a gentlemen's club, but don't bother with any of them unless you're into getting ripped off; there are plenty of places to get better food and cheaper beer. Instead, bring your own, or just enjoy the boats and buildings of this little slice of Copenhagen.

*i* Prices vary; wheelchair accessible

## TIVOLI GARDENS
Vesterbrogade 3; 33 15 10 01; www.tivoli.dk/en; open summer M-Th 11am-11pm, F 11am-midnight, Sa 10am-midnight, Su 10am-11pm

Tivoli Gardens is the second-oldest amusement park in the world, and it's thriving. There are copies all over Scandinavia, like **Gröna Lund** in Stockholm and **Tivoli Friheden** in Aarhus, but they can't hold a candle to the king. See, Tivoli is more than an amusement park; it's a true cultural hub, with top notch rides (for the nine-year-old in you), fine dining restaurants, and live music in every genre from big band swing to hard rock. And unlike Trix, Tivoli's not just for kids. Sure, there are plenty of stroller-pushing dads, but you'll also find elderly couples swinging away on the dance floor and teenagers just looking for a good place to rip through a pack of cigarettes.

*i* Admission DKK 120, DKK 160 on Friday after 7pm, DKK 23 ride ticket; ; wheelchair accessible

## VISIT CARLSBERG
Gamle Carlsberg Vej 11; 33 27 10 20; www.visitcarlsberg.com; open daily May-Sept 10am-8pm, daily Oct-Apr 10am-5pm

"Probably the best beer in the world," is Carlsberg's famous tagline. That claim is certainly debatable, but if you want to find out, try the Carlsberg "exbeerience" (yikes). This museum and temple to all things Carlsberg is housed in the original brewery, where you can learn about the history of the company, including how the original beer was a flop and that there was a the long and incredibly petty feud between the founder, **J. C. Jacobsen,** and his son. The museum also holds the world's largest collection of unopened bottles—to the confusion of every college kid, because why wouldn't you just open the bottle? Best of all, every admission ticket includes a free beer!

*i* *Admission (includes one beer) DKK 100, DKK 70 student; beer tasting DKK 75; guided tour DKK 50; beer tastings daily on the hour noon-6pm; guided tours daily on the hour 11am-6pm; last entry 30min. before closing; wheelchair accessible*

## LANDMARKS

### CHURCH OF OUR SAVIOUR

Sankt Annæ Gade 29; 32 54 68 83; www.vorfrelserskirke.dk; church open daily 11am-3:30pm, tower May-Sept open 9:30am-7pm, Su 10:30am-9pm, Jan-Apr, Oct-Dec M-Sa 10am-4pm, Su 10:30am-4pm

Staying in shape is tough while traveling. Gym access is pretty much zero, and sure, walking is good, but, if you're craving leg day, try climbing the tower of this church. It's one of the most recognizable of Copenhagen's many spires with its gilded staircase that spirals up outside the tower. There are over 400 steps in all, and the climb, while worth it, is not for the faint of heart. Be sure to arrive right at opening or risk long lines. For the aerially challenged, the church itself is also fantastic, with an altar featuring marble columns and life-sized statues. The facade of the massive pipe organ on the back wall is carved in Baroque style, and features a bust of King Christian V. Who else?

*i* *Admission M-Th adults DKK 40, DKK 30 student, F-Sa adults DKK 45, DKK 35 student; ; church wheelchair accessible, no wheelchair accessibility in tower*

### KRONBORG CASTLE

Helsingør; 49 21 30 78; www.kongeligeslotte.dk/en; open Jan-Mar T-Su 11am-4pm, Apr-May daily 11am-4pm, June-Sept 10am-5:30pm, Oct 11am-4pm, Nov-Dec T-Su 11am-4pm

Kronborg is probably etched somewhere in the back of your mind, even if you've never heard the name before. Located north of Copenhagen in the town of **Helsingør,** this famous Renaissance castle was **William Shakespeare's** inspiration for Elsinore, the Danish castle in every high school student's worst nightmare, *Hamlet.* The castle was built so the Danish kings could control trade in the Baltic Sea (read: tax the absolute shit out of just about everyone). Kronborg incorporates *Hamlet* differently each year, from offering guided tours from the prince himself (that must be depressing) to using a full cast to act out scenes. If you don't want scarring flashbacks to English class, explore the casemates, an underground network of tunnels with a statue of the local legend Holger Danske.

*i* *Admission June-Aug DKK 140, student DKK 130; off-season adults (18+) DKK 90, student DKK 80; tours June-Aug daily noon, 1pm, 3pm, and 4pm; last entry 30min. before closing time; limited wheelchair accessibility*

## MUSEUMS

### ◪LOUISIANA MUSEUM OF MODERN ART

Gammel Strandvej 13; 49 19 07 19; www.en.louisiana.dk; open Tu-F 11am-10pm, Sa-Su 11am-6pm

Despite the name, you won't find any creole or crawfish at Louisiana (so-named by the original owner of the estate, who married three different women, all named Louise). What you will find is Denmark's most-visited art museum, breathtaking panoramic views of the **Øresund,** and some of the strangest galleries you've ever seen. Past exhibitions have involved live, naked models, hallways filled with speakers projecting the sound of machine guns, and shoes made of rocks. It's all very confusing, but luckily there are also more traditional galleries featuring well-known artists like **Andy Warhol** and **Picasso.** Overlooking the Øresund is a beautifully landscaped sculpture garden, with works by **Alexander Calder** and other prominent sculptors. **Humlebæk** is near **Helsingør,** so consider pairing Louisiana with a visit to **Kronborg** or the **Maritime Museum.**

*i* *Admission DKK 125, DKK 110 student; wheelchair accessible*

## DESIGN MUSEUM
Bredgade 68; 33 18 56 56; www.design-museum.dk/en; open Tu 10am-6pm, W 10am-9pm, Th-Su 10am-6pm

The Danes are a famously beautiful people and Danish design is no different. The world of design is underappreciated, essential to daily life, and often completely ridiculous to normal people, and the Design Museum displays every aspect of Danish design, from the practical to the absurd. Consider, for instance, the Danish chair. Here, you can walk through a tunnel of 110 different chairs and watch the evolution of simple wooden stools into steel recliners and behemoths of oak and leather. Other exhibits showcase modern Danish designs with a focus on sustainability, with objects like bamboo bikes and Wi-Fi routers so good-looking you'd want to hang them on your wall.

*i* *Admission DKK 100, free student and under 26; guided tours Su 2pm; last entry 30min. before closing; Wheelchair accessible*

## NATIONAL MUSEUM OF DENMARK
Ny Vestergade 10; 33 13 44 11; www.en.natmus.dk; open daily 10am-5pm

This is Denmark's premier museum of cultural history, and damn does it cover a lot. It's definitely a history museum, but there's some pretty cool stuff in here. You'll find golden hunting horns for bougie Vikings, a room dedicated

## CHRISTIANIA

Mention Copenhagen to any twenty-something who has been there before, and he or she is almost guaranteed to mention Christiania: Denmark's own hippy commune turned social experiment. The area, formerly a military barracks, was taken over by squatters in the 1970s and has maintained a tenuous, if confusing, relationship with the city of Copenhagen.

Christiania is most famous for its open and very public cannabis trade (see why the kids love it so much?). While technically illegal, Copenhagen has decided it's better to concentrate such activity in a single, well-known place (aptly named Pusher Street and alternatively known as the Green Light District), rather than in seedy bars and back alleys in other parts of the city.

Christiania has sometimes been a politically turbulent place over the years, with a few incidents turning violent (this is perhaps not surprising in an area where illegal activity is a regular part of public life), but, in general, it's a very safe place to visit, and, in addition to almost every young tourist in Copenhagen, you'll see middle-aged couples, stroller-pushing mothers (how's that for alternative parenting?), and dreadlock-sporting locals. There are a few rules you should know, though. Don't take photos, especially around Pusher Street (surprisingly, people don't like being photographed engaging in illegal activity), and don't run (you could literally start a riot).

Obviously, Christiania's most notable attraction is weed, but there's a lot to appreciate for non-potheads as well. The independent lifestyle and society of the Christianites has led to a truly unique community within otherwise-heavily-governed Denmark. On the outskirts of the area, there are undeveloped patches of forest with walking trails along the canals, and you'll find ridiculously organic cafés, concert spaces, and alternative art galleries. Just walking among the houses can be interesting in itself, and there are some really wacky designs, often dubbed "architecture without architects."

Overall, Christiania is a different world from the rest of Copenhagen, and worth a visit for anyone interested in seeing the less-known reason the Danes are the happiest people on Earth. Just use common sense, and make sure you can tell the difference between a good cookie, and a really good cookie.

entirely to the "art" of cosplay, and one of the world's largest collections of rune stones (they actually exist). On the second floor, there's an exhibit called **Ethnographical Treasures,** which contains an incredible collection of artifacts from all over the world, including a case full of fur anoraks and entire suits of samurai armor. If that's all a bit too cultured for you, there's also an entire exhibit dedicated to toys, which might be more up your alley.

*i* *Admission DKK 75; tours July-Sept daily at 11am and 1pm; wheelchair accessible*

### THE CISTERNS

Søndermarken; 30 73 80 32; www.cisternerne.dk; open May Tu-Su 11am-7pm, June-July Tu-Su 11am-8pm, Aug Tu-Su 11am-7pm, Sept Tu-Su 11am-6pm, Oct Tu-Su 11am-5pm

The Cisterns are dank (in the literal sense; grow up). This massive, man-made cavern underneath **Søndermarken,** a park in **Frederiksberg,** used to hold fresh drinking water for the city, but thanks to modern technology it has been repurposed into a contemporary art exhibition. The Cisterns are dark, cool, and damp, and the exhibitions are similar, often focusing on themes of light, darkness, and water. Be prepared to walk over boardwalks and through clouds of mist, all in near-darkness. The exhibitions can be quite confusing, but at least it's nice and cool down there!

*i* *Admission DKK 60, DKK 50 student; no wheelchair accessibility*

## OUTDOORS

### CANAL BOAT TOUR

Nyhavn or Gammel Strand; 32 96 30 00; www.stromma.dk/en

Copenhagen is a city on the water, but a lot of that water is man-made. The canals that make up **Nyhavn** and **Christianshavn** were constructed by **King Christian IV,** who was trying to design the city to look more like Amsterdam to attract wealthy Dutch merchants. Spoiler alert: it didn't work. The Dutch aren't stupid and have no interest in Danish taxes, but the canals remain. That said, a canal boat tour is a great way to explore the city.

Multiple tours leave daily from a few spots, including Nyhavn, and pass by multiple sights, including the opera house, the famous *Little Mermaid* statue, and Paper Island. Just remember to duck going under the low bridges, or risk the wrath of the captain and a nasty knock on the head.

*i* *Most tours DKK 80; tours at least every 30-45min., starting at 9:30am, last tour varies, but as late as 9pm in the summer high season; no wheelchair accessibility*

## FOOD

### ⌧GRØD ($)

Jægersborggade 50; 50 58 55 79; www.groed.com/en; open M-F 7:30am-9pm, Sa-Su 9am-9pm

Grød's claim to fame is that it's the world's first porridge restaurant. Now, that may not sound exciting unless you're a bear or a curly-headed blonde girl lacking common sense, but Grød is a big deal. The morning menu (served until 5pm) mainly consists of the oatmeal-type breakfasts with toppings like homemade caramel sauce, fresh fruit, or *skyr* (everyone's favorite Icelandic pseudo-yogurt product), but the afternoon menu (served from 11am) is practically gourmet. Try fried risotto with apples, roasted nuts, and mustard vinaigrette, or Asian congee with ginger and peanuts. As you might expect from a porridge restaurant, Grød has the whole coffee-in-mason-jar vibe going and emphasizes its use of seasonal and organic ingredients.

*i* *Morning menu DKK 45, afternoon menu from DKK 65; vegetarian, vegan, or gluten-free options available; no wheelchair accessibility*

### ⌧NEXT DOOR CAFÉ ($)

Larsbjørnsstræde 23; 27 12 08 18; www.nextdoorcafe.dk; open M-F 7am-6pm, Sa-Su 9am-6pm

Too often, city center cafés are overpriced and underwhelming, filled with middle-aged tourist couples, reheated pastries, and generic jazz tracks. Not so with Next Door Café. This place is authentic, fun, and always hopping. The basement café is painted entirely in different shades of purple, and the young, tattooed staff bounces the music between pop and hip-hop favorites like Latch and Jason Drool (wait, is he still considered a favorite?). Grab an American-style breakfast of pancakes or a lunch sandwich on homemade bread, and squeeze in at one of the glass-topped tables proudly displaying a wild selection items like banknotes from around the world, hotel room keys, and boarding passes. Enjoy the youthful energy, but don't get carried away and join in by accidentally leaving behind something important!

*i* *Breakfast plates from DKK 40, lunch sandwiches DKK 50, coffee and espresso drinks DKK 20-35; vegetarian, vegan, and gluten-free options available; no wheelchair accessibility*

## PALUDAN BOG&CAFÉ ($)

Fiolestræde 10; 33 15 06 75; www.paludan-cafe.dk; open M-Th 9am-10pm, F 9am-11pm, Sa 10am-11pm, Su 10am-10pm

Picture an aspiring author, furiously scribbling away on a yellow legal pad, surrounded by books and empty coffee cups, and you already have a good idea of what Paludan is like. It's an all-day café and book store right in the heart of downtown Copenhagen filled with textured acrylic paintings, tables and decorations that toe the line between retro and shabby chic, and of course, books. All kinds of books, from paperback leaflets to leather-bound tomes, probably containing old secrets of alchemy, or unlikelier still, a proper English translation of *hygge*. The ground floor restaurant serves three meals a day, as well as a wide selection of coffee and espresso drinks, and since Paludan is right next to Copenhagen University, everything is reasonably priced.

*i* *Coffee/espresso drinks DKK 20-30, brunch plates DKK 60-100; vegetarian, vegan, and gluten-free options available; wheelchair accessible*

## TORVEHALLERNE ($$)

Frederiksborggade 21; www.torvehallernekbh.dk; open M-Th 10am-7pm, F 10am-8pm, Sa 10am-6pm, Su 11am-5pm

With Copenhagen Street Food shutting its doors for the foreseeable future at the end of 2017, multiple food halls are vying to take its place as the city's top food court. Torvehallerne is part artisanal food hall, part classic Danish bakery, and part gentrified street market. This upscale foodie-paradise stretches across two buildings, and houses hipster smoothie bars, fancy meat markets, and seafood stalls with fish caught in varying distressed expressions. The offerings are mostly expensive, but there are a few gems sprinkled in for around DKK 65, like the classic Scandinavian duck confit sandwich from Ma Poule, or a Vietnamese bánh mì from LêLê Street Kitchen. Be sure to check out some local favorites, like **Grød,** the world's first porridge bar, and **Mikkeller,** Copenhagen's hottest microbrewery.

*i* *Sandwiches and individual entrées from DKK 65, some vendors cash only; vegetarian, vegan, and gluten-free options available; wheelchair accessible*

# NIGHTLIFE

## ⬛BAKKEN

Flæsketorvet 19; www.bakkenkbh.dk; open W 9am-3am, Th-Sa 5pm-5am

Bakken is a no-nonsense, unpretentious nightclub in Copenhagen's meatpacking district in **Vesterbro,** home to some of the city's best nightlife. It's the kind of place where the bouncer gives you the once over, and then remembers that Bakken lets just about everyone in. Energy levels are high, thanks to the soul-shaking electronic and dance music pumped out by weekend DJs, and even the bartenders want in on the fun, often drinking with the customers, each other, or just about anybody who will join them. Don't expect to debate the finer points of philosophy here, but if you're looking for a place that will blow out your eardrums, Bakken is a go-to.

*i* No cover, beer from DKK 30, mixed drinks from DKK 60, shots from DKK 25; BGLTQ+ friendly; wheelchair accessible

## ⬛MIKKELLER BAR

Viktoriagade 8; 1655; 33310415; www. mikkeller.dk; open M-W 1pm-1am, Th-F 1pm-2am, Sa noon-2am, Su 1pm-1am

There are lots of microbreweries in Copenhagen, but Mikkeller is the darling of them all. It gained fame as a "gypsy" brewery (these guys are better at beer than at political correctness), meaning that it didn't actually own its own brewery and relied mainly on collaborations. Today, it has locations all over the world, including several in the US, but the original is still its **Vesterbro** location. This basement bar has 20 ever-changing craft brews on tap. The whitewashed brick beer mecca is the place where people come for a drink after a long, six-hour Danish work day, whether they want to talk about beer, or simply enjoy it.

*i* Beer from DKK 55, bar snacks from DKK 30; BGLTQ+ friendly; no wheelchair accessibility

## NØRREBRO BRYGHUS

Ryesgade 3; 35 30 05 30; www.noerre-brobryghus.dk/en; open M-Th noon-11pm, F-Sa noon-1pm, Su noon-10pm

It's Friday night. The clink of glasses and murmurs of light chatter filter their way downstairs, where candlelight flickers across exposed brick walls. Is it an Italian fine dining establishment, with copious amounts of red wine? Is it Noma, ranked as the best restaurant in the world four times? No, it's Nørrebro Bryghus, a microbrewery. This place isn't just for the casual beer lover, though. It's for people who love drinking good beer, and don't mind feeling classy while they do it. The whole place is dimly lit, in a somehow classy way, by bare, incandescent bulbs, and the ultramodern exposed ventilation ducts balance the retro feel of brick in the basement.

*i* Beer DKK 65; BGLTQ+ friendly; no wheelchair accessibility

## TEMPLE BAR

Nørrebrogade 48; 35 37 44 14; open M-W 3pm-2am, Th 3pm-3am, F-Sa 3pm-5am, Su 3pm-1am

Surprisingly, smoking indoors is not completely prohibited in Denmark; it's legal in establishments smaller than 40 square meters (nicotine's a hell of a drug). These bars have become local favorites all over Copenhagen, and Temple Bar is one of the best in **Nørrebro.** It's a proper dive bar right in the middle of one of the city's hip neighborhoods that flatly rejects the maddening principles of Scandinavian simplicity. Cheap drinks, a student special on beer, and a pool table on the smoky second floor draw crowds of young people looking for a low-key place to have a drink and smoke. If you don't want to smell like an ashtray until you do laundry next, the first floor is smoke-free.

*i* Beer from DKK 40, shots and mixed drinks from DKK 25; BGLTQ+ friendly; no wheelchair accessibility

# DENMARK ESSENTIALS

## VISAS

Denmark is a member of the European Union and is part of the Schengen Area, so US citizens can stay in Denmark for up to 90 days without a visa.

## MONEY

Denmark's currency is the Danish krone, officially abbreviated DKK and locally used interchangeably with kr.

**Credit/Debit Cards:** Like in Sweden and Norway, cards are accepted at the vast majority of establishments, and some are even cash free. However, in Denmark, you are more likely to be charged a small fee for using an international card. The fee is usually small (no more than 3-4% of the value of the transaction), but consider cash if you're worried, though it's worth noting you could be charged a similar fee for withdrawing from a foreign ATM. Check with your bank about foreign fees.

**Tipping:** Tipping in Denmark is neither expected nor required; in fact, a service charge is normally included in the bill at most restaurants. As always, a tip is appreciated, so if you feel you received exceptional service, feel free to round up the bill or tip 5-10%.

**Taxes:** Like it's Scandinavian neighbors, Denmark has a sky-high VAT rate of 25%, which is included in all prices. Tip: Some stores in Denmark, specifically those with a "Tax Free Worldwide" or "Global Blue" sticker, will refund the VAT for goods leaving the country. Be sure to ask at the counter for specifics, and to save receipts for any goods for which you hope to claim a refund.

## SAFETY AND HEALTH

Though there is technically no drinking age in Denmark, there are purchasing ages, as well as laws aimed at preventing minors from getting alcohol. You must be 18 to be served in a bar or restaurant, or to purchase anything stronger than 16.5% ABV in stores. To purchase beverages weaker than 16.5% in stores, you must be 16.

## BGLTQ+ TRAVEL

Denmark (and Copenhagen in particular) is very liberal in terms of BGLTQ+ rights. Hostels, restaurants, and nightlife establishments are very friendly towards the BGLTQ+ community, and cities like Copenhagen and Aarhus have extensive BGLTQ+ nightlife scenes.

# FRANCE

**France is like the popular student with prime real estate on the third page of the high school yearbook.** The nation has been involved in so many of the major world events you learned about in World History that you can't turn a corner in either its vibrant metropolises or idyllic country villages without bumping into something historic. World War II comes to life in Normandy, the extravagance that provoked the French Revolution provokes Versailles, and the jaw-dropping wealth of the upper class in the South is extremely prominent. The French capital itself, Paris, is renowned around the globe for its fame in fashion and food. In more recent years, Paris has been affected by the tragedies of the 2015 Charlie Hebdo shootings and 2017 attacks at Notre Dame and the Champs-Elysees. France has been at the center of global news networks, battling political unrest, inequality, and international conflicts. However, throughout its conflicts and challenges, the nation undoubtedly preserves its pride in being a center of history where life revolves around family, friends, food, and other simple pleasures that make life worth living. En bref, as the French would say, they work to live instead of living to work.

In the world's yearbook—not just your high school's—France would win superlatives like "Best Dressed" and "Most Likely to Become a Movie Star." It is a center for all the finer things in life: art, music, film, and food. It's a country that made the definition of chic from the cosmopolitan center of Paris to the beaches of Saint-Tropez to the small towns of Aix-en-Provence. Explore the beautiful country from the misty farms and orchards of the north to the dramatic cliffs and crystal blue water of the Riviera. To travel in France is truly to wish you were French.

# AVIGNON

Coverage by **Julia Bunte-Mein**

Avignon is a tranquil, medieval city in the Provence region of southern France that is a calm respite from the more bustling cities in France. Take a deep breath in this lavender-smelling walled destination and explore the Palais des Papes, Gothic cathedrals, and other Roman relics; all the sightseeing will, admittedly, take no more than one afternoon in this quaint town. You may be quick to say that you only need one day in Avignon, but its charm will grow on you and, if you stay a few nights, you'll experience its wild side. Avignon changed hands from conqueror to conqueror for thousands of years and once held an extreme amount of power as the seat of the Catholic Church in the fourteenth century. Today, the town is definitely tamer; there's no threat of the Roman or French empires invading, but you might have to look out for the breezy winds of Provence, known as *le Mistral,* which are fierce, unruly, and biting. Stay for a while, discover the history, and get to the nitty gritty of the subtle, understated culture of Avignon.

## ORIENTATION

The medieval, walled city of Avignon is dense and easily navigable on foot. **Le Gare Avignon Centre,** the main train station, sits just outside the towering wall. To enter the city, simply walk through the gates, **Porte de la République.** The main street, **Rue de la République,** runs straight through the city and is lined with commercial stores. At the end of the street lies **Le Place de l'Hortage,** the largest (but still pretty small) square in Avignon. Keep going up from there, past the carousel, to the massive **Palais des Papes.** This is a huge complex that connects in the back to the beautiful gardens, **Les Rocher des Domes.** At the far end of the gardens is a lookout that has a steep staircase down to ground-level where you can access **le Pont d'Avignon** over the **River Rhône.**

## ESSENTIALS

### GETTING THERE

Avignon has a small international airport (AVN), but flights may be cheaper out of nearby Marseille (MRS) or Montpellier (MPL). From Marseille, you can access Avignon via an easy train or bus ride. Trains arrive at Gare d'Avignon-Centre, which is just across the street from Avignon's old-city gates. TGV high-speed trains service the city from Gare d'Avignon TGV, which is a 5min. train ride from Gare Centre (€1.30).

### GETTING AROUND

Avignon has local buses running along the outskirts of the medieval walls, but everything you want to see is inside the walls and easily walkable. Use the blue line (#5) to get to the Fort Saint-André, which is 3km outside the city (€1.40 single journey).

### PRACTICAL INFORMATION

**Tourist Offices:** 41 Cours Jean Jaurès; 04 32 74 32 74; open M-F 9am-6pm, Su 10am-5pm; www.avignon-tourisme.com.

**Banks/ATMs/Currency Exchange:** BNP Paribas (39 Rue de la République; 0 820 82 00 01; open T-F 8:15am-12:15pm and 1:30-5:30pm, Sa 8:15-12:30pm).

**Post Offices:** La Poste (4 Cours Président Kennedy; open M-W, F 9am-6pm, Th 9am-12:15pm and 2pm-6pm, Sa 9am-noon).

**Internet:** There is free Wi-Fi in the tourist offices, as well as many surrounding cafés and restaurants.

**BGLTQ+ Resources:** www.gay-provence.org has tips on accommodations, restaurants, events and nightlife.

### EMERGENCY INFORMATION

**Emergency Number:** 112

**Police:** For non-emergencies, call the local police at 04 90 16 81 00.

**US Embassy:** The closest US consulate is in Marseille (12 Bd. Paul Peytral; 04 91 55 09 47; M-F 9am-noon and 2pm-5pm).

**Rape Crisis Center:** Rape Crisis Network Europe (www.inavem.org; 01 45 88 19 00).

**Hospitals:**
- Avignon Central Hospital (Centre Hospitalier Général, 305 rue Raoul Follereau; 04 32 75 33 33).

**Pharmacies:**
- Pharmacie Des Halles (52 Rue de la Bonneterie; 04 90 82 54 27; open M-Sa 8:30am-12:30pm and 2pm-7:30pm)

# ACCOMMODATIONS

### AUBERGE BAGATELLE ($)

25 Allée Antoine Pinay—Ile de la Barthelasse; 04 90 86 71 35; www.auberge-bagatelle.com

First things first, Bagatalle is primarily a campground, where many families stay in RVs or young people pitch tents. The hostel is definitely a large step up from sleeping outside, but it only comes with the bare minimum (no large storage lockers or blankets). White linoleum floors, happy-go-lucky murals, and bright bubble lettering on the walls makes it feel like it's designed for young kids, but many ignore this because of the ridiculously cheap prices. From its location across the river, you'll have great views of the old city at night.

*i* Dorms €13-15; towels included; wheelchair accessible

### POP' HOSTEL ($$)

17 Rue de la République; 04 32 40 50 60; www.pophostel; reception open 24hr

Right in the heart of Avignon, Pop will make your stay in Avignon convenient and pleasant. They offer clean, spacious bathrooms with individual toilets and showers, which is major key. The air-conditioned, carpeted dorms have modern bunks, each equipped with a privacy curtain, reading lamp, and two outlets. The balconies look right over the **Rue de la Republique** and the airtight windows do a good job of blocking out noise. Skip the €5 breakfast and instead come for the €1 wine during happy hour from 5-8pm in their colorful and modern bar/lounge area on the first floor. The one caveat is the strange, and very dysfunctional Wi-Fi system, which involves a complicated process to get online.

*i* Dorms from €24; reservation required during the Festival of Avignon in July; BGLTQ+ friendly; wheelchair accessible; Wi-Fi; towels for rent

# SIGHTS

## CULTURE

### CATHÉDRALE NOTRE-DAME DES DOMES D'AVIGNON

Pl. du Palais; 04 90 82 12 21; www.cathedrale-avignon.fr; open summer M-Sa 7:30am-8:30pm, winter M-Sa 8am-8:30pm, Mass M-Sa 7:30am-8:30am, Su 10am-11:30am

This pristine cathedral is like a twelfth-century Plaza Hotel. Built in three successive phases and renovated again in 1838, the cathedral underwent a major restoration in 2013, bringing it

to tip-top condition. After 30 months of work, the dazzling structure, also known as the Basilique Metropole, was re-opened in March 2016. The steadfast efforts clearly paid off, as the Romanesque nave, Gothic chapels, and ceiling frescos are truly marvelous. Check out the Baroque balconies, covered with angels and delicately carved leaves.

*i* Free; last entry 20min. before closing; wheelchair accessible

## LANDMARKS

### 🏛PALAIS DES PAPES

Pl. du Palais; 32 74 32 74; www.palais-des-papes.com; open daily July 9am-8pm, Aug 9am-8:30pm, Sept-Oct 9am-7pm, Nov-Feb 9:30am-5:45pm, Mar 9am-6:30pm, April-Jun 9am-7pm

Let's be honest: Palais des Papes is most likely the reason you're in Avignon. And yes, it's expensive. And yes, you've already seen ten other Gothic buildings on your European tour. But a visit here is simply non-negotiable. Built in 1335, this colossal fortress, now a **UNESCO World Heritage site,** is the largest Gothic palace in Europe and attracts over 650,000 visitors a year. With over 25 rooms decorated in beautiful frescoes and faded wall paintings, its visuals are stunning with contemporary African art that creates a juxtaposition of eras and cultures. We recommend snagging the audio guide for €2, so you can learn about what the palace looked like in its prime and hear about its drama-filled history soon to be adapted into the reality TV show: *Nine Popes, One Palace: Who Will Survive?*

*i* Admission €11, student €9, combined ticket with Pont d'Avignon €13.50, student €10.50; audio guide €2; last entry 1hr. before closing; wheelchair accessible

### PONT DU AVIGNON

Pont d'Avignon, Bd. de la Ligne; 04 32 74 32 74; www.avignon-pont.com/fr; open daily July 9am-8pm, Aug 9am-8:30pm, Nov 9am-7pm, Mar 9am-6:30pm, Apr-Jun 9am-7pm

The Pont d'Avignon, also called the Bridge of Saint-Benezet, wins the award for having the most confusing audio guide ever. As you walk on the old stones of this bridge to nowhere, listen to the legend of how a young shepherd, Benezet, received a divine order from God at age 12 to build a bridge in Avignon. The legend consists of Benezet developing superhuman

## DAYTRIPS FROM AVIGNON

**1. Arles:** This charming city is famous for its extensive Roman treasures, Saturday market, and inspiring many a Van Gogh painting (15-20min. train ride from Avignon €7.70, €5.80 student).

**2. Roussillon:** This tiny village always makes the "Top 10 Most Beautiful Villages in France." The church and clock tower are notable sites, but the real treasure is walking the streets themselves (2hr. bus ride via line #15, €2-4).

**3. Les Baux de Provence:** A forged cliff-side village with narrow, cobbled streets, light-sand colored ancient houses, and castle ruins, this is one of the most popular daytrip destinations in the summer (45min. bus ride via line #57, €7, taxi to les Baux after bus).

**4. Pont du Gard:** The site of the famous Roman aqueduct connecting Nîmes and Uzés, Pont du Gard provides for a day of swimming under the river, picknicking, or hiking the surrounding mountain trails (1hr. bus ride via Edgard Bus, round trip €3.50).

**5. Uzès:** Storybook-pretty village that used to serve as an important trading center. It is visited for its Renaissance architecture, cathedral, farmers market, and restaurants serving local cuisine (1hr. bus ride via Edgard bus, round trip €4).

**6. Cassis:** This adorable fishing port with terraced vineyards, beaches, and harbor-side restaurants is a wonderful place to kick back and relax (2.5hr TGV train, €19-34).

strength to complete the project. When completed, the bridge stood, but the river eventually washed it away, which prompted an effort from Avignon locals to rebuild it, and the cycle continued. In all honesty, you cannot get a good view of the bridge while standing on it, but, the history lesson is interesting.

*i* *Admission €5, €4 student, combined ticket with Palais des Papes €13.50, student €10.50; free audio guide*

## MUSEUMS

### MUSÉE DU PETIT PALAIS
Palais des Archevêques, Pl. du Palais; 04 90 86 44 58; www.petit-palais.org; open M, W-Su 10am-1pm and 2pm-6pm

This **UNESCO World Heritage** museum is home to one of the greatest collections of medieval art. Its permanent collection includes over 300 Italian pre-Renaissance religious paintings, containing works by **Botticelli, Carpaccio,** and **Giovanni di Paolo,** as well as Gothic and Romanesque pieces from the fine arts school of Avignon. Juxtaposed by the towering **Popes Palace,** this small palace looks like a dollhouse, but, once you step inside, the two inner courtyards and airy main gallery give it an inexplicably majestic feel. Admire the frescoed ceiling and the ginormous sculptures and pottery (we swear we saw a sculpture taller than Michael Jordan). The highlight, however, is Botticelli's *La Vierge et L'enfant* (1470).

*i* *Admission €6, €3 student; last entry 45min. before closing; guided tours available upon request; wheelchair accessible*

## FOOD

### 🍴L'AMISTA ($)
23 Rue de la Bonneterie; 06 19 24 15 47; open daily noon-10pm

At this small bistro in the heart of the old village, you can find traditional Catalan tapas like house favorite *patatas bravas con chorizo, pan con tomate,* and *gambas persillades.* Avignon's location in the south of France places it close to Catalonia, giving this place a more authentic vibe. Their most exciting offering is the *caisette de tapas,* which is a huge selection of tapas to share

(minimum two people) that is served in a wooden crate. The terrace seating, just next to an ancient archway, is lovely, but take a moment to peek inside the inside, which is decorated in a theme of the French children's book series "Martine." The bathroom is covered in pages from the picture book.

*i* *Tapas €3-6, charcuterie boards €8.50, large salads €14-16, sangria €3; happy hour Th-Sa 6:30pm-8pm; vegetarian options available; wheelchair accessible*

### E.A.T. ESTAMINET ARÔMES ET TENTATIONS ($$)
8 Rue Mazan; 04 90 83 46 74; www.restaurant-eat.com; open daily noon-2pm and 7pm-10pm

This lovely, secluded French restaurant is hidden on a tiny alleyway (follow the signs once you get to **Place Crillon**) and has only about a dozen tables, so you'll be lucky if you even score a seat. Their a-la-carte menu, which changes on the regular, serves hearty and homey dishes, usually a balanced composition of a protein, grain, and some fresh, seasonal veggies. The cozy and neutral-tone interior reflects their simple, but very tasteful menu. Try the tender veal braised with rosemary or asparagus wrapped in a blanket of prosciutto, sprinkled with sliced almonds and poached cherry tomatoes.

*i* *Entrées €10-13, dessert €6-7; reservation recommended; vegetarian options available; wheelchair accessible*

### LE VINTAGE ($$)
10 Rue Galante; 04 86 65 48 54; open daily 11:30am-2:30pm and 6:30pm-10:30pm

Le Vintage boasts quality *bistronomie Provençale,* serving traditional and modern French dishes of fresh and in-season produce. Serving over 60 types of regional wines, Le Vintage pairs its drinks perfectly with food of the highest quality made with only in-season fresh produce. We recommend coming for their set lunch menu, which is a bargain for the amount of food you get; the portion sizes are truly huge. If you're lucky, you'll snag a seat in the minuscule triangular square just outside the restaurant, although the air-conditioned interior is a nice break from the mid-August heat or windy fall

# ARLES

**Picture sunbaked houses on narrow cobbled streets with off-kilter wooden window shutter and pink and green flower boxes.** Fade-in on Arles and that's exactly what you get. Arles looks straight out of a nineteenth-century impressionist oil painting. And, hey, now that we think of it, we're feeling a little déjà vu because we actually have seen this scene before on a Van Gogh canvas. Van Gogh painted over 200 works around Arles, capturing its shady squares, Roman monuments, and lovely countryside. If that doesn't convince you that Arles is one of the most picturesque cities in La Côte d'Azur region, we don't know what will. And, if you, for some reason, still aren't sold, Arles also boasts a famous Roman arena where gladiators once fought to their deaths. We admit that the gory image we've just described is neither picturesque nor pleasant, but the ruins of the amphitheater are quite interesting and well-worth a daytrip.

The historic center of Arles is bordered by **Boulevard Georges Clemenceau,** which morphs into **Boulevard des Lices,** in the south. **Boulevard Emile Combes** constitutes the western border and the River Rhône runs on the northeastern edge of the city. The train station in the north is just a 15-minute walk from the entrance to Arles, which you will enter by passing a large roundabout and through **La Porte de La Cavalerie.** The main street from the gates leads you directly to the **Roman Amphitheater** (it's ginormous—you can't miss it). Continuing down **Rue de la Galade** will take you right to **L'Eglise de Saint-Trophime.** The **Place du Forum** is just a street away on your right, and the rest of sights are all within a few blocks from there.=

## GETTING THERE

There is a shuttle bus between Arles and Marseille-Provence Airport. Other nearby airports include Nîmes-Alès-Camargue and Montpellier-Mediterranee Airports. The Gare d'Arles (Av. Paulin Talabot) accepts high-speed (TGV) and regional (TEV) trains. The TGV is on the line from Paris-Lyon to Marseille-Saint-Charles train station. Paris-Arles direct trains connect Arles and Avignon (20min.), Marseille (50min.) and Nîmes (20min.). The fastest way to arrive from an international destination is via airplane to Marseille and connection to a train to Arles. is by airplane to Marseille. The main bus station on is Bd. De Lices.

## GETTING AROUND

Arles is easily walkable and requires no public transportation whatsoever. The tourist office provides maps that point out the best walking routes through the city to pass all the major sights. If walking isn't your thing, there is a train that offers a 40min. tour of all the sites with commentary in six different languages from April to October. You could rent a bike, but roads in Arles lend themselves to bumpy rides.

## Swing by...

### LES ARÈNES (ROMAN AMPHITHEATRE)

1 Rond-Point des Arènes; 08 91 70 03 70; www.arenes-arles.com; open daily May-Sept 9am-7pm, Nov-Mar 10am-5pm, Apr-Oct 9am-6pm

Welcome to the jungle—we mean the arena. You're standing smack dab in the middle of an enclosed sand pit and the stadiums are filled with 21,000 spectators. Let's hope you brought your strappy leather sandals and metal vest because today you'll be fighting against a fellow tourist... for an acceptable Instagram shot...to the death. The Roman amphitheater is where, centuries ago, gladiators fought bloody battles with wild animals before it became a fortress in the fifth century CE. Climb up the four towers added to each side of the oval for a great look down at the area and view of Arles on the opposite site.

*i* *Admission €9, €7 student; limited wheelchair accessibility*

## Check out...

### THÉÂTRE ANTIQUE (ROMAN THEATRE)
8 Rue de la Calade; 04 90 18 41 20; open daily Jan 9am-noon, Feb 10am-noon and 2pm-5pm, Mar-Apr 9am-noon, May-Sept 9am-7pm, Oct-Dec 9am-noon and 2pm-6pm

Eager for more oval-shaped, tiered Roman relics? You're in luck! Just around the corner from Les Arènes is the less visually impressive, but still historically fascinating Roman Theatre. The theatre—not to be confused with its neighboring relic—was built in the time of Augustus and had 33 tiers to hold 8,000 spectators. Unlike its amphi-counterpart, this theatre has had a much harder time holding up over the years, mainly because it was employed as a quarry in the Middle Ages to provide stone for the surrounding town wall. Save two, all the columns are mere stumps, giving the ruins an ancient Stonehenge feeling.

*i* *Admission €9, €7 student, with Liberty Pass adult €12, €10 student; wheelchair accessible*

## Grab a bite at...

### L'HUILE FAD'OLI
44 Rue des Arènes; 04 90 49 70 73; open daily noon-midnight

If you're looking for a delicious meal that won't break the bank, Fad'Oli is the spot. Just on the corner of Place du Forum, this brightly-colored, petite restaurant with four red and yellow tables outside serves gourmet baguette sandwiches, large "Fadola" sandwiches, and (perhaps strangely) sushi. Around the restaurant there are giant barrels of olive oil on tap since, if you couldn't tell from the name, olive oil is their specialty. Drizzled on top of salads and sandwiches (and let's hope not the sushi), this liquid gold adds rich flavor to even the simplest of ingredients. Inside, you can read the descriptions of each gold-medal winning oil (yes, there are competitions for these things), and you can even buy a bottle to-go.

*i* *Sandwiches €4-7, salads €6-8, sushi €10-12; vegetarian and vegan options available*

## Don't miss...

### FONDATION VAN GOGH
35 Rue du Dr Fanton; 04 90 93 08 08; open daily Apr-Sept 11am-7pm; open Mar Tu-Su 11am-6pm

Pronounced "vahn-saw van-gog" in Southern France, Van Gogh has fans by the dozens in Arles. In 1888, when the renowned artist left Paris behind for the South, Van Gogh welcomed the light, sun, and rugged landscapes of Provence. Here, he painted like wildfire, producing over 200 works in just a few years. Every year, the Fondation Van Gogh exhibits a rotating selection of his works. Only about ten are on display at once, but the small number allows you to really take in each one at full value as you stare at each saturated color, unusual perspective, and evidence of compositional genius. After you pay your respect to our dear Vahn-saw, tour the sleek, white galleries of Van-Gogh's contemporaries before heading to the geometric rooftop terrace.

*i* *Admission €9, €4 student; last entry 45min. before closing; 75min. guided tours daily at 11:30am and 3pm €4; wheelchair accessible* days of Southern France.

*i* *Entrées €12-17; vegetarian options available; wheelchair accessible*

# NIGHTLIFE

## AOC

5 Pl. Jérusalem; 04 90 25 21 04; www. aocavignon.fr; open M-T noon-2pm and 6pm-10:30pm, F-Sa noon-2pm and 6pm-11pm, Su noon-2pm and 6pm-10pm

AOC is a fabulous wine bar in the heart of Avignon. Boasting a cozy inside lined with wine bottles, a shaded outdoor tourist, AOC allows you to play the best game of pretend wine-connoisseur of your life. Here's how to play: 1. Listen to the waiter describe the subtle notes of melon or honeysuckle in such-and-such regional wine. 2. Pick up your glass (cup it from the bottom for red and hold it by the stem for white). 3. Stick your nose inside, gracefully. 4. Swirl it, take a small sip, don't swallow, but instead swish it in your mouth. 5. Watch the waiter's respect for you go up tenfold, we promise. Make sure to pair your wine correctly (red with meat, white with seafood), otherwise all your effort will go to waste.

*i* *Appetizers €10, main courses €15, lunch special €14.90, three-course lunch menu, snacks €5-9; vegetarian options available; wheelchair accessible*

## LALOGÈNE

1 Pl. Pie; 04 86 81 60 76; open daily 7:30am-1:30am

Lalogène is a lovely terrace café by day and the closest thing Avignon has to a club by night. Packed with locals and students, tourists are in the vast minority in this stylish, clean bar with blue lights, bumping beats, and extremely affordable drinks. Situated on the lovely **Place Pie,** either party inside or chill on the outdoor terrace, which is one of our favorite spots to spend a warm summer evening with old and new friends. The best part? Waiters constantly swing by to clear tables outside, so you won't have to worry about empty beer bottles lying around as you're trying to have a fun rendezvous at Lalogène.

*i* *Beer and wine €2.50, coffee €1.10*

# BIARRITZ

Coverage by **Julia Bunte-Mein**

This getaway in France's Basque country is aware of its elite status. Ever since Napoléon III and his Spanish wife, Empress Eugénie, started summering here in the mid-nineteenth century, it became the go-to beach resort for European royalty. Not much has changed. Today, the Hôtel du Palais still glimmers in the sunlight, and linen-clad Europeans shop at Goyard and Hermès. Despite its glamorous (read: expensive) reputation, Biarritz has at least one free source of entertainment: the ocean. Young travelers from all over the world come to cruise the swooping waves, filling up bars and clubs that would otherwise be empty.

## ORIENTATION

Biarritz has four main beaches that stretch from the **Pointe Saint Martin Lighthouse** to **Le Plage de Milady.** The downtown area is located along these beaches, and is the hub of activity in the immediate region. The seaside trail, **Le Circuit Bord de Mer,** will take you from the lighthouse to **Le Grande Plage,** Biarritz's most popular beach, passing the **Hôtel du Palais.** If you continue along the coast, past the **Port du Pecheûr** (Fisherman's Port), you'll run into the **Pointe Atalaye,** from which the **Virgin Rock** extends. On the southern side of the Virgin Rock lie the aquarium, **Plage Port Vieux, Plage de la Côte de Basques**—home to the best waves in town—, **Plage de la Marbella,** Plage Milady, and finally **La Cité de L'ocean,** the ocean-themed interactive museum. A few more miles south are the towns of Bidart and **Saint-Jean-de-Luz.** Just inland of the coast is **Rue Gambetta,** Biarritz's main drag, which leads to **Les Halles,** the central market.

Just beyond that is **Place George Clémenceau,** a neighborhood known for its great restaurants and exciting nightlife scene.

# ESSENTIALS

## GETTING THERE

Biarritz has its own airport situated just outside of town that receives international and domestic flights. From there, you can take Bus #6 into the city center. Gare de Biarritz is the town's central train station. From there, it is about a 10min. drive or 20min. bus ride (#8) into the city center. Regional buses connect Biarritz to neighboring destinations like Saint-Jean-de-Luz, Hendaye, and San Sebastian.

## GETTING AROUND

The city center of Biarritz is quite compact, and easily navigable on foot. However, the town is very hilly, and if you're not one to enjoy hiking up hills all day, consult the bus schedule. The public buses (1hr. ticket €1; 24hr ticket €2; purchase directly from driver), called Chronoplus, are the cheapest and most reliable way to get around Biarritz and the surrounding towns of Anglet and Bayonne. Bus #8 takes you from the train station to the center.

## PRACTICAL INFORMATION

**Tourist Offices:** Square d'Ixelles; 5 59 22 37 00; open daily 9am-7pm
**Banks/ATMs/Currency:** Barclays Bank; 7 Av. Edouard VII; 5 59 22 44 44; open M-F 9am-noon, 2pm-5pm
Post Offices: Correus (17 Rue de la Poste; open M-F 9:30am-5:30pm, Sa 9:30am-12:30pm).
**Internet:** Free, functional Wi-Fi is available in most restaurants and cafés.

## EMERGENCY INFORMATION

**Emergency Number:** 112
**Police:** The local police station is located 1 Av. Joseph Petit (5 59 01 22 22l; open 24hr).
**Rape Crisis Center:** Rape Crisis Network Europe (01 45 88 19 00; www.inavem.org).
**Hospitals:**
- Centre Hospitalier Côte Basque (13 Av. de l'Interne Jacques Loeb, Bayonne; 5 59 44 39 54).
- Clinic Aguilera (21 Rue de l'Estagnas; 825 13 50 64; open daily 24hr).
**Pharmacies:**
- Pharmacie de L'Océan (7 Pl. Georges Clemenceau; 5 59 24 00 08; open M-Sa 8:30am-8pm).

# ACCOMMODATIONS

### ⚑NAMI HOUSE ($$)
14 R. de Tartilon; 05 40 48 02 82; www.nami-house-anglet.fr; reception open daily 8am-noon and 2pm-5pm

Part Japanese Zen garden, part Hawaiian bungalow, and part Australian surfer hostel, Nami House feels more like a shared guest house than a dormitory. Oftentimes, the travelers who pass through Nami end up staying twice as long as they intended because of its tranquil ambiance. Nami's interior—decorated with orchids, succulents, paper lanterns, bamboo cabinets, and large murals—is quite a welcome surprise compared to its relatively unassuming exterior. Here, you can enjoy a glass of wine in a chaise lounge on the terraced veranda before heading upstairs for a comfortable night in one of Nami's spacious bunks.

*i* Dorms €28-40, private rooms available; reservation recommended; min. stay 2 nights; BGLTQ+ friendly; wheelchair accessible; Wi-Fi; lockers available; free breakfast

### SURF HOSTEL BIARRITZ ($$$)
27 Av. de Migron; 06 63 34 27 45; www.surfhostelbiarritz.com; reception open Apr-Oct daily 8am-noon and 2pm-5pm

Providing its guests with a restful night of sleep, filling continental breakfast (none of that meager bread and jam bullshit), and a complimentary board, Surf is more B&B than hostel. As its name implies, this establishment is really made for surfers, but don't be deterred if you lack shredding experience. Surf Hostel Biarritz recently partnered with a surf school; opt into taking a lesson or pester one

# ST. JEAN DE LUZ

**Just a 15-minute train ride from Biarritz, the small fishing port of Saint-Jean-de-Luz is more relaxed, humble, and charming than its northern counterpart.** Like, Biarritz, this village is an exclusive holiday destination, but, here, the wealth is not quite as in-your-face. Buildings are beautiful, but not luxurious, and streets are busy but not overflowing with tourists. It has a certain... douceuer de vivre, with its picturesque port, yellow-sand beach, narrow pedestrian streets, traditional baserris (farmhouses) and glorious history. Saint-Jean-de-Luz was founded as a fishing and whaling port, but rose up to the level of aristocracy after King Louis XIV and wife Maria Theresa wed here in 1660.

Only 10km from the Spanish border, this small Basque beach town is tucked between Spain's Hendaye and France's Biarritz. It shares a bus and train station (**Gare St. Jean de Luz-Ciboure**) with the city of Ciboure. The center of Saint-Jean-de-Luz is the area just between the fisherman's port to the southwest and Le Baie de St. Jean de Luz et Ciboure, around the northwest bend, and pressed up against **Le Grande Plage. Place Louis XIV** is the main square and Rue Gambetta, which runs parallel to the beach and is lined with specialty stores, is the town's main pedestrian thoroughfare. During your visit, walk **Le Promenade Jacques,** which starts at the lighthouse and continues down to a sprawling yellow-sand beach.

## GETTING THERE

The Saint-Jean-de-Luz train station is shared by Ciboure and receives local trains from surrounding towns, including Biarritz and Bayonne, and is included on the SNCF Bordeaux-Irun and high-speed TGV Paris-Madrid train lines. Buses run frequently between Saint-Jean-de-Luz and neighboring Bayonne, Biarritz, and Hendaye. Ouibus, TCRB, and Basque Bondissant are the major bus companies. Saint-Jean-de-Luz is only a 20min. drive from Biarritz and a 30min. drive from San Sebastian. It is located off the highway A-63.

## GETTING AROUND

You can walk from one side of Saint-Jean-de-Luz to the other in less than 20min., so your feet are all you need! However, if you want to check out the neighboring town of Ciboure, there is a shuttle bus, called Itzulia, that runs between the two towns all year round (tickets €1). Also, there is a free shuttle that arrives every 30min. (during the summer months) that connects the Chantaco and Parc des Sports parking lots in the outskirts of Saint-Jean-de-Luz to the town center.

## Swing by...

**MAISON LOUIS XIV**
6 Pl. Louis XIV; 05 59 26 27 58; www.maison-louis-xiv.fr; open July- Aug daily 10:30am-12:30pm and 2:30pm-6:30pm, Sept-Oct, Apr-June daily visits at 11am, 3pm, 4pm, and 5pm
Designed by ship-builder **Joannis Lohobiague,** this house was originally called the Lohobiague-Enea, changed to the Maison Louis XIV after the king stayed there for 40 days in 1660. It was here in 1659 that Louis signed the **Treaty of the Pyrenees** that ended the ongoing conflict with Spain, and also confirmed his marriage to the Spanish Infanta Maria Teresa. If only we could solve all of our 21st-century problems by joining

together warring nations through marriage (Ivanka Trump and Kim Jong-un? We'd ship it). Take a 40-minute guided tour to see the seventeenth-century furniture, splendid painted beams, and poodle-haired family portraits. In the bedroom, notice the table with human-like legs as well as the ridiculously short bed. Apparently, Louis XIV used to sleep half-sitting out of fear of suffocating to death while lying under sheets!

*i* *Admission €6, €3.80 student; guided visits only; tours every 40min. July-Aug, last tour 30min. before closing, arrive 5min. before tour starts; no wheelchair accessibility*

## Check out...

### L'EGLISE SAINT JEAN BAPTISTE

Rue Léon Gambetta; 05 59 26 08 81; open Apr-Sep M-Sa 8:30am-6:30pm, Su 8am-7:30pm; Oct-Mar M-Sa 8:30am-6pm, Su 8am-7:30pm

Just off the commercial pedestrian street **Rue Gambetta,** you'll find the historic church where Louis XIV and Maria Theresa tied the royal knot. Although the outside isn't that special, L'Eglise Saint Jean Baptiste's interior is definitely fit for an imperial marriage. As soon as you enter, your eyes will be drawn to the front of the church, where the central nave is decorated with intricate floral patterns, ornate carvings, and golden statues. Look up at the red and gold ceilings, stained-glass skylight, and fleur-de-lis adorned side chapels. In stark contrast to the front of the church, the back has a clear traditional Basque influence. There are three-tiered balconies of dark wood and a giant sailboat hangs from the ceiling.

*i* *Free; limited wheelchair accessibility*

## Grab a bite at...

### LA TAVERNE BASQUE

5 Rue de la République; 05 59 26 01 26; open Tu-Sa noon-2pm and 7pm-10pm, Su noon-2pm

**Rue de la République,** the little street between **Place Louis XIV** and **Le Grande Plage,** is the place to go for traditional Basque food, and of the many restaurants that line it, La Taverne Basque is the obvious choice. Enjoy a bowl of toro soup, split a Serrano ham charcuterie board, and savor a grilled duck with honey-balsamic glaze, and wash it all down with a pitcher of sangria (€10). The portions are large and the food is relatively inexpensive, but, if you find yourself craving more, stop in one of the street's many pastry shops to try a gateaux Basque, an almond-based cake filled with vanilla, rum, or cherry-flavored cream.

*i* *Three-course meal €19.90; vegetarian options available; limited wheelchair accessibilitye*

## Don't miss...

### LA GRANDE PLAGE

While Saint-Jean-de-Luz's port and pedestrian streets are admittedly adorable, it is the town's sandy shore that attracts thousands every summer. Unlike Biarritz, where you have a plethora of fantastic beaches to choose from, this is the beach to visit in Saint-Jean-de-Luz and, accordingly, it is usually packed during the summer months. Also, unlike Biarritz, it's as flat as a pancake. Nestled in a protected bay, you'll see lots of paddle boarders, swimmers, and motor boats gliding over the smooth water. Le Grande Plage is the picture of summer in France: a mosaic of striped rainbow beach umbrellas, topless ladies, and men in speedos framed by turquoise water.

*i* *Free; limited wheelchair accessibility*

# THE LEGENDARY WAVE OF HOSSEGOR

Just up the coast from Biarritz lies Soorts-Hossegor, a lesser-known beach town (or more well-known, depending on who you're talking to) that's earned a reputation as the surfing capital of France, and arguably the world. Any real surfer would agree that between Biarritz and Hossegor, the latter is the ultimate surfing locale, as it boasts enormous waves that have consistent breaks—a hard thing to find in Europe. The inexplicably perfect waves have been legendary for generations, but it wasn't until the 1960s that scientists discovered what makes them so great: an underwater ravine called the Gouf de Capbretons. This subterranean canyon, gouf meaning "pit" in English, is over 15,000-kilometers wide and 3,500-meters deep. Scientists, researchers, and oceanographers have been puzzling over the origins of this abnormal trench for years and have come up with countless theories, ranging from an ancient valley dating back to the Ice Age, a seismic fault from the Pyrenean fold, and tectonic plate separation. When it was discovered, thousands of surfers from the US, Australia, and Europe began flocking to this small southwestern coastal town in Landes, France. Today, surfers from the all over the world come for the Rip Curl Pro world surfing championship and Quicksilver annual pro competition. These waves are not for the feint-hearted; Hossegarians live and breathe surfing, spending upwards of ten hours a day in the ocean before hitting the bars and clubs. Hossegor's nightlife scene is one thing even the biggest "Barney" (read: someone who's bad at surfing) can enjoy. In the summer, the beach town is filled exclusively with tanned, toned surfer babes and bros, making for a great change of pace from Biarritz.

of your surfer bunkmates enough and you'll be on your feet in no time.

*i* Dorms €38-40; reservation recommended; min. stay 3 nights; Wi-Fi; laundry facilities; free breakfast; kitchen

# SIGHTS
## CULTURE

### CHAPPELLE IMPÉRIALE (PARISH OF NOTRE DAME DU ROCHER)
4 Rue Saint Martin; 05 59 23 08 36; www.paroisse-biarritz.fr/eglises/chapelle-imperiale.php; open Jun-Sep Th, Sa 2pm-6pm, Sept-Dec Sa 2pm- 5pm, Mar-Jun Sa 2pm-6pm

Built in 1864 near Napoleon III's summer villa, has a deep purple exterior that encases a Hispano-Moorish interior, decorated with wooden paneling and ornately-painted and tiled walls. Known as the "Jewel of Biarritz," the chapel was designed by French architect Émile Boeswillwald and can be toured by appointment only. The limited hours are tricky

to navigate, so make sure to plan accordingly in advance of your trip.

*i* Admission €3; wheelchair accessible; guided tours available by appointment

## LANDMARKS

### PHARE DE BIARRITZ
60 B Espl. Elisabeth II; 05 59 22 37 10; open daily 2pm-6pm

The Phare de Biarritz, which was constructed in 1834 and is still operational, stands a whopping 73-meters above sea level, offering stunning views of the Basque coast and Atlantic Ocean. The plot of the lighthouse is crawling with hydrangeas (and tourists, especially during sunset), peppered with tamarisk trees, and crisscrossed by a network of pebbled pathways. Pro-tip: arrive early to beat the lines.

*i* Admission €2.50; no wheelchair accessibility

### PORT DES PÊCHEURS
Allée Port des Pêcheurs; open daily 24hr

Biarritz's Port des Pêcheurs dates back to its humble fishing-village days. The port was rebuilt in the nineteenth century but it still has its original *crampottes,* the picturesque fisherman houses outfitted with wooden doors and colorful shutters. At low-tide, the port completely drains out, leaving a huge stretch of tide pools kids flock to with nets to catch crabs. To the right of the port is a small beach that provides a great alternative to the crowded **Grande Plage,** as well as a selection of delicious seafood restaurants. Before you leave, make sure to check out Crampotte 30, a tapas and wine bar housed in one of the original crampottes.

*i* Free; limited wheelchair accessibility

### ROCHER DE LA VIERGE
Allée Port des Pêcheurs; 05 59 22 37 10; open daily 9:30am-7pm

The Virgin Rock is the emblematic symbol of and largest tourist attraction in Biarritz. It's no Eiffel Tower, but the metal footbridge was designed by the landmark's namesake, which is close enough. Located between **Port-Vieux** and **Port des Pêcheurs** on the promontory of Atalaye, the bridge joining the rock formation to the mainland was originally wooden, built on the orders of **Napoleon III,** who decided to drill a tunnel through the formation and use it as an anchor point for the sea wall of the **Port du Refuge.** Despite enduring centuries of damage by the Atlantic, the monument, consecrated in 1865, still stands strong today. Walk across and behold the beauty of the ocean before you, statue above you, and city behind you.

*i* Free; no wheelchair accessibility

## MUSEUMS

### ⬛PLANÈTE MUSÉE DU CHOCOLAT
14 Ave. Beau Rivage; 05 59 23 27 72; www.planetemuseeduchocolat.com; open Jul-Sep daily 10am-7pm, Sept-July M-Sa 10am-12:30pm and 2pm-6:30pm

You could be like everyone else and go to the aquarium or **Cité de L'ocean,** but if you' aren't feeling particularly aquatic, we recommend heading to this adorable and hilarious chocolate museum. Upon arrival, you'll be handed a bag of chocolates (if that's not already enough of an incentive, we don't know what is). The tour begins with an educational video of the cacao bean, tracing its history from legend of the Aztec deity Quetzalcoatl to King Louis XIII obsession's with hot chocolate. All of the descriptions are in French, but the close-up shots don't need translation. The second half of the visit includes a trip to a sculpture gallery, some of which are quite scandalous (read: a chocolate rendition of *Désir* by Rodin), and cabinets full of bizarrely-shaped chocolate molds (read: rifles and llamas. How appetizing!).

*i* Admission €6.50, €5 student, €4.50 guided tour groups of 15+; ticket office closes at 6pm; wheelchair accessible

## OUTDOORS

### BIARRITZ BEACHES
Open daily 24hr (weather permitting)

You already know that Biarritz is famous for its beaches, but you may not know which one is best for you. **Le Grande Plage,** the closest one to the center of town, is popular among surfers and bathers alike for its easy access, broad swatch of sand, and huge waves. There is a narrow swimming area delineated by two flags; if you venture

outside of it, lifeguards will yell at you and chase you down (believe us, we tried). To the northeast is **Plage Miramar,** close to the rocky area just south of the **Phare de Biarritz.** Plage Miramar is also great for surfing, but a little more dangerous. Sandwiched between of the **Port des Pêcheurs** and Le Grand Plage is the quiet, small **Plage Port Vieux.** This protected spot is popular for families because it has no waves or wind it also boasts a convenient location adjacent to Biarritz's diving clubs and seafood bars. Around the Pointe Atalaye is the long, open **Plage Côte des Basques**—the ultimate surfing beach where you can rent a board or take a lesson. Note that during high tide, the beach is not open for lounging as the water brushes up against the cliffs.

*i* Free

# FOOD

### EDEN ROCK CAFÉ ($$)

6 Pl. Port Vieux; 659681824; open daily 11am-2am

Located just north of **Le Plage Port View,** this cliff-side restaurant dangles right over the shimmering ocean, with direct views of the **Rocher de la Vieux.** Eden Rock Café's menu is simple— chipirons (cuttlefish), chili, fries, beer, sangria—but extensive, and the food is much cheaper than other restaurants in the area. The true draw of Eden Rock, however, is not the food, but its canopied outdoor patio. Arrive early enough and you'll be able to snag a table on its perimeter, one of the best places, in our humble opinion, to watch the sun set in Biarritz.

*i* Sangria €3, cocktails €7.50, appetizers €8, entrées €12-14; vegetarian options available

### IL GIARDINO ($$$)

5 R. du Ctre; 05 59 22 16 41; www.ilgiardino-biarritz.com; open Tu-Sa noon-2pm and 7pm-11pm, Su 7pm-11pm

Come to Il Giardino to treat yourself to an exquisite meal that won't break the bank. This Italian restaurant serves homemade, melt-in-your-mouth pasta, along with all sorts of freshly-prepared meat, fish, and vegetable dishes. Take your pick of linguini, spaghetti,

gnocchi, or risotto—we loved the *linguine nero di sepia* (squid in its ink)—in the "simple" or "complete" size. For dessert, soothe your sweet tooth with the tiramisu and panna cotta they're both delicious.

*i* Appetizers €6-8, entrées €14-20, wine €5; vegetarian options available; wheelchair accessible; reservation recommended

### MIREMONT SALON DE THÉ ET PATISSERIE ($)

1bis Pl. Georges Clemenceau; 05 59 24 01 38; www.miremont-biarritz.fr; open daily 9am-8pm

This tearoom and pastry shop is truly the king of all bakeries. Dating back to the nineteenth century, the shop was frequented by European royalty like King Edward VII of England and King Alphonso XIII of Spain, the latter of which loved it so much that he appointed its founder to the country's Royal House. And the pastries truly do live up to their royal heritage. Miremont's display case features layered millefeuilles, macarons, lemon tarts, chocolate mousse delicacies, éclairs, and more, all topped with edible gold and Miremont's confectioner crest. The interior of the shop is equally over-the-top, featuring baby pink walls, crystal chandeliers, and grand siècle ceilings. Pastry prices are a bit steep, so we recommend ordering yours to-go, which will automatically knock €2 off the top.

*i* Cakes to-go €3.50, €5.50 to-stay

# NIGHTLIFE

### DUPLEX

24 Av. Edouard VII; 05 59 24 65 39; www.nightclub-biarritz.com; open daily 7pm-6am

The population in Biarritz consists of two very distinct crowds: posh vacationers and young surfers. As its name suggests, Duplex accommodates both by leaning into the city's naturally-occurring dichotomy, funneling anyone above the age of 25 upstairs to the "Cotton Club" and anyone below that age downstairs to "Pulp." Despite their absurd names, both floors are surprisingly lit. Cotton Club may be more chic with its arched ceilings, glowing blue bar, and VIP lounges, but Pulp is where the real party happens. Here, you can order a vodka and orange juice concoction that's almost as sugary as the daddies upstairs, and dance the night away under black nights to the rapid thumping of house music.

*i* *Cover €12 (includes one free drink), cocktails €1; wheelchair accessible*

## NEWQUAY BAR

20 Pl. Georges Clemenceau; 05 59 22 19 90; open daily 9am-midnight

A student hideaway in the middle of glitzy Biarritz, Newquay Bar is consistently packed with English-speaking Australians, Americans, South Africans, and tons of non-French-speaking Europeans. Unlike its neighbors, this pub is unpretentious, serving cheap beers, salty food, and ciders imported from Cornwall, England. It's the perfect a relaxed environment to meet other travelers, listen to live music, or watch the latest football match.

*i* *Beer €2-3, drinks €5-10; wheelchair accessible*

# BORDEAUX

Coverage by **Julia Bunte-Mein**

Let's play the word-association game. Paris? Baguettes. Lyon? *Bouchons.* Bordeaux? Wine. Holy grail of wine connoisseurs and wine moms alike, Bordeaux is world-renowned for having some of the world's best vineyards since before 71 BCE. However, Bordeaux, the sixth-largest city in France, has so much more to offer beyond its place as the wine capital of the world. The city, in a way, has undergone a twenty-first century Renaissance under Mayor Alain Juppé, who ordered that every single neoclassical limestone façade in the city be washed, rejuvenating the city with a fresh-old time look. This rejuvenation has also resulted in a more pedestrian-friendly city, which takes shape in the boardwalk at the Garonne riverfront, high-tech public transport system, and now-bustling industrial docks at Bassin à Flots. Bordeaux, which used to be affectionately called the Belle au Bois Dormant (the Sleeping Beauty), has woken up and blossomed into a dynamic, trendy city complete with vibrant nightlife scenes and priceless dining experiences. In all of its new vigor, however, Bordeaux is far from forgetting its roots; the entire city is designated as a UNESCO World-Heritage Site, as it houses remarkable eighteenth-century architecture characteristic of La Belle Époque and has incredible historical significance. These classic structures, juxtaposed by more modern buildings such as the decanter-shaped Cité du Vin, dot the banks of the Garonne River, which is also the site of outdoor concerts, ex-military camps, and art exhibition spaces. So swirl your glass of *Malbec* or *Sauvignon Blanc* and put on your walking shoes, Bordeaux is waiting for you.

## ORIENTATION

The city of Bordeaux is situated around the **Garonne River,** with its center on the western bank. The riverfront boardwalk, **Les Quais,** stretches between the two main bridges of the city. At the focal point of the boardwalk is **Le Miroir d'Eau,** behind which is **Le Place de la Bourse.** This is the main entry point into **La Vielle Ville** of Bordeaux, also called the **Saint-Pierre district. Promenade Sainte-Catherine,** the longest pedestrian shopping street in Europe, stretches from l**e Place de la Comédie** to **Place Victoire,** which are both dynamic hubs of the Old Quarter. To the north of the **Saint-Pierre quarter** is the **Triangle d' Or neighborhood** whose three main boulevards form a triangular shape with vertexes at **Le Grande Théâtre, Place Gambetta,** and **Place Tourny.** Much farther north of La Vielle Ville, still along the riverbank, is the Chartrons neighborhood. Even farther north is the recently transformed industrial area, **Bassin à Flot,** home to **La Cité du Vin** and the **Base Sous-Marine.** Jumping to the south side of the old city is the area called **Saint Michel.** Across the river, on Bordeaux's eastern bank is the **Bastide area.**

# ESSENTIALS
## GETTING THERE

The Bordeaux-Mérignac Airport is only 9km outside the city center. The Jetbus (€7) runs directly between the airport and Gare St-Jean, takes 30min. For a cheaper option, you can take the city bus Line #1 (€1.40) which runs every 10min. and takes slightly longer than the Jetbus. Trains to Bordeaux arrive at Gare St-Jean, the main train station. From there, tram line C will take you into the city center.

## GETTING AROUND

Bordeaux has a tram system, which is=most convenient form of public transport, as trams depart every 5min. or so from the many street-side stops (€1.50 single ride). Even better than the tram, though, are Bordeaux's city bikes, VCub. Get 24hr or seven-day access for an unlimited number of trips within the first 30min. of each trip.

## PRACTICAL INFORMATION

**Tourist Offices:** 12 Cours du 30 Juillet; 5 56 00 66 00; www.bordeaux-tourisme.com; open M-Sa 9:30am-1pm and 2-7pm.
**Banks/ATMs/Currency Exchange:** BNP Paribas Bordeaux (40 Cours du Chapeau-Rouge; 820 82 00 01; open M-F 9am-5:30pm).
**Post Offices:** La Poste Bordeaux (29 Allée de Tourny; open M, W-F 9am-6pm, Tu 10am-6pm, Sa 9am-noon).
**Internet:** Bordeaux is covered with public Wi-Fi spots. Simply click "Wifi Bordeaux" on your phone network. Free Wi-Fi is also offered in all municipal buildings, including the tourist office.
**BGLTQ+ Resources:** BGLTQ Association of Aquitaine; www.le-girofard.org.

## EMERGENCY INFORMATION

**Emergency Number:** 112
**Police:** Hôtel de Police (Commissariat central: 23 Rue François de Sourdis; 05 57 85 77 77; open daily 24hr).

**US Embassy:** US Consulate Bordeaux (89 Quai des Chartrons; 01 43 12 48 65).
**Rape Crisis Center:** Rape Crisis Network Europe; www.inavem.org; (0)1 45 88 19 00
**Hospitals:** Hôpital Saint-André (1 Rue Jean Burgue; 05 56 79 56 79; open daily 24hr)
**Pharmacies:** There is a 24hr pharmacy located at 30 Pl. des Capucins (05 56 91 62 66).

# ACCOMMODATIONS
### AUBERGE DE JEUNESSE BORDEAUX ($$)

22 Cours Barbey; 05 56 33 00 70; www.auberge-jeunesse-bordeaux.com/; open May 1-Oct 31 daily 24hr and Nov 1-Apr 30 closed 1pm-3pm

Before Hostel 20 popped up in 2015, Auberge de Jeunesse held a complete monopoly on Bordeaux's backpacker accommodation industry since it opened in 1964. Luckily, it subscribed to a benevolent form of economic tyranny and offers an excellent product for an extremely reasonable price. The bright pink and lime green common areas have comfy sofas. Furthermore, the kitchen comes equipped with everything you could possibly need. The dorms are less colorful, but they are spacious and clean. Although it's located in a somewhat quiet residential area, it is extremely close to the train station and only a 10-to-15-minute walk to the city center.

*i* Dorms from €27; reservation recommended; Wi-Fi; BGLTQ+ friendly; linens included; towels included; laundry facilities €4; breakfast €2

### HOSTEL 20 ($$)

20 Rue Borie; 06 65 52 16 80; www.hostel20.fr; reception open 24hr

Staying at Hostel 20 is like crashing at your second cousin's apartment-style dorm at his French university—very quirky, homey, and full of interesting people from all around the world. The private and shared rooms have all regular beds (i.e no bunks), giving it a more bedroom feel. By far the best

The Dune du Pilat is a 2,700-meter long, 500-meter wide, and 109-meter high pile of sand. Yes, a pile of sand is just a pile of sand, but this is the highest dune in all of Europe. Unless you're going to the Sahara Desert anytime soon, visiting the Dune du Pilat is your chance to be Lawrence of Arabia for a day. The golden dune is located next to the coastal town of Arcachon, a popular beach destination that has attracted bourgeois Bordelaise since the late nineteenth century.

The vast dunes seem to stretch on for miles, cascading down on one side to a lush green forest, and on the other to the glimmering ocean. Just above the distant wavy mirage, people hike along the dunes' crests and paragliders soar through the perfectly blue sky. Luckily, there's an embedded staircase in the dune to climb up, but even so, the climb is a real workout, especially in the blazing mid-day heat.

On the way down, skip the stairs and just run straight down, praying your legs will move fast enough to keep you from face planting, which wouldn't be so bad either. Even better, log roll down the entire way. Be careful not to drop your keys or phone because these dunes are like quicksand—they'll gobble it up in a minute.

If you feel like going for a swim, just be prepared to trek up the burning hot sand back to the top, as there's no staircase on the ocean-side. At the end of the day, the Dune du Pilat is really just a pile of sand, but a damn cool one that should not be missed if you're traveling through Bordeaux.

Arcachon is a 30 to 40-minute train ride from Bordeaux and the dune is an eight to nine-mile bicycle or bus ride (bus #1) from there.

**FRANCE BORDEAUX**

part of this boutique hostel though is the welcoming, international staff and their amazing sense of community. The eighteenth-century the hostel is housed in is not directly in the center of the old city, but in the cooler **Chartrons district,** which and is only a short walk or metro ride away from **Place de la Bourse.**

*i* Dorms from €24; reservation recommended; Wi-Fi; linens included; lockers available; full kitchen

# SIGHTS
## CULTURE

### BASILIQUE SAINT-MICHEL
Pl. Meynard; 05 56 94 30 50; open daily 8am-noon and 1pm-6pm

A **UNESCO World Heritage Site** and a stop on the **Camino de Santiago,** this fourteenth-century Gothic basilica is a nice visit if you are in the **St. Michel area.** Though its opening hours are tough to accommodate, it's not the end of the world because Saint-Michel's exterior is its most impressive aspect. The inside looks very similar to

the **Cathedral Saint-Andre,** with the same vaulted brick ceiling, but looks older and less clean. While you're there, climb the 114-meter tall **Fleche de St. Michel** (independent bell tower) for a panoramic view of the city and explore the crypt underneath. The adjoining square is lovely, surrounded by little cafés, restaurants, and an outdoor market on Sundays.

*i* Free, tower and crypt €5, €3.50 student; last entry 30min. before closing

### CATHÉDRAL SAINT-ANDRÉ
Pl. Pey Berland; 05 56 52 68 10; open June-Sept daily 10am-1pm and 3pm-7:30pm, except until 7pm on Su in July and Aug; Oct-May daily 10am-noon and 2pm-6pm and until 7pm on M, W, Sa, closed on M mornings year-round

The Cathédral Saint André is the city's never-ending pet project. It is considered one of the finest works of Gothic architecture, but it took thousands of years of constant renovations to reach its current state. Historians guestimate that construction began in the fifth or sixth century, after which it was destroyed a couple of times before being reconstructed in the eleventh

century. Over the following centuries, the Bordelaise made radical improvements to the flamboyant exterior, elevated the nave with pointed arches, and opened the **Royal Portal.** Sadly, all this beautification wasn't appreciated because (plot-twist!) the church became an animal feed store during the French Revolution. Take a loop around the dark wood choir, painted ambulatories, and pristine white chapels before taking a seat in one of the little wicker chairs to gaze up at the magnificent brickwork above you.

*i* *Free; last entry 30min. before closing; wheelchair accessible*

## LANDMARKS

### PLACE DE LA BOURSE
Quai du Maréchal Lyautey; open daily 24hr
The Place de la Bourse is Bordeaux's main square and its most dazzling attraction. Built during the eighteenth century in the neoclassical style for **King Louis XV,** it is very much a manifestation of his lavish tastes. The square features the **Bourse** (stock exchange), the **Customs Museum,** and a beautiful fountain of The Three Graces in its center. The coolest part of Place de la Bourse is the **Miroir d'Eau,** the world's largest water mirror spanning 37,000 square feet which is, located just up the street. It offers double the magic during the day, creating the illusion that the surrounding buildings are twice as large and is truly a spectacle to behold at dusk, when the facades glow with warm yellow light.

*i* *Free; limited wheelchair accessibility*

### TOUR PEY-BERLAND
Pl. Pey Berland; 05 56 81 26 25; www. pey-berland.fr; open Jan-May daily 10am-12:30pm and 2pm-5:30pm, June-Sept daily 10am-1:15pm and 2pm-6pm, Oct-Dec daily 10am-12:30pm and 2pm-5:30pm
The 233-step Tour Pey-Berland is the bell tower of Cathedral Saint Andre, but it really is a separate sight, or rather activity, in itself. This fifteenth-century Gothic bell tower was built independently from the cathedral to avoid vibrations in the main church, but, ironically, the bell tower lacked bells until 1853. Since it didn't serve a function other than casting an enormous shadow over half the city, it was divided into dwellings in the seventeenth century, and then turned into a factory for making shotgun pellets. Today, it has one single spiral staircase leading up to the highest viewpoint in Bordeaux that you can access. The panorama from the top is great, but be warned that it's a thigh-quivering climb to get there, and your trek back down to Earth will involve lots of butt-bumping and belly-rubbing.

*i* *Admission €6, €5 student, free EU residents 18-25 years old; last entrance 30min. before closing; no wheelchair accessibility*

## MUSEUMS

### MUSÉE DU VIN ET DU NÉGOCE
Cellier des Chartrons; 41 Rue Borie; 05 56 90 19 13; www.museeduvinbordeaux.com; open daily 10am-6pm
To learn the complete history of Bordeaux wine, head to the Musée du Vin et de Négoce in the **Chartrons**

**district,** which has been the center of Bordeaux's wine trade since the Middle Ages. The museum is housed in an original eighteenth-century building, and the visit includes a self-guided tour through three underground cellar. The museum itself is quite small, but offers a thick laminated binder tracing the evolutions of the wine merchants from the Middle Ages to the present day, going into extreme detail about the trading system and technical winemaking process. The best part comes in the form of an in-depth tasting experience, during which you'll learn about Bordeaux's different wine geographies and grape varieties and try two different types of wine with chocolate covered wine-raisins.

*i* *Admission €10, €5 student, includes two wine tastings; no wheelchair accessibility*

### CITÉ DU VIN

134 Quai de Bacalan; 05 56 16 20 20; www.laciteduvin.com/fr; open daily 9:30am-7:30pm

When glitzy La Cité du Vin opened in 2016, it quickly overshadowed nearby **Musée du Vin et du Négoce.** However, if you only have time to visit one or the other, we'd recommend visiting the latter. Yes, La Cité du Vin's decanter-shaped building is a stunning piece of modern architecture, but the museum is about wine in general, not Bordeaux wine specifically. Plus, you only get one wine tasting instead of two (#priorities). You'd think it'd be the other way around, considering entrance to La Cité du Vin costs twice as much as its predecessor.

*i* *Admission €20, €14 reduced; limited wheelchair accessibility*

## OUTDOORS

### 🏛DARWIN

t87 Quai des Queyrie; 05 56 77 52 06; www.darwin.camp; restaurant open M-F 8:30am-6pm, Sa- Su 10am-6pm

If you are at all into the alternative/vegan/street-art/skate-board/eco-friendly/craft coffee scene, head across the river to Darwin. This ex-military site turned sustainable development project on the right bank of the **Garonne River** is a great example

of how Bordeaux has adopted a radically new look. Just a few years ago, the **Bastide** area was an industrial wasteland, but now it is home to a complex of re-purposed industrial buildings fitted with a trendy café and restaurant, organic food shop, a vegetable garden, a skate-park, and street-art space. Don't miss the "sauvage" gorilla art installation on your right when you come in—very Charles Darwin-esque.

*i* *Free; limited wheelchair accessibility*

## FOOD

### 🍽L'OISEAU CABOSSE ($$)

30 Rue Sainte-Colombe; 05 57 14 02 07; open T-Sa 9:30am-7pm, Su 11:30am-5:30pm

This small terrace restaurant in the heart of Bordeaux's old city offers fresh, light, and varied dishes perfect for the summer. L'Oiseau Cabosse is famous for its Sunday brunch, but is a fantastic casual lunch or dinner option any day of the week. They offer small *assiettes* (think French tapas) of soups, salads, and savory tarts. For lunch, get two salads and one *assiette* of your choice for less than €10, or two plates for €14.50. We loved the zucchini goat-cheese tart, grilled eggplant and mozzarella bruschetta, polenta with chorizo, and baked Brie with honey.

*i* *Single-course set lunch €9.50, two-course set lunch €14.50, brunch €20, desserts €5; vegetarian options available; reservation recommended*

### CHEZ DUPONT ($$)

45 Rue Notre Dame; 05 56 81 49 59; www.chez-dupont.com/fr/restaurant_chez_dupont_bordeaux.html; open T-Sa 11:30am-2:30pm and 7:30pm-11pm

Even if you're not into the French's obsession with eating animal organs, Chez Dupont is the perfect restaurant to try typical Bordelaise cuisine, as it serves everything, including traditional veal, duck, *foie gras,* and steak with crispy *frites.* Come here for a cozy, high-end, but reasonably-priced dining experience away from the hordes of tourists. While you're there, be sure to try *la baba gourmand,* a sweet rum cake

There is not just one type of Bordeaux wine; there are countless varieties, blends, and growing methods that determine the recipe for this grape elixir. The complete explanation is very technical and detailed, but here are the basics:

Wine is almost never made with only one kind of grape. Bordeaux wines blend six different locally-grown grape varieties: Cabernet Sauvignon, Merlot, Cabernet Franc for reds and Sauvignon Blanc, Semillon, and Muscadelle for white wines. Each of these grape varieties require a different type of environment to grow, but luckily the terrain of the Bordeaux region is so varied that it can accommodate these differences. For example, the left side of the Garonne River is called the Medoc region. Here the soil is gravely and course—best for the Cabernet Sauvignon grape used in full-bodied red wines. On the right side of the River, in the St. Emillion region, the soil is full of clay and limestone, which is best for the Merlot grape. Wines made with Merlot are fruity, light, and best consumed in the same year of production.

served with a small glass of Havana Club whiskey.

*i  Starters €10-12, entrées €20-25; vegetarian options available; reservation recommended; wheelchair accessible*

### FUFU BORDEAUX ($)

37 Rue Saint-Rémi; 05 56 52 10 29; www.restaurantfufu.com; open M-F 11:30am-3pm and 6:30pm-11pm

FuFu Bordeaux, a Japanese noodle bar, has a local cult following. Every day, ramen and dumpling aficionados start lining up outside this tiny restaurant, ready to wait for more than 20 minutes for their eggy and delicious noodles, woks, and bouillon bowls. If you manage to snag a seat, you can watch the chefs make your meal from scratch right in front of you. The restaurant is hectic, loud, and full of steam, but if that's a little too much, you can order your meal to-go too. FuFu is so popular that they opened up another location, FuFu 2, just outside of the city center, where you're much more likely to get seated right away.

*i  Entrées €6-10; vegetarian options available; wheelchair accessible*

## NIGHTLIFE

### BAR NOTRE DAME (BRIT COLETTE)

82 Rue Notre Dame; 05 56 81 55 33; open daily 8am-10pm

To visit Bordeaux and miss the alternative and slightly bohemian neighborhood of **Chartrons**, however, would be a sin. **Rue Notre Dame,** is the neighborhood's main street and is filled with small boutique shops, salon de thés, and terrace bars. Our favorite of the offerings is Bar Notre Dame, located just around the corner from the **St. Louis Church** and covered market. Its green marble tabletops, blue and red tiled walls, and newspaper clippings from the 60s attract an older crowd, ranging 30-50s, but overall, Bar Notre Dame has a welcoming look that anyone would enjoy.

*i  Coffee €1, beer and wine €3, sandwiches €4; wheelchair accessible*

### LA CONSERVERIE—CONSERVERIE

18 Rue Notre Dame; 05 56 81 49 17; open Tu-W 11am-8pm, Th-Sa 11am-10pm

La Conserverie-Conserverie is an exceptional wine-bar, serving high quality Bordelaise wines in a rustic, charming environment that is almost exclusively occupied by locals. It has an understated entrance, but the interior, filled with patterned Moroccan rugs, stretches far back. Stay inside for a cozy, warm ambiance, complemented by comfortable armchairs, or head to the terrace courtyard.

*i  Wine €4-6, small plates €10; wheelchair accessible*

### SYMBOISE

4 Quai des Chartrons; 05 56 23 67 15; open M-Sa noon-2pm and 7am-2am

From the front, Symbiose looks like a fancy restaurant, but if you walk all the way to the back, through the grandfather clock on the back wall, you will be transported into the coolest cocktail bar in Bordeaux (and arguably all of France). With stone walls, low ceilings, and some crazy drinks (read: bacon-infused negroni or the "Forest Gump," served with a shitake mushroom), Symbiose exudes a speakeasy feel. This hidden bar is not advertised at all and you either need to hear about it from a local or stumble upon it by chance while looking for the bathroom after dining at the front restaurant.

*i* Cocktails €11, wine €6; wheelchair accessible

## THE STARFISH PUB

24/26 Rue Sainte Colombe; 05 56 52 88 61; open M-F 4pm-2am, Sa 2pm-2am, Su 2pm-midnight

On any night of the week, the Starfish Pub will be popping. It is the go-to spot for young Erasmus students, backpackers, and Bordey's alike for a fun night out. Come between 5:30pm and 8:30pm for the sweet happy hour deals and stay past sundown when it really gets crowded. Starfish loves hosting themed events like karaoke nights and jam sessions in its cool underground club.

*i* Drinks €3-6; wheelchair accessible

# CAEN

Coverage by **Emily Corrigan**

Caen left its impression in the annals of history long before there were students to invade it with their backpacks and travel guides in tow. It especially gained fame as the former home of William the Conqueror (known as William the Bastard to some), and his castle and other constructions still dominate the city's architecture. In more recent history, Caen played an important role in World War II. Not far from the landing beaches on the coast of Normandy, it's the perfect base for exploring the region and understanding its harrowing past. In the city, medieval streets lined with bars and restaurants mingle with shops in modern buildings (constructed after its near-complete bombardment in the war) and massive cathedrals. Add some regional cheese and cider specialties and you have yourself an extremely intriguing place.

## ORIENTATION

The city of Caen spreads over five main districts. Near the center of the city is **Caen Castle**, surrounded by the main hustle and bustle of the town. **Le Vaugueux,** the medieval district full of restaurants, lies just below it to the southeast, while the shop-lined pedestrian streets of **Saint-Sauveur** flank the castle to the southwest. The **Jardin des Plantes** district to the northwest showcases impressive nineteenth-century townhouses, while the peninsula district to the southeast is perfect for an evening stroll along the water. Don't miss the hippodrome towards the city's southern edge, or the historical beaches just a few miles north.

## ESSENTIALS
### GETTING THERE

Caen has its own small regional airport with some international flights from a limited number of other European cities. It's about 3mi. north of the city, so take a taxi. SNCF also runs high-speed trains out of Caen station.

## GETTING AROUND

Caen has a tram system that spans over two lines. Tickets cost €2 but depend on how far you're traveling. Caen has a convenient bus system that can also travel to other nearby towns. The main hub is Gare de Caen. Tickets are €1.50.

## PRACTICAL INFORMATION

**Tourist Offices:** 12 Pl. Saint-Pierre; 02 31 27 14 14

**Banks/ATMS/Currency Exchange:** Currency can be exchanged at the Bureau de Change; (115 Rue Saint-Jean; 02 31 30 18 87; www.change-caen.com; open M-F 9:15am-12:30pm and 2:15pm-6:30pm, Sa 9:15am-12:30pm and 2:15pm-5pm).

**Post Offices:** La Poste (2 Rue Georges Lebret, open M-F 8:30am-6:30pm, Sa 9am-12:30pm and 1:30pm-4:30pm).

**Internet:** Free public Wi-Fi is provided at six points around the city. A list of these points can be found here: http://caen.fr/capitale-vivre/wifi-en-acces-libre.

**BGLTQ+ Resources:** Centre BGLTQ de Normandie (74 Bd. Dunois, 06 89 49 40 56; www.centrelgbt-normandie.fr).

## EMERGENCY INFORMATION

**Emergency Number:** 112

**Police:** Police Nationale (10 Rue du Dr Thibout de la Fresnaye; 02 31 29 22 22)

**Rape Crisis Center:** In case of a crisis, cal RAINN (800 656 4673).

**Hospitals:** Hospital Center University De Caen (Av. de la Côte de Nacre; 02 31 06 31 06)

**Pharmacies:** Pharmacy Hastings (24 Rue Lanfranc; 02 31 74 75 24).

## ACCOMMODATIONS

**HÔTEL DU HAVRE CAEN CENTRE ($$)**
11 Rue du Havre; 02 31 86 19 80; www.caen-hotel.fr

Beds as soft as baby sheep covered in butter. Wi-Fi that works faster than the speed of light. The privacy of your own bathroom. In short, a weary traveler's oasis. This is how you will feel when you check in at Hôtel du Havre. Although Caen isn't exactly a young traveler's hub, the hotel provides the most comfortable and affordable accommodations near the city center. The staff is professional and knowledgeable, not just a teenager on summer vacation, and the fluffy (and FREE) towels feel like clouds

compared to your average hostel sandpaper.

*i* Rooms starting at €55; reservation required; wheelchair accessible; Wi-Fi

## SIGHTS
### CULTURE

#### ⊠HIPPODROME DE LA PRAIRIE
Bd. Yves Guillou; 02 31 27 50 80; www.letrot.com/fr/hippodrome/caen/1400; hours vary

Sure, every year you put on a pastel colored shirt and half-watch the Kentucky Derby while you play beer pong, and maybe you've even seen the movie Seabiscuit. But you'll experience much more authentic French horse-racing culture at Caen's very own hippodrome. The track features exclusively trotting races, meaning either the horses will remain in the trotting gait (if you know anything about horses) or it'll just look really weird (if you don't). Whether you want to bet on a horse, or just root for whichever one has the prettiest tail, one thing is certain: the fast-talking horse race announcing is even less comprehensible in French.

*i* Admission €3; wheelchair accessible

### LANDMARKS

#### ⊠CAEN CASTLE
02 31 30 47 60; www.musee-de-normandie.caen.fr/application-chateau; open daily 9:30am-6pm

The Castle of Caen looms over the city like a basketball player looms over an oompa loompa. Its construction began in 1060 by none other than William the Conqueror, who resided there when he wasn't launching conquests on England. It remains one of the largest fortified enclosures in Europe, with 800-meters of ramparts (on which you can walk, but mostly pretend to shoot arrows out of small slits and pose comically with large cannons). The castle has a moat, the ruins of a dungeon, portcullised drawbridges, the whole nine yards. But, if that's not enough to pique your interest, you can still visit the fine arts museum and the Museum of Normandy for free, provided you're under 25. That's ageism at its finest.

*i* Free admission to the castle, museum admission free under 25; tours Tu and F 11am and 4pm; wheelchair accessible

## ABBAYE AUX HOMMES

Esplanade Jean-Marie Louvel; 02 31 30 42 81; www.caen.fr/node/457; open daily 24hr

We've all been there. You went and married your cousin (despite what Dad said) and now you have to get yourself some insurance just in case the old man upstairs isn't too pleased with your incestuous behavior. William the Conqueror's solution for this all-too-relatable problem was to construct the enormous Abbaye aux Hommes (mens' abbey). Much larger and more resplendent than the womens' abbey—1063 was a little early for feminism—this abbey features a beautiful cloister with a manicured garden, as well as the tomb of the famed conqueror himself. It would be a lovely place for a wedding, say, to your cousin.

*i* Admission €7, €5.50 reduced, free under 18; tours M-F at 10:30am and 2pm; wheelchair accessible

## MUSEUMS

### ◾MÉMORIAL DE CAEN

Esplanade Général Eisenhower; 02 31 06 06 44; www.memorial-caen.fr; open daily 9am-7pm

You would be hard pressed to find a more personal, inspiring, haunting, and devastatingly sad take on World War II history than here. The museum emphasizes the costly toll the war took in terms of human life and confidence in humankind. Caen was one of the cities in Normandy occupied by Germans for the longest and later, hit by Allied bombardment during liberation the hardest. Not only does the museum explore combat, strategy, and politics, but it focuses on massacres, extermination, and the effects of waging invasive total war on all of its fronts. It would be difficult to leave the Mémorial de Caen without both a nuanced understanding of an event that altered the course of human

history and a heightened sense of your own humanity.

*i* Admission student €17; wheelchair accessible

## OUTDOORS

### ◾ÉTRETAT

Étretat; www.etretat.net

There should be a reality TV show called "Keeping Up with the Cliffs" because the cliffs at Étretat are as dramatic as they come. Turquoise water laps at the bottom of striped, white cliff faces hundreds of feet tall, topped with lush green grass as well as a spattering of handsome cows and a quaint church building. As if these gargantuan striped walls weren't enough, there are a number of physics-defying natural archways carved into the stone that you have to see to believe. Be sure not to miss the small trail down to the beach starting just past the church, as it leads to a long tunnel cutting straight through the stone.

*i* Free; wheelchair accessible

### SWORD BEACH

Colleville Plage, Ouistreham; www.ouistre-ham.mobi/en/today/sword.html

Sword Beach has a number of draws that nearly necessitate a trip from Caen to stroll the sandy shoreline. First of all, it's a beautiful, wide beach where locals dig for clams, dogs with lolling tongues sprint by, and friendly locals sell cheap crepes from beachside stands. It's also the most easily accessible **D-Day beach** to visit from Caen. A British landing beach near the strategically important **Pegasus Bridge,** the fighting that took place at this beach played a significant role in the outcome of the June 6, 1944 operation. To get there, just take the #61 bus about 25 minutes toward Ouistreham and get off at Colleville Plage.

*i* Free; wheelchair accessible

Someone can tell you that American soldiers climbed a 100-foot cliff under heavy German fire to take out important enemy guns on D-Day. But it's absolutely nothing like standing at the edge of that cliff, inside a German bunker, surrounded by bomb craters, and truly comprehending the enormous odds that were stacked against them. Someone can tell you that thousands of people died on Omaha Beach in just one day, but it's an entirely different feeling to stand on that beach, look out at low tide, and imagine just how far away safety must have seemed to the troops whose mission was to storm it. Visiting the region's important sites from D-Day and the Battle of Normandy, you'll encounter beautiful, haunting landscapes, stories of tragedy and triumph, and a new perspective on World War II that will certainly make you reevaluate the cost of war.

On June 6th, 1944, Normandy became the site of the Allies' major attack on German-occupied Europe. Hitler had ordered an "Atlantic wall" consisting of heavy fortifications be built along Normandy's coast, making the momentous task of breaking through heavy German defenses and liberating the region seem nearly impossible. On D-Day, the first stage of Operation Overlord, hundreds of thousands of American, Canadian, and British troops, backed by aircraft bombardments, naval power, and tanks, stormed five of Normandy's beaches (Utah, Omaha, Gold, Juno, and Sword). The German defenses inflicted massive casualties, especially at the American Omaha Beach. Yet despite the immense odds against the Allies, the Atlantic wall was breached in just one day.

At Pointe du Hoc, see the site of one of D-Day's most crucial operations and step inside the German fortifications of the Atlantic wall. You'll see the location of the bloodiest beach of D-Day at Omaha Beach. At the American cemetery, the immense human cost of the war will begin to be put into perspective. And at Gold Beach you'll see what remains of an engineering feat: the British artificial port. Normandy's history is both saddening and incredibly important; experiencing this trip to some of World War II's most momentous sites is something you certainly won't be able to forget, nor should you.

# FOOD

## ⚑SA-SE-SU ($)

156 Rue Saint-Jean; 02 31 91 83 43; www.sasesu14.fr; open M-Sa noon-2pm and 7pm-11pm, Su 7pm-11pm

Caen, at only 10,122 km away from Vietnam, is the perfect place to have fresh and authentic Vietnamese food! Don't let our sarcastic tone fool you; Sa-se-su actually validates this statement. Light salads at the outdoor tables are refreshing on hot summer days, but the bo bun (beef and noodle soup) is the winner for a hearty meal, for as little as €6. Snacking on amazing starters doesn't get cheaper than at Sa-se-su either, with appetizers for €3-5.

*i* *Starters €3-5, entrées €6-10; vegetarian, vegan, and gluten-free options available; wheelchair accessible*

## L'ATELIER DU BURGER ($)

27 Rue Ecuyere; 02 31 50 13 44; www.latelier-duburger.fr; open daily noon-2:30pm and 7pm-11:30pm

It may seem counter to your authenticity-seeking, off-the-beaten-path, traveler's attitude to come all the way to Caen, France and then go to a burger joint. I mean, come on, you have a "Not all who wander are lost" sticker on your guitar case and your Instagram bio is "I haven't been everywhere, but it's on my list." But L'Atelier du Burger isn't your average burger joint. They keep it simple: their menu consists of only five delicious burgers, one featuring the establishment's signature secret sauce. The only other option on the menu is to add fries and a drink for €3.

*i* *Burgers €7.50-7.90, combo add €3; vegetarian options available; no wheelchair accessibility*

## Ô CHATO ($$)

28 Rue du Vaugueux; 02 31 94 35 70;
open M-Th noon-2pm and 7pm-10pm,
F-Sa noon-2pm and 7pm-10:30pm, Su
noon-2pm and 7pm-10pm

Situated in the medieval part of town,
Ô Chato boasts both food and views
that you just can't find anywhere else.
It lies at the end of a busy restaurant-
filled street directly beneath Caen
Castle, meaning you'll be living
the fantasy of middle-aged moms
everywhere: drinking wine and eating
cheese with an unobstructed view of
a French castle. And presumably, you
don't even have screaming kids! The
restaurant serves Italian food alongside
irresistible local specialties. Just a few
miles from the beach, Caen suffers no
shortage of mussels, and Ô Chato is
the perfect place to try moules frites,
the traditional Norman dish of mussels
with fries. The fondue starter is another
regional gem, as Norman cheese is
difficult to beat.

*i* *Moules frites €12, dinner menu €15;*
*vegetarian, or vegan options available;*
*wheelchair accessible*

# NIGHTLIFE

## LE VERTIGO

14 Rue Ecuyere; 02 31 85 43 12; open
M-Sa 11:30am-1am

This gritty, cider-slinging pub seems
like the bar version of a Dungeons
and Dragons club with the added
advantage of being right down the
street from a real life dungeon (dragons
sold separately). Decorated like the
inside of a castle, complete with swords
and suits of armor, Vertigo hosts ye
olde happy hour from 7-9pm, when
ciders are only €2.10 and signature
beer cocktails start at €5 for a hefty
50cl pour. If this spot doesn't fit your
vibe, never fear. The bar is on Rue
Ecuyère, one of Caen's most animated
nightlife streets.

*i* *Beer cocktails €5-9 for 50cl, ciders*
*for €2.10 at happy hour; wheelchair*
*accessible*

## LE WHAT'S

1 Bis Av. de Tourville; 02 31 93 57 76;
www.lewhats.com; open W-Sa 11pm-6am

A night at Le What's is like hanging
out with a cool exchange student:
it's foreign and exciting but you're
never one hundred percent sure you
understand what's going on. Unlike in
larger French metropolises, this place
plays real French music, and unlike
in some cities that think they're too
cool *cough* Paris *cough*, everyone
actually dances too. Everyone else there
will seem like they've been a hundred
times (and they probably have), so to
avoid sticking out as the tourist you
are, keep a few things in mind: don't
come before midnight (or better yet
one or two), keep the receipt from
entry to redeem two included drinks,
and just smile and nod.

*i* *Entry €10 with two drinks included;*
*wheelchair accessible*

# CANNES

Coverage by **Alejandro Lampell**

Take out your sole pair of clean slacks, unpack the button-down shirt that's been
sitting in the bottom of your bag for weeks, straighten out the creases of your
giant pack, for you are in Cannes—a household name synonymous with affluence,
extravagance, and class. Unlike tourist-friendly Nice or metropolitan Marseille,
Cannes—the ritziest city in the Côte d'Azur —caters almost exclusively to, well,
an exclusive clientele. You need only take a stroll along the yacht-filled Old Port or
the diamond-encrusted storefronts at the Boulevard de la Croisette to understand
what we're talking about. As it is home to the infamous annual Film Festival,
visiting Cannes in May entails rubbing elbows with A and B-list celebrities. The
real draw of Cannes, however, is not the possibility of bumping into your celebrity
crush while walking along one of the city's sandy beaches, but the sandy beaches
themselves. They're a hot commodity in the French Riviera, and explain, in part,
why it's virtually impossible to find a place to stay for less than €40 a night. That

said, if approached intelligently, Cannes is actually a very manageable city, and with our recommendations, you'll be able to survive—thrive even—on a traveler's budget.

# ORIENTATION

Cannes' city center hugs the coastline of the Mediterranean, with suburbs stretching inland towards the French Alps. It's just a 30-minute train ride west from **Nice,** making it a great day trip destination for those who don't want to break the bank on accommodations. The **Vieux Port** marks the true center of town; here, you'll find the **Palais des Festivals et des Congrès,** the venue of the **Cannes Film Festival.** Just west of the Vieux Port is the **Old Town,** called **Le Suquet.** East of the city center lies the famous nightclub area and yet another yacht-packed port. Connecting these two areas are the **Boulevard de la Croisette,** a major thoroughfare that runs along the shore and is lined with name-brand stores, upscale restaurants, and art galleries, and the **Croissete is Rue d'Antibes,** Boulevard de la Croisette's inland counterpart.

# ESSENTIALS

## GETTING THERE

The nearest major airport is the Côte d'Azur Airport in Nice, located approximately 20 mi. east of Cannes. The smaller Cannes-Mandelieu airport, located 4 mi. from the city center, is much closer, but frequented exclusively by smaller private aircrafts. From the Côte d'Azur Airport, you can take a 20min. train ride to Cannes (€6). Cannes has two train stations, Cannes and Cannes la Boca. Make sure to get off at the former, as the latter is several miles east of the city center.

## GETTING AROUND

For us plebeians who cannot afford the luxury of wasting away our days bobbing on yachts on the Mediterranean, the most efficient means of exploring Cannes is by foot. The city is quite small—crossing it from east to west takes 40min., tops. Cannes also has a fairly developed public transportation system called Palm Bus, which consists of five bus lines. All five lines pass through the main Hôtel de Ville stop, adjacent to the Vieux Port. You can purchase tickets on the bus (single ride €1.50), from *tabac* shops, or from the tourist office on Boulevard de la Croisette (24hr ticket €4, 3-day ticket €7, week-long ticket €13.50, 10-trip ticket €12). Buses run daily from 6am- 9pm, but there is also a night line called Palm Night, which runs from 9pm-2am.

## PRACTICAL INFORMATION

**Tourist Offices:** Cannes' main tourist office (1 Bd. de la Croisette; 04 92 99 84 22; open daily Mar-Oct 9am-7pm, Nov-Feb 10am-7pm, July-Aug 9am-8pm) is located near the Palais des Festivals et des Congrès.

**Banks/ATMs/Currency Exchange:** Banks, ATMs, and exchange houses litter the city, but most are located close to the Palais des Festivals et des Congrès.

**Post Offices:** Cannes Croisette (22 Rue Bivouac Napoléon; 04 93 06 26 50; open M-F 9am-1pm, 2pm-6pm, Sa 9am-12:30pm). The postal code is 06400.

**Internet:** There is free Wi-Fi at the train station and central tourist office. You can rent a personal hotspot box at the Cannes Tourist Office (€7.9 per day, additional €3 upon return).

**BGLTQ+ Resources:** Centre BGLTQ Côte d'Azur (123 Rue de Roquebillière; 09 81 93 14 82; www.centrelgbt06.fr; open M, W, F 9:30am-8pm, Tu 9:30am-5:30pm, Sa 2pm-8pm).

## EMERGENCY INFORMATION

**Emergency Number:** 112

**Police:** Police Municipale (2 Quai Saint-Pierre; 0 800 11 71 18; open daily 24hr), Commissioner of Police (1 Avenue de Grasse, 04 93 06 22 22).

**US Embassy:** The nearest US Consulate is located in Marseille (Place Varian Fry; 01 43 12 48 85).

**Rape Crisis Center:** Institut National d'Aide aux Victimes et de Médiation (14 rue Ferrus; 01 45 88 19 00; open daily 9am-9pm).

**Hospitals:** Hôpital de Cannes (15 Av. des Broussailles; 04 93 69 70 00; open daily 24hr).

**Pharmacies:** Anglo-French Pharmacy Cannes (95 Rue d'Antibes; 04 93 38 53 79; open M-Sa 8:30am-8pm).

# ACCOMMODATIONS

## ⬛HÔTEL PLM ($$$)

3 Rue Hoche; 04 93 38 31 19; www. hotel-plm.com; reception open daily 9am-1pm and 3pm-7pmr

Hotel PLM is the clear winner in the race for value housing in Cannes. This small, yet modern two-star is located in Rue Hoche, a popular pedestrian area, and is within walking distance of some of city's best restaurants and nightlife. The well-lit rooms are clean and welcoming (unlike the staff, unfortunately), outfitted in sleek grey and white furniture—a sharp contrast from the décor of PLM's slightly more upscale neighbor, Hotel Villa Tosca.

*i* Basic single €30-45, basic single with en suite shower €46-69, double €59-89; reservation recommended; BGLTQ+ friendly; no wheelchair accessibility; Wi-Fi; linens and towels included; laundry facilities

## HÔTEL ATLANTIS ($$$)

4 Rue du 24 Août; 04 93 39 18 72; www. hotel-atlantis-cannes.cote.azur.fr; reception open 24hr

Frequented primarily by old-time beach-goers, Hotel Atlantis' rooms come equipped with beds, desks, showers, TVs, flower pots, and, perhaps most importantly, air conditioning. The walls are bright and the décor is uplifting, and although Atlantis doesn't offer the communal vibe that most European hostels exude, it does have a communal eating area that lends itself well to conversations with other travelers

*i* Rooms from €44; reservation recommended, especially during high season (May-June); wheelchair accessible; Wi-Fi; linens included; laundry facilities €10.50; breakfast €7-10

# SIGHTS
## CULTURE

### ⬛MARCHE FORVILLE

12 Rue Louis Blanc; 04 92 99 84 22; www.cannes.com/fr/decouvrir-cannes/visiter-cannes/marche-forville.html; open Sept 15-June 14 Tu-F 7am-1:30pm, Sa-Su 7am-2:30pm, June 15-Sept 14 T-Su 7am-2:30pm

The Marche Forville is a vestige of a foregone past—a time when fishing vessels lined the coastline instead of mega-yachts and quaint shops decked **la Croisette** instead of internationally-recognized stores. This market unites local fisherman and gardeners to sell their wares and evokes the Provençal, small-town feel you've been longing to find in the French Riviera. Walk along the wide lanes of the covered market, organized into different sectors according to produce type. If you are looking for something pre-made, the market also offers seasonal *socca*, paella, and hamburgers.

*i* Market prices vary; cash only; wheelchair accessible

### BOULEVARD DE LA CROISETTE

Bd. de la Croisette; street itself open daily 24hr, shop hours vary

The path to fame is lined with palm trees, brand-name stores, chic gallerias, and crêperies, if by fame you're referring to the hoard of A-list celebrities slinking along the red carpet at the **Palais des Festivals et des Congres** and by path you're referring to the Boulevard de la Croisette. Stretching from the **Old Port** to the **Cap de la Croisette,** this renowned street is not only Cannes' biggest thoroughfare, but also your best bet for ~casually~ running into your favorite celebrity. Stroll past the star-frequented Armani and Dolce and Gabanna stores, and, when you inevitably get tired of window shopping (read: walking into a store and becoming the subject of passive-aggressive stares), take a breather on one of the street's iconic blue chairs.

*i* Free; wheelchair accessible

## LANDMARKS

### ☑FORT ROYAL & MUSÉE DE LA MER

Saint-Marguerite Island; 04 89 82 26 26;
open daily Oct-Mar 10:30am-1:15pm,
2:15pm-4:45pm; Apr-May 10:30am-
1:15pm, 2:15pm-5:45pm; Jun-Sep 10am-
5:45pm

After spending a few hours walking
around Cannes, you'll see that the
city offers relatively few sources of
affordable entertainment—on the
mainland, at least. Enter St. Marguerite
Island, a tree-covered, yacht-flanked
oasis located 15min. (by boat) from
Cannes' sandy shores. Upon it rests
Fort Royal, a citadel built just before
the Spanish occupied the island in
1635 and extended in 1637 under the
direction of French military architect
Vauban. The citadel itself offers
astonishing views of the Mediterranean
and the mainland, and is just a short
walk away from the State Prison, which
held notorious felons such as the Man
in the Iron Mask. Also within walking
distance is the Musée de la Mer, which
offers a comprehensive overview of
the island's history as a Roman trading
post.

*i* Admission €6, €3 reduced, free for
students under 26, children under 18, and
disabled persons; limited wheelchair accessibility; last entry 5:30pm; guided tours
available upon request (04 93 38 55 26)

### PALAIS DES FESTIVALS ET DES CONGRÈS

1 Bd. de la Croisette; 04 92 99 84 00
The Palais des Festivals et des Congrès
is truly a spectacle to behold, especially
in May when movie projectors
and camera flashes set it aglow,
transforming the structure into a
beacon for artists, cinemaphiles, and
A-list celebrities alike. Designed by
architect and visionary Sir Hubert
Bennett and completed—initially—in
1949, this six-story glass complex
is the venue of (you guessed it) the
**Cannes Film Festival** and the **Cannes
Liones International Festival of
Creativity.** In the months between the
two, the Palais hosts a slew of cultural
events, some of which are open to the
public. The interior of the building is
accessible only by guided tour and slots
fill up quickly, so be sure to book well
in advance.

*i* Admission €6, free for children
under 16, half price for disabled persons;
reservation recommended; wheelchair
accessible

## OUTDOORS

### ☑PLAGE DU MIDI

Bd. Jean Hibert; open daily 9am-6pm
Can't bear to see one more damn
yacht? Looking for a classic, packed,
semi-nude beach that's basically the
human equivalent of a can of sardines?
Then look no further than the Plage
du Midi, the perfect place to spend
an afternoon on a hot summer day.
The 20-minute walk from Cannes'
city center may seem like a trek, but
the tan sand, clear coastal water, and
surrounding hills make up for it.

*i* Free; limited wheelchair accessibility

## FOOD

### ☑LA CREPERIE DE LA CROISETTE ($)

82 Bd. de la Croisette; 04 93 94 43 47;
www.creperiedelacroisette.com; open high

season daily at 9am, low season daily at 10:30am; by reservation only

Located on the infamous **Boulevard de la Croisette** and serving up a variety of sweet and savory crêpes, this lavender-clad locale is perfect for any meal. Each crêpe comes with a side salad, dollop of ice cream, or caramel drizzle. If you don't identify as a crêpe aficionado, La Croisette offers a small assortment of salads, cheese plates, snack-style pastas, sandwiches, and burgers as well.

*i* *Crêpes €4-8, main plates €8-12; card minimum €10; vegetarian options available; wheelchair accessible*

### LE TROQUET À SOUPES ($)

Prom. De la Pantiero; 04 93 38 43 4; open daily 9:30am-7pm

"All dishes are cooked with love," reads the bulletin above the doors. One slurp of Le Troquet à Soupes' famous Gazpacho will deem this externalization unnecessary. This small locale is run entirely by one woman, Sylvie, who's a jack-of-all-trades. Part owner, part manager, part waitress, and all chef, she'll set up the umbrellas on the patio, take your order, cook your food, and still find time to chat about life. We recommend starting your meal with a hearty bowl of soup and splurging on the plate of the day. A well-traveled woman herself, Sylvie likes to experiment, concocting dishes reminiscent of other cultures, including chili con carne and ceviche.

*i* *Soups €6, salads €7, main plates €10, plate of the day €13; vegetarian options available; limited wheelchair accessibility*

### PHILCAT ($)

Prom. De la Pantiero; 04 93 38 43 4; open daily 9:30am-7pm

A €4 panini in Cannes? At a restaurant located two minutes from the Palais des Festivals? No, you're not hallucinating. Philcat, a white and blue shack serving up a variety of sweet and savory sandwiches, stands defiantly on the expansive **Pantiero Promenade** and is truly a backpacker's blessing. Don't let the small interior dissuade you, as there is almost unlimited seating surrounding the **Old Port.**

*i* *Sandwiches €3-6; minimum card charge €15; vegetarian options available; wheelchair accessible*

# NIGHTLIFE

### ⚑MORRISONS IRISH PUB

10 Rue Teisseire; 04 92 98 16 17; open daily 5pm-2am

We know what you're thinking. *Another Irish pub?* Yes, another Irish pub. Cannes offers very little in terms of cheap nightlife, and of this small pool of establishments, Irish pubs just so happen to comprise the majority. And of all the pubs we visited, we liked this one—Morrisons—the best. It's spacious, but not so big that it feels hollow; loud, but not overwhelmingly so; and offers a wide selection of draft beers and mixed drinks. Both a great place to stop before going clubbing and one worth spending an entire night at, Morrisons will fulfill your nightlife needs while in Cannes, without breaking the budget.

*i* *Beers €3-7, drinks €8; minimum card charge €7; open mic on Tuesdays, ladies' night on Sundays*

### GOTHA CLUB

Pl. Franklin Roosevelt; 04 93 45 11 11; www.gotha-club.com; open daily midnight-7am

Recognized by nearly every Sperry-clad Hamptons crew as one of the best nightclubs in the world, Gotha is, well, an experience. It has a tight window of opening from midnight until about 12:30am, during which the bouncers pay little attention to attire, company, and level of intoxication. Arrive after 12:30am, however, and your chances of getting in will dwindle. Inside, living walls give way to a dimly-lit dance floor, strobe lights, large sofas, and VIP lounges. Drinks start at €12 and venture into the quintuple digits, so if you plan on drinking, it'd be best to do so beforehand. Don't go too hard, however, or you may be coaxed into splitting a €500 bottle of champagne with the son of a Russian billionaire.

*i* *Beer €12, alcohol €15; dressy attire recommended*

### QUAY'S IRISH PUB

17 Quai Saint-Pierre; 04 93 39 27 84; open M-Sa noon-2am

This English-speaking pub located on the bank of the Old Port is the perfect place to stop before spending an evening in one of Cannes' exorbitantly-priced clubs. Quay's interior is completely decked out with wooden planks, signed dollar bills, Irish flags, and sports memorabilia, and will effectively bring you back down to earth. And not just in the figurative sense! The drinks are so cheap (relatively speaking) that you'll be on your ass before you get the chance to sing along to a live cover of Billy Joel's "Piano Man."

*i* Beer €4-7, shots €5-7; minimum card charge €7; happy hour 5pm-8pm

# LYON

Coverage by **Alejandro Lampell**

Lyon is often overlooked as "that landlocked city smack in the middle of France." The unknowing traveler might scoff and move on, but luckily we're here to make sure you don't skip this wonderful city. Situated at the intersection of the Rhone and Saone Rivers, Lyon is packed with great food, beauty, and history that you would be a fool to skip it. Vocalize your gastronomical desires while in France, and Lyon will deliver in the form of cheese, bread, wine, sausage, or signature *bouchons*. And, once you've gorged on every consumable part of cows and pigs, you can take to the streets, roam large parks and discover countless ornate churches that display the heavy Catholic influence on Lyon. For those more historically inclined, explore the ruins of two Gallo-Roman amphitheaters constructed circa 15 BCE, located a 10min. walk away from Lyon's Old Town, which in itself is a UNESCO World Heritage site.

## ORIENTATION

Lyon is in the southeastern region of France, a few hours west of the border with Switzerland and Italy. The city is bound by two hills, to the north and west of the city, respectively. The western hill is **Fourvière,** which is the site of both the ancient city of **Lugdunum** and the **Basilique Notre-Dame de Fourvière.** The northern hill is **Croix-Rousse,** where the silk workers of the nineteenth-century lived. This "hill that prays" is the site of small alleys, old buildings, and the famous morning food market. The city is divided by the two rivers traveling north and south, the **Saône** and the **Rhône,** which converge at the southern tip of the city, creating the famous peninsula, **Presqu'île.** Lyon itself is divided into nine districts, known as arrondissements. The first and second arrondissements, located on Presqu'île, are home to the main shopping district, the opera, and the largest square in Europe: **Place Bellecour.** The fifth arrondissement, situated at the foot of the **Fourvière Hill,** houses the **Vielle Ville,** where you can find the **Cathédrale Jean-Paul Baptiste** and old medieval buildings.

## ESSENTIALS

### GETTING THERE

Lyon St-Exupéry is the closest airport is located 25km east of the city and connected to the city's main train station, Part Dieu, by an express tramway called Rhône express. The 30min. ride costs €15 for adults and €13 for individuals between 12-25 years of age. The tram runs daily from 4:25pm to midnight around every 15 to 30min. The cheapest option is to buy the ticket online (www.rhonexpress.fr), but you can also buy it at vending machines upon arrival. Lyon has two main train stations, Perrache, located in Presqu'île, and Part-Dieu, located in the commercial center of the city east of the Rhône. The other main station, Saint-Exupéry, is located outside the city. The cheapest way to travel to Lyon if you are in Europe is by bus. Most buses arrive at the Part-Dieu train station.

## GETTING AROUND

Lyon is easily walkable. If you'd like to bike, you can rent one with the Velo'v service. The first 30min. of each ride are free and there is an additional cost of €1 for every additional half hour for a max of 24 hours. A day-long ticket is €1.50. The city also has four metro lines, five tram lines, two funiculars, and over 100 bus lines. The buses operate from 5am-midnight and the metro from 4am-12:30am. Purchase your ticket at the bus or metro station or from the bus driver, but remember to validate your ticket before boarding. One-hour tickets are €1.80, but you can also purchase a 24hr pass (€5.60), 48hr pass (€11), or a 72hr pass (€15). There is also a ticket called Soirée that allows for unlimited travel from 7pm until the end of that day's service for just €3. Download the TCL app to help plan your routes, but keep in mind the Lyon transport system is not yet on Google Maps as of July 2017.

## PRACTICAL INFORMATION

**Tourist Offices:** Office de Tourisme et des Congrès du Grand Lyon (Pl. Bellecour; 04 72 77 69 69; open daily 9am-6pm).

**Banks/ATMs/Currency Exchange:** Banks and ATMS are ubiquitous. One of the better exchange houses is Global Cash (20 Rue Gasparin; 04 78 38 12 00; open M-Sa 9:30am-6:30pm).

**Post Offices:** Main post office (10 Pl. Antonin Poncet; 08 99 23 24 62; open M-F 9am-7pm, Sa 9am-noon).

**Internet:** You can rent out a pocket Wi-Fi from the Tourist Information Office for €4 with Lyon City Card (€8 regular price).

**BGLTQ+ Resources:** Ligne Azur is an organization that provides information and support to BGLTQ+ individuals (08 10 20 30 40; daily 8am-11pm).

## EMERGENCY INFORMATION

**Emergency Number:** 112
**Police:** Commissariat de Police, second arrondissement (47 Rue de la Charité; 04 78 42 26 56; open daily 24hr).
**US Embassy:** There is a US Consulate in Lyon (1 Quai Jules Courmont; 01 43 12 48 60; open M-F 9:30am-5:30pm).

**Rape Crisis Center:** National Federation Women Solidarity (3919), is available, but not an emergency number. In the case of an emergency, call the police.
**Hospitals:** Hôpital Edouard Herriot (5 Pl. d'Arsonval; 08 25 08 25 69; open daily 24hr).
**Pharmacies:** Great Pharmacy Lyonnaise (22 R. de la République; 04 72 56 44 00; open M-Sa 8am-11pm, Su 7pm-11pm).

# ACCOMMODATIONS

### SLO LIVING HOSTEL ($$)
5 Rue Bonnefoi; 04 78 59 06 90; www.slo-hostel.com; reception open 24hr
Take a break and live *slo*. A ten-minute walk from **Place Bellecour**, Slo Living Hostel boasts a prime location and still manages to cultivate a relaxing atmosphere. The courtyard is decorated with pristine artificial grass, twinkly Christmas lights, hammocks, and comfortable chairs, creating a space for travelers to socialize and kick back. Mingle with fellow guests during hostel-organized crêpe nights, or, if you're one to venture solo, peruse through the hostel's book of recommended activities.

*i* Dorms €20-35, privates from €90; reservation recommended; max stay 7 days; wheelchair accessible; Wi-Fi; linens included; breakfast €5

### ALTER HOSTEL ($$)
32 Quai Arloing; 04 26 18 05 28; www.alter-hostel.com; reception open 24hr
This bohemian hostel run by two friends, Sam and Alain, who backpacked around the world is truly ~alternative~. In establishing Alter Hostel, the pair aimed to create an ecologically friendly establishment with dry toilets, showers that turn off intermittently, and motion-detecting lights. Check out the themed rooms, decorated with paintings of tourist attractions, and the lounge area, filled with board games to foster a relaxed and comfortable atmosphere. The hostel is a ten-minute bus ride from the city center, but is a haven from Lyon's tourist-dense city center.

*i* Dorms from €19-27; wheelchair accessible; linens included; laundry facilities €3-4

### AWAY HOSTEL AND COFFEE SHOP ($$)

21 rue Alsace Lorraine; 04 78 98 53 20; www.awayhostel.com; reception open 24hr

You're not in Sweden, but this hostel is straight out of an IKEA catalogue. Away Hostel boasts clean, simple, and welcoming wooden interiors. The reception/coffee shop area has classic espressos and delicious pastries to jump start your morning. Centrally located next to the opera and Museum of Fine Arts, there's not much to complain about except the sound of cars passing on the street (pro-tip: grab a pair of free earplugs in the lobby). Be sure to take advantage of the free walking tours provided by the staff.

*i* Dorms from €24, privates from €65; reservation recommended; max stay 7 days; wheelchair accessible; Wi-Fi; laundry €5 for wash and dry, €1 detergent; breakfast 7am-10:30am

# SIGHTS
## CULTURE
...........................................

### ◾VIEUX VILLE

69005 Lyon 5ème; 04 72 10 30 30; open daily 24hr

The narrow cobblestone streets of Lyon's Old Town are as picturesque as Europe gets. Stand in the middle of the road, which used to be filled with sewage, and imagine carts led by horses trotting by and ladies throwing pots of dirty water out the window. At least that's how we picture the medieval ages. This **UNESCO World Heritage Site**, which is one of the most extensive remnants of a medieval city, has beautiful, tall, skinny buildings packed next to each other in an almost cartoonish way. You can get a lot of your sightseeing done in one day here with the **Cathedral of Saint John** and the famous **Musée des Gadagnes** located just minutes away.

*i* Price vary by store; limited wheelchair accessibility

### OPÉRA NATIONAL DE LYON

Pl. de la Comédie; 04 69 85 54 54; www.opera-lyon.com; ticket office open Tu-Sa noon-7pm; opera runs Sept-July

Housed within a magnificent glass-topped building right behind the **Hôtel de Ville,** the National Opera hosts an array of singing performances, dances, and concerts throughout the year. On summer nights watch the building light up from within as you sit on the steps and listen to suave jazz music. With leftover tickets as cheap as €5, you may be able to snag one before the show!

*i* Tickets €16-108, €5 tickets go on sale the hour before a show (if available); wheelchair accessible

### MARCHÉ DE LA CROIX-ROUSSE (CROIX ROUSSE MORNING FOOD MARKET)

Bd. de la Croix Rousse; open Tu 6am-1:30pm, W-Th 6am-1pm, F-Su 6am-1:30pm

In the wee hours of the morning, take a stroll along the Croix Rousse boulevard to be welcomed by the iconic stalls of the Marché de la Croix-Rousse. Pass by vendors with stands filled to the brim with all kinds of fresh fruits and vegetables, wide assortments of cheese, and meats to make the famous Lyonnaise *bouchon*. On Sundays, the market is full of life and stretches out over one kilometer from the Croix-Rousse metro stop. Swing by on a Tuesday for some clubbing—just kidding, you'll run into vendors selling fabric and clothes, including that chic flower dress you wanted for under €20!

*i* Prices vary by stand; cash only; wheelchair accessible

## LANDMARKS
...........................................

### ◾BASILIQUE NOTRE-DAME DE FOURVIÈRE

8 Pl. de Fourvière; 04 78 25 86 19; www.fourviere.org; basilica open daily 8am-6:45pm, Mass daily at 7:30am, 9:30am, 11am, 5pm, museum daily at 10am-12:30pm, 2pm-5:30pm

Perhaps obviously situated atop **Fourvière Hill,** this nineteenth-century church is, for lack of a better word, a house of gold. The massive white exterior, accented by Greco-Roman pillars, exudes a sense of majesty. Step into the church, which is covered in gold, mosaics, and painting depicting biblical scenes. Apart from its beauty, the church is historically and religiously iconic, dedicated to the

Virgin Mary by the city of Lyon for protecting them during the Franco-Prussian wars. For bonus points, explore the **crypt** below, which is even more ornate than the church naves.

*i* Free; discovery tour free Apr-Nov 9am-12:30pm, 2pm-6pm, unusual discover roof and places of basilica June 1-Sept 30 M-Sa 11am, 2:30am, 4pm, Su 2:30pm and 4pm adults €10, €5 children, free children under 5 and for Lyon City Card

### CATHÉDRALE JEAN-PAUL BAPTISTE
Pl. St Jean; 06 60 83 53 97; www. cathedrale-lyon.cef.fr; open M-F 8:15am-7:45pm, Sa 8:15am-7pm, Su 8am-7pm

At the heart of Lyon's historic center, St. John's Cathedral, also known as **"Primatiale"** is considered by some to be the seat of the French church. The sandstone exterior, adorned with three big red doors and a large flower window, is reminiscent of Paris' Notre Dame. The cathedral nonetheless has its own character and charm. The interior has much to offer including the **treasury,** which holds artifacts from the Byzantine Empire and an *horloge astronomique,* a clock that mimics the movement of the stars. Check out the **Chapel des Bourbons,** where beautiful panes of white and blue stained glass and a painting of baby Jesus await you.

*i* Free; no wheelchair accessibility

### PASSAGE THIAFFAIT
Between Rue René Leynaud and Rue Burdeau; open daily 24hr

In the heart of the **Croix Rous-se** district, Passage Thiaffait connects Rue René Leynaud to Rue Burdeau via two white staircases. The passage, named after the creative genius behind **Monsieur Thiaffait,** is filled with chic boutiques and artist workshops. A city renovation process during the early 2000s transformed it from a crime-filled alley to a serene courtyard within the middle of the Old Town. Walk through the portico

and feel engulfed by the surrounding pastel-colored buildings.

*i* Free; no wheelchair accessibility

## MUSEUMS

### MUSÉE DES BEAUX ARTS
20 Pl. des Terreaux; 04 72 10 17 40; www. mba-lyon.fr; open M, W-Th 10am-6pm, F 10:30am-6pm, Sa-Su 10am-6pm

In a city as culturally enriching as Lyon, you expect to find museums with world-class artwork. The Museum of Fine Arts, located in an impressive seventeenth-century Benedictine abbey, houses a large collection of art encompassing 70 exhibition rooms and covering everything from Ancient Egyptian frescoes to twentieth-century photography. Come hang with your renowned artist pals **Monet, Gauguin, Chagall,** and **Picasso.** The museum's garden and chapel possess an astounding collection of marble and plaster sculptures, featuring works by **Rodin.** Get through the museum and then go out for drinks with the likes of Claude and Pablo later—you've

seen enough of their work to warrant a couple rounds.

*i* Admission €8, €4 student; last entry 5:30pm; audio guide €1 in French, English, Italian; wheelchair accessible

## MUSÉES GADAGNE
1 Pl. du Petit Collège; 04 78 42 03 61; www.gadagne.musees.lyon.fr; open W-Su 11am-6:30pm

Two museums are housed in this magnificent seventeenth-century building: the **Lyon History Museum** and the **Puppetry Museum.** The former boasts 30 rooms and over 1000 exhibits that trace the rise of Lyon as the Roman city of **Lugdunum,** through the progression of Christianity, and to the technological advances of the twentieth century. The Puppetry Museum demonstrates the process of bringing inanimate objects to life (like Pinocchio) and houses a couple of creepy Guignol hand puppets. Why these two museums are in the same building befuddles even the best of us. Budget at least two hours for each of them if you intend on fully exploring both.

*i* Admission €6, €4 student, free under 18, admission during temporary exhibition adults €8, €6 student; last entry 6pm; tours M, W-F 10am-noon, 2pm4pm, Tu 2pm-4pm, must book in advance, €3, €1 children; wheelchair accessible

## MUSÉE GALLO-ROMAIN DE FOUR-VIÈRE
17 Rue Cleberg; 04 72 38 49 30; www.museegalloromain.grandlyon.com; museum open Tu-F 11am-6pm, Sa-Su 10am-6pm, archaeological site open Apr 15-Sept 15 daily 7am-9pm, Sept 16-Apr 14 daily 7am-7pm

Appropriately located next to the preserved remains of the Roman amphitheater and odeum, the Roman-Gallo museum is seamlessly engraved into the side of the hill, making it a bit of a hidden destination. Follow a slanted path into the museum to experience the life of Romans in **Lungdunum** through artifacts and ornate mosaics from its founding in 43 CE. From a large glass window, you can view the ruins in the comfort that is the pagan god of air-conditioning.

Apparently, there used to be a circus, but it hasn't been discovered yet.

*i* Admission €4, €2.50 reduced free under 18; last entry 5:30pm; wheelchair accessible

## OUTDOORS

### ◪PARC DES HAUTEURS
Montée Nicolas de Lange; 04 72 69 47 60; open daily 24hr

The Parc des Hauteurs, directly translated to the "park of heights," connects the top of **Fourvière Hill** to the cemetery of Loyasse. Follow the gold rose petal plate upwards towards the basilica or explore the rosary garden within the park itself. We recommend planning to trek up the hill, stop at intervals, sit on the beach, and take in the view. The park feels more like a hiking path, save the view of orange-tiled rooftops, the river, and downtown buildings.

*i* Free; no wheelchair accessibility

### PARC DE LA TÊTE D'OR
69006 Lyon; 04 72 69 47 60; www.loisirs-parcdelatetedor.com; mid-Apr-mid-Oct 6:30am-10:30pm, mid-Oct-mid-Apr 6:30am-8:30pm

Like New York City's Central Park, the Parc de la Tête d'Or was the Lyonnaise people's idea of creating a green space in a bustling urban metropolis. Two brothers, Denis and Eugène Bühler, took on this project to turn a 117-hectare plot into a park, just east of Old Town. Equipped with a goose-filled lake, rose garden, and zoo, the Park truly does provide solace from the chaos of the city. Small carousels, miniature train rides, and swing sets attract families with children. If lakes are your thing, you can find one here with a statue of a centaur fighting a lion in front of it.

*i* Free; wheelchair accessible

## FOOD

### ▧L'AUBERGE DES CANUTS ($$)
8B Pl. Saint Jean; 09 86 50 89 66; www.auberge-des-canuts.com; open daily 8am-midnight

Registered as one of the "Authentiques Bouchons Lyonnais," L'Auberge des Canuts serves traditional dishes from the region in a prime location facing the Saint-Jean Cathedral. Like other traditional *bouchons,* there are three set menus (€10-20), where you pick and choose the heavy meat dishes as main courses with accompanying appetizers and desserts. Expect to sit down for two hours if you pick the set menu, as the meals are slow to come and even slower to be taken away. The staff here truly wants you to enjoy your food at a leisurely piece.

*i* Main plates €14-17, prix-fixe menu €16-20; card minimum €20; vegetarian options available; limited wheelchair accessibility

### ▨LES HALLES DE LYON – PAUL BOCUSE ($$)

102 cours la Fayette; 04 78 60 32 82; www.halles-de-lyon-paulbocuse.com; open Tu-Sa 7am-10:30pm, most restaurants close around 6-7pm

We could easily place Les Halles under landmarks, but it's more a venue to carry out your quest for culinary perfection. Named after the iconic French chef **Paul Bocuse,** whose accolades include three star restaurants, this food market brings together some of the best produce from around the region. Be continuously tempted by enticing sausages at the charcuteries and mouthwatering cheeses around every corner. The restaurants and produce are slightly pricey, but that won't stop you from creating your own

perfect picnic for under €15 filled with wines, cheeses, breads, and sausages.

*i* Entrées €15-20, cheeses €4-6; limited wheelchair accessibility

### CAFÉ 203 ($$)

9 Rue de Garet; 04 78 28 65 66; www. moncafe203.com; open noon-1am daily

Although not an official *bouchon,* this popular restaurant—which is divided in half by a small street—serves classic and hearty Lyonnaise dishes. The cheesy *quenelle* and *croziflette* are house staples. Looking for something less foreign? Try the juicy burgers or the plat du jour (€11). While you wait, enjoy the complimentary tap water from a used wine bottle—it might just be the only time you get to drink water for free in Europe—and check out the posters plastered on the walls reading *beaut, audace,* and *bruit.* Stay classy.

*i* Entrées €12-16; vegetarian options available; limited wheelchair accessibility

### DEUX FILLES EN CUISINE ($$)

32 Rue des Tables Claudiennes; 06 10 77 23 92; www.2fillesencuisine.fr; open M-Tu, Th-F 11:45am-2:30pm

"Deux filles en cuisine" may sound like the next big sitcom and, boy, do we have a pitch for whatever the biggest television network in France is (Canal+, where you at?). Here, two ladies, Davia and Sophia, create delicious, creative food dishes on the daily. They serve up a different three-

## BOUCHON: THE WORKER'S RESTAURANT?

*Bouchon*—it's a word that comes up all the time when it comes to talking about Lyon. Pronounced "boo-chon," these classic restaurants are ubiquitous here. *Bouchons* were known as go-to places for Lyon's silk workers during the nineteenth-century. Unpretentious, simple establishments, *bouchons* are the perfect place to spend a couple of hours having a three-course meal with a bottle of wine. Finish it all off with a coffee and you will have truly enjoyed the ultimate Lyonnais gastronomical experience.

The main specialties at *bouchons* are hearty, meat-focused dishes. Staples include variations of pork and veal offal, the cheaper parts of the animal, which workers could easily afford in the nineteenth-century. With their increased popularity, however, don't expect to pay nineteenth-century prices. Catch lunch specials for €20-25, which have different options to pick from for each course. Our recommendation? The classic *quenelle* (meat dumpling), tripe stew, and literally every combination of cheese, wine, and bread possible. This is a rite of passion in Lyon.

course meal (€16.50) for each of the four days per week they're open for lunch. The meal includes appetizers, entrées, and desserts, so we venture to say it's a pretty good deal. Because its important to use only in-season local products, Davia and Sophia provide a detailed description of the daily menu's ingredients that will make you salivate upon sitting down. Dine either at the large wooden table inside or enjoy the exterior patio tables.

*i* Prix-fixe menu €16.50; limited wheelchair accessibility

# NIGHTLIFE

## ◪THE MONKEY CLUB

19 Pl. Tolozan; 04 78 27 99 29; www. themonkeyclub.fr; open M noon-2pm, Tu-W noon-2pm, 6:30pm-1am, Th-F noon-2pm, 6:30pm-3am, Sa 6:30pm-3am, Su 11am-4pm

Get fun and flirty here in this dimly-lit, Victorian-style club, with its mahogany bar and red velvet chairs. The Monkey Club exudes a vibe that makes it the perfect place for post-work drinks, as evidenced by the clientele who enjoys exquisite wine and bite-size snacks. It's so sophisticated that you might wish you had a job to wine—we mean whine—about too! The cocktails, or "prescriptions" as they are called, are pricey and sadly, half the glass will be filled with ice unless you tell the bartender otherwise. Channel your elegant Dr. Jekyll here and save your rager Mr. Hyde for a rowdier club.

*i* Cocktails €11, shots €5-6, beers €5-7; BGLTQ+ friendly

## BIG WHITE

22 Rue Lainerie; 04 78 29 54 53; open Tu-Th 5pm-1am, F-Sa 5pm-4am, Su 5pm-1am

To the traveling beer connoisseur, this is the holy grail of international fermented wheats. Offering bottled beers from more than 21 different countries and plenty of more draft options, Big White pulls out all the stops to enlighten your taste buds with exquisite brews. Sit under the guise of a circle of flags from around the world or strike up a conversation with the bartender in the wood-paneled bar as he explains the meaning of the name of that beer from Tahiti. More of a lean alcohol person? Try the signature cocktails or the even wackier shots. With shot names like "Kamikaze," "shit on the grass," and "alien brain," you better get ready for a wild night on the town.

*i* Beer €3.50-6.50, shots €3-4, cocktails €7-9; card minimum €8; no wheelchair accessibility

## LE SUCRE

50 Quai Rambaud; www.le-sucre.eu; open F 6:30pm-3am, Sa 11am-5am, Su 6:30pm-11pm

Located in a sugar factory, hence the name, Le Sucre is the go-to club in town. This four-story industrial complex rises from the ground with *gauche* and *droite* written on the two former-plant chimneys. Hang out on the upstairs rooftop area, filled with beach chairs, picnic tables, and plants growing out of the Havana Club wooden carts. It's the perfect place to crack a cold one but, if you're looking for a more of a clubbing experience, you can find that too in the lively smoke-clad interior. The cover fee may be on the steep side, but this is the night out you came to Europe for. Make sure to book in advance and arrive early to beat the line.

*i* Cover €10-20, shot €4, beer €4, cocktail €10; book in advance

# NICE

Coverage by **Alejandro Lampell**

If a backpacker-friendly city is what you seek, Nice delivers. It's the most affordable city in the French Riviera and somehow doesn't make you feel like you need to own three yachts to live here (looking at you, Saint-Tropez). You and thousands of other backpackers will fill the streets, keep the bars running until the early hours of the morning, and hang out in the magnificent beach-filled Côte d'Azur. Nice brims with buckets of history and culture. Check out everything from Roman ruins to decaying citadels, and eighteenth-century palaces that demonstrate the importance of Nice's former status as a major trading post. The city has a vibrant cultural scene that features dozens of new museums. And, with your handy-dandy student ID, you can get into ten of them, free of charge. At the end of the day, however, people come to Nice for the beach. Nothing beats the sapphire blue water in the Bay of Angels. Daytrips to Eze, Monaco, and Cannes make this the ultimate destination to budget properly; splurge on the daytrip and save on accommodations. Nice, isn't it?

# ORIENTATION

Bordering the **Mediterranean Sea,** Nice is 18 miles from the French-Italian border, close to where the Alps meet the sea. Tourists use Nice to commute **Monaco** (8mi.) or **Cannes** (16mi.) The city center is located north of the **Bay of Angels,** the beachfront stretching to **Castle Hill.** Hugging the Bay is the **Promenade des Anglais,** a four-mile walkway filled with cyclists, tourists, and ice cream lovers. One of the most famous pedestrian streets is **Avenue Jean Médicin,** which connects the city center to **Place Masséna. Vieux Nice** (Old Town) is located southeast of the city center at the foot of Castle Hill. **The Port,** located east of Castle Hill, hasn't been overrun by tourists like Vieux Nice. Slightly north of the city center is **Cimiez,** site of the former Roman city, **Cemenelum.**

# ESSENTIALS

## GETTING THERE

The most common way to get to Nice is via plane to Nice Airport, located 5mi. southwest of the city. To get to the city center from the airport, take the express buses #98 and 99 (€6),and which run every 30 minutes from 6am-midnight. Alternatively, you can walk 10min. from the airport to a small train station called Saint-Augustin, from which you are one stop away from Nice (€1.60). Another way to get to Nice is via the direct train that connects the Côte d'Azur from Monaco to the border with Italy. Trains are usually expensive, with tickets from Lyon priced around €60 and tickets from Paris around €100. If traveling via bus, one of the most popular bus lines is Ouibus.

## GETTING AROUND

Nice has an extensive public transport system called the Ligne d'Azur network that includes more than 130 bus routes in the Nice metropolitan area and a tram line that runs from 4:35am-1:35am. A solo ticket for one journey costs €1.50, a ten-journey ticket costs €10, and a day-long pass costs €5. Purchase tickets at tram stops and from bus drivers and make sure to validate your ticket every time you board the transport system. You can incur a hefty fine for not having the appropriate ticket. The T1 line makes a U-shape from the main train station through Place Masséna and up towards Old Town. If you prefer biking, there is a rental system known as Velo Blue. A day subscription costs €1.50 with the first half hour of travel free. An additional hour costs €1 and it costs €2 for every additional hour.

## PRACTICAL INFORMATION

**Tourist Offices:** Promenade des Anglais tourist information office (2, Promenade des Anglais; 08 92 70 74 07; www.nicetourisme.com).

**Banks/ATMs/Currency Exchange:** Banks and ATMs are ubiquitous throughout the city. If you are coming into the Nice airport, you can exchange money at InterChange (Terminal 1 and 2; 04 93 21 74 18; T1: open daily 6:45am-10:30pm, T2 open daily 6:45am-10pm).

**Post Offices:** The main post office is a 3-minute walk from the train station (21 Av. Thiers; open M-F 8am-7pm, Sa 8am-12:30pm).

**Internet:** The city offers free Wi-Fi at certain tourist offices and parks. If you need to use a computer, there are various cybercafés around the city. You can also rent out a Wi-Fi hotspot at the Tourist Office for €7.9 per day.

**BGLTQ+ Resources:** Centre BGLTQ+ Côte d'Azur (123 Rue de Roquebillière; 09 81 93 14 82; www.centrelgbt06.fr; open M, W, F 9:30am-8pm, Tu, Th 9:30am-5:30pm, Sa 2pm-8pm).

## EMERGENCY INFORMATION

**Emergency Number:** 112

**Police:** Central Police Station (1 Av. Maréchal Foch; 04 92 17 22 22; open daily 24hr, foreign visitor reception desk open daily 9am-5pm).

**Rape Crisis Center:** Call 115 in the case of an emergency.

**Hospitals:**
- Hôpital Pasteur (30 Voie Romaine; 04 92 03 77 77; open M-F 8am-6pm, Sa 9am-5:45pm).
- Lenval Hospital (57 Av. De la Californie; 04 92 03 03 03; open M-F 8am-6pm, Sa 8am-3:30pm).

**Pharmacies:** To find the nearest pharmacy, call 3237. The following are the pharmacies open daily 24hr.
- Pharmacie Masséna (7 Rue Masséna; 04 93 87 78 94).
- Pharmacie Riviera (66 Av. Jean Médecin; 04 93 62 54 44).

# ACCOMMODATIONS

### ⭐ANTARES HOSTEL ($$)
5 Av. Thiers; 04 93 88 22 87; reception open 6am-3am

Antares Hostel has its mind in the little things with small amenities that can go a long way for the weary traveler. Daily replenished soaps and shampoos, free breakfast, and air-conditioning are among its many benefits as well as a wide range of guests who come from all over the world. The best part? Antares Hostel shares a common room with Baccarat hostel, where you can party with its residents and then retire to your air-conditioned room. Let's say that again. Slowly. *Air. Conditioned.*

*i* Dorms €21-45, private €60-90; max stay 7 night; BGLTQ+ friendly; wheelchair accessible; Wi-Fi; linens included

### HOSTEL BACCARAT ($$)
39 Rue d'Angleterre; 04 93 88 35 73; reception open 7am-3am

When it comes to affordable cities in the French Riviera, Nice is the place to be. And when it comes to affordable party housing, Hotel Baccarat has you covered. Although it is always filled to the brim with party-crazed backpackers, Baccarat has a 3am-6am lookout to keep the drunks out or in their own beds. Partying aside, the Hotel has clean, well-maintained facilities, including an Internet room and common area. However, its strong suit is its management. The Baccarat team has a refreshing approach towards guests, frequently chatting and mingling to ensure a homey experience!

*i* Dorms €24, double €80, single €60; reservation recommended; BGLTQ+ friendly; no wheelchair accessibility; Wi-Fi; laundry facilities

### HOSTEL PASTORAL ($)
27 Rue Assalit; 04 93 85 17 22; reception open 24hr

The bonus to living in a residential building like Hostel Pastoral is that there's no curfew! That said, this hostel, which is just a large apartment, is located right next to the main train station. The old building gives way to a spacious modern-looking hostel, fully equipped with bathrooms and en-suite lockers. Boasting a great communal kitchen and open terrace spaces, Hostel Pastoral is packed with young travelers sharing stories of their adventures. Pick a seat on one of the red lounge chairs and kick back. The only trade-off is constantly holding on to each of your three keys to get back in at night.

*i* Dorms €12-25, private €40-50; BGLTQ+ friendly; wheelchair accessible; Wi-Fi; laundry facilities €10; linens included

# SIGHTS
## CULTURE

### CATHÉDRALE SAINT-NICOLAS DE NICE (RUSSIAN ORTHODOX CATHEDRAL)
Av. Nicolas II; 09 81 09 53 45; www.sobor.fr; open daily 9am-6pm, access restricted from noon-2pm for celebrations

This structure adorned with colorful, meringue-style cupolas would fit in better in Russia's Red Square than in the sunny coastal town of Nice. Dedicate at most an hour to touring around the grounds and examining the stunning architecture from every angle possible. The large influence of Russian aristocrats since the nineteenth century in Nice is ever-present at the Cathédrale Saint-Nicolas. Check out the small and ornate Russian icons and jewels. Note: there is a dress code, so make sure to cover both your knees and shoulders (no swimsuits here, save those for the beach).

*i* Free; wheelchair accessible

### PALAIS LASCARIS

15 Rue Droite; 04 93 62 72 40; Jan 2-June 22 M, W-Su 11am-6pm, June 23-Oct 15 M, W-Su 10am-6pm, Oct 16-Dec 31 M, W-Su 11am-6pm, closed Jan 1, Easter Sunday, May 1, Dec 25

Not quite the extensive garden-filled French palace you might expect, the Palais Lascaris in the middle of the **Vieux Nice** is just lavish and ornate inside. Built by the family of Jean-Paul Lascaris in the mid sixteenth-century, the building-turned-museum houses the second largest collection of musical instruments in France. Check out the lutes, flutes, and all the other instrumentutes in this museum. Full of paintings of wigged men and uncomfortable-looking furniture, the Palais is a typical aristocratic household. The two floors of the museum can be explored in less than an hour, so make sure to use the Nice municipal pass and visit some of the other museums in the area.

*i* Part of Municipal museums day ticket €10, 7-day ticket €20, day group ticket €8 per person, free children under 18, students, unemployed, disabled civilians, journalist; last entry 5:30pm; guided tours F at 3pm €6; no wheelchair accessibility

## LANDMARKS

### ▨MARCHÉ AUX FLEURS COURS SALEYA

Cours Saleya; 04 92 14 46 14; open Tu-Sa 6am-5:30pm, Su 6am-1pm

Let's hope you brought your allergy pills because the aroma of this flower market is strong. Everyone always talks about the wafting scents of

*boulangeries,* but nothing compares to the subtle hints of lavender, rose, or bouquets of flowers drifting from this hidden gem on the Cours Saleya, open most days of the week. Walk past stands filled with colorful flowers, flavored soaps, and every other wonderfully-scented object in between. If life on the road has been giving you massive bouts of BO, then rest assured that this market has the cure. Also, you shouldn't have forgotten deodorant. Rookie mistake.

*i* Prices vary by stand; wheelchair accessible

### COLLINE DU CHÂTEAU (CASTLE HILL)

Montee du Chateau; www.en.nicetourisme. com/nice/92-parc-de-la-colline-du-cha-teau; open Oct 1-Mar 31 8:30am-6pm, Apr 1-Sep 30 8:30am-8pm

A crumbling castle, a lofty hill, and an Ed Sheeran song come to mind as you make the 300-foot climb to the top. This site of the former Château de Nice, which was destroyed in the eighteenth century, features a maze of paths that weave through the lush greenery of the mountain. Stop at the **Bellana Tower** for a stunning view of **Bay of Angels**—the aptly-named gorgeous Nice seafront. If you're reluctant to engage in any form of cardio (because you do so much at home, right?), feel free to take the elevator three-quarters of the way up. Once you've made it through the last quarter, take advantage of the children's playground, more views of the port, and a roaring manmade waterfall.

*i* Free admission to the castle, museum admission free under 25; tours Tu and F 11am and 4pm; wheelchair accessible

### PLACE MASSÉNA

15 Pl. Masséna; 06 29 64 10 12; open daily 24hr

Place Masséna is the soul and beating heart of Nice and you will probably pass through it daily on your way to the beachfront. Surrounding by vibrant Pompeiian, eighteenth-century buildings and an imposing marble fountain of the Greek god **Apollo,** the square is full of life at all times of the day. Sculptures of seven naked men (whose mans?) on poles reside in Place Masséna and light up at night. Walk along **Avenue Jean Médicin** past the

# MONACO

**Many like to say that "size matters" and Monaco seeks to disprove them.** Monaco is second to none in class and style and is only a bit bigger than the Vatican City. Welcome to the tiny, two square kilometer Principality of Monaco, an independent city-state engulfed in French territory. Known as a private getaway for the affluent, mainly due to the no-income-tax rule for residents, Monaco calls to mind stacks of dollars, euros, pounds, pesos, or rupees. Housing the famed casino, Hôtel de Paris, and pavilions abundant with designer brand storefronts, the Monte Carlo neighborhood is the glam capital of the world. Stick to the army of tourists, avoid unwanted glances, and do a lot of eyeballing. They can't charge you for looking inside, right? Aside from Monte Carlo and the accompanying Grand Prix, however, Monaco has a stunning Old Town with a royal palace built on Le Rocher, which overlooks the Mediterranean Sea. The entire city-state can be knocked out in one day, if done properly. Get prepared, dear budget backpacker, you're entering high roller town.

Monaco is divided mostly into four different areas. Towards the western part of the city-state, on the **Rock of Monaco** is **Monaco-Ville,** the old, fortified part of the city. Here, you'll find the Prince's palace and some of the cheaper restaurants and shops. To the west of Monaco-Ville is **Fontvieille,** the newest areas, that houses the stadium of **AS Monaco** (yes, even this city-state has a football team. This is Europe). North of Monaco-Ville is **La Condamine,** which is right at **Port Hercule.** This is the starting point of the famed **Grand Prix.** Finally, east of Condamine is Monte-Carlo. Popularized by Selena Gomez, **Monte-Carlo** is the most luxurious and famous area of Monaco where you'll find the famous **Monte-Carlo Casino** and **Hôtel de Paris.**

## GETTING THERE

You can reach Monaco from the eastern port side of Nice, taking the #100 bus line, which only costs €1.50. Monaco is connected to the rest of the Côte d'Azur with a train line running from Ventimiglia to Marseille, so this train is another option if you are not coming from Nice.

## GETTING AROUND

Given Monaco's small size, you would save a ton just by walking. However, some parts of the city—like the palace—are built on a rock, so you will have to accept the fact that you'll spend a good portion of your day on an incline. There are seven public elevators that provide help with these hills. But, believe it or not, Monaco does have a transport system for people who don't own private helicopters or yachts. The public bus transportation consists of five bus lines. A one-way ticket is €2 on-board the bus and €1.50 if purchased in advance at a machine. The buses usually run from 6am-9pm. A night bus operates from 10pm-4am. There is also a boat bus that crosses the harbor for €2. Although the harbor is very small, so the boat ride is expensive relative to the trip.

## Swing by...

### CASINO DE MONTE CARLO
Pl. du Casino; 92 16 20 00; www.fr.casinomontecarlo.com; open 9am-1pm for touring, 2pm-4am for playing

Luxurious casinos frequented by millionaires isn't what comes to mind when you hear the word "backpackers." But we'll be damned if we don't try. Here's how to get in: 1. Pass the fortified barrier of Ferrari and Lamborghinis parked outside. 2. Avoid the snarky glances of doormen as they check your bag. You belong here. 3. Act the part. Be Jay Gatsby. Be James Bond. Be anyone but you! Once you've played this small melodrama in your head, realize you're surrounded by mobs of tourists like yourself who want to see how the other half lives. So, come early to explore the golden-clad walls, marble pillars, and magnificent chandeliers all while listening to the history of the casino with an audio guide. From 2pm onwards, the casino is 18+ and the gambling commences in a different renowned *salle*.

*i* Admission €12-17, €8-12 child (13-18), €6-8 child (6-12); audio guide available; wheelchair accessible

## Check out...

### OCEANOGRAPHIC MUSEUM

Av. Saint-Martin; 93 15 36 00; www.oceano.mc; open daily Jan-Mar 10am-6pm, Apr-Jun 10am-7pm, Jul-Aug 9:30am-8pm, Sep 10am-7pm, Oct-Dec 10am-6pm

Monaco is strangely filled with families and children who are young enough to be reckless, but not old enough to gamble. Meet the middle ground: the aquarium on the bottom floor of the Oceanographic Museum. We enjoy looking at fluorescent corals, lion fish, and Mexican salamanders as much as the next guy, but we actually enjoyed the upstairs museum Prince Albert envisioned as being a palace worthy of the ocean's treasures. This museum was also built into the side of the Rock of Monaco and therefore has a killer view of the ocean. See old time oceanographer's paraphernalia, including preserved ginormous and freaky-looking creatures. But, yeah, we'll go see the aquarium too because, you know, we're all kids inside.

*i* Admission €11-16, €7-12 child (13-18), €5-8 child (4-12), €7-12 student; last entry 5:30pm; limited wheelchair accessibility

## Grab a bite at...

### CRÊPERIE DU ROCHER ($)

12 Rue Comte Felix Gastaldi; 93 30 09 64; open daily 11am-11pm

When you're this close to Italy and France, the cheapest foods around are easily going to be either pizza or crêpes. Accept and embrace it. Luckily for us, Crêperie du Rocher specializes in these foods, sprinkled with some pastas, salads, and ice cream for a hot day. Right near the Royal Palace in the narrow streets of Old Town, the restaurant has tables on the patio so you can people-watch while enjoying a pizza. Break your preconceived notions of "thin pancakes" by trying the large variety of crêpes from salmon-filled to classic chocolate and bananas. It's the perfect way to not break the bank in Monaco.

*i* Pizzas €6-11, crêpes €5-8 ; vegetarian; no wheelchair accessibility

## Don't miss...

### JARDIN JAPONAIS

5 Av. Princesse Grace; 93 15 22 77; open Apr 1-Oct 31 9am-6:45pm, Nov 1-Mar 31 9am-5:45

The extravagance, the cars, the casinos...they can get tiring! And there's no better place to recharge and refuel than in this small, serene (read: less ostentatious) Japanese Garden. Filled with a tiny red bridge, stone paths, and blossoming flowers, this free (key word: free!) garden transports you to a simpler place. After walking through the pavilions and getting rejected from the Hôtel de Paris, it is great to feel welcomed somewhere with open arms. Walk around for a couple minutes admiring the precision of the garden and characteristic Zen. You are now recharged to enter high-end stores and not care what people think. Or maybe you've decided you're better off without them. Good for you.

*i* Free; wheelchair accessible

# EZE

You didn't know it, but you've been waiting for Èze for your whole life. Midway between Nice and Monaco, what Èze lacks in the party backpacker scene and glamour, it makes up for in natural beauty. To get here, you'll have to hike for about an hour up a steep hill from the train station, Èze Bord de Mer. Tourists who shy away from the hike opt to instead take the #100 bus line from Nice (€1.50), which provides amazing views of the coast as it climbs up the hill. Perched on the summit, Èze, an "eagle's nest" village, provides a breathtaking view of the Côte d'Azur down below.

Èze has two major selling points: the view and the architecture. To get to the summit, you must go through a maze of stone streets, small underpasses, yellow churches, and Provençal boutiques. Use the map provided by the tourist office, but don't be afraid to get lost in the village (it's that small). At the top of the hill, you'll find an exotic garden, which, for an entrance fee of €6, you can explore. Emerge from the stone walls to this open area teeming with succulent plants and a truly stunning panoramic view. It is here that you understand why celebrities like Walt Disney and Nietzsche frequented this small village.

Accommodations are expensive. Food is expensive. Pack a supermarket lunch and make your way up for a wonderful day trip. If you're feeling up to the task, take the Chemin de Nietzsche down to the Èze-Bord-de-Mer and spend some time at the quiet beach below.

chic boutiques, watch the street artists do their thing, and snag an ice cream along the way.

*i* Admission €7, €5.50 reduced, free under 18; tours M-F at 10:30am and 2pm; wheelchair accessible

## MUSEUMS

### ◪MUSÉE MATISSE
164 Av. des Arènes de Cimiez; 04 93 81 08 08; open daily Jan 2-June 22 11am-6pm, June 23-Oct 15 10am-6pm, Oct 16-Dec 31 11am-6pm

Housed in a bright red Genoese villa, this small museum possesses many of Matisse's earlier paintings, sculptures, and cutouts. Lacking most of the famous ones, the museum instead has exhibits on the artist's life and his time spent specifically in the French Riviera. The works can be knocked out in less than an hour, leaving time for you to admire the beautiful seventeenth-century structure the works are housed in or the surrounding **Arènes de Cimiez.**

*i* Admission student €17; wheelchair accessible

### MUSÉE MARC CHAGALL
36 Av. Dr Ménard; 04 93 53 87 20; www.muse-chagall.fr; open Nov 1-May 1 M, W-F 10am-5pm, May 2-Oct 31 M, W-F 10am-6pm, closed Jan 1, May 1, Dec 25

Whether you are an art connoisseur or a lowly student who barely passed Art History in high school, you can definitely appreciate the works of Marc Chagall and their soothing effects on the soul. Housed in the middle of a picturesque olive garden (without the unlimited breadsticks), the museum is the dream child of the artist himself, as Chagall designed it. The museum, with large open spaces, white walls, and lots of sunlight flooding inside, creates the "universe of light" Chagall deems necessary to appreciate his art (whatever that means). Admire the 17 biblical inspired paintings with the classic vibrant, yet calming colors or sit in the auditorium room surrounded by the artist's stained glass works.

*i* Admission €10, €8 reduced, free under 18, free admission first Su of month; last entry 5:30pm; audio guide available; wheelchair accessible

# OUTDOORS

## ◪PLAGE PUBLIQUE DE PONCHETTES

70 Quai des Etats Unis; lifeguards on duty
Jun 1-Sep 3 9am-6pm

Although Nice is a vibrant cultural
center, most people come for the
beaches. We don't blame you: nothing
is better than working on that tan
next to the enticing sapphire blue
Mediterranean. The beaches in Nice
are indeed pebbly, but this means that
you will never have to wash out the
sand from the crooks and crannies of
your body. If the rocks don't win you
over by the end of the day, head west to
**Antibes** for a beach more up your alley.

*i* *Free; no wheelchair accessibility*

## PROMENADE DES ANGLAIS

Promenade des Anglais; 07 12 34 56 78

Picture the Jersey Shore boardwalk, but
exchange the fake tans and blowouts
for short swimsuits and topless women.
A magnificently-paved seafront
sidewalk stretching from the airport all
the way to **Castle Hill,** the Promenade
is *the* place to be on a nice, sunny day,
which is every day in Nice. Special
lanes for cyclists make it the ideal spot
to rent a bike, take in the beach views,
and get in that much-needed cardio.

*i* *Free; wheelchair accessible*

# FOOD

## ◪CHEZ PIPO ($)

13 Rue Bavastro; 04 93 55 88 82; open
W-Su 11:30am-2:30pm and 5:30pm-
10pm

It's simple. You want the traditional
Niçoise *socca.* You've searched
everywhere for it and find that it is
indeed everywhere. But you want to
make sure you get the best one. And
for that, there's Chez Pipo. Frequented
by locals for almost 100 years, Chez
Pipo prides itself on sticking to its
traditional values and recipes. Order
*socca,* which comes fresh out of a large
oven in the middle of the restaurant.
Whether you're sitting on the outdoor
terrace or wooden tables inside, Chez
Pipo is guaranteed to be packed.
So, get there early and start up a

conversation with your neighbor as you
wait for your delicious meal.

*i* *Small appetizers €3-4, socca €3-6;
cash only; limited wheelchair accessibility*

## ◪SOCCA D'OR ($)

45 Rue Bonaparte; 04 93 56 52 93; www.
restaurant-soccador-nice.fr; open M-Tu
11am-2pm and 6pm-10pm, Th-Sa 11am-
2pm and 6pm-10pm

A restaurant with such a bold name
is bound to peak your interest and
Socca d'Or certainly does that job. The
restaurant serves Niçoise specialties,
specifically *socca,* a chickpea pancake
that originated in Genoa, large pizzas,
and elaborate salads. Sit on the terrace
area and watch the servers periodically
carve out pieces of the large *socca* on
display. Past the bar, the very narrow
interior has a modern touch and you
can gaze at paintings of the port as you
enjoy your meal.

*i* *Socca €3, pizzas €6-10; cash only;
vegetarian options available; limited wheelchair accessibility*

## BAGUETTES D'ARGENT ($)

26 rue d'Angleterre; 04 93 82 19 04;
open M 7pm-10pm, W-Th 7pm-10pm, F-Sa
11:45am-1:15pm and 7pm-10pm

No. Stop right there. This is not a
*boulangerie* and you cannot buy your
daily baguette here. We know, what
are the French thinking trying to
confuse poor foreigners like ourselves?
Instead of the small bread shop you
envisioned, Baguettes d'Argent is a
go-to Vietnamese restaurant near the
main train station. A hole-in-the-wall
exterior gives way to a more upscale
dining establishment with gilded walls
and oriental lamps hanging from the
ceiling. Try some tasty duck or, if you
want to be bold, the frog legs. The food
is tasty, but be warned that the
portions are deceptively small.

*i* *Entrées €9-11; cash only; vegetarian
options available; limited wheelchair
accessibility*

## FENNOCHIOS ($)

2 Pl. Rossetti, 6 Rue de la Fissonnerie; 04
93 80 72 52, 04 93 62 88 80; www.fenoc-
chio.fr; open daily 9am-midnight

It would be a huge oversight to forget
to include an ice cream parlor in a
town with a beachside location. So,

here it is. Family-run Fennochios is in the heart of **Vieux Nice**, a five minute walk away from the promenade. Let your head swirl as you pick from the 94 ice cream and sorbet flavors. You can go for the classic chocolate or vanilla, or opt for the cactus, thyme, or even tomato basil. Munch happily on your cone as you make your way through Vieux Nice to the other Fennochios store for your second scoop (you know you want it).

*i* *1 scoop €2.50, 2 scoops €4, 3 scoops €5.50, 15 scoops €23; wheelchair accessible*

#### PORTOVENERE ($$)
12 Rue Halévy; 04 93 88 24 92; www.portovenererestaurant.fr; open daily noon-3pm, 7pm-11pm

Just inward from the **Promenade des Anglais**, the Portovenere is the perfect place to sit down, enjoy traditional Italian dishes, and people-watch on the nearby street. You know that the food is authentic based on the way the chef meanders his way around the many tables, making sure his customers are not only stuffed, but satisfied. The pastas are simple. Choose your preferred noodle, glob on some sauce, and you're home free! But, if you're not feeling a night of ingesting mass amounts of carbs, order the seafood platter. Or, get the best of both worlds by ordering a combination of the two.

*i* *Entrées €14-18; both; vegetarian options available; wheelchair accessible*

## NIGHTLIFE
#### KING'S PUB
5 Rue de la Préfecture; 04 93 62 17 11; www.kings-nice.com; open daily 5pm-2am

When it comes to drinking, no venue will ever compare to a tavern in the Middle Ages. Or, at least that's what we know from our reliable sources (read: *Game of Thrones*). Regardless, this medieval-styled pub in the middle of **Vieux Nice** has all the ingredients: live rock music, cheap draught beer, and televisions to watch football (soccer) matches. Did they have these things in the fourteenth-century? Probably not the rock music. But with people tricking in from the pub next door, King's Pub comes alive around 1am,

and, on good days, people climb on tables to dance to the beats.

*i* *Shots €4, beer €4*

#### LE BLUE WHALES
1 Rue Mascoinat; 04 93 62 90 94; open daily 6pm-4:30am

Blue Whales is the old faithful diner-pub combination that serves drunk customers who trickle in during the early hours of the morning, whether they need food or more drinks. The staggered lounge area gives way to a bar serving affordable cocktails and draught beer. Happy hour is a very happy event indeed, as it goes on until 1am. And if you find yourself wanting to dance, there's a small area under a TV next to a DJ stand where you can bust a move. Through a side door are the red booths of the diner, where talented chefs serve classic comfort food (read: massive burgers).

*i* *Shot €4, beer €4-7, cocktails €6-10, food €10-13; card minimum €10; BGLTQ+ friendly*

#### WAYNE'S BAR
15 Rue de la Préfecture; 04 93 13 46 99; www.lwaynes.fr/fr/accueil; open daily 10am-2am

Switch your "*bonjour*" for a hearty "how you doin'?" in this English-speaking pub. Get ready for some sweaty elbow to elbow dancing on the sturdy wooden tables. The table dancing happens every night, and it's expected you dance on those tables with every fiber of your being. The daily live music (including bands from the UK and different DJs) is sure to get your muscles moving. Arguably the most popular bar in the area, Wayne's is a place you should aim to visit before 1am. If not, whip out the best British accent you can muster and hope they let you shimmy in.

*i* *Shots €6, cocktails €8, beers €3-5; BGLTQ+ friendly*

# PARIS

Coverage by **Emily Corrigan**

To the rest of the world, Paris can be surrounded by enigmas: where are people buying all those blue and white striped shirts? Why are their hats flat? How is that tower so sexy? Even beyond the warm glow of Hollywood-crafted romanticism, there is a contradiction. The city seems at once nostalgic and *à la mode,* classic and modern. Yes, well-dressed people sip espresso in wicker café chairs, buy baguettes at *boulangeries,* and kiss each other on both cheeks, but a more dynamic view of the city reveals neighborhoods with distinct characters and plenty of people who are not too chic to laugh when someone trips, spill drinks while singing karaoke, let their dog just go right there on the sidewalk, or eat chicken McNuggets. Paris hasn't been blissfully left in some golden age of the past; it faces contemporary challenges of globalization and immigration and confronts social issues like from wealth to race to religion. These factors combine with its rich history and tradition, creating a diverse city that's livable, evolving, and exciting. So, while its landmarks reflect ancient influences, its museums house works from old masters, and its wineries take advantage of thousands of years of knowledge, there are always new and unique parts of the city to meet and explore. *Enchanté,* Paris.

## ORIENTATION

They say that Paris is laid out like one of its famous escargots: unlike New York's its rigid grids, Paris's winding rues are divided into blob-shaped **arrondissements,** starting in the center and spiraling outward like a snail's shell. You'll always be able to tell which arrondissement an address comes from by looking at the last digits of its zip code (750 are the first three, followed by the number of the neighborhood). Arrondissements are also noted with the number and suffix -ème or -e (e.g. 8ème or 8e). The Seine River bends through the city's center, providing a frame of reference and historically separating the city into the **Rive Gauche** and **Rive Droite.**

The first arrondissement begins in the center of the city just north of the river. It's home to the big guns: the **Louvre,** the **Tuileries Gardens,** and **Place de la Concorde,** along with beautiful but bank-breaking shops. To its eastern end near **Les Halles,** however, you'll start to encounter more affordable living. Just north is the second, a small and trendy neighborhood defined by **rue Montorgueil,** a street lined with cafés, cheese shops, produce stands, butchers, clothing stores— you name it. The third and fourth arrondissements make up **Le Marais,** whose youthful and slightly hipster crowd means it can always be counted on for unique restaurants and bars.

Before crossing the river to the fifth, you'll encounter **Île de la Cité** and **Île Saint-Louis,** two islands in the middle of the Seine which hold **Sainte Chapelle** and **Notre Dame,** and are some of the oldest parts of the city. Students from high school (lycée) and university (like the area's **Sorbonne**) crowd into the fifth arrondissement, or the **Latin Quarter.** The **Museum of Natural History** and its surrounding **Jardin des Plantes** make up its eastern edge while the beautiful **Jardin du Luxembourg** defines its western boundary with the sixth. The sixth itself, **Saint-Germain-des-Prés,** is host to the old haunts of celebrated writers and intellectuals, making it a fashionable and expensive area with famous cafés and plenty of bookstores. The seventh is the stuff of postcards: clean, quiet, picturesque Paris streets, in some parts mixed with the grand display of the **Eiffel Tower** and **Champ de Mars.**

Back across the river to the north is the eighth, where stereotypes of impossibly sleek, black-clad, high-heeled Parisians come to life. The district is bisected by the famous wide avenue of the **Champs-Elysées,** with its endpoints at the **Place de Charles de Gaulle** (where the **Arc de Triomphe** stands) and the **Place de la Concorde** defining two of its corners and the lovely **Parc Monceau** lining its northern boundary. East of the eighth, you'll find the **Grands Boulevards** neighborhood of the ninth, where young people can find thriving nightlife on even the slowest of nights and large department stores attract shoppers in droves.

The tenth, where many hostels are located (along with the 18th), reveals a grittier side of Paris, but still doesn't lack in beautiful waterside views along the **Canal St-Martin.** The 11th has scores of small brasseries, hidden gems, and lively side streets, while the **Bastille** area in the 12th has more crowded bars. The 13th, 14th, and 15th are more residential neighborhoods, each with their own character: the 13th reflects significant Asian influences, the 14th has both cute sleepy streets and lively energy near Montparnasse, and the 15th holds hidden charm behind 1970s high-rises.

Continuing to spiral outward to the west, the 16th feels upscale, full of young professionals with seemingly important business. On the side facing the Seine you'll find interesting museums and the **Trocadero,** from which you'll find one of the best views of the Eiffel Tower the city has to offer. While the 17th is a haven for artists seeking pretty cafés, the 18th's **Pigalle** area is chock-full of sex shops and peep shows, and houses the **Red Light District** of *Moulin Rouge* fame. The 18th also features **Montmartre,** where **Sacré Coeur** beckons from the highest point in Paris and artists do sketches and portraits around **Place de Tertre.** Finally, **Parc des Buttes-Chaumont** is the highlight of the 19th, and the **Père Lachaise** cemetery makes a daytrip out to the 20th worth your while.

Paris may seem a daunting and large city, but its arrondissements are so diverse and distinct that you are certain to find one in which you feel right at home: all you need is a little time to explore.

# ESSENTIALS

## GETTING THERE

Coming into Paris, you can fly into either Charles de Gaulle or Orly airports. From Charles de Gaulle, take the RER Line B into the city. Some trains go directly to Gare du Nord, which is close to many of the city's hostels in the tenth arrondissement and connects to multiple other metro lines. The journey should take about 40min. and costs €10. From Orly, you can take RER Line C into the city for about €6, which will take approximately 30min. Most trains will either arrive at Gare du Nord or Gare de l'Est, both located in the 10th arrondissement. From there, you can take the metro to where you need to go.

## GETTING AROUND

The metro, SNCF, is definitely the easiest way to get around Paris. With tons of lines, it can get you anywhere you need to go. Tickets can be purchased in the stations, and get cheaper the more you purchase. Navigo passes can also be purchased at many stations for €5, and are valid on the metro, bus, and RER (the larger commuter trains). They can be charged with the weekly fare, about €22, or the monthly fare, about €73. Buses are also easy to take and provide an opportunity to get acquainted with the layout of the city above ground. Vélib, the Parisian bike sharing service, also has stations all over the city and bikes are available daily 24hr. Passes can be bought by the day for only €1.70 or by the week for €8. The first 30min. of a ride are always free.

## PRACTICAL INFORMATION

**Tourist Offices:** The main tourist office can be found at 25 Rue des Pyramides, 1e; (open daily 10:15am-7pm).

**Banks/ATMs/Currency Exchange:** Major French banks include BNP Paribas, Banque Populaire, Société Générale, Crédit Mutuel, and more. ATM fees will apply.

**Post Offices:** The La Poste Paris, Louvre location is open all night at 16 Rue Étienne Marcel, 2e. Other locations include 18 Bd. de la Chapelle, 18e and 11 Rue des Islettes, 18e.

**Internet:** Many businesses in Paris don't offer free Wi-Fi, so McDonald's is going to become your best friend when you're in a pinch. Free internet access is also provided at nearly all of the city's most frequented museums.

**BGLTQ+ Resources:** The Centre BGLTQ Paris-ÎdF (63 Rue Beaubourg, 3e; 01 43 57 21 47; open M-F 3:30pm-8pm, Sa 1pm-7pm).

## EMERGENCY INFORMATION

**Emergency Number:** 112

**Police:** Direction de la Police Judiciaire (36 Quai des Orfèvres, 1e; 01 53 71 53 71)

**US Embassy:** There is a US Embassy in Paris (2 Av. Gabriel, 8e; 01 43 12 22 22; open M-Th 7:30am-5pm, F 7:30am-12:30pm).

**Rape Crisis Center:** Institut National d'Aide aux Victimes et de Médiation (14 Rue Ferrus, 14e 01 45 88 19 00; 0884284637; help line open every day 9am-9pm).

**Hospitals:**
- Hôtel-Dieu de Paris (1 Pl. du Parvis de Notre-Dame, 4e; 01 42 34 82 34).
- Hôpital Saint-Louis (1 Av. Claude Vellefaux, 10e; 01 42 49 49 49).

**Pharmacies:**
- Pharmacie de Garde Auber Paris Opéra (01 42 65 88 29).
- Pharmacie Monge (01 43 31 39 44).

# ACCOMMODATIONS

## ⧫MIJE FOURCY FAUCONNIER MAUBUISSON ($$)

6 Rue du Fourcy, 4e; 01 42 74 23 45; www.mije.com/en/accueil; reception open 24hr

Staying at MIJE is a true French experience; you'll be living in one of its three seventeenth-century buildings in the **Marais,** one of Paris's most centrally located and trendy districts. There are plenty of picturesque cafés nearby, but it will be hard to leave the hostel with its free breakfast, lunch buffet, and full-service dinner. In true homey Parisian style, the front door opens onto a beautiful courtyard full of flowers and white tables. So say "bonne journée" to your elderly neighbor, grab your motor scooter keys and grocery bag and—wait you're forgetting you don't actually live here.

*i* *Dorms from €30; reservation recommended; Wi-Fi; luggage storage available; free breakfast 7am-10am*

## ⧫OOPS! DESIGN HOSTEL-LATIN QUARTER ($$)

50 Av. des Gobelins, 13e; 01 47 07 47 00; www.oops-paris.com; reception open 24hr

You may pull an "oops" by forgetting to come back to the hostel since its location in the fun-filled Latin Quarter means you won't want to spend any more time cooped up inside. The hostel is tucked between cafés on a busy flower-filled street, within walking distance of attractions like the **Panthéon** and **Luxembourg Gardens.** As much fun as you'll find in the area, though, the hostel provides plenty of services itself. Pick up groceries across the street to cook in the kitchen or rent a board game to play in the colorful common room. Despite its name, staying at Oops! is no mistake (unlike using its TV to watch a Nicholas Cage movie).

*i* *Dorms starting at €32; reservation recommended; cash only; Wi-Fi; linens included; luggage storage; lockers provided; free breakfast; kitchen*

## AUBERGE INTERNATIONALE DES JEUNES ($)

10 Rue Trousseau, 11e; 01 47 00 62 00; www.aijparis.com; reception open 24hr

"AIJ" is a true student hostel: there are no guests over 30, it's cheap as can be, and coffee is free. Even with some of the best rates in the city, this hostel still doesn't sacrifice its quality. A warm and inviting staff makes you feel at home, and the rooms are completely comfortable. The four-person maximum dorms and in-suite bathrooms are thoroughly cleaned between 11am and 3pm daily, but you'll have no trouble finding something to do outside the hostel during those hours. The **Bastille** area is full of bakeries, cafés, and shops, and there's even a small produce market just a block away.

*i* *Dorms from €15; reservation required; no wheelchair accessibility; Wi-Fi; towels for rent; luggage storage; free breakfast*

## GENERATOR HOSTEL ($$)

9-11 Pl. du Colonel Fabien, 10e; 01 70 98 84 00; reception open 24hr

If you enjoy breathtaking views but aren't willing to miss the birth of your child, that child's college graduation, and your own retirement party while waiting in the line at the **Eiffel Tower,** make your way over to Generator Hostel. Located in the tenth arrondissement like many of the city's more affordable accommodations, this hostel features a rooftop terrace with views of **Sacré Coeur** in the foreground and **La Défense** in the distance that are so nice you'll find yourself wondering where you can buy a postcard to send to your very bitter child. After watching the sunset from the terrace, retire to your clean and comfortable dorm room or take advantage of the first-floor club open until 2am

*i* Dorms €35-41; reservation recommended; wheelchair accessible; Wi-Fi; café open daily 24hrs, terrace 4pm-10pm, downstairs club 10pm-2am; laundry facilities; lockers available

## LE VILLAGE HOSTEL MONTMARTRE ($$)

20 Rue d'Orsel, 18e; 01 42 64 22 02; www.villagehostel.fr; reception open 24hr

You'll have to wade through the countless colorful fabric stores of **Montmartre** to get to this hillside hostel, but you'll be rewarded with a free shot upon check-in at the pub next door. The location will allow you to explore the historic neighborhood easily, and the terrace features a beautiful view of **Sacré Coeur.** The hostel serves breakfast for only €4.50, and you're also welcome to prepare your own food there after picking up some groceries conveniently across the street. No, your reservation doesn't come with fire insurance, so exercise caution.

*i* Dorms from €33; reservation recommended; Wi-Fi; kitchen, hairdryers and towels for rent, breakfast (€4.50)

## THE BIG SPLURGE: LOIRRE VALLEY CASTLES

Unless you have an insomniac neighbor who does chainsaw art, we know that you don't usually get up before 6am. As painfully early as the start time may seem for a sleep-deprived traveler, it's worth it for a full day of "oh la la-ing" at three of France's more than 300 extravagant historical châteaux. After a hotel transfer drops you off at the meeting point, you'll board a two-story tour bus that will transport you to the **Vallée Loire** (in English, beautiful lush valley with a whole goddamn lot of castles and stuff). The first stop is either **Amboise or Cheverny,** depending on the time of the year and day of the week. Your tour guide will outfit you with headphones as the group explores the first château in an approximately 45-minute guided session. After the guided portions at each chateau, you'll also receive plenty of free time to eat lunch, wander the mazes and gardens, and speculate about the psychological impact of having 200 people clamor into your bedroom just to watch you wake up every morning (à la Louis XIV) must have on an individual. At Amboise, see where Leonardo da Vinci lived out his last years, and where King Charles VIII died by hitting his head on a doorframe. The second stop is **Chenonceau,** France's second-most visited castle (after Versailles), dating from 1515. Chenonceau serves as a castle-bridge; the waters of the Cher flow underneath its five archways, providing it with ample insurance against revolutionary mobs, since they were unlikely to destroy their only place to cross the river. Finally, the bus will bring you to the largest and most spectacular of the three castles, **Chambord.** Started as a hunting lodge for King François I at the dawn of the French Renaissance, its architecture reflects a mix of Gothic and Italian influences. After your guided session, you can try to catch one of the spectacles with horses and birds of prey that take place on the castle's grounds. With interesting history, beautiful scenery, and spectacular châteaux, this all-day tour is well worth its price tag.

## SMART PLACE GARE DU NORD ($$)

28 Rue de Dunkerque, 10e; 01 48 78 25 15; www.smartplaceparis.com; reception open 24hr

Smart Place isn't just book smart (although they do have a book exchange). It's smart in a street-savvy, plays-the-guitar, wears-horn-rimmed-glasses kind of way, too. The human embodiment of these characteristics can often be found casually playing foosball in the lobby, whipping up dinner in the common kitchen (that's right, they're a good cook), or making moves on your girlfriend in the spacious dorm rooms. Smart Place is so smooth it'll even offer to buy you a drink (with a voucher upon check-in).

*i* Dorms €35; reservation recommended; BGLTQ+ friendly; wheelchair accessible; Wi-Fi; laundry; lockers available; reservation recommended

## VINTAGE HOSTEL AND BUDGET HOTEL ($)

73 Rue Dunkerque, 9e ; 75009; 140161640; www.vintage-hostel.com; reception open 24hr

The handyman of hostels, Vintage offers an array of services that would inspire jealousy in any toolbox-toting do-it-yourselfer. Direction cards to famous monuments, restaurant recommendations, weather information, museum hours and prices: there's nothing Vintage can't provide. Plus, as one of the rare hostels with a gym, it offers the opportunity to offset at least some small part of the damage the backpacking lifestyle is doing to your body. Or you can just play foosball, we won't judge you.

*i* Dorms €25-45; reservation recommended; Wi-Fi; reservation recommended; laundry available; towels for rent

# SIGHTS
## CULTURE

### ◾MARCHÉ AUX PUCES

30 Av. Gabriel Péri, Saint-Ouen; www.marcheauxpuces-saintouen.com; open M 11am-5pm, Sa 9am-6pm, Su 10am-6pm

Marché aux Puces, the largest antiques market in the world, combines a coppery vintage feel with unexpected gems like garden gnomes giving you the finger and life-sized silver sharks to suspend from your ceiling. You wouldn't be surprised to see a boy in a newsboy cap and suspenders yelling something like "R2D2 coffee tables! Get your R2D2 coffee tables here!" With over 1700 vendors, the outdoor market is like a small city, with neighborhoods of plant shops, art dealers, and general collections of, for lack of a better word, stuff. Located just north of Paris, the market is a metro ride away, the ideal place to escape the city and spend a weekend day trying to find that perfect lampshade made of peacock feathers.

*i* Prices vary by stand

### AVENUE DES CHAMPS-ÉLYSÉES

Eighth Arrondissement; open daily 24hr

This famous avenue began as an extension of the **Tuileries Gardens,** but by the eighteenth century, it became a fashionable street for shopping, strolling, seeing, and being seen. Stretching between the **Place de la Concorde** and the **Arc de Triomphe,** it has a parallel garden on its northeastern side. Events such as the annual Bastille Day parade and the final stage of the Tour de France draw huge crowds to the Champs-Élysées. In the winter, the avenue adopts a ferris wheel and an extensive Christmas market. On a daily basis, tourists flock to the Tiffany and Co. shop, check out French styles from Zadig & Voltaire and Maje, or nibble dainty pastries at famous bakeries like the macaron shop **Ladurée.**

*i* Free

### CHOPIN AU JARDIN

2 Rue Gazan, 14e; open summer Su 5pm-6pm

If you've ever fantasized about laying in a meadow with music softly caressing your eardrums and gentle horses nuzzling your face, you're not alone. While this dream may seem somewhat out of reach for those who don't live on a ranch in Candyland, Chopin au Jardin is certainly the next best thing. Every summer, renowned pianists give a series of free performances in **Parc Montsouris,** a beautiful green area on the southern edge of the city. Listeners crowd onto the nearby hill, shaded by large trees and featuring a beautiful view of the park's pond, to recline and relax. Children on stubborn ponies idle by periodically, but for the most part the audience is hushed, captivated by the beautiful music.

*i* Free; wheelchair accessible

## GALERIES LAFAYETTE
40 Bd. Haussmann, 9e; 01 42 82 34 56; www.galerieslafayette.com; open M-Sa 9:30am-8:30pm, Su 11am-7pm

Do you ever get frustrated that your mink scarf is no longer in season? Do you hate it when your Prada boots get a little scuffed? What about when you can't decide between colors of Gucci sunglasses so you have to buy all of them? No?? Well then, you won't have much in common with many of the shoppers perusing the designer racks at Galeries Lafayette, Paris's most famous department store. Visitors flock by the busload to throw euros at shoes, bags, suits, perfumes, just about anything that will scream, "My parents own a boat." But there's lots to see even if you're not being crushed under the weight of your expendable income.

Winter

window displays draw crowds, cafés serve steaming hot chocolate, and the rooftop offers a beautiful view of the city.

*i* Prices vary; wheelchair accessible

## JARDIN DES PLANTES
57 Rue Cuvier, 5e; 01 40 79 56 01; www.jardindesplantes.net; open daily 7:30am-8pm

It may seem repetitive to name a garden the "garden of plants." Here, though, it really is all about those beautiful rectangular-celled beings. Paris's own botanical garden features greenhouses growing tropical trees, shallow ponds full of water lilies, and gardens overflowing with beautiful flowers. A host of animals like leopards and wallabies lives in the menagerie, while a maze leads up to a small pagoda. Entrance to the garden is free, but its different components may have their own fees. If you're looking to relive your *Night at the Museum* fantasies, enter the **Museum of Natural History** housed in the garden to stare expectantly at life-like dioramas.

*i* Free entry to garden, but €9 to other areas of the garden for under 25; wheelchair accessible

## MARCHÉ DES ENFANTS ROUGES
39 Rue de Bretagne, 3e; 01 40 11 20 40; open Tu-Th 10am-8pm, F-Sa 8am-8:30pm, Su 8:30am-5pm

Despite the concerning literal translation (read: market of the red children), this outdoor market is innocent and charming. Among stalls selling meat, cheese, produce, and flowers are multiple excellent restaurants with outdoor seating. Although it's crowded at peak lunch hours, the wait is worth it. Don't miss the couscous royal (€12) from the Moroccan restaurant Le Traiteur

It's been employed by Iron Age people, the Romans, and the Vikings for important trade and transportation. It's the place where Joan of Arc's ashes were tossed away, and where athletes competed at the 1900 Olympic Games. Today, it's used by Parisian youths as a fun alternative to land for getting drunk: the Seine. Nightlife in Paris begins here, with the wide banks and bridges providing the perfect place to open a bottle of wine with friends and swing your legs over the water while you pretend not to notice the rats. The front tip of the Île de la Cité and the stretch near Pont Alexandre III are congregating places for food and drink around nine or ten in the evening before the scene moves either to land or to the various clubs floating on riverboats or hiding beneath the bridges. But people enjoy the Seine for much more during the day as well. Elderly men play petanque in sand courts near Pont Louis Philippe, children play on swing sets and pass soccer balls around the banks, and the more ambitious tanning crowd manages to take advantage of a narrow grass strip at Pont Au Change. Whether you're a lover looking to attach a lock to just about anything, an Instagram model searching for a dreamy sunset photo op, or that one guy who always pretends like he's going to push people into the water but then doesn't, the Seine is the place to go.

Marocain. An entertaining connoisseur at a shop just behind it painstakingly crafts excellent sandwiches, if you're willing to wait. And, to calm your fears, the name's roots lie in the clothing worn by children cared for at an orphanage nearby.

*i* Prices vary by stand

### PLACE DES VOSGES
Pl. des Vosges, 4e; open M-F 8am-6pm, Sa 8:30am-6pm, Su 9am-6pm

Formerly the **Place Royale** (the home of the French monarchy), the Place des Vosges is now surrounded by some of the best art galleries of **Le Marais.** With beautiful architecture, the omnipresent aroma of the shady linden trees, and a stunning fountain, it's a relaxing spot that you would never guess was the site of King Henri IX's untimely death (by a lance through his eye, brutal). Step through the courtyard of the Hôtel de Sully, lunch at a neighboring café, or enter (for free) the former home of **Victor Hugo,** author of *The Hunchback of Notre Dame* and *Les Misérables.*

*i* Free; last entry 5:40pm; wheelchair accessible

## LANDMARKS

### LES CATACOMBES
1 Av. du Colonel Henri Rol-Tanguy, 14e; 01 43 22 47 63; ; www.catacombes.paris.fr; open Tu-Su 10am-8:30pm

After waiting in line until you're almost ready to join the ranks of the deceased in the Catacombs yourself, you'll be welcomed into the chilly labyrinthine underground tunnels with the cheery inscription "Halt, this is the realm of Death." Beginning in the late eighteenth century, as graveyards closed for public health reasons, remains were moved to the Catacombs. Millions of skulls and bones are stacked in arrangements that are surprisingly pleasing to the eye, until you remember that they were once living breathing humans. It begs the question: how does one get into the bone-arranging line of work? Do you have to have an internship, or just be one of those kids that burned a lot of ants? In any case, underground Paris is not for the faint of heart.

*i* Admission €13, free under 17; last entry 7:30pm; no wheelchair accessibility

### NOTRE DAME
6 Parvis Notre-Dame, Pl. Jean-Paul II, 4e; 01 42 34 56 10; www.notredamedeparis.

fr/en; open M-F 7:45am to 6:45pm, Sa-Su 7:45am-7:15pm

"A long time ago" to some means when their dog was a puppy. To others, it means when Patricia stole their juice box in kindergarten. But the construction of the Notre Dame cathedral began a really long time ago, far before the development of modern juice box technology. Its first stage began in the 1160s and the façade was finally completed in 1215. Its French Gothic style incorporates flying buttresses, impressive stained glass rose windows, and a gallery of 28 statues of kings demonstrating the privileged relationship between the era's monarchy and the Church of Paris. Pro tip: check out the cathedral's crypt (located down a stairway outside in the square), the site of Paris's first fortifications from 308 when the city was still called Lutetia.

*i* Free entry to cathedral, audio guide €2, towers €10, treasury €5, crypt €8; wheelchair accessible

### ▨PÈRE LACHAISE CEMETERY

16 Rue du Repos, 20e; 01 55 25 82 10; open M-F 8am-6pm, Sa 8:30am-6pm, Su 9am-6pm

The Père Lachaise Cemetery, established in 1804, is the most visited cemetery in the world for a few reasons. First, as the largest green space in Paris, it's incredibly beautiful and serene. Signs claim that 4134 trees of 76 species grow there. Secondly, more than one million bodies have been buried there over the years, making navigating the elaborate and numerous headstones and monuments an interesting journey through time. Finally, seeing the graves of famous people like **Oscar Wilde, Edith Piaf, Frédéric Chopin,** and others will allow you opportunities to boast that you've "always loved the work of Delacroix" or suggest that you "discuss Proust's In Search of Lost Time, shall we?"

*i* Free entry; wheelchair accessible

### CHURCH OF SAINT-SULPICE

2 Rue Palatine, 6e; 01 42 34 59 98; open daily 7:30am-7:30pm

Despite terms like "French kissing" and *ménage à trois,* it's impossible to forget France's more pious traditions. With its age-old Catholic tradition, it's no surprise to find this church in the heart of the **Saint-Germain-des-Près** district. With foundations from as far back as the twelfth-century, it has stood the test of time as one of Paris's largest churches. Additions from the 1800s include famous paintings from Eugène Delacroix in its interior and an enormous organ spanning the length of the back wall. Today, you may recognize parts of the church from its use in the film *The Da Vinci Code.*

*i* Free; no wheelchair accessibility; must cover shoulders and knees to enter

### EIFFEL TOWER

Champ de Mars, 5 Av. Anatole, 7e; www.toureiffel.paris/en/; open daily 9:30am-11pm, mid-June to September 9am-midnight

The Eiffel Tower was supposed to be destroyed six months after its use for the **1889 World's Fair,** but a vote by Parisian citizens to keep it determined its fate as a setting for wedding photos, the site of the highest concentration of selfie sticks per capita in the world (we're assuming), and a source of inspiration for the more creative sex shops around the **Moulin Rouge.** Enjoy a picnic in the surrounding park if you're not willing to wait 45min. to 1hr. amongst the engaged couples, selfie-takers, and sex toy designers to actually get into the tower and see its incredible panoramic views. Just watch out for dangerously high wind levels caused by thousands of moon-eyed romantics collectively sighing.

*i* Lift to 2nd fl. €11, stairs to 2nd fl. €7, lift to top €17; last 2nd fl. lift 11pm, last summit lift 10:30pm, last stairs entry 6pm; wheelchair accessible; reserve tours online

### LE PANTHÉON

Pl. du Panthéon, 5e; 01 44 32 18 00; www.paris-pantheon.fr/en; open daily 10am-6:30pm, closed Jan 1, May 1, Dec 25

Originally intended by Louis XV as a dedication to Geneviève, the patron saint of Paris, this large domed structure eventually became the secular national pantheon. It pays homage to writers who died for France in WWI and WWII, and it hosts the tombs of scientists like **Marie Curie** (who was the first female professor at the neighboring **Sorbonne** university) and thinkers like **Voltaire** and **Rousseau.** Although her spotlight was stolen, Geneviève is still featured in many of the massive paintings covering the walls, ensuring that she's still on Paris's side. In the center of the transept you'll find **Foucault's pendulum,** which he used to prove that the Earth rotates around itself. Funny, we always thought it rotated around chocolate croissants.

*i* Admission €9; last audio guide issued 5:15pm; wheelchair accessible; tours available of the upper levels

### L'ARC DE TRIOMPHE
Pl. Charles-de-Gaulle, 8e; 01 55 37 73 77; www.monuments-nationaux.fr; open daily 10am-11pm

Assuming you played Little League, you are probably familiar with the concept that when you win something, you get a trophy. Usually it's a plastic statue in some sort of athletic stance, but add Napoleon to the mix (yes Napoleon, of the "Napoleonic complex") and you get a 50-meter high tribute to military victory. L'Arc de Triomphe honors the achievements of the Grande Armée and memorializes the **Unknown Soldier** with an eternal flame. It was built in what was originally named Place de l'étoile (meaning star) after the 12 large avenues that radiate from it, including the famous **Champs-Élysées.** The top of the arch has one of the best views in Paris, especially since it's open late for the sunset. Someone give this arch a plastic statue.

*i* Admission €9; wheelchair accessible

### PALAIS GARNIER: OPÉRA NATIONAL DE PARIS
8 Rue Scribe, 9e; www.operadeparis.fr/en; open Sept 12-July 16 10am-4:30pm, July 17-Sept 11 10am-5:30pm

Charles Garnier undertook this architectural feat in 1861 at the request of **Napoleon III,** building what is now considered one of the world's most beautiful theaters for the national opera. The elite opera-goers of years past and present have mingled in the **Grand Foyer** outside the most expensive boxes, admiring its high painted ceilings. Less elite civilians have just taken pictures of the chandeliers and called it a day. The

ballets and operas still taking place here are expensive, but those under 25 can see the theater and its museum and library with costume jewelry, set designs, books, and paintings for only €7.

*i* Admission €11, €7 ages 12-25; guided tours daily 11am and 2:30pm; last entry 4:30pm; wheelchair accessible

### SACRÉ COEUR
35 Rue de Chevalier de la Barre, 18e; 01 53 41 89 00; www.sacre-coeur-montmartre.fr; basilica open daily 6am-10:30pm, dome open May-Sept 8:30am-8pm, Oct-Apr 9am-5pm

From the laying of the first stone in 1875, Sacré Coeur has had at least one person praying inside at all times, day and night, for over 125 years. Its construction began after France's defeat in the 1870 war against Germany, a response to thoughts that France's troubles had spiritual roots. Signs prompting you to dress respectfully and be silent reinforce the solemn mood and religious history, but the touristy souvenir shops of the **Montmartre** neighborhood have even permeated inside the basilica. Here, have a souvenir coin with your dazzling mosaics and enormous angel sculptures.

*i* Basilica admission free, dome admission €6; no wheelchair accessibility

### SAINTE-CHAPELLE
8 Bd. du Palais, 1e; 01 53 40 60 80; www.sainte-chapelle.fr/en; open daily 9am-7pm

Most stains require the tough, grease-fighting cleansing power of a Tide pen. But in the thirteenth century, King Louis IX threw caution to the wind and hired some guys to just stain the living hell (pun intended) out of some glass, Gothic style. A reliquary and place of worship, this two-story chapel is home to a stunning collection of stained glass windows, each telling its own story. The mammoth windows, including an impressive rose one, flood the place with light, which glints off chandeliers and golden decorations inside. The chapel often holds cultural events such as concerts in the summer

# GIVERNY

**Giverny is only a 45-minute train ride from Paris, but it's an entirely different world.** Vines entirely cover medieval buildings, lazy green streams meander through fields of cattle, and life seems much simpler than usual, like it does in Disney Channel Original Movies. The small village, about 15-kilometers from Vernon, claims fame as the former home of Impressionist master Claude Monet. Visitors can walk through Monet's house and gardens, visit an Impressionist museum, and enjoy fantasies of being able to paint masterpieces rather than pathetically attempt shading in stick figures. Water lilies and floral compositions dot the landscape, making it clear why many famous American painters followed the lead of Monet, who discovered his love for the place out the window of a passing train. A visit to this magical spot is an ideal way to spend a dreamy long afternoon.

Vernon lies in the Normandy region, northwest of Paris about halfway to **Rouen.** The Seine makes its way along the northeast edge of the city, with the old mill across the river from the city's historic center, and just southwest, the train station at **Place de la Gare.** The village of Giverny lies to the southwest, across the river from the city. About 15-kilometers away, the journey will take you past farms where ostriches, llamas, horses, and cows roam over the lush green landscape. Once in Giverny, you'll find the main street, rue Claude Monet. The painter's house and gardens take up its eastern end, while walking further west will bring you to the tourist office, cafés, and eventually the **Museum of Impressionism.**

## GETTING THERE

From Paris, take the train from Paris St-Lazare station to Vernon-Giverny. The trains run approximately hourly, and take about 45min. Allow extra time to buy your tickets (about €15-20) at the station if you can't print them at your hostel. Save time and trouble by buying the return ticket at the same time. You will probably want to spend at least a few hours in Giverny.

## GETTING AROUND

Shuttles to Giverny depart from the train station in Vernon shortly after each train arrives. The round-trip costs €8. You can either take the large air conditioned buses or a smaller "train" service that will pass sights in Vernon as well and provide some historical narrative along the way. Make sure to check the return shuttle times in order to make it back to the train station on time. In Giverny, everything is within walking distance.

## Swing by...

### MONET'S HOUSE

We like to believe that if we had lived in Monet's former home and had been able to stroll the beautiful aromatic gardens surrounding it, we too would have become famous artists and avoided resorting to the lowly life of travel writing. In any case, entry to the property is only €5.50 for students, and you'll have access to the famous impressionist's personal home of over 40 years and his main sources of inspiration. In the house, Monet's own collections of Japanese prints hang in colorful sunlit rooms, and his former studio holds replicas of 59 of his paintings, displayed exactly how they once were in the room in which they were painted. The gardens are both a treasure trove of beautiful flowers and a dream come true for any

Monet fan. The lily ponds, framed by weeping willows, seem like old friends, familiar from the artist's most well-known paintings. You won't want to miss such an unbelievable indulgence.

## Check out...

### VERNON

Vernon is like Beyoncé's sister: amazing in its own right, but usually overshadowed by its close relation. A visit to Giverny necessarily takes you through this medieval town, whose history likely reaches as far back as the twelfth-century. Give yourself some time before heading out of its train station to marvel at the old buildings with exposed wooden beams, the large church Notre-Dame of Vernon, and the old mill that stretches into the Seine itself right next to the ruins of the city's formerly impressive bridge. You'll find cheaper food and drink options in the town than near the tourist-frequented sites of Giverny, and you'll experience the bucolic charm of an authentic medieval French city.

## Grab a bite at...

### TERRA CAFE

99 Rue Claude Monet, 27620 Giverny; 02 32 51 94 65; www.giverny.org/restos/terra; open daily 10am-6pm

There's something irresistible about shady trellises covered with vines, and something even more irresistible about sweet, sweet air conditioning. It can get hot in Giverny during peak summer months, and the café at the Museum of Impressionism provides a cool spot to take a break from wandering the gardens and cool off with a cold beverage or a scoop of ice cream. It's just a stone's throw from Monet's house. If you have time to kill before a shuttle brings you back down to Vernon, grab lunch or a crêpe here and peruse the next-door gift shop and a small free art exhibit downstairs. The museum itself is of course an option as well, at only €4.50 for students.

*i* Meals €13-18, beverages €3-7, crêpes €6-8; vegetarian options; wheelchair accessible

months, so be sure to check the schedule before you go.

*i* *Admission €10, free under 26; guided tours daily 11am-3pm; last entry 30min. before closing*

## MUSEUMS
..............................................

### ◾CENTRE GEORGES POMPIDOU
Pl. Georges-Pompidou, 4e; 01 44 78 12 33; www.centrepompidou.fr/en; Open M, W-Su 11am-9pm, closed May 1, Level 6 open Th until 11pm

Your first indication that the Pompidou is going to get weird and wild is the fact that you enter the museum through a large transparent tube and your next indication is that the art is bananas. We mean that in a figurative sense, but, after an hour at the Pompidou, you would no longer be skeptical if you were to see a bunch of bananas wearing little jackets with a sign that read something like "Costumed Fruit. 2011. Reinterpretation of light, fabric, and organic energy. Medium: bananas, polyester." As the largest collection of modern and contemporary art in Europe, works by Matisse and Picasso are displayed alongside sideways urinals and stained folding tables. Ahh, art.

*i* *Admission €14; tours Saturday at noon; last entry 8pm; wheelchair accessible*

### ◾MUSÉE DU QUAI BRANLY - JACQUES CHIRAC ($$)
37 Quai Branly, 7e; 01 56 61 70 00; www.quaibranly.fr/en/; open T-W, Su 11am to 7pm, Th-Sat 11am-9pm

We know, we know. All these museums are great but there are just not enough Yemeni feast dresses for your taste. Look no further: at this museum, you'll walk through a large display hall housing indigenous art from Africa, Oceania, Asia, and the Americas. Screens play footage of cultural ceremonies while visitors peruse Maori dugout canoes, Bedouin camel litters used in the Syrian steppes, Persian ceramics, Ethiopian prayer scrolls, and elaborate masks from all over the world. (And to think, we've just been using a brown paper bag!) Make sure to look up the temporary exhibits,

since they take up almost half of the museum's space.

*i* *Admission €10, access to temporary exhibitions €10; wheelchair accessible*

### ◾MUSÉE DE PICASSO
5 Rue de Thorigny, 3e; 01 85 56 00 36; www.museepicassoparis.fr; open Tu-F 10:30am to 6pm, Sa-Sun and French holidays 9:30am-6pm, closed Dec 25, Jan 1, May 1

For the artist with perhaps the most widely recognized name in the world, Picasso sure loved to paint in his underwear. We know this because the Picasso Museum, providing photo evidence, focuses as much on the master's life and influences as on his art. A well-crafted narrative guides visitors through the museum, with each step demonstrating chronologically how Picasso's relationships, setbacks, and passions (especially in his marriage and subsequent affair) manifested in his work and developed his artistic alter ego: a minotaur. It'll be difficult to leave, but, once you do, spend some time wandering through the small art galleries surrounding the museum.

*i* *Admission €12.50; tours €7; tours Saturday at 2pm; wheelchair accessible*

### FONDATION LOUIS VUITTON
8 Av. du Mahatma Gandhi, 16e; 01 40 69 96 00; www.fondationlouisvuitton.fr; open M, W-Th noon-7pm, F noon-9pm, Sa-Su 11am-8pm

The "museum of man" explores how humans have evolved, organized ourselves, migrated to colonize continents, and developed our own languages and cultures. It incorporates archaeological history, art, models, and nature, but in fun and interactive ways. You can squash your face to look like a Neanderthal, pull rubbery tongues sticking out of the wall to hear different languages, look at brains in jars, and press buttons that give off the scents of various cuisines. See the Peruvian mummy that inspired the famous painting *Scream*. And don't forget to grin smugly to yourself knowing that of all species of the Homo genus, we Sapiens are the last ones standing. Suck it, erectus.

*i* *Admission €14, €10 student; wheelchair accessible and free entry to disabled visitors*

## LE LOUVRE

Rue de Rivoli, 1e; 01 40 20 50 50; www.
louvre.fr/en; open M 9am-6pm, W 9am-
10pm, Th 9am-6pm, F 9am-10pm, Sa-Su
9am-6pm

The Louvre. Oh, you've heard of it?
Big glass pyramids, that one lady that
doesn't smile with her teeth, people in
scarves looking thoughtfully at things.
We're guessing you have the basic info
down, so here are some insider tips. Go
in the morning or buy a Paris museum
pass ahead of time to avoid lines.
When viewing the famous sculpture
*Winged Victory*, stand on the stairs from
a three-quarters angle on the left, the
vantage point from which its artist
originally intended it to be viewed. Go
to the **Pavilion to l'Horloge** to walk
in what used to be the moat of the
royal palace. Plan ahead: the massive
museum can be overwhelming if you
don't do your research. Unless of course
you're just there to see our gal Mona.

*i* *Admission €15; tour €12 and tickets
can only be purchased at the museum the
day of; wheelchair accessible*

## MUSÉE DE L'ORANGERIE

Jardin des Tuileries, Pl. de la Concorde, 1e;
01 44 77 80 07; www.musee-orangerie.fr/
en; open M, W-Su 9am-6pm

The highlight of the museum, located
at the edge of the **Tuileries Gardens,**
is the collection of eight huge water
lilies paintings by **Monet.** The rooms
in which the *Nymphéas* series are
installed were specifically designed with
input by Monet himself. The paintings
curve around oval rooms, encircling
the viewer and inviting them into the
beautiful natural scene. The other 145
paintings by famous artists like **Renoir,
Matisse,** and **Picasso** are located two
floors down. You know your museum
is pretty important when you have to
toss the Matisse in the basement.

*i* *Admission €9; tours €6; M 2:15pm and
Sa 11am; last entry 5:15pm; wheelchair
accessible*

## MUSÉE D'ORSAY

1 Rue de la Légion d'Honneur, 7e; 01 40
49 48 14; www.musee-orsay.fr/en/home.

## MUSEE DE LA GRANDE GUERRE

While it's a tough case to make that Paris doesn't have enough museums, it's true
that they tend to focus more on art than on history. France, whose first written
records appeared in the Iron Age, has been intimately involved in its fair share of
wars and disputes since its birth. It seems fair to take a half day to travel outside
of Paris to learn more about its role in one of the most monumental worldwide
events of modern memory: World War I.

The Musée de la Grande Guerre is located east of Paris in a city called **Meaux.**
To get there, take the train about 40 minutes out from Gare de l'Est (€8), and
then a ten-minute bus ride to the museum (€2). There, history buffs will have a
field day. The museum is largely uncrowded and allows you plenty of space to
roam the exhibits. It starts with a well-done video taking you back in time to
the 1870-1871 war between France and Germany and proceeds in chronological
order up to the end of the World War I. It extends further to even the conditions
and events following that set the stage for World War II. The exhibits walk
visitors through the array of motivations and complicated alliance systems that
precipitated the involvement of 32 countries in a massive and deadly worldwide
conflict.

The museum explores topics from camouflage to espionage (including the tale
of a prostitute that was shot for being a German spy), from the development of
tanks (of which they have a few) to chemical warfare. Screens play alarming real
footage of the trenches while you walk over ground that squelches to simulate
mud. You'll leave with a better understanding of the war from all sides: the motivations of nations, the conditions faced by soldiers, the outcomes of battles, and
the dehumanizing horrors that resulted in the loss of more than nine million lives.
It's a sobering yet profoundly interesting experience.

html; open daily 9:30am-6pm, Th 9:30am-9:45pm, closed May 1, Dec. 25

Housed in an old train station, the Musée d'Orsay takes advantage of an enormous main hall to display the largest collection of Impressionist masterpieces in the world. Between the huge landscapes, a polar bear sculpture, and masterpieces like the famous *Petite Danseuse* of **Edgar Degas,** the museum's scale can be overwhelming. Luckily, enormous clocks occupy some of the fifth-floor windows if you need to take a gaze-romantically-over-the-rooftops-while-imagining-you-lived-in-the-mid-nineteenth-century break.

*i* *Admission €12; tours €6 from 9:30am onward; last tickets entry 5pm, 9pm Th; wheelchair accessible*

## MUSÉE RODIN

79 Rue de Varenne, 7e; 01 44 18 61 10; www.musee-rodin.fr; open Tu-Su 10am-5:45pm

Rodin was a controversial sculptor in his day. Sometimes too provocative and erotic, he offended many and gained the loyalty and support of others. His statue of **Balzac** was first met with outrage, but is now considered the starting point for modern sculpture; who knows, maybe one day we'll realize that *Fifty Shades of Grey* was in fact the dawn of a new era of literature. Rodin's works are spread around a beautiful garden of roses and trees, from which the Invalides dome and the Eiffel Tower are both visible. An elegant mansion where Rodin once lived is also open to the public, although his most famous sculptures like *The Thinker, The Kiss,* and *The Gates of Hell* can all be found outside.

*i* *Admission €10, audio guide €6; last entry 5:15pm; wheelchair accessible, wheelchairs provided free of charge*

## PALAIS DE TOKYO

13 Avenue du Président Wilson, 16e; 01 81 97 35 88; www.palaisdetokyo.com/en

Nobody can claim that Palais de Tokyo isn't an immersive experience. The huge modern art museum just across the river from the **Eiffel Tower** displays enormous video screens in dark rooms, complicated dioramas viewed from multiple angles as you follow the path of the exhibit, and light displays accompanied by music. What is subjective, however, is the art itself. The video screens depict strange silver robot animals speaking German, the dioramas have live fish that look like something you've only seen in episodes of *Planet Earth,* and the lights and music are jarring and discordant. You'll likely leave being somewhere between inspired, dazed, and thoroughly confused.

*i* *Admission €12, €9 for under 25; tours conducted in French; wheelchair accessible*

## PETANQUE

It's no secret: the French love balls. Get your mind out of the gutter; of course, we don't mean basketballs. In any case, you may have wondered on more than one occasion what those old men throwing silver spheres into the dirt are doing. Well, they're engaging in one of the Parisians' most beloved games (right behind soccer and seeing who can drink their coffee the slowest while they judge the outfits of passersby): pétanque. Early forms of the game were played by the Ancient Greeks and Romans, and eventually found their way to France's Provence. In its current version, players stand in a small circle and compete to see who can toss their metal balls the closest to a smaller wooden one (the cochonnet, or piglet, awww). It's typically played on gravel or sand, and specialized pétanque areas have popped up all over Paris, including at public parks and at spots on the river. Even so, the game is such a part of Parisian culture that people will play just about anywhere. While traditionally played by elderly men (some of whom actually do wear berets), the game has picked up more of a hipster youth following within the past few years. Its governing body, the Fédération Française de Pétanque et Jeu Provençal (ahh yes the FFPJP,) has amassed hundreds of thousands of members, young and old.

## OUTDOORS

### JARDIN DU LUXEMBOURG

Rue de Médicis, Rue de Vaugirard, 6e

The Luxembourg Gardens stretch out in front of Luxembourg Palace, once the home of King Henry IV's widow Marie de' Medici but now the home of the French Senate. Hundreds of statues are scattered throughout the gardens along with tennis courts, greenhouses, cafés, ponds, and plenty of painters and writers. The greenery ranges from perfectly manicured in some areas to more natural in others, and there seems to be an unwritten code of conduct for where you can and cannot walk on the grass. A good rule of thumb: if it looks like that golf course your stepdad took you to once, you should probably find somewhere else to picnic.

*i* *Free; wheelchair accessible; hours subject to change*

### PARC DES BUTTES-CHAUMONT

1 Rue Botzaris, 19e; 01 48 03 83 10; open daily summer 7am-10pm, winter 7am-8pm winter

Paris' more touristy gardens achieve a manicured "wow" factor, but you may feel as if you have to hold your breath to prevent accidentally stirring a leaf from its rightful place. At Parc des Buttes-Chaumont, however, locals play soccer in the tall grass, people make out on blankets, giggling children try to outrun sprinklers, and nobody uses a measuring tape to make sure the bushes are all at regulation height. The site of a former gypsum quarry, the park was created by **Napoleon III** in 1867, complete with a waterfall, a cave, and a cliff with a white temple perched atop it. It's a more easy-going park for an easy-going traveler.

*i* *Free entry; wheelchair accessible*

### TUILERIES GARDEN

113 Rue de Rivoli, 1e; open daily 24hr

When the **Louvre** was still the royal palace, long before that large glass pyramid became the subject of countless gimmicky photos, the Tuileries were the gardens of kings, queens, courtiers, and the ever-present ducks. A wide white gravel path stretches from the Louvre all the way to the **Place de la Concorde,** punctuated

by large round fountains and hundreds of marble statues. While the main pathways can be packed, groves of trees on the sides provide more seclusion and a respite from the heat and dust of the day. Tons of green metal chairs let you relax in comfort, especially if you can snag one of the reclining ones. There's no doubt it's one of the most picturesque parts of Paris.

*i* *Free; wheelchair accessible*

## FOOD

### BOB'S KITCHEN ($$)

74 Rue des Gravilliers, 3e; 09 52 55 11 66; www.bobsjuicebar.com/kitchen.html; open M-F 8am-3pm, Sa-Su 8am-6pm

You know your vegan Aunt Lisa who teaches yoga and does water color paintings of vegetables? Bob's Kitchen is her dream come true. Ultra-flavorful veggie stew, gluten-free pancakes, avocado toast: it's a vegetarian oasis in a lamb kebab desert. Not only is everything instagramable, but it's delicious, full of texture, and healthy too. Have a sweet açai bowl or sip on kombucha or homemade mint lemonade at communal tables. Juices are made fresh and bagels are house-made every morning. You'll have to keep your eyes peeled though; the only indication of the restaurant is a white balloon in the window.

*i* *Breakfast €4-11, lunch €6-14; vegetarian, vegan, and gluten-free options available; credit card minimum €20*

### CAVE LA BOURGOGNE ($)

144 Rue Mouffetard, 5e; 01 47 07 82 80; open daily 7am-2am

There's no better place for traditional French staples (*croque monsieur, confit de canard, charcuterie*). Mountains of delicious salads (especially the warm goat cheese and honey one) are surprisingly a bargain. Aside from the top notch food, the ambiance is *très français* as well. Tables spill onto the lovely rue Mouffetard, overlooking a fountain surrounded by flowers. In the summer, Cave la Bourgogne is packed with locals looking for typical French fare. In the back of the restaurant, cozy

# VERSAILLES

The estate at Versailles has come a long way since it became a symbol of monarchical splendor and separation from the French people in the 1600s. It was first established by Louis XIII as a hunting lodge, but eventually grew under the reign of the three successive Louises. The Sun King, Louis XIV, moved the court to Versailles, making it home to about 10,000 family members, court members, servants and the like. In October 1789, Louis XVI and Marie-Antoinette were finally forced to leave Versailles for the last time as the revolutionaries took control of the country. Remarkably, the palace survived the Revolution and became a museum in honor of French glory. Now a popular tourist attraction, the vast estate is the perfect place to spend a day away from Paris learning about the history of the nation, wandering the gardens, or playing a game of "I Spy" in which every turn starts with "I spy something gold."

If you thought the Louvre was large, think again. With the main chateau, **Grand Trianon, Petit Trianon,** stables, and gardens it's nearly impossible to see everything at Versailles in a day. A good place to start is either the tourist office between the stables or the info desk and ticket office to the left as you enter the palace. After proceeding through the chateau, make your way outside to the gardens. The beautiful **Latona's Fountain** is directly ahead, but it's worth making a diversion to your left to look out across the **Lake of the Swiss Guards** before heading deeper into the gardens. An efficient way to see a lot is to head down the right-hand side of the gardens and groves and visit the **Grand Trianon, Petit Trianon, Queen's Hamlet,** and **Marie-Antoinette's estate** on the northwest side before heading back to the château on the other side. Once you leave the main palace, stop at the stables just across the parking lot from the **Honour Gate** if you have any gas left in the tank. From there, the train stations are just a short walk away (the Versailles—Chateau Rive Gauche station is to the East).

## GETTING THERE

From Paris, take the RER Line C to Versailles—Châteâu Rive Gauche. There are also two slightly further train stations, Versailles—Chantiers (departing from Paris Montparnasse), and Versailles—Rive Droite (departing from Paris Saint-Lazare.) You can also take Bus RATP #171 to Versailles Place d'Armes (departing from Pont de Sèvres).

## GETTING AROUND

It's easy enough to get around the grounds on foot, but there's also a mini train going between the main palace and the Trianon Estate for €4.

## Swing by...

### PALACE OF VERSAILLES

The chateau has played an important role in the history of both the French monarchy and the rise of the Republic. Louis XVI and Marie-Antoinette were married there in 1770. A museum dedicated to the glories of France was opened there in 1837, years after the court left for Paris following the French Revolution. Today, visitors can see the rooms of Louis XIV, the State Apartments, the Gallery of Battles, and the Mesdames' Apartments. The extravagance of the gold façade and the chandeliers of the Hall of Mirrors leave no questions as to why the peasants had no qualms when it came to beheading their former rulers. There's a room called the "Abundance Salon" for god's sake. Make sure to pick up a free audio guide; you won't want to miss such an unbelievable indulgence.

## Check out...

### 🏛TRIANON ESTATE

Made up of the Grand Trianon, Petit Trianon, Queen's Hamlet, and Marie-Antoinette's estate, this area to the northwest of the palace is a can't-miss. Far less crowded and equally historic and beautiful, it served as the quarters of the visiting Peter the Great and later as the separate residence of Marie-Antoinette. It makes sense: when your husband is Louis XVI, you want as much alone time as you can get. More natural gardens and meandering paths make this area magical to explore. You go, Marie.

## Grab a bite at...

### CREPERIE LA PLACE

17 rue Colbert, 78000, Versailles, Francwwe; 01 39 49 09 52; Open M-F 10am-3pm, 7pm-11pm, Sa-Su 11am-11pm

Versailles is so huge it can swallow you up and not spit you out until hours later when you've seen 146 different gold statues and made circles around the same fountain 16 times. It can be easy to get sucked into the expensive Angelina cafés and pond-side restaurants, but, getting a meal outside of the chateau will both save you money and remind you that actual people live in this town right next to a giant palace. La Place is still within sight of the chateau, so you can sit outside with a savory or sweet crêpe and continue to imagine yourself as Marie Antoinette. Let them eat crêpes!

*i* Savory crepes €8-10, sweet crepes €6-9, salads €9-14; vegetarian options; wheelchair accessible

## Don't miss...

### THE GALLERY OF COACHES

On the ground floor of the Great Stables is an impressive display of coaches, sedans, chariots, and all other kinds of horse-drawn transportation that can be gold-plated, embellished, and generally fancified. If you need any more convincing that these royal families lived ridiculously and extravagantly, just go watch some dressage and know that the place they built for their hoses is probably nicer than any home you will own.

booths make the restaurant great for a chilly evening too.

*i* *Entrées €10-18; vegan and gluten-free options available; wheelchair accessible*

## CHEZ JANOU ($$)

2 Rue Roger Verlomme, 3e; 01 42 72 28 41; www.chezjanou.com; open M-F 10am-3pm and 7pm-midnight, Sa-Su 7am-midnight

Ever since that Disney movie you've always wanted to try ratatouille, huh? Well Chez Janou is the place to do it. We're pretty sure that their chef is a person and not a small rodent, too. Serving traditional **Provençal** cuisine, they use plenty of fresh, light ingredients like crisp tomatoes, basil, and olive oil (not to mention the 80 or so different kinds of pastis, a typical Provençal alcohol). Try the duck, rabbit, or a beautiful goat cheese salad while you sit outside on a tree-lined **Marais** street corner. You'll want to go on the early side, though (meaning before 8pm), since the excellent food tends to draw crowds of locals later in the evening.

*i* *Entrées €16-25; vegetarian options available; wheelchair accessible*

## DERRIÈRE ($$$)

69, rue des Gravilliers, 4e; 01 44 61 91 95; www.derriere-resto.com/restaurant/paris/derriere; open M-Sa noon-2:30pm and 8pm-11:30pm, Su noon-4pm and 8pm-11pm

Sometimes you just have to wrap yourself in a silk diamond-studded bathrobe, put some cucumbers over your eyes, and get a hot stone massage. But then you remember that you're still slightly in touch with reality. A dinner, or just appetizers or a drink, at Derrière is the perfect way to treat yourself, and you don't even have to have parents that own exotic pets and summer in Capri. The restaurant is located in its own little courtyard in the **Marais,** where guests sit at colorful tables or around beds upstairs. A hidden passage through a mirrored armoire in the upstairs hallway leads to an extra bar area with a foosball table. High prices may deter more thrifty travelers, but then again, you're in Paris. Treat yo self.

*i* *Appetizers €12-18, entrées €22, lunch starter and main course €25; vegan options available; wheelchair accessible*

## SOURIRE ($$)

27 Rue Galande, 5e; 01 42 01 06 43; www.sourire-restaurant.com; open Tu-Su noon-2:30pm and 7:30pm-10:30pm

The staff at Sourire, a French tapas restaurant near the trendy **Boulevard Saint-Germain,** suggests you start with two plates and see what happens. And like going on a date at an oyster restaurant, it's hard not to let one thing lead to another. You won't want to stop ordering until you've sampled all the unique and complex miniature dishes: mint risotto, Thai chicken, French cheeses, and all the other magical wonders your heart doesn't know it wants yet. Pair these plates (€8-10) with some well-crafted

cocktails and a young, hip ambiance and you'll find out why the restaurant's name means "smile."

*i* Cocktails €9, tapas €8-10; vegetarian options available; wheelchair accessible

## BOLLYNAN ($)
12 Rue des Petits Carreaux Montorgueil, 2e; 01 45 08 40 51; open M-Sa 11am-11:30pm

Bollynan has all the understated charm of a common Parisian café: small outdoor tables spilling onto a lively pedestrian street, chic people smoking cigarettes, and a relaxed atmosphere. But you won't find any crêpes or croissants here. Unlike a Parisian café, this restaurant features more flavors than "bread" and "slightly sweeter bread." It's known for its variety of savory and sweet naan, going for just €2-4, as well as its other flavorful staples of Indian cuisine. For just over €10, build a combo with your choice of curry, rice, and sides like sweet potato or lentils.

*i* Naan €2-4, other food €8-11; vegetarian options available; wheelchair accessible

## CAFÉ DES CHATS ($$)
9 Rue Sedaine, 11e; 09 73 53 35 81; www.lecafédeschats.fr; open T-Th 12pm to 10:30pm, F-Sa 12pm to 11pm, Su 12pm-10:30pm

Café des Chats is a cat-lover's dream (and a dog-lover's nightmare). We're willing to bet that you've never seen so much tacky feline-themed artwork in one place before, but the real highlight is the pack of kitties dozing in the sun, snoozing on the furniture, and well, pretty much just sleeping everywhere as you sip rich hot chocolate and sample some cheesecake. The cats are docile, friendly, and amenable to being petted and sometimes held.

*i* Hot drinks €5, lunch €10-15

## LE BRAQUE ($$)
11 Rue de Braque, 3e; 01 40 27 86 63; www.lebraqueparis.com; open M-W 7pm-2am, Th-Sa 6pm-3am

The interior of Le Braque is where *Beauty and the Beast* meets Parisian chic. Candelabras decorate the tables while cool wallpaper lines the walls and a painting on the ceiling dares guests to "trust me, love me, fuck me." The

owner, Chris, will make your meal as much of an experience as the delicious and beautifully presented food and signature cocktails. Once you're done with your meal, head downstairs to the restaurant's club, where the floor is made of sand and the DJ plays throwback tunes that will get you moving. Son of a beach, this is a great place.

*i* Salads €10-13, entrées €16-24, cocktails €11; vegetarian options available

## L'ATELIER ARTISAN CRÊPIER ($)
10 Rue Mabillon, 6e; 01 43 26 30 05; www.artisancrepier.com; open M-Th noon-2:30pm and 7pm-10:30pm, F noon-2:30pm and 7pm-11pm, Sa 7pm-11pm

At L'Atelier, the crêpe-deliciousness to crêpe-expensiveness ratio is nice and high. In the typically ritzy and pricey **sixth arrondissement,** it maintains the trendy atmosphere (wicker chairs and colorful pillows, cool posters, jazz music, spheres of grass hanging from the ceiling) of the rest of the neighborhood but ditches the high price tags. Traditional crêpes are barely more expensive than at your typical take-away stand, and you'll have the added benefit of having them served to you by a waitress with a face tattoo or a waiter with great taste in shoes.

*i* Crêpes €4-9, waffles €9-12; vegetarian options available; wheelchair accessible

## MIZNON ($)
22 Rue des Ecouffes, 4e; 01 42 74 83 58; open M-Th noon-11pm, F noon-3:30pm. Su noon-11pm

This Israeli restaurant in the heart of **Le Marais** serves the best pita sandwiches around. Heck, they even have specially-made pita sandwich holders on the tables. But forget greasy kebab—Miznon's dishes taste fresh and complex. Self-serve sauces add interesting flavor to your meal. On the side, you can snack on a whole ear of corn, a garlicky artichoke, or a giant head of charred cauliflower. Piles of raw vegetables decorate every surface (because apparently perishable interior design is now a thing). A casual vibe accentuated by 80s tunes and friendly staff members makes Miznon a perfect lunch stop.

*i* Pita sandwiches €6-15, vegetables €3-7; vegetarian and vegan options available

## PIZZERIA POPOLARE ($)

111 Rue Réaumur, 2e; 01 42 21 30 91; www.bigmammagroup.com/fr/accueil; open M-W 11:45am-2:15pm and 6:30pm-10:30pm, Th-F 11:45am-2:15pm and 7pm-11pm, Sa noon-3:15pm and 7pm-11pm, Su noon-3:15pm and 6:30pm-10:30pm

Perhaps you're sick and tired of baguettes and *duck confit*. Maybe you need a healthy dose of mozzarella in your life. Or maybe you accidentally booked your flight to Paris instead of Palermo, Italy. Whatever your motivation, Popolare will satisfy your pizza craving in the most affordable way. Traditional pizzas starting from only €4 spill over the sides of their plates, full of fresh tasting cheese and tomatoes. Inside, you'll sit alongside locals at long tables or at counters by the open kitchen. You'll recognize the restaurant from the outside by its collection of liquor bottles lining the windows and the long line out the door. Don't be deterred though: the plethora of tables means you'll be seated in no time.

*i* Pizzas €4-12; vegetarian options available; no wheelchair accessibility

## PÉNICHE MARCOUNET ($$)

Port des Célestins, au pied du Pont Marie, 4e; 06 60 47 38 52; open M-Sa 10am-1am, Su 12pm-9pm

What do a woman on roller skates walking a dog, a tourist on a Seine cruise, and a French man who shouldn't be wearing a Speedo (but nevertheless is) have in common? They can all be seen from your vantage point at Péniche Marcounet. It's the perfect people-watching position: half of the restaurant's tables are on a boat on the Seine, meaning you'll mingle with those taking advantage of the river's cooling breeze and scenic view. Higher prices reflect the prime location, but a refreshing drink before you join the ranks of Speedo-clad men yourself is well worth it.

*i* Entrées €15, cocktails €10; vegetarian options available; wheelchair accessible

# NIGHTLIFE

## 🎵FAUST

Pont Alexandre III, Rive Gauche, 7e; 01 44 18 60 60; www.faustparis.fr; open M-Th 10am-2am, F-Sa 10am-6am, Su 10am-2am

You know it's been a fun night out when the only time you stopped dancing was when you tripped on a pineapple. At this large and populated late-night club under the bridge **Pont Alexandre III,** moving with the masses is a must. You'll return home from Faust with a sweaty shirt, a ketchup stain from the hot dog stand inside, and a revised definition of "bedtime." You'll also hold onto the memories of the mesmerizing light displays, the hypnotizing techno DJs, and the energetic crowd with as much strength as the cigarette smoke from the crowded outdoor smoking area will cling to your clothes.

*i* Cover €20, cocktails €12, shots €5

## 🎵CANDELARIA

52 Rue de Saintonge, 3e; 01 42 74 41 28; open daily 6pm-2am

Upon first glance, Candelaria has the same basic features as any tiny taco place: greasy meat, fluorescent lights, people sweating from hot sauce. But go beyond the store's front through an unmarked white door, and there you'll find a bumping bar full of Paris's "bobos" (read: hipsters). The music is electric, played by a DJ standing in a tiny corner with an impressive mustache and the walls are decorated with unidentifiable animal wool. Once you get to the bar though, since it's a while to get to the bar, a tasty Summer Wish will be well worth it. So, while you're welcome to scarf down a beef tongue taco on your way in, let's just say there's more than meats the eye.

*i* Cocktails €10-12, tacos €3.80

## 🎵LITTLE RED DOOR

60 Rue Charlot, 3e; 01 42 71 19 32; www.lrdparis.com; open M-W 6pm-2am, Th-Sa 6pm-3am, Su 6pm-2am

Beer? Never heard of it. Wine? Nope. Vodka Red Bull? Well yeah, but that's beside the point. At Little Red Door, nothing else flies. You must have one of their 11 extremely unique cocktails.

Each one was developed and then blind-tasted by a different artist, who created a visual representation of its flavor. Guests then pick whichever picture speaks to them the most. If you're not especially adventurous, you can check the description of the ingredients, but that doesn't exactly clear things up when the ingredients are things like fermented banana, panama wood, and green coffee. Its location can be difficult to find at first since it's unmarked, but just look for the little red door, Sherlock.

*i Drinks €13-15*

## AUX FOLIES

8 Rue de Belleville, 20e; 06 28 55 89 40; www.aux-folies-belleville.fr; open daily 7am-2am

Quick service is not only important in table tennis. At Aux Folies, you'll have a beer on the table before you can say, "Oh yeah, I forgot that was an Olympic sport." Cheap drinks are whisked to and from tables, which are full of chatting Parisians smoking cigarettes and having a rendezvous with friends. Open from early in the morning to late at night, it's a true neighborhood installment that's always packed with the local crowd. It's also a great place to try *pastis* for only €3. It's a traditional anise-flavored Provençal drink, served with water to dilute its powerful licorice taste.

*i Beer €4, pastis €3*

## BACARDI MOJITO LAB

28 Rue Keller, 11e; 01 75 77 23 95; www. mojitolab.com; open Tu-Th 6pm-2am, F-Sa 6pm-3am

At Bacardi Mojito Lab, get the alcoholic equivalent of dinner and a show. First, you'll pick one of the multitude of creative mojito variations on their photo-illustrated menu. These include twists like the smoky mojito, which looks like a middle school science experiment, the spicy mojito, and the *Star Wars* mojito, whatever that means. Then you'll be able to watch the servers create fizzy rum spectacles in front of your eyes; the trio requires the simultaneous pouring of three separate flavors from a series of stacked glasses, and the mojito aux effluves entails a tube plopping bubbles of smoke onto the top of the drink and creating a giant bubble dome.

*i Mojitos €10-15; no wheelchair accessibility*

## BESPOKE

3 Rue Oberkampf, 11e; 01 58 30 88 59; open Tu-Su noon-2am

Even though spiky cacti greet you through the window, Bespoke could not be warmer or more inviting. Small tables line candlelit walls and a collage of rich brown leather belts sets the mood. Not in a *Fifty Shades* way, more in a romantic and rustic way that makes you wish your family owned a saddle-making business. A cocktail menu full of unique infusions and ingredients beckons, and weekly specials mean you can visit again and again. Even better, though, is to tell the expert bartenders what you like; they're

more than happy to craft a custom-made drink.

*i* *Cocktails €8-14*

## DIRTY DICK

10 Rue Frochot, 9e; 01 48 78 74 58; open daily 6pm-2am

Formerly... umm... "hostess bar," this laid back lounge in Pigalle gives a nod to its former use in its name. These days, though, the bartenders wear Hawaiian shirts, tiki torches decorate the perimeter, and a large mural of a bikini-clad woman in the sunset dominates one wall. The drinks, however, are hands down the highlight. Like a contestant on Hell's Kitchen, Dirty Dick understands the importance of presentation. You can order a conch shell decorated with flaming limes and sugary sprigs of mint, but the bar is renowned for their volcanoes. The bartender lights flames all along it with his own finger before pouring in the delicious frozen "magma."

*i* *Volcanoes and shells €45-50 (for four people), other cocktails €10-12; no wheel-chair accessibility*

## LA FOURMI

74 Rue des Martyrs, 18e; 01 42 64 70 35; M-Th 8am-2am, F-Sa 8am-4am, Su 9am-2am

It's difficult to sit down in **Pigalle** without making yourself susceptible to a lap dance. La Fourmi is a safe haven for those located in the neighborhood who would rather chat with friends over some affordable beers than yell to each other over Nelly's "Hot in Here." Don't fear if you skipped dinner; La Fourmi serves food even past midnight, so you'll be able to snack on fries or a burger while you play foosball or hang at the bar. Just consider that those down the street are probably trying to figure out how this whole dollar-bill-in-the-underwear thing works with €1 coins.

*i* *Beers €3-12*

## LES BLOUSES BLANCHES

186 Rue du Faubourg Saint-Antoine, 12e; 01 43 73 70 58; open M-Sa 7am-2am, Su 7am-midnight

Grabbing drinks at this café-turned-hangout-spot feels like going over to your friend's basement where everyone would hang out in high school. You know, the friend that was popular and had arcade games and chill parents. With a very loose (and cheap) definition of "happy hour" and a great taste in music, Les Blouses Blanches attracts all the neighborhood cool kids with its €5 cocktails like the Zombie, Nurse, and Firefighter, and its abundance of comfortable leather couches. All you need to complete the vibe is a rousing game of Spin the Bottle.

*i* *Cocktails €5 at happy hour; wheelchair accessible*

## MOONSHINER

5 Rue Sedaine, 11e; 09 50 73 12 99; open daily 6pm-2am

Just this bar's name conjures up images of moonlit nights spent in secluded locations, where alcohol and adrenaline flow freely with the thrill of secrecy. The bar itself surpasses these expectations. An unassuming red-painted pizza restaurant called Da Vito marks its entrance. You'll have to weave through a sea of families splitting pepperoni pies and couples debating adding olives to push through a refrigerator door and come out on the other side in a dimly lit, jazz-playing, gin-serving cocktail lounge. It's probably the first time "crossing the Red Sea" could apply to marinara sauce. Although you'll physically remain in the 11th arrondissement, you'll suddenly feel transported to prohibition-era Hollywood.

*i* *Cocktails €10-1; wheelchair accessible*

## RAIDD BAR

23 Rue du Temple, 4e; 01 53 01 00 00; open M-Th 6pm-4am, F-Sa 6pm-5am, Su 6pm-4am

The high-energy crowd at RAIDD always comes out in full force, pun only slightly intended. You'll constantly be bumping up against the almost entirely male clientele, but only because everyone is dancing, chatting, and engaging with people around them. That is, until the shower show begins and all eyes turn. Yes, that's exactly what it sounds like. The drinks are a little pricey, but what can you expect when they have to constantly replenish their supply of body wash? Go, dance, drink, have fun, and then go home and take a shower; you'll be inspired.

*i* Shots €5, cocktails €10; limited wheelchair accessibility

### YELLOW MAD MONKEY
8 Rue de Lappe, 11e; 01 43 38 30 20; open M-Th 5pm-2am, F-Sa 5pm-5am, Su 5pm-2am

Located on a bar-lined street, Yellow Mad Monkey is the star of the show that is the **Bastille** area. It tends to stay open later than its neighbors and cultivates a rowdy dancing atmosphere with top hits. The decor is fun and unique: a large artificial tree is the bar's centerpiece, and the branches extend across the ceiling over chalk writing while assorted bras hang from a birdcage in the center, like a chandelier at Lady Gaga's house. The drinks are somewhat pricey for how strong they are, but there are plenty of other bars in the area where you can kick off your night.

*i* Drinks €5-10

# TOULOUSE

Coverage by **Julia Bunte-Mein**

Toulouse, France's fourth largest city, is one of the most beautiful, historic, vibrant, and underrated cities in France. It is known as "La Ville Rose" (the Pink City) for its ochre rooftops, blushing brick basilicas, and rose-tinted storefronts. Like a glowing pink jellyfish, its historic center is very dense, pulsing with life and light, but its tendrils stretch far and wide into a sprawling metropolis of residential areas. On every corner, you'll pass an exquisite southern French restaurant, ethnic food stand, *bar à vin*, or overflowing jazz, techno, or rock club. Home to one of the largest universities in France, Toulouse is a vibrant, animated, and extremely young city. Le Place Saint-George explodes with students at late-night clubs on the weekends. While Toulouse surely knows how to have fun, it has a tranquil ambiance and likes to get its beauty sleep on weekdays. That means from lundi to jeudi, you'll find more pleasure in enjoying many a morning croissant in the coral-colored Capitole square, indulging in lazy afternoons in green spaces, or having a glass of wine while watching the sun set over the illuminated Pont Neuf on the Garonne. The welcoming and friendly residents of Toulouse walk through life wearing rose-colored glasses, drinking rosé, and enjoying life's pleasures. Here, you too can live life in pink.

## ORIENTATION

**Le Vieux Quartier** (Old Quarter) is situated between the mighty **Canal du Midi** and bend in **Garonne River.** The entire Vieux Quartier is bound by an octagonal ring of streets, with **Boulevard de Strasbourg** at the top and flanked by **Saint-Michel** and **Catalans** on either side. In the middle, the **Pont Neuf** and **Le Pont St. Pierre,** form the main entrances to the heart of the city. The **Gare de Matabiau,** Toulouse's main train station, is just across the Canal du Midi and a 15-minute walk to the entrance of the old city. The majestic **Place de Capitole** and **Charles de Gaulle Square** mark the center of Toulouse, from which narrow cobblestone streets extend. Almost all of the major sights are within 10-minutes walking distance from here. **Rue de Saint-Rome** and **Rue d'Alsace-Lorraine** are on the right, lined with commercial streets. Restaurants and café are scattered throughout, but **Rue Leon Gambetta** leading to **Rue Reyrolières** is the area. **Place Wilson, Place Saint-Georges,** and **Place de la Trinité** are best for nightlife.

## ESSENTIALS
### GETTING THERE

Domestic and international flights arrive at Blagnac Airport, 11km west of Toulouse. To get to the city from the airport, you can take the airport shuttle bus to the Gare Matabiau (one way €8, round-trip €15). The main bus or train station or the Jean Jaures or Jeanne

209

d'Arc metro stations in the city center. Within 90min., you can use the same ticket for transfers on city buses and metros. Purchase tickets at the desk in the airport or on the bus. Alternatively, you can take the tramline T2 and then change to Metro red line A at Arenes station (€1.60 single ticket). This takes approximately 40min. Buy a ticket at the machine or in the airport ticket office. A taxi will cost about €20-25. Both SNCF, the regional intercity train in France, and TGV trains go to Gare Matabiau. Ouibus and Megabus are popular options for bus travel.

## GETTING AROUND

Toulouse is a large city, but the historic downtown center is quite small and best visited on foot. We also recommend renting a bike from any one of the 253 Velo Toulouse bike stations. For only €1.20, you get 24hr of bike-riding, the only catch is that if you don't return the bike to a station within 30min., you will be charge a small fee. A €150 hold is taken on credit cards, but it is only charged if the bike is not returned. The metro is small with only two lines going east to west and north to south. It operates from 5am-midnight during the week and until 3am on Friday and Saturday nights.

## PRACTICAL INFORMATION

**Tourist Offices:** Donjon du Capitole, Square Charles; 0 892 18 01 80; open M 10am-7pm; T-Sa 9am-7pm, Su 10am-6pm.

**Banks/ATMs/Currency Exchange:** BNP Paribas Centre (59 Rue d'Alsace Lorraine; 0 820 82 00 01; open M-W 8:45am-12:15pm and 1:45pm-5:30pm, Th 9:30am-12:15pm and 1:45pm-5:30pm, F 8:45am-12:15pm and 1:45pm-5:30pm).

**Post Offices:** La Poste Toulouse Capitole (9 Rue Lafayette; 0 810 82 18 21; open M-F 8:30am-6:3pm, Su 9am-12:30pm).

**Internet:** Cyber Copie (5 Pl. Peyrou; 05 61 21 48 80; open M-F 8:30am-7pm, Su 10am-7pm).

**BGLTQ+ Resources:** Arc en Ciel Toulouse (l'Espace des Diversités, 38 Rue d'Aubuisson, 05 81 91 79 60; www.acetoulouse.fr).

## EMERGENCY INFORMATION

**Emergency Number:** 112

**Police:** Central Police Station (23 Bd. de l'Embouchure; 05 61 12 77 77).

**US Embassy:** Consulat des Etats-Unis d'Amérique (25 Allée Jean Jaurès; 05 34 41 36 50; www.fr.usembassy.gov/fr/ambassades-et-consulats/toulouse-fr; open M-Th 7:30am-5pm, F 7:30am-12:30pm). Visit by appointment only, does not issue Visas

**Rape Crisis Center:** Rape Crisis Network Europe (www.inavem.org; 01 45 88 19 00).

**Hospitals:** Centre hospitalier universitaire de Toulouse (170 Av. de Casselardit; 05 61 77 22 33; www.chu-toulouse.fr; open daily 24hr).

**Pharmacies:** Pharmacie de Nuit (76 Allée Jean Jaurès; open daily 8pm-8am. 00 33 5 61 62 38 05).

# ACCOMMODATIONS

### 🔖LA PETITE AUBERGE SAINT SERNIN ($$)

17 Rue d'Embarthe; 07 60 88 17 17; www.lapetiteaubergedesaintsernin.com; reception open 10am-12:30pm and 2:30pm-7pm

This hostel may not seem like much when you arrive with its metal gate, small terrace with garden tools and empty paint cans, and packed dorm rooms with white tile floors. But, unless a new five-star hostel opened up since this was published, it is your best hostel option in Toulouse. Each dorm has its own kitchenette, including a stove, fridge, and microwave, but it's quite cramped, so we advise not venturing past microwaveable couscous. The rooms are cleaned daily, but pack your shower shoes since there's grime in the corners of the rooms.

*i* Dorms €22; reservation recommended; locks provided; kitchen; wheelchair accessible

### THE FRIENDLY AUBERGE ($$)

32 Rue Gilet; 05 61 42 24 92; www.friendsauberge.com/hotel; reception open 24hr

This boutique hostel in the recently-renovated Parc Hotel pushes the limits of what you'd consider a hostel. Located in a beautiful white house outfitted with a lush green garden and wood-planked kitchen, The Friendly Auberge provides a homey and luxurious atmosphere that couldn't be more welcoming. It even has an attached bar and restaurant that serves traditional southwestern French cuisine. The only downside: it's really far from the city center. The facilities are pristine, though, so we consider the 20-30min. ride via public transport to and from Toulouse's center a small price to pay. You'll come home to a communal dinner (€14) and comfortable bed waiting for you.

*i* *Dorms €18-25, triple €25, double €50; Wi-Fi; linens included; towel included; laundry facilities; shared dinner for €14*

# SIGHTS
## CULTURE

### ⚑BASILIQUE SAINT-SERNIN DE TOULOUSE
Pl. Saint-Sernin; 05 61 21 80 45; www.basilique-saint-sernin.fr; crypt open daily 10am-6pm; Su 11:30am-6pm
This fifth-century church and now **UNESCO World Heritage site** was built in memory of the martyr, Saint Saturnin, the first bishop of Toulouse, who died by being dragged through the streets by a sacrificial bull. This church is one of the main stopping points on the **Pilgrimage of Saint-Jacques de Compostelle.** This is a super warm cathedral with cream-colored stone and dusty red brick Romanesque arches. Restored in the ninteenth century by **Eugène Viollet-le-Duc,** the church's central nave is crowned by a mid-eighteenth-century Baroque dome of a beautiful night sky with gold-leafed stars.

*i* *Free; crypt admission €2.50, €2 student*

### COUVENT DES JACONBINS TOULOUSE
Rue Lakanal; 05 61 22 23 82; www.jacobins.toulouse.fr; open daily 10am-6pm
Visiting the Convent of Jacobins is like eating at a restaurant and expecting just one course, but ending with an eight-course meal. You'll enter the majestic church with geometric stained-glass windows of brilliant oranges and fiery reds that project onto the stone floor. To the right is *le palmier,* a soaring

92-foot tall column, which holds up the apse and branches out with beautiful red and green brickwork. In the center are the relics of **St. Thomas Aquinas.** Next, visit the cloister, where you can hang in the tranquil interior courtyard. To finish off, head into the large chapterhouse room where monks used to meet, the adjacent **Chappelle Saint Antonin,** and the large refractory where contemporary art exhibits take place.

*i* *Free admission to church, cloister admission €4, €2 large groups, free student; wheelchair accessible*

## LANDMARKS

### LA CAPITOLE DE TOULOUSE AND THE HENRI IV COURT
Capitole de Toulouse; 05 61 22 21 43; Capitole building open daily 8:30am-6pm
Le Place Capitole is the pulsing heart of the city. While the square is a sight in itself, there are a bunch of interesting things to check out here at various times of the day. During the day, it is filled with street performers and covered markets, but, at night, it comes alive with terrace restaurants facing the illuminated pink façade of the magnificent Capitole building. Blue and gold windows behind wrought iron balustrades, and eight pink marble columns, symbolizing the eight members of the municipal council. The sprawling brick Capitole building, the Buckingham Palace of Toulouse, is home to the city's **Town Hall,** inner courtyard, **Théâtre de Toulouse,** and the **Court of Henri IV,** but this last area is by far the best part. Inside, take *le grande escalier* to sumptuously decorated rooms and prepare yourself for some of the most beautiful frescos and murals you've ever seen.

*i* *Free; wheelchair accessible*

### PLACE DAURADE AND LE GARONNE
1 Bd. de la Croisette; 04 92 99 84 00
Just left of **Le Pont Neuf,** Place Daurade, the previously twelfth-century fortified Pont Daurade, is an absolute must-visit when in Toulouse. The square and boardwalk accompanying it are right next to the **Garonne River,** from which you will

**The Classics:**

*Croissant* — It's hard to go wrong with this flaky, buttery, crescent-shaped pastry. They're everywhere, usually cost about €1, and come in many varieties. Look for a croissant au beure for an extra gluttonous treat, or its cousins, pain au chocolat (chocolate stuffed croissant) and croissant amande (filled with almond paste and toped with sliced almonds and powdered sugar). Ever wonder why they're crescent shaped? Following the Muslim defeat in the Battle of Tours in 732, French bakers created the pastry to represent the Islamic crescent.

*Éclaire* — This oblong pâte à choux (a pastry with a flaky, doughy base) is customarily filled with coffee, vanilla, or chocolate-flavored cream. Occasionally, you'll encounter varietals filled with run, almond, or chestnut-flavored custard.

*Macarons* — These delicate sandwich-like pastries consist of two soft cookies glued together by a thin layer of icing. Made well, they are slightly crunchy on the outside, chewy on the inside, and come in dozens delectable flavors and colors.

*Profiterole* — These are basically cream puffs (read: short, squatty éclairs). The bold pastry is baked in the shape of a hollow ball, filled with custard cream, and iced with caramel or chocolate sauce.

*Mille-Feuille* — A decadent, striped puff pastry alternating between sweet-flavored cream and flaky sheets of dough, topped with iced sugar or fondant in swirling black and white patterns.

**The Specialties:**

*Canelé* — This small, ridged, cylindrical pastry is a specialty of Bordeaux. It has a thick, caramelized crust surrounding a tender and spongey center. The traditional Canelé d'Or is flavored with rum and vanilla, but you can often find pure vanilla and chocolate varietals.

*Gateaux Basque* — A crumbly, flour-based pastry with dense almond-flavored filling, topped with a cherry or raspberry garnish. These almond-based cakes dominate nearly every pastry shop in Basque country.

*Paris-Brest* — Essentially a doughnut, chopped in half lengthwise, filled with ornate swirls of praline cream, and topped with powdered sugar and sliced almonds.

*Gâteaux Opéra* — Consisting of an almond sponge cake soaked in coffee syrup and smothered in chocolate ganache, layered with coffee buttercream, and drizzled with chocolate glaze, this brick of rich chocolate and coffee is the ultimate gourmandize treat.

*Rum Baba* — A savarin cake soaked in rum syrup, topped with vanilla cream.

*Frasier* — A delightful strawberry cake infused with cream and covered with a thin layer of almond paste.

*Tarte Tatin* — This upside-down pastry was actually created by accident in the 1880s at the Hotel Tatin outside of Paris. Basically an apple pie gone wrong, the mistake is now a signature dish found at restaurants and pâtisseries throughout France.

have the best view of the sunset in all of Toulouse. Bring a bottle of wine, a picnic blanket, and food to settle down for the night. Starting in the early evening, young couples and friends flock to the banks to set up camp for sunset, so be sure to arrive a little early to snag a good spot. Watch as the towering **Dôme de la Grave** and giant Ferris wheel across the river become black silhouettes against a lilac sky and the water turn from dark indigo to shimmering gold.

*i* Free; in the summer months, lights turn on at 9:45pm

# MUSEUMS

### ◪LES ABBATOIRS
76 Allées Charles de Fitt; 05 34 51 10 60; www.lesabattoirs.org; W noon-6pm, Th noon-8pm, Su noon-6pm

Prepare yourself for possibly the strangest sensory experience of your life. Opened in 2000, Les Abattoirs has earned the renowned title of "Musée de France" and if being trippy earns you titles like that, we're truly astounded. Enter through the arched brick main gallery into what used to be a slaughterhouse into the museum, which consists of three floors of over 34000 pieces from the twentieth and twenty-first centuries. Check out the internal monologues of a paralyzed turtle and Barack Obama reconstructed as an automaton; in short, art you won't be able to begin to understand in one visit.

*i* Admission €7, €4 student, €2 Th night "nocturne" visit; last entry 30min. before closing; guided tours included with entry ticket W 2:30pm-4pm, Sa 3pm-4:30pm, first Su of the month 12:30pm-2pm; wheelchair accessible

### MUSÉE DES AUGUSTINS DE TOULOUSE (MUSÉE DE BEAUX-ARTS DE TOULOUSE)
21 Rue de Metz; 05 61 22 21 82; open M 10am-6pm, W 10am-9pm, Th-Su 10am-6pm

Housed in the former convent of the Augustins of Toulouse, le Musée des Augustins is a prime example of what we like to call artception: amazing works of art inside an amazing work of art. This fourteenth-century convent includes Romanesque sculpture galleries, a voluminous church, a cloister, and an interior courtyard. This museum boasts over 4000 works and is considered to have the richest collection of Romanesque sculpture in the world. Highlights include the gallery of Romanesque capitals suspended between blue and red striped pillars and brightly colored lamps (yes, you should

take a panorama), the thirteenth century howling gargoyles next to the courtyard, and the majestic red brick Darcy Staircase.

*i* Admission €5, €3 reduced; guided tours €3; Wednesday evening visit includes a free organ concert in the church included with entry ticket; wheelchair accessible

# OUTDOORS

### JARDIN ROYAL AND JARDIN DES PLANTES
Jardin Royal: Rue Ozenne; 05 62 27 48 48; open daily 7:45am-7pm; Jardin des Plantes: 31 Allée Jules Guesde; 05 62 27 48 48; www.jardindesplantes.net; open daily 7:45am-9pm

In the northwest corner of Toulouse's **Vieux Quartier,** just below **Canal du Midi,** are Toulouse's expansive green spaces, including the Jardin Royal and the Jarden des Plantes. The former is small and quaint, featuring a duck house, mossy bridge with a underpass, and a statue of St. Exupery holding the Little Prince. Although there's not a ton to see, you should stop here on your way to the impressive Jardin des Plantes. The latter garden features an arched bridge, large roundabout with a fountain, the **Natural History Museum,** and the **Henri Gaussent Greenhouse** in the botanical gardens. Merry go-rounds, bumper car rides, little ice cream stands, and a swing set can be found in the public park, where you can have a picnic near the duck pond and gazebo.

*i* Free entry, Grande Serres (Greenhouse) €7, €5 student; wheelchair accessible

# FOOD

### ◪LE FAIM DES HARICOTS ($$)
3 Rue du Puits Vert; 05 61 22 49 25; Open daily noon-2:30pm; 7pm-10:30pm

*Cassoulet, foie gras,* Toulouse sausage, beef tartare: all delicious, signature dishes of southern France. But, if you need a break from the typical, head to Le Faim des Haricots, an all-you-can-eat vegetarian buffet where you can get your entire trip's worth of veggies. You won't find a better deal anywhere else when you can take advantage of enormous salads, delectable pasta, and a grain bar. Check out the wide selection of quiches and savory tarts, soups, and a full dessert display. It's easy to spend a few hours in this warm and inviting restaurant—enough time so you can get hungry enough for round two. But, if you're not into the all-you-can-eat aesthetic, you can also take a box to go for just €1.25 per kilo, choosing from all the buffet options.

*i* One buffet €11, two buffets €12, three buffets €13, to-go box €1.25 per kilo

### AU POUSSIN BLEU ($)

45 Rue du Languedoc; 05 61 52 01 70; open M 10am-1:30pm and 3pm-7pm, Tu-Sa 8am-7pm, Su 8am-12:30pm

Whether you pass the dark blue awning by chance or you came to Toulouse specifically for this one pastry shop, once you see its storefront filled with a forest of macaroon trees, you won't be able to resist succumbing to this sugary temptation. Nor should you because this is the best *patisserie* in Toulouse. Known throughout the city as the cake, pastry, and chocolate experts, all of their homemade desserts and melt-in-your-mouth macaroons live up to their reputation. The hardest part of coming here is decided whether to try the fruit tarts, chocolate pastries, pralines, or buttery frangipane tarts. Better yet, don't choose. Just buy all of them! Embrace obesity. Just kidding—whatever you choose will be a treat and even Michelle Obama will be forgive you for racking up those calories.

*i* Pastries €1.80, cakes €3-5

### LE PETITE OGRE ($$)

1 Rue des Pénitents Gris; 06 95 33 33 18; www.restaurant-petit-ogre.com; open M-Th noon-11pm, F-Sa noon-midnight, Su noon-11pm

Like Shrek's moss-covered house, Le Petite Ogre can't fit more than a dozen people, has tree trunks stuck inside it, and is full of green (foods). This hippie eatery boasts all natural, local, and in-season produce bought fresh from the market each morning. For only €10 at lunch or €15 at dinner, you'll get nicely-sized portions of meat and vegetarian dishes served with warm grains and fresh salads. For a drink, try their artisan lemonade, *délicieuse* fresh juices, or regional wines and local beers. With only one chef and one waitress, the food and service have a clear, personal touch. Dine at one of the three little tables by the wooden bar or on the floor at one of the low tables in the upstairs "Moroccan living room."

*i* Lunch €10, dinner €15; vegetarian, vegan, and gluten-free options available

## NIGHTLIFE

### ☒LA CALE SÈCHE

41 Rue Léon Gambetta; open M-F 6:45pm-2am, Sa 6:45pm-3am

This all-rum bar is a great stop for all young travelers in Toulouse. It's the exact opposite of a terrace bar, as it looks and feels like a shoebox, containing all its noise and rambunctiousness in tinted-glass walls. From outside, you can just make out the outline of many dark forms and muffled noise. But, once you open the door, it'll hit you: rock music, skull and bones cross flags, and young people yelling *tchin tchin* as they clink their shot glasses together. Walk through a hollowed-out beer barrel into the dark, wooden bar and take your pick of one of their signature fruity, sweet, or spicy rums. Our favorites? Caramel, papaya, or litchi. You can also just point randomly and see what the bartender decides might fit your fancy.

*i* Rum shots €2.50, cocktails €5, beer €3; card minimum €10

### LE PETITE VOISIN

37 Rue Peyrolières; 05 61 22 65 22; open M-F 7:30am-2am, Sa 9:30am-3am

This student bar in the heart of **Vieux Quartier** is renowned for having over 50 different types of shooters, which are beefed-up mixed drinks taken as a shot. Start the night with a classic Kamikaze (vodka, Triple Sec, and lime juice), pay homage to Europe's transportation system with the **TGV** (tequila, gin, vodka), and then venture into signature recipes as the night gets wilder. We recommend the **Tsunami** (tequila, grapefruit juice, vodka, red hot chili pepper), but remember to check the blackboard for the cocktail of the night and shooter deals (6 shooters for €15!). The young tank-top clad bartenders dance along to the bumping beats as crowds play foosball and dance on the outdoor terrace.

*i* Shooters €3, cocktails €6, tapas, sandwiches, and charcuterie boards €5-10

### THE GEORGE AND DRAGON

1 Pl. du Peyrou; 05 61 23 16 22; open daily 5pm-1:30am

This lively, classic Irish pub, which is almost too classic (read: rugby on the telly, bartenders wearing vintage tweed hats, quiz nights, and "chips" with artisan IPA craft beers and draft ciders), is a hit for young English-speaking travelers. Their flipbook beer menu features banana bread beer, special London ale, and something called a "double chocolate stout." Although the drinks are a bit pricey, the bottles are twice the size of a regular beer so it's worth it. So make your way on over here, order a pint, and play beer pong at the table inside the bar. You know you miss it.

*i* Beer €4-5, cocktails €6, wine €3-4

# FRANCE ESSENTIALS

## VISAS

France is part of the European Union, so US citizens can stay in the country for up to 90 days without a visa.

## MONEY

France uses the euro and is a part of the "freedom of movement" zone of the European Union.

**Tipping:** By law, a service charge, known as "service compris," is added to bills in bars and restaurants. Most people do leave some change in addition to this (up to €2) for sit-down service and, in more upscale restaurants, it is not uncommon to tip 5% of the bill. For other services, such as taxis, a 10% tip is acceptable.

**Taxes:** The quoted price of goods in France includes value-added tax (VAT). This tax on goods is generally levied at 19.6% in France, although some goods are subject to lower rates. Non-EU visitors who are taking these goods home unused may be refunded this tax for purchases totaling over €175 per store. When making purchases, request a VAT form and present it at a Tax-Free Shopping Office, found at most airports, road borders, and ferry stations, or by mail. Refunds must be claimed within six months.

## SAFETY AND HEALTH

**Drugs and Alcohol**: There is no drinking age in France, but restaurants will not serve anyone under the age of 16. To purchase alcohol, you must be at least 18. Though there are no laws prohibiting open containers, drinking on the street is frowned upon. The legal blood-alcohol level for driving in France is 0.05%, which is less than that of the US, UK, and Australia. Possession of illegal drugs (including marijuana) in France could result in a substantial jail sentence or fine.

**Terrorism**: France has been subject to terrorist attacks in recent years, including the 2015 shootings at Charlie Hebdo and 2017 attack in Notre Dame. Our Researcher-Writer, Emily, was in Paris during the latter attack. Exercise caution when walking in large crowds and be vigilant of your surroundings.

# GERMANY

**Germany was once your high school's star quarterback, if your high school had a quarterback that was also the nexus of the Prussian Empire.** You see, this was back in the mid-to-late 19th century, when things were going great for the young hotshot—it became a global power and produced some incredibly important art and thinkers. But then, Germany went to college, and things got out of control. World War I was the gateway, then it started moving onto the harder stuff: World War II. Soon enough, Germany hit rock bottom. Goodbye World Cup career. Hello Cold War. Nowadays, Germany's back on its feet, and it's arguably doing better than ever. (Seriously, have you seen its economy? So robust.) Nonetheless, it's undoubtedly seen some stuff, and it's all the tougher—and stranger—because of it. While you'll see reminders from all periods of its history wherever you go, Germany is determined not to let its more recent and painful past define what it is today. Instead, the nation looks hopefully towards the future, paving a new path for other countries to trod down. The remnants of the Cold War also inject a punk attitude into Germany's metropolises. Berlin, Munich, Hamburg, and Frankfurt are young, vibrant, and multicultural cities, each with its own individual and artistic flair. Berlin, in particular, boasts an almost "poor but sexy" chic and practically frigid coolness. Some, however, might argue that the young and grungy Leipzig isn't too far behind. Locals are generally pretty helpful, and most have a working knowledge of English, making it easy to find someone who can recommend the best local beer and someone else who will immediately disagree.

217

# BERLIN

Coverage by **Nicholas Grundlingh**

Nearly everyone says that Berlin's the coolest city on the planet, but honestly we just don't see it. Sure, if you like history, Berlin can be cool, what with its Prussian palaces, World War II museums, and defining landmarks of the Cold War. But besides having been the center of not just European, but world history for the last 200-odd years, the city really doesn't have much going for it. Yeah, okay. Maybe it has one or two or twenty clubs that run non-stop from Friday at midnight to Monday at noon. But who would want to go to them? They're all old industrial plants and abandoned buildings overrun by the best DJs in the world. Thanks, but no thanks. And don't even get us started on the food. Every neighborhood is just a complete and utter wasteland full of cheap, delicious, and diverse dining options. In other words, prepare to starve. What about the city's celebration of liberalism and multiculturalism, you ask? Well, what about it? Berlin's multicultural and liberal identity is just one of the many countless features that make it a place unlike anywhere else in the world, in the sense that no other city is this bland and forgettable. Look, if you don't have anything better to do, it's worth a visit.

## ORIENTATION

Berlin, situated in the northeastern region of Germany, is a city full of cities, like a Russian nesting doll or a giant Transformer composed of many smaller Transformers. No single neighborhood is alike, and you could easily spend at least a week discovering the quirks and charms of each. As a general rule of thumb, the east side of the city, separated from the west by the **Spree River,** is younger, artsier, and has more of a gritty, industrial feel. This is where you'll find the best clubs, vintage stores, and cheap-eats. But if you're more interested in Berlin's famous landmarks, historical towns, or monstrously large **Tiergarten park,** the slightly more upmarket and touristy west is the place to be. However, in the likely situation that you're equally interested in gritty industrialism and large parks, and thus unable to decide which side sounds more appealing, head over to **Mitte,** the city center, which is split into two distinct districts. While a map of the public transport system may look like a pair of earphones that's been left in your pants pocket for 20 years, if you're equipped with Google Maps or a natural maze-solving ability, you'll be able to get wherever you want within a half hour.

## ESSENTIALS
### GETTING THERE

While the Capital Airport Berlin Brandenburg International (BBI), to be opened in 2019, undergoes construction, Tegel Airport will serve most international travelers. Schönefeld Airport is a smaller, second international airport serving mostly budget airlines. International trains pass through Berlin's Hauptbahnhof and run to nearby countries. Prices vary, depending on how far in advance tickets are booked, but typically range from €39 (advance) to €130-200 (standard). ZOB is the central bus station that links to all big cities in Germany and many regions in Europe.

## GETTING AROUND

The two pillars of Berlin's metro are the U-Bahn, the underground trains, and the S-Bahn, the above-ground trains. Trams and buses (U-Bahn) scuttle many of the city's corners. The U-Bahn runs from 4am-1am and the S-Bahn from 4:30am-1:30am. These lines run with 30min. intervals on Friday and Saturday night. When the train stops running, night buses take over, indicated by the "N" preceding the bus number. Berlin is divided into three transit zones. Zone A is central Berlin and the rest of Berlin is Zone B. Zone C covers the larger state of Brandenburg, including Potsdam. An AB ticket is the best deal, but a one-way ticket is good for 2hr. after validation (Zones AB €2.80, BC €3.10,

**1. Charlottenburg** — The kind of place where you're likely to find Billy Joel's eponymous "Uptown Girl," Charlottenburg is where the hipsters of Friedrichschain and Kreuzberg migrate once they give up their dreams of graphic design and become successful lawyers, bankers, or owners of expensive cafés. But what it lacks in youth and gritty charm, Charlottenburg makes up for in affluence and suavity. After all, the neighborhood was originally built around Friedrich I's palace in the west. Nowadays, however, you're more likely to find the rich and glamorous further east, prowling the streets of Kurfürstendamm, Berlin's Fifth Ave. equivalent.

**2. Schöneberg and Wilmersdorf** — Schöneberg and Wilmersdorf epitomize Berlin's lively yet laidback spirit. Situated between Charlottenburg and Tempelhof, and separated from Kreuzberg by the Landwehrkanal, the area is heavy on green spaces. A train to Nollendorf Pl. will find you at the meeting point of the two neighborhoods, as well as the heart of Berlin's BGLTQ+ scene. However, you might choose to ignore the cafés and nightlife altogether and just lounge the day away at Viktoria Park, or if you just want to get away from it all, the more out-of-the-way and consequently more serene Grunewald Forest.

**3. Mitte** — While most neighborhoods in the city require at most a day to explore, Mitte could easily take a week. Found at the base of the Tiergarten, the Pariser Platz area boasts the Reichstag, Brandenburg Gate, Jewish Memorial (among other Holocaust memorials), and the Victory Column. Not to be outdone, the six museums that comprise Museum Island—a 10-minute walk east—house incredible collections of ancient relics that'll put any nursing home to shame. While you'll find all these sights south of the Spree, the north is where you'll spend most of your time eating, unless the idea of bland and overpriced food excites you. Check out Prenzlauer Berg, which forms Mitte's northern border, for the Berlin Wall Memorial.

**4. Friedrichschain** — Berlin's answer to Outkast's perennial question "What's cooler than being cool?", Friedrichschain is the grungy and graffiti-strewn haunt of the city's artists, hipsters, and punks. Following the collapse of the wall, West Berliners flooded into this formerly Soviet-occupied region, turning every abandoned building into a café, bar, or nightclub and every café, bar, or nightclub into one of the city's trendiest destinations. Walking along the main street, Warschauer Str., you'll pass the East Side Gallery, the RAW site—an old train repair facility that now houses everything from art galleries to beer gardens—and eventually Grünberg Str., which will lead you to the best restaurants, cafés, and vintage stores Friedrichschain has to offer. With world-renowned clubs like Berghain, About Blank, and Salon Zur Wilden Renate, diving head-first into the nightlife of Friedrichschain is a totally non-optional experience.

**5. Kreuzberg** —Young, multicultural, and counter-cultural, Kreuzberg is Friedrichschain's even grittier counterpart. You'll find the same abandoned industrial plants-turned-clubs (Tresor, OHM) and the same 50-foot, graffiti-plastered walls (look out for the Cosmonaut) as you would just across the Spree in F'Hain. The area's abandoned buildings include a former international airport (Templehof), and its cheap eats have a chic "hole-in-the-wall" aesthetic: some of them are literal holes-in-the-wall (Maroush)—and all the better because of it.

ABC €3.40). Within the validation period, the ticket may be used on any S-Bahn, U-Bahn, bus, or tram. If you have a ticket but don't validate it, plainclothes policemen, who occasionally ride the BVG, will fine you €7. If you are caught without a ticket or with an expired one, you will be charged €60.

## PRACTICAL INFORMATION

**Tourist Offices:** Tegel Airport (Am Gate 1 Terminal A Flughafen Tegel; 030 25 00 25; open daily 8am-9pm), Schönefeld Airport (Terminal A, main hall, ground floor; 0331 200 47 47; M-F 9am-6pm).

**Banks/ATMs/Currency Exchange:** Although not fantastic, the best rates are usually found at exchange offices with Wechselstube signs outside, at most major train stations, and in large squares. However, provided that your overseas bank has a partner bank in Germany, it is best to withdraw from the ATM. For money wires through Western Union, use ReiseBank. (M: Hauptbahnhof 030 204 53 761. Open M-Sa 8am-10pm.).

**Post Offices:** Post (Frankfurter Allee 1; 228 4333112; open M-Sa 9am-1pm and 2pm-6pm).

**Internet:** Free internet with admission to the Staatsbibliothek. During its renovation, Staatsbibliothek requires €10 month-long pass to the library. (Potsdamer Str. 33; 030 26 60 Open M-F 9am-9pm, Sa 10am-7pm.) Most hostels and restaurants, and cafés, including Starbucks, provide free Wi-Fi.

## EMERGENCY INFORMATION

**Emergency Number:** 112

**Police:** 112; Polizeirevier Abschnitt 53 (Friedrichstaße 219; 30 4664553700).

**US Embassy:** Embassy of the United States of America Berlin (Pariser Platz 2; 30 83050; open M-F 8am-5:30pm).

**Rape Crisis Center:** LARA offers counseling for victims of sexual assault. (Fuggerstr. 19; 030 216 88 88; www.lara-berlin.de; open M-F 9am-6pm). Frauenkrisentelefon is a women's crisis line (030 615 4243; www.frauenkrisentelefon.de/en/home; open M 10am-noon, Tu 3-5pm W 7-9pm, Th 10am-noon, F 7-9pm, Sa-Su 5-7pm).

**Hospitals:** DRK Klinken Berlin Mitte (Drontheimer Str. 39-40; 30 30356000; open daily 24hr).

**Pharmacies:** Brandenburger Tor Apotheke (Under den Linden 69D; 30 39887448; open M-F 8am-7pm, Sa 9am-7pm, Su 10am-6pm).

# ACCOMMODATIONS

## ◼GRAND HOSTEL BERLIN ($)

Tempelhofer Ufer 14, Kreuzberg; 30 20095450; www.grandhostel-berlin.de/en; reception 24hr

Let's just say that, if Wes Anderson had known about this place, everyone would be raving about Ralph Fiennes' performance in *The Grand Kreuzberg Hostel*. And there would probably be some chatter about the lovely hostel interiors, as well. "There's no way bedrooms that nice could belong to a hostel," Peter Travers would write in his *Rolling Stone* review. And he'd be right. The high-ceilinged rooms are 100% bunk-bed free, and, as a result, extremely capacious—a word that we don't use lightly. What's more, each room comes equipped with an old nineteenth-century heater, which is as much a functional piece of machinery as it is a steampunk sculpture. The hostel's nightly events and inviting library/bar area make meeting people an easy and organic experience.

*i* Dorms from €10, singles from €20, doubles from €49; reservation recommended; BGLTQ+ friendly; wheelchair accessible; Wi-Fi; laundry facilities

## ◼KIEZ HOSTEL ($)

Marchlewskistrabe 88; 30 12036240; kiezhostel.berlin; reception open 9am-10pm

Kiez Hostel feels more like a boutique hotel than a hostel. Each room has its own theme, which, as opposed to being kitschy and gimmicky, lend them an understated and elegant touch. Furthermore, the rooms' large windows, which allow for ample sunshine, and spacious floor plans, give them a bright and airy feel. Every bed has its own light and electric outlet. Although the staff will do your laundry at a cost (€5), they'll recommend events to check out each day for free. Kiez Hostel is also ideally located, with **Berghain** and the **East Side Gallery** both within arm's reach (if you have 550-yard long arms).

*i* Dorms €22.50, doubles €49; reservation recommended; min. stay 3 nights; BGLTQ+ friendly; Wi-Fi; wheelchair accessible

## BAXPAX DOWNTOWN HOSTEL ($)

Ziegelstraße 28; 30 27874880; www.bax-pax.de/en/downtown; reception open 24hr

(To the tune of Fall Out Boy's "Sugar, We're Going Down.") Am I more than a bargain yet? / I've been dying to sell you another beer or coffee/'Cause that's what we do at our café-bar / Lie in our dorms* next to Museum Island / I'm just a conveniently-located hostel / But you're just a member of our typically younger clientele / Drop down in / Our bean-bag chairs / You're always hanging out, hanging out at our outdoor lounge / You're staying downtown at the Baxpax Hostel / Sugar, our downstairs club is popping / I'll change the Wi-Fi code every day** / A dorm that's not in suite,*** find it and book it.

*Clean and comfortable but with no reading light or bedside plug points.

**Slightly annoying but not a massive inconvenience.

***You might find it easier and less awkward to use a bathroom located outside rather than inside your room.

*i* Dorms €15, singles €49, doubles €35; reservation recommended; wheelchair accessible; Wi-Fi; linens not included; towels for rent

## ALETTO KUDAMM ($$)

Hardenbergstraße 21, Charlottenburg; 30 233214100; www.aletto.de/en; reception 24hr

As both a hotel and a hostel, Aletto Kudamm gives you the best of both worlds. When it comes to your dorm, you'll get the affordable prices of a hostel but the housekeeping services of a hotel. In fact, if you arrived wanting to check into the hostel, the lobby's bar, lounge, pool table and vending machines might lead you to think that you'd got the wrong place entirely. Of course, Aletto Kudamm consequently lacks the charm of a smaller hostel, but you'll be surprised by how trivial such an observation looks when viewed from the hotel's seven-story high rooftop bar.

*i* Dorms from €19, singles from €49, doubles from €59; reservation recommended; BGLTQ+ friendly; wheelchair accessible; Wi-Fi; laundry available, linens included

## EASTERN COMFORT HOSTELBOAT ($)

Muehlenstr. 73; 30 66763806; www.eastern-comfort.com; reception open 24hr

At first, the Eastern Comfort Hostel Boat might sound a little too good to be true. It floats on the gorgeous **Spree River.** It's located smack in-between **Friedrichschain** and **Kreuzberg.** And this boat, which not only adds a whimsical touch to the stay, gives guests the coveted opportunity to join the mile-low club. Although space is a little tight in the dorms, the rooms are clean and cozy. What's more, the boat hardly rocks, so the only reason you'll feel queasy at night is from drinking one too many drinks at the on-deck bar, which shares a bathroom with some of the dorms—not that it's too much of an inconvenience. Also, if camping's your thing, you can stay in a tent (€15 per night) on the boat's upper deck.

*i* Dorms €19, singles €44, doubles €50; reservation recommended; BGLTQ+ friendly; wheelchair accessible; Wi-Fi; linens not included, towels for rent

## HAPPY GO LUCKY HOTEL AND HOSTEL ($)

Stuttgarter Pl. 17, Kreuzberg; 30 32709072; www.happygoluckyhotel.com; reception open 24hr

We try not to judge a book by its cover (we prefer to do it by the author photo on the back), but when the cover is a graffiti-plastered five-story high façade, it's hard not to. The hostel's bubbly atmosphere continues in the reception area, which bustles with travelers and friendly staff. Although the €50 key deposit will send shivers down of the spine of the book you bought written by the handsome author, the quality of the rooms—basic, yet comfortable—will set you at ease.

*i* Dorms from €16, singles from €37, doubles from €52; reservation recommended; BGLTQ+ friendly; no wheelchair accessibility; Wi-Fi; laundry facilities; linens included

## U INN BERLIN HOSTEL ($)

Finowstraße 36; 30 33024410; www.uinnberlinhostel.com; reception open 8am-11pm

U-Inn Hostel is everything a good hostel should be. The rooms are clean and comfortable. The reception sells

snacks and essential travel amenities (read: toiletries and beer). Not to mention the cozy lounge and kitchen spaces create a social vibe among guests. Although the scarcity of electrical outlets in the rooms means you're likely to wake up to 0% battery after a big night out, you'll at least be able to recharge your body with €4 breakfast. Because the area between the hostel and the center of Friedrichschain can be quiet and poorly lit at night, if you're heading back alone, it's best to walk along Frankfurter Allee until you can turn right down **Finowstraße.**

*i* Dorms €15-21, singles €28-55, doubles €25-53; reservation recommended; BGLTQ+ friendly; wheelchair accessible; Wi-Fi; linens not included, towels for rent

## SIGHTS
### CULTURE

### VABALI SPA
Seydlitzstraße 6, Mitte; 30 9114860; www.vabali.de; open daily 9am-midnight

A spa? You're telling us to go to a spa? We came here to immerse ourselves in this one-of-a-kind city and now you're telling us to go to a freakin' spa? We, too, were skeptical at first. But after two different locals recommended this place as an authentic German experience, we threw caution and our clothing to the wind (Vabali is "textile-free") and decided to check it out. While the prices may make your eyes do that thing in cartoons where they spring out of a person's skull in shock, if you've got the cash to splash, the spa is an unforgettable experience. The 15 saunas, each of which is gender-neutral save one that's women-only, fall under the categories of hot, organic, steam, aromatherapy, or "Banja." And once you've rid your body of the toxins accumulated from successive nights out, take a dip in the pool. Vabali Spa isn't quite to Germany what bath houses are to Turkey, but the locals, young and old alike, seem to enjoy it all the same.

*i* Tickets 2hr. €20.50, 4hr. €27.5; wheelchair accessible

### KINO BABYLON
Rosa-Luxemburg-Str. 30; 30 2425969; www.babylonberlin.de; open daily 5pm-midnight

Kino Babylon is one of, if not the premier arts house cinema, in Berlin. Kino Babylon features national cinemas from around the world, cult classics, legendary directors, animation, shorts, and, of course, German film, making it Berlin's go-to place for film lovers and people who want to impress their dates from the nearby **Berlin Art Institute.** It boasts three theaters, most notably a 450-seat hall with a nearly 90-year-old organ that is still used to accompany free weekly midnight screenings of silent films. Keep a look out for the film festivals, as well. When we attended, Kino Babylon was scheduled to host Cuban, Southeast European, and Italian festivals all within the same month.

*i* Tickets €7-10.50; wheelchair accessible

## RAW FLOHMARKET

Revaler Str. 99; 17 78279352; raw-floh-markt-berlin.de; open Su 9am-7pm

The RAW site used to be the largest train repair facility in Friedrichshain, but nowadays it's known as a nightlife district that embodies Berlin's infamous "poor but sexy" attitude. However, every Sunday, this labyrinth of derelict and graffiti-covered warehouses blossoms into a flea market full of vintage goods and multicultural food. Selling everything from clothes and vinyl to action figures and Buddhist ornaments, the stalls are mostly family-run and attract locals and tourists alike, which really make the market feel like a tiny microcosm of the city as a whole. Even if you decide not to buy anything.

*i* Free; no wheelchair accessibility

## SPACE HALL

Zossener Str. 33, Kreuzberg; 30 53088718; spacehall.de; open M-W 11am-8pm, Th-F 11am-10pm, Sa 11am-8pm

While techno purists journey to Hard Wax—a fantastically curated, albeit small, collection of electronic vinyl—people interested in finding both the latest "12 from Berghain's Ostgut Ton" label as well as the new Carly Rae Jepsen LP (or, in our case, just the latter) head to Space Hall. With three large sections roughly divided between CDs, indie and rock vinyl, and electronic records, you're unlikely to be singing U2's smash-hit "I Still Haven't Found What I'm Looking For" any time soon, unless, of course, that song is on a record you bought. And if you're worried about how you're going to get a boatload of vinyl back home, you're wasting your time: Space Hall will ship it for you!

*i* LPs €10-30, CDs €10-20; wheelchair accessible

# LANDMARKS

## ✦EAST SIDE GALLERY

Mhlenstrae; 17 23918726; www.eastside-gallery-berlin.de; open daily 24hr

The East Side Gallery, a 1.3km-stretch of the Berlin Wall covered in over 100 murals by artists from around the world, is a testament to Berlin's uncanny ability to turn painful reminders of the past into contemporary symbols of hope and peace. Converted into the world's largest open-air art gallery following the fall of the wall in 1989, the Gallery is probably the most tourist-heavy spot east of the **Spree River,** but that's only because it's an absolutely essential component of any Berlin trip. The walk up and down the wall is roughly 45-mins long, but it can last an hour depending on the time it takes to find someone willing to recreate "the socialist fraternal kiss" in front of the famous mural.

*i* Free; wheelchair accessible

## BRANDENBURG GATE

Pariser Pl.; open daily 24hr

You're going to see this, regardless of what we say. It's big and impressive and the defining landmark of Berlin. It would be crazy if you didn't. While the Acropolis-inspired architecture is, indeed, striking, it's perhaps the gate's history that makes it such a permanent fixture in every tourist's schedule. Built by Friedrich Wilhelm II in the late eighteenth century as part of a system of city gates, the Brandenburg Gate is the only one that survives, although it's had a few close calls. Allied attacks inflicted significant damage during WWII, East German tinkering altered its quadriga (the thing on top) during the Cold War, and we accidentally bumped into a pillar during our visit. If you want to avoid the daytime infestation of tourists, pay a visit during the night, or better still, stop by on your way back from the club and watch the sunrise.

*i* Free; wheelchair accessible; private guided tours can be booked

## CHARLOTTENBURG PALACE

Spandauer Damm 20-24; 33 19694200; www.spsg.de/en/palaces-gardens/object/schloss-charlottenburg; open Apr-Oct Tu-Su 10am-6pm, Nov-Mar Tu-Su 10am-5pm

An old wise man once told us, "If you've seen one palace, you've seen them all." But the Charlottenburg Palace proves what we suspected all along: that old guy's absolute kook. Inside the palace, you might find yourself in the **White Room,** staring at the golden rococo patterns on the walls and ceiling, and think, "Wow, it doesn't get much better than this." But then you'll get to the **Golden Gallery** and hate yourself for being so foolish and naïve: the intricate, satin-covered walls in the private apartments and the collection of silverware, porcelain, and crown jewels will make you hate the Hohenzollern dynasty out of jealousy. Stroll through the sprawling palace gardens and visit the mausoleum, where various Prussian monarchs are buried in tombs that are works of art in themselves.

*i* *Admission €12, reduced €9; free audio guide; last entry 30min. before closing; ground floor and park are wheelchair accessible; guided tours by appointment only*

# MUSEUMS

### 🏛HAMBURGER BAHNHOF

Invalidenstraße 50-51, Mitte; 30 39783439; www.smb.museum/en/museums-institutions/hamburger-bahnhof; open Tu-W 10am-6pm, Th 10am-8pm, F 10am-6pm Sa-Su 11am-6pm

Housed in an old train station, Berlin's premier contemporary art museum is filled with permanent exhibits showcasing twentieth-century powerhouses such as **Warhol** and **Beuys.** It'll take a good three hours to fully absorb everything here, even counting the time saved by skipping the giant exhibit that attempts to dismantle capitalism by placing an axe next to a piano. Nonetheless, the most intriguing section of the museum is the adjacent warehouse full of nothing but installations. It's an area that invites intense contemplation as you walk through a football field-sized space. Because contemporary art reflects the contemporary world, and since the contemporary world is... complicated, today's art has to communicate that. That's why, although you probably won't comprehend the meaning behind half of the art in Hamburger Bahnhof, you'll find yourself unsettled by nearly all of it.

*i* *Admission €14, reduced €7; guided tours in English Sa-Su at noon; limited wheelchair accessibility*

### 🏛PERGAMON MUSEUM

Bodestraße 1-3; 30 266424242; www.smb.museum/en/museums-institutions/alte-nationalgalerie; open Tu-W 10am-6pm, Th 10am-8pm, F-Su 10am-6pm

If you were stuck on a desert island and that island had a lot of museums on it, and you could only pick one to visit, which would it be? If you answered with anything but the Pergamon, you're wrong. Even though its crown jewel—the **Pergamon Altar**—is under renovation until 2019, the museum still contains some truly awe-inspiring exhibits. 2,500-years-old and 100-foot-tall, the **Ishtar Gate** is comprised of some of the most miraculous tilework we've ever seen—and trust us, we've seen some tiles. Come for these exhibits, but stay for the **Museum of Islamic Art,** which, with its beautifully ornate and intricate artifacts, might just be the most pleasant surprise of Museum Island.

*i* *Admission €12, reduced €6, all exhibits on Museum Island €18, reduced €9; last entry 30min. before closing; wheelchair accessible*

### ALTE NATIONALGALERIE

Bodestraße 1-3; 30 266424242; www.smb.museum/en/museums-institutions/alte-nationalgalerie; open Tu-W 10am-6pm, Th 10am-8pm, F-Su 10am-6pm

Life is full of sad, unavoidable truths, but perhaps the saddest of them all is that, when you spend a day at **Museum Island,** there are only so many ancient relics you can see without wanting to plant your butt one of those oh-so-tempting benches in the center of each exhibit and just stay there. Luckily, the Alte Nationalgalerie is full of enough gorgeous nineteenth- and twentieth-century art to keep your booty high and tight as you hop from gallery to gallery. The collections of German Realism and Modernism are also highlights that might even inspire you to jot down the names of specific artists into your phone, which you will definitely refer back to and not forget about as soon as you leave to check out some more relics.

*i* *Admission €10, €5 reduced, all exhibits on Museum Island €18, €9 reduced; last entry 30min. before closing; wheelchair accessible*

# A BRIEF OVERVIEW: THE BERLIN WALL

While nowadays it may seem as if the only thing that could divide Berlin is a debate about where to find the best currywurst, it is a little known, kept-under-wraps fact that, for the majority of the last 60 years, a concrete wall split the city in two.

Following WWII, the Allies and the USSR carved up Germany between themselves, with the Allies gaining control of the west and the USSR, the east. However, even though Berlin lies in the east, the city's importance as the German capital meant that it too was divided in half, creating a small western stronghold within the Soviet bloc. It wasn't until 1961, once a collective total of 4 million Eastern Germans had fled to the west, that the East German government (the DDR), not wanting to seem weaker than its capitalist neighbor, decided to build a 93-mile wall overnight.

Soon enough, as tensions rose between the two sides, what started out as a single wall soon turned into two walls with a 300-foot wide "no man's land" between the two. Fortunately, nothing lasts forever and the USSR, suffering from a weakened Soviet bloc, opened the borders between East Berlin and West Berlin in 1989. In 1990, the wall fell.

The Berlin Wall Memorial in Prenzlauer Berg provides a comprehensive overview of the Wall's history and tells how the Wall impacted the daily lives of those in the immediate area. Similarly, the DDR museum focuses on life in East Germany under Communist rule and explores the USSR and the DDR's decline in a clear and lucid manner. The longest remaining stretch of the Wall, the East Side Gallery, aims to turn a symbol of division and hatred into one of unity and hope.

## BERLINER DOM

]Am Lustgarten; 30 20269136; www.berlinerdom.de; open M-Sa 9am-8pm, Su noon-8pm

Visit a church? On a day that's not a Sunday, Christmas, or Easter? Why, what an absolute treat! But, it gets better. The Berliner Dom isn't just any old church, it's one of the most breathtaking cathedrals in Europe. And once you've retrieved your breath, guess what else you can do? You can hike up a seemingly endless flight of stairs, walk around the very dome itself, and marvel at another breathtaking sight—the city of Berlin! At this point, if you're not writhing on the floor gasping for air, you're probably at the wrong church. We mean, Kaiser Wilhelm II built this thing to rival St. Peter's Basilica. He also buried his family right beneath it. Swing by their crypts on your way out!

*i* *Admission €7, reduced €5, audio guide €3; last entry 1hr. before closing; wheelchair accessible*

## C/O BERLIN

Hardenbergstraße 22-24, Charlottenburg; 30 28444160; www.co-berlin.org/en; open daily 11am-8pm

With three exhibitions running simultaneously, which usually feature a mix of world-renowned, local, and up-and-coming photographers, you're sure to find yourself struck by something in C/O Berlin. So, in short, photography nerds, come—it's a no-brainer. C/O's retrospectives (there's usually one going on at any given time) alone are a reason to visit for anyone: they not only present an overview of an important figure's work, but also do it in a way that allows you to understand why they were so important, and by extension, why photography is an important art form.

*i* *Admission €10, reduced €6; weekly guided tours in English Sa 6pm; limited wheelchair accessibility*

## DDR MUSEUM

Karl-Liebknecht-Str. 1; 30 84712373; www.ddr-museum.de; open Su-Fri 10am-8pm, Sa 10am-10pm

If you've ever wanted to know what life was like under Communist rule, but have never spent a weekend at my mother-in-law's, the DDR museum has you covered. Focusing on the public and private lives of Eastern Germans during the latter half of the twentieth century as well as the practices of DDR government, the museum uses interactive and detailed exhibits to make the past relatable today. In about 90 minutes, you'll walk through a kindergarten, cinema, Stasi prison cell, and even a full-scale replica of a typical East German apartment—far and away the museum's highlight.

*i* Admission €8.50, reduced €7.50; limited wheelchair accessibility

## MEMORIAL TO THE MURDERED JEWS OF EUROPE

Cora-Berliner-Straße 1, Mitte; 30 2639430; www.stiftung-denkmal.de/en/memorials/the-memorial-to-the-murdered-jews-of-europe; memorial open daily 24hr, information center open Apr-Sep Tu-Su 10am-8pm, Oct-Mar Tu-Su 10am-7pm

Just south of the **Brandenburg Gate,** a sea of grave-like concrete slabs serves as a memorial to the six million Jewish victims of the Holocaust. Described by the architect as representing "the innate disturbances and potential for chaos in all systems of seeming order," the memorial is a quiet and contemplative place. But once you reach its center and the slabs begin to tower above you, the memorial can become disturbing—which, of course, is the point. While it also provides a broad overview of the Holocaust, the information center focuses on telling the stories of the individual victims. Learn about the lives of families before the war, life inside the camps, and the devastating experiences of those who lost their lives. No two stories are the same but all resonate with an equally tragic weight.

*i* Free entry, audio guide €4, reduced €2; free guided tour in English Sa 3pm; wheelchair accessible

## NEUES MUSEUM

Bodestraße 1-3; 30 26 6424242; www.smb.museum/en/museums-institutions/neues-museum; open M-W 10am-6pm, Th 10am-8pm, W-Su 10am-6pm

Sure, everyone visits the Neues Museum to see the **bust of Nefertiti**—one of the world's most famous ancient artifacts. But once you've seen the Egyptian lady's clay head, have you seen everything the museum has to offer? No. In fact, the museum's expansive collection of sarcophagi, located in a crypt-like hall, is arguably more intriguing, if only because it serves as a reminder of how cool it would be to get buried in a sarcophagus.

*i* Admission €12, reduced €6, all exhibits on Museum Island €18, reduced €9; last entry 1hr. before closing; wheelchair accessible

# OUTDOORS

## 🏛TIERGARTEN

Straße des 17; 30 901833101; open M-W 9am-6pm, Th-F 9am-3pm

Similar to Monaco in size, but used as a stress-free haven instead of a tax-heavy one, the Tiergarten used to be a hunting grounds for Prussian rulers. Nowadays, it is home to some of Berlin's most well-known landmarks. The **Reichstag, Brandenburg Gate, Memorial for Murdered Jews, Victory Column,** and **Berlin Zoo** can all be found in or around the park. But the Tiergarten hasn't let such success get to its head—deep down it's still just a regular park where you can picnic, rent kayaks, and watch teens drown their angst with fizzy alcoholic beverages. While the park's renown means it's the most crowded one in town, this is a reason to visit rather than avoid it—everyone simply knows that an afternoon at the Tiergarten is an unmissable element of any trip to Berlin.

*i* Free

## STRANDBAD PLÖTZENSEE

Nordufer 26; 17 634418634; www.strand-bad-ploetzensee.de; open daily May-Sept 9am-7pm

Although we could spend all day praising the virtues of summer, we can only spend four words outlining its faults: it is very hot. Fortunately, when the sun becomes unbearable, Berliners have a contingency plan: they go to a lake, the closest and most convenient of which is the Plötzensee, a half-hour train ride from **Mitte.** While the lake has plenty of areas where you can swim for free, we recommend breaking out the ol' check book for the €5 (€3 reduced) entrance fee to StrandbadPlötzensee. A small resort on the lake, StrandbadPlötzensee comes equipped with a lifeguard, a volleyball court, table tennis, and restaurants, as well as sunbed and beach chair rentals.

*i* *Admission €5, reduced €3, sunbed €4, beach chair €3; wheelchair accessible*

## TEMPELHOF

Tempelhofer Damm; 30 700906616; open daily 6am-9:30pm

Templehof seems like it was designed in a lab focused on producing the most quintessential Berlin sight possible. Formerly an international airport until 2008, Templehof is now one of the most popular, and certainly the most interesting, parks in Berlin. Although it's still possible to receive tours of the building itself, most people are perfectly content to roam around the runway, which has since been converted into a wide walkway. For those who prefer to cycle, the nearby information center (open 10am to 7pm) makes renting a painless process. Since there's very little shade, a cool evening trip, equipped with a picnic blanket, dinner, and a portable speaker of sorts, is ideal.

*i* *Free*

## TREPTOWER

Alt-Treptow; 30 25002333; open daily 10am-1am

There are two main reasons to visit Treptower. Of course, it covers the traditional aspects of a park without much fuss, but so do most Berlin parks. What makes Trep-tower special is that

it's home to not just the intimidatingly large **Soviet War Memorial,** but also an abandoned amusement park. The former commemorates 6,000 USSR soldiers who fell during the Battle of Berlin, while the latter commemorates the poor financial prudence of Normann Whitte, whose bankruptcy in 2001 allowed Spreepark to become the dilapidated and endlessly fascinating sight it is today. You're technically not allowed into Spreepark without a guided tour, but if you manage to sneak in without alerting the patrol guards, hats off to you (not that we're advocating doing so).

*i* *Free*

## VOLKSPARK FRIEDRICHSCHAIN

30 25002333; open daily 24r

When it comes to large and central parks located east of the Spree, it doesn't get much larger, more central, and east of the Spree than Volkspark Friedrichschain. Beyond its centerpiece, the **Märchenbrunnen,** or "fountain of fairy tales," the space is more or less your typical park. Fun fact (well, not necessarily fun, but intriguing): the park's hills are actually landfills of rubble from bunkers destroyed during WWII. But the

that made us question just how deadly our deadly gluten intolerance really is.

*i* *Breakfast €10; vegetarian options available; limited wheelchair accessibility*

### CÔ CÔ - BÁNH MÌ DELI ($)

Rosenthaler Str. 2; 30 55475188; www.co-co. net; open M-Th 11am-10pm, Fri-Sa 11am-11pm, Su noon-10pm

Basically the Vietnamese-French version of Subway, Cô Cô - Bánh Mì Deli stuffs its sandwiches with liver patê, marinated pork, a homemade sauce that packs a punch, and traditional garnishes. To put it simply, it's the sandwich equivalent of a Vietnamese fresh spring roll, which is the spring roll equivalent of heaven, which is the Christian equivalent of Nirvana, the ultimate pinnacle of rock music. Sit inside surrounded by floral arrangements and jars of lemons, or outside amongst the vibrant goings-on of **Rosenthaler Platz.**

*i* *Sandwiches €5.50-9.50; vegetarian options available; wheelchair accessible*

intrigue of this fact pales in comparison to that of the park's summer open-air-movie screenings (€7.50), which range from newly released German films to recent, yet acclaimed English ones.

*i* *Free*

## FOOD

### CAFE KALWIL ($$)

Motzstr. 30, Schöneberg; 30 23638818; www.cafekalwilberlin.de; open M, W-F 9am-7pm

On Wednesdays, you wear pink? Nice try, *Mean Girls*. Café Kalwil wears pink every single day. With pink drapes adorning the entrance, pink sequined pillows, and pink light bulbs intertwined with pink fairy lights running along the awning, the café is impossible to miss. But let us be clear: Café Kalwil isn't tasteless or trashy. If you venture inside, you'll see it's less a Hello Kitty store vibe and more like an antique shop run by Hello Kitty. And it's not just a pretty face either: beside the usual café and breakfast fare, it has an incredibly detailed but pricey tea menu (€5.60 per pot), ice cream sundaes (€5), and a cake selection (€4)

### DAS EDELWEISS ($$)

Görlitzer Str. 1-3, Kreuzberg; 30 61074858; www.edelweiss36.com; open summer M-F 9:30am-last call, Sa-Su 9am-last call; open Winter M 10:30am-last call, Tu 5pm-last call, Th-F 10:30am-last call, Sa-Su 10pm-open end

In any other city, the sight of an old, graffiti-plastered building might only excite amateur ghostbusters and professional old building-hunters. In Berlin, however, it's almost a guarantee that whatever's happening inside is worth checking out. Das Edelweiss is no exception. A breakfast joint, bar, café, traditional German dining experience, and weekly jazz club (Tuesdays at 10pm), Das Edelweiss is as versatile as James Franco and as enjoyable as he is insufferable. We could spend the rest of the book singing the praises of the restaurant's

Görlitzer Park location, but we'd rather use that space to obsess over the tenderness and juiciness of its *Weißwürste* (traditional Bavarian sausage).

*i* *Sausage €5.90-16; vegetarian options available; limited wheelchair accessibility*

## INDIAN EXPRESS ($)

Kantstr. 74, Charlottenburg; 30 32301023; www.indiaexpress.de; open daily noon-11pm

Let's cut to the chase, and then we'll cut to the scene after the chase where we're all eating butter chicken at Indian Express. The thing is, Indian Express, at least from our experience, doesn't make the best naan bread. It's just a little undercooked, and when it comes to the cheese naan, you might as well be eating regular naan for all the difference it makes in taste. That said, we'll be damned if it doesn't make some of the most delicious butter chicken we've had. This chicken is so tender that it could be a Marvin Gaye song, which means that the Tandoori chicken and chicken tikka are definitely worth a try, as well. Of course, Indian food is much more than bread and chicken. And this family-run restaurant knows this, as proven by its 12-section menu that covers everything from duck specialties to vegan dishes. So what if the naan isn't great? You can literally order over 80 other things!

*i* *Starter and entrée €10; vegetarian options available; limited wheelchair accessibility*

## MAROUSH ($)

Adalbertstraße 93; 30 69536171; www.maroush-berlin.de; open daily 11am-2am

We believe its Webster's dictionary that defines "falafel sandwiches" as "delicacies perfected by Maroush." And after having eaten there ourselves, we have to say that these folks at Webster really did their research. As soon as you step into Maroush, you feel as if you've teleported to Beirut, in the sense that the restaurant seems like it has a population of 2,006,500 people. Not that this has any effect on your meal's preparation time. Within five minutes, three of which are spent grilling your order on a sandwich press, you'll receive a piping-hot pita filled to the brim with falafel, mint, parsley, radish,

cucumbers, and sesame sauce. Oh, and did we mention that it only costs €3?

*i* *Entrées €3-7; vegetarian options available; wheelchair accessible*

## GEMUSE KEBAB ($)

Mehringdamm 32, Kreuzberg; open M-Th 10am-2am, F-Sa 10am-5am, Su 10am-2am

O, Mustafa's! The most famous vendor of Berlin's favorite fast food: the döner kebab! How we wait in line for you! Your kebab, it is great and cheap! But your line, is it worth it? A 30-minute wait or more! O, Mustafa's! We have sights to see! We want not to doubt your greatness, nor to worship a false god! But we must ask: is there that great a difference between your kebab and that of another? Three kinds of sauces, O how they complement the chicken (or grilled vegetables)! And what is that taste? Feta salad? The warm bread? Potatoes? It weeps, my mouth, for it does not know where to focus! 'Tis o'erwhelmed. But is it worth the wait? If one's heart is set on this cultural icon, then yes! Alas, if one simply wants some good döner kebab, look elsewhere. For there are respectable rivals, with less fame but kebab of equal quality.

*i* *Kebab €3-4; vegetarian options available; limited wheelchair accessibility*

## PATTA ($)

Krossener Str. 16; 17 661918140; www.patta-berlin.de; open daily 12:30pm-10pm

Question: What kind of restaurant has the nerve to center its entire concept around baked potatoes? Answer: Patta. Patta has so much nerve that, when your dish arrives, the potato itself won't even be visible. Instead, it will be submerged in what looks like Jackson Pollock's best attempt at making a salad. And while you may be hesitant at first to disrupt the work of art in front you, your hunger will kick in and you'll smash through the edible paint that is the couscous, feta, roasted tomatoes, and your choice of chicken or tofu that smothers the potato canvas below. Suffice it to say that, if you choose to overlook Patta, we can only assume that you have a baked potato for a brain.

*i* *Entrées €6-7; vegetarian options available; wheelchair accessible*

## SCHEERS ($)

Warschauer Pl. 18; 15 788948011; scheers-schnitzel.de; open Su-Th 11:30am-10pm, F-Sa 11:30am-midnight

Not so much hole-in-the-wall as hole-underneath-the-autobahn, Scheers is an inexpensive, no-frills restaurant that serves some, to borrow an old German phrase, "gut schnitzel" ("good breaded pork"). For just €5.50, get a paper plate full of schnitzel, steak fries, and coleslaw, and for a little extra, a range of tasty toppings (go for the mushroom sauce). If you choose to sit inside, prepare yourself for an immersive visual experience: the only wall spaces not covered in crayon are plastered with old concert posters. If you choose to sit outside, prepare yourself for an immersive auditory experience: the sounds of cyclists whizzing by serves as the perfect accompaniment to Scheers' schnitzel-eating extravaganza.

*i* *Single schnitzel €5-7, double €9-10; vegetarian options available; wheelchair accessible*

## SCHWARZES CAFÉ ($$)

Kantstraße 148, Charlottenburg; 30 3138038; www.schwarzescafe-berlin.de; open daily 24hr except Tu 3-10am

At midnight, Schwarzes Café is relatively empty. But it's not winding down for the night: it's just getting started. A welcome respite from the city's other 24hr falafel-centric dining options, Schwarzes Café is the kind of place you'll arrive at just wanting to fill your stomach, but find yourself unwilling to leave. Whether it's packed with four people or 40, the café manages to maintain a warm and charming ambiance thanks to its antique décor, background jazz, and the general merriment that accompanies drunken people in search of a meal. The expansive menu, with nearly as many sweet options as savory, has something to satisfy anyone's cravings. However, if you're in the mood for steak, schnitzel, or salmon, you'd better be in the mood to fork over upward of €16.

*i* *Entrées €5.80-19; vegetarian options available; limited wheelchair accessibility*

## THE BOWL ($$)

Warschauer Str. 33; 30 29771447; www.thebowl-berlin.com; open M-Fri 11:30am-11pm, Sa-Su 10am-11pm

Berlin's first ever clean-eating vegan restaurant, The Bowl probably already has you eagerly wondering what the heck "clean-eating" even means. As your waiter will be happy to tell you, everything on the menu is 100% natural—no artificial additives, sugars, or fats here. Note, however, that this doesn't mean your food will be lacking in flavor. Once you finally reach the bottom of your salad bowl, you'll feel satisfied and stuffed, but, if your wallet allows it, treat yourself to a smoothie, as well. While The Bowl is a little pricier than Goodies—the more casual vegan option downstairs—it's larger portions and spacious dining area overlooking the lively **Warschauer Straße** will make you glad you chose something slightly more upscale.

*i* *Bowl €11.90; vegetarian options available; wheelchair accessible*

## WAWA ($$)

Grunewaldstr. 10, Schöneberg; 3065774230; wawaberlin.com; open daily 5pm-11pm

Borat's catchphrase may be "Wawa-wee-wa", but this Korean restaurant has us saying "Wawa-we-want-more"! While most good Korean food costs an arm and a leg, Wawa is a relatively inexpensive option in the heart of **Schöneberg,** but doesn't sacrifice quality for affordability. The Wawa Spezial (marinated beef, which can be subbed for tofu, vegetables, and rice) was perhaps our favorite meal we've had in a city where every meal could've been our favorite. It's clearly a local favorite as well, since we didn't hear a word of English spoken the entire time. But if you want to avoid a wait, make a reservation, arrive outside of peak meal times, or steal someone's plate as you walk by. Seriously, it's that good.

*i* *Entrées €10.50-15; vegetarian options available; limited wheelchair accessibility*

# NIGHTLIFE

## ⚑BERGHAIN

Am Wriezener Bahnhof; 30 29360210;
www.berghain.de; open Th 10pm-6am,
F-Su midnight-6am

A non-stop party from Friday night
until Monday morning, Berghain is the
most insane, mind-numbingly loud,
grungy, wild, and clothing-optional
place we've ever been. Here's how you
get in:

1. Wear dark colors, but nothing too
   warm.
2. Forget about going at night.
   Arrive between 6am and 8am or
   2pm and 4pm on a Sunday when
   the line is 15 minutes long.
3. Line up alone and act aloof.
4. When you get to the front, don't
   acknowledge the bouncers until
   they acknowledge you (unless they
   deliver a devastating burn as they
   turn someone away, in which case
   you have to give them credit).
5. Answer their questions politely
   and curtly.

By now, chances are you've made it
inside. And once you're in, you're in
for good (stamps are good for reentry
so you can return later at night
without having to queue). What makes
Berghain special isn't its exclusivity,
cathedral-like dance floor, unrivaled
sound system, or ice-cream bar; it's the
club's ability to allow everyone to shed
their self-consciousness and just be
themselves. So go ahead, let loose and
go crazy—we guarantee that everyone
else will.

*i* Cover €10-16, drinks €2.50-7; cash
only; BGLTQ+ friendly; closed-toed shoes,
dark colors recommended

## ⚑OHM

Kopenicker Str. 70; 17 78279352; ohm-
berlin.com; open F-Sa midnight-late

Located in a small room not unlike a
prison shower in the same abandoned
power plant that houses Tresor, OHM
is one of the best kept secrets of Berlin's
clubbing scene. Unlike Tresor or
Watergate, OHM attracts a younger
crowd of locals purely interested in
dancing to the most forward-thinking
electronic music around, regardless
of whether it's techno, house, or

something a little more genre-defying
and experimental. Although OHM
lacks the brain-melting volume and
lighting wizardry of larger clubs, the
intimate, communal feel of the venue
creates an environment where you can
feel free to let loose. If you've grown
tired of Berlin's more traditional techno
clubs, a night at OHM will restore
your faith in the city's nightlife scene.

*i* Cover €5-8, drinks €2-3; cash only;
closed toe-shoes only

## ABOUT BLANK

Markgrafendamm 24c; www.aboutblank.li;
open W-Su midnight-8am

Located in a grimy shack-looking
building, which almost seems a
prerequisite for East Berlin clubs,
About Blank is remarkable in that,
without having any apparent hook
(i.e., the space isn't particularly
impressive and the line outside is of
average length), it still manages to
find itself consistently ranked among
the best clubs in the city. But that's
simply because it attracts a dedicated
community of locals who, on most
nights of the week, are willing to
dance until the sun rises. When you
arrive, the bouncers will expect you to
know who's DJing, and if you can tell
them, you'll spend the rest of the night
gliding between three dancefloors.

*i* Cover €10-16, beer and shots €3,
mixed drinks €5-8; cash only

## GALANDER CHARLOTTENBURG

Stuttgarter Pl. 15, Charlottenburg; 30
36465363; www.stutti.galander-berlin.de;
open daily 6pm-2am

It's all well and good to subsist on
pilsner and vodka as you gallivant from
club to club, but when you want a
good, sturdy cocktail, where on earth
do you go? Well, you follow the hordes
of older, slightly better dressed adults
into Galander, where you can sink
into a red leather chair and pick your
poison from a carefully crafted cocktail
menu. The bar's smoky and old-
fashioned feel may lead you to think
that it's exclusively populated by "swag
is for boys, class is for men" types, but
thankfully such affectation is limited to
its décor. While most of the crowd is
30+ years old, the atmosphere remains
cozy and warm, rather than boring and

unwelcoming—although your wallet may disagree.

*i* Cocktails €8-12, long drinks from €7.50, beer from €3; cash only; BGLTQ+

### KITKAT CLUB
Köpenicker Str. 76; 30 78718963; www.kitkatclub.org; open M, Fri-Sa 11pm-late, Su 8am-7pm

A night at KitKat isn't for the faint of heart, but it is for anyone who wants an unforgettable experience and/or their coat checked by a topless woman who might playfully ask you to refer to her colleague, a man who's dressed just as provocatively, as "Mr. President." Known as Berlin's most infamous "sex club," KitKat attracts a crowd that a) disregards clothes in favor of leather or nothing at all, and b) embraces sex with a sense of adventure and experimentation. But don't worry—regular, clothed tourists are welcome. As long as you come with an open-mind and have no qualms about dancing next to naked people, you're guaranteed to have a night-out unlike any you've had before. That said, check the club's website beforehand to see if there's any dress code required on the night, because if you don't stick to it, you will, for better or worse, be turned away or forced to enter naked.

*i* Cover €8-€15; cash only; BGLTQ+ friendly; look at website for event-specific dress codes

### KNEIPE KLO
Leibnizstraße 57, Charlottenburg; 30 43727219; www.klo.de; open M-Th 7pm-2am, Fri-Sa 7pm-4am, Su 7pm-1:30am

People say you shouldn't poop where you eat, but they never mentioned anything about drinking, and Kneipe Klo (literally, "The Loo Bar") exploits this linguistic loophole to the fullest. At Kneipe Klo, your drinks will be served in urine collectors, which you can enjoy while sitting on a toilet and staring at the toilet-brush covered ceiling. Every inch of the interior not taken up by potty paraphernalia is plastered with a mix of Halloween decorations and nonspecific kitschy junk. The bar's a veritable madhouse—an impression only intensified by the mechanized tables and chairs that could, depending on the whims of the staff, give you quite the shock. The drink menu is nothing to write home about, but that's probably a good thing, since your family will be preoccupied with all your letters about the crazy toilet pub.

*i* Beer and liquor €4, long drinks and cocktails €5-10; no shorts or sandals allowed

### KUMPELNEST 3000
Lützowstraße 23, Wilmersdorf; 30 2616918; www.kumpelnest3000.com; open M-Thu 7pm-6am, Fri-Sa 7pm-8am, Su 7pm-6am

It's pretty high praise to say that, out of all the places we've visited in Berlin, Kumpelnest 3000 is certainly the strangest. And it's not just because it's located in a former brothel. Here, some sort of quirky-risqué fact is virtually a given about any nightlife spot. What makes this disco-themed dive bar so weird and fascinating is the crowd it attracts. At least, in a place like the sex club KitKat, everyone you see broadly fits the archetype of "A Person Who Would Go to a Sex

Club." But at Kumpelnest, there's no such consistency: underage teens, hipsters, 60-year-old hippies, lads on a pub crawl, tourists who look very confused to find that this isn't the Ritz Carlton—Kumpelnest welcomes everyone. And what's more, everyone seems to have a pretty good time.

*i* *Beer and liquor €2.50-4, mixed drinks €5.50-7.50; cash only*

# COLOGNE

Coverage by **Antonia Washington**

Now the fourth largest city in Germany behind Berlin, Hamburg, and Munich, Cologne dates back to the first century when it was established as a Roman territory. Fast forward almost 2000 years and Cologne was one of the most heavily bombed cities in Germany during World War II. By the end of the war, most of the city's population had fled and the vast majority of the city had been destroyed. At the time, Cologne was called the "world's greatest heap of rubble" by architect Rudolf Schwarz and the city then underwent some 50 years of rebuilding. About one million people now reside in the rejuvenated, reconstructed Cologne, which has a bustling city cafe. It boasts the largest BGLTQ+ community in Germany and is well-known for being one of the most socially open spaces in the country.

## ORIENTATION

Cologne sits on the banks of the **Rhein River** (Rhine River), which runs through the city roughly from north to south. The city center is concentrated on the west side. Cologne has its own version of a ring boulevard, surrounding the city center in a semi-circle closed by the river on the east side. Along it, **Zülpicher Platz** and **Friesenplatz** tend to be good places to get a drink or hit the clubs, while the area around **Rudolfplatz** along **Hohenzollernring** is lined with restaurants. Further east, at the center of the ring, the plaza around the **Cologne Cathedral** is one of the most significant centers in the city. Moving south from the cathedral, **Hohe Straße** is the city's most prominent shopping thoroughfare. The **Old Town** is concentrated in the few blocks extending west from the river between the **Hohenzollernbrücke** and **Deutzer Brücke bridges**.

## ESSENTIALS

### GETTING THERE

The Cologne Airport, called Köln Bonn Airport (or Cologne Bonn Airport), serves most European airlines and many others, making it reasonably accessible. The airport is located significantly southeast of the city, so you will need to take some secondary form of transportation from the airport into town. There is an S-Bahn line from the airport to the city center. If you are headed into town from elsewhere in the region, we recommend traveling by train, as the central train station, Köln Hauptbahnhof, empties onto a plaza that is linked to the plaza of the Cologne Cathedral.

## GETTING AROUND

Public transport in Cologne includes S-Bahn, U-Bahn, tram, and bus services, which all tend to be reliable. These can be very helpful getting to and from locations that are farther outside the city center. Within the city center, most things tend to be within about a half hour's walk. Much of the downtown area, especially the Old Town, is made up of pedestrian streets, so walking is often the best way to travel.

### PRACTICAL INFORMATION

**Tourist Offices:** Köln Tourismus tourist office in Cologne (Kardinal-Höffner-Platz 1; 0221 346430; open M-Sa 9am-8pm, Su 10am-5pm).
**Banks/ATMS/Currency Exchange:** You should expect to pay for most things

in Cologne with cash. There is an ATM just around the corner from the tourist office, across the street from the McDonald's.

**Post Offices:** The easiest post office to use is the one in the city center (Marspfortengasse 10; open M-Sa 9am-8pm).

**Internet:** Wi-Fi tends to be standard in accommodations in Cologne. There is also Wi-Fi available in some major city centers, such as the plaza surrounding the Cologne Cathedral. Look for the network "hotspot.koeln."

**BGLTQ+ Resources:** Köln Tourismus and Cologne Pride put together a pamphlet called "A survival guide for Cologne visitors," which contains all sorts of tips, activities, and resources for gay visitors. Jugendzentrum Anyway is an BGLTQ+ youth center (Kamekestr. 14; 0221 5777760; www.anyway-koeln.de).

## EMERGENCY INFORMATION

**Emergency Number:** 112

**Police:** Polizeiwache Stolkgasse police station near the central train station (Stolkgasse 47; 0221 2290).

**US Embassy:** The US Embassy in Germany is in Berlin, but there is a US Consulate near Cologne located in Dusseldorf (Willi-Becker-Allee 10; 40227 Düsseldorf; 211 7888927).

**Rape Crisis Center:** Frauen Gegen Gewalt runs rape crisis centers all over Germany. To find Cologne's nearest center to you, visit www.frauen-gegen-gewalt.de.

**Hospitals:** St. Marien Hospital (Kunibertskloster 11-13; 0221 16290; open daily 24hr).

**Pharmacies:** Dom Apotheke Köln (Bahnhofsvorplatz 1; 0221 20050500; open M-F 8am-6:30pm, Sa 9am-6:30pm).

## ACCOMMODATIONS

### STATION HOSTEL FOR BACKPACKERS ($$)

Marzellenstraße 44-56; 221 9125301; www.hostel-cologne.de; reception open 24hr

The Station Hostel in Cologne is one of the city's more social accommodations, though the staff reminisces about a time without

smartphones when the social scene was at its peak. This should be a hint that some of the hostel's staff has been around the block a few times, perfect if you're fishing for recommendations. Gather at the bar, in the beer garden, or in the lounge with cushy home-built looking sectionals and a string of rainbow pillows to kick back with your new hostel-mates. Downsides include toilets that sometimes smell a bit too removed from their last flush and the lack of a guest kitchen. The "pros" list, on the other hand, has one major factor working in its favor: no bunk beds.

*i* Dorms €18-26; reservation recommended; max stay 7 nights; BGLTQ+ friendly; no wheelchair accessibility; Wi-Fi; linens included, towels for rent €1, laundry facilities €4

### COLOGNE DOWNTOWN HOSTEL ($$)

Hohe Straße 30a; 22 12772950; www.downtownhostel.de; reception open 24hr

Cologne Downtown Hostel checks all the boxes: it's super clean, has spacious showers, and gives you towels. You don't have to make your own bed and reception is readily available round the clock. Still, there is something cold about the hostel (metaphorically as well as physically because sometimes the air conditioning is really cranking in the rooms). Maybe it's the neutral color scheme with slate highlights or the insistence on going through the hostel rules at check-in, but socializing here often feels more difficult.

*i* Dorms €20-27; reservation recommended; wheelchair accessible; Wi-Fi; linens included; towels included; laundry facilities; kitchen

## SIGHTS

### CULTURE

### COLOGNE CATHEDRAL

Domkloster 4; www.koelner-dom.de; open May-Oct M-Sa 6am-9pm, Su 1pm-4:30pm, Nov-Apr M-Sa 6am-7:30pm, Su 1pm-4:30pm

The Cologne Cathedral is a humongous Gothic cathedral that pretty much no one expected to be so big. The cathedral towers over the city and distinguishes the city's skyline. On the site of original ancient church construction, the foundation for today's High Gothic cathedral was laid in the mid-thirteenth century. Though the cathedral was extremely damaged by bombing in WWII, removing windows and sandbagging pieces in anticipation meant that no major works of medieval art were lost, but minor damage to the cathedral's stone work can be seen even today. The cathedral also possesses the **Shrine of the Three Kings,** said to contain the remains of the Biblical magi.

*i* *Free admission, English guided tours €8; tours M-Sa 10:30am and 2:30pm, Su 2:30pm, meet inside the main portal; tours M-Sa 10:30am and 2:30pm, Su 2:30pm, meet inside the main portal; wheelchair accessible*

### GROSS ST. MARTIN (GREAT ST. MARTIN CHURCH) ($)

Am Groß St. Martin; open daily 24hr

Another church shaping the city's horizon, Groß St. Martin is largely free of tourists, since most are drawn only to the cathedral. Well, that's fair enough. The interior isn't flashy by any standard. The true appeal of the St. Martin Church is the stone construction itself, which we know is ancient, but wow it really looks ancient. Today's Romanesque church building was constructed in the second half of the twelfth century on top of older Roman foundations, and, from within the chapel, visitors now can visit the Roman excavations underneath the church.

*i* *Free; wheelchair accessible*

## LANDMARKS

### ⬛HOHENZOLLERNBRÜCKE

50679 Cologne

This bridge crossing the **Rhine River** just behind the **Cologne Cathedral** is one of the city's most romantic treasures. Constructed in the early twentieth century, the bridge carries rail traffic to the central train station and has pedestrian walkways on either side. Along these walkways, you'll find padlocks covering the bridge's fencing, affixed by couples to eternalize their love. The locks are especially concentrated on the south side of the bridge, and there are so many of them that they seem to cascade off of the fencing in waves. Giant locks and bike chains hang on the bridge and smaller locks hang on those, with still smaller locks attached to the second layer in turn. The wall of multicolored, drawn-on, and even engraved padlocks are a beautiful sight for even the most jaded visitors.

*i* *Free; wheelchair accessible*

### EIGELSTEINTOR

Eigelstein; open daily 24hr

The Eigelsteintor is one of the last remaining pieces of the city's ancient fortifications. Erected in the late twelfth century, it was the city's northernmost gate in medieval Cologne. With its towers and tall stone archway, the gate stood guard around the city, protecting it from invaders. Though of course, Napoleon Bonaparte came through this very gate in his 1804 invasion of the city, so it's track record is a bit of a mixed bag (you can't win 'em all). And Napoleon was, like, a super-invader anyway, so that shouldn't even count.

*i* Free; wheelchair accessible

## MUSEUMS

### MUSEUM LUDWIG
Heinrich-Böll-Platz; 22 122126165; www. museum-ludwig.de; open Tu-Su 10am-6pm, 1st Th of month 10am-10pm

Cologne's Museum Ludwig is a major collection of modern and contemporary art from the turn of the twentieth century to the present day with a focus on the mid-century development of pop art. This style of art first bloomed in Great Britain and the United States as a commentary on mass production and consumerism in post-war society. Pop art's most famous contributor is **Andy Warhol,** and the museum has many of his works on display. All we have to say is that, artists of this style did a lot of weird things with doll heads. All the depraved things you did to your little sibling's Barbies as a kid don't even begin to describe how dolls are often used in pop art displays.

*i* Admission €12, €8 student, free under 18, first Th of month €7 starting at 5pm, tours €2; tour times vary, check the website; wheelchair accessible; audio guides downloadable online

### SCHOKOLADEN MUSEUM (CHOCO-LATE MUSEUM)
Am Schokoladenmuseum 1a; 22 19318880; www.schokoladenmuseum.de; open M-F 10am-6pm, Sa-Su 11am-7pm

Chocoholics beware: binging ahead. The chocolate museum pulls out all the stops with exhibits that take visitors through cocoa's origins in the Amazon and its spread across the globe, a greenhouse room where you can suddenly find yourself in a humid tropical garden, and the museum's own small chocolate factory. Be on the lookout for free samples. Don't pass by the giant chocolate fountain at the factory's end without picking up a freshly dipped wafer. Keep your eyes peeled for a small monkey decal that looks like Curious George really let himself go; he marks children's exhibits which are often more hands-on that the adult plaques.

*i* Admission €11.50, €9 student; guided tours can be booked in advance; chocolate production starts 30min. after opening, last entry 1hr. before closing; wheelchair accessible

## FOOD

### ⧫FRITES BELGIQUE ($)
Hohe Straße 96; 22 12 7121177; www. frites-belgique.com; open M-F 11am-8pm, Sa 11am-8pm, Su closed

If you find it frustrating that you can't have french fries conveniently in hand at all times, you may find a kindred spirit in Frites Belgique. Here, they've implemented a cardboard cone, which puts their hand-cut French fries right in your hand as you amble through Cologne's busy shopping streets and pedestrian areas. Better yet, the cone has an attached mini cone to hold Frites Belgique's homemade sauce, meaning fries and sauce can be carried in one hand, without the risk of the delicious treat becoming soggy potato mush. The shopping area where this storefront is located typically isn't the place to find food other than fast food

and French fry stands, but you should have an edible accessory while you shop.

*i* Fries €2.90-4, sauces €0.50-1.20, sausage €2.50-3; vegetarian options available; wheelchair accessible

### DON GELATI ($)

Am Hof 20; 22 127047950; www.don-ge-lati.de

If you have a breakfast sweet tooth, Don Gelati might be the place to soothe it. The café's specialty is, of course, gelato, so you can fill up on one of those towering monstrosities of gelato, fruit, chocolate, and candy that Europeans eat if they feel like slipping into a coma. The menu items that attract us most, however, are their waffles, crêpes and canolis. Get a Nutella waffle with ice cream and whipped cream. Or order a panino if you feel like rubbing your health in everyone's face. Otherwise, the best part about Don Gelati is its location. Situated just across the street from Roncalliplatz, effectively the south plaza of the Cologne Cathedral, you'll get a great view while sitting outside.

*i* Paninis €5.90-7.50, waffles and crêpes €4-9, fancy gelatos €5-10; vegetarian options available; wheelchair accessible

### HANS IM GLÜCK

Hohenzollernring 38-40; 22 129892163; www.hansimglueck-burgergrill.de; open M-Th noon-midnight, F-Sa noon-2am, Su noon-midnight, kitchen open M-Th noon-11pm, F-Sa noon-1am, Su noon-11pm

If you go for burgers at Hans im Glück, you must sit indoors and take advantage of the magnificent and ridiculous ode to nature they have created within. The potted plant sitting inside a tray carved from a section of tree, which also holds a selection of the restaurant's homemade ketchup and sauces, is just the beginning. Apparently, the restaurant decided that it really ought to feel like you're eating inside of an alder forest, so the thin, white-barked trunks of the tree stretch from floor to ceiling inside, winding their way through aisles and separating tables from each other. Our favorites from their burger menu include the Alsdann (€8.30), with fried pear, mild gorgonzola sauce, and walnuts, and the Geissbock (€8.80), with goat cheese, bacon, and fig jam.

*i* Burgers €7-9, lunch special of burger, drink, and side €5.50; vegetarian and vegan options available; wheelchair accessible

# NIGHTLIFE

### CENT CLUB

Hohenstaufenring 25; www.centclub.de; open M-W closed, Th-Sa 10pm-5am

Cent Club is a great place for a casual night out. We were told, "They let everybody in. The only thing they won't go for is athletic wear." While we think that's pretty unfair to the appropriate clothing genre athleisure (it's more than clothes really, it's a lifestyle), it means as long as your travel outfit looks intentional, you should be fine. The crowd is young enough to get wasted on free vodka energies and excited enough about each new song to yell out the first lyrics in harmony. The club doesn't start to get busy until about midnight. If you show up earlier, you'll probably have plenty of space to yourself on the dance floor and, depending on the night, it could also mean getting discounted or free drinks.

*i* Cover €5, drinks from €3, €0.50 deposit for your glass; cash only; BGLTQ+ friendly; wheelchair accessible

### DIAMONDS CLUB

Hohenzollernring 90; 17 85173273; www.club-diamonds.de; open Th-Sa 11pm-6am

Diamonds Club plays mostly hip-hop and reggaeton mixes, so if you're looking to drop it low and pretend you're Shakira, you made a great choice. In a haze of fog-infused air, get down in a t-shirt dress and your white Adidas sneakers (if that reference is dated by 2018 so be it, they made a comeback once, they can do it again) under the most arrogantly-sized disco ball we've ever seen. It's so big, it makes your mama look like a pygmy marmoset, and that's a size joke, not an ugliness joke, so if your mind went there, that's on you.

*i* No cover, required to spend a minimum of €5; cash only

# FRANKFURT

Coverage by **Antonia Washington**

If you expanded Wall Street into an entire city, it would be Frankfurt. Best known as a hub, Frankfurt is home to the seat of the European Central Bank, the German Federal Bank, and the Frankfurt Stock Exchange, among other similar institutions. Frankfurt is among the primary financial centers of the European continent and that said, you might wonder why parallels to huge feature films like *Wolf of Wall Street* and *The Big Short* haven't taken place here. A friend we made in a hostel who moved to Frankfurt from the United States summed it up to us by comparing it to more commonly visited tourist destinations. "When you think of Paris," he told us, "Even if you've never been there, you have something in mind… the Eiffel Tower, pastries, baguettes, or people wearing scarves. But when you think of Frankfurt, most of us don't have a first thought." And, according to him, even after living in Frankfurt for a few years, he felt the same way. Frankfurt is a big city where there is always something going on, but you can be as seen or as anonymous as you want to be. It gives you the blank slate to springboard off into some adventure.

## ORIENTATION

Frankfurt is split by the **Main River** (that's why you'll often see the city called "Frankfurt am Main"), which runs roughly east to west through the city, though in the city center it runs at more of an angle. To orient yourself, it helps to start with the **Frankfurt Hauptbahnhof,** the central train station. The train station sits north of the river and functions as the effective west end of the city center. If you walk east from the train station, you will find **Kaiserstraße,** a well-traveled area full of restaurants that runs through the heart of Frankfurt's Red Light District. Further east, you will cross through a small park and find yourself in the city center, which is ringed by parks on the north of the river; these are small, green city blocks that do not typically mark a significant change in environment. Within this central city ring, you will find Frankfurt's main tourist sites, including the **Kaiserdom Cathedral**. On the south side of the river, directly across from this central city area is the Museumsufer where you will find many of the city's principal museums. Near the south side of the "Alte Brücke" bridge, around **Große Rittergasse,** there are many bars and clubs.

## ESSENTIALS

### GETTING THERE

Because of its prominence in the business world, Frankfurt is easily accessible. The Frankfurt Airport is the largest international airport in Germany and services more passengers (read: men and women in suits) per year than any other airport in continental Europe. If you're coming into town from elsewhere in the region, we recommend travel by train to Hauptbahnhof because of how centrally located the central train station is. If you stay in a hostel in Frankfurt, chances are good that you'll be in one within a few blocks of the train station.

### GETTING AROUND

Similar to elsewhere in Germany, Frankfurt uses an S-Bahn and U-Bahn; both rail lines tend to be easy to find and run efficiently. Together with bus lines, most parts of the city tend to be easily reachable. Within the city center, most places are within about a 30min. walk, so travel on foot is our favorite way of getting around.

### PRACTICAL INFORMATION

**Tourist Offices:** There is a tourist office inside Hauptbahnhof. There is another in Römerberg square. It does not have Wi-Fi and it's not wheelchair accessible (Römerberg 27, 069 21238800; www.frankfurt-tourismus.de; open M-F 9:30am-5:30pm, Sa-Su 9:30am-4pm).

**Banks/ATMs/Currency Exchange:** Many places in Frankfurt do not take payment by card. ATMs are most accessible at banks. There is a Wells Fargo in the city center (An der Hauptwache 7; 069 2980270; M-F 8am-7pm).

**Post Offices:** Postbank Finanzcenter (Zeil 90, 60313 Frankfurt; 0228 55005500; M-F 9:30am-7pm, Sa 10am-2pm).

**Internet:** Wi-Fi is generally available at accommodations in Frankfurt. Wi-Fi is not available at the tourist office, but, when in doubt, Starbucks has your back.

**BGLTQ+ Resources:** For an orientation to BGLTQ+ life in Frankfurt, check out http://www.germany.travel/en/ms/lgbt/culture/frankfurt-and-the-center/frankfurt-and-the-center.html. The tourist information office also publishes a pamphlet called Gay Frankfurt, which includes many BGLTQ+ resources and venues. Frankfurt also has a Lesbian Information Center, which you can find at www.libs.w4w.net.

## EMERGENCY INFORMATION

**Emergency Number:** 112

**Police:** Polizeirevier Innenstadt (Downtown Police Station: Zeil 33; 069 755 10100).

**US Embassy:** Though the US Embassy in Germany is located in Berlin, there is a US Consulate in Frankfurt (Gießener Str. 30; 069 75350).

**Rape Crisis Center:** Frauen Gegen Gewalt, an organization from Berlin, has services available for victims of sexual assault in Frankfurt. Look into their locations and accessing resources at www.frauen-gegen-gewalt.de.

**Hospitals:** Burgerhospital Frankfurt (Nibelungen¬allee 37-41; 069 15000; open daily 24hr).

**Pharmacies:** Apotheke Hauptbahnhof (B-Ebene, at the central train station; 069; M-F 6:30am-9pm, Sa 8am-9pm, Su 9am-8pm).

# ACCOMMODATIONS

### FIVE ELEMENTS HOSTEL ($)

Moselstraße 40; 69 24005885; www.5elementshostel.de; reception open 24hr

The Five Elements Hostel in Frankfurt has a nicely balanced social scene, where most days there is someone working on their laptop in the common area and most evenings you can find groups crushing beers they picked up at the hostel bar and playing pool downstairs. Run by a young international staff, the hostel often puts on group activities, which range from movie nights to making crêpes or grilling burgers with the token (and often shirtless) American staffer on the Fourth of July. Plus, the breakfast buffet at the hostel includes seemingly endless Nutella, which is free when you stay at least three nights.

*i* Dorms €15-25; reservation required; BGLTQ+ friendly; limited wheelchair accessibility; Wi-Fi; laundry facilities €4.50; breakfast €4.50

### FRANKFURT HOSTEL ($$)

Kaiserstrasse 74; 69 2475130; www.frankfurt-hostel.com; reception open 24hr

Frankfurt Hostel is another good place to make friends on the road, with a bar where we ended up for drinks when we weren't even staying there! With a considerate bar environment to boot, there is a small second common room for people who need a quiet place to work and perhaps brush up on their consulting interview skills. Plus, the hostel serves a daily free pasta dinner where travelers can come together over their love of noodles and dedication to free food (the most universal of human qualities). Their claim about having "live music" is a little sketch though because that really translated to people hopping on the piano once in a while, but a little jazz never hurt anyone.

*i* Dorms €18-2; reservation recommended; max stay 2 weeks; Wi-Fi; laundry facilities €5; towels for rent €1

### UNITED-HOSTEL FRANKFURT CITY CENTER ($$)

Kaiserstraße 52; 69 256678000; www.united-hostel-frankfurt.com; reception open 24hr

The modern furnishings and panels of neon light in United-Hostel Frankfurt

City Center give off a spaceship vibe with lights beaming down on you and changing color when you least expect, like that shirt American Apparel used to sell that changed color in heat, which was a cool idea until we realized it meant having constant and aggressive pit stains. Dorm beds are pulled into the center of the room and built into their own nooks, which gives you an added sense of privacy. Though renovations have temporarily closed down the hostel bar, there are plenty of large common spaces to crack your own supermarket beers and a gigantic TV in the lounge.

*i* Dorms €17-30; reservation recommended; max stay 1 week; wheelchair accessible; Wi-Fi; towels €5; self-service laundry facilities wash €4, dry €2; breakfast buffet €4.50

# SIGHTS
## CULTURE

### ◼KAISERDOM (FRANKFURT CATHEDRAL)
Domplatz 14; 69 2970320; www. dom-frankfurt.de; tower access 9am-6pm
A grand red stone interior awaits visitors to the Frankfurt Cathedral, which today relies heavily on Gothic style, but includes other architectural elements picked up over the church's centuries-long history. Visitors can also climb the 95-meter tower. The tower staircase is a seemingly endless spiral, wrapping in circles as it carries you upwards with no view of anything but the curving walls surrounding you. It is a physically dizzying experience as much as it is an exhausting one (we all romanticize spiral staircases but we also forget the strange lateral exertion that they actually require), but, at the top, you are rewarded with truly incredible views of the city, worth every one of the 328 steps.

*i* Tower admission €3, student €1.50; wheelchair accessible

### KLEINMARKTHALLE
Hasengasse 5-7; 69 21233696; www. kleinmarkthalle.de; open M-F 8am-6pm, Sa 8am-4pm, Su closed
This indoor market in Frankfurt operates rain or shine, meaning there are opportunities to stock up on novelty cheeses and sausages as big as your forearm no matter what time of the year it is. Pop in for fresh produce from papayas to teeny tiny blueberries you can eat by the handful. With a few cafés and butcher stands happy to slice cured meats straight into sandwiches, Kleinmarkthalle is also a reliable place to come for a midday bite. Whether you walk out with a fresh, meaty sandwich or a bag full of groceries, you made a good choice. And another bonus: like Costco, several of the booths give free samples.

*i* Prices vary by stand, some stands cash only; wheelchair accessible

# LANDMARKS

### FRANKFURT STOCK EXCHANGE
Börsenplatz 4; 69 21111515; www.frankfurtstockexchange.de; open M-F 9am-5pm
To see one of the things that makes Frankfurt famous and lose yourself in an existential wormhole about how stocks really work, the Frankfurt Stock Exchange is a great place to swing by for a quick photo opportunity. Outside of the stock exchange there is a cool work of art posed for the world to see. No, not the trader in the gorgeous three-piece suit who spent the last 20 minutes chain-smoking and yelling into his cell phone. We're talking about the statues of the bull and the bear. Why are people drawn to the idea of placing metal sculptures, bulls in particular, in front of stock exchanges? We don't know, but we're into it.

*i* Free; plaza is wheelchair accessible

### RIVERFRONT PROMENADE
Untermainkai 17; open daily 24hr
The promenade that extends on either side of the **Main River** in Frankfurt is one of our favorite ways to see the city. Start at the **Holbeinsteg pedestrian bridge** if you are staying at a hostel in the **Red Light District** and walk a loop along the promenade crossing **Eiserner Steg,** the city's other pedestrian bridge further east. Eiserner Steg is known as destination where couples go to attach padlocks to the railings. The walk along the promenade is always well populated with plenty of green spaces to stop and hang out by the river. This will lead

you along the row of museums to the south of the river and **Old Town** to the north.

*i* *Free; wheelchair accessible*

## RÖMERBERG (RÖMER SQUARE)
Römerberg 27; open daily 24hr

Römerberg is the lasting façade of an old German town inside Frankfurt's urban center. With the spire of the **Frankfurt Cathedral** looming in the background, fairytale apartment buildings stand precariously wedged side by side (it's unclear if they would all domino to the ground if not for the super glue holding them together, or if they are secretly all one building sliced into thin sections). Römer square sits at the center of the **Altstadt** (Old Town). Opposite the apartment buildings, you will find the **Römer,** which is the several hundred-year-old **City Hall of Frankfurt.** You'll also find restaurants, bustling pedestrian walkways, and one of those street performers who pretends to be a statue moving around impatiently and gesturing at passersby.

*i* *Free; wheelchair accessible*

## MUSEUMS

### FILMMUSEUM
Schaumainkai 41; 69 961220220; www.
deutsches-filminstitut.de/en/filmmuseum;
open Tu 10am-6pm, W 10am-8pm, Th-Su
10am-6pm

The Frankfurt Filmmuseum is a small, but modern collection that takes visitors through the history and evolution of film. Beginning with the development of technology, learn about the use of still photos to create moving video, and tinker around with kaleidoscopes and early flip-book style movie boxes. Next, take a look at the construction of narrative. Our favorite display is a four-projector ensemble where movie scenes are shown on alternating screens, while neighboring screens juxtapose clips from other productions using similar visual or thematic elements. Here, you can witness **Martin Scorsese** become legend with his avant-garde filming in *Mean Streets,* see **Meryl Streep's** scope of characters, and rewatch the *Twilight* make out scene like never before.

*i* *Admission €6, student €3, special exhibitions €7, €5; wheelchair accessible*

### STÄDEL MUSEUM
Schaumainkai 63; 69 605098200; www.
staedelmuseum.de; open Tu-W 10am-6pm,
Th-F 10am-9pm, Sa-Su 10am-6pm

The Städel Museum is the major art museum in Frankfurt and one of the most important collections of art in Germany; the city's finance bros probably ignore it, but you shouldn't. Beginning with the Old Masters on the top floor, visitors will see pieces from **Rembrandt** and **Reubens,** as well as a significant display of early Dutch art, including pieces from **Jan van Eyck, Hieronymus Bosch** (though nothing as perverse as *The Garden of Earthly Delights*), and **Lucas Cranach the Elder.** In more modern sections, experience the transformation of art at the turn of the twentieth century, as artists like                    Claude

Monet and Max Liebermann turned towards Impressionism.

*i* *Admission €14, student €12; wheelchair accessible*

## OUTDOORS

### FREIBAD ESCHERSHEIM

Alexander-Riese-Weg; 69 2710892300; www.bbf-frankfurt.de; open M-F 10am-8pm, Sa-Su 9am-8pm

If you need a day to unwind, a trip to the pool Freibad Eschersheim is the thing to do. This huge public pool is surrounded by equally massive grass areas, so while it doesn't have lounge chairs to recline in, it is the perfect place to bring a blanket or a towel and lay out with a picnic, alternating between the cool water and hot rays. In fact, the pool is unheated, so we advise visiting on a hot day or amping yourself up to take the plunge all at once. The deepest part of the pool is only 1.6 meters deep. The edges are roped off where there aren't stairs, so you can't jump in, which we think is stupid, but relaxing beside an outdoor pool is always a net positive.

*i* *Admission €4.80, student €3.20; wheelchair accessible*

## FOOD

### ☑MEAT ROOM ($$)

Kaiserstraße 39; 69 87201927; www.meatroom.de; open M-F 11am-11:30pm

Amid furniture smoothed out of fork lift crates and a blazing fire roaring on a flat-screen TV in the back corner, the Meat Room truly lives up to its name with an array of meat dishes and a few salads for the veg-heads among us. Choose between steak and seafood, including T-Bones, lamb chops, salmon, and lobster. Then, pick a side and add one of the restaurant's specialty sauces. Looking for more traditional food? Meat Room also has a menu of German specials, a long list of pork dishes where we counted "Frankfurter," the region's legendary sausage style, in the name of no fewer than five dishes. Try handkäs with musik, which translates to "hand

cheese with music," a regional cuisine made of sour milk cheese.

*i* *Entrées €7-15; vegetarian options available; limited wheelchair accessibility*

### EBERT'S SUPPENSTUBE ($)

Grosse Bockenheimer Strasse 31; 69 20973877; www.ebert-feinkost.de; open M-F 11am-7pm, Sa 11am-6pm

This simple deli-style restaurant is a great place to stop in for the essentials, namely, soup and sausage, virtually the only things on the menu. Soups are Ebert's specialty; they did put "suppen" in their name. Still, their sausage is great and lots of their soups are sausage-based anyway, so, either way, you can't lose. The menu is not available in English, which can be daunting, but, when in doubt, simply ask for bratwurst. You'll be asked if you want beer or pork and then quickly handed your sausage in a bun, ready for mustarding at the self-serve pump. Soups are a little harder to navigate without being able to read the menu, but you can get clues from pieces of the names including wurst or *gulaschsuppe,* and vegetarian soups should usually say *vegetarische.*

*i* *Sausage and soup €2.50-6; vegetarian options available; wheelchair accessible*

### THAI FUN ($$)

Elbestraße 15; 69 26958430; www.thai-fun-halal.de; open daily 11am-11pm

If you're looking for a sit-down restaurant with atypical ambiance, you would probably have better luck finding a bite to eat around the corner on Kaiserstraß. Thai Fun has a few bamboo-themed decorations and satisfyingly smooth furniture, but the great thing about the restaurant is its attention to dietary restrictions. Beyond just vegetarian and vegan options, the Thai restaurant serves halal food, a great option for those travelers that need halal options, but have grown tired of roadside falafel stands (as much as we love quick access to *döner* boxes). Stop by Thai Fun for fried egg noodles with vegetables, pad thai with chicken, shrimp, or beef, or one of their many squid dishes.

*i* *Entrées €6-10; vegetarian, Halal, or vegan options available; wheelchair accessible*

## URBAN KITCHEN ORIGIN FOOD ($$)

Kaiserstraße 53; 69 27107999; www.
myurbankitchen.de; open M-F 11am-mid-
night, Sa 11am-open end, Su 11am-11pm

Urban Kitchen Origin Food has a
little bit of just about anything you
could want. On the menu, you'll
find burgers, pasta, pizza, steak, fish,
ambiguous Asian food, and even
sushi. We dove straight into their
salad section because, after weeks
on the road, we may be developing
scurvy. Other menu highlights
include ramen (€10-13), an upscale
wholesome version of everyone's
favorite microwave lunch (we love you
Cup Noodles, no shade), and pitas and
skewers (€9.90-11.5), available with
a variety of proteins, but also packed
with veggies and tzaziki, both feel-good
options for every occasion.

*i* Entrées €8-15, steaks and fish up to
€30, card min €25; vegetarian options
available; limited wheelchair accessibility

# NIGHTLIFE

## ⬛SHOTZ

Große Rittergasse 40; www.shotz-bar.com/
locations/frankfurt; open M-Th 8pm-1am, F
8pm-2am, Sa 8pm-3am

Shotz is the party spot for students
in Frankfurt. With more than 150
specialty shots, choose one with
an embarrassing title and see what
happens. Favorites include the Google,
with four layers of color, the Botox,
with alcohol squirted from a syringe,
the Psycho Killer, with a goldfish
cracker swimming inside, and the
Viagra, with a little blue pill (it's candy,
don't worry). Try one of their action
shots for a more involved experience
with titles like the Bangcock, though
the bartender made us swear we
wouldn't divulge the stunt and ruin
the surprise. When in doubt, the
Copacabana is a safe bet; it's creamy
and chocolatey liqueur on a fruity
mango base.

*i* No cover, mixed shots €2-2.50, straight
shots €2.50-3.50; cash only; BGLTQ+
friendly

## CITY BEACH

Carl-Theodor-Reiffenstein-Platz 5; 69
29729697; www.citybeach-frankfurt.de;
open M-Th 11am-11pm, F-Sa 11am-mid-
night

City Beach is a venue combining two
of our favorite things, rooftop bars and
artificial urban beaches. We have no
idea how they got sand on top of a six-
story building, but we're thankful they
did. At City Beach, you can recline
in a lounge chair, drink in hand, and
dig your toes into the sand looking
out on the Frankfurt skyline feeling
bad for all the sad financiers working
away in their tall office buildings. But
even if that's your work-week persona,
you're on vacation now, so live it up.
Take a dip in the pool and dry off in
the unencumbered rooftop sun with a
fruity cocktail on ice.

*i* No cover, drinks from €5; cash only

## PLANK

Elbestraße 15; 69 26958666; www.
barplank.de; open M-Th 10am-1am, F
10am-2am, Sa 11am-2am

Plank is a bar with an aesthetic that
might be the material incarnation of a
man-bunned IKEA designer wearing
a charcoal suit with a white v-neck
t-shirt and an Urban Outfitters scarf. A
mostly slate-grey interior carved into a
brick corner window front, the street-
level chairs out front are almost always
occupied, even in the bar's slowest
moments. Gather at Plank for drinks
and a relaxed place for conversation by
their open floor to ceiling windows.
Right around the corner from the
restaurant strip on Kaiserstraß, the
bar is a perfect after-dinner locale, but
worth a late-night trip, when its dark
walls seem to blend with the night.

*i* No cover, drinks from €5; cash only;
BGLTQ+ friendly

# HAMBURG

Coverage by **Antonia Washington**

Hamburg is the second largest city in Germany, behind Berlin. Connected to the North Sea by the Elbe River, it gained prominence as a center of trade in Europe beginning in the Middle Ages. This Hanseatic port city, in fact, was once known as the "gateway to the world." As water was the bestower of trade and expansion for most of Hamburg's history, the waterways permeate into the city's core, and because the city sits at the crux of a web of channels, it has bridges. A lot of them. Hamburg is home to more bridges than any other city in the world. With at least 2,300 bridges—though some estimates put it over 2,500—, the combined bridge score of Venice, Amsterdam, and London doesn't even begin to approach this number. If you need more than this deluge of canals to entice you to Hamburg, consider its history as a rebounding city. Structurally, Hamburg has been through a lot. It was burned almost entirely to the ground in the nineteenth century, bombed heavily in WWII, and inundated by floods that killed hundreds of people as late as the 1960s. After everything, Hamburg has always maintained the courage and the spirit to rebuild and look to the future, and that's something worth experiencing.

## ORIENTATION

The city center of Hamburg is a fairly small ring located north of the **Elbe River's** canals and just south of the **Außenalster lake.** A circular road winds around the area and the central train station borders it to the northeast. In the city center, you will find many of the historic sights, including the **Rathaus,** most of the historic churches, and many museums, as well as the corporate offices of modern companies like Google. To the west of the city center is the **St. Pauli district,** a hip, young neighborhood where it often feels like everyone could be a bassist in a punk band or a graphic designer. Important areas in St. Pauli include the **Reeperbahn** and surrounding streets, which are the center of the city's **Red Light district** and hotspots for clubbing and nightlife in the city. The Sternschanze area is in the north and, around **Schulterblatt street,** you will find tons of trendy restaurants and shops. To the east of the city center is the **St. Georg neighborhood,** the primary area for BGLTQ+ life in Hamburg.

## ESSENTIALS

### GETTING THERE

The Hamburg Airport is a major international airport north of the city. The airport is serviced by airlines from all over the world, so reaching Hamburg is simple by plane from just about anywhere. Direct flights to and from the United States tend to only be from New York City, so if you're flying from elsewhere, you may have a connecting flight. If you are traveling from elsewhere in the region, trains and buses are both great options for reaching Hamburg. The central train station, Hamburg Hauptbahnhof, and the central bus station, Hamburg ZOB, are right next to each other.

### GETTING AROUND

Hamburg is surprisingly walkable within neighborhoods, and things in the city center tend to be within about a 30min walk from each other. If you plan to move significantly between neighborhoods, it will be easier to use public transport. The S-Bahn and U-Bahn trains are both available as well as buses. We thought the U-Bahn was especially useful in Hamburg, particularly the U3, which essentially runs in a giant loop around the city center, with stops on the edges of the St. Pauli and St. Georg neighborhoods.

### PRACTICAL INFORMATION

**Tourist Offices:** St. Pauli Tourist Office (Wohlwillstraße 1; 040 98234483;

www.pauli-tourist.de; open M-Sa 10am-7pm).

**Banks/ATMs/Currency Exchange:** Most restaurants and many businesses in Hamburg only accept cash. Most ATMs are located in banks, which are readily available throughout the city.

**Post Offices:** There are post offices throughout the city. The following is located in the city center (Alter Wall 38; 0228 4333112; open M-F 9am-6:30pm, Sa 10:30am-1pm).

**Internet:** Wi-Fi is fairly standard in accommodations in Hamburg, but not often elsewhere. Many coffee shops in the city center have Wi-Fi.

**BGLTQ+ Resources:** The Hamburg tourist office publishes a pamphlet called "Hamburger Queer" with resources and suggestions for BGLTQ+ visitors. Many of the establishments along Lange Reihe in St. Georg also have all sorts of pamphlets and flyers with information on BGLTQ+ events and businesses in Hamburg.

## EMERGENCY INFORMATION

**Emergency Number:** 112
**Police:** Polizeirevierwache Rathaus. (Große Johannisstraße 1; 40 428 650).
**US Embassy:** The US Embassy in Germany is nearby in Berlin, but Hamburg also has its own US Consulate, listed here (Alsterufer 27/28; 040 411 71 100).
**Rape Crisis Center:** Emergency hotline for victims of sexual assault and rape (040 255566). Weißer Ring runs rape crisis centers in Hamburg. Call them at 040 2517680 or go online to www.hamburg.weisser-ring.de.
**Hospitals:** Universitätsklinikum Hamburg-Eppendorf (Martinistraße 52; 040 74100; open daily 24hr).
**Pharmacies:** Europa Apotheke (Bergstraße 14; 040 32527690; www.europa-apotheke-hamburg.de; open M-F 8am-8pm, Sa 9:30am-8pm).

# ACCOMMODATIONS

### ⛰MAC CITY HOSTEL ($$)
Beim Strohhause 26; 40 35629146; www.maccityhostel.de; reception open daily 8am-midnight

Rooms at the MAC City Hostel are clean and bright. They may be plain, but they are great places to wake up and stretch on a sunny morning before remembering that you're in a bunk bed and the guy sleeping above you is snoring. Still, it's great for a moment. The common areas at MAC City Hostel are very small, but maybe you can start hanging out with friends in the incredibly spacious shower rooms, where showers are standard-sized but an unnecessary amount of floor space sprawls in front of the sinks. Don't even try to lie and tell us you wouldn't love the space to just hang out in there with, like, any girl you've ever met in the bathroom at a party.

*i* Dorms €25-40; reservation recommended; wheelchair accessible; Wi-Fi; linens included; towels €2.50 deposit; laundry €5; kitchen

### BACKPACKERS HOSTEL ST. PAULI ($)
Bernstorffstrasse 98; 40 23517043; www.backpackers-stpauli.de; reception open Apr-Nov daily 8am-midnight, Dec-Mar daily 9am-10pm

Backpackers Hostel St. Pauli is not afraid of making a political statement. There is a small anti-Trump figurine standing atop a cabinet, and among the stickers plastering the bar, you'll find many with anti-racism slogans and things like, "refugees welcome," and "no human is illegal." At the heart of the matter, the hostel believes in welcoming with open arms anyone who is willing to do the same. Common areas are limited, but the guest kitchen has a massive couch to compensate, and if you hang out around the bar or the small backyard patio, you're bound to encounter some friendly faces.

*i* Dorms €15-25; reservation recommended; min stay 2 nights on weekends; no wheelchair accessibility; Wi-Fi; linens included; towels €1.50; lockers €5 deposit; breakfast buffet €5; kitchen

### INSTANT SLEEP BACKPACKERHOSTEL ($$)
Max-Brauer-Allee 277; 40 43180180; www.instantsleep.de; reception open daily 9am-10pm

Upon arriving at Instant Sleep Backpackerhostel in Hamburg, the first area you will encounter is the main hallway where flyers, announcements, and art plaster the walls. The rest of the hostel proceeds in the same fashion, with mismatched maps and art pieces scattered about, including in the rooms, which are spacious and clean. Instant Sleep sometimes hosts hostel-wide activities (group dinners, open mics, drinking games, etc.) where you'll get to hang out with other travelers, but don't expect those events to be regular occurrences. As we were told, "Whoever's working just does whatever they want with the guests." So, chat up the reception while you're there and you may be able to stir something up.

*i* *Dorms €24-€32; reservation recommended; min stay 2 nights on weekends; max 7 nights; not BGLTQ+ friendly; no wheelchair accessibility; Wi-Fi; linens included; towel rental €1; laundry facilities €3 wash, €3 dry; kitchen*

# SIGHTS
## CULTURE

### ▧ST. MICHAELISKIRCHE (ST. MICHAEL'S CHURCH)

Englische Planke 1; 40 376780; www.st-michaelis.de; open May-Oct daily 9am-8pm, Nov-Apr daily 10am-6pm

St. Michael's Church is a gorgeous Baroque church with a white and gold interior, and was one of our favorite visits in Hamburg. In contrast to narrow Gothic churches whose aisles are so narrow that you start having visions of that scene from *Harry Potter and the Prisoner of Azkaban* (HP fans, you know what we're talking about), the body of St. Michael's opens up on wide balconies that extend the length of the nave into a bright and yawning space. These balconies are the seat of the church's several organs, so snag a spot on a balcony pew before service starts if you want a prime spot next to the DJ. Visitors to the church can also climb the church tower, one of Hamburgs's most famous landmarks, and take a gander at the crypts.

*i* *Free entry tower €5, student €4, crypt €4, student €3, combination ticket €7, student €6; without prior registration church tours every second and fourth Sunday of the month at 3pm; last entry 30min. before closing; wheelchair accessible; tours available daily but must be booked at least 2 weeks in advance*

### ELBPHILHARMONIE

Am Kaiserkai 62; www.elbphilharmonie.com; plaza open daily 9am-midnight

Newly opened in January 2017, the Elbphilharmonie is a dazzling demonstration of architectural imagination. A futuristic work of glass, the building reflects the sky while simultaneously evoking waves with its shape, an ode to its position on the water's edge, with a plaza observation deck that peers out over Hamburg's many ports. Inside the concert hall, custom-surfaced walls are designed to reflect sound in every direction and ensure acoustic perfection, making this one of the most advanced concert venues in the world in terms of acoustic technology. Visit the plaza for views of the city or come to a concert to experience the superior orchestral sound (we know we said "acoustic" a lot of times, but don't start thinking that you're going to come watch Ed Sheeran strum on his guitar).

*i* *Free; wheelchair accessible; purchase concert tickets online or by phone at 040 35766666*

## LANDMARKS

### ▧PLANTEN UN BLOMEN

Planten un Blomen, St. Petersburger Straße; www.plantenunblomen.hamburg.de; open Apr daily 7am-10pm, May-Sept daily 7am-11pm, Oct-Mar 7am-8pm

This large park that sits between Hamburg's city center and the St. Pauli neighborhood stretches from the St. Pauli U-Bahn station at the east end of the **Reeperbahn** up past the north end of the city center. Here, you'll find open fields, flower gardens, and ponds meandering through the park where you can sit and read with your bike resting serenely against a park bench. We saw an old man doing just that when we visited. And even after an intense downpour, you'll find moms pushing strollers, kids running barefoot in the playground sand, and people dumping gravel out of their shoes.

*i* *Free; wheelchair accessible*

### RATHAUS

Rathausmarkt 1; open daily 8am-6pm

The Hamburg Rathaus is the political center of the city, home to the office of the Hamburg mayor, and the places of meeting for the city's parliamentary and senatorial bodies. Built at the end of the nineteenth century, the exterior of the city hall is an exemplar of Neo-Renaissance style, made to display Hamburg's prosperity, especially at the time of its construction. The sandstone building is particularly ornate as compared to styles typical of the region. If you watched *Home Alone 2: Lost in New York* and identified most with the lady in the park who had a deep spiritual affinity for pigeons, the plaza in front of the Hamburg Rathaus would be a great place to start amassing your pigeon army.

*i* *Free, tours €4; wheelchair accessible; call to book tours in English (040 4283124)*

## SPEICHERSTADT

Speicherstadt; www.speicherstadtmuseum. de; open daily 24hr

The Speicherstadt area is a small window into Hamburg's history as one of the world's great port cities. This warehouse district is the world's largest contiguous warehouse complex, designated as a **UNESCO World Heritage site** in 2015 and built on wooden piles in brick Gothic style. You might say, "they're literally brick buildings that you're raving about," but they're special brick buildings, and their reflection off the canal waters feels like a real slice of history. If you're looking for other historic neighborhoods to meander through and remark excitedly about the character of the buildings, the **Krameramtsstuben,** houses of the **Guild of Shopkeepers,** constitute the oldest lane of terraced houses in the world (Krayenkamp 10, 20459 Hamburg).

*i* *Free to visit; wheelchair accessible*

# MUSEUMS

### KUNSTHALLE MUSEUM

Glockengießerwall 5; 40 428131200; www.hamburger-kunsthalle.de; open Tu-W 10am-6pm, Th 10am-9pm, F-Su 10am-6pm

The Kunsthalle Museum is Hamburg's greatest collection of art, stretching from the Old Masters to contemporary exhibitions. As you wander from room to room and through time periods, it may feel a bit like an art history lesson, where slowly your understanding of art movements will begin to take form. From the Enlightenment collection, keep an eye out for the understated *View of the Tiber and Fidenae at the Acqua Acetosa Spring* by **Johann Christian Reinhart,** a picturesque scene that could have come straight from *Westworld.* (But the TV show or the theme park itself? You'll never know. Ha! Set design inception.) And from the Romanticism collection, we loved **Caspar David Friedrich's** piece, *Wanderer Above the Sea of Fog,* with a nineteenth-century Instagram aesthetic to make everyone jealous.

*i* *Admission M-F €12, student €6, Sa-Su €14, student €7, Th 5:30pm-9pm €8, student €4; tours €4; English tours Sundays at 11am; wheelchair accessible*

### MUSEUM FÜR HAMBURGISCHE GESCHICHTE (MUSEUM OF HAMBURG HISTORY)

Holstenwall 24; 40 428132100; www. hamburgmuseum.de; open Tu-Sa 10am-

5pm, Su 10am-6pm

The museum, founded in 1908, walks visitors through the history of Hamburg from its early origins to the political changes of the modern age. Of course, this has long been a port city, and you'll find plenty of ship reconstructions and dioramas here, documenting how industry flourished on its docks beginning with lumber milling and trade, filling barrels with all sorts of goods and stacking them in boats. But the museum doesn't just look at Hamburg as a port. Here, you will learn about the city's destruction in the **Great Fire of 1842**, life during the Baroque era, and even the history of the Jewish community in Hamburg. The museum itself is housed in a college-esque brick building overhung by trees, perfect to get you jazzed for learning!

*i* Admission €9.50, student €6; wheelchair accessible; tours can be booked in advance online at www.museumsdienst-hamburg.de or by calling 040 4281310

## OUTDOORS

### ALSTER LAKES

Alster Lakes; open daily 24hr, barring extraneous circumstances

The Alster Lakes are a paradise within the city. On the lakes, you'll find sail boats, pedal boats, paddle boards (yes, "pedal" and "paddle" are different; sometimes correct spelling is the bane of wordplay), and even inflatable rafts that people bring from home and plop down in the water. The **Binnenalster** is the smaller of the two lakes and sits within the city center, rimmed by cafés and marvelous city buildings reflecting off the water's surface. In the center, a huge fountain sprays water pointlessly high into the air. The **Außenalster,** the outer lake, is much larger, and it's here that you'll find the most boat activity. And even if you don't want to rent a boat, grab a soda or a snack at one of the boathouses or a dock-perched restaurant and dangle your feet in the water.

*i* Free; limited wheelchair accessibility

## FOOD

### ◪EDEL CURRY ($)

Große Bleichen 68; 40 35716262; www.edelcurry.de; open M-Sa 11am-10pm, Su noon-10pm

If you have any interest in sausage, Edel Curry is the place to go. It looks deceptively like it could be any random strip-mall chain restaurant. But it's not any random restaurant. Its beef is sourced from local grass-fed cattle and sausage is prepared by a local butcher. The potatoes used to produce their french fries are also local and fresh, and their sauces are homemade. It's not all just yuppie obsession with locally-sourced ingredients; Edel Curry has the chops to back up the "philosophy" section of their menu. Named "best french fries in Hamburg" three times, the restaurant has also been crowned "best *currywurst* in all of Germany." We walked away with a stomach full of currywurst, French fries, and beer, all for under €10.

*i* Currywurst €3.80, bratwurst €3.50, fries €2.80-4, specialty sauces €0.50-1.50; limited wheelchair accessibility

### FRAU MÖLLER ($)

Lange Reihe 96; 40 25328817; www.fraumoeller.com; open M-Th 11:30am-4am, F 11:30am-6am, Sa 11am-6am, Su 11am-4am, kitchen open M-Th 11:30am-1am, F 11:30am-3am, Sa 11am-3am, Su 11am-1am

One of our favorite restaurants in Hamburg, Frau Möller serves German cuisine in a restaurant that we would call a fun hodgepodge of antiquated items, from mismatched wooden furniture and intentional antiques like a wooden ship's steering wheel and old coffee cans to—perhaps even more dated—the CD collection behind the bar. But don't get your millennial knickers in a twist; if receding from the digital age tastes this good, we're all for it. Chow down on organic fried potatoes with onions, bacon, and three fried eggs (€5.90), or gobble up a chicken breast fillet with pepper cream sauce, fried potatoes, and salad (€8.50).

*i* Entrées €5-9; vegetarian options available; limited wheelchair accessibility

## BEAR CLAW ($)
Lange Reihe 1-5; 040 18040892; www.
bearclaw.de; open daily 11am-11pm

If you love pulled pork, first, we
completely agree with you, and second,
your mind is about to explode. At Bear
Claw, your meal starts with beef, pork,
or chicken, slow roasted for eight hours
to reach tender perfection. The meat
is "clawed" from the roast, swirled in
what we translated to "meat juices" but
might actually be gravy, and doused
in homemade sauce. Finally, it gets
plopped onto bread and served as a
sandwich, scooped into your desperate
hands, and gulped down in a frenzy.
This is pulled various-kinds-of-meat
done right.

*i* *Pulled-meat sandwiches €8-9; no
wheelchair accessibility*

## PAULINE CAFÉ ($)
Neuer Pferdemarkt 3; 40 41359964; www.
pauline-hamburg.de; open M-F 8:30am-
4pm, Sa 9am-6pm, Su 10am-6pm; Su
brunch 10am-12:15pm and 12:30pm-3pm

Pauline Café is a great spot
for breakfast in the **St. Pauli**
neighborhood. Start the day feeling
fresh with the "In a good mood"
breakfast (€8.40), which includes
yogurt with fruit and granola, vegetable
sticks with guacamole, and herb cream
cheese on wholesome, whole-grain
bread. Or, order up something sweet
with their French toast (€5.90), which
comes dripping with maple syrup
and piled high with fruit. If you're
not a coffee drinker, we recommend
ordering Pauline's sweet hot chocolate
(€3), which is foamy and delicious.
The whipped cream comes served on
the side in a small metal cup and we've
rarely felt so self-satisfied as we did
when transferring our whipped cream
into our cocoa with a parfait spoon.
If you want to try Pauline for Sunday
brunch, make sure to reserve a table
ahead of time.

*i* *Entrées €6-9; vegetarian and vegan options available; no wheelchair accessibility*

# NIGHTLIFE
## ⭐KYTI VOO
Lange Reihe 82; 40 28055565; www.
kytivoo.com; open M-Sa 5pm-varies, Su
2pm-varies

Kyti Voo is a large, chic gay bar. Too
chic maybe, because their logo of
a silhouetted cat with a handlebar
mustache and a bow tie just takes the
whole thing too far. The bar specializes
in craft beers and cocktails, and though
you may not be able to read the menu,
bartenders are more than happy to
make recommendations. Plus, the best
part is some drinks are served with
glowsticks in the glass, and if you can
move past the fact that your drink is
holding a vessel of literal poison, that's
an awesome touch! Especially on nice
nights, the bar is the place to be, as
people flock to the Kyti Voo patio for
drinks. And on the weekends, expect
the crowd to get younger, the music to
get louder.

*i* *No cover, cocktails €7-10; cash only;
BGLTQ+ friendly*

## 99 CENT BAR
Große Freiheit 31; www.bar-99.de; open
M-Th 8pm-2am, F-Sa 8pm-4am

In a sea of night clubs in Hamburg's
**Red Light District,** 99 Cent Bar
stood out to us because, well, we're
cheapskates at heart. This club is just
a small room, and on busy weekend
nights, there is no space for dancing. A
fun-loving and social bar, there is only
one real activity here, and that activity
is drinking, because the bar's name
is true. **All beers and shots are just
€0.99.** (Longdrinks are €2, but we're
not complaining.) Stop here to hang
out with a rowdy and rambunctious
crowd of students and gear up for a
wild night at the surrounding clubs.

*i* *No cover, drinks €1-3; cash only;
BGLTQ+ friendly*

## GOLDFISCHGLAS
Bartelsstraße 30; www.goldfischglas.de;
open daily 2pm-varies

If hipness and dim lighting are
correlated, then we've hit max capacity.
Named for everyone's favorite golden
cracker, or probably the real fish now
that we think of it, GoldFischGlas is lit
only by a low orange glow that makes
the bar feel a little like Halloween,

but we guess it's supposed to evoke goldfish. Free-standing booths and cozy nooks along the walls make this a great place to chat over drinks with friends, hostel-mates, or that guy with the short-on-the-sides, long-on-top haircut making eye contact with you from the bar. What do you mean you don't know which one we're talking about? Windows occupying most of the walls make the bar feel nicely linked to the street outside, and the vibe at the counter says young urban professional mingles with young urban would-be-professional-but-I'm-following-my-passions-right-now.

*i* No cover, drinks from €5; cash only

## HERZBLUT ST. PAULI

Reeperbahn 50; 40 33396933; www.herz-blut-st-pauli.de; open M-Th 5pm-open end, F 5pm-4am, Sa 1pm-4am, Su 1pm-varies

If you're looking to party on a weekday, do not come to Herzblut St. Pauli because it will feel like a sad Las Vegas with lots of empty seating and neutral tones. Even the rack of bras behind the bar are mostly black and nude, which is kind of a depressing sight in normal lighting. On the weekends, however, Herzblut St. Pauli transforms. Tables are cleared to create a dance floor and a young crowd comes to enjoy exotic cocktails and dancing with DJs and live music. So, if you're looking for a place to go out on the Reeperbahn, the street at the center of Hamburg's Red Light District, Herzblut St. Pauli isn't a bad choice. Just promise us that if you give them your bra, you'll spice things up with some bright colors or patterns.

*i* No cover, beers €3-5, cocktails €9

# MUNICH

Coverage by **Antonia Washington**

Compared to those of its eastern neighbors, Germany's cities are much more cosmopolitan. Munich, one of the country's largest cities with a population of 1.43 million, is especially so. As such, getting a handle on it, especially if you've spent the last few weeks in the Austrian countryside, can be a bit tricky. If you feel like you're struggling to understand Munich, lean into its Bavarian roots, which truly remain its lifeblood. Lounge in a few beer gardens and you will soon feel the city consolidating around you. If Vienna is the chic older sister of the German-speaking world and Berlin is the sister's edgy boyfriend who plays in a rock band and doesn't sleep before 4am, then Munich is the grandparent that gives you beer behind your parents' backs. Here, tradition matters. And as stereotypical as it may sound, we guarantee that while in Munich, you'll find plenty of people casually wearing lederhosen and subsisting on diet of beer (often cheaper than water) and pretzels.

## ORIENTATION

When trying to orient yourself in Munich, start with **Marienplatz.** This square in the middle of the city center will help you understand the city layout and is a great jumping-off point to get just about anywhere and do just about anything. The area surrounding Marienplatz is a hub for restaurants and shopping. In the surrounding blocks, you will find many of Munich's historic sites. To the south of Marienplatz, sites include **St. Peter's Church** and **Viktualienmarkt.** To the north of Marienplatz, sights include the **Residenz Palace.** The Residenz sits about equidistant between Marienplatz and the lower tip of the **Englischer Garten,** to the northeast. West of Marienplatz and ever so slightly north is another square called **Karlsplatz.** Traveling south from Karlsplatz, along **Sonnenstraße,** you'll encounter many popular bars and clubs. The main train station is just west of Karlsplatz.

# ESSENTIALS

## GETTING THERE

Munich Airport is a major international airport with services from most major airlines worldwide and airlines of all kinds in Europe. The central train station (hauptbahnhof in German, often written "Hbf") is on the northwestern edge of the main historic city center. The central bus station in Munich, often called Munich ZOB, is in a similar area, on the west end of the train station. Both stations are connected to the S-bahn public transport lines. The name of the S-bahn stop at the central bus station is Hackerbrücke.

## GETTING AROUND

Public transport is simple to use in Munich. It is important to keep in mind that if you plan to visit sites a little further from the city center, such as the BMW Welt and Museum, the Olympic park and stadium, or Dachau, you will likely need to use public transport. The S-Bahn and the U-Bahn are the primary subway train systems, will be a great resource during your time in Munich. Within the city center, the S-Bahn runs roughly northwest to southeast, and all the lines use the same route in this area.

## PRACTICAL INFORMATION

**Tourist Offices:** The central tourist office is located in Marienplatz. (Marienplatz 8; 089 23396500; www. muenchen.de; open M-F 9:30-7:30, Sa 9am-4pm, Su 10am-2pm).
**Banks/ATMs/Currency Exchange:** Many businesses in Munich only accept cash, but ATMs are usually easily accessible.
**Post Offices:** Postbank(Sattlerstraße 1; open M-F 9am-6pm, Sa 9am-12:30pm).
**Internet:** Internet is generally available at accommodations in Munich. Additionally, you can find free Wi-Fi in major city areas, such as Marienplatz.
**BGLTQ+ Resources:** For BGLTQ+ resources, check out these websites: www.munich.international-friends. net/lgbt-guide-to-munich and www. angloinfo.com/how-to/germany/ munich/family/lgbt/munich-gay-community along with the tourist office for information and resources.

## EMERGENCY INFORMATION

**Emergency Number:** 112
**Police:** Ettstraße 2; 089 29100
**US Embassy:** The US Embassy in Germany is located in Berlin, listed here, but there are consulates in Munich and Frankfurt that may be more easily accessible (Clayallee 170; 30 83050). The US Consulate General Munich is located at Königinstraße 5 (8928880).
**Rape Crisis Center:** Frauennotruf München (Saarstraße 5; 89763737; www.frauennotrufmuenchen.de; open M-F 10am-midnight, Sa-Su 6pm-midnight).
**Hospitals:** Schwabing Hospital (Kölner Platz 1; 89 3304 0302; www.klinikum-muenchen.de; open daily 24hr).
**Pharmacies:** International Pharmacy Hauptbahnhof (Bahnhofplatz 2; 89 599 890 40; open M-F 7am-8pm, Sa 8am-8pm).

# ACCOMMODATIONS

### ✎EURO YOUTH HOTEL ($$)

Senefelderstraße 5; 89 59900811; www. euro-youth-hotel.de; reception open 24hr

Housed in a wood-laden building that looks like an awful lot like a pub, Euro Youth Hotel claims it blurs the line between hotel and hostel by providing both comfortable rooms and a hostel atmosphere. By the time we checked out, our vision was admittedly hazy. You simply can't argue with complementary daily linen change; nor with weekly music performances. In the center of the in-house bar—the venue of the performances and the location of most hostel-sponsored activities— a pillar is wallpapered with currency from around the world and hand-written notes. We would've added to the collection, had we a dollar or two to spare.

*i* Dorms €30-40 summer; reservation required; max stay 7 nights; wheelchair accessible; Wi-Fi; towels €1.50; laundry facilities, €3 wash, €1.50 dry, €0.50 detergent packs; breakfast €4.90

## GSPUSI BAR HOSTEL ($)

Oberanger 45; 89 24411790; www.gspu-sibarhostel.com; hours vary

A hip hostel aesthetic awaits at the Gspusi Bar Hostel, with a heavy emphasis on wood and metal-work décor. Even the bar area, a small space packed with seating from a picnic table to bar stools, is wall-papered with repainted metal roofing panels, a surprisingly charming touch. In terms of amenities, Gspusi isn't trying too hard (if the early 2000s taught us anything, it's that trying hard is #lame). Instead, they provide the essentials: a place to sleep, to shower, and to get a drink before going out in earnest for the night. Because the bar is the central focus of the hostel, it's a great place to congregate and get to know other travelers. Situated just up the road from **Marienplatz,** the hostel is also exceedingly well located.

*i* Dorms €25-35; reservation recommended; wheelchair accessible; Wi-Fi; towels €2

## JAEGER'S MUNICH ($)

Senefelderstraße 3; 89 555281; www.jaegershostel.de; reception open 24hr

With a guest age limit of 18-35 years and a fleet of 260 beds, Jaeger's Hostel is a temporary home to slews of young travelers passing through Munich. Despite its massive size, the hostel continues to expand, with renovations going on throughout the day. Friendly and helpful staff pour free welcome shots at the bar and occasionally organize hostel-wide activities. The rooms are simple and generally clean, but your locker may look like it's suffered through years of graffiti-crazed tweens. And though we spotted some fungus and mildew on the edges of shower doors, by 2018 many of the accommodations will be brand new.

*i* Dorms €30-35 summer, €15-20 winter; reservation recommended; max stay 7 nights per month; wheelchair accessible; towels €1 per day; free self-service laundry facilities (kit with detergent €5); breakfast €4.90

## MEININGER MUNICH CITY CENTER ($)

Landsberger Straße 20; 89 54998023; www.meininger-hotels.com; hours vary

The Meininger hostel in Munich offers basic, clean accommodations.

Although, like many chain hostels, the common areas are distant and quiet during the day, interrupted only by the shouting of school groups, the crowd gets considerably more hostel-ish as the evening wears on. Groups of student-age travelers often gather on the patio and around the hostel bar at night before going out. If you've come with a travel buddy or if you can round up friends in your room, we recommend ditching the hostel bar for Augustiner Bräu directly across the street, the perfect place to pop over for a beer and a pretzel. The hostel is a little further from the historic center than the others we reviewed, but it's close to the **Oktoberfest fair grounds,** if you plan to splurge on the party of a lifetime.

*i* Dorms €20-35, privates €55+; reservation recommended; BGLTQ+ friendly; limited wheelchair accessibility; Wi-Fi; lockers provided; linens provided; laundry facilities; towels €1; breakfast €6.90

# SIGHTS

## CULTURE

..............................................

## ALTER PETER (ST. PETER'S CHURCH)

Perersplatz 1; 89 210237760; www.erzbis-tum-muenchen.de/StPeterMuenchen; open summer M-F 9am-6:30pm, Sa, Su, and holidays 10am-7pm; open winter M-F 9am-5:30pm, Sa, Su, and holidays 10am-6pm

Unlike many old European churches, Alter Peter has bright, white walls that reflect the sun throughout the long center aisle. Ceiling frescos painted in vibrant colors liven the dome and gleam down at parishioners, while the sides of the church are lined with tombs. After exploring the ground floor of the church, climb 300+ steps to the top of the tower through narrow passageways to find a sweeping view over the city.

*i* Free; last entry 30min. before closing; limited wheelchair accessibility

## ASAMKIRCHE (ASAM CHURCH)

Sendlinger Straße 32; 89 23687989

Though as intricate and ornate as the other churches we scoped out in Munich, the Asamkirche, constructed originally as a private chapel without a religious order, is relatively small in comparison. Sit in a pew and you may feel like the church is closing in on you slowly (in a cool way, not a you're-being-buried-alive way)—ornamental marble-work makes the walls feel heavy and balconies rounding the sides and nave of the church body narrow the space. Because the Baroque façade is built into the neighboring buildings, you may walk right by the church if you're not looking for it.

*i* *Free; no wheelchair accessibility*

### FRAUENKIRCHE (MÜNCHNER DOM)

Frauenplatz 12; 89 2900820; www. muenchner-dom.de; open daily 7:30am-8:30pm

As big as the Frauenkirche looks from the outside, the magnitude of its interior is downright confusing—its size amplified by the lack of ostentatious decoration. The cathedral's roof and massive towers are supported by smooth, white pilasters rather than darkened stone ones, and the simple webbed molding where the pilasters meet the ceiling makes the cathedral feel cavernous. Furthermore, Frauenkirche's large stained-glass windows don't resemble the typical Gothic windows of similar cathedrals, instead featuring a variety geometric shapes.

*i* *Free; tours €6; tours May-Oct Tu, Th, Su 3pm; wheelchair accessible*

### VIKTUALIENMARKT

Viktualienmarkt 3; 89 89068205; www. viktualienmarkt-muenchen.de; open M-F 10am-6pm, Sa 10am-3pm

Viktualienmarkt is the major outdoor market to be found in Munich, where local vendors set up to sell their wares every day of the week.

Booths overflow with fresh fruits and vegetables, spices, floral arrangements, and even small potted plants. One of our favorite features of the market are the booths selling arts-n-crafts style home decorations. Run mostly by crafty-grandma entrepreneurs, these booths sell everything from magnets to baskets to lavender plants, but we especially like the emphasis on hanging knickknacks. Spend your wad at these booths and you will also need to outfit your home with hooks and knobs so you have enough places to hang the many ornaments, wind chimes, mobiles, lantern boxes, and wooden heart-shaped cutouts. Of course, in true Bavarian form, that market is also a decent place to pick up sausage and beer.

*i* *Prices vary by stand; wheelchair accessible*

## LANDMARKS

### MARIENPLATZ

Marienplatz 1

Marienplatz square is the heart of Munich. Situated in the middle of the city center, the square is the crossing point of every person in Munich, visitors and locals alike. Named for the fountain at the square center, Marienplatz sits on the edge of Neues Rathaus, the new town hall, an imposing Neo-Gothic building with windows and archways often overflowing with flowers, and an 85 meter tower (with an observation deck accessible by elevator) and glockenspiel. Come by Marienplatz to grab some ice cream, eat at a slightly overpriced restaurant, stroll between groups of street performing musicians, or just

hop on the public transport because let's be honest, when we're abroad, we all latch onto one public transport station without which we would be completely lost.

*i* Free; wheelchair accessible

## DACHAU
Peter-Roth-Str. 2a; 81 31669970; www. kz-gedenkstaette-dachau.de

There is nothing cool or fun about visiting the Dachau concentration camp, but you would be remiss not to see the memorial site and museum during your time in Munich. The concentration camp at Dachau, a town just northwest of Munich, was the first such camp established under the Nazi regime, shortly after the election of Adolf Hitler in 1933. On this site, atrocities were committed and tested which would proliferate throughout Nazi occupied territories and lead to the murder and torture of millions of people. Today, the site holds tributes to the victims, remaining and reconstructed buildings from the camp, and a museum with an abundance of information on the history and events of the Dachau camp.

*i* Free entry, audio guide €3.50; limited wheelchair accessibility

## ENGLISCHER GARTEN
Englischer Garten

The Englischer Garten is one of the largest urban parks in the world, filled with grass lawns, overgrown trees, and plenty of water. It offers 48.5 miles (78 kilometers) of paths to be taken advantage of by cyclists, walkers, and joggers. Frankly, we think Ann Perkins said it best on Parks and Rec when she said, "Jogging is the worst, Chris.

## BECOME A BAVARIAN BEER-DRINKER

Upon arriving in Munich you'll undoubtedly be hit with a wave of desperation. Desperation to drink beer, that is. Thankfully, breweries abound in this city—a testament to its Bavarian roots. Beer here has a protected status as food and is taxed as such, making it extremely cheap, often cheaper than water. Munich's Oktoberfest, a folk festival that consumes the city each fall, attracts millions—yes, millions—of visitors from around the world, and has spurned imitation festivals in dozens of countries. Most people don't know that Oktoberfest's origins, in fact, were not a celebration of beer at all. Actually, the celebration began with a wedding. In 1806, when the region allied itself with Napoleon, it became the Kingdom of Bavaria. This made the new king's son Ludwig I the first crown prince of Bavaria, and when he wed his bride Therese in 1810, it was Bavaria's first royal wedding. The celebration was unlike any before it, and so Oktoberfest was born. Today, the festival is essentially a 20-day rager in the heart of Munich during which beer is siphoned from barrel to gullet as fast as you can tip the waiter enough to get his attention.

Festival aside, beer in Bavaria is truly special. Since 1516, Bavaria has employed a beer purity law, called "Reinheitsgebot," limiting the ingredients that can be used in the brewing process (this law dates to the late 1400s in Munich!). The law limits the ingredients in beer to three simple components: water, barley, and hops. Modern revision of the law has since allowed for the use of yeast, but the principle is the same. As a result of the strict attention to ingredients and tradition, there are only six major breweries in Munich today, most of which date back several hundred years. These breweries are Augustiner Bräu, Hofbräu, Hacker-Pschorr Bräu, Spatenbräu, Löwenbräu, and Paulanerbräu. With centuries of experience under their belts, the Big Six breweries have turned a short list of ingredients into an equally short list of beers, but they've perfected them. Still, Munich is a quantity-over-quality place. Beer is typically consumed by the liter, which, in Bavaria, is called a "Maß" ("measure" in English). One liter of beer is thus one standard measure. Grab a beer with friends from all over the world and set aside all your systems of measurement. There's no need to squabble over gallons and liters anymore: instead there is only the Maß.

I mean, I know it keeps you healthy, but God, at what cost?" But yes, people do jog here. Check out our listings on Chinesischer Turm and Urban Surfing to see what else the park has to offer. If you have hay fever, you may need to arm yourself with plenty of Benadryl in the spring, but the FOMO of not hanging out at the park with your friends will probably kill you before your allergies will.

*i* Free; limited wheelchair accessibility

## RESIDENZ MUNICH
Residenzstraße 1; 89 290671; www. residenz-muenchen.de

The seat of Bavarian rulership from 1508 to 1918, the Residenz is an expansive palace and garden complex on the northeast end of the city center, right between **Marienplatz** and the **Englischergarten.** The museum that inhabits the residence today takes visitors through the extravagant lives of Bavarian royalty. Long hallways, gold framed mirrors, and walls covered in velvets and silks to match the furniture define the Residenz passageways. It doesn't matter if wallpaper is long out of style, matching is always in. A throne room with over-the-top décor might make you think the throne itself looks like a small toy (like, you designed a whole room to show everyone how grand you were, but then you just sat in a chair?), but it's hard to be underwhelmed with the rest of the palace.

*i* Admission €7, student €6; last entry 1hr. before closing; wheelchair accessible

# MUSEUMS

## ⬛PINAKOTHEK DER MODERNE
Barer Straße 40; 89 23805360; www. pinakothek.de

The Pinakothek der Moderne is another major museum in the Pinakothek museum complex, the most important collection of art museums in the city. This one is dedicated to contemporary and modern art of the twentieth and twenty first centuries, including exhibitions on architecture and design, as well as fine arts installments. Made of four separate and interacting museums, the Pinakothek der Moderne is one of the largest museums with this artistic focus in the world. When we visited, there was an installment of larger-than-life Russian nesting dolls and we got to sit among them, trying to look rolley-polley to blend in.

*i* Admission €10, student €7; wheelchair accessible

## ALTE PINAKOTHEK
Barer Straße 27; 89 23805216; www. pinakothek.de

The Alte Pinakothek museum is the major collection of art by the Old Masters in the region, especially featuring European Renaissance paintings. With a substantial collection of works by Rembrandt and an impressive display of Rubens pieces as well, be on the look out for salient works in the history of Christian art. Here, you'll find one of our favorite Albrecht Dürer pieces, a self-portrait styled to appear as the image of Christ that looks like a mix between Chris Hemsworth and Orlando Bloom when he had long hair and a mustache. We would never wish to downplay the significance of this seminal work of art, but it's just a little *Snow White and the Huntsman,* if you know what we mean.

*i* Admission €4, student €2, Su €1; wheelchair accessible

## BMW WELT & MUSEUM
Am Olympiapark 2; 89 125016001; www. bmw-welt.com/de/location/museum/ concept.html

In a building seemingly from the year 3000, the BMW Welt and Museum is a tribute to the car company's development. Important to note, the exterior construction of the BMW Welt was actually completed in 2006, which was the same year the Jonas Brothers' smash hit *Year 3000* was released. Coincidence? We don't think so. The future is now. At the Welt, visitors can sit in Mini Coopers, wish they could sit in Rolls Royces, and shop the BMW lifestyle brand, while the museum presents exhibitions on the company's history, successes, and philosophies. As a corporate brand, don't expect the museum to linger on its mistakes (including its darker history as an automaker for the Nazi regime), but it's still a great opportunity to see the evolution of their cars from early models to their first electric cars and even designs based on art pieces.

*i BMW Welt free, museum €10, student €7; tour times vary based on events, check website; last entry to museum 30min. before closing; wheelchair accessible*

# FOOD

### ◪MARAIS GESCHMACKSACHEN ($)

Parkstraße 2; 89 50094552; www. cafe-marais.de; open Tu-Sa 8am-8pm, Su 10am-6pm

Serving cakes, croissants, and all sorts of coffee, Marais is a corner café frequented mostly by locals, with a menu entirely in German. But don't let that scare you off, "cappuccino" is the same in every language. Marais also offers paninis (€6.20) and more substantial breakfasts, but our favorite part of this café is its atmosphere, as it is also half antique shop. Almost everything in the café is for sale, so come here for coffee and you could end up buying a vintage tea kettle, dozens of new but old-looking postcards, or even the table where you sat down to enjoy your quiche.

*i Entrées €6.50-12.50, paninis €6.20; vegetarian options available; limited wheelchair accessibility*

### COTIDIANO ($)

Gärtnerplatz 6; 89 242078610; www. cotidiano.de; open M-Th 7:30am-10pm, F-Sa 7:30am-11pm, Su 7:30am-9pm

We ended up at Cotidiano when we were told that this was the best breakfast place in Munich. The café may be one more example of people abroad having no idea what an "American Breakfast" is, claiming that it's an oven-baked croissant filled with scrambled eggs and cheese, but we stuffed ourselves with that egg-filled croissant and loved every second of it (€6.90).

*i Entrées €10-15; vegetarian and vegan options available; limited wheelchair accessibility*

### HACKERHAUS ($)

Sendlinger Straße 14; 89 2605026; www. hackerhaus.de; open daily 10am-midnight, kitchen closes at 11:30pm

Hackerhaus is the restaurant of Hackerbräu, one of the major breweries in Munich. First given the name Hackerbräu for the last name of the owner in 1738, the brewery dates back originally to the fifteenth century. The Hackerhaus has been burned down, rebuilt, bought and sold again, changing hands between the Hacker and Pschorr families for more than 200 years. Eventually, Hackerhaus was renovated and reopened by the Pongratz family in the 1980s, a totally separate group from the other two from what we can tell. That one came out of left field for us, too. We recommend taking a look at their daily specials; that's where we found their homemade potato pancakes, served with thick, creamy apple sauce (€9.90). To feel like you're sitting in a Bavarian hunting lodge, we recommend sitting indoors.

*i Entrées €8-20; card minimum €15; limited wheelchair accessibility*

### LEDU HAPPY DUMPLINGS ($)

Theresienstraße 18; 89 95898460; www. ledu-dumpling.de; open M-Th 11:30am-9:30pm, F 11:30am-10pm, Sa noon-10pm, Su noon-9:30pm

A tiny storefront serving up big dreams (dumplings are always big dreams to us), LeDU Happy Dumplings uses fresh ingredients to make authentic Chinese dumpling concoctions that really will make you happy, unlike the hundredth time you heard Pharrell's "Happy" in a single day for the hundredth day in a row, throwback to 2014. Dumplings come in noodles and a variety of colors, and we haven't figured out the right order to elicit a multi-color spread, but we wish you luck with that endeavor. Put in an order for 10 dumplings (€7.90), decide whether you want them steamed or pan-fried, your fillings of choice, and soon you'll have a pile of piping hot, puckered noodles steaming in front of you.

*i 10 dumplings €7.90; vegetarian and vegan options available; limited wheelchair accessibility*

### ZUM FRANZISKANER ($)

Residenzstraße 9; 89 2318120; www.zum-franziskaner.de; undefined

Just across the plaza from the **Residenz palace,** Zum Franziskaner is a little expensive for a casual meal, but a great place to stop for appetizers to share. Our favorite is the *weißbier-obatzda* (white beer obatzda), a Bavarian cheese delicacy that is often a beer garden essential. The dish, made by mixing together an aged, soft cheese (Zum Franziskaner uses camembert, but we've seen recipes with others), butter, and seasonings such as paprika powder, and a little bit of beer into a soft schmear. Spread the cheese over bread, pile it high with onions, and take a bite, or slather it all over your body and just see what happens.

*i* *Appetizers €10-15, main dishes €11-20; cash preferred; vegetarian options available; limited wheelchair accessibility*

## NIGHTLIFE

### ☒CHINESISCHER TURM (CHINESE TOWER)

Englischer Garten 3; 89 38387327; www.chinaturm.de; open daily 10am-10pm

The Chinesischer Turm is our favorite beer garden in Munich. Planted in the middle of the Englischer Garten, the Chinesischer Turm feels like a real garden, completely outdoor, with immediate access to the park's many paths, swimming holes on the park's waterways, and expansive grass fields. The location encourages you to stroll through the park and take your time outdoors. The beer garden's namesake, the Chinese Tower, is a structure with pagoda-style architecture looming over the garden, built in the late eighteenth century. If you're headed for a picnic in the park, you might as well bring your food to the garden and add a fresh and frothy beer to the mix.

*i* *No cover, liter €6-8; cash preferred; wheelchair accessible*

### 089 BAR

Maximiliansplatz 5; 89 59988890; 089-bar.de; open Tu-Sa 9pm-7am

This bar is a great place to party with a young crowd, plus the occasional too-old-for-this man trying his best to blend in. Under the disco balls, a flooded dance floor moves along to DJs who play the hits. We came to the club sick of DJs who remix songs by slowing down the lyrics and speeding up the beat, a trend that we hope dies soon, and we didn't have to put up with any of that here. The DJs gave the people what they wanted. We even heard Chris Brown remixed into House of Pain's "Jump Around," to which the crowd went wild. There's no need to dress up, but we'd ballpark that when we visited around 50% of the men were wearing black jeans and white Calvin Klein t-shirts, so keep that in mind.

*i* *Cover €5; cash only; no wheelchair accessibility*

### HOFBRÄUHAUS

Platzl 9; 89 29013610; www.hofbraeu-haus.de; open daily 9am-11:30pm

The Hofbräuhaus in Munich is one of the cities largest and most frequented beer halls, packed with tourists, but worth a visit. Here, a lederhosen-clad band plays traditional Bavarian music while tourists clap along, swept up in the excitement of the accordion player, a relatable feeling, right? Although the beers are a little overpriced because of the tourist appeal, seeing the history of the famous beer hall that was open only to royalty until the late 1820s is worth a couple extra euro. A standard pour here is a full liter, and though they'll reluctantly serve you a half liter if you ask, you won't find smaller measures on the menu. We say, the bigger the better.

*i* No cover, liter beer €8-10

### MILCHUNDBAR

Sonnenstraße 27; 89 45028818; www. milchundbar.de; open daily 24hr

Milchundbar is just large enough to fit a fully stocked bar and just small enough that you'll get good and sweaty as soon as everyone starts moving. As you dance, steam is deployed through vents and descends to the dance floor, creating a colorful haze just thin enough to see the face of the person grinding next to you. If that's not enough, the DJ occasionally activates a smoke machine to cover the dance floor in a white cloud (hence the "milk" component of Milchundbar's name, which translates to "milk and bar"). Milchundbar is particularly popular on Wednesday nights and doesn't start getting busy until about midnight. Once it does, however, the party won't stop until 9am.

*i* Cover €5-8

# STUTTGART

Coverage by **Antonia Washington**

Admittedly, much of Stuttgart looks (and feels) like a corporate wasteland—an ocean of glass and metal looming over wide but largely deserted walkways. As home to the headquarters of Mercedes Benz, Porsche, and a collection of other internationally recognized companies, it makes sense. Today, Stuttgart is first and foremost a hub of enterprise, and most visitors come for business, not leisure. It is often difficult to see beyond the modern infrastructure, but if you look hard enough, you'll find indicators of a rich and dynamic history. One such indicator is Schlossplatz, Stuttgart Mitte's largest square (and one of its oldest, dating back to the late eighteenth century). In recent years, Stuttgart has become increasingly diverse. About 50% of the city's total population consists of immigrants or children of immigrants, many of which emigrated from the United States. As a result, it is not uncommon to hear English-speakers commiserating over work while you're out and about. Furthermore, perhaps because of Stuttgart's business draw, or maybe just because it's a German city, a good part of its population is young and down to party.

## ORIENTATION

The main areas of Stuttgart are very small, so navigating the city is fairly simple. **Schlossplatz** marks the center of the city, housing many of its monuments (including the **Neue Palace**), museums, shopping centers, and popular dining options. To the north of Schlossplatz is the central train station, **Stuttgart Hauptbahnhof,** and to the south of Schlossplatz, sandwiched between the park to the northeast and **Paulinenstraße** to the southwest, lies Stuttgart's "downtown," where you'll find most of the city's shopping, restaurants, and clubs.

# ESSENTIALS

## GETTING THERE

The central train station is the easiest access point to Stuttgart's city center, and trains run from all over the region. If you're coming from further away, the Stuttgart airport services flights from many European airlines and even a few international ones. From the airport, it is easiest to arrive in the old town via subway. There is an S-bahn stop inside on the ground floor of terminal 1. An S-bahn ticket from the airport to the Stuttgart Central Station (Hauptbahnhof) costs €4.10.

## GETTING AROUND

Stuttgart's central city is easily walkable, but exploration of the suburbs requires an extensive knowledge of the public transportation system. Construction often reroutes sidewalks and cuts off walkways, especially on the north side of the city center, so traveling to and from the suburbs on foot can easily take up more time than anticipated. If you intend to stay outside of the city center, we recommend picking up a map of the public transportation system at the tourist office (Königstraße 1A). The system itself is very comprehensive, and the stations near Schlossplatz and Hauptbahnhof are easily navigable.

## PRACTICAL INFORMATION

**Tourist Offices:** The tourist office is located right across from Stuttgart Hauptbahnhof (Königstraße 1A; 0711 22280; open M-F 9am-8pm, Sa 9am-6pm, Su 10am-5pm (10am-4pm Nov-Mar).

**Banks/ATMs/Currency Exchange:** Many businesses in Stuttgart only accept cash, so plan ahead. Most ATMs are located in banks, which are dispersed throughout the city.

**Post Offices:** There is a post office across the street from Stuttgart Hauptbahnhof (Arnulf-Klett-Platz 2; open M-F 7am-8pm, Sa 9am-2pm, Su 10am-3pm).

**Internet:** Internet is available at most accommodations and in major public areas such as Schlossplatz. Free Wi-Fi is occasionally available throughout the city center on the network UnitymediaWiFi.

**BGLTQ+ Resources:** For a list of gay establishments throughout Germany, ask for "Gab" magazine at the tourist office. More information is available at Weissenburg, a BGLTQ+ resource center in Stuttgart, www.zentrum-weissenburg.de.

## EMERGENCY INFORMATION

**Emergency Number:** 112
**Police:** Königstraße 1A; 0711 870350.
**US Embassy:** The US Embassy in Germany is located in Berlin, listed here, but there are consulates in Munich and Frankfurt that may be more easily accessible. (Clayallee 170; 30 83050).
**Rape Crisis Center:** Call Weisser Ring for assistance and resources relating to sexual assault (Victims call 116006; general phone 06131 83030).
**Hospitals:** Katherinen Hospital (Kriegsbergstraße 60; 0711 27801; open daily 24hr).
**Pharmacies:** Apotheke im Hauptbahnhof (Arnulf-Klett-Platz 2; 0711 2239430; open M-F 6:30am-8:30pm, Sa 8am-6pm, Su 10am-5pm).

# ACCOMMODATIONS

## 🏠HOSTEL ALEX 30 ($)

Alexanderstraße 30; 71 18388950; www.alex30-hostel.de; reception open 24hr

Hostel Alex 30 is about as close to Schlossplatz as any hostel, and it's easily accessible by public transport. The hostel's spaces are small, but clean, and what the rooms, bathrooms, and common areas lack in size, the lockers make up for. The hostel bar is a cozy place to start the night, but don't get too excited when you discover Alex 30 has a beer garden. The balcony space that constitutes the beer garden is to its namesake what dandelions are to real flowers. Otherwise, Hostel Alex 30 is charming, centrally located, and one of the better finds in Stuttgart.

*i* *Dorms €18-30; reservation recommended; no wheelchair accessibility; Wi-Fi; linens included; towels €5 deposit; breakfast €6*

### A&O STUTTGART CITY ($)

Rosensteinstraße 14/16; 71 125277401; www.aohostels.com; reception open 24hr

On the surface, A&O Stuttgart City has everything you need: the reception is open 24 hours, seven days a week, the nightly rate is relatively inexpensive, and the facilities are very clean, sterile even. And yet, we weren't exactly hot and bothered by our stay here. For one thing, the Wi-Fi is terrible. If you need to do work, you will probably find enough signal to send emails, do minor online research, and accomplish your basic mid-vacation goals. Trying to post an Instagram picture, on the other hand, is a nightmare, which we know is a big deal to twenty-first century travelers. Also of note: hostels belonging to the A&O brand charge for bed linens, which we think is a little bit soulless.

*i* Dorms €20-25; reservation recommended; wheelchair accessible; Wi-Fi; linens and towels not included

# SIGHTS
## CULTURE

### OPER STUTTGART (STUTTGART OPERA HOUSE)

Oberer Schoßgarten 6; 71 120320; www.oper-stuttgart.de; showtimes vary

The opera house's location is almost as breathtaking as its performances. Though less grand and ornate than the opera houses of larger cities in the region, the exterior of the house in Stuttgart makes a statement. Topped by statues and supported by massive pillars, it sits just on the edge of the **Eckensee**. The lights of the opera house glint off the surface of the water in the evenings and the **Neue Schloss palace** sits within a stone's throw. Take in one of the best shows in Europe at the opera, or go to the ballet.

*i* Price varies by show; wheelchair accessible

### STIFTSKIRCHE

Stiftstraße 12; 71 1240893; www.stifts-kirche-stuttgart.de

The poster child for architectural plastic surgery, Stiftskirche has undergone several reconstructions over the course of its long lifetime.

Originally built in the Romanesque style, the church that stands today is an amalgamation of genres—Gothic, classical, Baroque, you name it. Its last renovation took place during the early 2000s; however, most of the church's modern features were implemented just after WWII, when Stifskirche was effectively leveled.

*i* Free entry, information brochures €0.50; wheelchair accessible

# LANDMARKS

### ALTE SCHLOSS AND LANDESMUSEUM WÜRTTEMBERG

Schillerplatz 6; 71 189535111; www.landesmuseum-stuttgart.de; open Tu-Su 10am-5pm

Once the seat of Württemberg royalty, the Alte Schloss is now the home to the Landesmuseum Württemberg, a museum whose collection of regional art and artifacts dates back 80,000 years. (Yes, you read that correctly. They've got an axe used by Neanderthals during the Paleolithic era.) Highlights include the royal vault, a tomb which still holds several members of the royal family, their graves topped by life-size statues of the deceased resting peacefully on beds that really capture the gentle recline of modern-day hospital beds. As you make your way through the museum, keep an eye out for decals of a freckled red-head because she marks kid-friendly displays where you can touch crystals, hold animal pelts in your hands, and thumb through books from the early nineteenth century.

*i* Admission €5.50, €4.50 student; wheelchair accessible

### RATHAUS

Marktplatz 1; 71 12166736; open M-F 8am-5pm

The Stuttgart Rathaus is a monster of concrete, constructed in the giant, cubic, often unattractive style characteristic of the 1970s—the decade during which we poured concrete into square molds and convinced ourselves it was the look of the future. What we do love about the Stuttgart city hall, however, is its bell tower. The design of the clock itself is reminiscent of Art Nouveau, its open face revealing bells that put on quite a show when the clock strikes noon. Festivals during the summer months turn this bleak square into a buzzing microcosmic metropolis, attracting musicians and artisans from the surrounding region.

*i* *Free; plaza is wheelchair accessible*

## SCHLOSSPLATZ AND NEUE SCHLOSS
Schloßplatz; open daily 24hr

The Schlossplatz is where Stuttgart's corporate frigidity begins to melt away. The tall pillar in the center of the square stands unrivaled by adjacent buildings, alone and unhindered in the open air. Just as appealing, at the foot of the pillar, groups of students can often be seen passing around bottles of wine. The square's benches and plots of even, green grass are typically occupied by grown men reading graphic novels, couples taking selfies, and families enjoying the time they have together outside of the 9-to-5 grind. Around the square, at all hours of day, there are people mulling about, relaxing in the sun or ambling through the rain.

*i* *Free; wheelchair accessible*

# MUSEUMS

## KUNSTMUSEUM STUTTGART
Kleiner Schloßplatz 1; 71 121619600; www.kunstmuseum-stuttgart.de; open Tu-Su 10am-6pm, F 10am-9pm

The Kunstmuseum is a modern art museum that, in and of itself, will justify your visit to Stuttgart. More inviting than nearby office buildings but a stark contrast to its immediate surroundings on the **Schlossplatz,** the Kunstmuseum is an overpowering block of concrete and metal panels with glass, a vision both transparent and imposing. With fluorescent lighting scattered over the foyer like interwoven pick-up sticks, walkways that are ever-so-slightly geometrically askew, and creative ways

of playing with light and space, the building blends in with the exhibits themselves. Stop by the museum's bar to down some liquid courage before facing the inevitable few pieces composed of too-deep phrases written in neon lights.

*i* *Admission €6, €4 student; wheelchair accessible*

## MERCEDES-BENZ MUSEUM
Mercedesstraße 100; 71 11730000; www.mercedes-benz.com/en/mercedes-benz/classic/museum; open Tu-Su 9am-6pm

Sometimes visiting car museums just feels like walking through the set of a car commercial, but the Mercedes-Benz Museum, we have to admit, is a little different. Sure, the museum propagandizes the achievements of Mercedes-Benz, but there is something that sets them apart: they invented the automobile. Come learn about the history of the automobile, truly from start to finish, beginning with the lives of Karl Benz and Gottlieb Daimler, whose two companies would eventually become the Mercedes-Benz of today. Almost as cool, learn about Karl Benz' wife Bertha who pawned her wedding dowry to float her husband's

inventing, cranked the engine and pushed the car on their many secret test drives, and jerry-rigged the first ever long-distance drive in 1888.

*i* *Admission €10, reduced €5, kids under 14 free; last entry 1hr. before closing*

# FOOD

## BISTRO TERRAZZA ($$)
Königstrasse 28; 71 1290080; terraza-restaurant.de; open daily 9am-midnight

Bistro Terrazza is one of the restaurants inhabiting the palace-like shopping mall directly opposite the actual palace across **Schlossplatz square.** Bistro Terrazza serves mostly Italian fare, heavily favoring pastas and pizzas on its main dish menu. If you're looking for a full sit-down meal, then take a seat on the patio and enjoy the great people-watching opportunity it offers, but if you intend to buy pizza, we recommend skipping the full-pizza menu options. Instead, grab a slice (or several) from Bistro Terraza's to-go window (€3.50-4.10) and head deeper into the square to enjoy your wedge of spongey, cheese-laden pizza.

*i* *Pizzas €8.50-12, pastas €8.70-14; vegetarian options available; limited wheelchair accessibility*

## BLOCK HOUSE ($$$)
Arnulf-Klett-Platz 3; 71 1291770; www.block-house.de; open M-Sa 11:30am-midnight, Su 11:30am-11pm

Block House is a German steakhouse brand that's especially prolific in Hamburg and Berlin, but also one of few non-fast food style meals you'll find near the Stuttgart Hauptbahnhof. The Block House in Stuttgart has a classic steakhouse feel, with wood ceilings and deep-red walls accented with wine racks. Here, you'll feast on meat and potato dishes ripe for a king. Unless you're on a budget like us, in which case, we'll nourish ourselves with carbohydrates. We recommend skipping the steak section in favor of appetizers (baked potato €3.50) and pasta.

*i* *Entrées €14-34; vegetarian options available; no wheelchair accessibility*

## CAFÉ NAST ($)
Sporerstrasse 4; 71 12389716; www.cafenast.com; open M-F 7am-6:30 pm, Sa 7am-6pm

More intimate than the Starbucks and Nesspresso cafés nearby, Café Nast has made a name for itself in Stuttgart with a handful of locations in the city. If you're in the market for breakfast, we can assure you that there isn't anything "nast" about the establishment. It's hard to go wrong with the farmer's breakfast (€9.30), a classic ham and cheese plate kicked up a notch with Brie cheese, a soft-boiled egg, and a fresh roll with jam. If you're in the mood to forgo "protein," whatever that is (we've heard it's important, but sometimes we just couldn't care less), then take a gander at Café Nast's pastry case, which is overflowing with sweets.

*i* *Entrées €5-11, pastries and cakes €2.50-5; wheelchair accessible*

# NIGHTLIFE

## MATA HARI
Geißstraße 3; 71 150421479; open M-Th 3pm-2am, F 3pm-3am, Sa noon-3am, Su 3pm-2am

Mata Hari is a Mecca of endearingly crunchy 20-somethings and 30-somethings who still have roommates. No judgment, though, that'll be us in a few years. Men in flannels and jorts prop their bikes against the lamp posts outside, Lena Dunham doppelgangers with glasses abound, and people wear rock corduroy once more. Above the bar, a skateboard bears a photo of a cat with neon green orbs in place of its eyes. The bar offers a range of local German beers along with €2 "Lecker Mexikaner" tequila shots. Come here to remind yourself that mom jeans are hot, jean jackets are still very much in, and the man bun is an international trend. Everyone at this bar screams "chill vibes only" so much it's annoying, but not enough that you've stopped believing them, and you can't get enough.

*i* *Beer €3.20, shots €2; cash only; BGLTQ+ friendly; wheelchair accessible*

**TEQUILA BAR**
Steinstraße 15; 71 1232481; www.tequila-bar-stuttgart.com; open daily 24hr

Tequila is a regional drink native to Mexico and the American Southwest. Today, it's is a worldwide hit. So, to specialize in tequila in Germany, there's really no need to lean on the drink's regional origins. Along with the gecko on the bar's logo, décor includes a horse saddle, a sombrero, a small Mayan calendar, and, inexplicably, a pirate with a foot up on a barrel of what is probably rum. Close enough. Get a shot of tequila free with every beer purchase. Other house rules hang over the bar: never drink alone, go hard or go home, and pull the stick out of your butt.

*i* *Beer €5; cash only; BGLTQ+ friendly*

# GERMANY ESSENTIALS

## MONEY

**Tipping:** Service staff are paid by the hour, and a service charge is included in an item's unit price. It's customary and polite to tip your waiter normally. To tip, mention the total to your waiter while paying. If he states that the bill is €9, respond "€10," and he will include the tip, or just hand him a €10 and tell him to keep the change. It is standard to tip a taxi driver at least €1, and public toilet attendants around €0.50.

**Taxes:** Most goods in Germany are subject to a value-added tax or *mehrwertsteuer* (MwSt)—of 19%, which is included in the purchase price of goods (a reduced tax of 7% is applied to books and magazines, food, and agricultural products). Non-EU visitors who are taking these goods home unused may be refunded this tax for goods totaling over €25 per store. When making purchases, request a MwSt or tax-free form and present it at a Tax-Free Shopping Office. Refunds must be claimed within six months.

## SAFETY AND HEALTH

**Local Laws and Police:** City regulations might seem weird and unusual. Drinking in public is perfectly acceptable while jaywalking is practically unheard of (it carries a €5 fine).

**Drugs and Alcohol:** The drinking age in Germany is 16 for beer and wine and 18 for spirits. The maximum blood alcohol content level for drivers is 0.05%. Although drinking in public is legal, it's smart to avoid public drunkenness; it can jeopardize your safety and earn the disdain of locals. Needless to say, illegal drugs are best avoided. Possession of small quantities of marijuana and hashish for personal use is legal in Germany. Each region has interpreted "small quantities" differently (anywhere from 5 to 30 grams). Carrying drugs across an international border is a serious offense that could land you in prison.

**Prescription Drugs:** Common drugs such as aspirin (*Kopfschmerztablette* or Aspirin), acetaminophen or Tylenol (*Paracetamol*), ibuprofen or Advil, antihistamines (*Antihistaminika*), and penicillin (*Penizillin*) are available at German pharmacies. Some drugs—like pseudoephedrine (Sudafed) and diphenhydramine (Benadryl)—are not available in Germany, or are only available with a prescription, so plan accordingly.

# GREAT BRITAIN

**There's a good chance that you think you know Britain pretty well.** After all, it's the land of much-exported BBC dramas, a royal family whose every move is watched all over the world, and literature—from Shakespeare to *Harry Potter*—read in every corner of the globe. It's true that, for the English-speaking traveler, traipsing through Britain is a logistical breeze (although you may not be able to understand a word said in Glasgow). But what you'll find, should you venture to these historic Isles, is that Britain is still quite capable of producing shock and delight. Whether you go to Manchester for the football, Liverpool for The Beatles, Cambridge and Oxford for the learnin', or London for some of the best museums, theatres, and parks in the world, England will prove she's still got it after all these years. And, to the north, Scotland is downright seductive with its towering castles, jaw-dropping countryside, and museums that kick serious kilt-clad booty.

Britain is a land of great stories (just ask Walter Scott or Arthur Conan Doyle)—sometimes, as in World War II, it's been the protagonist, and other times, as in its days as an oppressive imperial power, it's stepped into the role of the power-hungry villain. While all this history is here for you to explore, Britain is still writing new stories. Political drama no longer revolves around succession to the throne—Brexit, immigration, and economic disparities as evidenced by the Grenfell Tower tragedy are today's hot-button issues gracing the front page of *The Daily Mail*. So, when you're here, don't just look to the past. Pick up a copy of that newspaper to read on the Tube and watch the next chapter unfold.

# EDINBURGH

Coverage by **Mia Karr**

Stand on the upper level of Edinburgh Castle, where you can see the whole urban sprawl of New Town and the mountains in the distance, and you'll feel it—magic. Okay, maybe we drank a little too much whisky or became delirious after walking up Edinburgh's many hills. Maybe, even, the constant bagpiping on the Royal Mile did something to our heads. Regardless, we think there's truly something magical about the Scottish capital that can't be denied by even the most haggis-scorning skeptic. If you do need convincing, walk through the cobblestoned Old Town, where all the architecture has a bit of castle in it, go to a museum or festival (this is an artist's paradise), or pick up something by Sir Walter Scott at a secondhand bookstore. There's so much to see and do, but merely being in Edinburgh is an experience in itself and not a wee one at that.

## ORIENTATION

The heart of Edinburgh is made up of the historic **Old Town,** where streets curve and twist without reason, and the perfectly planned Georgian **New Town. Waverley Station** straddles the two. To the south of Waverley is Old Town, home of the **Royal Mile,** which links **Edinburgh Castle** on the west and The **Palace of Holyroodhouse** on the east with **St. Giles Cathedral, The Scottish Whisky Experience,** and many tartan and shortbread shops in between. **The Grassmarket,** most of Edinburgh's museums, and many theaters are also in Old Town. To the north, Waverley borders **Princes Street,** the main shopping street in Edinburgh and the start of New Town. North of Princes Street, the streets form an even grid and are full of cool bars and shops. The **University of Edinburgh** is spread throughout the city, but many of its buildings can be found in the southeast city center, near the **Royal Museum of Scotland.**

## ORIENTATION

### GETTING THERE

Edinburgh International Airport is just west of the city, which you can access via tram, bus, taxi, or car after landing. Trams run every 10min. to the city center (single ticket £4.50, £2 child). You can take a train into Edinburgh from London Euston station, for example, into Waverly Station. Both National Express and Megabus offer bus services to Edinburgh as well.

### GETTING AROUND

Edinburgh has both a bus and a tram system. Tram tickets cost £1.50 for city-zone travel. The main line runs along Princes Street and terminates at Haymarket. The bus system, Lothian Buses, has several routes; the 24 is easiest for getting from the North Town to the Old Town (avoiding numerous hills in between).

### PRACTICAL INFORMATION

**Tourist Offices:** VisitScotland Edinburgh iCentre (3 Princes St.; 141 473 3868; open M-Sa 9am-7pm, Su 10am-7pm).
**Banks/ATMs/Currency Exchange:** There are ATMs up and down Princes Street, including a number of Royal Bank of Scotland ATMs. Bank of Scotland (43 Comely Bank, 131 456 8501; open M-Tu 9am-5pm, W 9:30am-5pm, Th-F 9am-5pm, Sa 9am-1pm).
**Post Offices:** The Inch Sub Post Office (68-70 Walton Scott Ave.; 131 664 3103; open M-F 8am-6pm, Sa 9am-4pm).
**BGLTQ+ Resources:** BGLTQ Health and Wellbeing (9 Howe St.; 131 523 1100; open M-F 9am-5pm).

### EMERGENCY INFORMATION

**Emergency Number:** 999
**Police:** Police Scotland (14 St. Leonard's St.; 1786 289070).

**US Embassy:** Consulate General of the United States (3 Regent Terrace, 131 556 8315).

**Rape Crisis Center:** Edinburgh Rape Crisis Centre (17 Claremont Cresent; 131 556 9437; open M-F 9am-7pm). Rape Crisis Scotland Helpline (08088 01 003 02).

**Hospitals:**
- Royal Edinburgh Hospital (Morningside Place; 131 537 6000; open daily 24hr.).
- Spire Murrayfield Hospital Edinburgh (122 Corstophrine Rd.; 131 334 0363; open daily 24hr).

**Pharmacies:** Boots Pharmacy (40-44 North Bridge; open M-F 8am-7pm, Sa 8:30am-6:30pm).

# ACCOMMODATIONS

### 🏚BUDGET BACKPACKERS ($)
37-39 Cowgate; 1312266351; www.budgetbackpackers.com; reception open 24hr

Great Scot, these rooms are cheap! You would never guess it, though, from the location. Budget Backpackers is super close to a hopping scene of restaurants and bars. Indicatively, though, there's a sign on the door that says "this is not a bar." Be aware that the cheapest dorms have you sleeping beside upwards of 20 people, but there's adequate space for everyone and their bags. There's also a bar/café for residents only, contrary to the sign. This is rare case where you get a little bit more than what you pay for and we love it.

*i* Dorms from £9.30; reservation recommended; no wheelchair accessibility; Wi-Fi; linens included

### COWGATE TOURIST HOSTEL ($)
96-112 Cowgate; 8081689610; www.cowgate.hostel.com; reception hours 8am-11pm

Cowgate isn't the most appealing name for a road, but names can be deceiving: it's just a block over from the **Royal Mile,** right next to **The Grassmarket,** and plenty of restaurants and bars. Cowgate Tourist Hostel takes advantage of this killer location by offering almost 200 beds to attract solo backpackers and rowdy stag and hen parties. While prices are good, the rooms are unfortunately a bit cramped and there's not a lot of head space for bottom bunkers. While maybe not your top hostel choice, it's still a good option.

*i* Dorms £12-15; reservation recommended; max stay 31 nights; Wi-Fi; linens included

### ROYAL MILE BACKPACKERS ($)
105 High St.; 1315576120; www.royalmilebackpackers.com; reception hours 6am-3:30am

The old real-estate refrain of "location, location, location" could not apply more to Royal Mile Backpackers: it's on the **Royal Mile** (duh) and only a few jaunty strides away from **Edinburgh Castle.** It's also on the smaller side, with a cozy dining room and lounge area. Unlike some hostels in the area, it explicitly caters towards backpackers, as it boasts free Thursday night pub crawls and assistance in booking excursions to the **Scottish Highlands.** Perhaps the only downside is the flight of stairs from the street to reception, but consider it training for Edinburgh's hilly streets.

*i* Dorms from £12-14; reservation recommended; no wheelchair acessibility; Wi-Fi; linens included; laundry facilities

# SIGHTS

## CULTURE

### ☑THE SCOTCH WHISKY EXPERIENCE

354 Castlehill; 1312200441; www.
scotchwhiskyexperience.co.uk; open daily
10am-6:30pm

You begin the tour strapped into a
moving barrel and end it sampling
whisky among the world's biggest
unopened collection of the drink, so
you could say it's a pretty wild time.
Whether you love whisky or can barely
get it down, the intricate details of the
whisky-making process in the first leg
of the tour (according to British law,
whisky must mature for at least *three
years*), the gorgeous images of Scotland
in the portion where you learn about
whiskies from different regions, and the
rows and rows of whisky in the vaults
are enough to make you want to pack
it all up and move to a distillery in the
Highlands. Or at least buy something
from the gift shop.

*i* *Silver tour adult £15, £13 student,
gold tour adult adult £26, £23.75 student;
wheelchair accessible*

### EDINBURGH FESTIVAL THEATRE

13/29 Nicolson; 1315296005; www.
edtheatres.com; open M-Sa 10am-6pm

Edinburgh loves the arts: it's a
**UNESCO** world city of literature, its
art galleries hold masterpieces, and
it hosts the biggest arts festival in the
world. If you can't make it to **Fringe,**
there are still plenty of opportunities
to see stellar performances. The
Edinburgh Festival Theatre is a good
place to catch a play, musical, ballet,
opera, or concert. While some tickets
are excruciatingly expensive, the theatre
has student standby tickets from £10
that can be purchased on the day of the
show from midday until half an hour
before curtain.

*i* *Ticket prices vary; shows take place
on the weekends and some weekday evenings; book wheelchair-accessible seats in
advance (limited number available)*

### THE GRASSMARKET

Grassmarket; www.greatergrassmarket.
co.uk; hours for stores and restaurants vary

The Grassmarket is truly the best
of the delightful clusterfuck that is
Edinburgh. As you stroll through
the historic shopping area centered
around Grassmarket Street, you'll get
a fantastic view of the ancient castle,
right above vintage shops hawking
hipster wares. You'll find touristy
shops blaring the bagpipes alongside

## THE FESTIVAL FRINGE

We were kind of bummed when we found out this wasn't a festival celebrating
tassles, until we learned that it's even cooler; Fringe is the world's largest arts festival. Months before performers from around the world take the stage in August,
the city begins hyping everybody up for this truly spectacular event. Programs are
available in businesses of all stripes and posters riddle walls and bulletin boards. If
you want to get in on the fun, you should think months ahead, too—hostel beds
fill up and prices are much higher than the rest of the year.

How did the festival get so bloody huge, you ask? By not turning anyone away.
The original Festival Fringe was formed by several performers who were rejected
from the Edinburgh International Festival and simply performed on its fring-
es—true to that spirit of inclusion, all are welcome to sing, dance, act, or bagpipe
their hearts out. Yes, this does mean that not every act is West End-quality, but
there are quite a few diamonds in the rough. Edfringe, thankfully, is no cousin
to Coachella when it comes to pricing. Tickets for shows are bought individually
starting as early as February. Some shows are free, and half-price tickets can be
bought on The Mound day-of. Edinburgh may not be the most tropical location
to spend the hottest of your summer months, but being part of a massive, messy,
mishmashy celebration of art ain't half bad.

independent boutiques; pubs that have been on the site for centuries next to new cafés and juice bars. And, to make things all the more intriguing, executions once happened on this site. It's a great hang (no pun intended) any day of the week, but Saturday adds a little extra flair with a street market from 10am-5pm.

*i* *Prices vary by store/restaurant; limited wheelchair accessibility*

## LANDMARKS

### ▨EDINBURGH CASTLE

Castlehill; 1312259846; www.edinburgh-castle.gov.uk; open daily 9:30am-5pm

Is the Edinburgh Castle expensive? Yes. Is it worth it? Absolutely. In fact, if you see one thing in Edinburgh, this towering fortress of Scottish should be it. There's so much to see: the Scottish crown jewels, the prisons of war, a war museum and memorial, the massive cannon Mons Meg, and sublime views of the city from every direction. Edinburgh is downright magical and nowhere is that more apparent than in these hallowed walls, even if the magic is diminished a little bit by a proliferation of selfie sticks. Oh, and it's oh-so-Scottish: the turrets practically play the bagpipes.

*i* *Admission £17, audio guides £3.50; limited wheelchair accessibility*

### PALACE OF HOLYROODHOUSE

Canongate; 3031237306; www.royalcollection.org.uk; open M, F-Su 9:30am-6pm

In 1603, The Union of the Crowns brought England and Scotland together under one monarch, so now the Queen of England has some sweet digs in Scotland in addition to her London residence. The Palace of Holyroodhouse is fairly small, as British palaces go, but steeped in history. The most interesting part is the bedchamber of **Mary Queen of Scots,** Scotland's poster girl. In addition to a recreation of her rooms, you can see various objects relating to her and the **Stewarts,** including a lock of her hair—perhaps this obsession is starting to border on creepy. Make sure to check out the gardens outside.

*i* *Palace and Queen's Gallery adult £17.50, £16 student, Palace adult £12.50,*

£11.40 student; limited wheelchair accessibility; the Palace is not open to visitors when the Queen is in residence

### ST. GILES CATHEDRAL

High St.; 1312254363; www.stgilescathedral.org.uk; open M-F 9am-7pm, Sa 9am-5pm, Su 1pm-5pm

St. Giles Cathedral is beautiful. Like okay, we know, a lot of historic churches are beautiful and if you're Church of Scotland HQ you should obviously pay attention to aesthetics. But any other word but beautiful doesn't really sum up the arched ceilings, the stained glass, the intricate little side chapels, and the monuments to Scots of the past. In fact, this might be one of those "a picture is worth a thousand words scenarios," but we can't help you there because you have to pay £2 to take pictures. So we'll just leave it at really, really beautiful.

*i* *Free admission, picture pass £2, self-guided tour £1; wheelchair accessible*

## MUSEUMS

### NATIONAL MUSEUM OF SCOTLAND

Chambers St.; 3001236789; www.nms.ac.uk; open daily 10am-5pm

The National Museum of Scotland seems to be several museums molded together: natural history, anthropology, fashion, technology, and a six-floor exhibit on Scottish history all vie for your attention. Unless you have unlimited time and incredible museum stamina you can't do it all, so here's our advice: breeze through (or skip) the whale bones and model trains that you can see at plenty of other museums and focus on the story of Scotland that no one can tell as well as Edinburgh. Oh, and try to make it down to see the millennial clock chime on the hour—it's morbid and wonderful.

*i* *Free admission, free tours; tours at 11am, 1pm, and 3pm; wheelchair accessible*

### SCOTTISH NATIONAL GALLERY

The Mound; 1316246200; www.nationalgalleries.org; open M-W 10am-5pm, Th 10am-7pm, F-Su 10am-5pm

If you're the capital of a European nation, you're expected to have a pretty bitchin' art gallery, and Edinburgh

# BARD OF THE SCOTS

When you arrive at Waverley station, one of the first things you'll see is a giant, blackened, tower-like structure. A quick peek at a labeled map will reveal that this is the **Scott Monument.** "Oh," you'll probably think. "I get it, we're in Scotland, so it's a monument to the Scottish People." But, alas, you are but a naïve newcomer to this linguistically confusing land. In a twist of fate—or perhaps a case of predestination—one of the most famous Scots is also a Scott. Sir Walter Scott, to be exact. If your image of Scotland involves rugged highland famers in kilts telling tales of ancient beasts and kings around a fire, you have old Walt to thank. Through his wildly popular novels and poems, such as *The Lady of the Lake* and *The Fair Maid of Perth*, Scott created the romantic and mystical Scotland of popular imagination and inspired a fascination in all things Scottish for many foreigners. Although his tales didn't bare much resemblance to the actual lives of most Scotlanders, they were happy to embrace his version of Scotland—if someone's painting your homeland as a beautifully romantic land of kings and warriors, you should probably just roll with it.

The people of Scotland did more than roll with it. They felt so indebted to Scott that, after his death, they built a monument to him in Edinburgh, his hometown. Today, you can climb to the top of the monument for a view of the city—it sits right across from **Edinburgh Castle** and **the Royal Mile.** The Scott Monument is actually the largest monument in the world dedicated to a writer, because usually these sorts of towering structures are reserved for kings or heroes. While Sir Walter wasn't a king or hero himself, he created kings and heroes and wielded a pen that proved just as mighty as a sword.

isn't going to disappoint. The National Gallery system also includes a portrait gallery and gallery of modern art, but the Scottish National Gallery is where you'll find all the golden oldies. From **Raphael** to **Peter Paul Rubens** to **Edgar Degas,** it's an absolute artistic smorgasbord. Right next to the free permanent collection, the Academy building holds temporary exhibitions, some of which are free. It's a good choice for your doctor-recommended daily dose of culture.

*i* *Free admission; wheelchair accessible*

## SURGEONS HALL MUSEUMS

Nicolson St.; 1315271711; www.museum. rcsed.ac.uk; open daily 10am-5pm

If you loved dissecting frogs in eighth grade biology class, this museum is for you. It's fascinating in a completely morbid, is-something-wrong-with-me-because-I-love-this kind of way: terrifying old surgical equipment, diseased hearts in jars, child skeletons, and early anesthetic equipment are some of the grim wonders on display. There's also a whole room full of seemingly infinite jars of diseased body parts, like feet with gangrene,

spines with severe scoliosis and skin: just pure, unattached skin. Admit it, you're intrigued. It's absolutely worth a visit—just don't plan to eat lunch right afterward.

*i* *Admission adult £6.50, £4 student; last entry 4:30pm; wheelchair accessible*

## FOOD

### ◼EL TORO LOCO ($)

60 Grassmarket; 1312902411; www. toroloco.co.uk; open M-Th 9am-11pm, F-Sa 9am-midnight, Sa 9am-11pm

Their motto is "Street food. No bull," but it could also be "Street food. I'm crying right now because this is so good and also so cheap." (Ours has a better ring to it, right?) Situated in the Grassmarket among pubs hawking Scottish delicacies, El Toro Loco is a little something different. Choose from a variety of dishes like burritos and quesadillas, pick your own protein (their meat is unreal) and fillings and sit outside if the weather isn't too grey. If this is what crazy tastes like, we're all for crazy.

*i* *Quesadillas and burritos £4-6; vegetarian options available*

### BRUNCH ($$)

37-39 George IV Bridge; 1312256690; www.brunchedinburgh.co.uk; open M-Th 8am-5pm, F 8am-9pm, Sa 9am-9pm, Su 9am-6pm

No, we didn't get super lazy and just suggest you eat brunch anywhere you damn well choose—Brunch is a transparently-named restaurant in Old Town. This may shock you, but Brunch does really good brunch. Their massive six egg omelette is a good choice or you can go for full-throttle with their full English. Oh, and there are pancakes. And drinks that come in mason jars. Play right into their eager hands, why don't you, because the brunch at Brunch is mmm-mmm good.

*i* *Entrées £6-10; vegetarian and gluten-free options available*

### TANJORE ($)

6-8 Clerk St.; 1314786518; open M-F noon-2:30pm and 5pm-10pm, Sa-Su noon-3:30pm and 5pm-10pm

When it comes to food, quantity has got to be almost as important as quality. Luckily, Tanjore provides both. They serve dinner, but the real product for your pound occurs at lunch on weekdays, where you can get a wide array of Indian delicacies for £8. Choose a starter, a curry, a bread, and a dessert and you're off—they also throw in a few other small dishes and a whole lotta rice. It's a perfect midday pick-me-up after losing your breath on Edinburgh's hilly streets.

*i* *Entrées £6-8; vegetarian options available; limited wheelchair accessibility*

### TING THAI CARAVAN ($)

Teviot Pl.; 1312259801; open daily 11:30am-10pm

Edinburgh is full of students and it knows how to cater to their needs—namely good, affordable food that you can grab in between a study sesh and a head-clearing emotional breakdown. Ting Thai Caravan is both tiny and very popular, which means you'll probably be sitting next to someone you don't know, but you'll both be too absorbed in delicious Thai cuisine for awkward small talk. Also, if you're a solo traveler, this is a place where "one, please" won't get you any weird looks. Which is a relief after certain pitying

glances from other waitstaff—you're just *independent*, okay!

*i* *Entrées £5-7; cash only; vegetarian options available*

# NIGHTLIFE

### ⬛THE LUCKY LIQUOR CO.

39a Queen St.; 1312263976; www.luckyliquorco.com; open daily 4pm-1am

Lucky Liquor Co doesn't have any Felix Felicis potion on tap, but they do have a range of specialty cocktails. It's kind of what they do. Because of the mile-long list of ingredients and crazy skills needed to make these concoctions (we assume) they're not cheap, but it's the perfect opportunity to treat yourself to something yummy and boozy in a cute, relaxed bar. It's definitely too small to rage, but just the right size for an intimate hang. If you're lost among the exotic drinks, just try whatever has the best name.

*i* *No cover, cocktails £6-8.50; limited wheelchair accessibility*

### BREWDOG

143 Cowgate; 1312206517; www.brewdog.com; open daily noon-1am

If you're anything like us, the extent of your beer knowledge is that PBR tastes better cold. At BrewDog, things are a little more (okay, a lot more) advanced. Each craft brew is tenderly described on their daily beer list as one might describe a loved one. Some of their brews even have t-shirts. It's okay if you're an amateur, though—the bartenders will help you out and they even host a "beer school." There's also live music and board games for your enjoyment. BeerDog is a far cry from some of the more tequila-soaked establishments on Cowgate and pretty smug about it too: just read their website.

*i* *No cover, pints £4.50-6, pizza £9; limited wheelchair accessibility*

### THE HOLYROOD 9A

9a Holyrood Rd.; 1315565044; www.theholyrood.co.uk; open M-Th 9am-midnight, F-Sa 9am-1am, Su 9am-midnight

You can run, but you can't hide from the pub life in the United Kingdom. While Edinburgh has a host of more hip and innovative bars, it's always worth stopping by a great pub classic like Holyrood 9A. Although they get zero points for name creativity, this Holyrood joint does score on the drinks front. There are tons of (affordable!) brews and wine and cocktails. In the evenings, it's crowded and friendly, with locals and tourists stopping by for a bite to eat or a pint at the bar. Cheers!

*i* No cover, beer and wine £3-5, cocktails £7

### THE POTTING SHED
32-34 Potterow; 1316629788; www. thepottingshededinburgh.co.uk; open M-W noon-11pm, Th noon-midnight, F-Sa noon-1am, Su noon-10pm

The Potting Shed is the bar equivalent of the college student who dyes their hair for theme parties. The whole place is a boozy garden wonderland: the wall decorations are gardening tools, the light covers are upside-down buckets, the seats are barrels, and every inch rocks the earth tones. For a botanist, it's probably a vision of heaven on earth. For everyone else, it's a good bar with a twist. The drink list is pages on pages and cocktails are 2 for £8 at all times. While you can also order classy pub grub for dinner, be aware that it's pretty pricey (£12-16 range) and the wait is often long.

*i* No cover, beer £3-5, wine £4-7, cocktails £7-8

# GLASGLOW

Coverage by **Mia Karr**

Edinburgh locals are fond of claiming that the best thing in Glasgow is the train to Edinburgh—and for travelers looking for the Scotland of castles, kings, and unsurpassed natural beauty, there may be some truth to it. But Glasgow is the type of city where people *live* just as much as people visit. It's an industrial stronghold that rose to prominence as "the second city of the empire," the home of 40 percent of Scotland's citizens, and a bit of a Cinderella story. After gaining infamy for overcrowding and poverty, Glasgow worked to turn its image around and become a city known for its art, sports, and culture instead. The twenty-first century traveler will encounter a city that's both aware of its past (see, for example, The People's Palace) and looking toward the future. Glasgow's official guide operates under the slogan "People Make Glasgow," and it's a smart pick—from architect Charles Rennie Mackintosh to scientist Lord Kelvin to the bagpipers on Buchanan Street, it's the people, not the kings, that make Glasgow a great place to experience Scotland.

## ORIENTATION

Glasgow is a big city—Scotland's largest, in fact. The **River Clyde** separates the city into north and south, and almost all tourist attractions are in the north part of the city. Just north of the Clyde is the city center, where you'll find the retail district, **City Chambers, Merchant City,** and bar-heavy **Sauchiehall Street.** Just east of the center, you'll find a small cluster of attractions around **Glasgow Cathedral,** on **Castle Street,** and **Glasgow Green** lies to the southeast. To the west of the city center is **Kelvingrove Park** and **The West End,** home of **Glasgow University** and several museums. To the eastern and southern reaches of the city lie the **East End** and **South End,** respectively, but the traveler staying only a few days in the city likely won't venture out to either.

# ESSENTIALS

## GETTING THERE

Glasgow's main bus station is Buchanan Street, right in the city centre. You can use Citylink buses to travel between cities in Scotland, or Megabus to travel within the UK. Glasgow's two main train stations are Glasgow Central and Glasgow Queens Street. Glasgow Central links Glasgow to every city in the UK. The nearest airport is Glasgow Airport. Your fastest option to get to the city center is the Glasgow Airport Express, which runs every ten minutes and costs £7.50 for a single ride. You can also take a train to Glasgow City Central, which will take 40-minutes to an hour and run you around £3.50.

## GETTING AROUND

Glasgow Taxis (http://www.glasgowtaxis.co.uk/) is the largest taxi company in Glasglow. All cabs are wheelchair accessible. Glasgow's tiny Subway (www.spt.co.uk) has only 15 stations and two lines, both of which run in a complete circle. Use it to get around the city center and the West End. Glasgow has an extensive bus network that runs on a zone system and most popular destinations are located within the first zone. Tickets for first-zone travel are £1.40.

## PRACTICAL INFORMATION

**Tourist Offices:** Visit Scotland Information Centre (Royal Exchange Square; open M-W 10am-4:45pm, Th 10am-7:45pm, F 11am-4:45pm, Sa 10am-4:45pm, Su 11am-4:45pm).
**Banks/ATMs/Currency Exchange:** Barclays Bank (St. Enoch Shopping Centre, 83 Argyle St.; 345 734 5345; open M-F 9am-6pm, Sa 9am-5pm).
**Post Offices:** Sauchiehall Street Post Office (177 Sauchiehall St.; 906 302 1222; open M-Sa 9am-5:30pm, Su 10:30am-2:30pm).
**BGLTQ+ Resources:** BGLTQ Youth Scotland (30 Bell St.; 141 552 7425).

## EMERGENCY INFORMATION

**Emergency Number:** 999
**Police:** Police Scotland (50 Stewart St.; 178 628 9070, 101 for non-emergen-

cies).
**US Embassy:** There is no US Embassy in Glasgow, but there is a Consulate General of the US in Edinburgh (3 Regent Terrace, Edinburgh EH7 5BW; 131 556 8315; open M-F 8:30am-5pm).
**Rape Crisis Center:** Rape Crisis Centre (30 Bell St.; 141 552 3201).
**Hospitals:** Glasglow Royal Infirmary (84 Castle St.; 141 211 4000).
**Pharmacies:**
- Superdrug (66 Argyle St.; 141 221 9644; open M-W 8am-7pm, Th 8am-8pm, F 8am-7pm, Sa 8am-6:30pm, Su 9:30am-6pm).
- Llyod's Pharmacy (147 Great Western Rd.; 141 332 1478; open M-F 9am-6pm, Sa 9am-5pm).

# ACCOMMODATIONS

### CLYDE HOSTEL ($)
65 Berkeley St.; 1412211710; www.clydehostel.co.uk; reception open 24hr

Oof. Clyde Hostel is proof you shouldn't believe everything you read on the internet. On paper, it seems like a decent, cheap hostel with a good location. In actuality, it's a poorly upkept building with gross-smelling bathrooms, showers that alternate between scalding and freezing, bunk beds that are one step away from a mattress on the floor, next to zero power outlets, and unprofessional staff. Unfortunately, Glasgow seems to suffer from a spate of similar hostels so your options for something better are few and far between. But you should honestly just stay in an Airbnb rather than this bargain basement accommodation. We suffered through this so you don't have to.

*i* *Dorms from £14; reservation recommended; no wheelchair accessibility; Wi-Fi; linens included; must be 18 or older to stay*

### EURO HOSTEL ($)
318 Clyde St.; 8455399956; www.euro-hostels.co.uk; reception open 24hr

You can spot a Euro Hostel from a mile away by the large "EH!" sign, which seems a weird expression of mediocrity mixed with enthusiasm. Euro Hostel is not mediocre—it's solidly "above average" or perhaps even "good." In short, it's not all that much to get excited about. The showers are warm and clean, the bunk beds are comfortable for both top and bottom bunkers, and an unusually elaborate hostel breakfast can be purchased at the bar every morning. Likely because the building resembles a hotel (nine floors, bland white walls) more than a hostel, there isn't much in the way of hostel community, and the bar is hardly bumpin'. But you could do much, much worse for accommodations in Glasgow.

*i* *Dorms from £10; reservation recommended; BGLTQ+ friendly; wheelchair accessible; Wi-Fi; linens included*

## SYHA GLASGOW ($$)

7-8 Park Terrace; 1413323004; www.syha. org.uk; reception open 24hr

The hostel scene in Glasgow can leave you wanting, but SYHA is a shining beacon of light in the budget backpacking darkness. It's everything a hostel should be: clean, welcoming, professional. The reception area is stocked with Scottish alcohol and sightseeing advice, visitors have access to a kitchen and TV room, and the neighborhood is beautiful. It's also a bit removed from the city center, which could be a pain, but trust us— sometimes good location just can't make up for a lack of comfort.

*i* *Dorms £18-22; reservation recommended; Wi-Fi; linens included; laundry facilities*

# SIGHTS
## CULTURE
....................................................

## BUCHANAN STREET

Buchanan St.; hours vary

Do you hear that? The ever-grinding wheels of commerce mixed with the sound of bagpipes from a kilt-wearing busker? You must be on Buchanan Street! From the indoor Buchanan Galleria on **Sauchiehall Street** all the way down to Argyle Street, Buchanan is the center of Glasgow's thriving retail district. Here you visit just about any big-name UK clothing store, and also stock up on the requisite "I love Scotland" keychains and postcards. The street is cobblestoned and pedestrian only, so starry-eyed outdoor mall-goers

don't have to worry about being run over by a bus as they stare longingly into the **House of Fraser** window. (We'll be back for you someday!)

*i* *Everything varies for the street in general, but here's some info for Buchanan Galleries in particular: buchanangalleries. co.uk, open M-W, F-Sa 9am-7pm, Th 9am-8pm, Su 10-6, wheelchair accessible*

## GLASGOW FILM THEATRE

12 Rose St.; 1413326535; www. glasgowfilm.org; box office hours open Su-F noon-15 minutes after start of final film, Sa 11am-15 minutes after start of final film

Going to a nice independent cinema is a little like experiencing the class of a live theatre performance at (almost) Cinemax prices. Set among the rowdy bars of **Sauchiehall Street,** Glasgow Film Theatre is the perfect location for an alternative night out. Here you can catch your art house darlings, foreign language films, and generally anything that will impress your snooty, film major friends. The cinema has two bars, and movie snacks here are more of the "glass of pinot grigio and assorted nuts" than "extra large coke and butter-slathered popcorn" variety. Glasgow Film Theatre also hosts the extremely popular **Glasgow Film Festival,** so check that out if you're visiting in February.

*i* *Adult £9.50, £7.50 student; film showings daily*

## WELLPARK BREWERY

161 Duke St.; 1414947145; www.tennentstours.com; open M-Sa 9am-6pm, Su 10am-6pm

Touring the Wellpark Brewery is a little like touring Willie Wonka's Factory, if he specialized in booze instead of chocolate. And although people from outside Scotland may not realize it, Tennant's beer is a little like Wonka chocolate in its massive, nation-wide popularity. On the tour, see where the magic happens, including learning what the hell "hops" are and watching beer can after beer can after beer can whiz by on a giant, mesmerizing assembly line. The best part might be the tasting, though: in addition to a pint of your choice, you get tastes of

# TOP 10 SCOTTISH CONTRIBUTIONS TO THE WORLD

Believe it or not, the Scots have done a lot more for the world than just make some baller whisky and bless us with bagpipe covers of pop songs (see: The Red Hot Chili Pipers). Although it has a population of just five million, Scotland has made its mark on everything from art to medicine. Here are ten reasons to thank your nearest Scot.

1. **Supply and Demand:** If you failed your introductory Econ course, you can blame Scot Adam Smith who basically invented the whole blasted field. Bad for our GPAs, good for our understanding of the world.

2. **Advances in surgery:** Hey, do you enjoy not dying from infection after surgery? Thank Joseph Lister, who developed antiseptic surgery techniques while at the University of Glasgow.

3. **Sherlock Holmes:** the famed detective is British, but his creator, Sir Arthur Conan Doyle, is Scottish, and he based the character on one of his professors at The University of Edinburgh.

4. **Literature in general:** Robert Burns, one of the most famous poets of all time, Sir Walter Scott, the ultrapopular novelist, and J.K. Rowling, who wrote about wizards or something, all hail from Scotland.

5. **Weird systems of temperature measurement:** Actually, U of Glasgow-bred Lord Kelvin did a lot more than lend his name to an obscure temperature scale; he was a huge pioneer in the field of thermodynamics

6. **Art:** The Glasgow Boys, or "The Boys," as they embarrassingly referred to themselves, were a group of innovative eighteenth or nineteenth-century artists who made a worldwide splash

7. **Scottish accents:** Och aye, yer aff yer heid—if you don't think this accent is wonderful.

8. **The world's best aquatic monster:** Has any creature of the deep captured hearts like Nessie? Bigfoot can't hold a candle to her.

9. **Scotch Whisky:** Yeah, you knew it would make the list. The earliest distillery records in Scotland date back to 1494 and the most recent whisky consumption records date to us, five minutes ago.

10. **The song "500 Miles" by The Proclaimers:** screw it, this should be number one. Not many countries can claim a jam so singable we've been singing it at the top of our lungs for decades. Honestly, Scotland, we're forever in your debt for this one.

various other brews. Not bad for a tenner.

*i* Adults £10, students £7; M-F 10am, noon, 2pm, 4pm, and 6pm, Sa 11am, noon, 2pm, 4pm, 6pm, Su noon, 2pm, 4pm; No wheelchair accessibility; hairnets or hats required inside brewery

## LANDMARKS

### GLASGOW CITY CHAMBERS
George Sq.; 1412872000; www.glasgow. gov.uk; open M-F 9am-5pm

Glasgow's most beautiful building is perhaps not a museum or a church, but the seat of its city government. Marble staircases, a Cinderella-worthy ballroom, and intricate ceilings put the party in Scottish National Party, and you can feast your eyes if you take a brief, free tour. Much of the tour focuses on the history of the building itself, and while we're all for architecture lessons, it's a little too brief on the, you know, *politics*. We're still not quite sure what it is city councillors do in this beautiful building—presumably not slide down the marble railings, but no one has told us otherwise.

*i* Free tours; tours daily 10:30am and 2:30pm; wheelchair accessible

## GLASGOW NECROPOLIS

Castle St.; 1412873961; www.glasgowne-cropolis.org; open daily 8pm-4:30pm

We see dead people—their tombstones, that is. Visiting a graveyard may seem a bit morbid, but the Glasgow Necropolis is totally chill. It was built for the merchant patriarchs of Victorian Glasgow, so some pretty prominent people are buried here, like chemist **Charles Tennant.** Confusingly, the cemetery's most striking monument is dedicated to someone who's mortal remains are elsewhere—**John Knox,** Protestant extraordinaire. The Necropolis is on a hill, making for some great views of Glasgow. And, while you're at it, you might as well stop by the (also free) Glasgow Cathedral for some sick stained glass.

*i* *Free admission; limited wheelchair accessibility*

## THE PEOPLE'S PALACE

Glasgow Green; 1412760788; www.glasgowmuseums.com; open M-Th 10am-5pm, F-Su 11am-5pm

Power to the people! In 1898, the People's Palace was established in **Glasgow Green** as a community space for the people of Glasgow. Today, in addition to keeping its doors open to Glaswegians, it tells the story of what life in the city was like, from the perspective of the regular ol' folk. Glasgow was once famous for overcrowding, poverty, and horrendous living conditions, so a large part of the exhibit is dedicated to the realities of life in a tenement. While this is fascinating, some of the museum is rather banal ("Old age can be lonely" a sign informs us). But, you can skip the boring parts and make time for the gift shop instead, which has a stellar collection of items relating to the infamous Glaswegian dialect.

*i* *Free admission; wheelchair accessible*

# MUSEUMS

### 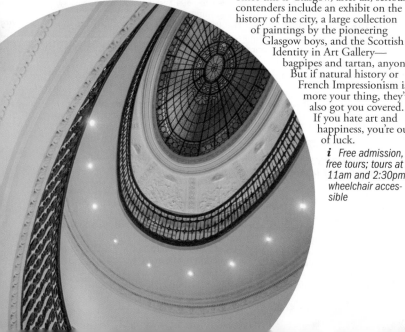KELVINGROVE ART GALLERY AND MUSEUM

Argyle St.; 1412769599; www.glasgow-museums.com; open M-Th 10am-5pm, F 11am-5pm, Sa 10am-5pm, Su 11am-5pm

Salvador Dali's *Christ of St. John on the Cross,* this is a fantastic museum! Although the curators act like Dali's famous painting is the most impressive part of the collection, we think there are too many wonderful paintings, artifacts, and exhibits to pick the best. Since this is Glasgow, after all, serious contenders include an exhibit on the history of the city, a large collection of paintings by the pioneering Glasgow boys, and the Scottish Identity in Art Gallery— bagpipes and tartan, anyone? But if natural history or French Impressionism is more your thing, they've also got you covered. If you hate art and happiness, you're out of luck.

*i* *Free admission, free tours; tours at 11am and 2:30pm; wheelchair accessible*

## HUNTERIAN MUSEUM AND HUNTERIAN ART GALLERY

University Ave.; 1413304221; www.glasgow.ac.uk/hunterian; open Tu-Sa 10am-5pm, Su 11am-4pm

Do you ever get the impulse to, like, travel the world and collect a bunch of random artifacts and then start a museum? William Hunter did, and thus began Scotland's first public museum. The modest collection of natural history, medical, and anthropological artifacts at the Hunterian Museum are presented in a way that focuses almost as much on their various collectors as on the objects themselves. There's some neat stuff, but it's a little uncomfortable to think about these Westerners traveling to less-developed parts of the world and removing important cultural artifacts to keep for their own purposes. Across the street, the Hunterian Art Gallery has a lovely collection of paintings and a slightly less white man's burden-y vibe.

*i* *Free admission; last entry 45min. before closing; wheelchair accessible*

## ST. MUNGO'S MUSEUM OF RELIGIOUS ART AND LIFE

2 Castle St.; 1412761625; www.glasgow-museums.com; open Tu 10am-5pm, F-Su 11am-5pm

St. Mungo's Museum—named for the patron saint of Scotland—is a relatively small, cathedral-adjacent museum about the world's six major religions. If you forgot what you learned about the Buddha and the Qu'ran in high school world history, this is a good chance to brush up on the basics and view a wide range of historical religious artifacts. Unfortunately, the museum's answer to tackling the incredibly vast subject of religion is to simplify. Religions with extreme varieties of difference are reduced to generalizations and much is glossed over—for example, a display on marriage in religion mentions nothing about the very pertinent issue of gay marriage in religious societies. Furthermore, Scotland's fascinating history of religious conflict is barely covered.

*i* *Free admission; wheelchair accessible*

## OUTDOORS

### KELVINGROVE PARK

Kelvingrove Park; 1413346363; www.glasgow.gov.uk; open daily 24hr

Glasgow is the most urban place in Scotland, so it's a relief to encounter some greenery among the cityscape. Kelvingrove has all the elements of a respectable public park: a river that winds through it (this is crucial), statues and memorials, play areas for the wee ones, sports pitches, and an art gallery. It borders the **University of Glasgow** and the chic West End and altogether it's a very pleasant part of the city. There's also a skateboard park if you're looking to shred, or whatever the people that know the first thing about skateboarding call it.

*i* *Free; wheelchair accessible*

## FOOD

### 'BABS ($)

49 W. Nile St.; 1414651882; www.babs.co.uk; open daily 11am-10pm

If you're visiting Scotland over the summer, 'Babs allows you to briefly forget that it's 60 and raining, because from the first bite of kebab, you're transported to a slice of Mediterranean heaven. These kebabs—"done right," as the restaurant claims—are of the fancy shmancy knife and fork variety. While there are lots of meats (and vegetarian options) to choose from, we humbly suggest you try the lamb, because it's flippin' delicious. 'Babs is BYOB, so don't expect any cocktails on the menu, but they do have a nice selection of coffees and desserts. One word: tiramisu.

*i* *Entrées £6-9; vegetarian options available; limited wheelchair accessibility*

### MAMAFUBU ($)

61 Glasford St.; 1415529798; www.mamafubu.com; open daily noon-10pm

You can only take so much pub grub, so Mamafubu had us at "Pan-Asian cuisine" and kept us all the way through to the caramel they left with the check. Because they gave themselves a whole continent to draw from, there are pages and pages of choices: fried rice, noodle dishes, seafood dishes, steamed bao buns, lots of meat and also things that are not meat. The service is fast, the prices ain't bad, and we genuinely don't have much to complain about. It's a good place to stop while you're shopping in the retail district.

*i* Entrées £7-9; vegetarian options available

## MONO ($$)

12 King St.; 1415532400; www.mono-cafebar.com; open M-Th 11am-11pm, F-Sa 11am-1am, Su 11am-11pm

Mono is not the place to declare your love for a big, dripping rack of ribs or state that you think vinyl is a silly hipster trend. It is, however, the place to eat good vegan food (pizzas, falafel, mac and cheese, etc.) in a welcoming atmosphere, or to catch a local artist while sipping an organic brew. Mono shares its roof with—you guessed it—an independent record shop, so there's plenty to do in that terrible lull between ordering food and delivering it to your mouth. And, if you're a skeptical meat eater, just remember that potatoes are vegan.

*i* Entrées £7-10; vegetarian, vegan, or gluten-free options available

## POMMES FRITES ($)

476 Sauchiehall St.; 1413320860; www.pommesfrites.uk.com; open M-Sa noon-4am, Su 1pm-midnight

If you go for a night out in Glasgow, there's a large possibility that you will find yourself on **Sauchiehall Street** in the wee hours of the morning. And, if this happens, there is an even larger possibility that you will feel an urge to down a large quantity of greasy food. Pommes Frites is the devil on your (less-than-capacitated) shoulder, urging you to go ahead and order the large fries with the extra sauce. And, oh hey, why don't you throw in a hot dog too? Give in to that sweet, sweet voice, because their fries (chips? frites?) are just what you need.

*i* Entrées £2-6; vegetarian options available

# NIGHTLIFE

## ⬛BAR HOME

80 Albion St.; 1415521734; www.craft-pubs.co.uk/homeglasgow; open daily 11:45am-midnight

Bar Home is soon to become one of your best Glasgow bar homies. The chic, two floor bar with book wallpaper, high ceilings, and plenty of intimate corners could always be a go-to, but, if you really play your cards right, and capitalize on their killer deals you'll love it even more. For example, £2.50 craft bottles from Sunday to Wednesday, £3.25 cocktails from Monday to Thursday, and two-for-one pizzas on Thursdays. And Sundays at Bar Home are "Lazy Sundays," with cheap brunch all day, a selection of newspapers, and Bloody Marys. So should you just go every day of the week? We're not saying no.

*i* No cover, drinks £3-8, food £3-9; wheel-chair accessible

## NICE N SLEAZY

421 Sauchiehall St.; 1413330900; www.nicensleazy.com; open M-Sa noon-3am, Su 1pm-3am

Nice N Sleazy is heavy on the nice (as in, high-quality) and just enough on the sleazy, making it a standout among Sauchiehall's plethora of places to drink the night away. Upstairs is for the more chill among us with plenty of space to stretch out and a disco ball that gently anoints the room with its light. Downstairs, however, is where things get more interesting—Nice N Sleazy frequently hosts live music acts, erring on the side of alternative. Relatively cheap drinks, fun hangs, and poor to middling decisions can be found on either floor.

*i* No cover, drinks £3-5; must be 18 to enter

## SLOUCH

203-205 Bath St.; 1412215518; www.slouch-bar.co.uk; open daily 11am-3am

If you're slouching toward central Glasgow, take a break at Slouch, a bar, kitchen, and music venue not far from Buchanan Street. No matter if you come for live folk music on Mondays, live jazz on Tuesdays, live blues on Wednesdays, or a DJ on the weekends, the tunes are sick and there's never a cover charge. Or you could just come for the lovely, subterranean bar which has puffy, furniture showroom-esque couches, lots of signature cocktails (and beer, duh), and general good vibes.

*i* No cover, drinks £4-7; no wheelchair accessibility

## WAXY O'CONNER'S

44 W. George St.; 1413545154; www.waxyoconners.co.uk; open M-Th noon-11pm, F noon-midnight, Sa 10am-midnight, Su 11am-11pm

The name makes a lot more sense once you find out that Waxy O'Conner was a candlemaker, and one that could really put away the liquor, apparently. His namesake pub is the Mother of All Pubs: we're talking three floors, six bars, and a very real chance of getting lost on the way back from the bathroom. Waxy's is ideal if you want some classic pub grub and a pint, but also a more rowdy (and diverse) crowd than the ten 50-year-old regulars that gather in the pub on the corner. You can also catch the latest football or rugby match on the giant flatscreen downstairs.

*i* No cover, food £8-10, drinks £4-7

# LIVERPOOL

Coverage by **Mia Karr**

The Beatles hit their prime 50 years ago (and this city'll be damned if they let you forget it!). That said, Liverpool still knows how to rock. Okay, so the Cavern Quarter now plays host to impersonation bands instead of the real deal and there are more department stores than record shops. But go out on a weekend night and you'll be surrounded by people looking to have a good time, including scads of stag and hen parties (is Liverpool the stag and hen capital of the UK? Maybe). In addition to the soon-to-be wedded off, old-timers parade in the streets belting out karaoke tunes. The Ropewalks bars are alive with activity at night and the museums are alive with culture vultures during the day. The docks are full of places to eat, learn, and relax; there's perhaps no easier city in which to spend half your salary (looking at you, Liverpool ONE!). All this to say that Liverpool isn't just a washed-up city profiting off Beatles nostalgia (although profit they do)—it's a worthwhile stop for anyone traveling through Britain.

## ORIENTATION

Liverpool's city center is nicely compact and walkable. **Liverpool Lime Street Station** is located in the northeast of the center, right across from the city's **"cultural quarter,"** which is home to several museums, historic theaters, and the central library. Bordering the cultural quarter and train station, **Liverpool ONE** shopping center takes up a lot of real estate in the center of the center and stretches almost all the way to the docks. Speaking of said docks, the **River Mersey** borders the center on the west and many of Liverpool's attractions, like the **Beatles Story** and **Maritime Museum,** are located on the docks, which stretch all the way to the south of the city center. In the southeastern part of the city center, the **Georgian Quarter** features beautiful architecture and several theatres, and the **Liverpool Cathedral** towers over the city. Beatles attractions like **Mendips House, Strawberry Fields,** and **Penny Lane** are a few miles outside the city center and best reached by bus.

# ESSENTIALS

## GETTING THERE

If flying into Liverpool, your closest airport is the aptly-named John Lennon Airport. To get into the city center, you can take a train, bus, or ferry: the Merseyside Travel Planner (www.jp.merseytravel.gov.uk) is a handy website that will allow you to plug in your travel details and find the best option. Liverpool Lime Street is the main train station and it's a short walk away from the city's major sights.

## GETTING AROUND

Most of Liverpool's major sights are within walking distance of the train station and one another. If that fails, take the bus: www.merseytravel.gov.uk has the details. You can buy a one-day solo ticket directly from a bus driver, or buy tickets at a travel center—there is one located in Liverpool ONE.

## PRACTICAL INFORMATION

**Tourist Offices:** Tourist Information Centre (Anchor Courtyard, Albert Dock; 151 707 0729; www.visitliverpool.com; open daily Oct-Mar 10am-4:30pm, Apr-Sept 10am-5:30pm).

**Banks/ATMs/Currency Exchange:** Banks and ATMs are easy to find in Liverpool, especially in and around Liverpool ONE. Barclay's Bank, Liverpool ONE (345 734 5345, open M-F 9:30am-5pm, Sa 9:30am-4pm).

**Post Offices:** Liverpool Post Office (1-3 South John St.; 151 707 6606; open M-Sa 9am-5:30pm, Su 11am-3pm).

**Internet:** Internet should not be a challenge. It's available in most cafés (and definitely in chains like Starbucks or Pret a Manger) and hostels.

**BGLTQ+ Resources:** The Armistead Project (151 227 1931) promotes sexual health and offers support and social groups.

## EMERGENCY INFORMATION

**Emergency Number:** 999

**Police:** Merseyside Police are located at Canning Pl. Their website is www.merseysidepolice.uk and for non-emergencies you can call them at 101.

**Sexual Assault Hotlines:** RASA Merseyside (www.rasamerseyside.org) provides support for survivors of sexual assault. Their helpline is 0151 666 1392 and is staffed Tu 6-8pm, Th 6-8pm, and F noon-2pm. Their general number is 0151 558 1801 and their address is Units 2 and 3 Stella Nova, Washington Parade, Bootle.

**Hospitals:**
- Royal Liverpool University Hospital (Prescot St.; 0151 706 2000; open daily 24hr).
- Broadgreen Hospital (Thomas Dr.; 0151 282 6000; open daily 24hr).

**Pharmacies:** Pharmacies are in abundance in Liverpool.
- Boots (0151 709 4711).
- Euro Chemists (0151 708 0778).
- Kays Pharmacy (0151 207 2212).

# ACCOMMODATIONS

### ⬛HATTER'S HOSTEL ($)
56-60 Hatters Hostel; 1517095570; www.hattershostels.com; reception open 24hr

Hatter's began in Manchester, but their Liverpool branch is more luxurious. Situated in a beautiful old building on a hill and located close to the train station and city center, Hatter's sweetens the deal further with free breakfast, a large bar that doubles as a lounge in the daytime, and a gregarious staff. Take advantage of their multiple activities, like a Friday night bar crawl, a Thursday night Beatles bar crawl, and **free food** on Tuesday evening. It may not quite be Wonderland, but it's not too far off, either.

*i* Dorms from £12, prices higher on weekends; reservation recommended; BGLTQ+ friendly; Wi-Fi; linens included; laundry facilities; free breakfast

### EURO HOSTEL ($)
54 Hostel St.; 8454900971; www.eurohostels.co.uk; reception open 24hr

There are two ways to look at Euro Hostel: a location that can't be beat right by the **Cavern Quarter** and **Liverpool ONE** with an exciting atmosphere buoyed by stag and hen parties on the weekends. Alternatively, an unwitting front-row seat to the touristy, commercial chaos that has overtaken The Beatles' old haunt and a night spent dealing with buzzed bridesmaids-to-be. Either way you take it, one undeniable perk of Euro Hostel is the nice beds with ample headroom on the bottom bunk (something so often overlooked) and plenty of power outlets.

*i* Dorms from £12.50, prices higher on weekends; reservation recommended; Wi-Fi; linens included; breakfast £4.50

# SIGHTS
## CULTURE
...................................................

### BOLD STREET
Bold Street; hours vary, but generally 10am-evening

Bold Street is the place to be if you're young, hip, and disagree with your parents on key political issues. Perhaps the ethos of the shop-heavy street is best summed up by **Soho's,** which manages to be a vintage clothing store, a record shop, and a tattoo parlor. Other highlights include **Resurrection,** which adds a coffee shop to the vintage store/tattoo parlor genre, **News from Nowhere,** a radical bookstore, and **Take 2,** a thrift shop with blissfully budget-friendly prices. You'll also want to stop for a bite to eat in between trying on leather jackets at one of Bold Street's A-plus eateries—vegans and vegetarians absolutely welcome.

*i* Prices vary by store; wheelchair accessible

### LIVERPOOL ONE
5 Wall St.; 1512323100; www.liver-pool-one.com; open M-F 9:30am-8pm, Sa 9am-7pm, Su 11am-5pm

Liverpool ONE is less of a shopping center and more of a small village. Smack dab in the city center, you

can't miss it, and, if you're suddenly surrounded by three-story stores and buskers strumming the guitar, you're probably already there. Perhaps its best feature (when it's not raining) is that it's pleasantly open air. You can buy a whole new wardrobe here and shoes to match, or just walk through on your way to the docks. Food options are rather chain-y, however, so it's probably best to eat elsewhere.

*i* Prices vary by store; wheelchair accessible

### THE BLUECOAT
School Ln.; 1517025324; www.thebluecoat.org.uk; open M-Sa 9am-7pm, Su 11am-6pm

The Bluecoat has the distinction of being both the oldest building in Liverpool's city center (and a lovely one at that) and the oldest arts center in the UK. It plays host to a king-sized range of arts activities such as film screenings, live performances in all genres, book fairs, and workshops—check their website to see what's coming up. It also opens its doors to the public every day, and anyone can walk through its art galleries for free or eat in the café. If nothing else, it's a great place to find people passionate about the arts and a good Wi-Fi connection.

*i* Free entry; wheelchair accessible

## LANDMARKS
...................................................

### PENNY LANE
Penny Lane, of "Penny Lane" infamy, is...a lane. Except every business makes reference to the street, from Penny Lane Flowers ("funerals and weddings!" it enthusiastically advertises) to Penny

Lane Surgery (apparently accepting new customers, if you're looking). There's also a barbershop, but the barber was not showing photographs as far as we could tell. The history of the place is neat—John Lennon and Paul McCartney used to meet here to take a bus into town—but the actual site is pretty underwhelming. It *is* a damn good song, though.

*i* Free; limited wheelchair accessibility

## MENDIPS

251 Menlowe Av.; 1514277231; www.thenationaltrust.org.uk/beatles

Lest you doubt that John Lennon actually grew up in Liverpool and think it's a vast conspiracy, you can visit his childhood home on Menlowe Av. and take a picture in front of the fence in the same spot where a scowling little John was once photographed. Want to go inside? There's a catch: you have to book in advance from the National Trust and buy an expensive combined ticket to visit Mendips and **Paul McCartney's home.** If you're a Beatles superfan, this is a chance for unparalleled insight into the childhoods of these two legends, but if you're more of a casual listener, perhaps you should just take the picture and "Let it Be." **Strawberry Field** is nearby if you want to snap a picture of the red gates.

*i* Adult admission £23; must book in advance; check website for tour times

## THE LIVERPOOL CATHEDRAL

St. James' Mt.; 1517096271; www.liverpoolcathedral.org.uk; open daily 8am-6pm

The Liverpool Cathedral wins the coveted *Let's Go* Award for Best Free British Church. As the largest Anglican church in the UK it packs quite a visual punch and holds its own against London's coffer-draining cathedrals. The inside is quite stunning, yet elegantly simple. There's not much in the way of historical plaques or famous tombs, but the aesthetics are enough. From 10am-5pm M-Sa and noon-4pm Su, you can go up the tower for a fantastic view of the city, but alas, you must finally open your tightly-clutched purse.

*i* Free admission; wheelchair accessible

## MUSEUMS

### ◪THE BEATLES STORY

Britannia Vaults, Albert Dock; 1517091963; www.beatlesstory.com; open daily 9am-7pm

If you're in Liverpool, you're either an avid Beatles fan or gradually resigning yourself to joining in the madness. Either way, you should probably go to The Beatles Story, the crowning jewel of The Beatles tourism empire. You'll wind your way through recreations of places relevant to the band like the **Cavern Club** and **Abbey Road Studios** (with accompanying soundtrack), and learn many bits of trivia. You gotta admit, the story of four talented boys from modest backgrounds who joined together and changed music history forever is rather inspiring. Just don't let them inspire you to spend £100 in the gift shop.

*i* Adult admission £15.85, £12 student

### MERSEYSIDE MARITIME MUSEUM

Albert Dock; 1514784499; www.liverpoomuseums.org.uk; open daily 10am-5pm

Life's a carnival down by the lovely River Mersey docks, but the Maritime Museum is here to remind us of the more serious side of sea travel. From the torpedo-ing of the *Lusitania* to the sinking of the *Titanic* (which was part of a Liverpool fleet), the maritime history of the city is enough to put anyone off boats for a good while. But it's also a story of triumph, as Liverpool established itself as an international trading port. The third floor of the museum explores the dark consequences of this triumph with the **International Slavery Museum.** It's an arresting attempt to memorialize the horrors of slavery and own up to Liverpool's part in the international slave trade.

*i* Free admission; wheelchair accessible

### WALKER ART GALLERY

William Brown St.; 1514784199; www.liverpoolmuseums.org.uk; open daily 10am-5pm

This is one of the most chronological art museums you'll ever find: clearly labeled rooms gently guide you from medieval depictions of Christ (who else?) to the oddities of the twentieth century. It's both a crash course in art history and a chance to take in a good-sized collection of beautiful paintings and sculptures. Highlights include that one really famous portrait of Henry VIII, known to anyone that's every cracked open a European history textbook, and an early self-portrait of Rembrandt.

*i* Free; wheelchair accessible

# FOOD

### DEATH ROW DINER ($$)
32 Hope St.; 1517091188; www.deathrow-diveanddiner.com; open M-Th 5-11pm, F 5-11:45pm, Sa noon-11:30pm, Su noon-11pm

We're guessing Death Row Diner's name alludes to its appropriateness for a last meal pick, but it could also refer to the fact that its meals move you incrementally closer to death. Seriously—there's no standard burger here. Everything is meat on more meat on even more meat, double patties, crazy additions (bacon onion rings? nachos on a burger?), and a little bit more meat to top it off. Truly the kind of crazy thing you would eat if your world was ending tomorrow. But hey, you're young, you can probably handle a meat-a-palooza every once in a while. If you really want to test fate, you can order a hard milkshake or cocktail to go with. But don't get cocky.

*i* Burgers £9-10.50; no wheelchair accessibility

### MOWGLI ($$)
69 Bold St.; 1517089356; www.mowglistreetfood.com; open M-Th noon-9:30pm, F-Sa noon-10:30pm, Su noon-9:30pm

Bold Street is a veritable cornucopia of Middle Eastern and South Asian cuisine (a.k.a paradise), but Mowgli stands out even in this crowd. The menu is happy to introduce you to the finer points of Indian street food and sass you a little bit while doing so: "Chicken Tikka Masala does not exist in India," they'll tell you matter-of-factly. The dishes are similar to tapas, in that you're expected to order multiple to constitute a meal—great for sampling the menu, but less great for your pocketbook (individual dishes

run around £5-7). Still, we think it's worth the splurge.

*i* Entrées £11-15; vegetarian and vegan options available; wheelchair accessible

### SHIRAZ ($)
19 N. John St.; 1512368325; www.shiraz-bq.co.uk; open daily 8am-11pm

This is the place to bring your friend who resents your attempts at adventurous eating—they can get a (super cheap) hamburger or calzone and you can go full Turkish. In addition to this wide variety of lunch and dinner options, Shiraz also has an extensive breakfast menu, and their full English is only £5.90. Although the low prices might suggest otherwise, the décor is nothing but class: red string lights and faux tree branches create a canopy on the ceiling and the color scheme is hot, hot, hot. Shiraz clearly has a loyal Liverpool following (the wait staff greets many a customer by name) and you, too, can become one of the groupies.

*i* Breakfast and burgers £3-6, kebabs 8-10; vegetarian options available

### TOKYO ($)
7 Berry St.; 1517086286; open daily noon-11pm

Tokyo may not be a city in China (we passed eighth grade geography with flying colors), but Tokyo is a restaurant in Chinatown. What sets it apart from other Asian eateries surrounding Liverpool's giant Chinese arch—apart from geographical confusion—is its prices. Entrées are food coma-inducing in size but still cheap. You could easily go halfsies on a noodle dish and an appetizer with a pal and be full—this type of restaurant is the bread and butter (spring rolls and soy sauce?) of budget travel.

*i* Entrées £5-8; vegetarian options available

# NIGHTLIFE

### BAA BAR
43-45 Fleet St.; 1517088673; www.baabar.co.uk; open M-Th 8pm-4am, F-Sa 6pm-4am, Su 5pm-4am

The base is bumping at Baa Bar and all of Liverpool has come out to dance. The building consists of two floors (drinking on the first, dancing and drinking on the second) and a courtyard where you can get some much-needed fresh air. You'll probably encounter quite a few stag and hen parties—this is Liverpool after all—and other youths just looking to have a good time in a popular club. Lace up those dancin' shoes! (Which can totally be sneakers because dress ranges all the way from casual to night-on-the-town).

*i* *No cover, drinks from £1 (shooters)*

## BAR CA VA

4A Wood St.; 1517099300; open M-Sa noon-2am, Su noon-12:30am

There are some things that are so much easier when you're young—climbing up stairs, remembering small details, taking multiple tequila shots without feeling the grim caress of death the next morning. Celebrate your youth while it lasts at Ca Va—the shots are so cheap and so plentifully-flavored you won't be able to resist, anyway. If you're feeling adventurous, you can even try bizarre flavors like coffee and baked bean. Yikes. As a relatively small and relaxed bar, it's a good early stop to get those inhibitions lowered before you embarrass yourself on the dance floor at a nearby club.

*i* *Tequila shots £1; no wheelchair accessibility*

## MOTEL

5-7 Fleet St.; www.motelbarliverpool.com; open Tu-Su 5pm-2am

A neon sign behind the bar proclaims that "sleep is the baby mama of death."

Other decorations include a mounted cow head and two pinball machines. The website consists of a picture of the bar and an address, nothing else. Are you intrigued yet? Motel bills itself as "dive bar tacos cocktails craft beer punk American garage psycho Billy," and we're honestly not going to try and top that. We will say that those cocktails they speak of are quite tasty and that it's a welcome reprieve from the many, many bad karaoke bars in the area. Check it out, as a sign in the window proclaims, "until then if not before."

*i* *No cover, drinks £4-7; no wheelchair accessibility*

## THE SHIPPING FORECAST

15 Slater St.; 1517096901; www.theshippingforecastliverpool.com; open M-W 10am-midnight, Th-Sa 10am-3am, Su 10am-midnight

Aye, what's the shipping forecast, matey? Good drinks, good tunes, and enough space to stretch your legs. Also live music acts, DJs, and the odd vintage fair on a Saturday. Adele came here once, apparently. The food is cheap and greasy. It has the laid-back vibe of a pub without a bunch of 50-year-old men drinking Guinness. Grab some friends, grab a pint, and hunker down on a comfortable sofa. Looks like smooth sailing to me!

*i* *No cover, drinks £4-7, food £5-7; BGLTQ+ friendly; wheelchair accessible*

# LONDON

Coverage by **Mia Karr**

Back before William met Kate, before a boy wizard named Harry Potter saved the world, before German bombs ripped through the city and Jack ripped through his victims, before Shakespeare's verses and Sherlock's cases and Henry's marriages, before the whole bloody thing burned down and was built up again, before anyone could have guessed what it would become, the Romans founded a small town on the River Thames and called it Londinium. Zoom forward about 2000 years to you, intrepid traveler, fresh off the Underground, sipping a pint in a pub and anxiously staring at a map of the massive city. The question is obvious: where to begin?

The official crown jewels are housed in the Tower of London, but cheaper treasures are nearly everywhere you look. There's the touristy but worthwhile spires of Buckingham Palace and St. Paul's Cathedral, theater in the West End and Southbank, vast and beautiful parks, and more art, literature, and greasy food than you can shake a crisp at. It seems as though every pub holds a wide-ranging history, and every museum a work of great cultural significance.

Connected by a network of convenient underground stations, containing individuals (and food!) of every race, creed, and religion, and bolstered by an eager-to-help tourism industry, London is a visitor's paradise. Go to museums all day or bars all night, stick to the well-trodden paths of Central London or venture into quirkier regions, stay for a weekend or stay for a year—the only mistake would be to stay home.

## ORIENTATION

London can sometimes feel more like a collection of cities than a city with any singular identity, given its multitude of distinctive neighborhoods. Perhaps the best place to start is the **City of London,** the square mile of oldest settlement just north of the Thames. High on history but low on actual residents, here you'll find the likes of the Tower of London and St. Paul's Cathedral. Just across the Thames is the neighborhood of **Southbank,** which was the sight of theaters like the Rose and the Globe back when it wasn't considered a part of London proper. Today, this theatrical spirit remains with the recreation of the Globe and historic theaters like the **Old Vic.** Moving West of the City, you'll find the **West End** and **Westminster,** two of the most tourist attraction-heavy neighborhoods of London. The West End is London's answer to Broadway, with shiny marquees on every street. It's also home to **Soho,** thriving enclave of gay culture. Westminster is the seat of government, with Parliament, Downing St., and Buckingham Palace all within walking distance of one another; expect crowds. Just north of the West End are **Marylebone and Bloomsbury** where you can find plenty of museums and the British Library. In the western part of central London, the well-coiffed neighborhoods of **Hyde Park, Notting Hill, South Kensington,** and **Chelsea** are some of the most pleasant places to visit. South Kensington and Chelsea are famous for their museums (The Victoria and Albert among them), and Hyde Park and Notting Hill houses its eponymous park and the beautiful rowhouses, respectively. Outside of central London lie the less well-defined neighborhoods of **East London, South London** (which would be more aptly named Southeast London), **North London,** and **West London.** Here you can visit the party center of **Camden Town** in North London, the impressive Hampton Court Palace in West London, **Greenwich** to the east, and **Peckham** to the south, but plan to spend lots of time on the Tube.

## ESSENTIALS

### GETTING THERE

London's main airport is Heathrow (www.heathrow.com, 0844 335 1801). To get from the airport to central London, you have several options: you can take the faster and more expensive Heathrow Express, which departs every 15 minutes, or opt for the much cheaper but slower Underground (see: Getting Around). You can also take a bus to Earl's Court or Victoria station. Another flying option is to arrive at Gatwick Airport, which has an express train to Victoria station. If arriving by train, London has multiple train stations that are connected to the Underground, making it easy to get to your ultimate destination easy.

National Rail (www.nationalrail.co.uk) connects cities throughout the United Kingdom.

### GETTING AROUND

By far the easiest, cheapest, and most quintessentially British way to get around the sprawling city of London is the Underground, or Tube. When you arrive, immediately pick up a wallet-sized Tube map (available at Heathrow and most hostels) and purchase an Oyster Card. This allows you to load money onto the card periodically and then tap in and out of the station to pay instead of buying a ticket every ride. Fares for individual routes depend on time of day and zone (the city is divided into nine zones, with one zone being the most central—you will probably rarely get outside of zone two). The Underground's website is www.tfl.gov.uk, and here you can find information about closures, although you'll rarely need to because they are announced frequently in the stations. You can also download the "Tubemap" app, which includes a route planner that will help you figure out where to change lines. The Tube runs about 5am-midnight M-Sa, with reduced service Su. Tube maps clearly indicate which stations are wheelchair-accessible, and this information can also be found on the website.

## PRACTICAL INFORMATION

**Tourist Offices:** City of London Information Centre (St. Paul's Churchyard, 020 7332 1456, open M-Sa 9:30am-5:30pm, Su 10am-4pm).
**Banks/ATMs/Currency Exchange:** Banks, ATMs, and currency exchange centers can be found on almost every street, so you should never find yourself cash-strapped—even then, almost everywhere accepts credit card. Withdrawing pounds is almost always cheaper than exchanging currencies, and be weary of enterprising currency exchange shops. Here are two centrally-located branches of Barclay's: 191 Earl's Court Rd, and 2 Victoria St., 0345 734 5345, both open M-F 9:30am-4:30pm.
**Post Offices:** Unsurprisingly, a city the size of London has quite a few post offices. Here are two: 167 Vauxhall Bridge Rd, Pimlico, 0845 722 3344, M-F 9:30am-5:30pm, Sa 9am-12:30pm; 6 Eccleston St., Belgravia, 0345 611 2970, M-F 9:30am-5:30pm, Sa 9am-12:30pm.
**Internet:** Free Wi-Fi is easy to find in London. Most cafés provide internet access, but, for a sure bet, Starbucks and Prêt à Manger (which is on every street) always have Wi-Fi. Public areas also sometimes have free Wi-Fi. Additionally, many of London's famous telephone boxes have upgraded for the twenty-first century and now provide Wi-Fi; this will be clearly indicated on their exterior.
**BGLTQ+ Resources:** There is an BGLTQ Tourist Information Centre on 25 Frith St. in Soho, a neighborhood famous for queer culture and gay bars. Its website is www.

gaytouristoffice.co.uk. Visit London, the city's official visitor guide (www.visitlondon.com), also has a section for BGLTQ+ travelers where you can find BGLTQ+ friendly hotels and ideas for things to do. In June, London goes all out to celebrate Pride, culminating in a massive parade.

## EMERGENCY INFORMATION

**Emergency Number:** 999
**Police:** There is a visible police presence in London, especially in crowded areas. For a non-emergency, they can be contacted via 101. More information and your nearest police station can be found at www.met.police.uk.
**US Embassy:** The U.S. Embassy in London is at 24 Grosvenor Sq., Mayfair. It can be reached at 020 7499 9000 or www.uk.usembassy.gov, and it is open M-F 8am-5:30pm.
**Hospitals:** London has many hospitals. Here are two:
• University College Hospital (235 Eudston Rd., 020 3456 7890, open 24hr).
• St. Thomas' Hospital (Westminster Bridge Rd., 020 7188 7188, open 24hr).
**Pharmacies:** Pharmacies are almost as ubiquitous as ATMs. Here are three:
• Boots (020 7262 7434).
• Zafash Pharmacy (020 7373 2798; open 24hr).
• Nelsons Pharmacy (020 7629 3118).

# ACCOMMODATIONS

### ⛿ASTOR VICTORIA ($$)
71 Belgrave Rd., Westminster; 2078343077; www.astorhostels.com; reception open 24hr

When we left Astor Victoria behind, we shed a single tear. Was it because of the gregarious staff and comfy lounge? The fast Wi-Fi and pet fish? No—while those were great, it was the beautiful, blissful, euphoria-inducing showers that did it. Do not underestimate the importance of clean walls and high water pressure to the weary backpacker. We would come back for that alone, but Astor Victoria is also located a few tube stops away from the sights of **Westminster** and piles on the free amenities. All in all, it's a steal.

*i* Dorms from £24.50; reservation recommended; BGLTQ+ friendly; no wheelchair accessibility; Wi-Fi; linens and towel included; laundry facilities

### ST. CHRISTOPHER'S INN GREENWICH HOSTEL ($)

189 Greenwich High Rd., East London; 2086002500; www.st-christophers.co.uk; reception open 7am-11pm

The brochure for St. Christopher's Inn Greenwich shows a hip couple glowing with youth and beauty—and perhaps you, too, could be hip, young, and beautiful if you stay in this hostel connected to a banging bar and use the money you save on their super low rates to buy moisturizer and avocados. St. Christopher and his partner in crime Belushi, of Belushi's bar, have a network of hostels all over Europe, and this installment is within spitting distance of Greenwich's major sights. Pro tip: book online for better rates and free breakfast.

*i* Dorms from £10-13; reservation recommended; Wi-Fi; breakfast included with online booking

### THE WALRUS ($)

172 Westminster Bridge Rd., Southbank; 2079288599; www.thewalrusbarandhostel. co.uk; reception open M-W noon-11pm, Th noon-midnight, F-Sa noon-1am

The Walrus is ostensibly a reference to a certain Beatles song, but it could also be that the funky, cuddly animal (walruses are funky and cuddly, right?) was chosen to represent the spirit of this hostel-above-a-bar (15% discount on drinks for guests!). If The Walrus were a person, she would be an art school student with several tasteful tattoos who doesn't have a cooler-than-thou attitude and is happy to share her towels, converters, lockers, and breakfast with you. Okay, that metaphor may have gotten away from us, but don't let the great deal that is the Walrus get away from you.

*i* Dorms £22-26; reservation recommended; Wi-Fi; linens provided; free breakfast

### ASTOR HYDE PARK ($$)

191 Queen's Gate, Hyde Park and Notting Hill; 2075810103; www.astorhostels.com; reception open 24hr

Oh, Astor Hostels, how do we love you; let us count the ways. In addition to the cleanliness and kind staff we've come to associate with the Astor brand, the neighborhood and building of Astor Hyde Park are beautiful. Every hostel—from **Central London** to the far reaches of **Underground Zone 6**—brags about their location, but this is the real deal: easy access to all the museums in **South Kensington,** and practically across the street from **Hyde Park.** The staff also hosts activities almost every day of the week, from wine and cheese nights to a watch party for London's naked bike race.

*i* Dorms £19-25; reservation recommended; Wi-Fi; linens included; laundry facilities; lockers provided; free breakfast

### BARMY BADGER BACKPACKERS ($$)

17 Longridge Rd., South Kensington and Chelsea; 2073705213; www.barmybadger.

com; reception open M-Sa 7:30am-5am, Su 9am-8pm

There are (sadly?) no badgers on the premises, but there are two dogs who have the run of the place. This is just one of the many touches that make Barmy Badger feel more like a home and less like a waystation than most other hostels. It includes in-suite bathrooms, coffee and tea served all day, free breakfast in the morning, and staff that is nothing short of motherly. Perhaps the only real downside is bunks stacked in threes, but large lockers help to alleviate space concerns. Then again, this review doesn't matter much, because if the name hasn't already convinced you, nothing will.

*i* *Dorms £22.50-27; reservation recommended; no wheelchair accessibility; Wi-Fi; linens included; laundry facilities; free breakfast*

### CLINK 78 ($)
78 King's Cross Rd., Marylebone and Bloomsbury; 2071839400; www.clinkhostels.com/london/clink78; reception open 24hr

Clink78 used to be a two-for-one courthouse and jail, and now it's a two-for-one hostel and place to rage. Blaring pop hits, a busy basement bar, and a generally raucous clientele make this one of the less relaxing hostel experiences—either terrible or great, depending on how much you like listening to Macklemore at midnight. Be warned that the bunks in the large dorms are a little too true to the building's prison origins—say goodbye to personal space and be prepared to fight your neighbor to the death to use one of very, very few outlets.

*i* *Dorms from £17-21; no reservation required; max stay 2 weeks; wheelchair accessible; Wi-Fi; laundry; linens provided; breakfast £1*

### SMART CAMDEN INN ($)
55-57 Bayham St, North London; 2073888900; www.smarthostels.com; reception open 24hr

If you're a dancing queen (of any age), the pubby, clubby **Camden** is a good place to headquarter your time in London. Smart Camden Inn isn't the height of luxury accommodations—we'd love to have a little chat with Smart Hostels about the concept of

space—but it is smack dab in the middle of party rocking Camden Town. There's also a very cute garden in the back of the hostel and a self-service kitchen, but, more importantly, rooms are at a true budget travel price.

*i* *£13-18; reservation recommended; Wi-Fi; laundry facilities*

### SMART HYDE PARK VIEW ($$)
16 Leinster Terrace, Hyde Park and Notting Hill; 2074024101; www.smarthostels.com; reception open 24hr

When you embrace the hostel lifestyle, you knowingly surrender some of your personal space—but, within reason. Smart Hyde Park View wins the dubious (okay, not so dubious) award for Most Cramped London Hostel. We're talking multiple three-high bunkbeds in a tiny room, too few outlets, and one in-suite bathroom for nine people. Slightly alleviating the situation are privacy curtains, and free breakfast and proximity to **Hyde Park** are serious perks. But Smart Hyde Park View lacks the kind of distinctive character that might lead us to overlook some of its shortcomings.

*i* *Dorms from £24-£27; reservation recommended; wheelchair accessible; Wi-Fi; linens included; laundry facilities; free breakfast*

### YHA LONDON OXFORD ST. ($$)
14 Noel St., West End; 2077341618; www.yha.org.uk; reception open 24hr

Exiting Oxford Circus Underground station puts you smack in the middle of West End tourist central, and it can all be a bit overwhelming. However, walk about seven minutes and you'll see the soothing green of the king of all British hostels, the YHA. If you're a needy person, YHA London Oxford St. has got you covered—24-hour reception, adorably dorky movie nights, discounted tickets to West End shows, a large, self-service kitchen. True to YHA form, its value lies in its reliability, rather than its funky freshness.

*i* *Dorms from £28; reservation recommended; wheelchair accessible; Wi-Fi; linens provided*

## YHA LONDON ST. PAUL'S ($$)

20 Carter Ln., City of London; 2072364965; www.yha.org.uk; reception open 24hr

Once a school for choir boys, this hostel now houses the very young, the very old, and those in the middle who can appreciate staff-mandated quiet hours after 11pm. The vast swatch of populace frequenting this massive (213 beds!) establishment is likely attracted by the two-minute walk to St. Paul's Cathedral, variety of family and solo traveler living arrangements, and 24hr access. This is certainly no place to rage, but seeing all the city has to offer will leave you ready to observe those quite hours and drift away into pure, choir boy-accompanied dreams.

*i* Single-gender dorms from £20-28; reservation recommended; Wi-Fi; laundry service; breakfast from £6.25, lunch and dinner available for purchase

# SIGHTS
## CULTURE
......................................................

### ⬛THE BARBICAN CENTRE

Silk St., City of London; 2076388891; www.barbican.org.uk; open M-Sa 9am-11pm, Su noon-11pm

So, you're going to give up pubbing for a night, put on something presentable, and experience some good ol' British culture. But where to possibly start? How about with *everything*? The Barbican Centre, founded by the Queen herself, is some kind of magical artist's paradise where visitors in the know can watch films, attend theater, dance, and music performances (this is home base of the **London Symphony Orchestra!**), and peruse art galleries. The venue also hosts an unreal number of events for culture lovers of all tastes, and has an open-to-the-public library. Thanks, Elizabeth!

*i* Library admission free; prices vary by performance

## CAMDEN MARKET

Camden Lock Pl., North London; 2037639900; www.camdenmarket.com; open daily 10am-7pm

If you're looking for a t-shirt with a crude slogan or a cheap oil painting of the Suicide Squad look no further— Camden Market is here to help. Although many of its wares are of the "who actually buys this tourist crap" variety, the magnitude and popularity of the market make it a fun place to check out. The main event, though, is the food. Cuisines from every corner of the globe compete for attention— which, praise be, often involves free samples—and a hearty meal is much cheaper here than in most London restaurants. We suggest taking a multiple course approach to lunch and not forgetting dessert(s).

*i* Prices vary by stall; limited wheelchair accessibility

## KING'S STREET SHOPS

King's St., South Kensington and Chelsea

Chelsea is almost as famous for its shopping as it is for its football, and King's Street is *the* posh place to shop. Just off the Sloane Square Tube station, King's street is positively riddled with places to blow your hard-earned cash:                      trendy

# SCREEN TO RE(E)L LIFE: *HARRY POTTER'S* LONDON

Visit any book or souvenir shop in London and you'll see that *Harry Potter* mania has not died down since the final book and movie about the boy wizard were released. Most recently, the J.K. Rowling-approved spinoff *Harry Potter and the Cursed Child* is a smash success in the **West End.** While you probably can't afford tickets unless you have Malfoy-family style wealth, you're soaking up some of the Harry Potter glow just by being in London. **King's Cross Station,** home of platform 9 ¾, now holds a *Harry Potter* shop with an insane queue, and yes, the scenes from the movie were filmed in this busy rail and Underground station. Movie crews also filmed in London for scenes where the characters enter the Ministry of Magic—just like the muggle government, wizard HQ is in Britain's busiest city. Harry and his friends can also be seen flying, via broomstick, past the famous Westminster skyline: the London Bridge, Big Ben and Parliament whiz past in *The Order of the Phoenix*. Other moments are subtler: The Leaky Cauldron Tavern, entrance to Diagon Alley, is alternately filmed in Borough Market and Leadenhall Market. Rowling has said she originally imagined it on Charing Cross Road, but its businesses make for more difficult filming. If you want to get super niche (by which we mean nerdy) you can stop by the Australia High Commission, a.k.a. Gringotts Bank, or Claremonet Sq., the inspiration for Grimald Place Finally, although not in the books, the Millenium Bridge is destroyed by Death Eaters in the beginning of *Harry Potter and the Half-Blood Prince*. Thankfully, it has since been restored.

boutiques, familiar chain stores, coffee shops, book stores, restaurants, a store (T2) devoted to tea and teapots, another (Tabio) advertising only of fancy socks. While some stores may seem too hallowed to even set your dirty backpacker foot in, there are plenty of more affordable options—and window shopping is highly cost effective.

*i* Prices vary by store; wheelchair accessible

### LLOYD'S OF KEW BOOKSHOP

9 Mortlake Rd., West London; 2089482446; www.lloydsofkewbooks. co.uk; open Tu-Sa 10am-5pm

There's a certain pleasure in a well-organized bookshelf, but there's a different pleasure in an absolute book tornado. Lloyd's of Kew prioritizes books over walking space and books over order and books over everything. There are ridiculous, haphazard piles of books on every subject imaginable, as well as antique books in glass cases, signed books, and first editions. And while some bookshops dare you to *breathe* near their wares, Lloyd's serves

coffee. This delightful disaster is just a short walk from Kew Gardens.

*i* Prices vary by book; no wheelchair accessibility

### ONE NEW CHANGE

1 New Change, City of London; 2070028900; www.onenewchange.com; open M-W 10am-6pm, Th-F 10am-8pm, Sa 10am-6pm, Su noon-6pm

If you thought you had left sprawling, multi-level displays of capitalism behind in the states, think again! One New Change, an outdoor mall within spitting distance of **St. Paul's Cathedral,** is here to serve every clothing, accessory, food, or beauty need you may have. Less expensive brands like H&M and Topshop coincide with the Pandoras of the world, and international mainstays like The Gap rub shoulders with local variants like Sweaty Betty, which stops sounding gross once you realize it's an athletic clothing store. Access it via Watling, Bread, Cheapside, or New Change (duh!) Street.

*i* Prices vary by store; wheelchair accessible

## PORTOBELLO ROAD

Portobello Rd., Hyde Park and Notting Hill; 2073613001; www.portabelloroad.co.uk; open M-W 9am-6pm, Th 9am-1pm, F-Sa 9am-7pm

Portobello Road is your one stop shop for first order bric-a-brac. Buy your mother an antique brooch, your sister a decaying copy of *Through the Looking Glass*, and your tacky aunt a hand-stitched double-decker bus pillow. You can also enjoy the wealth of oddities without spending a cent, merely wandering up the gently sloping market road. It's like an art museum for *things*. We strongly suggest coming hungry—the international street food is top notch and the fresh fruit can ward off the scurvy that poor, undernourished travelers are always on the brink of developing. There's really no better way to spend a few hours in **Notting Hill.**

*i* Prices vary by stall; wheelchair accessible

## ROYAL ALBERT HALL

Kensington Gore, South Kensington and Chelsea; 2075898212; www.royalalberthall.com

Victoria and Albert had a love story for the ages, and, like any good love story, it was tinged with tragedy—poor Albert kicked the bucket in 1861. Victoria then had the perfectly normal response of naming a gigantic concert hall in his honor. Since then, Royal Al has become one of the most famous performance venues in Europe, hosting an eclectic range of performances in every art form imaginable. While front-row seats are not budget-traveler friendly, arts-lovers can take a mid-priced tour of the facilities and learn more about their history or buy cheaper tickets for the balcony.

*i* Adult tours £13.27, £11.75 student, ticket prices vary; first tour 9:30am, last tour 4:30pm; box office open from 9am; wheelchair accessible

## THE CALDER BOOKSHOP AND THEATRE

51 The Cut, Southbank; 2076202900; www.calderbookshop.com; open M-Sa 11am-8pm, Su 1pm-6pm

From the street, Calder looks like a typical quirky, independent bookstore, but it's even better than that—it's a combination bookstore and theater! Although live performances aren't always showing—check the website for current details—the shop also screens movies free of charge. Or you could just come for the bookstore itself, which sells mostly plays and books about theater, politics, and philosophy. To further up its indie street cred, Calder buys and sells used books and rents out rehearsal space.

*i* Books range from £10-16; bookstore closes at 7pm when there is a performance, performance times vary

## THE GLOBE THEATRE

Cardinal Cap Alley, Southbank; 2079021500; www.shakespearesglobe.com; exhibition open daily 9am-5pm

The British have much to brag about—the creation of calculus and superior taste in tea, for example. But perhaps nothing compares in national pride to a little playwright named **William Shakespeare.** Today's Globe Theatre is unfortunately not an original, but a recreation—the violent delights of the two Victorian Globe Theaters had violent ends, the first at the hands of fire and the next at the hands of killjoy Puritans. Still, this modern-day recreation is worth visiting for an entertaining history tour or a show. "Groundlings" pay only five pounds to stand in front of the stage and brave the elements.

*i* Tickets for performances vary, but standing tickets are typically £5, tickets for exhibition and tour £16, £12.50 students; tours leave every 30 min between M 9:30am-5pm, T-Sa 9:30am-12:30pm, Su 9:30am-11:30am

## WEST END THEATRE

The Lodge, Leicester square (TKTS booth), throughout the West End; 75576700; www.tkts.co.uk; open M-Sa 10am-7pm, Su 11am-6:30pm

You can't go anywhere in the West End without either passing a theater marquee or a poster for a production in one of the district's many famous theaters. "Alas!" you might think to yourself, "If only I had the travel budget of a minor duke and not that of a hostel-bound commoner!" Fear not—if you're flexible about what show you're willing to see, you can get cheap day-of tickets at the TKTS booth in

**Leicester Square.** Prices can go as low as £15, although keep in mind that's probably not for the current blockbuster musical. But hey, it's the West End!

*i* Tickets range from £15-60

## LANDMARKS

### ◪TOWER OF LONDON

Tower of London, City of London; 2031666000; www.hrp.org.uk/tower-of-london; open M 10am-5:30pm, Tu-Sa 9am-5:30pm, Su 10am-5:30pm

The Tower of London is not a single tower but several; not a musty old relic but a time machine-cum-theme park-cum-museum-cum-*experience*. As you wander the bridges and parapets of the imposing fortress, you'll both long for the days when the monarchy was more than a figurehead and be thankful everyone's no longer just a catechism away from a beheading. (Although, executions took place at the Tower as recently as WWII!) If you don't want to grow grey waiting to see the crown jewels, there's plenty else to explore.

*i* Suggested donation £24.80, £19.30 student; last tour at 3:30pm; audio tours available; wheelchair accessible

### BIG BEN

Westminster; 2072194247; www.parliament.uk; open daily 24hr

Much like its West End cousin **Trafalgar Square,** Big Ben is one of those landmarks that you can't really *do* anything with, but if you're in London, you just gotta go. (Fun fact: it's said that if Big Ben ever chimes 13 times, the Trafalgar lions will get up and walk around.) Conveniently attached to the **Houses of Parliament,** this most famous of London sights presides majestically over the droves of tourists that walk through the area every day. As you become one of those tourists, make sure you snap a pic of ol' Ben—your Instagram followers are expecting it.

*i* Free; tours available for UK residents only

### BUCKINGHAM PALACE

Westminster; 3031237300; www.royalcollection.org.uk; Changing of the Guard daily at 11:30am

There's nothing that can whip a crowd of foreign tourists into a frenzy of photo taking like **The Changing of the Guard**—literally nothing. The fuzzy hats, the pomp and circumstance, the brass band, the perfectly executed square turns—it's almost too much to handle. Prepare to be pushed, stepped on, and ultimately mystified by this most ceremonious of ceremonies. (And, for the love of Elizabeth, get there early!) For a less mosh-pit-like experience, you can tour parts of the Palace like the **State Rooms** and **Royal Mews,** but only during certain parts of the year and for a hefty price.

*i* State Rooms tour £23, £21 student, full tour £39.50, £36.20 student; check website for seasonal tour times; limited wheelchair accessibility

### DR. JOHNSON'S HOUSE

17 Gough St., City of London; 2073533745; www.drjohnsonhouse.org; open May-Sept M-Sa 11am-5:30pm, Oct-Apr M-Sa 11am-5pm

Shakespeare may have added hundreds of new words to the dictionary, but the second-most quoted Englishmen, **Samuel Johnson,** wrote the dictionary itself. Johnson's dictionary wasn't the first English language dictionary, but it reigned supreme for over a century until it was finally eclipsed by the Oxford English Dictionary. You can marvel at this impressive feat as you peruse his home, complete with facsimile of the dictionary itself and handy info cards about his life. Johnson apparently surrounded himself with interesting people because he was afraid he would go mad if he was alone—something fun for the solo traveler to contemplate.

*i* Admission adult £6, £5 students; audio tour £2

### HAMPTON COURT PALACE

Molesey, West London; 8444827777; www.hrp.org.uk; open daily 10am-6pm

**Henry VIII** may primarily be famous for not fricking around about producing a male heir, but he also did not frick around with interior design. Hampton Court Palace was

# TOP TEN FREE THINGS TO DO IN LONDON

So, the price of London's got you down: Westminster Abbey lightened your wallet by 40%, it seems like you have to top up your Oyster Card after every other trip, and it takes British monarchy-style cash to get a decent Full English. Chin up, young traveler! As expensive as the cost of living can be, London has plenty of world-class attractions that are blissfully free. Here we compiled ten of the best:

1. **The British Museum:** How, you ask, could a museum of this magnitude and depth possibly be free? Scientists are still working on an answer to this difficult question. Just be thankful you can lay eyes on the Rosetta Stone without dropping a sixpence.

2. **The Royal Parks:** So many to choose from—Greenwich, Regent's, Hyde, Kensington Gardens, to name a few—and all these acres and acres of green are free and open to the public to frolic within as they see fit.

3. **The National Gallery:** Over in the United States, large art museums are happy to reach deep into your pockets. But the British just want you to waltz through rooms and rooms of medieval and Renaissance art until you collapse from exhausted joy.

4. **The Changing of the Guard:** We're honestly shocked they haven't monetized this yet, since it's one of London's most popular tourist attractions, but for a sacrifice of merely your time and personal space, you can see this famous spectacle of funny hats and high knees.

5. **The Victoria and Albert Museum:** This is a world-class museum in every sense, from the depth of its collections to the range of time periods and geographic areas it covers. It's no wonder people eagerly queue for free access.

6. **The British Library:** Okay, so being free is kind of a library's whole shtick, but when you've got documents of such importance on display you could stand to charge a few pounds. Lucky for us, the BL takes mercy on our parchment-craving souls.

7. **The Tate Modern and Tate Britain:** Two spectacular Tates for the price of one—or is that the price of zero, since they're both free? You don't have to be good at math to appreciate the collections in Westminster or Southbank.

8. **The Cortauld Gallery:** Gee, it doesn't take much cash to see good art in this town. Head on over to the gorgeous Somerset house to view all the famous Impressionist paintings your heart desires.

9. **Portobello Road:** This spectacular outdoor market could become not free very, very fast, but if you exercise self-control, browsing is almost as fun as buying.

10. **Take a walking tour:** Almost every hostel has some sort of free walking tour, and it's a great way to orient yourself to your surroundings and maybe even—gasp—make a pal or two along the way.

the sweet, sweet crib of Henry and several competing dynasties of kings to follow. Hampton Court also has a spectacular, shrubbery-laden garden and a host of knowledgeable staff in period costumes. But there's a catch—getting to the Palace requires venturing outside even the farthest reaches of the tube and takes considerable time and expense, not to mention the expense of the ticket itself (we're talking fare zone four, people). But if you're rolling in Tudor-like dough, this isn't a bad way to spend it.

*i Adults £20.90, £17.10 students; last entry 5pm; free audio guide; wheelchair accessible*

## HOUSES OF PARLIAMENT

Parliament Square, Westminster; 2072194144; www.parliament.uk/visit; *tours available Sa and M-F during recess*

Lots of countries have democratically elected lawmakers, but how many can

remain. In addition to this impressive distinction, the tower once held the official records of the **House of Lords.** Currently, it houses a modest exhibit about the history of **Parliament** that's worth a quick stop if you're looking for something less crowded to do in Westminster or want to see a really, really old building.

*i* *Admission £5, £4.50 student; last entry 30min. before closing; wheelchair accessible*

say their lawmakers meet in a building that looks like a castle? (Britain 1, America 0). The British Parliament has evolved into a thoroughly modern institution, but the ornate edifice of the Houses retains its history. For visitors wanting to soak up some of that history, tours and audio tours are available, but only on Saturdays or weekdays when the Parliament is in recess—book ahead if you don't want to be left sobbing by the statue of **Winston Churchill.**

*i* *Tours £28, £23 students; audio tours £20.50, £18 students (pre-book discounts); last entry 4:30pm; wheelchair accessible*

### JEWEL TOWER

Abingdon St., Westminster; 3703331181; http://www.english-heritage.org.uk; open daily Apr-Sept 10am-6pm, Oct 10am-5pm, Nov-Mar 10am-4pm

Much like Khloe Kardashian had someone build a closet to hold all of her on-brand exercise wear, **King Edward III** had someone (Henry Yevele) build a tower to hold all his treasure in 1365. This small tower, located just behind **Westminster Abbey,** is one of the only parts of the original **Westminster Castle** to

### KENSINGTON PALACE

Kensington Gardens, South Kensington and Chelsea; 8444827788; www.hrp.org.uk; open daily 10am-6pm

Buckingham may get top palace billing in London, but Kensington is half the price, less crowded, and chock-full of soap opera-worthy British history. It was built for William and Mary, who only got the throne in an act of shade-throwing toward all Catholics. With your ticket, you can see the rooms where kings and queens of yore lived and entertained the rich and powerful. Basically, your tour will let you trace the British monarchy through a few tumultuous generations. The palace is also located in the idyllic **Kensington Gardens,** an appropriately vast front yard for a king. (Important note: this is *still* a royal residence, so you tragically will not be able to wander into Prince Harry's bathroom.)

*i* *Admission adults £17, £13.50 student; last entry 5pm; wheelchair accessible*

### SPEAKER'S CORNER AND MARBLE ARCH

Northeast Hyde Park, Hyde Park and Notting Hill; www.royalparks.org.uk; open daily 24hr

In this pair of landmarks on the corner of **Hyde Park,** Speaker's Corner got the family brains and Marble Arch got the beauty. While the Corner has a fascinating history—**Orwell, Marx,** and **Lenin** are a few of the figures to take advantage of this government-designated spot for oratory—it's not much to look at. Marble Arch, right across the street, was intended to be the entrance to **Buckingham Palace,** before an expansion made that unfeasible. This now-pleasant area also has a dark past: it used to be the spot of the infamous **Tyburn Gallows,** and Londoners would buy tickets to watch the ghastly proceedings. Think about that the next time someone accuses millennials of being callous.

*i* Free admission; wheelchair accessible

## ST. PAUL'S CATHEDRAL

St. Paul's Churchyard, City of London; 2072468348; www.stpauls.co.uk; open M-Sa 8:30am-4:30pm

St. Paul's is just a slight 600 years younger than Jesus Christ himself, and this opulent center of British Christendom has seen it all, from the wedding of **Charles and Diana** to the execution of the infamous **Gunpowder Plotters.** Brave a claustrophobia-inducing staircase and you can look down at the Cathedral floor from the **Whispering Gallery.** Alternatively, stand on the floor and develop a minor neck problem from staring slack-jawed at the painted ceiling. Ideally, do both and stop by the tombs of some famous people, read about the church's history in the crypt, and visit the gardens outside while you're at it.

*i* Free for prayer, admission adult £18, £16 student, £8 child, group discounts; last entry 4:15pm; tours 90 min or 30 min; wheelchair accessible

## ST.-MARTIN-IN-THE-FIELDS

Trafalgar Square, West End; 2077661100; www.smitf.org; hours vary

Perhaps more aptly named St.-Martin-by-the-Square, this historic Anglican church is a bustling center of music and worship just across from the **National Gallery.** Good old Martin shared his cloak with a beggar, and then Christ appeared to him in a dream in the form of the beggar, prompting his baptism and subsequent rise through the Christian ranks. Today, his namesake church is a popular spot for visitors who want to take a look around the lovely eighteenth-century architecture or attend a performance. The church also holds regular services, and includes a café and gift shop in the crypt.

*i* Free; audio tours available; wheelchair accessible

## THE BRITISH LIBRARY

96 Euston Rd., Marylebone and Blooms-bury; 1937546060; www.bl.uk; open M-Th 9:30am-8pm, F 9:30am-6pm, Sa 9:30am-5pm, Su 11am-5pm

Everyone knows how to steal the Declaration of Independence, but to steal the **Magna Carta** you're going to have to come to the British Library. (Note: we do not endorse emulating the behavior of Nicholas Cage.) In addition to legal documents, the library's **Sir John Ritblat Gallery** holds a fascinating collection of old books, manuscripts, and documents, including a Gutenberg Bible, **Jane Austen's** notebooks, and the only surviving copy of *Beowulf.* The library also has above-average (even for a library) study spots and temporary exhibits on everything from The Russian Revolution to *Harry Potter* to the Gay Rights Movement in Britain.

*i* Free; wheelchair accessible

## THE ROYAL OBSERVATORY — EAST LONDON

Blackheath Ave., East London; 2088584422; www.rmg.co.uk; open daily 10am-5pm

It's the early 1700s, you're at sea, and you need to tell time—what do you do? Prayer is about the best you've got. The Royal Observatory's exhibits detail the wonder of John Harrison's 1761 marine chronometer, the creation of Greenwich Mean Time, and other aspects of measurement we tend to literally never think about. Once you're done being thrust into an existential crisis by the realization that time is oh-so-manmade, you can stand in a too-long line to view the **Prime Meridian Line,** or look at the wicked view from the hill for zero wait and zero dollars.

*i* Admission £9.50, £7.50 student; last entry 4:30pm; audio tours available; wheelchair accessible

# CAMBRIDGE

**Life in Cambridge sounds pretty good: the Cam River is flowing, church bells from countless chapels are ringing, and bicycles are whizzing over the cobblestone streets.** Tourists and university students pass each other in punts on the Cam and jostle for space in cafés along Trinity Street. Like its fellow college town and bitter rival, Oxford, Cambridge has quite the laundry list of history-making past residents—take King's College, brainchild of Henry VI and alma mater of Alan Turing, John Maynard Keynes and Zadie Smith. But don't think the gates to the city are locked until you score high on an IQ test: Cambridge is happy to have you explore its many museums, attend services in its churches, and patronize its pubs. Just don't wear an Oxford sweatshirt while you do so.

To reach the city center from the train station, walk about 20 minutes northwest, following the clearly marked signs. At the center, you will find the tourist office, post office, ATMs, public restrooms, and **King's College chapel** within a five-minute radius. Many of **Cambridge University's** colleges and museums are scattered around the city center. The **Fitzwilliam Museum** is about seven minutes southwest of the tourist office, on **Trumpington Street.** The River Cam cuts through the city center on the west and north; to reach areas for punting, travel southwest to the **Mill Pond** or northwest to **Quayside.** The Cambridge bus station is near the tourist office, on **Emmanuel Street.** Many intersections contain signs pointing toward major sights.

## GETTING THERE

The nearest major airports to Cambridge are London Stansted, London Heathrow, and London Gatwick. From Heathrow, take a train from King's Cross station or use the more expensive direct coach service. From Stansted, take a direct train or direct coach service. From Gatwick, take a train from King's Cross. If traveling by train, it's easiest to travel from King's Cross or London Liverpool Street stations in London, but there are also connections from Scotland and the north via Peterborough. The train station is conveniently located near the city center.

## GETTING AROUND

Many of Cambridge's major sights are clustered in the city center, making it easily navigable by foot. However, the local transport du jour is the bicycle. You can rent cycles (the British parlance) at City Cycle Hire on Newham Road (0122 336 5629); it's open M-Sa 9:30am-5:30pm. You can also take the bus. If you purchase a multibus ticket (£8 for a day, £33 for a week), you can travel on buses run by several different services without having to pay fares every time you change. For questions, call 34 045 0675. The Cambridge Bus Station is on Emmanuel Street.

## Swing by...

### KING'S COLLEGE CHAPEL

King's Parade; 0122 333 1212; www.kings.cam.ac.uk; open M-F 9:30am-3:30pm, Sa 9:30am-3:15pm, Su 1:15pm-2:30pm

In many ways, King's College Chapel is a microcosm of **Cambridge University:** beautiful architecture, rich history involving the monarchy, and source of fascination for travelers. Unlike most of Cambridge, you can visit both the chapel and, sometimes, the grounds of King's College itself (this is included in the ticket). The chapel was started by **Henry VI,** who later died in the Tower of London (real househusbands of the British monarchy brings the drama again), and finished by **Henry VIII,** he of the many wives. It's still very much a living church, and visitors can attend services and performances of its world-famous boys' choir.

*i* Adults £9, £6 students; last entry 3pm; tours (adult £6, £4 student) some Sa at 11am and noon; wheelchair accessible

## Check out...

### FTIZWILLIAM MUSEUM

Trumpington St.; 0122 333 2900; www.fitzwilliammuseum.cam.ac.uk; open Tu-Sa 10am-5pm, Su noon-5pm

No one would blame you for coming to the Fitzwilliam solely to see the suits of armor—we think we can all agree that knights are cooler than a brisk breeze off the Cam—but there are other, less dragon slaying-centric exhibits in store at this Cambridge University-affiliated museum. Think pottery, porcelain, Egyptian tombs, centuries-worth of paintings, and sculptures missing a limb or two. Less vast and less crowded than the **Ashmolian** in Oxford or the **Victoria and Albert** in London (but equally free!), this is a culturally-enriching way to spend a few hours in one of the brainiest cities in England.

*i* Free; tours Sa at 2:30pm for £6, self-guided audio tours £4; wheelchair accessible

## Grab a bite at...

### AROMI ($)

1 Bene't St.; 122 330 0117; www.aromi.co.uk; open M-Th 9am-7pm, F-Sa 9am-10:30pm, Su 9am-7pm

Not to worry folks, no "Italian" food here. This family-run Sicilian eatery makes pizza like your mama used to, if your mama was an accomplished Italian chef with a passion for sourdough and pastries. And, at less than £5 per a slice (and their slices are an absolute meal and a half), it's a true culinary bargain. If you're looking for Aromi pizzeria, don't get confused with the affiliated Aromi gelateria right next door—or absolutely do, if gelato is more your thing. Both are a hair's breadth away from **King's College chapel,** and when you take your first bite it's hard to know whether the angelic voices in the air are from the pizza or the choir boys practicing across the road.

*i* Pizza £4.90; vegetarian options available; limited wheelchair accessibility

## Don't miss...

### PUNTING ON THE CAM RIVER

Magdalene Bridge or Mill Lane; 122 335 9750; www.punting.co.uk; open daily 9am-dusk

Venice may have its gondoliers, but Cambridge has its punters. Punting, named after the canoe-like "punt boats," involves standing on the back of the boat, propelling with a big stick, and trying your darndest not to crash into the scores of other boats on the **Cam River.** If that sounds untenable, chauffeured tours are available and include an engaging history of the colleges along the river—you will learn more about bridges than you ever thought possible. If you think chauffers are for the weak, you can try punting yourself. Bringing along some booze seems a popular choice for the Cam's self-punters, although alcohol famously does not increase your likelihood of operating a moving vehicle without incident—the ducks have clearly had enough of this nonsense.

*i* Shared tour £19, £17.50 student; self-hire £27.50, £22 students; no wheelchair accessibility

## TOWER BRIDGE

Tower Bridge Rd., City of London; 2074033761; www.towerbridge.org.uk; open daily 10am-5:30pm

The Tower Bridge bills itself as "the most famous bridge in the world," and if you've been fascinated with bridges since you were a wee thing you'll likely want to give this one a try. You can shell out a few pounds to learn about its history and live out your stress nightmares on a vertigo-inducing glass floor. If that doesn't sound worth it, you can simply walk on to the bridge for free and enjoy a view of the **Thames.** Exiting the Tower of London conveniently puts you near the entrance to the bridge, so do both at once for the most tower-centric afternoon of your life.

*i* *Museum admission £9.80, £6.30 student*

## TRAFALGAR SQUARE

Trafalgar Square, West End; open daily 24hr

In the early 1800s, Admiral Viscount Nelson won victory at the Battle of Trafalgar and received the greatest military honor there is—having a square named in honor of your accomplishment. Statues of Nelson and other notable figures, two large fountains, and imposing stone lions occupy the square, which has historically been a center for rallies. Unfortunately, Nelson's square also attracts people who dress up in costumes and charge you to take pictures with them, drenching the atmosphere with tacky touristy-ness. Worth a quick visit, if only because it's right next to the National Gallery.

*i* *Free; wheelchair accessible*

## WESTMINSTER ABBEY

20 Deans Yd., Westminster; 2072225152; www.westminster-abbey.org; open M-Tu 9:30am-3:30pm, W 9:30am-6pm, Th-Sa 9:30am-3:30pm

The queue may be as long as the price is steep, but once you step into the resplendence of Westminster Abbey you'll understand why they can get away with this sort of thing. This masterpiece of Gothic opulence has an all-star cast of corpses (Mary, Queen of Scots! Geoffrey Chaucer!), is the site of coronations and royal weddings, and lays claim to London's "oldest door"

(we're just going to take their word for this one). You'll not so much wander as *be herded* through the chapels and monuments—with the help of a free audio guide—and emerge on the other side truly awed.

*i* *Adults £22, £17 student; 90min. tours throughout the day; wheelchair accessible*

# MUSEUMS

## CABINET WAR ROOMS, CHURCHILL MUSEUM

King Charles St., Westminster; 2074165000; www.iwm.org.uk/visits/churchill-war-rooms; open daily 9:30am-6pm

Like most good museums, the Cabinet War Rooms tell a story: one of bravery and perseverance under difficult circumstances, ingenuity in the face of war, and crazy spy shit so top secret James Bond would be jealous. The exhibit expertly recreates the life of **Winston Churchill** and his cabinet during World War II, when they lived, worked, and saved the world in a bunker underground. Fun fact: they managed to fortify the bunker without anyone suspecting what was really going on under **King Charles Street.** You can't make this stuff up. Connected to the war rooms is a meticulously detailed exhibit on the blood, sweat, toil, and tears of Churchill himself. Worth a visit, despite the long queue.

*i* *Adults £17.25, £13.80 students; last entry 5pm; wheelchair accessible; free audio tour*

## CARTOON MUSEUM

35 Little Russell St., Marylebone and Bloomsbury; 2075808155; www.cartoonmuseum.org; open Tu-Su 10:30am-5:30pm

Nope, this isn't an exhibit about your old Saturday morning faves, but rather a museum celebrating the paper and pencil kind of cartoon, and the British paper and pencil kind of cartoon, specifically. From political commentary to social satire to pure entertainment, the cartoon has a storied past which the museum explores. This is essentially a small art museum, except instead of staring at a painting of some tortured saint (no offense to tortured saints), you get to read framed comic strip after framed comic strip. Chuckling to yourself is not required, but highly encouraged.

*i* Admission £7, £3 student, free under 18; wheelchair accessible

## CORTAULD GALLERY
Somerset House, Strand, City of London; 2078481448; www.courtauld.ac.uk; open daily 10am-6pm

Cortauld Gallery may be small, but boy does it contain a star-studded cast of artists: **Van Gogh, Monet, Degas, Picasso,** and that's just the tip of the name-drop iceberg. It's also nestled within the gorgeous Somerset House, so you can watch children frolic in the courtyard fountains after you're done. What's more, if you're a student, all this art can be yours and more for the low, low price of zero dollars! There's really no excuse not to go—just remember that we are not liable if you get inspired by Van Gogh's famous "Self-Portrait with Bandaged Ear" and hack off a body part.

*i* Admission adults £6, free under 18 and students; last entry at 5:30pm; wheelchair accessible

## DESIGN MUSEUM
234-238 Kensington High St., South Kensington and Chelsea; 2074036933; www.designmuseum.org; open daily 10am-6pm

Hey now, what exactly is design? The better question: what isn't design? This underrated gem explores everything from typography (team serif for life) to drawing tube maps, punk fashion, and the evolution of Apple products. The museum just moved to a pretty rad building that's as aesthetically exciting and innovative as the exhibits themselves, and a straight shot walk from Earl's Court tube station. While you have to pay for some temporary exhibits (ah, don't you always) the free permanent installation is absolutely worth the trip.

*i* Free; last entry 5pm; wheelchair accessible

## HORNIMAN MUSEUM AND GARDENS
100 London Rd., South London; 2086991872; www.horniman.ac.uk; open daily 10am-5:30pm, gardens open M-Sa 7:15am-sunset

Brave the capricious **London Overground** and a calf-busting walk up a hill and you'll be rewarded with the collection at the Horniman Museum. Natural history, a huge collection of musical instruments, and taxidermy collide in a way that can only be described as...odd. But we like odd. A notable Horniman treasure is the Horniman Merman, a terrifying imitation merman from Japan. (The stuff of nightmares, people). The museum also houses an aquarium (£4) and temporary exhibits such as a zoo full of robotic animals—we repeat, nightmares. Perhaps most excitingly, the museum is planning to open a huge new "world gallery" in 2018.

*i* Free admission to museum, aquarium £4; wheelchair accessible

## IMPERIAL WAR MUSEUM
Lambeth Rd., Southbank; 2074165000; www.imw.org.uk; open daily 10am-6pm

Rarely does a museum manage to be as immersive as the Imperial War Museum: the exhibits combine film, primary sources, ominous war audio, artifacts of war, and oh so many propaganda posters to glorious effect, and there's something of interest for both amateur historians and those that just like looking at really big weapons. The comprehensive **WWI** exhibit and the **Holocaust** exhibit deserve special attention, with the latter including first person video narratives from survivors. There's extensive content on England's empire in the museum, but it doesn't always provide visitors with a discussion of the reality of life under British imperialism.

*i* Free; wheelchair accessible

## MUSEUM OF LONDON
150 London Wall, City of London; 2078145507; www.museumoflondon.org.uk; open daily 10am-6pm

As we were rounding the corner from prehistoric London into the Roman Age, we thought, "Wouldn't this be the perfect place for a fieldtrip?" Barely had the thought crossed our mind when suddenly appeared scads of school children and a few beleaguered guardians. Indeed, this museum is bloody educational, and a history nerd could spend hours taking in every detail. If you're not a history nerd and were just lured in by the free admission and equally free Wi-Fi, you can whiz through the centuries at a brisker pace and emerge assured that London, or Londinium as the Romans would say, is pretty dope.

*i* *Free; free tours throughout the day; wheelchair accessible*

### SHERLOCK HOLMES MUSEUM

221B Baker St., Marylebone and Bloomsbury; 2072243688; www.sherlock-holmes.co.uk; open daily 9:30am-6pm, closed Dec 25

Whiz detective Sherlock Holmes came up against some pretty terrifying situations in his day, and the Sherlock Holmes Museum aims to simulate that terror by charging £15 a ticket. With this hefty price, you have two options: if you're a Sir Arthur Conan Doyle-obsessed, Benedict Cumberbatch-worshipping traveler, pay the fare and view the small but immaculate recreation of Sherlock's flat. If you're a more casual fan, it might be better to just peruse the lovely Victorian gift shop, take a picture of the building, and tell friends and family later that you've visited the infamous 221B Baker St.

*i* *Admission adult £15, £10 child*

### SOUTH LONDON GALLERY

65 Peckham Rd., South London; 2077036120; www.southlondongallery.org; Tu-Su 11am-6pm, W until 9pm

No depictions of Christ and Hercules here: the South London Gallery is a fabulously odd art venue attracting pierced and pink-haired patrons and nary an "I Love London" t-shirt in sight. The museum has no permanent exhibits, so it's hard to know what you're in store for—to give you a taste, in June 2017, the main exhibit consisted of three films—one about cats—shown in a complicated architectural structure including a tunnel and a felt ramp. If you can't picture that, come see whatever's on yourself. It's bound to be a different world from the **National Gallery.**

*i* *Free; free tours at 1pm; wheelchair accessible*

### TATE BRITAIN

Millibank, Westminster; 2078778888; www.tate.org.uk; open daily 10am-6pm

Me oh my do we love free things, and this is an ultra-high-quality free thing. The Tate Britain, more buttoned-up cousin to the Tate Modern, is a gallery of British art spanning 1500 to the present day. And, if you thought this sort of thing was better left to the Italians or the French, think again. The museum has some stunning pieces, like **Millais'** famous depiction of Ophelia and a huge collection of art by **JMW Turner,** British artist so beloved that his self-portrait will feature on a new version of the £20 note. Easily reached by a ten-minute walk from Parliament down the **Thames.**

*i* *Free; collection highlights tour at 11am, noon, 2pm, 3pm; wheelchair accessible*

### TATE MODERN

Bankside, Southbank; 2078878888; www.tate.org.uk/visit/tate-modern; open M-Th 10am-6pm, F-Sat 10am-10pm, Su 10am-6pm

The Tate Modern has everything you would expect from a modern art museum: strange noises of origin unknown, confusing canvasses that make your grandfather proclaim that he could do that, and short, haunting films in dark rooms that play on continuous loop. If you're in to that sort of thing, you can happily explore floors and floors worth of free galleries. The Tate's architecture is as cutting-edge as its contents, with two strangely-shaped tall and skinny buildings connected by a bridge, so it's a sight to behold even if you don't set foot inside. A plus for confused travelers: orange signs mark a path to the museum starting about ten minutes away.

*i* *Free; wheelchair accessible*

### THE BRITISH MUSEUM

Great Russell St., Marylebone and Bloomsbury; 2073238299; www.britishmuseum.org; open M-Th 10am-5:30pm, F 10am-8:30pm, Sa-Su 10am-5:30pm

The British Museum is huge. You could spend days, nay, years here—subsist off food from the 500 cafés, read all the books in the 600 gift shops, raise a small family in the Enlightenment wing, grow old together, die, and join the mummies in the Egyptian exhibit. Alternatively, you could just spend an afternoon perusing the thousands of artifacts from around the world, guiltily avoiding the ever-present donation buckets, and snapping a pic of the Rosetta Stone for the old scrapbook. If you want a more targeted trip, audio guides are £5.50 for students and mysteriously sponsored by Korean Air.

*i* *Free; audio tours available £6, £5.50 student; wheelchair accessible*

## THE MUSEUM OF BRANDS, PACKAGING, AND ADVERTISING

111-117 Lancaster Rd., Hyde Park and Notting Hill; 2072439611; www.museumofbrands.com; open Tu-Sa 10am-6pm, Su 11am-5pm

For every famous and vast London museum, there must be an equal and opposite museum of small size and niche content: **The British Museum** looks at human history through ruins, art, and artifacts, and the Museum of Brands tells a story through...cereal boxes (and toffee tins and Victorian dolls and World War I board games with title like "Kill the Kaiser"). It turns out an awful lot can be learned through the magazines we read and the toys we play with—for one thing, every jubilee and royal wedding in Britain has caused an absolute frenzy of commercial activity. (Princess Diana Rubix Cube anyone?) While an old Paddington Bear may not have the draw of the Rosetta Stone, this is a quirky museum for the more adventurous traveler.

*i* *Adults £9, students £7; last entry 45min. before closing; wheelchair accessible*

## THE NATIONAL GALLERY

Trafalgar Square, West End; 2077472850; www.nationalgallery.org.uk; open M-Th 10am-6pm, F 10am-9p, Sa-Su 10am-6pm

Art-lovers can spend a pleasant afternoon wandering through the greatest thematic hits of Western art: lots of classical mythology, portraits of rich people, and rooms and rooms of Jesus and

Jesus's mom. The museum itself is free, but it's probably worth donating £1 for a map or resigning yourself to becoming hopelessly lost in the labyrinthine second floor galleries, which are allegedly organized by time period, but are possibly also organized for maximum confusion. (Have I been in this room before or is this a different portrayal of the immaculate conception?) Be sure to check out **Da Vinci's** *The Virgin of the Rocks* and **Van Gogh's** *Sunflowers,* if you can find them.

*i* *Free; audio tours available for £4, £3.50 students; wheelchair accessible*

## THE SERPENTINE GALLERIES

Hyde Park/Kensington Gardens, Hyde Park and Notting Hill; 2074026075; www.serpentinegalleris.org; open Tu-Su 10am-6pm

Today on Great Free London Art—Park Edition: the Serpentine and Serpentine Sackler Galleries are separated by the slithery Serpentine River in the heart of **Hyde Park/ Kensington Gardens.** Both pint-sized museums change their artwork every season—summer 2017 showcased two contemporary artists' works on politics and race. Both can be sampled in under an hour, and are an ideal place to take refuge lest the parks become drizzly. The bookstore in the Serpentine Gallery

also houses a great—if a bit pretentious—collection of art books.

*i* *Free; free cell phone audio tour; wheelchair accessible*

### VICTORIA AND ALBERT MUSEUM

Cromwell Road., South Kensington and Chelsea; 2079422000; www.vam.ac.uk; open M-Th 10am-5pm, F 10am-10pm, Sa-Su 10am-5pm

International travel is expensive (don't we know it), and time travel comes with all sorts of thorny logistical concerns, so why not just go to the Victoria and Albert Museum? The self-proclaimed "world's leading museum of art and design" is made for a wander: from the statues of ancient Rome, to the art and architecture of the Islamic world, to the works of Raphael, you'll find yourself turned around but not overwhelmed, content to let Vic and Al's lovingly presented collection reveal itself to you. Highlights include an awe-inspiring room of sculpture casts and the architecture of the building itself. Tickets are gloriously free, but temporary exhibits—like a massively popular 2017 exhibit on Pink Floyd—will set you back a few pounds.

*i* *Free admission; free introductory tours; tours 10:30am, 12:30pm, 1:30pm, 3:30pm; wheelchair accessible*

## OUTDOORS

### REGENT'S PARK

Chester Rd., Marylebone and Bloomsbury; 3000612300; www.royalparks.org.uk; open daily 5am-dusk

The 12000 roses in Queen Mary's gardens would smell as sweet by any other name, and how sweet they smell! The gardens are absolutely *gah-geous*, darling, and so is the rest of this Royal Park. An open-air theater, sports pitches, a boating lake, small children on scooters—this park has it all, ideal for pic snapping and duck watching. For those that would rather see their animals in cages, head on over to the London Zoo. All in all, a royally good time.

*i* *Free; wheelchair accessible*

### GREENWICH PARK

East London; 3000612381; www.royalparks.org.uk; open daily 6am-9pm

Just off the highly commercial, highly congested heart of Greenwich, Greenwich Park offers a refuge as only an urban park can. The **Royal Observatory** is likely the crown jewel of this royally-sponsored park, but there's lots else to do: visit the **Royal Maritime Museum,** stop for a tea or coffee, explore the remains of a **Roman Temple** (this park is old as heck), or just take a leisurely stroll through the beautiful greenery. Sturdy walking shoes and an appreciation for the glory of British nature are strongly advised.

*i* *Free*

### HYDE PARK AND KENSINGTON GARDENS

Hyde Park and Kensington Gardens, Hyde Park and Notting Hill; 3000612000; www.royalparks.org.uk; open daily 6am-dusk

Is there anything better than fresh air, beautiful greenery, and small British children riding scooters? All this and more can be yours at Hyde Park and Kensington Gardens, two royal parks that blend seamlessly into each other like botanic puzzle pieces. Particular bright spots include the swan-laden **Serpentine River** (someone get an Impressionist over here, stat!) and the Italian Gardens, which Prince Albert created for Victoria. Get you a Prince Albert, ladies—but maybe not your first cousin. You can also cue major childhood nostalgia by visiting a statue of Peter Pan or hitting up the playground.

*i* *Free; wheelchair accessible*

## FOOD

### SNACKISTAN AT PERSEPOLIS ($)

28-30 Peckham High St., South London; 2076398007; www.snackistan.co.uk; open daily 11am-8:45ish

Be advised: a meal at Snackistan may cause a moment of near transcendence: a glimpse at the afterlife, an outburst of uncontrollable weeping. It may, in fact, change your life. Perhaps this is a bit melodramatic (what? never!), but the sumptuous Persian fare at this **Peckham** café-within-a-market is *un. real.* It's also sold at totally reasonable prices in a tastefully decorated room. Because of Snackistan's ability to kick absolute culinary ass, you might want to make a reservation. You also might want to stay for dessert (a Turkish delight sundae?), stay for a year, and bring your vegan/vegetarian/even mildly sentient friends along for the ride.

*i* Entrées £5-9; vegetarian, or vegan options available; minimum £10 credit card charge

### CHEEKY CHICOS ($$)
8-12 New Bridge St., City of London; 2034415545; www.cheekychicos.co.uk; open M-F noon-10pm, Sa 5pm-9pm

The words "Cheeky" and "Chicos" are the opposite of a KFC/Taco Bell combo: two things from vastly different cultures that blend together beautifully. If the name doesn't draw you in to this small Mexican joint, then the lively, if stereotypical, décor will (read: wall of sombreros). But none of that matters if the British can't cook Mexican food...except it turns out they can, quite deftly, although don't expect the portions of an American burrito bowl or be surprised by a few divergences from typical Mexican fare, by which we mean sweet potato fries (?). Don't question, just enjoy!

*i* Entrées £10-15

### HOP POLES ($$)
17-19 King St., West London; 2087481411; www.craft-pubs.co.uk; open

M-Th 10am-11pm, F 10am-midnight, Sa noon-midnight, Su noon-10:30pm

Hop Poles isn't a suggestion to start doing some Olympic-style jumping, but rather **Hammersmith's** answer to good old pub grub. While all the classics are here, Hop Poles includes burritos on the menu (still making up our minds about this one) and a deliciously meaty loaded mac and cheese (£9.25). If you bring a buddy, or someone random you found on the street, you can get two meals from a select menu for £6 from M-Sa. Other than this bright spot, prices are average, but sometimes you just need a joint where the booze keeps flowin' and the cod keeps fryin'.

*i* Entrées £8-12; vegetarian options available

### KENSINGTON CREPERIE ($$)
2-6 Exhibition Rd., South Kensington and Chelsea; 2075898947; www.kensington-creperie.com; open daily 9:30am-11pm

If you're under the impression that a crepe is not a meal, come right on over to Kensington Creperie to be dispossessed of that misguided notion. Kensington's large crepes come in both savory—eggs, cheeses, vegetables, meats—and sweet—ever heard of a little thing called Nutella?—varieties. The popular restaurant also serves a variety of coffee drinks, smoothies, and alcoholic beverages. (Did someone suggest a boozy crepe brunch?) Because of its proximity to the South

## EAT LIKE THE BRITISH

"I went to Britain for the food!" ...said no one ever. The continent may have the poor old British Isles spanked in a taste test—*Great British Bake Off* notwithstanding—but there are wonders to be had and bellies to be filled in a British pub. A day of eating like a Brit starts, obviously, with a full English breakfast. Thought baked beans were for barbecues? Amateur! They're perfectly at home alongside scrambled eggs, toast, bacon, sausage, black pudding (less terrifying than it sounds, we promise), tomatoes and mushrooms. Ah, nothing like a proper fry-up! For lunch or dinner, go for the classic pub grub. The obvious choice is fish and chips—delicious fried-into-oblivion cod or haddock, and what we geographically-confused Americans refer to as "french fries." If seafood isn't your thing, try sausages with mash potatoes or a meat pie (sorry, vegetarians). Brits are also rather fond of "toasties," or toasted sandwiches—a "cheese toastie" is essentially a grilled cheese (mmmmm!). And of course, whatever your order, top it off with a pint of beer. Cheers!

# OXFORD

**Oxford is just your everyday college town—if your everyday college boasted alumni from J.R.R. Tolkien to Margaret Thatcher to Adam Smith, was built like a castle, and attracted visitors from around the globe willing to pay for a glimpse of its campus.** Despite the magnitude of the Oxford name, the town itself is small and concentrated enough to walk from famous sight to famous sight. From its bookshops, to its museums, to its 500 stores selling Oxford University sweatshirts, Oxford is the ideal place to get your nerd on—or at least pretend for a day.

Arriving to Oxford by train will put you in the western part of the city. From there, it's a short walk to **George Street** which turns into **Broad Street,** at the center of the city; along this road you'll find **Bodleian Library** and the **Tourist Office.** To the south, you'll find **Queen Street/High Street,** another commercial thoroughfare, and to the northwest **Beaumont,** home of the **Ashmolian Museum.** The city is prone to small alleys, but streets are well-marked and signs pointing towards various sights can be found at nearly every intersection. If you're looking to visit **Oxford University** itself, its various colleges are scattered around the city; **Balliol College** is on Broad Street and open to the public.

## GETTING THERE

Oxford Rail Station is located a 10min. walk from the city center, and therefore highly convenient. Trains from London are about 1hr. The closest airports are Heathrow and Gatwick. For the former, take a train from London, and for the latter, take a train from Reading, or take the airline coach service.

## GETTING AROUND

Most of Oxford's major sights are clustered together, so the city is walkable. If you'd rather not walk, use Oxford Bus Company (01865 785 400). You can get a 24hr unlimited travel pass for £4.20 or a week unlimited travel pass for £14.50.

## Swing by...

### BODLEIAN LIBRARY

Broad St.; 186 527 7094; www.bodleian.ox.ac.uk; open M-F 9am-5pm, Sa 9am-4:30pm, Su 11am-5pm

London may be the capital of *Harry Potter* mania, but Oxford can claim a piece of the boy wizard hype as well: **Bodleian Library,** the University of Oxford's majestic, 13-million-book library, was used in filming several scenes. Before its turn on the big screen, Bodleian was still super rad as the keeper of centuries of knowledge and a resource for centuries of Oxford-bred thinkers. Paying for the standard tour won't allow you to actually see much of the library, but you will learn a fascinating thing or two and get to visit **Duke Humfrey's** medieval library, where ancient tomes abound and talking above a whisper is considered high treason.

*i* Standard 60min. tour £8, extended 90min. tour £14, mini 30min. tour £6, self-guided Divinity School tour £1, 40min. audio tour £2.50

## Grab a bite at..

### JIMBOB'S BAGUETTES ($)

19 Magdalen St.; 186 524 5549; www.jimbobsbaguettes.co.uk; open daily
7am-10pm

Whoever Jimbob is, he's risen above his unfortunate name to create a real bargain of a sandwich shop. For around £5, you can snag a hearty sandwich (on a baguette, as the name would indicate), a snack such as a fruit or pastry, and a drink. Students also get a 10% discount in this student-saturated town. Since Oxford will practically charge you to merely gaze at its storied façades, it's nice to know there's a cheap lunch spot you can hit to compensate for the money you spent to observe smart people in their natural habitat.

*i* *Entrées £5-7 with a 10% student discount; Halal and vegetarian options available; wheelchair accessible*

## Check out...

### ASHMOLEAN MUSEUM

Beaumont St.; 1865 278 000; www.ashmolean.org; open T-Su 10am-5pm, also open bank holiday Mondays

"There are more things in [The Ashmolean Museum], Horatio, than are dreamt of in your philosophy"—Hamlet, probably. This massive, can't-read-all-the-plaques-in-a-lifetime museum of art and architecture has Egyptian mummies, Greek sculptures, Italian paintings, and quite a few other testaments to the artistic capabilities of mankind through the ages. What were the Greeks up to before they donned togas and built columns? How do we know what we know about ancient civilizations anyhow? If you're curious, stop by. Like most everything in the city, it's associated with the **University of Oxford** and located near the city center.

*i* *Free; audio tours; wheelchair accessible*

## Kick back at...

### THE EAGLE & CHILD ($$)

49 St. Giles St.; 01865 302925; open daily 11am-11pm

How would you like a side of literary history with your fish and chips? Very much so, thank you. The Eagle and Child was a favorite watering hole of the **"Inklings,"** a group of Oxford writers that included **C.S. Lewis** and **J.R.R. Tolkien**. The pub—which the group nicknamed "The Bird and Baby"—is quick to remind you of its history with quotes from the two most famous Inklings and a map of the Shire. However, it doesn't rest on its literary laurels, serving up tasty pub grub and pints—nothing to sell your family to the White Witch for, but pretty darn tasty.

*i* *Entrées £9-13*

Kensington museums it's no serene spot, but it turns out that a hearty bite of crepe tends to drown out ambient noise.

*i* *Entrées £8-12; vegetarian and Halal options available; wheelchair accessible*

## NOODLE TIME ($)

10-11 Nelson Rd., East London; 2083052109; open M-Th 11:30am-11pm, F-Sa 11:30am-11:30pm, Su 11:30am-11pm

Noodle Time satisfies the Holy Trinity of budget eating requirements: cheap, fast, and large. After a day traipsing around **Greenwich,** you can settle in for some classic Chinese food at the price of little more than a cheap glass of wine. Portions are generous, service is speedy, and the name reminds us to set aside some time for noodles every now and again. The menu proudly proclaims "Healthy eating, good food need not to be expensive." The health factor is dubious (chicken fried rice is the new salad?) but to the goodness of the food we say, "Amen!"

*i* *Entrées £5-7*

## PEYTON AND BYRNE ($)

224 Great Portland St., Marylebone and Bloomsbury; 2077475836; www. peytonandbyrne.co.uk; open M-F 7:30am-7pm, Sa 9am-6pm

Prepare to be lured inside by the sweet siren call of baked goods. Carrot cake, cinnamon buns, and cupcakes, oh my! Once this small **Marylebone** café has trapped you, give lunch a try: fresh sandwiches (avocado *mmmmm*), salads, and pies beckon. The green color of the walls is as fresh as the food, and it's almost as though you never left **Regent's Park** (a mere five-minute walk away). Peyton and Byrne is a tasty and cheap gem in an otherwise drab and pricey area, and—we promise—better than the food they'll try to sell you in the park.

*i* *Lunch £4-6, £2-4 breakfast and pastries; wheelchair accessible*

## THE ANCHOR & HOPE ($$$)

86 The Cut, Marylebone and Bloomsbury; 2079289898; www.anchorandhopepub. co.uk; open M 5-11pm, Tu-Sa 11am-11pm, Su 12:30-3:15pm

If you have an ampersand in your restaurant name, you're probably hip or trying really hard to be hip, and The Anchor & Hope is solidly in the first category. Although technically a pub, its fare is much classier than your typical fish and chips with dishes like *foie gras ballotine* and pot roast duck leg. (Pro tip: the duck hearts on toast are divine!) As such, it's also on the

# THE BEST UNDERGROUND STATION NAMES

Ah, the Tube: whiz at transport, hot and sweaty in the summertime (when they advise you to carry water at all times, you know it's bad), originator of the infamous phrase "mind the gap." London's signature underground network will take you all 'round the city and back again, but it will also do something much more important: provide entertainment in the form of oh so British station names. Here, we present the nine best Underground station names so you don't have to scour your own pocket map.

1. Brondsbury Park
2. Chorleywood
3. Dagenham Heathway
4. Elephant & Castle
5. Finchley Road & Frognal
6. Mornington Crescent
7. North Wembley
8. Pudding Mill Lane
9. Totteridge & Whetstone

pricier side, but vibrant artwork on the walls, an outdoor seating area, and proximity to the **Tate Modern** and **Old Vic Theater** might encourage a splurge.

*i* *Entrées £12-16*

### THE BREAKFAST CLUB SOHO ($$)

33 D'Arblay St., West End; 2074342571; www.thebreak-fastclubcafés.com/locations/soho; open M-Sa 8am-10pm, Su 8am-7pm

Is there anything better than breakfast for dinner? Yes: English breakfast for dinner. The Breakfast Club, however, does not limit your options: you can have English breakfast for breakfast, American breakfast for dinner, or (blasphemy!) dinner for dinner. Wherever your stomach leads you, you can't go wrong in this lively school-bus yellow restaurant, the original location in a small London-wide chain. Unfortunately, "Don't You (Forget About Me)" does not play on a loop.

*i* *Entrées £8-12; wheelchair accessible*

### THE CENTRE PAGE ($$)

29-33 Knightrider St., City of London; 2072363614; www.thecentrepage.co.uk; kitchen open 9am-9pm, pub open 9am-midnight

The Centre Page was once the Horn Tavern which was once a slightly different pre-Great Fire Horn Tavern. (As you'll find out from many similar histories printed on pub menus, the **Great Fire** really ripped London a new one.) If that isn't British enough for you, this restaurant—just a hop and a skip from **St. Paul's**—features pub grub of the most classic sort, pints of various kinds, and a TV for displaying none other than (British) football. Dig in to some of the more reasonably-priced fish and chips in town, especially if you opt for takeout—err, takeaway.

*i* *Fish and chips £10-13*

### THE NEW JOMUNA ($$)

74 Wilston Rd., Westminster; 718287509; www.thenewjomuna.com; open daily noon-3pm, 6pm-midnight

Move over old Jomuna, because there's a new Jomuna in town and it's serving up tasty curries, hearty vegetarian dishes, and mouthwatering naan in a little restaurant on Wilston Rd. This **Pimlico** Indian restaurant is, in a word, soothing—soothing music, soothing AC, the soothing smells of carefully-prepared food. Just be careful that you don't rack up a bill, because the staff is happy to bring you appetizers semi-against your will and slide in a side before you know what's happened to you. Or you could just give in to your rumbling stomach and soak up all the spicy goodness the menu has to offer.

*i* *Entrées £8-12; vegetarian and Halal options available*

### ULI ($$)

5 Ladbroke Rd., Hyde Park and Notting Hill; 2031415878; www.ulilondon.com; open M-Th noon-3pm and 6pm-midnight, F-Sa noon-midnight, Su noon-11pm

Uli is straight out of a Pinterest board—an outdoor terrace with comfy pillows, a chic blue and white color scheme, and plants hanging from the ceiling and on every table. There's really no better environment to consume mid-priced Asian food.

Uli draws on several Asian cuisines for its menu, so variety of flavor is as abundant as tiny decorative details. But don't think that just because the place exudes class they'll turn away a dirty backpacker. The staff will go so far as to remove your spoon from your soup for you after it falls in.

*i* *Entrées £9-11; vegetarian options available; limited wheelchair accessibility*

# NIGHTLIFE

## YE OLDE CHESHIRE CHEESE

145 Fleet St., City of London; 2073536170; www.cheshirecheeselondon. co.uk; open M-F 11:30am-11pm, Sat noon-11pm

Picture a British pub and you might inadvertently picture Ye Olde Cheshire Cheese: people sitting around wooden tables and sipping pints, a classic British figure or two claimed as a patron of days gone by, and an amiable wait staff with a few stories to tell. Rebuilt after the **Great Fire,** this pub once hosted **Charles Dickens** and **Samuel Johnson,** and was home to a parrot named Polly who (allegedly) died of fatigue after imitating the sound of a corkscrew popping one too many times. The network of small rooms allows it to hold many people while feeling just as cozy as it should.

*i* *Food £10, drinks £4*

## NOTTING HILL ARTS CLUB

21 Notting Hill Gate, Hyde Park and Notting Hill; 2074604459; www.nottinghillartsclub. com; open W-Sa 7pm-2am

Among the deeply conventional storefronts of banks and souvenir shops and London's 1001 Pret A Mangers,

two massive warehouse doors mark the entrance to the solidly unconventional Notting Hill Arts Club. If you can find the small underground bar and music venue, count yourself among the cool cats that stop by for sweet tunes, whether from a DJ or a live music act. Tickets to shows can be bought online in advance or at the door, but the former is cheaper—more money for beer.

*i* *Cover varies by show, usually £5-12; drinks £4-6*

## SCOOTER CAFFÉ

132 Lower Marsh, Southbank; 2076201421; open M-Th 8:30am-11pm, Fri 8:30am-midnight, Sat 10am-midnight, Su 10am-11pm

Scooter Caffé is the Clark Kent of late night spots: café by day, bar by night! Once the cape is on, it serves low-priced but good drinks in a setting that can only be described as *intimate*. Take a date downstairs and sit under the twinkly lights, or relax upstairs on an upholstered chair. Not the spot to party, party, party, but rather a venue for a sophisticated and *chill* glass of wine. Bonus features include a small outdoor patio, charmingly mismatched furniture, and a soundtrack as serene as the good vibes.

*i* *Wine by the glass £4-7*

## SIMMONS

7-9 Kentish Town Rd., North London; 2073771843; www.simmonsbar.co.uk; open M-Th 4pm-2am, F-Sa 4pm-3am, Su 4pm-2am

Teapots full of tea are great and all, but how about tea pots full of booze? At Simmons—a small bar near **King's**

**Cross Station**—you and your friends (or just you, I guess?) can order a teapot full of "G and Tea," "Long Island Iced Tea," or other punny cocktails, and then drink out of tea cups. Pinkies up! In addition to this absolute innovation, Simmons has a happy hour from 4-9pm everyday but Saturday, and serves up sick beats via a DJ on the weekends. This hip hang is rather tiny in size—intimate, yet personal space-invading.

*i* Cocktails £9-12, happy hour is M-F, Su 4pm-9pm with 2 cocktails for £10, or beer and wine £2.50; BGLTQ+ friendly; must be 18+ to enter

### THE DARTMOUTH ARMS
7 Dartmouth Rd., South London; 2084883117; www.thedartmouth.com; open M-Th noon-midnight, F-Sa noon-1am, Su noon-11pm

Despite its stodgy name, this is no stodgy pub. Décor highlights include succulents, book shelves, gloriously vintage wallpaper, and trendy screen prints for sale. But it's the booze you really care about, right? Fear not, the Dartmouth Arms serves up quirky cocktails like the blueberry and ginger mojito (a must-try) as well as beer and wine. And, once again proving its youth, the pub has a small menu of vegan food and drinks. Located in the hinterlands of Underground Zone three, this is the place to find a loyal local crowd quite different from the denizens of Central London's many touristy pubs.

*i* Cocktails £7; wheelchair accessible

### THE DRAYTON ARMS
153 Old Brompton St., South Kensington and Chelsea; 2078352301; www.thedraytonarmsSW5.co.uk; open M-Th noon-11pm, Fri noon-midnight, Sa 10am-midnight, Su noon-10:30pm

In today's installment of a theater where a theater is not expected to be, we bring you The Drayton Arms. Downstairs, this Old Brompton St. attraction is a classic pub with chic touches serving food, bar snacks (3 for £11) and the requisite booze. Upstairs, it's a black box theater with performances far cheaper than some of the city's more obvious performance venues. And, much like the mythical centaur, this unprecedented combination proves fairly magical. Unlike a centaur, it will not run away with the young maidens of your village—so it's a win-win in the books.

*i* Food £10-14, drinks start at £4, shows £10-12; wheelchair accessible

### THE LOOP
19 Dering St, West End; 2074931003; www.theloopbar.co.uk; open M noon-11pm, Tu noon-midnight, W noon-1am, Th-Sa noon-3am

At ground level, The Loop looks like a fairly typical bar, but descend into its depths and you'll find all sorts of flashy décor and things that light up or go dark. In similar style, a daytime lunch venue (doors open at noon) turns positively bumpin' once the sun goes down. Check the website for an events calendar, including "Boom vs. Carwash" parties, where an 80s and 90s pop DJ and an R&B DJ compete for the biggest dance crowd. If all this excitement is going to throw you for a loop, just come for significantly discounted drinks every day from 5-8pm.

*i* Drinks £8-10, food £9-12

### THE RED LION
48 Parliament St., Westminster; 2079305826; www.redlionwestminster.co.uk; open M-F 8am-11pm, Sa-Su 8am-9pm

There are pubs tucked away from visiting eyes, down allies that are hard to find, full of chic locals drinking chic drinks in a chic room. The Red Lion is not one of those pubs—if you walked in wearing a fanny pack, no one would bat an eye. But there's a reason for the tourist hype and a reason you should care, too. Because of its proximity to **10 Downing St.,** generations of Prime Ministers have dropped in for a pint. (As did **Charles Dickens,** quite frequently). Worth a stop, if only to look around.

*i* Drinks £3-9, food £10-15

### THE SOCIAL
5 Little Portland St., West End; 2076364992; www.thesocial.com; open M-W 12:30pm-2am, Th-F 12:30pm-1am, Sa 6pm-1am

If you're tired of pubs (but how could you be?) and want something a little more refined, The Social is a hip spot just close enough to the **West End** hubbub to be convenient and just far enough to get away from the shopping bag-toting crowds. Upstairs, strings of lights on the ceiling, wood-paneled walls adorned with art, and comfy couches make for a chill place to grab a pint or a cocktail (£9.50). Downstairs, things veer out of bar and into club territory for a more upbeat evening. The Social also hosts a variety of music acts.

*i* Cocktails £9.50, £3-7 beer and wine

### THE SOUTHAMPTON ARMS
139 Highgate Rd., North London; 7958780073; www.thesouthhamptonarms. co.uk; open M-Sa noon-midnight, Su noon-10:30pm

What's with the British obsession with arms? Can't a pub be named after *legs* for a change? Nomenclature aside, this is not your typical pub: it's your typical pub with a garden. Good drinks at good prices and a jolly cast of regulars make this neighborhood hangout a perfect stop on your **Camden** pub crawl. The garden closes at 10pm, so get there early for some fresh air with your Pimms.

*i* No cover, drinks £3-6

### VAULTY TOWERS
34 Lower Marsh, Southbank; 2079289042; www.vaultytowers.london; open M-W noon-11pm, Th-Sa noon-1 am, Su noon-11pm

A zebra, a light-draped tree, and a giant crescent moon cut out walk into a bar...no wait, that's wrong, they're already in the bar! Vaulty Towers looks like the brainchild of a mad, yet brilliant, interior designer, and you can sip your pint in an indoor treehouse or a greenery-curtained alcove, as God intended. The bar offers the unholy combo of burgers and tacos in the way of food, holds pub quizzes on Mondays (£2 to play), and hosts magic acts and comedy nights. They suggest you reserve a table (or "area"), because the wackiness is in great demand.

*i* No cover, food £5-8

# MANCHESTER

Coverage by **Mia Karr**

Manchester was the world's first industrial city, and pride in that legacy is represented in the worker bee symbol found on everything from trashcans to sweatshirts. But, somewhere in the midst of inventing the intercity railroad and the commercial computer, Mancunians also learned how to have fun. Hip pubs and boutiques in the Northern Quarter, raucous nightlife in the Gay Village, and two universities that continue to innovate make Manchester an ideal spot for the young and restless. While Manchester may have fallen from its international prominence in the Industrial Age, it still has plenty to offer the traveler who wants to go to a museum in the morning, have tea in the afternoon, and hang out in a bar until the middle of the night. Sadly, the city is now associated with the horrible terrorist attack of 2017, but its resilience following the attack has been evident. Perhaps a sign on Newton St. expresses it best: "Never mind the terrorists, we're Manchester."

## ORIENTATION

Manchester has a multitude of neighborhoods (helpfully color-coded on the official city map), but each is tiny, making the whole city much smaller than expected. **Piccadilly Station,** the city's main train station, is on the eastern side. Just north of Piccadilly, the hip **Northern Quarter** houses plenty of pubs and vintage boutiques; expect to spend a lot of time here. To the west side of Piccadilly lies Manchester's tiny **Chinatown** and the **Gay Village,** which is gay bar central. Right at the city center are the self-explanatory **Central Retail District** and the **Civic Quarter,** home to **Town Hall.** To the north of the city center, the Medieval Quarter holds old architecture and, further north, **Manchester Arena** holds rabid football fans. On the western side of the city, upscale **Spinningfields** and residential, quay-side **Castlefield** will probably not be your first stop, but are within walking distance from Piccadilly as well.

# ESSENTIALS

## GETTING THERE

From Manchester airport, trains run every 10min. to Manchester Piccadilly, located in the city center. The journey is about 20min. If traveling solely by train, the National Rail Service operates trains to Manchester Piccadilly from other locations in the UK.

## GETTING AROUND

Manchester is easily walkable: pick up a map at a hostel or the train station, and you can be on your way by foot. However, if walking isn't your style, the city also has two public transportation options. The metroshuttle bus is free and should get you where you need to go in the city center. It also has free Wi-Fi! Check www.tfgm.com for route information. The metrolink tram, also found on www.tfgm.com, is cheap but not free.

## PRACTICAL INFORMATION

**Tourist Offices:** The Manchester Tourist Information Centre (1 Piccadilly Gardens, Portland St.; 0871 2228223; www.visitmanchester.com; open M-Sa 9:30am-5pm and Su 10:30am-4:30pm).

**Banks/ATMs/Currency Exchange:** Banks and ATMs are easy to find in Manchester. Here are two banks:
- Virgin Money (1 Princess St.; 0161 834 9883; open M 9am-5pm, Tu 9:30am-5pm, W-F 9am-5pm, Sa 9am-1pm).
- Barclays Bank (88-86 Market St.; 345 734 5345; open M-F 10am-6pm, Sa 10am-4pm, Su 11am-3pm).

**Post Offices:** F4, Londis Store (Piccadilly Plaza, Portland St.; 161 237 1229; open M-F 6am-6pm, Sa 9am-5:30pm).

**Internet:** Internet is easy to come by. It should be available in most cafés (and definitely in chains like Starbucks or Pret a Manger) and hostels, as well as in some public areas. The free bus system also has Wi-Fi.

**BGLTQ+ Resources:** Manchester's The Proud Trust (www.theproudtrust.org) is the first fully publicly-funded gay center in Europe (49-51 Sidney St.; 7813 981338) Manchester has the largest BGLTQ+ population in the UK outside of London and is home to many BGLTQ+ establishments in the Gay Village neighborhood.

## EMERGENCY INFORMATION

**Emergency Number:** 999

**Police:** The website for the Greater Manchester Police is www.gmp.police.uk, and for non-emergencies you can call them at 101.

**Sexual Assault Hotlines:** The Manchester Rape Crisis Centre (60 Nelson St.; 161 273 4500; www.manchesterrapecrisis.co.uk; open M-Tu 10am-4pm, W-Th 10am-4pm and 6pm-9pm, F 10am-4pm).

**US Embassy:** The nearest US Embassy is located in London (24 Grosvenor Square London, WLA 2LQ; 020 7499 9000).

**Hospitals:**
- Manchester Royal Infirmary (Oxford Rd.; 161 276 1234; open daily 24hr).
- North Manchester General Hospital (Delaunays Rd.; 161 624 0420; open daily 24hr).

**Pharmacies:** Pharmacies are in abundance in Manchester.
- Boots (161 832 6533).
- Everest Pharmacy (161 273 4629).
- Lloyds Pharmacy (161 273 1327).

# ACCOMMODATIONS

### HATTER'S HILTON CHAMBERS ($)
15 Hilton St.; 1612364414; www.hattershostels.com; reception open 24hr

Hatter's basically runs the hostel scene is Manchester—after their original success on Newton St., they set up another branch just two minutes away. The two spots have a lot in common: great location in the **Northern Quarter,** free breakfast, and a schedule of nightly events like staff-lead pub crawls and movie nights. Hatter's Hilton's ongoing

renovation might just give it a leg-up over the Newton location: it already has some refurbished rooms that provide the ample outlet access that Hatter's Newton lacks. Unlike the older establishment, however, it is not connected to a bumping pub—take that as either a pro or a con, depending on your vacation style.

*i* *Dorms from £11, prices higher on weekends; reservation recommended; Wi-Fi; linens included; free breakfast*

### HATTER'S ON NEWTON ST. ($)

50 Newton St.; 1612369500; www.hatter-shostels.com; reception open 24hr

As far as location goes, Hatter's can't be beat: it's right in the buzzing **Northern Quarter,** a stone's throw away from both the retail district and quirky **Oldham Street.** Facilities-wise, things could be nicer, but they're clearly expecting you to be too sloshed to care about chipping paint or toilets from the Stone Age—and they're probably right. With the tagline "better beds, better buzz," Hatter's is an ultra-social hostel in an ultra-social part of town and having fun is pretty much mandatory. The **YHA** across town has nicer rooms, but all things considered Hatter's is the way to go for your Manchester stay.

*i* *Dorms from £11, prices higher on weekends; reservation recommended; Wi-Fi; linens included; free breakfast*

### YHA MANCHESTER ($)

Potato Wharf, Castlefield; 3453719647; www.yha.org.uk; reception open 24hr

Where there's a British city, there's a YHA hostel, and Manchester is no exception. This installment of the green-hued, children-and-elderly-accepting, generally chill hostel chain is located in a quiet part of the city and it can feel as though you're in the middle of nowhere instead of a bustling metropolis. But, if you want reliably clean and spacious rooms (with enough outlets!) it's a safe bet. The hostel won't throw anything except linens your way for free, but it has everything you might need at a reasonable price, and is a treasure trove of information about the city.

*i* *Dorms from £13-16, prices higher on weekends; reservation recommended; wheelchair accessible; Wi-Fi; linens included; laundry facilities; meals available for purchase*

## SIGHTS
### CULTURE

### AFFLECKS

52 Church St.; 1618390718; www.afflecks.com; open M-F 10:30am-6pm, Sa 10am-6pm, Su 11am-5pm

Have you ever wanted to start a coven? Did you secretly never recover from your goth phase? Have you always dreamt of making your own vegan shampoo? If you answered yes to any of the above, run-don't-walk to Afflecks, an indoor market and helluva time in the **Northern Quarter.** While it's so much more than the sum of its bizarre parts, here are some of the retail highlights: a breakfast cereal café, several "fancy dress" (read: costume) shops, a place offering half-priced corsets and tarot card readings, and a boutique specializing in dresses with funky prints like dinosaurs and unicorns. It absolutely takes the (vegan) cake for most interesting spot in Manchester.

*i Prices vary by store; some stores cash only; wheelchair accessible*

## MANCHESTER ARNDALE

Manchester M4 1AZ; 1618339851; www.manchesterarndale.com; open M-F 9am-8pm, Sa 9am-7pm, Su 11:30am-5:30pm

Socialism may have been invented in Manchester, but the clanging coffers of capitalism are alive and thriving at Arndale in the city center. This shopping center is the crown jewel of the ultra-commercial central retail district, and conveniently located across the street from a multi-story **Primark** if you aren't done shopping. All the classic British mall brands are out in full force, among cheap, greasy eats and the odd currency exchange. Marx may be rolling over in his grave, but don't let that stop you from having a good time—the proletariat can rebel tomorrow.

*i Prices vary by store; wheelchair accessible*

## ROYAL EXCHANGE THEATRE

St. Ann's Sq.; 1618339833; www.royal-exchange.co.uk; open M-Sa 9:30-start of show, Su 11-start of show

Back in the days when Manchester ran on cotton, its prominent businessmen would use the Royal Exchange as a forum to share ideas and probably smoke a lot of cigars. Since then, the Exchange has been destroyed and rebuilt multiple times, finally arriving in its present form as a theater. And a rather unique one: The Royal Exchange has an in-the-round audience set-up and stage, and the 700-member audience is enclosed in a crazy-looking contraption within the theater's grand hall. While front row seats aren't cheap, the theatre has a lot of student and youth discounts, such as day-of half-priced tickets. If you check the website and use your money-saving savvy, you should be able to see a good performance at a reasonable price.

*i Prices vary by show, students can pay as little as £7; open M-Sa 9:30-start of show, Su 11-start of show; wheelchair accessible*

# LANDMARKS

## MANCHESTER TOWN HALL

Albert Sq.; 1618277661; www.thetownhallmcr.co.uk; sculpture hall café open M-F 9am-4pm, Sa-Su 10am-4pm

Manchester is perhaps not the most aesthetic city—its symbol is the worker bee, not the pollinated flower—but the magnificent town hall is easy on the eyes. Walking down John Dalton St., you won't be able to miss this towering display of Neogothic architecture. During the day, you can enter the sculpture hall, home to commemorative busts of Manchester's finest (and a nice café). Unfortunately, that's about as far as you'll get before hitting ominous "closed to the public" signs. To get inside, you'll just have to book your wedding there—details are helpfully provided on the website.

*i Free admission; wheelchair accessible*

## THE JOHN RYLANDS LIBRARY

150 Deansgate; 1613060555; www.manchester.as.uk/library/rylands; open M noon-5pm, Tu-Sa 10am-5pm, Su noon-5pm

Neogothic architecture and ancient books are basically the peanut butter and jelly of the library world, and the John Rylands Library delivers. The majestic third-floor reading room is the grandest part of the building—and open to visitors to stay and work, if inspiration for that screenplay in the bottom of your backpack suddenly strikes. Down a floor, the arch-laden goodness continues, and the John Rylands Gallery showcases some of the coolest parts of the library's collection, like a piece of a manuscript that many believe is the earliest portion of New Testament writing ever found. The beauty here is truly biblical.

*i Free admission; limited wheelchair accessibility*

# MUSEUMS

## MANCHESTER ART GALLERY

Molsey St.; 1612358888; www.manchesterartgallery.org; open M-W 10am-5pm, Th 10am-9pm, F-Su 10am-5pm

Like many things in this proud city, the Manchester Art Gallery adopts a local focus, showcasing works by

Mancunians (we're not sure why they're called that, either) like **Joseph Parry** and **L.S. Lowry,** as well as works from the rest of Britain and Europe. One fun curatorial touch is to intersperse contemporary artworks that relate thematically in galleries focused on other time periods. The gallery also keeps itself young with exciting temporary exhibits as blissfully free as the rest of the museum. The space is large enough to get your fill of British art for the day without suffering from museum fatigue.

*i* Free; wheelchair accessible

### MUSEUM OF SCIENCE AND INDUSTRY

Liverpool Rd.; 1618322244; www.msimanchester.org.uk; open daily 10am-5pm

If you're tired of the "look, don't touch" vibe of most museums, the Museum of Science and Industry may be the answer to your itchy-fingered prayers. Not only are there plenty of interactive exhibits, but the museum is all about how Manchester has gotten its hands dirty in the pursuit of progress. From the days when it emerged as the world's first industrial city to its role in the invention of the first commercial computer, Manchester has made some pretty rad contributions to society. The museum is made up of multiple warehouses that maintain a very industrial, down-by-the-docks feel.

*i* Free admission; wheelchair accessible

### NATIONAL FOOTBALL MUSEUM

Cathedral Gardens; 1616058200; www.nationalfootballmuseum.com; open daily 10am-5pm

If you're a football fan (no, not that kind of football, you silly American), or at least mildly familiar with the sport, you've probably heard of a little team called **Manchester United.** Man Utd makes Manchester the perfect spot for a museum dedicated to the much-beloved national pastime. Part history lesson, part arcade, and part shrine, the National Football Museum is a loud, interactive extravaganza—music blares, football beckons. A definite stop for people with multiple stadium ticket stubs at home and a fun excursion for the rest of us.

*i* Free admission; wheelchair accessible

### THE PEOPLE'S HISTORY MUSEUM

Left Bank, Spinningfields; 1618389190; www.phm.org.uk; open daily 10am-5pm

Go to any of London's palaces and you'll get the picture that British History is just one all-out soap operatic battle for power. But it turns out that while the British elite were arguing over succession, a lot was happening in Britain's factories, town squares, and *reasonably*-sized houses. The People's History Museum is a detailed, fascinating, and unabashedly left-wing look at the past 400 years of working-and middle-class history, from the struggle for the common man to get the vote to more recent attempts to include BGLTQ+ citizens in the movement for workers' rights. Prepare to be schooled on a lot of stuff you never learned in history class.

*i* Free admission; wheelchair accessible

# FOOD

### ⬛COMMON ($)

39-41 Edge St.; 1618329245; www.aplacecalledcommon.co.uk; open daily 10am-late

Common has fried its way on to half a dozen city- and country-wide "best of" lists, and the hype is well-deserved. They've perfected brunch favorites like the Full English and avocado toast. Trust us, deciding which delectable option from their menu to choose is the hardest thing you'll do all morning. Common is also wonderfully hipster: its walls are adorned with colorful abstract art and its long list of events include art shows and a knitting workshop. You can eat and drink here until the ill-defined "late," but the real time to remember is 3pm, when brunch tragically grinds to a halt. Ah, parting is such sweet (and salty) sorrow.

*i* Entrées £5-8; vegetarian and vegan options available; wheelchair accessible

### COMPTOIR LIBANAIS ($$)

18-19 The Avenue, Spinningfields; 1616723999; www.comptoirlibanais.com; open M-F 8am-11:30pm, Sa 9am-11:30pm, Su 9am-10:30pm

Comptoir Libanais, which has a handful of locations throughout the UK, serves up truly delicious Lebanese food—and if you're not sure what that entails, all the more reason to give it a try. The ambiance is second only to the fare; it includes lively music, colorfully tiled walls and floors, an outdoor terrace, and intricately decorated teapots for sale. This is Britain, after all. Comptoir Libanais has a bar area with lots of wine and cocktails on the menu, if you want to make your fattoush a little more festive.

*i* Entrées £8-11; vegetarian and Halal options available; wheelchair accessible

### HAPPY SEASONS ($$)

59-61 Faulkner St.; 1612367189; open M-Th noon-11pm, F-Sa noon-11:30pm, Su noon-9:30pm

If you like Chinese food (in other words, if you are a rational human being), you can't really go wrong on Faulkner St., home of Manchester's tiny Chinatown. But if you're looking for a sure bet where non-MSG soaked portions are plentiful and the clientele are largely chopstick-wielding regulars, Happy Seasons can be your Chinatown stop. The menu is pages and pages long, and, if you're really hungry, they offer tantalizing multi-course meals for two or more people. The sheer volume of good food might knock you out, leaving you to lay dying by the giant golden arch above Faulkner.

*i* Entrées £8-11; minimum £15 credit card charge; vegetarian options available

### THE KITCHENS ($)

Irwell Sq., Leftbank; 8448267214; www.thekitchensleftbank.com; open M-Sa 8am-7pm

The Kitchens is a small food hub tucked away among massive apartment buildings that features a rotating cast of street food vendors. Past businesses have included a Polish breakfast and lunch joint and a Jamaican restaurant. If the whole concept sounds absolutely awesome (which it is), the prices are even more awesome. You could easily sample a little of each booth without breaking the bank. It's like an around-the-world budget travel experience for your stomach.

*i* Entrées £4-6; vegetarian options available; wheelchair accessible

## NIGHTLIFE

### NIGHT AND DAY CAFÉ

26 Oldham St.; 1612361822; www.night-nday.org; open M-Th 10am-2am, F 10am-4am, Sa 9am-4am, Su 9am-10:30pm

It's hard to choose the best bar in the **Northern Quarter** (have we mentioned that we love it yet?), but Night and Day Café is a serious contender. This Manchester mainstay has hosted big name music acts like **Jessie J** and **Arctic Monkeys,** and continues to offer first-rate live performances at budget-friendly prices. Its hours verge on perpetual, so you can come for breakfast in the morning and a killer show in the evening—night and day, right? We recommend looking up the performance schedule ahead of time, because tickets are often sold out night-of.

*i* Drinks £5-9; the cover depends on show; wheelchair accessible

### THE GAY VILLAGE

Princess St. to Minshull St., centered around Canal St.; www.canal-st.co.uk; hours vary

Manchester's Gay Village is one of the most lit parts of the city, both in the twenty-first century sense of the word and in the sense that there's a whole lot of neon. Centered around Canal Street, this is one of the UK's first and most famous enclaves of gay culture—you'll know you're there when every building has a pride flag. There's something for everyone: bars, cabaret bars, bars with signs that light up and whir, clubs. Check out **Vanilla**, a famous hub for gay women, **Oscar's**, which shows musical theater film clips, or **The Goose**, a gay pub (is there any better combination of words?).

*i* Prices vary; BGLTQ+ friendly

### THE LIARS CLUB

19a Back Bridge St.; 1618345111; www. theliarsclub.co.uk; open M-Sa 5pm-4am, Su 5pm-3am

The Liars Club does not go halfway on its tropical island theme—think palm tree everything, barrels for chairs, and the most orange you'll see outside of a Tropicana factory. Some might call it tacky or "trying too hard to escape a place where you need a jacket in June," but others would say it's just fun. You can decide for yourself who's the liar every night until the wee hours of the morning, or come earlier for deals on cocktails with names like "Floradita Swizzle" and "Suffering Bastard." Mmmmm, tropical.

*i* Cocktails £7-9; BGLTQ+ friendly; limited wheelchair accessibility

# GREAT BRITAIN ESSENTIALS

## VISAS

Britain is not a signatory to the Schengen Agreement, which means it is not a member of the freedom of movement zone that covers most of continental Europe. EU citizens do not need a visa to visit Britain, and citizens of Australia, Canada, New Zealand, the U.S. and many other non-EU countries do not need a visa for stays of up to six months Those staying longer than six months may apply for a longer-term visa; consult an embassy or consulate for more information. Because Britain is not a part of the Schengen zone, time spent here does not count toward the 90-day limit on travel within that area. Entering to work or study for longer than six months will require a visa. You can learn more at www.ukvisas. gov.uk. Although there is a lot of uncertainty surrounding the recent Brexit, this appears to only affect EU citizens living in the UK and not those who are just visiting.

## MONEY

**Tipping and Bargaining:** Restaurant servers are paid at least the minimum wage, so tipping is slightly different. If you receive table service, there may be a tip included in your bill. It will appear as a "service charge" and you do not need to tip on top of it. If there is no service charge, you should tip around 10%. You do not need to tip if you order at the counter, or in bars or pubs. If you are staying in a nice hotel (read: not a hostel), you should tip porters £1-2, and tipping the housekeeper is up to your discretion. For taxi drivers, it is customary to round up to the nearest pound, but you don't need to tip. Bargaining is not common in the UK and should probably not be attempted.

## TAXES

The UK has a 20% value added tax (VAT), a sales tax applied to everything but food, books, and children's clothing. The tax is included on the amount indicated on the price tag, and all prices stated in Let's Go include VAT. Upon exiting Britain, non-EU citizens can reclaim VAT (minus an administrative fee) through the Retail Export Scheme, although the process is time-consuming and can only be applied to goods you take out of the country. Participating shops display a "tax-free shopping" sign and have a minimum purchase condition, usually around £75. To claim a refund, you must fill out the form given to you in the shop (VAT 407) and this must be presented to customs when you depart. You must leave the UK for at least twelve months within three months of making the purchase to qualify.

## POLICE

Police are a common presence in Britain and there are many police stations throughout the country. There are two types of police offers in the UK: regular officers with full police powers and police community support officers (PCSOs), who have limited police power and focus on community and safety. The emergency number is 999, and the non-emergency number is 101. Find out more at www.police.uk.

## DRUGS AND ALCOHOL

The presence of alcohol is unavoidable in a nation famed for its pubs and distilleries. Remember that the British pint is 20oz. as compared to the 16oz. U.S. pint. The legal age at which you can buy alcohol in the UK is 18; expect to be asked for I.D. if you look under 25. Sixteen and seventeen-year-olds can drink beer or wine in a restaurant if they are accompanied by an adult and the adult makes the purchase.

The use, possession, and sale of hard drugs is illegal and can carry a penalty of up to seven years in prison for possession alone. Do not test this. Penalties for cannabis are less severe, but police can issue a warning or on the spot fine of £90 if you're found with it. Smoking is banned in enclosed public spaces, including pubs and restaurants.

## TERRORISM

The terrorist attacks of 2017 in Manchester Arena and London Bridge and Borough Market revealed that the UK is still susceptible to terrorism, despite the more stringent safety measures put in place after the 2005 London Underground Bombings. Expect thorough security checks in airports and do not pack any sharp objects in your carry-on luggage. Check your home country's foreign affairs office for travel information and advisories.

## MEASUREMENTS

Brits primarily use the metric system of measurement, and metric must be used when selling packaged or loose goods—the exception to this is beer or cider, sold in pints. However, road distances are always given in miles, not kilometers.

# GREECE

**To travel in Europe is to swerve between past and present, and, in Greece, the curves get tighter, more mythologized, and covered in an ancient alphabet.**
Greece is the Acropolis-crowned jewel in Europe's study of time contrasts, where remains from some of the oldest known civilizations in the world rub up against clubs playing the latest Rihanna hit. At the center of this time warp rests Athens, the sprawling capital of Greece, where the storied Parthenon towers over graffitied streets and raucous student bars. Once the stomping ground of Plato, Socrates, Aristophanes, and other intellectual luminaries of the ancient world, present-day Athens maintains its pull as a major cultural center in the Mediterranean, mixing ancient glory with modern art. Daily ferries leave the poured concrete of Athens behind for the sparkling white stucco of the Cycladic Islands, the vacationer's paradise renowned for sun, sea, blue-domed churches, and nonstop parties. Absorb the glitz and glitter of Mykonos and recover from sleepless nights among the eye-popping cliffs of Santorini. Or, take a trip north to the former Macedonian port of Thessaloniki, Greece's second-largest city and a cultural hub in its own right. Between numerous coffee breaks, Byzantine churches, and nightly club visits, Thessaloniki may require superhuman energy, though luckily the gods aren't too far away—their alleged home, Mt. Olympus, awaits you just a 90-minute bus ride south. From Zeus to Zedd, Parthenon to café patio, abandoned temple to abandoned warehouse bar, Greece will have you hanging on to every turn—though you may not remember what year it is.

# ATHENS

Coverage by **Adrian Horton**

The word "Athens" conjures images of spectacular history: the Parthenon towering over an ancient city, the original schools of democracy, and massive marble statues. Its reputation is merited: Athens is over 3400 years old, and remnants of the past appear seemingly every step (sometimes in a museum, sometimes next to an H&M). Classical Athens—the peak of the city-states civilization around 300 BCE—is, of course, the immediate draw, as the mind-bending array of temples, art, and history have overwhelmed travelers for centuries (even writers in Ancient Rome geeked out when they finally got to visit the Acropolis). Today, though, the classical era is but a part of a much longer story. With a population of nearly 3.75 million (roughly a third of Greece), Athens is very much a living, breathing, car-honking, expletive-shouting city, as evidenced by its omnipresent street art and stray cat army. Amid the tumult you'll find the *ouzerie* culture and alternative youth scene of modern Athens, which have their own feisty, yet laid-back, charm. Balance your shots of the Acropolis with some shots of *ouzo* at a local *taverna,* or a strong coffee in rebellious Exarchia. From museums to night clubs, parks to packed bars, flea markets to fat *souvlaki* pitas, Athens has both your inner-nerd and inner-socialite covered.

## ORIENTATION

The energy of central Athens flows around two main points: Monastiraki Square and, to its east down Mitropoleos Street, Syntagma Square, which is home to the Greek National Parliament. Due south of Monastiraki Square looms the Acropolis, which can still be seen from most points in the city and makes a great orientation point, especially at night. Wedged between Monastiraki and the Acropolis is the Plaka, the historic district that contains many hostels, monuments, tourist shops, and the famous neighborhood of Anafiotika. Just north of Monastiraki is the revitalized neighborhood of Psiri, which buzzes at night with Athens' thriving bar scene. Heading west from Monastiraki on Ermou Street (a ten-minute walk), you'll reach Gazi, a factory-zone-turned-home for touring DJs and late-night clubbers. Traveling north from Monastiraki on Athinas Street, you reach Omonia Square, a major metro stop. From Omonia, Metaxourgeio, a more working-class and less-visited area of Athens, stretches west; to the northeast lies the National Archaeological Museum and university hub Exarchia, which is more street art and apartment buildings than tourist traps and souvenir shops. Central Athens is about a half hour metro ride northeast of Piraeus Port, and a half hour tram ride west of the beach.

## ESSENTIALS

### GETTING THERE

After arriving at Athens International Airport (Eleftherios Venizelos), take the metro or bus downtown. A cab will also drop you in the city center for a set fare of €38. If arriving through Piraeus Port, take the green line downtown from Piraeus Port Station. If the metro is out of service, a cab from Piraeus to Monastiraki Square costs €15.

## GETTING AROUND

Athens is safe to explore on foot, especially in areas frequented by tourists, though, of course, be wary of walking alone at night. Most of the city is also accessible via the metro, which runs 5:30am-12:30am and until 2:30am on Friday and Saturday. Individual tickets cost €1.40; a day pass is €4.50. Tickets can be bought at kiosks located at each station, but make sure you validate your ticket or you could face a large fine. Buses also run throughout the day—see the routes on maps from the GNTO or Syntagma Station. Information on bus schedules and routes can also be found at www.oasa.gr.

## PRACTICAL INFORMATION

**Tourist Offices:** Greek National Tourism Organization (18-20 Dinoyssiou Areopagitou; 210 870 7000; www.visitgreece.gr).

**Banks/ATMs/Currency Exchange:** Check back in a year or so, but as of July 2017, Greece uses the euro (€). ATMs can be found throughout the city, especially in the tourist-friendly Plaka neighborhood and near all major museums and monuments.

**Post Offices:** Hellenic Post manages snail mail for Greece (www.elta.gr).

**Internet:** If you want Wi-Fi, you have to pay for it, and, even then, you may not get it. Solid Wi-Fi is a rare find in Athens, especially at well-frequented hostels. Your best bet is a trendy-looking café during off hours.

**BGLTQ+ Resources:** Homosexuality is decriminalized in Greece, but socially frowned upon in some areas of the country. In Athens, however, the culture is open and tolerant, and there is a thriving gay scene in some parts of the city, notably Gazi.

## EMERGENCY INFORMATION

**Emergency Number:** 166

**Police:** Dial 100 in emergencies; www.astynomia.gr; Tourist Police (1571, available daily 24hr).

**US Embassy:** US Embassy Athens (91 Vasilisis Sophias Avenue; 210 721 2951).

**Hospitals:** Athens General Hospital G. Genimatas (Mesogeion 154, 210 77012115).

**Pharmacies:** Locations throughout the city and especially near the Plaka area; they commonly close at 9pm.

# ACCOMMODATIONS

### ☒ATHENS BACKPACKERS ($$)
12 Makri St., Makriyanni; 210 9224044; www.backpackers.gr; reception open 24hr
Athens Backpackers has boiled hosteling down to a science: rooftop bar + spacious common area + large kitchen with a functional stove + sinks deep enough to fit your water bottle + Wi-Fi that works in your room + showers where you can stretch out AND

enjoy hot water = happy travelers. Additionally, the hostel offers walking tours of the city on most days, as well as access to its own laundromat. Oh, there are balconies, too, and it's all just a stone's throw away from some of the city's biggest monuments.

*i* Dorms from €24; reservation recommended; BGLTQ+ friendly; no wheelchair accessibility; Wi-Fi; luggage storage; laundry facilities; free breakfast

### ATHENSTYLE ($)
Agias Thekla 10, Monastiraki; 210 3225010; www.athenstyle.com; reception open 24hr
Renovated lounge area? Check. Electronic key card and locker system? Check. Rooftop bar with stunning views of the **Parthenon?** Check. Things have changed since your parents backpacked in the '80s and paid for a sleeping pad. To hostel in Athenstyle is to hostel, well, in style (sorry, it was too easy). With spacious, naturally lit bunk rooms, rooftop access, and a large community of travelers, Athenstyle puts a modern spin on experiencing Athens.

*i* Dorms from €18, studio rooms from €25; reservation recommended; BGLTQ+ friendly; Wi-Fi; laundry facilities; breakfast €3

### STUDENTS AND TRAVELLERS INN ($)
Kydathineon 16; 210 3244808; www.studenttravellersinn.com; reception open 24hr
In the heart of the **Plaka,** wedged between an upscale ice cream parlor and a boutique selling Greek goddess clothing, lies the marble entrance of Students and Travellers Inn. With its central garden courtyard, where guests chat over €2.50 beers at small plastic tables, Students and Travellers does not set the "hit-the-club" mood like some of Athens' bigger hostels do, but a friendly staff, worn-in furniture, and a steady stream of solo backpackers give this hostel its own unassuming charm.

*i* Dorms from €18, private rooms from €50; reservation recommended; BGLTQ+ friendly; no wheelchair accessibility; Wi-Fi; cash only; luggage storage; laundry for €8.50; linens included; breakfast €3.50-5.50

# SIGHTS

## CULTURE

### CHANGING OF THE GUARD AT SYNTAGMA SQUARE

Syntagma Sq.

He wears a tassel longer than most ponytails, pom-pom-festooned shoes, and more stoicism than half the marbles in the Archaeological Museum. In a feat of restraint, he has not wavered in the sweltering heat nor batted an eye at the group of American tourists zooming their cameras in on his face. Is he a marionette? No, he's one of the *Evzones* (Evzoni), the prestigious ceremonial unit of the Greek military that constantly guards the **Tomb of the Unknown Solider** in front of the Greek Parliament building. Dressed in traditional military costumes from southern Greece (very unclear how this outfit fared in battle), the *Evzones* put on a choreographed changing of the guard every hour, complete with gravity-(and hamstring) defying high kicks and loud scrapes of their *tsarouchia* clogs on the marble. For a grander show, stop by Syntagma on Sunday morning for a full unit procession.

*i* Free to the public; wheelchair accessible; hourly changing of the guard, full unit procession Su 11am

### MONASTIRAKI FLEA MARKET

Open daily May-October

Back in the day (a century or two ago, not Plato's day), **Monastiraki Square** was the gateway to a new life for those moving to Athens. Immigrants from across Greece and neighboring areas created a Balkan-style medina of shops, mosques, churches, workshops, homes, and inns—a mix of work and life to bring community to a new place. Today, though carriages no longer clog the thoroughfare, the Monastiraki Flea Market still maintains its old-time Ottoman feel, as Byzantine churches rub shoulders with cart vendors peddling antiques and homemade evil-eye bracelets.

*i* Free; limited wheelchair accessibility

### GREEK DANCING

Philopappou Hill; ticket office at Scholiou 8, Plaka; 210 3244395; www.grdance.org; shows W-F 9:30pm, Sa-Su 8:15pm

You know you've heard it before: the light twang of the lute strings slowly picking up tempo to a soft bass beat. It plays in every movie set on a Mediterranean island. It plays on Greek public buses and in the background of at least 65% of Greece's restaurants. It's Greek folk music, and it's given its proper space (i.e. not an elevator) at **Philopappou Hill.** Every Wednesday through Sunday at the old theater, across from the Acropolis, a crew of 75 professional musicians, singers, and dancers in traditional costumes (tights, aprons, pom-poms, tassels) treat crowds to a spectacle of regional culture.

*i* Tickets €15

## LANDMARKS

### THE ACROPOLIS

Dionysiou Areopagitou St.; 210 3222816; open daily 8am-8pm

What is there to say? One of the most iconic landmarks in the world and a universal symbol for Greece. Even in the

modern maze of Athens, the Acropolis still looms large over the city, day and night. Once an early settlement for the **Myceneans** and later the cradle for democratic government, the Acropolis has housed pagan idolatry, national treasures, and a Turkish garrison; it even briefly functioned as a mosque. Now, it is still the most sacred (and toured) site in Athens. Regardless of the heat and the overwhelming number of guided tour groups, the Acropolis commands respect—for the view, for the historical and cultural significance, and for the sheer awe of finally seeing the legendary hill in real life.

*i* *Tickets €20, €10 student; last entry 30min. before closing; wheelchair accessible; 5-day combination passes available (and highly recommended)*

### LYCABETTUS HILL

At 910 feet, Lycabettus Hill (mountain?) reigns as the highest point in Athens, topping even the **Acropolis.** Even better, a trip to the top reveals the whole of Athens around you, 360-degree style. Though supposedly once inhabited by wolves (*lykos*), Lycabettus is the subject of relatively few ancient stories. Instead, the hill is renowned today for its spectacular sunset views of the city (improved only with wine and a picnic dinner from the **Monastiraki** market). Prepare yourself for a 30min. zig-zag hike up the hill, or be practical and take the funicular from Ploutarchou Street (every 30 min. €7 up).

*i* *Wheelchair accessible via funicular*

### THE ANCIENT AGORA AND TEMPLE OF HEPHAISTOS

24 Adrianou St.; 210 3210185; open daily 8am-8pm

"Agora" translates to marketplace, but, for ancient Athens, this plain at the base of the Acropolis was more than just a space for buying and selling goods. It was the place to find the who's who of the city, where social status ruled and all the drama went down (Socrates' trial took place here). Basically, if ancient Athens were a middle school, the Agora was the mall. Today, the ancient Agora has been partly uncovered and converted into a walkable museum of temples, court buildings (basilica), merchant

stalls (*stoa*), and a public square. Pick and choose what catches your eye as you stroll through this forest of millennium-old marble ruins in the footsteps of **Plato, Aristophanes,** and other luminaries of the classical era.

*i* *Admission €8, €4 student; last entry 30min. before closing; wheelchair accessible; included on 5-day monument pass from the Acropolis*

## MUSEUMS

### ☒THE ACROPOLIS MUSEUM

15 Dionysou Areopagitou St. ; 210 9000900; www.theacropolismuseum. gr; open Apr 1-Oct 31 M 8am-4pm, Tu-Th 8am-8pm, Fr 8am-10pm, Sa-Su 8am-8pm; open Nov 1 - Mar 31 M-Th 9am-5pm, F 9am-10pm, Sa-Su 9am-8pm

The city of Athens will not be pleased if you skip its Acropolis Museum, which was conceived as a project of national pride and opened in 2009 to great fanfare (and controversy—it cost a hefty $200 million). Meticulously designed with an eye towards the international community, the Acropolis Museum boasts floor-to-ceiling glass walls, a café patio in the shadow of the **Parthenon,** and impressive exhibits on Athenian history. The well-preserved *kourai* (female figures) and *hippeis* (horse riders), once brightly painted, recall the groundbreaking talent of Greek sculptors, while the remains of the Parthenon friezes in the third floor gallery commemorate a raucous festival for the goddess Athena.

*i* *Admission €5, €3 student; wheelchair accessible; no flash photography or mobile phones*

### THE NATIONAL ARCHAEOLOGICAL MUSEUM

44 Patision St.; 213 2144800; www. namuseum.gr; open M 1pm-8pm, Tu-Su 8am-8pm

Sure, Athens has a lot of *old things,* but the National Archaeological Museum reveals just how much ground that term covers. The museum's massive collection spans millennia, from old (Byzantine jewelry, 1500 years ago), to really old (archaic Greek sculpture, about 2500 years ago), to really, *really* old (Egyptian masks, several millennia ago). When the painted vases

# THE ACROPOLIS: WHAT'S THE BIG DEAL?

You've been in Athens for ten minutes and already you're thinking "Enough of the Acropolis already!" It's old, it's important, I get it. Why is it such a big deal? Good question. To start, you have to mentally erase what you see of the Acropolis today. In the beginning, there was a flat-topped hill, a fertile valley, and a Mycenean temple. In other words, the Acropolis has been inhabited for nearly 5000 years, so stop saying that you're "getting so old."

Sometime after the end of Mycenean rule, Athenians dedicated the hill to the pagan goddess Athena and erected a set of religious structures on top of it. As Athens developed from dinky town to major trade port, the ruler Pericles decided to transform the Acropolis into a spectacle of city-state pride. Under Pericles' building program (during the Golden Age of Athens, 460-430 BCE), the Acropolis transformed from a collection of temples to an extravaganza of classical art and architecture.

First, there's the Parthenon—the crowd-pleaser, Pericles's pride, the most recognized symbol of Athens. Originally a far less impressive temple to Athena, the Parthenon was transformed by the greatest architects of Classical Greece into a massive colonnaded structure decorated with friezes (marble murals). The construction revolutionized architectural techniques at the time, resulting in some cool optical illusions: the outer columns swell in the middle to appear straight from a distance, and they tilt slightly inwards. At one point in the fifth century BCE, the Parthenon served as a treasury for the Delian League, an alliance of city-states. The temple has also served as a church, a mosque, and a storehouse for gunpowder during the Venetian siege of 1687, which resulted in half the building blowing up. Oops.

If walls could talk, you'd want to get coffee with the Erechtheion, which has been 1) a temple to Athena (duh), 2) a church, 3) a Turkish governor's harem, and 4) a bomb recipient. Ingeniously designed to make use of uneven ground and avoid old burial plots, the Erechtheion boasts the famous Porch of the Caryatids, whose columns are modeled on individual female figures.

Before you get to the Erechtheion, though, you must pass through the Propylaia, the grand entrance gate. One of the greatest examples of Doric architecture, which still greets all visitors to the Acropolis, the Propylaia was originally designed to extend outward with massive marble wings. These plans never materialized, as Athens instead went to war with (This! Is!) Sparta (431 BCE). Just outside the Propylaia gates rests the Temple of Athena Nike, an open-air sanctuary dedicated to the goddess of victory. This temple is notable for its easy access to the Athenian public, and for inspiring a shoe company you've never heard of.

Phew, that's a lot. You can get your selfie with the Parthenon now.

and homages to the male physique all start to blur together, try to find the personal touches that turn these pieces from antiques to remnants of lives past: a woman's special perfume bottle, hieroglyphic graffiti preserved in stone, the grave stele painted with the deceased man's telltale asymmetrical eyes. And ugh, fine, send a funny snap of the nude sculptures to your friends.

*i* *Admission €10, €5 student; wheelchair accessible*

## OUTDOORS

### THE NATIONAL GARDEN
Main entrance at Amalias 1; open sunrise to sunset

Under the lush green canopy of the National Garden, where the birds chirp so frequently that it sounds almost tropical, the bustle of the city seems far away. But look closely and the relaxed imperfection of modern Athens seeps through. Millennia-old ruins lie next to graffitied concrete. A woman sings a beautiful rendition of *Les Misérables*'s

"I Dreamed a Dream" under an empty trellis, a drained fountain her only audience. A message on a park bench reads "fuck the police" in thick black marker under an exquisite display of purple flowers. A barely-acknowledged Roman floor mosaic extends before you, but you must step over molding oranges to see it. Athens' National Garden, a park of 38 acres designed as a botanical escape, draws you in not because it is a reprieve, but because it is a work of art.

*i* Free; wheelchair accessible

# FOOD

## 🗷ATLANTIKO ($)
Avilton 7, Psiri; 213 0330350; open daily 12:30pm-1am

You know a place means business when there are five boiling pots on the stove and a huge rack of *ouzo* bottles above the bar. And you know a place means fish business when half the menu is handwritten fresh daily. Welcome to Atlantiko, *the* place to go for delicious and affordable seafood. Hidden in an alley just off the **Monastiraki Flea Market,** Atlantikos keeps it simple with nautical decorations, fresh seafood (grilled or fried), and *ouzo*. Their grilled sardines could win over even the biggest salty-fish skeptic, while also raising a series of uncomfortable questions: do you eat the head? Do you eat the bones? Do you eat the tail? Is the waiter judging me? The answer is yes to all of those questions. It's not pretty but it's damn delicious.

*i* Drinks from €4, fresh fish from €6; vegetarian options available; wheelchair accessible

## 🗷TAVERNA TOU PSIRI ($)
Eschilou 12; 210 3214923; open daily noon-midnight

Many of the restaurants in **Psiri** offer the look of an authentic taverna to attract tourists, but Taverna Tou Psiri actually stands by its name. Owned by the lovely Manolis, this traditional working-class taverna is bright and accommodating to locals and tourists alike, even if you roll in with a seven person crew a half hour before closing time. Start with the best grilled bread served in Athens (free!), then sample

some classic Greek *mezedes* (appetizers), especially the *keftedes* (meatballs) and *kolokithea keftedes* (fried zucchini balls with feta). For some much-needed protein, Taverna Tou Psiri's specialty, grilled meat fillets (€8-10), offer a flavorful alternative to street food grease and pita. Oh wait, it comes with french fries, too? And they're delicious? Damn. Athens gets the best of you again.

*i* Beer from €3, house wine €6, appetizers from €3, salads from €4, grill items from €8; no wheelchair accessibility

## ARISTON PITA BAKERY ($)
10 Voulis St.; 210 7223626; open M, W, Sa 7:30am-6pm, T, Th-F 7am-9pm

At some point during your time in Athens, your body will be mad at you. It will protest and shout at you something along the lines of "please sleep more," or "not another sandwich," or simply "STOP." When the street food's got you down but you're ballin' on a tight budget, what can you do? Switch up tactics, of course. Souvlaki may be renowned as the street food of Athens, but *spanakopita* (spinach and feta pie) is a cheap stomach-filler in its own right, and no one does the savory pastry better than Ariston Pita Bakery. Just two blocks from **Syntagma Square** and open since 1910, Ariston *understands* pies, from zucchini to eggplant to ham and cheese. For less than €2, you've got a meal.

*i* Baked goods from €1.80; wheelchair accessible

## KAFENEIO ($$)
1 Epicharmou, Plaka; 210 3246916; www.tokafeneio.gr; open daily 10am-1am

In Greece, eating and drinking are synonymous—you can't have one without the other. You may never want to drink *ouzo* again after last night, but for many Athenians it's the evening drink of choice, and you can't have *ouzo* without *mezedes* (small plates). Housed in an old coffee shop in the heart of **Plaka,** Kafeneio is a traditional *ouzerie,* a place where Athenians gather to sip *ouzo,* pace through small plates, and tip back laughing in their chairs. Any small plate from Kafeneio is a winner, but the **seafood meze** is particularly delicious. For the TV foodies out there, Jamie Oliver filmed a segment here, and he approves! We're not quite Food Network certified (see: street food budget), but the cozy café atmosphere and reasonable prices have us inclined to agree.

*i* *Drinks from €4, small plates from €6, large plates from €12; vegetarian options available; limited wheelchair accessibility*

# NIGHTLIFE

## ⊠CANTINA SOCIAL
Leokoriou 6; 210 3251668; open daily 24hr

A local favorite in up-and-coming **Psiri,** Cantina Social encapsulates non-Acropolis Athens: unpromoted, a bit gritty, somewhat intimidating, and way cooler than you expect. Though seemingly an industrial-style no-go from the front, inside, Cantina Social opens into a large, artfully lit garden space lined by a bar stocked with bottles for your choosing. You may be the only non-Greek speaker there though, as the clientele skews heavily local and alternative. Even on a summer Sunday night, you'll find Cantina Social crowded with youngish Athenians with tousled hair, ripped clothing, and a casual shrug at the workweek. Ah, so this is what being in-the-know feels like.

*i* *No cover, beer €4-5, spirits €6-9; BGLTQ+ friendly*

## A FOR ATHENS
2-4 Miaouli, Monastiraki; 210 3244244; www.aforathens.com

Long before the dawn of electricity, Pericles intended the **Parthenon** to

be a spectacular attention-whore. Today, the classical temple is beautifully spot-lit at night, and views of it can command top dollar. A for Athens, a sleek bar and café right on **Monastiraki Square,** is one of the more affordable places to see ancient Athens' pride in all its modern glory. The beers here may be more expensive than street-level options, but the rooftop seating is romantically lit, comfy, and neatly styled. And the view is, indeed, stunning. FYI: A for Athens is a smaller space, so accommodating larger groups can be tricky. If you're rolling with a hostel squad of over eight or so, plan ahead.

*i* *Cover €15; BGLTQ+ friendly*

## AKANTHUS
Pireos 104, Alimos; 210 9680800; www. akanthus.gr

Don't spend precious euro on ferry tickets to the islands for a beach party. Instead, cash out on a 30-minute metro ride and tropical drinks at Akanthus, Athens' wildest beach club. With neon lights, a steady lineup of touring DJs, and a spacious dance floor, it's not just club-hungry tourists flocking to Akanthus's all-night affair. Catch Athenians in all their crop-top and shades-at-night glory at Akanthus' signature "Sex Me Up" parties. Clothing is largely optional, but don't forget money for the cab ride back (unless, of course, you do Akanthus right and catch the morning metro back at 5:30am).

*i* *No cover, beer from €7, cocktails €12; BGLTQ+ friendly*

# MYKONOS

Coverage by **Adrian Horton**

Mykonos has a bit of a split personality. There's the "Mykonos: City of the Winds" side listed on tourist brochures and ritzy magazine ads—the Mykonos famed for its Cycladic windmills, postcard-ready white stucco buildings, and luxury shopping. And then there's "MYKONOSSSSSS." This is the Mykonos of half-naked recent college grads and girls with fanny packs, of heavy beats and heavier shots, and of parties that do not stop. To its credit, Mykonos makes the most of its two predominant resources: wind and sun. In the past, this translated into granaries and significance as an Aegean trading port. Today, the wind revitalizes those tanning on any of the island's many beaches. As the Cyclades's glitziest and wildest island, Mykonos attracts a crowd of both upscale leisure travelers and backpackers ready to pull their longest-ever all-nighter. Here, the UV exposure is high, the stress level low, and the energy anywhere between.

# ORIENTATION

At 40 square miles and about 10,000 residents, Mykonos is a fairly small island, and most of its activity is confined to the western side. The island's main settlement, the aptly-named **Mykonos Town,** faces the sea from two ports on the central-western coast. The **New Port** of Mykonos, which receives all ferry traffic, lies about a 45-minute walk to the north of the Town (it is also accessible by bus or sea taxi). The most popular party beaches in Mykonos—**Paraga, Paradise,** and **Super Paradise**—line the island's southern coast, and are a short and slightly terrifying bus ride away from town (to be a bus driver on the narrow roads of Mykonos is a craft). The rest of the island is comprised of less-travelled beaches, farms, old stone walls, and over 400 blue-and-white churches.

# ESSENTIALS

## GETTING THERE

Public buses run from Mykonos International Airport (JMK) to Mykonos Town (Fabrika Square) and the New Port hourly from 9am-8pm. Exact bus times are posted at each station. All ferries now dock at the New Port, which is about a 45min. walk from the Old Harbor in Mykonos Town. Taxis and private transfers are available at the port, and some hostels, such as Paraga or Paradise Beach Resort, provide their own transport free of charge. Otherwise, take the Sea Taxi (€2) from the ferry dock to Mykonos Town (10min.).

## GETTING AROUND

Public buses provide hourly transport between Mykonos Town (Fabrika Square) and other popular destinations on the island, such as Paraga Beach (daily 9:15am-12:15am), Paradise Beach (daily 7:15am-1:15am), and Elia. Tickets can be purchased at the station kiosk or on the bus. For those craving more independence, ATVs can be rented for €25-35 a day, depending on the model.

## PRACTICAL INFORMATION

**Tourist Offices:** Mykonos closed its brick-and-mortar tourist office; all information can be found online at www.mykonosnow.gr or through the MyMykonos app. For excursions or help with transportation, there are several private tourist companies in Mykonos Town.

**Banks/ATMs/Currency Exchange:** Check back in a year or so, but as of now, Greece uses the euro. ATMs can be found throughout Mykonos Town (it's a major shopping area, after all) and near popular clubbing areas such as Paradise Beach.

**BGLTQ+ Resources:** Mykonos is known as a party island with a thriving gay scene. There aren't specific BGLTQ+ resources but the island is clearly very comfortable with openly BGLTQ+ individuals.

## EMERGENCY INFORMATION

**Emergency Number:** 166
**Police:** 100; www.astynomia.gr; tourist police (1571; open daily 24hr).
**US Embassy:** The nearest US Embassy is in Athens (91 Vasilisis Sophias Avenue; 210 7212951).
**Hospitals:** SEA Medical Health Clinic (Aggelika 846 00, Mykonos, 228 9027350).
**Pharmacies:** Mykonos Pharmacy and Ornos Pharmacy (Karamanli Konstantinou, Mykonos; 228 907 8707; www.mykonospharmacy.com; open M-Sa 8am-11pm, Su 9am-9pm).

# ACCOMMODATIONS

### PARADISE BEACH RESORT AND CAMPSITE ($)
Paradise Beach; 228 9022852; reception open 24hr

Paradise is complete with loud music and so many mirrors (which may or may not be a good thing after a

Mykonos-style night out). It's more party complex than hostel—there are two mini-markets, a self-service dining area, and direct access to **Guapaloca** and **Tropicana** (literally the only functional Wi-Fi is on the dance floor, so you have to party)—and the living area is a sprawl of single and double cabins, private rooms, and sparse sleeping bag areas. The privacy is welcome, the showers are well-maintained, and the beds are spacious, but remember: this is a campsite, so there will be ants (and mosquitoes).

*i* Single/double cabins from €18; reservation recommended; no Wi-Fi; BGLTQ+ friendly; secure lockers available; linens included; laundry €5 wash, €1 per 10 minutes dry

### PARAGA BEACH HOSTEL AND CAMPSITE ($)
Paraga Beach; 228 9025915; reception open 24hr

You arrive at Paraga Beach and are immediately captivated. This water! This view! Oh, I'm sorry, I can't sit here? I need to buy something from the restaurant first? Ok, ok. But this pool! These people! Everyone here is dressed to the nines and staying up until 6am. Wait, I can't drink this tap water? I must buy bottled water from the hostel mini-market? Right. But this cabin! It smells like real pine! Oh, there's only two outlets for the six of us? There's only Wi-Fi by the hostel bar where you can't sit unless you buy a drink? Right. Paraga Beach Hostel and Campsite is both a slice of communal heaven and a total trap. You'll see beautiful views, you'll meet beautiful people, you'll party until break of dawn, but you'll pay for every moment of it.

*i* Cabins from €15, double cabins from €18; reservation recommended; no Wi-Fi; BGLTQ+ friendly; lockers available; linens included; laundry facilities €5 wash, €5 dry

# SIGHTS
## CULTURE

### CYCLADIC WINDMILLS
Boni Mill; 228 9026246; open daily July-Sept 4-8pm

A tall white cylinder with a thatched roof and 12 wooden spokes splayed out toward the sea. What is this odd structure that lines the **Old Harbor**? It's a Cycladic windmill, now defunct but still emblematic of Mykonos' rich agricultural past. Though today

---

## SCREEN TO RE(E)L LIFE: *MAMMA MIA!*

I say Greece and you conjure up images of white plaster buildings, blue windows, Mediterranean breezes, and…ABBA? Yes, to many, the tranquil beauty of the Aegean has become synonymous with the Swedish pop group, thanks to the smash Broadway musical *Mamma Mia*. ABBA's association with Greece has become even more entrenched since the film version of the musical was released in 2008. Audiences around the world, but particularly in the US and the UK, flocked to see Meryl Streep prove that she can sing, Pierce Brosnan demonstrate that he cannot, and Amanda Seyfried say "I Do, I Do, I Do," against the backdrop of turquoise water and Mediterranean sun. In the film's case, however, the setting was not a fictional island but a very real one: the tiny island of **Skopelos** (population: 5,000), which was hand-picked by the filmmakers. By all reports, Skopelos is the magical Greek paradise of your Dancing Queen dreams; it is one of the greenest islands in the Aegean, with beaches and over 360 churches to boot. Unfortunately, none of these churches exactly match the set design seen in the film, which has reportedly angered the influx of *Mamma Mia*-enthused tourists to the island. In fact, residents of Skopelos were less than pleased when the cult of ABBA drove throngs of *Mamma Mia* diehards to the island, driving up prices and clogging usually peaceful roads. PSA: you must be Greek Orthodox to marry in a church on Skopelos, so if you're a tourist looking for your dream ABBA wedding, find another island (there are plenty) and hire any cover singer. Guaranteed he'll hit the notes of "S.O.S." better than Pierce Brosnan.

these structures seem more tiki-grain silo than engine of renewable energy, these contraptions once ground the wheat and barley that drove the island's economy. From the sixteenth to the nineteenth century, Mykonos was the main Aegean producer of sea rusk, the hardened bread that could feed sailors for months at sea. Thankfully, Greek cuisine has improved a bit, but the mechanics behind this wind technology are still on display at the Boni Mill in Mykonos's **Agricultural Museum.**

*i* *Free; wheelchair accessible*

### MATOYIANNI STREET

Most stores open around 9am, and close around 1am during high season

What do you get when you combine an upscale suburban shopping mall with Mediterranean stucco and more jewelry boutiques than you've ever seen? Some people's definition of paradise, and also Matoyianni Street, the main shopping boulevard in Mykonos. A narrow cobblestone street lined with bougainvillea-covered buildings, Matoyianni and its neighboring alleys feature designer boutiques, numerous restaurants and gelaterias, and plenty of opportunities to take your next profile picture by a blue-painted door. During high season, some shops will stay open late, and the street will remain brilliantly lit well into the night.

*i* *Prices vary by store; limited wheelchair accessibility*

## LANDMARKS

### ◧CHURCH OF PARAPORTIANI

Mykonos Town Old Harbor

At first glance, the Paraportiani Church looks, well, kind of like your third-grade clay cities project: order and controlled effort in the front, slapdash shapes and lost patience in the back. This is not due to lack of effort on behalf of the Mykonians, but rather to Paraportiani's unique status as the Lunchables of churches—it took five less interesting churches of different styles and layered them together into a plastered whole. Originally intended to mark the side door of Mykonos Town's old fortress (hence the name

Paraportiani, which means "by the door"), the first iteration of the church was established in the fifteenth century.

*i* *Free admission; no wheelchair accessibility*

## MUSEUMS

### MYKONOS FOLKLORE MUSEUM

Mykonos Old Harbor (just north of Paraportiani Church); 228 9022591; open M-Sa 10:30am-2pm and 5:30-8:30pm

Five-hundred-year-old Venetian chest? Check. Old dolls used as mannequins for a nineteenth-century bedroom? Uh, check. Genuine and earnest attempt to communicate the history of Mykonian maritime and domestic life? Definitely, check. At just five rooms packed with antiques, the Mykonian Folklore Museum is not the bland, staid museum display you're accustomed to. In fact, it seems more passion project than coherent museum, which makes the full-size model of a Mykonian sea merchant all the more… interesting. Housed in one of the oldest buildings on the island (it dates back to the Byzantine era), the Mykonian Folklore Museum is a dust-covered step away from the luxury shopping and brand power of Matoyianni Street. The chests, armoires, votives, and ship fragments arranged here are probably worth more than that leather handbag, anyway.

*i* *Free admission, but a small donation is requested; no wheelchair accessibility*

## OUTDOORS

### ◧RENT AN ATV

For those fed up with the bus schedule and comfortable with narrow turns, renting an ATV presents the best and most efficient method to explore Mykonos. Moto rentals are a dime a dozen on the island and most hostels or accommodations will happily arrange a vehicle for you. (Most 24hr rentals cost about €25, depending on the model and your need for speed.) With a clutch and handbrake in your grip, follow your whims on the old roads of the island, past goats, small farms, snack shacks, and numerous unoccupied beaches. Reliable destinations include the beautiful beaches on the bay to the north and the sunset view from **Armenistis Lighthouse** in the northwest corner of the island. Remember, don't fall off, lean into turns, and do not try to speed past buses.

### TRIP TO DELOS

Delos Tours, Kastro Mykonos; 228 9023051; ferry service from Mykonos M 10am and 5pm, Tu-Su 9am, 10am, 11:30am, and 5pm

The island of Delos is barely a square mile in size, but has *casually* been witness to the birth of the god Apollo and his goddess twin Artemis, the meeting point of the Delian League (the alliance of powerful Greek city-states founded in 478 BCE), and the "purification" of dead bodies by cult leaders from Athens (?). Delos has been one of the most important excavation sites in Greece since the French School of Athens began digging in 1872, and you too can witness relics of the island's storied past through a short daytrip from Mykonos. The sights in Delos are numerous and span centuries of history. From the sixth-century BCE **Minoan fountain** to the **Doric Temple** of the Delians to the imposing Terrace of the Lions, Delos occupies a solid half-day of sight-seeing at least.

*i* Round-trip transportation €20, guided tours €20; guided tours available in English daily at 10am and 5pm; limited wheelchair accessibility

# FOOD

### ⬛GIORAS MEDIEVAL WOODEN BAKERY ($)

St. Efthimiou St.; 197; 228 9027784

Need a reminder that Mykonos is freakin' old? The wooden stoves in Gioras' basement bakery have been in commission since 1420. Now one of only a few wooden stoves left in the Cycladic islands, Gioras' whole building was shaped by hand from mud, hay, stone, and wood. If you ask politely, the bakery's owner, George, will show you the massive oven that his family has operated for the past 200 years (that's his grandfather baking bread in the photo above the register). The oven still bakes all of Gioras' homemade cookies and savory pies, and quickly evokes the horror of

*Hansel and Gretel* (*shudder*). On a far less terrifying note, everything looks scrumptious, but the powdered almond balls are especially a gem.

*i* Baked goods from €1, specialty coffees €3-5; vegetarian, or gluten-free options available; no wheelchair accessibility

### JOANNA'S NIKO'S PLACE ($$)

Megali Ammos; 228 9024251; open daily at 10am for drinks, noon-11pm for food

Joanna's Niko's Place is a rarity in Mykonos: an authentic restaurant with delicious, affordable food. This locally-owned taverna boasts a prime beach perch just five minutes from the **Fabrika bus station** in Mykonos Town. Specializing in seafood, Joanna's Niko's is your best bet for enjoying fresh Greek cuisine and the turquoise waves of the Aegean without blowing your Paradise Beach budget. The grilled seafood platter (€14) will feed two, while the fish fillet and vegetables special (€10) will leave you charmed (and a little sleepy) for hours. The side order of grilled pita with olive oil and spices for only €0.50 is a Mykonian treasure. And the sea breeze trailing through the bamboo-roofed porch? Divine. Life is good. Life is dang good.

*i* Salads from €5, entrées from €10, drinks €2-5, 1L house wine €10; vegetarian options available; limited wheelchair accessibility

### TASOS TAVERNA ($$)

Paraga Beach; 228 9023002; open daily 10am-11pm

You can't live on the Paraga hostel mini-market or the over-priced pizzas of Paradise Beach forever. Luckily, an alternative lies just steps away from the Paraga Beach campsite in the form of Tasos Taverna. By most metrics, Tasos is an unremarkable taverna, but compared to camp food, it's nearly luxurious. The seafood is decent, the entrées reasonably priced (for Mykonos, at least), and it's literally on the sands of Snap Story-worthy Paraga Beach. In short, Tasos provides a convenient and (depending on your order) nutritious option for those partying/recovering in the beach hostels who don't feel like weathering

another roller-coaster bus ride into town.

*i* *Appetizers from €5, salads from €9, entrées from €10, beer and wine €4-7; vegetarian options available; no wheelchair accessibility*

# NIGHTLIFE

## ARGO

Kouzi Georgouli 43; 695 7149413; open M-Sa 8pm-5am, Su 8pm-midnight

Bright-white walls to match the street outside. Panel after panel behind the bar stocked with bottles. Pounding music without blinding strobe lights. People spilling out of the door, dancing, at 3:15am. Welcome to Argo, the seemingly reserved yet most raucous late-night party in Mykonos. The drinks are strong, the staff welcoming, and the mood that euphoric feeling you get just before you realize how tired you are. Who ever said nothing good happens after 2am? Party on.

*i* *Drinks €7-9, cocktails €10; BGLTQ+ friendly; limited wheelchair accessibility*

## PARADISE BEACH

Tropicana Beach Bar: 228 9023582, Guapaloca Mykonos: 697 3016311; Tropicana Beach Bar open daily 10am-5am and Guapaloca Mykonos open daily 10am-4am

Anyone who's been to Mykonos will tell you that Paradise Beach is where the party happens. They're not wrong. During high season (end of June-Sept), the drinks pour and the beats pound from sun-down to sun-up and back again. Though technically divided into two establishments, Tropicana and Guapaloca, on a strip of Caribbean-style sand, the beach bars and their overpriced self-service restaurant run together, much like the endless cycle of remixes from the DJ booth. Shirtless men pour €14 cocktails at the Guapaloca bar. The DJ somehow fits a beat to even the most untouchable classic rock songs. Bikini-clad women cling to poles on Tropicana tables. And crowds of beach-goers from around the globe look as though they're having the time of their lives. Oh wait, that girl dancing on the bar lost her bikini top. She is unfazed. Welcome to Paradise Beach.

*i* *Tropicana Beach Bar: no cover, cocktails from €10, self-service restaurant entrées from €10; Guapaloca: no cover, cocktails from €13, beer €10; BGLTQ+ friendly*

## SKANDINAVIAN BAR AND DISCO

Georgouli; 228 9022669; open daily 8pm-6am (or when the crowd thins)

Skandinavian Bar and Disco is the island of Mykonos in miniature: a charming blue-and-white slice of the Aegean by day, and a raging party by night. The largest and most popular town-square-hangout-turned-bar-turned-club on the island, Skandinavian is the heart of the late-night scene in Mykonos Town, where hardcore clubs rub up against luxury shops and cheap gyro joints. Skandinavian's multi-story, L-shaped layout has a little bit for everyone: lose yourself to the beat drops and strobe lights at the club upstairs or lounge at the wooden tables outside.

*i* *Beer €6-7, spirits €9-10, cocktails €10, special shots €4-5; you must buy a drink to enter the club level upstairs; BGLTQ+ friendly; no swimsuits*

# SANTORINI

Coverage by **Adrian Horton**

There's no getting around the blue-and-white-stuccoed, cliffhanging truth besetting your eyes—Santorini is a visual wonder. Cycladic buildings and patios cling to the cliff face, hundreds of feet above the sparkling Aegean water. Donkeys carry goods (and people) through tight whitewashed streets as the setting sun illuminates the jostled homes of an old seaside village. In many snapshots—both the literal and the mental you take while strolling along the caldera's edge—Santorini seems like a fairy-tale place. At least, until the tour buses show up. Yes, the legend of Santorini's beauty stretches far and wide, drawing a horde of visitors to the once-sleepy island every summer. Though the crowds can be large and have pushed parts of Santorini (namely, Fira) to the outright bland touristy, Santorini remains a cultural and geographic treasure to be adored. So lounge in the sun, marvel at the cliffs, or find your own route to witness the famous sunset—the storybook magic of Santorini awaits, no matter how many random vacationers stray into your photographs.

## ORIENTATION

Santorini is shaped like a jagged, westward-facing "C" in the heart of the **Aegean Sea.** The island used to be circular, but a massive volcanic eruption thousands of years ago formed the caldera, a deep hole filled with sea water in the island's former center. The inner curve of the "C" traces the caldera and is lined with Santorini's famous cliffs. The port of **Thira** rests at the base of the cliffs in the center of the cresent. Switchback roads lead up and north from Thira to Santorini's capital city, **Fira,** which bumps up against the cliff edge at the midpoint of the "C." The famous sunset city of **Oia** also clings to the cliffs on the island's northwestern tip. On the other end of Santorini is **Perissa,** a beach town that faces south, away from the caldera. Santorini's airport lies on a flat stretch of grass on the island's eastern side, near the smaller resort town of **Kamari.**

## ESSENTIALS

### GETTING THERE

Public buses run from the Thera Port to Fira town roughly every hour. One trip takes around 40-50min. and costs €1.80. Private transport directly to a hostel or hotel can be arranged through numerous tourist companies at the port, and will cost about €15. Buses leave from Santorini Airport for Fira about every 90min. from 7:10am to 10:20pm. Check the bus schedule posted in the terminal for exact times. Tickets cost €1.80.

### GETTING AROUND

The major points of interest for tourists in Santorini—Perissa, Fira, Oia, Akrotiri, and Thera and Athinos ports—are connected by a public bus network with very talented drivers. Schedules are posted online at www.

ktel-santorini.gr and at bus stations. Most routes operate from about 7am-10pm, with tickets priced between €1.80 and €2.50. For questions or concerns, call the local bus network at 228 6025404. Other than by bus, the best way to explore Santorini is to rent a vehicle—bicycle, ATV, scooter, or car. Rental rates vary per company, but most will lease an ATV for 24hr (€15-€20).

### PRACTICAL INFORMATION

**Tourist Offices:** No central tourism office, but several private companies can help arrange tours or provide practical information, including Daktouros Travel in Fira (228 6022958) and Santo Sun in Perissa (228 6081456).

**Banks/ATMs/Currency Exchange:** ATMs are available across the island, especially in more crowded areas such as Fira or Oia. In addition, there are five banks with establishments on the island such as Agrotiki Bank (228 6022261) and Eurobank (228 6025851)

**Post Offices:** Hellenic Post (Oia 847 02; open M-Sa 9am-2pm).

**Internet:** Santorini provides public (functional) Wi-Fi in busy areas, such as the main shopping area of Fira and bus stations. Internet cafés are also popular and clustered around the caldera cities.

## EMERGENCY INFORMATION

**Emergency:** 166
**Police:**
- Thira: 228 602 2649
- Oia: 228 607 1954

**US Embassy:** The nearest US Embassy is in Athens (91 Vasilisis Sophias Avenue; 210 721 2951).

**Hospitals:** Health Center Central Clinic of Santorini, Fira (228 6021728)

**Pharmacies:**
- Fira: (228 6023444)
- Kamari (228 6032440)
- Oia (228 6071464)

# ACCOMMODATIONS

### ▨CAVELAND ($)

Karterados; 228 6022122; www.cave-land. com; reception open 8am-10:30pm

The name "Caveland" suggests an amusement park, which is appropriate for this playground of sun, caves, and relaxation. With two adorable hostel collies, spacious rooms built into old caves, and the best hostel shower we've ever seen, Caveland treats you far better than the grubby backpacker you are. Plus, there's a large pool with a view of the stucco-dotted hills sloping down to the sea. And, wait, Caveland offers yoga classes (€8) and private massages? *Is this a hostel or a retreat?* The only potential downside to staying here is that it's a 25-minute walk from the center of **Fira**. But after a few weeks on the road, you'll gladly walk a mile for all that shower space.

*i* *Dorms from €18, private rooms from €60; reservation recommended during high season; cash only; Wi-Fi; limited wheelchair accessibility; linens included; laundry facilities; free breakfast*

### FIRA BACKPACKER'S PLACE ($$)

Fira downtown, behind Coffee Island; 2286031626; www.firabackpackers.com; reception open 8am-11pm

For all its stunning daytime views and vacationing families, Santorini also knows how to throw down at night—a scene bolstered by the transient crowd at Fira Backpacker's Place. By day, the hostel functions as a convenient base for all of Santorini's sunlit activities, as it's located a few meters from a coffee joint, ATV rental companies, and **Fira's** numerous shopping streets. By night, Fira Backpacker's patio rings with laughter as newly acquainted travelers prepare to bar crawl through the city's few late-night stops. Although slightly more expensive than other Santorini hostels, Fira Backpacker's provides prime real estate and new friends to split your six-pack with over cards. Who needs good Wi-Fi when you have a game of Kings to play?

*i* *Dorms from €30, private rooms from €100; reservation recommended; BGLTQ+ friendly; no wheelchair accessibility; Wi-Fi; lockers provided; towels included; laundry facilities; kitchen*

# SIGHTS

## CULTURE

### SANTO WINERY

Pirgos, Thira; 228 6028058; open daily 9am-9pm

Like its tomatoes, Santorini's grapes present their own distinctive flavor (we detect a slight hint of smoke, perhaps?). These special grapes translate, naturally, into upscale wineries with cliff-side views of the island. If this sounds too upscale for your budget, don't fret—you and your slightly wrinkled clothing can still snag a seat at the glass patio table, as the flights at Santo Winery skew towards the relatively inexpensive end of Santorini's wine tasting spectrum. (Or, just order a coffee.) At Santo, you can tour the processing facilities, shop for local products, eat a more-expensive-than-necessary meal, or just brainstorm fancy adjectives for the *mellifluous* white wine you sip as you gaze across the Mediterranean.

*i* *Flight of six wines €14.50, €26 for 12 wines, €36 for 18 wines; pairing salads*

You can only get away with using "caldera" as a synonym for "sunset" or "view" for so long, so what exactly is every restaurant advertisement and earth science geek talking about? Technically, a caldera is a volcanic crater—like a cauldron formed when an explosion causes the peak of a mountain to collapse. Technically, Santorini is a collection of five islands formed by various eruptions of the same volcano. The main island, known as Santorini but actually named Thera, earned its half-moon shape in the eruption you've already heard so much about—the spectacular one that occurred 3,500 years ago, buried the flourishing Minoan civilization at Akrotiri, and probably altered climate patterns for a bit, as eruptions are wont to do. Thirasia and Aspronisi, two islands on Thera's periphery, were also shaped by this eruption, while minor volcanic activity in the sixteenth and seventeenth centuries gave rise to the two Kameni islands in the caldera's center

Wait, does this mean that modern-day Santorini rests on the lip of a living volcano? Indeed it does. There have been numerous earthquakes and smaller eruptions since the behemoth that dispelled Akrotiri, some more deadly than others. Since humans resettled on Thera, at least 11 smaller eruptions have toppled homes and scared people back to the mainland. The most recent event occurred in 1956, when a 7.7 magnitude earthquake—one of the biggest ever recorded in the Aegean reign—struck Santorini and seriously damaged its cliff-side villages. Over 300 homes were destroyed as landslides decimated the towns of Fira and Oia. The island has since recovered; however, since it rests above one of the most seismically active places in the world, another quake is, technically, only a matter of time.

If this freaks you out a bit, good! The earth is powerful. But don't worry too much—scientists track the area for signs of eruption, and crafty Greeks have reinforced their buildings with steel and concrete to better withstand the next quake. You're far more likely to enjoy the cliffs of Santorini with a strong cocktail than strong tremors.

*and entrées from €9; other drinks from €3; wheelchair accessible*

## LANDMARKS

### 🏛AKROTIRI
Thera; 228 6081366; open M-W 8am-8pm, Th 8am-3pm, F-Su 8am-8pm

Hostel "Never Have I Ever" games can get intense, but nothing tops the crazy story that Akrotiri has to share. The excavation site on Santorini's southern end used to be a flourishing settlement of about 30,000 people back when the island didn't have a caldera-shaped hole in the middle. About 3,500 years ago, the Minoans occupied Akrotiri with frecoses and pottery. Then—no one knows exactly when or why—the people disappeared. Then, the town disappeared, buried under volcanic ash from ancient **Thera's** massive eruption. Today, visitors can tour the excavation site, a Greek treasure and active investigation since 1967. Thanks to the preservative qualities of the ash, Akrotiri spills more secrets than less volcanic archaeological sites, and you can view remarkably intact frescoes and mosaics.

*i* *Tickets €12, €6 student; last entry 30 min. before closing; wheelchair accessible*

### ANCIENT THERA
Located on a ridge of the steep of Messavouno Mountain; 228 6032474; open Tu-Su 8am-3pm

Long after the volcano stopped **Akrotiri** in its tracks, ancient Thera took up the reins as the island's most active settlement. Founded by Doric settlers from (This! Is!) Sparta (!) 600 or so years after the dust settled on Akrotiri, Thera served as a garrison for the Ptolemaic (Egyptian) navy and a port for the Roman province of Asia. But, it wasn't easy lugging groceries up that hill. The area was abandoned in the eighth century CE and only uncovered by German archaeologists in 1895. Today, visitors can explore another iteration of the Roman agora, a second-century theater, sacred temple remains, and evidence of the Ptolemaic headquarters.

*i* *Tickets €4, €2 reduced; tours available every hour from 9am-1pm*

## OUTDOORS

### PERISSA BLACK BEACHES
Open daily 24hr

While the caldera half of Santorini is all cliff-hanging drama and rocky terrain, the eastern half of the island stretches horizontally into flat land and expansive beaches. But it can't be Santorini without some sort of environmental plot twist. That white color you're used to seeing along the shoreline? It's missing—replaced by a line of black sand (well, more accurately, bits of rock), courtesy of the island's volcanic past. Perissa's miles of dark coastline welcome vacationers looking for some sun and warmth without the chlorine of hostel pools. For even more natural wonder, check out Perissa's **Red Beach,** also a product of volcanic deposits in the soil. The Red Beach has been restricted since a landslide occurred in 2015, but can still be partially accessed from a road near the site of **Akrotiri.**

### SUNSET IN OIA

Odds are that you've seen a picture of the sunset over Santorini. Odds are even greater than that picture was taken from Oia, the gorgeous cliff town on Santorini's northwestern edge, where visitors flock each evening to witness the sun sink behind the caldera. People take this event so seriously—some even stake out spots hours ahead of time—that you wonder if, perhaps, it's a bit overhyped. The sunset is, indeed, beautiful, but there are plenty of other perches on the caldera edge from which to watch it (namely the lighthouse on the island's southwestern tip, frequented by more locals than tourists). There's something to be said, though, for the communal experience of dusk in Oia—the collective gasp when the sun skims the horizon, or the collective groan when a cloud blocks the view.

## FOOD

### KALIMERA KALINIXTA
Erythrou Stavrou, Fira; 228 6024194; open daily 8am-8pm (until midnight July/Aug)

There are, unsurprisingly, a very large number of potential dessert shops in Fira. Many are overpriced gelaterias, some are frozen yogurt shops indistinguishable from the ones found in your run-of-the-mill American mall. And then there's Kalimera Kalinixta, the new kid on the block with old-school Greek pastries, strong coffee, and underused balcony seating. Founded in early 2017 by pastry chef extraordinaire Markos, Kalimera Kalinixta specializes in a traditional creation of folded filo dough, some layered with sweets (chocolate, ground nuts, and syrup), others with savory (cheese, Markos' own mixture of ground meat). Its sleek interior speaks to a modern audience, but the secret behind the pastries' crunchy, melt-in-your-mouth brilliance is time. Watch Markos himself demonstrate for you using the fresh dough behind the register.

*i* *Pastries by weight, coffee €2.50-4; vegetarian options available; limited wheelchair accessibility*

### NIKOLAS TAVERNA
Erythrou Stavrou, Fira; 228 6024550; open daily 12pm-11pm

During the high season, the quiet town of Fira bustles with enough travelers to fill any number of restaurants, regardless of price or cuisine. Many establishments have transformed to cater to the crowds, but Nikolas Taverna, open since 1955, remains wed to a tried and true formula: quality food, not too expensive. Somewhat hidden on one of Fira's main shopping streets, Nikolas offers a peaceful atmosphere—pastel-colored interior, upstairs seating away from the street—without the price of a sunset view, which could cost you a night of accommodation, at least. The food is **classic Greek taverna,** which could get old unless done well; luckily Nikolas has a reputation for mastering the classics, particularly *moussaka* and grilled sea bream.

*i* *Starters from €6, entrées €8, drinks from €5; vegetarian options available; wheelchair accessible*

### ΨΗΣΤΑΡΙΑ Ο ΣΤΑΥΡΟΣ ("CROWN CROSS")
Epar. Om. Firon-Ormou Perissa; open daily until 11pm

Crown Cross lacks numerous restaurant features familiar to the Western traveler: a clear sign for its name, a list of regular hours, a searchable address on Google Maps, and a name that processes in Google Translate. What does it have? Twelve golden-brown chickens roasting in the window, a crowd of locals, and some curious tourists filling its patio. Here, the roasting spits are steaming, the portions heaping, and the staff gregariously Greek (though also a little overstretched—service can be very slow). The language barrier is alive and well here (so you know it's not a tourist trap) but do not fret—"souvlaki," "chicken," "pork," and "gyro" translate,

and you can trust that your €2.50 will be well-spent.

## NIGHTLIFE

### MURPHY'S SPORTS BAR
Erythrou Stavrou; 228 6022248; open daily noon-6am

On a weekend night during high season, Murphy's is packed—with backpackers, with bar crawlers, and tourists seduced by the tempting two-for-one cocktail advertisements. There's nothing groundbreaking or revelatory about Murphy's—it's an Irish sports pub, complete with dark wood furnishings, TVs blaring the latest sporting event, and a Jack Daniel's flag hanging from the rafters. It's appeal, however, with its watery drinks and greasy, non-Greek pub food (chicken nuggets, burgers), can at times be difficult to find. But the crowds keep coming, and they seem to have a good time.

*i* *No cover, shots €3-5, drinks €5-7, cocktails €9; cash only*

### TWO BROTHERS
Dekigala, Thera; 228 6023061; www.2brothersbarsantorini.com; open daily 5pm-when the crowd thins

Two Brothers does not let you escape its notice. "Three euro shots! LITs €5!" scream posters on its exterior. "Woohoo" and "ahhh!!" scream the people inside. Founded by—you guessed it—two brothers in 1983, this relatively small bar remains reliably packed on weekend nights, as an array of visitors dance and laugh under the United Nations of flags and old records. The drinks are cheap and highly encouraged by Two Brother's' affable bartenders, so chances are you'll be ready to join the crowd shortly after crossing the threshold.

*i* *Beer from €3, LITs and some cocktails €5, mixed drinks €3-7*

# THESSALONIKI

Coverage by **Adrian Horton**

Thessaloniki is that actor in every movie you can never place—you don't know his name, but his face is familiar, his character well-formed, and his performance memorable—the Stanley Tucci of cities, so to speak. When it comes to Greek cities, megawatt Athens usually steals the show, but second-fiddle Thessaloniki has built a name for itself, one Byzantine church, packed café, and raging nightclub at a time. Thessaloniki's colorful church mosaics and Turkish-influenced cuisine are but two windows into the city's pluralistic past. Since its founding, Thessaloniki has been home to numerous religious and cultural traditions, from pagan to Christian to Muslim, Greek to Turkish to Macedonian. Only a part of the Greek state for just over a century, Thessaloniki greets visitors today with its own curious mix of history and modernity—wide, centrally-planned streets lead to mazes with Ottoman castles while former port buildings pound with techno beats and neon lights. So catch the sunset from the old city walls, nurse a frappe with locals, find your new favorite cocktail at 5am, or all of the above—in Thessaloniki, it's not a story without a good plot twist.

# ORIENTATION

Thessaloniki faces southwest, with the popular harbor-front walk tracing a like from northwest to southeast. The flat area of Thessaloniki closest to the sea mostly burned down in a fire in 1917; as a result, this part of the city was rebuilt in a familiar grid layout. The center city of Thessaloniki is bounded by the former wharf area, known today as **Ladadika,** a popular clubbing neighborhood, and by the city's most prominent monument, **The White Tower.** In the middle of this harbor line is **Aristotelous Square,** the redesigned city center. Roman and Byzantine monuments dot the map northwest and east of Aristotelous Square. Encompassing Thessaloniki are the hills of **Ano Poli** (Upper Town), the formerly Ottoman neighborhood, which was spared by the 1917 fire and still confuses visitors with its maze of narrow, unmarked streets. Thessaloniki's suburbs extend along the coastline, particularly to the southeast, where the airport is located.

# ESSENTIALS

## GETTING THERE

From Thessaloniki International Airport (SKG), take the public bus line #78 or 78N towards the city center (such as Aristoleus Square, which is conveniently located for numerous public bus lines). Tickets cost €2 and can be purchased at the kiosk in the right of the bus stop when walking out of the terminal. Be sure to validate your ticket on the bus.

## GETTING AROUND

Thessaloniki has numerous public bus lines that form a web throughout the city. Buses run from 5am-12:30am and cost between €1.10-2.00 depending on the route. Be sure to bring coins to purchase tickets on the bus, and try to be exact—the machines don't give change. For more information, visit www.ktelmacedonia.gr or call 059 5533.

## PRACTICAL INFORMATION

**Tourist Offices:** The Tourist Information Booth is located in the center of Aristoleus Square (open M-F 9am-9pm).
**Banks/ATMS/Currency Exchange:** ATMs are available throughout Thessaloniki.
**Post Offices:** Hellenic Post (Tsimski 117; open M-F 8am-2pm).
**Internet:** There is no reliable public Wi-Fi, but Internet cafés abound.

## EMERGENCY INFORMATION

**Emergency Number:** 166
**Police:** Aristotelous 18; 231 0253341; emergency number 100
**US Embassy:** The nearest US Embassy is in Athens (91 Vasilisis Sophias Avenue; 210 721 2951).
**Hospitals:** AHEPA Hospital (Kiriakidi 1; 231 3303110).
**Pharmacies:** Pharmacies are located throughout the city. Typical hours are M-F 8am-2pm, 5pm-8:30pm, Sa 8am-2pm.

# ACCOMMODATIONS

### LITTLE BIG HOUSE GUESTHOUSE AND CAFÉ ($)

Andokidou 24; 231 3014323; www.littlebighouse.gr; reception open 8am-11pm

On a cobblestoned slope of Thessaloniki's **Old Quarter** and beneath an Ottoman castle resides Little Big House, a magical café-turned-hostel that is light on the wallet but heavy on the charm. Its front half is the cozy, homespun coffee shop you didn't know you missed, complete with artful sugar packet arrangements, acoustic Spotify playlists, and homemade apple pie. In the back half of the building, guests stay in rooms supplied with full kitchens, fridges, and functional Wi-Fi. Guests and locals alike sip frappes (free upon arrival) and lounge on the fabulously cozy rooftop patio.

*i* Dorms €17-19, private double €48; reservation recommended; BGLTQ+ friendly; no wheelchair accessibility; Wi-Fi; towels included; laundry facilities; free breakfast

### RENTROOMS THESSALONIKI ($)

9 Melenikou K. Street; 231 0204080; www.rentrooms-thessaloniki.com; reception open 8am-11:30pm

Amidst the multi-story apartment buildings and pedestrian traffic of Thessaloniki's center city, RentRooms provides a welcome (and caffeinated) respite from the city's miles and miles of pavement. Its apartment quarters sit atop a backyard café, which spills into the gardens surrounding the **Roman Rotunda** and features cushioned picnic tables, reliable internet, and ivy-covered walls. A stop at RentRooms checks every box in the Weary Backpacker's Recovery Kit: clean bed, room to stretch in the shower, a view of something very old, and strong coffee. Once you've recharged, walk south to the **White Tower** and seaside promenade, or west to the bars and cafés surrounding the old **Roman Agora**—they're all just five minutes away.

*i* Dorms €17-19, private rooms from €55; reservation recommended; BGLTQ+ friendly; no wheelchair accessibility; Wi-Fi; lockers provided; towels included; laundry facilities; free breakfast

# SIGHTS

## CULTURE

### ANO POLI

While the flat center of Thessaloniki stretches with the tropes of a modern city (grid layout, legible street signs, multiple Starbucks), the sloping neighborhood of Ano Poli barricades its tradition in the hills above town. Ano Poli was spared when the rest of the city burned down in 1917, and thus demonstrates the old Ottoman character that used to infuse much of Thessaloniki. Here, ochre and terracotta-colored homes mingle with antique Turkish lamps and *Rebetika* folk music. There are very few cars, plenty of cats, and several Turkish-influenced cafés on Ano Poli's steep streets. Looming above it all is the "Yenti Koule," the Ottoman fortress on the city's original walls that draws a crowd each evening for sunset.

*i* Free; limited wheelchair accessibility

## LANDMARKS

### ⬛THE AGIA SOPHIA

22 Agia Sofia; 231 0270253; www.agias-ophia.info; open M 1pm-7:30pm, Tu-Su 8am-7:30pm (there may be siesta breaks)

Thessaloniki offers an array of Byzantine structures (some marked, some not, some in the middle of busy intersections), but the Agia Sophia reigns as Queen Bee. Though smaller and less ornate than its predecessor in Istanbul, Thessaloniki's Agia Sophia still impresses with its copper dome, ceiling mosaics, and ridiculously ornate chandelier. An average Christian worship site when it was first built in the eighth century CE, the Agia Sophia became cool in 1205, when the Crusaders turned it into a cathedral. It had a phase as a mosque, then was converted back to a church after the Greek annexation in 1912. The Agia Sophia can be a pain to visit (see: neck cramp from looking at the ceiling), but it's far more enthralling than a museum.

*i* Admission €6, free student; wheelchair accessible

## THE WHITE TOWER

Thessaloniki; 231 0267832; open Tu-Su 8:30am-3pm

The White Tower is Thessaloniki's prized symbol, perhaps more for its multilayered cultural heritage than its height (at seven stories, it barely qualifies as a tower in the year 2017). What it lacks in stature, however, it recoups with its imposing history. Likely first constructed by the Venetians in the twelfth century, the Tower was officially built in 1430 by the Ottoman conquerors, who used it as a prison and execution venue. When Greece annexed Thessaloniki from the Ottoman Empire in 1912, they promptly whitewashed the building and its murderous past, adopting it as the symbol of the city. Today, the (off-) White Tower serves mainly as an oft-pictured orientation point along the harbor walk. It also houses a museum dedicated to the history of Thessaloniki.

*i* Free; limited wheelchair accessibility

# MUSEUMS

## ◪ARCHAEOLOGICAL MUSEUM OF THESSALONIKI

6 Manoli Andronikou Street; 231 3310201; www.amth.gr; open daily 8am-8pm

With its numerous churches and crumbling brick archways, Thessaloniki wears its Byzantine and Roman hearts on its sleeve. Lesser known is Thessaloniki's history as a prehistoric human settlement. The city's Archaeological Museum, based a few blocks from the **White Tower,** attempts to unspool the long thread of Macedonian history from cave people to **Alexander the Great** to wealthy Roman merchants who paid for their own public sculptures. The prehistoric section of the museum contains archaeological finds from the **Neolithic Era** (spears!), while the Macedonian section displays more familiar museum fare, such as Roman marbles, mosaics, and a second-century CE female skeleton with preserved hair.

*i* Admission €8, €4 student; wheelchair accessible

## THE MUSEUM OF BYZANTINE CULTURE

2 Stratou Avenue; 231 3306400; www.mbp.gr; open daily 8am-8pm

Thessaloniki throws around the term "Byzantine." a lot, which makes you wonder: what was the period actually like? Any building in the city (usually a church) or artwork (usually gold-plated) dates to the Byzantine Empire, a continuation of the eastern half of the Roman Empire after **Constantine** moved the capital to his namesake city, Constantinople, in 330 CE. The Byzantine era, which lasted until the Turks took over in 1453, witnessed the transformation of Greece from a pagan center to a stronghold of Christianity. The Museum of Byza ntine Culture traces this shift, as many Greeks said bye to Zeus and hello to Jesus while still maintaining numerous cultural traditions.

*i* Tickets €8, €4 student; wheelchair accessible

# OUTDOORS

## CLIMBING MT. OLYMPUS

One of the more endearing aspects of Greek mythology is how the gods, for all their might, could be irrationally, stubbornly human. They got jealous and cheated on each other. They got lustful and had ill-advised affairs with mortal farm boys. And they lived on a scalable mountain peak, Mt. Olympus, which even you—a mere mortal—can visit, so long as you have two days to spare, good shoes, and an ability to read trail maps. Buses from Thessaloniki run to **Litohoro,** a village at the base of Mt. Olympus, daily. Day trippers can hike from there to **Pironia,** a village 11km up the path, and head back to the city after inhaling some stunning views and mountainside coffee. More serious hikers can arrange to stay in one of the mountain refuge hostels for about €12 a night, then summit Olympus the next day (be sure to choose a path suitable to your hiking experience—one requires a helmet for loose rock).

*i* Bus, hostel, and rental prices vary; no wheelchair accessibility

# FOOD

## 🔖GARBANZO ($)

Agnostou Stratiotou 6; 231 3075892; open daily noon-midnight

Trying to save money but still craving something fresh and inventive? Well, Garbanzo is calling your name. Centrally located next to the old **Roman Agora,** this self-service start-up with window bar seating specializes in customizable falafel pitas—your combo, your way. Just pick the sauce (classics such as hummus and *baba gannouj,* or more daring options like the crazy house blend), add as many veggies and hot sauce squirts as you want, and voila! A filling vegetarian meal on the go, for only €2.80 (€4 if you skip the bread).

*i* *Sandwiches €2.80, platters €4, salads €4, beer €1.50, cocktails €4; vegetarian options available; wheelchair accessible*

## REDIVIVA CUCINA POVERA ($)

Alexandras Papadopoulou 70; 231 3067400; open daily noon-2am

While some restaurants tiptoe around a radically re-envisioned menu, Rediviva dives right in. Rediviva offers dense wheat bread with a variety of accompaniments, such as scrumptious eggplant salad, revamped *tzatziki* sauce, and freshly ground hummus. Seafood? Not merely grilled fish here, but sardines and pesto wrapped in vine leaves (€7), octopus salad with rock samphire and fennel (€8), and squid stuffed with pine nuts and raisins (€11). Rediviva's open kitchen and lightly-colored interior breathe easily, while its canopied patio across the street offers an intimate take on the old **Ano Poli** neighborhood.

*i* *Starters €3-7, entrées €6-12; vegetarian options available; wheelchair accessible*

## TAVERNA IGGLI'S

32 Irodotou; 231 3011967; open daily 12:30pm-12:30am

Taverna Iggli's appears almost out of nowhere in the maze of **Ano Poli.** There's a hill, a few TVs blaring from open apartment windows, a crew of cats, and then: Iggli's, chilling on a corner with its trellis-covered patio. If the antique lamps and open kitchen don't persuade you that Iggli's is the real Greek-taverna deal, then the **complimentary raki shots** and revelatory roasted zucchini salad will. The best part? Everything on the menu—Middle Eastern-inspired specials included—is €8 or less. Iggli's has built a reputation for serving up reliably satisfying local treasures. The dishes are memorable, the atmosphere intimate, and the staff disarmingly enthusiastic about their food.

*i* *Appetizers €3-5, specials €5-8, drinks €4-6; vegetarian options available; wheelchair accessible*

# NIGHTLIFE

## BERLIN

Chrisostomou Smyrnis 10; 231 0221223; open Su-Th midnight-9am, F-Sa 10:30pm-9am

Thessaloniki can be a leisurely city, from coffee breaks to long strolls along the harbor to the way its nightlife scene ambles slowly to bed around breakfast. While some bars attempt a normal schedule and die down around 2am, Berlin keeps the rock vibes jamming until late (early?) in the morning (night?). Named after the Lou Reed album, not the German capital, Berlin blends the two associations with its rock posters, extensive beer selection, well-loved wooden bar, and red-eye hours. The question of tourist or local is irrelevant at Berlin; if you're a fan of music from before the year 2000, come on in.

*i* *No cover, drinks €6-7*

## LA DOZE

1 Villara Street; 231 0532986; open daily 8pm-late

Part art gallery, part local bar, part cocktail factory, part dance club, La Doze is the oversubscribed student who still manages to excel at every extracurricular AND let loose on the weekends. Part of a stretch of bumping bars and clubs on **Valaritou Street,** La Doze mixes crowds and over 100 cocktails every night as one of Thessaloniki's hippest spots. The rotating art displays, mood lighting, and well-stocked bar draw in artists, drink enthusiasts, and R&B dance clubbers alike, so the vibe depends on the night. Keep an open mind, hold on to your cocktail, and keep up with the cool crowd, if you can.

*i* *Drinks €6.50-8, cocktails €7*

# GREECE ESSENTIALS

## MONEY

**Currency:** Although many are aware, few are keen to acknowledge that Greece is saddled in debt. This has led to much controversy over Greece's status in the eurozone. The country still uses the euro as of August 2017, but be sure to check the news before you go.

**Taxes:** Currently, the value-added tax (VAT) in Greece is 24%, with a 13% excise tax on tobacco, fuel, and alcohol.

## SAFETY AND HEALTH

**Local Laws and Police:** Many parts of Greece, especially Athens and the popular vacation islands, are accustomed to tourists, but make no mistake—illegal behavior will not be taken lightly. Don't drink and drive or behave indecently, as these actions could result in fines or imprisonment. Purchase of pirated goods (CDs, DVDs) can result in heavy fines, as does stealing rock or material from ancient sites. Though Greece decriminalized homosexuality in 1951, it is still frowned upon socially in some areas of the country. However, in urban areas and some islands, especially Mykonos, attitudes towards the BGLTQ+ community have changed rapidly, and gay and lesbian hotels, bars, and clubs have an increased presence.

**Drugs and Alcohol:** Attitudes towards alcohol are fairly blasé in Greece, and most visitors can obtain it easily. Drugs are a different story. Conviction for possession, use, or trafficking of drugs, including marijuana, can result in heavy fines or imprisonment. Authorities are particularly vigilant near the Turkish and Albanian borders.

**Natural Disasters:** Greece hovers above one of the most seismically active areas on Earth, and thus experiences (relatively) frequent and powerful earthquakes. Adrian, our Researcher-Writer, was in Greece during the last serious earthquake on June 12, 2017, which struck the island of Lesbos. The quake killed one, injured ten, and caused serious damage across the island. In sum: earthquakes can occur at random and at times in serious fashion. If one occurs during your visit, protect yourself by standing under a sturdy surface (e.g. doorway, desk, or table) and open a door to provide an escape route.

**Demonstrations and Political Gatherings:** Strikes and demonstrations occur frequently in Greece, especially during the ever-deepening debt crisis. Most demonstrations are peaceful but a few have escalated into more dangerous protests. A strike in May 2011, for example, degenerated into a summer of riots and violent clashes with police that involved tear gas and stun grenades. Public transport and air traffic control can occasionally halt without warning due to union strikes. If a demonstration or tense political situation does occur during your trip, it is advisable to avoid the area of the city where it is taking place and or head for the islands, where things are typically more peaceful.

# HUNGARY

**In Hungary you will find an amalgam of a place, constructed from the cultures that have collided here.** At the end of the ninth century, a federation of Hungarian tribes, nomads united under Árpád—the single-named precursor to the world's Madonnas and Chers, whose progeny would rule Hungary for the next near-millennium—conquered the Carpathian Basin and established Hungary as their own. Next, the country came under Ottoman rule for just over 150 years in the sixteenth and seventeenth centuries, before being seized by the Habsburgs. The Habsburg monarchy tightened the country's relationship to Austria, as well as the other territories under Habsburg rule, which today number parts of at least 13 modern countries. Finally, the Austro-Hungarian Empire established by the Habsburgs defined the region until its dissolution following WWI. As the territory changed hands, each new culture left a legacy in Hungary. The Hungarian tribes established an ethnic and cultural unity that gave form to early Hungarian identity; the Ottoman Empire left a land populated with Turkish bathhouses and thermal spas; and if not for trying to upstage the Austrians, the Hungarian State Opera in Budapest may never have been so opulent. These legacies also combined to have great influence on Hungary's architectural landscape. Heavily constructed in Baroque style, this aesthetic lovechild of a million affairs frequently incorporates Ottoman influences as well. The Hungarian Parliament Building, meanwhile, is a behemoth work of Gothic design. Especially in Hungary's urban centers, these historic forms sit beside works of modern design, skate parks, and several-story Coca-Cola super-billboards, so the country seems planted on a fault line between distant centuries. Walking the streets, you are as likely to stroll past old people smoking pipes and gossiping on benches as you are to pass trendy millennials with gauged ears and skateboards. (There is little obscurity like the existence of 45-year-olds in Hungary.) Spend your days soaking in thermal baths or public fountains, your meals pounding goulash and renowned wines, and your nights partying in Budapest's ruin pubs, the ultimate culmination of this age collision which merges the club scene with the vestiges of past architectural lives.

343

# BUDAPEST

Coverage by **Antonia Washington**

Budapest is a city that feels lived in: an urban center that isn't manicured, where the people you meet, even in the city center, are often as likely locals as visitors. It's a place where people unapologetically sit back and enjoy the summer, and although it has an inexplicable amount of advertisements for "Thai massage," it also has an optimistic amount of gelato stands. Budapest is a city where entire crowds spontaneously climb up and lounge upon the massive steel beams of Szabadság híd (Liberty Bridge). After witnessing such a scene, we're tempted to say, "Enough!" with all of the liability nonsense espoused in other countries. If people want to climb all over potentially dangerous public fixtures, then let the people climb! Spending a week scouting out Budapest's best places to kick your feet up and relax is the perfect way to start off a trip, for above all else, this city reminds you that every once in a while, it's okay to just stop and take a breath.

## ORIENTATION

The rule of thumb for orienting yourself in Budapest is to know your position in relation to the **Danube River**. If you know this, it's impossible to get lost. Street names in Budapest are sometimes hard to find, but are usually written on white tiles on the sides of corner buildings. Underneath the street name, there is a series of numbers with an arrow (8 ->12, for example). This indicates the address numbers found on this block. The city itself is split into two sides and is divided by the Danube River, with **Buda** located to the west and **Pest** to the east. While Buda contains popular tourist areas such as **Gellért Hill** and the **castle quarter**, Pest is truly the city center. **District 7** (in Pest) is home to much of the city's nightlife.

## ESSENTIALS

### GETTING THERE

Getting to Budapest is easy by plane, train, or bus. Planes fly into Budapest Ferenc Liszt International Airport, from which most city destinations can be reached via public transport. However, routes change frequently depending on destination, so check ahead. Taxis from the airport are safe, give a price estimate before the ride, and generally take cash or card (though we recommend keeping cash on you just in case). The airport offers shuttle services to the city center through miniBUD (www.minibud.hu), which can be booked in advance.

### GETTING AROUND

Budapest is a very walkable city, especially within the city center, and public transportation (the metro, trams, and buses) is fairly efficient. The city's public transportation authority BKV uses a ticket system, so each new ride requires a single ticket. Transfers between metro lines are free, but all other transfers are not. If you plan to travel by public transportation frequently, it may be worthwhile to purchase a 24-hour, 72-hour, or weeklong pass.

### PRACTICAL INFORMATION

**Tourist Offices:** Budapestinfo is the city's official tourist office, with information available online at www.budapestinfo. hu. Tourism stands also can be found throughout the city center selling Budapest Cards, which provide unlimited public transportation and free or reduced admission to many of the city's museums. However, we wouldn't recommend purchasing one unless you intend to use more than a handful of public transport rides or visit the majority of museums in a brief window of time.

**ATMs:** ATMs are available throughout Budapest and typically have options to perform transactions in English. Many show the exchange rate and withdrawal equivalency in U.S. dollars before concluding transactions. Currency exchange booths are also widely available.

**BLGTQ+ Resources:** www.budapestgaycity.net provides updates on BGLTQ+-friendly businesses in the city and is a hub for information on BGLTQ+ activities and events.

**Internet:** Wi-Fi is available throughout the city in accommodations, as well as often in restaurants and bars. Some major squares and tourist attractions also provide free public Wi-Fi.

**Post Offices:** Post offices in Budapest are run by Maygar Post. Information regarding shipping mail internationally can be found online at https://posta.hu. You can translate the site from Hungarian to English by clicking on a button located in the top right corner of the home screen.

## EMERGENCY INFORMATION

**Emergency Numbers:** General (112), police (107), ambulance (104), fire (105), English-speaking tourist hotline (14388080)

**Pharmacies:** Pharmacies are marked with a green "+" sign. Many are not open 24hr, but Deli Pharmacy (Alkotás út 1/B) and Teréz Pharmacy (Teréz körút 41) are two reliable stops.

**Hospitals:** The majority of medical centers in Budapest have English-speaking staff. The US Embassy keeps a list of English-speaking doctors as well.

**The US Embassy:** The American Embassy is located at Liberty Square. (Szabadság tér 12; 14754400; hungary.usembassy. gov.)

# ACCOMMODATIONS

### ADAGIO HOSTEL 2.0
Andrássy u. 2; 1 950 9674; www.ada-giohostel.com

Adagio Hostel 2.0 is very proud of its Hungarian heritage. Each room in the hostel is named after a different important Hungarian thing – a person, a dish, an invention (did you know the Rubik's Cube was a Hungarian invention?). On the wall adjacent to the reception desk, a computerized photo of **John von Neumann**, the conceptual inventor behind digital computing, hangs next to a photo of Mark Zuckerberg, who doesn't really have anything to do with Hungary (that we know of). Overall, it's a reliable hostel in a great location

between **St. Stephen's Basilica** and **Erzsébet Square.**

*i* 8 and 10-bed dorms €12-25; reservation recommended; BGLTQ+ friendly; Wi-Fi; reservation recommended; lockers provided; free coffee and tea

### HIPSTER HOSTEL
Baross u. 3; 1788 9441; hipsterhostel.com

If you worried that mustache humor died out in recent years, fear not, there is a place where it thrives. We counted no fewer than 18 handlebar mustache decorations at the Hipster Hostel. Unfortunately for their street cred, calling yourself "hipster" is decidedly not hipster at all. This hostel is a quiet, homey environment where high ceilings compliment spacious bedrooms and common areas in spite of its exceptionally squeaky floors. Despite its shabby-chic appearance (paint is peeling and the furniture is, shall we say, worn in), Hipster Hostel's staff cleans industriously and is eager to provide restaurant and nightlife recommendations.

*i* 10-bed dorm €8-18, 6-bed dorm €10-20, private bedroom €50-60, honeymoon suite with bath €60-70; reservation recommended; BGLTQ+ friendly; no wheelchair accessibility; Wi-Fi; linens, towel, and locker provided; cash only; reservation recommended

### HIVE PARTY HOSTEL
Dob u. 19; 3 082 66197; www.thehive.hu; reception open 24hr

If in visiting Budapest you hope to let loose with your friends and your friends happen to be named Jose Cuervo and Captain Morgan, Hive Party Hostel is the place for you. It's located in Budapest's party district and has recently installed a bar on the main floor that stays open late every night featuring live music and DJs. The accommodations are modern, but if you don't want to party, we'd recommend going with another option.

*i* 14 and 16-bed dorms €9-10, €15-16 on weekends; 6, 8, 10, 12-bed dorms €10-20 (female-only dorms are the same price as coed dorms), double bed private room €30-40, €70 on weekends; reservation recommended; BGLTQ+ friendly; Wi-Fi; reservation recommended; large lockers provided; in-house bar; hairdryers and irons available to borrow

## MAVERICK HOSTEL

Ferenciek Tere 2; 1 267 3166; maverick-lodges.com

Maverick Hostel seems to have thought of everything. It boasts a large luggage room, multiple common rooms, and kitchens for guests staying in rooms above the main floor. They hold events in the lobby every other night (past events include movie nights and wine tastings) and offer "intimacy kits" at the reception desk, not that we recommend picking up a stranger in a strange land. This hostel is comfortable, professional, and noticeably practiced.

*i* 10-bed dorm €10-15, 5-bed dorm €15-20, private suites €50-100; reservation recommended; BGLTQ+ friendly; not wheelchair accessible; Wi-Fi; reservation recommended; large lockers provid

# SIGHTS
## CULTURE

### HUNGARIAN STATE OPERA BUILDING

Andrassy u. 22; 1 814 7100, 1 332 8197; www.opera.hu, www.operavisit.hu; open daily 10am-8pm

Built in the late nineteenth century, the Hungarian State Opera is the birthplace of operatic rivalry between Hungary and Vienna. Said to be so beautiful that the Austrian king of the (then) Austro-Hungarian Empire refused to attend after its opening night in 1884, the opera house is a sight to awe both the devoted supporters of the arts and the casual tour-taker alike. Opera fans, you're in luck. The Hungarian opera is heavily subsidized by the state, so book ahead of time and

you could get tickets on the cheap for one of its 200 performances per season.

*i* Opera tickets range by show; tour tickets 2990HUF, 1990HUF reduced; mini concert 690HUF, camera ticket 500HUF; tours daily at 2pm (English), 3pm, and 4pm (English and a handful of other languages); wheelchair accessible

### MATTHIAS CHURCH AND FISHERMAN'S BASTION

Szentháromság tér 2; 1 488 7716, 2 095 94419; www.matyas-templom.hu; open M-F 9am-5pm, Sa 9am-12pm, Sa 1pm-5pm

Matthias Church is a mosaic masterpiece that no Pinterest board could have imagined in its wildest dreams. The inside is intricately painted, as opposed to carved and leafed, which gives the walls a soft quality, almost like they're thinly carpeted. Tickets to the upper level of Fisherman's Bastion (800HUF), the fortress-like terrace that rims the portico on the church's front façade, can be purchased with tickets to the church (1500HUF), but there are also great views from the ground (free).

*i* Church 1500HUF, 1000HUF reduced; bell tower 1500HUF, 1000HUF reduced; bastion 800HUF, 400HUF reduced

### ST. STEPHEN'S BASILICA

Szent István tér 1; 1 311 0839; www.bazilika.biz

Another day, another church, another dollar. Actually, lots and lots of dollars because the inside of this church is ridiculously beautiful. Visit St. Stephen's Basilica to experience one of the essential cultural sights of Budapest. Marvel at the gold-leafed walls and wonder how in the world people painted such intricate ceilings. The steeple is also open for visitors to climb and see the city from on high. Although there's a museum, we recommend prioritizing your visit to the actual tower.

*i* *Free to enter the church; panoramic tower 600HUF, 400HUF reduced; museum 400HUF, 300HUF reduced; wheelchair accessible*

## LANDMARKS

### ERZSÉBET SQUARE
Erzsébet tér; 2 025 47818; erzsebetter.hu; open daily 24hr

Erzsébet Square is a great place to take a break and absorb all that laid-back Budapest has to offer. Because let's be honest, we know it's our business, but being a tourist can be exhausting. So take off your backpack, take off your shoes, take off your socks, keep your pants on, and relax with your feet in the cool water of the park's central fountain. The square is also home to the country's largest seasonal Ferris wheel, the Budapest Eye (locally known as the **Sziget Eye**), which offers breathtaking views of the city below.

*i* *Free; wheelchair accessible*

### HEROES' SQUARE
Hősök tere; 1146 Budapest; open daily 24hr

The monument at Heroes' Square is another public fixture literally crawling with people. Tourists flock here to see (and climb on) its statues, including the seven chieftains of Magyars and the **Tomb of the Unknown Soldier**. So you can do as the tourists do and whip out your selfie stick, but we're here for the site's history, which will not disappoint.

*i* *Free; wheelchair accessible*

### HUNGARIAN PARLIAMENT BUILDING
Kossuth Lajos tér 1-3; 1 441 4000; http://latogatokozpont.parlament.hu/en; open daily Apr-Oct 8am-6pm, Nov-Mar 8am-4pm

The Hungarian Parliament Building is one of Budapest's few gothic buildings. Tours, which run daily, provide a snippet of historical context on everything from the era of kings to that of communism. You'll be awestruck as you gawk at the countless statues of chiefs and kings lining the walls and, if you're lucky, you'll catch a glimpse of the original Holy Crown of Hungary. Beyond the tour, stroll along the Buda side of the Danube after dark to witness the building – including its 96-foot-tall dome – come to life.

*i* *EU adults 2400HUF, EU students 1300HUF, other adults 6000HUF, other students 3100HUF; last entry depends on time of year and whether or not parliament is in session; wheelchair accessible (appointment necessary); free Wi-Fi available in Kossuth Square*

### LIBERTY SQUARE
Szabadság tér; open daily 24hr

A visit to Liberty Square is a quick way to explore the war-torn history of Budapest, which has endured centuries of political tension. Here, a monument implying Hungary's innocence in WWII has seen three years of frequent protests. On the south end of the square lies a row of personal items, flowers, and photos placed by Holocaust survivors and their families. Towards the back, a Soviet monument stands in front of the American embassy along with a **statue of Ronald Reagan**, which was erected after the fall of the Berlin wall in 1989.

*i* *Free; wheelchair accessible*

### SZÉCHENYI THERMAL BATH
Állatkerti krt. 9-11; 136 3210; www.szechenyibath.hu; open daily 9am-10pm

The Széchenyi Baths were the first of their kind established on the Pest side of the city. Originally called the **Artesian baths**, Széchenyi's hot spring wells were drilled at the end of the nineteenth century and opened to the public in 1881. The baths quickly became popular, and in 1909, the city council broke ground on building **Széchenyi palace**. The palace itself is extraordinary, featuring nearly 20 indoor pools, three large outdoor pools ranging from 81 to 101°F (27-39°C), ample space for tanning, and several bars. Additionally, there are several saunas and steam rooms available. Pro tip: bring your own towel to avoid queuing for one.

*i* *Ticket and locker 4900HUF, 5100HUF on weekends; last entry at 6pm; wheelchair accessible*

## MUSEUMS

### HUNGARIAN NATIONAL GALLERY

Szent György Tér; 1 201 9082; www.mng.
hu; open Tu-Su 10am-6pm

If you only go to one art museum in
Hungary, go here. Beginning in the
medieval and renaissance periods, the
permanent collections of the museum
take visitors through the history of
Hungarian art over time and in every
medium. The museum has something
for everyone: things to laugh at if you
"don't get" art and things to ponder
about if you do. One of our favorites
was Czimra Gyula's "Still Life in the
Kitchen" (1962). Most of the galleries
are housed in Buda Palace, and exhibits
showcasing the building's rich history
line the perimeter of the royal grounds.

*i* Permanent exhibitions 1800HUF, all exhibitions 2200HUF; wheelchair accessible

### TERROR HOUSE

Andrássy u. 60; 6 137 42600; www.hou-
seofterror.hu; open Tu-Su 10am-6pm

This museum takes visitors through
the experience of the Nazi and Soviet
occupations in Hungary, documenting
the history of Nazi concentration
camps, Soviet work camps, and Soviet
prisons. The path of Terror House
takes you progressively lower into the
basement of the building, which has
been converted into a reconstruction of
Soviet prison cells. Fair warning: this is
an intense and emotional experience,
so we'd recommend preparing yourself
accordingly.

*i* Adult 2000HUF, 1000HUF reduced (EU
citizens); wheelchair accessible

## OUTDOORS

### GELLÉRT HILL

Paths begin on the Buda side of Erzsébet
Bridge; open daily 24hr

For the outdoorsy and the athletically
inclined, Gellért Hill offers a fun,
short, and rewarding hike up the
highest hillside in Buda. The park's
many monuments are great places to
stop and catch your breath and will
keep even the least exercise-driven
motivated. At the top, look upon the
city from the citadel. Beware that the
park is a web of paths, but all of them
lead to the same place, so continue
uphill and you'll make it, we promise.

*i* Free; wheelchair accessible

## FOOD

### ALFÖLDI VENDÉGLŐ RESTAURANT ($)

Kecskemétu u. 4; 1053; 1 267 0224; open
daily 11am-11pm

Hungarian in every regard, Alföldi
Vendéglő is a dimly lit, relatively
inexpensive dinner restaurant. The cool
ambiance is accented by walls paneled
with strips of thin dark wood that
resemble stacked pretzel sticks. When
we visited, the wait staff consisted
of two men: one was older, a little
grouchy, and growled occasionally at
his younger counterpart, who was the
type to wink in an endearing, boyish
way instead of a creepy one—an
extremely difficult persona to master.
Also difficult to master: deep-frying
cheese, which, to our surprise, Alföldi
Vendéglő did with tremendous ease.

*i* Mains 1890HUF-8490HUF; wheelchair
accessible; Wi-Fi

### BONNIE ($$)

Ferenciek tere 5; 3 074 43555; bonnier-
estro.hu; open M-W 8am-1am, Th-F 8am-
3am, Sa 9am-3am, Su 9am-12am

For an establishment that's so clean-cut
and industrial, Bonnie has surprisingly
hearty, home-style food. Come here
for a nice dinner that may push the
budget boundary, but not by much.
On the menu, you will find goulash
(1550HUF), a traditional Hungarian
stew, as well as more modern dishes
such as bacon-wrapped chicken breast
stuffed with mozzarella, basil, and
roasted tomatoes (2890HUF). We
don't usually list ingredients in our
reviews, but...come on! Does that not
sound delicious?

*i* 1550HUF-5990HUF; vegetarian, or
gluten-free options available

### BUDAPEST HOT DOG COLD BEER ($)

Zrínyi u. 14; 17921702; open M-Th 11am-
3am, F-Sa 11am-6am, Su 11am-12am

Outside of St. Stephen's Basilica, amid
a sea of overpriced restaurants, there
is a sign with a simple promise: Hot
Dog Cold Beer. Every city needs a
good hotdog shop, and this one serves
dogs stacked high with toppings. A

first-hand tip: patrons with nose rings may want to remove them to better facilitate rapid consumption. If you feel like testing the limits of the human body, finish your meal with a sweet dog (790HUF), your choice of candy bar deep-fried and covered in powdered sugar.

*i* City dogs 990HUF, corn dog 790HUF, sweet dog 790HUF, tornado chips 490HUF, cold beer 490-790HUF; wheelchair accessible

### EL RAPIDO GRILL AND TEQUILA ($)
Kazinczy utca 10; 1 783 4627; http://www.tequilashop.hu/; open M-Th 11am-4am, F-Sa 11am-5am, Su 11am-3am

We reviewed this restaurant because we know that if you have taste buds, you have been asking yourself two questions: 1) What about Mexican food? And 2) Is Mexican food in Hungary any good? We wondered the same thing. Though the chefs are somewhat confused as to the difference between a burrito and a taco, El Rapido is a great place to stop for a quick bite of Hispanic flavors, especially late at night.

*i* 350HUF-1350HUF; vegetarian options available; wheelchair accessible

### FARGER KÁVÉZÓ ($)
Zoltán u. 18; 2 023 77825; www.farger.hu; open M-F 7am-9pm, Sa-Su 9am-6pm

Sandwiched between Liberty Square and the Hungarian Parliament Building, Farger is an affordable café with a specialty dish that we can get behind: sliders. The "Farger Plank" includes one of every variety that the restaurant offers and will leave you feeling more optimistic about the state of the world— until you remember that the beef industry is rapidly killing the planet, that is. Pair your meal with beer and wine, or try Farger's fresh squeezed juice, but make sure to specify that you want orange juice. If you don't, they'll bring you Orangina instead.

*i* Breakfast 610-1490HUF, two sliders 1190HUF, three sliders 1790HUF, four sliders 2380HUF; limited wheelchair accessibility

### VENDETTA PASTA E BASTA ($$)
Váci u. 16; 3 055 02645; www.vendetta-pasta.hu; open daily 11am-12am

Italian joint Vendetta Pasta e Basta is a perfect lunch spot to bask in the summer bustle of one of Budapest's major pedestrian thoroughfares and get caught up in the thrill of watching staff from the Ice Bar across the street harassing passersby with their latest promotions. Because of its prime location, Vendetta Pasta e Basta's food is, frankly, overpriced, but splitting a pizza with a friend can make for a relatively affordable lunch. Warning: the pizza does not hold up well after refrigeration.

*i* Pasta 2500-3900HUF, pizza 2700-4000HUF, lemonade 990HUF; wheelchair accessible

# SZENTENDRE

**Szentendre is a small town north of Budapest full of colorful sights and old buildings.** It has the vibe of an authentic little village turned tourist destination for both locals and visitors, not unlike Salem, Massachusetts, San Miguel de Allende outside of Mexico City, or basically any beach town in America. On the main streets of town, you'll find lively businesses and quaint decorations, but cut off the central drag and you'll encounter deserted cobblestone streets and walls overgrown with hanging vines. Szentendre is a place where it feels good, not overwhelming, to be a tourist.

## GETTING THERE

Szentendre sits on the west bank of the Danube River. Take the H5 train line from Budapest (part of HÉV public transport service). You can transfer to the H5 from metro line M2 at Batthyány tér station. To ride the H5 out of the city limits, you will need to add a suburban railway extension ticket to your fare. They do check tickets once you leave the city. When you get to the train station in Szentendre, walk through the pedestrian tunnel (it looks like a white metro station) to get to Kossuth Lajos utca. From there, walk north and you will hit the town center.

## GETTING AROUND

Szentendre is a small town, so unless you plan to leave the main attractions located in its center, you should stick to walking.

### Swing by...

#### BOARDWALK ALONG THE DANUBE
2000 Szentendre, Dunakorzó; open daily 24hr
The charm of Szentendre is especially poignant along the river, so don't be ashamed to flock to the boardwalk like every other tourist. Grab some langos, ice cream, or whatever your snack of choice may be, and meander lazily along the small waterfront park. Sit around and people watch, listen to kids play the saxophone for tips near the riverbed, and look out on boats coming up the river.
*i* Free; wheelchair accessible

### Check out...

#### CATEDRAL BEOGRADSKA SERBIAN ORTHODOX CHURCH
2000 Szentendre, Pátriarka utca 5; 26312399; open Tu-Su 10am-6pm
An ideal escape from the hustle and bustle of Szentendre's lively center, the walk to Catedral Beogradska will take you through smaller alleys. The church grounds are slightly dark and overgrown—just enough to feel ominous but still enticing. Inside the church is an altar of painted panels and a museum with eighteenth century art and artifacts from around Hungary.
*i* Museum and church 700HUF, photo ticket 700HUF (not recommended); cash only; no wheelchair accessibility

### Don't miss...

#### SZENTENDREI KÉPTÁR
2000 Szentendre, Fő tér 2-5; 207796657; open Tu-Su, 10am-6pm
Szentendrei Képtár is an art museum looking for attention—it boasts the single largest flat wall in Szentendre's center square, which is covered in advertisements for their latest exhibitions. For the museum's offerings, it is admittedly a little overpriced. A ticket to the main exhibit will let you into just three or four modestly sized rooms of art, so unless you stare at each piece for a full 60 seconds minimum, you'll run up quite a bill.
*i* All exhibits 1400HUF, 700HUF reduced; cash only; wheelchair accessible

# NIGHTLIFE

## PONTOON
Id. Antall József Rakpart; 3 065 22732;
www.pontoonbudapest.com; open daily
12pm-4am

Location, location, location. Situated
on the eastern bank of the Danube
River, Pontoon offers a stunning view
of the Széchenyi Chain Bridge and
ample outdoor seating. The drink
menu is extensive; the food menu…
not so much. But that's not to say
that what's offered isn't tasty. Sip your
wine from a plastic cup to the muffled
pulse of electronic music playing softly
in the background and soak in the
magnificence that is the Danube at
dusk.

*i* Beer/wine 400-1000 HUF; BGLTQ+
friendly; wheelchair accessible

## START HUNGARIAN CRAFT BEER
Kazinczy u. 20; 7 042 41727; open Su-M
5pm-12am, Th 5pm-2am, F-Sa 5pm-4am

For those of us from craft beer meccas
like the Pacific Northwest and Boston,
Start Hungarian Craft Beer Bar is a
refreshing reminder of home. Although
this bar has only five taps, it serves over
50 local bottled beers and a variety of
snacks, from french fries to popcorn.
Part surf shop, part old comic store,
Start's a fantastic place for anyone who
can get down with an inventive cold
brew.

*i* Beer/wine 500-1000 HUF; BGLTQ+
friendly; no wheelchair accessibility

## SZIMPLA
Kazinczy u. 14; 2 026 18669; www.szimp-
la.hu; open M-Sa 12pm-4am, Su 9am-5am

Szimpla is one of the largest and most
famous ruin pubs in Budapest. It's truly
a must-visit spot for anyone over the
legal drinking age. The eclectic mix of
decorative collections strewn about the
building looks like it came out of the
garden of a hoarder clown who played
in a punk band in his 20s and now
dabbles in local business and organic
farming. Host to DJs and live bands on
both weeknights and weekends and a
farmer's market on Sunday mornings,
Szimpla's got a little something for
everyone.

*i* Beer 400-600 HUF; main floor is wheelchair accessible; Wi-Fi

# GYÖR

Coverage by **Antonia Washington**

With its pedestrian streets, outdoor bistros, and fair share of river-front properties,
Györ is like a small-scale Budapest—and it's expanding quickly. Construction
crews hang out, and probably work sometimes, around every corner. So who
knows? Györ could be the next trendy town in Europe. The place is already
covered in bookstores. Also, the ice cream portions here are bigger and cheaper per
ounce than elsewhere in Hungary, so we're fans.

As for the architecture: it's mostly baroque and often painted yellow. Think a
combination of the life's work of a decorative molding devotee and the scene in
Juno when Vanessa can't decide which shade of yellow to paint the nursery. You
may not think there's a huge difference between paint swatches for custard and
cheesecake yellow, but it's called nesting, it's especially important for adoptive
mothers, and you would know that if you read the baby books and started pulling
your fucking weight, Mark.

## ORIENTATION

Györ is located in the northwest of Hungary, directly between **Budapest** and
**Vienna** and an hour south of **Bratislava, Slovakia**. It sits at the intersection of
the **Mosoni-Duna** and **Rába Rivers**, with the city center situated in the southeast
portion of this intersection. The best places to orient yourself within the city
center are Széchenyi tér, the main square with the **Benedictine church**, and
**Baross Gábor út**, a major pedestrian street that runs roughly north to south and
sits a couple of blocks west of the square.

# ESSENTIALS

## GETTING THERE

By train or bus, Györ is easily reachable from Budapest, Bratislava, and Vienna. The Györ train and bus stations are separate, but located next to each other at the south end of the city center. Most central accommodations are within walking distance. There is usually a taxi or two at the station, but if you plan to travel by taxi, calling ahead may be a good idea.

## GETTING AROUND

Györ, especially the city center, is small, so the easiest way to travel is usually by foot. Beyond the city center, walking is generally still the easiest form of transportation for able bodied individuals. Otherwise, buses sometimes travel within the city from the Györ bus station, or visitors can call a taxi service to request a ride (the most frequently used taxis in Györ are Duna Tele-4 Taxi; 96 444 444).

## PRACTICAL INFORMATION

**Tourist Offices:** There is a very helpful Tourinform office in the heart of the city center. (Baross Gábor u. 21; 96336817; open M-F 9am-5pm, Sa 9am-2pm, closed Su)

**Banks/ATMS/Currency Exchange:** While there may not be ATMs on every corner like in Budapest, they are available and many businesses accept cards.

**Post Offices:** There are multiple post offices in Györ, but the post office closest to the city center is near the National Theater of Györ (Bajcsy-Zsilinszky u. 46; 96547600; open M-F 8am-6pm).

**Internet:** Most accommodations in the area provide free wireless internet. It is rare to find elsewhere.

## EMERGENCY INFORMATION

**Emergency Numbers:** General (112), police (107), ambulance (104), fire (105)

**Police:** Police in Hungary are safe to call, but they are allowed to ask for paperwork and identification, so make sure to carry yours with you. There are no police stations in the city center, but there is one across the river to the west (Köztelek utca 4-6; 96520083).

**US Embassy:** Györ is almost equidistant between Budapest, Vienna, and Bratislava, Slovakia, each of which have U.S. embassies. Information for the embassy

in Budapest is as follows (1054 Budapest, Szabadság tér 12; 14754400; open M-F 8am-5pm).

**Rape Crisis Center:** There is no rape crisis center in Györ.

**Hospitals:** The main hospital in Györ is located substantially southeast of the city center (Petz Aladár Megyei Oktató Kórház: Vasvári Pál u. 2-4; 96507900).

**Pharmacies:** There are many pharmacies in Györ, but the most central one is run by the Benedictine church in Széchenyi square (Széchenyi Patika: Széchenyi tér 8; 96550348).

# ACCOMMODATIONS

Györ does not have much in the way of hostels, but there are some reasonable hotels, and visitors may have luck finding affordable accommodations on Airbnb. Accommodations labeled "panzió" are generally cheaper than those labeled "hotel."

### FEHÉR HAJÓ PANZIÓ

Kiss Ernö u. 4; 9 631 7608; www.feherhajopanzio.hu/; reception open 24hr

The Fehér Hajó Panzió is a good place to crash if all you're looking for is Wi-Fi and a bed (in that order). The rooms are small, it smells vaguely of cigarettes, and the toilet flushes by a pull-cord from the ceiling. All the fine comforts of home. No? Come on, we can't be the only ones who spent the first 11 years of our lives in a cupboard under the stairs. The duds here are not flashy, but it's a 5-min. walk to the city center and you've probably been staying in hostels for a while now, so how much do you care?

*i* Single room €25-30, room with a double bed €35-50; BGLTQ+ friendly; no wheelchair accessibility; Wi-Fi; reservation recommended; linens provided

### HOTEL FAMULUS

Budai u. 4-6; 9027; 9 654 7770; www.famulushotel.hu

If you looked up Hotel Famulus without reading this blurb, you probably rejoiced about what a treat it was to be able to afford such a nice hotel. Well, you should have kept reading. The main hotel is not affordable at all, but they offer small apartment style accommodations—much like college dorms—with a much lower price tag. This is a popular option for students, especially those taking summer classes in Győr. Hotel Famulus offers short-term housing, which is a great deal if you can snatch it! Rooms are suite-style and very small, but include a kitchenette.

*i* One bed in 4-person suite 3300 HUF, personal suite 5700 HUF; reservation recommended; not BGLTQ+ friendly; wheelchair accessible; Wi-Fi; reservation recommended; wheelchair accessible

# SIGHTS

## CULTURE

### LOYOLAI SZENT IGNÁC TEMPLOM (BENEDICTINE CHURCH ST. IGNATIUS OF LOYOLA)
Széchenyi tér; 9 651 3020; bencesgyor.hu; open M-F 9am-5pm, Sa 9am-1pm, Sunday mass (time varies)

Though this church is small compared to many of the behemoths you'd visit in more traditional backpacking destinations, it was built to impress, with carved wooden pews, ornate ceiling frescos, and an overwhelming amount of gold leaf. Visiting the church is free; however, because it is an active place of worship, it's recommended to double check hours before entering. If that seems like too much work, you can do as a Research-Writer does and enter the front hall enthusiastically, realize where you are and watch your optimism fly out the clerestory windows, then quickly panic-moonwalk from the scene and pray no one noticed.

*i* Free; limited wheelchair accessible

### NATIONAL THEATER OF GYŐR
Czuczor Gergely u. 7; 9 652 0611; www.gyoriszinhaz.hu

Offering a smattering of performances in the classical arts and a slightly wider repertoire than other Hungarian theaters like the **Hungarian State Opera** in Budapest, the National Theater of Győr is a must-see for those who consider themselves arts fanatics. The building itself dates to 1978 and reflects many of the architectural trends of the decade—brutally clean lines, lots of reinforced concrete, and a sweeping façade. It is an imposing

cornucopia of creativity, serving as a striking antithesis to Győr's somewhat homogeneous cityscape. Catch one of their performances during the September to May season.

*i* Prices vary by show; wheelchair accessible

# LANDMARKS

### ARK OF THE COVENANT STATUE
Gutenberg tér

A stunning piece of baroque sculpture with a healthy dose of gold leaf, the Ark of the Covenant statue in Győr was once a gate to the citadel. Today, it's a work of art for visitors to admire and a convenient place to sit and hang out—particularly important because of its central location between several nearby ice cream shops. Take in the significance of historic monuments, but never without sweets.

*i* Free; wheelchair accessible

### COLUMN OF ST. MARY AT SZÉCHENYI TÉR
Széchenyi tér

A towering column stands watch over the main square in Győr. The Column of St. Mary, erected in the late seventeenth century by the Bishop of Győr, offers another opportunity to struggle to get a decent photo featuring a really tall thing (we all do this). Our visit to the fountain in front of the monument taught us that no matter how many times you've watched that three-year-old in his underwear clap his hands over the bubbling fountain and try desperately to get the water to do what he wants, you will watch when he does it again 30 seconds later.

*i* Free; wheelchair accessible

### THE BOATMAN FOUNTAIN
Baross Gábor u.

This statue and fountain, located right in the middle of Győr's major pedestrian street, gives a great sense of the spirit of the city. On nice days, musicians often sit on the rim of the fountain and play wonderfully accented versions of songs by The Beatles, Bruno Mars, and The Script. The songs they chose tend to be of a genre we call, "These haven't been relevant for a while, so maybe you won't notice when I don't actually know the words." A beloved genre overall, but we were 13 years old when The Script's "Breakeven" came out. *We know all the words.*

*i* Free; wheelchair accessible

## MUSEUMS

Many of the museums in Győr, including those at the Bishop's Castle and the Cathedral of Győr, have been shut down due to construction. Most are scheduled to reopen in 2018, but contact the tourist offices for up-to-date information.

### BORSOS HOUSE

Király u. 17; 9 631 6329; open T-Su 10am-6pm

This art exhibition displays the work of Miklós Borsos, a Hungarian sculptor who worked in a range of mediums, creating figures, busts, and medals. His works explore grief, fertility, and perfection, as well as more abstract themes. If you're interested in contemplating the significance of an artist's not having fully carved the details of a woman's face, Borsos House is the place to do so.

*i* 700 HUF, student 350 HUF; no wheelchair accessibility

### KOVÁCS MARGIT PERMANENT EXHIBITION

Apáca u. 1; 9 632 6739; open T-Su 10am-6pm

If you took a ceramics elective in school like we did, you'll be thrilled to learn that there's a place in Győr where you can judge your work against one of the most celebrated ceramic artists in Hungary: Margit Kovács. Her permanent collection consists of a sizable number of small figurines (first floor) of everything from soldiers to women with elegant up-dos. Move on to the second floor to see some of Kovács' larger pieces. But we must say, detail work is truly where Kovács shines. The gallery itself can be easy to miss, so look out for a marker above a door on the right side of the building.

*i* 700 HUF, student 350 HUF; no wheelchair accessibility

## OUTDOORS

### RÁBA RIVER

Running north to south through Győr is the Rába River, in the middle of which lies Radó Island. Both the island and the banks of the Rába feature extensive networks of walking paths which, barring the weather is nice, are a great means of checking out the city. The northern section of Győr (along the north bank of the Mosoni-Duna River and west of Jedlik Ányos Bridge) has a grassy shoreline and sandy beach complete with volleyball courts. Come lay out in the sun or lounge in a lawn chair in the shade of a big tree.

*i* Free; wheelchair accessibility varies by location

# FOOD

### DUNA DÖNER GYŐR ($)

Széchenyi tér 7; 9 631 0325; zeugmakebap.com; open Su-W 11am-10pm, Th 11am-11pm, F-Sa 11am-11:45pm

Duna Döner is one of the cheapest and most delicious take-out restaurants on Széchenyi tér. Their specialty is the Döner Box (990HUF), which consists of a pile of French fries covered in spicy sauce (don't fret, the sauce isn't *that* spicy), a hearty portion of freshly-carved (chicken or beef), and fresh slices of tomato, onion, and lettuce.

*i* Döner Box 990 HUF; vegetarian options available; wheelchair accessible

### ISTAMBULDA ÉTTEREM ($)

Baross Gábor u. 30; 9 625 4761; open M-Th 10am-12am, F-Sa 10am-4am, Su 10am-9pm

Despite the fact that Istambulda's only outward-facing signage features a picture of a hookah, tobacco in Hungary is highly regulated and only available at specific tobacco shops. So, while said hookah is a fun reminder of Turkish culture and of Hungary's multicultural history, you will not casually smoke with your lunch at Istambulda Étterem. What you will find in Istambulda is a fast-food counter style restaurant that puts Turkish food in your hands right when you need it.

*i* 700-1800 HUF; wheelchair accessible

### PIZZA PICCOLINO ($)
Kazinczy u. 16; 9 631 4461; open daily 12pm-9pm

There are two kinds of foods that are especially abundant in Hungary: Hungarian food and pizza. However, many Hungarian pizzerias are sit-down restaurants, where you order pizzas in full instead of by the slice. Pizza Piccolino is the first old-fashioned pizza counter we encountered on our trek, and we eagerly grabbed a slice (or three—man this place is tasty), payed in cash, and were on our way in a matter of minutes. Pizza varieties include (but aren't limited to) Hungarian favorites such as ham, corn, and ham with corn.

*i* One slice 200-400 HUF; vegetarian options available; wheelchair accessible

## NIGHTLIFE

### DIVINO GYÖR
Széchenyi tér 7; 9 631 0342; gyor. divinoborbar.hu; open M 4pm-12am, Tu-Th 4pm-2am, F 4pm-4am, Sa 2pm-2am, Su 2pm-12am

Visiting a wine bar basically anywhere can make you feel like a chic, urban 20-something. That said, DiVino Györ's clientele spans a fairly wide age range. In Hungary, wine is a crowd favorite. But fear not, students of the world and those of you afraid to talk to old people, the music gets louder and the crowd gets younger as the night wears on. Oh, and not to mention the wine only gets more delicious.

*i* No cover, drink from 300; BGLTQ+ friendly; wheelchair accessible

### YOLO PUB GYÖR
Baross Gábor u. 5; 3 025 20100; open Tu-Th 8pm-1am, F-Sa 8pm-2:30am, closed Su-M

Do not walk into the Yolo Pub at opening on a Tuesday and expect to see anyone but the bartender—weekdays tend to be a little slow. Weekends, on the other hand, are bumpin'. Every Friday, Yolo Pub's staff clears out all of the furniture to make space for a dance floor and cranks up the music, which ranges from old-school funk to current pop hits. Crowded and shrouded in neon light, Yolo Bar is an ideal place to embarrass yourself on the dance floor and debut those "signature moves" you rehearsed in the mirror when your roommate wasn't home. #Yolo.

*i* Drinks from 450 HUF; cash only; BGLTQ+ friendly; no wheelchair accessibility

# TIHANY

Coverage by **Antonia Washington**

In Tihany, a fairytale town on a hillside in rural Hungary, you will find straw-roofed cottages, sweeping views of Lake Balaton, and very little English. Tihany and Balatonfüred, both towns on the edge of Lake Balaton, are hubs for domestic tourism. While Balatonfüred is a larger resort town, Tihany has more of a vacation home vibe. Tihany sells itself on being "quaint," so if you're looking for photo-ops of your weekend trip to the nineteenth century, this is the place. Come for the history, the lavender festival, or the open-air shops, and end up with everybody else, picnicking on the grass promenade and staring out across the strikingly blue water of Lake Balaton.

## ORIENTATION

Tihany is situated on a southern-facing peninsula, so **Lake Balaton** surrounds it from all sides except the north. The center of the town is located on a hillside, and is concentrated on the east side of the peninsula. The main street through Tihany, **Kossuth Lajos utca**, runs northwest to southeast through the center of town. Other important roads include **Batthyány utca**, which has some shops and restaurants, and **Pisky sétány**, a popular promenade with views of the lake. Both streets run more or less parallel to Kossuth Lajos utca.

# ESSENTIALS

## GETTING THERE

Tihany is reachable from Budapest by train or bus. The main nearby train hub is Balatonfüred station, a short distance from Tihany. Taxis are available at the train station.

## GETTING AROUND

Once in Tihany, getting around is easy. It's small, so the easiest way to travel is often by foot. Bike paths are also widely available through the towns surrounding Lake Balaton and can be a great way to explore the area.

## PRACTICAL INFORMATION

**Tourist Offices:** Tourinform runs the tourist office in Tihany. It is located smack in the middle of the town center, next to the Tihany Abbey (Kossuth Lajos u. 20; 87448804; tihany@tourinform. hu, www.tihany.hu ).

**Banks/ATMS/Currency Exchange:** Many of the established businesses in Tihany accept cards (especially restaurants), but do not expect that they all will. Smaller businesses, museums, food carts, and ice-cream stands only take cash. ATMs are not readily available, so bring cash with you.

**Post Offices:** The post office in Tihany is located on the main road (Kossuth Lajos u. 3; 87448119; open M-F 8am-4pm, closed for lunch 12-12:30pm).

**Internet:** Internet access is common at accommodations in and around Tihany and occasionally at cafes, but rarely elsewhere.

**BLGTQ+ Resources:** No specific resources found.

## EMERGENCY INFORMATION

**Emergency Number:** General (112), police (107), ambulance (104), fire (105)

**Police:** Police in Hungary should be safe to call, but they are allowed to ask for paperwork and identification, so make sure to have yours with you. There is not a police station in Tihany. To call the police, dial 107.

**US Embassy:** The nearest U.S. embassy is in Budapest (1054 Budapest, Szabadság tér 12; 14754400; open M-F 8am-5pm).

**Rape Crisis Center:** There is no rape crisis center in Tihany. In case of emergency, dial 112.

**Hospitals:** The nearest hospitals to Tihany are located in Balatonfüred.
- Állami Szívkórház (Gyógy tér 2; 8 758 4584; open daily 6am-9pm)

**Pharmacies:** Rozmaring Gyógyszertár (Csokonai u. 2; 87448480)

# ACCOMMODATIONS

Finding and booking accommodations in Tihany is tricky. Because it is a popular vacation spot for locals, couples, and families, hotels in Tihany rarely charge less than the equivalent of $50 per night. Often, they charge much more. Visitors to Tihany may have luck finding affordable accommodations on Airbnb, or staying in Balatonfüred, a larger town just northeast of Tihany, also on the edge of Lake Balaton. From Balatonfüred, it is possible to visit Tihany by car or bike.

# SIGHTS

## CULTURE

### TIHANYI BENCÉS APÁTSÁG (TIHANY ABBEY)

I. András tér 1; 8 753 8200; www.tihany. osb.hu; open M-Sa 9am-6pm, Su and holidays 11:15am-6pm

The Tihany Abbey, home to a league of Benedictine monks and established in 1055, is an imposing sight on Óvár Hill, visible from almost anywhere in town. Just like we all learned the mitochondria is the powerhouse of the cell, we all learned 90% of an iceberg's mass is below the surface. The same, apparently, is true of churches. Winding its way through tunnels and back halls, the abbey's museum will have you questioning where you are and how you got there. Not unlike your typical Sunday morning.

*i* Adult 1200 HUF, 700 HUF student, audio-guide 500 HUF; last entry a half hour before closing time; no wheelchair accessibility

## LANDMARKS

### THE STATIONS OF THE CROSS MONUMENT

8237 Tihany; open daily 24hr

Don't we all like to feel the imposing force of the death of Christ staring down at us on a casual Sunday stroll? This 1927 monument, with artistic depictions of Christ in the hours before his death, is the most notable monument in Tihany. A series of small pillars line either side of the front lawn, leading the viewer up to a large crucifix. Though it may be considered a sin to take photos in the grass, if you choose to do so, we won't rat you out to the big guy.

*i* Free; no wheelchair accessibility; the pedestrian street between Alsóóvári utca and Visszhang utca, one street west of where they intersect

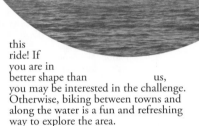

## ÓVÁR HILL
Path 2

Tihany sits on the southeastern edge of Óvár Hill, which features some of the town's many hiking trails and hidden sights. Over the hill and through the woods, you'll come across stunning views of Tihany, lavender fields, and the surrounding lakes and find yourself surrounded by butterflies. On the trail, you can see the remnants of man-made caves dug by eleventh-century Russian monks, whose bodies archaeologists found as late as the 1990s. This is a great chance to feel like Lara Croft, if you happen to have brought tight black tank tops, a holster, and knee-high combat boots on your trip.

*i* Free; no wheelchair accessibility; Path 2, which leads through Óvár Hill, begins on the promenade by the Tihany Abbey. At the north end of the promenade, follow markings for trails 1 or 2 to find the path on Óvár Hill. You can also find the path behind the Stations of the Cross monument.

## OUTDOORS

### LAKE BALATON BIKE PATHS
Lake Balaton; www.balatonbike.hu; open 24hr, but not recommended after dark
A huge web of well-marked bike paths encircles all of Lake Balaton, connecting the surrounding towns. Rent a bike (or mooch one off your Airbnb host), and the world becomes your oyster. Cycling all the way around the lake is a journey of about 130 miles. Doing so would be amazing (we think), but we are very aware of our physical limits, so we did not attempt

this ride! If you are in better shape than us, you may be interested in the challenge. Otherwise, biking between towns and along the water is a fun and refreshing way to explore the area.

*i* Rental costs vary; wheelchair accessible

## FOOD

### BALATONI HÁZ RESTAURANT ($$)
Halász köz 9; 8 744 8608; www.balatoni-haz.eu; open daily Easter-Oct 10am-10pm
Serving Hungarian fare, this dinner spot overlooking Lake Balaton won't break the bank. Balatoni Ház's vibe is upscale picnic, though we saw some patrons wearing cycling gear, so maybe it just feels upscale because we're not used to restaurants with table cloths. The staff does not speak much English, but if you're willing to point and mime your way through the menu, it may be one of the best meals you eat while in town.

*i* 1800-3900 HUF; vegetarian options available; no wheelchair accessibility

### CAFÉ FEELING ($)
Batthyány u. 1-3; 7 028 46705; www.tihanyinfo.com; open T-Su 9am-6pm
This is one of the cheapest places to eat in Tihany, which may feel especially important if you splurged on accommodations. However, if

357

# TIHANY'S LAVENDER OBSESSION

In and around Tihany, lavender fields stretch as far as the eye can see—an expansive purple blanket that hugs the curves of the surrounding terrain and crinkles up along the grassy shores of Lake Balaton. The scene is a lux swirl of pastels—here a stroke of azure, there a stroke of chartreuse, with a healthy splatter of lavender to top it off. The purple herb grows all over Tihany's main peninsula wild and in droves, peeking out around every bend of its winding cobblestone streets. Throughout town, shops sell lavender-inspired goods including teas and herbal remedies, as well as more unconventional items like crushed ice, ice creams, and beer.

Lavender has historical significance in Tihany. The Benedictine monks of Tihany Abbey, which was founded in the mid-eleventh century, have long been involved in the tradition of lavender farming, and they still, to this day, view it as one of their most important duties. The plant is one of Tihany's greatest treasures, and try as we might to come up with a joke about it, we couldn't. We decided lavender is just too wonderful and wholesome to poke fun at, sort of like losing your virginity at prom or *My Neighbor Totoro*.

In June, when lavender is in full bloom, Tihany hosts an annual lavender festival celebrating the season. The festival brings together local artisans and encourages visitors to participate in the lavender harvest, so if you have a particularly smelly travel partner, this may be a solution to your problems (see: "Showering in Rural Hungary: Pros and Cons"). If you don't happen to be in town during the festival, you can get up close and personal with this ambrosial purple plant on any of Tihany's walking paths (we recommend Path 3, which cuts along the edges of the lavender fields).

you like your bacon crispy or your burgers "thicc," we suggest you choose something else on the menu – like pizza or gyros. Chase it down with home-brewed lavender beer. Otherwise, it's a chance to fill your stomach for around $5 USD. PSA: Café Feeling also gets its side hustle on with an ice cream stand, so stop by if you feel so inclined.

*i* 800-2000 HUF; vegetarian options available; wheelchair accessible

### TÜZKERT ÉTTEREM ($)
Batthyány u. 15; 7 051 98513; www.tuzkert.hu; open daily 12pm-9pm, winter months F-Su 12pm-8pm

If you're looking to enjoy Hungarian specialties in a traditional setting, this restaurant is a top contender. Serving refined versions of Hungarian home cooking like homemade pasta with ratatouille at a decent price, Tüzkert is truly a cottage-style restaurant. Outside on the patio, visitors dine at picnic tables nestled between neat piles of chopped wood, small flowerboxes, and the woven floor rugs we all wanted in college until we realized our dorm room floor was way too disgusting to make it work.

*i* 1200-3500 HUF; vegetarian options available; no wheelchair accessibility

## NIGHTLIFE
Primarily a quiet destination for families and couples to relax, you won't find any raging clubs or even mildly populated bars in Tihany. Instead, alcohol is generally consumed with meals—you can purchase a drink at most restaurants any time of day. Some even offer home-brewed lavender beer, an exciting new taste that we'd recommend everyone try at least once.

# HUNGARY ESSENTIALS

## MONEY

**Tipping:** Tipping in Hungary is most common at restaurants, where it is standard to tip about 10% and not more than 15%. Often, the tip will be included in the bill, in which case the menu and/or bill will state that there is a 10% service fee. It will generally suffice to tip bartenders by rounding above the cost of your drinks to the next 100-forint denomination. In restaurants and bars, it is common to tell the server how much to charge total with the tip, or instruct them how much change you want back, instead of leaving a tip on the table. Usually taxis should be tipped 5-10%.Public restrooms often will charge a fee of 100-200 forints to pay restroom attendants as well.

**Taxes:** Most goods in Hungary are subject to a value added tax (VAT) of 27%, included in the purchase price of goods. The 27% VAT is a standard rate, though it fluctuates based on the goods bought, so you should ask the retailer for exact rates. Non-EU visitors taking these goods home unused can apply for a VAT refund for goods totaling more than 55,000 HUF at one retailer. To apply for this refund, ask the store for a VAT refund form, sometimes called a tax-free form, and carry your passport with you as retailers may ask to see it. Present the refund form and be prepared to show the unused goods you are exporting at the customs office at your point of departure from the EU, regardless of country. Once your paperwork has been approved by customs, present it at a Tax-Free Shopping Office, also at the point of departure, to claim the refund. Refunds must be claimed within 90 days of the original purchase.

## SAFETY AND HEALTH

**Local Laws and Police:** Police in Hungary can generally be relied upon if you need help, but always have your passport with you, as they are entitled to ask for your documentation.

**Tobacco, Drugs, and Alcohol:** The drinking age in Hungary is 18. Drinking in public is illegal, and there is a zero tolerance policy on alcohol and drinking. If you are found driving with a BAC of even 0.001%, you could be in serious trouble. Tobacco is tightly regulated in Hungary. Only official tobacco shops are licensed to sell any tobacco products at all, though these shops are easy to find. They are marked by signs with the number 18 inside of a circle and labeled "Nemzeti Dohánybolt." The signs are brown with red and green. Persons under the age of 18 are not allowed to enter these stores.

# ICELAND

**Do Iceland wrong, and you'll find yourself languishing in an overpriced Reykjavík hostel, struggling to fall asleep as the midnight sun streams through the paper-thin curtains and that middle-aged guy two beds over snores like an Icelandic horse.** You'll head out to book a minibus tour to the South Coast only to remember you blew $50 on a few shitty beers at the bar last night. You'll aimlessly wander the streets of the capital, surrounded by super jeeps and backpackers, catching snatches of conversation about black-sand beaches and snowcapped mountains while you dream of the lands beyond the city. Do Iceland wrong and you'll spend a lot and see very little.

But do Iceland right, and you'll have the adventure of a lifetime. You'll stay up late to sit on the shore and watch the sun as it sets behind the distant mountains at 11:45pm. You'll feel the raw power and majesty of this planet as you swim in the frigid water between two tectonic plates sitting just meters apart. You'll drive up mountain roads that seem to ascend into the clouds and through fjords with slopes of scree on one side and boundless sea on the other.

This country develops further each year. Hotels and gift shops sprout up around once-unknown waterfalls, and camper vans and coaches cover every kilometer of the Ring Road. But drive long enough, and the buses will become few and far between; climb high enough, and the tourists will shrink like ants below you; walk far enough and you'll find yourself alone with the sand or the trail and the sky. Iceland's untouched beauty is still out there.

Do Iceland right, and you'll discover what so few have found.

# REYKJAVÍK

Coverage by **Eric Chin**

Everything about Iceland's capital city just *feels* expensive and purposely built for tourists. Information and booking centers line the main streets, menus in restaurant windows showcase some eye-opening cuisine (and even more eye-opening prices), and even the street art is in a league of its own. What's more, despite being Iceland's largest city by a big margin, Reykjavík doesn't even feel like the island's main attraction. Talk to fellow travelers and their primary question will not be "Have you tried fermented shark yet," but rather "What tours of the island have you done so far?" as if the only thing to do once you get to Reykjavík is leave it.

Was Reykjavík the artistic and cultural hub of Renaissance Europe? No (it wasn't even a city back in the days of Michelangelo). Did it command a vast global empire and help lead Europe into the modern era? Not really (it wasn't even fully independent until 1944). Does it have an entire museum about penises with almost 300 biological specimens? Absolutely. (Oh, so now you're intrigued?) Reykjavík is a different breed of city—one that is modern and completely unapologetic about its many oddities. It's the kind of city that you *actually* want to visit. The museums are unpretentious and genuinely interesting (sometimes shockingly so), the nightlife is thriving and without the usual pressures of dress codes and exorbitant cover charges, and, in the summer at least, daylight never fades.

Do take tours to see the astounding natural beauty of Iceland, and do plan for only a few days in the city itself, but don't overlook Reykjavík as nothing more than a gateway to the island. There is more here for you than meets the eye.

## ORIENTATION

The **BSÍ Bus Terminal** is located at the very southern tip of the city center. Tourist information centers, shops, restaurants, and bars can be found on **Laugavegur,** which turns into **Bankastræti** and then **Austurstræti** as it stretches west. These streets are generally touristy during the day and are crowded late at night, especially on weekends. They also house the city's post office and many ATMs. Head uphill from Laugavegur to reach **Hallgrímskirkja,** Reykjavík's iconic church, and the statue of **Leif Erikson** which looks out over the city. North is the ocean, along which a paved walking and biking path runs west, past the statue **Sólfar, Harpa,** and the harbor at the northwestern end of the city.

## ESSENTIALS

### GETTING THERE

Iceland is, well, an island, meaning that air travel is inevitable. Most international journeys go through Keflavík International Airport (KEF). Your best bet is Icelandair, though WOW Air is always an option, provided you don't mind paying for a carry-on and a reserved seat in addition to your ticket. Keflavík is about 30 miles southwest of Reykjavík, so take a bus ("transfer," as it's called) to the main city. The Flybus will take you to Reykjavík's BSÍ Bus Terminal, about a 45-minute trip, for 2500 kr, and has

free Wi-Fi. Note: most flights from America are red-eyes, but the airport is open and busy even in the mornings.

### GETTING AROUND

Reykjavík is an easily walkable city; it's less than a half hour walk across at its widest point. There is a city bus service, Strætó, but note that you must buy a ticket in advance (sold at a number of shops) or pay with exact change on the bus, in cash! If you plan to use the bus a lot, the 1-day (1560 kr) and 3-day passes (3650 kr) are a better value. Taxis are also available, and rates are standard. Try Hreyfill (588 5522) or

BSR (561 0000). In such an expensive country, though, walking is a great way to save some money.

## PRACTICAL INFORMATION

**Tourist Offices:** Reykjavík's official information center is located in City Hall (Tjarnargata 11, 101 Reykjavík; 411 6040; open daily 8am-8pm).

**Banks/ATMs/Currency Exchange:** Banks are mostly closed on weekends, but ATMs are common on main streets. You can exchange currency upon arrival at the airport or in any bank, but cards are accepted almost everywhere (Landsbankinn: Austurstræti 12, 101 Reykjavík; 410 4000; M-F open 9am-4pm).

**Post Offices:** Pósthússtræti 5, 101 Reykjavík; 580 1000; open M-F 9am-9pm.

**Internet:** Free Wi-Fi is available at most cafés and public spaces, as well as at City Hall.

**BGLTQ+ Resources:** Iceland is one of the most progressive countries in the world with regard to BGLTQ+ rights and was the first country to openly elect a gay head of state. Reykjavík, like the rest of the country, is so well integrated that specific BGLTQ+ spaces are hardly necessary, though a few exist (Samtökin '78 is the National Queer Organization at Suðurgata 3, 101 Reykjavík; 552 7878; www.samtokin78.is; open M-F 1-4pm, open house 8-11pm).

## EMERGENCY INFORMATION

**Emergency Number:** 112

**Police:** Icelandic police are known for being friendly and fun-loving. Check out their Instagram (@logreglan) to see how they've been cracking down on crime among the snowman population (113-115 Hverfisgata, 105 Reykjavík; 444 1000).

**US Embassy:** Laufásvegur 21, 101 Reykjavík; 595 2200 (595 2248 after hours and weekends); M-F 8am-5pm.

**Rape Crisis Center:** A special emergency unit is located in the Emergency Department at Landspítali University Hospital, Fossvogur (108 Reykjavík; 543 2085; open daily 24hr).

**Hospitals:** The main hospital is located outside the city center. If urgent care is required, call 112 for an ambulance (Landspítali University Hospital, Fossvogur: Bráðamóttaka, Fossvogi; 543 2000; open daily 24hr).

**Pharmacies:**
- Lyfja (Laugavegur 16; 552 4045; M-F 9am-6pm, Sa 11am-5pm).
- Lyfja (Lágmúla 5; 533 2300; daily 8am-midnight).

# ACCOMMODATIONS

### ◪HLEMMUR SQUARE ($$)
Laugavegur 105; 105; 415 1600; www.hlemmursquare.com; reception open 24hr

Look, it's expensive to stay in Reykjavík. So, if you're going to spend the money anyway, treat yourself and book a room at Hlemmur Square. It's a combination hotel/hostel, and, while dorm prices are average for this city, the amenities are top-notch. Dorm rooms are spacious and include couches and sinks. The restaurant in the lobby offers a special "Square Meal" (1100 kr) Tuesday through Saturday. Sit at a communal table with other travelers and enjoy a selection of Icelandic cuisine. Seating begins at 6pm, but come early as it's first come first served.

*i* Hostel dorm rooms from 4800 kr, private double with shower from 19000 kr, private quad from 32400 kr; reservation recommended; BGLTQ+ friendly; Wi-Fi; linens included; laundry facilities (1500 kr); breakfast 7:30am-10:30am (1800 kr); luggage storage

### ODDSSON ($$)
Hringbraut 121; 101; 511 3579; www.oddsson.is; reception open 24hr

ODDSSON is a hotel/hostel, creatively marketing itself as "Ho(s)tel." Dorm rooms are standard issue, but the common spaces are some of the best you'll find, including a lobby with bare neon lights, a yoga studio, and a rooftop with a hot tub. Located right next to Reykjavík's harbor, it puts long strolls on the coast and midnight sunset walks just outside your door. Although it's a little far from town, you'll love being right by the beach. When the tide is low, there may even be a few patches of black sand exposed on the rocky shore.

*i* Dorms from 5500 kr, private from 15000 kr; reservation recommended;

BGLTQ+ friendly; Wi-Fi; linens included; lockers (500 kr); towel rental; laundry facilities (1500 kr)

# SIGHTS

## CULTURE

### HALLGRÍMSKIRKJA
Hallgrímstorg 1; 101; 510 1000; www.en.hallgrimskirkja.is; open daily May-Sept 9am- 9pm, Oct-Apr 9am-5pm, closed for Sunday morning mass

Situated high on a hill in the center of Reykjavík, Hallgrímskirkja stands tall and proud over the city. Finding this contemporary Lutheran church is easy, as its 74.5-meter tower can be seen from ground-level throughout the city. The design evokes Iceland's mountains, glaciers, and volcanic rock, and the result is what must be one of the world's most striking concrete structures. Inside, wander through the cavernous yet comfortable sanctuary, which contains **Iceland's largest instrument:** a 25-metric-ton organ composed of 5000 pipes. The church organist sometimes practices during the day, and you can listen for free. For a fee, take the elevator up to the top of the tower for a vertigo-inducing view of downtown Reykjavík and the ocean beyond.

*i* Church admission free, tower 900 kr; tower closes 30min before church; wheelchair accessible

### HARPA
Autobrake 2; 102; 528 5000; www.en.harpa.is; open daily 8am-midnight

Outside, it looks like the Water Cube's trendy younger cousin. Inside, it's like standing in a giant kaleidoscope. Overall, it's the essence of Iceland (read: aesthetically pleasing) captured in stone and glass. Harpa is officially a conference center and concert hall, home to the **Iceland Symphony Orchestra** and the **Icelandic Opera,** but it also hosts many lesser-known artists, cultural performances, and comedy shows. For 4500 kr, try *How to become Icelandic in 60 minutes*, a production which promises to have you feeling "100% Icelandic."

## WALL POETRY

Spend enough time wandering around downtown Reykjavík and you're bound to notice the street art. It's everywhere and comes in all forms, from American-esque graffiti, probably painted while the cops weren't looking, to larger, half-wall paintings of cityscapes and the like. But a few pieces—huge murals scattered seemingly randomly across the city—are different. They're unmissable, taking up entire walls with vibrant colors and scenes ranging from majestic to psychedelic: weather-beaten ship captain at the helm of his boat, positioned so that he stares out over the open sea; black unicorn with a yellow bolt of lightning tattooed across its face leaping in front of a dripping rainbow; lines of ghostly human figures pacing across a black background. They're stunning to say the least.

It turns out that the project is a coordinated effort, sponsored in part by the city itself. URBAN NATION, a German street artist collective, partnered with the Icelandic Airwaves music festival two years ago to expand the project known as Wall Poetry. Each musician chosen to participate picks or composes a song and is paired with a street artist who paints his or her interpretation of that song on a wall.

The result is art that you *actually want to see.* If you wanted to see renaissance oil paintings and beautiful wooden frames in a stuffy, pretentious art museum, you would have gone to Paris, right? But you're here, where the art is out in the open and always on display. Visit www.icelandairwaves.is/wall-poetry for a complete list of addresses for all 20 pieces, and hit the streets. Start on the west side at the harbor or at Hlemmur Square on the east, and get a full tour within an hour or two. Or, for more adventure, pick a starting point and wander until you've seen all you can.

If only it were really that easy...

*i* *Free, show prices vary; paid guided tours available regularly in summer, winter M-F 3:30pm, Sa-Su 11am and 3:30pm; wheelchair accessible*

## LANDMARKS

### ◪SÓLFAR (SUN VOYAGER)

Sæbraut; open daily 24hr

You're in Iceland. Expectations for your Instagram posts have never been higher, but there's already a 100-person line in front of **Leif Erikson** (Eiríksgata; open daily 24hr; wheelchair accessible)! Fear not, Sólfar delivers. The platform on which this dreamboat statue sits juts away from the otherwise uniform coastline, with the ship's bow extended proudly toward the sea and the mountains beyond. Though it looks something like a jungle gym, most viewers stay back, snapping clear shots from every angle. There's really no bad time to visit, but we'd recommend going at sunset.

*i* *Free; wheelchair accessible*

### REYKJAVÍK CITY LIBRARY

Tryggvagata 15; 101; 411 6100; www. borgarbokasafn.is/end; open M-Th 10am-7pm, F 11am-6pm, Sa-Su 1-4pm

Not the most interesting spot in the city—it is a library after all. But the City Library is a great spot for strong Wi-Fi access and outlets for your phone, laptop, portable battery, camera, and whatever other gadgets you're dragging around. The space is modern with lots of natural light and several types of seating (beanbag chair anyone?). The upstairs level houses the kids' section where you can let loose your inner child in play spaces with cushioned reading nooks, comic and picture books, and an entire shelf of board games

*i* *Free; wheelchair accessible*

## MUSEUMS

### ◪ICELANDIC PUNK MUSEUM

Bankastræti 2; www.thepunkmuseum.is; open M-F 10am-10pm, Sa-Su noon-10pm

The Icelandic Punk Museum has established itself below street level in an abandoned city restroom. Rent must be pretty cheap down there, except everything is expensive in Iceland. Everything about the IPM screams "anarchy," and it's not just the anarchy symbols painted just about everywhere you look. It's also the punk music blaring from street-level speakers, eliciting disgruntled looks from patrons of a nearby seafood restaurant, and the child-sized blue M&M statue sporting a mohawk and an ammo belt. Downstairs, travel through the history of this famously Icelandic genre from the first appearance of punk in 1974 through its current evolution. If you're feeling brave (or rebellious), listen to famous punk hits from the array of headsets or try out the electric guitar and drum kit for yourself.

*i* *Admission 1000 kr*

### ◪THE ICELANDIC PHALLOGICAL MUSEUM

Laugavegur 116; 105; 561 6663; www. phallus.is

Now that you know it exists, you *have* to go, right? This well-endowed museum boasts a collection of over 280 specimens from more than 90 species (including species of "folklore," how Icelandic), ranging in size from a few millimeters to several feet.

Yes, feet! If you're getting overwhelmed by penises dried, stuffed and mounted, or preserved in formaldehyde, check out the museum's even bigger (by quantity at least) assortment of penis art and "practical utensils." Prepare to learn more fun (or maybe not fun) phallus facts than you ever wanted from a series of panels in Icelandic and English. And while it can be difficult to stay composed when learning about the "surprisingly high motion control" that an elephant has over its member, please try to stay classy.

*i* Admission 1500 kr; wheelchair accessible

### ÞJÓÐMINJASAFN ÍSLANDS (NATIONAL MUSEUM OF ICELAND)

Suðurgata 41; 101; 530 2200; www.thjod-minjasafn.is; open T-Su 10am-5pm, closed Sept 16-Apr 30

If your parents are expecting to hear about museums, this one's a no-brainer. Iceland's National Museum covers over 1000 years of Icelandic history, from the first settlement of the island by the Norse to the establishment of the modern republic in 1944 and to present day events. Check out the collection of ancient drinking horns and gawk at an entire fishing boat annotated with complete, syntactically convoluted English translations. (Ever heard of an "unruly reformation" before?) For a break, head to one of the "Hands-On Rooms," where you can grab a comfy reading nook or try on a selection of traditional Icelandic clothing.

*i* Admission 2000 kr, 1000 kr student, seniors and under 18 free; tours only for groups of 10+ and booked in advance; audio guide 300 kr; wheelchair accessible

## OUTDOORS

### THE BLUE LAGOON

240 Grindavík; 420 8800; www.bluela-goon.com; open Jan 1-May 25 8am-10pm, 7am-11pm, June 30-Aug 20 7am-midnight, Aug 21-Oct 1 8am-10pm, Oct 2-Dec 31 8am-8pm

If you want the ultimate in Icelandic tourism, look no further (and that's saying a *lot*). Along with large quantities of geothermally-heated water and steam, the Blue Lagoon oozes luxury. This pristine spa has everything from a steam cave to a man-made waterfall. It even has a bar in the lagoon itself where you can charge in-water drinks to your Star Trek-style wristband. None of this comes cheap, though, and it shows. You'll be sharing the enormous pool with wealthy couples, foreign tourists, and lots of families with kids (they get in free under 14). The Blue Lagoon is about an hour from Reykjavík, so you'll have to arrange bus transit as well. Depending on how early you book, it can be cheaper and easier to book through an independent tour company.

*i* Book in advance; admission 6100 kr; price goes up during high season; from Reykjavík/airport 4500 kr; towel/bathing suit (700 kr ); robe/slippers (1400 kr); last entry 1hr before close; wheelchair accessible

# FOOD

### ◾BÆJARINS BEZTU PYLSUR (THE BEST HOT DOG IN TOWN) ($)

Tryggvagata 1; 101; 511 1566; www.bbp.is; open M-Th 10am-1am, F-Sa 10am-4:30pm, Su 10am-1am

That's right, this hot dog stand is open later than most bars in America. The menu is simple, too. Hot dog: 450 kr. Soda: 250 kr. So easy you'll still be able to understand it even after a few too many *brennivín* shots at the bar. This tiny hot dog shack's unassuming appearance belies its deliciousness and popularity; it's been around since 1937, giving its staff a lot of time to perfect their single item. Apparently, Bill Clinton was here once, and judging by his picture on the wall, they've done a damn good job.

*i* Hot dog 450 kr, soda 250 kr; wheelchair accessible

### ◾BRAUÐ & CO ($$)

Frakkastígur 16; 101; www.braudogco.is; open M-F 6am-6pm, Sa-Su 6am-5pm

You can't miss Brauð & Co, but by its appearance alone you won't recognize it as a bakery. What gave it away to us was the smell of freshly-baked pastries wafting out of the front door. The building's façade, just a short walk from Reykjavík's main shopping street, is painted in a kaleidoscopic rainbow

# WAIT, THEY EAT *WHAT* HERE?

If you choose to come to Iceland, chances are it isn't for the food; it's to see hot springs and glaciers. Iceland's cuisine isn't known all over the world like that of France, Italy, or Thailand, but, with dishes like these, it should be. Here are five dishes you have to try in Reykjavík, in ascending order of shock factor:

1. **Meat Soup:** It's often said that there are more sheep in Iceland than people, so it comes as no surprise that lamb is one of the main proteins. There's no better way to try it than in meat soup, where it is traditionally accompanied by fresh vegetables and simmered for hours. A great way to warm up on a cold Icelandic winter (or summer) day.

2. **Plokkfiskur:** Don't be alarmed by the name; this is just fish stew. It's the Icelandic equivalent of meat and potatoes. (Well, they have that too, but you get the point.) It's made from fresh-caught fish – often cod or haddock – potatoes, vegetables, and enough butter to make Paula Dean wince. The result is a stew hearty enough to be a full meal. Often served with rye bread.

3. **Hot Dogs:** It feels a little bit wrong to think of hot dogs as representative of any cuisine (except American of course), but the Icelandic version deserves it. They're made with lamb, which is sure to add a delicious twist to your first bite. Try *eina með öllu* (translation: one with everything) to get the full assortment of toppings: ketchup, sweet mustard, crisp fried onion, raw onion, and remoulade.

4. **Hákarl:** Now this is getting weird. Perhaps the most infamous Icelandic dish, Hákarl is a type of putrescent ("fermented" is probably more appropriate) shark meat. It is traditionally prepared by burying a Greenland shark under a heavy weight to press out the fluids, which are poisonous. After a few months, the shark is cut into strips and hung to dry for a few more weeks prior to being served. It's traditionally taken with a shot of *brennivín*, Iceland's signature schnapps.

5. **Svið:** It's a boiled sheep's head. Well, half a sheep's head. And the brain is removed. Oh yeah, they singe off all the hair first. Still not convinced? Svið comes from a time when no animal part could go to waste, and it has stuck around until today. Apparently many Icelanders consider the eyes to be a delicacy…

that belongs on the set of a psychedelic Beatles music video. Inside, most of the square footage is behind the counter, where you can watch as the bakers mix, pour, knead, and shuffle trays full of warm buns, crossiants, and their **signature cinnamon rolls** and **sourdough bread** in and out of ovens. The place is understandably busy, but don't be fooled by a long line; it's worth the wait for a delectable cinnamon bun or famous sourdough loaf.

*i* *Individual pastries 500 kr; vegetarian and vegan options available*

### 🥐CAFÉ BABALÚ ($$)
Skólavörðustígur 22; 101; 555 8845; www. babalu.is
Nothing in Café Babalú makes sense. The tables and chairs don't match, the advertised opening time is 11am, but it often opens earlier, and the music unexpectedly switches from Journey to polka. But, in a way, everything does makes sense: décor is so eclectic that nothing looks out of place, not even the entire shelf of *The Flintstones* merchandise. Babalú makes you think, "Well, why wouldn't there be a New York license plate hanging next to a clock made entirely of plastic forks?" Drinks are in the 500 kr range, and food varies from the sweet (the signature cheesecake, 990 kr) to the savory (traditional lamb soup, 1690 kr). Oh, and the bathroom is Star Wars themed and mysteriously playing the soundtrack when you enter.

*i* *Coffee/tea 400 kr, coffee 500-600 kr, sweet crepes 890 kr, cheesecake 990 kr; vegetarian and vegan options available; wheelchair accessible*

## NOODLE STATION ($$)

Laugavegur 103; 551 3198; www.noodles-station.is; open M-F 11am-10pm, Sa-Su noon-10pm

It's late, the grocery stores are closed, and the line for the hostel kitchen is way too long. How are you going to get the daily dose of ramen that college kids and budget travelers need for survival? Head east, away from downtown Reykjavík to Noodle Station. There's only one item on the menu: noodle soup (beef, chicken, or vegetable), and, at 1580 kr, it's one of the cheapest meals in town. You'll feel right at home among a crowd of younger travelers grabbing a quick meal before a night out. Select a spice level (spicy packs a punch without being overpowering) and then adjust to taste with fish sauce, hot chili oil, and salt.

*i* Soup 920-1580kr, drinks 300kr; vegetarian and vegan options available

## ÍSLENSKI BARINN ($$$)

Ingólfsstræti 1a; 101; 517 6767; www.islenskibarinn.is; open M-Th 11:30am-1am, F-Sa 11:30am-3am, Su 11:30am-1am

If you find yourself with a little bit of extra cash (unlikely as that is) and want to try some strange Icelandic food in a decidedly not-strange setting, try Íslenski Barinn. The menu features all the greatest hits, including shark, fish stew, and meat soup. As a bonus, the bar is stocked with almost every alcohol produced in Iceland, you know, for when you get bored of Viking beer and *brennivín*. Retro décor, unlike in your grandmother's house, is done well, in a wallpaper-without-the-mold kind of way.

*i* Beer 900-1300 kr, spirits 800-1200 kr, entrées from 2850 kr, burgers from 2500 kr; vegetarian, vegan, and gluten-free options available; no wheelchair accessibility

# NIGHTLIFE

## ⬛KIKI QUEER BAR

Laugavegur 22; 101; www.kiki.is; open W-Th 8pm-1am, F-Sa 8pm-4:30am, Su 8pm-1am

In a country as progressive as Iceland in terms of BGLTQ+ rights, it's surprising that there's only one **queer bar.** Maybe it's because Kiki would drive any others out of business. Up the rainbow stairs are two small bars that fill up quickly on the weekends. Pro tip: show up before 11pm to beat the crowds and take advantage of one of the best happy hour deals around (beer and shots from 500 kr). Bring friends or make new ones in a diverse crowd of people of all stripes: young, old, gay, straight, or somewhere in between. The atmosphere is a mélange of bar and club, but always upbeat thanks to a DJ who indulges all of your guilty pleasures (come on, you know "Take on Me" never gets old).

*i* No cover, beer 1000 kr, mixed drinks from 1500 kr; happy hour 8-11pm (500 kr beer/shots); BGLTQ+ friendly

## HRESSÓ

Austurstræti 20; 101; 561 2240; www.hresso.is; open M-Th 9am-1am, Sa 10am-4:30am, Su 10am-1am

In America, people with man buns don't normally mix well with those who wear camo. At Hressó, the guys with man buns also wear camo. Hressó is a full-service restaurant during the day and a hot local venue at night. In the early hours of the evening, the courtyard is often bumping with locally produced hip hop mixtapes. After midnight, the party moves inside to a live DJ. It's a fantastic spot for feeling out the local scene or potentially scouting the next great Icelandic music star, but if you're after something upbeat, look elsewhere.

*i* No cover, beer 1250 kr, mixed drinks from 1650 kr; BGLTQ+ friendly

## PRIKIÐ

Bankastræti 12; 101; 551 2866; www.prikid.is

Don't be fooled by Prikið's daytime alter-ego of "oldest café in Iceland;" this place shines after dark (err, in the evening?). After the kitchen closes at 9pm, the tourists clear out and Prikið makes the typical Icelandic switch from coffee shop to late-night hangout. The DJ's loud hip hop selections keep the crowd casual, young, and quite local, and two bars and an outdoor courtyard provide ample space to mix, mingle, and marvel at the amount of sunlight present at 1am on a summer night.

*i* No cover, mixed drinks from 1500 kr, happy hour 4-8pm (600 kr beer), burgers 2000kr; BGLTQ+ friendly

# RING ROAD

Coverage by **Eric Chin**

"**Hringvegur.**" "**Þjóðvegur.**" "**Route 1.**" Each of these names refers to the same 1332 kilometer stretch of asphalt and gravel winding its way in a lazy circle around Iceland. Most know it simply as the Ring Road.

Though its fame and popularity grow each year, a road trip on the Ring Road is still the ultimate way to experience as much of Iceland's raw beauty as you can at your own pace. Sure, a guide can explain what makes geysers erupt or why all the beaches have black sand, but no bus driver will pull off the road every 10 minutes to let you gawk at and photograph the newest scenery. Nor will any tour drive you through the most remote regions of the island least touched by society, like the East Fjords or the highlands of the north. Only getting behind the wheel yourself will enable you to immerse yourself in Iceland's glaciers and volcanoes, its black beaches and waterfalls, and its peaks and fjords.

But it won't be easy. You'll be jockeying with other tourists for the best photo angles one day and aching to see a fellow traveler the next. You'll cross a lifetime of one-lane bridges in a span of just days. You'll struggle to find accommodations priced so you can also afford to eat. The road will just wear you down.

But if you want to have the adventure of a lifetime, it's all worth it. There's no better place and no better way. Here's how to do it.

## BEFORE YOU GO

**Renting a Car:** If you're going to drive the Ring Road, you'll need a car; that much is non-negotiable. But you do have options. In the summer when road conditions are good, just about any car will be suitable for the journey, and your cheapest option will be a subcompact. These tiny things are cheap to rent (under $500 for a week-long rental) and very fuel efficient. Here are a few technicalities:

- In order to rent a car in Iceland, you must be 20 years old and have held a valid driver's license for over a year. The minimum age for many companies is 21.
- Like in the United States, you'll need a credit (not debit) card in the main driver's name.
- For any car rental, **make sure you have insurance. If your insurance does not cover you abroad, buy insurance.** This trip is long and hard on vehicles. In short, just get the insurance.
- Most cars in Iceland are manual transmission. Renting an automatic will probably be more expensive. (Get a friend to teach you to drive manual; it will save you a lot of money!)

**Driving in Iceland:** The vast majority of Route 1 is a paved, undivided highway with one lane traveling in each direction. Lanes are added near Reykjavík and in some larger towns. Most of the road has little or no shoulder, but there are frequent pull-offs where you can get out, stretch, and take pictures. One section of the Ring Road in East Iceland, and many of the roads branching off of Route 1, are gravel.

- Like in the United States, cars drive on the right side of the road in Iceland.
- The speed limit is 90 kph (about 56 mph) on paved roads and 80 kph (about 50 mph) on gravel roads.
- Your headlights must be on at all times and seatbelts are mandatory in all seats.
- Most towns have gas stations, but these can be few and far between, especially in the eastern region. A good rule of thumb is to refuel whenever your tank

drops below half-full, but be warned: gas is expensive in Iceland—around $7 per gallon.

**Navigation:** The nice thing about driving on the Ring Road is that it's tough to get too lost; it's just one road! Okay, it's not quite that simple. While many stops are directly off Route 1, you will need to take other roads to get to some areas of the country. To avoid using international data (expensive) or renting a GPS (not worth it), the following strategy with Google Maps is usually plenty effective:
- Decide on your start/end points for the next day and star them in Google Maps.
- Star all the sights you might want to visit between those two points. Seriously, star everything!
- Google Maps will allow you download entire portions of maps for offline use. Download the area covering your two endpoints and the entire section of road in between. Most of Iceland is pretty empty, so downloads are generally a reasonable size.
- Most waterfalls, mountains, and other attractions are already labeled by name in Google Maps. If not, the coordinates can be looked up online and plugged in.

**Accommodations:** This is probably the piece of your trip that requires the most planning, and you have two basic options:
- **Camping.** There are designated campsites all over Iceland, allowing almost unlimited customization of your route. Campsites charge fees, but for 18900 kr the Camping Card (www.campingcard.is) gives you access to over 40 of these sites. If you don't want to lug your own gear all the way to Iceland, many companies in Reykjavík rent out tents, sleeping bags, and other supplies.
- **Not camping.** This is doable, but requires serious preparation to be cost-effective. True hostels are somewhat rare on the road, and the ones that exist aren't cheap. Failing hostels, Airbnb can be a good option, but be sure to book early.

**Food:** Eating out in Iceland is expensive, and, on the road, it's no different. To save money, it's a good idea to stock up on food in Reykjavík at Bónus or a similar discount store, as groceries are more expensive outside the city. If you're camping, it's not a bad idea to bring or rent a camp stove.

**Trip Length:** Driving the Ring Road is possible in five days, but only if you want to spend (even more) hours a day in the car, driving past beautiful sights you wish you could stop at. A week is more reasonable, allowing you to pull over and take photos when you want to, throw in a spontaneous extra stop or hike, and retain some semblance of sanity.

**Packing:** It probably shouldn't come as a surprise that a country called "Iceland" is cold. Summer temperatures often sit in the 50s during the day and can drop to the low 40s at night. If you plan on camping, thermal layers and a sleeping bag are a must. Rain is fairly frequent, and wind is almost constant outside Reykjavík, so a raincoat or light shell is a good idea, even if just to break the wind. A sturdy pair of hiking boots or shoes is also necessary.

**Bring a friend!** A solo trip of the Ring Road can be incredibly rewarding. It can also drive you insane. Going with a friend allows you to split up the driving, have some much-needed human contact during the loneliest times, and split the cost of the car, tent, campsite, and so on more effectively. Plus, Icelandic radio is great (if spotty in places), and you wouldn't want to have to sing along by yourself!

Iceland can be divided very roughly into six regions, one of which won't be covered here (the **Westfjords** are sparsely populated, tracked with rough roads, and seldom traveled). Here are the five regions of Iceland you should hit on your trip:

# THE GOLDEN CIRCLE

The Golden Circle is, you guessed it, a circle. Starting from Reykjavík, it winds through West Iceland's mountainous landscape, hitting several of Iceland's most famous natural and historical landmarks before returning to the capital or continuing to other regions of the country. It's a logical first day for a Ring Road trip, but it can also be booked as a day trip through any of Reykjavík's tour agencies. The waterfalls and geysers are breathtaking, but be prepared to battle crowds all day.

## SIGHTS

### ÞINGVELLIR NATIONAL PARK

482 3613; www.thingvellir.is/english; visitor center open June-Aug 9am-8pm, Sept-Apr 9am-6pm

Þingvellir has something for everyone. History buffs will appreciate the fact that Iceland's parliament, the Alþing, was established here in 930 CE. Science and nature geeks will appreciate the fantastic natural phenomena created by Þingvellir's location on the edge of the North American and Eurasian tectonic plates. Everyone else will enjoy the easily accessible hiking trails that crisscross the park. For a truly unforgettable, if somewhat cold, experience, sign up for a tour to snorkel in Silfra, a crack between the tectonic plates found in Lake Þingvallavatn.

*i* Free admission, parking 500 kr per day; from Reykjavík, head north on Route 1 for about 35km. At traffic circle, turn right onto Þingvallavegur (Route 36), following signs for Þingvellir. Park will be about 30km on the right.

### SILFRA

Þingvellir National Park

You don't have to be a scientist to know that tectonic plates are pretty damn big, and nowhere but Iceland gives you the chance to stand between them. In the northern part of Lake Þingvallavatn lies Silfra, a fissure between the North American and Eurasian plates. Water from a glacier melts and trickles through an underground aquifer of volcanic rock for decades before finally being released into the giant crack. The result is some of the clearest, purest water to be found anywhere on Earth. Oh, and it's also 2-4°C year-round, a temperature known in Iceland as "really fucking cold." But when has a little bit of glacial water stopped humans from appreciating the beauty of nature before, right?

Your guides will layer you up in a puffy thermal suit before stuffing you into a thick drysuit. (Ever wondered what a hybrid of Iron Man and a marshmallow would be like? No? Well now you know.) It's hard not be anxious about the frigid waters, but once you're in, the view is all you'll be able to think about. The water is so clear and the colors so vibrant that it makes the air seem dull. The depths of Silfra are a deep blue, the jagged boulders that make up the walls of the tectonic plates seem to glow red and green, and the long strands of algae, affectionately called "troll's hair," stand out a vibrant green. The buoyant drysuits seal out the cold (er, mostly) and keep you afloat so you can enjoy the view as you drift through Silfra Hall and the majestic Silfra Cathedral (where the walls of the plates can reach 20 meters in depth) and end in the wide expanse of Silfra Lagoon. Head back to the parking lot (pro tip: keep your gloves on for this bit), where most tours will regroup with hot chocolate and cookies, or similar goodies.

*i* Book a tour in advance, most tours over 15000 kr, cheaper if you don't need transportation from Reykjavík

### HAUKADALUR

Haukadalur is home to the famous Geysir. That's right, one of the first geysers known to Europeans, and the one that gave us the word "geyser" in the first place. Some sources say its spray can reach 80 meters high. Oh, and it's broken. Seriously, the Great Geysir has been dormant since the early twentieth century. Conveniently, though, a second geyser named Strokkur is right next door, and spouts to heights of 15- to 20 meters every five to ten minutes. The area also contains a number of steaming hot springs and fumaroles. When you can't bear the smell of rotten eggs anymore (nobody ever tells you how bad these things smell), head back over to the visitor center, where you can join throngs of tourists at restaurants and a gift shop.

*i* From Þingvellir National Park, head northeast on Route 36. In 15km, stay straight onto Route 365. In 15 km, stay straight through roundabout onto Route 37, which becomes Route 35. Stay on Route 35 for 5 km and you'll arrive at Haukadalur.

## GULLFOSS
www.gullfoss.is

Gullfoss is the first of countless waterfalls you'll encounter along the Ring Road, and it starts things off with a bang. Easy hikes will take you from the parking lot to several viewpoints (ideal for picking the best Instagram angle). To hike the trail closest to the falls, bring raingear because the spray reaches high enough to soak the trail. Like every stop on the Golden Circle, Gullfoss is often overrun with tourists, but don't lose hope! You're driving the Ring Road! You'll leave these amateurs behind soon enough.

*i* From Haukadalur, head east on Route 35 for about 9 km. Parking will be on your right.

## KERIÐ CRATER
Another great stop on the Golden Circle is Kerið Crater (55 km south of Gullfoss on Route 35), a collapsed volcano which now holds a strikingly blue lake. After touring the Golden Circle, spend the night in Reykjavík or at Midgard Adventure for a head start on the South Coast.

*i* 400 kr; from Gullfoss, drive 55 km south on Route 35, and the parking lot will be on the left.

# SOUTH COAST
The term "South Coast" most commonly refers to the region between Reykjavík and the southern city of Vík. This heavily traveled section of the Ring Road includes waterfalls, rock formations, and several of Iceland's famous sand beaches. Like the Golden Circle, tours of the south coast from Reykjavík are popular, so the area is quite busy.

## SIGHTS

### ◼SELJALANDSFOSS AND SKÓGAFOSS
Gullfoss was just the beginning. The south coast is home to these two popular waterfalls, each with a different claim to fame. At Seljalandsfoss, suit up in your raingear and take a very wet, if short, hike into a cave behind the pounding falls. Half an hour east is Skógafoss, where you can climb a man-made staircase to an aerial viewing platform. From here, you can escape the selfie stick-wielding crowd by taking a bit of a hike up the ridge for panoramic views of the ocean, snow-capped mountains, and, in all likelihood, a good number of sheep. They're everywhere.

### BLACK BEACH
Vík

It's a lot like any other beach you've ever visited, but the water is way too cold for swimming. Oh, and the sand is black, but you've probably figured that bit out by now. A good rule of thumb for any outdoor sight is that the farther you go from the parking lot, the fewer tourists you'll encounter, and it holds true here. If you head all the way down the left side of the beach and around the point (accessibility changes based on the tide), you'll find another beach, just as beautiful, but significantly less crowded.

*i* Take Route 215 from the Ring Road until you reach the beach parking lot.

### OTHER SIGHTS ON THE SOUTHCOAST
If you're looking for an incredible photo spot and are up for a bit of a hike, visit Sólheimasandur to see the wreckage of a United States Navy DC plane that crashed on the beach. If you plan on continuing around the Ring Road after traveling the South Coast, try camping at Skaftafell Campground in Vatnajökull National Park, or finding other accommodations in the Skaftafell area.

# EAST ICELAND

If you've made it this far, congratulations! Welcome to the solitude, the untamed wilderness, and the stunning beauty that is East Iceland. You've made it where even Reykjavík's endless tour buses can't reach. Just you, the sheep, and the road. And the road is glorious out here. It winds by the massive glacier Vatnajökull, past ethereal glacier lagoons, and through the majestic East Fjords. The drive is long and lonely, but you won't want to miss a mile.

## SIGHTS

### VATNAJÖKULL NATIONAL PARK, SKAFTAFELL REGION

Route 998; 470 8300; www.vatnajokulsth-jodgardur.is/english; open Jan 10am-4pm, Feb-Apr 10am-5pm, May-Sept 9am-7pm, Oct-Nov 10am-5pm, Dec 11am-5pm

If you took up the mantle of driving the Ring Road, chances are you're into flannel, recycling, and nature. Well here's your big chance to get up close and personal with some of Iceland's best, all walkable from the Skaftafell visitor center. Svartifoss, a waterfall framed by sheer cliffs of columnar basalt, is one of the area's main attractions and a quick 5.5km loop. From there, trails feature every variation of length and difficulty, all the way up to a nearly-30km haul around the park. Another unforgettable (if a bit expensive) tour opportunity leaves right from the visitor center: a chance to hike on one of Europe's largest glaciers.

### GLACIER HIKE

Vatnajökull National Park; tour leaves from Skaftafell

You've probably heard of glaciers before: they're basically just big ice cubes on mountains, right? But how big, exactly? Find out for yourself with this once-in-a-lifetime (seriously, they're disappearing at an alarming rate) chance to hike on one of Europe's largest glaciers, Vatnajökull. Included with your tour is a badass set of gear, including crampons, ice axe, harness, and helmet (bring your own raincoat, rain pants, boots, food, and camera) to make you feel like the mountaineer you could never be. After a short bus ride and hike out to the tongue of the glacier, strap on your spikes and follow your guide up onto the ice.

Oh right, the guides! They're incredibly friendly and knowledgeable about all things glacier, and each one carries an enormous, 3-foot beast of an axe used to clear the trail. The path winds up the slope and down into crevasses (not "crevices;" this is the big leagues), some which are just a few feet wide. The longer, half-day tours go all the way up to the edge of the icefall, which is just as cool as it sounds—a jagged cliff of ice formed by chunks falling from the main glacier above. Your guide will show you arches and caves, as well as glacial clay—a fine black silt, reportedly excellent for the skin. Seriously, they sell mud masks of the stuff. Most tours will spend around 1.5 or 3.5 hours on the glacier itself, and it's impossible not to be awed and humbled by nature at its purest.

*i Tours are frequent during the spring/ summer season and generally start from about 10000 kr for 3-hour tours and 15000 kr for half-day tours.*

### JÖKULSÁRLÓN GLACIER LAGOON AND DIAMOND BEACH

About 50 km east of Skaftafell is Jökulsárlón Glacier Lagoon. It's basically a lake full of icebergs—but big, scary, Titanic-sinking icebergs is what you're probably picturing. These are much more manageable, and unlike in Titanic, you can safely travel among them. Boat tours start at 5500 kr for large boats, or 9500 kr for a nimbler Zodiac. Just across the road from Jökulsárlón is Diamond Beach, a black-sand beach named for the tiny icebergs dotted across its shores like, well, diamonds. Walk among the smaller chunks higher on the beach; just don't try standing on them.

### OTHER SIGHTS IN EAST ICELAND

The drive through the East Fjords is one of the most beautiful sections of the entire Ring Road, winding up the coast with sheer cliffs on one side and the vast ocean on the other. It's also the emptiest and contains a few gravel sections. The gravel roads are well-maintained, but use caution. Finding a place to spend the night out here can be tricky, so be creative. Your best bet is to look in the area around Alistair, the largest town in the region.

# NORTH ICELAND

And just like that, you're back to civilization. From Egilsstaðir, Route 1 turns west and away from the coast. You'll head up into the gorgeous highlands of Iceland's northeastern interior, before descending into the Mývatn area, safely back into tourist territory.

## SIGHTS

### ◣KRAFLA

If you're driving in from the east, this is the first big stop in the Mývatn region, and it's a can't-miss. Krafla is a volcanic crater (a caldera, to be pedantic) that still exhibits lots of geothermal activity, even though it hasn't actively erupted in a while. Yes, this sounds boring, but trust us, it's better for you that way. Check out Víti, another of those utterly-Instagram-able crater lakes with impossibly blue water. The road leads right up to the edge, and it's a short hike around the lip of the crater. From the lower parking lot, a more substantial hike will take you to the Leirhnjúkur lava field. Walk among jagged spikes of cooled lava, many still spewing sulfurous steam, and look out over a milky blue hot spring.

### HVERIR

Just past the road to Krafla is Hverir, a huge geothermal area that feels more like an artist's rendition of the surface of Mars than a naturally occurring landscape. Cracked yellow earth, bubbling pits of dark mud, and rock chimneys spewing steam so vigorously you can hear it all lie beneath the red mountain Námafjall. Great for a quick pit stop, but if you just can't get enough of the smell of rotten eggs (hey, no judgment) hike up Námafjall for an incredible view of the whole area.

### MÝVATN NATURE BATHS

Office 464 4411; www.myvatnnaturebaths. is; open May 15-Sept 30 9am-midnight, Oct 1-May 14 noon-10pm

It would be a shame to come to Iceland and not bathe in one of the country's famed geothermal pools, but you also don't want to hurt your wallet or your reputation as a savvy traveler by going to the Blue Lagoon. Enter the Mývatn Nature Baths. It's like the Blue Lagoon's lowkey little brother who just wants to hang out. The warm, milky blue water gives you all the best parts of a hot tub without having to awkwardly squeeze yourself between wrinkly old men in "European-style" bathing suits.

You know what we're talking about. It's certainly not a steaming pool out in the middle of the forest, but it's been a long trip. Don't you deserve a little bit of pampering?

*i* Admission May 15-Sept 30 adults 4300 kr, 2700 kr student, Oct 1-May 15 adults 3800 kr, student 2400 kr, towel/ swimsuit rental 700 kr each, bathrobe rental 1500 kr; last entry 30min. before close

### OTHER SIGHTS IN NORTH ICELAND

The volcanic lake Mývatn was formed in the aftermath of an eruption, so it's no surprise that the surrounding landscape is rich in volcanic landforms like Dimmuborgir, a lava field with especially strange spires of rock, and the Skútustaðir pseudocraters, a field of craters formed not directly by volcanic eruptions, but by steam. Route 1 stays on the north side of the lake, while Route 848 loops around to the south before rejoining the main road. Akureyri, the first real city since Reykjavík, is a good spot to spend a night or two to recharge.

# AKUREYRI

Akureyri's population of just under 20,000 people makes the city a thriving metropolis by Iceland's standards—the country's second-largest, in fact. It certainly doesn't have the attractions and landmarks of a major city, but it is an excellent spot to take a day to rest, resupply, and generally reconnect with civilization. There's a Bónus where you can restock on all your favorite Icelandic groceries at a reasonable (for Iceland, at least) price, and Akureyri Backpackers is an excellent hostel, with a restaurant and bar that serve as a hub for the whole town. Akureyri is the main tourist hub outside of Reykjavík, and some of the most popular offerings include whale watching and horseback riding.

## ACCOMMODATIONS

### ⛔AKUREYRI BACKPACKERS ($$)

Hafnarstræti 98, 600 Akureyri; +354 571 9050; www.akureyribackpackers. com; reception open M-F 7:30am-11pm, Sa-Su 7:30am-1pm (late check-in can be arranged)

They say that first impressions matter, and Akureyri Backpackers nails it by giving you a free drink at the bar when you check in. Everything that follows is similarly fantastic. The vibe is upbeat and energetic, the clientele tired from packed days yet adventurous and excited for what tomorrow will bring. Pro tip: stop by the tour desk to book a whale watch or super jeep trip. A prime location in the middle of "downtown" Akureyri (if such a thing exists) keeps the street-level restaurant and bar alive with a mix of backpackers and locals all day and into the evening. Akureyri, and indeed the entire north of Iceland, seems to live and breathe through this hostel.

*i* *Dorms from 4500 kr, privates from 16000 kr; reservation recommended; Wi-Fi; BGLTQ+ friendly; pillow included but not duvet (1100 kr for whole stay), sleeping bags allowed, free sauna, continental breakfast buffet 1215 kr if booked in advance, laundry services, security lockers*

## FOOD

### DJ GRILL ($)

Strandgata 11, 600 Akureyri; 462 1800; open M-F 11:30am-9:00pm, Sa-Su noon-9pm

Sometimes the only thing to fill you up is a nice hot meal, especially if you've been pounding PB&Js on the road for the past few days. Whether you're in Akureyri for days or just a few hours, stop by Dj Grill for the greasy, delicious burger you've been dreaming of. A cheeseburger is just 690 kr, but you can add patties, toppings, and sides to bring the price into more familiar Icelandic territory. Just a short walk from the center of town, Dj Grill is also a convenient takeout spot, with locals popping in and out during dinner hours.

*i* *Burgers 690-2000 kr, sides 400-800 kr*

# SNÆFELLSNES PENINSULA

From Akureyri, it's a bit of a drive to the Snæfellsnes Peninsula, the last big stop on the Ring Road. Route 1 cuts inland a bit, only navigating one or two fjords before reaching Snæfellsnes. This area is sometimes called "Iceland in miniature" by various tour agencies, because it features many of Iceland's main attractions—waterfalls, volcanoes, beaches, and glaciers—in a small, easily drivable area.

## SIGHTS

### ⛔KIRKJUFELL

Kirkjufell is one of the most photographed mountains in Iceland (that Dr. Seuss-like one that shows up in every search for "Iceland"). Sweet, sounds touristy, move on. Oh wait, you can climb it? Better switch out your fanny pack for a CamelBak—this is a proper adventure now. The ascent isn't long, but it's certainly not easy; the trail is ill-defined and without distinct markers, and features a fair bit of slippery scree on the way up. Oh, and the ropes. The locals have fixed (only slightly frayed) ropes to large boulders to help in the ascent and descent of three particularly dicey scrambles. If you're bold (or slightly stupid?) and reach the peak, the reward is huge. Though only 1500ft., a long ridge along the summit affords unobstructed views of the sea on one side and snow-capped mountains to the other.

*i* *Park in Kirkjufellsfoss parking lot. Walk up the road toward Kirkjufell and turn right up a driveway leading toward a few guesthouses. The trail heads straight up toward the front of the mountain before reaching the guesthouses*

### ⛔RAUÐFELDSGJÁ

Fantasy novels abound with scenes of overgrown grottos buried deep under mighty mountains, but unless you're actually Gollum you've probably never been inside one. Rauðfeldsgjá is your chance. It's a huge fissure in the cliffs on the southern coast. Just inside the mouth of the gorge is a large, mossy chamber with plenty of standing room. Most people stop here, but, if you're not afraid of a bit of water, the ravine goes much further. You may have to hike a bit through the shallow river and past more than a few bird carcasses, but eventually you'll find a waterfall you can climb with the help of, you guessed it, a sketchy rope! Sure, you'll get soaked, but you'll travel even further into Lord of the Rings territory.

## GATKLETTUR
Arnarstapi

Just minutes from Rauðfeldsgjá is the tiny fishing village of Arnarstapi, a town made relevant only by the fantastic rock formations carved out of its cliffs. The most famous, Gatklettur, is a huge, moss-covered stone arch, perpetually pummeled by waves on one side and flashbulbs on the other. Walk left along the paths to reach several smaller arches, which are not freestanding but part of the cliffs themselves.

This means you can walk over them (cool!), but also that you can't actually get a good view of them (less cool). If the cliffs aren't enough, though, there's also a fish and chips food truck.

## OTHER SIGHTS ON THE SNÆFELLSNES PENINSULA

Snæfellsnes has countless attractions beyond those listed here, including Snæfellsjökull National Park, where you can book a snowmobile or lava cave tour, the Lóndrangar rock pillars, and Skarðsvík Beach, a rare white sand beach. The Harbour Hostel, located in the town of Stykkishólmur on the northern coast of the peninsula, is an excellent place to stop for the night or to use as a base for an extra day of exploring.

You're in the home stretch now! From Snæfellsnes, it's just a two-hour drive back to the capital. The road is busy in this last segment, and there's a tunnel under a fjord that requires a toll. But through the anticipation of arriving back in Reykjavík and returning to civilization for real, be sure to enjoy these last kilometers. Who knows what they'll look like if you ever return?

# ICELAND ESSENTIALS

## VISAS

Iceland is part of the Schengen Area, meaning that US citizens do not need a visa for visits of up to 90 days. Note that your passport should be valid for at least three months after your planned date of departure from the Schengen Area.

## MONEY

Iceland's currency is the Icelandic króna, abbreviated as ISK officially and as kr locally. As an island, Iceland has to import a lot of goods, raising prices. The Icelandic króna has also gained strength in recent years relative to the dollar, driving prices even higher for American tourists. Long story short, this place is expensive!

**Tipping:** Tipping is not expected in Iceland. All prices, including at stores and on menus, include all service charges. That said, tipping is not rude or offensive, as is sometimes claimed. If you want to leave a tip for excellent service, more power (and an even emptier wallet) to you.

**Taxes:** Bad news. Iceland's standard VAT rate is 24%. The rate is reduced to 11% for a number of relevant services, including hostel rooms, food, and travel agents. Taxes are always included in prices, so what you see is what you pay. You can have your VAT refunded for goods leaving the country with you, like souvenirs, as long as the total spent is over 6000 kr. You must present the goods for which you are claiming a refund, as well as the receipt from the time of purchase.

## ALCOHOL

The legal drinking age in Iceland is 20. The only alcohol sold in grocery stores is low-alcohol beer (ABV 2.25% or below). Anything stronger can be purchased in state-owned liquor stores called Vinculin or at restaurants and bars. Drinking in the streets is legal and very common (especially on Friday and Saturday nights), being a drunken mess less so, you degenerate. Driving under the influence is a serious offense in Iceland. Drivers can be charged with a BAC as low as 0.05%. Just don't do it.

## WEATHER/CLIMATE

Iceland lies just south of the Arctic Circle, the implications of which are twofold. First, that means it's cold. Even in summer, temperatures rarely rise above the 60s. Second, it leads to the midnight sun. Through much of the summer, though the sun will set and rise (often just a few hours apart), it will never be truly dark. No matter how prepared you are for it, you may not get used to walking out of the bar at 1am into broad daylight.

## LANGUAGE

Iceland's official language is Icelandic, but English is spoken almost everywhere. Avoid trying to pronounce Icelandic words at all costs. (Seriously, you'll just make a fool of yourself.) If you have to try and say a street name though, be aware that the non-English letters eth (Ð,ð) and thorn (Þ,þ) are both pronounced with a "th" sound, crudely speaking.

# IRELAND

**If your knowledge of Ireland comes from St. Patrick's Day parades and childhood tales of leprechauns hoarding pots of gold, you'll be quite surprised to find that the Emerald Isle is not a mystical land, but a real one.** Yes, it's green and beautiful and the Guinness flows freely, but this tiny country with a disproportionate hold on Western culture is so much more than that. While the country's two capitals, Dublin in the Republic and Belfast in the north, have a history of being at odds, they have two things in common: a pride in what Ireland has contributed to the world and a willingness to engage with the bloodier parts of their history. And bloody it's been. From the fight for Irish independence in the early twentieth century to the conflict between Catholic nationalists and Protestant unionists known as "The Troubles," which ended just two decades ago, the question of what it means to be Irish has been asked and answered in lives. While this may not seem particularly relevent to the traveler that plans on journeying to Ireland's castles and carousing in its pubs, you'll find that this not-so-ancient history is ever present, and you may leave the country a certified Irish history geek. It's not all tragedy and trauma, of course. In Dublin especially, the country celebrates the incredible authors, artists, and politicians that Ireland has produced and continues to produce. There's plenty of opportunities in both the north and the south to appreciate this culture in museums, theaters, and, in the case of music, in pubs on city streets. There's no doubt about it, Ireland is a fun and enriching place to be—even if it's not entirely what you were expecting.

# BELFAST

Coverage by **Mia Karr**

Belfast is on the up and up—after the dark decades of The Troubles in the late twentieth century, Northern Ireland's capital city has refashioned itself as a destination for culture-seekers and party goers alike. It's the mother of ships (one ship in particular: the *Titanic*) and a university town, a jumping off point for the natural wonders of the north and a city of beautiful architecture. You're not going to find many shamrocks here—Belfast feels similar in many ways to the rest of the United Kingdom, and it will never be as emblematic of Ireland as its southern cousin, Dublin. But that's no reason to skip it, especially as it continues to innovate in order to attract adventurous visitors precisely like yourself.

## ORIENTATION

Belfast's attractions are a bit more spread out than in many cities of similar size, so get ready to become best friends with the bus system. A good place to start is the city center, which is just west of the **River Lagan.** Here you'll find **City Hall, the Grand Opera House,** a tourist information center, and lots of places to shop. Just to the east of the Lagan and a bit to the north is the Titanic Quarter, home to all the *Titanic* attractions the city has to offer (and there are many). To the south of the city center is the **Queen's Quarter,** a district full of coffee shops, college students (Queen's University is located here) and youth hostels. To get to **Belfast Castle** and **Cave Hill Park, Crumlin Road Gaol,** or the **Museum of Orange Heritage,** you'll have to venture to the far north, northwest, and southeast of the city center, respectably. (Again, love the buses).

## ESSENTIALS

### GETTING THERE

Belfast International Airport is the city's major airport. To get to the city center, you can take the Airport Express 300 (£7.50) or catch a bus or cab in front of the terminal building. If you're travelling from the U.K., taking a ferry is cheaper than flying. Popular ports include Liverpool and Cairnryan, a small village on the Scottish coast. Belfast Central is Belfast's main train station. If you're traveling from the Republic of Ireland, you'll likely have to change trains at Dublin because there are different service providers in the north and south.

### GETTING AROUND

Belfast's bus system, called Translink Metro, is the simplest way to get around the city. A single-day ticket (£3.70) can be purchased on-board. The Metro has 12 lines that run to various parts of Belfast and all converge in the city center. If you don't feel like figuring out which one you need to take, the people in the information centre in Donegall Sq. (across from City Hall) will be happy to help.

### PRACTICAL INFORMATION

**Tourist Offices:** The Belfast Information Centre (9 Donegall Sq. N; 028 9024 6609; open M-Sa 9am-5:30pm, Su 11am-4pm).

**Banks/ATMs/Currency Exchange:** There are banks and ATMs all over Belfast. Here's one in the city center (Ulster Bank, 11-16 Donegall Sq. E; 0345 948 2222; open M-F 9:30am-4:30pm, Sa 10am-1pm).

**Post Offices:** Belfast City Post Office (12-16 Bridge St.; 0345 611 2970, open M 9am-5:30pm, Tu 9:30am-5:30pm, W-Sa 9am-5:30pm).

**Internet:** Most restaurants and cafés in Belfast have Wi-Fi. Belfast City Council also provides free Wi-Fi (BelfastWiFi) at 109 hotspots around the city.

**BGLTQ+ Resources:** The Rainbow Project is the largest LGBT organization in Northern Ireland (23-21 Waring St.; 028 9030 9030;

www.rainbow-project.org; open M-F 10am-5:30pm).

## EMERGENCY INFORMATION

**Emergency Number:** 999
**Police:** Police Service of Northern Ireland (Upper Lisburn Rd.; 0845 600 8000; www.psni.police.uk)
**US Embassy:** The US Consulate General (223 Stranmillis Rd; 028 9038 6100; www.uk.usembassy.gov/embassy-consulates/belfast; open M-F 8:30am-5pm)
**Rape Crisis Center:** Nexus NI (119 University St.; 028 9032 6803; www.nexusni.org; open M-Th 9am-5pm, F 9am-3:30pm)
**Hospitals:**
• Belfast City Hospital (Lisburn Rd.; 028 9032 9241; open daily 24hr).
**Pharmacies:**
• Urban Pharmacy (028 90246336).
• MediCare-Fitzroy Pharmacy (028 90230170).

# ACCOMMODATIONS

### ◩GLOBAL VILLAGE ($)
87 University St.; 289 031 3533; www.globalvillagebelfast.com; reception open 24hr

The name may be hippy dippy, but the living conditions are far from a tent at Woodstock. Global Village accomplishes the extremely rare trifecta of good location, comfortable dorms, and social atmosphere. The nearby **Queen's Quarter** is a coffee shop and restaurant mecca not far from the city center. The level of personal space and allotted storage space is exceptional. The hostel has enough space for you to jam in the kitchen with some newfound pals. But, if that isn't enough, there are hostel-sponsored social activities almost every night of the week.

*i Dorms £14-17; reservation recommended; Wi-Fi; linens included; laundry facilities; free breakfast*

### VAGABONDS HOSTEL ($)
7 University Rd.; 289 023 3017; www.vagabondsbelfast.com

The vibes here are chiller than chill: guitar jam sessions, lounging in front of the TV, and rowdy drinking games are typical features of a Vagabonds day.

The beds are pretty tightly packed in the dorms, but under-bed bins are a nice organizational feature. Like many Belfast hostels, Vagabonds is in the lovely **Queen's Quarter,** home of the university, but it's also a super quick walk to the city center—if you ever manage to pry yourself away from the large couch and hearty free breakfast, that is.

*i Dorms from £15; Wi-Fi; BGLTQ+ friendly; linens included; lockers included; laundry facilities; free breakfast*

# SIGHTS
## CULTURE

### ◩THE QUEEN'S FILM THEATRE
20 University Sq.; 289 097 1097; www.queensfilmtheatre.com; doors open 30min. before the first screening of the day

We may or may not have watched a foreign language cat documentary here and it may or may not have been glorious. The Queen's Film Theatre is a quirky independent cinema where you can get your fill of the aforementioned genre as well as buzzy indie films and old-school classics, like *The Graduate.* QFT stays socially-conscious by applying as "F" label to any film that is directed or written by a woman, or features "significant women on the screen in their own right." Unlike massive chain movieplexes, it's a venue you can feel good contributing a few pounds to.

*i Tickets £6.70 after 5:30, £5 before 5:30, students £4 all day; show times vary, check website; wheelchair accessible*

### GRAND OPERA HOUSE
2-4 Great Victoria St.; 289 024 1919; www.goh.co.uk; box office open M-Sa 10am-5pm

Don't worry if opera isn't your thing—Northern Ireland's flagship theatre also hosts musicals, plays, dance performances, and programming for the kiddos. Located in the city center, the Grand Opera House has stood through the trials and triumphs of the twentieth century, from hosting Dwight Eisenhower after the end of World War II to sustaining significant damages from bombing during **The Troubles.** Today, absent of war and unrest, the theatre lifts the curtain almost every night of the week. While prices ain't cheap, there is a student discount—if you come after 6pm on Monday to Thursday, you can get whatever tickets are left for the night's performance at half-price.

*i* *Prices vary by show from £16-60*

## ST. GEORGE'S MARKET

12-20 East Bridge St.; 289 043 5704; www.belfastcity.gov.uk/markets; open F 6am-3pm, Sa 9am-3pm, Su 10am-4pm

St. George's Market has a lot going for it—adorable Belfast grandmas, knick-knacks galore—but perhaps the best part is that there are as many free samples here as there are at Costco. As you wander among the food booths, it's easy to snag a little honey here, a piece of cake there, some fudge. At some point, you'll stop even pretending that you're considering buying something. This is also the place to get all of your Belfast souvenirs—if you ever wanted a mug/shirt/coaster/toilet cover that says "What's the craic?" now's the time. The market is, tragically, only open Friday through Sunday, so plan accordingly.

*i* *Prices vary by stand; wheelchair accessible*

## LANDMARKS

### ⬛BELFAST CASTLE

Antrim St.; 289 077 6925; www.belfast-castle.co.uk; open M 9am-6pm, Tu-Sa 9am-10pm, Su 9am-5:30pm

When the third Marquis of Donegall decided to build a castle on **Cave Hill,** he probably didn't imagine that it would come to be used primarily as a wedding venue. But, ah, how time marches on. You won't find the historical room recreations or elaborate architecture of many of the castles in the United Kingdom, but you should still give Belfast Castle a chance. Not only is it free, but the views from the hill are absolutely spectacular. It's too far to walk from the city center, but you can take **bus #1** for a fairly quick ride.

*i* *Free admission; limited wheelchair accessibility*

## BELFAST CATHEDRAL

Donegall St.; 289 0328 332; www.belfast-cathedral.org; open M-F 9am-5:15pm, Su 1pm-3pm

Belfast's biggest cathedral (also called **St. Ann's**) is absolutely striking from the outside, but less so from within. No one would blame you for just admiring the architecture and skipping the small entrance fee, but if you decide to take a look inside, you will get to learn a lot about the cathedral's history and take pictures of beautiful stained glass. The cathedral is such a prominent feature of Belfast that a whole quarter is named after it, to the north of the city center, so it's worth a walk-by at least.

*i* *Admission £5, £4 student; tours £6*

## CRUMLIN ROAD GAOL (CRUMLIN ROAD JAIL)

53-55 Crumlin Rd.; 289 074 1500; www.crumlinroadgaol.com; open M-Su 9am-5pm

If you want to get in touch with your slightly morbid side—come on, we've all got one—make the trek to Crumlin Road Gaol, a recently-closed prison turned tourist attraction. The 75min. tour takes you through the spooky tunnel connecting the prison and the courthouse, in cells recreated to match various points in the prison's history. The tour continues into the condemned man's cell and hanging chamber where the majority of the prison's 17 executions took place. By all means, go just to satisfy your curiosity, or to learn more about Belfast's history through an unusual lens—during **The Troubles,** both loyalists and republicans were interned here.

*i* *Admission £9, £8 student; daily 75min. tours from 10am until 4:30pm; limited wheelchair accessibility*

## MUSEUMS

### THE TITANIC BELFAST

1 Olympic Way; 289 076 6386; www.titanicbelfast.com; open M-Su 9am-7pm

The ill-starred *Titanic* was built in Belfast, a fact permanently emblazoned into the mind of any visitor to the city. The culmination of Belfast's *Titanic* obsession is this museum, or, as they aptly put it, "experience." With

# A WEE HISTORY LESSON

So you've arrived in Belfast, which you know—you geographic genius, you—is in Ireland. But there are British flags flying from buildings, you're paying for your coffee in pounds, not euros, and—wait, is that "God Save the Queen?" you hear in the distance? Here's the thing. Belfast is the capital of Northern Ireland, which is part of the United Kingdom. The Republic of Ireland, led by Dublin, is a different country. Now you're probably wondering how this divided arrangement came to be. The short answer: not in the greatest way. If you're going to Belfast, we recommend you read up on its fascinating history from an actual historical source (we can't do everything over here), but here's the short version.

Those who've done a little reading on world history will recognize two common story lines here: "Catholics and Protestants couldn't get along if their lives (literally) depended on it" and "England makes everything worse for everyone by being a power-hungry colonial machine." In 1921, Ireland was partitioned into Northern and Southern entities by the British parliament. The North was primarily Protestant and Unionist, meaning they wished to stay within the U.K., while the South was primarily Catholic and nationalist. The original plan was for both countries to remain in the U.K., but the south seceded after the Irish War of Independence. While it might seem like everyone ultimately got what they wanted for a hot second, the Emerald Isle proved too small for both unionists and nationalists, who wanted Northern Ireland to reunite with the south and separate from Britain.

From roughly the late 60s to the late 90s, Northern Ireland became the site of "The Troubles," and a lot of that trouble occurred in Belfast. Essentially, what started out as a non-violent protest over treatment of Catholics in the North escalated into a pseudo-war. Nationalist and Unionist paramilitaries and police forces violently clashed for three decades—it was complicated, bloody, and morally ambiguous. Civilians died, cities were damaged, and Belfast was certainly not the tourist destination it is today. The Troubles ended with the Good Friday Agreement of 1998, but there's still a lot of bad feeling.

So, there you have it, folks—the all too brief explanation of why you can't take a direct train from Belfast to Galway. At least we're no longer living in such troubled times.

video simulations of the inside of the *Titanic*, a theme park ride that takes you through a mock shipyard, and recreations of first-, second-, and third-class living quarters, this is—dare we say it—the *Titanic* of museums. They go absolutely all-out to tell the story, from the ship's construction to the government inquiry into what went wrong. It's the priciest attraction in Belfast, but if you're even mildly interested in the ordeal, you should go.

*i* *Admission £18, £14.50 student; last entry 5:15pm; wheelchair accessible*

### THE ULSTER MUSEUM
Botanic Gardens; 289 044 0000; www.nmni.com; open Tu-Su 10am-5pm
The Ulster is a most excellent specimen of the Great European Catch-All

Museum. Here, you'll find art, nature, and history, all with a distinctly Irish bent. If you start at the top, you can work your way down through Irish and British modernist paintings and models of Irish wildlife and then get to the really good stuff: a walk through Irish history from early settler of the island to **The Troubles.** If you're still confused about what exactly transpired in **Northern Ireland** a few decades ago, this is the place to get all of your lingering questions answered. This is perhaps the best free thing you'll do in Belfast.

*i* *Free admission; wheelchair accessible*

## OUTDOORS

### CAVE HILL PARK
Antrim Rd.; 289 077 6925; www.belfastcity.gov.uk/parks; open daily 24hr

Humans have been wandering the paths on Cave Hill since the New Stone Age—there are remains of a settlement on the summit dating back to 4500-2500 BCE. Early man may have flocked to it because the steep terrain kept away invaders, but there are reasons to pay a visit even in the absence of clan warfare. First of all, the views. Get those panoramas ready, because this is one beautiful look at the city. Secondly, the trails. If you love to hike or if you're taking a brief break from couch potatodom, there are trails at a variety of different levels of difficulty, but they all get up close and personal with nature. And finally, there's a castle on the grounds. Casual.

*i* Free admission; no wheelchair accessibility

# FOOD

### ACTON AND SONS ($$)
17 Brunswick St.; 289 024 0239; www.actonandsons.com; open M-Th 11:30am-9:30pm, F-Sa 11:30am-10pm

If you're looking for a restaurant smack dab in the middle of the city center, Acton and Sons is a good choice. They serve lunch, dinner, brunch on Saturdays, and have a separate vegetarian menu, along with many gluten-free options. Food here is of the seafood, meat dishes, sandwiches, and salads variety, and they also do a mean **avocado toast,** which you will surely enjoy if you're as basic as we are. A full bar means you can also get a little bit tipsy with your tenderloin, if you so desire.

*i* Lunch £6-10, dinner £10-20; gluten-free and vegetarian options available

### BUBBACUE ($)
12 Callender St.; 289 027 8220; www.bubbacue.com; open M-Sa 11:30am-8pm, Su 1-6pm

Bubbacue imports two grand American traditions—the made-to-order dish and slow-cooked barbecue—and truly does the U.S. proud in the process. First you choose a delicious meat (or halloumi, poor vegetarians), some toppings, and throw in a side like french fries or mac and cheese. Then, you mix in whatever sauces your heart desires from the bottles circulating among the tables. It's filling, cheap, and quite different than most of the fare in the area. A win-win-win, we say!

*i* Dishes £4-7; vegetarian options available

### CONOR ($)
11a Stranmillis Rd.; 289 066 3266; www.cafeconor.com; open M-Sa 9am-10pm, Su 9am-9pm

Ahh breakfast all day—the answer to the prayers of those who love eggs and bacon but can't get their shit together by actual breakfast time. Conor does fabulous eggs benedict (£6.50), as well as other decadent breakfast favorites like waffles and (duh) the full English. Or you could order something boring like a burger or fish and chips, if you must. Either way, you get to enjoy your meal in a lovely converted artist's studio with Penguin book cover posters, exposed brick walls, and a high

ceiling with skylight. Conor is also conveniently located across from the **Ulster Museum** and a stone's throw away from several hostels.

*i* *Entrées £6-10; vegetarian options available*

## SLUMS ($)

25 Bruce St.; 289 031 5164; www.slums.co; open M-Sa 12pm-9pm

The food here is more yummy than slummy. Mix and match rice, meats, toppings, and sauces and you're all set with a made-to-order Indian street food meal. This is much cheaper than many of the U.K.'s boutique Indian street food eateries and the portions are far from tapas-sized. It's almost as though they're specifically catering to students, which they just might be, given their proximity to the **Queen's District.** Don't worry if city center is more your style, though, because Slums is located halfway in between the two districts. With such prime real estate, it's a wonder they can keep those prices so low.

*i* *Entrées £5-6; credit card minimum of £10; wheelchair accessible*

# NIGHTLIFE

## FIBBER MAGEE

38-42 Great Victoria St.; 289 024 7447; www.fibbers.robinsonsbar.co.uk; open M-Sa 11:30am-1pm, Su 12:30pm-midnight

There's a little-known law that any visitor to Ireland must spend at least one night in an Irish pub. Okay, we lied, but what are you even doing with your life if you don't? Despite its central location, Fibber Magee is full of locals, rather than tourists, and they sure know how to dance. Come equally for the live Irish music and the chance to have your mind blown by over-the-

hill bar-goers showing off their best moves. You're probably not going to find someone to take you home, but it's some of the most fun you'll have in the city. And—provided you've got a pint of Guinness in hand—also the most Irish you'll feel.

*i* *No cover, pints £4-6*

## THE FILTHY QUARTER

45 Dublin Rd.; 289 024 6823; www.thefilthyquarter.com; open M-Sa 1pm-1am; Su 1pm-12am

The Filthy Quarter is the Choose Your Own Adventure of bars. You've got **Filthy McNasty's,** a charmingly decorated little bar, which opens up into a beer garden (creatively named **The Secret Garden**), which then turns into **Filthy Chic,** cocktail HQ, or, alternatively **The Gypsey Lounge,** your place to get down on the dance floor. It's ideal for one of Belfast's many rainy nights—you can experience a whole range of night life without venturing out into the drizzle. For whatever reason, everyone here seems to be under 25—take that information as you will.

*i* *Drinks £3-8; cash only*

## THE NATIONAL GRANDE CAFÉ

62 High St.; 289 031 1130; www.thenationalbelfast.com; open M-Sa 9am-1pm, Su 9am-12am

It's national. It's grand. And it's a café.../club/bar/beer garden. The National Grande Café is housed in a beautiful former Victorian bank and it's quite a popular spot from breakfast until the wee hours of the morning. You can enjoy classy drinks in the first-floor bar, get a little outdoorsy in the expansive beer garden, or get your club on upstairs. The cocktails are stupid expensive, but otherwise it's an A-plus night out.

*i* *No cover, cocktails £9-11, beer £4-6*

# DUBLIN

Coverage by **Mia Karr**

James Joyce famously said he would have Dublin written on his heart when he died, and, while you'll likely get sick of seeing this sentiment pasted on gift shop magnets, after spending some time in the city, it may apply to you as well. Dublin is a monumental city, in the literal sense. It refuses to let you forget that some of the world's most famous verses and paragraphs were composed here, that freedom was died for and won here, and that hardship—in the case of the famine memorial, for example—and triumph exist side by side in this complex capital. It's not all about the past, though. Dublin's arts offerings are as vibrant as ever, and a day spent wandering through museums is best followed by a night spent wandering through pubs. Dublin is famed as a city of beer, a city of rebellion, and a city of Riverdance. It looms large in popular imagination, and, since Joyce and his fellow literary revivalists, much ink has been spilled about the Irish capital—but you'll just have to see it for yourself.

## ORIENTATION

Dublin falls into the popular European category of "cities divided by rivers," in this case the **River Liffey.** At the center of the city and to the south of the Liffey is the **Temple Bar** area, land of shops, pubs, churches, and **Dublin Castle.** To the east of **Temple Bar,** commerce is replaced by culture in the form of several grand museums and **Trinity College,** as well as **St. Stephen's Green.** To the north of the Liffey and east of Temple Bar is **O'Connell Street,** another highly commercial area that leads to a cluster of museums around **Parnell Square The Guinness Brewery** is to the southwest of the city, a bit removed from the action.

## ESSENTIALS

### GETTING THERE

If you're flying, you'll find yourself in Dublin Airport. To get to the city center, your best bet is probably to take the Dublin Bus (Airlink 757 or Airlink 747), which stops at most of the city's major sights, including Temple Bar. An adult ticket is €7 one-way and €12 return. If you're traveling to Dublin from elsewhere in Ireland, you can take Bus Eireann or Irish Rail.

### GETTING AROUND

Dublin is totally walkable, but if you would rather take public transportation you have two main options. The Dublin Bus (www.dublinbus.ie) has a route planner on its website, and one ride will cost you around €2-3, depending on where you want to go. You can also take the light rail tram (www.luas.ie) for between €2-3 a ticket.

### PRACTICAL INFORMATION

**Tourist Offices:** Dublin Visitor Centre (17 O'Connell St.; 01 898 0700; www. dublinvisitorcentre.ie; open M-F 9am-5pm, Sa 9am-6pm, Su 9am-4pm).
**Banks/ATMs/Currency Exchange:** Banks and ATMs will not be hard to find. Try Ulster Bank (105 Grafton St.; 01 672 4747; open M-F 9am-5pm, Sa 10am-1pm).

**Post Offices:** Dublin's Central Post Office on O'Connell St. actually doubles as a tourist attraction. If you're just interested in sending mail, try 5 Usher's Quay (01 677 9201, open M-F 9am-5:30pm, Sa 9am-1pm).
**Internet:** Internet is available in most restaurants and cafés. There is also internet in all of the Dublin City Public Libraries.
**BGLTQ+ Resources:** Outhouse is an BGLTQ community resource center (105 Capel St.; 01 873 4999; www. outhouse.ie.; open M-F 10am-6pm)

### EMERGENCY INFORMATION

**Emergency Number:** 112 or 999
**Police:** The Dublin police (An Garda Siochana) headquarters are in Phoenix Park (01 666 0000; www.garda.ie).
**US Embassy:** The US Embassy, Dublin (42 Elgin Rd.; 01 668 8777; www. ie.usembassy.gov; open M-F 9am-5pm).
**Rape Crisis Center:** The Dublin Rape Crisis Centre (70 Leeson St. Lower; 01 661 4911; www.drcc.ie; open M-F 8am-7pm, Sa 9am-4pm). The national, 24hr rape crisis helpline is 1800 77 8888.
**Hospitals:**
• Beaumont Hospital (Beaumunt Rd., Beaumunt; 01 809 3000; open daily 24hr).
• St. James's Hospital (James's St.; 01

410 3000; open daily 24hr).

**Pharmacies:**
- Boots (01 873 0209).
- Patrick St. Pharmacy (01 4544897).

# ACCOMMODATIONS

### ABIGAILS HOSTEL ($$)

7-9 Aston Quay; 1677 9300; www.abigailshostel.com; reception open 24hr

Abigails Hostel is right on the **River Liffey,** which is ideal for accessing both the north and south sides of the city, but slightly less ideal if you're trying to get to bed without the sweet lullaby of drunken revelers outside. Noise problems aside, this is a very good hostel—en-suite bathrooms, under-bed storage, personal outlets in the dorms, free breakfast in the large dining area, and Wi-Fi so fast it should enter the Olympics. And, if you haven't had enough of Dublin's memorializing, the walls are covered with colorful murals of Irish greats, including one which (quite accurately), calls **Oscar Wilde** the Paris Hilton of the nineteenth century.

*i* Dorms €17-30, higher on the weekends; reservation recommended; BGLTQ+ friendly; wheelchair accessible; Wi-Fi; linens included; free breakfast

### EGALI HOSTEL ($)

146 Parnell St.; 1558 0882; www.egalihostel.com.br; reception open 24hr

The reception area of Egali Hostel is decorated like the put-together dorm room down the hall that fills you with jealousy: there are string lights and photos hanging on the wall and colorful signs that say "hello" in multiple languages. It gets even better downstairs, with a lounge and expansive kitchen. The dorms aren't bad either—in fact, they could even be called spacious, which is not something you hear often about hostels. A glance at a map might fool you

into thinking Egali is farther from the main action (a.k.a **Temple Bar**) than it really is. Just ten minutes, people, you can do it.

*i* Dorms €18-30; reservation recommended; 3 weeks max. stay; Wi-Fi; linens included; laundry facilities; free breakfast

### SPIRE HOSTEL ($$)

90-93 Marlborough St; 1873 4173; www.spirehostel.com; reception open 24hr

If you aspire to a great stay in Dublin, this could be the hostel for you. (We know, we hate puns too). In terms of location, it's adjacent to O'Connell St. Spire (duh), close to **Temple Bar,** and the closest hostel to the **James Joyce statue,** which yes, should totally make or break your decision to stay here. Amenities are solid: free breakfast, copious outlets in the dorms, clean bathrooms. The most unique feature is the wealth of social spaces. With two lounges, a terrace, and a kitchen, there's a lot of opportunities to make awkward small talk with other travelers. You can lessen the awkwardness—or at least make it more bearable—by catching up over **free drinks** in the hostel on Saturday nights.

*i* Dorms €30-40 with higher rates on week-

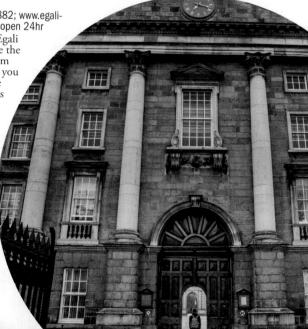

ends; reservation recommended; Wi-Fi; linens included; free breakfast

## TIMES HOSTEL CAMDEN PLACE ($$)

8 Camden Pl.; 1475 8588; www.timeshostels.com; reception open 24hr

Times Hostel Camden wins the Most Purple Irish Hostel Award, no-contest. Jury's out on if this is a good or bad thing, but, regardless, it does have plenty of other merits: a large kitchen, cozy lounge areas, and squeaky clean bathrooms to start. The best part about Times Camden, though, is its nightly activities: Monday ice cream parties, Tuesday wine and cheese nights, and Wednesday free dinners oh my! There's also **nightly pub crawls,** because they're really invested in you never leaving. The downside is that all of this comes at a pretty steep price, even for Dublin, and the location is a little far removed—but if you're more interested in going to museums than **Temple Bar** pubs, that won't be a problem.

*i* Dorms from €25, higher rates on weekends; reservation recommended; Wi-Fi; linens included; laundry facilities; free breakfast (when you book directly with the hostel)

# SIGHTS
## CULTURE

### GUINNESS STOREHOUSE

St. James's Gate; 1408 4800; www.guinness-storehouse.com; open daily 9am-6pm

Like pilgrims to a religious sight, Dublin visitors from all over the world flock to the Guinness Storehouse. It's something of a spectacle—there are videos at every turn describing some

aspect of the beer-making process, a whole floor is dedicated to the history of Guinness advertising, and everything is treated with the deepest solemnity. There's a catch, though—it's one of the most expensive things to do in Dublin. If you have your heart set on learning how to pull your own pint, go right ahead, but you could probably just bribe a bartender at the pub next door for less. This is a fun way to dive right in to Dublin's Guinness obsession, but by no means a must-see if you'd rather spend that money on actual beer.

*i* Admission €20, €18 student; wheelchair accessible

### NATIONAL LIBRARY OF IRELAND

Kildare St.; 1603 0200; www.nli.ie; open M-W 9:30am-7:45pm, Th-Sa 9:30am-4:45pm, Su 1pm-4:45pm

In the 1800s, the (not so) terrible beauty of the National Library was born, and it remains open to both intrepid researchers and curious tourists looking to photograph some bomb mosaics. On the first floor, you can visit an exhibit on *the* **W.B Yeats**—he's kind of a big deal here—and see handwritten drafts of poetry, his Nobel prize, and other artifacts. Head upstairs to the reading room, which we recommend seeing during the week so you don't have to endure a boring architecture tour to get inside. If your grandmother has always dubiously claimed that your family is descended from Irish royalty, you can fact-check this at the library's **Geneaology Advisory Service** (just

let her believe what she wants to, though).

*i* *Free admission; various themed tours available, check website for the day's offerings*

## TEMPLE BAR

Temple Bar; open daily 24hr

By the time you've read three hostel descriptions that say "and we're only x-minutes away from Temple Bar!" you'll start to wonder about this "Temple Bar" business. If you're interested in art, fashion, or beer, you won't be disappointed. The neighborhood—next to the **Liffey** and centered around **Temple Bar St.**—is Dublin's mecca for vintage clothing shops, small, independent art galleries (if you're looking for an independent cinema, check out the **Irish Film Institute** on 6 Eustace Street), and popular bars and restaurants. While you're trying not to spill gelato on your new band T-shirt, check out the **Icon Walk,** a series of murals around the area that depict famous Irishmen (and Irishwomen!). You will almost certainly end up in Temple Bar on a night out, but you should also come during the day before all the stores close.

*i* *Prices vary by store*

## THE ABBEY THEATRE

26/27 Abbey Street Lower; 1878 7222; www.abbeytheatre.ie

Like any self-respecting one-time European Capital of Culture, Dublin has a lot of theaters. Seriously, a lot. If you're paralyzed by your options, why not try the Abbey—it's considerably less grand than venues like the **Gaiety Theatre,** but in terms of history it can't be beat. The Abbey was a hugely important part of the **Irish Revival** in the early twentieth century, and its creation was spearheaded by absolute badass **Lady Augusta Gregory** and one **William Butler Yeats.** It's transitioned from showcasing Irish playwrights and themes to a variety of theater acts (*Waiting for Godot* was in their 2017 season, though, so they haven't strayed too far).

*i* *Ticket prices €25-40; limited wheelchair accessibility*

# LANDMARKS

## CHRISTCHURCH CATHEDRAL

Christchurch Pl.; 1677 8099; www.christchurchdublin.ie; open Jan-Feb M-Sa 9:30am-5pm, Su 12:30-2:30pm, Mar M-Sa 9:30am-6pm, Su 12:30-2:30pm, 4:30-6pm, Apr-Sept M-Sa 9:30am-7pm, Su 12:30-2:30pm, 4:30-7pm, Oct M-Sa 9:30am-6pm, Su 12:30-2pm, 4:30-6pm, Nov-Dec M-Sa 9:30am-5pm, Su 12:30-2:30pm

Christchurch Cathedral is Dublin's oldest cathedral, but much has changed over the years, including most of the architecture and, oh yeah, the religion practiced there. As the church of the English ruling elite, when **Henry VIII** peaced out of Catholicism, Christchurch came with and became a part of the Church of Ireland. Complicated stuff. We recommend watching the history video in the crypt, an expansive underground lair that also features the church's "treasures" (gold plates galore!) and a mummified cat and rat. The church itself is, naturally, quite beautiful and they don't begrudge you a picture or twenty.

*i* *Admission €6.50, students €5, tours €4; tours available roughly every hour; last entry 45min. before closing*

## DUBLIN CASTLE

Dame St.; 1645 8813; www.dublincastle.ie; open M-Sa 9:45am-4:45pm, Su noon-4:45pm

Ah, an Irish castle—probably deep in the green countryside, surrounded by sheep and maybe a leprechaun or two? Actually, it doesn't get more urban than Dublin Castle. Once the home of the royally-appointed British viceroy who exercised colonial authority, the castle was handed over to Irish leadership when the country gained independence and, now, the President is inaugurated there every seven years. You can either take a self-guided tour of the sumptuous royal apartments or take a (slightly more expensive) guided tour that will also get you into the **cathedral** and medieval **undercroft.** The free **Chester Beatty library** is also on the castle grounds.

*i* *Self-guided tour €7, €6 student, guided tour €10, €8 students; tours available every 30min.*

# THE LIST WITH THE GIST

Dublin loves its statues and monuments—politicians, artists, and fictional characters are immortalized in stone and spread throughout the city to appear in tourist selfies and be pooped on by pigeons forevermore. While any official map will point them out for you by their proper names, the famously wicked Irish wit has bestowed many of the city's famous monuments with more cheeky monikers.

1. **The Tart with the Cart:** The Molly Malone statue is one of the city's best-loved. Miss Malone is the tragic heroine of a popular Irish folk song, and also a prostitute; hence, the tart business.

2. **The Prick with the Stick:** James Joyce appears near O'Connell St. with his famous walking stick, and anyone who writes something like *Finnegan's Wake* has to be a bit of a prick.

3. **The Stiffy at the Liffey:** You really can't miss the giant spire on O'Connell St. as you cross the Liffey, which was built to replace the blown-up Nelson Pillar. Alternatively, it's the "erection at the intersection"—Dublin was really asking for it by building something this phallic.

4. **The Hags with the Bags:** Near the Ha'Penny Bridge (so named because that used to be the price to cross it) there are two regular women having a neverending chat. They have bags, because all women must have bags.

5. **The Ace with the Base:** This decidedly more charitable nickname is for the staute of Phil Lynott, former Thin Lizzy frontman.

6. **The Floozy in the Jacuzzi:** You can thank The Prick with the Stick for this one. Dublin's statue of Anna Livia, a character in Joyce's *Finnegan's Wake* who is meant to be a personification of the River Liffey, is not immune to the rhyming game.

## GLASNEVIN CEMETERY

Finglas Rd.; 1882 6550; www.glasnevin-museum.ie; open daily 10am-6pm

Glasnevin Cemetery is essentially a "who's who" of Irish corpses. The likes of Eamon de Valera, Charles Stewart Parnell, Daniel O'Conell and Countess Markievicz are buried here—and if you're too embarrassed at this point in your Dublin stay to ask who these people are, the 90-minute guided tour will answer all your questions. The tour, which also gains you admission to the small museum, is very interesting, but you can also wander around by yourself, with or without the assistance of a €3.50 map. The cemetery holds more bodies than the current population of Dublin, so lace up your walking shoes.

*i* *Free admission to cemetery; guided tour with museum entry €13, €10 student; tours hourly from 10:30am-3:30pm; limited wheelchair accessibility*

## ST. PATRICK'S CATHEDRAL

St Patrick's Close; 1453 9472; www.stpatrickscathedral.ie; open M-F 9:30am-5pm, Sa 9am-6pm, Su 9-10:30am and 12:30-2:30pm and 4:30-6pm

Sorry **Christchurch,** but in a Clash of the Cathedrals we'd put our money on Pat. In size alone, it towers (literally) over every other church in Ireland. Bring your camera (everyone is doing it) for the gorgeous stained glass, especially in the **Lady Chapel,** and for various monuments to people involved in the church's rich history. One such person is **Jonathan Swift,** wildly known as the author of *Gulliver's Travels,* who also served as dean of St. Patrick's for a few decades. You can reflect on this feat of multitasking by visiting his grave in the chapel and getting slightly creeped out at the cast of his skull. **St. Patrick's Park,** right outside, is also a great (and perhaps less grim) way to spend some time on a sunny day.

*i* *Admission €6.50, €5.50 student; audio guide €5; free tours every 30min.; wheelchair accessible*

## TRINITY COLLEGE

College Green; 1896 1000; www.tcd.ie;
open M-Sa 8:30am-5pm, Su 9:30am-5pm

Trinity College is both a world-class
institution of higher learning and a
smashing success as a tourist attraction.
It's also one of the rare cases in which
you should probably cough up money
for the guided tour, because otherwise
the buildings will be just that to
you—buildings. The guides are *real
live* Trinity students and know a thing
or two about the college's somewhat
contentious history (Catholics vs.
Protestants round 50,000,000) and
wacky traditions. The tour also gives
you admission to the **Book of Kells,**
the oldest, best-preserved Bible in the
world, and the jawdropping old library.
It's a bit of a tourist feeding frenzy (you
literally cannot move in the gift shop),
but a worthwhile one.

*i* Free admission to campus; guided tour
and Books of Kells €14, €13 student; tours
every 20min. from 9am-4pm; wheelchair
accessible

## MUSEUMS

### 🖼NATIONAL GALLERY OF IRELAND

Merrion Sq. W; 1661 5133; www.national-
gallery.ie; open M-W 9:15am-5:30pm, Th
9:15am-8:30pm, F-Sa 9:15am-5:30pm,
Su 11am-5:30pm

If you have any doubts that Dublin
is a European cultural capital, just
visit the positively lovely National
Museum of Ireland. There's art for
all European tastes here, but the
collection of Irish art is, predictably, a
highlight, especially the collection
of paintings by **Jack B. Yeats,**
kid brother to **W.B.** Although
it sounds underwhelming,
the best gallery may well
be the **National Portrait
Gallery,** a room dedicated
to creative and revealing
portraits of Ireland's greats
in politics, art, sports, and
other fields. **The Grand
Hall,** where breathtaking
architecture threatens to
upstage the art on the
walls, is also a must-see.

*i* Free admission; last entry
15min. before closing; wheelchair accessible

## DUBLIN WRITERS MUSEUM

Rotunda; 1877 2077; www.writersmu-
seum.com; open M-Sa 10am-5pm, Su
11am-5pm

After an entirely non-exhaustive survey,
we've concluded that no city honors
its literary heritage better than Dublin.
Whether you're an Irish literophile
or you're confused about who the
**Samuel Beckett Bridge** is named
after, you should definitely go to the
Dublin Writers Museum. Downstairs
is a physically small but highly detailed
account of Irish literary history: spoiler
alert, there's a lot of it. Upstairs, there's
a portrait gallery of Ireland's writers
and a small library. If you haven't had
enough, the **James Joyce Centre** is
also nearby. Do Irish writers rock? Yes
they do yes they do yes!

*i* Admission €7.50, €6.30 student; last
entry 4:15pm

## EPIC THE IRISH EMIGRATION MUSEUM

CHQ Custom House Quay; 1906 0861;
www.epicchq.com; open daily 10am-
6:45pm

It took us until the gift shop to
realize that "EPIC" is an acronym
for "Every Person is Connected," but
we were convinced before then that
this museum is pretty darn epic. It
starts with the reasons for emigration
from Ireland, from                famine to

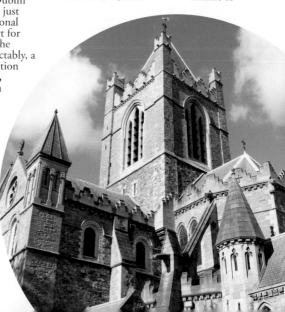

persecution, and then transitions to a more upbeat series of rooms about the contributions of Irish emigrants to every cause and field under the sun. Every exhibit is interactive and features videos, like our personal favorite, a dance battle between a tap dancer and an Irish dancer. It's fancy and comes with a fancy pricetag, but what better way to celebrate the Irish people? Except for drinking Guinness of course, but the two are not mutually exclusive.

*i* *Admission €14, students €12; last entry 5pm; audio guide €1, but primarily for non-English speakers; wheelchair accessible*

### NATIONAL MUSEUM OF IRELAND: ARCHAEOLOGY AND HISTORY

Kildare St.; 1677 7444; www.museum.ie; open Tu-Sa 10am-5pm, Su 2-5pm

The National Museum has four branches: Archaeology, Natural History, and Decorative Arts are in Dublin, and Country Life is, appropriately, not in Dublin. While you can visit all of them and museum your heart out, the Archaeology Museum has an interesting exhibit dedicated to the remains of ancient Irishmen brutally murdered and then left in bogs. It's grisly, but also pretty rad—from an archaeological perspective, of course. Other gems include metalworking from the "Golden Age of Irish art," medieval weapons, and an elaborate tile mosaic underfoot.

*i* *Free admission; limited wheelchair accessibility*

## OUTDOORS
. . . . . . . . . . . . . . . . . . . . . . . . . . . . . . .

### ☘ST. STEPHEN'S GREEN

St. Stephen's Green; 1475 7816; www.ststephensgreenpark.ie; open M-Sa 8am-20min. before dark, Su 10am-20min. before dark

Today, St. Stephen's Green is all swans and roses and delightfully shady reading spots, but, in 1916, **Easter Rising** rebels used it as a stronghold, only ceasing fire for one hour each day so the groundskeeper could feed the ducks. There are still ducks, and also plenty of monuments to the nationalist cause—this is where Dublin's obsession

with commemorating things in stone reaches its frenzied peak. (Joyce and Yeats, obviously, both have memorials in the park). But even if you care not one whit for this history—which actually isn't going to fly in Dublin, so let's hope you do—the park is green and glorious and perfect in summer, which is, as Dubliners say, "the best day of the year."

*i* *Free admission; wheelchair accessible*

### ☘GARDEN OF REMEMBRANCE

Parnell Sq. E. ; 1821 3021; www.opwdublincommemorative.ie/garden-of-remembrance/; open daily 8:30am-6pm

The fact that it's a tour bus stop aside, the Garden of Remembrance is an excellent spot for quiet contemplation. Appropriately placed on **Parnell Square,** the garden commemorates those who died in the struggle for Irish freedom. If there's one thing nearly half of the world can appreciate, it's the struggle for freedom from colonial oppression, so—whatever your nationality or thoughts on **Oliver Cromwell**—stop by to enjoy the cross-shaped reflecting pool, roses, and towering sculpture. Or visit just for the rare sense of calm in the midst of metropolitan Dublin, perhaps with an Irish-authored book in hand.

*i* *Free admission; wheelchair accessible*

## FOOD

### ☘GOOSE ON THE LOOSE ($)

2 Kevin St. Lower; 86 152 9140; no website; open daily 8:30am-5pm

If ever a place were to sell green eggs and ham, it would be this playfully named café. Unfortunately, you'll just have to settle for an expertly-crafted full Irish breakfast, custom-made omelette, or crepe. Goose on the Loose has developed a loyal following among locals who stop in for breakfast and the latest *craic* (gossip), and it's a refreshing change from more tourist-frequented places—the prices are refreshing as well. It's positively happenin' in the morning, but you can get breakfast until closing, all under the watchful eye

# THE 2018 *LET'S GO* OFFICIAL DUBLIN PUB CRAWL™

A lot of Irish stereotypes ring false. The Emerald Isle is not, in fact, one big green field where all the clovers are four-leaved, the sheep dance with the leprechauns around pots of gold, and potatoes grow on every tree. But popular imagination does get one thing about Ireland, and, by extension, Dublin, right—there are A LOT of pubs. No trip to the capital would be complete without a pub crawl, so we've thoughtfully constructed one for you. Drink responsibly, kiddos.

1. First, we'll get the ball rolling at the sure-to-please **P. Mac's on Drury Lane.** Settle in, grab a craft beer or two, and maybe something off their food menu as well. It's important to fortify ourselves for the night ahead. And, while we're all still sober, there's a selection of board games to act as a social lubricant if we're crawlin' with new pals.

2. Okay, let's try something a little more traditional, shall we? **Hairy Lemon** is right across the road on **Carnaby Street.** The décor is classic Guinness Kitsch and there are both booths and booze galore. If Guinness isn't your thing, 1) don't admit it, and 2) try a Bulmers, Ireland's favorite cider.

3. Gear up for a bit of a walk—five whole minutes to **The George on S. George St.** We're all loosened up and ready to get a little dancey at this thoroughly festive gay club.

4. Okay, okay, mixing it up by walking two seconds to another more traditional joint. You'll know **The Mercantile** by the Easter Rising mural on its façade. At this point we're *a few* pints deep and not in the best place to think about political turmoil, but pour at least one out for Patrick Pearse while you're there.

5. Now it's time to cross **Dame St.** and head for the beery mecca that is **Temple Bar.** And we are going to *the* Temple Bar itself for some live music, Irish dancing, and statues of famous Irish figures. Is it touristy? Yes. Do we care at this point? No.

6. Okay folks, we did it, we traversed the streets of Dublin in search of the perfect pint. All that's left to do is get drunk food, and luckily there's a **Supermac's**—basically an Irish Sheetz that serves Papa John's pizza—a few meters away. Thanks for crawling and good night!

of the duck in aviator goggles hanging from the ceiling.

*i* Entrées €4-7; vegetarian and gluten-free options available; wheelchair accessible

### ACAPULCO ($$$)
7 South Great Georges St.; 1677 1085; www.acapulco.ie

Acapulco is all about the color, from their brightly painted chairs to the bell peppers in their fajitas. Not your cheapest Mexican dining option in Dublin, to be sure, but considerably better than a lot of the chain burrito joints. If you're passionate about enchiladas, this is the place to splurge. Of course no Mexican meal would be complete without a margarita, and these margaritas are no joke—the menu warns that "you will feel it."

We suggest going on a Wednesday, when margs are €6.50 after 5pm. There's no shame in planning your day around discounted alcohol. In fact, we encourage it.

*i* Food €15-19, margaritas €9.50; vegetarian options available; wheelchair accessible

### CORNUCOPIA ($$)
19-20 Wicklow St.; 1677 7583; www.cornucopia.ie; open M-Sa 8:30am-10pm, Su noon-10pm

It can be hard to eat well while traveling, and sometimes after the thirtieth consecutive day of consuming both Nutella (it's European!) and French fries (they sound healthier when you call them crisps!), you feel the need to atone for your greasy sins. In that moment, Cornucopia is there—

perhaps a little self-righteously, perhaps a little too salad-y, but she's there. Hipsters and health-freaks alike flock to her quinoa-laden gates for large portions of vegetarian fare in a building just off of the anything-but-all-natural **Grafton Street**. It's a worthwhile, if a bit expensive, change of pace from typical Irish food—just don't bring any carnivorous pals.

*i* *Lunch €9-10, dinner €13-14; vegetarian and vegan options available*

### FUSCIARDI'S ($)

10 Capel St; 1441 1333; no website; open M-Th 9am-10pm, F-Sa 9am-1am, Su 9am-10pm

Fusciardi's lurks behind an unassuming storefront on Capel St., and the food and ambiance aren't particularly flashy—they're just good. If you want pizza, a burger, or an Irish favorite like fish and chips or churry with chips (we're sensing a theme here), Fusciardi is your guy. The prices are an anecdote to Dublin's attempts to break our banks and spirits with overpriced cuisine, despite the restaurant's central location. It's a perfect lunch stop if you're doing some shopping on **Henry Street.**

*i* *Entrées €5-10; vegetarian options available; wheelchair accessible*

### LILY'S CAFE ($)

3A Cavendish Row; 1872 9379; no website; open M-F 7:30am-5pm, Sa 8am-5pm, Su 9am-4pm

If you're looking for a place to eat on the north side of Dublin—near the **Parnell statue,** specifically—Lily's Café is great choice. Their specialty is breakfast food, especially scrumptious eggs benedict served with smoked salmon, but sandwiches and salads are also on the menu for reasonable prices.

*i* *Entrées €5-8; vegetarian options available; wheelchair accessible*

# NIGHTLIFE

### P. MAC'S

Dessie Ellis, 30 Stephen St. Lower; 1475 8578; no website; open M-Th noon-midnight, F-Sa noon-1am, Su noon-midnight

This is the type of pub to which we would bring a date, if we had any idea how to procure one of those. The dripping candlesticks on every table and mood lighting keep things intimate, and there are even booths with fully closing doors if, well, you get the idea. That's not all, though—choosing a pub that's on the quirky side (china cabinets? board games?) shows that you are a real person of taste, yet still respect Irish drinking culture. We suggest getting a quick primer on the many, many craft brews from the gregarious staff while your date is in the bathroom so you look like you know a thing or two about beer. Feel free to send us an invite to the wedding!

*i* *Drinks €5-9*

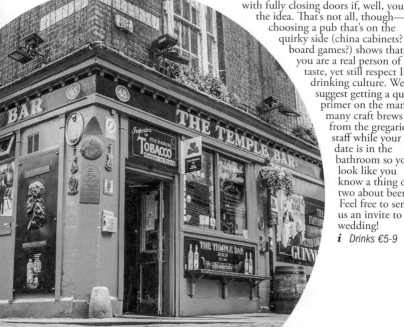

## ⬛WHELAN'S

25 Wexford St; 1478 0766; open M-Sa
5pm-3am, Su 5pm-2am

Whelan's is quite possibly the hippest
music venue in town, and it wears
its cool well. There's something fresh
going on almost every night—expect
act descriptions to contain phrases like
"experimental duo." To make sure you
get a spot, you can buy tickets online
or call their box office. They also host
a silent disco every Monday, Tuesday,
and Wednesday and entry is free. Even
if you don't make it to a performance
or event, Whelan's is super fun when
it's wearing its "regular bar" hat as well
and (as expected) they know how to
make a stellar night-out playlist. For
a similar experience at a slightly lower
price (and age) point, check out **Bad
Bobs** on Essex Street.

*i* Tickets €8-25, drinks €5-8

## O'NEILL'S PUB AND KITCHEN

2 Suffolk St; 1679 3656; www.oneillspub-
dublin.com; open M-Th 8am-11:30pm,
F-Sa 8am-12:30am

The name should assure you that this
pub is as Irish as it gets, but, if you
still need convincing, the selection of
whiskeys and live Irish music should
do the trick. In addition to some good
old fiddlin', Irish dancers show off
their mad skills and then get the crowd
on their feet—don't stand too close if
you're not interested in being pulled
into an impromptu jig. There's also a
rooftop beer garden, so you can take
the Guinness-fueled revelry outside,
horrendously fickle Irish weather
permitting.

*i* Drinks €6-9

## THE BLACK SHEEP

61 Capel St.; 1873 0013; galwaybaybrew-
ery.com/blacksheep

Put on the €6 sheep socks you bought
at Carroll's gifts and head over to this
chill North Dublin pub for a pint of
something yummy. The atmosphere
here—from the pride flag hanging
in the window to the proliferance of
board games available to borrow—is
welcoming and relaxed. If you spend
more than a few seconds staring at
their extensive list of craft brews, they'll
start offering free samples and won't
stop until you find the right one. You
can also munch on some pub grub, but
the food prices are the only *meh* thing
about the place.

*i* Drinks €5-8, food €13-14; BGLTQ+
friendly; wheelchair accessible

## THE GEORGE

89 South Great George's St.; 1478 2983;
no website; open M-F 2pm-2:30am, Sa
12:30pm-2am, Su 12:30pm-1:30am

The George has long been a major
component of Dublin's gay scene and
it continues to be a hip nightlife spot
for party people of all sexualities. You'll
know it by the massive pride flags
and the neon sign, and the flashiness
continues in the interior with a disco
ball, and some sort of pink flame
ordeal. While some guests just curl
up on the couches with a craft brew
or cocktail, as the night wears on,
the dancing starts up. The George
also hosts now-iconic Sunday bingo
nights hosted by drag queen "Shirley
Templebar." Get it?

*i* Drinks €5-8; BGLTQ+ friendly

# GALWAY

Coverage by **Mia Karr**

Many a traveler to Galway drops their bags and rushes off to the Cliffs of Moher
or the Aran Islands, and, while Galway is an apt headquarters for Western Ireland
wilderness adventures, don't sleep on the city itself. Rarely will you find a tourist
destination so convenient—the bus and train stations are both within the city
center, the major attractions bump shoulders, and you'll never be bereft of places
to eat or drink. You can do it all in a few days, and do it you should. At the heart
of Galway there is music, both from buskers on the streets and fiddlers in the
pubs. The waterfowl on the River Corrib get in on music-making, too. If you
want to explore Ireland, the "most Irish city" is the place to fall in love with the
Emerald Isle.

# ORIENTATION

Galway is split down the middle by the **River Corrib,** which empties into **Galway Bay.** Most of the action is to the east of the river, where you'll find the **Latin Quarter,** the **Galway City Museum, St. Nicholas' Collegiate Church,** and pubs and hostels galore all within five minutes of one another. The coach and train stations and the tourist information center are also on this side of the river, to the northeast of the Latin Quarter, near **Eyre Square.** The west side of the river is much quieter, but you can visit for the **Galway Cathedral** and several small parks.

# ESSENTIALS

## GETTING THERE

The nearest airports to Galway are Knock Airport and Shannon Airport, which are both 1hr. away from the city. Once there, you can get into the city via Bus Éireann. If flying internationally, you're probably more likely to fly into Dublin Airport, which is 2.5hr. away via Citylink or GoBus. If you're already on the island, you can travel via bus or train into Galway Coach Station and Ceannt Railway Station, respectably. If you're traveling from Northern Ireland, there isn't a direct bus or train so you'll have to connect at Dublin or Dublin Airport.

## GETTING AROUND

Galway is quite easily accessible on foot. If you need to get to the far reaches of the city, there is a bus and you can find timetables at www. galwaytransport.info. One ticket will cost you about €2-3.

## PRACTICAL INFORMATION

**Tourist Offices:** The Galway Tourist Office (Forster St.; 091 537 700; www. galwaytourism.ie; open M-Sa 9am-5pm).
**Banks/ATMs/Currency Exchange:** Ulster Bank (33 Eyre Sq., 091 562 910; www.digital.ulsterbank.ie; open M-Tu 9:30am-4:30pm, W 10am-4:30pm, Th-F 9:30am-4:30pm, Sa 10am-1pm).
**Post Offices:** An Post (3 Eglington St.; 091 534 727; www.anpost.ie; open M-Sa 9am-5:30pm).
**Internet:** Most restaurants and cafés in Galway have Wi-Fi. If you don't want to buy anything, you can pop into Eyre Sq. Shopping Centre and connect to their Wi-Fi for up to an hour.

**BGLTQ+ Resources:** AMACH! BGLTQ Galway Ltd. "represents and advocates on behalf of" members of the BGLTQ+ community in Galway (1 Victoria Pl., Merchants Rd.; www. amachlgbt.com). There is an BGLTQ+ helpline at 1890 929 539.

## EMERGENCY INFORMATION

**Emergency Number:** 112 or 999
**Police:** Galway Garda Station (Mill St.; 091 538 000; www.garda.ie)
**US Embassy:** The US Consulate General (223 Stranmillis Rd; 028 9038 6100; www.uk.usembassy.gov/ embassy-consulates/belfast; open M-F 8:30am-5pm)
**Rape Crisis Center:** Galway Rape Crisis Centre (Forster Ct.; 091 564800; www.galwayrcc.org). Their helpline is 1800 355 355 and is open M-F 10am-1pm.
**Hospitals:**
* University Hospital Galway (Newcastle Rd.; 091 524 222, open daily 24hr).
**Pharmacies:**
* McAnena's Pharmacy (091 381 900).
* Boots (091 561 022).

# ACCOMMODATIONS

### ▓GALWAY CITY HOSTEL ($$)
Frenchville Ln., Eyre Sq.; 9153 5878; www. galwaycityhostel.com; reception open 8am-10pm

This is a hostel that pays attention to the little things, like spacious under-the-bed bins, bunks with curtains and power outlets, superb Wi-Fi, and free breakfast that doesn't even remotely suck. (Trust us, it can suck). Galway City Hostel is also located approximately 30 seconds from everything in the city and from both the train and coach stations. It's not the cheapest hostel in the world, but it can be so nice to just kick back and relax. And, although it's less homey than many smaller, independent hostels, there are staff-led activities like pub crawls and dinners every night.

*i* *Dorms from €25; BGLTQ+ friendly; Wi-Fi; linens included; laundry facilities*

### SNOOZLES ($)

Forster St.; 9153 0064; www.snoozleshostelgalway.ie; reception open 24hr

Usually, picking the first hostel you see after you roll out of the bus station is a recipe for sad facilities and even sadder prices, but Snoozles defies this pattern with gusto—come on, could a place called *Snoozles* rip you off in any way? The outside of the building looks more hotel than hostel-like, but once you walk inside the furniture-filled lounge and breakfast area will assure you that this is, indeed, a hostel. All the dorms are en-suite and the beds come with those super dope under-the-bed bins. Thanks for having our back, Snooze.

*i* *Dorms from €17; Wi-Fi; laundry facilities; free breakfast*

# SIGHTS

## CULTURE

### ⛫THE LATIN QUARTER

The Latin Quarter; www.thelatinquarter.ie; open daily 24hr

The Latin Quarter is thus named (we presume) because it culminates in Galway's **Spanish Arch,** but "The Celtic Quarter" would be a more apt choice: from the countless shops selling wool scarves and Claddagh rings to the pubs with unpronounceable Gaelic names to the fiddle-playing buskers, this is the area that truly makes Galway feel like Ireland's most Irish city. At least half of the things to see and do in Galway fall within this group of cobblestoned streets and you will not leave hungry or confused about what a stereotypical Irish

souvenir looks like. This is that rare beast, the overcrowded tourist area that deserves to be an overcrowded tourist area.

*i* *Prices vary by store*

### CHARLIE BYRNE'S BOOKSHOP

Cornstone Mall, Middle St.; 9156 1766; www.charliebyrne.com; open M-Sa 9am-6pm, Su noon-6pm

We think even Stephen Dedalus would approve of this overstuffed city center bookshop. Charlie Byrne's has it all—despite several rooms of shelves, it's still necessary to have suitcases of overflow on the floor—but it really shines in the Irish department. Follow the signs (in English and Gaelic) to piles of books about Ireland's history, geography, and literary greats. And, of course, there's the Irish literature itself—try not to swoon next to the stacks on stacks of **Joyce** and **Yeats.** If you're totally lost, the staff recommendations in the front of the store are a good place to start. As **Oscar Wilde** once possibly said, go read the shit out of some books.

*i* *Book prices vary*

### TOWN HALL THEATRE

1 Courthouse Sq.; 9156 9777; www.tht.ie; open daily M-Sa 10am-7pm

The name has probably already given it away, but                    this

nineteenth-century building used to serve as Galway's town hall. Now the only politicians who come through its doors are here to see a play, film, concert, or dance performance. The theatre also serves as a venue during Galway's many arts festivals, like the **Galway International Arts Festival** and **Galway Film Fleadh,** both of which happen in the summer. For a city of its size, Galway is impressively invested in the arts and this theatre is a crucial part of that.

*i* *Prices vary by show; show times vary, most evenings there is a performance*

## LANDMARKS

### ◪CLIFFS OF MOHER

Co. Clare; 6570 86141; www.cliffsofmoher.ie; open daily Jan 9am-5pm, Feb 9am-5:30pm, Mar M-F 9am-6pm, Sa-Su 9am-6:30pm, Apr M-F 9am-6:30pm, Sa-Su 9am-7pm, May M-F 9am-7pm, Sa-Su 9am-7:30pm, June M-F 9am-7:30pm, Sa-Su 9am-8pm, July-Aug 9am-9pm, Sept M-F 9am-7pm, Sa-Su 9am-7:30pm, Oct M-F 9am-6pm, Sa-Su 9am-6:30pm, Nov-Dec daily 9am-5pm

One of Galway's most popular tourist attractions isn't actually in Galway, but, once you get to the Cliffs of Moher, you'll see why scads of tourists leave the city to see this natural wonder. This is the Ireland of popular imagination— wild, ancient, and oh so green. The photos practically take themselves. If you have access to a car, you can drive about an hour and a half, but the easiest way is to take one of the buses that leaves Galway every morning in the summer. This way, you get the bonus of other, short stops along the journey, such as a brief jaunt around **Dunguire Castle.**

*i* *Admission to the Cliffs €6, students €4.50, admission to the Cliffs and bus tour €30, €25 student; bus tours leave daily at 10am in the summer; if you are not with a tour group, staff advises you to arrive after 4pm for guaranteed entry; last entry 20min. before closing; wheelchair accessible*

### GALWAY CATHEDRAL

River Corrib West Bank; 9156 3577; www.galwaycathedral.ie; open daily 8:30am-6:30pm

The Renaissance architecture and killer stained glass might fool you, but this cathedral is actually an infant in Church years—it arrived on the scene in 1965. If it's any consolation, Catholicism has been in Galway for a lot longer than that. In fact, visiting a Catholic church is a lot more Irish than buying a shamrock keychain, and this is particularly beautiful specimen, even if it's not particularly rich in history— yet. (While you're at it, make sure to swing by **St. Nicholas' Collegiate Church** on Lombard Street to cover all your bases.)

*i* *Suggested donation of €2; wheelchair accessible*

## MUSEUMS

### ◪GALWAY CITY MUSEUM

Spanish Parade; 9153 2460; www.galwaycitymuseum.ie; open Tu-Sa 10am-5pm, Su 12pm-5pm

Future cartographers and historians, lovers of the deep sea, and aspiring Galway girls (and boys), make your way to Galway's only multi-floor museum, pronto. Here you will find a look at Irish history with a distinctly Galwegian focus, from the early days of kings and clans through the tumult of the early twentieth century. While a lot of the major political action happened in **Dublin** (capital cities always get to have all the fun, don't they?), Galway has been a pretty significant player on the Emerald Isle. After you've become an **Easter Rising** expert, you can wander up to the third floor for a highly interactive ocean exhibit.

*i* *Free admission; wheelchair accessible*

## OUTDOORS

### GALWAY BAY

Galway Bay; open daily 24hr

Ah, Galway Bay—more like Galway Bae, amirite? Start in the city center on the west side of the **River Corrib.** There's a lovely walking and biking trail that takes you along the bay for quite a while. There are a few small sandy beaches if you fancy a longer stop, and, in order to get real up close and personal with the water, you can walk out on the **Mutton Island Causeway.** Unfortunately, **Mutton Island** itself is closed to visitors, but the causeway provides some great photo-taking and nature-communing opportunities. On the way back, the **River Corrib** is great for swan-watching. Just don't be that tourist who loses an eye trying to feed them.

*i* *Free; wheelchair accessible*

# FOOD

### DELA ($$)
51 Lower Dominick St.; 9144 9252; www.dela.ie; open M-Th 11:30am-3pm, 6-10pm, F-Sa 10am-3pm, 6-10pm, Su 10am-4pm

This **West End** gem serves delicious brunch into the afternoon (until 3pm) and then reopens for dinner on most evenings. The décor is as stylish as the option to add avocado to your dish— ornament and light-laden tree branches dominate the interior, one wall is exposed limestone, and there's a book shelf for pre-pancake browsing. Or pre-eggs benedict, pre-breakfast burrito, or pre-fry up browsing. Dela also offers a large selection of brunch cocktails and their fresh-sqeezed orange juice is divine—with or without champagne.

*i* *Entrées €9-11; vegetarian options available; wheelchair accessible*

### JUNGE CAFÉ ($)
29 Forster St.; 9156 2858; open M-Sa 9am-6:30pm

Many vacation buzzwords apply to Galway, such as "charming," "vibrant," and "picturesque." "Tropical," however, does not—until you walk into Jungle Café. They've created an outdoor eating area with copious plants, couches, jungle-y murals and a delicious amount of orange. The food, also, isn't bad, although the options are pretty limited. But you can get an eggy breakfast dish or a sandwich, wash it down with a coffee, and pretend that you're in the midst of a Rudyard Kipling novel.

*i* *Entrées €4-7; cash only; vegetarian options available; wheelchair accessible*

### PASTA FACTORY ($$)
13 Mary St.; 9139 2551; open M-Sa 12pm-9pm, Su 12pm-7pm

If you're in Ireland, chances are you haven't had a good pasta dish in a while. (No, sad pub spaghetti, you do not count). All this is about to change when you walk into the pasta paradise that is The Pasta Factory. You choose your style of pasta, your sauce (chorizo, veggies, or clams, perhaps?), and whether you want to make a minor (€7.50) or major (€10.50) sacrifice to the pasta gods. Yes, this is a temple of tagliateli and you're about to be converted.

*i* *Small plate €7.50, large €10.50; vegetarian options available*

### PIE MAKER ($$)
10 Cross St. Upper; 9151 3151; www.thepiemaker.ie; open daily 11am-10pm

Who doesn't love a hearty mix of meat and vegetables baked into a savory crust, slathered in gravy, and topped with mashed potatoes and peas? The name says it all—they make pies. Real good pies. Pie Maker is in the **Latin Quarter,** so it can be tough to get a table in its tiny interior. But, if you do, said interior is pretty great. It's decorated quite miscellaneously with various types of hats, old clocks, and a picture each of Ireland's two favorite J's: John F. Kennedy and Jesus Christ.

*i* *Pies €12-13; vegetarian options available; wheelchair accessible*

# NIGHTLIFE

### KASHAH WINE BAR
17 Cross St.; 9156 8820; www.tighneach-tain.com; open M-Th 10:30am-11:30pm, F-Sa 10:30am-12:30am, Su 10:30am-11:30pm

It takes a lot of maturity to admit it, but sometimes you just get sick of beer and, yes, pubs. If you're looking to have a drink somewhere where you can actually talk to one another without screaming over live music, Kasbah Wine Bar is for you. It's connected to a traditional pub, but its second-floor perch is as serene as the swans in the **River Corrib.** You can browse through an impressive list of international wines before picking the cheapest and then settle back for some good conversation accompanied by the (gentle) sounds of buskers in the street below.

*i* *Wine by the glass €6-8*

## ROISIN DUBH

9 Dominic St. Upper; 9158 6540; www. roisindubh.net; open M-Th 5pm-2am, F-Sa 3:30pm-2am

Just across the river from the concentration of pubs in the **Latin Quarter,** Roisin Dubh sits aloof and cool. You have beer? She says, offering you a cigarette. We have beer *and* comedy *and* music *and* **Two Door Cinema Club** played here once *and* we're kind of a Galway cultural institution. Roisin Dubh is, indeed, a cultural institution. Come for the **silent disco** on Tuesdays, the **Roisin Dubh Comedy Club** on Fridays, periodic **open mic nights, film screenings,** and **live music** of various stripes pretty much every night in-between. If you're especially looking for alternative vibes, check out "Strange Brew" on Thursday. Oh, and **Ed Sheeran** has played here but they're too cool to list him first under their list of notable past performers.

*i* *Tickets €5-30, drinks €5; BGLTQ+ friendly*

## THE QUAYS

11 Quay St.; 9156 8347; www.louisfitz-gerald.com/quaysgalway; open M-Sa 10:30am-2am, Su 12pm-midnight

The Quays is so quintessential Galway that its recognizable mermaid sign shows up on postcards. As you can imagine, it's no hidden gem—nothing in the **Latin Quarter** is remotely hidden at all—but it is a necessary stop on your quest to conquer Ireland one pub at a time. The beer is a'flowin, there's a distinct smell of fried fish in the air, and live Irish music is on daily from 7pm.

*i* *Pints €4.60-5.40*

# IRELAND ESSENTIALS

## VISAS

Citizens of almost all developed countries (including Australia, Canada, New Zealand, and the US) do not need visas to visit the Republic of Ireland for up to three months. Note that the Republic of Ireland is not a signatory of the Schengen Agreement, which means it is not part of the freedom of movement zone that covers most of the EU. Accordingly, non-EU citizens can visit Ireland without eating into the 90-day limit on travel in Schengen areas, but will be subject to border controls on entry.

Citizens from the aforementioned developed countries do not need visas for long-term study or work in the Republic of Ireland, although they must have proof that they are enrolled in a course or proof of employment, and apply for permission to stay and register with immigration authorities upon arrival. For more information on this, consult www.inis.gov.ie.

Citizens from the EU do not ever need a visa to come to Ireland—but it is unclear exactly how U.K. citizens wishing to stay in Ireland will be affected by Brexit. Since Northern Ireland is in the United Kingdom, its visa rules are the same as for Britain. For more information on these policies, see the Great Britain chapter.

## MONEY

**Tipping:** Ireland does not have a strong tipping culture. In sit-down restaurants, there may be a service charge already figured into the bill. If not, you can tip 10-15 percent. In bars, tipping is not expected and even looked down upon. Tipping taxi drivers is also not expected, although it's standard to round up to the nearest euro. Hairdressers are generally tipped 10 percent.

**Taxes:** The Republic of Ireland had a standard 23 percent value added tax (VAT), although some good are subject to a lower rate of 13 percent. Northern Ireland shares the United Kingdom's 20 percent VAT. The prices in *Let's Go* include VAT unless otherwise noted.

## SAFETY AND HEALTH

**Drugs and Alcohol:** Ireland is a land famed for its beer and pub culture, so it's not surprising that alcohol is a common presence in the county. The legal drinking age is 18 in both the Republic of Ireland and Northern Ireland, and this is more strictly enforced in urban areas. Both regions regulate the possession of recreational drugs, with penalties ranging from a warning to lengthy prison sentences. In the Republic, possession of cannabis can result in a quite hefty fine, and repeated offenses can result in imprisonment. Check the Great Britain chapter for more detailed information on drug laws in Northern Ireland.

**Taxes:** Although Ireland has a long history of sectarian violence and terrorism, the situation has improved considerably in the last 15 years. It's still good to be aware that tensions linger, and that this is not ancient history but rather something that many Irish citizens lived through. One thing to look out for is the annual parade held by the Orange Order on and around July 12. The Orange Order is a Protestant group and the parades celebrate the defeat of the Catholic James II by the Protestant William III—as you can imagine, many Catholics and nationalists are not a big fan, and the parades have a history of turning into riots.

# ITALY

**When it comes to art, architecture, history, picturesque landscapes, food, and living *la dolce vita,* Italy has more stars than a movie premiere.** The boot-shaped peninsula dazzles with some of the most famous sights and delectable dishes in the world, making it a must-see destination for visitors to Europe year after year. Every genre of Instagram-worthy landscape appears in Italy, from snow-capped Alps in the north to sun-drenched beaches on its southern coast. Like a true Renaissance man, Italy does it all: ancient ruins, Medieval palaces, Baroque marble, and the works of the actual Renaissance men. And then there's the food, which needs no introduction. Pizza, pasta, gelato, an array of carb-loaded and deep-fried fare—Italy dominates in international symbols of the good life, and there's a reason people flock here to gain ten pounds.

Italy's take on the European blend of old and new mixes great power with understated back roads, screensaver scenery with life's little pleasures. Every region offers a different perspective on *la dolce vita,* in part because nearly every region developed separately. Italy as a country was not established until 1861, when the existing principalities united to form one monarchy. Prior to that, multiple principalities split the peninsula and its surrounding islands, bowing, of course, to the power of the Popes in Rome. There's mountainous Turin to the northwest, with its chocolate-filled cafés. Business and fashion capital Milan impresses with its ornate Duomo, while Venice beckons with its maze of canals. The Apennine Mountains trace the spine of the country, which spills into the rolling hills of Tuscany and Florence, the birthplace of the Renaissance. Further south lies Rome, a living museum of glory—imperial, papal, and sculptural. Meanwhile, Naples basks in the glory of marinara and mozzarella, and in the shadow of Mt. Vesuvius. Closest to the equator resides Sicily, the largest island in the Mediterranean and a blend of cultures, lively markets, and fresh food. Whether you go for the legendary sights or an evening of fine wine and twice your daily calories, Italy rolls out a red carpet of treasures.

# CATANIA

Coverage by **Adrian Horton**

Some cities have loose lips about their drama; their streets bear the scars of the past openly, or veer from medieval to ancient to modern in a single block. And then there are places like Catania, which has a smooth rhythm to its daily life—small *piazzas* with relaxed cafés, bars that hum in the evening, a castle here and there to tour on quiet afternoons. But this placid hub of Baroque architecture will divulge its secrets, if you look hard enough. The omnipresent flourishes of marble belie the fact that nearly the entire city was destroyed in a 1693 earthquake. The numerous dedications to Vittorio Emanuele II hint that Catania was one of the first cities in Sicily to submit to Italian unification. And the neighborhoods surrounding the Castello Ursino remind us that this fortress once overlooked the sea—until it was surrounded by lava. A blend of explosive and peaceful, easygoing and resilient, Sicily's second-largest city has emerged from the shadow of Mt. Etna as a worthy destination in its own right. Etna's lava oozes at the slow but steady rate of a meter or so per hour, and Catania operates at a similar pace. It won't reach out to grab you, but the city is used to playing a long game. Poke around the markets, stare in awe of the airy frescoes, and let Catania work its way with you one chapel, fish stand, and volcanic crater at a time.

## ORIENTATION

Catania resides on the east coast of the island of **Sicily.** Its greater metropolitan area is bound by the Mediterranean on the east, its airport (Catania Fontanarossa) to the south, and by the smoldering **Mt. Etna** to the north. Trains arrive at **Stazione Centrale Catania,** on the city's east end, directly north of Catania's two main ports, **Porto Vecchio** and **Porto Nuovo.** The **Cattedrale,** also known as the Duomo, marks the heart of the city center at the intersections of **Vittorio Emanuele II** and **Via Etnea** (Etna). Heading south from **Piazza Duomo,** you reach the old fish market and the imposing **Castello Ursino.** Via Etnea, the main shopping street of Catania, heads north from Piazza Duomo towards the rest of the city. Side streets from Via Etnea lead east to the **Teatro Massimo Bellini** and its neighborhood of clubs and bars, or west to the **Via Crociferi** and its line of Baroque churches. The main tourist attractions are located in this central area, though suburbs of the city continue to sprawl along the coast.

## ESSENTIALS

### GETTING THERE

The public bus, Alibus, runs from Catania-Fontanarossa Airport to the city center (near Piazza Duomo) every 20min. between 5am-midnight. Tickets cost €4 and can be purchased on the bus. Taxis to and from the airport cost around €20. Catania's main train station, Stazione Catania Centrale, is a manageable walk from the city's attractions. Most bus lines depart from the lot directly in front of Stazione Centrale's doors. If you want to walk to the city center, turn left outside the station and proceed down V. VI Aprile. When you reach a large roundabout (P. dei Martiri), turn right onto Via Vittorio Emanuele II (note: if you find a street with this name in Italy, it leads somewhere important). Follow Vittorio Emanuele II until it runs into the unmistakable P. Duomo.

### GETTING AROUND

Catania has a bus system that reaches most of the city with tickets costing €1. Tickets last 90min. and can be purchased from *tabacchi* (tobacco shops) or AMT kiosks. If you're planning on traveling for more than 90min., you can purchase a day pass for €2.50. The subway system is the shortest metro system in the world, boasting a mere six stations. Tickets cost €1 and the trains run every 15-30min. daily from 7am-8:45pm. Radio

Taxi Catania (095 330 966) operates daily 24hr and is a helpful resource that might help you get to Mt. Etna.

## PRACTICAL INFORMATION

**Tourist Offices:** Tourist Info Stop (V. Etnea 63; 0957367623; open M, W, F 9am-noon, Tu, Th 3pm-6pm).
**Banks/ATMs/Currency Exchange:** ATMs are available throughout the city, particularly on main thoroughfares such as V. Etnea or V. Vittorio Emanuele.
**Post Offices:** Mail is handled by Poste Italia. Two post offices convenient for most accommodations can be found at V. Vittorio Emanuele II 347 (095 316955) and Corso Sicilia 25 (095 316 957).
**Internet:** Catania does not offer public Wi-Fi, but many restaurants and cafés offer a strong connection. Look for complimentary Wi-Fi advertisements.
**BGLTQ+ Resources:** Though rural areas in Sicily may have less tolerant attitudes, Palermo and Catania have thriving gay scenes and a popular pride parade in the summer (www.cataniapride.it). For additional resources and support, check out www.arcigay.it or Coordinamento Lesbiche Italiano (Italy's largest lesbian activist organization; www.clrbp.it).

## EMERGENCY INFORMATION

**Emergency Number:** 112 (general emergency), 115 (fire brigade), 118 (ambulance).
**Police:** Polizia Di Stato Questura Catania (P. Santa Nicolella, 8; 095 736 7111).
**US Embassy:** The nearest US Consular Agency is in Palermo (V. G.B. Vaccarini, 1; 091 30 5857 (call between 10 a.m. and noon); USCitizensPalermo@state.gov)
**Rape Crisis Center:** TelefonoRosa, based in Rome, provides support and resources at telefonorosa.it as well as a help line at 0637518282.
**Hospitals:**
- Ospedale Vittorio Emanuele (V. G.Clementi; 0957431111).
- Ospedale Garibaldi Centro (P. S. Maria di Gesù, 5; 095 7591111; open daily 24hr).
**Pharmacies:** Farmacia Consoli (V. Etnea 400; 095 448317; open M-F

8:30am-2pm, 4-8:30pm, Sa 8:30am-1pm).

# ACCOMMODATIONS

### OSTELLO DEGLI ELEFANTI ($)
V. Etnea, 28; 952265691; www.ostellodeglielefanti.it; reception open 24hr
Ostello degli Elefanti picked an apt inspiration for its name, because the hostel hasn't forgotten anything. Complimentary breakfast with coffee cake fresh out of the oven? Check. Spacious rooms with the remains of an old palace fresco on the ceiling? Check. Access to the rooftop bar? Check, with five-euro cocktails coming right up. This guesthouse, centrally located just north of the **Piazza Duomo** on Via Etnea, has the look and service of a hotel, with the laid-back air of a hostel. The common areas offer ample space to meet fellow travelers (or screen *Game of Thrones*), and the rooftop bar provides one of the best views in the city of **Mt. Etna.** Did we mention there's a 20% discount on drinks? Oh, we forgot? Well, Ostello degli Elefanti did not.

*i* Dorms €23-26; reservation recommended; BGLTQ+ friendly; Wi-Fi; luggage storage; linens included; laundry facilities; free breakfast; kitchen

### CITY-IN HOSTEL B&B CATANIA ($)
V. Grimaldi 2; 95341450; www.cityinhostel.it; reception open 9am-11pm
There's nothing that stands out about City-In Hostel's name (do they mean "In the City?"), which is indicative of this indistinct hostel a short walk from the fish market. The rooms are fine—clean, colorful, with enough room to spread out—but unremarkable in character. City-In does provide a courtyard patio and second floor porch, though the space is quiet and not often used. To City-In's credit, the facilities are solid, the price one of the best in Catania, and the location convenient for the **Piazza Duomo** and other nearby sights. But memorable, it is not. We hope you have more to say about Catania than this accommodation.

*i* Dorms from €16, private rooms from €20 per person; cash only; reservation recommended; BGLTQ+ friendly; no wheelchair accessibility; Wi-Fi; linens included; laundry facilities; kitchen

# SIGHTS
## CULTURE

### ◼VIA DEI CROCIFIERI
Via Crocifieri; street open 24hr

Via dei Crocifieri is Sicilian Baroque in concentrate form—ornate facades and marble-columned balconies bottled up and contained. This stretch of road has been designated a **UNESCO World Heritage Site** for its cluster of picturesque churches and obsessive detail. A short walk, beginning at the Piazza San Francesco d'Assisi, will cover enough ornamented pediments to last you a lifetime. First, you'll pass the **Church of St. Benedict,** with its adjoining monastery, then the **Church of St. Francesco Borgia.** Additional stops include the **Church of San Giuliano** and the **Basilica St. Camillus.** The stroll down Baroque lane ends with the **Villa Cerami,** once a lush mansion for Catania's aristocracy. Today, it's home to Catania's College of Law and is a popular outdoor study space.

*i* Free; limited wheelchair accessibility

### BASILICA DELLA COLLEGIATA
V. Etnea 3; 95313447; hours vary

In 1693, a massive earthquake decimated Catania and the surrounding towns, reducing much of the existing architecture to dust. This was bad luck for the residents of eastern Sicily but fortunate for you, because the money of the aristocracy survived and funded the Basilica della Collegiata to rise as a phoenix from the ashes. This compact church represents the epitome of the Sicilian Baroque style, which flourished under the island's Spanish rule for a half century following the earthquake. Essentially, local architects modified the ornate style popularized in Rome with their own touch of concave façades, decorative *puttis* (Cupid figures, often supporting a balcony), and flamboyant sculptures. Basilica della Collegiata displays all of these elements in spades, as well as airy frescoes and gilded columns in the nave. **Mt. Etna** may be powerful, but it can't keep naked babies and marble balustrades down.

*i* Free entry; wheelchair accessible

## LANDMARKS

### DUOMO (CATTEDRALE DI SANT'AGATA)
V. Vittorio Emanuele II 163; 95320044; open daily 7am-noon and 4pm-7pm

It's not an easy time, living in the shadow of **Mt. Etna.** Thanks to the area's tectonic activity, Catania's Duomo, a cathedral dedicated to the patron Saint Agatha, has experienced almost as many reinventions as Madonna (the singer, not Jesus's mom). The OG Duomo, built in the eleventh century over the ruins of the **Roman Achillean Baths,** was reduced to rubble in 1169. The Duomo rebounded under the Normans, only to be struck down again by the famous 1693 earthquake. Today's Duomo was constructed in the Baroque style, as conveyed by the curved façade and marble figures. The interior of the church impresses with its tall cupola (dome) and distinct pulpit, which seems to surge from the heart of the building. Stare and admire, but don't call it a comeback.

*i* Free entrance to the cathedral, €1 to view the "terrace" (glorified porch, not worth it); wheelchair accessible

### TEATRO MASSIMO BELLINI
V. Giuseppe Perrotta 12; 957306111; www.teatromassimobellini.it; open Tu-Th 9am-noon

It's not a Sicilian city without a lavish opera house, and it's not a Sicilian opera house without a story of delay, disruption, and funding issues. The plans for an opulent public theater in Catania began shortly after the devastating earthquake in 1693, but the municipality took their sweet time in hashing out the details; the cornerstone of the theater wasn't laid until 1812, and it took another 78 years to complete the structure. Today's Teatro Massimo seats 1,200 in plush red velvet, and takes its name from the local hero of opera, **Vincenzo Bellini.** The theater is open to the non-opera attending public for limited hours each week, which reserves most of its energy for what really matters: the show.

*i* Ticket €6; guided tours available in English between 10am and 11:30am; wheelchair accessible

## TEATRO ROMANO DI CATANIA (ROMAN THEATER AND ODEON)

V. Vittorio Emanuele II 266; 957150508; open daily 9am-1:30pm, 4:30 until 1hr. before sunset

Though long buried by earthquakes and eager church-builders, glimpses of Catania's Roman past still peek through the cobblestones, most prominently at the Roman Theater, just off Vittorio Emanuele II near the **Benedettini monastery.** Catania's theater, which likely held up to 15,000 people, is Roman ruins without makeup—casual, unkempt, still in clothing from the night (or couple centuries) before. Opening hours are sporadic but the weeds covering the old concrete are not. This Colosseum prototype lacks the crowds of its famous descendant, which makes visiting this theater an eerie tour through empty archways and abandoned seats. A note: the Teatro Romano, a semi-circular theater, can be confused with the remains of the Roman amphitheater farther north, off Via Etnea. Those ruins are mostly obscured by the street, though a portion (specially, one fourth) of the amphitheater, located below street level, is open to the public each day.

*i* Free; no wheelchair accessibility

## MUSEUMS

### MUSEO CIVICO AL CASTELLO URSINO

Piazza Federico di Svevia 24; 95345830; open daily 9am-7pm

Like any good humanities major, the Civic Museum in Castello Ursino has many great ideas but no idea who it wants to be. A museum of Greek vases and Roman sculpture? Perhaps—the museum has intriguing works from antiquity, particularly a collection of emotional grave inscriptions from the late Empire. A repository of Christian relics and medieval art? Maybe, as several rooms house more takes on the Madonna and Child and the plight of Saint Sebastian. A display for local talent? Potentially, part of the museum is devoted to Catanian artists. The Civic Museum attempts combinations others would forego—ancient figurines and a provocative, modern painting titled "The Effects of Hashish." Not everything sticks (and not every lighting installation actually illuminates the art), but you have to give Museo Civico credit for trying.

*i* Tickets €6, €3 student; wheelchair accessible

### MUSEO DIOCESANO CATANIA

V. Etnea 8; 95281635; open M, W, F 9am-2pm, Tu, Th 9am-2pm and 3pm-6pm, Sa 9am-1pm

Housed just off the **Piazza Duomo,** Catania's Diocesan Museum serves as a testament to the longstanding influence of the Catholic Church in Sicily. The museum displays a series of valuable church relics—altarpieces, antiquities, and commanding views of the city— but an understated presentation and lack of English subtitles obscures most of their significance. Visitors of a religious bent may find the Catholic treasures enthralling, but others will breeze through the rooms quickly. However, tickets recoup value for the secular with access to the **Achillian Baths,** the remains of a Roman-era

thermal bath systems that resides beneath the museum.

*i* *Tickets €6 (includes Achillian Baths); last entry 30min. before closing*

## OUTDOORS

### CATANIA FISH MARKET

V. Pardo 29; open M-Sa 6am-1:30pm (restaurants and food counters open later)

Catania's fish market has learned a thing or two over the years. This outdoor series of shops, hawking the port's fish hauls since medieval times, knows how to chop up a swordfish. It knows how to drain buckets of octopi and scoop barrels of squid. And it knows how to shout at you in wildly gesticulated Italian, in a way that doesn't make you run for the hills. This fish market keeps it old-school, from the lack of decoration or printed labeling to the fishermen's calls that you *must* try this shrimp here or that sardine there. It's a fishy, briny jungle out there—an authentic and lively one that you want to at least stroll through for a taste (and smell) of Catania's mix of past and present.

*i* *Free to visit; limited wheelchair accessibility*

### MT. ETNA

Etna Cable Car (Funivia dell'Etna, Stazione Partenza): Parco dell'Etna, Nicolosi, Piazzale Rifugio Sapienza, Nicolosi, CT; 95914141; www.funiviaetna.com; open daily 9am-4:15pm

Don't let the numerous "Etna" name drops and postcards fool you: this is not a casual mountain. Sicily's most famous volcano, which towers over Catania and the neighboring coast, has been very active throughout the centuries. It buried part of Catania in 1669, nearly scalded a town in 1993, and exploded on a BBC camera crew as recently as March 2017. It can also be climbed, if you have euro and a day to spare. Hiking on Etna requires advance planning and is subject to the whims of the mountain, so double check schedules ahead of time. First, take the AST bus from Catania's central station at 8:15am (tickets €6.60 each way, buy from the station in advance). The bus will arrive at **Refugio Sapienza,** the mountain's base camp (altitude 2,000

meters) around 10:15am. From there, you can hike the next 1,000 meters to the summit; or, you can ride the cable car to a stop 500 meters from the top. Be sure to bring a jacket, sunscreen, and a camera.

*i* *Bus tickets €6.60 each way; cable car tickets €30; last ride 4:15pm; hiking essentials sold at Refuge Sapienza*

## FOOD

### FUD ($)

Via Santa Filomena 35; 957153518; www.fud.it; open daily 12:30pm-1am

Most nights after 8pm, the narrow, quiet Via Santa Filomena transforms into a purgatory of people with flashing blinkers, waiting for their turn at FUD. This experimental kitchen has earned a reputation for its fresh ingredients, gargantuan portions, and damn good food. Despite the hype, FUD keeps its décor debonair—simple café tables lining the small patio, large family-style tables, barstools, and signs encouraging you to eat inside. What's not understated? The quality of their dishes, from skyscraping burgers to artfully-seasoned fries to Naples-quality pizza. The ingredients may be top-tier but your manners need not be; go ahead and smear the ketchup on your nose, pool the olive oil on your plate, and share a fry or two with your (elbow-bumping) neighbor—no one's here to judge you.

*i* *Pizza from €8.50, paninis and burgers €7-9, salads €10, chips €3-5; vegetarian options available; wheelchair accessible*

### SCARDACI ICE CAFÉ ($)

V. Etnea 158; 95313131; open daily 11am-11pm

It's just too easy to end up in a gelato shop when strolling through Catania. The question is not if you will get gelato but where, and for what price. Scardaci Ice Café aces both of those queries, with its prime location (on Via Etnea) and unbeatable scoop-per-euro ratio. For a mere €1.90, you can try two of Scardaci's many flavors, including its signature "Etnea," a combination of pistachio and almond. Scardaci offers both indoor and patio seating, as well as coffee, pastries, and other frozen treats, but let's not get distracted from the main point: a medium cup (three scoops) of very good gelato for less than a specialty gelateria's kiddie portion. If you're not aiming for the crème de la crème of Catanian gelato (they're all good, if we're being honest), then gelato shopping means striking the perfect balance between quality and volume. Scardaci hits the jackpot here, not your wallet.

*i* *One scoop €1.90, three scoops €2.30; wheelchair accessible*

# NIGHTLIFE

### LA CHIAVE
V. Landolina 70; 347 948 0910; open M-Sa 4pm-3am, Su 4pm-midnight

Most nights, the area surrounding **Piazza Bellini** resounds with club beats and amped up renditions of "Despacito." Out of the fray of neon lights and club promoters emerges La Chiave, a laid-back bar which, on the right night, puts on its own low-key show. There's one guy on the bass, one on the tuba, one stroking the ivories, one singing a scat mix of English and Italian into the mic. It's a down-home, real jazz show, witnessed by a small crowd with spritzes in-hand. Inside,

La Chiave holds a trove of bottles and barstools, but that doesn't matter to most when the real attraction keeps the beat outside. On a summer night, try your luck at La Chiave's patio; like the best improvisational jazz, some great things can't be planned, but it's worth a shot (and another spritz).

*i* *Aperitivi starting at €3, cocktails €5-6, beer €3-5; BGLTQ+ friendly*

### RAZMATAZ
V. Montesano 17/19; 95311893; open M-Sa noon-4pm and 7pm-1am

Razmataz has a lot going on—rhythm in its name, cooks in its kitchen, people on its patio, frames on its walls. There's enough happening in this bohemian wine bar to make your attention zig from the French cartoon on the right to the full menu of daily specials on the left. Antique goods loom from the wooden railings above, while vintage Coca-Cola advertisements peer at you from the walls below. Cheerful, tipsy patrons pack the bar at night, sharing space with large plates, strong cocktails, and cheekily-censored sexual drawings. Anything goes here, whether you're looking for dinner, a rowdy pint, or a long evening of good conversation.

*i* *Wine starting at €4, beer €3-5, cocktails €6-7; wheelchair accessible*

# FLORENCE

Coverage by **Joseph Winters**

Although the Medici family is long gone, their legacy lives and breathes in every nook and cranny of Florence. From the Uffizi Gallery (the family's personal art collection, now one of the most famous museums in the world) to the Boboli Gardens (a once-private 11-acre maze of hedges, roses, fruit trees, and fifteenth-century statues), few parts of the city's history evolved without some Medicean influence. Today, the city is understandably a huge tourist attraction; it'd be hard to find a higher density of famous monuments, pieces of art, and historical objects, in any other world city. Brunelleschi's Dome ("The Duomo") is stunning enough to put Florence on the map on its own, but the city is blessed with a treasure trove of other fantastic architecture like the Palazzo Pitti, as well as iconic artwork like Botticelli's *Birth of Venus*. Intensely proud of their heritage, Florence natives effortlessly mesh modernity with tradition. ATMs are embedded into ancient marble edifices and free Wi-Fi is accessible at the world-renowned Piazza del Duomo. Unfortunately, the beauty of Florence is prone to dissolution amongst the hordes of tourists looking for their own special slice of Tuscan culture, but there's plenty to go around, depending on where you look for it. From a perch at the top of the Bardini Gardens or the stairs at Piazzale Michelangelo, you may be able to feel for yourself what Florence is all about.

# ORIENTATION

Most of Florence's sights lie north of the **Arno.** The **Piazza del Duomo** is the most central square and is home to the most impressive architecture. Just north of it are the **Mercato San Lorenzo** and **Mercato Centrale,** a bustling foodie hotspot and a good option for cheap (and unfortunately cheaply-made) souvenirs. To the east of the is **Santa Maria Novella,** the city's main train season. You may find yourself staying just north of this area, as many budget hostels can be found here (especially on/near Via Nazionale). Still north of the river on the eastern side of town is the **Santa Croce** area. In the main piazza is a stunningly fame-filled church (burial place to Galileo, Dante, and Michelangelo, to name a few), and a few blocks away is the **Mercato Sant'Ambrogio.** From the Piazza del Duomo, tourists spill across the river via the **Ponte Vecchio** (literally "Old Bridge") to the Oltrarno to see monuments like the **Palazza Pitti** and **Boboli Gardens.** East of the Ponte Vecchio is the **Piazzale Michelangelo,** high above Florence, but west of the bridge is the most up-and-coming part of the city, with the streets near **Piazza Santo Spirito** offering many options for artisanal souvenirs and budget-friendly food (better quality, too).

# ESSENTIALS

## GETTING THERE

Planes arrive in Florence at the Amerigo Vespucci airport. From there, catch the VolainBus shuttle to Santa Maria Novella train station for €6. Shuttles leave every 30min. from 6am-8:30pm and every hour from 8:30-11:30pm. Taxis to the city are €25. The Santa Maria Novella train station is located in the northwestern part of Florence and also serves as the main bus terminal. Tickets to destinations like Bologna (€19, 40min.), Milan (€44, 2hr), Rome (€34, 1hr 300min.), Siena (€9, 1hr, 45min.), and Venice (€40, 2hr) can be purchased at self-service kiosks at the *biglietteria*. The main bus terminal area is found left of the main entrance to the train station. For buses to Siena, Chianti, and other parts of Tuscany, look for SITA buses (www.sitabus.it). For Lucca and Pisa, check with Lazzi. There is also a FlixBus station on the other side of the train station—enter through the main entrance and turn right immediately (it'll seem like you're going towards the train terminal), walking until you reach an off-ramp that takes you back onto the street. Check online for updated timetables and ticket prices.

## GETTING AROUND

Unlike Milan or Rome, where a metro pass is pretty much a necessity, Florence is incredibly walkable. To be fair, a stroll from the northwestern train station to the southeastern Piazzale Michelangelo might take you around an hour (but this isn't a trek you'll be making too many times; all of Florence's sights and monuments lie between these two points). If you need to get somewhere in a hurry, Florence does have some alternatives. Buses connect the outskirts of Florence to the central areas. You should buy tickets before you get on, although it's possible to do so on board. There's either a single-ride ticket or a four-ride pass (90min.) for €1.20 and €4.70, respectively. If you're going to pay on the bus, either have exact change or expect to overpay. Once you have your ticket, make sure to stamp it on the bus—otherwise, you could be landed with a €50 fine. The C1 goes north-south from Piazza Libertà to the Palazzo Vecchio, the C2 covers the busiest downtown area north of the river (east to west from Beccaria to Leopolda bus station), C3 crosses goes east to west, but crosses south of the river to hit the Palazzo Pitti, and the D Line goes west-south-east from the train station to Piazzale Michelangelo. Bikers in Florence either have their own dedicated bike lanes or absolutely nothing, having to nearly plow into groups of tourists in order to navigate the maze-like city center. If you're up for it, though, bikes can give you a broader view of the city, and there's a very ridable bike/walking path that runs far along the Arno.

## PRACTICAL INFORMATION

**Tourist Offices:** Uffizi Informazione Turistica (V. Manzoni 16; 055 23320; www.firenzeturismo.it; open M-F 9am-1pm).

**Banks/ATMs/Currency Exchange:** The highest concentration of ATMs are along V. Cavour and Piazza del Duomo. BNL ATM locations are on V. Giuseppe Giusti 2, V. dei Cerretani 28, and V. dei Sparaco Lavagini 27.

**Post Offices:** Poste Italiane (V. Pellicceria 3; 055 273 6481).

**Internet:** There is free Wi-Fi accessible in many public areas, including Piazza del Duomo.

## EMERGENCY INFORMATION

**Emergency Number:** 112

**Police:** Emergency number 118, but there is a station at V. Pietrapiana 50R (055 203911; open M-F 8am-2pm). You can also reach the police daily 24hr at their urban helpline (055 3283333).

**US Embassy:** There is a US Consulate General in Florence (Lungarno Vespucci, 38; 055 266 951). The nearest US Embassy is located in Rome (V. Vittorio Veneto 121, 00187 Rome; 06 46741).

**Rape Crisis Center:** RAINN (800 656 4673).

**Hospitals:**
- Santa Maria Nuova Hospital (P. Santa Maria Nuova, 1; 055 69381; open daily 24hr).
- Ospedale San Giovanni di Dio (V. Torregali, 3; 055 69321; open daily 24hr).

**Pharmacies:** Pharmacies, known as *farmacias*, are marked by bright-green light-up crosses (Firenze Santa Maria Novella, P. della Stazione; 066 389435; open daily 24hr).

# ACCOMMODATIONS

### 🏨PLUS FLORENCE ($$)

V. Santa Caterina D'Allesandria 15, 17; 554628934; www.plushostels.com; reception open 24hr

If you're looking for a hostel to go with your free-spirited, minimalist, roughing-it backpacker lifestyle, Plus Florence is not for you. The sign at the front reads: "Trust me, it's paradise," and that's not totally wrong. Featuring its own rooftop terrace, full-service restaurant, pool tables, and swimming pool (indoor and outdoor!), this hostel feels more like a resort than anything else. With all its amenities and all the other travelers to meet, you could probably have the vacation of your life without ever leaving its two buildings.

*i* Dorms €30; reservation required; wheelchair accessible; Wi-Fi; laundry facilities

### HOSTEL ARCHI ROSSI ($)

V. Faenza 94R; 55290804; www.hostelarchirossi.com; reception open 24hr

There's the **Uffizi Gallery** and the **Galleria Dell'Accademia,** but there's also enough Renaissance artwork in the Hostel Archi Rossi to make a night in feel like a trip to the museum (without Ben Stiller and his monkey pal, though). The counter staff can be a little cold, but the breakfast isn't. Indulge in a full buffet with American, Italian, and Japanese-style options, as well as a free espresso machine. Rooms are basic, but comfortable, with airy outdoor common areas (watch out for mosquitoes, though!).

*i* Dorms from €23; reservation recommended; BGLTQ+ friendly; wheelchair accessible; Wi-Fi; free breakfast

### OSTELLO GALLO D'ORO ($$)

V. Cavour 104; 555522964; www.ostellogallodoro.it; reception open 24hr

Snugly fit in the first floor of an apartment-style building a few minutes away from the **Duomo,** Ostello Gallo d'Oro is a hidden gem that's almost too hidden; you may end up walking around the block a few times before you see the actual place. Then, you'll enter a building, walk past an odontologist office (just in case you need a forensic investigation during your stay), and then head up the stairs, where you will finally find reception on the right. From there, navigation is easy: "what you see is what you get," the owners write on the web. But when what you see is free breakfast, unlimited coffee, dinner, towels, and a quiet common space for some post-tourism relaxation (no golden rooster, though), there's not much to complain about.

*i* *Dorms from €35; reservation recommended; wheelchair accessible; Wi-Fi; towels included; free breakfast*

### WOW FLORENCE ($)

V. dei Mille, 14; 55579603; www.wowflorence.com; reception open M 10am-9pm, Tu 2pm-11pm, W 10am-9pm, Th-Su 2pm-11pm

If superheroes stayed in hostels, WoW Florence would probably be their go-to. Thankfully, they have The Bat Cave, Stark Tower, and Krypton among other planets, leaving us the spacious hostels and comic book-themed decorations plastered onto the walls of WoW Florence. Centrally located, it has plenty of airy common rooms, free food at random hours, free sunset yoga, and lots of superhero posters (fan-favorites include Batman, Thor, and Spiderman). A word of warning: the décor is pretty Spiderman-heavy, so if you're more of a Batman geek, you might want to look for one of Florence's other superhero-themed budget hostels (good luck finding one).

*i* *Dorms from €20, single from €50; reservation recommended; wheelchair accessible; Wi-Fi; towels included; laundry facilities €8 (€1 detergent); free breakfast; kitchen*

# SIGHTS
## CULTURE

### ⬛MERCATO CENTRALE

V. dell'Ariento; 552399798; www.mercato-centrale.it/en; open 8am-midnight

Also called the Mercato di San Lorenzo, the Mercato Centrale has three distinct sections. Surrounding the building are open-air vendors selling souvenirs and doodads, including enough leather products to drive a significant cow population into extinction. The ground floor of the warehouse-like building is home to lots of market vendors selling fruits, veggies, cold cuts, or traditional organ meat sandwiches. Upstairs, though, is the real jewel of the market; since 2014, a project by **Umberto Montano** (the guy behind Milan's Vittorio Emanuele II mall) has been housed

here. The first floor of the market has housed hand-picked vendors from around Florence. Find anything from street food delicacies (squid ink *arancine*, anyone?) to pizza to caprese salads.

*i* *Prices vary by stand, some stands cash only; wheelchair accessible*

### LA COMPAGNIA

V. Cavour 50R; 55268451; www.cinema-compagnia.it; hours vary

In a city where authenticity can be hard to come by, La Compagnia is a refreshing break from the its neighboring tourist traps. Appealing to "those who cultivate passion for the documentary experience," the organization shows **documentary films** on edgy subjects. Past showings have included *I am Not Your Negro* and *Liberame*. There's also the very hipster **Ditta Café** attached, serving up aperitivos with your film screening (€10) or even a whole dinner (€15). Tickets without food are €6 (but kale pesto quinoa really enhances the "audiovisual culture in all its forms").

*i* *Tickets €6, €5 reduced, cinema and dinner €15; wheelchair accessible*

### MERCATO SANT' AMBROGIO

P. Lorenzo Ghiberti; 552343950; www.mercatosantambrogio.it; open M-Sa 10am-2pm

Much smaller than the better-known **San Lorenzo market,** the Mercato Sant'Ambrogio is probably reminiscent what San Lorenzo used to look like before tourists found it. Prices remain firmly rooted in reality, there are no T-shirts emblazoned with "I <3 Firenze," and locals might actually go there for their groceries (imagine that!). Look for fewer trinkets, more fruits and veggies and meats (including many gruesomely recognizable, fleshy pig body parts).

*i* *Prices vary by stand; wheelchair accessible*

### PONTE VECCHIO

Ponte Vecchio; open daily 24hr

Despite being almost 700 years old (the original Roman one was washed away in a flood in 1117), the structural integrity of the Ponte Vecchio is most likely completely sound. Merchants have peddled their wares from the bridge for centuries, and today is no different; both sides of the Ponte are lined with expensive jewelry and leather bag shops. In the middle is a gap in the storefronts, offering a picturesque view of the banks of the **Arno.** Besides the jewelry, there are some cheap souvenir salesmen, so you can get a €2 Pinocchio pencil or "Firenze" tank top (to go with your €18,000 Yacht Master Rolex from next door).

*i* *Free to cross; wheelchair accessible*

## TEATRO DEL SALE
V. de' Macci, 111r; 552001492; www.teatrodelsale.com/en; open Tu-F noon-5pm, Sa-Sun noon-3pm

Although the Medici family is long gone from Florence, there's a new supreme ruler in town (or at least in the Sant'Ambrogio neighborhood), and his name is Fabio Picchi. In this area, there's not one, not two, not three, but four Picchi restaurants, ranging from ultra-fancy Italian black-tie to Italian-Chinese fusion. The Teatro del Sale is just another piece of Picchi's empire, a "cultural association" to which you have to apply for membership. Once you're in "The Club," you're allowed to attend the 200+ events hosted by Teatro del Sale: comedies including Picchi's wife, musicals like *Mamma Mia,* and music nights. It'll cost (€35), but the slice of Florentine life (and maybe torta?) is probably worth it.

*i* *Membership fee €7, €30 additional per person for dinner buffet and show, lunch €15; shows daily at 9:30pm; wheelchair accessible*

## LANDMARKS
......................................................

### ◪PIAZZA DEL DUOMO
P. del Duomo; piazza open daily 24hr, cathedral open M-W 10am-5pm, Th 10am-4:55pm, F 10am-5pm, Sa 10am-4:45pm, Su 1:30pm-4:45pm, closed Jan 1, Epiphany, Easter, Dec 25; dome open M-F 8:30am-7pm, Sa 8:30am-5:40pm (last entry 40min. before close); bell tower open daily 8:15am-6:50pm

Christmas just came early...or, at least that was our first thought when we stepped into the massive Piazza del Duomo, the home of the **Cathedral**

**of Santa Maria del Fiore,** one of the most beautiful and awe-inspiring feats of mankind. The thirteenth-century cathedral itself is wonder with olive green, pink, and white pattern designs (colors we think that clash but somehow happened to look good when you put them together here). The interior of the cathedral is admittedly a little underwhelming compared to the majesty of its exterior design, but nonetheless stunning. If you're in the mood for some cardio, climb the accompanying 463-steps of the **Dome** of Piazza del Duomo or the nearby 414 steps of the **Bell Tower.**

*i* *Free entrance to cathedral, entrance to Dome and Bell Tower €15 with Duomo ticket; dome last entry 40min. before close*

### ◪PIAZZALE MICHELANGELO
Piazzale Michelangelo; open daily 24hr

There's no elevator to the best panoramic view of Florence, just massive stairs. *Massive.* But that's okay, because the view is worth the labor. And this isn't just the view of the superhumanly toned David (a bronze replica of the original); from the *piazza,* you can see the **Duomo, Palazzo Vecchio, Bargello,** and the **Ponte Vecchio** bridge over the Arno. Fun fact: the huge David statue was brought up the hill in 1873, pulled by oxen! This is definitely a good place for sunsets or a glass of champagne with your newfound Italian *amore.*

*i* *Free; no wheelchair accessibility*

### BASILICA DI SAN LORENZO
P. San Lorenzo; 55216634; open M-Sa 10am-5pm, Su 1:30pm-5pm, closed Su Jan-Feb and Nov-Dec

Oldest church in Florence? Consecrated in 393 CE by Saint Ambrose of Milan, the Basilica di San Lorenzo was actually outside city limits at the time. Regardless of geographical controversy, though, it's still pretty cool, as the basilica holds works by a host of art world celebs like Donatello, Filippo Lippi, Varocchio, and so on. Check out the Sacristy, as it serves as the tomb of Lorenzo the Magnificent and was designed by Michelangelo. Pretty much all the other members of the Medici family are buried here as well, including Cosimo the Elder

# MALTA

**Malta plays a long game.** This tiny island archipelago nation, a republic since only 1974, has withstood centuries of bombardment and besiegement. Before that, it weathered the Roman empire and the Phoenicians, who dotted the island with tombs. And even before that, this speck of land in the middle of the Mediterranean—lodged on a map between Sicily and Libya—supported some of the earliest human settlements known in the world, as evidenced by the limestone temples at Hagar Qim and Qrendi. Now, at only 122 square miles and 445,000 people, Malta has built a reputation for sun and sport, making it an ever more popular tourist destination. In Malta, you can float on the surface, or dive deep. The country's cinematic natural landmarks, such as the Blue Grotto or the Blue Lagoon, shimmer in the year-round sun, while some of Europe's best scuba diving rests just off the coast. The beaches, trendy restaurants, and thumping bars and clubs of Malta's active social scene live in the moment, while its temples and foundations pull you six thousand years back in time. The island's numerous pubs, coffee joints, and English-language signs point to its recent history as a strategic port in the British Empire, while the gargle of letters in Maltese relay the island's longstanding Arabic, Italian, and French influences. In densely populated Malta, everything swirls together like the ancient markings on its signature limestone. Take a meat pie with your Baroque churches, combine cliff jumping with clubbing, and a catch a fort with your beach trip. Through it all—and there's been a lot, as its long list of conquerors suggests—Malta plays it cool, but knows how to make an impression. Just don't expect to master its language anytime soon.

The tiny country of Malta consists of three main islands. From east to west: **Malta** (the big island), **Comino,** and **Gozo.** Gozo is a holiday resort island renowned for diving, and is accessed by ferry from Malta's **Cirkewwa port.** Comino has very few full-time residents; the island receives mostly day visitors there to see its famed **Blue Lagoon** and sea caves. Most of the country's human action occurs on the island of Malta, which contains the capital, **Valletta**, and its airport, in **Luqa.** Most accommodations reside on shore of the hammerhead-shaped bay in and around Valletta. The capital itself lies along a peninsula on the island's northeastern side. The city is relatively small—its narrow streets, set along a grid, contain classic restaurants, churches, and white apartment buildings. To the northeast of Valletta is **Sliema,** a town full of more places to eat, drink, and sleep. (In any other place, Sliema would be a neighborhood of Valletta). The cheaper, livelier town of **St. Julian's** lies further up the coast from Sliema, and is popular with students. The northernmost part of St. Julian's, a peninsula known as **Paceville,** teems with clubs and bars, particularly on **St. Georges Street.** From Valletta, buses proceed to other notable towns on the island, including **Mosta** to the west, **Mdina/Rabat** to the southwest, and **Marsaxlokk** to the southeast.

## GETTING THERE

**From Malta Luqa International Airport LQA:** The "X" bus lines (X1, X2, X3, and X4) run from outside the baggage terminal to Malta's hubs (Valletta, St. Julian's, Paceville, and Sliema). X4 heads directly to Valletta, X2 to St. Julian's and Sliema, and X1 to destinations across the island, including the ferry port (Cirkewwa) to Comino and Gozo. Tickets cost €3 and can be purchased on the bus. Though Valletta and the neighboring cities aren't far, in distance, from Luqa, the journey can take more than an hour, depending on traffic.

**From Valletta waterfront (ferry dock):** Ferries arrive at Valletta's eastern harbor, which is connected by bus to most points on the island. Check routes and schedules at www.

publictransport.com.mt or call +356 212 2000. Tickets cost €3 and can be purchased on the bus.

## GETTING AROUND

Though often incredibly inefficient, public transport does connect most of the popular destinations in Malta. Buses fan out from the central station in Valletta to stops across the island. Routes and schedules vary, but most run from about 8am until 10pm. Tickets cost between €1.50-3, depending on the route. You can pay with cash on the bus or purchase a Tallinja card at the station. For more information, visit www.publictransport.com.mt or call +356 2122 2000. To get from Sliema to Valletta, it is most efficient to take the ferry, which runs every half hour from 7am until 11pm (on the 00/30 from Sliema, on the 15/45 from Valletta).

## Swing by...

### FORTIFICATIONS OF VALLETTA
Surrounding Valletta

A summary of Valletta's history sounds pretty standard for a European city: fortified, invaded, convulsed with religious purpose, refortified, life goes on, etc. But Valletta—its shape, its creation, and its battle-scarred history—is far more unusual than what comes across on paper. For a visual understanding of Valletta's singularity, take a stroll along its fortifications, which still outline the upper end of its peninsula. First built in 1488, Valletta's outermost defenses have seen their fair share of defeat: first, in 1551, when the Ottoman toppled a tower, and again in 1565, when the Turks sieged the **Fort of St. Elmo** for four months. The current walls were built under the tutelage of Jean de Valette, who imposed a grid and his name on the new capital city. Today, the limestone walls spend far more time glowing in the sun than defending the city, which is great news for your Facebook album. The fortifications still have the military on their mind, though—a walk along the walls will lead you to Malta's **National War Museum** and to the secret **Lascaris War Rooms of WWII.**

*i* Malta's National War Museum: Fort St. Elmo, Valletta; 2123 3088; open daily 9am-6pm; Lascaris War Rooms: St. James Ditch, Valletta; 212 34717; www.lascariswarrooms.com; open daily 10am-5pm (last entry 4:15pm); tickets €10

### HAGAR QIM TEMPLES
Triq Hagar Qim, Qrendi; 21424231; www.heritagemalta.org; open daily Apr-Sept 9am-6pm, Oct-Mar 9am-5pm

You'd expect Hagar Qim, at over 5,600 years old, to quake with age. Yet it stands resolute on Malta's southern edge, demonstrating that Stonehenge's status as the symbol of *the oldest of old* is merely great marketing. For those keeping score, this temple complex, built around 3,600 BCE, is the oldest religious site in the world, predating even the Egyptian pyramids. Without context, Hagar Qim looks as if a kindergartener built a parking garage out of dominoes. This is in part due to the ivory color of Malta's globigerina limestone, which composes most of the island and all of Hagar Qim. This is also due to the arrangement of the buildings, which consist of entrances and circular recesses made from large slabs. Visitors to the complex can stroll in and around the weathered remains of these devotional buildings, which have been studied and debated for—you guessed it—centuries. Most of the complex's treasures (statuettes, pots) now reside in the museum in **Valletta,** but a few decorative limestones are on display at the site. Bring water, a hat for shade, and an appreciation for the longevity of mankind.

*i* Entrance adult €10, €7.50 student; audio guide €1; Apr-Sept last entry 5:30pm, Oct-Mar last entry 4:30pm; wheelchair accessible

## MDINA

Only a Maltese city could take abandonment issues and turn them into a selling point. Mdina, Malta's former capital, has guarded its hilltop perch in the center of Malta for over 4000 years. First founded by the Phoenicians, Mdina once bustled with merchants, the island's 1% and the territory's provisional government, but declined when all the resources were diverted to **Valletta.** Now, only three hundred or so full-time residents live in the walled "Silent City," though the villas of the past's elite are still on view. Mdina is a place to wander—through cream-colored alleyways, around sixteenth-century corners, and into **Baroque St. Paul's Cathedral.** Mdina's subdued monasteries, palaces, and gardens seem trapped in a fantasy world. This isn't completely inaccurate, as Mdina played King's Landing in the first season of *Game of Thrones.* When you play the game of thrones, you either win, or you die—or, in Mdina's case, you keep on standing silently, raking in those photo ops.

*i* Free to visit, excluding the cost of travel St. Paul's Cathedral admission €5

# Grab a bite at...

### ⟨MINT ($)

Triq Windsor, Sliema; 2133 7177; www.mintmalta.com; open W-Su 8am-4pm
In a culinary world where "cheap" is often synonymous with fat, fried, or simply not filling, Mint appears like a healthy, affordable, delicious Narnia near the waterfront in **Sliema.** This nature-themed eatery, owned by a couple from New Zealand, tempts with two glass displays full of freshly-designed delicacies. The Chronicles of Mint cover most of your healthy-ish food cravings with items like tofu noodle salad (€4.90), a grilled chicken and mushroom quesadilla (€4), and a chicken and brie sandwich with homemade kiwi relish (€5.80). The play is simple, quick, and easy: order your combination of goodies from the counter, take a seat at their expansive patio, and enjoy a warm meal with a complimentary side salad. Mint also offers numerous vegan, gluten-free, and dairy-free baked goods, for those craving a dosage of oats and chocolate. But never fear, fans of the fat and filling—there's still our favorite, "mega double chocolate brownie with warm chocolate sauce and vanilla ice cream" (€5.80).

*i* Baked goods €1-4, entrées €4-9; vegan, vegetarian, and gluten-free options available; wheelchair accessible

### CAFFE CORDINA ($$)

224 Republic Street, Valletta; 2123 4385; www.caffecordina.com; open M-Sa 7:30am-7:30pm, Su 7:30am-3pm
Caffe Cordina isn't modest about its status as a Maltese landmark. In business since 1837, this salon-style restaurant and bakery presides over one of Valletta's main streets, with an eye for business and self-promotion. "Buy Cordina to try Maltese," its advertisements implore, with pictures of their signature honey rings and savory pies. To its credit, Cordina's efforts—the slogans, the crisply attired wait staff, the excess of marble tabletops—contribute to a generally positive experience. The traditional pea-stuffed pie, at only a euro, is flaky and filling, and their selection of cakes, cookies, and various sweets is unparalleled in Valletta. It's a task to get beyond the options peering through the long glass counter, but those that do will find a menu stocked with sandwiches, salads, and savory appetizers. No matter your choice, Caffe Cordina, with its nineteenth-century flourishes, provides enough elegance to make any stop in its large hall look classy.

*i* Egg breakfast (until noon) €5.50-8, entrées €7-10, platters €10-14, ice cream sundaes €2.50-7, pies €1-2, cocktails €6; vegetarian options available; wheelchair accessible

## HAVANA CLUB

St. Georges Street, Paceville; 2137 4500; open daily 24hr

On St. George's Street, the question is not where to go but what order to go in. Borderline underage kids start with pitchers at **Qube**, while mid-twenties folks mingle on the balcony at **Native.** But at one point or another, everyone passes through Havana. This dance club brings in everyone with its buy-one-get-one-free shot cards, from kids who may or may not have their driver's licenses to probably alcoholic old men. Not that you'll be taking in the crowd, though, when you're jiving to the latest "Shape of You" remix and or screaming "I love it!" about crashing your car into a bridge. Simply put, Havana is a textbook club, one with multiple bars, a "throwback" section for 90s hip-hop, and plethora of cheap tequila shots. Feel the beat, let your hair down, and forget all the people you need to email—at Havana, one must prioritize correctly to have a good time.

*i* *No cover, shots €2, mixed drinks €4, cocktails €4-6; BGLTQ+ friendly; wheelchair accessible*

# Rest your head at...

## MARCO POLO HOSTEL

Triq Ross, San Ġiljan; 2700 1430; www.marcopolomalta.com; reception open 24hr

Opened a few years ago by the same management as **Hostel Malti,** Marco Polo is Malti's cooler, fashionable younger brother who gets invited to more parties. It's similar to its predecessor but with brighter colors, a bigger rooftop, and more socializing over cheap beers. Located closer to the nightlife in Paceville than Malti, Marco Polo's rooftop, with its pillowed lounge chairs and bar, has become a prime pre-game spot for both hostels. It's a development the management welcomes, hosting barbecues for all guests on Fridays and joining forces for excursions to nearby attractions. Marco Polo runs more expensive than its brother hostel for similar lodging, though its rooms are, to be fair, nicer—cleaner, larger, with outlets and privacy curtains, and arranged so everyone gets a quality dose of natural light. A little sibling rivalry doesn't hurt, though in the end, the choice between the two comes down to how much you're willing to pay.

*i* *Dorms €27-33, private rooms from €90; reservation recommended; min stay two nights; BGLTQ+ friendly; wheelchair accessible; Wi-Fi; linens included; laundry available; kitchen*

# Don't miss...

## THE BLUE GROTTO

Boat Service: Qrendi; 2164 0058; open daily 9am-5pm

Since the collapse of the **Azure Window** in March 2017, the Blue Grotto has assumed the position as Malta's most recognizable natural landmark. The Grotto resembles the departed Window, but with more rock and less *Game of Thrones* recognition. Located just southeast of the **Hagar Qim Temples,** the Blue Grotto frames the bright Mediterranean waters with a series of limestone sea caverns. You could just look up a picture, but why not snap your own? Visitors can get a glimpse of the Grotto from atop a lookout, or get a closer look through an official 20-minute boat tour. To get to the Blue Grotto, arrange private transport, rent a car, or take the 30-minute bus route #74 from Valletta.

*i* *Tickets for 20-minute boat ride €8; wheelchair accessible; weather permitting* (known as "Father of the Nation"—a pretty important dude).

*i* *Free; wheelchair accessible*

## BASILICA SANTA TRÌNITA
P. di Santa Trinita; 55216912; www.diocesifirenze.it; open daily 7am-noon and 4pm-7pm

The relative plainness of the Basilica Santa Trìnita is actually a boon, as it keeps tourists away, offering a respite from Florence's more crowded attractions. Founded in the eleventh century by Vallombrosan monks and rebuilt in the Gothic style during the thirteenth and fourteenth-centuries, the basilica houses a plethora of fifteenth-century paintings, sixteenth-century sculptures, and a particularly notable Barbieri's *Pietà*. It's a good warm-up for the more famous **Basilica di San Lorenzo** or the **Duomo.**

*i* *Free entry; wheelchair accessible*

## CAPELLA BRANCACCI
P. del Carmine; www.museocivicifiorentini.comune.fri.it; open M, W-Su 10am-5pm, closed Jan 1, Jan 7, Easter, May 1, July 16, Aug 15, Dec 25

The Medici may have been the most powerful Florentine family of the Renaissance, but they weren't the only powerful family. Felice Brancacci was an outspoken enemy of the **Medicis** (fun fact: this didn't really work out well for him, as he was soon exiled to Hungary). However, it seems that, regardless of who hated whom, everyone could agree on spending a ton of money making really impressive churches; the Cappella Brancacci is one of the first churches to have Renaissance-style fresco paintings, featuring **Masolino, Lippi,** and **Masaccio,** who inspired **Michelangelo.**

*i* *Admission W-F €6, €4.50 reduced, Sa-M €7, €5.50 reduced; reservations recommended; ticket sales end 45min. before closing; wheelchair accessible*

## PIAZZA DELLA SIGNORIA
P. Della Signoria; piazza open daily 24hr, Loggia open daily 8am-7pm

When you see Michelangelo's *David*, don't get too excited; it's a replica. The real one's in the **Accademia,** but you can still ogle the many other nude statues showcased in the Piazza della Signoria. There's the **Fountain of Neptune** (essentially Neptune taking a shower in public), *Cellini's Perseus with the Head of Medusa*, and Bandinelli's *Hercules and Cacus*. A walk through the Loggia is highly recommended; some of the statues have been showcased there since 1582.

*i* *Free; piazza wheelchair accessible, no wheelchair accessibility in Loggia*

# MUSEUMS

## MUSEO DEGLI UFFIZI
P. degli Uffizi; 55294883; open Tu-Su 8:15am-6:50pm

This is pretty much the Louvre of Italy, and the greatest danger of perusing the halls of the Uffizi is that you might accidentally miss a world-famous work of art. There's a lot to see, and just because you don't know the name of one of the pieces doesn't mean it won't be familiar. From thirteenth-century triptychs (that were almost definitely in your eighth-grade history textbook) to late-Renaissance masterpieces, the Uffizi really is worth the long lines and potentially confusing ticket system. Just to name-drop a little, artists include: **Botticelli** (*Birth of Venus* is the main attraction), **Raphael, Michelangelo, da Vinci, Dürer,** and **Rembrandt** (convinced yet?).

*i* *Admission adult €8, €4 reduced, during special exhibits admission adult €13, €6.50 reduced; wheelchair accessible*

## GALLERIA DELL'ACCADEMIA
V. Riscoli, 58/60; 552388609; open Tu-Su 8:15am-6:50pm

They might try to pretend otherwise, but this museum was made to show off *David*. He's undoubtedly the star of the show with a high-vaulted, rotunda-like ceiling just for the larger-than-life statue. 360 degree views are absolutely included (yes, all his muscles are toned)—so, feel free to linger. Other than *David*, the museum is actually quite small. It has a room dedicated to busts and sculptures (whose eyes follow you creepily as you shuffle through the displays), the notable *Rape of the Sabine Woman,* and some unfinished **Michelangelo** pieces. Best to book tickets in advance, as it can get pretty crowded.

*i* *Admission €8, €4 reduced; last entry 6:20pm; wheelchair accessible*

## MUSEO DI FERRAGAMO

Palazzo Spini Feront, P. di Santa Trinita, 5/R; 553562846; www.ferragamo.com/museo/en/usa; open daily 10am-7pm

When you think of Italian history, the 1920s surely isn't the first decade that comes to mind (real talk: it's not even in the top ten). Nonetheless, that's the entire premise of the Ferragamo museum: "1927: The Return to Italy." The museum puts a spotlight on how the 1920s shaped the lifestyle Italians are renowned for. You know, fishing, relaxed beachside living, high fashion. A small museum, this is a fun afternoon activity if you happen to be in the **Palazzo Vecchio** area or are interested in fashion history. The exit is through the gift shop, but the only souvenir you'll find are pairs of multi-thousand euro shoes.

*i* *Admission adult €8, free under 10 or over 65, free with Firenze card and on first Su of the month; wheelchair accessible*

## MUSEO DI SANTA CROCE

P. Santa Croce; 552466105; www.san-tacroceopera.it/en; open M-Sa 9:30am-5:30pm, Su 2:30pm-5:30

"What'd you do on vacation?" your distant cousin asks. "Oh, you know, I saw Galileo, Michelangelo, and Dante's tomb," you reply, only listing things housed in the Museo di Santa Croce. The €8 admission is well worth the price, just for the name dropping you'll get to do when you're through, but, if you really need more convincing, there's also a crucifix by **Donatello** and a chapel designed by **Brunelleschi** in the mix. Of course, there's also historical value to the basilica itself. It was home to Florence's first symbolic banner from the end of the thirteenth century,

and its background is interestingly intertwined with a conflict between the Pazzi and Medici families.

*i* *Admission adult €8, €6 reduced; last entry 5pm; wheelchair accessible*

# OUTDOORS

## BARDINI GARDENS

Costa S. Giorgio, 2; 5520066206; open daily Jan-Feb 8:15am-4:30pm, Mar 8:15am-5:30pm, Apr-May 8:15am-6:30pm, June-Aug 8:15am-6:50pm, Sept-Oct 8:15am-6:30pm, Nov-Dec 8:15am-4:30pm, closed first and last M of each month, Jan 1, May 1, Dec 25

Just east of the **Boboli Gardens** are the less-famous Bardini Gardens. The views aren't quite as good, but the garden itself is beautiful and a little more secluded. If you start at the entrance on **Via de' Bardi,** you'll climb through rows of roses, hydrangeas, azaleas, fruit trees, and more, arriving at a Renaissance-era loggia at the top, where—conveniently—there's a little café/restaurant and an overlook. From there, you can get exit onto **Costa San Giorgio** for easy access to the **Forte di**

**Belvedere** and the Boboli Gardens for even more sweeping views of Florence.

*i* Admission adult €8, €6 reduced, free Florence residents, price subject to increase if there is a temporary exhibition adult €10, €5 reduced; last entry 30min. before closing; wheelchair accessible

## BOBOLI GARDENS

P. Pitti 1; 552298732; open daily Jan-Feb 8:15am-4:30pm, Mar 8:15am-5:30pm, Apr-May 8:15am-6:30pm, June-Aug 8:15am-6:50pm, Sept-Oct 8:15am-6:30pm, Nov-Dec 8:15am-4:30pm, closed first and last M of each month, Jan 1, May 1, Dec 25

Here's the run-down: it's 11 acres of an outdoor museum—nymphs and cupids dating back to the 1500s line the garden's walkways and a grotto holds works by **Michelangelo** (now replaced with replicas). Interestingly, in the past, it was only open to the immediate members of the **Medici family** and wasn't even used for events (what a waste of space). For your visit, plan plenty of time (several hours) to meander through the many paths that will call to mind images of Disney castle gardens. The highlight is the **Fountain of Neptune** at the top of a giant hill (yes, the climb is worth it); it's a great spot to whip out that selfie stick. Or, you know, just ask someone else to snap your photo...

*i* Admission adult €7, €3.50 reduced, free first Su of the month and Florence residents, price subject to increase if there is a temporary exhibition adult €10, €5 reduced; last entry 30min. before closing; wheelchair accessible

# FOOD

## ALL'ANTICO VINAIO ($)

V. dei Neri, 74R; 552382723; www.allanticovinaio.com/it; open daily 10am-10pm

Fortunately for you, Florentine street food involves face-sized *focaccia* sandwiches full of smearable deliciousness and thin-sliced meats, served for only €5 a sammie at All'Antico Vinaio. Unfortunately for you, the rest of the world is onto this amazing opportunity; All'Antico's website boasts that it was the most reviewed restaurant in the world in 2014. The classic flavor has slices of

*sbriciolana* (Italian salami), artichoke sauce, and spicy grilled eggplant, but you probably can't go wrong with any of the seven or eight flavor combos.

*i* Sandwiches €5; wheelchair accessible

## DA NERBONE ($)

Mercato Centrale; 55219949; open M-Sa 8am-2pm

When a hole-in-the-wall style restaurant can get people to line up for tripe and other miscellaneous offal, you know they must be doing something pretty special. That's the case with Da Nerbone—located on the ground of floor of **Mercato Centrale.** You're pretty much guaranteed a long line between you and your organ meat (whether that's in sandwich, soup, or pasta form). That's how it's been since 1872, when Da Nerbone first set up shop. They have some more familiar fare, as well, so no worries if you're weak-stomached.

*i* Entrées €3.50-7; vegetarian options available; wheelchair accessible

## GELETARIA DE' MEDICI ($)

P. Beccaria 7r; 553860008; www.geletariademedici.com/en; open Tu-Su 9:30am-midnight

Okay, so it isn't the oldest gelato shop in Florence (that prize goes to **Vivoli** est. 1929), but kudos to Gelateria de' Medici for being the most creative. Flavours like limone, crema, and pistachio are ubiquitous to Florentine gelato shops, but you'd be hard-pressed to find someone else serving scoops of ricotta-pear, gorgonzola, fig-cream, or "inferno," which incorporates candied lemon and rum into thick dark chocolate. Well-loved by Florentine students, cones are dirt-cheap compared to gelaterias closer to the main piazzas from the tiny €1.80 cone (perfect for sampling) to the molto grande €4 cone (which is still probably only as big as an American small).

*i* Scoops €1.80-€4.00; vegan and vegetarian options available; wheelchair accessible

## IL VEGETARIANO ($$)

V. Delle Ruote, 30R; 55475030; www.il-vegetariano.it; open M 12:30pm-2:30pm,

Tu-F 12:30pm-2:30pm and 7:30pm-10:30pm, Sa-Su 7:30pm-10:30pm

Vegetarian food in Florence often comes with an overdose of American hipster vibes—impersonal white walls, spirulina, and mysterious soilless plants have popped up throughout Florence's winding streets and *piazzas*. But Il Vegetariano is actually something of a legend for staying away from that trend; theirs is the only *trattoria* specializing in vegetarian fare that still feels like a regular *trattoria*, with the same traditionally-laid tables, Italian-only menus, and dimly-lit atmosphere. So, you can still get classic pastas, and lasagnas, just without the meat. There's also a nice salad bar, and they give you that traditional, unsalted bread that is so ubiquitous to Florence, on the house. Definitely a winner, whether you're vegetarian or not.

*i* Entrées €8-15; vegan and vegetarian options available; wheelchair accessible

# NIGHTLIFE

### BAR KITCH DEVX

V. San Gallo, 22R; 554684551; www. kitschfirenze.com; open daily 6pm-3am

You've always wanted to party inside an elegant museum like the Uffizi, and now you can! Sort of. Bar Kitsch DevX can't really decide what to be—décor includes red velvet-y chairs, ornate gold mirrors, Renaissance-style statues, and lots of green neon lights. The one thing Kitsch DevX definitely is: a very economic late-night hangout for loud music, beer, and a ton of food (drinks come with unlimited access to buffet-style aperitivo offerings like pizza, rice dishes, and curries). Hey, after a day spent paying to shuffle through half a gazillion museums, every euro counts!

*i* Cocktails all under €10

### THE MAYDAY CLUB

V. Dante Alighieri 16R; 552381290; www. maydayclub.it; open Tu-Sa 7pm-2am

There's no bartender at the Mayday Club. Instead, the mixologist and owner of 16 years calls himself an "alchemist," stirring up intriguing blends and, in general, "serving awesomeness since 2001." The bar is off the main streets, tucked into a small piazza with other nightclub hotspots, but this one's special. It's not like every nightclub serves artichoke vermouth or "Antico Toscano Liqueuer" (infused with Tuscan cigars). The entire menu (over 40 cocktails) changes every year, so you'll have to stop by yourself to see what the alchemist has been up to.

*i* No cover, cocktails €8; wheelchair accessible

### IL TRIP PER TRÉ

Borgo Ognissanti, 144R; 550988177; open M-Th 6pm-2am, F-Sa 6pm-3am, Su 6pm-2am

Il Trip per Tré is like a panacea for the homesick; you're bound to feel the sweet pangs of familiarity brought on by Il Trip per Tré's mélange of culture. "Come," the bartender will tell you, putting an arm around your shoulder, his face just a little uncomfortably close to yours. "Only rock music!" he'll grin. It's true: no pop songs allowed, and Trip per Tré has not one, but *multiple* Rolling Stones shrines. "And," the bartender will whap your chest as he happily gestures to the TV "*Always* soccer!" There's beer flowing for relatively cheap (€5 a pint before 9:30pm), served from a positively jolly bartender who may or may not have already enjoyed a pint (or two). Truly a no-frills institution, but highly homey and very comfortable.

*i* Pints €5.50, half-pints €3.50 (happy hour €5 and €3); wheelchair accessible

# MILAN

Coverage by **Joseph Winters**

If you accidentally packed those green velvet Prada sandals with the hand-embellished sequins instead of the calf leather Bottega Veneta ones with the intrecciato borders that you meant to grab, you'll probably be able to buy a new pair once you get to Milan. Industry, particularly fashion, lives side-by-side with history here, and the dynamic duo will permeate every part of your touristic experience. Go about your day, casually sightseeing your way from the grandeur of the fourteenth century Duomo to other marvels of the Renaissance, like da *Vinci's The Last Supper.* At any point, look up and *voilà*—chances are, you'll be face-to-face with another ultra-fancy boutique. Just be sure to save some money for the real cultural experiences: a night of *aperitivos* (appetizers and tapas), creative cocktails, and the hottest beats in one of Milan's famous nightclubs.

# ORIENTATION

Milan is roughly circular; it spreads outwards from the center, where most of the historic sites are located, like the **Duomo, Galleria Vittorio Emanuele II,** and **Teatro alla Scala.** Beyond those, there are many broad *piazzas* (plazas), each bringing a defining characteristic to their neighborhood. The most popular neighborhoods are **Brera, Centrale, Isola,** and **Navigli.** Isola is renowned for alternative culture, Navigli for nightlife, and Brera for high-end shopping. To get the full Milanese experience, we'd recommend spending at least a day in the historic **Duomo and Castello district,** then picking out a couple areas to really delve into for the remainder of your stay.

# ESSENTIALS

## GETTING THERE

Milan has two international airports: Malpensa Airport (MXP) and Linate Airport (LIN). The former carries more flights from areas outside of Europe while the latter mostly handles domestic and international flights within Europe. You can also take the train into Milan, docking at Milano Centrale. The station receives trains from both MXP and LIN every 20-30min. and cities such as Florence, Geneva, Paris, Nice, and Rome. It also has connections to Milan's metro system. Bus operators such as Ouibus also serve Milan, docking at the Autostradale Viaggi Lampugnano Coach Station.

## GETTING AROUND

The metro will be your ever-faithful best friend in Milan. Tickets are €1.50 per ride within the urban city limits (you probably won't do much outside in the "hinterlands"—as the information sign calls it—anyway), but the best deals are either a 24hr or 48hr ticket, for €4.50 and €8.25, respectively. There's also a carnet of 10 tickets (€13.80), or a nighttime ticket for unlimited use between 8pm and the end of that day's service (€3). You can buy any of these ticket options inside the metro, but the carnets cannot be purchased self-serve. Pick those up at the ticket office. The metro consists of the M1 (red), M2 (green),

M3 (yellow), and M5 (purple). There are easy-to-read signs at every station and in every metro car, so navigation should not be a hassle. While planning your Milanese adventures, plan your nights so you don't get stranded far from your hostel after the metro stops running; the M1, M2, and M3 run from 6am-12:30am, and the M5 goes from 6am-midnight. You can catch a night bus every 30min. while the M1, M2, and M3 are on break.

## PRACTICAL INFORMATION

**Tourist Offices:** Galleria Vittorio Emanuele II, P. della Scala; 02 8845555; www.turismo.milanoit; open M-F 9am-7pm, Sa 9am-6pm, Su 10am-6pm.

**Banks/ATMs/Currency Exchange:** There are ATMs throughout the city, so you should have no problem finding one. Here's the address of HSBC in Milan (V. Mike Bongiorno, 13; 02 7243741).

**Post Offices:** Poste Italiane (Milano Centrale, P. Duca d'Aosta; 02 6707 2150; open M-F 8:20am-7:05pm, Sa 8:20am-12:35pm).

**Internet:** There are Wi-Fi hotspots in public squares throughout Milan.

**BGLTQ+ Resources:** Centro d'Iniziativa Gay—ArchiGay Milano (V. Bezzeca 3; 02 5412225; www.arcigaymilano.org).

## EMERGENCY INFORMATION

**Emergency Number:** 112

**Police:** 112 for *carabinieri* or 113 for local police. Police headquarters (V.

Fatebenefratelli, 11; 02 62261; www.
questura.poliziadistato.it/milano).

**US Embassy:** The nearest US Embassy
is located in Rome (V. Vittotio Veneto
121; 06 46741). However, there is a
US consulate in Milan (V. Principe
Amedeo, 2/10; 02 290351).

**Rape Crisis Center:** RAINN (800 646
4673) and National Coalition Against
Domestic Violence (303 839 1852).

**Hospitals:**
- Ospedale Niguarda Ca'Granda (P.
  dell'Osepedale Maggiore, 3; 02
  64441; open daily 24hr)
- Milan Medical Center S.R.L. (V.
  Mauri Angelo, 3; 02 4399 0401;
  open M-F 9am-6pm)

**Pharmacies:**
- Della Cittadella (Corso di Porta
  Ticinese, 50; 02 832 1584; open
  M-Sa 7am-1am, Su 8pm-mid-
  night).

# ACCOMMODATIONS

### ⚑OSTELLO BELLO ($$)
V. Medici 4; 236482720; www.ostellobello.
com; reception open 24hr

According to the counter staff, "this
hostel is more of a bar." Named the
best hostel in Italy by Hostelworld,
Bello is truly much more than just a
hostel. Aside from the bar, there's a
big breakfast buffet, free dinner, and a
fridge stocked with food for the taking.
They even offer Wi-Fi modems to
take with you throughout your days
pedaling through Milan's streets. Plus,
it's the most centrally-located hostel
in Milan, just a few blocks away from
the Duomo, near a sort of Bohemian
neighborhood full of niche bookstores,
cafés, and nightclubs.

*i* *Dorms from €45; reservation recommended; wheelchair accessible; Wi-Fi;
reservation recommended; linens included;
towels included; lockers provided; free
breakfast*

### MADAMA HOSTEL AND BISTROT ($)
V. Benaco 1; 3663107485; www.madama-
hostel.com/en; reception open 24hr

Something of an oasis in the middle
of an otherwise unremarkable part of
Milan, Madama Hostel and Bistrot
makes up for its location with the
amenities it provides. Free breakfast in
the morning, *aperitivos* in the evening,
free entrance to the affiliated club,

morning yoga, African dance classes,
and poetry readings, just to name a
few. The staff are both friendly and
knowledgeable, which helps as the
bistrot gets surprisingly busy at night.
It serves hostel-goers, clubbers, and
other passersby who are up for some
cheap eats and maybe a final shot (of
espresso) before bedtime.

*i* *Dorms €25; reservation recommended;
BGLTQ+ friendly; wheelchair accessible; Wi-
Fi; linens included; towels included; lockers
provided; laundry facilities €3 wash, €3
dry; free Italian breakfast*

### QUEEN HOSTEL ($)
V. Regina Margherita, 9; 236564959; www.
queenhostel.com; reception open 24hr

Part hostel, part local college student
study spot, Queen Hostel is the new
kid on the block. The common areas,
with a pool, foosball tables, and punk
rock instruments strewn about, make
you feel like you're in an underground
lounge. This might be because you're
so far most of the other notable
nightlife in Milan, although the metro
isn't too far away. Plus, whatever
Queen Hostel lacks location-wise, it
makes up for in its amenities: daily
events at the bar, a stocked guest
kitchen (meaning flour, sugar, salt,
spices, etc.), free towels upon request,
and complimentary breakfast. They
have a bit of fun with the word
"breakfast," though, as they really mean
a croissant, some "rusks" (croutons in
a bag), and coffee. Thankfully, grocery
stores abound in this neighborhood.

*i* *Dorms €24-35; BGLTQ+ friendly; wheelchair accessible; Wi-Fi; linens included;
towels included; lockers provided, padlock
€3; free breakfast*

# SIGHTS
## CULTURE

### FIERA DI SINIGAGLIA FLEA MARKET
Ripa di Porta Ticinese; open Sa 8am-3pm

When the Milanese aren't perusing the
**Vittorio Emmanuel Mall** for a new
pair of diamond-studded, crocodile
skin stilettos (that's a thing, right?),
you might find them doing normal
people things, like haggling over a
head of cabbage at a street market.
It really can't get more authentic

than the market on the edges of the **Parco Baravalle,** which is open every Saturday from around 8am to 3pm. There are killer deals on veggies, fruits, cheeses, fish, and even some prepared street food delicacies like *arancini di riso.* Pro-tip: swing by at 4pm when the vendors are almost done packing up—lots of the fresh stuff can't be resold at the next market, so oftentimes you can pick up food on the cheap.

*i* *Prices vary by stand; some stands cash only; wheelchair accessible*

### NAVIGLI

Navigli District; open daily 24hr

Canals? In Milan? They aren't the canals of Venice, but Milan has its own set of boutique and restaurant-lined waterways in the Navigli District, south of the **Duomo.** Home to not one but three universities, students and tourists flock to the area after sunset for some cocktails and *aperitivos.* Pros include quality seafood, beautiful sunsets, and flea markets on the weekends. Cons include having to discern which places are the tourist traps and which are the local joints. The best advice: use your instincts; if a place is serving "Tradishonal Milan Cuisine," chances are it might not be as "tradishonal" as they'd have you believe.

*i* *Prices vary by store; wheelchair accessible*

### PORTA VENEZIA

Porta Venezia; open daily 24hr

Navigli is generally the first place people think of when it comes to Milanese nightlife and culture, but Porta Venezia, on the opposite side of town, offers a different genre of entertainment. Unlike Navigli, which caters to larger hordes of unknowing tourists, you won't find as many Americanized places like "Pizzeria Manhattan" in Porta Venezia. Instead, look for tons of hipster cafés, ethnic restaurants, clubs, and a thriving BGLTQ+ nightlife scene. There's also an interesting park full of science-y attractions, like the **Museum of Natural History** and a **Planetarium,** which offers pretty much the only way

to see the stars in Milan due to urban light pollution.

*i* *Prices vary by store; wheelchair accessible*

## LANDMARKS

### THE DUOMO

P. del Duomo; 272022656; www.duomo-milano.it/en; church open daily 8am-7pm, museum open daily 10am-6pm

It's not like you're going to miss it, since it's pretty much the center of the whole city and reaches a gargantuan height of 158 meters, but the Duomo—the fifth largest cathedral in the world—is non-negotiable as far as tourist destinations go. It took nearly 600 years to build and has since attracted thousands of tourists on the daily, including Mark Twain and Ernest Hemingway (yes, celebrities can be tourists, too). The interior is breathtaking, but, for the real deal, clamber onto the rooftop terraces for a panoramic view of Milan. Pro-tip: there's little information to be found, so we advise that you buy an audio guide, tour the museum, or research its architectural style to give the Duomo historical context. Or, you know, there's also Wikipedia.

*i* *Admission to church, terrace, and museum €12, €16 with combination ticket with elevator to terraces; tours every 90min.; wheelchair accessible*

### THE LAST SUPPER

P. Santa Maria della Grazie, 2; 292800360; www.cenacovinciano.net; open Tu-Su 8:15am-7pm, closed Jan 1, May 1, Dec 25

For some reason, no one ever tells you that *The Last Supper* isn't some painting hanging on a curator's wall, but rather an enormous, **15-foot-high fresco** that completely covers one side of a Dominican monastery. **Da Vinci** used an avant-garde technique called "dry" painting in order to make changes as he went, but it actually ended up making the fresco really hard to preserve. Way to go, Leo. To get in, you'll have to book tickets online way in advance, or hope someone canceled their reservation. Best to play it safe:

your trip to Milan pretty much won't count if you skip **The Last Supper.**

*i* *Admission adult €25 plus €2 booking tax, €5 plus €2 booking tax EU citizens, free under 25 plus €2 booking tax, €3.50 guided tours daily every 15min.; last entry 6:45pm; wheelchair accessible*

### GALLERIA VITTORIO EMANUELE II
P. del Duomo; open daily 24hr

Instead of exhausting your brain through intense study of Renaissance painting or Gothic architecture, invest time into the history behind the world's oldest malls: the Galleria Vittorio Emanuele II. Crash course: the building, completed in 1877, was named after the first king and its architecture makes it a must-see. Stroll through two massive glass-paned hallways that meet in the centrally-located glass dome. Once you've snapped a few photos, there's plenty of perusing to do in—you guessed it—high fashion stores. That isn't to say there aren't some trinket shops and cheap eats sprinkled here and there. Fun fact: There was a McDonald's until 2012, until it was booted out by Prada.

*i* *Prices vary by store; wheelchair accessible*

### L.O.V.E.
P. defli Affari; open daily 24hr

L.O.V.E. might seem an inappropriate name for a statue of a hand flipping the bird, but, in this case, it stands for *Libertà, Odio, Vendetta,* and *Eternità* (Freedom, Hate, Vengeance, and Eternity). It was provocatively added to Piazza Degli Affari, the center of the Italian stock exchange, in 2010. Ever since, hordes of tourists with Gucci handbags bursting with designer clothes and sunglasses have stopped by to snap a picture of this anti-capitalist symbol. The piazza itself is actually relatively quiet—L.O.V.E. will never reach **Duomo** status as a tourist destination—but it offers a worthwhile change of scenery from the more commercial piazzas that surround it.

*i* *Free; wheelchair accessible*

# MUSEUMS

### CASTELLO SFORZESCO MUSEO
P. Castello; 288463700; www.milanocastel-lo.it/en; open Tu-Su 9am-5:30pm

Castello Sforzesco Museo is an... eclectic mix of Italian art. Seriously, one second you'll be appreciating **Michelangelo's** *Pietà Rondanini,* and the next you'll be admiring a decorative set of silverware from the 1980s. There's the **Museum of Ancient Art, the Museum of Musical Instruments, an Egyptian Museum,** and so on. The best strategy is to select just a few areas, and explore them thoroughly, rather than try to hopelessly sprint through the entire museum to see everything in one shot (we found out the hard way). Don't miss the **da Vinci** museum, though—unfortunately, you won't see THE *Last Supper,* but there's an entire room full of replicas, some nearly as old as the original. You'll turn corner after corner, thinking, "this has got to be the last *Last Supper.*" It won't be.

*i* *Admission €5, €3 reduced; last entry 5pm; wheelchair accessible*

### MUSEO DI STORIA NATURALE DI MILANO
Corso Venezia, 55; 288463337; open Tu-Su 9am-5:30pm

Many, many years ago, before its conquest by the Romans in 222 BCE, and before being captured by the Celts in 400 BCE, and right around the years 1000 to 4.5 billion years B.D.G. (before Dolce and Gabbana), Milan had a pretty rich natural history. The Museo di Storia Naturale di Milano showcases it expertly with an impressive density of dioramas featuring animals and skeletons by region of origin. They even have an entire section devoted to the wildlife of Italy—something often forgotten by the average city-going tourist. Granted, sometimes, the taxidermists were a little too ambitious in planning some of the dioramas; keep your eyes peeled for a particularly wonderful display of two marmosets in the midst of a fierce battle. *Nota Bene:* most of the exhibits are labeled only in Italian, so be prepared to admire the displays

# PISA

**A four-degree tilt has stolen Pisa's cultural identity and made the city a famous get-in, get-out tourist destination.** Of course, the Piazza dei Miracoli, with its UNESCO-grade marvels (the Baptistery, Camposanto, Cathedral, and Tower are found here) is a stunning and non-negotiable tourist destination, but the rest of Pisa's history shouldn't lie obscured in the shadow of the tipping tower. An important trading center since antiquity (even the Romans thought Pisa was an old city), Pisa has a large student population (it's home to three universities, one of which was founded by Pope Clement VI in 1343) and everything that comes with it: ethnic street food, flea markets, and a fair share of nightlife options. So snag your Tower selfie and explore the main Piazza, but save at least half a day for the winding streets that lie to the south, especially near the riverbanks.

For the most dramatic first view of the Leaning Tower, you'll want to plan your route to the Piazza dei Miracoli. The lean is most visible when you come in from the **Porta Santa Maria** on the western side of the Piazza, as opposed to the **Via Santa Maria** (which makes the tower look disappointingly normal). Once you're in the Piazza dei Miracoli, you're perfectly placed to check out the other sights: the Baptistery, Cathedral, Camposanto, and Museum. There are a few student hangouts in the piazzas just north of the river (south of the Tower), particularly **Piazza Garibaldi, Piazza dei Cavalieri,** and **Piazza San Omobono.** The banks of the Arno are also popular nightlife areas. Once you cross the river, you'll find the main shopping area on **Corso Italia** (pretty much the whole street, all the way to the **Pisa Centrale** train station). To either side of this street are some cheaper, less crowded dining options.

## GETTING THERE

Trains to Pisa stop at the Pisa Centrale station, which is a 20-minute walk south of the Piazza dei Miracoli. Trains arrive from Florence (€9, 1hr 15min), Rome (€30-50, 3hr), and Lucca (€4, 30min). There's also a smaller train station in the northwest corner of the city. Buses from Florence to the Galileo Galilei airport are operated by SITA (043 6228048; www.sitabus.it) and Terravision (44 6894239; www.terravision.eu). Lazzi (058 3584876; www.lazzi.it) and CPT (050 505511; www.cpt.pisa) run buses that go from Florence's Santa Maria Novella station to Pisa's Piazza Sant'Antonio.

However, bus tickets are usually more expensive than the train (€10, and the bus is less frequent).

## GETTING AROUND

Pisa is highly walkable. From the train station, walk north on Corso Italia, which then turns into Borgo Stretto once you cross the Arno. After taking a left on Via dei Mille, travel north on Via Santa Maria all the way to the Piazza dei Miracoli. LAM Rossa buses do a loop around the city every 20 minutes, stopping at major destinations like the Tower, train station, airport, and others. Tickets are €1 for an hour, and can be found at most tabaccherias or at the train station or airport.

## Swing by...

### THE LEANING TOWER

Piazza del Duomo; 050 835011; www.opapisa.it; open Tu-Su 10am-6pm

Depending on how you get to the tower, your initial reaction may actually be disappointment; from Via Santa Maria, it actually looks pretty vertical. But once you get a little closer and look at it from the left (near the Duomo), you'll see the tower in all its precarious glory. Fun fact: its lean is only four degrees, but, over such a tall height, this means that the short side is almost an entire meter shorter than the tall side! Granted, its construction began in 1173, so maybe we need to cut it some slack. Either way, climbing the tower is a required tourist activity for Pisa visitors. You'll get to scale the 296 stone steps, then admire the cityscape from 55.86 meters up (or 56.67, it depends)!

*i* *Admission €18, includes ticket to cathedral; last entry 5:30pm; wheelchair accessible*

## Check out...

### PIAZZA DEI MIRACOLI

Piazza dei Miracoli; Baptistery, Camposanto, and Sinopie Museum open daily 8am-8pm

This is *the* tourism piazza of Pisa. It's flooded with visitors on the daily and you'll question if you'll ever get a moment yourself with the Sinopie Museum, Camposanto, Baptistery, Cathedral, and—of course—the Leaning Tower. If you get the timing right, you can probably even snag a photo of yourself propping the tower up without a half a dozen other tourists photobombing your photo as they strike the same classless pose. Apart from your ticket up the Tower, you can buy a pass for 1, 2, or 3 of the monuments (€5, €7, and €8, respectively, and the Cathedral is included in the purchase of any ticket). Obviously, the best deal is to go for all three, but if we had to pick favorites, the Battistero has an upper gallery with a view, and was part of the "liturgical path" that led to the cathedral, the "place of the Eucharistic celebration." Speaking of the Cathedral, it's home to a little-known painting on wood that has survived in pristine condition since the year 1226, despite being paraded around the city during times of celebration.

*i* *Admission to all three monuments €8, includes ticket to cathedral; tours every 90 mins; limited wheelchair accessibility*

## Grab a bite at...

### AL MADINA ($)

Via San Martino, 41; 050 20409; www.ristorantealmadina.it; Tu-Sa 11:30am-3pm and 7pm-11:30pm, Su 7pm-11:30pm

Middle Eastern food and college students are nearly inseparable in the college towns of Italy, and Pisa is no exception. Al Madina is the perfect place for those with big appetites and light wallets; your precious euros will get you much more falafel than fettuccine. Sit among Persian carpets and Arabic décor, sheeshas and mosque selfies, and grab a wrap or hummus mezze. Or, for the best deal, there's the legendary "mix plate": a small mountain of hummus, baba ghanouj, falafel, tabbouleh, Greek salad, tomatoes, salsa, pita, and whatever else they have lying around in the kitchen. Maybe it's best to save this "truly special dish" (according to the counter staff) for after the strenuous hike up the Leaning Tower.

*i* *€3.5-10; vegetarian and vegan options available; wheelchair accessible*

## Don't miss...

### ORTO BOTANICO

Via Luca Ghini, 13; 050 221 1310; www.sma.unipi.it/it/orto-e-museo-botanico. html/; open daily 8am-8pm

The oldest botanical garden in Europe (founded in 1543), the Orto Botanico of Pisa is just a stone's throw away from the Piazza dei Miracoli, and is definitely worth a visit if you're wondering what to do after the Tower. They suggest walking along the "Ancient Trees Path," which takes you past magnolias, camphor trees, a gingko, and a "European hackberry" (whatever that is). There's also a botanical museum with cross-sections of mushrooms, recreated botany labs from the sixteenth century, and pressed flowers from over two centuries ago.

*i* *€4, €2 student; last entry 1hr. before closing; limited wheelchair accessibility*

# THE LOCAL FARE: *APERITIVOS IN MILAN*

Just like their espresso, the Milanese like to eat their food little by little. Maybe it helps them fit into their designer skinny jeans. Either way, food culture in Milan dictates that thou shalt not eat dinner before the sun has set and you've eaten at least three kinds of carbs, one of which absolutely must be pasta. Thus, 6-9pm is the time for the *aperitivo*. Originally invented in Milan, *aperitivos* are a magical, mouth-watering mélange of the concept of the hors d'oeuvre, tapas, and bar food, but they're more about socializing than about the food itself. Chat while nibbling on simple plates of olives and nuts, or sometimes on dishes as involved as a full-on Italian lasagna. Either way, *aperitivos* help you whet your appetite while you sip a cocktail or two in preparation for a late-night dinner (basically, *aperitivos* remove the stigma of the midnight pizza run). Some tourists don't really understand this concept (ahem, Americans) and do *aperitivos* like they're at a buffet, indulging in a small mountain of chicken tikka masala while the savvy travelers around them are picking at their three or four cubes of buffalo mozzarella. To blend in better, order a cocktail (we recommend the Negroni) and grab a few bites to get those digestive juices flowing.

without really understanding what's going on.

*i* Admission €3, €1.50 reduced; last entry 5pm; wheelchair accessible

## MUSEO TEATRO ALLA SCALA

Largo Ghiringhelli 1, P. Scala; 288797473; www.teatroallascala.org; open daily 9am-5:30pm

Step into the shoes of the Milanese elite (like Armani or Prada) at the Museo Teatro alla Scala and look onto the stage, home to some of Italy's most renowned performing artists, from a third-story box. Imagine it's 1776 and you're settling down for a nearly endless showcase of supersonic arias and unintelligible cantatas. Thankfully, you can snap yourself out of that fantasy by checking out the museum's musical artifacts —of particular note is a copy of **Verdi's** *Requiem Mass* and **Franz Liszt's** piano, gifted to him by Steinway and Sons themselves in 1883.

*i* Admission adult €7, €5 student, group, and over 65, free under 12 and disabled; audio guide €7; wheelchair accessible

# OUTDOORS

## LAKE COMO

Como, Italy; open daily 24hr

A mere hour-long train ride away from **Porta Garibaldi** or **Cadorna Station** (€4.80), Como is a playground for the uber-rich. Prices are sky-high for

everything, the streets are pristine, and the typical tourist carries a different pair of sunglasses for every hour of the day. If you make the trek to Como, do a quick walk-through of the streets, checking out some historical sites (like its own Duomo—much smaller than Milan's), and soak in some beautiful views of the water. You can take a ferry ride to one of the smaller villages further north. **Bellagio,** the "Crotch of Lake Como" (because Lake Como is shaped like a pair of pants) is very popular, but it's a whole notch (or three) more tourist-y than Como.

*i* Free admission, train from Garibaldi or Cadorna Station €4.80, speed ferry to Bellagio €14.80, regular ferry €10, bus round-trip to Bellagio €3.60; wheelchair accessible

## PARCO SEMPIONE

V. Wolfango; open daily 6:30am-8:30pm

Just behind the grandiose **Castello Sforzesco** is Parco Sempione, Milan's largest urban park, home to lots of hidden gems like the **Arco della Pace** (Arch of Peace), an Arc-de-Triomphe-style tribute to Napoleon Bonaparte's victories; the **Arena Civica** (Civic Arena), a sports and music venue built in the early 1800s; the **Acquario Civico** (Civic Aquarium); the **Torre Branca,** a tower you can ride an elevator to the top of for €4; and the **Palazzo dell'Arte,** home of the International Exhibition of Decorative

Arts. If none of that piques your interest, it's always nice to sprawl out in the grass and soak up the Milanese sun while locals walk their dogs through the park.

*i* Free admission; wheelchair accessible

# FOOD

## FLOWER BURGER ($$)

V. Vittorio Veneto 10; 239628381; www.flowerburger.it; open daily 12:30pm-3:30pm and 7pm-11pm

"Don't be a fool, nutrition is cool!" reads a sign on the wall at Flower Burger. Even though you may have come to Milan for the hunks of breaded meat fried in butter that they call *alla Milanesa*, it's not like that's what the Milanese eat at every lunchtime; if they did, they wouldn't fit into those teeny cars. At Flower Burger, however, the Milanese have struck a mouthwatering balance between health and flavor; the six burgers served are all vegan, cooked on black, yellow, or pink buns and slathered with delicious homemade "cheese" or "mayo" concoctions, spicy salsas, and—of course—topped with a hearty dose of veggies. There's no Wi-Fi, but that's okay because you'll be too busy devouring your burger to check Facebook anyway.

*i* Burgers €6.50-9, 10% lunch discount; wheelchair accessible

## IL MASSIMO DEL GELATO ($)

V. Lodovico Castelvetro, 18; 23494943; www.ilmassimodelgelato.it; open Tu-Su noon-midnight

With a gelateria on literally every street corner, it can be hard to separate the fantastico from the average. Try to restrain yourself from the allure of the first one you spot and seek out Il Massimo del Gelato—the difference in quality is well worth the wait. Self-described as having been "created to conquer the eyes," Il Massimo offers "voluptuous" flavors like 100% dark chocolate, Aztec (chocolate with chili pepper), and classics such as pistachio and gianduja (hazelnut). A surprising favorite: the *limono*, which might just be more lemon-y than sucking on an actual slice of fresh lemon. There are a couple different locations—the original

one in the northwest part of Milan has the most flavors, but there's a smaller store right by the **Duomo.**

*i* Scoops €2-5; card minimum €10; vegetarian options available; wheelchair accessible

## PAVÉ ($$)

V. Felice Casati, 21; 294392259; www.pavemilano.com; open Tu-F 8am-8pm, Sa-Su 8:30pm-7pm

"Sex, love, and *pannetone*" are apparently the ingredients to a life of bliss, according to one of the many typographic posters adorning the walls of this hipster coffee joint. The *pannetone* doesn't disappoint, and it's certainly served with a lot of love (but you'll need to look elsewhere to complete the happiness trio). Expect deliciously rich shots of espresso brewed with "traditional values" and "raw materials value." Bad translations aside, it's worth coming for the funky vibes and free Wi-Fi. You might even meet a fellow traveler at their communal table. Serendipitous meetings are encouraged, as Pavé's menu reads "By the way, you should know your greatest love was a stranger once." Maybe that bite of *pannetone* really could lead to love, which could lead to... Well, you get the idea.

*i* Entrées €6-12, pastries €5, coffee €1-3, wine €20; vegetarian options available; wheelchair accessible

## PIZZA AM ($$)

Corso di Porta Romana, 83; 25110579; www.pizzaam.it; open Tu-F noon-3pm and 7pm-11:30, Sa noon-3:30pm and 7pm-11:30pm, Su 7pm-11:30pm

The Italians know they're famous for pizza, and you'll get the feeling everyone is trying to jump on the pizzeria bandwagon whether it makes sense or not. Use your discerning eye and say no to "Kebab Pizzeria" or similar jack-of-all-trades places like "Pizzeria Restaurante Café Internet!"; there are better places out there, we promise. Pizza AM, with its bright colors, creepy marionettes, and world flags galore, boasts a mere six—but highly sought-after—flavors. In the evenings, hungry patrons form lines that extend down the street. Waiting may not be so bad, though, as the owner appeases hungry soon-to-be customers by offering them free beers and much-needed *aperitivos*.

*i* Slices €6-9; vegetarian options available; wheelchair accessible

# NIGHTLIFE

## FRIDA

V. Pollaiuolo, 3; 2680260; www.fridaisloa.it; open M-F 10am-3pm and 6pm-8pm, Sa 6pm-2am, Su noon-1am

Just north of the ultra-polished shopping mall at **Piazza Gae Aulenti** is a grungier student hangout called **Isola,** where chain stores and clean-cut sidewalks are replaced with hole-in-the-wall bars and urban patches of greenery. Here, you'll find Frida, a café/bar/nightclub/shop hybrid with a lovely patio area surrounded by vine-covered walls and geometric graphic art. Frida boasts an ability to cater to all palettes, so whether you're looking for a simple Mai Tai or more creative creations like the "Puppa Puppa" with vodka, peach juice, and passion fruit, this is the place to be.

*i* Small plates from €5-10, beer €5-6, wine €7-12, cocktails €7, gin or rum or whiskey €9; wheelchair accessible

## VINILE

V. Alessandro Tadino 17; 02 36514233; www.vinilemilano.com; open Tu-Su 6:30pm-2am

Ideal wine night partners: Chewbacca, Prince, and Pikachu. Where can you find them? Vinile—a wine bar for those with oddly specific tastes.

Beyond wine, enjoy beer or "Mixing Desk Specials," as well as a Jazz Menu replete with Soul Salads, Rock Snacks, and Funky Sandwiches named after rock and pop legends like Beyoncé. If you're already dizzy from an overdose of eclectic-ness and groovy live music, try to avert your eyes from the disco ball that dimly illuminates the bar. Side note: pretty much every piece of Vinile's décor is for sale, so the fun doesn't ever have to end. If you buy the life-sized R2-D2 replica, our editorial staff would be highly appreciative of a photo.

*i* Wine €5-8, beer €5-12, cocktails €7-10, Wine €5-8, beer €5-12, cocktails €7-10, entrées €7-15; vegetarian options available; wheelchair accessible

## GINGER COCKTAIL LAB

V. Ascanio Sforza, 25; 33 55690779; open Tu-Su 6pm-3am

Who said being vegan was supposed to be boring? At Ginger Cocktail Lab, a tiny bar adorned car hoods and antique furniture, carnivores and vegivores alike can both nosh on traditional Milanese *aperitivos* gone animal-free while sipping on specialty cocktails with names like Jekyll and Hyde. There are also some more traditional drinks like caipirinhas or mojitos for the less adventurous. For the even less adventurous, there's a pharmacy across the canal where you can sip vitamin water or prepare for the next morning's epic hangover.

*i* Drinks €6-9; vegan and vegetarian options available

# NAPLES

Coverage by **Adrian Horton**

You've probably heard some rumors about Naples. "It's incredible!" some say, citing the city's energy, authenticity, and pizza (a recurring theme, for good reason). "It's so dirty!" others claim, put off by the port's crowded apartment buildings, overstuffed trash bins, and grit-stained sidewalks. Naples has a mixed reputation, beloved by some for its unpretentious treasures and culinary wonders, written off by others for its rampant garbage and overwhelming congestion. Churches and palaces abound in Naples but Rome, it is not. Rather, Naples has its own unpolished take on the living history museum—medieval buildings teem with people and televisions, apartments rest upon Roman ruins, and restaurants serve up recipes perfected over generations. Once a Roman resort city, later a jewel in the French and Spanish crowns, and formerly the second largest city in Europe, Naples wears its turbulent past on its sleeve. It also bears the scars of

Italian unification, which decimated its economy. The twin thorns of poverty and pollution still burrow into Naples' side, though conditions have improved in the past couple decades. Don't be deterred by the word on the street, though—Naples doesn't hide, and neither should you.

# ORIENTATION

Though on the west coast of Italy, Naples actually faces south; its coastline on the Gulf of Naples is bookmarked by the town of **Pozzuoli** to the west and the storied **Mt. Vesuvius** to the east. **Napoli Centrale Station** and the overrun **Piazza Garibaldi** greet visitors at the east end of the center city. The historic center of Naples, **Centro Antico,** lies just west of Piazza Garibaldi and is framed by two major streets. The first, **Via Tribulani**—commonly known as "Speccanapoli," meaning "Split Naples"—runs west from **Castel Capuano** to **Piazza Dante** and provides the main artery through which Centro Antico's towering apartment buildings, artisan shops, and most famous pizza joints flow. The second, **Via Toledo,** runs from Piazza Plebescito on the harbor, through Piazza Dante and towards **Capodimonte** in the north. Across Via Toledo lies the Spanish Quarter, a maze of narrow streets, laundry lines, and scooters that do not look before they power around corners. The Spanish Quarter slopes upward towards the **Vomero Hill,** home to the star-shaped **Castel Sant'Elmo.** Along the coast to the south of Vomero is **Chiaia,** where many bars, upscale restaurants, and some clubs can be found.

# ESSENTIALS

## GETTING THERE

From Naples International Airport, "Alibus" connects the airport with Napoli Centrale Station. Buses run from 6:30am-11:50pm from the station just outside the terminal. One-way tickets cost €4. From Napoli Centrale Station (Piazza Garibaldi), trains from other cities and surrounding areas arrive at Napoli Centrale, also referred to as Garibaldi Station. Napoli Centrale is east of the city center, so most visitors will need to hop on the metro (downstairs in the station; follow signs from the train platforms) to reach their final destination.

## GETTING AROUND

Naples is, for the most part, navigable on foot (though the hills are a challenge), but recent investment in public transportation provides visitors with several less strenuous options. Naples's metro caters mostly to suburban commuters, though the two main lines span large portions of the city. Line 1 connects Napoli Centrale to the east with the Vomero hill to the north, and weaves through popular stops such as Piazza Dante, Via Toledo, and the Archaeological Museum

(Museo). Line 2 mirrors the coast, running from Centrale in the east to the Stadio San Paolo in the west. Single metro tickets cost €1.10 and are valid for 90min. A day pass costs €3.10. The metro runs from 6am-11pm. Bus routes can occasionally provide efficient service to areas not as well-reached by the metro. Tickets cost €1.20 and are valid on any changes for 90min. Not the most efficient, though certainly the most fun form of transportation, Naples's four funiculars have ferried passengers up and down the hills of the city for decades (and you can tell). There are four funiculari routes, all of which serve the Vomero hill: Centrale, Chiaia, Mergellina, and Montesanto. The funiculari save you some walking (the average ride time is ten minutes) and make for great pictures. All four are open daily 7am-10pm except for Chiaia, which remains open until 2am on Saturdays. Tickets cost €1.20.

## PRACTICAL INFORMATION

**Tourist Offices:** There are numerous tourist information centers across the city, including Garibaldi Station (081268779), P. del Gesú (0815512701), and P. dei Martiri (0814107211).
**Banks/ATMs/Currency Exchange:** As in most large Italian cities, ATMs are

431

common throughout the popular areas and deliver cash in euros.

**Post Offices:** Besides PosteItalia centers, international stamps can be purchased at tourist information centers in Naples.

**Internet:** Naples does not offer reliable public Wi-Fi, but many restaurants and cafés do.

## EMERGENCY INFORMATION

**Emergency Number:** 113 (general emergency), 118 (ambulance).

**Police:** Headquartered at the Palazzo della Questura, via Medina 75 (081 794 1111); call 112 for police (carabinieri) emergencies.

**US Consulate:** P. della Repubblica 2; 081 5838111; open daily 9am-8pm.

**Rape Crisis Center:** For English-language support, contact RAINN (Rape, Abuse, and Incest National Network) at 1-800-656-4673. The hotline, supported by the American Victims Assistance Programs, is toll-free and available 24hr.

**Hospitals:**
- Cardinale Ascalesi (V. Egiziaca a Forcella 31, 80139; 081 254 2111; open daily 24hr; located near Garibaldi Station).
- Primo Policlinico di Napoli (P. Luigi Miraglia 2, 80138; 800 177 780; open daily 24hr; located near Garibaldi Station).

**Pharmacies:** As in most big cities, pharmacies are a dime a dozen in the heart of Napes.
- Farmacia Internazionale (V. Calabritto 6, 081 7643444).
- Farmacia Mezzocannone (Corso Umberto I, 43, 081 5517488).

# ACCOMMODATIONS

### GIOVANNI'S HOME ($)

V. Sapienza 43; 8119565641; www.giovannishome.com; reception open as long as Giovanni is awake (he will stay up for you but prefers to close shop at 11pm)

Giovanni doesn't mess around. When he says "home," he means it—the hostel is literally his house, a medieval building converted into cozy bunk rooms with bathrooms, a common area, a patio, and a kitchen. When he advertises hospitality, he means it—he will stay up late into the night to greet incoming travelers, arrange transportation for guests, and cook fresh pasta for new arrivals. (When asked if he likes to cook, Giovanni shakes his head firmly. "No," he says, "I like to eat.") And when he promotes Naples, he means it—travelers who reveal they've never been to the former capital city are treated to a 45-minute tutorial on its importance, complete with picture books and a Google Earth geography lesson.

*i* Dorms €16; reservation recommended; min stay 2 nights; BGLTQ+ friendly; no wheelchair accessibility; Wi-Fi; laundry facilities; kitchen

### NEAPOLITAN TRIPS HOSTEL AND BAR ($$)

V. dei Fiorentini 10, 18366402; www.neapolitantrips.com; reception open 24hr

Sturdy metal-frame beds? Check. High ceilings, complimentary lockers, and repurposed game tables? Naturally. Neapolitan Trips Hostel and Bar definitely took the intro class on the Art and Architecture of Modern Hostels, and earned all the cheeky posters, sleek style, and electronic key-card credentials needed for a good time. In fact, with a full-service bar, a piano, and a refurbished stone and wood interior, we'd say it aced the course. Extra credit points go to its local accents, such as the decorations documenting the history of Italian soccer (er, football), central location off of Via Toledo, and winning staff with the best food recommendations in town.

*i* Dorms €22-25; reservation recommended; BGLTQ+ friendly; wheelchair accessible; Wi-Fi; towels included; laundry facilities (€4 per machine); kitchen; free breakfast

# SIGHTS

## CULTURE

### CAPPELLA SAN SEVERO

V. Francesco de Sanctis 19; 815518470; www.museosansevero.it; open M, W-Su 9:30am-6:30pm

Housed within the chapel of San Severo, built in 1590, this museum houses objects of the bizarre, otherworldly, and downright confounding. The chapel's sculpture collection astounds, with pieces that make a mockery of the limitations of stone. A man peaks out from under netting in one, and cloth clings lightly to a woman in another. The star of this stock-still show, and arguably of Naples's art collection, is **Giuseppe Sanmartino's** *Veiled Christ*, a virtuosic work that defies the weight of marble. If you're still not dumbfounded, head down to "anatomical exhibits" in the museum's basement. The two creepy skeletons that reside there have perfectly preserved (or constructed, it's still unclear) circulatory systems, and stare down at you from upright models. How? Why? We don't know, either.

*i* *Tickets €7, €5 under 25; last entry at 6pm; wheelchair accessible*

### PIO MONTE DELLA MISERICORDIA
V. dei Tribunali 253; 81446944; www.piomontedellamisericordia.it; open M-Sa 9am-6pm, Su 9am-2:30pm

A small, unassuming church from the outside—especially compared to the nearby **Duomo**—Pio Monte della Misericordia holds firm on its trump card: **Caravaggio's** *The Seven Works of Mercy*. This work is considered one of the most important religious paintings of the seventeenth century; or, in non-technical speak, another example of Caravaggio being an art celeb who mastered the compare/contrast concept better than anyone else. His beautiful rendering of a man who's clearly done a lot of push-ups (oh, and his use of light and shadow) cannot be ignored, though the church hangs the painting front and center, just in case. There's not a ton to see for the ticket price, but it does pay off to casually drop the word *chiaroscuro* in conversation.

*i* *Tickets €7, €5 reduced; audio guide €2; wheelchair accessible*

## LANDMARKS

### CASTEL SANT'ELMO
V. Tito Angelini 22; 812294459; open daily 8:30am-6:30pm (access to Piazza d'Arma and Spalti on Tu only)

On a map, it's impossible to miss the star-shaped Castel Sant'Elmo. First built in the fourteenth century by King Robert of Angou, then enlarged into

its distinctive shape by the sixteenth century, the Castel Sant'Elmo looms over Naples from the **Vomero Hill.** It's role in past and present is more difficult to pinpoint, however. The defensive fortress witnessed little fighting, though it has seen death—a lightning-sparked explosion killed 150 people within its walls in 1587. Today, it rotates through temporary art and museum exhibitions of varying interest. The spectacular view of Naples from its ramparts (the Piazza d'Arma) remains a constant gem, and is accessible by lift.

*i* *Tickets €5, €2.50 reduced (EU residents 18-24) on W-M €2.50 on Tu, combined ticket for the Castel Sant'Elmo, Museo di Capodimonte, Certosa e Museo San Martino, and Villa Pignatelli €10 (valid for two consecutive days); last entry 1hr. before closing*

### NAPLES UNDERGROUND
San Gaetano 68; 81296944; www.napoli-sotterranea.org; hours vary

A Naples underground tour, officially operated by the company Napoli Sotterranea, explores the vast network of tunnels and ancient remains that honeycomb the city about 35 meters below the current street level. Dating back to the Roman times, these streets, later tunnels, were in and out of use for centuries before being overhauled in WWII as a citywide bomb shelter for air raids. Visitors today have far less to fear when venturing down the steps (unless you don't like cool, dark spaces) and plenty to see, including the remains of a Greco-Roman theater, a water-filled Roman cistern, and the shelters themselves.

*i* *90min. tour €10.50; daily tours in English every two hours from 10am-6pm; last tour begins at 6pm; no wheelchair accessibility*

### PALAZZO REALE
P. del Plebiscito 1; 815808255; open Th-Tu 9am-7pm

Though not associated today with the sumptuous tastes of kings and queens, Naples was once quite the coveted royal residence, as the Palazzo Reale reminds you. The Palazzo Reale, which dominates the **Piazza del Plebiscito** in central Naples has catered to the whims of rulers since the Spanish first built the sprawling building in the

# POMPEII AND HERCULANEUM

**Though nearly two millennia have passed, the story of August 24, 79 CE is still hard to fathom.** That morning, the Roman city of Pompeii and resort town of Herculaneum went about their usual business—eating, trading, drawing erotic graffiti on the bathhouse walls. By the next morning, it was all gone, buried under meters of pumice, ash, and pyroclastic sludge. The two cities remained locked in time and molten earth—their locations and histories lost for generations—until excavations began in the eighteenth century.

Today, the tale of Pompeii and Herculaneum still fascinates, though the sites themselves elicit mixed opinions. To enjoy your day trip to these archaeological wonders—and they are wonders—you should know what you're getting into ahead of time. First, remember that the most interesting artifacts from Pompeii and Herculaneum aren't there anymore; they're in Naples at its **National Archaeological Museum.** The sites themselves display the cities' skeletons—a framework of their previous shape and scope. Second, know that a visit to these sites involves a fair amount of walking, sun exposure, and imagination. Herculaneum, the smaller and better preserved of the two sites, displays colorful mosaics and an idea of how Romans filled their seaside villas. Pompeii is a vast maze of mundane buildings (homes, shops, toilets) and grand public spaces (the forum, an amphitheater). In short, the entire spread of a Roman city, calcified and emptied out for you to explore. Visit one on a whim, or combine the two for a full-day experience. If you intend to see both, buy the combined ticket (€20, reduced to €10 for EU citizens 18-24), which is valid for three days and also includes entrance to one of the other three "Pompeii Sites": Oplontis (a well-preserved mansion built in Rome's version of the Riviera), Stabiae (more villas—seriously, this was Rome's Riviera), and Boscoreale.

## GETTING THERE

**From Napoli Centrale:** Follow signs for the Circumvesuviana line (www.vesuviana.it, trains run daily from 5am until 10pm). Make sure to check which train you board—not all follow the same route around Vesuvius. Take the train to Sorrento or Poggiomarino (via Pompei) and disembark at the station called Pompei Scavi. Tickets cost €2.80 each way and the journey takes approximately 45 min.
**For Herculaneum (Ercolano):** As with Pompeii, board a Circumvesuviana train to either Sorrento or Poggiomarino, but disembark at the station called "Ercolano Scavi." The entrance to the excavation site is about a 10min. walk downhill, along the main street of Ercolano.

## GETTING AROUND

The entrance to the Pompeii excavations is right across from the train station, and can only be accessed on foot. To reach the modern city of Pompei, follow the road outside the Pompei Scavi station to the east.

## POMPEII

First things first, be sure to get an audio guide. For a city with such an explosive history, the intrigue of Pompeii doesn't translate well to visitors. There are no guides throughout Pompeii's 163 acre spread, nor are there many signs (and the ones that do exist are mostly in Italian). Today's Pompeii is like a beetle's exoskeleton, or the skin of a snake—you can see the shape of the former inhabitants, but none of the color or vibrancy. Without an audio guide, Pompeii's story fades quickly into a monotonous route of bricks, arches, and uneven roads. The cost may seem steep on top of the entrance ticket, but an audio guide earns will tell you exactly where you are, what these rows of doorways mean, and why we care about the House of the Faun.

It is also important to note that in terms of food, the cheapest and possibly most satisfying option is to plan ahead and pack a lunch, as food options near the excavations are limited and overpriced. There is a cafeteria within the park that serves sandwiches, pizza, coffee, gelato, and other standard lunch foods for somewhere between eight and 15 euros. The street between Ercolano Station and the archaeological site is lined with typical restaurants and takeaway places, all similarly priced and geared towards tourists.

## Don't miss...

### THE HOUSE OF THE FAUN
One of the largest and most lavish of Pompeii's Hamptons-esque villas, the House of the Faun offers a glimpse of rustic luxury in the Imperial era. The famous faun statue fountain greets visitors to the sprawling complex, which contains mosaics, frescoes, and plenty of breathing room for Rome's 1%.

### THE AMPITHEATER
It can be difficult to envision, but all of these empty rooms used to contain thousands of real, raucous people, and they enjoyed having a good time. Specifically, they enjoyed the gladiatorial games synonymous with Ancient Rome, as evidenced by Pompeii's amphitheater, which predates the Colosseum and could hold about 15,000 people. Mt. Vesuvius pummeled the former crowds here but did preserve some of the benches, which make for a nice resting place as you figure out how to get back to the entrance from this corner of the park.

### THE GARDEN OF FUGITIVES
It's the question on your mind and on the lips of every over-eager child: "Where are the bodies? I thought there were plaster casts?" Yes, in this case, Google Images didn't lie; there are plaster casts of the unfortunate souls who perished hiding from the wrath of Vesuvius, and they're in the Garden of the Fugitives. If there's one part of the park that can bring the horror of the eruption to life, this is it.

# HERCULANEUM

## Don't miss...

### THE HOUSE OF NEPTUNE AND AMPHITRITE
A beautiful gold and blue mosaic—still glowing in color despite enduring centuries caked in volcanic sludge—resides in this house-turned-shop. Many Roman homes during this period doubled as storefronts, a trend recalled here.

### THE HOUSE OF THE WOODEN SCREEN
How can wood withstand a volcanic eruption whose heat wave instantly killed everyone within its radius? Good question. Science is weird, but seeing very old wood in its original location is, indeed, very interesting. The screen in the back hall of this house gives a better impression of how homes were styled in Pompeii than any other on-site artifact.

### THE HOUSE OF THE BLACK SALON
Not everything in Campania is terracotta-colored. Though sleepier than Pompeii, Herculaneum attracted a crowd of glitzy Romans to its shores, which is reflected in this home's lavish decor.

1600s. Given that it was occupied for several generations by the same dynasty that commissioned Versailles (the Bourbons), it's unsurprising that Palazzo Reale's interior luxuriates in marble, exquisite draping, gold trim, more marble, and Baroque art. The ostentatiousness of royal spending habits—lots of frescoes, chandeliers, did we mention the marble?—assaults the senses at times.

*i* *Admission €4, €3 reduced (includes audio guide); wheelchair accessible*

# MUSEUMS

### MUSEO ARCHEOLOGICO NAZIONALE

P. Museo 19; 814422149; www.museoarcheologiconapoli.it; open M, W-Su 9am-7:30pm

It's an open secret—yet one that still escapes some tourists—that the best parts of Pompeii actually reside in Naples, in their renowned Archaeological Museum. Though not necessarily the best promoted nor the most streamlined (in the way of the Acropolis Museum in Athens, for example), Naples's Archaeological Museum maintains one of the finest troves of Greco-Roman treasures in the world. Remnants of Pompeii's mosaics are given a second life; sculptural wonders such as the Farnese Bull marble finally secure their rightful space. The museum winds through masterful bronze figures (some with stirring inlaid eyes), Egyptian sarcophagi, marbles of Hercules and Atlas, and one sensual, semi-naked model of Venus. Don't miss the so-called "secret cabinet," the museum's collection of erotic art from **Pompeii and Herculaneum,** which has only been open to visitors since 2005. Turns out that the Romans were ahead of their time in raunch and R-ratings, as well.

*i* *Tickets €12, €6 reduced (EU citizens aged 18-24); last entry at 6:45pm; wheelchair accessible*

### MUSEO NAZIONALE DI CAPODIMONTE

V. Miano 2; 817499111; www.museocapodimonte.beniculturali.it; open M-Tu, Th-Su 8:30am-7:30pm

The museum in the **Palazzo Capodimonte,** a former Bourbon dynasty palace, presents a masterclass in detail. The folds of bedsheets in Titian's *Danaë* catch every possible beam of natural light. The hands in Parmagianino's *Antea*—one bare, one gloved—reflect the genteel steeliness of the woman's face. And the bulbous noses in numerous portraits of the Bourbons demonstrate that you did not need to be Prince Charming to be royal and very, very rich. Capodimonte's museum, one of the largest in Italy, fills vast gilded halls with collections ranging from thirteenth to eighteenth-century paintings to the Roman marbles of the famed Farnese collection. Many of the Renaissance and Baroque A-listers get a byline—**Raphael, Titian, Caravaggio, El Greco,** and **Botticelli,** to name a few.

*i* *Tickets €8, €4 for visitors aged 18-24, free for under 18; last entry 6:30pm (galleries begin closing at 7pm); wheelchair accessible; for guided tours, call 0639967050*

# OUTDOORS

### 🏔PARCO NAZIONALE DEL VESUVIO

V. Palazzo del Principe, Ottaviano; 818653911; www.vesuviopark.it; open daily 9am-4pm (until 6pm July-Aug)

One of the most famous volcanoes in the world, claimer of thousands of lives, and the hulking backdrop of Naples—all in a half day's hike? Though intimidating when viewed from sea level, Mt. Vesuvius isn't as tricky (or dangerous) to ascend as one might assume. The National Park Authority has established clear paths to the crater rim, which presents stunning views of both the volcano's hidden middle and the city of Naples beyond. To reach Vesuvius from Naples, take the Circumvesuviana train from Garibaldi Station towards Sorrento or Poggiomarino (via Pompeii). Disembark at Ercolano Scavi, and take a public bus from the square in front of the station to Vesuvius. Buses depart about every 30 minutes, and the journey takes about the same time. Once at the Vesuvius park entrance, begin brainstorming Instagram captions. Assess your energy level and footwear situation. Select your path (treks range from an easy hour to a moderate three-hour excursion on "Il Gran Cono," the standard trail). Ascend! Determine what is harder: the hike or settling on a caption. Take photos. Descend. Find clever ways to boast about your adventurousness. Impress everyone. Just another day at the office, right?

*i* Tickets €8, issued by the Vesuvius National Park Authority for access to the crater; no wheelchair accessibility; bring layered clothing on spring and autumn days; no wheelchair accessibility

# FOOD

## L'ANTICA PIZZERIA DA MICHELE ($)
V. Cesare Sersale 1; 815539204; www. damichele.net; open M-Sa 11am-11pm

If you can endure the crowds long enough to snag a table at da Michele's or even just peek inside, you'll see a sparse white interior, a glowing oven, and a framed picture of Julia Roberts chomping down on a slice of pizza from the movie *Eat, Pray, Love*. For some, that's enough to trust that this Neapolitan establishment, in business since 1870, represents the holy grail of pizza. If you're not persuaded by Hollywood or bestselling memoirs, well, we don't know what it will take to convince you. The constant line? The small army of pizza soldiers who constantly tend the smoldering oven? The smiling man who kneads pizza dough with the finesse of a practiced craftsman? The simplicity of options— margherita or marinara?

*i* Pizza €4-5, drinks €2-3; limited wheelchair accessibility

## PIZZERIA GINO SORBILLO'S ($$)
V. dei Tribunali 32; 81446643; www. sorbillo.it; open M-Sa noon-3:30pm and 7pm-midnight

In the *Game of Margherita Thrones* that is Neapolitan pizza, Gino Sorbillo is a fierce competitor. A celebrity within and now beyond Naples, Sorbillo's builds on a family legacy of pizza-making (Gino's father was the nineteenth of twenty-one siblings, all in the business) with award-winning pizza, global accolades, and crowds of hungry fans. Notoriety aside, Sorbillo's knows and serves exceptional pizza— thin, flavorful, inventive, and defiant of science or any American imitation. The hype and wait time, which can be as long as a couple hours, is too much for some. But if the art of pizza is your calling, consider picking Sorbillo's, which manages to deliver despite having half of Naples eyeing its crown. Winter seems nowhere in sight for Sorbillo's, though it will have to adjust to the colder temperatures of New York City, where Gino is set to open a location later this year.

*i* Pizza €8-19; vegetarian options available; wheelchair accessible

## SCATURCHIO ($)
P. S. Domenico Maggiore 19; 815517031; www.scaturchio.it; bakery open daily 8am-9pm, restaurant open W-Su 12:30-3:30pm

Naples has built a global reputation on savory, but it still knows how to sweet talk. Specifically, the city has developed its own signature pastry, *sfogliatella* (sfoy-AH-tell-uh), a mastery of light pastry and dense filling (usually orange-flavored ricotta cream or almond paste). *Sfogliatella* requires a delicate layering of dough, resembling

# "WAIT, BOURBON'S NOT JUST A DRINK?"

### *So who the hell were the Bourbons?*

First of all, yes, bourbon is a drink—it's a type of barrel-distilled whiskey, frequently associated with Kentucky and college boys who want to seem sophisticated. "Bourbon" also refers to the French dynasty, which produced European monarchs for eight centuries. The Bourbons originated in France in the 1200s, spread their influence to Spain, and eventually held claims to the thrones in Sicily, Naples, and Parma, as well. Naples was once the capital of the Kingdom of Naples (the southern half of the Italian peninsula), which passed between French and Spanish hands for generations. It gets confusing because a lot of cousins married cousins—you know, the usual—but basically this means: fancy palaces were built in Naples. This is the family that made Versailles, after all. The Bourbons were pushed out of power when the Kingdom of Sardinia annexed Naples in 1860, but buildings such as the **Palazzo Reale** and **Palazzo di Capodimonte** still reflect their influence today.

### *People keep referring to the Kingdom of Two Sicilies, but there's only one Sicily...?*

Yes, there is only one Sicily—the largest island in the Mediterranean—and it serves fabulous seafood. But for a time, there were two Sicilies—the Kingdom of Sicily and the Kingdom of Naples, combined on paper in 1808, in practice in 1815. Actually, depending on who you ask, there were two Sicilies since the sixteenth century, when the War of the Sicilian Vespers separated the rulers of the island from the rulers of the peninsula. Technically, the mainland rulers occupied the Kingdom of Naples, but they enjoyed being annoying and continued to refer to their land as the Kingdom of Sicily. Confused yet? So are we, as were half of Italy's citizens. What you need to know is that all of the kingdoms—Sicily, Naples, and the Two Sicilies—ceased to exist in 1861, when the nationalist state of Italy was formed.

### *Why didn't I know that Naples used to be the second most populous city in Europe?*

Most people don't! Perhaps this is because Naples is now just the fourth largest city in Italy. But in the seventeenth century—the age of the great painters in Rome—Naples teemed with 250,000 people, second only to Paris in population. Unfortunately, the crowded conditions eventually took their toll on the city; bubonic plague wiped out nearly half the inhabitants in 1656, while typhoid and cholera killed over 48,000 people between 1834 and 1884. Naples endured, however, and was still Italy's largest city by the end of the nineteenth century. But economic sluggishness and emigration slowed growth, leading to Naples's reputation today as a mid-size European city.

### *Why do I keep hearing the phrase "used to be"?*

Because Naples's fortunes took a hit after Italian unification in 1861, which significantly dented its economy and political importance. "Unification" refers to the annexation (or "invasion," depending on who you ask) of the Kingdom of Two Sicilies by the Kingdom of Sardinia. **Garibaldi** and **King Victor Emmanuel II** spearheaded this consolidation of power, which is why you see their names everywhere in Italy. They also required the former Kingdom of Naples to empty their coffers for the new Italian state—some 443.2 million ducats. Unsurprisingly, Naples's economy faltered, causing many residents to emigrate (four million between 1876 and 1913, by some estimates). Though the state of Italy altered Naples's trajectory, the city has rebounded over the past decades into a major center of culture, food, and history in the Mediterranean.

a lobster's tail—a feat few perform better than Scaturchio. Open since 1905, this establishment in Naples' ancient center offers arguably the city's best iteration of *sfogliatella*—warm, flaky, and somehow light yet very filling. Scaturchio also specializes in its original *ministeriale* pastry, a medallion of chocolate-covered liquored cream that may have you leaving dough behind.

*i* Baked goods €2.50-5, restaurant dishes €6-12; wheelchair accessible

# NIGHTLIFE

## L'ANTIQUARIO

V. Vannella Gaetani 2; 817645390; open daily 7:30pm-4am

Italy had the good sense to avoid America's experiment with Prohibition (we can't say the same for organized crime, though), but a speakeasy can still flourish in the land of pizza. L'Antiquario, opened by celebrity bartender **Alex Frezza,** takes its cocktails as seriously as any bootlegger found in *Boardwalk Empire.* Frezza's colorful, generous, expertly crafted drinks will make the transition back to rum and Coke difficult, as will the staggering array of alcohol bottles rising like the Great Wall above the bar. You might miss this swanky cocktail lounge, with couches upholstered in red, if you're not in the know; like any good speakeasy, L'Antiquario doesn't have any signage. You must ring the doorbell to gain admittance, which leaves ample time to ask yourself the question: "Am I cool enough to be here?" We cannot answer that for you, but knowing the difference between liquor and liqueur is a good start.

*i* Cocktails €10-12; snacks and small plates €7-12; BGLTQ+ friendly; cocktail attire recommended

## DANTE 43

P. Dante 43; 3349578690; open daily 7am-midnight

Despite its reputation as the Italian version of happy hour, *apertivi* is oftentimes hard on the wallet. This is not the case at Dante 43, where aperol spritzes go for a cool €3 for most of the evening. You won't be skimping on location, either; Dante 43 rings its eponymous piazza on main shopping drag Via Toledo, offering great views of the square. Just across the piazza lies the **Porta Alba,** a gate to the old city that dates from 1625 and now welcomes a secondhand book market. Whether or not you're on the hunt for vintage Italian children's literature, stop by Dante 43 in the early evening to take advantage of the price, before you move on to better cocktails and bigger bills.

*i* Aperitivi €3-4, snacks €5-6; wheelchair accessible

## SHANTI ART MUSIK BAR

V. Giovanni Paladino 56; 80134; 8118525911; open Tu-W 10am-2am, Th-Su 11am-3am

The Tibetan flags, wooden-palette couches, and mason-jar salads don't scream "Italy." The American jazz soundtrack and fruit-inspired cocktail menu don't feel like Naples. Yet, on any given summer night, the patio of Shanti Art Musik Bar finds locals and tourists reveling in all this Italian city has to offer, enjoying time with friends, light drinks, and elephant pillows. A bar inspired by the Himalayas is probably not the alcoholic pit-stop you intended to make here, but it's hard to resist the energy of Shanti. The place is breezy and relaxed by day, laughter-filled and raucous by night, with refreshingly clean food and a staff that knows how to rock statement jewelry.

*i* Coffee €1-3, breakfast €2.50-5, salads in a jar €5-8, beer €3-5, cocktails €6-8; BGLTQ+ friendly

# PALERMO

Coverage by **Adrian Horton**

On an island as quaint, traditional, and rustic as Sicily, Palermo strikes an odd note. The former capital city sprawls along Sicily's northern coast, paints the night with music and dancing, and bustles with cars, and is filled with weathered apartment buildings. Palermo is a modern city—Italy's fifth largest, with the requisite cafés and designer stores—that wears centuries of history on its sleeve. Massive wooden doors lead to the foundations of twelfth-century Norman structures. Markets tingle with the same energy (and fishy smell) that wafted through medieval times. Landmarks are tattooed with insignia from various cultural chapters—Arab, Norman, Spanish Gothic, French—lest you ever forget the trials and tribulations of this city. Palermo puts on a show, but doesn't put on airs. This lively and spontaneous mix of old and new finds the wizened local chatting with the eager traveler, the youth-filled piazzas layered with centuries-old dust, and three hundred-year-old shops hosting freshly caught octopus. Palermo doesn't hold back, or hold its nose (though you might want to, on occasion). Check your hat, your diet, and a few of your inhibitions, and enjoy the ride.

## ORIENTATION

The bay of Palermo takes a bite out of Sicily's northern shore, though the city itself faces northeast, towards the sea. Ferries dock at the port on the east side of the city, while trains arrive at **Stazione Centrale,** south of the city center. From Stazione Centrale, two main thoroughfares extend north to form the main arteries of the city: **Via Roma** and **Via Maqueda.** Both streets cross the main east-west road, **Vittorio Emanuele,** in the center of Palermo's shopping district. The intersection of Maqueda and Vittorio Emanuele, known as "Quattro Canti," marks the center point of the city. From here, Albergheria forms the southwest quadrant with its narrow streets and Arab-style markets, including the famous Ballarò street. Monte di Pieta forms the northwest quadrant, just above the landmarks of Palazzo Normanni and Cattedrale. To the northeast is **Castellamare,** with its collection of restaurants, churches, and former castles. North of that is **Borgo Vecchio,** a more residential and shop-filled area. The southeast quadrant houses **Kalsa,** an older neighborhood that contains nightlife hub Vucciria, as well as smaller piazzas where people gather to mingle, eat, and drink. Popular day trips include beach ventures to Mondello, which is northwest of Palermo central, and to **Cefalú,** which is an hour east by train.

## ESSENTIALS

### GETTING THERE

Take the Prestia Comandé bus (€7) from outside the terminal, which leaves every 30 minutes and arrives at Palermo's Stazionale Centrale.
Bus #139 runs from the ferry dock to Stazionale Centrale. Tickets cost €1.40 and must be purchased in a tabaccherie or kiosk, not on the bus. Many accommodations are located within walking distance of Stazionale Centrale. To reach the center of the city, follow the street Via Roma, which continues straight ahead as you exit the front of the station. Numerous bus lines also leave from the front entrance and lead to various parts of the city.

### GETTING AROUND

Palermo is larger than you think, but by sticking to the main thoroughfares (Maqueda, Vittorio Emanuele, and Roma), most of it is accessible by foot. Palermo's AMAT provides transportation (by bus) across the city and to nearby points of interest, such as Monreale and Mount Pellegrino. For a map of routes and schedules, check kiosks at major bus stations (basically, points of interest in the city), or www. amat.pa.it. Tickets cost €1.40 and must be purchased before you board the bus at a nearby tabaccherie or small shop. Buses run from 6am until around 9:15pm. For questions or concerns, contact AMAT Palermo S.P.A. (Via Roccazzo 77) at 091 350 111.

### PRACTICAL INFORMATION

**Tourist Offices:** Servizio Turismo Comune di Palermo (Via A. Salinas #3, Villa Trabia; 091 740 5924; www. turismo.comune.palermo.it).
**Banks/ATMs/Currency Exchange:** ATMs are dispersed throughout the city, particularly on main shopping

streets such as Vittorio Emanuele, Maqueda, and Via Roma.

**Post Offices:** Poste Italia handles mail in Sicily. The central post office in Palermo is located at Via Roma 320 (open M-Sa 8:30am-7pm).

**Internet:** Palermo does not have strong public Wi-Fi. For Internet access, look for cafés or restaurants with complimentary Wi-Fi.

**BGLTQ+ Resources:** Though attitudes in rural areas may be less tolerant, Palermo and Catania both have thriving BGLTQ+ populations and large pride parades during the summer. For assistance, support, or resources, check out www.palermopride.it, www.arcigay.it, www.arcigaypalermo, wordpress.it, or call ArciGay Palermo's helpline at 344 0123880.

## EMERGENCY INFORMATION

**Emergency Number:** 112 (general emergency), 115 (fire brigade), 118 (ambulance).

**Police:** State Police/Questura Palermo (Via Della Vittoria 8; 091 210111).

**US Embassy:** US Consular Agency (Via G.B. Vaccarini 1; 091 30 5857, call between 10 a.m. and noon; USCitizensPalermo@state.gov).

**Rape Crisis Center:** TelefonoRosa, based in Rome, provides support and resources at telefonorosa.it as well as a help line at 063 751 8282.

**Hospitals:** Ospedale Civico (Off Via Carmelo Lazzaro; 091 606 1111; open daily 24hr).

**Pharmacies:** Farmacia della Stazione Centrale (Via Roma 1, 90100; 091 616 7298; open 24hr).

## ACCOMMODATIONS

### A CASA DI AMICI
Via Dante 57; 091 765 4650; www.acasa-diamici.com; reception open 24hr

On Google Maps, "A Casa di Amici" translates to "At Friend's Place," which is not linguistically correct, but accurate in spirit. This multi-story hostel and guesthouse, located a 10-minute walk northwest from Teatro Massimo, strikes a balance few hostels achieve: fresh and clean facilities that still feel personal and well-loved. The owner, Santos, doubles as a drum maker and has filled A Casa di Amici

with his musical instruments—a unique touch that brings guests and staff together on the patio for impromptu concerts (with drinks from the hostel's bar, of course). A Casa di Amici exudes an easy, welcoming rhythm, from the pillowed lounge couches, from the free breakfast and tea area, to the informal group bar crawls that wind late into the night.

*i* Dorms €20-22; payment on arrival; reservation recommended; BGLTQ+ friendly; no wheelchair accessibility; Wi-Fi; linens provided; laundry facilities available; free luggage storage

### SUNSHINE HOSTEL
Via Lincoln 97; 3238 327 9897; reception open daily 8am-11pm

Finished in 2017, Sunshine is Palermo's newest hostel and has put its best brightly-painted, well-priced foot forward. The facilities are small—only a few rooms and one common area—yet immaculate, with the courtyard patio offering extra seating away from the bustle outside. The staff, led by owner and manager Francesco, do their best to welcome you to Palermo by offering restaurant and day tour recommendations, complimentary breakfast, and free shots of limoncello. Sunshine Hostel's location near the **Botanical Gardens**, a five to 10-minute walk from **Stazione Centrale,** makes it easy to reach most of the city's sights, as well as Palermo's lively food and drink scene near the harbor.

*i* Dorms starting at €15; reservation recommended; BGLTQ+ friendly; no wheelchair accessibility; Wi-Fi; laundry services available; free breakfast; kitchen; free luggage storage

## SIGHTS
### CULTURE

### ◪MERCATO BALLARÒ
Via Ballarò; 091 616 1966; open daily 8am-2pm

Mercato Ballarò provides fish for ten holiday dinners, a mess for your kitchen, and a feast for your eyes. This Arab-influenced street market, which dates to medieval times, is a visual cacophony. Sausages hang from the rafters and spill over counter. Raw octopus and chunks of fish dot the tables. A price list is affixed to the nose of a recently beheaded swordfish. A man guts a shark before your eyes. Welcome to Sicily, where "fresh" means straight from the water bucket and into your bag. Ballarò occupies several blocks northwest of **Stazione Centrale,** and assaults your senses with the smell of seafood and the shouts of vendors hawking their wares. For the look, taste, smell, and song of authentic Sicily, wander through Ballaro's maze of counters.

*i*  *Free to visit; limited wheelchair accessibility*

### TEATRO MASSIMO

Piazza Verdi; 091 605 3267; www.teatromassimo.it; open daily 9:30am-6pm

1870 marked the start of a pivotal decade for Palermo. Several years earlier, in 1861, the former Kingdom of the Two Sicilies was absorbed into the new Italian state. Palermo, the former capital, was still the second largest city in Italy (following Naples). The thriving arts and culture scene in Sicily demanded a venue of global import. Thus, Palermo's mayor commissioned Giovan Battista Filippo Basile to build the biggest opera house in Italy. It took twenty-three years and, sadly, Basile's life, but the Teatro Massimo finally opened as the third largest opera house in Europe in 1897. Since then, the Teatro Massimo has ridden a wave of artistic highs and corruption-riddled lows. Tickets to a show today can cost you an arm and a leg, but you can still tour all 1,350 of the theater's plush seats, as well as it's backstage area and posh cocktail lounge for a few euros.

*i*  *Guided tours (30 minutes) €8, €5 reduced, plus an additional €5 for the backstage tour; wheelchair accessible*

## LANDMARKS

### PALAZZO NORMANNI AND CAPPELLA PALATINA

Piazza Indipendenza 1; 091 626 2833; www.fondazionefedericosecondo.it; Palatine Chapel and Royal Palace open M-Sa

8:15am-5:45pm, Su 8:15am-1pm; Royal Apartments closed Tu-Th

Pop quiz: when you successfully invade England and Sicily in the same decade, do you a) convert the existing Muslim palace into your own crib, b) transform said Muslim palace into a masterpiece of medieval Christian iconography, or c) all of the above. If you have learned anything in Sicily, you know the correct answer is, well, a version of "c)"—ball out with conquered territory as much as possible. Which is exactly what the Normans did when they claimed Sicily in 1072. Today, you can walk through the rooms of the Norman Palace complex, which display a mix of architectural styles—Norman, Aragonese, Bourbon Renaissance— typical of Palermo. The main draw, however, is the **Palatine Chapel,** built by King Roger II in 1132 and the best example of Norman-Byzantine church decoration in Sicily. Translation: gold on gold, a lot of Latin and geometric mosaics, and a bevy of important Christian figures staring down at you from the ceiling.

*i*  *Tickets €12, € 10 reduced (EU residents 18-24); €10, €8 on Tu-Th, when Royal Apartments are closed; last entry 5pm M-Sa, noon on Sunday; wheelchair accessible*

### CATTEDRALE

Piazza di Cattedrale; 091 334373 or 329 3977513; www.cattedrale.palermo.it; cathedral open daily 9am-5:30pm; tombs and roof open M-Sa 9am-5:30pm, tombs open Su 9am-6:45pm

Compared to its baroque counterparts in Rome, the Cattedrale's style is all over the place, from twelfth-century Norman towers to a Renaissance cupola to the Quranic inscriptions of an older mosque. This isn't due to a lack of taste but rather centuries of revisions and renovations at the hands of Palermo's many rulers. Today's Cattedrale dates principally to 1184, when the Normans reclaimed an existing mosque and put up the structure's original rectangular walls. Since then, the Spanish added Catalan Gothic porches, while Bourbon rulers furnished the interior with Renaissance-style frescoes. It takes time, a guide, and a discerning eye to work through the Cattedrale's details, so come prepared. For a few euros, you can also visit the crypt, tour the Cattedrale's collection of crowns, and trek up to the **Duomo terrace** for a panorama of Palermo.

*i* *Free entrance to the Cathedral; roof access €5, treasury and crypt €2, royal tombs €1.50; combo ticket without roof access €3, €7 with roof access; roof access scheduled for every half hour; last entry at 5pm; roof and tombs not wheelchair accessible*

## MUSEUMS

### 🏛PALAZZO CHIARAMONTE
Piazza Marina 61; 091 343616; open Tu-Su 10am-7pm

Many medieval palaces conceal sordid pasts—torture, incarceration, takeover, the usual—but Chiaramonte does not shy away from its demons. Rather, they are painted floor to ceiling on its former prison walls, accessible to you by guided tour. Constructed in the fourteenth century as a lavish home for a Sicilian lord, the palace was converted in the sixteenth century into the HQ of the Spanish Inquisition. Before the reign of terror ended in 1782, nearly 8,000 men and women were imprisoned in Chiaramonte. Today, the cell walls, stripped of plaster, reveal extraordinary hints of the souls lost to religious tyranny in the form of Christian imagery, poetry, and even explicit cartoons of the inquisitors.

*i* *Tours depart every hour on the hour for €8, €5 reduced; cash only; no wheelchair accessibility*

## FOOD

### ANTICA FOCACCERIA SAN FRANCESCO ($)
Via Alessandro Paternostro 58, 90133; 091 320264; www.anticafocacceria.it; open daily 11am-11pm

There's a reason brides travel for miles to have their pictures taken in front of Antica Focacceria San Francesco's storefront. This institution of Sicilian cuisine, open since 1834, has built a reputation for serving some of the best food, fried and otherwise, in Palermo. Order a selection of street food (arancini, focaccia/flatbread, more fried things) from the counter, or dine

al fresco with San Francesco's classier menu of pasta and meat dishes. The piazza seating area—definitely one of the more picturesque in Palermo—and selection of salads cater to tourists, but that's hardly a complaint when faced with a plate of delectable swordfish pasta.

*i* *Street food €3-4, entrées €8-15; wheelchair accessible*

### MOUNIR ($)
Via Giovanni da Procida 19, 90133; +39 091 773 0005; open daily 7pm-midnight

Nested in an alley between the main drags of Via Roma and Via Maqueda, Mounir attracts a large crowd of street revelers in Palermo with its killer portions and light price. Mounir makes its pizzas fresh to order and, in case you need a reminder that Palermo isn't Naples, loads them with toppings—prosciutto, *cappricciosa,* and piles of cheese, to be specific. There's also Mounir's famous kebab pizza—literally, a kebab on a pizza (minus the stick) drenched in yogurt sauce. This monster makes pizza purists shudder but provides enough fuel to keep dancing all night long.

*i* *Pizza and kebabs €4-8; wheelchair accessible*

## NIGHTLIFE

### TAVERNA AZZURRA
Via Maccherronai 15; Vucciria; 091 304107; open M-Sa 9am-5am

Though cocktail lounges and wine bars pepper Palermo, the real party occurs outside, on streets or in markets filled with music and the cheapest drinks you'll find in Italy. At the heart of Vucciria, Palermo's largest meat and fish market, lies Taverna Azzurra, a family-run establishment that hosts informal dance parties on its front stoop. Beneath the barrels once used to ferment its own alcohol, Azzurra serves one euro beers and mixed drinks to a raucous, nightly crowd. The price is a godsend, because you'll need a few to loosen up for the impromptu limbo games you're bound to partake in later in the evening.

*i* *Beer €1, mixed drinks €2; cash only; BGLTQ+ friendly*

## MONKEY PUB

Piazza Sant'Anna 19; Piazza Sant'Anna;
open Tu-Su 8:15am-2am

It's late on a Saturday night, and the pounding stereo of Vucciria has your head spinning. You leave the house music and strobe lights behind in search of a more placid scene. Enter Piazza Sant'Anna, a large church square by the Galleria D'Arte Moderna that teems with young people, plastic cups, and one guy playing "Despacito" from a speaker rigged to his bike. Huddled in a corner of the fiesta is MONKEY Pub, a British-themed establishment that, despite its small size, manages to supply drinks to most of the party. Revelers fill the dark wood and bottle-cap adorned MONKEY to the brim, yet the bartenders keep a pace faster than the classic rock music playing in the background.

*i* Beer €2-3, mixed drinks €4; cash only; BGLTQ+ friendly

# ROME

Coverage by **Adrian Horton**

You know the legacy of Rome well, though you may not realize it. It's there when you check the date, or celebrate a birthday in October. It's there when you add "etc." to the end of a text instead of continuing *ad nauseam,* or take a sip from a public drinking fountain. And it's there when you see a fish fry during Lent, or say "when in Rome…" before doing something ill-advised. Rome looms heavily in the global imagination, and for good reason. The Eternal City—officially founded in 753 BCE but likely settled earlier—forms the bedrock of our concept of Western civilization. Rome's 2770-year-old résumé puts most other cities to shame, and includes casual stints as seat of one of the largest and most powerful empires the world has ever seen, patron saint of Baroque art, headquarters of one of the world's most popular religions, and now the destination for lovers of *la dolce vita* everywhere.

And those are just a few of the highlights. Rome has led more lives than there are enemies of Julius Caesar, and has enchanted visitors for centuries to study, eat, admire, pray, and wander in its well-trod streets. Today, modern Rome attracts millions of tourists every year, which results in the formation of daunting crowds—they're particularly dense near the big monuments (the Colosseum, the Vatican), especially during the sweltering summers. Even if you can't handle the lines, though, Rome still charms with an extensive offering of museums, churches, excavation sights, galleries, and sorry, pasta repurposed remains. Oh, and the food—cafés, pasta restaurants, pizza joints, trellis-covered *trattorias,* and gelato stops galore. Go ahead and enjoy that third scoop, because if there's one place that understands indulgence—imperial, papal, dietary—it's Rome. Take a deep breath and take in the Roman sunset as it lights up the ochres, burnt oranges, and pinks of the city—you don't have to be an arts and culture buff to appreciate that.

## ORIENTATION

Rome has been planned, built, re-planned, rebuilt, and revitalized continuously for over 2770 years, so it's no wonder that old and new meld together throughout the city. While other major cities possess a grid layout or distinct districts, in Rome many of the neighborhoods flow together in a mix of marble, terracotta, tight streets, and churches. Though it's hard to get too disoriented, it can be difficult to discern where one neighborhood ends and another one begins, especially in the old-city area between **Termini Station** and **the Tiber.** To complicate matters, the official districts of Rome (*riones*), first delineated by Augustus and revised every couple centuries thereafter, don't correspond perfectly to common names for different sections of town. Technically, Rome has twenty-two *riones,* each with their own coat of arms. Knowing them makes for impressive trivia but, as a tourist, you're better off remembering the unofficial, colloquial terms for different areas, which usually refer to famous landmarks nearby or their geographic locations.

If Rome were the four-quadrant graph from sixth grade math, the **Foro Romano** (Roman Forum) would mark the origin point, which is fitting, since the Foro Romano was the heart of the ancient city. The area surrounding the Forum, known colloquially as the **Ancient City,** contains, unsurprisingly, the headliners of Imperial Rome: the **Capitoline Hill** and its world-class museum on the Forum's western edge, the **Palatine Hill** and its former palaces to the south, the Circus Maximus behind the Palatine, and the **Colosseum** to the east. Directly west of the Ancient City is the old historic center of Rome, known as **Centro Storico,** around which the Tiber River bends westward like an elbow. Centro Storico is Rome at its most classic and picturesque—cobblestone streets, buildings that glow in evening sunlight, apartment buildings and ristorantes that bump up against Baroque fountains and medieval churches. This area, about fourteen square kilometers in total, breaks down further into neighborhoods focused on certain monuments: to the northwest, **Navona,** near the elliptical Piazza Navona and the **Pantheon;** to the south, the narrow streets and squares of **Campo de'Fiori;** to the southeast, the old **Jewish Ghetto;** and to the north, the luxury shops and crowds of **Spagna.**

Heading west across the Tiber on the **Vittorio Emanuele II bridge,** you reach the walled **Vatican City,** which is technically its own country (with its own post office!). To the north of the Vatican sprawls **Prati,** known for its cheaper accommodations and restaurants. To the south rests **Trastevere,** the former artisanal/working-class neighborhood that is now a top tourist destination due to the area's quaint restaurants, centuries-old buildings, and ivy-lined streets. Starting again from the Forum and heading south along the east bank of the Tiber, you reach the Aventine Hill, sight of beautiful sweeping views of the city, expensive homes, and not much to eat. Further south lies the neighborhood of **Testaccio,** known for its energy and collection of fine restaurants. Just north of the Forum lies **Monti,** a combination of the Esquiline, Quirinale, and Virinale hills that buzzes with hip cafés, popular aperitivo bars, and boutique shops. Continuing north from Monti is the **Borghese area,** near the Borghese gardens and several notable churches. **Termini Station,** Rome's main transportation hub, resides northeast of Monti and the Ancient City. Most of the city's hostels surround Termini and its nearby streets, as do cheap tourist shops, international chain restaurants, and mini-markets. The area in and around Termini marks a gritty break from the other districts of Rome (and is a frequent complaint of unprepared tourists). The streets heading northeast from Termini go toward the blocks with the most popular hostels. Heading southeast, you reach **San Lorenzo,** home to Rome's **Sapienza University,** bars with attitude, and affordable housing. The list of areas may sound daunting, but don't worry—you will develop confidence in your navigational skills as your trip goes on. Rome was designed to be explored by foot (or Vespa, but that requires technique we cannot assume you possess), so strap on those €15 gladiator sandals and get walking. You're bound to find a Baroque *piazza,* narrow street, or enticing café that moves you.

# ESSENTIALS
## GETTING THERE

**From Leonardo da Vinci Airport/ Fiumicino** (FCO, www.adr.it, +39 0665951): Known commonly as Fiumicino, Rome's main airport resides on the coast, 19mi. southwest of the city. The Leonardo Express train runs between the airport and track 25 at Termini, Rome's main train station; the ride takes 30min. and costs €11.

Another train, the FM1, stops in Trastevere.

**From Ciampino Airport** (CIA, +39 06794941, www.adr.it)**:** Rome's other airport lies 9mi. south of the city center and mainly draws budget airlines. There are no direct train links from Ciampino to the city, but express buses leave every half hour or so and run directly to Termini. Tickets cost €4.90 and can be purchased at the information desk to the right as you're walking out of the terminal. The ride takes approximately 50min., depending on traffic.

**By rail:** State-owned Trenitalia (+39 892 2021 in Italy, +39 06 68475475 from abroad, www.trenitalia. it) operates trains out of Termini, Tiburtina, Ostiense, and Trastevere stations. Termini is open 4:30am-1:30am and its bus stop at Piazza del Cinquecento connects with most bus lines in the city. For those arriving in the wee morning hours, the night bus #175 runs from Tiburtina and Ostiense to Termini.

## GETTING AROUND

Rome is a relatively compact city, and the best way to explore its cluster of monuments, churches, and narrow streets is by foot. There are various options for public transportation, however, all operated through ATAC. One ticket costs €1.50 and is valid for 75min. on any combination of vehicles.

**By metro:** Though not comprehensive for the entire city, the most efficient way to travel to the most popular sights in Rome is by the metro. Rome has two metro lines that intersect at Termini Station. Line A, the "tourist line," runs from Battistini to Anagnina and passes through Piazza di Spagna, the Trevi Fountain, and the Vatican Museums (Ottaviano). Line B runs from Laurentina to Rebibbia, and passes through the Colosseum, Ostiense station, and the Testaccio District. Stations are indicated by the red letter "M" on a pole. Tickets can be purchased inside; a single ride costs €1.50 (valid for 60 min.) and a day pass costs €7 (€18 for a 3-day pass and €24 for a week). The metro operates 5:30am-11:30pm and is open until 1:30am on Sa night.

**By bus:** Buses cover more of Rome than the metro, but are less straightforward to use. ATAC operates city buses 5:30am-midnight, plus a network of night buses (notturno). Check routes and schedules at www.atac.roma.it (on the site, look for the Italian flag in the upper right corner to change the language to English). Tickets, valid for 75 minutes, cost €1.50 and can be purchased at tabaccherias, kiosks, and storefronts but NOT on the bus itself. Enter from the rear of the bus,

immediately validate your ticket in the yellow machine, and proceed towards the middle.

**By tram:** The trams, also operated by ATAC, make more frequent stops than buses and can be useful getting to and from Trastevere. As on the buses, tickets cost €1.50 and must be purchased ahead of time (consider buying several to have on you, in case a ticket station is hard to find in a pinch). Useful lines include: #3 (Trastevere, Aventine, Piazza San Giovanni, Borghese Gallery), #8 (Trastevere to Largo Argentina), #9 (Piazza Venezia, Trastevere), and #19 (Ottaviano, Villa Borghese, San Lorenzo).

**By taxi:** Taxis should be reserved for emergencies or pressing situations. It is technically against the law to hail cabs on the street, but they may still stop if you flag them down. They also wait at stands and can be reached by phone (+39 066645, 063570, 064994, 065551, 064157). Only enter cabs with the marking "Servizio Pubblico" next to the license plate. Be sure to ask for your receipt (ricevuta) to confirm the price.

**By bike:** ATAC operates bike-sharing. Purchase a rechargeable card from any ATAC station in the city. The initial charge is €5, with a €0.50 charge for every additional 30min. Bikes can be parked at stations around the city. Alternatively, companies such as Bici & Baci (+39 01683230567, www.bici-baci.com) loan bikes and mopeds and have stations by the major metro stops (Colosseo, Repubblica, Spagna).

**By scooter:** The honking, buzzing Vespa is ubiquitous in Rome, as are the daring yet helmeted people who ride them. You can join in on the fun (and chaos) by renting a two-wheeler, provided you show a valid driver's license and can handle the stress of Rainbow Road on MarioKart. Rates vary by the company, but start at around €30 for 4-8hr.

## PRACTICAL INFORMATION

**Tourist Offices:** Comune di Roma is Rome's official source for tourist information. Green PIT information booths, located near most major sights, have English-speaking staff and sell bus and metro maps and the Roma pass (V. Giovanni Giolitti 34; 060608;

www.turismoroma.it; open daily 8am-8:30pm).

**Post Offices:** Poste Italiane are located throughout the city (800160000; www.poste.it), but the main office is located at Piazza San Silvestro 19 (0669737216; open M-F 8:20am-7pm, Sa 8:20am-12:35pm).

**Luggage Storage:** Termini Luggage Deposit (Termini Station, below Track 24 in the Ala Termini wing; 064744777; www.romatermini.com; open daily 6am-11pm; bags max. 22kg; max. 5 days; 5hr €6, €0.90 per hr for hrs 6-12, €0.40 per hr thereafter).

## EMERGENCY INFORMATION

**Emergency Number:** 112, 118 (medical emergencies).

**Police:**
- Police Headquarters (V. di San Vitale 15; 0646861).
- Carabinieri have offices at V. Mentana 6 (near Termini; 0644741900) and at P. Venezia 6 (0667582800).
- City police (P. del Collegio Romano 3; 06468).

**Hospitals:**
- Policlinico Umberto I. (Vle. del Policlinico 155; 0649971; www.policlinicoumberto1.it; open 24hr; emergency treatment free).
- International Medical Center (V. Firenze 47; 064882371, 060862441111; www.imc84.com; call ahead for appointments).

**Pharmacies:** The following pharmacies are open 24hr.
- Farmacia Internazionale (P. Barberini 49; 064871195).
- Farmacia Risogimento (P. del Risorgimento 44; 0639738166).

# ACCOMMODATIONS

## ☒THE BEEHIVE ($$)
V. Margherita 8; 644704553; www.the-beehive.com; reception open daily 8am-11pm

If the interchangeability of IKEA furniture and persistent odor of sweaty travelers has you down, then The Beehive should be your first stop out of **Termini Station.** With pristinely clean floors, wall of framed family photos, and warm staff (the owners are frequently present and very sweet), the Beehive layers on character with a personal touch few hostels can match (especially if you're lucky enough

to be there for monthly storytelling night). The Beehive stretches the title of hostel well into the hotel realm, with a basement café (breakfast €2-7) and a clientele that favors families and couples more than rowdy students.

*i* Dorms €25-35, private rooms €70-90; reservation recommended; no wheelchair accessibility; lockers; linens provided; laundry services available; in-house café; massage and tour booking available at front desk

## ☒THE YELLOW ($$)
V. Palestro 51; 64463554; www.the-yellow.com; reception open 24hr

If you tell a fellow backpacker that you're headed to Rome, there's a 50% chance that they'll respond, "Oh, you must be staying at the Yellow!" The place has a reputation, and not without reason. A multi-building hostel, bar, restaurant, and tour guide service, the Yellow occupies nearly an entire block in the **Termini neighborhood** and is basically the hostel version of an all-inclusive resort. The Yellow has identified everything a social traveler might want—24hr bar, exceptionally clean rooms, cooking classes, comfy common areas, cheerful staff with great party recommendations, and friendly bartenders who make American-style iced coffees (€2). The Yellow can be a trap, but it's the most fun trap in Rome (if you can afford it). And even with all that space, the Wi-Fi still works, although you won't need it when you're so busy making friends.

*i* Dorms from €30, private rooms from €120; reservation recommended; limited wheelchair accessibility; Wi-Fi; luggage storage; small safe and towels provided; breakfast €3-5; in-house bar open 24hr; option to book cooking classes and excursions

## ALESSANDRO DOWNTOWN HOSTEL ($)
V. Carlo Cattaneo 23; 644340147; www.hostelsalessandro.com; reception hours vary

Night out on the river on Tuesday, sangria night on Wednesday, wine happy hour on Monday, Wednesday, and Friday, club night in Rome on Saturday. Got it? Good. You're ready for Alessandro Downtown. Like its companion hostel on the other side of **Termini Station, Alessandro Palace,**

447

the Downtown Hostel encourages partying and makes sure you don't miss one poster or promo video for it. With its large dorm rooms and seating area that rotates Top 40 music videos on a flat screen (Despacito strikes again!), Downtown Hostel caters to a younger crowd of backpackers—the kind willing to shell out €20 upfront for drinking games and bar entrance and will have the best night ever doing it.

*i* *Dorms €25-32, private rooms €80-90; lockers €2; linens provided; laundry available (€4 wash, €4 dry); breakfast €5; kitchen available noon-10pm; hostel-sponsored bar crawls most nights*

### FREEDOM TRAVELLERS ($)
V. Gaeta 23; 648913910; reception hours vary

There's little that would distinguish Freedom Travellers in a hostel line up, but when accommodations in Rome range from questionably sanitary to nearly €40 per night, that's not necessarily a bad thing. Housed in an old apartment building a stone's throw from **Termini Station,** Freedom Travellers checks most of the boxes for a quality hostel stay: convenient location, lively neighborhood (the party hostels are just around the corner), high ceilings, showers with elbow room, a common garden space. The hyper-social vibe found in nearby hostels is missing, however, and there's a reason why the complimentary wine at happy hour is free. (It's poured from a bottle, but is it really from a bottle?) What it lacks in atmosphere, though, Freedom Travellers recoups in affordability and location.

*i* *Dorms €18-25, private rooms from €60; reservation recommended; no*

wheelchair accessibility; linens provided; laundry services available; free croissant and coffee breakfast; outdoor patio

### HOSTEL DES ARTISTES ($)
V. Villafranca 20; 64454365; www.hostel-rome.com; reception hours vary

For those preferring a quieter, more private hotel feel rather than the communal parties of the neighboring **Yellow** and **Alessandro Palace,** Hotel Des Artistes offers tidy, two to six-person dorms and private rooms with the dignified air of the artists adorning its walls. The hostel section of Des Artistes sits atop the three-star Des Artistes hotel, which means the clientele here is more Disney movie than shots at midnight. But close proximity to a nice hotel has its perks—namely, very clean rooms, an expansive rooftop patio, and FaceTime-quality Wi-Fi at all times of day.

*i* *Dorms €22-30, private rooms €80, with en-suite bath €100; luggage storage available; linens provided; laundry services available; breakfast buffet €10; microwave available for use; 24hr common area*

## SIGHTS
### CULTURE
.............................................

### ◼BASILICA SAN CLEMENTE
V. Labicana 95; 67740021; www.basilicasanclemente.com; open M-Sa 9am-12:30pm and 3pm-6pm, Su 12:30pm-6pm

Ancient Rome consisted of thousands of buildings and palaces—a thriving city that Jupiter didn't just zap off the earth when he fell out of favor. Today's Rome was built on the foundations of earlier structures, resulting in a city of layers stratified by century. Today's Vespa traffic drives on top of medieval ruins, which in turn rest on the streets and homes of the ancient city, buried some twenty to thirty feet underground. Basilica San Clemente takes a knife to this lasagna of history, if you will, revealing three distinct eras of Rome's past. The current basilica was built in the twelfth century, and contains typical Renaissance decorations. One floor down lies the original fourth-century church, with its ghosts of eighth-century frescoes. Another staircase leads down to the first century AD, with the remains of Roman homes, alleys, and spring water faucets. If you thought the ancient city surrounded the Colosseum, think again—it's snaking beneath you.

*i* Free entrance to the basilica; tickets for the excavation site are adults €10, €5 student; last entry M-Sa 12:15pm and 5:30pm, Su 5:30pm; limited wheelchair accessibility

### ⬛ BASILICA SANTA MARIA DELLA VITTORIA

V. 20 Settembre 17; 642740671; open M-Sa 8:30am-noon and 3:30pm-6pm, Su 3:30pm-6pm

Between the **Borghese Gardens** and the front of **Termini Station,** the Basilica Santa Maria della Vittoria showcases Bernini at his most whimsical. The church, considerably smaller than Santa Maria Maggiore or St. Peter's, was designed to resemble a theater, with dozens of flying naked babies and marble likenesses of the wealthy Cornaro family. Bernini's playfulness rises throughout the church—literally, the ceiling, which transitions seamlessly from wood pediment to fresco painting, appears to float away in a haze of pink clouds. Closer to earth, the front of Santa Maria della Vittoria holds the masterful *Ecstasy of St. Theresa,* Bernini's depiction of female pleasure disguised as religious symbolism.

*i* Free; wheelchair accessible

### ⬛ SISTINE CHAPEL

Musei Vaticani, Vatican City; 669884676; www.museivaticani.va; open M-Sa 9am-6pm

The Sistine Chapel is basically the sixteenth century Olympics of Renaissance painting—you win just by being included, though the gold medal goes, of course, to Michelangelo's ceiling frescoes, whose technical virtuosity overshadows the other masterful works from Pinturicchio, Perugino, Botticelli, and Ghirlandaio. Begun in 1508, Michelangelo's defiance of gravity was intended to grace Pope Julius II's private chapel, but the Tuscan artist's stupidly impressive achievement has since gone viral—it's estimated that the Sistine Chapel's paintings are viewed by over 15000 people *per day.* And a majority of those visitors do not follow the no talking rule (or no photos, for that matter). But no matter how packed the room or how weak people's attempts to hide their selfies, the Sistine Chapel will command your attention, and also leave you baffled by Michelangelo's ability to endure neck cramps.

*i* Access to the Sistine Chapel comes with a ticket to the Vatican Museums; adults €16, €8 reduced; first entry promptly at 9am; ticket office closes at 4pm; wheelchair accessible; proper dress (covered shoulders, clothes to the knees) is required for the Vatican, though they may let skirts slightly above the knee pass; no photos or talking allowed, or you will be shushed/reprimanded

### ⬛ ST. PETER'S BASILICA

P. San Pietro, Vatican City; 669882350; www.vaticanstate.va; open Apr-Sept daily 7am-7pm, Oct-Mar 7am-6pm

As one of the most important examples of Renaissance architecture and one of the most visited pilgrimage sites in the world, St. Peter's Basilica needs no help fighting for attention. St. Peter's, built over the legendary tomb of the Christian martyr whose name it bears, is the culmination of the Church's power and patronage in the sixteenth and seventeenth centuries. The basilica is the final-exam group project of the biggest names in Baroque art—Michelangelo, Bernini, Maderno, Bramante, and whoever laid the incomprehensible amount of precious marble everywhere. It also exemplifies Rome's commitment to recycling: some of St. Peter's marble comes from the Colosseum, while Bernini's stunning *baldacchino* (altar piece) was cast using 927 tons of metal removed from the Pantheon roof. Words fail to describe the staggering impression of St. Peter's interior, just as human eyes fail to process the sheer amount of wealth and beauty within it. Most days, you will need to wait a crazy amount of time to witness the excess of St. Peter's, though your chances are better if you arrive before 9am or after 5pm.

*i* Free admission, but up to 3-4 hr. wait; wheelchair accessible; covered shoulders, clothes to the knees required for entry; audio guides available (reserve at 0669883229); the dome can be climbed daily 8am-6pm—entrance is at the portico (porch) of the Basilica

## ALTARE DELLA PATRIA
Piazza Venezia; 6699941; open daily 9am-5:30pm

This monstrosity of white marble (many Romans refer to it derisively as "the wedding cake" or "the typewriter") is also known as the Monumento Vittorio Emanuele II or "Vittoriano." It was constructed in the late nineteenth century as a testament to, you guessed it, King Victor Emmanuel II, who was elevated from King of Sardinia to the first ruler of a unified Italy. More broadly, the bombastic monument was erected to symbolize the aspirations of the nascent Italian state, which was riding the waves of intense nationalism that swept across Europe in the late nineteenth century. Regardless of your aesthetic judgment of the building, Vittoriano offers quality views from the top (if you don't mind stairs) and a chance to see Italy's version of the Tomb of the Unknown Soldier. Inside the monument and to the right is the more reserved **Museo di Risorgimento,** which traces the history behind Italy's unification.

*i* Adults €7.50, €3.50 under 18; wheelchair accessible

## BASILICA DI SANTA MARIA MAGGIORE
P. di Santa Maria Maggiore 42; 669886800; open daily 7am-7pm

You don't have to be a church person to appreciate the magnificence and ambition of Santa Maria Maggiore. It's not St. Peter's, but Santa Maria Maggiore's mind-clobbering attention to detail and commitment to purple marble (some of the most expensive in the world—it's the signature of the popes in stone) will leave you needing a seat in one of the nave's temporary chairs. Between gilded columns, a gold-pediment ceiling, and another painted altar masterpiece, Santa Maria Maggiore communicates all you need to know about the spectacular effort poured into Rome's churches during the Renaissance. Santa Maria Maggiore also features a museum of relics and an archaeological excavation for a couple extra euros, but the main show is free and worth a good, long, air-conditioned sit.

*i* Free; museum costs €3 for relics, €5 for excavations; wheelchair accessible; shoulders must be covered and clothes to the knees for entry (wraps provided free at the entrance)

## PALAZZO VENEZIA
V. del Plebescito 118; 669994388; www.museopalazzovenezia.beniculturali.it; open Tu-Su 8:30am-7:30pm

It takes the eyes a second to adjust to the Palazzo Venezia. Hard corners? No marble? No columns? Where are we? Venice? Well, close. The Palazzo Venezia was indeed gifted to the Venetians in 1564 by Pope Pius IV (gotta keep those relations tight), hence its medieval style that looks nothing like any of its neighbors. Located just north of the **Capitoline Hill,** the Palazzo Venezia has stood as a symbol of power for over 700 years. Mussolini adopted the palace as his headquarters and office; you can still see the balcony where he delivered most of his speeches, including his declaration of the Italian Empire on May 9, 1936. Today, the balcony appears unadorned, as Rome downplays its fascist past. The focus is instead placed on the Palazzo Venezia museum, which houses frescoes, pottery, and sculpture from the early Christian years to the Renaissance.

*i* Adults €14, €7 reduced (EU citizens 18-25); ticket also valid for the Museo Nazionale di Castel Sant'Angelo; free to see the balcony, on the right side of the palace if you're facing with your back to the Altare *della Patria; last entry 6:30pm; wheelchair accessible*

## PORTA PORTESE
Piazza di Porta Portese; open Su 6am-2pm

Porta Portese provides a break from all of the lavish tourist attractions found throughout Rome. This outdoor market, open only on Sunday mornings, specializes in the cheap, eclectic, and unpolished—things with value in the eye of the beholder. Here, you can find antiques, knick-knacks, cards, figurines, souvenirs as cheap as €1, and racks of clothing to replace the smelly, wrinkled shirts lumped in the bottom of your pack. Located along the Tiber to the south of the city center, Porta Portese lacks the glamour of Rome's monuments, but it attracts a mixed crowd of locals and visitors and will reveal aspects of the city that the Vatican will not.

*i* *Prices vary by stand; limited wheelchair accessibility*

## VILLA FARNESINA
V. della Lungara 230; 668027268; www.villafarnesina.it; open M-Sa 9am-2pm

When you're a rich banker from Siena, how do you make your presence known in Rome? Build a lavish summer villa and borrow the pope's favorite fresco painter (Raphael), of course. Agostino Chigi completed his mansion at the peak of Renaissance style in 1511, complete with floor-to-ceiling frescoes, the typical marble showcases, and airy porticoes. Chigi further cemented his status as the Gatsby of Rome by throwing extravagant parties, during which he allegedly encouraged guests to toss their silver into the Tiber (which he then fished out with a net). These indulgences didn't work out so well for Chigi, as the home was sold to the Farnese family by the end of the sixteenth century. But it works out great for you, old sport, as you can stroll through the still outlandishly-decorated halls and light-toned *loggios* like the Leonardo DiCaprio film extra you long to be.

*i* *Adults €6; last entry 2pm*

# LANDMARKS

## ◪FONTANA DEI QUATTRO FIUMI (AND PIAZZA NAVONA)
P. Navona; open daily 24hr

Like your best night-out stories, the Fontana dei Quattro Fiumi (Fountain of the Four Rivers) is all drama and excess. Designed by **Bernini** for Pope Innocent X, the fountain features a skyscraping Egyptian obelisk atop a pyramid pattern of rocks, cascading water, one roaring lion, and four nude river gods. Bernini designed the fountain as a celebration of four continents, with each god representing the Ganges, the Nile, the Danube, and the Rio de la Plata. Apparently North America was not important enough in 1651 to warrant a shout-out, but judging by the number of English menus on the surrounding Piazza Navona, people today have taken note of America. Ochre-colored apartments, purplish shutters, and flowering window boxes ring the elliptically shaped Piazza Navona, making it one of the more picturesque piazzas in the city and a rewarding stop on any walking tour of Rome.

*i* *Free; wheelchair accessible*

## ◪THE COLOSSEUM
Piazza del Colosseo 1; open daily 8:30am-7:30pm

The Colosseum has over two thousand years of experience at keeping people entertained. It held naval battles, featured wild beasts, and absorbed the blood of thousands of gladiators. It contained 80,000 people and then spit them out in less time than it takes you to get dressed in the morning. It inspired your favorite sports team arena and one historically inaccurate but highly quotable Russell Crowe movie. And now it hosts upward of 9000 visitors a day, making it Rome's top tourist attraction. To visit the Colosseum, you can book a tour or skip-the-line pass from one of the numerous companies operating in or around it. Or, muster more patience than Emperor Joaquin Phoenix in *Gladiator* and brave the line. The games are long gone, but the Colosseum still captivates.

*i* Tickets €12, valid for two consecutive days at the Roman Forum and Palatine Hill; limited wheelchair accessibility; last entry 1hr. before sunset; tickets at the Forum or Palatine Hill

## ⚨THE PANTHEON

P. della Rotunda; open daily 9am-7:30pm

The Romans may have had the most powerful empire of their time, but it can be difficult to see the architectural genius through so much crumbling marble. And then there's the Pantheon, one of the best-preserved symbols of the Eternal City (thank you, very rich popes), here to remind you that the Romans really were ahead of their time. This marvel still dazzles with its enormous, perfectly proportioned concrete dome, which is still the largest in the world a whopping 1,890 years later. The optical illusion of the ceiling—a series of square pediments in concentric circles surrounding the oculus (opening)—will make your head spin (don't worry, there's free seating). The Pantheon's lavishly marbled ground-floor, consecrated today as a Catholic sacred space, also offers its fair share of treasures: **Rafael** is buried here (specifically, creepily exhumed,

confirmed dead, and reburied), as well as national hero **King Vittorio Emmanuel II.**

*i* Free; last entry 7pm; wheelchair accessible; entry may be restricted depending on crowd size

## ⚨THE ROMAN FORUM

V. della Salara Vecchia; open daily 8:30am-7:15pm

On a surface level, the Forum appears to be a series of marble things at various stages of decay. Once the Times Square of Ancient Rome, the Forum has persevered through more than nine lives, including "stage for Cicero," "public looting ground," "Catholic Church reclamation area," "demolition zone for Mussolini," and now "the largest outdoor museum in the world." A visit to the Forum begins with the **Arch of Titus**—notable for its clear depiction of the sack of Jerusalem in the first century CE—and weaves through the remains of temples, basilicas (public buildings), the **House of the Vestal Virgins,** and marketplaces. As most of what we see today forms only the corners, slices, or skeletons of the original buildings, a visit to the Forum requires some imagination to fully appreciate its significance. But as the epicenter of Ancient Rome's power and the heart of the old city, the Forum is a must-see in Rome.

*i* Tickets €12, valid for two consecutive days at the Colosseum and Palatine Hill; last entry 7pm; wheelchair accessible

### PIAZZA DI SPAGNA

P. di Spagna; open daily 24hr

Despite its butterfly shape, the Spanish Steps is a monument of circular reasoning. Why see the Spanish Steps? Because they're famous and important, you say. Why are they famous and important? Because... they're the Spanish Steps? Yes, it's a set of steps (a very manageable 135 of them) leading from Bernini's least

impressive fountain below to a church of moderate importance above. In the past, the Spanish Steps served a logistical purpose—connecting the Spanish Embassy with the church—and as a functioned as a symbol of the Bourbon family's wealth (the guys who also funded Versailles). Today, the money is housed in the luxury shops lining the Piazza di Spagna, while the steps have become a hub for the Senate and for people-watching. By Roman ordinance, you can't each lunch here, but you can take five on the smooth marble steps.

*i* Free; P. is wheelchair accessible

## THE ARCH OF CONSTANTINE

V. di San Gregorio; open daily 24hr

When you've consolidated power, drowned your rival in the Tiber, and paraded his head through the streets of Rome, what's the natural next step? Build a gigantic arch with no practical use, of course. Technically gifted by the (mostly defunct, at this point) Senate of Rome to the emperor Constantine I, Rome's largest triumphal arch still stands beside the Colosseum as a reminder of what would happen if Ancient Rome wanted your money. Though completed in 315 CE, the arch contains details from earlier works also dedicated to the military booty seized by emperors such as Hadrian and Trajan. See Constantine's Arch if you're interested in 3D friezes and the spoils of war, skip it if the coolest thing about an arch to you is walking through it (as this one is fenced off).

*i* Free; wheelchair accessible

## THE CAPITOLINE HILL

P. del Campidoglio; open daily 24hr

Simultaneously the smallest of Rome's seven hills and its most sacred, the Capitoline Hill has upgraded over the years from the city's mint and political center to the home of two massive naked men and their horses (statues, of course). The pair boldly welcomes you to the Piazza di Campidoglio, designed by **Michelangelo** in the fifteenth century and the entrance to the **Capitoline Museums,** the world's oldest public collection of ancient art. The Capitoline today testifies to the egos of past Roman and Italian leaders—an impressive bronze statue

of **Marcus Aurelius** dominates the piazza, though it is dwarfed by the neo-Baroque monument to **Vittorio Emanuele II** behind it. You can climb this "wedding cake" building for a heightened view, or look onto the Forum for free from the back end of the Capitoline.

*i* Free; limited wheelchair accessibility

## THE PALATINE HILL

Palatine Hill; open daily 8am-7:30pm

Once upon a time, a she-wolf rescued abandoned twin babies—Romulus and Remus—on the Palatine Hill, and nursed them in a cave. One of them (Romulus) went on to found the city of Rome, then killed Remus out of… let's call it brotherly love. Whether or not you believe the founding legend of Rome, it's fact that the Palatine Hill has been inhabited since at least 1000 BCE, and that people likely pulled a Romulus to live there in the years since. During its heyday as the Beverly Hills of Rome in the Republican and Imperial eras, the Palatine Hill was populated with the who's who of the city and adorned with mansions for the emperor and his family (hence, the word "palace"). Visitors today can use their combined Colosseum-Forum-Palatine ticket to visit the **Palace of Domitian,** the remains of **Augustus's house,** and the **beautiful frescoes** in his wife's villa.

*i* Tickets €12, valid for two consecutive days at the Colosseum and Roman Forum; last entry 1hr. before sunset; wheelchair accessible; entrance on V. San Gregorio, as well as through the Roman Forum

## THE TREVI FOUNTAIN

P. di Trevi; open daily 24hr

You know you need to see the Trevi Fountain, but you're not sure why until you're there—it is impressive. It is massive. It commands the square. It is Baroque architecture at its finest, in that it's beautiful and knows it and will beat you over the head with it (not that you'll mind). By day, the Trevi Fountain, completed in 1762 as a celebration of Agrippa's ancient aqueducts, is a spectacle of excess—money (popes again!), marble, symbolism, people, selfies. By night or dawn, however, the smaller details of Nicola Salvi's artistic triumph trickle through—the precise definition of Poseidon's horses, the strategic pour of water over the rocks, the still edges of the pool, and of course the sound of running water filling the square. Close your eyes, toss a coin, and wish for fifty first dates with Fontana di Trevi. You'll meet a different fountain each time.

*i* *Free; wheelchair accessible*

## THEATER OF MARCELLUS

V. del Teatro di Marcello; www.tempietto.it; open daily 24hr

Rome displays a constant contradiction between past and present, and few buildings in the Eternal City demonstrate this odd symbiosis better than the Theater of Marcellus. Inaugurated by **Augustus** in 12 BCE, the Theater of Marcellus has been confusing tourists ever since with its passing likeness to the Colosseum. To be fair, it is a large entertainment venue—older and better preserved than the Colosseum, at that—but it is semi-circular whereas the Colosseum is 360 degrees, and your taxi driver will know the difference. Over the years, the structure has served as an apartment building, fortress, quarry, inspiration to Christopher Wren, and glory project for Mussolini. Today, the Theater of Marcellus straddles the gaps between public and private, ancient and modern; the bottom half of the structure—restored in recent years—hosts live musical performances in the summer (check online for schedules), while the top half is composed of privately owned and occupied apartments. Thus, you have two options to access the theater: see a show outside its walls, or somehow befriend the person who reportedly shelled out $10 million last year to live there.

*i* *Free to see the exterior, undetermined how much it costs to befriend the people who live there; wheelchair accessible*

## TRAJAN'S COLUMN

V. dei Fori Imperiali; open daily 24hr

A short walk from the Colosseum, Trajan's column in the Imperial Forum seems a bit unimpressive at first, especially compared to the **Vittorio Emanuele II monument** across the street. But this 126-foot-tall stone spire is actually one of the most important artifacts from Ancient Rome, and has stood for over 1900 years. Spiraling around the column from bottom to top are 155 friezes depicting Emperor Trajan's victory in the Dacian Wars (in present day Romania), a story which goes like this: Trajan musters thousands of soldiers to cross the Danube, destroys the Dacians, then uses all of their money to build a gigantic column in which he appears as hero/conqueror 58 times. Trajan is not renowned for his subtlety, but his column (seriously, not subtle) is highly regarded today for its detailed depictions of second-century war.

*i* *Free; wheelchair accessible*

# MUSEUMS

## ⬛BORGHESE GALLERY

Piazzale Scipione Borghese 5; 68413979; www.galleriaborghese.it; open Tu-Su 9am-7pm

The Borghese Gallery, located at the northeastern end of the **Borghese Gardens,** imparts a few inescapable lessons, including that money makes the seventeenth-century art world go 'round, Caravaggio was the original master of shade, and Bernini knew a thing or two about rippling muscles (and marble, too). Housed in Scipione Borghese's former party villa (because you're no one until you have a papal party villa on the edge of town), the private collection is now a must-see museum for Baroque art, with notable works from **Caravaggio, Bernini, Titian, Rubens,** and other titans of excessive detail. Finding a time to visit can get tricky; technically, ticket reservations must be made online for two-hour visiting slots, but they can also be purchased onsite if there are any left-over (though don't expect the staff to be pleased about this). The Borghese Gallery is worth the hassle, though, for a chance to witness what Google Images still can't capture: the virtuosity of Baroque A-listers.

*i* *Adults €15 (including €2 reservation fee), €8.50 reduced (EU students only); though you can try your luck with buying tickets at will call, visiting the Borghese Gallery requires a ticket reservation, which can be bought online or by phone (+39 06 32810); the Gallery admits 360 ticket holders every two hours starting at 9am,* and all guests are required to leave the Gallery after their two-hour tour is up; first entry 9am, ticket office closes at 6:30pm; wheelchair accessible

## ▨CAPITOLINE MUSEUMS

P. Campodoglio; www.museicapitolini.org; open daily 9:30am-7:30pm

As you have probably figured out by now, Imperial Rome was not subtle about its accomplishments (see: Colosseum, Trajan's Column, every marble frieze of military takeover). As the house of some of the greatest hits of Roman art, the Capitoline Museum puts on a show of size. Visitors are welcomed by the massive feet of Constantine, whose marble toe is the size of your head (because big feet, well... you know). The museum winds through the large (bronze she-wolf of Rome, exquisite statue of Venus), the huge (remains of Greek bronzes, entrancing bust of Brutus), and the downright colossal (bronze of Marcus Aurelius on a horse, Constantine's head). The classic **marble statues** and **bronze casts** steal the show, but you can get your dose of Renaissance and Caravaggio in the Capitoline's picture gallery and rooms furnished by, you guessed it, the popes.

*i* Tickets €15, video guides €6; last entry 1hr. before closing; wheelchair accessible, call 0667102071 for directions and assistance

## ▨PALAZZO MASSIMO (MUSEUM OF ROME)

Largo di Villa Peretti 1; 639967700; www.archeoroma.beniculturali.it; open Tu-Su 9am-7:45pm

Today, Ancient Rome is often summed up by its monuments, mighty ruins, and impressive concrete. But there would be no Colosseum, Forum, or aqueducts without the many ordinary people who worked, wined, dined, shopped, and lived in the city, a fact showcased in the exceptional Palazzo Massimo, a segment of the Museum of Rome next to the entrance of **Termini Station.** A visit to the Palazzo Massimo conjures the recognizably human ghosts of Ancient Rome: take in the colors of the restored full-room fresco from the **Villa of LiV,** then see how busts depict the change of style over time (beards only became a thing

because of Hadrian, for example). Don't miss the outstanding **"Boxer at Rest" bronze,** marked with cuts and bruises from an exhausting fight. In the basement, an extensive collection of coins traces the flow of commerce in Italy over centuries, while a display of jewelry confirms that chokers have been going in and out of style for millennia.

*i* Adults €7, free for visitors under 18; ticket valid at all National Roman Museum sites (Baths of Diocletian, Palazzo Altemps, and Balbi Crypt), ticket office closes 1hr. before closing; advanced ticket sales not necessary, but can be booked at www.coopculture.it; wheelchair accessible

## MUSEO DELL'ARA PACIS

Lungotevere in Augusta; en.arapacis.it; open daily 9:30am-7:30pm

While most celebratory arches in Rome are all about the "booty booty booty booty rockin' everywhere" (the spoils of war, that is), the Ara Pacis marks a change of pace. Literally translated to "Altar of Peace," the Ara Pacis was commissioned by Augustus in 13 BCE to commemorate an era of uncharacteristic peace and prosperity for Rome. With its scenes of bounty, fertility, and the Imperial family, the Ara Pacis also worked to visually establish a new civic religion for the recently imperialized Roman state (because if you're Augustus, it's not enough to be military conqueror and emperor—you must be father of the people, as well). Restored and now displayed in the Museo dell'Ara Pacis next to the Tiber, the Ara Pacis demonstrates that it was possible for Rome to produce exquisite sculptures without crushing another state first (actually, that's a lie, Augustus was fresh off a campaign in Gaul. But it's the thought that counts?).

*i* Adults €10.50; last entry 1hr. before closing; wheelchair accessible

## THE BATHS OF DIOCLETIAN

V. Enrico de Nicola 79; www.archeoroma.beniculturali.it; open Tu-Su 9am-7:30pm

Across the street from Termini Station, the remains of Diocletian's baths remind you that public nudity was all the rage back in Ancient Rome, at least in the bathhouse. Today, this mega-complex of personal hygiene, part of the National Roman Museum, houses an exhibit on the written communication of Rome (not that engaging), a room on inscriptions from the Roman republic (somewhat engaging), and **Michelangelo's Cloister,** a garden lined with sculptures of various quality (not necessarily interesting, but very peaceful). The baths themselves are difficult to find within the museum—you have to go left from the bookstore, not out the back door of the Cloister that locks behind you and won't let you back in.

*i* *Adults €7, free for under 18; ticket valid for three consecutive days at all National Roman Museum sites (Palazzo Altemps, Palazzo Massimo, and Balbi Crypt); last entry 1hr. before closing; wheelchair accessible*

### THE VATICAN MUSEUMS
V.le Vaticano; 669884676; www.museivaticani.va; open M-Sa 9am-6pm, last Su of every month 9am-2pm

A visit to the Vatican demands preparation. You can reserve tickets to skip the line, bring an umbrella to weather the heat, and wear proper shoes to endure the nearly seven kilometers of exhibits. But for all your thinking ahead, nothing can deflect the overwhelming power of the Vatican's opulence. The Vatican has zero chill when it comes to wealth, with over 70000 works of art (20,000 on display)—including some of the most recognizable pieces in the world—and an exorbitant amount of rare marble. The human mind cannot comprehend the sheer amount of detail, talent, luxury, and, of course, power housed in the Vatican. But you can give yourself a few hours to try. Follow the crowd through the **Pinacoteca,** down the intricately tiled and painted hallways and past the map collection. Take in what you can. This is the one of the most extensive and significant collections of art in the world, and even a sliver of it will impress.

*i* *Adults €16, €20 booked ahead, €8 reduced (students, religious seminaries, disabled persons), €12 booked ahead, free last Su of the month; tickets include entrance to Sistine Chapel, and are only valid for the date and time issued; book online to avoid waiting in line for 2-3 hours; tours*

begin every half hour starting at 9am; last entry 4pm; wheelchair accessible

## OUTDOORS

### AVENTINE HILL
V. di Santa Sabina; open daily Apr-Sept 7am-9pm, Oct-Mar 7am-6pm

According to legend, **Romulus'** settlement on the Palatine defeated **Remus'** camp on the Aventine for the founding of Rome, but the Aventine has since recouped its losses in the form of views of the city and sun-kissed gardens. A 10-to 15-minute hike from the path along the Tiber, the Aventine features the **Giardino degli Aranci** (Orange Garden), which smells of pine and flower blossoms and offers one of the best sunset perches in the city. From the balcony at the edge of the park, just past the evergreen trees and peaceful fountains, you can see sun-drenched Rome stretch before you, from the Altare della Patria on the right, to the **Vatican** beyond, to **Trastevere** on the left. You may also see some serious PDA, a few selfie sticks, and perhaps a guitar player welcoming the evening with an acoustic rendition of U2's "One."

*i* *Free; wheelchair accessible*

### GIANICOLO HILL
Open daily 24hr

Gianicolo Hill is to the seven hills of Rome what Lake Champlain is to the Great Lakes—too far away to ever be included, but with enough perks to make a claim. Across the Tiber from the actual hills of Rome (which, really, is not far away at all), Gianicolo is the second-tallest hill in the city, and arguably its greatest vantage point for views of the ancient center, if you can find a spot to look between the trees. Though outside the limits of the Imperial city, Gianicolo has since been embraced by Rome, as signified by its Baroque fountain (the **Fontana dell'Acqua Paola**) and its church. Getting to the top of Gianicolo requires some focus, but if you can manage the roadblocks, confusing street signs, and allure of bar patios, the piazza provides a worthwhile peek at the pink-tan city sprawled across the Tiber.

*i* Free; wheelchair accessible

## VILLA BORGHESE GARDENS
Open daily 24hr

The Villa Borghese Garden is not a destination, but a place to wander. The Garden's maze of gravel paths, less official dirt paths, steps, and occasional roads were designed to get you lost, but that's not at your expense. First designated by Cardinal Scipione Borghese in 1605, and thus the oldest public park in Rome, the Villa Borghese Garden has since filled in with towering trees, overgrown grasses, villas, too many fountains to keep straight, and of course the **Borghese Gallery.** Casual wanderers will also stumble upon some of the lesser known yet still intriguing sights, such as a group of high school kids up to no good, several elderly ladies yelling colorful Italian at their dogs, and a couple of brave joggers attempting to work off the day's pasta lunch.

*i* Free; wheelchair accessible; entrances include: Porta Pinciana, V. Belle Arte, V. Mercadante, and V. Pinciana

## CAN I DRINK THIS? ROME'S PUBLIC WATER SUPPLY

To the left of a monumental church, there's a spigot. At the top of some steps at the **Piazza del Spagna,** a quickly-flowing trough. At a random street corner, a running faucet. Are these architectural mistakes? A colossal waste of natural resources? A discarded Bernini knockoff? No, these are three of the *nasoni* ("big noses"), a system of public drinking fountains, and they are your best friend on a steaming summer day in Rome.

When the sun beats down, the heat overwhelms, and all you can think about is how badly you want to cannonball into the **Trevi Fountain,** don't go spending your euros on bottled water at the nearest kiosk. It looks far more badass to roll up to one of the wolf-head *nasoni* faucets, lean over, and take a drink of the refreshingly cool water that streams from it. Implemented in 1874 as a way to clean Rome's street markets, the *nasoni* flow with ice cold fresh water with more reliability than even Rome's best Wi-Fi spots. And though they are no Berninis—most are about three feet tall, understated, and possibly covered in graffiti—by Jove, you will admire that there are now nearly 2,500 *nasoni* faucets throughout the city.

Still not convinced? Yes, it's safe (though not for phones—multitask at your own risk). All of the water originates from the huge Peschiera reservoir nearly seventy miles away, and is funneled directly to Rome through a complicated series of aqueducts and underground pipes (hence, the cool temperature). If you *must* know, Rome's water quality is regulated and the *nasoni* pipes are tested hundreds of times throughout the year, so, seriously, you're all good. And for your green friends concerned about the waste (yet still buying bottled water?), all of the *nasoni* water left unconsumed by cranky tourists goes toward nourishing Rome's greenery and garden spaces.

It's not like Rome doesn't know how to handle all this H2O—they've been funneling in natural spring water from far outside the city walls for millennia. Though most of the ancient aqueducts (multistory with arches—you've seen photos) fell into disrepair in the years following the Goth invasion, they were restored during the Renaissance to supply Rome's growing quantity of demanding Baroque fountains. Today, the repaired version of Agrippa's OG aqueduct (Aqua Virgo, now **Virginale**) still feeds the Trevi Fountain, to the delight of coin tossers everywhere. And, yes, you can drink its water, too.

# FOOD

## BARNUM CAFÉ ($)

V. Del Pellegrino 87; 64760483; open
M-Sa 9am-2am

Open for the better part of the day,
Barnum Café shapeshifts from trendy
breakfast spot to studious work café to
popular aperitivo bar over the course of
your waking hours. Like its eponymous
circus entertainer, Barnum has many
acts, but it always remains a full-time
creative space and frequent hangout for
Rome's freelancers, alternative types,
and internationally-minded crowd.
Situated in the heart of the rose-tinted
**Centro Storico neighborhood,**
Barnum specializes in artful salads,
cocktail creations, and actually cold
iced coffee (served in a martini glass,
no less). Go for a snack, go for a spritz
and a bruschetta, or go for an hour of
focused laptop time—regardless, you'll
feel cooler for doing so.

*i* Daily specials €6-10, coffee €1.50-3,
juices €4, desserts €5, cocktails €7-9;
vegetarian and vegan options available;
wheelchair accessible

## BISCOTTIFICIO ARTIGIANO INNOCENTI ($)

V. della Luce 21; 65803926; open M-Sa
8am-8pm, Su 9:30am-2pm, closed Aug

Though its exterior beckons to no one,
Biscottificio Artigiano Innocenti's one-
room interior projects all the signs of
serious bakery business: a huge oven,
baskets of cookies in the window, a
large scale to accurately weigh your
haul of cookies, and store plaques
plastered on top of American political
campaign signs from the 1970s. The
vintage look isn't a show: the bakery
has been operated by the same family
for over 50 years, and is subject to the
usual non-corporate whims (such as
closing the whole month of August for
vacation). Innocenti delivers on a wide
range of baked goods, but specializes
in traditional Italian nut cookies, such
as hazelnut bites (*brutti ma buoni*) or
almond wedges (some with chocolate).
Running about €2 for six or so, you
can afford to try a few (or 20).

*i* Biscuits and cookies by weight (about
6 cookies per €2); vegetarian options
available; wheelchair accessible

## BONCI PIZZARIUM ($$)

V. della Meloria 43; 63974516; www.bonci.
it; open M-Sa 11am-10pm, Su 11am-4pm
and 6pm-10pm

Sure, the Vatican contains the wealth
of a country a hundred times its size,
but the real treasure might be just
outside its walls. We're talking about
Bonci Pizzarium, located a five-minute
walk from the Vatican Museums,
and arguably the best takeaway pizza
in Rome. Founded by famed pizza
connoisseur Gabriele Bonci, the
Pizzarium seems more like a pizza art
museum than a fast food joint, as the
crusts are loaded with Willy Wonka-
style portions of toppings—mounds of
mozzarella, piles of sautéed veggies, and
even heaps of seared tuna. (Haven't you
heard? Margherita was *so* last season). A
word of warning: some gourmet slices
(yes, that tuna one) can run several
euro more per slice, so check the labels
before you accidentally end up with a
€15 takeaway pizza bill.

*i* Pizza €4-6 per slice, €7-10 per slice
for gourmet varieties; vegetarian options
available; wheelchair accessible; to-go
only; small counter space provided

## GELATERIA DELLA PALMA ($)

V. Della Maddalena 19-23; 668806752;
www.dellapalma.it; open daily 8:30am-
12:30am

Gelateria Della Palma's rainbow palm
tree logo doesn't scream "GOOD
GELATO," but don't be fooled by the
neon: this shop takes gelato as seriously
as the color spectrum. Della Palma,
on the corner of the Pantheon plaza,
specializes in the wacky and wonderful,
with over 150 flavors ranging from
Kiwi Strawberry to Kit Kat to Sesame
and Honey. Yes, it's swimming with
people all taking too much time to
make a flavor decision, but the quality
of gelato and heaping portions render
the hassle irrelevant. Plus, there are
numerous soy/rice milk and yogurt
options for those challenged by dairy
and full fat. If you're going to ball out
on gelato in Rome (and you should),
this is center court.

*i* Gelato from €2.30; wheelchair accessible

## ⚑PIANOSTRADA ($$)

V. della Zoccolette 22; 689572296; open Tu-Su 1-4pm and 7pm-11:30pm

Recently relocated from Trastevere to a quiet corner of **Monti**, Pianostrada puts a fresh spin on familiar Italian staples. Their menu presents a tour de force of re-energized dishes, from refined street food (i.e., fried everything), to stir-fried veggies with pine nuts and raisins, to the best damn focaccia in Rome. The old trattoria provides inspiration for Pianostrada's pizzas, focaccias, and small plates, but their salads, fried dishes, and flavor combinations defy classification. Ristorante, this is not. And though it occupies the tail end of the student budget spectrum, Pianostrada's daring take on Italian cuisine, sprightly interior, and spacious back patio justify the cost.

*i* *Primi €12-18, secondi €12-20, sides €8-16, wine €6-10 per glass; vegetarian and vegan options available; wheelchair accessible*

## COURT DELICATI ($)

Vle. Aventino 41; 65746108; open Tu-Su noon-3pm and 7:30-11pm

There's a group of Italian friends laughing their way to wine bottle #2, a couple on a date, and a mom and daughter sharing a giant plate of noodles. Just another Roman ristorante? Nope, it's Malaysian fusion at lunchtime. With its extensive menu of Southeast Asian specialties (emphasis on spice, if you ask for it), Court Delicati draws a crowd of local foodies and a few stray tourists to its simply decorated yet homey perch, a 10-to 15-minute walk south from the **Circus Maximus.** The flavorful dishes—ranging from bean sprout stir fry to roast duck, spring rolls to steamed rice cakes—mostly fall under €10, making Court Delicati an ideal place to swap olive oil for teriyaki.

*i* *Apps €2.50-5, specials €7.50-12, wine by the bottle €14; vegetarian, vegan, and gluten-free options available; wheelchair accessible*

## FORNO CAMPO DE' FIORI ($)

Vicolo del Gallo 14; 668806662; www.fornocampodefiori.com; open M-Sa 7:30am-8pm

There are numerous *fornos* (bakeries) throughout Rome, which can make it difficult to choose one that doesn't hand you a bag of dried-out cookies or surprisingly charge you €4 for a couple biscotti. And then there's Il Forno Campo de'Fiori, which catches your gaze with its bright sign, yet soothes you with sweet, sweet sugar (specifically, a hefty bag of lemon cookies and biscotti for under €2). Il Forno Campo de'Fiori can also tempt you with savory treats, as its paninis, *piadinas,* and various other combos of sliced things and bread are delicious, filling, and mercifully cheap. No seating for this meal; you can pace yourself to all the nearby monuments one chocolate-dipped almond biscuit at a time.

*i* *Biscuits and cookies by weight, sandwiches €3-6; vegetarian and vegan options available; wheelchair accessible*

## LA CARBONARA ($$)

V. Panisperna 214; 64825176; www.lacarbonara.it; open M-Sa 12:30-2:30pm and 7pm-11pm

La Carbonara strikes a hard pose against the games of tourism, starting with a "No TripAdvisor" sign on the door. It's a bold play for a dining scene that runs on reputation and recommendations, but judging by the walls filled with notes and signatures of satisfied patrons, La Carbonara has earned enormous confidence. This no-frills trattoria on one of Monti's wider streets keeps its memories close—a case of used wine corks over here, a framed moon chart from a decade ago over there—and its pasta secrets closer. TripAdvisor or no, the reviews are in: the *cacio e pepe* under this framed record and shelf of wine bottles earns five stars (or, perhaps more appreciated, a sincere *grazie* to the waiter).

*i* *Primi €6-12, secondi €8-22; vegetarian options available; wheelchair accessible*

## QUE TE PONGO? ($)

V. Della Dogana Vecchia 13; 668803029; open M-Sa 9am-8pm

"Que te pongo? What would you like?" A small, understated "salmoneria"

# SCREEN TO RE(E)L LIFE: THE MOVIES OF ROME

Even to first-time visitors, many elements of Rome can feel familiar, and it's not just because half of all travel books don their covers with images of Colosseum. Dozens of movies have been made in or about Rome, so even those with just a partial knowledge of cinema have probably viewed a scene or two featuring a scooter and ruins. If you're wondering why people are watching YouTube clips by the Trevi Fountain or shouting "Are you not entertained?!" at the Colosseum, we've got you covered. Here are some of the most famous films set in Rome:

*1. Roman Holiday* (1953)—This classic romantic comedy, starring stand-outs Audrey Hepburn and Gregory Peck, told the very relatable story of the relationship between a princess-gone-rogue in Rome and the reporter determined to help/woo/interview her. The film's iconic scene set on the **Spanish Steps** cemented the landmark in American popular culture. *Roman Holiday* also features an iconic montage in which Audrey Hepburn and her insanely tiny waist drive a scooter around the city.

*2. La Dolce Vita* (1960)—Federico Fellini's achievement (many critics consider it one of the best films of all time) depicts an ideal week in the young sweet life—if your ideal consists of murder, doubt, existential crisis, and an intrusive photographer named Paparazzo (yes, this is where it comes from). To be fair, lead character Marcello does get to frolic in the Trevi Fountain with stunningly gorgeous Anita Ekberg (who, like a champ, filmed the scene on location in the middle of winter). Authentic Italian scooters abound in *La Dolce Vita*.

*3. Gladiator* (2000)—Are. You. Not. *Entertained?!* To many in 2001, the answer to Russell Crowe's question was "Yes, continue. Two thumbs up." This blockbuster about Ancient Rome's blockbusters has serious historical issues (the thumbs up/down was not a thing back then), but few seem to care. Audiences still flocked to see badass Russell Crowe wield a sword (or two) and show up bratty Emperor Commodus (Joaquin Phoenix). Shockingly, there are no scooters in this movie.

*4. The Lizzie McGuire Movie* (2003)—Reliable sources report that this is the best movie made about Rome. In this masterpiece, Disney Channel star Lizzie McGuire (Hilary Duff) flies to Rome for a middle school field trip, falls in love with an international pop star, exposes said pop star as a fraud, then launches her own pop star career. She also rides on the back of a Vespa in what is undoubtedly the greatest scooter scene in film history.

*5. Angels and Demons* (2009)—Tom Hanks stars in this Vatican version of *National Treasure*. The plot involves a giant nuclear fusion plant, anti-matter, murdered cardinals, pope problems, and some mystery that can only be solved by Harvard "symbologist" Robert Langdon (Hanks). Though set in Rome (and now the subject of some specialized tours), *Angels and Demons* was primarily filmed on staged sets because—surprise, surprise—the Vatican wasn't down to have its name linked to the Illuminati. This didn't stop film staff from (reportedly) posing as tourists to snap pics of the Sistine Chapel for research. Spoiler: Robert Langdon cracks the code but he doesn't drive a scooter.

around the corner from the Pantheon asks you. *Hmm...a sandwich,* you think, *one that is not 80% bread and has some flavor and enough protein to fuel these 16,000-step days.* "We've got you," the smile from behind the counter seems to say, and the menu confirms it. There are no slim prosciutto pieces here.

Specializing in fish of the smoked, pickled, or marinated variety, Que Te Pongo? delivers in taste and quantity where other sandwich shops skate by on a baguette. Their extensive list of sandwich options—combinations of fish, vegetables, and homemade sauce—sell for the respectable price of

€5-6 and can also be converted into a salad (€7.50-9). There's minimal seating, so opt for takeaway between monument stops. We hope the lunch sticks with you longer than the smell of salmon on your breath.

*i* *Sandwiches €5-8.50, salads €7.50-10, platters €10-12; wheelchair accessible*

# NIGHTLIFE

### 🏳️BAR DEL FICO

P. Del Fico 34/35; 668861373; www. bardelfico.com; open daily 7:30am-2am

To be in Rome is to blend living and leisure, and the city's nightlife generally holds to that mantra. Rome's scene is not the work hard, play hard of many American colleges, or the all-night raging of European club cities. In Rome, it's smooth, easy, and continuous—good food, soothing drinks, fun company, and establishments that shift from café to restaurant to bar throughout the day. Bar del Fico represents the best of these multitasking hangouts, with a consistent crowd of young professionals from morning espresso, to early evening spritzes, to late night cocktails. Taking up half a square in **Centro Storico,** Bar del Fico's packed wrap-around patio sets the tone for nights out in the surrounding restaurants and bars: not rowdy, but definitely not quiet, with plenty of drinks and fresh food to go around.

*i* *Beer €4-5, cocktails €8, food €6-15; wheelchair accessible; one of the few restaurants in Rome that serves Su brunch*

### 🏳️BLACKMARKET

V. Panisperna 101; 3398227541; www. blackmarketartgallery.it; open daily 7:30pm-2am

BlackMarket is Rome's angsty art school student who matured into a retro hipster with some business sense. Behind a heavy door and curtain on one of **Monti's** busier streets, this combo bar and art gallery keeps things dark—shaded lamps, mahogany-polished furniture, and the pitch black of late nights. It's too moody, from the outside, for some tourists, but its creative cocktail menu has stirred enough buzz to draw both visitors and some locals. A little edgier than

your standard wine bar and a little more rebellious than your classy patio cocktail, BlackMarket marks the second or third stop on a night out, when you're ready to upgrade from a small café table to a swanky velvet couch (cocktail glass delicately in hand, of course).

*i* *Beer €4-6, cocktails €10; limited wheelchair accessibility*

### 🏳️FRENI E FRIZIONI

V. del Politeama 4-6; 645497499; www. freniefrizioni.com; open daily 6:30pm-2am

If you're walking along the Tiber outside **Trastevere** on any given summer night, you'll inevitably be stopped by the sight of a square full of people, mostly mid-20s, lounging outside a restaurant. People drape over the stone walls and down the steps. A man breaks out some John Lennon on his guitar. Plates and wine glasses dot the tables. "I have to be a part of this,"you say, without thinking. Welcome to Freni e Frizioni, Trastevere's go-to spot for aperitivos, drinks, and blending into the scene. There's beer, wine, and croquettes aplenty, but Freni e Frizioni sets a new standard with its cocktails—please see the print-out menu of their creative creations, disguised as album covers. You know what's far cooler than being a Green Day fan in middle school? Sipping a Green Day cocktail on a piazza in Rome while watching the sun brighten every reddish paint job in Trastevere.

*i* *Beer €6, long drinks €7 (decrease by 1€ after 10pm), cocktails €8-10; aperitivo (7-10pm): wheelchair accessible; casual, hip attire*

### CELESTINO

V. degli Ausoni 62; 645472483; open daily 7:30am-2am

At Celestino, the glass display of old liquor bottles and array of psychedelic rock posters celebrate the hard drinking of days past, but the crowd only knows Jimi Hendrix from their parents (or grandparents). Located a short walk from **Sapienza University** campus, Celestino draws a youthful, predominantly local crowd, at prices friendly to students. Celestino serves coffee and sandwiches throughout the day, as well as beer (€2.50) and aperitivos (€3.50), but concentrates in cocktails. Take your pick from creations featuring whiskey, gin, rum, and coffee, or try your chances with "The Long Drink," (€3.50) marked with a skull and crossbones and a long-legged woman falling into a martini glass.

*i* No cover; coffee €0.60-2, cocktails €4-8, shots €1.50-4, sandwiches €2-4, beer €2.50-4; wheelchair accessible

## CUL DE SAC

P. di Pasquino 73; 668801094; www.eno-tecaculdesac.com; open daily noon-4pm and 6-12:30am

If you thought "go big or go home" was confined to America, then you haven't seen Cul de Sac's wine selection. Some wine bars offer a booklet; Cul de Sac ups the ante to encyclopedia. The phone book-thick wine list here ranges from Italian, of course, to American and French, and manifests in an extensive collection of bottles lining the walls of Cul de Sac's narrow interior. Come for cured meat and cheese aperitivos, stay for an education in the global expanse of wine and the indulgent ambiance of an Italian evening.

*i* No cover, wine glasses from €4, cured meat and cheese €7-13, primi €8-10, seconding €7-12; wheelchair accessible

## EX DOGANA

Vle. dello Scalo S. Lorenzo 10; 3343849185; www.exdogana.com; open Tu-W noon-10pm, Th-F noon-1am, Sa 10am-1am, Su 10am-10pm

It takes effort to prove that Ex Dogana is not too cool for you. The former 1920s train depot in **San Lorenzo** is more complex than nightclub, which requires navigation. It's a mostly local, university-student hangout, which requires either understanding Italian or accepting you're the only one who doesn't. It's located southeast of the

**Termini** hostel neighborhood, which means you'll be trekking a good twenty minutes through Rome's less picturesque streets to get there. And the venue hosts primarily live music events, which requires knowing what is going on and when (and not knowing any lyrics). If you think you can hang, then check the lineup of acts online and hit up Ex Dogana's electronic dance floor, outdoor lounge area, and themed parties. And congratulate yourself on infiltrating one of Rome's edgiest, most energetic, and unapologetically coolest night spots, though it's probably still too cool for you.

*i* Free, depending on event; some areas reportedly charge €12 for entrance; wheelchair accessible; check online for upcoming concerts or music festivals, which occur frequently throughout the summer

## THE YELLOW BAR

V. Palestro 40; 649382682; www.the-yellow.com; open daily 24hr

Rows of beer on tap, plastic-cupped cocktails spilling on to the dance floor, and not a word of Italian in earshot—what's the difference between the Yellow Bar and the old familiar college one? Not much, especially that rough tequila shot you just got roped into taking with the new hostel bunk mates. But when the mostly international crowd is as new to Rome as you are and eager to make friends, trying to find the hot underground local spot suddenly seems like a far less important priority. The Yellow is travel partying at its freewheeling and familiar finest (or worst, depending on your comfort level with sweaty and PDA-packed dance floors). A raucous hours-long trap for some, a night-starter for others, the Yellow will induct you into the traveler's scene one way or another.

*i* No cover, beer €5, cocktails €7; wheelchair accessible; DJ starts around 12:30am; serves coffee and breakfast

# VENICE

Coverage by **Joseph Winters**

Within minutes of your first steps through the narrow streets of the canaled city, you'll realize why it's the romantic capital of the world. Couples abound, cuddling on guided gondola tours, sipping glasses of wine at canal-side trattorias, or hugging tight while taking a vaporetto ride across the lagoon. And you? Well, your backpack will have to be company enough.

The romanticism of Venice is evidently present in the minds of those who visit: with 20 million visitors coming each year, Venice is one of the most popular tourist destinations in Italy (and the world—Venice is even considering instituting a tourist cap to limit the number of annual visitors), making many of the city's squares feel alarmingly like mosh pits rather than the far-flung getaways they were designed to be. In fact, the city was established by Romans for the very purpose of being inaccessible and inconvenient: they were fleeing from Barbarians (specifically, the Huns), and, upon reaching the area that would become Venice, they decided to start building on top of a seemingly-uninhabitable lagoon. By pressing wooden posts into the marshy wetland, they created the foundation of what would become one of the most powerful cities of the Middle Ages.

Thankfully for you, you're not in danger of an Attila attack, but you may still need to flee from other tourists. Strolling through St. Mark's Square is a must— the Palazzo Ducale, the Royal Palace, and the Campanile are unquestionably the city's most awe-inspiring landmarks—but you'll need to do a bit more digging to discover what it is that makes Venice so special. Put your map away and roam, far away from the crowds. You may find it in the twisting alleys of Cannaregio, on the nearly-uninhabited island of Troncetto, or on a lagoon-side park near the Arsenale.

# ORIENTATION

You (and everyone else) will enter Venice from either the **Ferrovia** (the train station) or **Piazzale Roma** (the bus stop) in the part of Venice called **Santa Croce**. From there, there are signs clearly marking the route to the two major hubs of the city: **Per Rialto** ("to Rialto") and **Per San Marco** ("to San Marco"). Follow these, or just let yourself be carried by the river of tourists flowing towards these tourist-dense destinations. The **Rialto Bridge** neighborhood is called **San Polo**, and the **St. Mark's Square** area is, believe it or not, **San Marco**. Venice wraps itself around the Grand Canal, which serves to connect all its major islands.

To the south of these areas is **Dorsoduro**, where you'll find the **Gallerie dell'Accademia** and the Peggy Guggenheim Collection, as well as some lovely lagoon-side restaurants facing the island of **Guidecca**. This is a good spot to get away from tourists (except for those staying in Giudecca's famous five-star resort).

To the northwest is **Cannaregio**, the historic Jewish Ghetto (the first official ghetto, actually); this is your best bet for what little nightlife can be found in Venice, as well as local restaurants and cicchetti (the Venetian equivalent of bar food). On the northeasternmost reaches of the island you'll find **Castello**, home to the Biennale's world-renowned art pavilions, the Byzantine shipyard, cheaper accommodations, and cheap eats (and a much sparser tourist density).

There are three main island destinations for Venice's tourists: **Lido**, **Murano**, and Burano. Lido, to the east, has a small airport and is known for good beaches (the island is really just a massive sandbar). Murano, a ten-minute vaporetto ride from Cannaregio's **Fondamente Nove**, is the island most famous for its glass production: all of Venice's glass-blowing factories were moved here in 1295 to prevent the spread of fires throughout the rest of Venice. Burano is a bit more far-flung (about 45min by vaporetto, including stops) and is known for lace-making and brightly-colored pastel houses.

When you're getting ready to leave Venice, the same helpful signs helping you navigate "Per San Marco" will help you find your way back to the Piazzale Roma or the Ferrovia.

# ESSENTIALS
## GETTING THERE

If you're flying into Marco Polo airport, you have a few options. Taxis take around 15min. (Radiotaxi Venezia, 041 936222, €35) to get to Piazzale Roma. There are also two bus services. ATVO buses are more expensive, leaving the airport every half hour (5:20am-12:20am daily, www.atvo.it/index.

php?lingua=en, €15), whereas ACTV buses (the public buses, Line 5) go for €8,and there is an option to get an extended ticket that will let you use the public transportation system in Venice for an extended period of time (http://www.veneziaunica.it/it). If you're coming in by train, you'll get off at the Santa Maria Lucia station (not Venezia Mestre), which is just steps away from the Venetian canals. There's also luggage storage just left of the station, open daily 6am-midnight).

## GETTING AROUND

Maps will be your best friend in Venice: the city of canals was obviously not designed for intuitive navigation. Just try to look up every now and again to appreciate the cityscape. It is highly recommended that you spend at least some time exploring Venice by foot—it's the best way to escape the most touristy areas. You might come up on some dead ends (some streets just end at the edge of a canal), but don't resort to swimming: there's almost always a bridge in the vicinity. Another option is to take a water taxi. Apparently, there are 159 kinds of water craft that paddle the canals of Venice, all operated by ACTV (the biggest public transportation provider). City Center lines (1 and 2) leave from Tronchetto and Piazzale Roma, and crisscross the main parts of Venice along the Canal Grande and the Giudecca Canal. City Circle lines (3, 4.1, 4.2, 5.1, 5.2, and 6) go to slightly more far-flung destinations like Murano and Lido, and the Lagoon lines (12, 13, 14, and 19) can get you as far as Chioggia, Fusina, San Guilano, Punta Sabbioni, Treporti, and Marco Polo airport. You can buy a 1-, 2-, 3-, or 7-day unlimited water taxi pass (one day starts at €20) at http://www.veneziaunica.it/en/.

## PRACTICAL INFORMATION

**Tourist Offices:** Tourist offices are just about as plentiful as tourists, so you should have no trouble finding one regardless of which island you happen to be on. Check www.turismovenezia. itfor more information. Stazione Ferroviaria (Santa Lucia, 30121, open daily 8am-6:30pm); Piazzale Roma Tourist Office(Piazzale Roma Garage ASM, 30135, open daily 9:30am-

3:30pm); San Marco Tourist Office (71/f, San Marco, 30124, open daily 9am-3:30pm).

**Banks/ATMs/Currency Exchange:** Venice wants you to spend your money. A lot of it. It shouldn't be too hard to find a bank, ATM, or currency exchange center (or all three, right next to each other) in any of the city's neighborhoods.
- BNL Venice (Rio Terà Antonio Foscarini, 877/D, 30123; 060060; M-F 8:35am-1:35pmand 2:45pm-4:55pm).

**Post Offices:** Look for Poste Italianes throughout the islands (bright yellow and blue signage).
- Poste Italiane Dorsoduro (Dorsoduro, 1507, 30123; 041 520 3218; open M-F 8:20am-1:35pm, Sa 8:20am-12:35pm).
- Poste Italiane San Marco (Merceria S. Salvador, 5016, 30124; 041 240 4149; open M-F 8:20am-7:05pm, Sa 8:20am-12:35pm).

**Internet:** There is a Wi-Fi network called VeniceConnected that works throughout the five main neighborhoods of Venice. You can purchase a special code for 24hr (€5), 72hr (€15), or a week (€20) at www.veneziaunica.it. A 24hr pass is also included with the Rolling Venice three-day public transportation package (students 26 and under €29).

**Wheelchair Accessibility:** Venice's streets are especially narrow and its many canals require climbing flights of occasionally steep stairs. This is an important note for travelers who require a wheelchair, as they will need assistance navigating around Venice's islands.

## EMERGENCY INFORMATION

**Emergency Number:** 113
**Police:** As in other Italian cities, there are both the local police and the Carabinieri. Either can help in case of an emergency.
- Carabinieri Piazzale Roma (Piazzale Roma; 041 523 53 33).
- State Police, Santa Croce (Sestiere di Santa Croce, 500, 30135; 041 271 5586; open M-F 8am-10pm, Sa 8am-2pm).

**U.S. Embassy:** There is no US consular embassy in Venice; the nearest ones are in Milan (V. Principe Amedeo,

2/10, 20121 Milan; 02 290351) and Florence(Lungarno Vespucci, 50123 Florence 38; 055 266 951).

**Hospitals:** Hopefully you won't need to find one, but Venice has two good options for hospitals, one of which is open for 24hr emergency care. Your next best bet is the hospital in Mestre, a bus ride away from Piazzale Roma or a train ride away from Santa Lucia station.
- Ospedale SS. Giovanni e Paolo (Castello 6777; 041 5294111,open M-F 3pm-4pm and 7pm-8pm, Su 10am-11:30am and 3pm-7pm).
- Ospedale San Raffaele Arcangelo (Fatebenefratelli)(Dell'orto,30100, Campo Madonna, 3458, Venice; 041 783111; open daily 24hr).

**Pharmacies:** There aren't any 24hr pharmacies in Venice, but there are a few that are open 9am-7pm daily. For pharmacies open on Su, check the updated roster compiled at www. farmacistivenezia.it.
- Baldisserotto al Basilico (Castello):041 5224109.
- Marangoni Internazionale, Lido (041 5260117).
- Zamboni San Francesco, Santa Croce (041 5286936).

# ACCOMMODATIONS

### ◩BACKPACKERS HOUSE VENICE ($)
Campo Santa Margherita, Dorsoduro 2967/a; 3294724966; www.backpackers-housevenice.com; reception open 24hr

If you want to stay in Venice proper, your euros won't get you the fancy schmancy accommodations you might be used to in less popular destinations like Bologna or even Milan. At Backpackers House Venice, you're paying for an incredible location—**Campo Santa Margherita** is pretty much in the heart of the residential part of the city, minutes away from the **Rialto Bridge** or the **Gallerie dell'Accademia**. But the charming college grad manager/receptionist comes for free (just beware of his nap schedule). Despite the lack of free breakfast, laundry, or personal space, the hostel's 24 beds fill up really quickly. Best to book well in advance.

*i Dorms in the summer €45, winter €20; reservation recommended; Wi-Fi; no wheel-*

chair accessibility; towels included;free locker storage

### ◩GENERATOR VENICE ($$)
Fondamenta Zitelle, 86; 418778288; www. generatorhostels.com/destinations/venice; reception open 24hr

Self-described as an "experience and design-led hostel," Generator Venice feels more like Venice Beach, California, than Venice, Italy. Between the vegan bagel sandwiches and **throwback karaoke nights**, the whole place feels remarkably modern. Behind the reception counter is a spacious common area where nightly events are held, bringing the late-night scene into an otherwise quiet part of town. Sometimes it seems like they're trying too hard ("Make some *noise*! Get *craaaaazy!*" the guitarist yells one night to an audience of six 40-year-olds who are clearly busy making light conversation amongst themselves at the bar counter), but they're well-intentioned. Compared to the lobby and café, rooms are pretty basic, but your eyes are closed while you sleep anyways, right?

*i Dorms summer €40-50; Wi-Fi; wheel-chair accessible; linens included; towels in-cluded; free luggage storage, locker storage €1; laundry facilities €3.50 wash,€3.50 dry; breakfast €4-4.50*

### PLUS CAMPING JOLLY ($)
V. Giuseppe de Marchi, 7; 041 920312; reception open 24hr

When you see how expensive the most basic accommodations in Venice are, you may end up fleeing the city to the far-flung PLUS Camping Jolly. If you can say its name with a straight face, the €12per night for a bed in a "tent" is probably the best deal you'll get around Venice. Don't worry—it's not real camping, and the tents' flimsy doors lock completely if you back into them. There's also a giant pool, two hot tubs, a bar/restaurant, and a supermarket all owned by PLUS, so you won't feel like you're depriving yourself too much. Just make sure you calculate the cost of getting to and from Venice every day—€3 total by public transport or €5 total by PLUS's private bus.

*i Tents from €12, private bungalows from €65; Wi-Fi; wheelchair accessible; linensin-*

cluded; laundry €5 wash, €4.50 dry, buffet
breakfast €6.50,free computers

# SIGHTS

## CULTURE

### ◙JEWISH GHETTO

Cannaregio; open daily 24hr

In the year 1516, the Venetian Doge
forced the city's Jewish population to
move the northwesternmost corner of
the island, in the area today known as
**Cannaregio**. The result: the world's
first official ghetto (the word "ghetto"
comes from *geto* from the Venetian
dialect), closed off from the rest of the
city. Today, it's just another Venice
neighborhood (Napoleon incorporated
it in 1797), but the area still retains
certain characteristics that differentiate
itself from the rest of Venice. Apart
from the five synagogues and the
annual conference on Hebrew Studies,
the area boasts some of the best food
and nightlife in Venice. Look for the
classic Venetian *cicchetti* and wine (at
a reasonable price, too), but keep an
eye out for the international flair in its
streets.

*i* Free entry; prices vary by establishment; wheelchair accessible

### ◙MURANO

Murano Island; open daily 24hr

If Venice had a suburbia, this might
be it. But instead of cookie-cutter
picket fences, they have glass-blowing
furnaces (which is way cooler). Due
to Venice's unlucky history with fires
(that's what you get when you combine
tightly-packed wooden buildings
with glass factories), in 1295, the city
decided to move all of its glass-blowing
production to the island of Murano.
Today, Murano is world-famous for
the glass it produces; just walk through
the town and you'll see *fornace* after
*fornace* (furnaces), as well as an entire
museum devoted to the art of glass.
Murano is also a little more real than
the mainland; here, you can escape
the tourist traps and walk through real
neighborhoods, cemeteries, and parks
where real Venetians play pick-up
soccer games.

*i* Free; vaporetto from Fte. Nove roundtrip
€15; wheelchair accessible

### ◙TEATRO LA FENICE

Campo San Fantin, 1965; 41786511;
www.festfenice.com/en; open daily
9:30am-6pm

The name "The Phoenix" is both
appropriate and ironic—yes, the
sumptuous theater rose from the ashes
of devastating fire (1774) to live again,
but fire also ravaged the theater in
1836, and yet another fire completely
destroyed the theater in 1996. Since
then, it has been rebuilt (all over
again) to look exactly as the previous
one did—solid gold-lined parapets
and all. Thanks to this painstaking
restoration, the history of the theater
has been largely preserved, and you
can now walk through the grand
foyer, the reception areas, and even the
theater itself. Musicians like **Rossini**,
**Stravinsky**, and **Verdi** have all written
works specifically for La Fenice, and it
is still a world-renowned opera house,
perhaps one of the most famous in the
world.

*i* Admission €10, €7 reduced; free audio
guide; book "Walk to the Theater" tour in
advance via phone or email (visite@fest-
fenice.com); wheelchair accessible

## LANDMARKS

### ◙BASILICA DI SAN MARCO

San Marco, 328; 412708311; www.
basilicasanmarco.it/?lang=en; open M-Sa
9:45am-5pm, Su 2pm-5pm

When they say San Marco, they're
talking about none other than *the* Saint
Mark. He's kind of important to the
Christian religion, as he casually helped
write the Christian Bible. His bones
were brought from Alexandria (stolen?)
in 828, and they helped put Venice
on the map, giving the city power and
prestige. Since then, the Byzantine-
style building has experienced
influence from the ages it has lived
through, from the height of the Gothic
era's popularity to the emergence of
Renaissance painting, making the
basilica one of the most complex and
magnificent in all of Italy. It's free to
admire the interior, but make sure to
bring some extra money in with you
if you want to see the **museum**, the

loggia, and the **Pala d'Oro** (which contains the relics).

*i* *Free entry; St. Mark's Treasure €3, reduced €1.50, Pala d'Oro €2, reduced €1, Museo, Cavalli, and Loggia €5, reduced €2.50; free tours M-Th 11am in basilica atrium; last entry M-Sa 4:45pm, Su 4:15pm; wheelchair accessible*

## ◨PALAZZO DUCALE

S. Marco, 1; 412715911; www.palazzoducale.visitmuve.it; open daily 8:30am-7pm

The history of the Palazzo Ducale alone makes it a must-visit Venetian landmark and museum. First built in the tenth century, its primarily gothic architecture shows hints of Renaissance and Napoleonoic influence. It had a specific room for every body of the Venetian government, which you can walk through yourself on the museum's preplanned itinerary. The most impressive is the **Chamber of the Great Council**: a 53m by 25m room fit to hold 2000 noblemen. It's one of the biggest rooms in all of Europe, and it's home to the longest canvas painting in the world, **Jacopo Tintoretto's** *Paradiso*. From there, cross the **Bridge of Sighs**, which feels like finding yourself onstage during a production of *The Merchant of Venice*.

*i* *Admission adult €20, reduced €13; last entry 6pm; wheelchair accessible; tours must be booked in advance online for €20, English tour at 11:45am, "Secret Itineraries" tour at 9:55am, 10:45am, 11:35am*

## BASILICA DEI FRARI

San Polo, 3072; 412728611; www.basilicadeifrari.it

If you haven't gotten sick of basilicas yet, the Basilica dei Frari in the **San Polo** district is one of the city's most impressive. It even has its own **campanile** (not as high as the St. Mark one, though). Since the façade is done in the Gothic style, it might seem a little plain from the outside, but once you enter you'll be able to see the stunning gilded choir stalls. Singers, along with the basilica's multiple organs, occasionally fill the church with ghostly Italian chorales (they don't take song requests, so don't bother asking). Also, **Titian**—one of Venice's most famous Renaissance painters—is buried

here, which means you can check out his artwork and then his monument.

*i* *Admission €3, €1.50 reduced; 5:30pm; wheelchair accessible; book tours in advance via email at basilica@basilicadeifrari.it*

## RIALTO BRIDGE

Sestiere San Polo; open daily 24hr

Chances are, you'll cross the Rialto Bridge at some point during your stay in Venice. It's one of four bridges that crosses the **Grand Canal**, connecting the **San Marco** neighborhood to the **San Polo** neighborhood. It's also one of Venice's most popular landmarks—so get ready to wade through a sea of other tourists. The current stone structure was built in 1588, but there were other previous iterations of a bridge, including a floating bridge (1181) and a wooden one (1255). Take note of the ultra-expensive diamond and jewelry shops along either side. Fun fact: these kinds of shops aren't there only to take advantage of the hundreds flush tourists that clamber over the bridge; rather, the high rent for their coveted location helps pay for the bridge's maintenance.

*i* *Free; limited wheelchair accessibility*

## MUSEUMS

### ◨GALLERIE DELL'ACCADEMIA

Campo della Carita, 1050; 415222247; www.gallerieaccademia.it; open M 8:15am-2pm, Tu-Su 8:15am-7:15pm

This is classic museum material: pre-nineteenth century artwork, airy rooms, full of roaming bespectacled fine art students with sketchbooks in hand. Housed in one of the ancient *Scuoli Grandi* ("big schools"—founded in 1260) of Venice, the Accademia is an important center for art restoration and preservation. If you aren't sick of them yet, take some time to stroll through the triptychs of the Virgin Mary, a giant *Last Supper* that was deemed heresy by the Church, and works by **Bellini**, **Tintoretto**, and **Titian**. Or, you know, you can just book it for da Vinci's *Vitruvian Man* and call it quits; no one's judging you.

*i* *Admission €12, €6 reduced; last entry 45min. before closing; wheelchair accessible*

# VERONA

**To the Veronese, a night at the theater is usually more of a cultural experience than a 3D showing of *Kung Fu Panda III* in Theater 4A.** We're talking the likes of *Aida* and *Carmen*, shown in amphitheaters that outdate the Roman Coliseum. During your visit, you'll definitely want to check out the historical Arena in the city center, as well as the Roman Theater just across the Adige River via the Ponte Pietra (literally "stone bridge"). The rest of the historic city center feels surprisingly quaint in comparison to the grandeur of the Arena. Medieval streets crisscross all the way to the banks of the powerful Adige, flanked by—big surprise—lots of churches, a tower or two (or, like, a dozen), and the Castelvecchio, a fourteenth-century fortress that straddles an L-curve of the river. As you explore, note the *Romeo and Juliet* references you'll see everywhere. Apparently, Verona is the historical home of the Cappello (not "Capulet") and Montague families.

If you're getting to Verona by bus—the most convenient way to arrive—you'll find yourself south of the historic city center at the Stazione Porta Nuova. From here, follow the signs saying "Centro Storico" along the Corso Porta Nuova until you reach Verona's main square, the **Piazza Brà.** Here, you'll find sights like the arena, **Palazzo Barbieri,** and **Palazzo Gran Guardia,** as well the high-end fashion retail and gelato joints that you've come to know and love. The touristic route of Verona will take you north along some intricate streets until you reach the small but shop-lined **Piazza delle Erbe**. Along the river to the east is the **Veronetta neighborhood,** where you'll find more greenery, most notably the **Giardini Giusti.** To the west of Piazzale Brá is the fortress of **Castelvecchio,** an impressive Romanesque castle with its own bridge crossing the Adige. The area south of the river is known as **San Zeno** (named after Verona's patron saint), and to the north is the neighborhood of **Borgo Trento,** home to some lovely gardens and public parks.

## GETTING THERE

Trains arrive at the Stazione Porta Nuova, which is ten minutes south of the historic city center. Hop on a train from Milan (€12, 1hr 50min.), Venice (€9, 1hr. 20min.), Rome (€60, 3hr.), or Florence (€10-20, 1hr. 30min.). You can also take a bus to Verona, which will also leave you at the Stazione Porta Nuova. In general, you can get to Verona from Milan (€9-15, 2hr. 20min.), Venice (€10, 2hr.), Rome (€15-25, 7-10hr.), or Florence (€10, 3hr. 45min.). If you're flying into the Verona Airport, you can take the bus (€6) to the train station starting at 5:35am, at 6:30am, and then every 20min. until 11:10pm.

## GETTING AROUND

The historic center of Verona is pretty small; it takes less than 20 minutes to walk from one side to the other, so you'll probably be on foot most of the time. Buses tickets cost €1.30 (€2 if purchased on board) and are valid for 90min. Day passes cost €4. There are multiple bike companies offering hourly, daily, or weekly rentals starting at €10.

## Swing by...

### ▧ANFITEATRO ARENA
P. Brà, 1; 045 800 5151; www.arena.it; open M 1:30-7:30pm, Tu-Su 8:30am-7:30pm

Built in the first century CE, the Veronese Arena is actually older than the Roman Coliseum (they point this out wryly in the arena's entryway). Today, the theater is famous for opera, but it's only been used as a theater since the fourteenth century. Before then, the Arena was famous for being the site of *munera* (gladiator fights) and *venatione* (man versus exotic beast). But it's housed many tamer events, as well, including horseracing, dances, plays, and parades. Our favorite is bingo. Or maybe a "greasy pole climbing" show (which, embarrassingly, we might be more willing to pay for than *Carmen*). A ticket gets you entry into the stands: modern red chairs at the bottom, Roman stone seats at the top.

*i* Admission €10, €7.50 reduced; last entry 6:30pm; limited wheelchair accessibility

## Check out...

### MUSEO CIVICO DI CASTELVECCHIO – IL CASTELLO E IL PONTE SCALIGERO
Corso Castelvecchio, 2; 045 8062611; http://museodicastelvecchio.comune. verona.it; open M 1:30-7:30pm, Tu-Su 8:30am-7:30pm

The weapons and armor collection is impressive, but the best part about the museum itinerary is access to the keep and some parts of the roof. This was meant to be the final stronghold of the fortress, the duke's final retreat in case of an attack. Here, from above the **Ponte Scaligero,** you can see across the **Adige** toward the **Borgo Trento,** all the way to the western edge of the historic city center. When you're done, cross the medieval stone bridge for yourself. The path is a popular haunt for street musicians, and the accordion gives it a particularly romantic Italian feel.

*i* Admission €6, €4.50 reduced; last entry 6:45pm; limited wheelchair accessibility; book tours in advance via email at segreteriadidattica@comune.verona.it

## Grab a bite at...

### OSTERIA AL DUCA ($$)
V. Arche Scaligere, 2; 0 45 594474; www.osteriaalduca.it/osteriaalduca; open M-Sa 10am-3pm and 6:30pm-midnight

If you've ever wanted to try horse meat, look no further: Ostaria al Duca has you covered. A mom-and pop-style restaurant in what they claim used to be **Romeo's house,** they serve horse preserved in alcohol, braised with corn grits, as tartare with mustard, covered with parmesan, or as a straight-up horse meat steak. We hear it tastes like chicken. Despite your initial reaction, this place is actually one of the most popular restaurants in Verona. The €18 menu includes one primi and one secondi. If you're not into the whole horse meat thing, they also serve bigoli with donkey meat (chicken and non-meat options are available, too).

*i* For a fixed menu including a primi, secondi €18; vegetarian options available; wheelchair accessible

## Don't miss...

### 🖼MUSEO ARCHEOLOGICO AL TEATRO ROMANO
Boat Service: Qrendi; 2164 0058; open daily 9am-5pm

Although the **Arena** is obviously Verona's best performance venue, there's another Roman theater in the north of the city, just across the **Ponte Pietra.** Like the Arena, this one hosts modern performances and events, but usually not opera. Jazz, pop, and rock are popular here, making a night at this theater a little more accessible to the everyday traveler (who probably doesn't have the patience for a four-hour *Carmen* showing). There's also a museum attached to the theater—archaeological finds are scattered throughout a fifteenth-century convent on the hill above the stage. They have a great exhibition on Roman life in the area, and the view of the city from the terrace gardens is excellent.

*i* Prices €4.50, €3 reduced; last entry 1hr. before closing; wheelchair accessible; book tours in advance via email at segreteriadidattica@comune.verona.it

## ⬛LA BIENNALE DI VENEZIA

Campiello Tana, 2169/F; 415218711; www.labiennale.org/en/biennale/index. html; open Tu-Su 10am-6pm, F-Sa 10am-8pm

Every two years, La Biennale di Venezia coordinates a monumental showcase of the world's best modern art and design. In between art years, the association organizes a similarly groundbreaking collection of modern architecture. From May to the end of November, the Biennale takes over nearly the entire northeastern corner of Venice in the **Arsenale** and the **Giardini**. Walking through all the exhibits is a day hike in itself; wear a comfy pair of shoes because you'll be doing a lot of shuffling. It might be good idea to wear the froofiest getup you packed; lots of inconvenient lace and ridiculous sunglasses will help you blend in with the other locals. No guarantees that it'll help you understand the artistic significance of a video showing a man slicing an apple with a MacBook Air, though.

*i* 48hr ticket €30, €22 reduced, 24hr ticket €25, €15 reduced ; last entry 15min. before closing; wheelchair accessible

## ⬛MUSEO CORRER

Piazza San Marco, 52; 412405211; www. correr.visitmuve.it; open daily 10am-7pm

It doesn't mean "to run" (that's *correre*), but you might need to run if you plan on getting through the Museo Correr's massive collection of Venetian art and historical artifcats in a timely manner. Housed in the palatial building that encircles **San Marco Square**, a walking tour will take you through the gluttonously posh life of the Venetian elite, from the cream-colored *marmorino* of the Emperor's bathroom to the "**Dining Room for Weekday Lunches**." There's also a picture gallery that highlights the emergence of international Gothicism in Venice, as well as some really intriguing Venetian artifacts, like an early form of high-heeled shoe that *did* have a functional purpose: to keep women's feet clean as they strolled the muddy streets of Venice.

*i* Admission €20, €13 student; last entry 6pm; wheelchair accessible

## ⬛PEGGY GUGGENHEIM COLLECTION

Dorsoduro, 701-704; 412405411; www. guggenheim-venice.it; open daily 10am-6pm

The Guggenheim Collection is one of those museums that makes you question what exactly defines art. Is a blank canvas art? Does *Curved Black Line*'s curved black line count? What about *The Way West*, which is literally "uncarved wooden blocks"? Either way, the museum is one of Venice's most popular tourist attractions. The building used to be Peggy Guggenheim's house, so it has a sort of quaint, homey feel. That is, if you consider a mini-mansion on the banks of the Grand Canal to be quaint. Whether you go to ponder the avant-garde art (or should we say "art"?) or to say you saw works by **Picasso**, **Jackson Pollock**, and **Joan Miró**, the Collection is definitely an unmissable Venetian attraction.

*i* Admission €15, €9 student under 26; 90min. tours for €75 booked in advance via email at prenotazioni@guggenheim-venice.it; last entry 5:30pm; wheelchair accessible

## OUTDOORS
......................................................

## ⬛GIARDINI DELLA BIENNALE

Sestiere Castello; 415218711; open Tu-Sa 10am-6pm

If you stick to the **San Polo** and **San Marco districts**, you might think all of Venice is devoid of trees. But the northeastern Giardini della Biennale (Gardens of the Biennale) more than make up for chlorophyll-deprived city center. First set up during **Napoleon**'s reign, the gardens have been a key part of the Biennale di Venezia's biannual international art exhibition since 1895. Inside the ticketed area are 29 pavillions, each devoted to groundbreaking artwork from a single country. But the gardens' reach extends far beyond the international pavilions; there are public spaces where you'll find people sprawled out on the grass, walking their dogs, or tossing frisbees. It may not sound like much, but this kind of public space is a rarity in Venice, making the Giardini quite special.

*i* 48hr ticket €30, €22 student under 26, 24hr ticket €25, €15 student under 26; tours must be booked in advance via email at booking@labiennale.org; wheelchair accessible

# FOOD

### ACQUA E MAIS ($)

Campiello dei Meloni, 1411-1412, San Polo; 412960530; www.acquaemais.com; open daily 9:30am-8pm

Despite the "Pizza Kebab" places at seemingly every street corner, there actually is a more traditional Venetian street food. Called *scartosso*, it's named for the paper cone that the dish is served in. At Acqua e Mais (literally "Water and Corn"), they fill the *scartosso* with polenta and heap crispy veggies, cod, or black cuttlefish on top—your choice. There's also a cold bar with mixed seafood salad or the no-frills but classic *baccalà*, which is just salted fish whipped with oil to form a pasty cream (it sounds grosser than it is). Perfect for a speedy (and cheap) lunch.

*i* Cones of polenta with toppings €3.50-8, polenta and wine €10; vegetarian, vegan, and gluten-free options available; wheelchair accessible

### CANTINE DEL VINO GIÀ SCHIAVI ($)

Dorosduro, 992, Fondemanta Nani; 415230034; www.cantina-schiavi.com; open 8:30am-8:30pm

Whether you're feeling pecking or penniless on your Venetian adventure, Cantini del Vina già Schiavi (literally "Wine Cellars Already Slaves") is worth a visit. They are legendary for serving dozens of kinds of Venice's famous *cicchetti* (basically mini bruschettas) on the daily, all of which are painstakingly prepared by a little old

lady with a penchant for salty cheeses and buttery purees. On any given day, you might find flavors like pumpkin-ricotta-parmesan, tuna-tartare-cocoa, or dried cod cream with garlic and parlsey. At €1.20 a pop, a nice-sized plate of these *cicchetti* won't break the bank. Plus, you can take your plate outside and eat on the banks of the canal, just to the side of a high bridge.

*i* Cicceti €1.20, sandwiches €3.50-4.50; vegetarian options available; wheelchair accessible

### LE SPIGHE ($)

Castello Via Garibaldi, 1341; 415238173; open M-Sa 10:30am-2:30pm, 5:30-7:30pm

Although you probably couldn't call her cooking "traditional," Doriana Pressotto's organic-vegetarian-fair trade dishes come with a hefty serving of traditional Italian attitude, completely free of charge. "This sytem, this is brain washing us!" she'll exclaim, pointing dramatically to the grocery store across the street while loading your plate with her own, more virtuous vittles. To Pressotto, it's all about the *ennergia* of the food, which is why she's been serving wholesome, affordable, and delicious meals

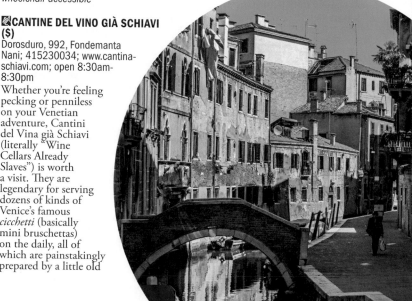

in the vegetable-starved **Castello** area since 2008. Every morning, she prepares around eight different dishes and serves them deli-style until the end of the evening. You can also take your meal to go and have a picnic in the park next door.

*i* Small plates €6-8, medium plates €8-10, large plates €10-12; vegetarian, vegan, and gluten-free options available; wheelchair accessible

## GELATERIA ALASKA ($)

Santa Croce, 1159; 41715211; open daily 11am-7pm

Finally, a gelato place serving more than just a cup of ice cream. At Gelateria Alaska, gelato comes with a smile (imagine that!) and a story (sometimes a very long one). Mr. Pistacchi, the owner of this 26-year-old creamery, is passionate about quality. All of his flavors are made with seasonal ingredients collected from the Venetian street markets; for example, when he finds apricots, apricot gelato appears on the menu. He doesn't use any artificial ingredients, either (so don't expect green pistachio gelato). Mr. Pistacchi also likes to experiment with off-the-wall flavors like "rocket salad" or "asparagus," which are highly recommended, although Rose Water is a good bet as well, with the flower petals coming from his own garden.

*i* Scoops from €2.50-4.50; vegetarian, or vegan options available; wheelchair accessible

# NIGHTLIFE

## AL TIMON

Cannaregio, 2754; 415246066; open daily 6pm-1am

Don't be alarmed if the bartender gives you a *bacio* or two when you walk into this **Cannaregio** area establishment; kisses on the cheek are the Italian equivalent of the handshake. They happen all the time at Al Timon, because the staff seems to know everyone who walks in. Customers line up for a heaping plate of *cicchetti* (€1 each, and you can choose up to ten per group—which works out great if you're solo or coming with a single friend) and a glass of wine, and then migrate outside to sit on Al Timon's two boats.

The soulful Italian jazz, wooden barrels, and melting Venetian sun make for quite a romantic atmosphere.

*i* No cover, cicchetti €1 (max of 10 per group), wine by the glass €3-4.5

## BACARO JAZZ

San Marco, 5546; 415285249; www.bacarojazz.com; open M-Th noon-2am, F-Sa midnight-3am, Su noon-2am

In a city where nightlife is sparse, Bacaro Jazz fills the late-night void with a bizarre mix of classy cocktails and autographed bras. Lots and lots of bras. For 13 years, this cocktail bar/restaurant/jazz club has encouraged visitors to leave behind signed bras as souvenirs, which are then hung from the ceiling in tightly-packed rows. Not all the bras are deemed suitable to go up, though. "These aren't even all of them," the bartender explains. It's anyone's guess where the unhung bras go. As for the food and drink, Bacaro Jazz is more of a bar than a restaurant, serving lots of cocktail-seeking Americans classic and signature drinks for a fair price. Plus, there's BOGO happy hour from 4-6pm.

*i* No cover, pastas and soups (primi piatti) €12-16, cocktails €4-10

## VENICE JAZZ CLUB

Dorsoduro, 3102, Ponte dei Pugni; 415232056; www.venicejazzclub.com; open M-Sa 7pm-11pm

Is there anything more authentically Venetian than a night of spicy bossa nova and smooth Charlie Parker? Probably, but the Venice Jazz Club is still one of the city's nightlife gems. The club has its own quartet of musicians who play international jazz standards, often joined by musicians and groups from around the world. The €20 cover fee pays for your place at a table, as well as your first drink. The space is pretty small, making this a cozy place to spend a relaxing night out (this also means no space for dancing, though). So, if seventh chords and esoteric jazz lingo are your thing, we'd definitely recommend getting down in this crib so you can hear these 18-karat cool cats and finger zingers get crazy with...uh, their instruments?

*i* Cover €20 (includes first drink), aperitivos €5, beer €4-6, long drinks €8,

*liquor €5-6, wine €4; semi-formal dress;*
*wheelchair accessible*

# ITALY ESSENTIALS

## MONEY

**Banks and ATMs:** To use a debit or credit card to withdraw money from a *bancomat* (ATM), you must have a four-digit PIN. If your PIN is longer than four digits, ask your bank whether you can use the first four or if they'll issue a new one. If you intend to use just a credit card while in Italy, call your carrier before your departure to request a PIN. The use of ATM cards is widespread in Italy. The two major international money networks are MasterCard/Maestro/Cirrus and Visa/PLUS. Most ATMs charge a transaction fee, but some Italian banks waive the withdrawal surcharge.

**Tipping:** In Italy, a 5% tip is customary, particularly in restaurants. Italian waiters won't cry if you don't leave a tip; just be ready to ignore the pangs of your conscience later on. Taxi drivers expect tips as well, but luckily for oenophiles, it is unusual to tip in bars.

**Bargaining:** Bargaining is appropriate in markets and other informal settings, though in regular shops it is inappropriate. Hotels will often offer lower prices to people looking for a room that night, so you will often be able to find a bed cheaper than what is officially quoted.

## SAFETY AND HEALTH

**Local Laws and Police:** In Italy, you will encounter two types of boys in blue: the *polizia* (113) and the *carabinieri* (112). The *polizia* are a civil force under the command of the Ministry of the Interior, whereas the *carabinieri* fall under the auspices of the Ministry of Defense and are considered a military force. Both, however, generally serve the same purpose: to maintain security and order in the country. In the case of an attack or robbery, both will respond to inquiries or requests for help.

**Drugs and Alcohol:** The legal drinking age in Italy is 16. Remember to drink responsibly and to never drink and drive. Doing so is illegal and can result in a prison sentence, not to mention early death. The legal BAC for driving in Italy is under 0.05%, significantly under the US limit of 0.08%.

**Travelers with Disabilities:** Travelers in wheelchairs should be aware that getting around in Italy will sometimes be extremely difficult. This country predates the wheelchair—sometimes it seems even the wheel—by several centuries and thus poses unique challenges to disabled travelers. Accessible Italy (378 941 111; www.accessibleitaly.com) offers advice to tourists of limited mobility heading to Italy, with tips on subjects ranging from finding accessible accommodations to wheelchair rentals.

# THE NETHERLANDS

**To travel a great distance in the Netherlands means to stray father than your bike ride to the supermarket.** Yet, this small country is good for much more than its legal substances and for jokes about "your mom's nether lands" (grow up, by the way). Each city and neighborhood within them is exquisite with its own distinguishable accent, customs, and people. This deep, centuries-old heritage makes for a wealth of regional festivals, cultural events, and local specialties. That's not to mention the country's impressive line-up of influential artists from Rembrandt to Van Gogh to M.C. Escher.

Beyond the rich history and thriving traditions, experiencing the fun and carefree student life here is easy. The country has small and navigable cities with blissfully flat bike paths, crowded cafés, and canal-side bars. Its filled with plenty of young people with progressive and easygoing attitudes (and impressive fluency in English). While the Dutch are straightforward and practical, a visit during King's Day, the Amsterdam Dance Event, or, well, pretty much any weekend for proof that everyone from rural farmers to university students are the world's most passionate partiers. Even though only about half the country is a meter above sea level, there's no better place to get high on life.

# AMSTERDAM

Coverage by **Emily Corrigan**

When you say you're going to Amsterdam, a lot of people raise their eyebrows, smile knowingly, and say "oh Amsterdam huh?" It's a city known for its legal prostitution, "coffee shops" selling more popular plants than just coffee beans (marijuana, for those who need it spelled out), and its wild nightlife. With an annual tourist population larger than its actual population, Amsterdam can be subject to misrepresentation by the weekend-trip frat bros, the nearly adulterous bachelorette parties, and the "I've never done it, but it's Amsterdam!" crowd. Amongst the madness, though, is a city with much more real character than first meets the eye. In terms of culture, practicality and efficiency meet relaxed social attitudes and an unmatched ability for leisure and fun. Scenic canals flanked by narrow buildings and a constant stream of bikes make up the cityscape. Cafés, tons of electronic music festivals, and a surprising number of all-you-can-eat sushi restaurants join the ranks of the "coffee shops" as gathering places. World-renowned art museums are tucked next to shops selling Dutch snacks out of cubbies in the wall, like *frikandel* and *kroketten* (find these at the Febo chain). Amsterdam is perhaps best described by the non-translatable Dutch word which describes something cozy and easy to relax into, a warm feeling, a nice day with friends or a date gone well: It's *gezellig*.

## ORIENTATION

Arriving at **Centraal Station,** you'll be on the northern side of the city. A ferry across the harbor to the north will bring you to **Amsterdam Noord,** an upcoming neighborhood featuring the new **Eye Film Institute** and a multitude of cafés overlooking the harbor. South of the station are some of the more touristy parts of town: the **Red Light District** is a center for nightlife, popular among tourists for its more debaucherous reputation ("red light" comes from the red lights that indicate the windows of prostitutes). In the city center, you'll find **Leidseplein,** the site of many clubs and restaurants frequented by tourists and locals alike, and the first location of the **Bulldog,** Amsterdam's oldest coffee shop. **Rembrandtplein, Leidseplein's** even more touristy counterpart, is also close by. The city center is also where you'll find many quaint canals and terraces on narrow houses, the classic Amsterdam views. East of the city center are the "nine streets," full of cute shops and small restaurants. Southwest in **Oud-Zuid** lies **Vondelpark,** the city's largest park, as well as **Museumplein,** a large grassy area with a stunning view of the **Rijksmuseum** as well as two of the city's other most famous museums. Oud-Zuid is also home to some of the city's wealthiest residents, leafy streets, restaurants, and boutiques. **Jordaan** is the home of cool traditional bars frequented by longtime Amsterdammers, and in **De Pijp** you'll find upscale young hipster places along with evening and early-night locations like restaurants and chatty bars, as well as one of the city's most famous markets. **Amsterdam Oost** in the east is spacious and green. Finally, visit **Amsterdam West** for an up and coming nightlife scene, trendy design stores, excellent restaurants, and hip hangouts.

## ESSENTIALS

### GETTING THERE

Buses, taxis, and trains are all available from the international airport, Schiphol. The Schiphol Airport train station is just below the airport and buses leave from directly outside the arrivals area. On the train, you'll arrive at Central Station, the main stop of the metro system. It lies on the harbor and it's easy to walk into the city center.

### GETTING AROUND

Amsterdam has excellent public transport, from buses to trams to a metro system to ferries. All public transportation in Amsterdam can be accessed with an OV-Chipkaart or temporary travel card, which can be purchased at vending machines in the main stations. A variety of options are available, from personalized rechargeable chip cards to single-use or 24hr tickets. You can also consider purchasing the "i amsterdam" City Card, which provides free entry to the top attractions, a canal cruise, and free public transport. It can be purchased for 24hr, 48hr, 72hr, and 96hr durations on www.iamsterdam.com. Bikes are also a popular way to get around Amsterdam. Bike rental shops are all over the city, the most popular being MacBike (red bikes) and Yellow Bike (obviously yellow bikes).

## PRACTICAL INFORMATION

**Tourist Offices:** Stationsplein 10; 020 702 6000; open M-Sa 9am-5pm.
**Banks/ATMs/Currency Exchange:** Damrak 86; 020 624 6682; open M-Sa 9am-8pm, Su 11am-6pm.
**Post Offices:** PostNL (Overtoom 8; 900 0990).
**Internet:** There are internet cafés and Wi-Fi hotspots available to the public throughout Amsterdam.
**BGLTQ+ Resources:** A complete list of Amsterdam's BLGTQ+ resources can be found here: www.iamsterdam.com/en/see-and-do/whats-on/gayamsterdam/resources.

## EMERGENCY INFORMATION

**Emergency Number:** 112
**Police:** Politiebureau Centrum-Jordaan (Lijnbaansgracht 219; 0900 8844).
**US Embassy:** US Consulate General (Museumplein 19; 020 575 5309; open M-F 8:30am-4:30pm).
**Hospitals:**
- OLVG, location Spuistraat (Spuistraat 239; 020 599 4100; M-W, F 8:30am-4:30pm, Th 8am-7:30pm).
- Amsterdam Tourist Doctors (Nieuwe Passeerdersstraat 8; 020 237 3654; open daily 24hr).

**Pharmacies:**
- Leidsestraat Pharmacy (020 422 0210; open M-F 8:30am-8pm, Sa 9am-8pm, Su 11am-8pm).
- Amsterdam Central Pharmacy (020 235 7822; M-W, F 7:30am-9pm,

Th 7:30am-10pm, Sa-Su 10am-8pm).

# ACCOMMODATIONS

### ◧COCOMAMA ($$)
Westeinde 18; 1017 ZP Amsterdam; 206272454; www.cocomamahostel.com; reception open 9am-9pm
At Cocomama, you'll feel like it truly is your mama's house. From family dinners to the many social activities, the sweet staff, and the adorable cat, Joop, this place is easy to call home. The dorm rooms are clean and comfortable (and Dutch-themed) and the outdoor garden and living room are cozy places to hang. A non-smoking hostel, this is the place to find the laid-back crowd that's in for the real Amsterdam, not just the touristy party scene. An included breakfast, cheap dinner nights, and a fully stocked kitchen will save you money on food, especially if you shop at the nearby market of **De Pijp**. With such a cute warm atmosphere, you would never guess that this place used to be a brothel.

*i* *Dorms from €39; reservation required; no wheelchair accessibility; Wi-Fi; laundry facilities; towels for rent; free breakfast*

### ◧THE FLYING PIG DOWNTOWN HOSTEL ($)
Nieuwendijk 100; 1012 MR Amsterdam; 204206822; www.flyingpig.nl; reception open 24hr
If you said you'll love a hostel when pigs fly, this place makes it possible. It's a social backpacker's heaven: a bar open until 3am hosting activities like quiz nights, a pool table, a communal kitchen and included breakfast as well as a smoking lounge. A fun and laid-back staff greets you at the door, which is off one of Amsterdam's busiest shopping streets. It's a busy area with lots of tourists, but the more easygoing Amsterdam is always accessible by foot and the security at the hostel is top notch. It's truly a great place to stay, regardless of our all too obvious flying pig joke.

*i* *Dorms from €32; reservation required; no wheelchair accessibility; Wi-Fi; towels for rent; lockers provided; free breakfast*

## THE BULLDOG HOTEL ($)

Oudezijds Voorburgwal 220; 1012 GJ Amsterdam; 206203822; www.hotel. thebulldog.com; reception open 24hr

Maybe you're telling people you're coming to Amsterdam for the art, culture, and a picture of yourself wearing clogs in front of a windmill. Or maybe you just want to get high and engage in debauchery. If the latter is more your style, you need to stay at the Bulldog Hotel. The Bulldog is the oldest and most famous "coffee shop" in Amsterdam, and its various locations now dominate the **Leidseplein** and the **Red Light District.** The hotel is next door to one of the "coffee shops," and even has its own smoking lounge and bar. Even if your stay isn't all about the Devil's lettuce, other aspects of the Bulldog make it an appealing accommodation. Breakfast is included, security is tight, and the Red Light District is right in the thick of things, albeit noisy.

*i* *Dorms from €38; reservation required; min stay 2 nights; wheelchair accessible; Wi-Fi; laundry facilities; luggage storage; free breakfast*

# SIGHTS

## CULTURE

### ◪EYE FILM INSTITUTE

IJpromenade 1; 1031 KT Amsterdam; 205891400; www.eyefilm.nl; open daily 10am-7pm

The Eye is all about films: how the art form developed, how film is created and projected, and stunning examples of color, editing, music, and more. The building itself is a striking work of architecture and features a gorgeous café on the water and four large cinemas. It highlights influential directors and a permanent presentation in the Panorama explores the creation and history of film. Visitors can sit in the mini cinemas, make their own flip books, create a film on the green screen (which usually consists of people laughing and posing awkwardly while appearing to be on the moon or in a comic strip), and sift through the institute's enormous film archives.

*i* *Film tickets online adult €10, €8.50 student, at the door adult €10.50, €9*

student; exhibitions and permanent presentation adult €13, €11.50 student; wheelchair accessible

### ◪GEITENBORDERIJ RIDAMMERHOEVE

Nieuwe Meerlaan 4; 1182 DB Amstelveen; 206455034; www.geitenboerderij.nl

When one thinks of Amsterdam, one usually pictures light reflected off of canals, old slightly-crooked buildings, and flowers decorating vintage bicycles. But life isn't all flowers and cityscapes. At this working goat farm in the beautiful forest **Amsterdamsebos,** you'll get a taste of real rural Dutch farm life. Visitors can pet friendly pigs, cows, and baby goats, hold chickens, and sit on tractors (for free)! The farmers are happy to let you watch them milk the goats, and you can even buy fresh goat cheese and homemade goat's milk ice cream in the farm's store. Whether you're an animal lover or a city slicker, this farm will make you fall in love with the pastoral side of the city.

*i* *Free admission; limited wheelchair accessibility*

## BOOM CHICAGO

Rozengracht 117; 1017 LV Amsterdam; 202170400; www.boomchicago.nl/en; hours vary

This fun comedy club is beloved by Dutch locals and humor-loving visitors alike. Reserve a small table beforehand and grab a bucket of Heinekens to loosen your giggles and you'll find yourself in tears of laughter. **Improv nights** in English involve the audience, and some routines by the ex-pat comedians poke fun at the particularities of Dutch culture as well as American and Dutch politics and current events. Make sure you stick around at the bar afterward; you'll probably be able to chat with the comedians themselves.

*i* *Tickets €15, €7.50 student, pre-order beer buckets (6 beers) €15; shows at 8pm, check website for details; wheelchair accessible*

## LANDMARKS

### ◪NEMO SCIENCE MUSEUM ROOFTOP

Oosterdok 2; 1011 VX Amsterdam; 205313233; open daily 10am-5:30pm

While we would equally recommend

a visit to the inside of the NEMO Science Museum on Amsterdam's eastern harbor side, it's worth the trip just for the roof. The top of the building is long and slanted, making it easy to walk up the long flat steps to the top. Water features cascade down the stairs, and binoculars let you closely examine the spectacular view of the harbor and the city. Purchase a lemonade or a snack from the cool café at the top and sit on the benches or the rotating circular pods. Check out the many sailboats and ships below but don't be deceived; the large old-looking ship that you see across the water is actually a replica made of concrete. Not very effective as an actual boat.

*i* *Free admission; no wheelchair accessibility*

### BLOEMENMARKT

Singel; 1012 DH Amsterdam; open M-Sa 9am-5:30pm, Su 11am-5:30pm
Stereotypes have never been more pleasant and colorful. The world famous Dutch tulips and clogs abound at this floating flower market that stretches along a canal between **Muntplein** and **Koningsplein.** Flower bulbs fill the stalls along with seeds, souvenirs, and plenty of other plants like succulents and cacti. You may not be able to bring dozens of live plants home on the plane—and you shouldn't try to pack a cactus next to your sweater anyway—but a walk along the market to peruse the plants is certainly time well spent anyway.

*i* *Prices vary by stall; wheelchair accessible*

### WESTERKERK

Prinsengracht 279; 1016 GW Amsterdam; 206247766; www.westerkerk.nl/english; open M-Sa 11am-4pm
Westerkerk can often be found telling people that it "isn't like other churches." Unlike the totally not-chill European cathedrals with their flying buttresses and their try-hard stained glass windows, Westerkerk knows how to keep it classy and has been doing so since 1631. Simple white walls allow all attention to be focused on the church's organ, which is used for free concerts every summer (mostly Bach music) on Fridays at 1pm. The church also features a tall tower that

can be accessed for €8 in small groups of six. Because of the small size, you may have to put your name down and return later in the day. From the top, you'll find a panoramic view including the **Prinsengracht canal** and the surrounding **Jordaan** neighborhood.

*i* *Church admission free, tower admission €8; tower tours every 30min.; church wheelchair accessible, tower no wheelchair accessibility*

### WINDMILLS AT ZAANSE SCHANS

Schansend 1; 1509 AW Zaandam; 756810000; www.dezaanseschans.nl/en; open daily 24hr
Many visitors to the Netherlands are taken with the idea of nostalgic windmills surrounded by happy, round-faced people wearing wooden shoes. "Ah, simpler times they were," they might sigh after buying a souvenir tulip bulb. The windmills at Zaanse Schans are bound to satisfy these idyllic dreams with a classic Dutch landscape. The windmills, mostly originals from the area, date as far back as the sixteenth century and were relocated here in the sixties, to a neighborhood of **Zaandam** that's been made to look like the typical Dutch village of old. Even with the knowledge that the neighborhood isn't in its original form, there's still plenty of history. Note the oil mill **De Bonte Hen** of 1693 that has survived multiple lightning strikes in its long life.

*i* *Free; limited wheelchair accessibility*

## MUSEUMS
..............................................

### ⚑ANNE FRANK HOUSE

Prinsengracht 263-267; 1016 GV Amsterdam; 205567105; www.annefrank.org; open daily 9am-10pm
The clear, young voice of Anne Frank has touched millions of people around the world. Her diary, written as a Jewish girl in hiding in Amsterdam during Nazi occupation, is powerful and tragic, a reminder not to forget the atrocities of the **Holocaust** and the many innocent lives that it touched. Even though Anne's life was eventually claimed, her father Otto made sure her diary was published in order to illuminate the horrifying reality of life under Nazi rule. At the Anne Frank House, visitors can see the small annex

that concealed the Frank family for two years before their discovery and arrest in 1944. This museum will not only give you a new perspective on Anne Frank, but also deliver a powerful message that you won't be able to ignore.

*i* *Admission €9; last entry 30min. before closing; limited wheelchair accessibility; from 9am-3:30pm the museum is only open to people with online tickets for a specific time slot. After 3:30pm tickets can be purchased at the museum entry; online tickets become available two months in advance.*

### MOCO MUSEUM

Honthorststraat 20; 1071 Amsterdam; 203701997; www.mocomuseum.com; open daily 10am-6pm

In 2017, the Moco Museum, set in a beautiful twentieth-century townhouse in **Museumplein,** displayed exhibitions from famous yet anonymous street artist **Banksy** and artist **Salvador Dalí,** whose surrealist work is only rivaled by his iconic mustache and his quote "I don't do drugs, I am drugs." The Moco Museum highlights specific artists rather than a collection of works. They tend to focus on artists that have carved new paths in their fields and approach society with a fresh voice and with a sense of irony. Banksy, for example, is cynical toward capitalism and once sold pieces of his artwork, each worth tens of thousands of dollars, on the streets of New York City for $60 a piece. At the Moco Museum, you're sure to find niche art and artists, curated well and displayed in an intimate setting.

*i* *Admission adult €12.50, €10 student, €7.50 under 16; audio guide €2.50; to*

*skip the line, purchase tickets online; limited wheelchair accessibility*

### VAN GOGH MUSEUM

Museumplein 6; 1071 DJ Amsterdam; 205705200; www.vangoghmuseum.nl; open M-Th 9am-6pm, F 9am-10pm, Sa-Su 9am-6pm

With his bold and colorful work, it's hard to imagine Van Gogh as a tortured artist plagued by inner turmoil and, eventually, the author of his own death. Not only does this museum display around 200 of his paintings, more than 500 drawings, and almost all of his letters, but it acquaints you with the Dutch painter's eventful life as well. It traces his studies in Antwerp and Paris, his friendships with other artists, and the extremely productive period (averaging a painting per day) that occupied the few months before his death. Plus, his many self-portraits are much more interesting than Kim Kardashian's selfie book. Be sure to buy your tickets online the day before in order to bypass the long ticket line.

*i* *Admission €17, free under 18; wheelchair accessible; no photography allowed*

### RIJKSMUSEUM

Museumstraat 1; 1071 XX Amsterdam; 206747000; www.rijksmuseum.nl; open daily 9am-5pm

With more than 8,000 artifacts of art and history, the Rijksmuseum is one of Amsterdam's finest attractions. It houses paintings from **Vermeer, Lucas van Leyden, Van Gogh,** and **Rembrandt** (including the masterpiece *Night Watch,* painted with no preliminary drawings). A centuries-old Shiva statue, an elaborate model of a warship, and a dollhouse with marble floors and real china commissioned by the **Dutch East India Company** (costing as much as an actual house on the **Herengracht** at the time) are all on display as well. In order to really delve into the artwork—instead of doing the classic "walk by slowly with slightly glazed eyes and hands behind your back"—download the free Rijksmuseum app, full of virtual guided tours of varying lengths and themes.

*i* *Admission adult €17.50, free under 18, multimedia tours €5; wheelchair accessible*

## OUTDOORS

### VONDELPARK
West from the Leidseplein and Museumplein; www.amsterdam.info/parks/vondelpark; open daily 24hr
Vondelpark takes up a good portion of the southwest side of Amsterdam. Ponds and weeping willows make for scenic lunches in the grass (and plenty of tourists smoking). 'T Blauwe Theehuse, a nice tea house and café, can be found closer to the center if you're looking for a fresh mint tea. Go further southwest away from the city center for a more natural, less crowded part of the park. Watch out for all the bikes, especially during rush hours when the paths running through the park are regular bicycle highways. One of the summer highlights of Vondelpark is the free **concert series** that takes place at its open-air theater on weekend afternoons. The events are popular, so check online for the schedule. For a less famous but equally beautiful outdoor experience, head to **Oosterpark** instead, where locals play soccer, jog, bike, and do yoga.

*i* *Wheelchair accessible*

## FOOD

### ⬛RESTAURANT THT ($)
Silodam 386; 1013 AW Amsterdam; 204422040; www.tht.nl; open daily 11am-4pm, 5:30pm-10pm
This trendy restaurant and bar lies across the water from the city center, making it accessible by ferry. A large outdoor patio overlooks the harbor, so you can watch the steady flow of boats trundling by from your vantage point

above the water. The restaurant is hip with a touch of hipster; the wall of the interior is covered in live plants while succulents and cacti rest on the colorful outdoor tables. Apart from the out-of-the-box location and design, the food itself also makes this place appealing. At lunch, THT serves sandwiches, salads, excellent soups, and Dutch specialties. Their menu elucidates the sources of their fresh ingredients and nearly everything can be made gluten-free. For such a hip restaurant, the prices are still astonishingly affordable.

*i* *Entrées €6.50-9.50; card only; vegetarian, vegan, and gluten-free options available; no wheelchair accessibility*

### ⬛THAI BIRD SNACKBAR ($)
Zeedijk 77; 1012 AS Amsterdam; 204206289; www.thaibird.nl; open M-Th 1pm-10pm, F-Su 1pm-10:30pm
You'll want to get to Thai Bird Snackbar a bit early, since it really is the size of a snack bar. Just walking across the tiny restaurant requires a chorus of "excuse me" and a great reshuffling of chairs and belongings. Once inside though, you'll be able to choose from the wide array of incredibly tasty curries, soups, pad thai, and other super-tasty Thai dishes. For such low prices, the food is both top-notch and plentiful. A €10 curry comes with a heaping plate of rice and is nearly enough for two meals. Luckily, handy to-go boxes mean you can enjoy it all over again back at your hostel.

*i* *Starters €4-5, soups €5-6, entrées €10-12; vegetarian and gluten-free options available; limited wheelchair accessibility*

### BULLS AND DOGS ($)
Van Woustraat 58; 1073 LN Amsterdam; open M-W 4pm-10pm, Th noon-10:30pm, F-Sa noon-11pm, Su noon-10pm
This restaurant's name is both a nod to Amsterdam's most famous coffee shop, **The Bulldog,** and a play on words. Elaborate hot dogs (beef, pork, veggie, and more) for €5-7 make up the menu, from the **Dutch Delight** to the **Spicy Texas Dog.** Fries on the side can be topped with truffle sauce or feta, and you can add a specially selected beer to complete the combo. The restaurant is hip and unique, and its food is as yummy as it is photogenic. You may have to make another trip back for

What seems sinful to some is quotidian in Amsterdam. Young Dutch kids are confused to learn that elsewhere, prostitution is illegal. It's a daily occurrence that visitors of coffee shops (for marijuana) or smart shops (for "magic mushrooms") wander past with glazed eyes. Yet, the truth is that these "sinful" industries are largely, even mostly, supported and perpetuated by the city's many tourists. After all, to the average Amsterdammer, they're no forbidden fruit. That's why you'll find the Red Light District—home to many coffee shops, erotic shows and stores, and lingerie-clad women behind red-lit doors—constantly swarming with tourists. Buying a penis-shaped lollipop, a marijuana-patterned pair of socks, or an explicit deck of cards here is a common way for visitors to end their stay. It's up to you if a potentially hilarious gag gift is worth the inflated price tag and the "T" for "Tourist" emblazoned upon you like a scarlet letter. Here's what you need to know about the Red Light District to avoid the wide-eyed look that accompanies first-timers.

Yes, those "peep shows" are exactly what you think. Most of the time they consist of a circular room surrounded by smaller stalls with viewing windows that can be unlocked for a few minutes for a couple of euros. Make sure you understand the implications of supporting this sort of industry, and remember: what you see can't be unseen. Dipping down a small alleyway from one of the Red Light District's main streets will probably find you surrounded by women trying to entice you inside the rooms behind the famous red-lit doorways. Although it's an unfamiliar sight, be respectful and refrain from jeering or taking photos, which is not allowed. Finally, when it comes to drug use, it may be legal in Amsterdam but it's generally never a good idea to experiment in a foreign country. If you do choose to partake, make sure you're with someone who knows what they're doing, you're in a safe place, and you know where it comes from. Never buy drugs from someone off the street, only in a licensed shop. These can be identified by the green and white "coffee shop" sign. Typically, you'll find more relaxed and less expensive coffee shops away from the Red Light District anyway.

their incredible milkshakes; you'll need to whip out the trampoline and the lawn furniture because they will bring the boys to your yard.

*i* Hot dogs €5-7; vegetarian options available; limited wheelchair accessibility

## SIR HUMMUS ($)

Van der Helstplein 2; 1072 PH Amsterdam; 206647055; www.sirhummus.nl; open Tu-F noon-8pm, Sa-Su noon-5pm

This isn't your average "we needed a vegetarian option at our barbecue so we put some celery sticks and hummus" hummus. Sir Hummus makes only one meal, done extremely well: the delicious vegan Middle Eastern classic with chickpeas, veggies and pickles, warm pita bread, and your choice of topping. A small version is a perfect afternoon snack while a large will quell the tempers of even the hangriest guests. The free "secret sauce" (also vegan) on the communal tables knocks the spice up a notch. For cheap and healthy eats in **De Pijp,** this is the place to go.

*i* Large bowl €7.50, small bowl €6.50, toppings €1-3; card only; vegetarian, vegan, and gluten-free options available; limited wheelchair accessibility; will sometimes close earlier if supply runs out

# NIGHTLIFE

### ▓COOLDOWN CAFE ("KLEINE COOLDOWN")

Lange Leidsedwarsstraat 116 3 BG; 1017 NN Amsterdam; 204212284; open M-Th 10:30pm-4am, F-Sa 10:30pm-5am, Su 10:30pm-4am

Known affectionately to locals as the "Kleine Cooldown" or just the "Kleine," this place beats any famous touristy club for a crazy night. With wild bartenders flipping between hit songs, Dutch folk songs, and electronic music every thirty or so seconds, ringing loud bells, and passing out Santa hats whether or not it's December or July, this is where real Amsterdammers go. A true Kleine Cooldown experience means showing up super late on a weekday, dancing like crazy, essentially washing your clothes in beer, and not leaving until you've ensured that the next day (or more accurately later that day because you'll be leaving in the early to late hours of the morning) is thoroughly ruined. If you're lucky, you'll even wake up in a Santa hat. A free souvenir!

*i Free admission; limited wheelchair accessibility*

### VOLKSHOTEL

Wibautstraat 150; 1091 GR Amsterdam; 202612100; www.volkshotel.nl/en; open Su noon-6pm

Things young budget travelers usually don't come across too often: free stuff, luxury rooftop bars, hot tubs. Things that Volkshotel has: all of the above. Normally the rooftop hot tub and bar areas are restricted to guests, but entry is free to the public on Sundays from noon to 6pm, so grab your swimsuit and towel and head up for the spectacular views, tasty drinks, and even a little sauna. The hot tubs are small, so you'll get a chance to bump shoulders with real Amsterdam residents. After your relaxation time, you can easily transition to dinner or a drink at the hotel's restaurant, where live DJs play, or later on, head to its nightclub. This gem of a spot is one of the city's best kept secrets.

*i Free entry; limited wheelchair accessibility; bring your own towel and swimsuit, showers provided*

### WATERKANT

Marnixstraat 246; 1016 TL Amsterdam; 207371126; www.waterkantamsterdam.nl/nl/index.html; open M-Th 11am-1am, F-Sa 11am-3am

Waterkant has perfected the recipe for attracting trendy young people: start with a beautiful but slightly strange and out of the way location, mix in a bunch of outdoor and indoor picnic tables, and top it off with plentiful beers. Dutch locals pack this cool waterside bar, even during the week, to hang their legs over the picturesque canal, watching the sunset in a friendly and chatty atmosphere. As the night wears on, it gets increasingly lively, making it a great place for pre-drinks and snacks or a stand-alone spot for a night out. The coolest part? Tourists tend to miss it because it's underneath a parking garage.

*i Beers €2.75-5; limited wheelchair accessibility*

### PIANOBAR MAXIM

Leidsekruisstraat 33; 1011 CR Amsterdam; 630364965; www.pianobarmaxim.com; open M-Th 9pm-3am, F 5pm-4am, Sa 9am-4am, Su 9pm-3am

Piano bar is fairly straightforward: it's a bar where there is a piano. The performer can do it all; request a classic song by writing it on a coaster and, in a few minutes, the whole bar will be singing and dancing along. By "the whole bar" we mean a cluster of people of all ages, drunk moms out with their friends and rowdy teens coming from nearby clubs alike. Whether you're starting the night off with some live music or you feel like yelling out some familiar songs after exploring other bars is of little importance. There is a cover but don't let it deter you. It's only €1, a small price to pay for the amount of times you'll request "The Piano Man."

*i Cover €1, beers €3.50; wheelchair accessible*

# UTRECHT

Coverage by **Emily Corrigan**

Even though Utrecht is often overshadowed by its larger neighbor Amsterdam (remember, even Beyoncé has a sister), it's a can't-miss stop for students who love the relaxed and honest Dutch culture, beautiful canals, and fun cafés, but don't care for the tourist-filled madness. This medieval city was once considered the most important city in the Netherlands, and continues to be a religious center as well as the host of countless cultural events. It holds the tallest church tower in the country, nice shopping areas and markets, boats gliding over flat water, and canal-side restaurants accessed by stairs. It has small-town charm and can be easily navigated on foot, and the relative scarcity of tourists makes it feel traditional and authentic. Yet the presence of Utrecht University also means there are always plenty of young people biking through town and packing the popular bars.

## ORIENTATION

The medieval city center is dominated by **Dom Tower** and the neighboring cathedral. Surrounding **Dom Square,** you'll find many of the city's shops and restaurants, as well as **Utrecht University.** East of the city center are a number of small parks and green walking paths along the large canal, which also bends around its northern end and to the south past the observatory. Near the observatory, you'll find a number of the city's other popular museums and the beautiful neighborhood of **Lange Nieuwstraat.** Farther west is the train station, **Utrecht Centraal.** Finally, a trip farther east will take you to the university's beautiful botanic gardens and historic buildings.

## ESSENTIALS

### GETTING THERE

To get to Utrecht by plane, you will have to fly in to Schiphol Airport in Amsterdam. Trains leave directly from the airport to Utrecht Central Station. The train station is located very close to the city center, within walking distance of most accommodations and sights.

### GETTING AROUND

Most attractions in Utrecht are within walking distance. However, buses and trams also run throughout the city. Tickets cost €2.70 either on the bus or tram or at a vending machine in the station. One-day passes can be purchased for €6. There are also numerous bike rental shops around the city.

### PRACTICAL INFORMATION

**Tourist Offices:** Domplein 9, 3512 JC Utrecht; 0900 1288732; open M noon-5pm, Tu-Sa 10am-5pm, Su noon-5pm.

**Banks/ATMs/Currency Exchange:** Western Union (De Lessepsstraat 59, 3553 RJ Utrecht; 030 244 4333; open M-F 8:30am-6pm).

**Post Offices:** Voorstraat 3 (Open M-Sa 8:30am-5pm).

**Internet:** The city of Utrecht provides free Wi-Fi nearly everywhere.

### EMERGENCY INFORMATION

**Emergency Number:** 112

**Police:** Politie Utrecht Bureau Kroonstraat (Kroonstraat 25, 3511 RC Utrecht; 0900 8844).

**Rape Crisis Center:** Centrum Seksueel Geweld Utrecht (Postbus 85090, 3508 AB Utrecht; 88 755 5588).

**Hospitals:**
- University Medical Center Utrecht (Heidelberglaan 100; 088 755 5555; open daily 24hr).

**Pharmacies:**
- Apotheek Binnenstad (Van Asch van Wijckskade 30; 030 232 6010; open M-F 8am-6pm).

# ACCOMMODATIONS

### ⚑HOSTEL STROWIS ($)
Boothstraat 8; 3512 BW Utrecht; 302380280; www.strowis.nl; reception open 8am-1am

Staying at Hostel Strowis feels much more like crashing at a friend's house than renting a bed at a hostel. A large and secluded garden with a long picnic table encourages a friendly social scene, as do the communal kitchen and cozy living room with bright colors and plenty of light streaming through tall windows. You're greeted with a cup of coffee or tea and you have plenty of extra amenities at your disposal, like free earplugs, books, and games. The hostel is in an excellent location in the center of the city, making it super easy to explore. If that's not enough, there are free concerts in the garden every Sunday.

*i* Dorms from €20; reservation required; no wheelchair accessibility; Wi-Fi; lockers available; laundry facilities

### STAYOKAY UTRECHT ($$)
Neude 5; 3512 AD Utrecht; 307501830; www.stayokay.com/nl/hostel/utrecht-centrum; reception open 24hr

Walking into Stayokay you'll think you're in the wrong place. That's because it looks more like a large hipster café—we're talking plants, strange artwork, copper pipes, exposed bulbs, people wearing glasses—than it does a hostel lounge. The bar is professional, and you can grab a fresh snack from the small restaurant area. The hostel is on the edge of the **Neude,** one of Utrecht's nicest squares. Even with such a central location, the hostel offers bicycle rentals for enjoying the rest of the city.

*i* Dorms from €32; reservation required; wheelchair accessible; Wi-Fi; laundry facilities; lockers provided; towels for rent

# SIGHTS

## CULTURE

### SONNENBORGH OBSERVATORY
Zonnenburg 2; 3512 NL Utrecht; 308201420; www.sonnenborgh.nl/page=site.home; open T-F 11am-5pm, Su 1pm-5pm

Sonnenborgh, meaning "fortress of the sun," is an apt name for this observatory, built on the site of a sixteenth-century bastion used for defending the city with cannons. While much of the museum portion of the observatory seems to cater to Dutch children, you'll still be able to find highlights like footage of the 2012 Curiosity landing on Mars, enormous telescopes, and a 115-kilogram meteorite. Even better attractions, however, are the star-watching and sun-viewing events held at the observatory. On summer "Sun Sundays," a guide can help you view the sun through a special telescope that protects your eyes, and from September to April, you can view stars with the help of one of the pros.

*i* Admission adult €7, €4.50 for students; sun viewings Su 2pm and 3:30pm; no wheelchair accessibility

### VREDENBURG MARKET
Vredenburg; 3511 AG Utrecht; open W 10am-5pm, F 10am-5pm, Sa 8am-5pm

On Wednesdays, Fridays, and Saturdays, in a square surrounded by busy stores, you'll find the Vredenburg Market. Here you can find everything from fresh fish to shampoo to books, records, cheese, and food stands selling tasty snacks. Local vendors often offer free samples of their goods, making it fun and filling to wander the stalls. For a jam-packed Saturday, check out more of Utrecht's street markets, like the colorful and aromatic **Janskerkhof Flower Market** or the **Breedmarkt Fabric Market.**

*i* Prices vary by stall; wheelchair accessible

## LANDMARKS

### DOM TOWER
Domplein 21; 3512 JC Utrecht; open M noon-5pm, Tu-Sa 10am-5pm, Su noon-5pm

The people of Utrecht really wanted to make a statement back in 1321 when they started work on Dom Tower, the highest tower in the Netherlands. *Cough* Compensating for something? The tower, once attached to the neighboring church, is over 112 meters tall, making for a long climb to the top for #views. Buy your tickets at the tourist office in the square before joining a tour. You'll be able to stand right under the enormous bells, many dating back to 1505, and watch the upper musical bells chime out a melody. For a tower experience even from the ground, just hang around the area on Monday at 8pm; the city's carillon player gives bell concerts of anything from David Bowie to Radiohead.

*i* *Tickets (with guided tour included) adult €9, €7.50 student, €16 student combination ticket; tours every hour on the hour; no bags allowed inside, but lockers are provided for free; no wheelchair accessibility*

### SAINT MARTIN'S CATHEDRAL

Achter de Dom 1; 3512 JN Utrecht; 302310403; www.domkerk.nl; open M-Sa 10am-5pm

This stunning cathedral is located at the heart of a Roman fort founded around 43 AD. Originaly Catholic, it became Protestant during the **Reformation of 1580**, and that's not the only change that has occurred since its construction. It was once connected to Dom Tower through a nave, which was destroyed in a tornado in 1674 and never rebuilt. Citizens even waited about 150 years to clear out the rubble, like teenagers hoarding dirty dishes in their rooms. Don't miss the gorgeous fifteenth-century courtyard, where the life story of Utrecht's patron saint, **Saint Martin**, is told in reliefs.

*i* *Free admission; tours available upon request; wheelchair accessible*

## MUSEUMS

### CENTRAAL MUSEUM

Agnietenstraat 1; 3512 XA Utrecht; 302362362; www.centraalmuseum.nl; open T-Su 11am-5pm

Centraal Museum has it all, in a thrilling and confusing way. It starts with a huge fashion collection, including some clothes that you have to already know are clothes in order to recognize them as such. The numerous expositions continue in seemingly random order. One moment you can be looking at a panel painting from 1363 and then turn around and see a room full of modern chairs, lifesize sculptures made of molten plastic, or a sweater made of human hair. Tucked in the basement almost as an afterthought

## DE HAAR CASTLE

Located a short trip away from Utrecht's city center, Kasteel de Haar (De Haar Castle) looks like something out of a six-year-old's princess fantasy. And like a princess fantasy, much of it is a myth. The original castle dates all the way back to 1391 under the De Haar family, but the buildings and beautiful towers on-site today were constructed during an 1892 restoration project. To initiate the restoration, the grounds were passed to the Van Zuylen family when one of its members married Baroness Hélène de Rothschild. Even without its original buildings, however, the enormous castle and its grounds provide for stunning views and a pleasant walk. In such a romantic and fantastical spot, you're sure to run into some lovebirds scoping out wedding locations, but the solo traveler can also enjoy the reflections on the moat, the manicured flower gardens, and the wide grassy park (and think about how you're alone and without love and single and...you know the rest). Inside are tapestries, a great dining room, and impressive woodwork.

The park is open from 9am-5pm, while the castle itself is open from 11am-5pm. However, it's a good idea to check online before you go to make sure the castle isn't closed for holidays or private events. Entrance to the castle is €16 and includes entrance to the park. An audio guide can also be rented for €1. Entrance to the park alone is €5. From Utrecht Centraal, you can take a sprinter to Vleuten, leaving every 15 minutes. From there, take Bus 111 to Kasteel de Haar. The trip takes about half an hour. You can also ride a bike there in about 40 to 45 minutes.

is an enormous, thousand-year-old ship found by archaeologists. The museum seems to embrace its strangeness; one sign reads, "What kind of morons are the people who come up with these objects and art works?... You need to cast aside the rules of how things 'should be done' in order to see the world with fresh eyes and an open mind."

*i* *Admission adult €12.50, €5 student; wheelchair accessible*

## MUSEUM SPEELKLOK

Steenweg 6; 3511 JP Utrecht; 302312789; www.museumspeelklok.nl; open T-Su 10am-5pm

Having a guided tour of clocks and organs may not immediately sound appealing to a young and adventurous traveler. Yet, this museum of self-playing instruments is about much more than just those creepy music boxes with spinning clowns. The tour guide will demonstrate instruments from moving-picture clocks to the ancestor of the karaoke machine to enormous traditional Dutch moving organs, which people would roll between neighborhoods to start impromptu block parties. One instrument even automatically plays multiple violins. The tickets are on the pricey side, but it's impossible to have a bad time at this cheerful museum.

*i* *Tickets €12, combination tickets for museum and Dom Tower €16; tours every hour on the half hour; wheelchair accessible*

## OUTDOORS

### ◪UTRECHT UNIVERSITY BOTANIC GARDENS

Budapestlaan 17; 3584 HD Utrecht; 302531826; www.uu.nl/botanischetuinen; open daily 10am-4:30pm

Walking through these extensive botanic gardens, you'll find yourself wondering why birds aren't tying bows in your hair and small doe-eyed forest critters aren't singing to you about love. That's because this place is truly magical. It holds a butterfly house, an apartment complex for solitary bees, a vegetable garden, massive orchids, and a section of particularly aromatic flowers and herbs. Even a cannabis plant has made its way into the gardens

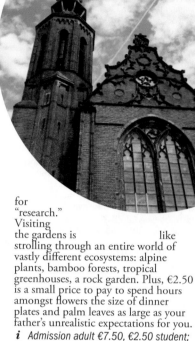

for "research." Visiting the gardens is like strolling through an entire world of vastly different ecosystems: alpine plants, bamboo forests, tropical greenhouses, a rock garden. Plus, €2.50 is a small price to pay to spend hours amongst flowers the size of dinner plates and palm leaves as large as your father's unrealistic expectations for you.

*i* *Admission adult €7.50, €2.50 student; wheelchair accessible*

# FOOD

### ◪KIMMADE VIETNAMESE FOOD VILLAGE ($$)

AC, Oudegracht aan de Werf 61; 3511 Utrecht; 37370281; www.kimmade.nl/food-village; open daily 8am-10pm

If this place is a real village, we want to move there, start a family, get a house with a tire swing, and never leave. Everything about Kimmade is appealing, from its location on a canal to its speed and visual appeal to its specialties like rice paper rolls and satisfying noodle soups. Light vegetarian and vegan meals are easy to find here, as are tender beef, spicy broths, and delicious soups. Stop by for lunch or come for dinner, when an extended menu offers even more Vietnamese delicacies.

*i* *Rice paper rolls €5.50, entrées €13-14; vegetarian and vegan options available; wheelchair accessible*

## ⬛VISJES ($)

Twijnstraat 24; 3511 ZL Utrecht;
302333944; www.kokenmetvisjes.nl; open
M noon-7pm, Tu-F 10am-7pm, Sa 9am-
5pm, Su noon-5pm

*Kibbeling* is a traditional Dutch snack
consisting of battered and fried chunks
of fish smothered in a delicious special
sauce. And nobody does *kibbeling*
better than Visjes; they even won the
2017 Utrecht-area **Kibbeling Cup** (a
competitive and prestigious honor).
Other Dutch specialties like herring are
served alongside seafood paellas, fried
mussels, shrimp, and more. You can
also purchase raw fish, the fresh goods
that the restaurant uses itself. Even
though it's such an acclaimed spot,
you would have to search hard to find
anything on the menu over €5.

*i* *Kibbeling €2.75-3.75, other entrées
under €5; wheelchair accessible*

## 'T OUDE POTHUYS ($$$)

Oudegracht 279; 3511 PA Utrecht;
302318970; www.pothuys.nl; open M-T
3pm-2am, W-Sa noon-3am, Su noon-midnight

This candlelit, wine-cellar-esque
restaurant placed classily along a
romantic canal could easily fall under
"food" or "nightlife." That's because
a late dinner transitions easily into
live musical performances, many
by students from the **Utrecht's
Conservatorium.** A small stage in an
intimate setting is the focal point of
the restaurant, whose walls are decked
out with all kinds of instruments.
Prices are on the slightly higher end for
budget travelers; after all, they include
dinner and a show. If you're not up for
the full dinner menu, just grab some
less-expensive snacks or starters at the
beginning of the performances.

*i* *Snacks and starters €3.50-7.50, entrées €14-19; vegetarian options available;
no wheelchair accessibility*

# NIGHTLIFE

## ⬛FEESTCAFÉ DE KNEUS

Nobelstraat 303; 3512 EM Utrecht;
302318799; http://www.feestcafedekne-
us.nl/; open daily 8pm-5am

Feestcafé de Kneus is where sobriety
goes to die. You'll only find Dutch
students in this late night "party café,"
where everyone knows the bartenders,

each other, and the mostly Dutch
songs (hip hop, electronic, or folk, with
the occasional appearance of crowd-
pleasers like "Unwritten" or "Breaking
Free" from *High School Musical*). It's
not a glamorous place—tacky lights
and a smoking area make it look like an
alley where people leave the furniture
they don't want anymore, but, boy,
does it have character. You won't find
any attention-seeking bottle buyers,
confused tourists (except for you),
or meek and self-conscious dancers
here. At Café de Kneus, nobody cares
if you're a terrible singer or you keep
spilling beer on them. They probably
won't remember anyway.

*i* *Beer and shots €2.50; no wheelchair
accessibility*

## BELGIAN BEER CAFÉ OLIVIER

Achter Clarenburg 6a; 3511 JJ Utrecht;
302367876; www.cafe-olivier.be; open
M-W 11am-midnight, Th-Sa 10am-2am, Su
11am-midnight

For some, "church" means a place
where their mother gets mad at them
for texting. For others, it's a place
of religious devotion or just another
building. At Café Olivier, it's a place
to drink beer. Under the high ceilings
of this former Catholic Church and
the watchful eyes of the statue of
Mother Mary, the bartenders proudly
serve more than 200 Belgian beers to
a predominantly older crowd. At first,
you'll keep expecting to hear music
from the giant organ and be shushed,
but soon you'll get accustomed to the
large bar's poppin' atmosphere. All it
takes is a Belgian beer and a healthy
sense of irony.

*i* *Beers from €3.60; limited wheelchair
accessibility*

## GRAND CAFÉ LEBOWSKI

Domplein 17; 3512 JD Utrecht;
302315217; www.grandcafelebowski.nl;
open M-Th 11am-1am, F 11am-2am, Sa
10am-2am, Su 11am-midnight

Although the outdoor seating at
Grand Café Lebowski is hard to beat
(meaning a stone's throw from **Dom
Tower**), the interior is interesting
enough to warrant some time
exploring. Made to look like a hunting
lodge, the bar probably single-handedly
keeps Utrecht's taxidermy industry in
business. After all, their centerpiece is a
real stuffed giraffe acquired for €6700.

Besides the various rabbits and even an ostrich overseeing your drinks, you'll find an old-school pinball machine, doll heads, and various other eccentric decorations. Since Lebowski closes at 1am, it's not the perfect place for late night dancing, but an ideal place to start.

*i* *Drinks €4-10; limited wheelchair accessibility*

# NETHERLANDS ESSENTIALS

## MONEY

**Tipping:** In The Netherlands, a service charge of usually 5% is often included in menu prices, so there is no need to worry about tipping extra. If you received really good service, it might be nice to round up the bill or leave a small tip, but you are not expected to do so even if there isn't a service charge included. A service charge is sometimes included in taxi fares, but drivers will appreciate if you round up the bill as well. Paying the exact amount, however, is never offensive.

**Taxes:** The marked price of goods in The Netherlands includes a value-added tax (VAT). This tax on goods is generally levied at 21%. Non-EU citizens who are taking these goods home unused may be refunded this tax at the end of their trip. When making purchases, be sure to ask and fill out a VAT form and present it to a Tax-Free Shopping Office, found at most airports, borders, or ferry stations. Refunds must be claimed within six months.

## SAFETY AND HEALTH

**Drugs and Alcohol:** The Dutch are liberal towards alcohol, with the drinking age set at 16 for beer and wine and 18 for hard liquor. Public drunkenness, however, is frowned upon. When it comes to drugs other than alcohol, consumption of marijuana and things like hallucinogenic mushrooms (which fall under "soft drugs") are legal. Consumption isn't limited to coffee shops and smart shops, just purchasing is.

**Prostitution:** Prostitution flourishes in The Netherlands, particularly in Amsterdam's Red Light District. Legal prostitution comes in two forms: window prostitution, which involves peeps shows, and legalized brothels. This term usually refers to an establishment centered around a bar. Women or men will make your acquaintance and then are available for hour long sessions. The best place to go for information about prostitution in Amsterdam is the Prostitution Information Centre (Enge Kerksteeg 3 in the Red Light District; 020 420 7328; www.pic-amsterdamn.com).

**BGLTQ+ Travelers:** The Netherlands are accepting of homosexuality and Amsterdam is a center thought of as a haven of homosexual tolerance. It was the first capital city to legalize gay marriage, and there are many parts of the city with BGLTQ+ nightlife establishments.

**Minority Travelers:** Despite Amsterdam being known for its openness, there's a lot of conversation around ethnic minorities coming into the Netherlands. Immigrants are not always welcomed with open arms. Although foreign tourists might be approached with suspicion, regardless of background, non-white visitors might encounter more hostility.

# NORWAY

**At first glance, Norway seems like another one of those Scandinavian utopias that always lands near the top of those "World's Happiest Countries" rankings.** And it's easy to see why when you look at the country's extensive welfare state, featuring universal healthcare and free public universities, and a ridiculously high standard of living. But things are a bit more complicated than that; society in Norway today is far from harmonious. While it's true that the country makes impressive use of renewable energy, especially of hydroelectric power, Norway also has enormous fossil fuel reserves, which are a considerable source of revenue for the government. Though Norwegians are willing to pay the sizable taxes levied by a bureaucracy often labeled as socialist, they are unwilling to buy into the biggest bureaucracy of all: the European Union. The best way to figure out the ins and outs of Norway is to pay a visit yourself. Its rich cultural history is inextricably tangled with nature, from the fearsome Vikings who used the sea to discover North America centuries before Columbus to the snow-capped mountains that lead to the country's dominance in winter sports. While its cities can't quite rival the vibrancy of Stockholm or Copenhagen, Norway boasts national treasures you can't afford to miss.

# BERGEN

Coverage by **Eric Chin**

Being a tourist in some cities is too easy, especially in Scandinavia. Credit cards and American dollars are accepted everywhere, menus and museum panels are printed in English, and Segway tours are maddeningly popular. Not in Bergen. Sure, it's a popular tourist destination, especially in the summer. But it's the kind of city where the woman behind the counter at the coffee shop will watch you stare vacantly at the Norwegian menu, prompt you a few times in Norwegian, and then ask, feigning surprise, "Oh, you don't speak Norwegian, do you?" It may seem stiff, but it's honestly a refreshingly authentic experience. Prices in Bergen are somewhat lower than in Oslo, especially for accommodations, and the city center is easily walkable, so you won't need to shell out for public transportation. Instead, use that cash to experience the surprising amount that such a small city has to offer. Take to the high seas to see why Bergen is called "The Gateway to the Fjords," or splurge on some of the freshest seafood (a lot) of money can buy at the Fish Market. If hiking is more your thing, The Seven Mountains, within which Bergen rests, offer trails to suit all abilities, and views to impress anyone. At the end of the day, you're still a tourist, but being in Bergen can help you forget, for a few days at least.

## ORIENTATION

Downtown Bergen is situated around the main square, **Torgallmenningen,** where you'll find expensive stores and chain restaurants. Just north is Bergen Harbor, where the **Fish Market** and **Tourist Information Center** sit on the east end of the harbor. North of the harbor is the historic **Bryggen district** and **Bergenhus Fortress,** which is the sight of **Rosenkrantz Tower** and Haakon's Hall. Just east of Torgallmenningen is **Byparken,** a large green with walking trails around a lake. The KODE art museums can be found along one side of the park. And to the south is the University of Bergen. The area between the square and the university is a hotspot for student nightlife.

## ESSENTIALS

### GETTING THERE

Bergen Lufthavn, Flesland (BGO) is Bergen's international airport, which receives regular flights from many European cities. From the airport, the easiest way to get to the city center is the Flybussen (www.flybussen. no, NOK 100, NOK 80 student) to Bergen bus station (20min.). The train between Oslo and Bergen, a journey of almost 7hr., is famously one of the most scenic rides in Europe (NOK 950, NOK 713 student). Trains arrive at Bergen Station.

### GETTING AROUND

Bergen is a compact city, and the city center is easily walkable. Most hostels and guesthouses are also centrally located, so public transportation is often unnecessary. Skyss is Bergen's public transportation system, consisting of buses and light rail. Single tickets can be bought in advance (NOK 37), on board (NOK 60), or for periods of 24hr (NOK 95), 7 days (NOK 245), or longer. Tickets can be bought at transportation stops. Bergen Taxi (07000, bergentaxi.no) is the largest taxi company in the city. Rates vary wildly, depending on the day of the week, and the time of day.

### PRACTICAL INFORMATION

**Tourist Offices:** Bergen Tourist Information Center (Strandkaien 3;55 55 20 00; open daily June-Aug 8:30am-10pm, May and Sept 9am-8pm, Oct-Apr M-Sa 9am-4pm).

**Banks/ATMs/Currency Exchange:** You can use a credit or debit card almost everywhere in Bergen, but if you need cash, ATMs, known as Minibanks, can be found on the street and in stores like 7-Eleven in the Fish Market area.

**Currency Exchange:** It's often best to withdraw cash directly from an ATM, but you can change currency at the Bergen Tourist Information Center.

**Post Offices:** Bergen Sentrum Postkontor (Småstrandgaten 3; 91 23 35 11; open M-F 9am-8pm, Sa 9am-6pm).

**Internet:** Free Wi-Fi is widely available around Bergen at cafés, bars, and the Tourist Information Center. Internet is also available at the Bergen Public Library (Strømgaten 6; 55 56 85 00; open M-Th 10am-6pm, F 10am-4pm, Sa 10am-3pm).

**BGLTQ+ Resources:** Bergen Pride (Strandgaten 6; 40 45 65 00; open M-F 9am-3pm www.bergenpride.no).

## EMERGENCY INFORMATION

**Emergency Number:** 112

**Police:** Bergen Sentrum Politistasjon (Allehelgens gate 6; for emergencies call 112, for non-emergencies call 02800).

**US Embassy:** The nearest US Embassy is in Oslo (Morgedalsvegen 36, 0378; 21 30 85 40).

**Hospitals:**
- Haukeland University Hospital (Haukelandsveien 22; for emergencies call 113, for non-emergencies call 05300; open daily 24hr).

**Pharmacies:**
- Apoteket Nordstjernen (55 21 83 84; M-Sa 8am-11pm, Su 1pm-11pm).

# ACCOMMODATIONS

### BERGEN YMCA HOSTEL ($)
Nedre Korskirkeallmenning 4; 556 06 055; www.bergenhostel.com/en; reception open 7am-midnight

If this was an episode of *House Hunters,* Bergen YMCA's selling point would be "Location, location, location!" And it's true, it doesn't get much better than this. It's a two-minute walk to the **Fish Market,** five minutes from **Bryggen,** and less than ten minutes from some of Bergen's best nightlife, all at a price that's hard to beat. Oh yeah, about the price. How is it so low? Well, what Bergen YMCA has in location, it lacks somewhat in amenities. The rooms,

though comfortable enough, are small, so don't expect a hot tub or anything crazy. Overall though, it is indeed fun to stay at the YMCA.
*i Dorms from NOK 215, singles 600 NOK; reservation recommended; 7 nights; BGLTQ+ friendly; wheelchair accessible; Wi-Fi; linens included; lockers available*

### MARKEN GJESTEHUS ($)
Kong Oscars gate 45; 553 14 404; www.marken-gjestehus.com/home; reception open May-Sept daily 9:30am-11pm, Oct-Apr 9:30am-4:30pm

Marken is located a bit farther from the city center, just enough to be in a quiet area while still feeling very much downtown. The building itself shows signs of age (the elevator has an upholstered bench, what?), but the rooms and common spaces are very clean and well-kept. Dorms include storage lockers big enough to hide a body, but outlets are somewhat scarce. If you're arriving late at night after reception is closed, reach out about late check-in before your arrival; through some sort of wizardry, your credit or debit card will then work seamlessly as a key card, so you can pass out on freshly-starched sheets. Goodness, what will they think of next?
*i Dorms from NOK 250, singles NOK 575; reservation recommended; Wi-Fi; linens included; towel rental NOK 20; lockers provided; kitchen*

# SIGHTS
## CULTURE

### 🐟FISH MARKET
Bergen Harbor; hours vary

Never been to an open-air market before? Definitely head over to Bergen's famous Fish Market for a welcoming, if somewhat tame, experience. The atmosphere is busy but relaxed, vendors aren't too pushy, and samples of caviar, reindeer sausage, and a mysterious jam made from cloudberries are plentiful. If you've been saving room in your stomach (and hopefully a big wad of cash) for some of Norway's best fresh fish, you won't be disappointed. Take your pick of salmon, shellfish, and live king crab or lobster, and the vendors will cook it and serve you at a table

### HÅKONSHALLEN (HAAKON'S HALL)
Bergenhus; 479 79 577; www.bymuseet.no/en; open daily summer 10am-4pm, winter noon-3pm

Haakon's Hall is the other major building in the **Bergenhus Fortress** complex, and it's perfect if you're tired of poking around the dingy, cobweb-filled rooms of **Rosenkrantz Tower.** Originally a banquet hall constructed in the thirteenth century, the building suffered damage from several major fires (seems to be a recurring theme in Bergen), and has been restored more than once. The dimly-lit rooms are decorated with colorful tapestries, and the cavernous great hall is set with a high table. Today, Haakon's Hall still hosts official dinners and events, for which the dress code includes battle axes and horned helmets (we think).

*i Admission adult NOK 80, NOK 40 student; guided tours NOK 20; tours at 10am and 2pm from June 24-Aug 15*

### ROSENKRANTZ TOWER
Bergenhus; 479 79 578; www.bymuseet.no/en; open daily summer 9am-4pm, winter noon-3pm

Rosenkrantz Tower is the most visible piece of **Bergenhus Fortress,** sitting proudly at the entrance to **Bergen Harbor** like a shorter, slightly stubbier, less humanoid Statue of Liberty. The tower was originally a thirteenth-century keep, but has expanded since into its present form. Inside, you can tour the whole building starting with the basement, where the dungeon sits empty, except for an original, thirteenth-century electric dehumidifier. From there, climb through the tower's many rooms: guard rooms, bedrooms, chapel rooms, rooms with cannons, you get the point. Learn about the single battle in which Bergenhus Fortress was involved before stepping out onto the roof and taking in views of Bergen and the harbor.

*i Admission NOK 80, NOK 40 student, guided tours NOK 20; tours at 10am*

overlooking the harbor. How's that for farm (er, sea?) to table?

*i Prices vary by stand; wheelchair accessible*

### BRYGGEN
Bergen Harbor

Want to feel cultured without having to set foot in a museum? A walk through Bryggen is your best bet. This historic district on the north side of the harbor is immediately recognizable by its traditional red and yellow wooden buildings and the swarms of tourists walking on the street nearby. The buildings were originally used by traders of the **Hanseatic League** as storehouses. Today, they're mostly shops, where modern merchants loosely adhere to the Hanseatic tradition, peddling not stockfish and cereals, but Norwegian flags and Christmas sweaters. It's not immediately apparent from the main street, but you can walk through the front row of buildings and into the alleyways of Bryggen for more interesting and authentic options, like a moose leather shop.

*i Prices vary by shop; wheelchair accessible*

*and 2pm June 24-Aug 15; no wheelchair accessibility*

## MUSEUMS

### KODE 4
Rasmus Meyers allé; 530 09 704; www.
kodebergen.no/en; open daily 11am-5pm

Art museums are confusing; they're huge, overwhelming, and it's impossible to see everything. Bergen's art museum, KODE, is different. It's composed of four smaller buildings, KODEs 1, 2, 3, and 4 (not a very creative naming scheme for a bunch of art people), each with different galleries and exhibitions, so check the website to pick the best one for you. Each bite-sized museum is easy to walk through in an hour or two. KODE 4 starts off in classic form: lots of oil paintings of landscapes and church figures. But don't worry, the top floor is devoted to contemporary "art" like a box lined with seal teeth and a giant, plush model of the female reproductive system suspended from the ceiling. Avant-garde?

*i Admission NOK 100, NOK 50 student; tour times vary based on exhibit/museum. Check the website for details.; wheelchair accessible*

## OUTDOORS

### ⬛MOUNT ULRIKEN
Open daily 24hr

What's that? Oh, you really like hiking, but you're allergic to cable cars? Good news! For true outdoorsy types, it's possible to walk to the base of Mount Ulriken, though it may take over 45 minutes. There are multiple routes to the top of varying difficulty, and, on clear days, the trails will be packed with active types of all sorts. Once you reach the peak, enjoy panoramic views of Bergen or grab a snack at the summit restaurant. If you still haven't broken a sweat, there are more trails from the cable car station, the king of which is a 13-km haul over to the summit of **Mount Fløyen**. This is a challenging hike, so if you want to attempt it, consider using the cable car after all. You deserve it.

*No wheelchair accessibility*

# FOOD

### ⬛HORN OF AFRICA ($$)
Strandgaten 212; 954 25 250; www.
hornofafrica.no

For almost all of human history, we have eaten with our hands. Why this sudden (in an evolutionary sense) fascination with utensils? Like your My Chemical Romance obsession, it's probably just a phase. Stay ahead of the curve at Horn of Africa, an Ethiopian/Eritrean restaurant that eschews fork and knife in favor of nature's own finely-crafted utensil: your ten fingers. Choose from a selection including sinus-tingling beef tips and buttery chicken wet, and get ready to get down and dirty. The concept of eating with your hands seems pretty self-explanatory, but, just to be sure, the host will demonstrate the nuances of scooping up the spiced meat stews and vegetables with *injure,* a spongy and slightly sour bread that accompanies all entrées.

*i Entrées NOK 150-190, combo platters NOK 215-260, beer NOK 60-70; vegetarian options available; wheelchair accessible*

### ⬛PINGVINEN ($$)
Vaskerelven 14; 556 04 646; www.
pingvinen.no

Pingvinen means "penguin" in Norwegian, and that's just about the only animal you won't find on the menu. This gastropub feels like a low-key bar, with ugly wallpaper on one wall and exposed brick on another, but you won't find nachos and wings here. If you can grab a table, ask for an English menu and choose from potato dumplings with mashed *swede* (a root vegetable, not a jab at Norway's neighbor to the east), wild boar, and even reindeer neck, all prepared to perfection. If you have a bit of extra cash to spend (in the name of cultural immersion, of course), go full-on Norse with a beer from Pingvinen's impressive spread of local brews.

*i Entrées NOK 169-249, beer NOK 80-100; wheelchair accessible*

### TREKRONEREN ($)
Kong Oscars gate 1; hours vary

Bergen doesn't have much of a street food scene, especially outside the Fish Market. Trekroneren is the one, juicy

# BERGEN'S FJORDS

Bergen's nickname, among tourism officials at least, is the Gateway to the Fjords, and it's easy to understand why. One of the best ways to see the fjords up close is to get out on the water yourself, and for this you have many options, from short, hour-long rides in a Zodiac, to 12-hour odysseys involving large catamarans and buses. To get your money's worth, try Rødne's three-hour cruise from Bergen to Mostraumen (NOK 550, daily at 10am and 2pm), which departs from right behind the Fish Market. You'll drive 27 kilometers from Bergen, up to the base of Osterfjorden, through some of Europe's most dramatic terrain. Be sure to grab a spot up front on either deck when the fjord begins to narrow and the music straight out of the Shire starts to play. A clear day is ideal, but there aren't too many of those in Norway so don't be disappointed if it clouds over as you cast off; the fjords have a majesty of their own even when shrouded in fog. No matter the weather, it gets cold out there with the wind and probable rain, so be sure to bring layers! Book at the Tourist Information Center or online at www.rodne.no.

exception. It's a counter-service sausage stand in the heart of downtown, and an establishment in its own right. Select from over ten varieties, from the familiar *bratwurst,* to the slightly enigmatic "wild game" sausage. But nothing can top the **reindeer sausage,** topped with mustard, crispy onions, and lingonberry jam. Somehow it works, okay? Just stay away from Rudolph at the Christmas store for a while. It's still a bit of a sore subject for him.

*i No cover except for special events, drinks from NOK 50; BGLTQ+ friendly*

*i 150g sausage NOK 60, 250g sausage NOK 90; wheelchair accessible*

# NIGHTLIFE

## GARAGE

Christies gate 14; 553 21 980; www. garage.no; open M-F 3pm-3am, Sa 1pm-3am, Su 5pm-1am

Some of Norway's most famous musical exports are in the rock and metal genres, and Garage is the place to tap into that scene. It feels like one of the first venues you perform at in *Guitar Hero*—dim lighting, album covers and old set lists plastered on the walls, and an eclectic crowd composed of middle-aged men trying to relive the glory days and college kids hopelessly lost in the wrong decade. Look out for live shows on the weekends, but, even if there's nothing happening on stage, the bar has a great spread.

*i No cover, beer and shots from NOK 70; BGLTQ+ friendly; wheelchair accessible*

## KVARTERET

Olav Kyrres gate 49; 555 89 910; www. kvarteret.no; open M-W 11:30am-10pm, Th-F 11:30am-3:30am, Sa 2pm-3:30am

If you want to find the best local spots and cheapest drinks in any city, it's never a bad idea to follow the local students. In Bergen, they all head to Kvarteret, the city's student culture house. It's run by student volunteers and attracts young people from both near and far. Drinks are reasonably priced in the warehouse-style bar where you'll probably walk into special events like quiz nights, concerts, wine and cheese shindigs, or poetry readings. If you're bold (or bored) enough to go out on a Monday night, swing by Kvarteret's Mikromandag (Micro-Monday) to try local Norwegian microbrews at reduced prices.

*i No cover except for special events, drinks from NOK 50; BGLTQ+ friendly*

# OSLO

Coverage by **Eric Chin**

Of the three Scandinavian capitals, Oslo is definitely the youngest child. While Stockholm and Copenhagen were busy inventing dynamite and opening the world's best restaurant, Oslo was crashing and burning (literally) with a fair amount of sailing and hiking thrown in the mix. The result is a cultural diversity all its own. Oslo's museums are interesting, but not pretentious; its landmarks are grounded in reality, not extravagant. The river running through the middle of the city separates wealthy, established houses and cultural landmarks from the young, international neighborhoods to the east. And within just a few kilometers of it all are mountains for skiing, fjords, and islands for exploring. All this variety doesn't come cheap, though. Since Oslo isn't Scandinavia's go-to destination for young travelers and backpackers, the hostel scene is sparse and high prices can make it difficult to experience all there is to offer. At the same time, crowds are smaller overall, making it easy to make the most of every museum, sculpture, and restaurant.

## ORIENTATION

Oslo's city center sits right on the **Oslofjord,** into which jut the piers in front of City Hall. Just to the east is the **Opera House,** which is easily the most recognizable building in the city. The main street, **Karl Johans gate,** runs straight through the middle of downtown, from the **Royal Palace** on its eastern end to **Oslo S** and the **Tiger statue** to the west. Along **Karl Johans gate** are landmarks like the National Theater, and the seat of Norway's Parliament. A short bus ride to the west brings you to **Bygdøy,** a large peninsula with beaches, walking and biking trails, and several of Oslo's most famous museums. The **Akerselva River** runs north from the city center, effectively dividing the rest of Oslo in two. To the west are parks and wealthier residential neighborhoods. To the east are younger, more diverse areas that house most of Oslo's nightlife, including **Grønland,** and a little farther north **Grünerløkka,** a veritable hipster's paradise. Far to the northwest is **Holmenkollen,** home to the only steel ski jump in the world.

## ESSENTIALS

### GETTING THERE

Oslo Airport, Gardermoen (Oslo Lufthaven) is Norway's main international airport. The airport is about 50km north of the city itself, and the easiest way get to the city center is the Flytoget Airport Express (20min. to and from Oslo S), which leaves from Oslo Sentralstasjon, better known as Oslo S, the main train station, every 10-20min. (NOK 180, NOK 90 student). Tickets kiosks are located at the airport and Oslo S. The Flybussen also travels between downtown Oslo and Oslo Lufthaven, but the journey is closer to 40min. from Oslo Bus Terminal, which is behind Oslo S (adult NOK 160, NOK 90 student). Trains to other Norwegian cities from Oslo S are operated by NSB (www. nsb.no). SJ also operates express trains between Oslo and Stockholm. The station is open daily 3:45am-1:30am.

### GETTING AROUND

Public transportation in Oslo is operated by Ruter, and utilizes buses, trains, ferries, and the metro. The system is divided into zones, but Zone 1 covers the city center as well as the whole metro service, so it should be enough to get you pretty much anywhere. Tickets can be purchased at stores including Narvesen, 7-Eleven, and at kiosks at some stations (single ticket NOK 33 in advance, NOK 55 onboard). If you plan on using public transportation frequently, consider a 24hr pass (NOK 90) or a 7-day pass (NOK 240). Your ticket is not active until you validate it. When you buy a new ticket, make sure you scan it the first time you use it or it doesn't count. Ticket officials will board random trains or buses and check tickets. The fine for being caught without a valid ticket is NOK 1150 (NOK 950 if paid on the spot).

## PRACTICAL INFORMATION

**Tourist Offices:** The Oslo Visitor Center is located in Østbanehallen, next to Oslo S (81 53 05 55; open May-June daily 9am-6pm, July-Aug M-Sa 8am-7pm, Su 9am-6pm, Sept daily 9am-6pm, Oct-Dec M-Sa 9am-6pm, Su 10am-4pm)

**Banks/ATMs/Currency Exchange:** Credit and debit cards can be used almost everywhere in Oslo, but, if you need cash, currency exchange and ATMs (called "Minibanks") can be found in Oslo S and on Karl Johans gate (Forex Bank: Oslo S; 22 17 22 65; open M-F 7am-9pm, Sa 9am-6pm, Su 10am-5pm).

**Post Offices:** Tollbugata 17; open M-F 7am-5pm

**Internet:** Wi-Fi is widely available in Oslo, both in cafés and restaurants, and in public settings like the Opera House and museums. Some networks may require a code sent via SMS.

**BGLTQ+ Resources:** FRI is the national BGLTQ+ organization in Norway (Tollbugata 24; 23 10 39 39; open M-F 10am-3pm).

## EMERGENCY INFORMATION

**Emergency Number:** 112

**Police:** Grønlandsleiret 44, 0190; 22 66 90 50

**US Embassy:** Morgedalsvegen 36; 21 30 85 40; check no.usembassy.gov for details

**Rape Crisis Center:** DIXI is a free and confidential resource for victims of sexual assault (Arbins gate 1; 22 44 40 50; Weekdays 9am-3pm).

**Hospitals:**
- Oslo Emergency Ward is open daily 24hr (Storgata 40; 113 (emergencies only), 116117 (non-emergencies)).

**Pharmacies:** There are pharmacies all over the city center. Pharmacies are called *apotek* in Norway,
- Jernbanetorvets Apotek (Jernbanetorget 4B; 23 35 81 00; open daily 24hr).
- Apotek 1 (Storgata 40, 22 98 87 20; open daily 24hr).

# ACCOMMODATIONS

### ◢SAGA POSHTEL OSLO ($$)

Kongens gate 7; 231 00 800; www.sagahoteloslocentral.no; reception open 24hr

One of Saga Poshtel Oslo's claims to fame is that it's the first hostel in Oslo to call itself a "poshtel," and it's easy to see why. If you can get past the ridiculous name, you'll find that the poshtel is one of the best accommodations in Oslo. It is a bit pricier than more traditional hostel options, but it's worth every krone. Included in the price are linens, towels, and a breakfast buffet; you'd have to take out a second mortgage to afford an all-you-can-eat, hot breakfast elsewhere in Oslo. The brand new building also has a great location downtown, just a few minutes from the **Opera House, Karl Johans gate,** and **Oslo S.**

*i Dorms from NOK 395; reservation recommended; BGLTQ+ friendly; wheelchair accessible; Wi-Fi; linens included; towels included; laundry facilities NOK 30; free breakfast*

### EKEBERG CAMPING ($$)

Ekebergveien 65; 221 98 568; www.ekebergcamping.no/en; open June-Aug

If you have your heart set on camping but turn up your nose at the anarchy of **Langøyene,** Ekeberg Camping offers a professional, structured option. The campsite has about 600 sites, so you shouldn't have a problem finding a place, even though reservations aren't allowed. Facilities include drinking water, restrooms, and paid showers, but they don't come cheap. By the time you pay for a tent site, snacks, and a shower, you're looking at the price of a hostel.

*Tent for 2 people NOK 200, shower (6min.) NOK 15; reservation recommended; BGLTQ+ friendly; wheelchair accessible;*

### LANGØYENE CAMPING ($)

Langøyene Island

Camping on Langøyene Island is free. That's right, free! But as they say, you get what you pay for. There's no source of clean drinking water on the island and compost-style outhouses may not be your preferred option for restrooms. The house rules are simple enough (yes there are rules; what do you think this is, *Lord of the Flies?*):

clean up after yourself, don't light fires (that hasn't worked out well for Oslo in the past), and don't be an asshole to your fellow campers (paraphrasing, of course). Easy, and as long as you don't mind roughing it a bit, Langøyene has lots to offer, including a nude beach, hiking trails, and easy ferry access to the mainland.

*i* *Free; reservation recommended; BGLTQ+ friendly; wheelchair accessible; no Wi-Fi; bring your own tent, food, and drinking water; accessible via the B4 Ferry, which leaves from City Hall Pier 4*

# SIGHTS
## CULTURE
......................................

### NOBEL PEACE CENTER
Brynjulf Bulls Plass 1; 483 01 000; www.nobelpeacecenter.org/en; open May-Aug daily 10am-6pm, Sept-Apr Tu-Su 10am-6pm

Two interesting facts about the Nobel Peace Prize: it's the only one of the five annual prizes not presented in Sweden and it was established by funds from the invention of arguably un-peaceful dynamite. The **Peace Prize** is awarded each year in Oslo's **City Hall,** just across the street from the Nobel Peace Center. This museum features exhibitions about the most recent laureate as well as about the tumultuous current events worldwide. The heart of the museum is The Nobel Field, an exhibit dedicated to all past laureates. A sea of waist-high lights interspersed with tablets are dedicated to every winner of the Nobel Peace Prize. Occasionally, the ethereal music pauses as an excerpt plays from a **Nobel Lecture.**

*Admission NOK 100, NOK 65 student; tours daily 2pm, 3pm; wheelchair accessible*

### OSLO FREE TOUR
The Tiger, Jernbanetorget; www.freetouroslo.com

Yeah you perked right up when you saw the word "free," right? It's an uncommon term in Scandinavia, but this tour is a gem. The meeting point is the **Tiger statue** next to the Ferris wheel in front of **Oslo S.** From there, your guide will lead you around to all the major landmarks and historical sites in downtown Oslo, including the **Opera House, Akershus Festning,** and **City Hall.** Along the way, you'll hear stories of the devastating fires that forever robbed Oslo of wooden buildings and how a ridiculous royal moved the city center on a whim. Though the whole thing is technically free, you'd have to be stingier than Scrooge not to tip after this two-hour tour.

*i* *Free, though tipping is expected; tours M, Th-Su 10am and 4pm; wheelchair accessible*

### ROYAL PALACE
Slottsplassen 1; www.royalcourt.no; changing of the guard daily at 1:30pm

Among the great palaces of Europe, Oslo's Royal Palace is something of a youngest child. Sure there's a resemblance to Versailles and Buckingham Palace—it stares imposingly down a long gravel drive, has a big statue of a guy on a horse, and is surrounded by guards in funny costumes—but it doesn't take itself too seriously. The gardens are open for sunbathing (though it is allegedly the only park where you can't do so topless), and you barely have to try to get the guards to move. Slottsparken, the large park surrounding the palace, is free, but if you want to see inside, you'll have to pay for a guided tour.

*i* *Park admission free; guided tours adult NOK 135, NOK 105 student; tours daily at noon, 2pm, 2:20pm, 4pm June 24-Aug 17; wheelchair accessible*

## LANDMARKS
......................................

### HOLMENKOLLEN
Kongeveien 5; 229 23 200; www.skiforeningen.no/en/holmenkollen; open Jan-Apr 10am-5pm, May 10am-5pm, June-Aug 9am-8pm, Sept 10am-5pm, Oct-Apr 10am-5pm

Norway has many proud traditions that have stretched back centuries: seafaring, not joining the European Union, and skiing. If you've ever watched the Winter Olympics, you're likely familiar with Norway's dominance on snow, and Holmenkollen, Oslo's ski jump, is where the magic happens. Situated on a high hill, the jump serves as a training ground during the winter and a tourist attraction in the summer, where visitors flock to jump. At the ski museum, learn about the history of skiing. An elevator goes to the top of the jump tower, where you'll find a zip line (expensive) and a viewing platform that looks out over Oslo and the fjord beyond (priceless).

*i* *Ski Museum/jump tower adults NOK 130, NOK 110 student, additional NOK 600 for zip line; wheelchair accessible*

## OPERA HOUSE
Kirsten Flagstads plass 1; 214 22 121; www.operaen.no/en
In a city that was once built mostly of brick in fear of fire, Oslo's Opera House sticks out. Designed to resemble a glacier, the angled marble structure seems to rise right out of the fjord like the real glaciers did millennia ago. But, like the rest of Oslo, it doesn't take itself too seriously; you can walk all over it, literally. The roof is open for visitors, and serves as the perfect place for views of the Oslofjord and the many tourists who continuously get in your pictures.

*i* *Free admission; adult tours NOK 100, NOK 60 student; M-F, Su 1pm, Sa noon; wheelchair accessible*

## MUSEUMS

### 🛶 KON-TIKI MUSEUM
Bygdøynesveien 36, Bygdøy; 230 86 767; www.kon-tiki.no; open daily Jan-Feb 10am-5pm, Mar-May 10am-5pm, June-Aug 9:30am-6pm, Sept-Oct 10am-5pm, Nov-Dec 10am-4pm
The Kon-Tiki Museum follows the journey of Thor Heyerdahl, who sailed ("floated" is more accurate) from Peru to Polynesia in 1947 on a balsa raft. It's a lot like *Moana,* but instead of an intrepid Polynesian girl setting off to fight the evils of the world, the protagonists of Kon-Tiki were six white guys and a parrot who wanted to spite a bunch of ivory-tower academics. The main hall features the original Kon-Tiki raft, along with panels about the expedition itself, from how the food was stored to Thor's fear of water and surprising lack of swimming skills. Downstairs, check out *Ra II,* a boat made of Papyrus reeds that Thor

captained across the Atlantic, because, you know, the Pacific was just too easy.

*i* *Admission NOK 100, NOK 60 student, joint ticket for Kon-Tiki, Fram, and Norwegian Maritime museums adult NOK 270, NOK 100 student; wheelchair accessible*

### 🖼 NATIONAL GALLERY
Universitetsgata 13; 219 82 000; www.nasjonalmuseet.no/en; open Tu-W 10am-6pm, Th 10am-7pm, Sa-Su 11am-5pm
It certainly isn't the prettiest building on the outside (no glass pyramid or marble columns like you'll find at the Louvre or the British Museum), but inside, the National Gallery is a manageable museum with works you'll recognize even if you don't own a beret. Does *The Scream* ring a bell? There's even a bench in front of a cast of *The Thinker,* where you can sit and, well, think. But where the National Gallery really shines is in its organization. It's not a labyrinth of hallways that split in two or lead to dead ends; the rooms are arranged chronologically (and numbered) to show you art from the earliest Greek and Roman sculptures to the movements of Romanticism and Realism, and everything in between.

*Admission adult NOK 100, NOK 50 student, free under 19 and every Th; audio guide NOK 50; wheelchair accessible*

### NORWAY'S RESISTANCE MUSEUM
Akershus Festning; 230 93 138; www.forsvaretsmuseer.no/hjemmefrontmuseet; open June-Aug M-Sa 10am-5pm, Su 11am-5pm, Sept-May M-F 10am-4pm, Sa-Su 11am-4pm
Germany had a habit of invading neutral countries during World War II, and Norway was no exception. The Nazis came knocking in 1940 and, probably enamored with the high standard of living, decided to stay for awhile. As Norway's Resistance Museum shows, though, their occupation was anything but easy. The museum details every bit of Norway's involvement in the war, from life during the five-year German occupation, to the inner workings of the Norwegian resistance movement. Check out the huge collection of news clippings, artifacts (including the remains of an actual Tallboy dropped by the Allies), and painstakingly constructed dioramas of specific

battles. The exhibit is fairly short, but packed with information on every facet of the war.

*i* Admission NOK 60, NOK 30 student; wheelchair accessible

## OUTDOORS

### OSLO SOMMERPARK

Tryvannsveien 64; 221 43 610; www. oslosommerpark.no; hours change several times over the course of the summer; be sure to check the website

Not content to sit at the top of **Holmenkollen** and just look at the view, but too cheap to crack open the piggy bank for the zip line? Head north on the 1 train to Oslo Sommerpark instead. It's a huge aerial ropes course with enough elements and routes to make Tarzan jealous. Climb as high as 20 meters into the treetops on a combination of bridges, ladders, and steel cables before swinging from one tree to the next on a network of zip lines. This is a must for any adventure-seeker looking to ditch the city and remember what those opposable thumbs were for in the first place.

*i* Admission NOK 375; last entry 2hr. before closing; wheelchair accessible

### VIKING BIKING

Nedre Slottsgate 4; 412 66 496; www. vikingbikingoslo.com; open daily 9:30am-6pm

Biking is always an excellent option for seeing a lot of city in minimal time, but honestly, city bikes are the worst! How the hell are you supposed to do anything fun with just one gear? Fortunately, the aptly/ unfortunately named Viking Biking has you covered. Full-day (9:30am-6pm) rentals for students start at just NOK 140 (NOK 160 for adults) for a real bike (with gears!), and a horned helmet. Not kidding. Wander the city and the surrounding area on your own, or, if you need a little more structure in your life, consider joining one of Viking Biking's

guided bike tours, which include a variety of routes.

*i* Guided tours (including rental) adult from NOK 350, NOK 280 student; check website for guided tour times; limited wheelchair accessibility

## FOOD

### ⬛MATHALLEN ($)

Vulkan 5; 400 01 209; www.mathallenoslo. no/en; open Tu-W 10am-7pm, Th-F 10am-8pm, Sa 10am-7pm, Su 11am-6pm

"Mathallen" translates to "food hall," and that could not be more accurate. Think Boston's Faneuil Hall or Philadelphia's Reading Terminal Market, then Scandinavianize it. The real treat is inside Mathallen; restaurants run the gamut from sushi stands to microbreweries, and market stalls sell fresh fish and Scandinavian sausages and jams (look out for free samples). Sitting down for a full meal can get pricey (surprise!), but there are plenty of great options for under NOK 100, like Ma Poule's duck confit sandwich (NOK 89), or the pulled chicken from Strangeriet (NOK 85).

*i* Prices vary, sit-down meal NOK 100-200; vegetarian, vegan, and gluten-free options available; wheelchair accessible

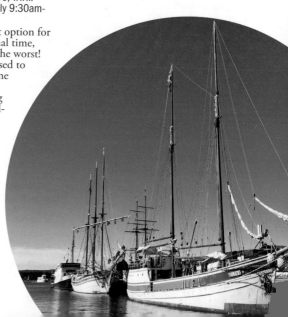

## TUNCO ($$)

Bjerregaards gate 2a; 400 98 690; www.tunco.no; open M-F 11:30am-10pm, Sa-Su 1pm-10pm

It's always tough to find a restaurant with quality food and a great atmosphere at a reasonable price, but TUNCO does it all and adds a global awareness that most restaurants don't. This new concept restaurant serves up delicious woks, with a selection of proteins and noodles large enough to satisfy even the pickiest eater. Pick a sauce to match your spice tolerance, but what will really give you the warm and fuzzies is TUNCO's "Meal for Meal" program. For every meal purchased, TUNCO donates money to charity to give a meal to a child in need. It's like the TOMS of the Oslo food scene, and it's sure to become just as popular.

*i* Entrées NOK 150, beer from NOK 79; vegetarian, vegan, and gluten-free options available; wheelchair accessible; card only

## ILLEGAL BURGER ($$)

Møllergata 23; 222 03 302; open M-Th 2pm-11pm, F-Sa 2pm-1am, Su 2pm-10pm

Illegal Burger is exactly the kind of place you want to go when you just can't take another day of the Scandinavia traveler's diet of herring, grocery store sushi, and regret. The burgers are juicy and generously portioned, the prices reasonable (or at least competitive), and the menu full of teenage angst (featuring a tomato wearing a bandit mask). Keep it simple with the Cheese Royale, or branch out with the Hot Mama (barbecue sauce and jalapeños) or the Illegal Spessial (chorizo and guacamole). Seating is limited, but you can still sit under the watchful gaze of a David Bowie poster while you wait for takeaway.

*i* Single burgers NOK 100, double burgers NOK 140, potatoes NOK 42; vegetarian, vegan, and gluten-free options available; no wheelchair accessibility

## PASTEL DE NATA ($)

Kongens gate 10; www.pasteldenata.no; open M-F 11am-6:30pm, Sa-Su 11am-4:30pm

Your first instinct when you see the price for individual pastries at Pastel de Nata (NOK 35) will be to run as fast as you can, but don't be so hasty.

The coffee prices are some of the best around (NOK 20-30), and for a reasonable NOK 55, you can get a coffee and pastry of your choice. That, and you get to hang out in the airy café for a while. The pastries are also top-notch, especially their namesake *pastel de nata,* a traditional Portuguese egg tart.

*i* Pastries NOK 35, coffee/espresso drinks NOK 20-30; wheelchair accessible

# NIGHTLIFE

## CROWBAR AND BRYGGERI

Torggata 32; 213 86 757; www.crowbryggeri.com; open M-F 3pm-3am, Sa 1pm-3am

No need to lock up your valuables; Crowbar has nothing to do with armed robbery. It's a bar and microbrewery in Grünerløkka with a slightly wacky theme: crows. The beer is excellent in terms of taste, variety, and naming (try the "Yellow Ferrari" or the 3.7% ABV "Featherweight"), but Crowbar isn't just for middle-aged guys with a knack for misusing the word "hoppy." It's the kind of place where the bartender drinks kombucha, and it attracts a young crowd to match. The multi-floor venue is packed on the weekends, both downstairs at the bar and upstairs where the kitchen serves all your drunk favorites like kebab wraps, quesadillas, and pork cracklings.

*i* Beer NOK 80-100; BGLTQ+ friendly; wheelchair accessible; age limit 23 F-Sa

## SCHOUSKJELLEREN MIKROBRYGGERI

Trondheimsveien 2; 213 83 930; www.schouskjelleren.no; open M-Tu 4pm-1am, W-Th 4pm-2am, F 3pm-3:30am, Sa 4pm-midnight

Sure, Coors is "The Banquet Beer," and PBR must have won that blue ribbon for something, but haven't you ever wondered what it's like to try beer that you can't buy in a 30-pack? Schouskjelleren, easily one of Oslo's best microbreweries, is your place. The bartenders know every hop and spice that goes into the selection of brews on tap. To top it all off, the bar is in a vaulted brick cellar that feels like a Viking banquet hall, complete with stained glass windows and high-backed booths. There really is something for everyone here, from IPAs like "Empress of India" and "No Means No," to stouts so rich they taste like chocolate syrup. Just don't try to pronounce the name; nobody can help you with that.

*i Draft beers NOK 80-100; BGLTQ+ friendly; no wheelchair accessibility*

## DATTERA TIL HAGEN

Grønland 10; 221 71 861; www.dattera. no; open M 11am-midnight, Tu-W 11am-1am, Th 11am-2am, F-Sa 11am-3am, Su noon-midnight

Club going up on a Tuesday? Probably not in Oslo, but, if it were, it would definitely be this one. Located in the young, diverse Grønland neighborhood, Dattera is a favorite among locals and tourists alike. The two floors and courtyard provide something for everyone, regardless of whether you'd prefer to get (maybe a bit too) cozy on the upstairs dance floor in front of a live DJ or sit in the courtyard to marvel at the sea of Norwegian man buns.

*i Cover NOK 10, drinks from NOK 80; BGLTQ+ friendly; wheelchair accessible*

# NORWAY ESSENTIALS

## VISAS

Norway is not part of the European Union, but it is part of the Schengen Area, so US citizens can stay in Norway for up to 90 days without a visa.

## MONEY

**Tipping:** Norway's currency is the Norwegian krona, officially abbreviated NOK or kr. Tipping in Norway is not usually expected or required, though if you have received excellent service in a restaurant, it is not uncommon to round the bill to the nearest NOK 10, or leave a tip of 6-10%.

**Taxes:** Norway's standard VAT rate is an eye-popping 25%, with a few patently Norwegian exceptions like raw fish, which is taxed at only 11.11%. However, tax is included in all advertised prices. Pro-tip: Some souvenir shops in Norway, specifically those with Global Blue or Tax Free Worldwide stickers, will refund the VAT for goods leaving the country with you. The protocol can vary, so ask at the store for instructions to claim your refund.

## SAFETY AND HEALTH

**Alcohol:** The legal drinking age is 18 for beverages below 22% ABV and 20 for anything higher. Drinking in public is technically illegal, but it's not uncommon to see beer and wine outside, especially in parks. Grocery stores only sell alcoholic beverages below 4.75% ABV; everything else must be bought from government-owned liquor stores called *Vinmonopolet*. Norway's taxes on alcohol are extremely high.

**Weather/Climate:** As you may have noticed, Norway is pretty far north. Much of the northern region lies within the Arctic Circle, leading to long hours of daylight during the summer and seemingly endless night during the winter, even in southern cities like Bergen and Oslo.

**BGLTQ+ Travel:** Like most of Scandinavia, Norway is very liberal in regard to BGLTQ+ rights. In 1981, Norway became the first country in the world to explicitly ban discrimination in places of employment based on sexual orientation, and that momentum can still be felt today.

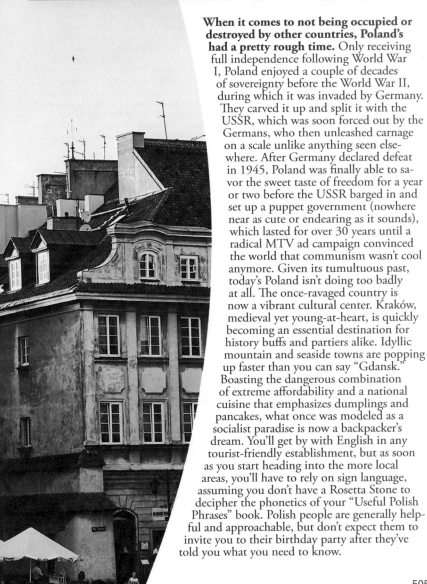

# POLAND

**When it comes to not being occupied or destroyed by other countries, Poland's had a pretty rough time.** Only receiving full independence following World War I, Poland enjoyed a couple of decades of sovereignty before the World War II, during which it was invaded by Germany. They carved it up and split it with the USSR, which was soon forced out by the Germans, who then unleashed carnage on a scale unlike anything seen elsewhere. After Germany declared defeat in 1945, Poland was finally able to savor the sweet taste of freedom for a year or two before the USSR barged in and set up a puppet government (nowhere near as cute or endearing as it sounds), which lasted for over 30 years until a radical MTV ad campaign convinced the world that communism wasn't cool anymore. Given its tumultuous past, today's Poland isn't doing too badly at all. The once-ravaged country is now a vibrant cultural center. Kraków, medieval yet young-at-heart, is quickly becoming an essential destination for history buffs and partiers alike. Idyllic mountain and seaside towns are popping up faster than you can say "Gdansk." Boasting the dangerous combination of extreme affordability and a national cuisine that emphasizes dumplings and pancakes, what once was modeled as a socialist paradise is now a backpacker's dream. You'll get by with English in any tourist-friendly establishment, but as soon as you start heading into the more local areas, you'll have to rely on sign language, assuming you don't have a Rosetta Stone to decipher the phonetics of your "Useful Polish Phrases" book. Polish people are generally helpful and approachable, but don't expect them to invite you to their birthday party after they've told you what you need to know.

# GDANSK

Coverage by **Nicholas Grundlingh**

When naming this town, did the King of Poland accidentally add a "g" at the start and an "s" near the end? Probably not! Nonetheless, if you're into medieval streets, World War II history, Soviet-era Poland, seafood, Ferris wheels, and using words like "dank," you'll undoubtedly find Gdansk to be very dank, indeed. A small naval town founded in the tenth century, Gdansk became decisively less boring when its Westerplatte region witnessed the first shots of WWII. In the wake of the war and during the dawn of communism, large shipyards were established in the town. Shipyard strikes in the 70s and 80s were pivotal to the Polish independence movement and the collapse of the Eastern bloc. The town looks back upon these events with its Museum of the Second World War and European Solidarity Center, both of which are undoubtedly some of the finest museums in Europe. Today, Gdansk's historic Old Town is teeming with tourists, particularly young students and elderly tour groups. But that's not to say it lacks excitement. Bars and clubs are everywhere, and the nearby town of Sopot boasts a vibrant nightlife scene as well. The town also hosts many music and theater festivals on an annual basis, so make sure you keep an eye on a local events calendar, unless you deliberately want to look like an uncultured yahoo.

## ORIENTATION

Unless you traveled via a pirate ship or pirated a ship of your own, your first taste of this idyllic, seaside town will be its unimpressive and landlocked central railway and bus station. But before you become disappointed and catch the next train out, fear not—the medieval **Old Town,** the one plastered across Polish travel brochures, is just a 10-minute walk away. Thankfully, this will be one of longest walks during your stay. With the exception of a few museums and landmarks, you'll find everything you need in the Old Town. **Ul. Piwna** and **ul. Dulga,** lined with cafés and restaurants, are the town's busiest streets. On the former, you'll find the tallest structure in the region, **St. Mary's Basilica,** and along the latter, you'll run into **Fontana di Neptune,** Gdansk's own Trevi fountain (much less impressive but just as much of a source of pride). Both roads, among many others, will lead you to the harbor front, which contains the expected number of seafood restaurants as well as Gdansk's unofficial symbol, the Crane. In between the Old Town and the more modern and residential area across the harbor lies an island, which is only significant thanks to its sizable Ferris wheel. Buses that run along **ul. Olawska,** which marks the end of the Old Town, will take you to the **Westerplatte ruins** as well as the nearby towns of **Sopot** and **Gdynia.**

## ESSENTIALS

### GETTING THERE

Trains and buses arrive at Gdansk Glowny station, a 15min. walk from the center of the Old Town. From the station, Bus #111 or Trams #8 or 9 will take you along the western and southern perimeters of the Old Town. From any point on the perimeter, it's a 7min. walk to St. Mary's Basilica, which serves as the center of the Old Town. Planes arrive at Gdansk Lech Walesa Airport, 15km (9mi.) west of the Old Town. Trains from the airport travel to Gdansk Glowny (3.80zł),

taking around 30min. A taxi from the airport costs around 60zł.

### GETTING AROUND

If you're spending most of your time in and around the Old Town, you should be able to walk to any given destination in less than 15min. But, if you're choosing to explore the tri-city area, then Gdansk's public transport system will be more than adequate. The public transport system is comprised of buses and trams, respectively known as the ZTM and ZKM, and serves the tri-city area of Gdansk, Sopot, and Gydnia. Google Maps hasn't yet incorporated the local public transport into their navigation system, but this website (www.jakdojade.pl/trojmiasto/trasa) allows you to select a start point and destination and shows you the best bus/tram route to take. The ticket options include: single (3.20zł), single on night or fast services (4.20zł), 1hr (3.80zł), 1hr on night or fast services (4.80zł), and 24hr (13zł). Local trains run between the three cities every 15min. from 5am-7pm, and less frequently from 7pm until 4am. Prices range from 4.20zł to 6.20zł. Be sure to validate your tickets in the yellow boxes. Plainclothes police officers will fine you if you're caught traveling without a validated ticket. Elite Airport, Hallo, Monte, and Neptun are reliable taxi companies.

## PRACTICAL INFORMATION

**Tourist Offices:** The three main tourist information centers are found in ul. Długa (Długi Targ 28/29, 58 301 43 55; open daily summer 9am-7pm, winter 9am-5pm). The official tourism site is www.visitgdansk.com.

**Banks/ATMs/Currency Exchange:** ATMs can be found all around the Old Town. ING Bank branches are located inside Madison Shopping Gallery (Rajska 10; 571 203 119; open M-Sa 9am-9pm, Su 10am-8pm). The Old Town is full of currency exchanges, known as "kantors." We recommend using ATMs, but if you have to exchange cash, avoid changing at airports, any exchanges labeled "change" instead of "kantor," and any exchanges that remain open until late. A safe option is the Poczta Polska post office that also exchanges money, located a third of the way down Ul. Długa (Długa 23/28; 58 301 80 49; open daily 24hr).

**Post Offices**: Poczta Polska (Ul. Długa 23/28; 58 301 80 49; open daily 24hr).

**Internet:** Most cafés, restaurants, and fast food restaurants have free Wi-Fi.

**BGLTQ+ Resources:** Although Poland's government doesn't offer many legal rights and protections for the BGLTQ+ community, the people of Gdansk are generally open-minded and all the accommodations and nightlife locations listed are BGLTQ+ friendly. Here are some resources.
- Campaign Against Homophobia

Warsaw Headquarters (22 423 64 38).
- Poland-wide BGLTQ+ helpline Lambda Warszawa (22 628 52 22; open M 6pm-10pm, Tu 6pm-9pm, W 6pm-10pm, Th 6pm-10pm, Tu, F 6-9pm).

## EMERGENCY INFORMATION

**Emergency Number:** 112; Poland Tourist Emergency Hotline (22 278 77 77, 608 599 999; open daily Oct-May 8am-6pm, Jun-Sept 8am-10pm).

**Police:** 997; headquarters (ul. Nowe Ogrody 27; 58 321 62 22; open daily 24hr).

**US Embassy:** The nearest US Embassy is in Warsaw (22 504 2000; open M-F 8:30am-5pm).

**Rape Crisis Center:** The Feminoteka Foundation (helpline: 731 731 551; admin: 720 908 974; open Tu-Th 1pm-7pm).

**Hospitals:**
- Copernicus Podimiot Leczniczy (Copernicus Hospital) (Nowe Ogrody 1-6; 58 764 01 00; open daily 24hr).
- Uniwersyteckie Centrum Kliniczne (University Clinical Center) (Dębinki 7; 58 727 05 05; open daily 24hr).

**Pharmacies:** Pharmacies are identifiable by the green cross on or protruding from their façade, and are known as *aptekas*. Most operate daily from around 8am-8pm.
- Apteka Dr. Max (Pańska 6; 58 778 90 37; open M-F 8am-8pm, Sa 9am-4pm).
- Apteka-Rajska (Rajska 10; 58 304 98 93, open M-Sa 9am-9pm, Su 10am-8pm).

# ACCOMMODATIONS

### 🏠MIDTOWN HOSTEL ($)
Podwale Staromiejskie 105/106/1; 587 105 057; www.midtownhostel.pl; reception open 24hr

Small and quaint. Simple but elegant. Quiet and clean. Modern yet homey. Any of these descriptions could easily apply to Midtown Hostel, and goddamn it, we're gonna apply them! Tucked just inside the Old Town, the hostel makes what's already a painless place to navigate even more so. With only eight rooms, the largest of which is a six person dorm, it's also a reprieve from the crowded and busy streets surrounding it. What's more, each of the dorms include a sink inside the room, which makes getting up in the middle of the night to fill up your water balloons that much less of an ordeal.

*i* *Dorms from 45 zł, doubles from 115 zł; reservation recommended; BGLTQ+ friendly; no wheelchair accessibility; Wi-Fi; reservation recommended; linens included; laundry facilities available*

### GRAND HOSTEL ($)

Świętojańska 43/44; 666 061 350; www. grandhostel.pl; reception open 24hr

Even the world's most brilliant city planner Andrés Duany, of Miami, couldn't have found a better location for Grand Hostel. It's not only right on the harbor front, but also within a very impressive long-jump's distance of the town's iconic and profoundly peculiar **Crane.** The hostel's décor matches its nautical location. Each room is painted in a baby blue and includes nice touches like posters of naval designs and an old sea captain who could tell you a tale or two about the South China Sea. If you're looking for a place to stay in Gdansk, Grand Hostel— with a buffet breakfast included as well as a small art gallery and bar forthcoming—is a pretty unbeatable choice.

*i* *Dorms from 39 zł, doubles from 120 zł, singles from 120 zł; reservation recommended; BGLTQ+ friendly; no wheelchair accessibility; Wi-Fi; linens included; laundry facilities available*

# SIGHTS

## CULTURE

### GDANSK SHAKESPEARE THEATRE

Wojciecha Bogusławskiego 1; 583 510 101; www.teatrszekspirowski.pl

As much a historical site as it is an architectural landmark, the Gdansk Shakespeare Theatre stands on the same site that hosted traveling English theater troupes in the seventeenth century. In fact, it was the only Shakespearean theater outside of England in existence at the time. Four hundred or so years later, this 95 million zł fortress-like structure is home to one of the most renowned Shakespeare festivals in the world, held in the first week of August. But when it's not telling the tales of star-crossed lovers or a brooding prince that wants to get with his mom, it's a popular local theater and concert space. Even if you can't make a show, the theatre offers tours in English every day at 3pm.

*i* *Tours 14 zł, 8zł reduced; check website for upcoming events and tickets; wheelchair accessible*

### MARKET HALL

pl. Dominikański 1; 583 463 133; www. teatrszekspirowski.pl; open M-F 9am-6pm, Sa 9am-5pm

An old Dominican monastery turned railway station turned food and clothing market, Market Hall is a wonderland of all things good and cheap. Inside, you'll find food on the first floor—meats, cheeses, chocolates, etc.—and clothing—mostly women's—on the second. However, the **outdoor fresh produce** area is where the magic really happens. Blueberries, strawberries, cherries, kiwis and nectarines—you name it and some vendor will inevitably be selling it, and you can almost guarantee that "it" will be fresh, juicy, and delicious. Because most vendors can't speak English, your purchases will probably be made through pointing and typing numbers into a calculator, but this isn't too inconvenient, especially given the odd satisfaction you'll get from looking at your too-good-to-be-true prices on a digital screen.

*i* *Prices vary by stand; limited wheelchair accessibility*

## LANDMARKS

### ST. MARY'S BASILICA AND NEPTUNE'S FOUNTAIN

Podkramarska 5; 583 013 982; www. bazylikamariacka.gdansk.pl; open M-Sa 8:30am-6:30pm, Su 11-noon, 1pm-6:30pm

Found on neighboring streets, St. Mary's Basilica and Neptune's Fountain, together with the **Crane,** make up the "Terrific Trio of Gdansk"—a term we just made up for the town's famous landmarks. The tallest structure in the tri-city area,

**St. Mary's Basilica** is particularly impressive. The view from the top is absolutely breathtaking, not that you'll have much breath left after climbing 400-odd steps. The church's astronomical clock is also a sight to behold, although not for its creator, whose eyes were gouged out so he'd never be able to design a better clock (yikes!). The nearby Neptune Fountain is the center of **Długi Targ**, or the Long Market.

*i* Church admission 4 zł, 2 zł reduced, viewing tower admission 8 zł, 4zł reduced; limited wheelchair accessibility

### ZURAW (CRANE)
Szeroka 67/68; 583 016 938; www. en.nmm.pl/crane; museum open Tu-Su 10pm-4pm

Zuraw, or the Crane, is probably Gdansk's most famous landmark. At the very least, it's certainly its weirdest. Resembling a gigantic bat perched along the harbor front, the Crane looms over passersby, giving it a rather sinister feel that belies its actual history and purpose. Built in the middle of the fifteenth century, the Crane, originally the largest of its kind in the world, used to transfer cargo to and from ships but today houses the **Polish Maritime Museum.** The museum's exhibits are exclusively in Polish, but if you fancy checking out the inside of the crane, the 8 zł entrance fee isn't anything to lose sleep over.

*i* Free to observe, museum admission 8 zł, reduced 4 zł; limited wheelchair accessibility

## MUSEUMS
......................................

### EUROPEAN SOLIDARITY CENTER AND MONUMENT TO THE FALLEN SHIPYARD WORKERS OF 1970
pl. Solidarności 1; 587 724 112; www.ecs.gda.pl; open daily winter 10am-5pm, summer 10am-7pm

Before you reach the European Solidarity Center, you'll come across a statue of three enormous crosses with anchors attached to each of their intersections. You'll quickly discover that the edifice before you is in fact the Monument to the Fallen Shipyard Workers of 1970, but many questions

will continue to linger. *Who were the workers? How did they fall? Why did they fall?* If you walk towards the huge rust-colored structure behind it, all these questions (and more) will be answered. The European Solidarity Center focuses on Poland under communist rule and the resistance movement that eventually led to the country's liberation. Its immersive exhibits are remarkably well put-together, engaging you in a subject that you likely knew or cared little about beforehand.

*i* Admission 20 zł, 15 zł reduced; wheelchair accessible

### MUSEUM OF THE SECOND WORLD WAR
pl. Władysława Bartoszewskiego 1; 587 600 960; www.muzeum1939.pl; open Tu-Su 10am-7pm

You'd need a museum the size of a football stadium to even begin to provide a comprehensive overview of World War II. Luckily, Gdansk has one. Covering everything, and we mean everything, from the end of the First World War to the post-WWII climate that ushered in the Cold War, the museum, despite its expansive focus, still manages to shine a light on how the war affected both Poland and Gdansk. The museum is so chock-full of highlights that it's almost futile to single out any specific ones. However, all we can say is that the two to three

hours you'll spend here will probably be the some of the best you've spent inside a museum ever.

*i* *Admission 23 zł, 16 zł reduced, audio guides 5 zł (recommended); last entry 2hr. before closing; wheelchair accessible*

# FOOD

### ◪NOVA PIEROGOVA ($$)

Szafarnia 6; 516 414 200; open daily noon-10pm

What dumplings are to China, *pierogis* are to Poland, which is pretty obvious considering *pierogis* are just traditional Polish dumplings. You'll see them on the menu at just about any Polish restaurant, but it'll be tough to find a place that does them better than Nova Pierogova. Nestled on the harbor front on the less historic side of town, the nautical-style restaurant specializes in an exhaustive range of delectable meat and vegetarian *pierogi*. Ten *pierogis* will be more than enough to fill you up, which means you'll somehow need to find some extra stomach space for the sweet varietals. We can't stress how important this is—the **apple and cinnamon pierogi** was one of the best desserts we've had in Europe.

*i* *6 pierogi 16-19 zł, 12 pierogi 18-32 zł; vegetarian options available; wheelchair accessible*

### ◪TURYSTYCZNY BAR MLECZNY ($)

Szeroka 8/10; 583016013; www.barturystyczny.pl; open M-F 8am-6pm, Sa-Su 9am-5pm

Of all the corrupting effects *A Clockwork Orange* has wrought upon society, the worst is undoubtedly the perception that a milk bar is a bar that specializes in milk, when, in reality, it's a Soviet-era cafeteria-style restaurant that specializes in traditional Polish cuisine. And while some may find the idea of a commie canteen unappealing, it's perhaps the most cherished kind of culinary institution in Poland. Once you reach the front, point at the menu until the old Polish woman behind the counter understands your order. After having paid, rejoice that your wallet is (at most) only 14 zł lighter.

Besides having your country destroyed by Germany and the USSR, visiting a milk bar is the quintessential Polish experience.

*i* *Entrées 6-14 zł; vegetarian options available; wheelchair accessible*

### ORIGINAL BURGER ($)

Długa 47/49; 583 067 763; www.original-burger.pl; open M-W 12:30pm-11pm, Th-Sa 12:30pm-12:30am, Su 12:30pm-11pm

When you tire of Gdansk's delicious, but relentless assault of meat, potatoes, and *pierogis,* Original Burger will welcome you with open arms and big, juicy burgers. Located on the town's main street, **ul. Długa,** the restaurant is an Eastern European fantasy of what a typical American burger joint would look like. Movie posters and LP sleeves plaster every inch of wall space and the menu itself is styled as a vinyl record. Original Burger radiates a certain charm, which is also in no small part due to the deathly comfortable leather car seats scattered around the inside.

*i* *Burger 18-27 zł, burger and beer combo 25 zł; vegetarian options available; wheelchair accessible*

# NIGHTLIFE

### ◪PUB LAWENDOWA

Lawendowa 8; 531 194 277; www.lawendowa8.ontap.pl; open M-W 3pm-1am, Th 3pm-2am, F-Sa 3pm-3am, Su 3pm-1am

Pub Lawendowa doesn't look too different from your average "cool" bar. It's got gritty exposed brick walls, David Bowie blasting out of the speakers, and an arcade machine—the holy trinity of hip. It undoubtedly fits a certain aesthetic, especially with its emphasis on craft beer, but it isn't necessarily a place you'll remember based on looks alone. However, who needs looks when you've got the kind of drinks and service that'll make folks weak at the knees. The range of craft beers on tap is stellar, and if you're having any trouble deciding what to drink, your bartender will go out of their way to ensure that you make the right choice. *

*i* *Beers 6-21 zł; BGLTQ+ friendly*

## BUNKIER CLUB

Olejarna 3; 531 711 207; www.bunk-ierclub.pl; open M-Th 7pm-1am, F-Sa 7pm-5am, Su 7pm-1am

An old air-raid shelter built in 1942, Bunkier Club, from the outside, is a hulking concrete monolith. However, once you waltz through the entrance, paying the bouncers nothing except a courteous smile (there is no cover fee), you'll discover five whole floors of madness that would give any military general worth their salt a heart attack.

The venue plays your typical Top-40 fare with a Euro trash banger slipped into the mix every now and again, and its general accessibility attracts all kinds of people. Wander around the space and you'll find decorative motorcycles, tables set up inside prison cells, and numerous sculptures of naked women's torsos. However, on weekend nights, the club gets so full that you might not have the luxury of doing so.

*i* No cover, beer 6.5-12 zł, spirits 10-12 zł; BGLTQ+ friendly

# KRAKOW

Coverage by **Nicholas Grundlingh**

Your grandmother visits Kraków for the medieval architecture. Your grandfather? For the Wawel Castle and its medieval history. Your UNESCO World Heritage Site-obsessed sister? She can't wait to check out the Wieliczka Salt Mine. Your brooding teenage cousin who believes the only salvation in life is art? He should be left at the hostel so you can enjoy the city's numerous galleries and museums in peace. Kraków, as small as it seems, has something to offer everyone. If you're into your facts and figures, you'll find yourself astonished that Kraków was named after a lowly peasant who slayed a fearsome dragon. And if you're a fan of myths and legends, you won't help but be amazed that Kraków once served as the Polish capital back when kings ruled and peasants drooled—a period that most historians agree ranges from the fourteenth to seventeenth century. The city, and the Old Town in particular, is populated with all kinds of historic landmarks, such as the world's oldest shopping mall (in Main Market Square), Europe's largest golden altar (found in St Mary's Basilica), and Poland's only fire-breathing dragon (the Wawel Dragon Statue). Auschwitz-Birkenau, the largest of the former Nazi concentration camps, lies an hour and a half outside of Kraków, and Schindler's Factory can be found in the city's Podgórze district. Widely regarded as the new Prague, Kraków hasn't been this hot since the days of that fearsome dragon.

## ORIENTATION

If ye wish to elude the mighty **Wawel dragon,** harken here! Just kidding, there's no such thing. But getting lost in Kraków is just as bad as being incinerated and then having each limb ripped off by a pair of razor-sharp dragon fangs. You need to be familiar with two areas, the medieval **Stare Miasto** (Old Town) and the more rugged and hip **Kazimierz district.** The Old Town is bound by a ring made of grass called **Planty Park.** In the center, you'll find the **Main Market Square.** A walk down **ul. Grodzka** will lead you to **Wawel Castle.** A tram line, which borders the east side of Planty Park, will take you into Kazimierz, either via **Stradomska** or **Starowiślna,** the latter of which is closer to the **Jewish Quarter.** In between these two streets lies **Plac Nowy**—a hotbed of bars and restaurants. **Schindler's Factory** and the **Museum of Contemporary Art** both share the same complex and are located across the river from Kazimierz in the **Podgórze/Zabłocie district.** Northeast of the Old Town, **Kraków Główny**—the main railway and bus station—awaits, ready to transport you out of the city to the **Wieliczka Salt Mine** (by train) or **Auschwitz** (preferably by bus).

# ESSENTIALS

## GETTING THERE

Kraków Airport is 15km (9mi.) west of the city, and trains run every 30min. from 4am-midnight from the airport to Kraków Glowny, the main train and bus station, which is a 10min. walk north of the Old Town. The journey is 17min., and tickets (9zł) can be purchased on the platform or on-board. Buses #208 and 252, and night bus #902 (4zł) run from the airport to the city center and take around 40min. If you're traveling to Kraków by bus or train, you will arrive in Kraków Glowny. The bus terminal is on the east side of the station, and you should exit on the west side to walk to the Old Town.

## GETTING AROUND

Kraków's public transport system consists of buses and trams. Regular service runs from 5am-11pm, with night buses and trams continuing less frequently afterwards. You can plan your journeys using www.jakdojade.pl/Krakow/trasa. 20min. (2.80zł), 40min. (3.80zł), and 1hr. (5 zł) tickets are available, as well as 24hr (15zł), 48hr (24zł), 72hr (36zł), and 7-day (48zł) options. Tickets can be purchased at bus and tram stops, and 1hr. tickets can be purchased from the driver. Tickets must be validated on-board, and inspectors will fine you if they find you have not done so. No public transport runs within the Old Town, but the area is very walkable and can be crossed by foot in about 20min. Trains to the Wiezlecka Salt Mine and buses to Auschwitz-Birkenau run from Kraków Glowny. Train tickets for the Salt Mine can be purchased at ticket machines or onboard the trains, which means you do not need to queue in line for domestic tickets.

## PRACTICAL INFORMATION

**Tourist Offices:** InfoKraków is the official city information network run by Kraków (hotline 124 320 060; open daily 9am-5pm), with five information centers in the Old Town (ul. Św. Jana 2; open daily 9am-7pm).

**Banks/ATMs/Currency Exchange:** ATMs are found throughout the city,

especially in the Old Town. In the city, currency exchanges are known as "kantors," some of which give better rates than ATM machines. Avoid kantors with English names, such as Western Union and Interchange, and those in touristy areas, such as the Old Town Square and ul. Florianska. Kantors along ul. Slawkowska usually provide reasonable rates.

**Post Offices:** The main office is just outside the eastern perimeter of the Old Town (Westerplatte 20; 12 421 44 89; open M-F 8am-8:30pm, Sa 8am-3pm).

**Internet:** Most cafés, restaurants, hostels, and fast food restaurants provide free Wi-Fi. Public libraries, identifiable by the phrase "Biblioteki Publicznej," also provide free Wi-Fi. The Arteteka Wojewódzkiej public library (Józefa Szujskiego; 12 375 21 40; open M-F 10am-7pm, Sa 11:30am-7pm, Su 10am-4pm).

**BGLTQ+ Resources:** Although Poland's government doesn't offer many legal rights and protections for the BGLTQ+ community, Kraków is generally considered an BGLTQ+ friendly city. Here are some resources:

- The Campaign Against Homophobia can be reached for any BGLTQ+ queries (22 423 64 38) and provides a list of therapists in Kraków online (kph.org.pl/pomoc/pomoc-psycho-logiczna).
- Poland-wide BGLTQ+ helpline Lambda Warszawa (22 628 52 22; open M, W, Th 6pm-10pm, Tu, F 6-9pm).
- Poland's first transgender member of Parliament Anna Grodzka offers free psychological consultations in her Deputies' Office for transgender people (biuro@annagrodzka.pl).

## EMERGENCY INFORMATION

**Emergency Number:** 112; Poland Tourist Emergency Hotline (22 278 77 77 and 608 599 999; open daily Oct-May 8am-6pm, Jun-Sept 8am-10pm).

**Police:** Rynek Główny 27; 12 615 73 18.

**US Embassy:** US Consulate General is located east of the Old Town Square (Stolarska 9; 12 424 51 00; open M-F 8:30am-5pm).

**Rape Crisis Center:** The Feminoteka Foundation serves as Poland's primary rape crisis helpline, providing legal and psychological support to victims of all kinds of violence (731 731 551 (helpline/support), 720 908 974 (admin); open Tu-Th 1pm-7pm).

**Hospitals:** The following 24hr hospitals have emergency wards that are obliged to help anyone who arrives regardless of nationality or health insurance.

- University Hospital of Kraków (Mikołaja Kopernika 36; 12 424 70 00).
- Health Care Ministry of Internal Affairs and Administration (Kronikarza Galla 25; 12 662 31 50).

**Pharmacies:** Pharmacies are identifiable by the green cross on or protruding from their façade, and are called aptekas in Polish.

- DOZ Apteka (Mikołajska 4 12 431 10 19; open M-Sa 8am-8pm, Su 10am-6pm).
- Apteka Pod Złotym Lwem (Długa 41 12 422 62 04; open M-Sa 8am-8pm, Su 8am-2pm).

# ACCOMMODATIONS

### ⬛SECRET GARDEN HOSTEL ($$)

Skawińska 7; 124 305 445; www.thesecretgarden.pl; reception open 24hr

Although we never found the secret garden (we spent most of our time in the one right by the entrance), we did find plenty to enjoy about our stay at this hostel. Let's talk about the rooms—each is assigned a theme like "Frozen Cranberry," which gives this relatively large hostel a personal feel. The location is (insert a fire emoji so hot it melts this book); the hostel's a leisurely stroll or a short tram ride to the **Old Town.** Unfortunately, a single traveler in need of a bed in a dorm will have to search elsewhere. However, a single traveler looking to bring back a hot date to a chic-looking room will feel right at home.

*i* Singles from 90 zł, twins from 150 zł; reservation recommended; not BGLTQ+ friendly; wheelchair accessible; no Wi-Fi; reservation recommended; linens included; laundry facilities; kitchen

### BUBBLE HOSTEL ($)

Basztowa 15; 500 498 100; www.bubble-hostel.krakówhotels.net; reception open 24hr

Unlike the housing market circa '08, this bubble is something we hope will never burst. While the hostel's fifth-story view of **Planty Park** is a treat in itself, the real cause for celebration lies just behind the park, where the **Old Town's** best cheap restaurants and bars can be found. The hostel's rooms are basic, yet clean and comfortable, and the fact that the entire establishment occupies just a single floor gives it a cozy and intimate feel. And if you like your hostels how you like your trains (near a train station), then you're in luck—the main Kraków station is just a five-minute walk away.

*i* Dorms from 45 zł, doubles from 160 zł; reservation recommended; limited wheelchair accessibility; linens included, laundry available; kitchen

### CRACOW HOSTEL ($)

Rynek Główny 18; 012 429 11 06; www.cracowhostel.com; reception open 24hr

If you're looking to stay in a fourteenth-century building right in the heart of Kraków, look no further than this hostel. Because of its superb location, the hostel attracts backpackers from around the world, which imbues it with a vibrant atmosphere and makes it an easy place to meet people. The bathrooms are clean, the clientele young, the Wi-Fi strong, and the views of **Main Market Square** spectacular—all factors that ensure Cracow Hostel isn't only a place to rest your head, but also an unforgettable part of your trip. Only potential downside: because of its killer location, Cracow's dorms can get quite noisy.

*i* Dorms from 45 zł, twin from 160 zł; reservation recommended; Wi-Fi; BGLTQ+ friendly; no wheelchair accessibility; linens included, laundry facilities

# SIGHTS
## CULTURE

### UNSOUND FESTIVAL

www.unsound.pl; occurs early to mid-Oct

For about a week in October, Kraków's cathedrals, factories, cinemas, salt mines, and brutalist Soviet-era hotels are overtaken by the world's most forward-thinking electronic DJs and producers. Since its creation in 2003, Unsound has transformed from a small underground festival to one of the most respected electronic music events in the world. It emphasizes collaboration between the international acts and the Polish arts community, so it's not uncommon to see a Kraków ballet company dancing to dubstep, or a local symphony orchestra backing a techno set. With a week-long pass costing the equivalent of $123 USD (for comparison, a three-day Coachella ticket is $400 USD), the festival is unlike any other you've ever attended and engenders a cult-like loyalty from fans across Europe.

*i* *Week pass 470 zł, event-specific tickets also available*

## LANDMARKS

### ◪WIELICZKA SALT MINE

Daniłowicza 10; 12 278 73 02; www.wieliczka-saltmine.com; open daily 7:30am-7:30pm

Attracting over a million tourists per year and listed as a **UNESCO site,** the Wieliczka Salt Mine certainly has a bit of a reputation. But does it live up to the hype? At first, a 90-minute guided tour of the mine might sound like a trade-off. But luckily, the engaging guides, animatronic exhibits, and small-scale mine replicas make salt-mining more interesting than it frankly has any right to be. The **Chapel of St. Kulga,** far and away the tour's highlight, is breathtaking and contains a salt replica of *The Last Supper* and a salt statue of **Pope John Paul II,** as well as majestic salt chandeliers. The **Tourist Route** is a favorite, but if you're feeling brave, a Miners' Route, which takes you deep into the darkness of the mine's oldest shaft, is also available.

*i* *Tours regular 84 zł, 64 zł reduced; last tour 7:30pm; limited wheelchair accessibility*

### GHETTO WALL FRAGMENT AND GHETTO HEROES SQUARE

Wall: Lwowska 29/Limanowskiego 60/62; pl. Bohaterow Getta; Wall and Square open daily 24hr

The **Podgorze district** is home to two important symbols relating to the persecution of Cracovian Jews during World War II—a fragment from the wall surrounding the Jewish Ghetto and the Ghetto Heroes Square memorial. In 1941, the Nazis imprisoned nearly 20,000 Jews in Podgorze, and over the next few years, **plac Zgody** became the Ghetto's social hub as well as the site of deportations and executions. The Ghetto Wall Fragment located along ul. Lwowska isn't as significant, but a longer stretch of wall can be found nearby behind the school at ul. Limanowskiego 60/62, providing an eerie contrast to its playground setting. The Ghetto Heroes Square is located closer to the river on plac Zgody. Here, you'll find **33 empty bronze chairs** representing the absence of the Ghetto's victims.

*i* *Free; wheelchair accessible*

### ST. MARY'S BASILICA

pl. Mariacki 5; 124 220 737; www.mariacki.com; basilica open M-Sa 11:30am-6pm, Su 2pm-6pm; Mariacki Tower open M-Sa 9:30am-5:30pm, Su 1pm-5:30pm

Even if you've seen a thousand churches and think you can miss this one, it's time to think again, because St. Mary's Basilica is something special. The church's ostensible highlight is its golden Gothic altarpiece, the largest of its kind in Europe, but we found ourselves more impressed by its starry, deep blue ceilings, which wouldn't look out of place in a Van Gogh painting. You have to pay a small fee to look inside the church, and an additional one to ascend the **Mariacki Tower,** which overlooks the **Main Market Square.** However, you could just wait outside the church to hear the famous **Hejnał Mariack**—the hourly bugle call that commemorates the thirteenth-century trumpeter, who was shot in the neck while warning the city of an impending Mongol attack.

*i* *Admission 10zł, 5zł reduced; last entry 15min. before closing; limited wheelchair accessibility*

Located an hour and a half from Kraków, Auschwitz-Birkenau is the largest, and most well-known, of the Nazi concentration camps. The name "Auschwitz" is the German translation of **Oscwiecim,** the town where the camp was situated, and collectively refers to three camps: **Auschwitz I,** which greeted prisoners with the message of "Arbeit Macht Frei" ("Work Sets You Free") looming above its entrance; **Auschwitz II-Birkenau,** whose "Gate of Death" and railway have become symbols of the Holocaust; and **Auschwitz III,** which is not open to the public. Nazi authorities at these camps murdered approximately 1.1 million people, the majority of which were Jewish, but also included Sinti and Roma Poles and other political prisoners. Since 1947, Auschwitz I, and, to a lesser extent Auschwitz II-Birkenau, has served as a museum, documenting the Nazi occupation of Poland, the establishment of Auschwitz-Birkenau, life at the camps, the horrific experiments carried out on prisoners, and many personal accounts of the prisoners' suffering and courage. Auschwitz II-Birkenau, while still containing information boards about its various structures, is primarily the site of the monument to the victims of Auschwitz. The site represents one of the greatest tragedies in human history, and although everyone's experience at Auschwitz is personal, it is an unquestionably harrowing and emotionally draining visit.

Entry to both camps is free, but a 3.5 hour guided tour—which covers the main exhibits at Auschwitz I before visiting Auschwitz II-Birkenau—is 40zł (30 zł reduced) and must be booked at least a few days in advance online. Although the guided tour—available from 10am-3pm—offers a valuable insight into the history of the camps that goes beyond what you could glean on your own, a self-guided tour is sometimes preferred by those who want to walk through the museum and the memorial at their own pace, which can allow for a more personal experience. If you wish to do a self-guided visit—possible during the 8am-10am and 3pm-8pm time slots—you are able to arrive at Auschwitz I without having made any prior reservations and receive a ticket to the museum. However, you may have to wait one or two hours before entering the museum—during which time you could take the free shuttle to Auschwitz II-Birkenau, entry to which is not ticketed—or face the possibility that there are no more tickets available for that day. To rule out that possibility, it is safest to reserve a ticket for a self-guided visit online in advance. Those doing a self-guided visit of the Auschwitz I museum should make sure to begin their tour at Block 4 and continue in a clockwise direction. In addition, a purchase of "The Auschwitz-Birkenau Memorial: A Guidebook" (15 zł) will provide more information about your visit, especially at Auschwitz II-Birkenau, which is less comprehensively sign-posted.

You'll undoubtedly see many private tours of Auschwitz advertised in Kraków; we advise against these. Firstly, while these tours guarantee you'll receive a guided tour, a regular Auschwitz Museum and Memorial guide, instead of a private one, will conduct the tour. Secondly, the majority of the cost of the private tour will go towards private coach transport and a meal, both of which are quite unnecessary.

## WAWEL DRAGON STATUE

Stare Miasto; open daily 24hr

The story of Kraków is a classic dragon-meets-village, village-fears-dragon, man-kills-dragon-by-feeding-it-sulphur-stuffed-lamb-causing-it-to-explode-and-as-a-reward-gets-to-marry-the-princess tale, which is remembered by the statue of the Wawel Dragon at the foot of **Wawel Hill.** You'll either encounter the statue once you've exited the **Dragon's Den** as part of your Wawel Castle visit, or you'll pass it as you stroll along the **Vistula River** on your way to see the world-famous Kraków **Walk of Fame** (compare your hand prints with Professor Lupin's!). Regardless, this prickly creature is definitely worth seeing, if only for the

flames that burst out of its mouth every five minutes.

*i* *Free; wheelchair accessible*

## MUSEUMS

### MUSEUM OF CONTEMPORARY ART IN KRAKÓW

Lipowa 4; 122 634 000; www.en.mocak.pl; open Tu-Su 11am-7pm

MOCAK provides a fascinating insight into Polish culture that is difficult to find elsewhere, as well as serving as a meta-critique of art itself. And while we can already hear the retching noise that the phrase "meta-critique" is likely to incite, the exhibits—which include a painstakingly recreated work of nineteenth-century realism ripped to pieces and a real-life video recording of an artist trying to steal the *Mona Lisa*—are (mostly) devoid of pretension and just plain hilarious. Since many believe that modern art is confusing, the very idea of the MOCAK might be an automatic turn-off. But we can assure you, even the most uncultured Neanderthal can find something to appreciate about a blown-up photo of an anonymous person wearing nothing but a pair of EU flag-print underwear.

*i* *Regular 14zł, 7 zł reduced; last entry 1hr. before closing; wheelchair accessible*

### NATIONAL MUSEUM IN KRAKÓW

al. 3 Maja 1; 124 335 500; www.mnk.pl/branch/main-building; open Tu-Sa 10am-6pm, Su 10am-4pm

When in a place as historic as Kraków, it might seem like a waste of a precious few hours to visit an art museum, which, in a broad sense, contains the same kind of work you're likely to find in similar museums around the world.

And if your interest in expressionism is solely limited to expressing how boring expressionism is, this museum won't change your mind. That said, any art-lover or art-curious individual will find this assortment of late eighteenth, nineteenth, and twentieth-century Polish art unquestionably worth their time. The galleries focusing upon Polish impressionism are particularly stunning.

*i* *Main building admission 11 zł, 6 zł reduced; all-branch pass 35 zł, reduced 28 zł; free on Su; wheelchair accessible*

## OUTDOORS

### KOSCIUSZKO MOUND

al. Waszyngtona 1; 124 251 116; www.kopieckosciuszki.pl; open daily 9am-dusk

Kosciuszko Mound is one of the most beloved spots in the city, but we're not sure if this is because of or in spite of the fact that it looks like an enormous grassy nipple. Following the death of Tadeusz Kosciuszko, leader of the Polish army and soldier in the American Revolutionary War, in 1817, citizens from across the country flocked to Kraków to build this mound in tribute to their hero. A few decades later, Austrian authorities constructed a brick fortress around the mound, which, today, makes your visit to the mound feel like a kind of invasion. However, once you reach the top of the mound, any imperial guilt will be replaced with an imperial enjoyment of the magnificent views of the **Old Town** and **Wawel Castle.**

*i* *Normal 12 zł, 10 zł reduced; wheelchair accessible*

# FOOD

### ⬛KANTON DIM SUM HOUSE
Węglowa 2; 882 020 402; open Tu-F noon-8pm, Sa-Su 10am-9pm

Having read that it's one of the best Chinese restaurants in the city, you might walk into Canton Dim Sum House, take one look at the kitchen personnel, and think you've been hoodwinked. They're all Polish! With the first criteria for authenticity already out the window, it's understandable that you might want to throw yourself out one as well, but resist the urge, because you've got another surprise right around the corner. The food, against all odds, really is delicious. Although the menus are Polish-only, the staff will be able to help you, an ignorant foreigner, decide what to eat.
*i* *Dumplings 14-17 zł, ramen 26-32 zł; vegetarian options available; wheelchair accessible*

### ⬛POD WAWELEM ($$)
Świętej Gertrudy 26-29; 012 421 23 36; www.podwawelem.eu; open M-Sa noon-midnight, Su noon-11pm

As close as you'll come to a Polish feast without traveling back in time to **Wawel Castle** c. 1200, Pod Wawelem is one of the best dining experiences you'll have in Kraków. If you arrive around peak time (7-9pm), don't be deterred by the waiting time—it's worth it. The restaurant serves delicious Polish cuisine that, once you take into account the enormous portions, is an absolute steal. Although the inside is perfectly nice, the outside veranda looking out onto **Planty Park** is nothing short of idyllic, and you should absolutely demand to be seated there. And while the in-house jazz trio is a nice touch, you'll wish the restaurant had spared the expense and bought each of its customers a larger pair of pants for optimal post-consumption comfort instead.
*i* *Entrées 23-26 zł; vegetarian options available; wheelchair accessible*

### KAWIARNIA LITERACKA ($$)
Krakówska 41; 513 158 167; www.kawiarnia-literacka.pl; open daily 11am-11pm

After a long, exploratory stroll from the **Old Town** through the **Kazimierz district,** you'll feel exhausted—physically (from all the walking), mentally (from the all the sights), and spiritually (from being a person living in a twenty-first-century world). Chances are, you'll need a drink. And this café's selection of beer, wine, liquor, and coffee might just do the trick. If it doesn't, its cozy suede couches and bean-bags chairs certainly will. And if it turns out that the concept of certainty no longer exists today, then maybe you can grab a book from one of Kawiarnia Literacka's many bookcases to take your mind off things.
*i* *Coffee 10-15 zł, alcohol 8-16 zł; vegetarian options available; no wheelchair accessibility*

### ZAPIEKANKI KROLEWSKIE ($)
Plac Nowy 4; open daily 10am-2am

We've said it once and we'll say it again: after sundown, **Plac Nowy,** the beating heart of the Kazimierz district, is the place to be. But while it's criminally easy to find a good bar, where can you find a hearty meal? Truthfully, there are quite a few sit-down places that'll get the job done, but every Pole on planet earth knows that it's not even a discussion: Zapiekanki is the way to go. Essentially a 15-inch toasted baguette covered in mushrooms, cheese, and your choice from an exhaustive list of toppings, Zapiekanki is the Subway-pizza combination that you didn't know was missing from your life. **The Royal** (bacon, chicken, lettuce, sweet corn, tomato and chives, 10zł) is the crowd favorite, and with good reason—it tastes good!
*i* *Zapiekanki 7-11 zł; wheelchair accessible*

# NIGHTLIFE

### ALCHEMIA ($)
Estery 5; 012 421 22 00; www.en.alchemia.com.pl; open M 10am-2am, Tu-W 9am-2am, Th 9am-3am, F-Sa 9am-4am, Su 9am-2am

Even if Alchemia weren't **the most lively and vibrant bar we visited in Kraków,** we'd recommend it purely based on its gritty bohemian furnishings, candlelit ambiance, and eclectic food menu, which includes fish and chips, falafel, pad thai, and everything in between. You'll struggle to find a table on most nights of the week, but if you're lucky enough find a seat or smart enough to steal someone else's, you're likely to have a memorable night, provided that you can still remember it in the morning (less a consequence of drinking, and more of falling off the tables, which double as a dance floor). The cellar regularly hosts DJs and live music acts, which are guaranteed all-night long affairs.

*i* Beer 7-11 zł, cocktails 10-22 zł, food 19-28 zł

### PROZAK 2.0
pl. Dominikański 6; open Su-Th 10pm-6am, F-Sa 10pm-8am

If you want the proverbial "big night out," head straight to Prozak 2.0,

which, on any weekend night, is packed to the gills with what seems like the entirety of Kraków's local and tourist population. Your typical brick-walled, black-ceilinged basement space—save for the neon signs all over the place—Prozak won't be a nightlife experience, but it will be fun. With four bars, three dance floors, and the best sound system money can buy, it caters to music-purists, party-pedants, and fast food enthusiasts (it's directly below a McDonald's) alike. The bar doesn't have a menu, so make sure you know the prices before you order. On the big nights, the lines don't seem to have an end, so make sure you arrive early, get stamped, and come back later.

*i* Cover 10 zł, beer 10 zł, cocktails 20-30 zł

# WARSAW

Coverage by **Nicholas Grundlingh**

While certainly not an eye-sore, Warsaw probably won't make you go back home to report, "It's certainly one of the better-looking places I saw" while eating your mom's homemade cole-slaw. But what the Polish capital—whose proper name is the much less pun-centric *Warszawa* (var-sha-vah)—lacks in architecture it makes up for in history and a relaxed, vibrant atmosphere. A city that was effectively leveled during World War II and lost nearly 30% of its population in the Holocaust, the Warsaw you see today is a replica of its former self, reconstructed and ruled, along with the rest of Poland, by a communist government until 1990. Institutions such as the Warsaw Rising and History of Polish Jews museums remember the war, and many of the buildings, most noticeably the Palace of Culture and Science, serve as relics to the period of Soviet influence. With over a thousand years of history but only around three decades of independence, Warsaw is an exciting blend of old and new. It's just as easy to find a vegan burger place as a traditional Polish restaurant, a futuristic one meter-wide house as a royal castle, a man wearing regular shorts as a man wearing early-2000s three-quarter jean shorts. Spend your days roaming around museums, parks, and cafés, your nights along the Vistula River, and the months afterwards thinking how stupid you were to judge this place by its looks.

## ORIENTATION

Just like your guidance counselor in high school, nearly every neighborhood in Warsaw is worth visiting at least once. Along the west bank of the Vistula River—which separates the more metropolitan part of the city from the grungy, less glamorous (but arguably cooler) **Praga district**—you'll find the Old Town (entirely rebuilt after WWII), the **Powisle district** (the student district), and **Lazienki Park** (filled with palaces, Chopin, and an art museum). **Powisle,** in particular, contains some of the best restaurants in the city as well as **Plac Zabaw,** which refers to a bunch of bars and food trucks on the river. Head further west into the city from Powisle to enter the city center, which subtly announces itself with the towering **Palace of Culture and Science.** If you follow **ul. Marszaalkowlska** south in the direction of hipster haven **Plac Zbawciela,** restaurants and bars will jump out as if you're walking through a very un-scary haunted house. Trams run horizontally and vertically along most main roads, and two metro lines, one adjacent to the river and the other perpendicular to it, intersect at **ul. Swietokryzska,** one street north of the aforementioned palace.

# ESSENTIALS

## GETTING THERE

From Chopin Airport's Terminal A, take the SKM S2 train to the Środmieście station and the S3 to Warszawa Centralna station (single-trip public transport tickets 4.40zł). From the budget airline-friendly Warsaw-Modlin Airport, take one of the green or yellow shuttles to Modlin Train Station, from which trains run into Warszawa Centralna station. If you're traveling by train, you'll likely disembark at Warszawa Centralna station as well. A bus journey into Warsaw will drop you off at the main bus station along Aleje Jerozolimskie, which is either a 15min. train ride from the nearby Warsaw West station or a 12min. bus ride (#127, 158, 517) east into the city center.

## GETTING AROUND

The public transport system consists of trams, buses, and two metro lines running north-south (blue line M1) and east-west (red line M2). A night bus runs after 11pm until 5am, and the metro runs from 5am until 11am on weekdays, and until 3am on Friday and Saturday. Public transport tickets (single ride 4.40zł) are valid for all three modes of transport, and can be purchased from green and yellow kiosks or anywhere with a "Bilety" ("ticket") sign. Unless you're traveling to the outskirts of Warsaw, you'll only need a Zone 1 ticket, which includes the Chopin Airport. 24hr (15zł), 72hr (36zł), and weekend (24zł) tickets are also available. You cannot board the metro without validating your ticket, but this isn't the case when riding a bus or tram. However, if a plainclothes police officer catches you without a validated ticket, you will be fined 266zł. Ubers are available in the city, and reliable taxi companies include Glob Cab Taxi (666 009 668) and VIP Taxi Warsaw (791 550 525).

## PRACTICAL INFORMATION

**Tourist Offices:** Old Town (Rynek Starego Miasta 19/21/21a; open daily May-Sept 8am-7pm, Oct-Apr 8am-6pm).

**Banks/ATMs/Currency Exchange:** ATMs are found throughout the city at most banks and by the arrival terminal at the airport. Use ATMs instead of currency exchanges at the airport. In the city, currency exchanges are known as "kantors," some of which give better rates than ATM machines. Avoid kantors with English signs and those in touristy areas. The kantors in Złoty Tarasy and Arkadia shopping malls offer reasonable rates.

**Post Offices:** Poczta Polska, and two branches are located near to aleje Jerozolimskie, right next to the Palace of Culture and Science.

**Internet:** Most cafés, restaurants, and fast food restaurants have free Wi-Fi available. This website (www.wifispc.com/poland/mazowieckie/warsaw) provides a map of all the available Wi-Fi hotspots in the city.

**BGLTQ+ Resources:** Although Poland's government doesn't offer many legal rights and protections for the BGLTQ+ community, Warsaw is generally considered an BGLTQ+ friendly city. Here are some resources:

- Counseling for BGLTQ+ people at the offices of the Campaign Against Homophobia (ul. Solec 30A; 22 423 64 38; kph.org.pl; bezpieczny@kph.org.pl).
- Poland-wide BGLTQ+ helpline Lambda Warszawa (22 628 52 22; open M W Th 6pm-10pm, Tu-F 6-9pm).

## EMERGENCY INFORMATION

**Emergency Number:** 112; Poland Tourist Emergency Hotline (22 278 77 77 and 608 599 999; open daily 8am-6pm, June-Sept 8am-10pm)

**Police:** Komenda Główna Policji (Puławska 148/150; 22 621 02 51).

**US Embassy:** There is a US Embassy in Warsaw (al. Ujazdowskie 29/31; 22 504 2000; open M-F 8:30am-5pm).

**Rape Crisis Center:** The Feminoteka Foundation serves as Poland's primary rape crisis helpline, providing legal and psychological support to victims of all kinds of violence (731 731 551 (helpline/support), 720 908 974 (admin); open Tu-Th 1pm-7pm). The foundation is based at ul. Mokotowska 29a, nearby plac Zbawiciela (open M-F 11am-7pm).

**Hospitals:**
- Szpital Kliniczny Dzieciątka Jezus (Children's Hospital of Jesus) (Williama Lindleya 4; 22 502 20 00; open daily 24hr).
- Lux Med. Al. Jerozolimskie 65/79 (Nowogrodzka 45; 22 33 22 888 (general hotline); open M-F 7am-8pm).

**Pharmacies:** Pharmacies are identifiable by the green cross on or protruding from their façade, and are called *aptekas* in Polish.
- Apteka Franciszkańska (ul. Franciszkańska 14 lok. 102; 22 635 35 25; open daily 24hr).
- Apteka Mirowska (pl. Mirowski 1; 22 620 02 66; open daily 24hr).

# ACCOMMODATIONS

## ◙OKI DOKI HOSTEL ($)
pl. Dąbrowskiego 3; 22 828 01 22; www.okidoki.pl; reception open 24hr

Although it's the only hostel in Warsaw to be recognized as a member of Europe's Famous Hostels, Oki Doki doesn't have any pretensions or airs about it whatsoever. The rooms are homey, the bar, where you'll find 5 zł (!) beers during happy hour, is always packed and in high spirits, and the nightly events are well-attended and welcoming. What's more, when you check in, you'll receive an Oki Doki wristband that entitles you to discounts at restaurants, bars, and sights across the city. Suffice it to say, the hostel, which is just a street away from a metro station, is a backpacker's wet dream.

*i* Dorms from 29 zł, doubles from 128 zł, singles from 100 zł; reservation recommended; Wi-Fi; BGLTQ+ friendly; no wheelchair accessibility; linens included; towels included

## EMKA HOSTEL ($$)
Kopernika 3; 22 657 20 04; www.emka-hostel.com; reception open 24hr

Unlike the famed astronomer, Nicolas Copernicus, whose initials (MK in Polish) give the hostel its name, EmKa won't change the way you think about the universe, but it will provide you with a very comfortable stay and a rather convenient location. Although it doesn't necessarily have a "unique personality," the hostel does have clean and modern bedrooms, a large common space, and incredibly spacious bathrooms—and at the end of the day, what more could you ask for? The hostel also makes navigating Warsaw a trouble-free experience, with the **Nowy Siat metro,** the cheap eats-lined **ul. Foksal,** and the alternative nightlife strip **Smolna** all just a three-minute walk away.

*i* Dorms from 50 zł, doubles from 200 zł, singles from 140 zł; reservation recommended; Wi-Fi; BGLTQ+ friendly; limited wheelchair accessibility; linens included; towels included

## WARSAW DOWNTOWN HOSTEL ($)
Wilcza 33; 22 629 35 76; www.warsaw-downtown.pl; reception open 24hr

You can tell a lot of effort has been put into this place to make it as warm and inviting as possible. In the common spaces, blackboards display the schedule of daily hostel-organized events, posters highlight staff recommendations for things to do in the city, and two separate maps document the hometowns of previous guests as well as those of current ones. The rooms are clean and each has a view of a quaint courtyard. It's very difficult to fault this hostel, but thanks to our millennial cynicism, not impossible: the rooms are just a little small.

*i* Dorms from 42 zł, doubles from 106 zł; reservation recommended; BGLTQ+ friendly; no wheelchair accessibility; Wi-Fi; reservation recommended; linens included; towels included; kitchen

Upon arriving in Warsaw, you'll quickly learn that 80% of the city was destroyed during the Second World War. In fact, Warsaw suffered the most damage out of any capital city during the war. How did this happen?

Well, even before the war began, the Nazis had set their sights on demolishing the city and rebuilding it as a small German town. As soon as the Nazis had invaded Poland and captured Warsaw in late 1939, they began to displace the city's population, using Varsovians for slave labor or sending them to concentration camps. In 1940, the Warsaw Ghetto was established, which effectively imprisoned over 400,000 Polish Jews, and in 1942, over half of the Ghetto residents were sent to Treblinka extermination camp.

Although the city had suffered constant bombardment throughout the war, Warsaw's systematic destruction began in the wake of the Warsaw Ghetto Uprising in 1943, the largest Jewish rebellion during the war. Following the uprising, the Ghetto was razed, and in its place, a concentration camp was erected.

A year later, the Polish resistance—knowing that the USSR, who were approaching from the East, would "liberate" (read: capture) Warsaw from the ever-weakening Nazis—attempted to drive the Germans out of the city before the Red Army troops arrived. Even though their troops were needed on both the Eastern and newly re-opened Western fronts, the Nazis concentrated their resources on ruthlessly crushing the uprising, which was the largest military effort undertaken by a European resistance movement.

Following the uprising, SS chief Heinrich Himmler, on the topic of Warsaw's future, stated, "the city must completely disappear from the surface of the earth and serve only as a transport station for the Wehrmacht." The Nazis used flame-throwers and explosives to inflict what was, later in 2005, estimated to be USD $56 billion worth of damage upon the city, leaving only a few Polish hideaways, known as the "Robinson Crusoes of Warsaw" to live amongst the rubble and ruins.

Thus, after the Nazi's defeat, the Polish people began to reconstruct the city from scratch—a process that ended in the early 70s. Amazingly, since the city received no foreign aid, reconstruction of Warsaw was solely financed by donations from the Polish people. As such, the city became a socialist symbol.

If you want to learn more about the German occupation, the Warsaw Uprising, and the context that produced it, visit the Warsaw Rising Museum.

# SIGHTS
## CULTURE
. . . . . . . . . . . . . . . . . . . . . . . . . . . . . . . . . . . . . . .

### CHOPIN CONERTS IN ŁAZIENKI PARK
Chopin Statue in Łazienki Park; 22 506 00 24; www.lazienki-krolewskie.pl/en/wydarzenia/koncerty-chopinowskie-2; summer concerts Su at noon and 4pm

While women around the world be shoppin', Varsovians be Chopin. More specifically, they be Chopin in Łazienki Park, which, every Sunday at noon and 4pm, hosts a free Chopin concert to celebrate the city's prodigal son. Appropriately held right next to the park's Chopin monument, the concerts are packed with people eager to hear some of the freshest beats and dirtiest drops in all of classical music. You can come and go as you like, although if you want a good place to sit, it's best to arrive early. And if you find such a place, it's likely that there won't be much shade, so definitely bring some sunblock, a hat, and a book of Chopin insults so you can throw some shade of your own.

*i* Free; wheelchair accessible

### SOHO FACTORY
Mińska 25; 22 323 19 00; www.sohofactory.pl; hours vary

Frustrated by the lack of a dedicated artistic area in Warsaw, a group of creatives decided to re-purpose an old manufacturing plant and turn it into a cultural hub. Today, SOHO Factory is the permanent home of many design, film-production, and publishing firms, and holds a variety of cultural events on a biweekly to monthly basis. The factory's center is often used as a gallery space, most famously displaying a 21m nude balloon sculpture of famed Polish artist Pawel Althamer in 2012. With the exception of the **Neon Museum** and a few modern art sculptures scattered around the place, there isn't much to see if you're not here to check out a specific event. Keep an eye on the SOHO Factory Facebook page for all the latest goings-on.

*i* *Events may be ticketed; limited wheelchair accessibility*

## LANDMARKS

### PALACE OF CULTURE AND SCIENCE

pl. Defilad 1; 22 656 76 00; www.pkin.pl; observation deck open daily 10am-8pm

As if a Soviet puppet government weren't enough, Stalin also decided to gift Poland the enormous Palace of Culture and Science. Constructed in the early 1950s, the building is the tallest in the country, the center of the city, and a source of mixed feelings among

locals. Some see the palace as a painful reminder of communism—others are willing to say "history shmistory" and simply enjoy its malls, cinemas, theaters, and museums. Nonetheless, just about every person in Poland would agree that a trip to the Palace's observation deck is a must. From the 42nd story, you'll receive panoramic views of the city that make even a place as ordinary-looking as Warsaw seem spectacular.

*i* *Admission 10 zł, 15 zł reduced; wheelchair accessible*

### ROYAL CASTLE

pl. Zamkowy; 22 355 51 70; www.zamek-krolewski.pl; open summer M-W 10am-6pm, Th 10am-8pm, F-Sa 10am-6pm, Su 11am 6pm, winter Tu-Sa 10am-4pm, Su 11am-4pm

Destroyed by the Germans during World War II, the Royal Castle, while still containing many of its original furnishings, is almost entirely reconstructed. It still looks impressive, but you can tell that it's just not the real deal. The castle's most memorable rooms involve either exceedingly opulent rococo decor or gigantic paintings in ornate, gilded frames. Additionally, the series of video exhibits on the castle's turbulent twentieth-century-existence—like the two Rembrandts downstairs—is deeply fascinating. But beyond such features, you'll find that many rooms are quite ordinary. If this is the only opportunity you'll have to see a castle or palace in Europe, then we encourage you to visit. But if it isn't, then we promise that you won't lose any sleep over passing.

*i* *Admission 30 zł, 20 zł reduced, free on Su; audio guides 17 zł, 12 zł reduced; last entry 1hr. before closing; wheelchair accessible*

## MUSEUMS

### CSW ZAMEK UJAZDOWSKI (UJAZDOWSKI CASTLE CENTRE FOR CONTEMPORARY ART)

Jazdów 2; 22 628 12 71; www.u-jazdowski.pl;

open Tu-W noon-7pm, Th noon-9pm, F-Su noon-7pm

Situated on a hill overlooking Łazienki Park, this sixteenth-century Baroque castle turned contemporary art gallery emphasizes interdisciplinary forms of art, hosting everything from video installations to experimental theater performances. When we attended, the primary exhibition, which ran for five months, presented a mix of paintings, installations, and theater and film projects that dealt with Poland's national identity in the twenty-first century. When you purchase your ticket, you're given a guidebook that contains at least a paragraph worth of information on every single piece in the gallery. The book's effect on your experience at the gallery is transformative. As soon as these challenging and abstruse works are contextualized and explained by critics and sometimes the artists themselves, the gallery becomes an immensely different invaluable experience.
*i* *Admission 12 zł, 6 zł reduced; wheelchair accessible*

## POLIN MUSEUM OF THE HISTORY OF POLISH JEWS

Anielewicza 6; 22 471 03 01; www.polin.pl; open M 10am-6pm, W 10am-8pm, Th-F 10am-6pm, Sa-Su 10am-8pm

Built on the site of the former **Warsaw Ghetto,** this museum provides a comprehensive look at the history of the Jewish community in Poland. Consisting of eight galleries, the core exhibition not only gives insight into the evolution of social, political, and religious components of Jewish life, but also explores the nature of the anti-Semitism and persecution that Jews faced for centuries prior to the **Holocaust.** The exhibits are often confusing to navigate, making the audio guide (10 zł) a very worthwhile expenditure. While some may find the museum a little dry and overwhelming, anyone with an active interest in Jewish or European history will find themselves endlessly engaged.
*i* *Admission 25 zł, 15 zł reduced; audio guide 10 zł; last entry 2hr. before closing; wheelchair accessible*

## OUTDOORS

### THE FILM SUMMER CAPITAL

Various locations across the city; 22 826 83 11; www.filmowastolica.pl; occurs daily late June-late August

It's common knowledge that the only people who like watching movies indoors are agoraphobes and those whose faces are too hideous to be seen in the light of day. With this in mind, Warsaw's annual Film Summer Capital festival is the perfect opportunity to prove that you don't have any intense fears and that your face is, at the very least, not hideous but just plain old ugly. From late June until the end of August, various parks around the city will host free film screenings daily. Historically, the festival has had an incredibly diverse program, ranging from cult classics to animation to various subgenres of Chinese cinema.
*i* *Free; wheelchair accessible*

## FOOD

### ⬛KROWARZYWA BURGER ($)

Hoża 29/31, Marszałkowska 27/35A; www.krowarzywa.pl; open daily noon-11pm

It says something about the quality of Krowarzya that it's not only one of the top vegan restaurants in the city, but one of the best burger joints as well. Now if we could only figure out what it says about the quality, then everything would make sense. But we're tempted to guess that it means that these vegan burgers are really, really good. At least, our experience there would indicate as much. With six different kinds of patties available, four of which are gluten-free, vegans, for possibly the first time in their lives, are spoilt for choice. Beyond the vegan components, the burger buns are toasted and warm, and once the patty is in place, dolloped with a healthy dose of fresh garnishing.
*i* *Entrées 13.50-16.50 zł; vegetarian and vegan options available; wheelchair accessible*

### ⬛ZAPIEKANKI REGIONALNE AND BUBBLE WAFFLE ($)

Chmielna 2; www.bubblewaffle.com; ZR open M-Th 11am-11pm, F-Sa 11am-2am,

Su noon-2am; BW open M-W 9am-10pm, Th-Su 9pm-midnight

Hey wise guy, you want the perfect fast food-dessert combo? Well then, listen up and listen good, because what you're going to do is this: head down ul. Foksal until you find a place called Zapiekanki Regionalne. Bright rainbow colors on the awning—you can't miss it. Once you're in, order a traditional Polish pizza kind of dish. A toasted baguette, some mushrooms, cheese, some toppings—bada bing bada boom, it's a *zapiekanki*. Then without even giving it a moment's thought, go next door to Bubble Waffle—and guess what, genius? You're going to order a bubble waffle. It's ice cream inside a waffle with bubbles on it. But what do you think's inside the bubbles? Whatever you want. Chocolate sauce, strawberries, bananas—the sky's the limit. Are the calories worth it? Buddy, these things could give me a freakin' heart attack and they'd be worth it.

*i* Large zapiekanki 10-15 zł, small 7-11 zł, bubble waffle 15-17zł; wheelchair accessible

### BAR PRASOWY ($)
Marszałkowska 10/16; 666 353 776; www.prasowy.pl; open M-F 9am-8pm, Sa-Su 11am-7pm

One of the few communist-era relics that people cherish, milk bars are no-frills canteens that serve the cheapest Polish cuisine in town. They're a requisite experience for any visitor to Warsaw and thus the question remains, which is the best one to visit? And while we're no experts, the common consensus amongst Varsovians is that Bar Prosowny is the milkiest bar of them all. Although recently revamped, it retains its original charm, possessing a similar atmosphere to a classic American diner. And with everything under 10 zł, you could eat three very filling meals for the price of a single dish at most restaurants in the city.

*i* Entrées 5-6.90 zł; vegetarian options available; wheelchair accessible

### GOSCINIEC POLSKIE PIEROGI ($$)
Podwale 19; 22 400 79 23; www.gosciniec.waw.pl; open M-Th 11am-10pm, F-Sa 11am-10pm, Su 11am-10pm

There's a famous statistic that states, in New Zealand, there are four sheep to every person. And in Poland, we imagine that something similar is true of dumplings, which, over here, are known as *pierogis*. You'll find these little guys everywhere, and truthfully the quality is fairly consistent. After all, they're just different combinations of meat, vegetables, and potatoes steamed inside a dough casing. That being said, if you're interested in chomping on some 'rogis in a scenic setting, then Gosciniec, a quaint place with walls featuring murals, is tough to beat.

*i* Nine pierogis 19.90-20.90 zł; vegetarian options available; limited wheelchair accessible

# NIGHTLIFE

### ⬛PLAC ZABAW AND BARKA
Podgórska 16; 796 122 108; PZ open M-Sa 11am-2am, Su 11am-midnight; BarKa open M-Th 11am-midnight, F-Sa 11am-6am, Su 11am-midnight

It's no exaggeration to say that there aren't many better ways to spend a summer's night than at Plac Zabaw and BarKa. Right next to the **Vistula River,** Plac Zabaw is a beer garden-esque area filled with bars and food trucks, which overlooks **BarKa,** a floating café-club on the river itself. Both places are operated by the same people who run the perennially hip **Plan B,** and although the crowd's a little more diverse in terms of age, the atmosphere's just as lively and vibrant. Start off your night at Plac Zabaw, sitting on the riverbank with a beer in one hand, a burger in the other. Once you're sufficiently well-fed and tipsy, head down to BarKa, where the DJ's warm, tropical house will take care of you until sunrise.

*i* Food 15-25 zł, beer 10zł, cocktails 15-27 zł

### CLUB LUZZTRO
Aleje Jerozolimskie 6; www.luzztro.com; open W-Th 10pm-10am, F-Sa midnight-2pm

A more alternative option to the mainstream clubs that line **Mazowiecka,** Luzztro is a dark and grimy venue filtered through pulsing red hues. A comically large disco ball hangs above the main house-focused dance floor—a Persian-carpeted platform. Head upstairs to find various nooks and crannies fitted with red leather couches, or slip off to the side and enter a no-frills, black-walled room blasting punishing techno. It's not for everyone, but if you're tired of dancing to radio pop while surrounded by a bunch of dudes who looked like they just stepped off the set of *Entourage*, then Luzztro might just be the place for you.

*i* Cover 20 zł, shots 10 zł, cocktails 22-30zł

## PLAN B

aleja Wyzwolenia 18; 503 116 154; open M-Th 11am-2am, F-Sa 11am-4am, Su 11am-2am

Plan B is so drenched in hipsters that even its name is ironic. Because, when it comes to a night out in Warsaw, this place is obviously Plan A! Easily differentiated by the sizable crowd congregated outside its doors, the bar has a grungy, laid-back aesthetic, which stands in sharp contrast to the early 2000s pop playing out of its speakers. The drinks are basic and cheap and there are a few couches and tables scattered around the inside, and depending on how late it is, a small to fairly reasonable amount of people on the dance floor.

*i* Beer 10zł, cocktails 15-27 zł; BGLTQ+ friendly

# POLAND ESSENTIALS

## VISAS

Poland is a member of the European Union, and the Schengen area. Citizens from Australia, Canada, New Zealand, the US, and many other non-EU countries do not require a visa for stays up to 90 days. However, if you plan to spend time in other Schengen countries, note that the 90-day period applies cumulatively to all Schengen countries.

## MONEY

Although Poland is a member of the EU, it is not in the Eurozone and uses the Polish złoty (zł or PLN as currency). Currency exchanges are known as "kantors," and those with signs in English, or which are located in airports or touristy areas, should be avoided. The best are those that advertise the "buy" and "sell" rates, which let you calculate exactly how much you will receive. To find out what out-of-network or international fees your credit or debit cards may be subjected to, call your bank.

**Tipping:** In restaurants, tips are not included in the bill, so it's customary to tip 10% or 15% if the service was exceptional. Be careful with saying "Thank you" to the waiter when they collect the bill, as it means that you don't want any change back. In taxis, tipping is not expected, but you can tip 10% for good service. ATMs in Poland can be found in shopping malls, banks and most public spaces in urban areas.

## SAFETY AND HEALTH

**Drugs and Alcohol:** The minimum age to purchase alcohol in Poland in 18. Remember to drink responsibly and never to drink and drive. The legal blood alcohol content (BAC) for driving is under 0.02%, which is significantly lower than the US limit of 0.08%. The possession of any quantity of drugs, including marijuana, is penalized with up to 3-years imprisonment.

# PORTUGAL

**If you could walk Portugal's cobble-stones from top to bottom, from the wine-drenched north to the sun-drenched south, you'd encounter more than ten centuries of rich history, massive amounts of seafood caught daily and served at your table, and locals singing in the streets.** Portugal's main cities dot its stunning, cliffy coastline and many beautiful rivers, with the nation's capital, Lisbon, standing as a proud, strong, and vibrant hub in the center of it all. As Europe goes, Portugal is inexpensive, making it a haven for backpackers and young travelers, yet the natural beauty and exciting culture draw in travelers of all demographics. It's praised for being a panacea of sorts for vacation-planners: mountainous regions, major international cities, endless activities, and some of the most beautiful beaches in the world are all readily available. Couple that with warm climate, and it's hard not to book a ticket in a millisecond. So begin with a glass (or four) of the Douro Valley region's famous port wine as you cruise along the vineyard-lined river, then make your way to the historic gem of Porto before winding your way down the coast to buzzing, shining Lisbon. Don't miss majestic beaches of the Algarve, where you'll swim, climb, and beach-nap off all the wine you drank along the way. It'll be a journey you'll never forget and one you'll catch yourself recommending to everyone the moment they mention they're booking a trip.

# LAGOS

Coverage by **Emma Scornavacchi**

If Portuguese cities were a family, Lagos would be the super-tan cousin who never wants to leave the beach and always has a beer in hand. A sunshine-filled, endless party of a city, Lagos offers cliffside vistas, crazy backpacker bars, and even upscale restaurants and shops that work together to create the ultimate beach vacation. A favorite amongst vacationers from nearby European countries, Lagos also draws backpackers from Canada, Australia, and the US, to name a few, which means the party is always international. And the beaches are as diverse as the community—some beaches are only accessible via wooden stairs, others only by kayak, but all of them are gorgeous. Lagos is the vacation spot of your dreams, waiting for you on the often-overlooked Portuguese coast.

## ORIENTATION

Located in southwest Portugal, the town of Lagos sits on the **Ribiera de Bensafrim,** while the famous local beaches dot the coastline. The town center of Lagos is a network of walk-only cobblestone streets lined with bistros, bars, and shops; it's small enough that you can walk it end to end in just 10-15min. The **Forte da Ponta da Bandeira** blends the town into the water. Other historical sites such as the **Igreja de Santo António** are located in the same area. All roads don't lead to Rome in Lagos; they connect to **Praça de Gil Eanes.** Popular beaches such as **Praia Dona Ana** and **Praia do Camilo** require a bit of a walk, bike, or taxi, and even more remote beaches can be found along the coastline if you're willing to make the trek. Lagos is walkable enough that you'll feel familiar with the geography in a day, leaving you room to explore outward and discover even more of the magic of **the Algarve.**

## ESSENTIALS

### GETTING THERE

Lagos is located about an hour west of Faro international airport, which services the entire Algarve. The airport does not have a public transportation hub within it, so in order to travel outside Faro, you must get a bus or taxi to the city of Faro itself before taking public transportation from there. Trains run to Lagos regularly from both Lisbon and Faro. Times and fares can be found at Portuguese Railway's website: www.cp.pt. Rede-Expressos (www.rede-expressos.pt) and RENEX (www.renex.pt) both operate bus service to Lagos that can be booked online.

### GETTING AROUND

The town of Lagos is small and very walkable, and his limited public transportation for this reason. The Algarve does have a network of trains servicing Lagos to Faro with five stops in between. The main way to get to beaches and cliff hikes surrounding Lagos is by rental car or taxi.

### PRACTICAL INFORMATION

**Tourist Office:** Praça do Giraldo 73; 266 777 071.

**Banks/ATMs/Currency:** Santander Totta (R. da Porta de Portugal 19; 282 770 940; open daily 24hr).

**Post Offices:** The Posto de Correios de Evora is on Rua Olivença (266 745 480; open T-F 8:10am-6:30pm).

Emergency Information

**Emergency Number:** 112

**Police:** 266 76 04 50

**Hospital:** Hospital do Espírito Santo (Lg. Senhor Jesus da Pobreza; 266 74 01 00) is located near city wall at the intersection of with R. Dr. Augusto Eduardo Nunes.

**Pharmacies:** Check the doors of pharmacies for each night's "farmacia de serviço."

### EMERGENCY INFORMATION

**Emergency Number:** 112

**Police:** N125 20; 282 780 240

**US Embassy:** The nearest US Embassy is in Portugal's capital, Lisbon (Avenida das Forças Armadas 133C; 21 727 3300; open M-F 8am-5pm).

**Rape Crisis Center:** APAV, Victim Support Portugal, provides support to all types of victims including sexual violence victims (21 358 79 00; www.apav.pt).

**Hospitals:** Hospital S.Gonçalo (Av. Dom Sebastião 129; 800 224 424; open daily 24hr).

**Pharmacies:** R. Henrique Correia da Silva 1; 282 760 556; open M-Sa 9am-11pm.

# ACCOMMODATIONS

### CAMONE HOSTEL
R. Primeiro de Maio 36; 28 208 55 88; camonehostel.com

Camone Hostel is owned by a Portuguese husband and wife duo, and their welcoming, family-style hospitality sets the tone for the entire hostel experience. Located in a spectacularly decorated building in the heart of old Lagos, Camone Hostel has everything you want (rooftop terrace! Yoga classes! Free breakfast spread! Air conditioning!). Their staff will book you the paddleboarding excursion of your dreams and answer all your questions while also sharing a beer and a story with you on the rooftop terrace after dinner. You'll feel like family by the end of your stay.

*i* Dorms €31-39; reservation recommended; BGLTQ+ friendly; Wi-Fi; free breakfast; luggage storage

### RISING COCK HOSTEL ($$)
Tv. do Forno 14; 28 208 76 30; www.risingcock.com/

Rising Cock is the first privately-owned hostel in Portugal, but it's more commonly known for a name that elicits giggles worldwide. Boasting 13 years of lively atmosphere, large common spaces, and fun activities such as barbeques and booze cruises, the Rising Cock wins the hearts of backpackers everywhere. Though it's certainly a party hostel, the Rising Cock exudes a family vibe, complete with a "momma" who endearingly makes crepes for guests each morning. Bedrooms and bathrooms are standard, so with a price above the average in Lagos, it's clear that what you pay for is the crazy fun atmosphere and social experience.

*i* Dorms from €38-42; reservation recommended; BGLTQ+ friendly; Wi-Fi; free breakfast

# SIGHTS

## CULTURE
......................................

### ◤CAPE ST. VINCENT
N268

As the southwesternmost point in Europe, Cape St. Vincent was literally believed to be the end of the world until the fifteenth century discovery of North America. Today, the point serves as a scenic viewpoint that still feels a bit like sacred ground. Shrouded in the history of religious practices, naval battles, and various cultural beliefs (the Romans believed the point was holy and that the sunset there was larger than anywhere in the world), the spot stands out among the Algarve coast's many stunning viewpoints. Complete with a lighthouse (one of the most powerful in Europe) along with food and market stands, Cape St. Vincent is worth the trip from Lagos.

*i* Limited wheelchair accessibility

## PRAÇA GIL EANES
Pr. Gil Eanes

Praça Gil Eanes is as cosmopolitan as this small beach town gets. Shops, bistros, tourist stands, and street performers surround a circular plaza with a ringed black-and-white tile pattern. Streets reach out like tentacles from the square itself, extending towards the water and back up into town. The square's location right by the Marina and the pier walkway makes it the perfect spot for kayak tour offerings and market stands.

*i* Free; limited wheelchair accessibility

## LANDMARKS

### ◪ANTIGO MERCADO DE ESCRAVOS (ANCIENT SLAVE MARKET)
Pr. Infante Dom Henrique

The first slave market in Europe was based at the Antigo Mercade de Escravos in August 1443, ushering in a practice that would take centuries to abolish. The exhibit here is informative, though, at times, more focused on the facts of the trade than the lives of the people who suffered. Still, through ancient artifacts, interactive tablets, and quotes sourced from the time, the exhibit manages to communicate the pain and injustices created by the slave trade. Though this exhibit can be difficult to consider on a beach vacation, historical context is crucial everywhere, and this is a piece of history not to be forgotten.

*i* Admission €3, €1.50 student

## MUSEUMS

### MUSEU MUNICIPAL DR. JOSÉ FORMOSINHO
R. General Alberto da Silveira s/n; 28 276 23 01; open Tu-Su 9:30am-5pm

An eclectic mix of archaeological artifacts and intricate miniatures representing life in the Algarve, the Museu Municipial leaves no shell, rock, or shard of clay pot left undisplayed. Built in 1930, the museum represents different periods in Lagos' history through mismatched objects and in-depth descriptions. As you wander through the detailed, miniature fishing boats and the exhaustive coin collection, you'll realize that

the ethnography of Lagos and its surrounding region is quite literally in full view within these cases.

*i* Admission €3, €1.50 student

## OUTDOORS

### ◪PONTA DA PIEDADE
Estr. da Ponta da Piedade

Ponta da Piedade will take your breath away, give it back, then take it away again. It's not just because the pathways and stairs will tire you out. A famous viewpoint atop a mini peninsula outside Lagos, Ponta da Piedade offers 360-degree views of the most spectacular rock formations, clustering of caves, and sparkling turquoise water you've ever seen. A snack bar offers food and drinks at the point of entrance, and though plenty of people will be around picnicking and taking photos, the paths don't feel too crowded. Walk to this point for photos the folks back at home won't believe and climb down the nearby stairs to Camilo Beach to get your breath back.

*i* No wheelchair accessibility

### PRAIA DO CAMILO
Estrada Ponta da Piedade

Down winding, steep steps built into a cliff and nestled among more rocky cliffs and caves, Praia do Camilo offers a small beach full of umbrellas and bikini-clad visitors. Though crowded, the beautiful Camilo Beach makes up for it with sparkling water, cave passageways, and unreal views of Lagos' coastline. Visitors will spend an afternoon or a whole day here, swimming, tanning, snorkeling, and taking extensive photos. A smaller option than some more famous beaches, Praia do Camilo offers a more intimate experience with the stunning scenery of the Algarve.

*i* Free; no wheelchair accessibility

### PRAIA DONA ANA
Alameda Dr. Armando Soares Ribiero

If your friend went to Lagos and sent you a postcard that looked too heavenly to be real, it was probably of Praia Dona Ana. Dona Ana's status as the go-to beach spot means it can get crowded (and the beach itself isn't that big), but somehow the clusters of brightly-colored umbrellas add to the charm. Bright blue water laps against gold sand coastline and cliffs that tower above the land. Hundreds of stairs have been built in to transport visitors up and down, so you'll get a nice workout even as you lounge on the sand.

*i* Free; no wheelchair accessibility

# FOOD

### 🏮DRAGON JAPANESE AND CHINESE RESTAURANT ($)

R. Marreiros Netto; 28 279 23 32; www. dragonlagos.pt/en_GB; open daily 11am-3pm and 5:30pm-midnight

If you're a fan of sushi, you came to the right place: in this neighborhood, there's a sushi restaurant on every other block. Even better, a full plate of sushi at Dragon will set you back just €6. Cheaper than most meals in Lagos, and cheaper than a single grain of rice at an American sushi restaurant, you'll love the bargain as much as the chance to enjoy a cuisine outside the Portuguese norm. Bonus points for all-you-can-eat offerings at both lunch and dinner (€11.90 and €13.90, respectively).

*i* Entrées €6; vegetarian options available

### MAR D'ESTÓRIAS ($$)

R. Silva Lopes 30; 28 279 21 65; www. mardestorias.com; open M-Th 10am-10pm, F-Sa 10am-midnight

Mar D'Estórias is a converted church that is now home to "Portuguese Essence," a market selling local artisan products like pottery and clothes, with a café and rooftop terrace to boot. The latter is a hip but still homey joint serving up delicious meat dishes, fresh seafood, and salad options. For starters, order the Algarve carrots (don't be fooled—veggies can taste great too) and then continue with a seafood and vegetable combo.

*i* Entrées €7-15; vegetarian options available

### HE GARDEN ($$)

R. Lançarote de Freitas 48; open daily 1pm-midnight

Tucked away in a plant-filled patio where tropical music is bumping and lanterns hang over outdoor tables, The Garden is a popular spot to grab a snack. The ribs and the garden burger are to die for, proving that both carnivores and vegetarians alike will be able to find a common ground. Other perks: the drinks are fruity, the outdoor grill smells great, and the lounge area means dinner can become after-dinner drinks without even leaving the patio.

*i* Entrées €3-8; vegetarian and vegan options available

# NIGHTLIFE

### 🏮JOE'S GARAGE

R. Primeiro de Maio 78; 91 725 28 09; www.joesgarage.eu.com

The party experience to end all party experiences, Joe's Garage is a hotspot for both traditional bar nights and parties with wild, original themes. From foam parties to flaming shots to jello wrestling, Joe's Garage does all the things you see in frat movies—and does them well. Centrally located and popular for visitors and locals alike, their friendly staff will supply you with drinks all night long while you dance, laugh, and theme-party the night away. Prepare to get sweaty (and no promises you won't get beer to the head), but if you're ready for it, Joe's Garage will provide a hilarious party night that doesn't take itself too seriously.

*i* Drinks €2-10

### INSIDEOUT BAR

R. Candido dos Reis 19; open 9pm-4am

Known for fishbowl cocktails and staying open later than any of its neighbors, InsideOut is a classic rager night in the making. The two-for-one before midnight special means people will be sitting around sipping fishbowl cocktails and more as soon as InsideOut opens, but the large dance floor and colorful lights will start up later in the night and keep people there until closing. InsideOut is a local favorite and is bound to turn what seems like a typical night into a memorable one.

*i* Drinks €2-6

### WHYTES BAR

R. do Ferrador 7; 92 906 14 07; www. whytesbar.com; open daily 7pm-2am

Free drinks? Check. Full bar? Check. Sweaty, busy dance room? Check.

An unassuming spot that's already packed when everywhere else is just starting up? Check. That's what you get at Whytes Bar. Employees in red tank tops may lure you in with the promise of free drinks if you can "Beat the Bartender" by rolling a higher number with a pair of dice. They're not kidding: it's that easy. The free drinks draw people in at all times, so Whytes will be a go-to stop for you whenever you need it.

*i* Drinks €2-8

# LISBON

Coverage by **Emma Scornavacchi**

Less traveled than other bigger, more well-known European cities, Lisbon feels like the continent's best kept secret. We almost don't want to rave too much (the waiting-to-be-discovered feel is part of what makes Lisbon so special), but we simply can't help ourselves: it's an absolutely incredible city. Somehow managing to blend the international with the distinctly Portuguese, Lisbon has everything a world traveler dreams of along with plenty of unique culture and style. The smells of the city's sardines, *bacalhau* (codfish), *bifana* (pork sandwiches), and *pastel de nata* (egg pastries) waft throughout, and these incredible foods are sold both as grilled-in-front-of-you street food and delicacies at the nicest of Lisbon's restaurant scene. String lights and decorations criss-cross narrow streets lined with colorful houses and overflowing flower boxes. Every square bustles with energy, the hum of animated Portuguese, and the buzz of a good wine-fueled night.

## ORIENTATION

Situated on the banks of the **Tagus River,** Lisbon's biggest square, **Praça do Comércio,** beckons visitors in from the water to explore the city. The eastern part of the city is occupied mostly by **Alfama.** More toward the center of the city lies **Baixa-Chiado,** a hip, popular area full of bistros, boutiques, and more international shopping. **Bairro Alto** lies to the west of Baixa and operates on a narrow grid system with shorter blocks than most of the city: home to cheap food during the day, Bairro Alto is the main spot for bars and street parties at night. Finally, toward the north lies **Avenida de Liberdades,** Lisbon's tree-lined luxury street, which leads straight into **Rossio Square.**

# ESSENTIALS

## GETTING THERE

Lisbon Portela Airport is Portugal's largest airport and the main HQ for airlines such as TAP Portugal. Located about 5mi. from the city center, the drive is about 20min. To get in from the airport via metro, take the Red Line and switch to the Green Line. By bus, take #708 or 744 into the center. Lisbon's Santa Apolonia Train Station is the city's largest station; Rossio, Barreiro, and Cais do Sodre are also major stations. Santa Apolonia is the main terminal for domestic travel as well as international destinations in Spain and France. ]The main bus terminal for domestic travel is Rios Bus Station located at R. Prof. Lima Basto 133.

## GETTING AROUND

Lisbon's metro operates on four lines—Blue, Yellow, Green, and Red—and connects the city center with surrounding suburbs. The metro operates from 6:30am-1am and trains come every 5-10 min. Single tickets are €1.45 and an unlimited 24hr travel ticket is €6.15. Metro is the easiest way to travel between Lisbon's neighborhoods. Lisbon's bus system covers the entire city.

## PRACTICAL INFORMATION

**Tourist Offices:** Lisbon's main tourist office (look for the purple "Ask Me Lisboa" logo) is located at Terreiro do Paço (Pr. do Comércio; 210 312 810; 9am-8pm).

### Banks/ATMs/Currency Exchange:
Banco de Portugal (R. Comércio 158, 21 313 0000). Except on special occasions, all banks are generally open M-F 8:30am-3pm.

**Post Offices:** Correios (Pr. dos Restauradores 58; 21 323 8971; open M-F 8am-10pm, Sa 9am-6pm).

**Internet:** Hostels and cafés throughout the city offer free Wi-Fi. Biblioteca Municipal Camões also offers free public internet access (Pr. dos Restauradores 58; 213 422 157; www. blx.com-lisboa-pt).

**BGLTQ+ Resources:** BGLTQ+ resources can be found at www.ilga-europe.org. Lisbon Beach offers BGLTQ+ geared tours of Lisbon as well as tips and other resources (www.lisbonbeach.com).

## EMERGENCY INFORMATION

**Emergency Number:** 112

**Police:** Lisbon's Tourism Police Office is located next to the Pr. dos Restauradores tourism office (Pr. dos Restauradores 58; 213 421 624).

**US Embassy:** There is a US Embassy in Lisbon (Avenida das Forças Armadas 133C; 21 727 3300; open M-F 8am-5pm).

**Rape Crisis Center:** Victim Support Portugal (APAV; 21 358 7900; www. apav.pt).

**Hospitals:** The main hospital in Lisbon is Hospital de São José (R. José António Serrano; 308 802 678; open daily 24hr; www.hospitaldesaojose. com).

**Pharmacies:** Pharmacies are all over Lisbon and operate on a shift schedule, posted outside every pharmacy, to determine which are open late. All pharmacies are marked by a blinking green cross.

# ACCOMMODATIONS

### GOODMORNING HOSTEL
Pr. Dos Restauradores 65; 21 342 11 28; www.goodmorninghostel.com; reception open 24hr

You've just gotten to Lisbon and want to meet people, but also go to bed early. How does "Community Tapas" sound? You slept in today and are ready to rage with new friends tonight. How about "Pub Crawl, free sangria?" Goodmorning Hostel offers amenities beyond a traveler's wildest dreams, in a central location just off of **Rossio Square.** Their colorful common spaces and dorms create the perfect atmosphere for fun of all kinds, and their staff is cheery and friendly to an extreme. Did we mention there are free waffles?

*i* Mixed dorms €14-18, private €55-65; reservation recommended; BGLTQ+ friendly; Wi-Fi; luggage storage; free breakfast

### GSPOT PARTY HOSTEL
Tr. Fala-só 24B; 21 825 33 44; www. gspothostels.com; reception open 24hr

The ultimate experience in party hostel-ing, GSpot in Lisbon is as out-there and ready to have a good time as its provocative name suggests. Whenever you arrive, you'll be greeted by friendly front-desk staff and travelers in the lounge drinking beers (whether it's 10am or 10pm). A cartoon movie is playing, someone is discussing the drinking game rules papered on the walls, and a French bulldog is dodging feet. GSpot has a distinct frat vibe (but better cleaning services!), with nightly pub crawls, wild parties, and a constant stream of backpackers arriving at the bar, looking to knock back a few. Some of the dorms are a little cramped, though, so it might not be your most comfortable stay.

*i* Dorms €18-24; reservation recommended; BGLTQ+ friendly; Wi-Fi; luggage storage; laundry facilities; free breakfast

### LOST INN LISBON
Beco dos Apóstolos; 21 347 07 55; www. lostinnlisbon.com; reception open 24hr

Striking the ideal balance between luxurious amenities and a friendly atmosphere, Lost Inn Lisbon will change the way you experience hostel living. Rooms are airy and beautiful, and the same key card will open your locker, dorm, and the front door to the hostel. High ceilings, rustic wooden furniture, and traditional Portuguese tiles decorate both the common spaces and living areas, making the hostel historic but also homey. Lost Inn offers recommendations for everything from excursions to budget eats from their knowledgeable staff.

*i* Mixed or female dorms €17-23, private €62; reservation recommended; BGLTQ+

friendly; Wi-Fi; free breakfas;, laundry facilities; luggage storage; airport shuttle

## URBAN GARDEN HOSTEL

R. Camilo Castelo Branco 2; 21 193 32 11; www.urbangardenhostel.com; reception open 24hr

Urban Garden lives up to its name. Located right off **Avenida de Liberdades,** the hostel puts you right in the middle of Lisbon's busy, urban culture. When you enter, though, the hardwood floors, green furniture, and combo of indoor and outdoor spaces will make you feel as if you've entered a garden oasis. The friendly and knowledgeable staff will answer all your questions and even invite the solo traveler to join in on some of their many fun after-work plans. Dorm rooms can get a little hot in warmer weather (opening a window helps), but, for the most part, the rooms are clean and comfortable.

*i* Dorms €10-23; reservation recommended; BGLTQ+ friendly; wheelchair accessible; Wi-Fi; reservation recommended; free breakfast

# SIGHTS

## CULTURE

### ROSSIO SQUARE (PRAÇA DOM PEDRO IV)

Pr. Dom Pedro IV; open daily 24hr

The beating heart of this vibrant city has to be Rossio Square. The statue of **Dom Pedro IV** stands imposingly over the square, which is home to shops, bistros, and guided tour groups strolling along the famed wavy tile patterns. Though the square's official name has been **Praça Dom Pedro IV**

since the statue's inauguration in 1874, residents have stayed strong-willed as ever about the history of their city, continuing to refer to the square by its original name. Rossio Square is the perfect spot to stop and eat a snack, hear about the history of Lisbon, or wander in and out of shops.

*i* Free; wheelchair accessible

### TEATRO NACIONAL D. MARIA II (PORTUGUESE NATIONAL THEATER)

Pr. D. Pedro IV (Rossio Square); 21 325 08 00; www.tndm.pt

A haven of the arts housed inside a renovated 200+ year old Neoclassical palace, the Portuguese National Theater takes up an entire end of **Rossio Square** with its grandiose dedication to dance, theater, and music. The National Theater is host to operas, art galleries, dance performances, and a general constant influx of art to Portugal's cultural capital. Centrally and conveniently located, its position in the city highlights Portugal's steadfast dedication to the arts.

*i* Ticket prices vary; tour tickets €8; guided tours M at 11am except Aug; wheelchair accessible

## LANDMARKS

### CASTELO DE SAO JORGE

R. de Santa Cruz do Castelo; 21 880 06 20; www.castelodesaojorge.pt; open daily Mar-Oct 9am-9pm, Nov-Feb 9am-6pm

If you're expecting just another crumbling castle when visiting Castelo de Sao Jorge, you're in for an exciting treat. The hidden, hilltop structure was built to be inaccessible to enemy militaries, and today, tourists trying to navigate the surrounding twisting alleyways will understand the struggle. Beyond just a castle, though, the gates open on to an eleventh-century world still very much intact. Walk under stone arches and duck around landscaped corners to find every bit of history that has accumulated here since the Moorish castle was a neighborhood for the royal elite.

*i Admission €8.50, €5 student; last entry 5:30pm; free guidebook available in English*

### MOSTEIRO DOS JERÓNIMOS (JERÓNIMO'S MONASTERY)

Pr. do Império; 21 362 00 34; www.mosteirojeronimos.pt; open Oct-May Tu-Su 10am-5:30pm, May-Sept T-Su 10am-6:30pm

Dedicated thematically to the voyages that funded its creation, the Jerónimos Monastery is a beautiful church and cloister combination with historic architecture, centered around Lisbon's dedication to global exploration. High, arched ceilings and stained glass windows surround tombs and a majestic altar inside the church, where ancient pictograms tell stories of religion and travel. Entrance to the cloister outside is pricey, but its intricate archways and courtyard are a sight to behold.

*i Cloister admission €10, church admission free; last entry 30 min. before closing*

### SANTA JUSTA LIFT

R. do Ouro; 21 413 86 79; open daily Mar-Oct 9am-11pm, Nov -Feb 9am-9pm

One of the most famous structures built by architect **Gustave Eiffel** (if we're not counting that tower in France), the dark-metal Santa Justa Lift is a striking sight against the backdrop of Lisbon's criss-crossing, cheery streets. For those tired of climbing historic towers, the lift offers a monument whose entire purpose is an elevator—so you can save the sweat and ride along quite literally inside a piece of history. The lift offers incredible panoramic views of Lisbon (once you pay the fee and wait in the 5 to 15-minute line). We recommend going at night to see the lift in all its illuminated glory. *Ding ding ding*, going up!

*i Admission €5.15; no wheelchair accessibility*

### TORRE DE BELÉM (BELÉM TOWER)

Av. Brasília; www.torrebelem.gov.pt; open Oct-Apr 10am-5pm, May-Sept 10am-6:30pm

Set aside some time for a visit to Belém Tower if you want wide-ranging views of the **Tagus River** and Lisbon's sprawling city center, but don't sweat it if you're sick of waiting in lines: looking up at the tower from the shoreline is an equally awe-inspiring (and less time-consuming) sight. Belém Tower has been around for over 500 years, attesting to Lisbon's centuries of maritime exploration and discovery. Now, it lends tourists glimpses into this historical connection to the ocean. A trip to the top will take at least an hour (and perhaps two), as lines are slow and the 93 winding stairs are narrow.

*i Admission €6, €3 student; large group private tours €500-1000*

## MUSEUMS

### MUSEU CALOUSTE GULBENKIAN

Av. De Berna 45A; 21 782 30 00; www.gulbenkian.pt; M, W-Su 10am-6pm

When you've made your money on Persian Gulf region oil exploration and have become one of the wealthiest individuals on earth, what else is there to do but open a private foundation and art museum in Lisbon? Nothing at all, we say. Back in 1956, **Calouste Gulbenkian** agreed. These days, the Gulbenkian Museum features two collections—the **Modern Collection** and the **Founder's Collection** of historic art—connected by stunning, overgrown, shady gardens. The two impressive collections feature a wide range of art, suited to groups with diverse tastes, or individuals whose tastes change as quickly as it takes to walk the hidden garden pathways. The delicious café with outdoor seating, for when you're tired of ogling paintings, is an added bonus.

*i Collections and exhibits €11.50, €10 collections only, €5 for under-30 years old; last entry 5:30pm; wheelchair accessible*

## MUSEU DE ARTE, ARQUITETURA E TECNOLOGIA (MAAT)

Av. Brasília; 21 002 81 30; www.maat.pt; open M, W-Su noon-8pm

Modern art like you've never seen it before: the MAAT took over a former power station and reinvigorated the waterfront space with contemporary exhibits and architecture. The building itself blends curved and straight lines with reflective tiles reminiscent of the sun glinting off the **Tagus River** just outside. Inside, the MAAT uses media and space to innovatively address themes of humanity, technology, and urban planning. You'll definitely need time to ponder the cutting-edge and contemporary exhibits, so stroll onto the roof of the museum itself (accessible on either side by a sloping ramp and stairs) to breathe in the sea air and take a moment to relax before diving back into the exhibits.

*i* Admission €5, €2.50 student; limited wheelchair accessibility

## MUSEU NACIONAL DE ARTE ANTIGA

R. das Janelas Verdes; 21 391 28 00; www.museudearteantiga.pt/english; open T-Su 10am-6pm

Housed inside a seventeenth century palace, the MNAA displays ancient art, from paintings and sculptures to gold and silver, from Portugal and around the world. Like many Portuguese museums, the MNAA does not draw large crowds of tourists, so there's no rush as you wander through the exhibits. The museum features an impressive amount of decorative art, much of it religious. Situated over the Doca de Santo Amaro in Lisbon's port, the museum opens right up to waterside cafés.

*i* Admission €6, extra charge varies by exhibit; 1hr and 4hr tours available; wheelchair accessible

## OUTDOORS

### MIRADOUROS DE LISBOA (VIEW-POINTS OF LISBON)

Open daily 24hr

The top of every Lisbon hill—which is to say, the top of every Lisbon street—offers spectacular views of sea, castle, or cityscape. These *miradouros* have been unofficially dubbed the seven best lookouts. Grab a glass of wine on the street (remember: no open container laws!) and get ready to climb to photo-taking glory at sunset. Miradouros da Senhora do Monte, São Pedro de Alcantara, Santa Catarina, Graça, and Santa Luzia along with special *Miradouros* from **São Jorge Castle** and the **Santa Justa Lift**, will all offer stunning vistas of Lisbon. All are easily navigable by GPS and marked on maps, but if you're alone and need to find a *miradouro*, just climb until you can't climb anymore. Chances are, you've found one.

*i* Free; limited wheelchair accessibility

# FOOD

### PASTEIS DE BELÉM ($$)

R. de Belém 84; 21 363 74 23; www.pasteisdebelem.pt; open daily 8am-11pm

How does Pasteis de Belém get their renowned *pastel de nata* pastry to taste so perfect—so flaky, gooey, and sweet? Maybe it's because this historic pastry shop in the Belém neighborhood is the birthplace of the famous Portuguese pastry itself, and has been baking them using a secret recipe to glazed, sugared perfection since 1837. The to-go line can get long, but there's plenty of seating inside the café as an alternate option. As soon as you sprinkle a little powdered sugar on top of the *pastel de nata's* delicious glaze and bite into the eggy-sweet pastry, you'll understand why Pasteis de Belém is so protective of their precious recipe.

*i* Pastel de nata and drink €6

### PONTO FINAL RESTAURANTE ($$)

R. do Ginjal 72, Cacilhas; 21 276 07 43; open M, W-Su noon-11pm

Just a quick ferry ride from **Cais do Sodré** and a 15-minute walk along the water leads you to one of Lisbon's best-kept secrets: Ponto Final. Ponto Final seems to emerge from the water of the **Tagus** and the surrounding abandoned buildings: a beacon of hope, wine, and grilled fish on the less-visited southern bank. As you sit down with the sun setting behind the **Ponte 25 de Abril,** you'll feel like you're the only people for miles. Well-loved for its generous portions of authentic Portuguese food, sardines, cod, and potatoes all star on the menu, alongside wine that only comes by the bottle. The outdoor patio gets windy, but the restaurant has a stock of fleece blankets on offer—they know what they're doing.

*i* *Entreés €12-19, specials €30*

### POP CEREAL CAFÉ ($)
R. do Norte 64; 21 131 72 11; www.pop-cereal.com; open daily 8am-midnight

Relive your childhood even better than the first time around (no judgment on your childhood, we just promise this is better!) at Pop Cereal Café, located right in **Bairro Alto** and offering over 100 types of cereal in every combination possible. With quirky pop art, bunk beds, chairs on the ceiling, and an entire wall of cereal boxes, Pop Cereal offers pre-made mixes, milkshakes, and ice cream. Check out the international cereals, traditional Portuguese cereals, and every flavor, style, type of mix or topping available. Making these trays is slow (it's a process!), but once you taste that first spoonful of cereal-chocolate-strawberry-almond milk-crunchy goodness, you'll realize just what a special place you've stumbled upon.

*i* *Cereal tray €3-5; vegetarian options available; wheelchair accessible*

### TIME OUT MARKET (MERCADO DA RIBEIRA) ($$)
Av. 24 de Julho 49; 21 395 12 74; www.timeout.com/market; open M-W, Su 10am-midnight, Th-Sa 10am-2am

An Italian is ordering sushi. A Belgian is ordering *"pastel de nata."* A French family is ordering Chinese food. Time Out Market is as international as it gets. High ceilings cover organized stands, many run by Lisbon's most esteemed chefs and restaurateurs, themed in the market's black and white décor. Though it's more upscale, standardized, and global than the authentic hustle and bustle of a traditional Portuguese market, you're guaranteed to find whatever meal you've been craving in top-notch quality here. Blurbs in both Portuguese and English flank each stand, helping you decide whether you'd rather have the ceviche from **Sea Me** or the burger from **Honorato**.

*i* *Prices vary by stand; vegetarian options available; wheelchair accessible; some stands cash only*

## NIGHTLIFE

### LUX CLUB
Av. Infante D. Henrique; 21 882 08 90; www.luxfragil.com; open Th-Su 11pm-6am

A bit of a quirky playground for the elite of Lisbon's club scene, Lux has all the trappings of a classic nightclub, and then some. Think mechanical polar bears, a giant rotating ball above the staircase, and an upstairs bar with giant lounge chairs for groups. The colorful lights and multiple bars will keep the night going, but the seemingly random amenities and rooftop views make Lux feel *lux*-urious. Gaining admittance without an absurd fee is contingent on the bouncer liking you (or liking your look), and this practice has led to negative experiences for some. Those who choose to try out Lux for the night, though, will surely find their experience everything they dreamed of and more—because who dreams of mechanical polar bears on the way to club bathrooms?

*i* *Cover varies about €8-12, drinks €5-10; upscale dress*

### PARK BAR
21 591 4011; open Tu-Sa 1pm-2am, Su 1pm-8p

Park Bar makes you work for your fun. For starters, it's notoriously hard to find—with no official address, the listed one gets you close and then you have to look for the looming parking garage. Take the dingy elevator to the fifth floor and climb the following flight of stairs to emerge from a bleak garage to a hip, trendy haven of a bar. Its location on the roof of this garage grants Park panoramic views of the city, the river, and the **Ponte 25 de Abril.** Drinks are pricey, so consider drinking before arriving if your budget is tight, but either way the fresh and fun atmosphere of Park will absolutely make you want to revisit.

*i* *Drinks €6-15; wheelchair accessible*

**PENSÃO AMOR**

R. do Alecrim 19; 21 314 33 99; open M-W noon-3am, Th-Sa noon-4am, Su noon-3am

When in Lisbon, order your next drink at a brothel. Wait—what was that? Oh, right: a converted brothel. Converted as it may be, Pensão Amor has kept the themes of sex and love alive and well in this eccentric bar. There will be a line to get in as the night goes on, but once you enter through the stairwell, lined with street-art, you'll enter a world of funky fantasy. Hazy rooms with plush lounge seating surround a pink-walled erotic library, a mini-storefront selling lingerie and sex toys, a terrace, and the bar room tightly packed with a crowd swaying to the often-live entertainment. Pensão Amor attracts a bit of an older crowd (groovy, dude!), but will be an experience for anyone looking to feel some type of way.

*i* *Cover varies, drinks €2-10*

# PORTO

Coverage by **Emma Scornavacchi**

Winding down seemingly secret cobblestone streets that just keep getting steeper, the smell of *alheira* (traditional sausage) mingles with the faint sound of shouting in Portuguese from behind a pale pink door. The petals of the purple jacaranda trees fall alongside a blue-and-white tiled building; vendors in the street market sell cork-themed souvenirs against the backdrop of the Douro River. This is Porto, the city also known as "Cidade Invicta" or "Unvanquished City," a character trait locals will tell you if you ask, and even if you don't. In Porto, you'll experience windy vistas, countless historical landmarks, and some of the most authentic and unpretentious Portuguese food anywhere. But "não quebrar um prato" (literally "don't break a plate," or "don't panic" in Portuguese slang) if you don't get a chance to experience everything Porto has to offer. If the city's history of standing strong and proud says anything about its future, Porto will be waiting for you when you return.

## ORIENTATION

Begin exploring Porto with the historical **Ribeira** region along the **Duoro River.** Climb up the steep hill into the hip and constantly changing **Baixa downtown,** filled with shops and modern restaurants, or avoid the urban area and cross the **Dom Luis Bridge** instead to the **Vila Nova de Gaia** suburb for wine-tasting on the banks. A 30-minute drive will get you out to the seaside **Foz region.**

## ESSENTIALS
### GETTING THERE

Porto Airport, officially Francisco Sa Carneiro Airport, is located about 6mi. from the city center. To get into the city center from the airport, take either the metro (purple E line into Trinidade, €2-3 including cost of Andante card), an AeroBus (STCP bus system to Praça de Liberdade; pay by Andante card), or a taxi from outside the airport (€20-25). Main train stations are São Bento station and Campanhã station. For in-country bus travel, the Rede Espressos terminal is located at R. Alexandre Herculano 366. For international travel, buses leave from the Casa de Música metro stop.

### GETTING AROUND

Porto's above-ground tram system is considered state-of-the-art. The system's six lines are organized by both color and letter and connect the city's center with its outskirts. Metro tickets and Andante passes (€0.60) can be purchased in any stations or tourist office. Tourist travel cards can be purchased (€7 per day, €15 per 3 days) for unlimited travel on metro and buses. Bus travel is also relatively cheap and easy; Andante cards can be used (€1.20 for a trip) and purchasing on board is also possible (€1.80). Andante cards must be validated at the station before they can be used.

## PRACTICAL INFORMATION

**Tourist Offices:** Porto's main tourist office is just across the street and west from City Hall (R. Clube dos Fenianos 25; 223 393 472; open daily May-Oct 9am-8pm, Aug 9am-9pm, Nov-Apr 9am-7pm).

**Banks/ATMs/Currency Exchange:** Caixa Geral de Depositos (22 209 8100; Av dos Aliados 106; open M-F 8:30am-3pm). ATMs are called "Multibanco," and are a better bet for exchanging currency than airports or hotels, which will charge commission fees.

**Post Offices:** The most centrally located is the Post Office Allied (storefront CTT Correios) on R. Dr. António Luís Gomes (www.ctt.pt, open M-F 8am-9pm, Sat 9am-6pm).

**Internet:** Many cafés and hostels offer free Wi-Fi, and there is free city Wi-Fi in major neighborhoods and squares as well.

**BGLTQ+ Resources:** BGLTQ+ resources can be found at www.ilga-europe.org. Porto hosts an annual Pride March in July.

## EMERGENCY INFORMATION

**Emergency Number:** 112

**Police:** The tourism police station is located next to the main tourist office on R. Clube dos Fenianos and handles tourist-specific cases (222 092 006; open daily, 8am-midnight).

**US Embassy:** The nearest US Embassy is in Portugal's capital, Lisbon (Avenida das Forças Armadas 133C; 21 727 3300; open M-F 8am-5pm).

**Rape Crisis Center:** Victim Support Portugal (APAV, 21 358 7900, www.apav.pt).

**Hospitals:** Hospital da Ordem Do Carmo (Praça de Carlos Alberto 32; 22 207 8400).

**Pharmacies:** Most pharmacies, marked by neon green crosses, are open M-F 9am-7pm and Sa 9am-1pm. Pharmacies operate on a shift system to determine late hours; the pharmacy on duty will be open 9am-11pm and will have someone on duty 24hr. Pharmacy Dos Clerigos (22 339 2370).

# ACCOMMODATIONS

### ◪PILOT DESIGN HOSTEL AND BAR ($$)

Largo Alberto Pimental 11; 22 208 43 62; www.pilothostel.com; reception open 24hr

A spot as social as it is accommodating, Pilot has everything the young, traveling backpacker needs. Dorm-style comfortable beds, knowledgeable front desk staff, daily breakfast spread, and even a free nightly shot for guests at 10pm. The free-flowing alcohol speaks to the vibe of the hostel—music blasts nightly from the bar just downstairs from the dorm rooms (so avoid first floor rooms if you're planning on sleeping early), guests use the available kitchen to cook and share their own meals, and everything from the lobby to the bathroom stalls are adorned with inspirational travel quotes. Not all who wander are lost, but you'll never get lost staying at Pilot.

*i* *Dorms €18-20; reservation recommended; BGLTQ+ friendly; wheelchair accessible; Wi-Fi; linens included; luggage storage; breakfast €3*

### PORTO REPUBLICA HOSTEL AND SUITES ($$)

Pr. da República 38; 22 201 12 70; www.portorepublica.com; reception open 24hr

Located right on the **Praça da República** in a building constructed in 1883, **Porto Republica** is grounded firmly in history, but located just five-minutes walking from everything you want to access in modern-day Porto. The luxurious hardwood floors, crisp white linens, and antique furniture feel more like a boutique hotel than a pit stop for backpackers, but prices for shared dorms are only barely above more typical places. Note that there are only three bathrooms (each private), so you may face a wait during busier hours but, luckily, you'll have crown molding and elegant decorations to distract you from the inconvenience.

*i* *Dorms €22-28; private 2-bed suite €112; reservation recommended; BGLTQ+ friendly; Wi-Fi; linens included; luggage storage; free breakfast*

# SIGHTS
## CULTURE

### ⬛LIVRARIA LELLO (LELLO BOOK-SHOP)

R. das Carmelitas 144; 22 200 20 37; www.livrarialello.pt; open M-F 10am-7:30pm, Sa 10am-7pm, Su 11am-7pm

Entering **Livraria Lello** is like stepping into a fairytale. An intricate storefront, wood-paneled interior, and splendid red staircase create a magical aura. The shop is crowded, but it's worth weaving through to witness all of Lello's exquisite beauty. It's a small nuisance that there's an entrance fee (€4) to access Lello's glory, but you'll forget all about the hassle when you're marveling the endless shelves of books. And, if you feel like owls should be swooping in during your visit, your *Harry Potter* senses are spot-on: J.K. Rowling lived in Porto for a time while creating the *Harry Potter* series, and is said to have drawn inspiration from Lello. Wicked!

*i* Entrance fee €4; wheelchair accessible

### CAIS DE RIBEIRA

Cais de Ribeira, Duoro River; hours vary by store

The most iconic taste of the city lies along the waters of the **Duoro,** and the Cais de Ribeira is as Porto as Porto gets. Cais de Ribeira, which translates essentially to "river pier" in English, is the concrete walkway lined with market stands, restaurants, and bars that separates the Duoro River from the city. Entertainment comes in the form of live musicians and artists, as well as the extreme force with which vendors will shout at you to buy their rope bracelets and tile magnets. You'll get the most culturally complete experience if you stop for an hour or so, order a drink at one of the many bars, and people-watch carefully.

*i* Prices vary by store

### CASA DA MÚSICA

Av. Da Boavista 604-610; 22 012 02 20; www.casademusica.com

Designated by some as the crowning achievement of architect **Rem Koolhas,** the Casa da Música would be famous even if nothing happened inside. Luckily for you, there's much to explore: orchestras, a cultural institution, a restaurant, and countless performance days throughout the year. Casa da Música is right on the **Jardim da Rotunda da Boavista** and is easily accessible by public transportation or taxi, as it's a mere 20-minutes from the city center. Though performance days boast the concert hall's finest moments, guided tours revealing beautiful and innovative decoration are themselves reason to go.

*i* Free entry; guided tour €7.50, ticket prices vary based on exhibit/performance; tours in Portuguese and English daily 11am, 4pm

### IGREJA SÃO FRANCISCO (SÃO FRANCISCO CHURCH)

R. do Infante D. Henrique; 22 206 21 00; open daily Nov-Feb 9am-6pm; Mar-Apr 9am-7pm, May-June 9am-7:30pm, July-Sep 9am-8pm, Oct 9am-7pm

You think you've seen impressive Baroque architecture, and then you step foot in the Igreja São Francisco and realize you know nothing. The walls and ceilings are covered, seemingly impossibly so, with gold, three-dimensional artwork depicting biblical figures and stories. In the **catacombs** beneath the church, walk not just beside graves but also on top of them, and the musky, unpleasant smell will confirm that you are, indeed, surrounded by death. It feels a bit like you'll never make it out, but, once you do, the magnificence of the church will jolt you back to the world of the living.

*i* Entrance fee €4.50, €3.50 student

## LANDMARKS

### ESTAÇÃO DE SÃO BENTO (SÃO BENTO TRAIN STATION)

Pr. Almedia Garrett

Only in Porto would something as practical as a train station be as stunning as the São Bento Train Station. Walk into the massive entrance hall and find yourself surrounded by blue and white tiles stretching high up toward the ceiling, which were installed in 1916. Though this design is ubiquitous throughout the city, São Bento is the spectacular crown jewel of such displays. Inside the open-air station itself, ticket offices offer maps, guides, information, tours, and travel cards to create a one-stop center for travel to, from, and within Porto.

*i* *Free entry*

## MOSTEIRO DA SERRA DO PILAR

Largo de Aviz, Vila Nova de Gaia; 22 014 24 25; open Tu-Su 10am-5:30pm

Did you exercise yet today? No? Same here. Don't have the cash for a gym membership? That's okay! Just cross the **Dom Luis Bridge** and take one of the many winding streets up to the Serra do Pilar Monastery. Designated as a **UNESCO World Heritage site** in 1996, the huge, round structure can be seen from many vantage points on the bridge and around the city, but the real winner is the view looking out from the monastery itself. Though you may battle high winds that make it chilly even in the summer, you'll find this spot worth the workout.

*i* *Free entry*

## PONTE DOM LUÍS I

Ponte Luis I

Hold onto your hats, it's breezy up here! A double deck metal arch bridge connecting the official city of Porto with **Vila Nova de Gaia,** the Dom Luis Bridge provides views of grassy hillsides, terracotta roofs, and boats on the river. While the top level is reserved for pedestrians and trains, vehicles travel along the lower level flanked by two narrow sidewalks. Stroll across the upper level for a less close-to-roadkill experience; just be wary of seagulls swooping low and keep in mind the steep descent you face on either side of the impressive structure.

*i* *Free; wheelchair accessible*

## SÉ DO PORTO (PORTO CATHEDRAL)

Terreiro Da Sé; 22 205 90 28; church open Apr-Oct M-Sa 9am-7pm, Nov-March M-Sa 9am-12:30pm, 2:30pm-6pm; Su and religious holidays 9am-noon, 2:30-6:30pm

Standing majestic atop yet another hill, the city's revered Cathedral overlooks the city in a fortress-like manner, welcoming visitors inside yet simultaneously warning foes. The cathedral is situated in the square **Terreiro Da Sé,** which offers incredible views at sunset and a general open-air feel all day long. Inside the church

itself, hushed tones, a gilded interior, and impossibly high arched ceilings remind you just how special it is. Be wary of the Cathedral's unpredictable hours; it's worth going at a time when you can enjoy both the airy outside and the awe-inspiring inside.

*i* *Free entry to church*

## TORRE E IGREJA DOS CLÉRIGOS (CLÉRIGOS TOWER AND CHURCH)

R. de São Filipe de Nery; 22 200 17 29; www.torredosclerigos.pt; open daily 9am-7pm

Though you may feel unholy as you shove people aside at the top of **Clerigos Tower,** camera in hand and poised to get that panorama, the view and historical experience will make up for your unsettled conscience. Originally completed in 1763 by legendary architect **Nicolau Nasoni,** the Baroque bell tower and accompanying church was once the tallest building in all of Portugal. Swing by the museum exhibit, which is complete with touch screens detailing the history of the structure. If you're just into the climb though, you'll be rewarded with unparalleled views of the city.

*i* *Tower and exhibition entrance €4; €6 guided tours daily 9am-7pm*

# MUSEUMS

## MUSEU NACIONAL DE SOARES DOS REIS

Palácio dos Carrancas, R. D. Manuel II; 22 339 37 70; www.museusoaresdosreis.pt; open Tu-Su 10am-6pm

Founded in 1833, Museu Nacional de Soares dos Reis boasts its status as Portugal's very first art museum. The museum, now housed in the **Palace of Carrancas,** is a historical stop in itself. Check out the permanent collection of nineteenth and twentieth-century Portuguese art and the well-curated collections of furniture, china, and tapestries. As you stroll through the often empty, chandelier-lit rooms, you'll feel like you're living in Renaissance Portugal, just with cleaner air and no threat of war.

*i* *Admission €5, €2.50 student, free first Su of month; last entry 5:30pm; wheelchair accessible*

## MUSEU SERRALVES

R. Dom João de Castro 210; 22 615 65 00; www.serralves.pt; open Apr-Sep Museum and Park M, W-F 10am-7pm, Sa-Su and holidays 10am-8pm, Oct-Mar M, W-F 10am-6pm, Sa-Su and holidays 10am-7pm

Serralves is more of an institution than a single spot. It's a foundation, museum, and park and has a café and library, making it a one-stop shop for all your possible needs. Featuring both indoor and outdoor exhibits, its light-hearted, airy rooms lend backdrop to shifting exhibits of impactful contemporary art. Additionally, in June, the museum hosts an annual city-wide festival: **Serralves em Festa,** which is a lively mix of live performances, special exhibits, and carnival-like stands enjoyable for all ages.

*i* Museum and park admission €10, park admission €5, free admission first Su of the month 10am-1pm; tours of exhibitions Sa 5-6pm, Su 12pm-1pm

# FOOD

### ✥PORTA'O LADO ($)

Campo Mártires da Pátria 49; 91 844 69 77; www.portaolado.com; Tu-W noon-midnight, Th-Sa noon-2am, Su noon-11pm

The sun starts to set, the sounds of **Fado music** drift through the alleyways, and you're famished from a day of climbing Porto's cobblestone hills. Where do you want to be? In the shadow of the **Clérigos Tower,** sitting in front of a beer and a sandwich at Porta'o Lado (clearly). Here, choose from an array snacks, boards, and sandwiches. If you want something hearty and wholeheartedly Portuguese, the **Prego** (steak sandwich) and the aptly named **Gift of** *Alheira* (traditional sausage wrapped in bacon) will do the trick, plus some potato wedges if you're left wanting more.

*i* Sandwiches and snacks €3-5, drinks €1-5; vegetarian options available; wheel-chair accessible

### CASA MARLINDO ($$)

R. de Trás 15; 22 328 67 64; open M-Th 11am-midnight, Fri-Sat 11am-2am, Su 11am-midnight

Located just up a side street so steep the entire restaurant feels slanted, Casa Marlindo presents you with a drink menu handwritten on cork board upon arrival. Are you enchanted yet? We were. If the open-air seating and charming ambiance wasn't enough, the food is exceptional. Their specialty is **"Bochecha de Porco Preto"** (which is—not kidding—Pork's Cheek), but, for the less adventurous, Casa Marlindo also offers hearty cheese plates, *alheira* sandwiches on fresh, fluffy rolls with runny yolk, and more.

*i* Appetizers and sandwiches €5-9, bigger plates €10-15; vegetarian options available; wheelchair accessible

### DATERRA ($$)

R. de Mouzinho da Silveira 249; 22 319 92 57; www.daterra.pt; open daily noon-11:30pm

Take a break from traditional Portuguese sausage and sink into the best vegan spot in town: **Daterra.** With three locations in Porto (the newest in the heart of **Baixa**), Daterra threatens to challenge tradition with its flavorful vegetarian buffets of soups, salads, spring rolls, potato wedges, and quiche. Though their prices are more expensive than grabbing a sandwich on the streets, catch their great all-you-can-eat deal, where the options change both daily and seasonally. If you happen to be there when they have *crème de ervilhas e hortelã* (pea and mint soup), don't miss out.

*i*  *Lunch buffet €7.50, regular buffet €9.90; vegetarian options available; wheelchair accessible*

## NIGHTLIFE

### ADUELA
R. das Oliveiras 36; 22 208 43 98; open M 3pm-2am, Tu-Sa noon-2am, Su 3pm-midnight

Aduela creates an exception to the everything-starts-late-in-Europe rule. A hopping, busy, energetic buzz of a scene from early dinner time until the wee hours of the night, it's the place to start, continue, or end your night—maybe even all three. Local beers on tap and wines are the specialties, with small plates to accompany the drinks, meaning there's no reason to worry if all the beer or the latest **FC Porto** game leaves you hungry. Swing by to enjoy both the drinks spilling out of their glasses and the people spilling out onto the streets, expanding the cozy atmosphere into the night air.

*i*  *Drinks €3-10*

### ESPAÇO 77
Trav. de Cedofeita 22; 22 321 88 93; open M-Sa 10am-4am

A night out and a nightcap wrapped into one, Espaço 77 is a tried-and-true Porto favorite for good reason. One part bar and one part café, Espaço 77 is a one-stop shop for those leaving the clubs, which means you'll love its infectious energy and riled-up, fun crowd. Espaço 77 prides itself on their "minis," tiny beers which cost only €0.50. The size of the minis may be to curtail the drunken revelry of those who have been out all night, or it might just be because they're cute, but either way they set this bar apart as the spot to be all night long. Greasy pizza and traditional Portuguese *Bifana* will look like heaven and will make it your go-to as many nights as possible.

*i*  *Drinks €.50-5, snacks €2-5*

### PETER CAFÉ SPORT
Cais da Ribiera 24; 93 943 51 05; www.petercsporto.com; open M 10am-midnight, Tu-Su 10am-2am

Peter's (as the locals call it) offers live music, an incredible atmosphere, and what they claim is the best gin in the world. Their **house gin** is, in fact, exceptional—so order a gin and tonic before even sitting down. When you've downed your cocktail, though, choose from their other drinks and cocktails, accompanied by killer bar snacks and some larger plates to suit anyone's fancy; Peter's is the authentic fisherman's pub experience.

*i*  *Drinks €3-6, small plates €2-9*

# PORTUGAL ESSENTIALS

## MONEY

A 13% tax (known as value added tax) is included on all restaurants and accommodations in Portugal. A 20% tip is never necessary, though Portuguese restaurants may expect more from you than from a local if they deem you a tourist.

## SAFETY AND HEALTH

**Police:** Guarda Nacional Republicana (GNR) covers 98% of Portuguese territory, especially urban areas. GNR are military personnel. Polícia de Segurança Pública (PSP) is a civilian police force based in more populated areas. Not all officers speak English.

**Drugs and Alcohol:** Using or possessing drugs is illegal in Portugal, but, in 2001, the charge was changed from criminal to administrative, meaning more community service and less (usually no) jail time. The legal drinking age in Portugal is 18.

# SLOVAKIA

**Slovakia has not been its own country for long.** Ethnic Slavs immigrated to the current-day Slovak Republic during the fifth and sixth centuries, but by the turn of the millennium, the territory had been annexed by the Kingdom of Hungary, and later by the Austro-Hungarian Empire. Following the partition of the Austro-Hungarian Empire at the end of WWI, Czechoslovakia emerged as the home of the Czechs and Slovaks, until 1992 that is. Despite this muddled history, Slovakia remains a place where the culture still feels unified. You'll notice this culture in the historic architecture, in a national anthem based on a traditional folk song, and in cuisine rooted in a deep appreciation for potatoes. We should pause here because Slovakian cuisine is wholly underrated. More comfort food than fine dining, expect pork, poultry, and always, always spuds—roasted, boiled, dumpling-ed, you name it. If you're traveling in the wake of a breakup and looking for a menu to soothe your aching soul, If you walk away from Slovakia without having tried *bryndzové halušky,* you've made a grave mistake. Now un-pause because this country has a lot more going for it than potatoes. Home to some of the most beautiful castles in all of Europe (there's more than 300 of them!), Slovakia is a country punctuated by royal ruins. Many of the castles are sprawling stone fields of rubble, situated high on hills, built to defend and impress. Meanwhile, some fortress monstrosities like the Bratislava Castle stand intact. And while Bratislava is a small urban haven for backpackers a mere hour from Vienna, outside the city visitors will find a vast countryside with rolling pastures and soaring mountains. Roughly 40% of Slovakia is forested land, and national parks such as Tatras and Slovak Paradise offer an opportunity for great hikes.

# BRATISLAVA

Coverage by **Antonia Washington**

Bratislava is a backpacker's paradise. Scenic but small, the city is cheap and much less crowded than many other European capital cities. There is enough sightseeing to keep visitors busy for several days of touring if they so choose, with a collection of castles, towers, and museums on nearly every historical subject, but not nearly as many as places like neighboring Vienna. Amid historic buildings spanning fourteenth to eighteenth-century architectural styles interspersed with communist-era urban designs, you'll find thrift shops, trendy vegan stands, and bars buried in alleyways like rabbit holes. See Bratislava with friends or hostelmates and, before long, you'll start to feel at home.

## ORIENTATION

Most of the sights and action in Bratislava are concentrated in **Old Town,** called "Staré Mesto" in Slovak. This area is situated north of the **Danube River** and east of the **Most SNP** (UFO bridge). It is bordered by **Námestie SNP** to the north and **Štúrova** to the east, but these streets are more general points within which Old Town is concentrated than hard neighborhood borders. Important streets in the area include **Hviezdoslavovo námestie,** which is a major pedestrian area, and Námestie SNP. The main square of Bratislava, called "Hlavné námestie" in Slovak, is located roughly in the center of Old Town. Streets like Ventúrska and Rybárska brána run roughly north to south connecting these areas and are lined with restaurants. **Obchodná** is a major street for tramlines and a place to find more fast-food style restaurants.

## ESSENTIALS

### GETTING THERE

Bratislava has an airport, serving mostly European airlines, and a train station. Often, the most convenient way to get to Bratislava is by train or bus. One of the main bus stations (Bratislava Most SNP) is located in the city center just on the western edge of Old Town. Visitors to Bratislava from outside of Europe may find it easier to fly into Vienna, and then take a bus or train to the city.

### GETTING AROUND

If you are staying in or around the city center in Bratislava, walking is often the simplest way to travel. The city center is relatively small and most of the city's historic sights, resources, and nightlife are also in this area. Public transport to locations further from the city center (such as Devín Castle, a nearby lake, or the airport) tends to be efficient and far-reaching. Single tickets cost less than €1; be aware that ticket machines at public transport stops only accept coins.

### PRACTICAL INFORMATION

**Tourist Offices:** Tourist Information Centre (Klobučnícka 2; 25 441 9410; open M-F 8am-4:30pm).
**Banks/ATMs/Currency Exchange:** Slovakia uses the euro. Many businesses accept cards, though some, especially small restaurants and tourist sights unaffiliated with the Bratislava Tourist Board, may not. ATMs are readily available. Banks and currency exchanges are often unwilling to exchange Hungarian forints.
**Post Offices:** Pošta Bratislava 1 (Námestie SNP 35; 02 5443 0381; open M-F 7am-8pm, Sa 7am-6pm).
**Internet:** Wi-Fi is widely available in accommodations throughout Bratislava, but rarely elsewhere.

### EMERGENCY INFORMATION

**Emergency Number:** 112
**Police:** 158 (City police, mostly for public order and transit violations: 159); there tends to be less crime of

all kinds in Bratislava as compared to other major European cities and tourist destinations, though there is occasional scamming and pick-pocketing of foreigners in tourist areas. Much of the city center is monitored by police cameras (Šasinkova 23; 09 6103 1905; open M-F 8am-6pm).

**US Embassy:** The US Embassy in Slovakia is located in Old Town, just off one of the main pedestrian areas, a couple of blocks from the river. (Hviezdoslavovo nam 4; 02 5443 3338; open for routine consular services M-F 8am-11:45am and 2pm-3:15pm by appointment).

**Rape Crisis Center:** No specific center found. For information on resources for women experiencing violence, visit www.zastavmenasilie.gov.sk.

**Hospitals:** Old Town Hospital (Mickiewiczova 13; 02 5729 0111; open daily 24hr).

**Pharmacies:** Lekáreň Pokrok (Račianska 1/A; 02 4445 5291).

# ACCOMMODATIONS

## A WILD ELEPHANTS HOSTEL ($)

Františkánske námestie 8; 90 882 1174; www.elephants.sk; reception open 24hr

The Wild Elephants Hostel brings travelers and staff together from all over the world to create a misfit band of renegades searching for the next adventure, the next friendly face to indoctrinate into their ragtag group, and the next poor sucker to take a shot of Slovak spirits. Run mostly by staff who arrived at the hostel as guests and then just never left, the Wild Elephants Hostel is truly a success story of traveler camaraderie with community dinners every night (€3-5). Pub crawls and in-house beer pong tournaments happen nightly, but dorms are usually quiet. Admittedly, common areas are far from sterile, but cleaned frequently.

*i* Dorms €8-25; reservation recommended; BGLTQ+ friendly; no wheelchair accessibility; Wi-Fi; towel for rent €1; laundry facilities €5; dinner €3-5

## ARTS HOSTEL TAURUS ($)

Zámocká 2327/24; 22 072 2401; www.hostel-taurus.com; reception open 24hr

The theme of the Arts Hostel Taurus is music, and each room is named after a different genre because, apparently, the hostel's owners are involved in music recording. Perks of this hostel include free breakfast, huge lockers, no more than two dorms per bathroom, and a couple of electric guitars available for guests to use while hanging out in the common room. Located halfway up the hill to the **Bratislava Castle,** this hostel can mean convenient picnics on the castle grounds with a view of the city, or it can mean lots of exercise walking up and down from the center of **Old Town.**

*i* Dorms €9-19, private rooms €30-74; reservation recommended; BGLTQ+ friendly; no wheelchair accessibility; Wi-Fi; towels included; laundry facilities €5; free breakfast

## CITY HOSTEL ($$)

Obchodná 38; 25 263 6041; www.cityhostel.sk; reception open 24hr

The City Hostel offers a place to sleep in basic accommodations for a price that won't run you dry, but isn't super wallet-friendly either. Really more of a hotel than a hostel, this establishment only offers private rooms, but charges per additional guest. So, although singles and doubles are the exact same room, doubles cost an extra €10. You will find little community or personality here. Think of all the criticism the first *Twilight* movie received; you could substitute the hostel name for "Kristen Stewart" without losing much accuracy. That said, splitting a room between two people will land you a nice bed, a couple nights to yourself, and a good location in the city center.

*i* Single €30, additional €10 per person (up to 4 per room); reservation recommended; limited wheelchair accessibility; Wi-Fi; linens included

# SIGHTS
## CULTURE

### 🏛ST. MARTIN'S CATHEDRAL
Rudnayovo námestie 1; 25 443 3430; www.dom.fara.sk; open for non-mass visitors M-F 9am-11:30am and 1pm-6pm, Sa 9am-11:30am, Su 1:30pm-4:30pm

Known for being the coronation church of the Kingdom of Hungary from the mid-sixteenth to the early nineteenth centuries, St. Martin's Cathedral is a cool work of Gothic architecture featuring long stained-glass windows and an imposing spire lined with gold and topped with a replica of the **Crown of St. Stephen** (the real crown is on display in the Hungarian Parliament building in Budapest). Visitors to the church, if they're lucky, may get to see the boys' choir during their rehearsal. The soloist practicing while we were there had the voice of a legitimate angel...a small angel who walks around singing all day while the other angels look very annoyed and very bored, as did the non-soloists in the choir. It's hard to stand so close to the limelight.

*i* Free; no wheelchair accessibility

### STARÁ TRŽNICA (OLD MARKET HALL)
Námestie SNP 25; 90 370 7913; www.staratrznica.sk/eng; food market Sa 10am-3pm, July-Aug Sa 8am-3pm

Old Market Hall houses a variety of cultural attractions. It's almost as multifaceted as Tim Allen in the 2002 holiday family favorite, *The Santa Clause 2*. Old Market Hall's building itself is historic, constructed in 1910, but it offers much more. In the square just in front of the building, food carts set up shop with all sorts of quick bites. On Saturday mornings, the main doors open up to a food market, where you can buy your fill of produce, pastries, and cheeses. Old Market Hall also serves as a venue for all kinds of concerts and performances.

*i* Prices vary by stand; wheelchair accessibility

### SYNAGOGUE OF BRATISLAVA
Kozia 18; 25 441 6949; www.synagogue.sk; museum open May-Oct F 10am-4pm, Su 10am-4pm, closed on Jewish holidays

Visiting the Synagogue of Bratislava, an active synagogue and a feat of Cubist architecture, is an experience which gives guests a personal look into the life of Bratislava's Jewish community. Depending on the staff working the entrance and museum, they may talk to visitors personally about how the synagogue functions and what it means to them. Upstairs, in the Bratislava Jewish Community Museum, displays document the history of Judaism and of its role in the city dating back centuries. Our favorite exhibits, however, are the ones showing the Jewish community in Bratislava today, their daily lives, and their family histories.

*i* Admission €6, €3 student; synagogue wheelchair accessible, no wheelchair accessibility in museum

## LANDMARKS

### 🏛STARÁ RADNICA (OLD TOWN HALL) AND THE MAIN SQUARE OF BRATISLAVA
Hlavné námestie 501/1; 25 910 0847; www.museum.bratislava.sk; open Tu-F 10am-5pm, Sa-Su 11am-6pm

One of the oldest stone buildings standing today in Bratislava and the oldest city hall in Slovakia, the Old Town Hall building dates back to the fourteenth century when the tower was erected in the Gothic style (though it later underwent Baroque renovations). The building now houses the **Museum of City History,** which also allows visitors to climb the tower and look out on Old Town. In front of Old Town Hall is the main square of Bratislava. Here you can sit by the fountain, scope out some restaurants, and maybe, at night, you might witness a reckless band of hooligans whooping and yelling on a nude run around the fountain (but that's highly classified, so don't press us for details).

*i* Museum admission €5, €2.50 student; last entry 30min. before closing; limited wheelchair accessibility

## SLAVÍN
Pažického; open daily 24hr

A memorial to the nearly 7,000 soldiers who died liberating Bratislava from Nazi occupation in WWII, the Slavín monument is the highest point in the city. This means, upon getting there after a long and winding upward trek, everyone will sit down immediately. After you regain your composure, take in what amounts to a beautiful tribute to the heroes of war and the sacrifices of battle. A huge stone courtyard surrounds the burial sites of the soldiers, while an obelisk towers over the north end, depicting a soldier holding a flag and standing on the broken remnants of a swastika.

*i* Free; wheelchair accessible via a ramp around the left from the main stairs

## VYHLIADKOVÁ VEŽA UFO (UFO TOWER)
Most SNP; 26 252 0300; www.U-F-O. sk; open daily 10am-11pm

The UFO Tower stands atop **Bratislava's Nový Most bridge.** The bridge, itself a landmark example of an early asymmetrical suspension bridge, is the only bridge to be included in the **World Federation of Great Towers** alongside towers the likes of the Empire State Building and the Eiffel Tower. Visit the disk at the top of the tower to eat at a restaurant with a serious view, or climb to the observation deck above the disk to look out on the city 360-degree style.

*i* Admisson €7.40, €4.95 student; no wheelchair accessibility

## MUSEUMS

### ▓BRATISLAVA CASTLE & SLOVAK NATIONAL MUSEUM OF HISTORY
Zámocká 862/2; 25 935 6111; www. bratislava-hrad.sk, www.snm.sk; castle grounds open daily 9am-1am, museum exhibitions open summer Tu-Su 10am-6pm, winter Tu-Su 10am-5pm

The goal of the Museum of History, administered by the Slovak National Museum, is to preserve and document "the development of society in Slovakia from the Middle Ages until the present." The goal of the writer creating this listing is to make it through one more year of college and maybe even come out the other side with a job. So, we're both setting goals on a similarly grand scale. The museum's exhibits include natural history, arts, and culture, among other collections. The castle itself, an amalgamation of Gothic, Rennaissance, and Baroque styles after many renovations, sits atop a hill overlooking the city. Visit

its large gardens modeled after the **Schönbrunn Palace** in Austria.

*i* *Admission €8, €4 student; last entry to museum 5pm; winter season (Nov 1-Mar 31) museum closes 1hr. earlier; wheelchair accessible*

### MICHAEL'S GATE AND MUSEUM OF ARMS

Michalská 390/22; 25 910 0811; www.muzeum.bratislava.sk; open Tu-F 10am-5pm, Sa-Su 11am-6pm

Michael's Gate is the only remaining gate of the original city wall and fortress that protected the city center through the medieval period. In its heyday, the gate even had a moat and drawbridge, so we think it's only fitting that the current structure contains the Museum of Arms. It all feels very King Arthur, although to be honest, we don't remember if that legend actually included a moat. The museum includes a beautiful collection of swords and engraved weaponry, and leads visitors gradually up the tower to a view overlooking **Old Town.**

*i* *Admission €4.50, €2.50 student; no wheelchair accessibility*

## OUTDOORS

### RUSOVSKÉ JAZERO (LAKE RUSOVSKÉ)

Rusovské jazero; open daily 24hr

Lake Rusovské is clear, blue, and as fresh as all those stock photos floating around the internet of white women with hilarious salads. If you're into nude swimming, strip down and join the locals basking in the grass, but nudity is not required. To get there from the city center, take bus #91 towards **Čunovo** from the **Most SNP** station. Ride the bus about 20 minutes to the Vývojová stop. Take a left at the café on the corner. Follow the bike paths northeast and you'll see a path into a wooded park (the street is Irkuská, but several surrounding streets bear the same name). From there, the trail wraps all the way around the lake, and you can plop down at any spot that suits your fancy.

*i* *Free; limited wheelchair accessibility*

## FOOD

### BRATISLAVA FLAGSHIP RESTAURANT ($)

Námestie SNP 8; 91 792 7673; www.bratislavskarestauracia.sk; open M 10am-11pm, Tu-Sa 10am-midnight, Su noon-11pm

At Bratislava Flagship Restaurant, guests can enjoy traditional Slovak food in what feels like the most traditional Slovak setting of all: a castle. Visitors must pass through stone hallways before stepping into the huge dining room decorated with coats of arms. Here, you will find similar dishes to Flagship's sister restaurant, the Slovak Pub. We recommend the garlic soup served in a bread bowl (€3.90). Pro tip: don't get too caught up in the rip 'n dip. The best bites come from scraping the side of your spoon against the inside of the bread bowl to pick up the saturated bread innards.

*i* *Entrées €5-9; vegetarian options available; no wheelchair accessibility*

### CARNEVALLE MEAT RESTAURANT AND BAR ($)

Hviezdoslavovo nám. 20; 22 086 3637; www.carnevalle.sk; open M-Sa 11am-midnight, Su 11am-11pm

To pull a quote from the restaurant itself, "Carnevalle is, first and foremost, a celebration of meat in all its forms." As a rule, we think anything that calls itself a celebration of any other thing in all its forms means serious business. The menu at Carnevalle takes shape from what it seems to regard as The Four Pillars of Meat-dom: beef, lamb, pork, and veal. Of course, the restaurant does not discriminate against any type of meat, and most can be found on the menu (read: everything from chicken to sashimi). If you are ambitiously honing your craft as a grill person, Carnevalle has its own meat market with butchers doing what they do best and experts available to give advice and answer questions.

*i* *Entrées €7-17; no wheelchair accessibility*

### LINOS BISTRO & COFFEE SHOP ($)

Panská 19; 91 715 7735; www.linoscafe.
sk; open M-Th 9am-12am, F 9am-1am, Sa
10am-1am, Su 10am-12am

Like a moth to a flame, or more accurately like a college student who spent too much money last night looking for something wholesome to put in their stomach, we gravitated to this café on a Saturday during our quest for €5 breakfast food at noon. Linos far surpassed our time table, serving breakfast until 10pm. Though we gorged ourselves on scrambled eggs , Linos also serves an array of sandwiches, burgers, pastas, and salads.

*i* *Breakfast €3.50; vegetarian options available; wheelchair accessible*

### RE:FRESH RESTAURANT AND MUSIC CLUB ($)

Ventúrska 5; 90 171 4339; www.refresh-
club.sk; open M-Tu 8am-1am, W 8am-2am,
Th-Sa 8am-4am, Su 10am-1am

If you've been traveling for a long time, chances are you've been eating at restaurants, subsisting on breaded chicken, potatoes, and the occasional lettuce garnish that you probably weren't actually supposed to eat, but you briefly lost control of yourself when you saw it, ravenous as you were even for the mediocre taste of lettuce. Just us? Well, for a helping of healthy, vegetable-filled, wholesome choices (though, not exclusively) that the student traveler does not often treat themselves to, we couldn't pass up Re:Fresh. We're pleased to report that the vegetables in our Greek salad were crisp, the chicken was lean, and the cheese was light. The restaurant also offers vegan and gluten-free options. At night, Re:Fresh turns into a bar with an underground dance floor and, often, live music.

*i* *Entrées €6-12; vegetarian, vegan, and gluten-free options available; no wheelchair accessibility*

### TULIPÁN KEBAB ($)

Obchodná 37; 91 180 7081; open M-F
8am-midnight, Sa-Su 9am-midnight

The three main attractions at Tulipán Kebab are location, price, and speed. Situated on Obchodná street, the restaurat is just north of the most concentrated area of Old Town. As for price and speed, it's cheap and

fast. Beyond kebabs, they serve pizza, sandwiches, and pastas. Meals come in large portions served on cafeteria trays, so you can flash back to your freshman year of college when you still thought trays were socially acceptable. Personally, we're convinced that the "Freshman 15" is a psychological effect of cafeteria trays on the relative appearance of normal portion sizes.

*i* *Entrées €3-8; vegetarian options available; no wheelchair accessibility*

## NIGHTLIFE

### KC DUNAJ~

Nedbalova 3; 94 826 2643; www.kcdunaj.
sk; open M-W noon-1am, Th noon-3am, F
noon-4am, Sa 4pm-4am, Su 4pm-midnight

KC Dunaj~ is a nightclub trying to do way too much, and we love it. While the venue is a nightclub first and foremost, it also features a large seating area and outdoor terrace where couples sip drinks calmly amid the hurricane of bodies flying back and forth between the dance floor and the bathrooms. The dance floor is, of course, the main attraction. Here we tossed back shots, played an "I Spy" game of hostel hookups, and kept our fingers crossed that nobody ruined the night by starting a dance battle.

*i* *Cover €5 starting at 9pm, €1 deposit on cups/glasses; cash only; no wheelchair accessibility*

### SLOVAK PUB

Obchodná 62; 25 292 6367; www.
slovakpub.sk; open M 10am-11pm, Tu-Th
10am-midnight, F-Sa 10am-2am, Su
noon-11pm

Beer here is a big deal. The Slovak Pub stores its beer in a brick cellar to ensure proper temperature and freshness. Though the method they use of sealing beer inside plastic bags within their metal kegs is a concept that reminds us suspiciously of boxed wine, it's all very scientific and legit. Their house-brewed beer has a robust wheat taste and a distinct hoppy flavor that isn't overwhelming. Even the foam is full-bodied and soft. If you feel like ordering food, the pub claims to have the best *halušky* in town, and we can confirm they have the locals on their side. This potato-dumpling-with-sheep-cheese dish, typically served with bacon garnish, will make you both disappointed and relieved that you didn't know about it through your last breakup.

*i* *No cover, beers €1.30-4*

## ŠTARTÉR PUB

Obchodná 521/36; 90 322 8887; www.starterpub.sk; open M-F noon-midnight, Sa 3pm-midnight

Venue appeal: getting beat handily at foosball over and over again by a couple of German guys. We have never seen the downright evisceration of an opposing foosball team happen so quickly or so casually. As even the bar's website admits, Štartér Pub is frequently thought of as an ideal pre-game hangout. They propose simply that you start your night with them, (hence the name), have a couple of drinks, vow to practice foosball every day, and then move on to other parties if you so choose. Another venue appeal: most pints of beer cost less than €1.

*i* *No cover, most beers under €1; cash only; BGLTQ+ friendly; no wheelchair accessibility*

# LOW TATRAS

Coverage by **Antonia Washington**

Low Tatras National Park is a testament to the beauty of Slovakia's wild lands. The park holds mountains high enough, valleys low enough, and rivers wide enough for just about anyone to find themselves in awe of their surroundings. Low Tatras is like an extreme hackeysacker, entrancing and impressive, but nothing if not laid back. Though the mountains of Low Tatras are certainly out-mountained by the peaks of High Tatras National Park to its northeast, this region is a skier's haven, and, in the summer, hikers will find a network of trails to keep them busy. The park also boasts some of Slovakia's monstrous ice caves. The highest peak in Low Tatras National Park is Mt. Dumbier, whose summit offers views of the High Tatras range. When looking in the other direction on a clear day, you can see all the way to the Hungarian border.

## ORIENTATION

Low Tatras National Park sits more or less in the center of the country, about four hours northeast of Bratislava by car, and southwest of **High Tatras National Park,** Low Tatras' older sibling of sorts. The most important roads to keep in mind in Low Tatras are the freeways. **Route E77** borders the park to its west and E50 runs along its northern edge. The freeways intersect at the park's northwest corner, and both can connect drivers to Bratislava (the former through E58 and the latter through E75). Towns border the park all along its northern and southern edges. On our own visit, we stayed in **Demänovská Dolina,** a ski town tucked deep in the park from its northern rim, just south of **Liptovský Mikuláš.**

## ESSENTIALS

### GETTING THERE

Drive! Though there are a few buses that stop through the national parks, once you arrive, anything you want to do, including activities and eating food, will probably necessitate driving. The price of renting a car in Slovakia is relatively affordable, so even on a student budget, this is an option worth looking into.

## PRACTICAL INFORMATION

**Tourist Offices:** The nearest tourist office in the area is run by Travel Slovakis, situated by the park's southwest corner in Banská Bystrica (Starohorská 14, 974 11 Banská Bystrica; 905594240; www.travelslovakia.sk; open M-F 9am-5pm).

**Banks/ATMs/Currency Exchange:** Many of the businesses in the area accept cards, but we would suggest having a reserve of cash because you will not easily come by a bank or ATM.

**Post Offices:** We've listed the nearest post office to Demänovská Dolina, but there are multiple in Liptovský Mikuláš and many in the towns surrounding the park, so check the area where you're staying if you plan to use postal services (Kamenné Pole 4447, 031 01 Liptovský Mikuláš; 445528337; open daily 9am-noon and 12:30pm-7pm).

**Internet:** Do not expect there to be Wi-Fi anywhere but your accommodation! You're going off the grid! Aren't you glad you brought us along now?

## EMERGENCY INFORMATION

**Emergency Number:** 112

**Police:** The information listed is for the police station in Liptovský Mikuláš (Kolská 120/6, 031 01 Liptovský Mikuláš; 961451111; open M-F 8am-6pm).

**US Embassy:** The nearest US embassy to Low Tatras National Park is in Bratislava (Hviezdoslavovo nam 4, 811 02 Bratislava; 25 443 3338; open for routine consular services M-F 8am-11:45am and 2pm-3:15pm by appointment).

**Hospitals:** During ski season, there are emergency medical centers at the major ski slopes. In case of an emergency, you should always call 112.

**Pharmacies:** Pharmacies are located in each of the major towns surrounding the park. We recommend bringing any medications you might need with you when you visit the park.

## ACCOMMODATIONS

### APARTAMANY JASNÁ ($$)

Biela Púť, 031 01 Demänovská Dolina; 90 807 2411; www.apartamany-jasna.sk; reception open M-F 9am-4pm, ask in advance if you need to check in or out during non-business hours

Apartamany Jasná is part of a business run by two brothers that is also part gear rental, part ski school, and part souvenir shop. Situated directly at the bottom of one of Jasná's main ski runs, visitors can ski right up to the front door in the winter or walk straight into the woods in the summer. The rooms, though basic, are comfortable and include a kitchenette. The ability to cook your own food like a full-fledged adult is crucial if you plan on hitting the trails early in the morning before nearby restaurants open their doors for the day.

*i* Studio apartment winter €60-105, summer €10-15, 4-bed apartment winter €120-210, summer €10-20; reservation required; BGLTQ+ friendly; limited wheelchair accessibility; Wi-Fi; linens included; towels included

## FOOD

### PENZIÓN JAKUB ($)

Demänovská dolina 277, 032 51 Demänovská dolina; 90 538 9510; www.jasnavj.sk; open Tu-Su 9:30am-2:30pm

The Penzión Jakub, tucked just south of the more visible parking lot and entrance for Riverside Hotel and Restaurant, lies buried in the trees. Inside, a wood stove heats a dining room with four tables. We know what you're thinking: quaint little cabin,

# IN THE BELLY OF DEMINOVSKI ICE CAVE

Visiting the Demänovská Ice Cave is the perfect activity for a day on which you'd intended to hike, but the conditions weren't ideal. Maybe you woke up a little late. Maybe the weather predictions are showing a huge thunder storm beginning at 2pm and hiking in the rain honestly just sounds exhausting, let alone potentially dangerous. At least, that's what drove me to the cave on this Tuesday morning. I found the cave about ten minutes north of where I was staying at Apartamany Jasná (about 7km south of the turnoff from the E50 freeway). From the parking lot to the ticket stand on top of the hillside, it is about a 20-minute uphill trek that's just taxing enough to feel like a feat, but brief enough that it's hard to call it a hike in earnest.

Once at the top, the ticket booth opens 15 minutes before each hour, and the tour enters the cave every hour on the hour. Though at first I was disappointed that visitors can't explore the cave without a guide, the truth is an unregulated setting would quickly leave the cave trashed. Plus, that place is so creepy! The size of the cave itself is unbelievable, and without the tour's lights to show the way, it'd be easy to get lost in the dark abyss. Truly one of my favorite parts of the tour was looking into the cave as the guides turned the lights off—20 seconds of equal parts thrill and terror, tightly gripping the safety rail of a secure metal stairway installed for tourists.

As the tour group assembled at our first stop on the trip through the cave, I quickly realized this tour would be given entirely in Slovak. This wasn't too disappointing because walking through and seeing the cave itself was all I really wanted. If you speak English, the company will give tours in English to groups of at least 12 English speakers. Otherwise, you can read through one of the brief information brochures on display at the ticket counter. Don't make the same mistake we did and crumple it up in your pocket without thinking, only to realize later it would have made your presence at the tour much less awkward. If you speak Slovak, I'm sure you will learn a lot about stalagmites and stalactites from a guide who is, apparently, the next great comedian of our time. I couldn't understand a word he said, but the crowd went wild every time he spoke.

A last word of advice, bring layers. The caves hover around freezing, so you will want warm clothes, but the moment you step out into the sun, you will have to strip as close to naked as you can to survive the heat.

right? Wrong. Forget the wood interior and plaid curtains, they have two hulking bean bag chairs available for guests to lose themselves in and there's nothing more hip and modern than that. As for the food, expect a menu of mostly potato dumplings. *Bryndzové halušky,* our favorite Slovak comfort food, also makes an appearance.

*i* *Entrées €2-7; vegetarian options available; no wheelchair accessibility*

### RESTAURANT 3 DOMKY ($)
Demänovská Dolina 180, 031 01 Demanovska Dolina; 94 809 3370; open daily 11am-9pm

While you're in the countryside, you should feel like you're in the countryside. At this restaurant, you'll sit in booths covered with sheepskin rugs at barn-wood tables in a room with floral wallpaper. Top that. Potatoes feature heavily on the menu and come in some form—boiled, roasted, french—with just about every dish. They can also be ordered as a side if you are unsatisfied with your starch intake for the day. For dessert, get the sweet potato dumplings with breadcrumbs, walnuts, butter, and chocolate sauce (€3.50). We know we've now suggested you add a side of potatoes to a meal with potatoes and finish things off with a potato dessert, but the dessert portion is a bargain for its price, and you deserve to treat yourself.

*i* *Entrées €6-10; vegetarian options available; no wheelchair accessibility*

# SLOVAKIA ESSENTIALS

## MONEY

**Tipping:** Tipping in Slovakia is common only at restaurants and bars. In restaurants, it is customary to tip about 10%. The tip will usually not be included in the bill. In bars, it is standard to tip if you are receiving table service, and the rate should be about 5-10%. In restaurants and bars, it is common to tell the server how much to charge total with the tip, or instruct them how much change you want back, instead of leaving a tip on the table. Do not say "thank you" until after you have gotten change, otherwise it can indicate to the waiter that they should keep the change as tip.

**Taxes:** Many goods in Slovakia are subject to a value-added tax (VAT) of 20%, included in the purchase price of goods. The 20% VAT is a standard rate, though it fluctuates based on the goods bought, so you should ask the retailer for exact rates. Non-EU visitors taking these goods home unused can apply for a VAT refund for goods exceeding €175 at one retailer. To apply for this refund, ask the store for a VAT refund form, sometimes called a tax-free form, and carry your passport with you as retailers may ask to see it. Present the refund form and be prepared to show the unused goods you are exporting at the customs office at your point of departure from the EU, regardless of country. Goods must be exported within 90 days and refunds must be claimed, usually from the seller of the goods, within six months of the original purchase.

## SAFETY AND HEALTH

**Local Laws and Police:** Police in Slovakia can generally be relied upon if you need help, but always have your passport with you when interacting with them, as they may ask to see it. Note that if you are over 15, you are required to carry a valid passport at all times in Slovakia.

**Drugs and Alcohol:** The drinking age in Slovakia is 18. Drinking in public is illegal, and there is a zero-tolerance policy on alcohol and driving. If you are found driving with a BAC of even 0.001%, you could be in serious trouble. Use or possession of illegal drugs in Slovakia can also come with stiff penalties. Smoking is fairly widespread in Slovakia and tobacco is available at most grocery stores and markets. It is illegal to sell tobacco to persons under the age of 18.

**Emergency Medical Services:** If you do not have Slovak medical insurance, ambulance service generally starts at about €120 (but can be more expensive) and is often expected paid in cash at the time of transport. For anyone staying in Slovakia for greater than 90 days, purchase of Slovak health insurance is required.

**Prescription Drugs:** Carry any prescription medications in their original packaging. Common over-the-counter drugs can be purchased at pharmacies in Slovakia, though they may not be out on shelves, in which case you'll have to ask for them from the pharmacist.

# SPAIN

**Wherever you are in Spain, there will be people sitting in metal chairs on outdoor patios in the bright sunshine and dry air, catching up over a glass of sangria and a plate of flavorful tapas.** The country of Spain is vast, diverse, and complete with no two identical cities. But, this scene is ubiquitous whether you're in the pristine northern beaches, to the major cities of Barcelona and Madrid, or the impossibly sunny southern streets of Seville and Malaga.

This is Spain. Its two major cities—sunny, beachside, culture-drenched Barcelona and urban, history-rich, vibrant Madrid—spark countless debates over which is the premier, but we're more than content to enjoy the endless energy and constantly evolving scenes of both. This exquisite culture does not exempt the country from strife; Spain is far from perfect, as highlighted by the movement to secede by the region of Catalonia, whose capital is Barcelona. A Catalan independence referendum on October 1, 2017 will determine the future of Spain as it currently exists.

But what exists today certainly has its gems outside of the two major hubs: between the caves of Grenada, beach parties of Ibiza, ancient relics of Toledo and Córdoba, sunny squares of Valencia, and sheer natural beauty of all the countryside in between, it's clear that hardly a square foot of Spain isn't touched by influences of history, beauty, and culture. There's something to see round every corner, even if it's just another group of friends finishing off a pitcher of sangria.

557

# BARCELONA

Coverage by **Julia Bunte-Mein**

Perhaps you know Barcelona perhaps for its pristine beaches and rambunctious party scene. Maybe you know it as the home of one of the top football clubs in the world: FC Barcelona, a basecamp for world-class players like Lionel Messi and Andres Iniesta. Or perhaps you're an architecture connoisseur who loves the works of Antoni Gaudí, who designed the world-famous La Sagrada Familia and Park Güell. Wherever or however you know it (whether it's mainstream Ed Sheeran songs or lowkey beats by George Ezra), Barcelona, the capital of Catalonia, is one of the most beautiful, lively, and vibrant places in not just Europe, but the world. Walking through its streets is to be washed over in a sea of color, mouthwatering aromas of seafood and tapas, and serenaded by the melodies of Catalan as you walk past its churches, boutiques, and bars. Barcelona, for all its beauty in the aquatic shades of blue, turquoise, and green, isn't without a storied past and current strife. Its role as the capital of Catalonia puts it in an important position regarding the future of Spain, there is an active independence movement from Spain. The modern independence movement began in 2006 and will be decided in October 2017. In this vein, Barcelona is a city full of people proud of their unique culture—a mixture of Spanish and Catalan traditions. Maybe you'll pick up some of this pride during your visit to Barcelona as you watch the sun set with panoramic views sitting on the Bunkers of Carmel or relaxing on Plaça del Sol with a few *estrellas* or embracing the coastal breeze that fills Barcelona's lungs with enough air to laugh, scream, and enjoy life.

## ORIENTATION

Barcelona is a sprawling city with a vast number of diverse neighborhoods that each bring their own character to the city. Noteworthy areas include **Las Ramblas**, which starts by the harbor at the **Plaça Portal de la Pau** and continues north to **Plaça de Catalunya**. This is the most central part of the city, complete with metro and bus connections to the airport, bus, and train stations. To the north of Las Ramblas lies **El Raval** to the left and the **Gothic Quarter** to the right. Continuing past the Gothic Quarter is **La Ribera**, which includes the trendy **El Born** neighborhood that houses many boutiques and restaurants. South of that is **Barceloneta**, the triangular-shaped neighborhood located next to the beach. **Passeig de Gracia** is a main street that leads north close to **La Sagrada Familia** past the quirky, more suburban district of **Gracia** to **Park Güell**. The mountain of **Montjuic** is to the southwest, past the neighborhood of **Poble Sec**.

## ESSENTIALS

### GETTING THERE

Aeroport del Prat de Llobregat (El Prat Airport) has international and domestic flights with two different terminals. There is a free bus shuttle between the terminals. To travel to the city from the airport, there are a few options. The Aérobus service is an express bus from Pl. Catalunya to both Terminals 1 and 2 that comes every 5min. and takes about 35min. (single ticket €5.90, €10.20 round trip). Buses take 40min. (single ticket €2.15, €4.30 round trip). You can also take the metro directly from El Prat airport to Estació Sants, Pg. De Gràcia, or El Clot for €4.50 and it takes about 40min. The train only departs from Terminal 1, but there is an overpass to access it from Terminal 2. Estacío Barcelona-Sants serves the most domestic and international traffic while Estació de França serves mostly regional destinations. RENFE (www.renfe.es) runs to Bilbao, Madrid, Sevilla, and Valencia. The main bus terminal is Estació d'Autobusos Barcelona Nord (www.barcelonanord.com), located close to Arc de Triomph. Buses also depart from Estacío Barcelona-Sants and the airport. ALSA (www.alsa.es) is Spain's main bus line.

## GETTING AROUND

The fastest way to get around the city is by metro (single ticket €2.15, €9.90 T-10 Zone 1 ticket). The latter gives you ten journeys on the metro. Metro rides have free transfers and work for all forms of transport, including the three-different metro/tram/train companies and buses. Metro lines are identified with an L and tram lines with a T. Metros and trains run M-Th 5am-midnight, F 5am-2am, Sa 24hr, Su 5am-midnight. The bus, however, offers a more scenic journey and also travels to more remote places than the metro. The most important bus is the NitBus, which runs all night after the metro closes. In the neighborhoods far from the center, the tiny BarriBus that has only 10 seats takes people through narrow streets.

## PRACTICAL INFORMATION

**Tourist Offices:** Plaça de Catalunya (Pl. De Catalunya; 17 932 85 38 34; www. barcelonaturisme.com; open 8:30am-9pm daily).
**Banks/ATMs/Currency Exchange:** Deutsche Bank Filliale (Pg. de Gràcia, 112; 934 04 21 02; open M-F 8:30am-2pm). Currency Exchange Ria—La Rambla (La Rambla, 56. 933 02 86 96; M-F 9am-10pm, Sa-Su 10am-10pm).
**Post Offices:** Correos (Pl. Antonio López; 93 486 83 02; www.correos.es; open M-F 8:30am-9:30pm, Sa 8:30am-2pm).
**Internet:** There is free public Wi-Fi at over 500 locations, including museums, parks, and beaches. Everywhere you see the blue "Barcelona WiFi" symbol on a sign, you can use it for free after accepting the terms and conditions through your browser.
**BGLTQ+ Resources:** Gay Barcelona (www.gaybarcelona.com) has up-do-date tips for BGLTQ+ restaurants, bars, and publications. Casal Lambda is a non-profit association in Spain offering a community space for socializing, center for information and documentation, as well as counseling (Callis, 10, Verdaguer; 933 195 550).

## EMERGENCY INFORMATION

**Emergency Number:** 112
**Police:** National Police: 091 (V. Laietana, 43. 932 903 000).

**US Embassy:** There is a US Consulate in Barcelona (Pg. de la Reina Elisenda de Montcada, 23; 932 80 22 27; open M-F 9am-1pm).
**Rape Crisis Center:** The Center for Assistance to Victims of Sexual Assault (CAVAS) (C. Alcalá, 124, Madrid; 91 574 01 10). CAVAS has a branch in Barcelona that can be reached via the Madrid branch.
**Hospitals:** Hospital Clínic i Provincial (C. Villarroel, 170; 932 27 54 00)
**Pharmacies:** Farmacia Bonanova (P. Bonanova, 6; 934 178 032; open daily 24hr)

## ACCOMMODATIONS

### AMISTAT BEACH HOSTEL BARCELONA

C. Amistat, 21-23; 932 213 281; www.amistathostels.com/barcelona; reception open 24hr

Summer in Barcelona is all about the beach days; and by virtue of it's location, Amistat Beach Hostel encourages you to go live your best life in the sand and ocean blue. Buy one of their neon Amistat tanks at reception and head directly across the street to **Playa Marbella** (read: the less crowded and nicer beach than **Playa Barceloneta**) for a morning dip before city exploring, beach volleyball, or a seaside *siesta*. Amistat is in the quiet neighborhood of **Poble Nou**, whose **Ramble de Poble Nou** has a full selection of locally-owned terrace restaurants where you can enjoy a quiet drink on a cool evening. If you want a little more dance action, though, the beach clubs are just a short walk east on the boardwalk.

*i* Dorms €49; reservation recommended; no Wi-Fi; breakfast €4 from 7:30am-11am

### BLACK SWAN HOSTEL

C. d'Alí Bei, 15; 932 311 369; www.black-swanhostel.com; reception open 24hr

From the fun staff to the seemingly endless perks included in your stay (read: walking tours, paella cooking classes, free breakfast, and movie nights), this four-story hostel knows how to cater to the backpacking crowd. The dorms are simple with as little as three and as many as 14 beds, and the hallways are decked out in black and white pop art. Situated on a quiet street in the center of the city, it is just a five-minute walk to the Arc de Triomf metro station. Start the night learning how to cook classic paella and then fill up on the delicious saffron rice to prepare for the nightly pub crawl that guides you to four bars around the city.

*i* Dorms €40-47; reservation recommended; linens included; luggage storage; lockers provided; laundry facilities; kitchen; free breakfast

### CASA GRÀCIA

Pg. de Gràcia, 116; 931 874 497; www.casagraciabcn.com; reception open 24hr

One night at Barcelona's first boutique hostel and you'll never go back to the bare-boned, fluorescently-lit, graffiti-covered hostels of yester-year. Vaulted ceilings, parquet wood flooring, and Corinthian white columns await you. Take the iron-barred elevator or winding marble staircase to the first floor with its large dining room, modern kitchen, lounge area, and outdoor patio. Don't miss their free buffet breakfast, yoga classes, downstairs restaurant, or cocktail bar.

*i* Dorms from €35, private rooms from €120; reservation recommended; Wi-Fi; free breakfast; lockers provided; luggage storage

### HOSTEL ONE RAMBLAS

C. d'Albareda, 6-8; 934 431 310; reception open 24hr

With young, social, and fantastic facilities, Hostel One has it all. The hostel offers dorm rooms with four, six, eight, or ten beds and, while it seems the four-bed room will give you more privacy, things are a little more complex than that. We recommend you take a larger room to experience their super cool, innovative "box bed" system, resembling the kind of beds on cruise ships. These beds provide more privacy with thick curtains and ample space to store your luggage. If you're not enamored by the sleeping accommodations, check out the airy

## NIT DE SANT JOAN

Every year, on the eve of June 23, Barcelona erupts into flame celebrating the wildest and loudest festival of the year: La Festa de Sant Joan. It is a night of fire, fireworks, Coca cakes, and Cava—basically anything but sleep. Thousands flood the streets and the beaches to party on the shortest night of the year; in short, the summer solstice in Barcelona is a coalescence of fire, light, renewal, and vitality. Explosions and white bursts of light erupt from every direction, burning your eyes and making you jump every second. Picture the rebirth of a phoenix. Now picture the rebirth of a city.

By far, the craziest midsummer celebrations occur on Barcelona's beaches. Around midnight, the metros (which run all night for Festa de Sant Joan) shuttle crowds to Mar Bella and Bogotell beaches, squeezing every adult, teenager, Spaniard, and international into cars like sardines. An estimated 70000 people flock to the sand each year to make bonfires by the coast, take midnight swims in their underwear, and send candlelit lanterns off into the sky. In a spirit of new beginnings, people are said to write down a wish on a piece of paper, throw it in the fire, and jump three times. A more dangerous tradition is to hold hands with a loved one and leap over the bonfire seven times, but we don't recommend trying this; many a drunken fire jumper has ended up with badly burnt limbs and a trip to the ER.

During the day, bakeries made special *coques*, which are brioche cakes made of sweet, light bread topped with candied fruits and pine nuts. Throughout the day, the festivalgoers enjoy these treats before heading to the beach to watch the sunrise and to spend June 24 as a public holiday.

This night is an unforgettable experience in Barcelona. If you happen to be there for this heartwarming, exhilarating, and mesmerizing night, remember to say "Bona Revetlla!," which means "Enjoy the Eve!"

lounge downstairs and the roof garden terrace.

*i* *Dorms from €33-€55; reservation recommended; Wi-Fi; lockers available; linens included; towels for rent*

### KABUL PARTY HOSTEL

Plaça Reial, 17; 933 185 190; www.kabul. es; reception open 24hr

If Barcelona's nightlife is your priority, look no further than Kabul Party Hostel. As Barcelona's first hostel, it goes way back having hosted sailors and prostitutes before they were replaced by today's backpackers and tourists. Kabul's staff hits a different club every night, so whatever day (or night) you arrive, brace yourself for a night to remember. From four beds all the way up to 22, the shared dorms squeeze in a lot of beds, but you probably won't be sleeping in them much anyway. With an unbeatable location, looking over the iconic (**Plaza Reial**), and the fantastic rooftop views, this hostel is not one to miss.

*i* *Dorm €32-37; reservation recommended; wheelchair accessible; lockers available; free breakfast*

### SAN JORDI HOSTEL

C. de Terol, 35; 933 424 161; www.sant-jordihostels.com/hostel-sant-jordi-gracia; reception open 24hr

There are four different San Jordi Hostels around Barcelona, and each offers the same quality services: impeccably clean facilities, hot showers, blasting air-conditioning, strong Wi-Fi, and a lively social scene. The Gràcia location is petite, with only 36 beds. Hang out in the bean bag chairs in the lounge, chill in the lower courtyard, or take a snooze on the day bed up on the roof (bring sunscreen because there's no shade!). All of their many social events are run by in-house staff, which means the nightly pub crawls are yours for the taking. The only nuisance: there aren't male and female showers on every floor, so you might have to walk down a flight of stairs to be squeaky clean.

*i* *Dorms €30-40; reservation recommended; Wi-Fi; free linens; towel rental €2; laundry facilities*

### URBANY HOSTEL

Av. Meridiana, 97; 932 458 414; www. urbanyhostels.com/barcelona-urbany-hostel; reception open 24hr

Young backpackers flock to Urbany Hostel for its cheap prices, prime location, and clean rooms. Just a short walk from **La Sagrada Familia**, the hostel is also situated next to metro stations that will take you anywhere in the city. And, when you're ready to get some shut-eye after a long day of sightseeing, Urbany's 16-bed rooms are quite spacious, equipped with reading lights, large lockers, and a plethora of charging outlets. Chill on the large rooftop terrace or on one of their colorful couches in the lounge, pool area, or pool table room with a cartoon mural of **Park Güell**. There's also a bar where you can make tons of friends in no time at all.

*i* *Dorms and privates €38-49; reservation recommended; wheelchair accessible; Wi-Fi; lockers available; luggage storage; kitchen; breakfast €4*

# SIGHTS
## CULTURE

### BASILICA OF SANTA MARIA DEL MAR

Pl. de Santa Maria, 1; 933 102 390; www. santamariadelmarbarcelona.org; open M-Sa 9am-1pm and 5-8:30pm, Su 10am-2pm and 5-8pm; daily mass 7:30pm

The Basilica of Santa Maria del Mar, in the **El Born** district of **La Ribera**, is somewhat in the shadow of the grandiose **Cathedral of Barcelona,** but it is a stellar example of fourteenth-century Catalan Gothic architecture. While the **Cathedral of Santa Eulalia** may be the more prestigious of the two, this Basilica, named "Our Lady of the Sea," is known as the "church of the people," since it was built from the ground up by local merchants who donated money and townspeople who transported stone from Montjuïc on their backs. Sadly, the interiors aren't as impressively decorated as they used to be, due to the 1936 fire that burned for 11 days straight, destroying everything but the walls and the upper stained glass windows.

*i* *Free entry; guided tour of rooftop, crypt, and chapel €8*

## CASTELL DE MONTJUÏC

Ctra. de Montjuïc, 66; 932 564 445; www.
bcn.cat/castelldemontjuic; open daily
Jan-Mar 10am-8pm, Apr-Oct 10am-8pm,
Nov-Mar 10am-6pm

Looming in the southern hills of
**Monjuïc Mountain,** the Castell de
Montjuic is a fortress dating back to
the late-seventeenth century. It has a
dark past, as it was used as a political
prison, execution ground, and a
lookout to watch over the city. Despite
its storied past, however, it is now
one of the most popular tourist stops
because of the sweeping views of the
sea and city atop the ramparts. This
can be one of many stops on your tour
of the mountain, which also includes
the **Botanical Gardens, Olympic
Stadium,** and **Miró Fountain**. We
recommend making your way up here
by the Telefèric cable car that carries
you to the *castell* via the *mirador*
(€6.80) or the Aeri cable car from
Barceloneta (€11 one-way, €16.50
round-trip)

*i* Admission €5, €3 student, free Su
*after 3pm, first Su of the month; last entry*
*7:30pm; wheelchair accessible*

## GRAN TEATRE DEL LICEU

Las Ramblas, 51-59; 934 859 900; www.
liceubarcelona.cat

This horseshoe-shaped Baroque
auditorium takes performance to a
whole new level from its location
on **Las Ramblas**. It is the opera
headquarters of Barcelona and
dates back to 1847, although it was
renovated in 1999 after a fire destroyed
most of the interior. Although the
renovation happened fairly recently,
the gold balustrades and 2300 velvet
red seats exude a beautiful antiquity.
If you can't catch a performance,
you can still enjoy the space with
the 20-minute architectural tour
that takes you through the black and
white marble foyer and ornate **Sala
de Espojos** (Room of Mirrors). If you
want an even cooler experience, book
the behind-the-scenes tour to glimpse
the backstage area, the dressing rooms,
and rehearsal areas that are normally
off limits to the public.

*i* 45min. express tour €9, €7.50 student,
*30min. express tour €6, €5 student, guided*
*tours €16, €12 student, backstage tour*
*€18, €12 student*

## LA CATEDRAL DE BARCELONA (CATHEDRAL OF SANTA EULALIA)

Pl. De la Seu, 3; 933 428 262; www.
catedralbcn.org; open M-F 8am-12:45pm,
1-5:30pm, and 5:45pm-7:30pm, Sa
8am-12:45pm, 1-5pm, and 5:15-8pm,
Su 8am-1:45pm, 2-5pm, and 5:15-8pm;
cloister open M-F 8am-12:30pm, Sa 8am-
12:30pm and 5:15-7pm, Su 8:30am-1pm
and 5:15-7pm

The Cathedral of Barcelona is a
Gothic masterpiece dating back to
the thirteenth century, even though
its more recent nineteenth-century
addition includes a Neo-Gothic main
façade with large wooden doors. Enter
past the guards, who actually enforce
the dress code—save the miniskirt
and linen shirts for clubbing—and,
inside, admire the spires, arched
ceiling, and over 500-year-old stained
glass windows. Plan to visit when
the secluded Gothic cloister is open
so that you can admire the 13 geese
that call the interior gardens home.
The Cathedral also holds masses in
the morning, which are an impressive
experience.

*i* Free entrance; choir €3, €3 roof; tour
*€6; last entry 5min. before closing; wheel-*
*chair accessible; long sleeves and long*
*pants required for entry*

## MERCAT DE LA BOQUERIA

La Rambla, 91; 933 182 584; www.boque-
ria.info; open M-Sa 8am-8:30pm

La Boqueria lies on Las Ramblas, the
most famous street in Barcelona, and
is a wonderful mélange of dazzling
displays of fruit, nut, vegetables, meat,
and every type of fish you can imagine.
What is now a covered market with
enthusiastic merchants used to be an
open-air market started unofficially
by merchants in 1217. The name of
the market comes from the word *boc*,
meaning goat, since that was the most
popular meat sold back then. Over
the centuries, however, the market has
expanded and now features to-go stalls.
Most of the vendors today are fourth-
generation merchants upholding the
traditions of their families, which
brings something wholesome to this
wonderful place.

*i* Prices vary by stand; wheelchair
*accessible*

## PALAU GÜELL

C. Nou de la Rambla, 3-5; 934 725 775; www.palauguell.cat; open daily Apr-Oct 10am-8pm; Nov-Mar 10am-5:30pm

**Gaudí** has footprints all over Barcelona, he even left his mark in **Raval** with the ominous Palau Güell. The main façade holds two towering, somewhat jarring iron-mesh gates reminiscent of a Moorish architectural style. A highlight of this peculiar palace is the parabolic dome in **El Saló Central,** where a series of small openings and a central oculus allow light to pierce into the central hall. Concerts were often held here, which created a chilling surround-sound effect as guests set on the ground level while the orchestra played on the floor above, followed by singers, and finally the organ pipes on the top. The visuals alone are dizzying, but you can experience the spectacular audio element if you attend **Les Nits del Palau Güell** to hear a concert.

*i* Admisson €12, €8 student; free first Su of the month, Nights at Palau Güell €35; free audio guide; last entry 1hr. before close; wheelchair accessible; group reservations call 2 days in advance

## PLAÇA REIAL

Pl. Reial, Gothic Quarter; open daily 24hr

Retreat from the bustling tourists and hounding street vendors of **Las Ramblas** to the nearby Plaça Reial. This extremely photogenic square is surrounded by nineteenth-century neoclassical buildings, has a lovely fountain in its center, and is dotted by palm trees. Not only is it Barcelona's only porticoed and closed square, but, more importantly, it's home to two iron lampposts that are original Gaudí creations. A closer look at the swirling top and six-armed red extensions will reveal Gaudí's subtler styles that later became his trademark. This is one of the most significant squares in the city, named after King Ferran VII who reigned during its construction. But history aside, it's a delightful spot to sip on a cocktail in one of the many bars and eateries surrounding it.

*i* Free; wheelchair accessible

## POBLE ESPANYOL

Av. Francesc Ferrer i Guardia, 13; 935 086 300; www.poble-espanyol.com; open M 9am-8pm, Tu-Th 9am-midnight, F 9am-3am, Sa 9am-4am, Su 9am-midnight

Poble Espanyol, meaning "Spanish Village," is one of the few relics from Barcelona's 1929 International Exhibition. This open-air museum was the brainchild of *modernista* celebrity **Puig i Cadaflach,** designed to synthesize the monumental soul of Spain into one unified space. With the help of three other architects, Cadaflach erected the Poble Espanyol with 117 full-scale buildings. Given Catalonia's strong desire for independence, its continued existence is somewhat controversial, but the tourist industry makes a ton of money, so it's not going anywhere for now. That said, locals from Barcelona wouldn't be caught dead in the tourist hub of Poble Espanyol, but there are many shows, concerts, open-air film festivals, and three nightclubs that attract all sorts.

*i* Admission €14, €10.50 student, night ticket €7, Poble Espanyol and MNAC €26; wheelchair accessible; 10% discount with tickets bought in advance

# LANDMARKS

## ▨LA SAGRADA FAMILIA

C. Mallora, 401; 935 132 060; www.sagradafamilia.cat; open Apr-Sept daily 9am-8pm, Oct-May 9am-6pm, Dec 25-Jan 6 9am -2pm

If there's one mandatory visit in all of Barcelona, this is it. From any high lookout point in Barcelona, you can see the basilica, emerging from the cityscape in all its glory. Antoni Gaudí's crowning masterpiece features extensive and intricate carvings that are sure to stun. La Sagrada Familia was Gaudí's lifelong project, but it was only one quarter completed when he died in a tram accident. It's still incomplete, as evidenced by the cranes and scaffolding on the basilica's exterior, and it's not expected to be fully finished until 2026. The inside, however, is somehow even more breathtaking than the outside. Light colored columns branch like towering trunks in a forest, exploding into a canopy of white and red leaves. The interior is illuminated by breathtaking blue and green daisies in stained glass windows. If you were to lie on your back in the center of the nave, the ceiling resembles a kaleidoscope.

*i*  *Individual ticket €15, ticket with audio guide €22, elevator to Nativity Tower €4.50; last elevator to the Nativity Tower 15min. before closing, last elevator to Passion lift 30min. before closing; wheelchair accessible ; reservation recommended*

## ◼PARQUE GUELL

Off C. d'Olot, entrance via Carrer de Larrard, Carretera del Carmel, n° 23, Passatge de Sant Josep de la Muntanya; www.parkguell.cat; park open daily Jan 1-Mar 25 8:30am-6:30pm, Mar 26-Apr 30 8am-8:30pm, May 1-Aug 27 8am-9:30pm, Aug 28-Oct 28 8am-8:30pm, Oct 29-Dec 31 8:30am-6:30pm

Park Güell is a real-life Candyland designed by none other than—you guessed it—Antoni Gaudí, Barcelona's hero. This **UNESCO World Heritage Site,** designed in the 1910s, will blow your mind with its life-size gingerbread houses and jelly-bean bright tiled mosaics. Located in **El Carmel** in **Gràcia,** it features an expansive garden, museum, and the Monumental Zone that contains a concentration of impressive sights. The latter is the only part of the park you'll need to pay to enter. The main entrance, from **Career d'Olot** leads you to a grand dragon stairway with a twin fight of cascading steps. An iconic mosaic salamander known as **El Drac** basks in the sunny center. Our favorite part of the park was the esplanade known as the **Greek Theatre** or **Nature Square,** where you'll find the best views of Barcelona city. It's definitely touristy, but it's a great spot to take pictures with the **Porter's Loge** and **Gaudí House Museum** in the background.

*i*  *Online ticket €7, door ticket €8, free if you enter before the ticket office opens*

## ARC DE TRIOMF

Pg. de Lluís Companys; open daily 24hr

Standing grandly on the wide, sand colored boulevard in front of **Park Ciutadella** is Barcelona's Arc de Triomf. Like its counterpart in Paris, this arch serves as an icon of the city, but was constructed 80 years after its twin. Designed by architect Josep Vilasec as the gateway to the **1888 Universal Exhibition,** the Arc de Triomf has a sculpture frieze inscribed

with the phrase "Barcelona welcomes the nations." We interpret that as Barcelona saying "We love tourists," so just remember that every time a local food vendor glares at you for saying "I quiero esto sandwich."

*i*  *Free; wheelchair accessible*

## CASA BATLLÓ

Pg. De Gràcia, 43934 88 06 66; 934880666; www.casabatllo.es; open daily 9am-9pm

Casa Batlló stands tall on Pg. De Gracia, a pearl in the heart of Barcelona. Built between 1904 and 1906, this is the most emblematic work of Gaudí: fantastical and daring to dream. It was originally built by Emilio Salas Cortes, but was redesigned by the brilliant Catalan architect for the wealthy Batlló family in the luxurious neighborhood of **l'Eixample.** True to Gaudí's style, this house has almost no right angles or straight lines, reflecting the organic forms of nature. Specifically, this house is an ode to the marine world with an exterior that undulates like ocean waves, walls hand-painted like fish scales, and turquoise stained glass windows resembling bubbles. Check out the main long gallery, called the Noble Floor, which offers a panoramic view of the street.

*i*  *Regular ticket €23.50, €20.50 student; last entry 8pm; wheelchair accessible*

## CASA MILÀ (LA PEDRERA)

Pg. De Gràcia, 92, C. Provença, 261-265; 902 202 138; www.lapedrera.com; open daily 9am-8:30pm and 9-11pm

Popularly known as "La Pedrera," meaning "stone quary," Casa Milà is an essential piece of architecture and culture in Barcelona. The nickname comes from the cliffs that served as Gaudí's inspiration for the house, now making it the most famous example of Catalan Modernism. It marks his last civil work before his beloved **Sagrada.** A **UNESCO World Heritage Site,** it draws in crowds every year, even though it is still an apartment building for the rich, famous, and very patient hopefuls on the three-decade long waitlist. A visit to the building comes with a tour of one of the apartments, decorated with haughty period furniture, and **L'Espai Gaudí,** an arched attic space which serves a mini-museum of Gaudí's models. Don't miss the night performances; the hefty price tag is worth it for the lively jazz recital.

*i* *Admission €22, €16.50 student; night show €34, day and night visit €41; free audio guide*

## COLUMBUS MONUMENT

Portal de la Pau; open daily 8:30am-8:30pm

Soaring 60m high at the coastal tip of **Las Ramblas** stands the Columbus Monument, constructed in the 1880s for the city's **World's Fair** in commemoration of Columbus's return from America (or "India," rather). The statue is intended to point west to the Americas, but it actually points east toward Christopher Columbus' hometown of Genoa. The reliefs around the base depict Columbus' journey. Pro-tip: take the elevator up to the **Mirador de Colom** to escape the noisy traffic and experience the breathtaking panoramic views of the city and port.

*i* *Free; wheelchair accessible*

## HOSPITAL DE LA SANTA CREUI I SANT PAU

C. Sant Antoni Maria Claret, 167; 932 919 000; www.santpaubarcelona.org; open Apr-Oct M-Sa,10am-6:30pm, Su 10am-2:30pm; Nov-Mar M-Sa 10am-4:30pm, Su 10am-2:30pm

This impressive Art Nouveau architectural complex, just a short walk from **La Sagrada Familia**, was designed by the renowned **Lluís Domenech i Montaner,** who also designed the lavish **Palau de la Musica** in **El Born.** Despite its name, this Modernist enclosure is not actually a hospital but a "knowledge center," where cutting-edge institutions in sustainability, health, and education research how to solve modern-day challenges. It did, however, serve as a hospital in 1401 when six smaller hospitals merged into this monster. Perhaps the majestic façade, tiled domes, and interiors with red stone and white marble looked too nice for the ill, so now it welcomes tourists instead of patients to the 48 large pavilions connected by underground tunnels and bedazzled with modern sculptures and paintings.

*i* *Admission €13, guided tour €19, €9.10 student (12-29), €13.30 guided tour; English tours daily 11am, Spanish tours daily noon, free first Su of the month*

## MAGIC FOUNTAIN OF MONTJUÏC

Av. de la Reina Maria Cristina; open Apr-May Th-Sa 9-10pm; Jun-Aug W-Su 9:30-11:30pm; Sept-Oct Th-Sa 9-10pm; Nov-Mar T-Sa 8-9pm

Crowning Av. de la Reina Maria Cristina, in front of the grand façade of the **Palau Nacional,** is the Font Màgica de Montjuïc. At night, the fountain erupts in a sound and light show that is mesmerizing (think: a smaller version of **Fantastia**). For an hour, your eyes will be glued to the cauldron of color and jumping torrents of water that sync with the classical music playing from surround-sound speakers. Like at a fireworks show, crowd coos with *oooohs* and *ahhhhs*. Bring your                    special

someone to kiss under the misty red light and hold hands under the stars.

*i* *Free entry; wheelchair accessible*

## PALAU DE LA MUSICA CATALANA

C. Palau de la Música, 4-6; 932 957 200; www.palaumusica.cat; box office open daily 9:30am-3:30pm

Gaudí may be the attention hog of Barcelona, but don't miss out on the renowned architect **Lluís Domènech I Montaner's** spectacular music palace. The architectural jewel of Catalonia, covered head to toe in organic motifs, the Palau de la Musica Catalana is a **UNESCO World Heritage Site.** Take a small guided tour through the Rehearsal Hall, up the green grand staircase with ornate floral decorations and a ribbon of green carpeting iron and glass banisters. Then, explore the large balcony with mosaic columns and the Concert Hall, which has a radiant stained glass ceiling in the shape of an inverted dome. For the grand finale, the tour ends with an acoustic performance on the 3772-pipe organ.

*i* *Guided tours €18, €11 student; 55min. English tours daily 10am-3:30pm every hour, Catalan and Spanish every 30min., guided tours schedule varies by season*

## MUSEUMS

### FUNDACIÓ ANTONI TÀPIES

C. d'Aragó, 255; 934 870 315; www.fundaciotapies.org; open Tu-Su 10am-7pm; library open Tu-F 10am-3pm and 4pm-7pm, by appointment only

If you're in **l'Eixample**, look for the wild ball of aluminum wire and ragged metal netting crowing the top of a building—it's pretty unmissable. This *modernista* building, previously a Montaner publishing house, is now a contemporary art shrine to the daring **Antoni Tàpies** (who recently died in 2002). Tàpies himself put the ball of metal on the roof, declaring it a sculpture titled **Núvol i Cadira** (Cloud and Chair). Tàpies first jumped full throttle into the 1950s-art scene with his 3D paintings that incorporated waste paper, mud, and rags. That escalated to whole pieces of furniture and moving elements. Intrigued? Come inside the exposed brick and iron space for even crazier art pieces by Tàpies

and other temporary exhibitions by renowned contemporary artists.

*i* *Admisson €7, €5.60 student; last entry 15min. before closing; wheelchair accessible*

### FUNDACIÓ MIRÓ

Parc de Montjuïc; 934 439 470; www.fmirobcn.org; open Jan-Mar T-W 10am-6pm, Th 10am-9pm, F 10am-6pm, Sa 10am-8pm, Su 10am-3pm, Apr-Oct T-W 10am-6pm, Th 10am-9pm, F 10am-6pm, Sa 10am-8pm, Su 10am-3pm, Nov-Dec T-W 10am-6pm, Th 10am-9pm, F 10am-6pm, Sa 10am-8pm, Su 10am-3pm

This foundation in the mountain of **Montjuic** holds the greatest single collection of Joan Miró, the twentieth-century artistic genius. It's airy and light-filled building designed by Josep Lluis Sert, a close friend of Miró, is considered one of the most outstanding examples of museum architecture (take that, Guggenheim). Step inside the Lego-esque buildings of sharp angles and soft curves and contemplate contemporary art. Is it just a random collection of splashes and scratches of paint or is it representing something larger? Open to interpretation. The museum also contains other artists such as the legendary Calder, Duchamp, Oldeburger, and Leger.

*i* *Permanent collection and temporary exhibition admission €12, student €7, temporary exhibition admission €7, €5 student, Espai 13 €2.50, sculpture garden free, annual pass €13; audio guide €5; last entry 30min. before closing; wheelchair accessible*

### MACBA (MUSEU D'ART CONTEMPO-RANI)

Pl. dels Àngels, 1; 934 120 810; www.macba.cat; open M, W-F 11am-8pm, Sa 10am-8pm, Su 10am-3pm

If you can handle feeling stupefied in front of contemporary art that goes clearly over the majority of our heads, take a very worthwhile visit to the MACBA. Just across from the twelfth century **Cathedral of Barcelona**, a visit to both of these will give you a healthy dose of really old, and then really, really new. We shouldn't assume though, maybe you are an art connoisseur and fit in with the other circle-glasses-clad *artistes* that take modern art very seriously. Regardless, as you navigate the cryptic minimalism of **Richard Meier's** icebox-like interior, a safe bet is to just assumes that everything is a critique of contemporary culture. On your way out, stop in the gift shop to buy a "graphic" tee with nothing on it to fit in with the other modo-arto aficionados. Since it opened in 1995, the MACBA has become a dominant player in Barcelona's modern art scene.

*i* *Guided tours in English M 6pm; Permanent and temporary exhibitions admission €10, €8 student, temporary exhibitions €6, €4.50 student; free first Su monthly; wheelchair accessible*

### MUSEU DE CARROSSES FÚNEBRES

C. de la Mare, Deu de Port, 56; 934 841 920; open Sa-Su 10am-2pm

Unless you're reading **Atlas Obscura,** you'd be hard pressed to find this museum on a list of top-ten history spots in Barcelona. This funeral hearse museum, located inside the **Montjuïc Cemetery,** is by far the most bizarre and random visit you can do in Barcelona. It displays the finest in cadaver transportation, mostly funerary carriages of *rococo* style, but also different horse-drawn escort vehicles. Apparently nineteenth-century Spaniards were so classy, they even traveled in style on their way to their deathbeds. If you're feeling a little morbid, or think your hotshot friend needs a reminder that no one is invincible, this museum will definitely do the job. Iconographic symbols of mortality are everywhere you look, representing from hourglasses slowly losing sand to Greek omega symbols, meaning the end.

*i* *Free; guided tours Sa noon; wheelchair accessible*

### MUSEU NACIONAL D'ART DE CATALUNYA (MNAC)

Palau Nacional, Parc de Montjuïc; 936 220 360; www.museunacional.cat; open Jan-Apr Tu-Sa 10am-6pm, Su 10am-3pm, May-Sept Tu-Sa 10am-8pm, Su 10am-3pm, Oct-Dec Tu-Sa 10am-6pm, Su 10am-3pm

Built for the 1929 World Exhibition, the majestic Palau Nacional perches on the slopes of **Monjuïc,** standing grandiosely over **Placa España** and resembling the home of a Spanish monarch. A cascading waterfall leads up to the main domed entrance, bordered by manicured gardens and a never-ending flight of steps (don't worry, there's an escalator for you lazy travelers). The castle houses the collection of MNAC, which features mostly Catalan art, ranging from the Middle Ages to early twentieth century. Highlights include the impressive collection of Romanesque frescos and stadium-like **Oval Hall.** For those of you more interested in the art of your time, check out the Modernist and Noucentisme work, dotted with handcrafted Gaudí furniture and Picasso's cubist works.

*i* *Admission €12 (valid for two days during a month from the purchasing date), €8.40 student, temporary exhibitions €4 or €6, rooftop access €2; audio guide €4*

### MUSEU PICASSO

C. de Montcada, 15-23; 932 563 000; www.museupicasso.bcn.cat; open Tu-Su 9am-7pm, Th 9am-9:30pm

There are Picasso museums all around the world, but Barcelona arguably has the best one. Tucked into a tiny street in **El Born** and located in a restored medieval building, the museum houses an extensive collection of Picasso's works, many of which you would never guess were painted by this renowned abstract artist. Picasso spent his youth in Barcelona and this museum contains highlights from his formative years as well as works from the **Blue Period** and the preparatory sketches for his famous tribute to **Velasquez's Las Meninas.** Wander from room to room to see the technical and realistic paintings and fast-forward through Picasso's illustrative life.

*i* *Permanent collection €14, permanent collection only €11, temporary exhibitions only €6.50, free student and under 18, €7 ages 18-24, free first Su of each month 7am-9pm, free after 3pm other Su; free guided tours; last entry 30min. before closing; wheelchair accessible*

## OUTDOORS

### BUNKERS OF CARMEL

MUHBA Turó de la Rovira, Carrer de Marià Lavèrnia; open daily 24hr

A trip to the natural wonder of the bunkers of Carmel is imperative for anyone traveling in Barcelona. In the district of **El Carmel,** abandoned bunkers built during the Spanish Civil War sit on the summit of **Turó de la Rovira** (Rovira's Hill). This remote spot offers stellar panoramic views of Barcelona and, every night, hundreds of 20-somethings make the trek to this viewpoint to watch the sunset. Groups of friends or couples come to watch the sunset, prepared with a picnic blanket, bottle of wine, and some baguettes and cheese. From the summit, the views include l**a Sagrada Familia, Tibidau, MAPFRE tower,** and the **Torre Agbar**. Be careful to not have too much wine, because the hike down in the dark is a little treacherous.

*i* Free; no wheelchair accessibility

## PARC DE LA CIUTADELLA

Pg. De Picasso, C. Pujades, and C. Wellington; 638 237 115; open daily 9am-9pm

Come for a picnic, a leisurely stroll, or a romantic lakeside rowboat ride at Barcelona's central urban green, Parc de la Ciutadella. Its main entrance in **La Ribera** is the **Arc de Triomf.** Not only will you be spending the day in the great outdoors, but you'll get your daily dose of history, as this was the site of the **Universal Exhibition of 1888.** There is also a zoo, regional parliament, and several museums located in the park. Don't miss the beautiful fountain with winged houses spewing water behind the lake, which apparently was one of **Antoni Gaudí's** favorites.

*i* Free

## ROSALEDA DE CERVANTES

Av. Diagonal, 706; www.bcn.cat/parc-sijardins; open daily Apr-Oct 10am-9pm, Nov-Mar 10am-7pm

Roses are red, violets are—nope, roses are blue too, and yellow, and white, and every other shade of pink, in the Rose Garden of Cervantes. It takes a tad bit of work to get here, but the Parc de Cervantes in the district of **Pedralbes** is remarkably beautiful. There are over 10,000 rose bushes of some 2,000 species. Because of Barcelona's mild climate, the flowers are in bloom from April to November, but, in the flowering season between May and July, there are over 150,000 in bloom. Every year, the garden hosts an international rose competition where new species are presented. Aside from the rose garden, the rest of the park has many grassy areas and paths perfect for jogging, biking, or simply contemplating life's beauty.

*i* Free entry; wheelchair accessible

## SITGES

Located only a 30-minute train ride from **Barcelona Sants Station,** this white-washed, wind-swept costal paradise has the best beaches in the region with none of that towel-to-towel business you'll find see at the more packed beaches. Spend the day admiring the twinkling turquoise water and tanning on one of the 17 white sand beaches. Sitges is often called the "Spanish Saint-Tropez," and for good reason. The ones closer to the center have facilities such as showers, toilets, and bars, but the secluded beaches in coves are real beauties. Our favorites: **Platja Sant Sebastía,** and **Platja de Terramar.** There are also family and

volleyball-friendly (Fragata), BGLTQ+ (Rodona), and nude (Balmains) beaches, so there's something for everyone.

*i* *Free entry; limited wheelchair accessibility*

# FOOD

### 🔖EL PACHUCO ($)
C. de Sant Pau, 110; 931 796 805; open Tu-Su 1:30pm-2:30am

You know Mexican food is good when you overhear a girl from Southern California say this is the best Mexican food she's ever had. El Pachuco is a Mexican tapas bar serving quick tacos, quesadillas, guacamole, and Mexican beers. The entrance may be hard to find, but it's usually overflowing with people, and, if you see a chalkboard sign that says "Keep Calm and Shut the Fuck Up," you've found the right place. As soon as your oozing cheese quesadilla order comes out, you'll for sure shut up, as you'll be too focused on devouring the Mexican goodness to talk. Before you leave, check out the cool bathroom covered in posters of the Meixcan lucha wrestler, El Santo.

*i* *3 tacos €6.70, 5 tacos €8.70; vegetarian options available; no wheelchair accessibility*

### BODEGA LA PENINSULAR ($$)
C. del Mar, 29; 932 214 089; open daily 11:30am-midnight

If you're looking for possibly the best seafood in Barcelona, look no further. It is pricier than the neighboring local tapas bars, but La Peninsular's *tapes marines* (seafood tapas) are a must. You'll be hard pressed to decide between the grilled cuttlefish and the marinated anchovies, as there's a large selection of tapes marines (seafood) or classics, including *patatas bravas* (potatos in sauce), *tortillas espanolas* (Spanish toritilla), or chorizo. Pro-tip: come any day but Sunday or Monday, as there is fresh seafood Tuesday through Saturday. Another pro-tip (because we like you so much): make a reservation, unless you want to sit at the bar (which wouldn't be so bad, considering it's white marble). And a bonus one, for you, dear reader: they'll only serve paella if you call ahead, so make that damn reservation.

*i* *Tapas €7-10, glass of wine €3; wheelchair accessible ; reservation recommended*

### BUN BO VIETNAM ($$)
C. dels Àngels, 6; 934 121 890; www.bunbovietnam.com; open M-Th noon-midnight, F-Sa noon-1am, Su noon-midnight

You might be surprised to find yourself eating spring rolls and slurping Vietnamese noodle soups in the middle of Barcelona's **Old Quarter**, but you'd also be surprised by the city's enormous number of modern and ethnic restaurants. Bun Bo offers a great alternative if you want to take a breather from Catalan tapas. Decorated with colorful paper lanterns and Asian masks, it's a popular spot for young people enjoying their absurdly cheap cocktails and delicious Vietnamese coffee with condensed milk. Both the **Raval** and **El Gotico** locations offer affordable menus of the day with Vietnamese-inspired dishes ranging from traditional *pho bò* to their version of Spanish *bocadillos*, i.e, the bánh mì sandwich.

*i* *Cocktails €3.50, menu of the day €9, entrées €8-10; vegetarian and vegan options available*

### CAFÉ CAMÈLIA ($)
Carrer de Verdi, 79; open daily 9:30am-midnight

It's cafés like this that make you fall in love with the charming neighborhood of Gràcia—quirky, healthy, reasonably priced, and serving all homemade recipes. Decorated with floral placemats and checkered green and white floors, Café Camèlia is the place for a fresh juice concoction (try *el Picantet* for a kick of ginger and red pepper), afternoon coffee, or freshly baked pastry. Check out their vegetarian lunch menu of the day, for those who don't dabble in Spain's carnivorous diet. They also have live music nights Thursday through Sunday. With one long common table down the middle and smaller two-person tables on the side, it's perfect for small groups or "parties" of one.

*i* *Fruit juices €3.50, salads €6.50, cakes €4, vegetarian menu of day €10.50;*

*vegetarian and vegan options available; wheelchair accessible*

### CHÖK—THE CHOCOLATE KITCHEN ($)
C. del Carme, 3; 933 042 360; www.chok-barcelona.com; open daily 9am-9pm

For all you chocolate lovers (sweet-tooth travelers) out there, this is your dream come true. Just off **Las Ramblas** in **El Raval**, rows and rows of donuts, kronuts (mixtures of croissant and donut), truffles, and more fill the dazzling display of this chocolate kitchen. One look at this modern chocolate kitchen and you'll start salivating like a dog. Unlike a dog, though, you can eat as much chocolate as you'd like and it won't kill you (within reason), so here's your chance to go crazy. Our favorite: their signature kronuts. Imagine: a fluffy base filled with cream and coated in your choice of icing and toppings. Sure, it's heart disease in a bite, but it'll satisfy even the most intense sweet tooth craving.

*i Brownies €3, kronuts €3.95, muffin €2; wheelchair accessible*

### EL REBELOT COCKTAIL AND FOOD ($$)
C. del Baluard, 58; 932 219 581; www.rebelotbcn.com; open daily 11am-2am

Get ready for some seriously mouth-watering food that will also make you feel great about yourself at El Rebelot. Right next door to its fancy sister restaurant, **Somorrostro,** El Rebelot is the cozier, more casual version that offers the same exquisite quality without the need for reservation. Both restaurants specialize in slow food, which is food prepared with a commitment to healthy, clean, and fair consumption by working directly with local farmers and fishermen. Their main menu features scrumptious salads and burgers. For vegetarians, try the burrata burger. The most popular dishes are actually not on menu, but rather the daily tapas menu hand scrawled on a chalkboard. These dishes are meant to be savored, so even though it's not what slow food means, please do eat your food slowly.

*i Tapas €8-12, burgers and salads €6-8; vegetarian options available*

### FEDERAL CAFÉ ($$)
C. del Parlament, 39; 931 873 607; www.federalcafé.es/barcelona; open M-Th 8am-11pm, F 8am-1pm, Sa 9am-1pm, Su 9am-5:30pm

If you put an egg on top of any food, does that officially make it a brunch option? Federal Café thinks so! This Aussie-run restaurant is heaven for brunch enthusiasts. It is a bright space with large windows, two floors, and clean environment. Go crazy with their breakfast burger, eggs benedict/Florentine, or Shakshuka. Their avocado toast on sourdough is like a Peruvian landscape, sliced and layered like the vibrant green terrace fields of Machu Pichu with a soft-boiled egg running like a yellow waterfall. Go check it out yourself to see what other landscapes you can explore through their brunch concoctions.

*i Breakfast dishes €7-9, toast and pastries €2-3; wheelchair accessible*

### KITSUNE SUSHI BAR ($$$)
C. el Montseny, 13; 620 666 885; www.kitsunesushi.com; open daily 1-3:45pm, 8-11:45pm

Getting a little tired of *jamón iberico* and *croquetas*? Switch is up for some refreshing Japanese cuisine at Kitsune Sushi Bar. Hidden in the tiny street of **Monteny,** this simple and functional restaurant feels very authentically Japanese. Although there are other sushi restaurants in **Gràcia,** Kitsune offers by far the best deal in teams of quality-price ratio. If you're at a loss staring at their menu, order the *aaburi shoga*, some *uramiakis* (inside-out sushi) with some spicy sake, or try the degustation menu for €22 and they will give you five to six dishes based on your taste preferences.

*i Sushi rolls €6-9, tasting menu €22; wheelchair accessible; reservation recommended*

### NABUCCO TIRAMISU ($)
Pl. de la Vila de Gràcia, 8; 932 176 101; www.nabuccotiramisu.com; open M-F 8:30am-10:30pm, Sa-Su 9:30am-10:30pm

As you roam through Gràcia, stop at this adorable café and let yourself be tempted by their delightful pastry display. Inside, the café is airy and light, with white brick walls that stretch far back. Start your day with an espresso and take advantage of the quiet atmosphere and Wi-Fi to spend a morning working and treating yourself to a thick hot chocolate or their delicious cakes, fruit tarts, or, of course, their specialty tiramisu. If you want more brain food, try their fresh fruit juice, avocado toast, or large salads.

*i* *Drinks €1-2, pastries €3, salads and sandwiches €6-8; wheelchair accessible*

## QUIMET & QUIMET ($)

C. del Poeta Cabanyes, 25; 934 423 142; open M-F noon-4pm and 7pm-10:30pm

This five-generation-old establishment is so famous that they don't even have to open on weekends to sustain their business. They offer assorted plates of meat, seafood, or cheese, but *bocadillos* (small sandwiches) are their star dish and for good reason. These tiny sandwiches of crunchy, yet fluffy bread have toppings that look like sculptures, and the gastronomic explosion in your mouth is the truly a work of art. Try anchovies and goat cheese, salmon, yogurt, and truffle honey, or the tuna belly and sea urchin sandwich, which are just a few of their delicious options. The restaurant itself is very small, so don't come during the lunch or dinner rush because you'll be waiting for hours. But, sometimes, a Spanish band will serenade you while you eat, which makes the whole experience just that much cooler.

*i* *Tapas €2.50-3.25, beer €5.75 per bottle; vegetarian options available*

## RISTORANTE GRAVIN ($$$)

C. de Rera Palau, 3; 932 684 628; www.gravinristorante.com; open M 7:30-11:30pm, Tu 7:30-11pm, W-Su 1-4:30 and 8-11:30pm

Mmm... Italian AND Catalan food?! This gastronomical fusion is like putting ice cream on a Belgian waffle and root beer float—two amazing things—even better. Ristorante Gravin is in a quiet plaza in **El Born,** with tables on the cobblestone streets under an umbrella. The Italian menu offers delicious fresh pastas as well as traditional Catalan tapas. In an ode to

*i* *Entrées €15.45, beer €2, tapas €6; vegetarian options available; wheelchair accessible; reservation recommended*

# NIGHTLIFE

## CDLC

P. Marítim de la Barceloneta; www.cdlcbarcelona.com; Open daily midnight-5am

CDLC, short for Carpe Diem Lounge Club, is a chic venue out on the seafront promenade. Outside, on its bleached wooden planks, a palm-tree framed terrace has low sofas that seat the uber-tanned, international elite. People who look like models, and who are probably models, sip pricey cocktails as the DJ pumps house music and crowd pleasers. This club has a capacity of only 500, and, during the day, serves as a nice restaurant. Girls, bring out the platform heels and the bronzer. Boys, tuck in your button down, but unbutton it a little more—you don't want to get turned away for a wardrobe faux-paus. If you're lucky, the might may end with a stroll on the beach with someone equally as attractive as the sunrise.

*i* *Cover €5-10*

## JAMBOREE

Plaça Reial, 17; 933 191 789; www.masimsa.com/jamborree

It's time to get down and dirty in the brick cave in the Gothic quarter that is Jamboree. Although it's been around for half a century, it still is the best hip-hop and R&B club, playing jazz, blues, afro beats, and Latin tunes. Rock your white Adidas sneakers and flat cap as you krump, jerk, and pop-and-lock on the dance floor. We recommend you look these moves up on YouTube before coming here; you don't want to show up without knowing your stuff. Check Jamboree out for "BCN or Die" with Flavio Rodrigues on Thursdays, DJ Yoda on Friday, and Bulma Beat on Wednesday.

*i* *Cover €10-20, drinks €5-10*

## LA TERAZZA (POBLE ESPANYOL)

Av. Marquès de Comillas, 13; 932 105 906; www.laterrrazza.com; open May-Sept F-Sa 12:30-6am

For almost two decades, the glamorous La Terrazza Club has been throwing the hottest summer parties. This beautifully designed, open-air dance club lights up **El Poble Espanyol** after the tourists and artisans leave the miniature Spanish city. It hosts renowned international and local DJs, pumping commercial house hits that guarantee a good time. The price of drinks reflects its elegant décor, so it might be a good idea to pregame at a cheaper bar before going. However, La Terazza is notoriously hard to find, so before you get too drunk, scrawl the address on your hand to show your taxi driver.

*i* Cover €18, including 1 free drink, beer €5-10, mixed drinks €8-12

## MOOG

C. de l'Arc del Teatre, 3; 933 191 789; www.masimas.com/moog; open daily midnight-5am

Moog may be small, but it has a big reputation. Electronic music lovers from all over the city flock to this tiny club just off **Las Ramblas**. Pump your fist to house and techno beats in the dark downstairs space with red and blue spotlights swirling around. The sunken dancefloor is lined with cabinets of spirit bottles, and has an elegant wooden bar at the far end. It gets packed as soon as the clock strikes 12, so get there early to skip the line. For less hardcore electro-heads, the smaller mirrored room upstairs plays a mix of pop and 80s music and all the hits in between, so you can't be disappointed.

*i* Cover €5, drinks €5-10; BGLTQ+ friendly

## PANIKA

Pg. de Joan de Borbó, 9; 655 108 920; open daily 10am-2am

Opened in April 2017, Panika is the new kid on the block and everyone wants to meet him. Situated on the main drag of **Port Vell**, on the way to **Barceloneta beach**, it gets a ton of street traffic. Think of it like a jack-of-all-trades, transforming from a calm breakfast spot for *pan con tomate* to a popping bar at night. One of their specialty cocktails is more expensive than those of the beer bar next door, but it is more than a drink—it's an experience. Here's a challenge: see if you can identify their "secret ingredient" mixed in with the swirling lemon peel in their classic Gin Sour.

*i* Cocktails €7-12; wine by the glass €4.5; beer €2-5; BGLTQ+ friendly; wheelchair accessible

## RAZZMATAZZ

Carrer dels Almogàvers, 122; 933 208 200; www.salarazzmatazz.com; open Th midnight-3:30am, F-Sa midnight-5:30am

Razzmatazz is five clubs in one, offering a classic live-music and clubbing scene with irresistible techno music in the loft room upstairs and indie-rock in the Razz Club below. Erasmus students flock to Wednesday night ragers, meaning that anyone over 30 will look like a lost chaperon here. The amazing sound system reverberates throughout the cavernous industrial warehouse, bouncing off the steel ceilings and energizing the crowd. Be prepared to be dance until the early hours of the morning, and, since Razzmatazz doesn't have any places to sit, your legs will be so tired that you may as well stay until the Barcelona metro opens shop again at 5am.

*i* Cover €12-32, drinks €7

# CORDOBA

Coverage by **Emma Scornavacchi**

On the plains of the Guadalquivir River, among the reeds where the water melts into a shade of pale green, sits Córdoba, Spain. Córdoba was once a great Roman city, until it became a stronghold during the Middle Ages, and, later becoming predominantly Catholic during the Reconquista. It now stands strong as one of the main Islamic cities of the Andalusian region. Today, Córdoba blends these different cultural backgrounds seamlessly, representing the heritage of each in a city that is growing more modern every day. The Mezquita, a main attraction in the city, exemplifies this, a beautiful, spiritual place representing different types of worship and cultural history. A small city that still feels metropolitan on the main streets and plazas, Córdoba's real magic lies in its roadways where cobblestone paths are bordered by white walls and flowers. Fresh fruit and authentic tapas stands reside on every corner. Eating Tapas breakfast, lunch, and dinner (and even second dinner) is encouraged, just make sure you save at least one meal for the Puente Romano, its vantage point provides a mesmerizing nocturnal view of the ancient city lit up from across the river.

# ORIENTATION

Córdoba is cohesive and easily walkable—nothing is ever more than 20 minutes away from anything else. If you begin at the train station, you'll find yourself at the corner of a large, grassy park which parallels **Avenida de la República Argentina** and **Paseo de la Victoria,** respectively. To the east is the more cosmopolitan which is mostly centered around the **Plaza de las Tendillas.** Here, you'll find bistros and shops surrounding a lively square, with side streets branching out in all directions. Head south to meet the **River Gudalquevir** as it trickles through green shrubbery, and you'll find the historic Mezquita just before the iconic **Puente Romano** (Roman Bridge) and its accompanying tower. Córdoba's official reach is far wider than these key features but most of what attracts visitors to the city lies within the confines of the center of the city, creating a small-town feel with big-city beauty.

# ESSENTIALS
## GETTING THERE

The closest airport to the city of Córdoba is Seville Airport (SVQ), which services over 40 destinations around Europe. From Seville, it is easiest to take a train to Córdoba, which will take about 45min. Sevilla Airport is a pivot point for many budget airlines such as Ryanair and Vueling. AVE railway line connects Córdoba to Seville, Barcelona, Madrid and more destinations quickly. Tickets can be purchased online at www.renfe.com and should be sought out in advance during high season when seats may sell out. Bus lines like Alsa and Socibus service the Córdoba Bus Station, which is next to the train station. Buses arrive regularly from destinations throughout Spain and neighboring countries.

## GETTING AROUND

Aside from taxis, buses are Córdoba's main form of public transportation and are operated through the local Aucorsa company. Both the urban and peripheral lines intersect and serve the inner parts of the city as well the outskirts. Taxis are readily available in Córdoba, and are most concentrated on bigger streets and near the train station. Bike rental companies such as Ride Me! Córdoba (located at C. Azonaicas 5) and Duribaik Bicicletas (C. Sevilla 13) offer easy rental processes.

## PRACTICAL INFORMATION

**Tourist Offices:** There is a tourist information at the RENFE train station (902 20 17 74; open daily 9am-2pm and 4:30pm-7pm)

**Banks/ATMS/Currency Exchange:** Deutsche Bank Filiale (C. Concepción 4; 957 47 87 37; www.deutsche-bank.es); Bankia (C. Conde de Gondomar 9; 957 49 70 24; www.bankia.es)

**Post Offices:** Correos (C. José Cruz Conde 15; 902 19 71 97; www.correos.es)

**Internet:** Wi-Fi is accessible in many independent cafés and restaurants.

**BGLTQ+ Resources:** There is no specific center for BGLTQ+ services and www.gayiberia.com and www.gayinspain.com.

## EMERGENCY INFORMATION

**Emergency Number:** 112
**Police:** Cuerpo de Policia Cordoba 2 (Av. Del Mediterráneo; 957 59 45 70; www.policia.es). Cordoba Police Emergencies (092).
**Hospitals:** Hospital Reina Sofía (Av. Menéndez Pidal; 957 21 70 00).
**Pharmacies:** Farmacia Concepción (C. Concepción 6; 957 47 02 72; www.farmaciaconcepcion.com).

# ACCOMMODATIONS

## ⊠OPTION BE HOSTEL

C. Leiva Aguilar 1; 661 420 733; www.
bedandbe.com; reception open 24hr

The cleverly named Option Be seems
to sparkle from top to bottom. The
giant skylight above the common room
and kitchen lights up the fresh, modern
décor. The bedrooms and bathrooms
are spacious and clean, making you feel
as if you are staying in a hotel. Hostels
are what now? The kitchen is stocked
with breakfast food all day long and
the rooftop terrace even boasts a
small pool for guests. Option Be also
hosts nightly excursions for guests
to restaurants and bars, led by their
knowledgeable staffers.

*i* *Dorms €18-22, private rooms €69;*
*reservation recommended; wheelchair*
*accessible; Wi-Fi; luggage storage; laundry*
*facilities; free breakfast*

## BACKPACKER AL-KATRE

C. Martínez Rucker 14; 626 389 706; www.
alkatre.com; reception open 9am-11pm

Backpacker Al-Katre sits comfortably
on the smaller, less social end of the
hostel spectrum, and provides a nice
space for travelers to relax. Authentic
tile decorations line the open common
space, which contains an orange
canopy that lends the whole room a
dim, pink-ish glow. Bedrooms and
bathrooms are fairly standard, but
the bonus amenities of the hostel—
meditation space, book exchange, small
rooftop patio— are nods to its slow-
paced, family-oriented experience. Staff
are lovely and accommodating, and
free walking tours are available daily.

*i* *Dorms €17-19, private rooms €40-42;*
*reservation recommended; Wi-Fi; luggage*
*storage; towels for rent €2; breakfast €2*

# SIGHTS

## CULTURE

## ⊠PUERTA DEL PUENTE

C. Ronda de Isasa; open M-F 11am-2pm
and 5pm-7pm, Sa-Su 11am-2pm

In 1572, Córdoba's mayor decided the
city needed a door. Thus, the Puerta
del Puente, translated as "Bridge
Door," was built. The Puerta del Puente
doesn't open, close, lock, or hinge (it
doesn't quite do its job as a door),
but it does function as a majestic and
statuesque gateway into the city. The
gate separates Córdoba from the wide-
open river plains of the **Guadalquivir
River**. The famous "door" now
includes an exposition and a balcony
viewpoint to observe both the city and
surrounding nature.

*i* *Tickets €1*

## LANDMARKS

## ⊠ALCÁZAR DE LOS REYES CRISTIA-
NOS

Pl. Campo Santo de los Mártires; 957
420 151; open Tu-Sa 8:30am-3pm, Su
8:30am-2:30pm

The authentic luxury of Córdoba's
Alcazar de Los Reyes Cristianos means
it is as mindblowing to visitors as it is
interesting to history-lovers. Having
changed hands throughout history and
influenced by Muslim and Christian
cultures, the Alcázar is now mostly
a tourist attraction consisting of the
palace and its surrounding manicured
gardens. Several flights of stairs to one
of the palace's towers offer 360-degree
views of the city and mountains
beyond. Pro-tip: take your time
strolling in the gardens, which have
water features, flowers, and meticulous
landscaping to make yourself feel royal.

*i* *Tickets €4.50, €2.25 student; last entry*
*30min. before closing; limited wheelchair*
*accessibility*

## MEZQUITA-CATEDRAL DE CÓRDOBA

C.del Cardenal Herrero 1; 957 470 512;
www.mezquitadecordoba.org

Dating back to 786, the Mezquita is a
structure recognized as both a mosque
and a cathedral. It holds centuries of
worship, spirituality, and history inside
its walls and arches. The Mezquita is
massive, with red-and-white-striped
arches, with the intricately detailed
**Mihrab** on the south wall. Smaller
chapels line the rest of the perimeter,
and one part of the structure even
displays exhibits with artifacts in cases.
Some parts are bathed in sunlight,
while others feel dark and eerie,
which creates an especially dynamic
experience for guests exploring
the Mezquita. Admission is on the
expensive side, but doors open for

free at 8:30am while the building is still being cleaned.

*i* *Tickets €10, free 8:30am-9:20am; €35 tour M 11:30am Mezquita and Jewish Quarter, €40 tour Tu-Sa at 10am of Mezquita, Alcazar, Jewish Quarter, Synagogue; hours of operation subject to change with special event; dress code: cover shoulders and knees; last entry 30min. before closing time; wheelchair accessible*

## MUSEUMS

### MUSEUM OF FINE ARTS OF CÓRDOBA

Pl. del Potro 1 ; 057 103 659; open Jan 1-June 15 Tu-Sa 9am-8pm, Su 9am-3pm, June 16-Sept 15 Tu-Su 9am-3pm

Modest in size, Córdoba's Museum of Fine Arts features mainly local paintings, drawings, and sculptures. Art collections span centuries, displaying both ancient and contemporary art. Córdoba's main art museum was founded in 1814 and continues to draw art fans to its comprehensive collections that scrutinize the city of Córdoba and the Andalusian region. Most plaques next to the works don't include an English translation, however, so you may be left up to your own interpretation.

*i* *Tickets €1.50, free for EU citizens*

## OUTDOORS

### PUENTE ROMANO AND TORRE DE LA CALAHORRA

Puente Romano; 957 293 929; www. torrecalahorra.es; open daily May-Sept 10am-2pm and 4:30pm-8:30pm, Oct-Apr 10am-6pm

The legendary Puente Romano is where everything comes together in Córdoba, the urban streets meet the river, history meets modern city, and mountain views meet the horizon line. The bridge, called "Romano" for the Romans who constructed it, and its connecting tower were erected to defend the city in the twelfth century and now constitute many famous

*vistas.*
The museum housed in the Torre de La Calahorra is intriguing, but the view from the top is the real gem—though you have to pay for both. The bridge is worth a visit during the daytime, but as locals will tell you, it's the most stunning when lit up against the backdrop of the metropolitan landscape at night.

*i* *Tickets €4.50, €3 student*

### CALLEJA DE LAS FLORES

Calleja de las Flores (off of Calle Velázquez Bosco); open daily 24hr

A photo opportunity and enjoyable stroll wrapped into one, Calleja de las Flores is one of many quaint, historic streets in Córdoba featuring white walls, cobblestones, and colorful accents. What sets this street apart are the flower pots covering the walls and windowsills—the abundance of blue pots overflow with geraniums, brightening up the street. The roadway's beauty makes it crowded with tour groups. A new and colorful side street lies around every corner in Córdoba, so for those looking to beat the crowds, Calleja de las Flores can be abandoned in favor of an expedition into many of the city's neighborhoods.

*i* *Free; wheelchair accessible*

# FOOD

## ✎LA BICICLETA ($)

C. Cardenal Gonzalez; 666 544 690; open daily noon-1am

Behind a small, unassuming storefront lies La Bicicleta, a restaurant serving authentic Spanish food and simple, healthy options amongst mismatched décor and friendly staff. *Tostas* are the menu's staple and are served with tomato, avocado, ham, cheese, salmon, and more, but this is just a portion of the impressive menu. Larger plates, many different drinks, and even fresh-squeezed juice are up for grabs. La Bicicleta manages to go beyond the basics while serving options and combinations impossible to find elsewhere.

*i* *Tostas €4-6, platos €4-13; vegetarian options available; wheelchair accessible*

## ✎LA TRANQUERA ($$)

Corregidor de la Cerda 53; 957 787 569; www.la-tranquera.es; open daily 1:30pm-4:30pm and 8:30pm-12:30am

Once you've gotten lost among the arches of the **Mezquita,** it's time to get lost in the crispy and flaky crust of empanadas at nearby La Tranquera. An authentic spot deep in the maze of city side streets, La Tranquera attracts locals for its Latin American influenced tapas and cozy, unassuming atmosphere. The red walls are filled with framed pictures, showcasing old time Spanish celebrities, bullfighting paraphernalia, and local art. Polish off the meal with a large pitcher (yes, large pitcher) of sangria and a dulce de leche and you've just covered miles of Spanish ground in one swoop.

*i* *Entrées €8-14; vegetarian options available*

## ✎MERCADO VICTORIA ($$)

Paseo de la Victoria; 957 290 707; www.lasalmoreteca.com; open M-W 9am-1am, Th-Sa 9am-2am, Su 9am-1am

As the night goes on, the buzz of Mercado Victoria hums louder. It started earlier, sure—the market, which is situated right on the river, is a popular spot for meals throughout the day, but the evenings are when the smörgåsbord of food options become popular quickly, fueled by the beer and wine stands within the large space..

From sushi to skewers to traditional *jamón* to Argentine food (try the oxtail empanada if you're feeling adventurous!), Mercado Victoria has never-ending choices and an ambiance that'll keep you sipping and browsing for hours.

*i* *Prices vary by stand; some stands cash only; vegetarian options available; wheelchair accessible*

# NIGHTLIFE

## ✎GLACE LOUNGE BAR

C. Escultor Fernández Márquez 9; 957 403 876; www.glace.es; open M-Th 9am-2am, F-Sa 9am-3am, Su 9am-2am

A wacky custom cocktail bar, Glace is an unexpected gem of a nighttime spot. Glace's owner/bartender is known to interact with guests and sit down to talk cocktails before preparing the ultimate in custom creativity to suit anyone's tastes. Think: it's like a really fun doctor writing a prescription. The white bar lined with endless bottles also adds to the clinical vibe, but it'll be like no doctor's office trip you've ever experienced when your colorful cocktail, topped with fresh fruit (or a lollipop, or nutmeg, or even an edible decoration) arrives at your table. Admire it, oogle it, take a picture (we won't judge), then bottom's up. You'll be looking for a prescription refill in no time.

*i* *Drinks €5-15; wheelchair accessible*

## CERVECERÍA CALIFA

C. Juan Valera 3; 678 428 330; www.cervezascalifa.com; open M-Th noon-4pm, 6:30pm-midnight, F-Sa noon-1:30am

Cervecería Califa is quite simply living the dream, a craft brewery in the heart of historic Córdoba, it provides an experience scarce in Cordoba. and boy, does the city appreciate it. Cervecería Califa specializes in their own line of beers brewed in their local factory, but also sells an incredibly wide range of beers both domestic and international. Pair it with some *tapas;* the *tostadas* are renowned for being the perfect complement to Califa beer and the modest prices are high value. Celebrating local beer of good character while also wiling the night away at a beautiful bar? Brew-tiful.

*i* Beer €2.50-3.50

# GRANADA

Coverage by **Julia Bunte-Mein**

Although famed for its extravagant Alhambra, Granada has much more to offer than this one landmark. Compared to its more raucous, fun younger sister, Málaga, Granada is the mysterious, romantic older sister with a complicated past. As the last Moorish stronghold in Western Europe, this cultural mixing pot has a dense history. Moorish architecture and teterías line the entrance to El Albaicín, Granada's Muslim quarter, and white-washed walls stand grandly in al Realejo, the Jewish quarter. Transport yourself back to the time when Catholic monarchs dominated the region by visiting El Capilla Real, or admire the work of graffiti artist El Niño de las Pinturas when strolling through El Realejo. Although the tapas scene is lively in the evening, the city goes to bed at around midnight. Granada is a place for day-time activities, such as exploring El Albaicín, hiking in the Sierra Nevada, or lounging on terraces in the shade of a flower-covered trellace. Granada is best explored by impulse. Once you've read this chapter, put down your book and follow your intuition. Soon enough, you'll find yourself gazing out at the Alhambra from El Mirador San Nicolas, watching the sunset from San Miguel Alto in Sacromonte, experiencing a deeply-moving flamenco performance, or simply stuffing your face with tapas. "Granada," meaning "pomegranate," is a unified whole made of many sweet parts. What follows are some of the sweetest.

## ORIENTATION

Granada is located in the crook of the **Sierra Nevada Mountain Range** in Andalucía, Spain and is the meeting point of four rivers. The bus and train station is located about 20 minutes northwest of the city center. From the station, a public bus will drop you off at a stop called "Catedral," located on **Calle Gran Vía de Colón,** which divides El Albaicín. El Centro contains Granada's ancient landmarks, including the **Cathedral of Granada** and **Capilla,** or Royal Chapel. This area, especially around **Plaza Bib-Rambla,** consists of cobblestone streets and is packed with tourists. As you head farther south, the city becomes more urban and modern. Here you'll find establishments that cater to your logistical needs (banks, pharmacies, contemporary clothing stores). Northeast of El Centro, next to el **Albaicín** is **El Realejo.** It is in this region that you will find the **Alhambra** and **Generalife Gardens.** El Albaicín is situated on a hill, and if you hike upwards, you'll reach **El Sacromonte,** which is home to the gypsy caves, the Sacromonte Cave Museum, El Abadia el Sacromonte, and San Miguel Alto, which offers the best views in all of Granada.

## ESSENTIALS

### GETTING THERE

The bus station is located at Carretera de Jaén (95 818 50 10). AlSA buses (www.alsa.es) run within Andalucía (95 818 54 80) and connect to the Madrid and Valencia-Barcelona lines. Transportes Rober runs regular services between the station and the city center. To get to the city center form the bus station, take bus SNI and get off at the Cathedral stop. The main train station (95 827 12 72) is located at Av. De los Andaluces. RENFE trains (www.renfe.es) run to and from Barcelona, Seville, and many other smaller cities. Aeropuerto Federico García Lorca is located about 15km. outside the city. A taxi will take you to the city center (€25) or directly to the Alhambra (€28). Call Radio taxi in advance at (60 605 29 25) or wait in line at the airport. The bus company Autocares José González offers a direct service between the airport and the city center (€3; 95 839 01 64 www.autocaresjosegonzalez.com; every hour daily 5:20am-8pm).

## GETTING AROUND

Trasportes Rober runs almost 40 bus lines around the city as well as smaller direct buses to the Alhambra, the Albaicín, and the Sacromonte (€1.20 per ride, €5 for seven rides; 90 071 09 00; www.transportesrober.com). The tourist lines are #30, 31, 32, and 34. The circular lines (#11, 12, and 23) make full loops around the city. Rober also runs a special Feria line (€1.40). When most lines stop running at 11:30pm, the Búho lines pick up the slack (€1.30; #111 and 121; daily midnight-5:15am).

## PRACTICAL INFORMATION

**Tourist Offices:** Main tourist office (el Ayuntamiento, or City Hall, Pl. Del Carmen; 958 248 280; www.granadatur.com; open M-Sa 9am-8pm, Su 9am-2pm).

**Banks/ATMS/Currency Exchange:** Most ATMs are located in the modern center of the city, especially lining Calle Gran Vía de Colón. Interchange is a money-exhange office that provides services for all major credit cards, including American Express (C. Reyes Catéolicos, 31; 958 22 45 12; open M-Sa 9am-10pm, Su 11am-3pm and 4-9pm).

**Post Offices:** Puerta Real (Puerta Real, 2, at the intersection of C. Reyes Católicos and Acera del Darro; 902 19 71 97; open M-F 8:30am-8:30pm, Sa 9:30am-2pm). Granada's postal code is 18005.

**Internet:** Biblioteca de Andalucía has eight desktop computers that you can use for free for up to one hour (C. Prof. Sainz Cantero, 6; 958 02 69 00; open M-F 9am-2pm). Idolos and Fans has photocopying, fax, scanning, and Wi-Fi (Camino de Ronda, 80; 958 52 14 96; open daily 10am-midnight).

**BGLTQ+ Resources:** Andalucía Diversidad offers information, social care service, counseling, legal advice, and other resources to municipalities

(C. Victoria, 8.: 951 00 38 14; info@andalucialgbt.com).

## EMERGENCY INFORMATION

**Emergency Number:** 112

**Police:** Local police headquarters located at C. Huerta Del Rasillo (958 20 68 78; open daily 9am-2pm). For major issues, head to the Granada Police Station (Pl. de los Campos (Barrio Realejo); 958 808 800; open daily 9am-2pm).

**U.S. Embassy:** The nearest US Consulate is in Málaga (Av. Juan Gómez Juanito, 8; 952 47 48 91; open M-F 10am-2pm).

**Rape Crisis Center:** Call Granada Police Station at 958 808 800.

**Hospitals:** Hospital Universitario Vírgen de las Nieves (Av. de las Fuerzas Armadas, 2; 958 02 00 00; open daily 24hr).

**Pharmacies:** There are a few 24-hour pharmacies around the intersection of C. Reyes Catéolicos and Acera del Darro, including Farmácia Martín Valverde (C. Reyes Católicos, 5; 958 26 26 64).

# ACCOMMODATIONS

### ◾MAKUTO BACKPACKER'S HOSTEL

C. Tiña, 18; 958 80 58 76; www.makuto-hostel.com/en; reception open 8am-midnight

Stop. Look no further. Makuto, located in el Albaicín, is the best hostel in Granada for young backpackers. This hostel is not just a hostel. We'd almost go as far as to say it's a cult, or maybe a commune, because of the strong community it fosters. Don't get freaked out though—it's not actually one. Despite Granada's endless attractions and activities, many guests choose to never leave the lovely confines of Makuto, playing guitar and singing in the tree house (a pomegranate tree grows through the hostel, from which hammocks dangle), sipping sangria at the tiki bar, playing cards on the patio, reading or watching movies in the "chill-out" room, and conversing over home-cooked dinner (daily at 10pm, €6-8). Despite its many common areas, Makuto is housed in a relatively small building, but it manages to squeeze in a ton of people with its innovative layering bunk system (we hope you're not scared of heights!) and space-saving coed bathrooms.

*i* Dorms from €20; reservation required; Wi-Fi; linens included; laundry €8; lockers provided; free breakfast

## BACKPACKERS INN GRANADA
C. Padre Alcover, 10; 958 26 62 14; reception open 24hr

Backpackers Inn Granada is the hostel you turn to when all the others are full. Not because it's crappy, but because it's enormous. Located outside of the cramped Albaicín quarter in the southern portion of El Centro, Backpackers Inn has a capacity in the hundreds, opening up some great opportunities for socializing, or conversely, for flying anonymously under the radar. Still, it maintains a certain charm with its grand interior courtyard, long wooden tables, and stone mosaics. Whether or not you stay at this hostel, it is a fantastic one to know about because it offers Alhambra tickets (€18.90), which will save you from getting up at 4:30am to queue for a ticket, if you hadn't already reserved one two months in advance.

*i* Dorms €14, apartment €180; wheelchair accessible; Wi-Fi; linens included; laundry facilities; kitchen

# SIGHTS
## CULTURE

### ⬛EL ALBAICÍN QUARTER
Though the Alhambra may draw you to Granada, El Albaicín may make you want to stay. Put down your map and get lost in the web of winding cobblestone streets of the city's old Moorish quarter, now a designated **UNESCO World Heritage Site.** The Albaicín is situated on a hill and filled to the brim with tapas bars, restaurants, and white-washed carmens—traditional open-floorplan houses with thick walls—and overflowing with flowers. Notice the small wall holes packed

## THE GYPSY CAVES OF SACROMONTE

One of Granada's most intriguing (yet often overlooked) cultural sites is Sacromonte, the mountainous region looking over the city. It's filled with caves that were decorated by gypsies and date back to the fifteenth century. While they admittedly don't come close to the Alhambra in terms of grandeur, they are *fascinating*, and certainly warrant a visit if you're spending more than a day or two in Granada. With curved ceilings, small adjoining rooms, and round doors that blend into the mountainside, they closely resemble hobbit homes, and their interiors feature rudimentary carvings—some of which document the region's complicated history.

Sacromonte was originally inhabited by Arabs who fled to the mountains following the Catholic conquest of Granada in 1492. The Catholics followed and eventually drove out the Moors completely, leaving the caves empty. In the fifteenth century, the Roma population, colloquially referred to as "gypsies," migrated to the area and inhabited them. Of Indian descent, these gypsies speak their own language, "el cali," and have managed to maintain a tight-knit and autonomous community. Many nineteenth-century artists used the caves as a source of inspiration, including Federico García de Lorca, who described the population's history in his famous "Romancero Ginato."

Today, the Sacromonte area is mostly inhabited by Roma, though hippies and **Senegalese** immigrants also squat in abandoned caves. The main street, el Camino de Sacromonte, is a popular destination for visitors, as it's lined with caves that you can peer into for free. Large groups of young people clamor up the mountain to watch the sunset from San Miguel Alta, enjoy the panoramic views of el Albaicín and the Alhambra, and experience traditional *zambra* performances. If you're interested in finding more out about the culture of the cave dwellers, check out the open-air **Sacromonte Cave Museum.**

with pieces of gum—they used to hold candles that lit the streets at night. Highlights of El Albaicín include Gypsy Square and Mirador San Nicolas, the latter of which offers stunning views of the Alhambra and surrounding city.

*i* *Free; no wheelchair accessibility*

## LE CHIEN DE ANDALOU (FLAMENCO)

Carrera del Darro, 7; 617 10 66 23; shows daily at 8pm and 10pm

Take a break from clubbing and watch someone else dance for a change. Granada is home to a variety of flamenco performance venues, but Le Chien de Andalou, located at the base of **El Albaicín**, offers the best bang for your buck. Cave performances, while enticing and well-reviewed, are triple the price, and because flamenco is such an intense, consuming dance in and of itself, the environment will command little to none of your attention. Arrive early to claim a seat and a drink before the performance starts.

*i* *Wine €2.50, regular seating €9, front-row seating €11, additional €1 when booked through hostel; arrive 30min. early*

# LANDMARKS

## CATEDRAL DE GRANADA

C.Gran Vía de Colón, 5; 958 222 959; open Mar-Aug M-Sa 10:45am-6:45pm, Su 4pm-6:45pm

The Cathedral of Granada was the first cathedral built after Catholics defeated the Nasrid Muslim Dynasty in 1492, and is essentially the architectural equivalent of the middle finger. A symbol of power and affluence, it boasts soaring white Corinthian columns, explosions of colorful ornamentation, tons of gold leaf, baroque paintings, and imposing organs. Complementary audio guides are provided near the entrance of the cathedral; if you don't have much time, we recommend listening to tracks 1,4,6, and 9 for an overview of the history of the region.

*i* *Admission €5, €3.50 student, free on Su if you buy your ticket online; last entry 6:15pm; limited wheelchair accessibility*

## LA ALHAMBRA

C. Real de la Alhambra; 958 027 971; www.alhambradegranada.org; open Tu-Sa 9am-3:30pm

Getting into La Alhambra is like getting into one of Manhattan's most cutting-edge nightclubs—either you have your shit together and breeze right through or you have the right connections and can finagle your way inside. With over 6,000 visitors traipsing through daily during the summer months, you need to reserve your tickets weeks—sometimes months—in advance; unless, of course, you enjoy waking up at 4:30am and standing in a line for 3+ hours. Arguably the most impressive UNESCO site of them all, La Alhambra consists of 142,000 square meters of gardens, fountains, fortifications, and stunning Islamic architecture. In order to make the most of your visit, we recommend reading up before you arrive so that you can take in the Alhambra's full visual beauty without any distractions. If you don't get the chance to do so, audio guides (€6) are available to rent and provide comprehensive descriptions of each room.

*i* *Tickets can be purchased online, at the Corral de Carbon, or at any La Caixa Bank ATM in Granada (€15.40) and include entrance to the Museo de la Alhambra and Museo de Bellas Artes; many parts of the Alhambra including the Plaza de los Alijbes can be accessed free of charge; arrive at 4:30am if trying to buy a ticket day-of; 30min. tours meet at Nasrid Palaces*

# MUSEUMS

## CAPILLA REAL GRANADA

C. Oficios; www.capillarealgranada.com; open Mar-Aug M-Sa 10:15am-1:30pm and 4pm-7:30pm, Su 11am- 1:30pm and 2:30pm-6:30pm; Sept-Feb M-Sa 10:15am-1:30pm and 3:30pm-6:30pm

For you crime-show/forensic-science lovers, the Capilla Real Granada provides the ultimate opportunity to see some dead people. And not just any dead people, Queen Isabella of Castille and King Ferdinand of Aragon! These Catholic monarchs were quite sensible and planned ahead for their deaths, ordering the construction of this lavish chapel to be their burial place. Unfortunately, they didn't plan far enough in advance, as they both died before construction finished, but that's okay because they chilled in the Alhambra until it was ready—not a bad place to push daisies either. Once you get inside, you'll understand why the Capilla Real Granada took so long to build—five centuries of history are catalogued in the paintings, sculptures, and elaborate silverwork that adorn the interiors.

*i* Admission €4; wheelchair accessible

## OUTDOORS

### ☝HIKING IN SIERRA NEVADA

Feel like you haven't sweat enough already? Take a trip to the Sierra Nevada Mountain Range, only a 20-minute bus ride away (bus #183 from Granada to Monachil), and you'll be losing bodily fluids by the liter. This hike will take you through dry, open landscapes as well as lush forests, and will lead you to a small waterfall, where you can rinse off and cool down. Hostels often offer guided tours of the region (€12), but the trails are easy to navigate, so no need to incur the expense if you're open to hiking on your own.

*i* Bus €1.50, guided hostel tour €12; bus runs hourly in both directions; no wheelchair accessibility

# FOOD

### ☝A LOS BUENOS CHICOS ($)

C. Elvira, 70; 663 68 18 09; open M-Th 5pm-2pm, F-Sa noon-3pm, Su noon-2pm

Feeling a little lonely? Grab a few hostel buddies and head to A Los Buenos Chicos for some tapas that are "made with love." This homey establishment located on the border of El Albaicín offers dishes like cheesy gnocchi, vegetarian lasagna, and *tubo*, or "beer on tap," for just two euros. Save yourself the brainpower required to translate the extensive menu and let the servers take the reins—they know what's best and, considering A Los Buenos Chicos has a total of five tables, tend to have time on their hands.

*i* Tapa and drink combo €2; vegetarian options available

### ☝CAFÉ - BAR REINA MONICA ($)

Panaderos, 20; 633 21 71 18; open daily noon-midnight

The five words you've been longing to hear ever since you left the states: all-you-can-eat buffet. Fatten up at Café Bar Reina Monica, where you can eat as much food as your stomach can hold, sip on a drink, and scarf down a desert for only €10. This beacon of hope/symbol of what's wrong with the world is only a few minutes from **el Mirador de San Nicolas**, on a side street of **Plaza Larga**. With over 30 varieties of tapas, you won't be able to resist this amazing deal. Grab a plate of saffron paella, pasta salad, roasted vegetables, eggplant parmesan bites, spinach couscous, and traditional *toasta*—the carbohydrate equivalent of a kabob—, and head outside, where you can admire the blue potted plants draping over the white walls of El Albaicín.

*i* Buffet €10, individual bocadillos €3-4; vegetarian and vegan options available; wheelchair accessible

### LA BODEGA CASTAÑEDA ($)

C. Almireceros, 1-3; 958 21 54 64; open daily 11:30am-1am

A good tapas bar meets at least one of three criteria: 1) it offers standing room only, 2) napkins litter the floor, or 3) you have no control over which tapa comes with your drink. La Bodega Castañeda was one of the only tapas places we visited in Granada that met all three. You can't miss this old-fashioned pub located just off of Calle Elvira, designated by a pair of massive wood doors and a black, scroll-shaped sign with gold lettering. Inside, you'll find huge hams hanging from the ceiling, beer barrels stacked behind the bar, and a boar's head towering over a crowd of lively locals. Lose track of time and of how many tapas you've consumed as you yell *salut* over and over again. Best to arrive after 10pm.

*i* Tapa and drink combo €2, larger appetizers €3.50; vegetarian options available

## CAFETERIA CHURRERIA ALHAMBRA GRANADA ($)

Pl. de Bib-Rambla, 27; 958 52 39 29; cafeteria-alhambra.com/spain/; open daily 8am-11pm

Did someone say fried dough? Heck yes. Fried dough dipped in chocolate? Oh, baby! Like Switzerland's raclette, churros are Spain's trademark, and legend has it they originated right here in Granada, specifically the Plaza Bib-Rambla. They are commonly enjoyed in Andalucía for breakfast, or, alternatively, as a merienda, or afternoon snack. Cafeteria Churreria Alhambra Granada is located adjacent to the birthplace of the churro, on the edge of the plaza. "Why wouldn't you recommend the latter?" you ask. One word: price. For a measly €3.80 you'll receive a bag of five freshly-fried doughnuts (€1.80 if you order to go) that are just as good as, or maybe even better than, the originals.

*i* Five doughnuts €3.80; vegetarian options available

# NIGHTLIFE

### ⚑EL BAR ERIC

C. Escuelas, 8; 958 27 63 01; open daily 9am-2am

Owned by Eric Jiménez, lead drummer of Los Planetas, this small bar in the center of Granada is rock-and-roll themed, with a red accent wall plastered with photo art, posters, and tickets—and offers surprisingly delicious tapas. If you want to get a taste of its trendy fusion food (highly recommended for vegans), arrive before 10pm. Once the clock strikes, this bar transforms into a vibrant performance venue, hosting artists from the local community. Pick from a wide selection of wines and cocktails, kick back, and enjoy the show.

*i* Wine €2.80, coffee €1.30, ice cream €3.90, main dishes €6-12; vegetarian and vegan options available

### BOOM BOOM ROOM GRANADA

Calle Cárcel Baja, 10; 608 66 66 10; open F-Sa 3pm-7am, Su-Th 3pm-6am

As Granada's biggest and baddest nightclub, Boom Boom Room Granada plays host to what seems like the region's entire millennial population. It recently replaced Granada 10, and now boasts chic white and gold décor, spotlights, and VIP suites. Throw on the nicest shirt in your pack and join Granada's glam crowd for a night of excess: savoring your overpriced drink, bopping to mainstream music, and grinding on the person sweating profusely next to you.

*i* Cover €10 with one drink included; drinks €10

# IBIZA

Coverage by **Julia Bunte-Mein**

*I took a pill in Ibiza to show Avicii I was cool*—oh, wait, that wasn't us. That was Mike Posner. We've all heard the tracks about Ibiza's club scene, among them Swedish House Mafia's "Miami 2 Ibiza" and Mike Candy's "One Night in Ibiza" (it's not like you were the first, Mike Poser—we mean, Posner). The point is, we get the hype: their songs aren't too far off reality. Ibiza is a holy ground for clubbers, boho-cool hippie models, sexy beach bums, and the hottest DJs on the planet. There are parties everywhere—the day-party at Ushuaia, a boat party just off the coast, a water fight at Es Paridis, an all-night-and-morning 24hr rager at Pacha. Everywhere. Take pictures to show your friends you know how to have a good time, but be prepared to spend some big bucks for those obscene covers. But don't fall into the trap of thinking Ibiza's just about the *thwump-thwump-thwump* of some party. Hike up the stunning Sa Talaissa mountain, relax on the white sand beaches, and explore the historic D'Alt Vila. Or, you know, just party, if that's what you're into.

# ORIENTATION

Ibiza is a Spanish island in the Mediterranean Sea, the third largest Balearic island after Mallorca and Menorca. The island has three hubs: **Elvissa** (Ibiza Town), **San Anotni de Portmany** (San Antonio), and **Santa Eularia des Riu.** Elvissa is just north of the airport and holds the historic walled town, **Dalt Villa.** This cobblestone labyrinth is situated on a hilltop and offers superb views of the coast. Nearby, in the direction of the harbor, is **Sa Penya,** which has narrow streets with whitewashed houses, restaurants, and shops. Passeig de Vara de Rey is another main street that connects Avinguda d'Espanya with Sa Penya. The top nightclubs line Elvissa's **Playa d'en Bossa,** but San Antoni attracts a younger crowed with its own nightlife scene. You can watch the sunrise in Elvissa and the sunset in San Antoni.

# ESSENTIALS

## GETTING THERE

There are two ways to get to Ibiza (not including swimming): by plane and by boat. Regular flights leave from Barcelona to Ibiza and are considerably cheaper and shorter than going by ferry, especially if you book at least a few weeks in advance. It is also cheaper to fly during week days or the off season. Budget airlines including Ryanair, Spanair, Iberia, Air Europa, and Vueling fly regularly to the airport, which is just south of Ibiza Town. Taking a ferry is considerably slower, but it might be cheaper than a plane for last-minute bookings. Ferries leave every day from Barcelona and Valencia, normally late at night, timed to arrive in Ibiza Old Town Port at around midday the following day. There are a few companies that operate the ferries. Their respective websites: www.trasmedi-terranea.es, www.balearia.com, and www.iscomar.com.

## GETTING AROUND

Bus #10 runs from the airport to Ibiza Town year-round. You should get off at the port rather than the bus station in order to avoid schlepping your bag through town. There are also summer-specific bus routes from the airport to San Antonio, San José, Cala Nova, Es Caná, and Santa Eulalia. The Ibiza Town bus leaves every 15-20min., while the San Antonio bus leaves hourly. Buses run from 7am to midnight. After dark, the "Discobus Ibiza" picks up the slack and transports club hoppers to their next party for €3-3.50. Taxis are also an efficient way to get somewhere fast but, in the summer months, expect to wait in a long taxi line unless you try (fruitlessly) waiving down a taxi yourself. Fare starts at €3.65 if you hail it off the street and €4.95 if you call ahead.

## PRACTICAL INFORMATION

**Tourist Offices:** Visit the tourism outlet at Ibiza Airport (www.ibiza.travel/en). The main branch in Ibiza Town is Vara de Rey (Paseo Vara de Rey, 1; 971 301 900; M-Sa 9am-8pm, Su 9am-2pm).

**Banks/ATMs/Currency Exchange:** CaixaBank (Av. D'Isidor Macabich, 62, Ibiza Town; 971 80 96 60; open M-Sa 8am-2pm).

**Post Offices:** Correos (Av. d'Isidor Macabich, 67, Ibiza Town; 902 19 71 97; open M-Sa 8:30am-8:30pm).

## EMERGENCY INFORMATION

**Emergency Number:** 112
**Police:** 091
**Hospitals:** Hospital Can Misses (C. de Corona, Eivissa. 971 39 70 00; open daily 24hr
**Pharmacies:** In the port area of Ibiza, there is a spot known as "The Chemists' Street," at Annibal and Antoni Palau streets, lined with pharmacies.

# ACCOMMODATIONS

### GIRAMUNDO BACKPACKER'S HOSTEL
C. Ramon Muntaner, 55; 971 307 640; http://www.hostalgiramundoibiza.com/en/ubicacion-ibiza

For all you globetrotting young party animals out there, look no further than Giramundo Backpacker's Hostel for a good time. Giramundo, meaning "globetrotter" in Italian, is a party destination in itself—bring back a bottle of wine and talk all night at the low sidewalk tables without hitting the clubs at all. With three floors

cemetery of **Puif des Molins** are also must-sees at this site

## LANDMARKS

### CATEDRAL DE EIVISSA (IBIZA CATHEDRAL)

Pl. de la Catedral, D'Alt Villa, Ibiza Town; 971 312 773; open Apr-Oct Tu-Su 10am-2pm and 5pm-8pm, Jul-Aug 6pm-9pm

At the tippy top of **D'Alt Vila** sits the Cathedral of Ibiza. The original fourteenth-century Gothic building was reformed in the eighteenth century, taking on a more Baroque style. It has a stone exterior with strong buttressing, and the white interiors mirror the whitewashed walls of the D'Alt Villa houses. It might not be a very impressive church in terms of decoration, but if you made it to the top of the Old City you might as well go inside, catch your breath while sitting on a pew, and light a candle for one of the saints for €1.

*i* Free

### PORTAL DE SES TAULES (SES TAULES GATEWAY)

D'Alt Villa, Ibiza Town; 971 399 232; open daily 10am-5pm

Remember that scene in *Lord of the Rings* when they dramatically open the gates to the walled city and the soldiers cross the drawbridge over a moat of sharks and crocodiles? Picture that in real-life, with a reduced drama factor, and you get the Ses Taules Gateway. This sixteenth-century, Renaissance-style entrance is the starting point for your exploration of the D'Alt Villa. Crowned by an imperial coat of arms, the crown leads to Amoury Court, which has an arcade of ten round arches.

*i* Free

## OUTDOORS

### IBIZA'S BEACHES

How can one tiny place have so many beaches? Take your pick of dozens of different beaches, depending on what you're into. The **Figueretes** beach, for example, is closest in location to the urban center for when you're looking

connected by an outdoor staircase, Giramundo named each room after a different country, reflecting an international community. This is the perfect environment for solo travelers, as you'll need to try really hard not to make friends to hit Ibiza's clubs with.

*i* Dorms from €40-50, private rooms €100; reservation recommended; Wi-Fi; free breakfast; linens included; towels included; luggage storage; lockers provided

## SIGHTS
### CULTURE

### D'ALT VILA (OLD CITY)

In Ibiza Town, Eivissa in Spanish, lies the ancient walled city and UNESCO World Heritage Site called D'Alt Vila. Start at the ramparts and take the adorable winding cobblestone streets past the **Church of Santo Domingo** and **Town Hall.** Stop at **El Mirador Rey Jaume** for some incredible views of the city. Continue up to the *Catedral* and the old bastions with cannons. At the bottom of the Old City, there are plenty of nice restaurants and clothing stores selling white linen and knitted clothing. D'Alt Vila, the best preserved coastal fortress in the Mediterranean, is the most impressive historical site, but Phoenician remains of **Sa Caleta** (in Sant Josep) and the Phoenician-Punic for a taste of beach city life. **Platja d'en Bossa** is full of young people enjoying the seemingly endless sun. The most stunning, more secluded beaches, however, are located on the San Antoni side of the island. Embrace nature at **Playa Es Cavallet,** Ibiza's nudist beach. Other must-sees are **Playa Salinas** and **Cala Compte**. The lesser-known, off-the-beaten-path beaches include **Buda Beach** and **Cala Secreta.**

*i* Limited wheelchair accessibility

# FOOD

### CAN GOURMET ($)
C. de Guillem de Montgrí, 20; 685 603 409; open M-Tu, Th-Su 9:30am-10pm

Ibiza may be famous for partying, but it is also a pro at draining your wallet. For a cheap-eats hidden gem, look no further than Can Gourmet in the Marina of Ibiza Town. Stop at this tiny eatery serving traditional *bocadillos* (little sandwiches), godsends not only for your taste buds but also for your wallet. With just one table inside and one outside, you'll be standing up as you enjoy a craft bottled beer, cheese squares, and Iberian ham. The plethora of chalkboards with hundreds of tapas variations can be overwhelming, but just ask for the most popular dish and you can't go wrong.

*i* Bocadillos and tapas €6-8; vegetarian options available

### EL PLAYA ES CAVALLET, SAN ANTONIO ($$$)
971 395 485; www.elchiringuitoibiza.com; open daily 10am-midnight

So you've found your soulmate in the clubs of Ibiza, but now you just need to find the right place to propose. El Chiringuito, nestled in the rocky landscape right on **Playa Cavallet**, is the ultimate romance destination. Picture white sofas, bamboo chairs, and an open kitchen with professional looking cooks in white shirts and chef's hats. Lights twinkle in the trees, which perfectly frame the view and a thin layer of white sand coats the floor. The food is exquisite but expensive; but it's worth the splurge for that special someone. Keep in mind that everyone

has the same idea as you, so it's best to call in case it's reserved for a wedding.

*i* Entrées €16-22, wine €4; no wheelchair accessibility

### PASSION CAFÉ – PLAYA D'EN BOSSA ($$)
Playa d'en Bossa, opposite Space Club; 971 305 130; www.passion-ibiza.com; open daily 9am-12am

After a few days of Ibiza-party lifestyle, your body will be begging you for some healthy food. Recover with a New York style breakfast, an energizing smoothie, or Passion Café's famous chicken burger. Passion Café is the trendiest health spot on the island, and has become so popular in recent years that there are now five different locations. They serve Instagramable smoothies with green super foods like spirulina and maca that can make you grow locks of real gold. Sure, there's no hard evidence to prove that, but, regardless, people rave about it. Expensive, true, and perhaps slightly overrated, it's a go-to for those times when you just need to feel healthy again (or, you know, cure that hangover).

*i* Coffee €3, smoothie bowl €10.50, full breakfast €14

# NIGHTLIFE

### AMNESIA
C. Ibiza a San Antonio Km R, San Rafael; www.amnesia.es; open daily midnight-6am

Amnesia, contrary to its name, provides an unforgettable experience. Hypnotic techno and trance beats reverberate through your body as you fist pump to DJ legends like **Paul Van Dyk** and **Éric Prydz**. Spotlights traverse the huge concert hall, which is covered with a greenhouse-like glass ceiling. Big nights include Cocoon (Mondays), Cream (Thursdays) and foam-party La Espuma (Wednesdays and Sundays).

*i* over €35-75 €10-15 drinks

### PACHA
Av. 8 d'Agost; 971 313 612; www.pachaibiza.com/es; open M-Sa midnight-6am

Although Pacha has many discos around the world, its Ibiza location is the original glamour club, going strong since 1974. Housing over 3000 people, this cavernous club has a full schedule of different music every night. Get ready for a long night of dancing in the main dance room filled with shimmering disco balls, or get some fresh air on the terrace. Pick your favorite night or try them all: "Fuck Me, I'm Famous" on Thursdays with **David Guetta**, house music with **Martin Solveig** on Wednesday, or "Flower Power hippie throwbacks" on Mondays.

*i* Cover €20-70, drinks €10

### USHUAÏA

Playa d'En Bossa, 10; 917 396 710; www. ushuaiaibiza.com; day party 5pm-midnight

No one can say it—Ushiaaaa, ushy, umbrella....it sounds like someone trying to say "your shower" with a mouthful of toothpaste. It's actually pronounced "boo-sh-why-ahh," but if you say anything that sounds remotely similar, everyone will know what you mean. Ushuaïa is the number one open-air club in Ibiza. At night, shimmering blue pools reflect the glowing letters of the Ushuaïa radiating from the stage while dancers in five-inch heels and crazy headdresses twist and turn to the music on white stepping stones in the middle of the water. This ice-cool hotel and club boasts big DJ names like **David Guetta, Martin Garrix,** and **Avicii.** Come just for the party or stay at the minimalist chic hotel for poolside lounging in canopy beds (they even have swim up rooms).

*i* Cover €20-70 (usually €50 in high season), drinks €10

# MADRID

Coverage by **Emma Scornavacchi**

It's a Sunday morning at the iconic El Rastro flea market. Hanging side by side at one of the market's many stands are two t-shirts. One reads: "Madrid: City of Joy;" The other, "Madrid is a Mixtape." Amid the shouts of vendors, the crooning piano of street performers, and the bustling energy of a city waking up, the t-shirts prove that there isn't a better way to describe Madrid than this: a joyful mixtape. Many of Madrid's neighborhoods couldn't be more different from one another—from the edgy, youthful energy of Chueca and Malasaña to the quieter, polished, and upscale Salamanca and Chamberí, one street over can feel like a different world. In reality, though, each neighborhood works in tandem to make the mixtape. The city itself wouldn't be as exciting and wholly alive without the medley of difference. All this ensures you'll find world-famous art, from the Prado to the Reina Sofía and beyond, a fantastic food scene on the rise and constantly evolving, and one of the most open and accepting communities in all of Europe. That's what's remarkable about Madrid. Though so different across its various *barrios*, the city is community-based in a way that's proud and accessible to locals and first-timers alike. This much is clear: all it will take is a morning walk through El Retiro park, an afternoon shopping spree through the bustling center of Sol, and an evening over beer and tapas in Chueca, and you'll be pressing "replay" on the mixtape that is Madrid faster than you can say "*Más, por favor.*"

## ORIENTATION

The best way to understand the city's diverse and complex makeup is to start from the center and spiral outwards. Starting from the center means starting from **Sol,** which is where everything from Spain's highway system to the city's metro begins. Sol is Madrid's bustling central square, home to department stores and the famous bear statue. It is also a convenient starting point to walk to many of Madrid's biggest attractions like **The Prado Museum, Plaza Mayor,** and the **Royal Palace.** Using Sol as our center, we'll start to the south and spiral clockwise. Just south of Sol is **Lavapies,** a melting pot of international cultures that has begun to attract a young, trendy crowd. Just clockwise from Lavapies is **La Latina,** home to Madrid's oldest architecture (the name is synonymous with "Latin Quarter") as well as streets overflowing with tapas and beer. Continuing to the northwest corner of the city, you'll find **Moncloa** and **Arguelles,** areas in proximity to the famous University. As the spiral continues, we arrive at **Malasaña,** the hip and happening area just north of Sol. Malasaña has leafy plazas, independent stores with quality, hidden-gem shopping, and bohemian cafés. North of Malasaña is Chamberí, which we can think of as the slightly older, more polished sibling. With its quieter streets, authentic architecture, and people in business suits along the tree lined avenues, Chamberí will serve you a delicious glass of wine for dinner and then probably go to bed early. On the contrary, no one in **Chueca** (the next neighborhood) has ever gone to bed before 8pm. Chueca is Madrid's hippest, most exciting neighborhood, teeming with busy, hipster bars and one-of-a-kind shops. As historically the gay district of Madrid, it remains true to its heritage with an abundance of BGLTQ+ references and celebrations. As we move east, we arrive at **Salamanca:** Madrid's crème-de-la-crème of upscale living. Completing the spiral, back in the southeast of the city, we find **Retiro** and **Las Letras.** Retiro is mainly home to Madrid's famous and fantastically beautiful park, **El Retiro,** while Las Letras is a small neighborhood named after famous writers of Madrid such as **Lope de Vega** and **Cervantes.** These days, Las Letras retains its starved-bohemian-writer feel with arts and culture events, cobblestone streets, and gritty independent stores. You've now made it back to Sol (didn't we tell you that's how it works?), completing a voyage through the neighborhoods of Madrid.

# ESSENTIALS

## GETTING THERE

Madrid-Bajaras Airport (MAD) is Madrid's international airport. From the airport, which is about 9mi. away from the city center, taxis are available, but taking the metro is an easy and cheap option. Metro stops are at Terminal 2 and Terminal 4, and the Nuevos Ministerios line will go straight to Madrid's center in under 15min. If you're not flying in, you can easily get to Madrid via train, as it is the hub of Spain's entire RENFE train system. Atocha is the city's main railway station, followed closely by Chamartín. Most trains depart from and arrive to one of these two stations. If you are arriving via bus, you will most likely arrive in Estación del Sur (Méndez Álvaro). Buses from all over Spain as well as several international stations travel through Madrid. Many different companies service the station, but tickets can be bought in one place at www.movelia.es.

## GETTING AROUND

Madrid's city bus system is called Empresa Municipal de Transporte (EMT), and operates 6am-9pm M-F with some exceptions. The bus system is extremely widespread, operating 214 lines and covering the entire city and beyond. Buses do not stop automatically at every stop; they must be flagged down. Buses are bright red and blue (older, diesel buses are red; newer, hydrogen buses are blue) so they are easily spotted. Madrid's Metro is a complex, rapidly-growing system of 13 lines and 301 stations connecting all of Madrid and the surrounding area. The Metro operates 6am-1:30am daily. A single trip ticket costs €1.50, and zone or region Tourist Passes can be bought for either one day or one week. The metro is fairly simple to navigate; within the city, you are never more than five or so minutes from a station, and each station has a map either outside or within it. Madrid is also full of taxis, which can be found on every main street, square, and landmark, as well as in lesser-populated areas. A green light indicates the taxi is free. Madrid's bike share system is called BiciMAD and has approximately 120 stations around the city. This is the easiest way to get around the city by bike, as access stations are available in many locations and bikes can be rented for as little as two hours.

## PRACTICAL INFORMATION

**Tourist Offices:** Plaza Mayor Tourist Information Centre (Pl. Mayor 27; 915 787 810; www.esmadrid.com; open daily 9:30am-9:30pm).

**Post Offices:** Palacio de Cibeles (Pl. Cibeles; 914 800 008; open daily 1:30-4:30pm and 8pm-midnight).

**Internet:** There is free Wi-Fi from Grupo Gowex in newspaper kiosks and municipal buses, plus some restaurants and shops. You'll also find free Wi-Fi hotspots at many cafés and local businesses

**BGLTQ+ Resources:** www.gayiberia. com and www.gayinspain.com are great resources for travelers in the BGLTQ+ community

## EMERGENCY INFORMATION

**Emergency Number:** 112
**Police:** National Police Headquarters Madrid (Av. Del Federico Rubio y Galí 55; 913 223 400).
**Rape Crisis Center:** RAINN National Sexual Assault Hotline: 800-656-HOPE
**Hospitals:** Hospital Universitario HM Madrid (Pl. del Conde del Valle de Súchil; 902 08 98 00; open daily 24hr).
**Pharmacies:** Farmacia Abelló (C. de Fuencarral 114; 914 472 374; open daily 9:30am-9:30pm)

# ACCOMMODATIONS

## CAT'S HOSTEL

C. Cañizares 6; 913 692 807; www.cat-shostel.com; reception open 24hr

If kegs of sangria on a random Wednesday night are what you seek, Cat's Hostel is the spot for you. A bona fide party hostel that still manages to have quality amenities, Cat's is the music-blasting, pub-crawling, bar-partying hotspot. Rooms are standard, but the courtyard is historic and beautiful, making it a stand-out. From pub crawls to tapas tours, happy hours to paella parties, Cat's is a bustling, exciting spot to ensure a rowdy and fun stay in Madrid.

*i* Dorms €14-22, private rooms €60-70; reservation recommended; wheelchair accessible; Wi-Fi; luggage storage; laundry facilities

## FAR HOME ATOCHA

C. de Atocha 45; 916 217 542; www. farhomehostels.com; reception open 24hr

Far Home Atocha is a special kind of hostel. On the surface, it has everything a really high-quality European hostel has: great location, big common spaces, a bar, clean and spacious rooms. But then the hostel goes one step further. Dedicated to being "hostel conscious," the Far Home Atocha's staff plans and hosts events such as lectures, conferences, and photography exhibits intended

to let guests think, learn, and enjoy. Everything from astrophysics to art is presented by the incredibly friendly staff, all against the backdrop of a relaxed space along one of Madrid's coolest streets.

*i* Dorms €21-27, private rooms €66-100; reservation recommended; wheelchair accessible; Wi-Fi; luggage storage; laundry facilities

## MAD4YOU HOSTEL

Costanilla de San Vicente; 915 217 549; www.mad4youhostel.com

A relaxing, chill place to stay in the trendy **Malasaña** area, MAD4YOU is a great spot to experience whichever version of Madrid you want. The hostel provides a laid back atmosphere, with outdoor common spaces and free sangria many weekend nights, but, if it's more of a busy social scene you're looking for, the surrounding area will provide nightlife in abundance just minutes away by foot. MAD4YOU is clean and serves free daily breakfast, which are major bonuses in the big city. Hallways are outdoors and all look out over the courtyard, which can be tricky in extreme heat. Luckily, though, all the rooms are air-conditioned.

*i* Dorms €15-21; reservation recommended; Wi-Fi; luggage storage, laundry facilities

## MOLA! HOSTEL

C. de Atocha 16; 663 624 143; molahostel.com; reception open 24hr

Like a miniature hotel in the middle of the city only three minutes away from **Sol,** Mola is the ideal hostel for a trip to Madrid. Both rooms and bathrooms are thoroughly clean, and the wooden bunk structure of the beds offers the extra benefit of privacy. The basement common space is lively and spacious, with social activities available for all guests. The best part of Mola, though, is its location. Whether it's a bar, restaurant, café, grocery store, theater, shopping center, gym, or landmark that you're after, it will all be right outside the front door, and Mola's wonderfully friendly staff and sparkling lobby will be there to welcome you when you return.

*i* Dorms €20-33; reservation recommended; BGLTQ+ friendly; wheelchair *accessible; Wi-Fi; laundry facilities; luggage storage*

## THE HAT MADRID
C. Imperial 9; 917 728 572; www.thehat-madrid.com; reception open 24hr

Stepping through The Hat's doors, you'd probably think you had the wrong spot if it weren't for the neon sign advertising the hostel's name behind the front desk. The Hat looks more like a hip, well-decorated coffee shop than a typical hostel, but, lo and behold, you're in the right place. With a subway-tiled bar, bright and clean boutique-y rooms, and a rooftop terrace so beautiful people come from the outside to hang, The Hat provides a space not only aesthetically pleasing but also high-quality when it comes to amenities. Nightly meetings for visitors include drinks, mini Spanish lessons, and a pub crawl with other hostels, but, if you're not down to socialize, it's also a relaxing place to chill.

*i Dorms €16-19, private rooms €60-80; reservation recommended; wheelchair accessible; no Wi-Fi; laundry facilities; luggage storage*

## U HOSTELS BY SAFESTAY
C. de Sagasta 22; www.uhostels.com; reception open 24hr

U Hostels is one of the most popular and well-known hostels in Madrid, and for good reason: it's huge (five-stories-filled-with-rooms huge) and features every amenity a traveler could want and then some. A big common room with a bar and foosball, a TV room with Netflix, kitchen and laundry facilities and a big hotel-esque front desk occupy just the first floor. The hostel feels like the child of a boutique hotel and college dorm building, with bunk rooms and big bathrooms down the hall, yet everything is pristinely clean. The sheer size of the hostel can make it feel a little impersonal, but offerings like daily breakfast and bar crawls can provide more of a community feel if that's what you're after.

*i Dorms €26-37, private rooms €119-127; reservation recommended; BGLTQ+ friendly; Wi-Fi; luggage storage; laundry facilities*

# SIGHTS
## CULTURE
.................................................

### ⬛CHANGING OF THE GUARD AT THE ROYAL PALACE
C. de Bailén; open Jan-June W 11am-2pm, Sa 11am-2pm; July W, Sa 10am-noon; Aug-Dec W, Sa 11am-2pm

Madrid may function like the utmost modern-day city, but the formalities of its monarchy still sometimes work exactly as they did in yesteryear. The Royal Palace hosts a changing of the guard every Wednesday and Saturday of the year every half hour for several hours in the morning, where uniformed guards holding rifles and cavalry on horses march in formation to the tune of a man yelling commands. The first Wednesday of every month there is a "Solemn" Changing of the Guard that draws big crowds: an almost hour-long ceremony that often culminates in a concert on the plaza. Most weeks, though, the ceremony is quick—ten minutes at best—and happens routinely throughout the morning to the amusement and appreciation of onlookers.

*i Free; changing of the guard occurs on the half hour; wheelchair accessible*

### ⬛CHUECA DISTRICT
Chueca; 28004

Whether you're looking for shopping, bars, people-watching, or cultural celebrations, the young and hip people of Madrid will point you in one direction: to Chueca. Chueca is historically the city's gay district, and to this day is adorned with rainbow flags on every other balcony and plays hosts to some of the world's most famous Pride celebrations in June and July. Chueca is not only a haven of acceptance and celebration, but also of fantastic shopping, art, and nightlife throughout the week and especially on weekends. A walk through Chueca will always yield something new and exciting: a trendy, minimalist café, a colorful mural or a bar with a new friend.

*i Prices vary by venue*

## PUERTA DEL SOL
Pl. de la Puerta del Sol

Puerta del Sol is not only the center of Madrid, but also the center of the entire Iberian Peninsula. It marks kilometer 0 for Spain's entire road network. As a result, Puerta del Sol is a wildly busy, bustling square that is a center for shopping, eating, and meeting up as well as for transportation. Directions in Madrid are often given from Sol, so make sure you know where this buzzing, shining, hectic spot is as soon as you arrive; it's the first step to pretty much everything.

*i* Free; wheelchair accessible

## GRAN VÍA
Gran Vía; open daily 24hr

The combination of architecture, shopping, and musical culture keeps this street busy at all time. It may not be New York City, but it quite literally never sleeps. The Gran Vía is popular for its offerings: giant, popular stores, exciting nightlife, and theaters with musicals that earned it the name "Spanish Broadway." Also a showcase of early twentieth-century architecture, the Gran Vía features endless white, beautifully-detailed buildings including the famous **Metropolis Building.** Though the street is exciting during the day, its energy hums incessantly long after the sun has set.

*i* Free; wheelchair accessible

## PLAZA DE ESPAÑA
Pl. de España

The Plaza de España isn't about to let the center of the city have all the fun. Located north of the center, by the Palacio Real and several peaceful parks, the Plaza de España is one of Madrid's most famous squares and a popular walk-through, talk-through, and snack-through place. It's an interesting combination of urban and natural, though it is surrounded on all sides by some of Madrid's most imposing skyscrapers. The square itself is tree-filled and its central fountain makes it feel idyllic, providing a break from Madrid's cosmopolitan culture.

*i* Free; wheelchair accessible

## SANTIAGO BERNABÉU STADIUM
Av. de Concha Espina 1; 913 984 300; www.realmadrid.com

Knowing Spain is equivalent to knowing soccer (sorry, *fútbol*), and **Real Madrid** is one of the top clubs in the world. With a cultlike following, Real Madrid inhabits the Santiago Bernabeu Stadium in the **Chamartín** area of Madrid and attracts visitors from all over the world to gaze at its grassy, trophy-winning, "Cristiano-Ronaldo-breathed-this-air" glory. Tours of the famous stadium can be purchased online or at the box office upon arrival, granting access to everything from exhibit rooms to panoramic views to the dressing rooms, a true superfan's dream. From the youngest toddler in a jersey to the old ladies who put on their best dress for the occasion, the Real Madrid stadium attracts everyone and is a cultural experience just a quick cab ride from the center of the city.

*i* Tours €25; tours on non-match days M-Sa 10am-7:30pm, Su 10:30am-6:30pm, tours available until 5hr. before the beginning of the game; parts of the tour wheelchair accessible

## TEATRO REAL
Plaza de Isabel II; 915 160 600; www.teatro-real.com; open M-F 10am-2pm, 4-8pm

Teatro Real was opened in 1818 and has been one of Europe's leading opera houses ever since. Not only home to opera, though, the famous theater situated directly on the Plaza Isabel II also hosts festivals, musicals, tributes, and daily guided tours to the public. The theater rotates through seasons of shows it hosts, but at any given time you may catch a combination of Shakespeare, contemporary playwrights, rock music, traditional opera, and more all on rotation at this arts and music behemoth.

*i* Ticket prices for tours and shows vary; guided tours M-Su every 30min. 10am-1:30pm; wheelchair accessible

## LANDMARKS

......................................

### 🏛PALACIO DE CRISTAL
Paseo República de Cuba 4; open daily
10am-10pm

Almost exactly at the center of **El
Retiro's** shady, tree-lined paths sits
the Palacio de Cristal, a miniature
version of London's **Crystal Palace**
that houses art exhibits sponsored by
the **Reina Sofía Museum.** Whether
you meant to come across the Palacio
de Cristal or not, it's a welcome sight:
beautiful, intricate glass panels create
a blindingly-bright structure that can
house art exhibits, given the amount
of space and light available for use.
The palace looks and feels like a
greenhouse– and indeed was originally
built to exhibit horticulture–but now
uses the intense light for the effects of
shadows and heat on art exhibits.

*i* Free admission; wheelchair accessible

### 🏛PLAZA DE ORIENTE
C. de Bailén 17; open daily 24hr

A landscaped half-moon facing the
**Royal Palace,** the Plaza de Oriente
is a beautiful place for a stroll or
momentary break in sightseeing.
Statues of Gothic kings overlook
the pathways while hedges are
meticulously cut into swirls, spheres,
and other designs that give the park
an extravagant flair. Though there isn't
always accessible shade on hot days
(and bench space will fill up fast!), just
a walk through the green park provides
an opportunity for a deep breath before
or after exploring the wonders of the
Royal Palace.

*i* Free; wheelchair accessible

### 🏛PUERTA DE ALCALÁ
Pl. de la Independencia 1; open daily 24hr

If you want to witness what feels like
the city of Madrid physically living and
breathing, take a moment to observe
the Puerta de Alcalá. Built in 1778 as
the gateway to the city, the arch now
sits at the center of a busy intersection
and rotary connecting four of the city's
main streets at one of the corners of
**El Retiro** park. Cars circle around the
monument in constant motion, an
endless loop of energy. And, if you feel
like you could be in Paris looking at
the **Arc de Triomphe,** remember the
Puerto de Alcalá came first (take that,
France)!

*i* Free; wheelchair accessible

### 🏛SAN FRANCISCO EL GRANDE
San Buenaventura 1; 913 653 800; open
winter Tu-Sa 10:30am-12:30pm and 4pm-
6pm; summer Tu-Sa 10:30am-12:30pm,
5pm-7pm

From the outside, you may pass the
San Francisco Basilica and think it's
just another monument in the old **La
Latina** neighborhood. The outside is
impressive, sure, and clearly represents
importance both historic and religious,
but the real treasure is the inside. A
dome more than 100ft. high features
gorgeous, colorful paintings including
works by **Goya,** and is shockingly
stunning when paired with the gold
columns that reach up from the
ground. The basilica still hosts religious
ceremonies as well as guided tours,
staying rooted in its original purpose
while presenting itself as a historical
artifact to the public.

*i* Tickets €3, €2 student; wheelchair
accessible

## ⬛TEMPLE OF DEBOD
Calle Ferraz 1; 913 667 415

On your trip to Egypt, you'll probably see—oh, wrong book? No, not the wrong book. Madrid's Temple of Debod was quite literally transplanted from Egypt, an authentic Egyptian relic now located in the heart of Spain's capital. The Temple of Debod was built in 200 BC in Upper Egypt and has seen an unfathomable amount of history: from the hands of Egyptian Pharaohs to Roman Emperors.

In 1960, **UNESCO** deemed this temple at risk of ruin due to natural conditions in the area, and, in 1968, it was dismantled and rebuilt in Madrid's **Parque del Oeste** as a gesture of thanks to Spain for helping to save other Egyptian temples.

*i* *Free admission*

## CENTROCENTRO CIBELES/PLAZA CIBELES
Pl. de Cibeles 1; 914 800 008; www. centrocentro.org; open Tu-Su 10am-8pm, observation desk open Tu-Su 10:30am-1:30pm and 4pm-7pm

Close your eyes and imagine what a "city center" looks like. Got it? CentroCentro at Plaza Cibeles is probably the picture you just had in your head, but even cooler. Housed inside a giant, historic palace, the center has lounges, cafés, information headquarters, a bookstore, entire floors of exhibition areas, and an observation deck on the eighth floor with city-wide views of Madrid. The palace is used to display the city's commitments to different movements, from a giant gay pride flag to a "Refugees Welcome" banner, and ultimately serves as both the seat of Madrid City Council and

# PLAZAS OF MADRID

In Spain, when they say "plaza," they don't always mean plaza. Directly translated, the word means "square," but more colloquially it's used to mean a number of things: square, oval, rectangle, park, open-air-space, patio-that-has-a-couple-buildings-near-it—you get the gist. Madrid is the ultimate city of plazas: it seems that everywhere you walk you're passing through plazas, being redirected to a plaza, or on your way to a plaza. Here we've unpacked some of Madrid's plazas, what they really mean, and what they're all about:

- **Plaza de Cibeles:** Actually a large traffic circle and fountain bordered by a massive, intricate palace. Connected to the Bank of Spain and an intersection of many major Madrid avenues, Plaza de Cibeles is a landmark of city government as well as a tourist attraction. Not really a plaza, though.
- **Plaza de la Villa:** Actually an open-ended quadrangle, Plaza de la Villa is situated right in the center of old Madrid and is home to the former Town Hall as well as an entire configuration of important medieval buildings leading to narrow, cobblestone streets. Plaza de la Villa is full of important ancient history for the city, but is it really a plaza?
- **Plaza Mayor:** OK, we'll give Madrid this one. Pretty square-like in formation, Plaza Mayor is one of the city's most famous landmarks and now serves as an open-air, pedestrian shopping and eating area that also hosts concerts and events. A plaza for sure, we concede.
- **Plaza de España:** Actually a big rectangular park, Plaza de España is one of Madrid's attractions, but is pretty far from a square. That being said, it's home to long, tree-lined pathways, a famous fountain, and views of some of the city's biggest and scariest skyscrapers. The stately city park is pretty cool, but not if you think of it like a plaza.
- **Plaza Oriente:** OK, this is getting ridiculous. So far from a square it's practically a half-moon, Plaza Oriente is beautiful, manicured, and super enjoyable…Unless you're expecting a square, in which case it is a severe letdown. The "plaza" faces the Royal Palace, creating a stunning view for a stroll, yet it's so far from being a square it's almost hard to focus. Can we get a name change?

the heart of the city itself. Stop in here for a workspace, a coffee, a view—quite literally anything you need—and get caught up on everything the city provides for residents and visitors.

*i* *Free, observation deck admission €2; wheelchair accessible*

## PALACIO REAL DE MADRID (ROYAL PALACE OF MADRID)

C. de Bailén; 914 548 700; www.patrimonionacional.es; open daily Oct-Mar 10am-6pm; Apr-Sept 10am-8pm

The Palacio Real is royal in the purest sense of the word: think of a royal palace and, after you've tossed aside Cinderella's Castle, the next in line is the Palacio Real de Madrid, complete with gold details, stately gates, imposing towers, and all. The palace is officially the residence of the Spanish royal family, but they only use it for state ceremonies. This makes it all feel special and a bit like you're intruding on royal life. Famous, important rooms (like the "**Hall of Columns**" where the formal signing of the king's abdication in 2014 was held) are wide open and are subject to exploration. The inside is the peak of luxury; Carlos III's dressing ceremony room, among others, will blow your mind.

*i* *Tickets €11, €6 student, free Oct-Mar M-Th 4pm-6pm, Apr-Sep M-Th 6pm-8pm; wheelchair accessible*

## PLAZA MAYOR

Pl. Mayor; open daily 24hr

The Plaza Mayor recently celebrated its 400th birthday, but it doesn't look a day over 399. The thriving, busy square is one of Madrid's main commercial spots, with a completely pedestrian interior and famous statue of Philip III in the center. Red painted apartments and offices line all four sides of the square, adorned with wrap-around balconies and spired towers. The square is full of cafés and souvenir shops, but also functions as a venue for concerts and other events year-round, which are often open to the public.

*i* *Free; wheelchair accessible*

# MUSEUMS

## CAIXAFORUM MADRID

Paseo del Prado 36; 913 207 300; www.madrid.caixaforum.com; open daily 10am-8pm

A museum and cultural center sponsored by La Caixa, one of Spain's largest financial services, CaixaForum is a work of art in itself that houses rotating contemporary exhibits. Constructed out of an old electrical station and completed in 2007, the building has geometric, modern stairways and a vertical garden right next door. Located on **Paseo del Prado,** the lush street of the famous **Prado Museum,** CaixaForum uses prime real estate to create an exciting contrast with the nearby ancient, classic art. Contemporary exhibits along with programs held regularly for both adults and kids make this not only a museum, but also a center for learning, artistic exploration, and community building.

*i* *Admission €4; last entry 30min. before closing*

## MUSEO NACIONAL CENTRO DE ARTE REINA SOFÍA

C. de Santa Isabel 52; 917 741 000; www.museoreinasofia.es; open M-Sa 10am-9pm, Su 10am-7pm

This four-story museum contains a wildly impressive amount of twentieth-century Spanish art, featuring everything from post-modernism to pop art in mediums such as film, photography, art, drawing, and sculpture. As makes sense contextually given Spain's twentieth century, many of the museum's collection feature protest art heavily, detailing a history of activism, war, and unrest. The avant-garde, provocative works featured in many of these collections show the true underbelly of Spain's culture and history.

*i* *Admission €10, free M, W-Sa 7pm-9pm; wheelchair accessible*

## MUSEO NACIONAL DE CIENCIAS NATURALES

C. José Gutiérrez Abascal 2; 914 111 328; www.mncn.csic.es; open Tu-F 10am-5pm, Sa-Su 10am-8pm

Lions and whales and bears, oh my! We may have minorly modified that classic phrase, but at the MNCN, Spain's museum dedicated to natural sciences, you could have filled in the blanks with virtually any animal native to the country, as well as many others. The MNCN has an unbelievable collection of specimens—over six million, to be exact—which means you can see everything from the smallest beetle to the largest African elephant during your visit. The museum is popular with families (what little kid doesn't love giant whale skeletons?) but is an exciting trip for anyone, especially with the slew of rotating exhibits that tackle different issues and themes in the art and science worlds.

*i* *Museum tickets €6, student €3, museum and exhibition €3, €5.50 student; wheelchair accessible*

## MUSEO NACIONAL DEL PRADO

Paseo del Prado; 913 302 800; www. museodelprado.es; open M-Sa 10am-8pm, Su 10am-7pm

Spain's premier art museum houses one of the world's most renowned collections of art, and is an experience as awe-inducing for first-time foreigners as for long-time patrons. The museum boasts a staggering 75 rooms, each of which feels significant in its own right. The comprehensive, expert curation makes each room work as a cohesive whole while still flowing into the next. The sheer number of paintings and sculptures, both large-scale and small, would be impressive on its own even if these works weren't beautiful and by famous artists like **Goya, Velazquez, and El Greco**. Prepare to be blown away by this gem.

*i* *Admission €15, free student, admission free M-Sa 6-8pm, Su 5-7pm; ; last entry 30min. before closing; wheelchair accessible*

## MUSEO NACIONAL DEL ROMANTICIS-MO

C. San Mateo 13; 914 481 045; www. mecd.gob.es; open Nov-Apr T-Sa 9:30am-6:30pm, Su 10am-3pm; May-Oct 9:30am-8:30pm, Su 10am-3pm

Floors are creaking, clocks are ticking, and it feels like someone is about to come home in a ball gown and start eating off the china that's laid out on the table. The Museum of Romanticism is dedicated to

showcasing life during the Romantic period—from paintings to furniture to entire complete bedrooms—inside a mansion typical of the era. The luxurious collection is less popular than many other museums, so it is rarely crowded. Make the trip, however, and you'll get to observe all the harps, busts, and dollhouses you've ever wanted in close proximity.

*i* *Tickets €3, free student, free Sa-Su from 2pm-close; wheelchair accessible*

## MUSEO THYSSEN-BORNEMISZA

Paseo del Prado 8; 917 911 370; www. museothyssen.org; open Tu-Su 10am-7pm

The final point on what is sometimes called the "Golden Triangle" of Madrid's art museums (along with the **Prado** and **Reina Sofía**), the Thyssen is also wildly impressive in its own right. With both Spanish and international art, from Impressionism to Post-Impressionism and beyond, the Thyssen is made even more interesting by the fact that it was once a private collection, the second largest in the world. Now open to the public, the museum still includes messages from the founders on its walls. Pale pink walls throughout tie the museum together, and the deliberate progression through different time periods, themes, and parts of the world make exploring the Thyssen an exciting trip.

*i* *Admission €12, €8 student*

# OUTDOORS

## ◪MADRID RÍO

Puente de Toledo; www.esmadrid.com; open daily 24hr

Madrid isn't a city on the water, or, at least you don't think of it that way. But then the natural serenity of the Madrid Río park reminds you that a river can run through even the most urban of cities. This four-mile park offers grassy landscapes, exercise paths, historic bridges, and sports areas for activities. Walking out of the center of the city can get you to certain places on the river in just 15 minutes, making the Madrid Río park a perfect natural respite in the big capital city.

*i* *Free; wheelchair accessible*

## PARQUE BUEN RETIRO

Pl. de la Independencia 7; open daily 24hr

The second you think you've seen everything Buen Retiro Park has to offer, you'll stumble across something else: a rose garden? A rowboat-filled fountain? A library? Retiro has it all. Retiro belonged to the Spanish throne until only a couple hundred years ago, and now reigns as a public favorite. Any given pocket of the park may host yoga and picnics under shaded pathways, cafés and stands among along the central walkway, or art exhibits by the Crystal Palace.

*i* *Free; wheelchair accessible*

## REAL JARDÍN BOTÁNICO

Pl. de Murillo 2; 914 203 017; www.rjb. csic.es; open Jan-Feb 10am-6pm, Mar 10am-7pm, Apr 10am-8pm, May-Aug 10am-9pm, Sept 10am-8pm, Oct 10am-7pm, Nov-Dec 10am-6pm

If you can think of any concept more beautiful than a garden that characterizes itself as a museum of flowers, you've got us beat. Adjacent to **Retiro Park,** the Botanical Gardens have endless grid-like pathways through fields of ferns, manicured hedges, and colorful displays of flowers that attract butterflies and seem to attract sunshine itself. The gardens have greenhouses and a miniature museum tucked away between their peaceful paths, so the possibilities for exploration are endless. Our recommendation? Don't even look at a map. Tune out all distractions and wander the paths with no aim in particular.

*i* *Admission €4, €2 student; wheelchair accessible*

## CASA DE CAMPO

Paseo Puerta del Angel; 915 298 210

If you're the Spanish royal family and they tell you to stop using your favorite centrally-located seven-square-mile park as your personal hunting ground, what do you do? Turn it into a massive public park, of course. This is what happened with Casa de Campo, which means "Country House" in Spanish. The former royal hunting ground was transformed into the city's largest park, which now contains an amusement park and zoo inside, plus wide expanses of paths, ponds, and wildlife. The park has had issues in the past with illegal practices, so stay smart and safe, especially at night. This is the much bigger and unrulier older cousin of the classic **El Retiro.**

*i* *Free; wheelchair accessible*

## ENRIQUE TIERNO GALVAN PARK

C. Meneses 4; open daily 24hr

Filled with culture, events, and activities, the Enrique Tierno Galvan Park is as much a venue for the culture of the city as it is a relaxing park in its own right. Though the grassy park is sometimes no more than a place to stroll or enjoy relaxing, it really shines when it hosts concerts (every summer boasts the "Brunch in the Park" series), shows (the IMAX theater and Planetarium are both inside the park), athletic meet-ups (there's a mini

outdoor gym, too!). There's no shortage of things to do here.

*i* Free; wheelchair accessible

# FOOD

## CHOCOLATERÍA SAN GINÉS ($)

Pasadizo de San Gines 5; 913 656 546; www.chocolateriasangines.com; open 24 hours daily

This iconic churro/chocolate joint opened in 1894 and has been open ever since. It literally has been open 24/7 since 1894. Chocolatería San Ginés also happens to have what the locals will tell you are the best churros in all of Spain. The menu is simple, and most customers just order churros (sold either thin or thick) and hot chocolate, which isn't the type of hot chocolate you drink, but instead rich, thick, creamy, melted chocolate. The mirrored walls and quaint marble counters give the tucked-away chocolatería a classic feel, but the real secret behind the spot's longevity is the moment you dunk that crispy churro into the cup of chocolate and take a bite because that's something anyone would want for another 124 years.

*i* Churros and chocolate €3; wheelchair accessible

## IL TAVOLO VERDE ($$)

C. Villalar 6; 918 051 512; www.iltavoloverde.com; open M-Th 9am-8pm, Sa 10am-8pm

Tucked away in the upscale residential area of **Salamanca** sits Il Tavolo Verde: an organic café/antique market hybrid that reminds us all that sometimes unexpected combinations produce the best results. Il Tavolo Verde's menu changes every day, but you can expect any mix of salads, pastas, quiches, and vegetable dishes—all organic, and all mouth-wateringly delicious. The rustic benches, exposed brick, and plants throughout the store create a calm and natural vibe, while the antique store located in the back is full of phenomenal (though expensive!) treasures. It doesn't get more zen than this dining experience, and we promise you'll be dreaming of the pesto

zucchini pasta or its daily equivalent long after you've left.

*i* Prices vary with menu changes- mid-level expensive; vegetarian and vegan options available; wheelchair accessible

## LATERAL ($)

Pl. Santa Ana 12; 914 201 582; www.lateral.com; open M-W noon-midnight, Th-Sa noon-2am, Su noon-midnight

Sometimes all you want is high quality, upscale but not pretentious, really shockingly delicious tapas. That's what Spain is supposed to be all about, right? Lateral thinks so. The gold-foil, patterned artwork adorning the walls and attractive atmosphere means you expect prices to be higher, but it's a pleasant surprise when they're squarely average. It's high value for a menu that has everything from spring rolls to gazpacho to various flavorful *croquetas*, plus a particularly robust cocktail menu. Cheese plates and passionfruit mojitos and vegetable lasagna, oh my!

*i* Tapas €3-9, entrées €7-15; vegetarian options available; wheelchair accessible

## MERCADO DE SAN MIGUEL ($$)

Pl. de San Miguel; 915 424 936; www.mercadodesanmiguel.es; open M-W 10am-midnight, Th-Sa 10am-2am, Su 10am-midnight

Every Spanish city has a major indoor market, but Madrid's feels the most worn-in. This isn't to say the Mercado de San Miguel is run-down or old in any way. On the contrary, it sparkles with shiny countertops and gleaming display cases. Tapas reigns supreme in this market, which features authentic Spanish food heavily though it still has various international options. Mercado de San Miguel is the ultimate spot for tapas-hopping without having to move more than a few feet: an empanada here, stuffed olives there, a *jamón tosta* across the way all under one (beautiful and intricately decorated) roof.

*i* Prices vary by stand; vegetarian options available; wheelchair accessible

## SAINT GEORGE'S CAFÉ ($)

C. del Cardenal Cisneros 62; 671 150 697; open M-F 8am-5pm

A tiny, narrow storefront in a busy area of the **Chamberí** neighborhood reads "Saint Georges," with just enough space for the 12 letters. Enter and find the magic exposed brick/subway tile combination serving as the backdrop for a miniature coffee shop that offers pastries, all types of specialty coffee, and one table with two small stools. Saint Georges was born of the coffee culture in Australia, and serves options like "bulletproof" coffee and various coffee infusions unusual to find in Europe.

*i* *Coffee €2-4; vegetarian options available; wheelchair accessible*

### BAR EL TIGRE ($)

C. de las Infantas 30; 915 320 072; open M-Th noon-1:15am, F-Sa noon-4am, Su noon-1:15am

Step one: walk into the bustling bar. Step two: order a drink. Step three: watch and wait as a large plate teeming with typical, gritty Spanish tapas is brought to your table. Step four: only pay for the drink. Sound too good to be true? It's not; it's just how things work at El Tigre. For every drink you order, the bartenders bring an accompanying plate of tapas—*patatas bravas, jamón, croquetas*—that changes with every round and is always completely free. El Tigre is popular (who doesn't love free food?) so it's not always easy to find a spot, but the bustling Madrid staple is the best way to try the ultimate in greasy Spanish tapas without spending more than the change in your pocket.

*i* *Drinks €5, free tapas; vegetarian options available; wheelchair accessible*

### CELICIOSO GLUTEN-FREE BAKERY ($$)

C. del Barquillo 19; 915 322 899; www.celicioso.es

Celicioso advertises as a gluten-free bakery, but it's really beyond that. It's a bright meeting point, a healthy and delicious lunch or dinner spot, or a coffee or juice haven. Celicioso wears enough hats that the list could go on. The gluten-free menu means exciting options for those with dietary restrictions, but there's hardly a noticeable difference for gluten-eaters in Celicioso's flavorful and diverse menu. Though they specialize in pastries and cakes, Celicioso also has a full range of sandwich, salad, and snack options, plus drinks to keep you fueled all day long.

*i* *Pastries €2-20; wheelchair accessible*

### MERCADO DE LA CEBADA ($)

Pl. de la Cebada; 913 666 966; www. mercadodelacebada.com; open M-Sa 9am-2pm and 5:30-8:30pm

An urban market in the heart of the trendy, historic **La Latina** neighborhood, Mercado de la Cebada has its roots in the sixteenth century. Now indoor and closed-in, the market smells faintly of fish and offers visitors a wide range of food and drink options. Unlike some more streamlined markets, Mercado de la Cebada is a mismatched collection of stands, a delicious mix of gourmet and gritty authentic. The market is particularly popular on Saturdays, when every stand opens to offer fresh tastings, an experience easily paired with a colorful walk through the surrounding area.

*i* *Prices vary by stand; vegetarian options available; wheelchair accessible*

### OVEN MOZZARELLA BAR ($)

C. de Atocha 114; 910 531 246; www. oven.es; open daily noon-1:30am

At Oven Mozzarella Bar, the menu's unifying factor is cheese, but it seems as if every dish could be special as a stand-alone masterpiece. The cuisine calls itself Italian (and, indeed, a map of Italy on the wall shows you where your cheese comes from), but both Spanish and international influences sneak their way onto the impressive burlap-covered list of dishes. *Burratas*, pastas, pizzas, and salads are offered, with an extensive wine list, in this beautiful, subway-tiled ambiance. Tomato truffle *burrata,* goat cheese salad, *tagliatelle* Bolognese: the possibilities are endless, no matter what your taste buds desire... and now we're hungry again.

*i* *Entrées €10-15; vegetarian options available; wheelchair accessible*

### PLATEA MADRID ($$)

C. de Goya 5; 915 770 025; www.platea-madrid.com; open M-W noon-12:30am, Th-Sa noon-2:30am, Su noon-12:30am

Platea Madrid, a gourmet food court of sorts, is housed in an old cinema and continues to play up that old-timey, glamorous charm while using the stage as a venue for nightly live performances. Multiple levels offer different types of dining, either sit-down menu ordering or choose-your-own-tapas wandering, but the whole hall is unified with the common thread of phenomenally high-quality food and an upscale ambiance. Though stands differ in price, food is quite pricey (as you'd expect from a spot that feels like you just stepped into a 1960s awards show), so keep your wallet in mind before you order the octopus, *jamón* tapas, sushi, AND the pizza. That said, if you're up for the splurge, there's quite literally no better place to do it.

*i* Prices vary by stand; vegetarian options available; limited wheelchair accessibility

# NIGHTLIFE

### ◪JOY ESLAVA
C. del Arenal 11; 913 665 439; www.joy-eslava.com; open M-Th midnight-5:30am, F-Sa midnight-6am, Su midnight-5:30am

Joy Eslava is a classic on the Madrid clubbing scene and one of the city's few major disco clubs open during the week in addition to weekends. Think of it as both a go-to and a fallback ever since it opened in 1981. Located in a historic part of the city right next to the famous 24hr churro shop **Chocolatería San Gines** (did someone say 5am churros and chocolate?), the club features a huge dance floor, multiple levels with bars, and special events throughout the year.

*i* Cover €20, drinks €8-20

### ◪TEATRO KAPITAL
C. de Atocha 125; 914 202 906; www.grupo-kapital.com

There's a reason Kapital has a reputation whispered from club-enthusiast to study-abroad-student throughout the city and beyond. A titan among nightclubs, Kapital has seven stories, each with different vibes and music, showcasing raging dance floors with diverse genres of the hottest beats interspersed with lounge areas and more intimate bars. On any given weekend night, it's almost guaranteed that all seven floors will be packed, mostly with foreign visitors

(the mainstream reputation means Kapital is less frequented by locals). As with most massive nightclubs, it's not rare for Kapital to have issues with purported rude or drunk behavior, so keep your wits about you as you dance and drink the night away under the fog, confetti, and blaring bass.

*i* Cover including one drink €20-50; upscale dress; limited wheelchair accessibility

### 1862 DRY BAR
C. del Pez 27; 609 531 151; open M-Th 3:30pm-2am, F-Sa 3:30pm-2:30am, Su 3:30pm-2am

1862 is that classy cocktail bar your favorite character orders a martini from in the movies: an upscale, but wholly unpretentious spot that attracts a low-key yet sophisticated and fun crowd. Early in the night or during the week, 1862 is a spot where you can sit and talk over drinks with friends, before it becomes a louder, standing-room only joint on the weekends. Effortlessly cool vibes ooze from the décor and attitude of the airy bar, and the cocktails are of an incredible quality, even topped with extra goodies like dried oranges and brown sugar.

*i* Drinks €9; wheelchair accessible

### CORAZÓN
C. de Valverde 44; 910 257 896; www.saloncorazon.com; open daily 7pm-3:30am

Whispered about by Madrid's glamorous, never-mainstream-but-always-drinking crowd, Corazón is a dark and moody bar with fantastic cocktails. Animal heads on the walls, wood-paneled ceilings, plush seating surrounding flickering candles: the entire bar simmers with seductive intrigue. Drinks are on the expensive side, but are worth the splurge, as they are simply phenomenal. Corazón is a busy spot for a younger crowd on Thursdays and Friday, but has a much quieter, laid-back vibe on other days of the week, so you have the option to experience the alluring bar and its many cocktail offerings whichever way you'd like.

*i* Drinks €9-12; wheelchair accessible

### NOMAD CLUB

C. de Manuel Fernández y González; 915 226 805; open M-Th 10:30pm-5:30am, F-Sa 10:30pm-6am, Su 10:30pm-5:30am

Disclaimer: Nomad is one of those spots the guys who promote clubs throughout **Sol** and other major plazas will send you to if you look like you're in the market for a night out. Despite that, this place is actually fun. A medium-sized club with an atmosphere that lends itself to dancing, Nomad is your classic post-dinner drinks-and-dancing spot, as long as you had dinner at 10pm. The swanky bar and flashing lights bring people in, and drinks are reasonably priced—not cheap, but not absurd. Music features everything from US Top 40 to Latin American hits, creating a blend enjoyed by locals and tourists alike.

*i* *Drinks from €4; wheelchair accessible*

### PONZANO STREET FESTIVAL

C. de Ponzano; every Sa in July

If all that was breezy and summery about parties came together—outdoor environment, live music, free-flowing drinks, chattering friends it would create the Ponzano Street Festival. Held on each of the four Saturdays of July, the festival on C. de Ponzano opens up the street's restaurants, shuts down the street, and offers tapas and *grande* drinks at picnic tables, all against the backdrop of local live music. The Ponzano Street Festival feels like everyone young and beautiful in Madrid had the same idea, and that idea was to snack on delicious tapas under the stars while sipping cocktails out of giant plastic cups at 11pm.

*i* *Drink prices vary by location; wheelchair accessible*

### THE PASSENGER

C. del Pez 16; 911 694 976; open M-Th 8pm-3am, F-Su 4pm-3:30am

All aboard! Tickets please! Just kidding—we'll stop messing around and let you order that cocktail. The Passenger is an old-timey bar shaped like a train car and even has window-like screens on the walls that play train journeys, transporting you from Japan to Chicago and back without ever leaving the dark-wood-paneled room in **Malasaña.** Think *Murder on the Orient Express* without the murder and expert deduction by Hercule Poirot. Drinks are on the more expensive side and there's only really a crowd on weekends, though, so the Passenger might not always attract the liveliest group. That said, the cocktails are excellent, so get on the train, grab a gin and tonic, and enjoy the ride.

*i* *Drinks €9-15; wheelchair accessible*

# PAMPLONA

Coverage by **Emma Scornavacchi**

Though Pamplona is known worldwide for its annual San Fermín festival (also known as Running of the Bulls), the northern city is full of surprises. A historical city center nestled in a valley surrounded on all sides by nature trails and viewpoints, Pamplona merges urban with rural unlike any other. Pamplona was once under Roman rule, with the Roman citadel to prove it, a landmark which, alongside Pamplona's famous Gothic cathedral and many other structures, speaks to the centuries of history woven into Pamplona's streets. The city hums with the memory of Ernest Hemingway, the American novelist who saw a spark in Pamplona when hardly a tourist had ever ventured into the area. Hemingway walked Pamplona's narrow streets and social squares, taking his coffee at Café Iruña and other local establishments before putting Pamplona on the international map with his 1926 novel *The Sun Also Rises*. His novel also popularized San Fermín for groups outside of Spain, celebrating the festival's excitement and writing it into worldwide fame. San Fermín, of course, remains Pamplona's greatest claim to fame because no matter how many churches or nature walks the city may have, in the end, it's all about the bulls.

# ORIENTATION

Pamplona is a small city, walkable and with a homogenous feel, but can be vaguely split into two parts, separated by the presence of the city's giant, grassy **Citadel**. To the north of the citadel lies the metropolitan area: **Avenida de Carlos III** with its major shopping venues, **Plaza del Castillo** just north with its historic cafés, and many ancient monuments including the legendary bullring and a smattering of iconic churches. To the south of the Citadel, you'll find **Barrio Iturrama**, a residential area with high rises that allows it a higher population density than the rest of the city, along with various places of education. Though there are nature trails and exploration options close to the city, one of the **Navarra** region of Spain's most beautiful outdoor areas lies just over an hour outside of Pamplona, at the **Urbasa y Andía Natural Park**, a respite for when you're tired of the cosmopolitan life or the festival craze.

# ESSENTIALS

## GETTING THERE

Pamplona has a small local airport that connects mostly to domestic airports such as Madrid and Barcelona but also makes international flights. The Pamplona airport is 15-20min. by taxi from the center of the city. Both Bilbao and Zaragoza airports are also close by and you can reach Pamplona via train. Trains run daily between Pamplona and many Spanish cities including Madrid, Barcelona, and Zaragoza. Tickets can be bought online at www.renfe.com, or directly from RENFE at a station. Buses run daily between Pamplona and Madrid, Barcelona, Zaragoza, and many other cities. Buses are a cheaper option than trains, and tickets can be purchased online through Alsa or at any bus stations.

## GETTING AROUND

Pamplona's city bus network, also known as Villevesas, is extensive and comprehensive. If you don't want to walk in Pamplona, the bus system will get you anywhere efficiently. Plus, it's almost always the city's cheapest option. The entire system is comprised of 33 lines that serve the city and its surrounding area. More commonly used lines run as often as every five minutes, while some less used lines run hourly. During San Fermín, the bus system remains a reliable and cheap way to get around the city. Taxis frequent Pamplona's busier streets and are relatively easy to find.

## PRACTICAL INFORMATION

**Tourist Offices:** Pamplona Tourist Information Centre (C. San Saturnino 2; 948 42 07 00; www.turismodepamplona.es; open M-Su 9am-2pm and 3pm-8pm).
**Post Offices:** Post Office (Pablo Sarasate 9; 948 20 72 17; open M-F 8:30am-8:30pm, Sa 9:30am-1pm).

## EMERGENCY INFORMATION

**Police:** Policía Municipal (Monasterio de Irache 2; 948 42 06 40).
**Pharmacies:** Farmacia Autobuses (C. Yanguas y Miranda 2; 948 21 31 07; open M-F 9am-2pm, 4pm-8pm, Sa 10am-2pm).
**Rape Crisis Center:** RAINN National Sexual Assault Hotline (800 656 4673).

# ACCOMMODATIONS

### ALOHA HOSTEL PAMPLONA

C. de Sangüesa 2; 948 153 367; www.alohahostel.es; reception open 24hr

With a colorful, bright social space, a sunny terrace filled with plants, and a friendly and accommodating team of staff, it will feel great to say "Aloha!" to Aloha Hostel in central Pamplona. Bedrooms, bathrooms and kitchen are all painted white, leaving a crisp and clean feeling and a comfortable atmosphere for breakfast (which is free every day). Aloha is one of the only hostels in Pamplona that sits firmly in the "hostel" camp, so expect a social backpacker atmosphere, but also a potential difficulty booking during high season.

*i* Dorms €15-18, private rooms €40; reservation recommended; Wi-Fi; no cancellation for San Fermín bookings; laundry facilities; luggage storage

## HOSTEL HEMINGWAY

C. de Amaya 26; 948 983 884; www.hostelhemingway.com; reception open 24hr

Maybe Hostel Hemingway's popularity comes from the name. Maybe it comes from the homey, clean common spaces adorned with posters and maps where visitors can pin their hometowns. Maybe it's the clean, comfortable bedrooms, or the location just minutes from Pamplona's famous bullring. We're not quite sure what serendipitous combination of these things makes Hostel Hemingway so popular, but we do know that sometimes it's booked years—yes, years—in advance. This means that if you're planning a trip way early or happen to get lucky with an opening, the comfortable, fun, friendly hostel experience at Hostel Hemingway is the one for you. Otherwise, it's just a dream.

*i* Dorms €15-19, private rooms €32-40; reservation recommended; Wi-Fi; free breakfast

## XARMA HOSTEL

Av. De la Baja Navarra 23; 948 046 449; www.xarmahostel.com; reception open 24hr

At Xarma Hostel, colorful and cheery décor greets guests while providing a relaxing atmosphere for a deep, mid-travel breath. Bright rooms are home to standard bunks, but few bathrooms shared between many rooms means a possible wait time. An outdoor patio is situated next to a parking lot, but the effort is still there to make it enjoyable: string lanterns and clean landscaping lend to the pleasant ambiance. Xarma is about ten minutes from the city center, and while common rooms are pleasant, the hostel is more focused around relaxing than social experiences.

*i* Dorms €15-16, private rooms €40; reservation recommended; wheelchair accessible; Wi-Fi; laundry facilities; luggage storage; free breakfast

# SIGHTS
## LANDMARKS

### CATEDRAL DE SANTA MARÍA (PAMPLONA CATHEDRAL)

C. Curia; 948 212 594; www.catedraldepamplona.com; open Mar-Oct M-Sa 10:30am-7pm, Oct-Mar M-Sa 10:30am-5pm

The Catedral de Santa María is a gothic church, built on the ruins of a Roman church, built on what archaeological evidence has suggested are the ruins of two other churches. Pamplona's cathedral is clearly built on seemingly endless religious history, and the structure that exists today represents that in the most spectacular way possible. The church is narrow and long, with high ceilings and low hanging chandeliers, giving the place the feeling of a medieval great hall. The cloister features unimaginable detail as it

# THE RUNNING OF THE BULLS

There is nothing in the world quite like the festival of San Fermín. Sometimes known colloquially as the Running of the Bulls, this week-long festival is a wild, dirty, city-wide party. Locals and visitors alike don traditional white outfits with red bandanas and take to the city center, as well as bars, restaurants, and squares surrounding the iconic bullring with drunken enthusiasm and unparalleled levels of excitement. The events begin each year at noon on July 6, no matter what day of the week July 6 falls on, with the launching of a rocket (*chupinazo*) from the city hall balcony. Pamplona parties non-stop until midnight on July 14 (when people light candles and sing the melancholy Pobre de Mí to mark the festival's end). We've experienced the adrenaline-rush-legendary-party-why-am-I-doing-this week that is San Fermín, and we have a few tips:

**Accommodations:** Booking somewhere to stay for San Fermín is nearly impossible, unless you did it a year ago. Hostels and Airbnbs will be booked up months in advance, save for pricey options that go on the market later in the hopes of luring in last-minute purchasers. If you can book early, do it. A centrally-located hostel, cheap hotel, or Airbnb is easily the best option. If you don't happen to plan your trips months in advance, booking a hotel off the beaten path (there are options within the 15-30 minute drive range) is a good option if you're willing to pay the daily taxi fare and general inflated fees. Prepare to spend more money on San Fermín accommodations than is typical of a few nights in Europe– they know people will come to the festival no matter what, so they aren't shy about jacking up prices. If all else fails, just don't sleep.

**Where to watch:** Everyone's big question is: where do I actually watch the bulls run? There are a couple options here, and they're all just as exciting as the next. The first is to watch from the street, while sprinting and screaming for your life, as 12 large bulls chase after you. We're not going to say we condone participating in the actual run (it's extremely dangerous, and many are injured every year), but for those in tip-top athletic condition with a flair for adventure, running with the bulls can be the choice of a lifetime. Another option is to watch from the street behind the wooden wall that's put up– but you most likely have to be there before 6am to have any kind of view from this spot. Above the streets themselves are balconies owned by homeowners and businesses that will rent viewing spots out to spectators for a large sum, depending on the view and how close to the festival you're purchasing. These views are epic, but only worth considering if you have the extra cash. It's worth noting that both watching from the street and from a balcony mean only two or three minutes of action; once the bulls run, your view is over. The final option is to watch from inside the bullring. This one comes with a bit of a tradeoff– you don't see the bulls running through the streets (though it's all broadcasted live on a giant screen), but you see their entrance into the stadium along with the exciting aftermath that lasts almost another hour. Tickets for stadium seats can usually be purchased outside the stadium the morning of for €6-8. For the value, we dub this the best option.

**Alcohol:** If you can avoid buying drinks out all day, do it. If this means bringing your own cheap alcohol into the stadium or on the streets, that's fine and normal; no establishment or officials will complain for a second if you're parading a handle or a cup of beer around the city. Grabbing a round of drinks at a local bar won't kill you, but if you end up buying drinks throughout the entire day at festival prices you'll regret not bringing your own, cheaper alcohol while you could. You'll see local pros with grilled food and pitchers of sangria and beer packed in coolers; some even bring champagne flutes.

**Safety:** San Fermín is a spectacular week of fun, but it's fun built around danger and personal safety should always come first. Only run if you've really considered and researched the process, keep your wits about you when alcohol is involved, and stick with friends throughout the festivities.

wraps around a beautiful courtyard and features a work of sculpture art telling the entire story of the Virgin Mary's life. Attached to the cathedral is the small **Diocesan Museum,** which visitors can check out, but that isn't covered in the cathedral's free admission.

*i* *Free admission*

## PLAZA DEL CASTILLO
Pl. del Castillo; 948 420 100

Stroll through a Hemingway story in the Plaza del Castillo, Pamplona's central square, flanked by historic buildings and constantly a bustle of pedestrian energy. The square is closed off to cars, making it a wide-open space that serves as a meeting place for everything from shopping trips to coffee dates to tour groups. The historic **Café Iruña** dominates one side of the square, but each balcony-lined building seems to hold more nineteenth-century charm than the last. At the center of the square lies the iconic bandstand, recently restored and now host to performances, speeches, and spectacles alike.

*i* *Free admission; wheelchair accessible*

## OUTDOORS

## CIUDADELA PAMPLONA (CITADEL)
Av. Ejército; park open daily 24hr; exhibition rooms open M-F 7:30am-9:30pm, Sa 8am-9:30pm, Su 9am-9:30pm

A massive, carefully landscaped fortification structure and surrounding park in the shape of a five-point star, the Citadel was built during the Renaissance to defend and fortify the city. Pamplona never quite needed defending, but the structure stayed under military use until midway through the twentieth-century, when it was converted for public use and is now a massive outdoor space and historical monument complete with exhibition rooms inside. The Citadel is the site of much of **San Fermín's** nightly revelries as crowds gather to watch the fireworks show, and, during the rest of the year, functions as a grassy, serene park and a main point of the city's makeup.

*i* *Free admission; wheelchair accessible*

# FOOD

## ★CAFÉ IRUÑA ($$)
Pl. del Castillo 44; 948 222 064; www.cafeiruna.com; open M-Th 8am-11pm, F-Sa 8am-1:45am, Su 9am-11pm

Ernest Hemingway seems to whisper his presence in every corner of Pamplona—the cobblestone streets he wrote about, the scenes of festivals he described, and the attitude of the people he helped to make famous. Opened in 1888, Iruña is where Hemingway sat to write while sipping on either coffee or wine. It's a café so influential that he wrote it directly into *The Sun Also Rises* (1926), where protagonist Jake Barnes sits on the wicker furniture with his socialite crew. Iruña is proud of its Hemingway-infused history with a steady flow of locals who still sit at the café to observe the comings and goings of the **Plaza del Castillo** over coffee. True to the story, Café Iruña also turns into a lively bar atmosphere during San Fermín.

*i* *Meal €14-20; wheelchair accessible*

## BAR CASA JESUS MARI ($)
C. San Agustín 21; 948 229 396; www.casajesusmari.es; open M-Th, Su 12:30pm-1am, F-Sa 12:30pm-3am

Anywhere you turn in Pamplona will serve you a *bocadilla*, but nowhere will they be as high value as Casa Jesus Mari. Their specialties are *bocadillas* and *tostas*, sandwiches in either snack or meal size s made up of fresh bread and high quality ingredients. Unlike many typical Spanish joints, it offers an entire range of gluten-free options, making it a favorite among travelers with dietary restrictions. Fill your *bocadilla* with everything from *jamón* to chicken to *chorizo* to roasted vegetables, and enjoy this gem that's managed to blend authentic Spanish cuisine with consistently high-quality elements.

*i* *Sandwiches €5; vegetarian and gluten-free options available; wheelchair accessible*

## RODERO ($$)
C. de Emilio Arrieta 3; 948 228 035; www.restauranterodero.com; open M-Tu 1:30pm-

3:30pm, 9pm-10:30pm, W-Sa 1:30pm-3:30pm, 9pm-10:30pm

The fine dining pride of Pamplona, Rodero has a **Michelin Star** and is widely renowned as the restaurant experience of the region. From the white tablecloths to the food served in small portions on glass plates, this restaurant gives off the vibe of luxury and cozy extravagance, and you will be hard pressed to forget that the food you're eating is of the highest quality. Menu standouts include trout, tortilla with potatoes and black truffle, and sirloin, and there are just as many mouth-watering vegetarian options. Rodero is the perfect spot for that birthday dinner, milestone celebration, or—dare we say it—second date.

*i* *Entrées €15-25; vegetarian options available; wheelchair accessible*

# SEVILLE

Coverage by **Emma Scornavacchi**

Bursting with vibrant music, layers of history, and temperatures that threaten to skyrocket, Seville is the capital of Andalusia, located on the plain of the River Guadalquivir, and a city that never ceases to amaze. Cobblestone streets that turn from wide to unsettlingly narrow in one block host souvenir shops, bistros, cafés, and shopping both upscale and discount. In the summer, Seville gets hot, hot, hot–luckily, though, even outdoor areas are shaded by massive awnings and most establishments will have air conditioning… no matter what, the city has your back. Home to the largest cathedral in the world, along with the spectacular Alcázar and legendary bull ring Maestranza, Seville also boasts unreal paella and endless meat/cheese combinations to satisfy you whether you end up at an upscale eatery or a local hole-in-the-wall. Seville holds down the anchor as Southern Spain's metropolitan capital and will surprise you with every stomp of its flamenco-dancing-shoe.

## ORIENTATION

Beginning from the center and moving outward, Seville's **Casco Antiguo** is the old quarter, featuring main attractions such as the famous cathedral and **Alcázar** flanked by bustling streets. Casco Antiguo blends into the **South District**, which gives way to overgrown parks, beautiful streets, the famous **Plaza de España**. The **Parque de María Luisa**, the largest park in the city, dominates much of this area. To the north is **La Mararena**, another historic district, and finally, the historically separate **Triana,** known for its vibrant pottery and flamenco culture.

## ESSENTIALS

### GETTING THERE

Sevilla Airport is located about 6mi. (15min.) out of the city and taxis or cars will take you to the center for a flat rate. Sevilla Airport is the main airport serving Andalusia and Western Spain and is a base for budget airlines like Ryanair and Vueling. The airport connects to 42 destinations in Europe and Northern Africa, but can only be accessed by connecting flight from North America. Santa Justa station, Seville's main train station, provides trains to stations throughout Andalucía as well as further destinations such as Madrid and Barcelona. AVE and RENFE trains use this station and tickets can be booked online or at the station. Bus lines such as ALSA come in from destinations across Spain and other European counties to Seville's central Plaza de Armas bus station.

### GETTING AROUND

Seville is a fairly well-connected city with integrated metro, bus, and tram systems. Seville's bus system (www.tussam.es) is run by Tussam and operates daily from 6am-11:30pm There are over 40 lines connecting much of the city, with stations Puerta de Jerez and Plaza Ponce de Leon acting as hubs. The city has circular buses (C3 and C4) that circle around the city center, while C5 follows a smaller route within the center. Fares are €1.20. Seville's metro has one line with 22 stops and runs 11mi. throughout the city and its metropolitan area. Alternatively, use the city tram (MetroCentro), which runs through the city center. It leaves from Pl. Nueva and follows Av. De la Constitución past the cathedral, stopping at Archivo de Indias and then at San Fernando (PuertaJerez). It terminates at the Prado de San Sebastián. Fares cost €1.20.

## PRACTICAL INFORMATION

**Tourist Offices:** Oficina Sevilla Centro (Pl. de San Francisco 19; 955 471 232; open M-F 9am-7:30pm, Sa-Su 10am-2pm).
**Post Offices:** Correos (Av. De la Constitución 32; 902 197 197; open M-F 8:30am-8:30pm, Sa 9:30am-1:30pm).
**Internet:** There are many plazas in the city that offer free Wi-Fi. Check out Plaza Salvador, Plaza del Pan, Plaza de la Pescadería, Plaza Alfalfa, and Plaza de la Encarnación.
**BGLTQ+ Resources:** There is no specific center in Seville, but some great online resources are www.gayiberia.com and www.gayinspain.com.

## EMERGENCY INFORMATION

**Emergency Number:** 112
**Police:** Patio de Banderas 4; 954 564 767; open daily 9am-9pm
**Rape Crisis Center:** RAINN National Sexual Assault Hotline (800 656 HOPE).
**Hospitals:** Hospital San Juan de Dios (Av Eduardo Dato; 954 93 93 00; open daily 24hr).
**Pharmacies:** Farmacia Neto Del Rio (C. Castillo de Constantina 4; 954 610 437; open daily 24hr).

# ACCOMMODATIONS

### ⚑OASIS BACKPACKERS' PALACE SEVILLA
C. Almirante Ulloa 1; 955 262 696; www.oasisseville.com/palace-hostel; reception open 24hr
This palace lives up to its name with hanging plants reaching down to tiled

floors, an ornate staircase (plus an elevator), and even a small pool on its luxurious rooftop terrace. Natural light filters in through a skylight, lending the common areas and hallways a sunny glow. Breakfast is a hit– choose from English, Spanish, or Healthy (we won't even try to pretend an English or Spanish breakfast is healthy) for a fixed price, and catch up with friends as you plan another day in beautiful Seville.
*i  Dorms from €18-24; reservation recommended; BGLTQ+ friendly; wheelchair accessible; Wi-Fi; luggage storage; laundry facilities*

### LA BANDA ROOFTOP HOSTEL
Calle Dos de Mayo 15; 955 228 118; www.labandahostel.com; reception open 24hr
A boutique hostel with a hotel feel, a focus on arts and music, and a friendly, social vibe, La Banda creates an ideal experience for Seville travelers. Common spaces are big, bedrooms are spacious, and the rooftop has cathedral views that glow up at sunset. Pro-tip: enjoy La Banda's bar and nightly home cooked dinner (fixed price) with new friends on the rooftop. Admittedly, there can be traffic for the bathroom in the bigger dorms where only one bathroom is en suite, but other bathrooms are available on other floors and it's a small price to pay for the hostel's general comfort. Activities like afternoon jazz and open-mic nights all tie into the arts vibe and will keep you humming along your entire stay.
*i  Dorms €26-34; reservation recommended; BGLTQ+ friendly; wheelchair accessible; Wi-Fi; luggage storage; laundry facilities; free breakfast*

# SIGHTS
## CULTURE

### ⚑PLAZA DE ESPAÑA
Av. de Isabel la Católica; open daily 24hr
Built for the **1929 Ibero-American Exposition** to showcase Spain's industry and improve global relations, Seville's Plaza de España has kept visitors gawking for almost 90 years. This Seville must-see is a marvelous half-circle of buildings and towers representing different styles of Spanish architecture throughout history. As if

of fights, the ring and museum will close early.

*i* Tickets €8, €5 student, free M 3pm-7pm; guided tours available with a tour every 20min.; wheelchair accessible

## LANDMARKS

### ▪ALCÁZAR OF SEVILLE

Patio de Banderas; 954 502 324; www.alcazarse-villa.org; open daily Oct-Mar 9:30am-5pm, Apr-Sept 9:30am-7pm

The Alcázar of Seville is the city's main tourist attraction: a network of tiled plazas, soaring archways, and lush gardens combining amount to royal palace with a history of renovations dating back to the tenth century. The palace opens up to expansive, tropical gardens that exude paradise, and the intricate details with nods to both Gothic and Moorish architecture throughout are wondrous. The palace's popularity means it's worth getting a ticket ahead of time online (there are separate lines for advance reservation and ticket purchase), but there's a chance you will wait in high season even with advance purchase.

*i* Tickets €9.50, €2 student, free under 16; tours available with private companies, book tickets online

### SEVILLE CATHEDRAL

Cuesta del Rosario 12; 954 787 578; open M 11am-3:30pm, Tu-Sa 11am-5pm, Su 2:30pm-6pm

Seville Cathedral is the largest cathedral in the world, and will make you feel like the tiniest person in the universe upon entering. Feel your smallness increase as you take in its impossibly high ceilings and gold decals. Everywhere you look, you think you're seeing "the" main part of the cathedral, until you turn around and spot something equally majestic. Lines can stretch, but advance tickets can be bought at the nearby **El Salvador Church** to skip the line. Supposedly,

that wasn't enough, it's also lined with a moat and surrounded by a wide-open plaza where fountains bubble and flamenco dancers perform. The plaza is worth a stroll around, but if you're not up to be on your feet, you can rent rowboat to see it from the moat.

*i* Free; wheelchair accessible

### PLAZA DE TOROS (ROYAL BULLRING)

Paseo de Cristóbal Colón; 954 224 577; www.realmaestranza.com/index-iden-idht-ml.html; open daily Apr-Oct 9:30am-9pm, Nov-Mar 9:30am-7pm, Good Friday and Bullfighting days 9:30am-3pm

Glory, danger, maybe even pain. That is what awaits you when you step inside Seville's epic, 12,000-person-capacity bullring. Oh, wait– you're not a bullfighter? You're just visiting? Either way, the massive white, yellow, and red ring lined with sand and bathed in sun is pretty cool. From the open-air stadium, you'll see the various gates both **matadors** and bulls enter and exit—whether in triumph or defeat—through, as well as the Royal Box for the Royal Family. If you're interested in seeing a fight, the season generally runs April to October and fights often take place on Sunday nights. On days the creators of the Seville Cathedral wrote they would build a church "so good that none will be its equal," and just about 600 years later, we daresay they succeeded.

*i Admission €9, €4 student, admission with audio guide €12, €7 student; wheelchair accessible*

## MUSEUMS

### ◼MUSEO DE BELLAS ARTES

Pl. del Museo 9; 955 542 931; www.juntadeandalucia.es/cultura/museos/MBASE/?lng=es; open Sept 16-June 15 Tu-Sa 9am-8pm, Su 9am-3pm, June 16-Sept 15 Tu-Su 9am-3pm

Seville's premier art museum, the Museo de Bellas Artes features collections of Spanish artwork and open-air gardens and courtyards, all housed inside a majestic pink structure dating back to 1594. High ceilings and ornate ceilings characterize the inside of this museum masterpiece as the interior itself becomes part of the artwork, and the meticulous landscaping of the outside spaces only contribute further to the feeling that every detail of the museum is, indeed, fine art.

*i Tickets €1.50; wheelchair accessible*

### ◼MUSEO DEL BAILE FLAMENCO

C. Manuel Rojas Marcos 3; 954 340 311; www.museodelbaileflamenco.com; open daily 10am-7pm

The Flamenco Dance Museum is a museum and performance house combination that boasts three floors of exhibits and daily shows year-round. For those looking for an easy and comprehensive way to understand the culture and history of flamenco dance, this is a one-stop-shop. Museum exhibits display flamenco photography, costumes, videos, and interactive galleries, while the performances are intimate and exciting at the same time. Show up early for front row seats and the chance to experience the emotion, passion, and music of flamenco close-up.

*i Museum admission €10, €8 student, show tickets €20, €14 student, museum and show ticket €24, €18 student*

## OUTDOORS

### ◼PARQUE DE MARÍA LUISA

Paseo de las Delicias; open daily 9am-10pm

For a breath of fresh air in the busy city of Seville, Parque de María Luisa offers a beautiful, natural haven in a central location. Seville's largest park lies adjacent to **Plaza de España** and draws visitors who wander through both. Wide, straight paths criss-cross and lead to fountains, miniature plazas, and endless meticulous landscaping. Whether you're in the mood for sunbathing, reading, picnicking, or just walking through between destinations in the city, Parque de María Luisa is the outdoor wonder for that moment of peace.

*i Free entry; wheelchair accessible*

### METROPOL PARASOL

Pl. de la Encarnación; 954 561 512; open M-Th 10am-11pm, F-Sa 10am-11:30pm, Su 10am-11pm

A newcomer on Seville's architecture scene, Metropol Parasol (sometimes called **Las Setas**, or the Mushrooms) was completed in 2011 and has taken the city by storm since. An impressive wooden structure with an elevator to the winding walkways on top, it offers some of the best views of Seville and is especially popular at sunset. The structure feels as if you're walking on clouds, and your entrance ticket grants you a free drink at the top. Ticket offices and the elevator are in the basement (look for the **Antiquarium** sign), where you'll also find a mini shopping center. Metropol Parasol is a photo-taking, city-marveling, breeze-enjoying must for those who love the city of Seville.

*i Tickets €3; last entry 30min. before closing; wheelchair accessible*

## FOOD

### ◼LA BRUNILDA TAPAS ($$)

C. Galera 5; 954 220 481; www.labrunildatapas.com; open daily 1pm-4pm, 8:30pm-11:30pm

Highly recommended and therefore often filled with tourists, La Brunilda is still way worth the hype. Tucked away down a side street yet bustling with the hum of tapas-fueled chatter, it has rustic decor and a menu filled with flavorful options, either tapas or entrée size. There will likely be a wait for dinner, but putting your name down is worth it for the delicious meal—menu favorites include salt cod fritters, duck confit, and *burrata*, proving the restaurant's flawless blend of authentic Andalusian food and international flavor delights.

*i* *Tapas €4, entrées €14; vegetarian options available; wheelchair accessible*

### MERCADO LONJA DEL BARRANCO ($$)

C. Arjona; 954 220 495; www.mercadolon-jadelbarranco.com; open M-Th, Su 10am-12am, F-Sa 10am-2am

White subway tiles and gold light fixtures set the backdrop for Mercado Lonja del Barranco, Seville's trendy, upscale one-stop-shop for every type of food imaginable. A fruit stand specializing in smoothies neighbors a taco stand, which just blends into crepes, sandwiches, seafood, sushi, and more as you continue. The high ceilings and plentiful seating options add to the atmosphere and the market's location right on the river makes for good nearby activities. Whatever you're craving, you'll find it in Mercado Lonja del Barranco—and it'll be high quality, quick, and delicious.

*i* *Prices vary based on stand; vegetarian options available; wheelchair accessible*

### BODEGA SANTA CRUZ ($)

C. Rodrigo Caro 1; 954 211 694; open daily 11am-midnight

Sometimes Spanish food is a complex, upscale flavor mash-up, and sometimes it's basic like the food at Bodega Santa Cruz. A watering hole for locals and passers-by alike, it offers indoor/outdoor seating while the chalkboard menu offers *montaditos*, miniature Spanish sandwiches, and an entire list of tapas. Hardly anything costs over €2. Foaming beer on tap will be served at the wooden bar within seconds of you asking the raucous bartenders. Seating is limited, but the food is easy to take and on the road, and it's an authentic Seville experience to leave

this local gem and stroll through the streets, tapas in hand.

*i* *Snacks and meals €2; wheelchair accessible*

# NIGHTLIFE

### LA CARBONERÍA

C. Levíes 18; 954 214 460; open daily 7pm-2am

Around or a little before midnight every night, something akin to magic happens at La Carbonería. The garden bar atmosphere quiets down, the people sitting on long wooden benches stop sipping pitchers of beer to crane their necks, and the lights dim. The flamenco performance begins. It's one of the most authentic performances to be found in the city. The bar itself is tucked away in what seems like a quieter area, but the crowd's enthusiastic clapping each night makes more than enough noise to direct visitors into the spectacle.

*i* *Drinks and food €11-20; free flamenco shows nightly; wheelchair accessible*

### THE SECOND ROOM

C. de Placentines; 602 628 759; open M-Th 3pm-2am, F-Sa 3pm-3am, Su 3pm-2am

This trendy, upscale spot in an area packed with bars and pubs will reel you in with its hip atmosphere, and keep you for hours after a sip of one of their carefully crafted cocktails. The drinks are extremely high quality, and, though the crowd is more older-twenty-something-young-professional than traveling-backpacker-looking-for-a-beer, everyone deserves a really good cocktail once in a while. The bar is nice and seating options are available, making the spot perfect for before or after dinner.

*i* *Cocktails €8-12; wheelchair accessible*

### MANHATTAN SEVILLA RIVER BAR ($)

Pasaje Las Delicias; 637 691 542; open Tu-Su 12pm-4pm

Right on the canal, at the end of a tree lined walkway, lies Manhattan Sevilla River Bar, a trendy outdoor/indoor bar with a wide range of drinks and a boisterous crowd all night. Walk along the river for a while and you'll hear Manhattan before you see it, but, once you see the colorful lights, you'll know you've arrived. The numerous seating options, and a light-up bar are nods to Seville's hip persona and the location right on the water creates a lively ambiance. They also get major bonus points for having a live DJ every night of the weekend.

*i* *Drinks €2-10; wheelchair accessible*

# VALENCIA

Coverage by **Julia Bunte-Mein**

Valencia is Spain's third largest city (after Madrid and Barcelona), and often comes third in order of visiting preference, but it is not to be missed for its thriving cultural, eating, and nightlife scenes. It is a city for all the senses—the gushing fountains of Plaza da la Virgen, the scent of orange trees in the breeze, warm sand beneath your toes on the sprawling Playa Malvarossa, the saffron-infused paella sitting warmly in your full stomach. The urban park running like a green ribbon across the entire city resembles a time machine. Get off in the Old City to roam the ancient cobblestone streets with flowers dangling off all the balconies, enter through the Roman gates dating from 138 BCE, then be transported to the year 3000 CE in the futuristic metropolis of La Ciudad de las Artes y las Ciencias, which is home to architect Santiago Calatrava's greatest architecture, the Museum of Science, and the Oceanogràfic (Europe's largest aquarium). Next, jump back a few centuries to the time of free roaming wild animals in the Bioparc. Forget what day, or even year, you actually live in as you dance the night away in one of Valencia's nightclubs. Finally settle for right here, right now in 2018, as you enjoy the beach and hot sun.

## ORIENTATION

Valencia is on the eastern coast of Spain. The city is traversed from east to west by **Los Jardines del Turia,** which was formerly the riverbed of the **River Turia** before the letter was diverted. The historic center is the main attraction of the city. The **Torres de Serranos**, in the northern area of the old city, next to the **Turia Gardens. C. Colón** is the main street with bus and metro stations that lead into the Old City. The center of the old city is **Plaza de la Virgen,** and all major sites, including **el Mercado Central** and la **Catedral,** are within a few minutes walking. The east end of the gardens of Turia leads you to **La Ciudad de las Artes y Ciencias** (City of Arts and Sciences). Continuing along **Calle Menorca,** to the northeast, and then turning right onto **Avinguda del Port,** will lead you directly to the **Port of Valencia.** Continue along the coast to reach **Playa de las Arenas, Playa de la Malvarossa,** and **Playa de la Patacona,** in order. The west side of the city is where you can find the **Bioparc.**

## ESSENTIALS

### GETTING THERE

Buses arrive at the bus station across the river (Av. Menéndez Pidal, 13; 96 346 62 66). Bus #8 runs between the bus station and the Pl. Reina and the Pl. Ayuntamiento. Valencia has two trains stations: Estación del Norte, which receives regular and domestic trains (C. Xàtiva, 24. 90 243 23 43; ticket windows open daily 8:45am-10:10pm) and the Estación de Joaquín Sorolla, which receives high-speed and international trains (C. San Vicente Mártir, 171; 90 243 23 43; ticket windows open daily 7am-10pm). Free shuttle buses run between the two stations. Flights to the Valencia region arrive in the Aeropuerto de Valencia, also known locally as the Aeropuerto de Manises (VLC; 91 321 10 00; www. aena.es), 8km. from the city. Getting between the airport and the city center is fairly straightforward: city bus #150 runs between the airport and the bus station (€1.35) and Metro lines #3 and #5 go between the airport and C. Xàtiva, near the train station.

## GETTING AROUND

The old quarter of Valencia is walkable, but the rest of the city is quite expansive, and walking everywhere would be inconvenient. Because the Jardines del Turia cut through the entire city, renting a bike is a fantastic way to explore and get around. There are bike rental shops scattered all around the old city, the port, and near the gardens. Buses run all around the city until about 10pm, with various night services continuing until around 1am. Buses to Malvarrosa and Arenas beaches are lines #1, 2, 19, 20, 23, 29, 31, 32 and 95. All of them have some stop along the Paseo Marítimo. From Colón, take #95 to the City of Arts and Sciences and #32 to the beach. The tram lines #4 and #6 in Valencia also go to the beach at stops Dr. Lluch and Les Arenes. Metro lines 5, 7 and 8 also go to station Marítim-Serrería near Malvarrosa beach.

## PRACTICAL INFORMATION

**Tourist Offices:** The municipal tourist office (Pl. Reina 19, 96 315 39 31, open M-Sa 9am-7pm, Su 10am-2pm).
**Banks/ATMs/Currency Exchange:** There are many banks on C. Pascual i Genis, including Deutsche Bank (C. de Pascual i Genís, 12; 963 98 70 80; open Tu-Th 8:30am-4:30pm, F 8:30am-2:30pm).
**Post Offices:** Valencia's main post office is so stunning it's worth going to even if you're all set with stamps (Pl. de l'Ajuntament, 24; 902 19 71 97; www.correos.es; Open M-F 8:30am-8:30pm, Sa 9:30am-2pm). Postal Code: 46002
**Internet:** Free Wi-Fi is available in public places denoted on the tourist office map with a Wi-Fi symbol, including the Jardines del Real and the Jardines del Turia near the Palau de la Música. Free Wi-Fi and free computers with internet access are also available at the Biblioteca Pública de Valencia (C. de l'Hospital, 13; 962 56 41 30; www.portales.gva.es/bpv).

## EMERGENCY INFORMATION

**Emergency Number:** 112
**Police:** Municipal Police (Av. Cid, 37. 092).
**US Embassy:** Dr. Romagosa, 1. 963 516 973. M-F 10am-2pm by appointment
**Hospitals:** Hospital General Universitari

(Av. Tres Cruces, 2. 96 197 20 00. Bus #3).
**Pharmacies:** Farmacia Corts Valencianes (Av. Les Cortes Valencianas, 48, Beside the Palacio de Congresos; 963 463 360; open daily 24hr).

# ACCOMMODATIONS

### ⬛RIVER HOSTEL

Plaça del Temple, 6; 963 913 955; reception open 24hr

Sure, the name is a little misleading since there's absolutely nothing river-related about this hostel, but, once you get over it, you'll realize you've hit the jackpot. Enjoy the light and airy downstairs common room stocked with a full kitchen and bakery (banana bread, anyone?). Dorms come equipped with high ceilings, privacy curtains, and large luggage drawers underneath each bunk (a storage game changer, we're telling you). And, if you ever tire of the great indoors, retire on your balcony as the sun sets over Valencia. The grand, historical exterior, impeccable cleanliness, central location, and seemingly unlimited amenities would make you think the rooms are really expensive, but they're actually some of the most affordable in town.

*i* *Dorms from €15; reservation recommended; wheelchair accessible; Wi-Fi; linens included; towel included; full-service kitchen; breakfast buffet €2.90*

### RED NEST BACKPACKER'S HOSTEL

C. De La Paz, 36; 963 427 168; www.nest-hostelsvalencia.com; reception open 24hr

With locations throughout Spain and two hostels in Valencia alone, Nest Hostels are experts in the business—and Red Nest doesn't disappoint. Perfect for the social solo traveler, Red Nest has great amenities (read: you will thank your lucky stars for the air conditioning) and helpful staff. Take the winding marble staircase with red graffiti walls up to their expansive kitchen, computer lounge, and rooftop terrace. In addition, there are many hostel events including a free walking tour of the old city and their nightly pub crawl. Never fear if you feel like staying in—there's always a group on the rooftop enjoying the in-house bar (beer €2, cocktails €4) and trading travel secrets.

*i* *Dorms from €16; reservation recommended; Wi-Fi; linens included; towels €2; lockers available; laundry facilities*

# SIGHTS
## CULTURE

### CUIDAD DE LAS ARTES Y LAS CIENCIAS (CITY OF ARTS AND SCIENCES)
www.cac.es; hours vary by museum

The City of Arts and Sciences, designed by the local legend and architect **Santiago Calatrava,** is just so…cool. There's no other way to describe the masses of concrete and glass that rise out of the turquoise water, connecting with shapes that form arches and bridges. Rent kayaks, rowboats, or water bikes that look like elliptical machines to admire the buildings from a different angle. Although the city's construction was controversial among Valencians because of the huge expense, you might as well enjoy the many activities here like the **Oceanogràfic,** Europe's largest aquarium, and the **Hemisfèric,** or **IMAX theater.** Unfortunately, entry to these venues is expensive and not especially worth the admission fee (with the exception of the aquarium, which, of course, is the most expensive).

*i* *Hemisfèric €8.80, science museum €8, oceanogràfic €28.50, combined admission €37*

## LANDMARKS

### CATEDRAL DE VALENCIA
Pl. de l'Almoina; 963 918 127; www.catedraldevalencia.es; open Mar 20-Oct 31 M-Sa 10am-6:30pm, Su 2pm-6:30pm, Nov 1-Mar 19 M-Sa 10am-5:30pm, Su closed from 2pm-5pm

This gothic cathedral isn't any more impressive than others in Spain, but it's still worth a visit because locals claim they have *the* Holy Grail. Yeah, that one from *Monty Python.* We're a little skeptical—over a dozen other cathedrals around the world claim the same thing, so unless Jesus played some chalice-pong before he peaced out for heaven, someone's lying. Whether or not you believe it, follow the masses of tourists to see the special cup surrounded by an impressive alabaster relief. But even if you're not convinced, check out the bright blue Renaissance frescoes of the 12 angelic musicians in the dome of the chapel or head up the **Miguelete Tower** (€2) on the Pl. de la Reina side for indisputably the best views of Valencia.

*i* *Admission €7, €2 tower*

### LA LONJA DE SEDA (THE SILK EXCHANGE)
Lonja, 2; 962 084 153; open M-Sa 9:30am-7pm, Su 9:30am-3pm

This **UNESCO World Heritage site** is a jewel of civil Gothic architecture, designed by the master builder and architect **Pere Compte.** It originally served as Valencia's silk and commodity exchange. There are four sections, but the highlights are the **colonnaded hall** with its forest of palm-tree shaped columns and the first floor, **Consulado del Mar,** with its coffered ceiling. Don't forget to recline in the lovely, pungent orange grove before taking a look at the façade overlooking the historic **Plaza del Mercado.** You'll be shocked to see the R-rated gargoyles performing various obscene actions Oh, what was that? Now you're interested. Well, now you have to go.

*i* *Admission €2, €1 student, free on Su*

## MUSEUMS

### ALMONIA ARCHAEOLOGICAL MUSEUM
Pl. de la Almoina; 962 084 173; open M-Sa 9:30am-7pm, Su 9:30am-3pm

You might think the sparkling pool of water in the **Plaza de la Almonia** is just a fancy urban decoration, but take closer look, and, through the clear water, you'll see archaeological ruins dating from Roman, Visigoth, and Arab periods. For a better view, visit the museum and admire the old ruins, artifacts, and pottery. For you architecture nerds, there are models of the original building and life-size drawings that depict what it would have looked like to be there in its prime. The museum is more a

30-minute activity, so don't budget the whole day just for this.

*i* *Admission €2, free Sa-Su; wheelchair accessible*

### EL MUSEO DE LAS BELLAS ARTES
C. de Sant Pius V, 9; 963 870 300; www.museobellasartesvalencia.gva.es; open Tu-Su 10am-8pm

This fine art museum is a castle housing masterpieces from Spain's Golden Age, including famous works by **Velazquez, Goya,** and **El Greco.** If you've never heard of any of those guys (which we would find hard to believe), here's your chance to learn some art history with minimal investment—the entire museum is free! Spend an hour or a whole afternoon looking at the paintings of the Virgin Mary holding baby Jesus, or if that's not your cup of tea check out the realistic portraits and impressionist scenes of Spanish culture in the side rooms.

*i* *Free; wheelchair accessible*

# FOOD
### ⬛BAR ALMUNDÍN ($$)
Carrer de l'Almodí, 14; open daily except Tu 1-4pm, 7-11pm

Imagine the cutest restaurant in Paris, but its Spanish sister. Red and green everything, checkered tablecloths, and eclectic decorations. The terrace seating is lovely for a cool evening, but you'll also love the cozy interior with dark wood, Art Nouveau chandeliers, and doily placemats. The second floor offers a particularly great view of the mesmerizing bar, stocking an impressive variety of vermouth. Try the tapa tasting menu for €16 if you're really hungry or get paella—served traditionally in the pan to share.

*i* *Tapas €5-12, paella €14, degustation menu €16; vegetarian options available*

### ⬛EL TROCITO DEL MEDIO ($)
Carrer de Blanes, 1; 620 677 881; open daily 5am-4pm

Want to live the high life in Valencia? Come to El Trocito for a one-of-a-kind personal chef experience. Located right outside the back entrance of **el Mercado Central**, this traditional Valencian restaurant will cook whatever meat, fish, or shellfish you buy from the market for only €4 (plus a free side salad)! They also offer three-course paella for only €10, as well as traditional Mediterranean tapas and sandwiches. Pro tip: try their grilled sardines with garlic and oil or stuffed baguette sandwich with octopus in olive oil and herbs.

*i* *Only open during hours of the market; call ahead to make a reservation for the personal chef experience*

### KIMPIRA ($)
C. Convento San Francisco, 5; 963 923 422; www.kimpira.es; M-Th 8:30am-4pm, F-Sa 8:30-midnight, Su 8:30am-4pm.

Feel refreshed and energized after eating a 100% vegan, organic, natural meal at Kimpira in the downtown area of Valencia. This gourmet health restaurant specializes in macrobiotic cuisine and can make even the most dedicated carnivore turn vegan. The nature of the food permeates the restaurant itself, with the building's airy interiors, white brick walls, rose wallpaper, plants, and antique clocks. Every day, Kimpira offers a different menu based on local, seasonal produce. It includes a soup, main dish with grain, vegetables or vegetable protein (such as seitan), dessert, and tea. The set menu is a great bargain, and it's guaranteed to fill your stomach.

*i* *Set menu M-F €13.50; vegan options available*

# NIGHTLIFE
### EL CAFÉTÍN
Pl. de Sant Jaume, 2; 652 383 228; open daily noon-1:30am

El Cafétín serves an amazing *agua de Valencia* for a reasonable price. On cool evenings, their small outdoor terrace is the perfect place to enjoy cheap drinks with friends in a quiet area of the **Old City.** If it's super-hot, though, we recommend sitting inside and admiring their floral wallpaper, antique chandeliers, gold framed photos on maroon colored walls, and a small upright piano in the corner. El Cafétín doubles as a place to trade in your rough backpacker lifestyle for elegant afternoon tea in ceramic pots.

*i* *Caña and tapas €2*

## L'UMBRACLE - MYA CLUB

Av. Del Saler, 5; open Th-Sa midnight-7am

If you only have one night in Valencia, this is the place to get the full experience. It's actually two separate nightclubs in one. Upstairs is l'Umbracle Terraza, an open-air club under the white arches of l'Umbracle Park; downstairs is the more clubby Mya. L'Umbracle's grand entrance is lined with palm trees in pink light, offering spectacular views of **El Palacio** de **Las Artes** and **El Hemisférico**. Dress up for this chic evening, as you might see a celebrity or two. Stay outside with the mass of people mingling under the covered patio or head downstairs via two circular white staircases to Mya's techno, hip-hop, or Latin-music rooms. You might want to stop at a local bar first to avoid paying for overpriced drinks.

*i* Cover €16 with one free drink

# SPAIN ESSENTIALS

## VISAS

Spain is a member of the European Union and is part of the Schengen Area, so US citizens can stay in Sweden for up to 90 days without a visa.

## MONEY

**Tipping and Bargaining:** Native Spaniards rarely tip more than their spare change, even at expensive restaurants. Don't feel like you have to tip, as the servers' pay is almost never based on tips. Bargaining is common and necessary in open-air and street markets. Do not barter in malls or established shops.

**Taxes:** Spain has a 10% value added tax (IVA) on all means and accommodations. The prices listed in Let's Go include IVA. Retail goods bear a much higher 21% IVA, although the listed prices generally include this tax. Non-EU citizens who have stayed in the EU fewer than 180 days can claim back the tax paid on purchases at the airport.

## SAFETY AND HEALTH

**Local Laws and Police:** There are several types of police in Spain. The policía local wear blue or black uniforms, deal more with local issues, and report to the mayor or town hall in each municipality. The guardia civil wear olive-green uniforms and are responsible for issues more relevant to travelers: customs, crowd control, and national security. Catalonia also has its own police force, the Mossos d'Esquadra. Officers generally wear blue and occasionally sport berets. This police force is often used for crowd control and to deal with riots.

**Drugs and Alcohol:** Recreational drugs are illegal in Spain, and police take these laws seriously. the legal drinking age is 16 in Asturias and 18 elsewhere. In Asturias, it is still illegal for stores to sell alcohol to those under the age of 18.

**Terrorism:** In August of 2017, a terrorist attack in Barcelona, Spain left 13 people dead and over 100 injured. *Let's Go* recommends travelers avoid large crowds and remain aware of their surroundings at all times.

# SWEDEN

**Many things that people traditionally associate with Scandinavia, like ABBA, IKEA, and Swedish Fish, are actually Swedish.** And, if you had to pick a Scandinavian country, Sweden is the one to see. It's Scandinavia's most populous country; it contains its largest city, boasts its tallest skyscraper, and houses the largest scale model of the solar system in the entire world. You can't make this stuff up! Sweden lies between Norway and Denmark geographically, but also ideologically. Sweden is laid-back enough to just suck it up and join the European Union (unlike Norway), but not so laid-back that drinking in the streets is commonplace (unlike Denmark). And don't worry, they haven't completely sold out to the EU anyway; they still refuse to adopt the euro. It will come as no surprise that Sweden isn't cheap, but it might be worth shelling out a little extra cash. There are museums dedicated to everything from ancient ships to liquor, palaces and gardens fit to rival any in Europe (as long as you haven't been anywhere else in Europe), and the hostels you've always dreamed of (you know, the ones where the kitchen is just as rowdy as most of the bars in the area). Sweden is a country of paradoxes. It's a country where everybody bikes but nobody wears a helmet, a country renowned for its healthy population but where tobacco use is relatively high, and a country with an enormous weapons industry, despite being famously neutral and peace-loving. So, what is the real Sweden like? Pack up your IKEA bag—you might have to assemble it first—and find out.

# MALMÖ

Coverage by **Eric Chin**

Sweden and Denmark have spent more time fighting throughout history than you and your roommate when there's only one free shower right before your 9am class. Though not official, it's widely believed that no two countries have gone to war as often as these, and Malmö was right in the thick of it all. Positioned just across Oresund from Copenhagen, the city changed hands multiple times, eventually falling under Swedish control for the long haul. The resulting city is diverse and independent with visible reminders of its Danish past such as Malmöhus Castle and the occasional *smørrebrød* restaurant. It's also increasingly young and modern, especially since the completion of the öresund Bridge, which connects Malmö to Copenhagen. From ancient Gothic churches to Scandinavia's tallest skyscraper, American-style burger joints to New Nordic Cuisine, and swing dancing bars to hard-charging nightclubs, Malmö has it all. The small city vibe is real here, but, if you ever get bored, Copenhagen is just a short, border control-free (how civilized!), train ride away. That probably won't be necessary, though. Malmö has sights ranging from brick-building-lined squares to absolutely baffling modern art exhibitions. And for those of you who accidentally booked a ticket to Sweden instead of Spain, fear not: there are beaches here, and two of them are nude. That's Malmö for you.

## ORIENTATION

Though Malmö doesn't have the vast, diverse neighborhoods of a city like Stockholm, there are still distinct areas. The heart of the city is **Gamla Staden,** which contains **Malmö C,** as well as most of the city's cultural and historical landmarks, like **Malmöhus Castle** and **Lilla Torg.** To the west is **Ribersborg,** home of Malmö's main beach and open-air bathhouse, **Ribersborgs Kallbadhus.** North of the city center is the exclusive neighborhood of Västra Hamnen, which claims to be Europe's first entirely carbon-neutral district. It's also home of Turning Torso. Things get a bit more residential south of Gamla Staden, but no less fun. **Möllevången,** known by the cool kids (and you want to be a cool kid around here) as **Möllan,** is Malmö's hip, no-hands-bike-riding, polaroid-camera-wielding, beanie-in-the-summer-wearing neighborhood. Catch a live show at **Folkets Park,** choose from a huge variety of international cuisines, or just head out for a stroll through the cultural spectrum that is Malmö.

## ESSENTIALS

### GETTING THERE

Malmö Airport (MMX), sometimes called by its old name, Sturup, is a small airport about 30km east of the city center. It connects to a number of major cities in Europe, especially in central Europe. Flygbussarna Airport Coaches travel regularly between the airport and city center, and can be purchased online (www.flygbussarna. se) for SEK 105. Also consider Copenhagen Airport (CPH), which flies to far more cities, including a few in North America. Malmö's train station is Malmö Central Station (Malmö C). Trains to destinations throughout Sweden are operated by SJ. Malmö C is open M-F 4:40am-midnight, Sa-Su 6am-midnight.

### GETTING AROUND

Malmö is super walkable. If you want to use public transportation, your best bet is to buy a Jojo card (available at Malmö C), which can be used on buses and trains (1-day pass SEK 65, 3-day pass SEK 165). You can also load money onto the card, in which case (single-fare SEK 17). Malmö is another bike-friendly Scandinavian city, and city bike stations can be found all over the city center (1-day pass SEK 80, 3-day pass SEK 165). They can be purchased online (www.malmobybike. se). Rentals are for 1hr. each.

## PRACTICAL INFORMATION

**Tourist Offices:** Malmö has no dedicated tourist office. Instead, maps, informationcan be found at "InfoPoints" around the city. Look for a green "i" logo in shop windows. The closest InfoPoint to Malmö Central Station is Travel Shop (Carlsgatan 4; 040 330 570; open M-F 9am-5pm, Sa-Su 10am-5pm).

**Banks/ATMs/Currency Exchange:** Credit and debit cards can be used almost everywhere in Malmö. If you need cash, ATMs (Bankomat in Sweden) can be found on the street, and currency exchange is possible at banks like Forex (Malmö Central Station; 10 211 1664; open M-F 7am-8pm, Sa-Su 10am-6pm).

**Post Offices:** PostNord Postombud at ICA Malmborgs Caroli (Stora Kvarngatan 59; 020 23 22 21; open M-F 8am-8pm, Sa 8am-6pm, Su 11am-6pm).

**Internet:** Free Wi-Fi is available at most cafés, including independent shops and chains like Espresso House. Malmö Central Station and the City Library also offer free Wi-Fi.

**BGLTQ+ Resources:** RFSL is the Swedish Federation for Lesbian, Gay, Bisexual, Transgender, and Queer Rights (Stora Nygatan 18; www.malmo.rfsl.se).

## EMERGENCY INFORMATION

**Emergency Number:** 112
**Police:** Malmö Porslinsgatan (Porslinsgatan 4B; 77 114 14 00; open M-F 7am-10pm, Sa-Su 8am-5pm).
**Hospitals:** Skåne University Hospital (Södra Föstadsgatan 101; 040 33 10 00).
**Pharmacies:** Apoteket Gripen (Bergsgatan 48; 0771 450 450; open daily 8am-11pm).

# ACCOMMODATIONS

### RUT & RAGNARS VANDRARHEM ($)
Nobelvägen 113; 406 116 060; www.rutochragnars.se; reception open 9am-1pm

Though the name makes it sound more like a Viking alehouse, Rut and Ragnars is the cheapest hostel you'll find in Malmö. The street entrance is unassuming, but inside there are definitely some features that elevate this place above your normal budget hostel. Check out the two kitchens, a lounge with TV, and free coffee and tea. The dorm rooms have couches and wall decorations to keep them from feeling too prison-like, and beds are equipped with privacy curtains to maximize your personal space. Don't expect anything too fancy, like a five-star breakfast buffet, but Rut and Ragnars is a solid choice for its asking price.

*i* Dorms from SEK 200, SEK 180 student, singles SEK 430, doubles SEK 590; reservation recommended; max stay 7 nights; BGLTQ+ friendly; wheelchair accessible; Wi-Fi; linens SEK 50; laundry facilities SEK 50

### STF VANDRARHEM MALMÖ CITY ($$)
Rönngatan 1; 406 116 220; www.swedish-touristassociation.com/facilities/stf-malmo-city-hostel

Small cities often don't have great hosteling culture, and Malmö is no exception. It just doesn't draw the hordes of backpackers required to sustain vibrant hostels. With that in mind, STF Vandrarhem is definitely your best bet in the city. While it's not a continuous party like you'll find in Stockholm, it definitely has a social atmosphere, especially on the weekends, and the facilities, including a kitchen and outdoor courtyard, are vague. The breakfast buffet, though a bit expensive for non-STF/HI members, is an excellent way to start the day.

*i* Dorms from SEK 270, privates from SEK 560, additional SEK 50 per night for non-STF/HI members; reservation recommended; max stay 5 nights; BGLTQ+ friendly; wheelchair accessible; Wi-Fi; linens included; lockers provided; breakfast SEK 65 for members, SEK 80 for non-members

# SIGHTS
## CULTURE

### FOLK Å ROCK
Lilla Torg, Skomakaregatan 11; 40 781 03; www.folkarock.se; open M-Sa 10am-10pm, Su noon-6pm

Like that kid in high school whose parents told him he could be whatever he wanted, Folk å Rock is a little bit of everything—part café, part bar, and part record store. Its abundance of indoor and outdoor seating is great for a steaming latte on a rainy afternoon or a cold beer on a sunny evening, but the upstairs music store is good for browsing all the time. Shelves of CDs and vinyl skew heavily towards your dad's favorites (Hendrix, Aerosmith, the Grateful Dead, you name it), but poke around a bit and you'll find timeless classics from **ABBA** to the Beatles, and even some contemporary artists, like Adele and Lana Del Rey.

*i* *Coffee and espresso drink SEK 20-40, pastries and cakes SEK 20-50, beer from SEK 60; wheelchair accessible*

### RIBERSBORGS KALLBADHUS

Limhamnsvägen, Brygga 1; 040 260 366; www.ribersborgskallbadhus.se; open M-Tu 9am-8pm, W 9am-9pm, Th-F 9am-8pm, Sa-Su 9am-6pm

For the full Swedish spa experience, Ribersborgs Kallbadhus is the go-to. This open-air bathhouse pokes out into the sea on its own pier, giving it an exclusive and private feel, which is good, considering that clothes are banned here. That's right, this place is completely nude. With separate areas for men and women, each side features an enclosed swimming area and saunas of varying temperatures. With ample deck space, you're guaranteed not only to snag a place to get your perfect tan, but also to see way more old man/lady junk than you've ever wanted. Don't worry, though; much like Planet Fitness, this is a judgment-free zone.

*i* *Admission SEK 65; swimwear prohibited in the sauna*

## LANDMARKS

. . . . . . . . . . . . . . . . . . . . . . . . . . . . . . . . . . . . . . . .

### HARBOR SCULPTURES

Posthusplatsen

The entire city of Malmö is overrun with sculptures (though admittedly, there are worse things with which to be overrun), depicting everything from the classic old man on a horse, to a slightly cartoonish marching band headed down one of the main streets. But some of the most interesting statues can be found along the harbor right next to **Malmö Central Station.** Here, you'll find works ranging from straightforward, but poignant, like

*Non-Violence* (a large, bronze revolver with its muzzle twisted in a knot), to the absolutely psychedelic, like *Spectral Self Container* (a mind-bending rainbow piece that looks more like it belongs in a college-level topology textbook). Don't think too hard; just enjoy.

*i* *Free; wheelchair accessible*

### LILLA TORG

Lilla Torg; open daily 24hr

Its name may literally translate to "Small Square" but don't tell that to Lilla Torg; this little square has a big personality and big-time bragging rights. Surrounded by old-looking brick and wooden buildings, the cobblestone streets are packed from dawn to dusk on most nights. These buildings house everything from the kind of rock and roll club/bar your dad and his buddies would love to steakhouses frequented by Italian men with chihuahuas. Ample outdoor seating makes Lilla Torg the perfect place to enjoy a coffee in the afternoon, a beer in the evening (or afternoon, if that floats your boat), and a good dose of sun and people-watching at any time of day.

*i* *Prices vary; wheelchair accessible*

### TURNING TORSO

Lilla Varvsgatan 14; open daily 24hr

Turning Torso is Scandinavia's tallest skyscraper, towering like an enormous middle finger to the rest of the world's conventional, straight-sided buildings. The building itself is composed of nine cubes with curved edges, stacked one on top of the next, each offset slightly from the one below. The result is an elegant tower that looks more like it belongs in Dubai than in the third-largest city in Sweden. Don't bother going inside, as it's mostly residential, but the Turning Torso Gallery next door has a natural, Whole Foods-y kind of market, and the whole neighborhood is a nice place for a wander.

*i* *Free; wheelchair accessible*

# THE SWEDISH SAUNA

Sweden has lots of traditions, from summertime crayfish parties to trying to take over Denmark, but none is quite like the Swedish Sauna. It's a place where you can sweat out toxins, bad vibes, and any lingering alcohol leftover from last night. Saunas in Sweden aren't just a relaxation tool though; they're a way of life. Entire Swedish hotels are centered around spas, and saunas are main attractions at places like Ribersborgs Kallbadhus in Malmö. City Backpackers Hostel in Stockholm even runs a Viking Sauna Tour during the winter months. Like any ancient tradition, though, there are rules, both written and unwritten. Here are a few you should know:

1. **Get ready to get naked.** Finally. A situation in which you can take the lyrics of Nelly's "Hot In Here" to heart! Bet you never thought you'd read a sentence like that, but it's strangely relevant here. Most Swedish saunas require you to be nude, either by rule, or by custom. This is almost always true in single-gender saunas, though towels or swim wear may be allowed in mixed-gender saunas. Oh yeah, those are a thing.

2. **Bring a towel.** Being nude is one thing; leaving a sweaty butt print all over the sauna seat is another. Just bring a towel.

3. **Eyes up!** Can it be awkward to make eye contact with a naked stranger? Absolutely; but not as awkward as if he catches you staring somewhere else… Better yet, look out the window, and enjoy the beautiful Swedish scenery.

4. **Blend in.** Sauna etiquette varies based on where you are. When in doubt, just do what everyone else is doing. Or better yet, ask!

## MUSEUMS

### 🏛SCIENCE AND MARITIME HOUSE
Malmöhusvägen; 40 344 438; www.malmo.se; open daily 10am-5pm

This is a fun science museum, probably in part because it seems to be aimed towards children, if the bright colors, playful font choices, and interactive exhibits are indicative of anything. But that doesn't mean you can't enjoy it too, right? You're probably young at heart, and that's what counts. Check out the explanation about the future of nanotechnology and seriously silly rooms full of simple games, like a hydrogen rocket, to help illustrate complex concepts. The star of the show, though, is the **U3 submarine** on display in the courtyard. Visitors can go inside the sub to view the cramped quarters, endless dials, and tiny control room. There are guided tours led by some of the sub's original crew members. As Confucius once said, "Damn the torpedoed; full speed ahead!"

*i* Admission to Malmö Museum and Science and Maritime House adults SEK 40, SEK 20 student, free 19 and under; U3 submarine tours Tu and Su 1pm-4pm; wheelchair accessible

### MALMÖ MUSEUM
Malmöhusvägen; 40 344 437; www.malmo.se; open daily 10am-5pm

Denmark and Sweden fought constantly in the Middle Ages (seriously, didn't they ever get bored?), and Malmö was often right in the thick of it due to its location. Thus, it needed a castle, which was cleverly named **Malmöhus Castle.** Today, the castle serves not only as a historical building, but also as the city's museum. Some castle rooms have been preserved, (like one of the cannon towers, which chronicles Sweden and Denmark's perpetual bickering), but you'll also find temporary exhibits, art galleries, and even a natural history museum and aquarium. It sounds like a lot, but none of the exhibits is particularly long, so you'll have plenty of time to look at paintings or jellyfish.

*i* Admission to Malmö Museum and Science and Maritime House SEK 40, SEK 20 student, free 19 and under; Malmöhus Castle tours July 5-August 27 W-Su 3pm; wheelchair accessible

# OUTDOORS

## RIBERSBORGSSTRANDEN
Open daily 24hr

Ribersborgsstranden is the place to get that much-needed dip in the Scandinavian sea. It's a long stretch of beach and green space just west of the city center that provides numerous swimming options for the general public, as well as a pier designed specifically for visitors with disabilities. There's also a nude beach (how European), in case you just can't resist the call of the wild, but **Ribersborgs Kallbadhus** is too gentrified for you.

*i* Free; wheelchair accessible

# FOOD

## ☪SALTIMPORTEN CANTEEN ($$)
Grimsbygatan 24; 706 518 426; www.saltimporten.com; open M-F noon-2pm

Saltimporten Canteen may just be Malmö's best lunch spot. They only use the freshest ingredients, the atmosphere is upbeat, and, at SEK 95 for an entrée, the price is tough to beat. So, what's the catch? It's only open weekdays noon-2pm. The rotating menu features a single dish each day; some examples include beef tartare with mushrooms and hazelnuts and lamb with new potatoes and fennel. But no matter what's being served, you can bet it will be elegant and executed to perfection. The restaurant itself is bright and modern with exposed ventilation ducts and an aggressive number of windows. Perfect for the solo traveler, the long communal tables bring together people who would venture all the way out to this pier to eat pretentious food.

*i* Lunch SEK 95; vegetarian options available; wheelchair accessible

## ☪SURF SHACK ($$)
Västergatan 9; 761 764 080; www.surfshacksmashburgers.com; open M-Th 11am-9pm, F-Sa 11am-10pm; Su noon-8pm

It's a bit gimmicky to open a surf-themed burger joint when you're closer to the Arctic Circle than the equator, but there are so many dudes in Sweden with long blond hair that it works. Surf Shack draws a hungry crowd at mealtimes, and it's easy to see why: these burgers are massive. The "Mini Burger" weighs in at 115g and constitutes a meal in itself, but, if you're feeling ravenous, make it a double with the "Surf Burger"—a tower so high, it has to be held together with a skewer. Keep it classic with free toppings like grilled onions and mayo, or go full Hawaiian with pineapple and teriyaki sauce. Surf Shack even features milkshakes spiked with whiskey or rum, as an adult twist on a diner favorite.

*i* Single burgers from SEK 70, doubles from SEK 95, fries SEK 25, spiked milkshakes SEK 110; vegetarian, vegan, and gluten-free options available; limited wheelchair accessibility

## LILLA KAFFEROSTERIET ($$)
Baltzargatan 24; 40 482 000; www.lillakafferosteriet.se

The concept of size in Malmö must be a bit different than in the rest of the world, because, like **Lilla Torg,** Lilla Kafferosteriet, (literally "small coffee roasters"), is anything but small. This café sprawls across multiple rooms on two floors, an outdoor patio, and a courtyard. The décor is rustic, with exposed beams, peeling paint (it's charming...somehow), and rough-cut wooden counters that look like they were placed by Paul Bunyan himself. There's ample seating, which is good, because Lilla Kafferosteriet draws everyone from business meetings well-supplied with espresso, to family breakfasts featuring grumpy children and numerous chocolate croissants. You're sure to fit right in.

*i* Coffee and espresso drinks SEK 20-40, pastries SEK 20-50

# NIGHTLIFE

## BABEL
Spångatan 38; 40 579 896; www.babel-malmo.se

For a small city, Malmö doesn't disappoint with its club scene, and Babel is a prime example. Open late Wednesday through Saturday, this nightclub, housed in a converted church, is a hit with young crowds from around the world. An outdoor patio and multiple floors with spinning lights, blaring speakers, and a fog machine provide lots of options for enjoying (tolerating?) reggae, house, EDM, or whatever the music of the night may be. Drinks are reasonably priced, and you'll even find some of your American favorites like PBR and Angry Orchard, just in case the whole experience is a bit too foreign otherwise.

*i* Cover SEK 60-120 depending on night, beer from SEK 60, mixed drinks and shots from SEK 80; BGLTQ+ friendly; no wheelchair accessibility

## MALMÖ BREWING CO. & TAPROOM
Bergsgatan 33; 733 921 966; www.malmobrewing.com; open M-Th 4pm-midnight, F 4pm-3am, Sa noon-3am, Su 2pm-10pm
This is it: Malmö's only microbrewery, and it doesn't disappoint. Downstairs in the rustic brick basement that houses the bar is a board listing over 30 different beers on tap, with clever (or maybe just ridiculous) names like **"Janky Stout"** and **"Kitten in Trance."** The atmosphere is casual, with laid-back hip hop and R&B, and the crowd a mix of older guys who would probably say they "dabble" in brewing, and young people getting a cold beer while their tastes are still discerning enough to appreciate it. If you get here early, don't miss the BBQ menu, with classics like ribs, brisket, and pulled pork so good, you'll forget that you're thousands of miles from the American Midwest.

*i* Beer from SEK 70, entrées SEK 100-200; BGLTQ+ friendly; no wheelchair accessibility

# STOCKHOLM

Coverage by **Eric Chin**

You came to Scandinavia expecting great things: meatballs, IKEA, ABBA, Vikings, and of course, meatballs. Well congratulations, you've made it to Stockholm: the biggest, baddest, and brightest city in the north. You've seen the fjords in Bergen and joined the hordes of cyclists in Copenhagen, but now it's time to move up to a true metropolis, or, at least, a city with a real subway system. Stockholm is a Scandinavia-traveler's dream. It's a bustling city where oxford-clad businessmen in Östermalm rub elbows with hipsters in Söder, where the museums range from old-fashioned (The Nordic Museum) to positively psychedelic (ABBA: The Museum), and where the world's first bar made from ice coexists with a luminescent tiki bar. Stockholm is the city to visit in Scandinavia, and it draws a crowd to match. Spend some time in one of the city's numerous hostels (which are the best in Scandinavia), and you'll meet every kind of traveler, from backpackers who packed three pairs of socks to child millionaires with more suitcases than can fit under a dorm bed. No matter where you fall in the duffel bag vs. three suitcase debate, you'll find something in Stockholm. Foodies can choose between gourmet coffee and pickled herring, history buffs from crown jewels and ancient cannons, and outdoor adventurers from kayaks and bicycles. One thing's for sure, though: no matter what you choose, you'll never be bored.

## ORIENTATION

Stockholm is the biggest city in Scandinavia and is truly urban with an extensive and highly efficient public transportation system and many neighborhoods with distinct character. At the center of it all is the bustling **Norrmalm district,** where you'll find **Stockholm Central Station** and the busy shopping street, **Drottninggatan.** Norrmalm is flanked to the west by **Kungsholmen,** a growing residential area home to City Hall, and to the east by Östermalm, Stockholm's most extravagant neighborhood. Östermalm is filled with expensive stores, Ferrari dealerships, and cafés rampant with suit-clad men who carry briefcases (not just because they're European, but also because they're rich). To the south are several notable islands, housing **Gala Stan, Södermalm,** and **Djurgården.** Djurgården has many interesting museums and cultural sights like **ABBA The Museum, Gröna Lund, the Vasa Museum,** and **Skansen.** Gamla Stan, just south of

Norrmalm, is the **Old Town,** where you'll find narrow, cobblestone streets packed with tourists, restaurants for tourists, and shops for tourists, as well as the **Royal Palace.** Finally, just south of Gamla Stan is Södermalm (usually shortened to Söder), an old working-class neighborhood-turned hipster hangout spot.

# ESSENTIALS

## GETTING THERE

Stockholm's main airport is Stockholm Arlanda, located about 40km north of the city with flights to most major European cities, as well as a few airports in North America and Asia. The easiest way to get between Arlanda and Stockholm Central Station is the Arlanda Express, a 20min. train ride with departures every 15min. most of the day. One-way tickets cost SEK 280 for adults (26 and older), SEK 150 for people 25 and under, and SEK 140 for students, and can be booked online at www.arlandaexpress.com. Stockholm Central Station (Stockholm C) is the main train station in Stockholm. Trains to destinations around Sweden are operated by SJ. The main hall is open daily 5am-1:15am, though parts of the station open earlier.

## GETTING AROUND

Public transportation in Stockholm includes buses, a metro system (called Tunnelbana), trams, and ferries around the city. Tickets can be purchased on the SL app or at ticket kiosks. Tickets cannot be purchased on board buses or trams. If you plan on using public transportation more than a few times, it makes sense to purchase a travel card for SEK 20. With the card, you can buy a pass for 24hr (SEK 120, SEK 80 discounted), 72hr (SEK 240, SEK 160 discounted), or one week (\SEK 315, SEK 210 discounted). Stockholm has a city bike program with over 100 stations across the city. A 3-day rental costs SEK 165 and can be purchased at most tourist centers. Bikes can be taken from any stand and returned to any stand, but each individual bike must be returned within three hours.

## PRACTICAL INFORMATION

**Tourist Offices:** Stockholm Visitor Center (Kulturhuset, Sergels Torg 3-5, 8 508 28 508; open May 1-Sept 15 M-F 9am-7pm, Sa 9am-4pm, Su 10am-4pm; Sept 16-Apr 30 M-F 9am-6pm, Sa 9am-4pm, Su 10am-4pm).

**Banks/ATMs/Currency Exchange:** If you need hard currency (unlikely), exchanges are available at Arlanda Airport and Stockholm Central Station, though you may be better off just finding an ATM (Bankomat in Swedish) on the street.

**Post Offices:** Sweden's postal service is called PostNord, and doesn't have many brick-and-mortar locations. Letters can be mailed on the street, or at private mail centers like Mail Boxes Etc. (Torsgatan 2; 8 124 494 00; open June 26-Aug 21 M-F 10am-6pm, Sa 10am-2pm, Aug 22-June 25: M-F 8am-7pm, Sa 10am-2pm).

**Internet:** The Stockholm Visitor Center, Arlanda Airport, and Stockholm Central Station also have Wi-Fi.

**BGLTQ+ Resources:** RFSL is the Swedish Federation for Lesbian, Gay, Bisexual, and Transgender Rights (Sveavägen 59; 08 501 62 950; www. rfslstockholm.com).

## EMERGENCY INFORMATION

**Emergency Number:** 112. For 24-hour non-emergency health advice, call 1177.

**Police:** Norrmalm Police Station (Kungsholmsgaten 43; 114 14; open daily 24hr).

**US Embassy:** There is a US Embassy in Stockhom (Dag Hammarskjölds Väg 31; 08 783 53 00; open M-F 8am-4:30pm).

**Rape Crisis Center:** Södersjukhuset, one of Stockholm's main hospitals, has a 24hr telephone hotline and an emergency clinic for rape victims on the second floor (Sjukhusbacken 10; 08 616 46 70).

**Hospitals:**
- Karolinska University Hospital, Solna (Karolinska vägen; 8 517 700 00; open daily 24hr).
- Södersjukhuset (SÖS) (Sjukhus-backen 10; 8 616 10 00; open daily 24hr).

**Pharmacies:** Pharmacies in Stockholm (called apotek) are widely available and generally open between 10am and 6pm. There is a 24hr pharmacy right across the street from Stockholm Central Station.

- Apoteket C W Scheele (Klarabergsgatan 64, open daily 24hr).

# ACCOMMODATIONS

### ⬛CITY BACKPACKERS HOSTEL ($$)
Upplandsgatan 2a; 8 206 920; www.citybackpackers.org; reception open 8am-midnight

There are only two reasons that you should ever consider a hostel in Stockholm other than City Backpackers: it's absolutely booked solid, or you hate good times, friendship, chocolate, weekends, and all else that is good in the world. The beds are soft as clouds, the décor looks like it was picked out by a hipster from the 1950s—complete with cartoon posters of snowboarding monks and retro TV sets—and the guests are overwhelmingly young and outgoing. The kitchen and common room are often so full on Friday and Saturday nights that the party sometimes never even leaves the hostel, though it may move upstairs into the outdoor courtyard and bar.

*i* Dorms from SEK 300, privates from SEK 820; reservation recommended; 7 nights; BGLTQ+ friendly; no wheelchair accessibility ; Wi-Fi; linens SEK 24; laundry facilities SEK 50; breakfast SEK 65, SEK 55 if booked at check-in

### CITY HOSTEL ($)
Fleminggatan 19 ; 8 410 038 30; www.cityhostel.se/en; reception open 9am-6pm

City Hostel is a solid choice, with a prime location downtown and a slew of amenities, including an enormous kitchen, and bathrooms fitted with speakers blaring The Strokes all night long. The clientele falls all over the age spectrum, but it shouldn't be hard to find other young travelers happy to check out the long list of nightlife recommendations posted by the staff. Alcohol isn't permitted in the hostel, though, so don't expect any of the debauchery you'll find down the street at City Backpackers.

*i* Dorms from SEK 240, privates from SEK 495; reservation recommended; BGLTQ+ friendly; no wheelchair accessibility; Wi-Fi; linens included; laundry SEK 30

### SKANSTULLS HOSTEL ($)
Ringvägen 135; 8 643 03 04; www.skanstulls.se/en; reception open 9am-8pm

You simply can't go wrong hosteling in Stockholm, and Skanstulls certainly lives up to the hype. Its prime location in **Söder** means you're never far from some of the city's best (and cheapest) bars, the kitchen and lounge are decked out with plush chairs and plenty of cooking space, and free pasta means you'll never go hungry, even as a backpacker on a budget. It's also right next to the **Skanstulls subway station,** keeping you connected to **Gamla Stan** and the city center.

*i* Dorms from SEK 235, privates from 540; reservation recommended; max stay 7 nights; BGLTQ+ friendly; Wi-Fi; linen SEK 50; lockers provided; breakfast SEK 75

# SIGHTS
## CULTURE

### ⬛STOCKHOLM PALACE
Slottsbacken 1; 8 402 60 00; www.kungahuset.se; open July-Aug daily 9am-5pm, May-June/Sept daily 10am-5pm, Oct-Apr Tu-Su 10am-4pm

Now before you jump up and rush over here to meet the king and queen, there are two things you might want to know: the royal family doesn't actually live here and this isn't the original palace (that one, you'll be surprised to hear, burned down in 1697). But it's not as boring as it sounds. Since the royals aren't around, much of the palace is open to the public. Guided tours of the **Royal Apartments** are available several times daily through the summer, and the treasury houses, well, treasures, like **Gustav Vasa's** sword of state and **Erik XIV's** orb, whatever the hell an orb is.

*i* Admission SEK 160, SEK 80 student, guided tour SEK 20; tours daily May-Sept: Royal Apartments 10:30am, 1:30pm, 3:30pm; Treasury 11:30am; limited wheelchair accessibility; different parts of the

tour SEK 30; check website
for seasonal tour times; no
wheelchair accessibility

### GRÖNA LUND
Lilla Allmänna Gränd 9;
010 708 91 00; www.
gronalund.com; open
daily 10am-11pm

Gröna Lund is
Stockholm's answer
to Six Flags, Lake
Compounce, or
whatever your local
version of a hot, sweaty
amusement park packed
with too many strollers,
ill-fitting tank tops, and
screaming kids happens to be
called. It has all your favorite
vomit-inducing favorites, like the
carousel and teacups, but it also has
real roller coasters. Multiple streets
are lined with carnival games and
food stands, and the park even hosts
concerts through the summer, with
big time artists like the 1975 and Zara
Larsson, as well as your dad's washed
up favorites like Elton John and Alice
Cooper.

*i* Admission SEK 115, rides SEK 25-75
each, all-day pass SEK 330; wheelchair
accessible

## LANDMARKS

### CITY HALL
Hantverkargatan 1; 8 508 290 58; www.
international.stockholm.se/the-city-hall;
open daily 9am-4pm

Much like you during your freshman
year of college, Stockholm's City Hall
has a bit of an identity crisis. It has
a garden filled with fountains and
marble statues and an area surrounded
by columns and painted with symbols
from Roman mythology in the style
of a grand palace—an idea only
slightly undercut by the fact that
the rest of the building is made of
red brick. Regardless, City Hall is
right downtown, and its garden is a
great spot to relax and enjoy views of
Stockholm's skyline. You can pay for a
tour up into the tower, which rises over
the city.

*i* Guided tours Apr-Oct SEK 110, SEK 90
student, Nov-Mar SEK 90, SEK 70 student;

palace
complex have different
hours, so check online; ticket valid for one
week

### DROTTNINGHOLM
178 02 Drottningholm; www.kungahuset.
se; open Jan 1-Jan 7 daily noon-3:30pm,
Jan 8-March Sa-Su noon-3pm, Apr daily
11am-3:30pm, May-Sept daily 10am-
4:30pm, Oct F-Su 11am-3:30pm, Nov-Dec
10 Sa-Su noon-3:30pm, Dec 31 noon-
3:30pm

Drottningholm is the reason the royals
abandoned the **Royal Palace** and
it's not hard to see why. This palace
is just as impressive, but everything
is quieter since it's outside the city.
Drottningholm, a **UNESCO World
Heritage site,** has a proper palace
that the Swedes proudly describe as
their "answer to Versailles," though
that seems a bit presumptuous. It can't
really compare to the great gardens of
Europe, but it's certainly a beautiful
place to walk around, especially if the
weather decides to cooperate. For a fee,
you can visit the **Chinese Pavilion,**
which was an eighteenth-century king
gave to his queen as a gift. Apparently,
the offering of a small Chinese palace
was a pleasant surprise.

*i* Palace admission SEK 130, SEK 65
student; palace and Chinese Pavilion admission SEK 190, 90 SEK student; guided

tower ticket SEK 50; guided tours every 30min. from 9am-3:30pm (last tour at 4pm from June 7-Aug 27), tower tours every 40min. from 9:10am-5:10pm (last tour 3:50pm May-Sept); wheelchair accessible

## FREE TOUR STOCKHOLM

Sergels torg; www.freetourstockholm.com

Imagine you've just arrived in Stockholm after touring some of Scandinavia's quieter towns. All of a sudden, you're overwhelmed. Stockholm is big; it has multiple neighborhoods—multiple islands even! Be honest, you probably haven't planned very much, but your solution is simple: a free tour. Free Tour Stockholm offers tours every day to three different parts of the city, perfect for getting your bearings. The City tour hits all the basics: **Hötorget** (the open-air market), the **Concert Hall,** and the main shopping streets. The **Old Town tour** dives a bit more into history, with stops at the **Royal Palace** and several old buildings of note. If you're too trendy for that, the **Söder tour** takes you to the area sometimes called "Stockholm's Brooklyn." You can be the judge of that.

*i* Free, but tip the guide; city tour 10am, Södermalm tour 1pm, Old Town tour 4pm; only city tour is wheelchair accessible;

tours are 2hr; City and Old meet at the top of a large staircase by Sergels torg, Söder tour meets outside Slussen metro entrance by Södermalmstor

## GLOBEN

77 131 00 00; www.stockholmlive.com/en; open daily July 3-Aug 13 10am-8pm, Aug 14-July 2 M-F 10am-6pm, Sa-Su 10am-4pm

Next time you're at a Sweden-themed trivia night, remember Globen. It's the world's largest hemispherical building, and it also represents the sun in the **Sweden Solar System,** a scale model of the solar system (also the world's largest) that stretches across the entire country. Surely everyone's favorite narcissist, **Gustav Vasa,** would be happy to learn that Stockholm is indeed at the center of the universe. Globen is mainly used as a concert venue, but it's popular with travelers because of **SkyView,** a ride in a glass-walled gondola that travels up and over the top of the dome, providing some of the best aerial views of Stockholm.

*i* Admission SEK 150; last ride leaves 10min. before closing; wheelchair accessible

## IKEA

Ask most people what they know about Scandinavia, and they're likely to at least mention IKEA in their answer. Though it seems cheesy at this point, there's good reason for it: the furniture giant changed the (somewhat niche) world of ready-to-assemble furniture forever. And while the jury's still out over whether the company recently evaded about €1 billion in taxes, spend any time in Scandinavia and you're going to become quite familiar with its products. Hostels are full of IKEA merchandise, from bunks and mattresses to plates, cups, silverware, and just about everything else in the kitchen.

Stockholm is something of the epicenter of the global IKEA empire. Indeed, the Nordic Museum's exhibit on furniture seems like a thinly-veiled attempt to show off some of the country's finest design. IKEA's largest European store is just south of Stockholm in Kungens Kurva, and if you grew up in the kind of household that would take family trips to IKEA (wait, other families don't do that?), you just might enjoy paying it a visit. The Swedish meatballs are just a little bit more Swedish, and the plastic furniture shines just a little bit brighter than everything else, but don't worry; that damn desk is just as impossible to assemble as in the rest of the world.

Free shuttle buses leave hourly on weekdays from a stop across from Stockholm.

# UPPSALA

Today, **Uppsala is Sweden's fourth-largest city and often appears as nothing more than an interestingly-named blip on the map.** But until relatively recently, the city held a few very important distinctions. It was the site of the coronations of Swedish kings and queens until the eighteenth century, and today its cathedral is the center of Church of Sweden. Aside from its cultural significance, Uppsala is also one of the original college towns. Uppsala University was founded in 1477, and, much like the mob in early-twentieth-century New York, seems to have a hand in the workings of the city to this day. It runs a number of museums and gardens around Uppsala, and even accounts for a substantial portion of the population during the year with its enrollment of over 40,000. With that many students around, you can expect an abundance of coffee shops, cheap lunch deals, and a more relaxed atmosphere. Uppsala is a sleepy town, especially in the summer, but that could be just what you need after a few exhausting days in Stockholm.

Uppsala is a small city. The **Centrum district** contains **Uppsala Central Station,** as well as much of the city's shopping and restaurants. Most of the cultural sights and landmarks, along with **Uppsala University,** are across the river to the west. Here you'll find **Uppsala Castle** and **Uppsala Cathedral, Gustavianum,** and the **Botanical Garden.**

## GETTING THERE

Uppsala is less than 45min. from Stockholm by train. Trains between Stockholm and Uppsala, operated mostly by SJ, are frequent throughout the day, and round-trip tickets can often be purchased for less than SEK 200, either online (www.sj.com) or at Stockholm C and Uppsala Central Station (Uppsala C).

## GETTING AROUND

Uppsala is easily walkable from one end to the other. There is a bus system, called UL, that covers the city center. Single tickets cost SEK 28 if purchased in advance, or you can buy a 24hr pass for SEK 88.

## Swing by...

### UPPSALA CATHEDRAL

Domkyrkoplan; 1 84 30 36 30; www.uppsaladomkyrka.se; open daily 8am-6pm

Okay, it's a church. Surely, you've seen enough churches, right? Wrong. Uppsala Cathedral is the most important church in Sweden, as the seat of the **Archbishop of Uppsala,** and the tallest in all of Scandinavia. It's also probably the most interesting and recognizable building in the whole city, with its unusual combination of Gothic architecture and brick materials. Under the vaulted ceilings, frescoes, and stained-glass windows, the cathedral houses a huge collection of artifacts, as well as tombs of famous Swedes. The legendary king **Gustav Vasa** is buried here, and, if you're at all familiar with royal egos, it won't surprise you to learn that his tomb is decorated with a thank you letter to himself.

*i* Admission and cathedral tour free, tower and treasury admission SEK 50; summer tours Cathedral tour M-Sa 10am and 2pm, Su 3pm, treasury tour daily 4pm; wheel-chair accessible

## GUSTAVIANUM

Akademigatan 3; 1 847 175 71; www.gustavianum.uu.se; open June-Aug Tu-Su 10am-4pm, Sept-May Tu-Su 11am-5pm

You guessed it; this museum is named after a king named Gustav. You probably shouldn't be surprised at this point. The building has served a number of purposes for Uppsala University over the years, including dorm and classroom space, but today it functions as the university's history museum. The eclectic collection includes exhibits about ancient Egypt, Vikings, and (nerd alert) a room full of heavy duty scientific artifacts from physics, chemistry, and astronomy. But the centerpiece of the museum is the university's old anatomical theater, a steep, octagonal amphitheater where pre-meds of old would observe dissections of human cadavers.

*i* Admission adult SEK 50, student SEK 40; tours daily 1pm; wheelchair accessible

# Grab a bite at...

## DYLAN'S GRILL ($)

Vaksalagatan 10; www.dylansgrill.se; open M-T 11am-8pm, W-Sa 11am-10pm, Su 11am-8pm

With so many college students in such a small town, you're pretty much guaranteed a cheap burger joint, and Dylan's doesn't disappoint, with options like the Cowboy (with jalapeños and barbecue sauce) and the Farmer (with a fried egg). A double burger and fries cost less than SEK 100, so the broke student vibe is real here, especially with the cheap-but-charming orange and blue plastic furniture. Much like the '70s, it somehow all works out, you're just not sure how.

*i* Single burgers from SEK 60, doubles from SEK 75, fries SEK 20, shakes SEK 45; gluten-free and vegetarian options available; wheelchair accessible

# Don't miss...

## BOTANICAL GARDEN

Villavägen 6-8; The Park open May-Oct daily 7am-9pm, Nov-Apr daily 7am-7pm, Tropical Greenhouse June-Aug M-F 9am-3pm, Sa-Su 11am-4pm, Sept-May Tu-F 9am-3pm, Sa-Su noon-3pm

It's tough to make it big as a botanical garden in Europe; you have to compete with Versailles and the Kew Gardens, just to name two. Uppsala's answer? A rainforest. That's right; even though this dark horse of a garden may not have the fountains and peacocks of some of its southern counterparts, Uppsala's Botanical Garden has an entire greenhouse that mimics a tropical climate, in order to grow all sorts of plants that wouldn't last up north. In the unlikely event that you just can't get enough of that fine Swedish weather, another outdoor park has a wide variety of native plants and plenty of hidden benches where you can sit and contemplate life, or whatever it is that botanical gardens are for.

*i* Tropical Greenhouse SEK 50; park and garden tours June-Aug Sa-Sun 2pm; limited wheelchair accessibility

# STOCKHOLM'S SUBWAY ART

Most subway stations around the world aren't anything to write home about. But, in Stockholm, the standard of living is so damn high that the metro stops are works of art. Seriously, many of the underground stations are designed to look like grottos hewn straight from the bedrock and are painted with fantastic colors and murals. You'll probably stumble across a few on your own, but here are five you can't miss:

**1. Kungsträdgården (Blue Line):** This cave-like station is designed to look like an archaeological dig and features so many partially-unearthed sculptures and columns that you'll wonder why your ninth-grade history teacher somehow forgot to mention the Roman conquest of Sweden.

**2. Stadion (Red Line):** Stadion's sky-blue walls are webbed with gold veins, and the station is adorned with colorful pieces, including a spectacular and frequently photographed rainbow arching over the platform.

**3. Universitet (Red Line):** You may think you're on vacation from school, but Universitet station has other ideas. It contains tile mosaics displaying a collection of knowledge exceeding that of most libraries, from a map of ancient global spice trade routes to a detailed diagram of the human eye.

**4. Solna centrum (Blue Line):** Another cavernous station, this one featuring green forested landscapes against a blood red sky. The place is practically a museum and features a number of dioramas, including one of a large moose. You know, because nature.

**5. T-Centralen (All Lines):** This maze of a station has multiple themes, but the best is a rocky, blue-and-white platform with blue vines climbing the walls and silhouettes of construction workers still at work on the station. As if you weren't already seeing enough construction outside...

## RIKSDAGSHUSET (PARLIAMENT HOUSE)

Riksgatan 1; 8 786 40 00; www.riksdagen.se

This is where all the magic happens, folks. Here, that 25% value-added tax is levied, the socialist safety net constructed, and the blond-hair-and-blue-eyes mandate enacted. The Riksdaghuset's **Public Gallery** is open whenever the Riksdag is in session, so that Swedes and visitors alike can directly observe the political process. How refreshingly democratic! Guided tours are also available on weekdays during the summer, and weekends during the rest of the year, which provide more information about how the Riksdag works and about the buildings themselves and their history.

*i* Free; tours June 26-Aug 18 M-F noon, 1pm, 2pm, 3pm; wheelchair accessible

## MUSEUMS

### ABBA THE MUSEUM

Djurgårdsvägen 68; 7 717 575 75; www.abbathemuseum.com/en; open May 29-Sept 3 daily 9am-7pm, Sept 4-Oct 1 M-Tu 10am-6pm, W-Th 10am-7pm, F-Sa 10am-6pm, Oct 2-Oct 29 M-Tu noon-6pm, W-Th 10am-7pm, F-Su 10am-6pm, Oct 30-Nov 5 M-Tu 10am-6pm, W-Th 10am-7pm, F-Su 10am-6pm, Nov 6-Dec 31 M-Tu noon-6pm, W-Th 10am-7pm, F-Su 10am-6pm

ABBA: performers of "Dancing Queen," inspiration for *Mamma Mia!*, and that thing that happens when one of your parents gets hold of the aux cord. The museum is masterfully designed to make your heart ache for the days of bedazzled bodysuits and platform boots, regardless of whether or not you lived through them in the first place. See stage outfits worn in concert, a complete replica of ABBA's recording studio, and all sorts of authentic props and instruments from a more flamboyant time in music history. Get in on the action by hopping on the stage and singing along to an ABBA classic, alongside holograms of the bandmates (or at the very least, try and figure out who let their mom give it a try).

*i Admission SEK 250; last entry 90min. before closing; wheelchair accessible; card only; best to book visit online*

## NORDIC MUSEUM

Djurgårdsvägen 6-16; 8 519 546 00; www.nordiskamuseet.se/en; open daily June-Aug 9am-6pm, Sept-May M-Tu 10am-5pm, W 10am-8pm, Th-Su 10am-5pm

Despite being called the Nordic Museum, this museum focuses almost exclusively on Sweden. It covers over 500 years of Swedish history and looks at many different aspects of life, like furniture in the *Homes and Interiors* exhibit, the contemporary section of which is basically a giant temple to IKEA, and *Table Settings,* which depicts the transition of Swedish cuisine from lowly dishes like roast suckling pig to its ultimate form: meatballs. Another object of interest is a collection of Sweden's oldest dollhouses, which were apparently meant for adults.

*i Admission SEK 120; free audio guide; tours daily at 11am and 2pm; wheelchair accessible*

## VASA MUSEUM

Galärvarvsvägen 14; 8 519 548 00; www.vasamuseet.se/en; open daily June-Aug 8:30am-6pm, Sept-May M-Tu 10am-5pm, W 10am-8pm, Th-Su 10am-5pm

Many Scandinavian museums follow a similar plan. Take a boat, build a house around it, and voila: museum. The ship in question is the *Vasa,* named by and for one of those kings of the most egotistical Vasa dynasty, **Gustavus Adolphus.** Unfortunately for him, it turned out that the *Vasa* wasn't something you wanted to have your name on; it capsized and sank just 30 minutes into its maiden voyage. Today, you can learn about everything from its construction, to how it was sailed (briefly) and how it (would have) performed in battle. Vasa is the most visited museum in Scandinavia, so anticipate crowds.

*i Admission SEK 130, SEK 110 student; tours daily June-Aug every half hour from 9:30-4:30; wheelchair accessible; free audio guide*

# OUTDOORS

## ARCHIPELAGO BOAT TOUR

Strandvägen Berth 15-16; 8 120 040 45; www.stromma.se

Throwback to your fifth-grade geography class: "archipelago" is just a fancy word for a big group of islands. You've probably seen a few of the main ones, like **Djurgården,** home of the **Vasa** and **ABBA museums,** and **Södermalm,** but the islands extend far to east, all the way out into the Baltic Sea. In all, the Stockholm Archipelago consists of about 30,000 islands. You'll never come close to seeing them all, but a good place to start is with a boat tour. Sit back and relax as you cruise out of Stockholm and into the islands. Your guide will explain the history of certain buildings, as well as how some of the sillier names came about, like a group of islands named Monday, Tuesday, Wednesday, etc. Creative.

*i Tours from SEK 280; 2.5-3hr tours run at 10:30am, noon, 1:30pm, and 3pm; limited wheelchair accessibility*

## SJÖCAFÉET KAYAK AND BIKE RENTAL

Galärvarvsvägen 2; 8 660 57 57; www.sjocafeet.se; open daily Apr-Sept 9am-9pm

Tour agencies like to call Stockholm the "Venice of the North," due to the large network of canals and islands that make up the city. That may be a bit of an overstatement, but if you want to get closer to the water than possible on a big motor boat or cruise ship, kayaking is a great option. Sjöcaféet is a café located conveniently on the north shore of the island Djurgården that offers kayak, bicycle, and even peddle boat rentals for anyone who can't decide between the two.

*i Bicycle SEK 80 per hour, SEK 275 per day, kayak SEK 125 per hour, SEK 400 per day; no wheelchair accessibility*

# FOOD

## ◪KAJSAS FISK ($$)

Hötorgshallen 3; 8 20 72 62; www.kajsas-fisk.se; open M-Th 11am-6pm, F 11am-7pm, Sa 11am-4pm

Kajsas Fisk is located in the basement of **Hötorgshallen food hall,** surrounded by artisanal butchers and fish vendors selling things that look more like ET than fish. Most of the other restaurants around are too expensive to consider, but Kajsas Fisk has one of the better deals in the city with its fish soup: a big, steaming bowl, chock-full of fish, mussels, spices, shrimp, and a dollop of secret sauce. Plus, help yourself to unlimited bread and salad. For just SEK 110, it might be the best deal since the Louisiana Purchase.

*i Entrées SEK 100-150, beer from SEK 55; wheelchair accessible*

### JOHAN & NYSTRÖM ($$)

Swedenborgsgatan 7; 8 702 20 40; www. johanochnystrom.se; open M-F 7am-8pm, Sa-Su 8am-7pm

In a neighborhood like **Södermalm,** it takes a lot to stand out as a coffee shop. "Hip, young café," describes just about every establishment around, but Johan & Nyström might be the best one. An apron-clad barista will fix you up a cappuccino from the rainbow-striped espresso machine or a cup of coffee so smooth that even the most devoted Starbucks latte-lover will think twice before asking for milk and sugar. The outdoor seating area is shaded, so you can break out your denim overalls, Södermalm style, without breaking a sweat, even on the sunniest Stockholm day.

*i Brewed coffee SEK 40, espresso drinks, tea, and tea-based drinks SEK 30-50*

### NYSTEKT STRÖMMING ($)

Södermalmstorg; open daily 11am-9pm

Scandinavia is sorely lacking in the street food department, especially compared to Southeast Asia, the Middle East, and, frankly, the rest of the world, but, if you're committed to delicious, cheap meals prepared in questionably sanitary conditions, there's only one place for it: Nystekt Strömming. This food cart right outside the **Slussen subway station** offers a few seafood options, but if it's local street food you want, there's no question about it. You have to get the fried herring: three pieces of breaded and fried fish (significantly more palatable than its fermented counterpart), sweet pickles, and a scoop of mashed potatoes big enough

to make a starving Viking tear up with joy.

*i Entrées SEK 50-100; wheelchair accessible*

# NIGHTLIFE

### ◪AIFUR

Västerlånggatan 68b; 8 20 10 55; www. aifur.se; open M-Th 5pm-11pm, F-Ss 5pm-1am

Spend more than a few days in any Nordic country and, like the coastal farmers of medieval Europe, you'll be sick of Vikings. Aifur wants you to give them a second chance (though it might be a bit tougher convincing those peasants). It's a restaurant and bar designed completely in the Viking tradition with replicas of spears and shields and proudly serving mead from earthenware mugs. There's live music, even on weeknights, from a variety of performers on fiddles and hand drums, all dressed the part. To top it all off, the whole place is in a vaulted cellar designed to look like an ancient mead hall. The place couldn't be more Nordic even if Thor himself was lounging in his favorite IKEA chair in the corner.

*i Mead from SEK 90, beer from SEK 70; BGLTQ+ friendly; wheelchair accessible*

### ◪BREWDOG

Ringvägen 149b; www.brewdog.com; open M-Th 4pm-midnight; F-Sa 2pm-1am; Su 2pm-11pm

Whether or not that thing in the logo can really be called a dog is still an open question, but what's not up for debate is the quality of the beer at BrewDog, a hip microbrewery in an even more hip neighborhood: Söder. Pick from a rotating carousel of house and guest brews with the inventive names you've come to expect. Forgot your overalls and man bun? Get the same effect with a glass of the Colonial Hipster, a New England IPA. Looking for something familiar? You can't go wrong with the PBR (Perhaps Blue Ribbon; get your head out of the frat house). BrewDog has something for everyone, and a casual atmosphere perfect for nights when you want to drink, chat, and not be hungover in the morning.

*i* Beer SEK 70; BGLTQ+ friendly; no wheelchair accessibility

### ICEBAR
Vasaplan 4; 8 505 635 20; www.icebar-stockholm.com; open M-Th 11:15am-midnight, F-Sa 11:15am-1am

You'd think that the novelty of a bar entirely made of ice would be somewhat lost in a place like Sweden, but apparently it isn't. In fact, Icebar was the world's first such establishment, and it's still going strong. The dress code is very strict: a furry poncho with attached gloves (don't worry, it looks equally ridiculous on everyone), and a glass made of ice (don't break it, or you'll have to pay for a replacement). As advertised, the walls, bar, and seats are all hewn straight from the ice, and the temperature is maintained at a positively balmy 19oF. Gimmicky? Definitely a little, but that doesn't mean you can't still have a good time.

*i* Admission (includes first cocktail) SEK 199 pre-booked, SEK 210 at the door, cocktails SEK 95, shots SEK 75; BGLTQ+ friendly; wheelchair accessible; last entry 45min. before closing

# SWEDEN ESSENTIALS

## VISAS
Sweden is a member of the European Union and is part of the Schengen Area, so US citizens can stay in Sweden for up to 90 days without a visa.

## MONEY
Sweden's currency is the Swedish krona, officially abbreviated SEK and locally used interchangeably with kr.

**Tipping**: Tipping in Sweden is neither expected nor required; a gratuity is often included in the service charge at restaurants. If there is no service charge, or if you received particularly excellent service, feel free to tip 5-10%, or to round the bill to the nearest SEK 10.

**Taxes:** Sweden's standard VAT rate is a steep 25%, and is included in all posted prices. Some stores in Sweden, specifically those with Global Blue stickers, will refund the VAT for goods leaving the country with you. Be sure to ask at the counter for specifics, and to save receipts for any goods for which you are claiming a refund.

## SAFETY AND HEALTH
**Alcohol:** There is technically no purchasing age for beverages under 2.25% ABV, though stores will often set their own age limits. Alcohol stronger than 2.25% ABV is strictly regulated. It is sold in bars and restaurants, where it cannot leave the premises and the purchasing age is 18, and in government-owned stores called Systembolaget, where the purchasing age is 20.

**BGLTQ+ Travel:** Like the rest of Scandinavia, Sweden is very liberal when it comes to BGLTQ+ rights. Hostels, restaurants, and nightlife establishments are very friendly towards the BGLTQ+ community, and many Swedish cities have dedicated BGLTQ+ nightlife venues.

# SWITZERLAND

**Switzerland jams to a different beat than the rest of Europe.** A collection of Confederate states in the middle of the European continent, it's surprisingly diverse, both culturally and linguistically—you'll find yourself speaking English, French, and German during your stay here… maybe even during the same day! Switzerland's cultural diversity lies, in part, in the interplay of religions between neighboring lands. Both the Zwingli Protestant Reformation and Calvinist movement took place in Zurich and Geneva, respectively. Switzerland's rich history has been enhanced by a commitment to neutrality amidst world conflict, as evidenced by the country's actions during the First and Second World Wars. Visiting Switzerland comes with a hefty price tag, as it happens to be one of the most expensive countries in Europe, but, if we had to pick a place to cash out, this is it.

More than just cheese, watches, chocolate, skiing, and Roger Federer, Switzerland boasts a kind of natural beauty that's hard to find in Europe. Your visit to Switzerland will, without a doubt, be augmented by breathtaking views of pristine lakes and snow-capped mountains. Whether you're coming in the summer to paraglide in Gimmelwald or in the winter to ski on Jungfrau, you've come to the right place. Hike the cow-covered trails in the mountains. Watch majestic glaciers crash, creating spectacles you could never make up. Take to the streets and explore the Lac Léman area in the student-filled city of Lausanne. Pretend to be a United Nations diplomat in Geneva while simultaneously admiring one of the grandest mountain ranges on the planet. We can't guarantee that you'll see Roger during your trip, but you never know who's on the trail with you.

633

# GENEVA

Coverage by **Alejandro Lampell**

A cosmopolitan city with a vibrant international community, Geneva is the indisputable belle of Switzerland. Situated on the shore of Lac Léman (Lake Geneva), the city is surrounded by towering, stately French Alps on all fronts, meaning that wherever you are, you'll have an unparalleled view of them. Geneva was originally established as a Roman outpost and the city has a strong historical significance. Well-preserved buildings like St. Pierre's Cathedral litter the Old Town. The cathedral, a European heritage site, served as a refuge for Jean Calvin; it was here that he professed his Calvinist ideas of austerity and advocated for returning to basic interpretations of the Bible itself. Geneva's proximity to France resulted in an influx of Counter-Reformation ideas and to the city, which in turn led to a mix of culture and belief still present today. Home to more than 22 international organizations including the International Committee of the Red Cross, the World Health Organization, and—how could we forget—the United Nations, the city has established itself as a powerhouse on the international stage.

## ORIENTATION

The city of Geneva is located in the westernmost region of Switzerland on the southwestern shore of **Lac Léman** (Lake Geneva), with suburbs extending into neighboring France. The city is split by the **Rhône River**—which transports the water from Lac Léman to the Mediterranean Sea—into **Rive Gauche,** the left bank, and **Rive Droite,** the right bank. The Rive Droite is the area of the city north of the Rhône River; here you'll find the main train station, the headquarters of several international organizations, and the airport. The **Pâquis District,** close to the main train station, is filled with international restaurants and upscale hotels, and is where the city's prostitution and drug markets are most concentrated. The **Vieille Ville** (Old Town), whose center is the picturesque **Place du Bourg-de-Four,** is located on the Rive Gauche and filled with chic bistros. **Rue du Rhône** is one of the main shopping streets in the city, filled with upscale shops and the equivalent of Swiss shopping malls. To the northeast of the city center is **Collonge-Bellerive,** Geneva's most expensive residential area. In this neighborhood stands the **Villa Diodati,** where Mary Shelley worked on her seminal work, *Frankenstein*.

## ESSENTIALS

### GETTING THERE

Geneva has the second largest international airport in Switzerland after Zurich. The airport is located 4km from the city center and is easily accessible via the public transportation system. Upon arrival at the airport, you can collect a free, 80-minute public transportation ticket that covers Zone 10, Tout Genève. In order to use this ticket, you have to provide a valid plane ticket. Take the tram to the main train station, Gare de Cornavin. The main bus station is Gare Routière de Genève, located a 5-minute walk from the Gare de Cornavin. This station

serves both domestic and international travel. Buses are typically cheaper than trains, but may not be as reliable.

### GETTING AROUND

Most of Geneva can be covered on foot or bike. You can rent a bike from the Genève Roule stops for four hours of free bike-riding with a 2CHF deposit. There are six stations around the city. Geneva has a fairly efficient public transportation system (Transports Public Genevois) that includes buses, trams, and boats. Download the TP app to view the bus and tram schedule. The public transportation system is divided into different zones. Zone 10 is the zone for Tout Genève, the proper city of Geneva and suburbs. Zones 21, 22, 81, 82, 84, 85, 86, 87, 88 and 90 are the regional zones outside the city, some in the Canton of Geneva and others in France. As of 2008, public transport is free if you are staying at a hostel or hotel in the area. You will receive a Geneva Transport Card, which is valid for the duration of your stay (maximum 15 days). If you are planning to use the public transport system and do not have the Geneva Transport Card, then you must buy a Tout Genève pass. A one-hour ticket costs 3CHF.

## PRACTICAL INFORMATION

**Tourist Offices:** Geneva Tourist Information Office (Rue du Mont-Blanc 18; 022 909 70 00; open M-W 9am-6pm, Th 10am-6pm, F-S 9am-6pm, Su/public holidays 10am-4pm).

**Banks/ATMs/Currency Exchange:** There are banks and ATMs all over the city. One of the best currency exchange houses is Migros Change (Rue du Mont-Blanc 16; 058 573 29 40; open M-F 8:30am-6:30pm, Sa 9am-6pm).

**Post Offices:** There are many different post offices throughout the city, but the largest one is located by the main train station (Rue des Gares 16; 0848 888 888; open M-F 9am-7pm, Sa 9am-noon).

**Internet:** The city of Geneva boasts more than 78 spots with free Wi-Fi. You can get a map at the Tourist Information Office with all of the locations. You can also rent out a Wi-Fi router at the Tourist Information Center (3 days 39.90CHF, 7 days 64.90CHF, 15 days 129.90CHF).

**BGLTQ+ Resources:** The main BGLTQ+ helpline in Switzerland is 080 013 31 33.

## EMERGENCY INFORMATION

**Emergency Numbers:** General (112); police (117); fire department (118); ambulance (144); Swiss Helicopter Rescue Service (1414)

**Police:** Fondation Privée de secours du Syndicat de la Police Judiciaire (Blvd. Carl-Vogt 17; 022 427 81 11; open M-F 9am-4pm).

**US Embassy:** Consular Agency in Geneva (Rue Versonnex 7; 22 840

51 60; open M-F 10am-1pm, by appointment only).

**Rape Crisis Center:** Rape Centre (Pl. des Charmilles 3; 022 345 20 20; information for different types of hotlines in Geneva can be found at www.angloinfo.com/how-to/switzerland/geneva/healthcare/support-groups).

**Hospitals:** The Geneva University Hospital is the biggest in the country (Rue Gabrielle-Perret-Gentil 4; 022 372 33 11; open daily 24hr).

**Pharmacies:** Pharmacie Amavita Gare Cornavin (Gare Cornavin; 058 878 10 00; open M-Sa 7am-11pm, Su 9am-11pm).

# ACCOMMODATIONS

### ◪GENEVA HOSTEL ($$)
Rue Rothschild 28-30; 022 732 62 60; www.genevahostel.ch; reception open 24hr

Wedged between the lake and a collection of international organization headquarters, Geneva Hostel has a very lean, clean look and boasts all of the amenities required while on the road: spacious rooms, sturdy wooden bunks, an attentive and welcoming staff—you name it. The modern, cubic lounge chairs in the lobby are consistently occupied, as is the upstairs terrace, which provides a stunning view of the city.

*i* *Dorm 36CHF; reservation recommended; max stay 6 nights; wheelchair accessible; Wi-Fi; linens included; laundry 8CHF*

### CITY HOSTEL GENEVA ($$)
Rue Ferrier 2; 022 901 15 00; www.cityhostel.ch; reception open 7:30am-noon, 1pm-midnight

City Hostel Geneva provides some of the only affordable housing in this city and is usually full. It attracts a diverse community of travelers, from students on class trips to retirees celebrating dipping into their life savings. Don't let City Hostel's dilapidated block façade fool you; the inside of the hostel is very modern, boasting several useful amenities such as a laundry room, a TV room (which tends to be underutilized), and free Wi-Fi. The hostel provides a free city transportation card for the duration of your stay and the friendly staff will eagerly provide recommendations for things to do in the surrounding area.

*i* Dorm 37-41CHF, single room (shared bathroom) 80-115CHF, single room (private bathroom) 90-135CHF, double room (per room, shared bathroom) 86-115CHF, double room (per room, private bathroom) 96-135CHF, parking per night 11CHF; reservation recommended; max stay for dorm 8 days, max for private 21 days; BGLTQ+ friendly; no wheelchair accessibility; Wi-Fi; laundry 8.50CHF, detergent 1CHF

# SIGHTS

## CULTURE
........................................................

### PLACE DU BOURG-DE-FOUR
Place du Bourg-de-Four; open daily 24hr

Formerly a cattle marketplace and a Roman forum, the Place du Bourg-de-Four is now a lively square in the middle of **Old Town.** Enjoy an espresso on the patio of one of various cafes and relax in the shadows cast by eighteenth-century buildings, squeezed tightly together along the perimeter of the square. At night, the square glows a pale yellow—lit up by vintage bistro lights and the laughter of patrons.

*i* Price varies by restaurant; limited wheelchair accessibility

## LANDMARKS
........................................................

### JET D'EAU
Central Lake Geneva (corner of Quai Gustave Ador and Rue du 31); Jan 2-Mar 5 open M-Su 10am-4pm, Mar 6-Apr 30 open M-Th 10am-sunset, F-Su 10am-10:30pm, May 1-Sept 10 M-Su 9am-11:15pm, Sept 11-Oct 29 M-Th 10am-sunset, F-Su 10am-10:30pm, Oct 30-Nov 15 annual maintenance, Nov 16-Mar 4 10am-4pm

Originally built to control the excess pressure from a hydraulic plant, this stunning fountain has become a symbol of innovation and progress. With water leaving the sprout at a velocity of 200km per hour and reaching a height of 140 meters, the fountain is a striking reminder of both the power of the natural world and of the human mind. Situated right at the harbor where the **River Rhône** meets the lake, the enormous stream is visible from almost anywhere in the city. After

sunset, lights illuminate the water, creating a surreal display of colors. Make sure to bring a bathing suit if you plan to get up close and personal; the wind tends to change quickly by the waterfront, and what appear to be dry docks could become soaking wet in a matter of seconds.

*i* Free; wheelchair accessible

### PALAIS DES NATIONS
Pregny Gate (Av. de la Paix 14); 022 917 12 34; www.unog.ch/visits; open Sep-Mar M-F 10am-noon and 2pm-4pm, Apr-Aug M-Sa 10am-noon and 2pm-4pm

At the Palais des Nations, the only thing keeping you from the paradise that is the thought of tangible social progress is an airport-style security checkpoint. Contrary to what one might assume, tours of this complex begin at the back of the palace, not the flag-lined main entrance. If you visit during a conference, you may have the rare opportunity of sitting in on an actual **United Nations** meeting. If your timing does not line up, rest assured that you'll still be able to explore the very same rooms that have hosted some of the greatest debates in human history. Make sure to check out the **Broken Chair Sculpture,** a monument imagined and constructed in the adjacent plaza by Swiss artist **Daniel Berset** after the passing of the **Ottawa Treaty,** on your way out.

*i* Admission adult 12CHF, 10CHF student, children 7CHF; wheelchair accessible; tours at 10:30am, noon, 2:30pm, and 4pm; visitors must check luggage and large personal items

### CATHÉDRALE ST. PIERRE
Place du Bourg-de-Four 24; 022 311 75 75; www.cathedrale-geneve.ch; open June 1-Sept 30 M-F 9:30am-6:30pm, Sa 9:30am-5pm, Su noon-6:30pm (bell ringing 5pm, organ concert 6pm), Jan 10-May 31 M-Sa 10am-5:30pm, Su noon-5:30pm

The place of **John Calvin's** revolutionary sermons, St. Pierre's Cathedral—a **European Heritage Site**—is located in the heart of Geneva's old city. The building's ornate façades contrast sharply with its simple Protestant interior—a physical testament to the city's diverse cultural composition. Two towers jut from the roof of the church: the southern-facing one holds five bells, while the northern one boasts a stunning panoramic view of the city and of the **Jet d'Eau** in the distance.

*i* *Church entrance free, entrance to tower adult 5CHF, 2CHF under 16; last entry to tower 30min. before closing; limited wheelchair accessibility*

## MUSEUMS

### MUSÉE INTERNATIONAL DE LA CROIX-ROUGE ET DU CROIS-SANT-ROUGE

Avenue de la Paix 17; 022 748 95 11; www.redcrossmuseum.ch; open Nov-Mar Tu-Su 10am-5pm, Apr-Oct Tu-Su 10am-6pm

The Musée International de la Croix-Rouge et du Croissant-Rouge addresses three of the largest problems facing modern society—defending human dignity, reconstructing family links, and reducing natural risks—through a series of eye-opening exhibits and testimonials from those suffering from different forms of marginalization or displacement. Appropriately located near the headquarters of the **Red Cross Organization,** this museum is a necessary and worthwhile stop on any tour of Geneva.

*i* *Adults 15CHF, 7CHF student and senior (65+); wheelchair accessible*

### MICROCOSM MUSEUM (CERN)

Route de Meyrin 385; 022 767 84 84; www.microcosm.web.cern.ch; open M-F 8:30am-5:30pm, Sa 9am-5pm, closed May 1st, May 25th, June 5th; Universe of Particles exhibition open M-Sa 10am-pm

At the edge of the Swiss country lies the CERN Large Hadron Collider, one of the largest research institutes in the world. At the Microcosm Museum, you'll learn all about the technology behind the equipment, the discoveries, and life at CERN

from video testimonials. Just across the French border is the **Universe of Particles,** an interactive exhibit that describes the beginning of the universe and the composition of matter in a futuristic-style room. The 30-minute ride from the city might seem long, but these fun—and most importantly free—museums can keep people of all ages entertained the whole day.

*i* *Free; limited wheelchair accessibility; guided tours at 11am and 1pm*

## OUTDOORS

### JARDIN D'ANGLAIS

Quai du Général-Guisan 34; www.ville-geneve.ch/plan-ville/parcs-jardins-plages-bains-publics/jardin-anglais; open daily 24hr

Inspired by the landscape architecture characteristic of English gardens, this small park overlooking Lake Geneva and the famous Jet d'Eau provides a relaxing and jovial respite from the city. Highlights include the **Flower Clock,** which consists of more than 12,000 individual plantings, and the **National Monument,** which honors

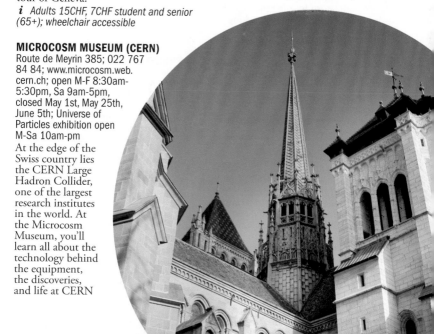

Geneva's incorporation into the Swiss confederation.

*i* *Free; wheelchair accessible*

# FOOD

### BIRDIE ($$)
Rue des Bains 40; 022 320 29 00; www.birdiecoffee.com; open T-F 8am-6pm, Sa-Su 10am-6pm

A small coffee shop that offers all of the staples—cappuccinos, lattes, macchiatos, espressos, and the like—Birdie was one of our favorite hubs of grub/workplaces/caffeination stations in Geneva. Brunch-style meals are offered every day between 8:30am and 2:30pm, and if you don't happen to like the beans Birdie keeps in stock, you can ask a barista to grind your own beans for you. Sip away to the tune of smooth jazz and indulge in even smoother Wi-Fi.

*i* *Coffee 4-6CHF, entrées 16-20CHF; vegetarian options available; wheelchair accessible*

### BOKY ($)
Rue des Alpes 21; 022 738 37 94; open M-Sa 11am-11pm

Boky does Chinese comfort food and does it well. With heaping plates and prices geared towards a backpacking budget, this is a great place to come with friends and sample several dishes. Swing by on weekdays at noon for all-you-can-eat buffet (22.50CHF) of fried noodles, dumplings, and Beijing duck; you'll leave with enough food in your belly to last you the day .

*i* *Appetizers 8CHF, entrées 16CHF; vegetarian options available; wheelchair accessible*

### INGLEWOOD ($)
Blvd. du Pont-d'Arve 44; 022 320 38 66; www.inglewood.ch; open M-Sa 11:30am-2:30pm and 7pm-10pm

Why someone would want to name a restaurant after the city of Inglewood escapes us. What doesn't escape us is the memory of sinking our teeth into Pasadena for the first time. *No, not the city, silly. The burger!* If you haven't already caught on, Inglewood's menu consists primarily of burgers

named after cities in California. Unlike the drought-stricken state, these puppies are *juicy*—no dearth of moisture here. Like the Golden State, however, Inglewood's buns are smooth and tan, grilled to perfection before functioning as the capstones to each delicious package. Make sure to flash your student ID at the registe—it may qualify you for a free drink.

*i* *Burger meal 15-18CHF; vegetarian options available; wheelchair accessible*

### WASABI 4 ($$)
Rue du Mont-Blanc; 022 732 36 38; www.wasabi-sushibar.com; open M-Sa 10am-11pm

Eleven iterations of this Japanese food chain litter this city. You heard that correctly: 11. There are more Wasabi restaurants in Geneva than there are McDonalds. Don't let the chain-ness of these restaurants scare you though, the food is tasty and the prices are even tastier. After 6pm, bento boxes come with a free drink (with student ID). If you're looking for something a bit less processed, opt for a classic roll or sushi burrito, both of which are fresh and filling.

*i* *Bento boxes 16-20CHF, soup 14CHF, rolls 8CHF; vegetarian options available; wheelchair accessible*

# NIGHTLIFE

### BARBERSHOP
Blvd. Georges-Favon 14; 022 320 71 92; open M-W 11:30am-midnight, Th 11:30am-1am, F 11:30am-2am, Sa 6:30pm-2am

Step into Barbershop and you'll find yourself questioning your whereabouts. This bar is decorated with objects you're likely find in any American frat house—empty liquor bottles, inflatable objects, signposts, and posters line the walls, creating an eccentric, yet welcoming environment. An obvious favorite among students, Barbershop is the place to go if you're looking to meet locals and try some out-of-the-box cocktail concoctions.

*i* *Beers 5-9CHF, shots 5CHF, cocktails 15CHF; BGLTQ+ friendly; wheelchair accessible*

## LE KRAKEN

Rue de l'École-de-Médecine 8; 022 321
59 41; www.lekrakenbar.ch; open M-Th
11am-1am, F 11am-2am, Sa 1pm-2am

With mahogany walls, velvet chairs,
and traces of aged whiskey, Le Kraken
looks more like a CEO's study than
a bar. Tattoo-clad bartenders move
quickly but quietly behind the large
bar, serving up classic and novel
concoctions like piña coladas and
spiked ginger lemonade, respectively. If
nothing on the menu is to your liking,
a bartender will whip up something
satisfying on the spot. Grab your drink
and head out back, where you'll find a
small secret garden.

*i* *Shots 5-7CHF, cocktails 15CHF, beer
5-7CHF*

## L'ELÉPHANT DANS LA CANETTE

Av. du Mail 18; 022 321 70 70; www.
elephantdanslacanette.ch; open M-Tu
11am-1am, W 7am-1am, Th 11am-1am,
F 11am-2am, Sa 7am-2am, Su 4pm-mid-
night

Ever thought about what would
happen if you downed a hundred
shots in a single night? Well, you
could theoretically find out the answer
to that question at L'Eléphant (100
shots, 300CHF), but after conducting
our own research, we strongly advise
against it. Whether you're looking
to party or kick back with a pitcher
of beer (1.5L, 14CHF) and a couple
friends, L'Eléphant dans la Canette,
with its wide variety of cocktails,
relaxed ambiance, and dirt-cheap
booze, is sure to fulfill your nightlife
needs.

*i* *Beer 3-5CHF, cocktails 8-12CHF, shots
5CHF; BGLTQ+ friendly; no wheelchair
accessibility*

# GIMMELWALD

Coverage by **Alejandro Lampell**

"You're going to Gimmelwald? You probably mean 'Grindelwald!'"

"No, *Gim-mel-wald*."

"Are you sure?"

This is the default conversation you will have with most Swiss people, who
are convinced that you want to go visit Dumbledore's childhood friend-turned-
nemesis. Stand your ground and tell them proudly it is, without a doubt,
Gimmelwald that you seek. This is a small village, and, when we say small, we
mean population-of-130-people small. Here, locals are outnumbered by livestock.
Together with the neighboring village of Mürren, these gems are some of the last
traffic-free towns in Switzerland, situated a mile off the ground at the base of the
Bernese Alps.

With miles and miles of hiking trails and countless activities from paragliding
to biking and climbing, Gimmelwald presents the perfect getaway for the
adventurous backpacker. During the winter, these towns double as ski resorts—
picturesque wooden cabins once decorated with colorful flowers are blanketed
with a thick layer of powdery snow. It puts the renowned ski destinations of the
United States to shame; Colorado and Vermont look like washed-down waterways
in comparison to the pristine slopes of the Jungfrau ski region. Granted, the trek
to get here might be difficult, but the views, wide array of outdoor activities, and
unique culture justify the trip.

## ORIENTATION

Gimmelwald and Mürren are on the area known as the **Berner Oberland**
(Bernese Highlands), which are the highest mountains in the canton of **Bern**,
south of **Interlaken.** The mountain on which these two towns are located—
**Schilthorn**—is southwest of the **Jungfrau, Eiger,** and **Mönch,** facing the valley
where **Stechelberg** is located. Gimmelwald and Mürren are located approximately

45 minutes apart by foot, with an altitude increase of 1000 feet between the two, respectively (facing Schilthorn, Mürren is located upwards to the right of Gimmelwald.). The Schwarzmönch mountain blocks the view of the Jungfrau, Eiger, and Monch; however, if you take a hike towards **Grütschalp,** they soon come into view. The **James Bond Museum** and **Piz Gloria** are located at the top of the Schilthorn, at an elevation of 9744ft.

# ESSENTIALS
## GETTING THERE
..........................................

Getting to Gimmelwald is a trek, but is well worth the hassle. The Bernese Oberland region is accessed almost exclusively from Interlaken, the closest major city. Many cities around Switzerland and neighboring countries connect Interlaken via train. From Interlaken Ost (there are two train stations in Interlaken, one in the eastern part of the city and the other in the west) take a 20-minute regional train ride to Lauterbrunnen. From here, take a train to Grütschalp and a cable car to Mürren. To reach Gimmelwald, you can take a subsequent cable car or hike downhill 45 minutes. Another way to get there involves taking a 10-minute bus ride from Lauterbrunnen to Stechelberg. The bus is located outside the train station                and there are

instructions to the bus area, which is usually in front of a bakery. Once you have made it to Stechelberg, take the cable car up to Gimmelwald (10 minutes). If you are driving, you can park your car in Lauterbrunnen or Stechelberg at one of the designated car parking spots and then follow the aforementioned steps. Mürren and Gimmelwald are not accessible by car or any other conventional method not listed here.

## GETTING AROUND
..........................................

The primary (and cheapest) way to get around is by hiking. From Gimmelwald to Mürren, it is a 45-minute uphill hike. There are even trails to go all the way to Schilthorn or down to Stechelberg. These trails are very difficult and it is advised to take precautions before attempting them. The most convenient method of transportation is through cable car. Gimmelwald has only one cable car station whereas Mürren has both a cable car station and a train station (bahnstation). The cable car follows the Stechelberg-Gimmelwald-Mürren-Birg-Schilthorn route, so you must get off at each station and board a different cable car. There are connections every 30 minutes from Stechelberg, with departures from 7:25am-4:25pm. Departures to the peak from the valley occur every 25 and 55 minutes past the hour. Departures to the valley from the peak are every three and 33 minutes past the hour. The last ride departs at 5:55pm.

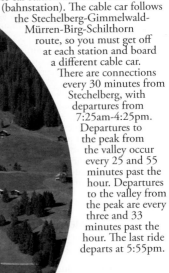

Last departure for Stechelberg-Gimmelwald-Mürren is at 11:45pm on Su-Th and at 12:55pm F-Sa. There are extended sunrise and sunset times during July and August. For an adult, the Stechelberg-Schilthorn roundtrip is 84CHF and Mürren-Schilthorn roundtrip is 66CHF. For children (6-16) the Stechelberg-Schilthorn roundtrip is 42CHF and the Mürren-Schilthorn roundtrip is 33CHF. The cable car is occasionally closed for maintenance during the spring and fall seasons, so make sure to check beforehand.

There is a train connecting Mürren, Winteregg, and Grütschalp. (From Grütschalp, a cable car can be taken to Lauterbrunnen.) The train travels through towns in the mountain, whereas, in the other path, you should take a bus to cross the valley. A ticket from Lauterbrunnen to Mürren costs 25.20CHF roundtrip, while that from Interlaken Ost to Mürren costs 40.40CHF.

In this region of Switzerland, transportation is more expensive than you would think, so you should consider the different options available at the SBB train company. You might consider getting a half-fare card for one month for 120CHF (applies to all public transport) or the Swiss Travel Pass (216-458CHF depending on duration of your stay), which provides free access to public transport (often including funiculars and boats) and free entrance to museums. Another options is the Tell Pass, which is great for this Alps region as it includes travel on all trains, buses, boats and aerial cable ways for two days (180CHF), three days (210CHF), four days (230CHF), five days (220CHF), or ten days (360CHF).

Besides those options, there are some more particular to the region. You can get the Ferienpass Mürren-Schilthorn, which allows as many trips as desired on Schilthornbahn Cable Car, bus line Lauterbrunnen-Isenfluh, and cableway Isenfluh-Sulwald, 4 days (adults 140CHF kids 93CHF) or 6 days (adults 160CHF, kids 103CHF). Alternatively, the Regionalpass Berner Oberland includes tickets for transportation by train, boat, bus and cable car on selected routes in Bernese

Oberland 4 days (250CHF), 6 days (310CHF), 8 days (350CHF), 10 days (390CHF). The Swiss Travel Pass and half-fare card will decrease these costs.

## PRACTICAL INFORMATION

**Tourist Offices:** The nearest tourist information center is in Mürren, a 45-minute hike north of Gimmelwald (3825 Mürren; 033 856 86 86; open mid-June-mid-Oct open 8:30am-6:45pm, mid-Oct to mid-Dec daily 8:30am-noon, 1pm-5pm, mid-Dec-mid-Apr daily 8:30am-7:45pm, mid-Apr-mid June daily 8:30am-noon, 1pm-5pm).

**Banks/ATMs/Currency Exchange:** The nearest ATM is located at the cable car station in Mürren (Schilthornbahn). The closest bank is in Lauterbrunnen (Bank EKI Cooperative; Railway station 473a; 033 855 36 55; open M-F 8am-noon, only M and F 2pm-5pm).

**Post Offices:** Post agency in Coop store (Dorfstrasse 1032; 033 225 29 70; open M-F 8am-noon and 1:45pm-6:30pm, Sa 8am-noon and 1:45-5pm).

**Internet:** There is free Wi-Fi in the Tourist Information Center in Mürren and in the cable car station in Mürren (Schilthornbahn), not in the station in Gimmelwald. Visitors can rent pocket Wi-Fi hotspots at Mürren for 3 days (39.90CHF), 7 days (64.90CHF), 10 days (83.40CHF), or 15 days (129.90CHF).

## EMERGENCY INFORMATION

**Emergency Numbers:** General (112); police (117); fire department (118); ambulance (144); Swiss Helicopter Rescue Service (1414)

**Police:** Lauterbrunnen (Stutzli 466; 033 356 85 01; "appointment agreement by telephone").

**US Embassy:** The nearest US Embassy is located in Switzerland's capital, Bern (Sulgeneckstrasse 19; 031 357 70 11; appointments are available M-F 9am-11:30am, speak to representative M-F 2pm-4pm).

**Hospitals:** The closest doctor is in Lauterbrunnen and the closest hospital is in Interlaken.
- Caremed Praxis (doctor) (Dokter-huus, Lauterbrunnen; 033 856 26 26)
- Regionalspital Interlaken Hospital (Weissenaustrasse 27, Unterseen;

033 826 26 26; open daily 24hr for emergencies)

**Pharmacies:** Wengen Apotheke (Wengiboden 1412E; 033 855 12 46; open M-F 8am-noon and 2-6:30pm, Sa 8am-noon and 2pm-6pm, Su 4-6pm).

## ACCOMMODATIONS

### ⛰MOUNTAIN HOSTEL ($$)

Nidrimatten, Gimmelwald; 338551704; www.mountainhostel.com; hostel open Dec 1-Mar 30, mid-Apr-Oct 31; reception open daily 8:30am-10pm

Rise and shine to stunning views of the **Bernese Alps** in this hidden gem of a hostel. Providing the most affordable accommodations in the region, Mountain Hostel will not disappoint with its rustic, camp-ground vibe. You would be hard-pressed to find a homier place that attracts more genuine and down-to-earth people passionate about the outdoors. It's a little surprising that the hostel doesn't have keys, but no keys, no problem, we say! This is an extremely safe area. Live carefree in the mountains with incredibly helpful staff who help you make the most of your time in Gimmelwald.

*i* *Bunks 45CHF; reservation recommended; BGLTQ+ friendly; no wheelchair accessibility; Wi-Fi; linens included; laundry 5CHF; cleaning lockout 9:30am-11am including the bathroom; quiet hours begin at midnight*

### EIGER GUESTHOUSE ($$$)

Aegerta 1079E; 338565460; www.eigerguesthouse.com; reception open 8am-11:30pm

Striking a fine, middle-ground line between an upper-tier hostel and lower-tier hotel, the Eiger Guesthouse boasts a prime location and stellar amenities. Situated on the lower street of Mürren, directly in front of the train station, Eiger Guesthouse, not to be confused with its next-door neighbor, Eiger Hotel, has a diverse guest community. The classic wooden façade gives way to colorful green walls, yellow doors, and different images of the typical Alp outdoor activities: paragliding, skiing, air balloon rides. The four-bunk bedrooms are clean and have pretty patios that offer breathtaking views. If you're looking

to upgrade your stay, select a "superior room" with a television.

*i* *Budget room 60CHF, double 160CHF; reservation recommended; BGLTQ+ friendly; no wheelchair accessibility; Wi-Fi; linens included*

## SIGHTS
## CULTURE

### UNTERSEEN

Unterseen; open daily 24hr

Situated on the eastern bank of **Lake Thun,** Unterseen, meaning Lower Lake, is the historic old town area of Interlaken, filled with classic timber-framed, flower-covered buildings. Stroll along the aqua-colored River Aare, passing by a thirteenth-century church and bell tower, and make a trip to the **Tourism Museum,** where you can discover how much tourism has influenced Interlaken (spoiler alert: a lot).

*i* *Prices vary by store or restaurant; free walking tours of Interlaken; tours most days at 5:45pm; limited wheelchair accessibility*

## LANDMARKS

### ⛰SCHILTHORN AND BIRG

Schilthorn; 338260007; www.schilthorn.ch/en/welcome; daily ascents every half hour from Mürren to Schilthorn 7:25am to 4:25pm, last descent 5:55pm; maintenance of cable car Nov 13-Dec 8, Apr 23-Apr 27, Nov 12-Dec 10

"The name's Bond. James Bond." Venture to Blofeld's Research Museum, hidden at the top of Schilthorn, with nothing other than an expensive cable-car ride, long wait, and crowds of tourists to slow your ascent. Confused? The top of the mountain was the set of some of the most iconic scenes of *On Her Majesty's Secret Service* (1969), one of the classic Bond movies. Apart from access to **Bond World 007,** a museum that describes the film's production in tremendous detail, the expensive cable car ride gives you access to Birg, which is close to the summit and includes a "thrill walk" over a glass bridge and down a fenced path that hugs the mountain. Above the clouds, Schiltorn

and Birg provide superb views of the Bernese Alps.

*i* Stechelberg-Schilthorn roundtrip 105CHF, Mürren-Schilthorn roundtrip 82.20CHF; limited wheelchair accessibility

## OUTDOORS

### 🪂PARAGLIDING

Company headquarters in Fuhren, for paragliding, meet at the Mürren train station; 792478463; www.airtime-paragliding.ch; book appointments online

Sometimes you skip things to save money. Sometimes you splurge for worthwhile experiences. Do you cash out for a potentially life-changing adventure? It's a difficult question to answer, but we can settle this one for you: Cash. Out. *Now.* From Mürren, lift off and embark on a paragliding journey, gliding from side to side (and upside-down) as you experience the valleys and mountains of the Alps—Eiger, Mönch, and Jungfrau included—from a completely different perspective. The guide who accompanies you (and keeps you safe) will take pictures and video during your flight for a hefty price tag, but let's be real, you'll want to document it. It's exhilarating, thrilling, and unparalleled; imagine feeling simply weightless mid-air. At the end of the day, you'll remember how it felt to fly, not how it felt when money flew out of your pocket.

*i* Paragliding 170CHF summer from Mürren, 180CHF winter from Mürren, 280CHF from Birg or Schilthorn; photos with GoPro 30CHF, photos and videos 40CHF; no wheelchair accessibility

### VIA FERRATA

Lower part of Mürren; 338568686; www.klettersteig-muerren.ch/index.php/en; open mid-June-mid-Oct

For the thrill-seekers who are not satisfied with hiking, follow the Via Ferrata, which translates to "the way of the iron" in Italian. Both poetic and thrilling, the Via Ferrata involves following a protected climbing route while being harnessed on to an iron rope on a mountainside. Unlike most "iron ways," this one travels downward instead of upwards, from its starting point in Mürren down to Gimmelwald, and covers over 2.2km. Be warned: this is not an easy trail and, for first-timers, it is best to book a guided tour at the Tourist Office.

*i* Free admission; equipment rental at Intersport Stäger Sport 25 CHF or Alfred's Sporthaus 22CHF; book guided tours with Schweizer Bergsportschule Grindelwald-SPORTS (33 854 12 80); no wheelchair accessibility

### MOUNTAIN VIEW TRAIL

www.gimmelwald.ch/e/activities/summer/hiking.htm

Baby, *this* is what you came for. After countless hours of travel and expensive transportation, you've made and it, now, you can enjoy nature's beauty at no cost whatsoever. There are over 800km of footpaths in the **Jungfrau** mountain region, many of which are easily accessible from Gimmelwald and Mürren. Whether you're a novice or a well-worn expert, you'll find a path suited to your ability, each with its individually breathtaking view. We recommend the Mountain View Trail, which departs from Mürren, travels along the ridge of the mountain, and winds through meadows and forests.

*i* *Free; no wheelchair accessibility*

## TRÜMMELBACHFÄLLE

Trümmelbachfälle, CH-3824 Trümmelbach; 338553232; www.truemmelbachfaelle. ch; open daily mid-Apr-June 9am-5pm, July-Aug 8:30am-6pm, Sept-early Nov 9am-5pm

Feel tiny and powerless at this UNESCO **World Natural Heritage Site** as 20,000 liters (per second) of melted glacier come crashing down in front of you. The Trümmelbach Falls are a set of ten waterfalls that exclusively drain the water coming down from the glaciers on the **Eiger, Mönch,** and **Jungfrau** mountains. The rails and tunnels that meander through the mountains provide astounding views of the crashing water. Not down for hiking, but still up for the views? Take the elevator up to the sixth waterfall and walk your way down.

*i* *Adult admission 11CHF, 4CHF child (6-16years); last elevator ride 30min before closing; limited wheelchair accessibility*

# FOOD

## EIGER GUESTHOUSE RESTAURANT ($$$)

Aegerta 1079E, Mürren; 338565460; www. eigerguesthouse.com; open daily from 11:30am-10pm

Located in front of the main train station, this locale offers a wide variety of food—from pasta and pizza to Swiss specialties and *bratwurst*—for reasonable prices. Opt for the 23.50CHF per person fondue, arguably the best quality-quantity ratio in Mürren.

*i* *Entrées 18-22CHF; card min of 20CHF; vegetarian options available; wheelchair accessible*

## RESTAURANT MOUNTAIN HOSTEL ($)

Nidrimatten, Gimmelwald; 338551704; www.mountainhostel.com; open daily 11am-8pm

Why leave the comfort of your hostel when it offers delicious pizza right downstairs? Call ahead and order a basic margherita pizza (16CHF) or a

pie with mixed toppings (19CHF), both of which are big enough to feed two hungry hikers. If you're not in the mood for pizza, the daily specials range from a big plate of spaghetti á la Bolognese to a Swiss specialty of *raclette* with potatoes. Sit at the familial picnic tables inside or, if the weather permits, the ones outside, with a clear view of the **Schwarzmönch mountain** up ahead.

*i* *Pizza 16-19CHF, entrées 18-20CHF; vegetarian options available; no wheelchair accessibility*

## SNACKBAR BERRY ($$)

Bir Schiir 1056, Mürren; 077 496 14 36;open M-Tu, Th-Su7:30am-5:30pm

Snackbar Berry is a do-it-all store, complete with strong coffee, scrumptious noodles, juicy hamburgers, Dutch delicacies called stroopwafel, and complimentary Wi-Fi! When we visited, the staff members were super accommodating—eager to discuss our mountain odysseys and provide recommendations for activities.

*i* *Dishes 10-12CHF; cash only; vegetarian options available; limited wheelchair accessibility*

## THAM CHINESE RESTAURANT ($$$)

Rouft 1067A CH-3825, Mürren; 338560110; www.tham.ch/chine-sisches-restaurant/chinese-food.html; open daily noon-9pm

Up in the Alps, where livestock outnumber humans and mountains tower above you, the last thing you expect to find is a Chinese restaurant. Tham serves typical Chinese fare from fried rice to Szechuan beef and duck, all for a reasonable price tag. A family business, this small locale has comfortable wooden tables and chairs and an open kitchen. Let the swinging paws of the doll cats lure you in and stay for the comfort food.

*i* *Entrées 18-22CHF; vegetarian options available; wheelchair accessible*

## NIGHTLIFE

### MOUNTAIN HOSTEL BAR

Nidrimatten, Gimmelwald; 338551704; www.mountainhostel.com; open daily 11am-10pm

The options for nightlife are limited in a 130-person village, but fear not, dear backpacker, there are ways to turn up even here. Pop by the reception-turned-bar at Mountain Hostel, where weary backpackers gather to kick back, share a brew, and recount crazy stories. The bar has two different tap beers, dark and light, and shots from bottles hung wrong-side-up from the ceiling. If you are up for the challenge, ask for the 1-liter beer boot, or, if you really dare, its big-footed 2-liter sibling.

*i* *Beer 5.50CHF, shots 5CHF; BGLTQ+ friendly; no wheelchair accessibility*

### TÄCHI BAR (HOTEL EIGER)

Aegerten; 338565454; www.hoteleiger. com/en/taechi-bar; open M-Th 11:30am-11:30pm, F-Sa 11:30am-noon

Below one of Mürren's most prestigious hotels, Hotel Eiger, Tächi Bar looks like an upscale ski cabin and is the closest you will get to nightlife in Mürren. An illuminated bar stocked with the likes of Grey Goose and Bombay lines the back wall and is attended to by friendly bartenders in red vests and bowties. With decorations of skiing equipment and seating around a fireplace, the mountain cabin feel permeates this joint. On weekends, Tächi hosts DJs and opens up the speckled dancefloor, attracting a slightly younger clientele than it would on the weekdays.

*i* *Beer 4.50-6.50CHF, shots 6.50CHF, mixed drinks 12CHF-17CHF; BGLTQ+ friendly; wheelchair accessible*

# LAUSANNE

Coverage by **Alejandro Lampell**

Usually overlooked by its neighboring, French-speaking counterpart Geneva, "Laussane-geles," as the young locals jokingly call it, is a university town with a bustling cultural life and fascinating history. Lausanne, originally called Lousonna, was founded as a Roman military camp over a Celtic settlement in 15BCE and has seen large amounts of structural and cultural changes throughout the ages. Most of the changes come from the influence of the Zwingli Protestant Reformation and the counter reformation; the former is more prominent in the eastern part of the city while the later manifests in the French-speaking regions. Lausanne's Ouchy district, located on the shores of beautiful Lac Léman, has served as the headquarters for the International Olympic Committee since 1915, while the Flon district boasts a vibrant nightlife scene and is the hub of the first fully automated metro in Switzerland.

## ORIENTATION

Lausanne is in Switzerland's western, French-speaking region, at the northeast shores of **Lac Léman.** The city is built on the southern edge of a plateau and slopes downward towards the lake. Centuries ago, affluent residents owned homes on the plateau to avoid diseases, which is why you'll find most of the main tourist attractions, including the **Cathédrale,** on a hillside overlooking the rest of the city. The center of the city covers part of an ancient river called the **Flon,** upon which the **Rue Centrale** now runs. This is especially confusing because maps do not show the different levels, so you can get lost trying to determine whether to stay on the lower road or take an upper bridge connecting different neighborhoods. The city is divided into different districts. The **Vieille Ville** district (Old Town) is where you'll find the **Cathédrale, St. Francis Church,** and the **Rue de Bourg,** a major shopping area. To the south of **Vieille Ville** is the **Flon District,** which has recently undergone major renovations and now houses the city's nightlife and different cultural events. The two metro lines intersect at the Flon stop. The **Ouchy District** is the most scenic part of the town, home to the renowned

**Olympic Museum** and located adjacent to the lake. Here, you can rent a paddle boat to experience the city from a different vantage point or recline on the beaches located slightly west of the district. Just inland of the **Plage de Vidy** lies the **Université de Lausanne** and the **École Polytechnique Fédérale de Lausanne.**

# ESSENTIALS
## GETTING THERE

Most travelers travel to Lausanne via the Swiss Federal Rail System (SBB). The main train station (Lausanne Gare) connects to Geneva, Zurich, Bern, and several other cities (both domestic and international) with trains running between 4:45am and 1:30am every 30min. There are direct trains from Geneva Airport to Lausanne (45 min.). Check out super-saver tickets, which offer reduced fares (50%-off) for SBB train rides. The closest international airport to Lausanne is in Geneva, which has daily international connecting flights to the United States. Although uncommon, you can take a boat ride from Geneva to Lausanne during high season, which costs around 45CHF and takes 4 hours. Buses connect Lausanne to major Swiss, French, and Spanish cities. These are usually cheaper, but take longer than a train ride. If you manage to score a deal on a train ticket, opt for that over a bus.

## GETTING AROUND

Lausanne is easily walkable, as many landmarks and sites are close to the main train station in Vieille Ville. Since much of the city is located on a hillside, there are different levels to streets. Almost all accommodations give out the Lausanne Transport card, which grants free public transport (bus, train, and metro for a maximum of 15 days) in zones 11, 12, 15, 16, and 18 and discounts on museums tickets and boat rides. Lausanne has a small subway system with only two metro lines, both of which intersect at the Flon station. The M1 line runs to the west towards University of Lausanne and the Ecole Polytechnique Fédérale de Lausanne, while the M2 line runs north-south, from Epalignes to Ouchy, right next to Lac Léman. You can buy tickets (1hr 3.60CHF, 1 day 9.30CHF) at blue machines at bus/train/metro stations; remember to validate your ticket before Buses run from 5am until midnight. There are additional late-night buses on F, Sa, and Su from 1am-4am.

## PRACTICAL INFORMATION

**Tourist Offices:** Tourist Information Center (Pl. de la Navigation 6; 021 613 73 21; high season open daily from 9am-7pm, low season 9am-6pm).
**Banks/ATMs/Currency Exchange:** ATMs are easily accessible throughout the city. Here's the information for one bank, Cembra Money Bank AG Lausanne (Av. Louis-Ruchonnet 1; 21 310 40 50; open M-F 9am-6pm).
**Post Offices:** Av. de la Gare 43B; 0848 888 888; open M-F 8am-8pm, Sa 8am-4pm, Su 4pm-7pm).
**Internet:** Wi-Fi is available throughout the main train station, but you need a Swiss number to access it. Free Wi-Fi is available at tourist information centers, in front of the lake, and in the main areas of the city.
**BGLTQ+ Resources:** The main BGLTQ+ helpline in Switzerland is 080 013 31 33.

## EMERGENCY INFORMATION

**Emergency Numbers:** General (112); police (117); fire department (118); ambulance (144); Swiss Helicopter Rescue Service (1414)
**Police:** There is a city and a canton po-lice. The city police are easily accessible (Hôtel de Police de Lausanne; Rue Saint-Martin 33; 021 315 15 15; open daily from 6am-9pm; 24hr emergency services available).
**US Embassy:** The closest Consular Agency in located in Geneva (Rue Versonnex 7; 22 840 51 60; open M-F 10am-1pm, by appointment only).
**Rape Crisis Center:** The domestic abuse hotline for all of Switzerland is 147.
**Hospitals:** Centre Hospitalier Universi-taire Vaudois (Rue du Bugnon 46; 021 314 11 11; open daily 24hr).
**Pharmacies:** Pharmacie 24 (Av. de Montchoisi 1; 021 613 12 24; open daily 8am-midnight).

# ACCOMMODATION

### LAUSANNE GUESTHOUSE AND BACKPACKER ($)

Chemin des Epinettes 4; 021 601 80 00; www.lausanne-guesthouse.ch; reception open 7:30am-noon and 3pm-10pm

In terms of location it doesn't get much better than Lausanne Guesthouse and Backpacker, which is a 5-minute walk away from the main train station at the heart of the city. The hostel is currently housed in a block building with pale yellow walls and baby blue window shutters, but there are plans to move to a new building in 2018 near the **Cathédrale.** Current amenities include large common rooms, a garden, a piano room, brightly-colored décor, and great views of **Lac Léman.** Make sure to check out the plans for the new building on Lausanne Guesthouse and Backpacker's website before booking.

*i Dorms from 36CHF, doubles from 80CHF; reservation recommended; wheelchair accessible; Wi-Fi; linens included; laundry facilities 3CHF per load, 3CHF per dry, 1CHF per detergent*

### YOUTH HOSTEL - JEUNOTEL ($$)

Chemin du Bois-de-Vaux 36; 021 626 02 22; www.youthhostel.ch/en/hostels/lausanne; reception open 24hr

Away from the bustle of **Vieille Ville** and just steps from the very popular **Plage de Vidy,** Youth Hostel Jeunotel practically skims the water of **Lac Léman.** This concrete and glass behemoth seems more like a hotel than a hostel as it's always well-staffed and frequented by a wide range of people—families, school groups, and everything in between. Despite the fact that it's outfitted with ping pong tables, volleyball courts, and a pool table, Jeunotel lacks a backpacking culture. But, if you're just looking for a place to kick back, work on your tan, and figure out Lausanne's map system, Youth Hostel Jeunotel may be the option for you.

*i Dorms from 46CHF, doubles from 107CHF-135CHF; reservation recommended; max stay 7 nights; BGLTQ+ friendly; limited wheelchair accessibility; Wi-Fi; linens included; laundry facilities (8CHF wash and dry, detergent 2CHF); free breakfast*

# SIGHTS

## LANDMARKS

### CATHÉDRALE DE LAUSANNE

Pl. de la Cathédrale; 021 316 71 60; www.cathedrale-lausanne.ch; open daily Oct-Mar 9am-5:30pm, Apr-Sept M-Sa 9am-7pm, Su 10am-6pm, Prayer service M-F 7:30am, tower visit M-Sa 9:30am-5:30pm, Su 1pm-5pm

On a hilltop overlooking the city, the Cathédrale de Lausanne stands tall as the religious hub of the French-speaking part of Switzerland. From the inside, the cathedral's high arching ceiling produces a belittling effect. The stalls, located in what used to be the main entrance, display fading colored sculptures, a sign of the Catholic roots of the Cathédrale before the influence of Zwingli's Reformation struck. Take the set of winding stone steps to the top of the tower for a stunning view of the city, lake region, and collection of bells that dates back to the thirteenth-century.

*i Free, tower admission adult 5CHF, student 3CHF; last entry 30min. before closing; limited wheelchair accessibility*

### CHÂTEAU SAINTE MARIE

R. du Port-Franc 18; 021 316 40 40; exterior open daily 24hr

The Château Sainte Marie is a beautiful medieval castle that was commissioned by the Bishops of Lausanne in the fifteenth century and has undergone a series of refurbishments in recent years. The bishops chose this location—atop a massive hill—to dissuade peasants from squatting on its doorstep. Today, it does just the opposite, attracting tens of thousands of tourists each year. Unfortunately, the interior is still not open to the public, meaning you won't be able to catch a glimpse of the pristine frescoes nor the members of the cantonal government, who use the castle as a meeting place. You will, however, be greeted by some seriously impressive architecture and sweeping views of the city below.

*i Free; interior closed to the public; limited wheelchair accessibility*

### ÉGLISE SAINT-FRANCOIS (CHURCH OF ST. FRANCIS)

Pl. St-Francois; 021 331 56 38; www. sainf.ch; open Tu-F 10am-noon and 4pm-6:40pm

Tucked among the chic boutique stores of the **Place St-Francois,** you'll find this large Franciscan-monetary-turned-Protestant-church. Dating back to the thirteenth century, the Church of St. Francis has gone through countless renovations; it currently serves as a cultural center for concerts and art exhibitions. Attend one of the **Saint Francis Concerts** (every Saturday) to hear the organ boom and swing by the outdoor market on your way out.

*i* Free; no wheelchair accessibility

## MUSEUMS

### COLLECTION DE L'ART BRUT

Av. des Bergières 11; 021 315 25 70; www.artbrut.ch; open Sept-June Tu-Su 11am-6pm, open July-Aug daily 11am-6pm, closed on holidays

"Art Brut is art brut and it is well understood everywhere. Not that well? Well, that is why we are curious to go and see for ourselves."- **Jean Debuffet,** the creator of the **Art Brut** movement. This quote, plastered on the outside of the museum, describes a movement composed of art created by historically marginalized individuals. The works are distinguishable by their use of bright colors, abstract images, and incomprehensible symbols, and typically touch upon themes of loss, hospitalization, and abandonment.

*i* Admission 10CHF, 5CHF student, 5CHF per person in groups of 6, children under 16 free admission, first Saturday of the month free admission; last entry 5:30pm; no wheelchair accessibility

### MUSÉE DE L'ELYSÉE

Av. de l'Elysée 18; 021 316 99 11; www. elysee.ch; open Tu-Su 11am-6pm

A dark room is illuminated with projections of photographs and filled with the sounds of acoustic music. Every few seconds, the images switch, in sync with each strum on the guitar. This is the scene at Musée de l'Elysée, Lausanne's only museum dedicated entirely to photography. New exhibitions pop up every couple of months and delve into the art of photographing, incorporating key aspects of history and interpretation. In the attic, the museum has an interactive station that offers you a chance to listen to professionals' interpretations of the photographs, as well as a chance for you to test your hand with a camera.

*i* Combined entrance and magazine 15CHF, entrance to museum 8CHF, seniors 6CHF, students 4CHF, free for art students, kids under 16, and everyone the first Saturday of every month; last entry 5:30pm; free tour first Sa of month at 4pm; limited wheelchair accessibility

## OUTDOORS

### ESPLANADE DE MONT-BENON

Allée Ernest-Ansermet 3; open daily 24hr

Pristine green lawns, well-kept bushes, and blossoming flowers make up the Esplanade de Montbenon, which boasts a view of the houses next to the lake below. An unkempt vineyard in the

fourteenth century, this (now) public park has developed with the city—the introductions of the **Palais de Justice** and the Casino in the nineteenth and twentieth centuries, respectively, brought with them the introduction of flower patches and chestnut trees. This is a popular hangout for students and families alike, so if you find yourself in need of a break from monument-hopping, make like a Lausannean and plant yourself down in the shade of a tree for some well-deserved R&R.

*i* *Free; limited wheelchair accessibility*

# FOOD

### BLACKBIRD ($$)

R. Cheneau-de-Bourg 1; 021 323 76 76; www.blackbirdcafé.ch; open M-F 7:30am-3pm, Sa 8am-4pm, Su 9am-3:30pm

Breakfast all day, every day—exactly the way it should be. Blackbird is the "Breakfast Club" of Lausanne. Antique bottles and black and white paintings of black birds give this locale an alternative feel. Enjoy culinary classics from around the world: a spicy breakfast burrito, pancakes and eggs, and even Nordic smoked salmon.

*i* *Entrées 14-18CHF; vegetarian options available; limited wheelchair accessibility*

### BURRITO BROTHERS ($)

R. du Grand Pont 4; 078 851 88 53; www.burritobrothers.ch; open M-W 11am-4pm, Th-Sa 11am-10pm

Staying true to its Mexican roots, Burrito brothers serves some of the best Tex-Mex food on this side of the planet. Founded by two brothers, Fernando and Cesar, the locale has grown to become a popular Swiss food chain, affiliated with **Holy Cow!** Departing from the mainstream build-your-own model, Burrito Brothers has a set of signature dishes, with classic names like "Mission Dolores" and "Divisadero." The creations are affordable and extremely filling.

*i* *Burrito 12-14CHF, nachos 5-6CHF; vegetarian option available; no wheelchair accessibility*

### CARROUSEL BURGER ($)

1006 Lausanne; open daily 10am-midnight in summer, shorter hours in winter

Named after the iconic children's **Carrousel d'Ouchy,** this small restaurant offers a wide variety of fair fare to enjoy next to the aqua-colored **Lac Léman.** A favorite among families and students, the menu includes an array of ice cream flavors and "granite" (flavored shredded ice), perfect for a hot summer day. In the mood for a larger meal? Enjoy a cheeseburger on a baguette or a classic croque-monsieur. If you're anything like us, you'll gobble it up within minutes of receiving it, if not out of hunger then out of the desire to avoid the predatory glances of the ducks and birds swarming around your feet.

*i* *Entrées 10-12CHF; vegetarian options available; wheelchair accessible*

### PZ PIZZA ($$)

R. Grand-St-Jean 5; 021 312 82 82; www.pzpizza.ch; open M-Sa 11:30am-10:30pm

The periodic table is missing an element: Pz. But Pz Pizza has the world of chemistry covered. The restaurant plays on the element theme by asking you to pick a basic base (type of sauce, type of cheese) and toppings designated by chemical symbols. The toppings are even divided into groups, much like a periodic table. Would you like a noble gas or a halogen today? Keep in mind that some elements are more expensive than others.

*i* *Entrées from 12-16CHF; vegetarian options available; limited wheelchair accessibility*

# NIGHTLIFE

### LES ARCHES

Route de Bel-Air; www.lesarches.ch; open M-W 11am-midnight, Th 11am-1am, F-Sa 11am-2am, Su 1pm-midnight

Located under the **Grand Pont,** Les Arches is open all day, meaning you can slowly transition from enjoying a powerful espresso to a smooth mojito without ever leaving the comfort of your chair. At night, the understaffed bartenders tend to be attacked from all sides by thirsty customers, so make sure to get there early, order a drink, and reserve a good seat to enjoy the cool night breeze and live music in the **Place de l'Europe.**

*i* *Shots 6CHF, beer 5-9CHF, cocktails 9-15CHF; wheelchair accessible*

## XOXO BAR

R. des Côtes-de-Montbenon 20; 021 311 29 55; open Tu-W 11:45am-2pm and 6pm-midnight; Th 11:45am-2pm and 6pm-1am, F 11:45am-2pm and 6pm-2am, Sa 6pm-2am

Located on a rooftop and outfitted with chic lounge chairs and cream-colored patio umbrellas, Xoxo Bar is *the* place to be whether you want to enjoy a coffee during the day or a cocktail at night. With 38CHF cocktail pitchers large enough to satisfy 4-5 people, the locale is perfect for lounging with friends and watching the sun set over the Lausanne skyline. If you're looking to drink underground, visit the basement's dimly-lit bistro—perfect for a low-key night with friends.

*i* *Beer 4.50-9CHF, cocktails 15CHF, cocktail pitchers 38CHF*

# LUCERNE

Coverage by **Alejandro Lampell**

In the heart of Switzerland, skirting a (you guessed it) pristine lake and nestled into the foothills of the Alps, is the gorgeous city of Lucerne. A lot smaller and less chaotic than other major Swiss cities, it has historically been used as a stop on the way to the impressive mountains of Pilatus, Rigi, and Stanserhorn. However, because of its impressive legacy—the myths and legends of the surrounding area and the beauty of the city—Lucerne has become a popular destination for tourists looking for that quintessential, one-with-nature Swiss experience. This "city of swans" is quite sizeable and has its own distinct character, which is reflected in details as minute as the vibrant hues of the buildings and intricate woodwork of its bridges. Lucerne, along with Uri, Schwyz, and Unterwalden, was one of the Swiss cantons that formed the "eternal" Swiss Confederacy. History, like the gushing Reuss River, flows through the city—the current is particularly strong in the Altstadt (Old Town), which has the oldest wooden bridge in Europe, Kapellbrücke, and one of the best preserved medieval fortifications in Switzerland, Museggmauer. Like Zürich, Lucerne is a large cultural hub, hosting several major music and art festivals as well as a poppin' nightlife scene. The city is also famous for Fasnacht, an annual carnival held before the start of Lent.

## ORIENTATION

An hour train ride southwest of Zürich, Lucerne is smack in the middle of Switzerland, on the northwestern shore of Lake Lucerne. River Reuss cuts through the city of Lucerne on a northwest-to-east trajectory. The **Altstadt** (Old Town) is right at the mouth of the river with the Kapellbrücke crossing the Reuss diagonally. To the north of the city is **Museggmauer,** the old city's fortifications. The major mountains **Pilatus, Stanserhorn,** and **Rigi** are located south and east of the city, respectively. To visit **Mt. Pilatus,** the closest mountain, take a boat to **Alpnachstad,** a train to its summit, and a cable car to Kriens.

## ESSENTIALS

### GETTING THERE

The closest international airport to Lucerne is located in Zürich. From the Zürich Airport, you can take a direct train to Lucerne main train station. This train runs at least once an hour and takes around 60 minutes. You can also rent a car and drive down to Zürich (50min.); however, available parking spots are few and far between. The most common way to arrive at the city is, by far, via train. You can see whether there is a train from different cities to Lucerne on this website: www.fahrplan.sbb.ch.

## GETTING AROUND

Most of the old city can be explored on foot and lends itself to very scenic walks—the distance from the historic city wall to the train station and Kapellbrücke area is less than 1km. Within the city, the public transport is dominated by buses and local trains. The regional area is divided into zones and the city of Lucerne proper is zone 10, which is where you will probably spend the most time. Travel within the city limits is included a zone 10 ticket. A day pass for zone 10 is 8.20CHF, and a single ticket for 1hr is 4.10CHF. Short-distance tickets valid for up to six stops (or 30min.) are 2.50CHF. Public transport runs roughly 5am-12:30am, and night buses (*nachtstern*) run F and Sa nights. As with other Swiss transport, you must validate your ticket either at the stop prior to boarding or on the bus itself.

The state-run SBB train company is exorbitantly priced, so it's worthwhile to purchase SuperSaver tickets—these are up to 50% off popular routes at off-peak times. Select the SuperSaver option at sbb.ch. If you're traveling around Switzerland a lot, you might want to consider getting a half-fare card for one month (120CHF, applies to all public transport) or the Swiss Travel pass (216-458CHF, depending on duration). If you're visiting the Alps as well as central Switzerland, consider the Tell Pass—it includes travel on all trains, buses, boats, and aerial cable ways (including Pilatus, Rigi and Titlis) for two (180CHF), three (210CHF), four (230CHF), five (220CHF), or 10 (300CHF) days. This is the best deal for traveling through the Lucerne Lake area. Boat travel ranges from 3-45CHF, bike travel about 20CHF per day, and taxis 3.50CHF/km.

Tickets for boat rides on the vast Lake Lucerne range from 3-45CHF, depending on duration. Get tickets at the blue stand at Schwanenplatz, across from the train station. Note there is no Uber coverage in Lucerne.

## PRACTICAL INFORMATION

**Tourist Offices:** Several tourist offices are located in Lucerne's central train station. They offer brochures and pamphlets on different outdoor excursions, as well as suggestions of things to do in the city (Zentralstrasse 5; 0 41 227 17 17; summer M-F 8:30am-7pm, Sa 9am-7pm, Su 9am-5pm winter M-F 8:30am-5:30pm, Sa 9am-5pm, Su 9am-1pm, Apr M-F 8:30am-5:30pm, Sa-Su 9am-5pm).

**Banks/ATMs/Currency Exchange:** ATMs can be found outside of and near banks. Closest to the station are UBS and Credit Suisse, both just across the bridge and on the left. Use CHF to avoid poor exchange rates.

**Post Offices:** There are many post offices around the city. Postselle Universität has longer hours (Frohburgstrasse 3; M-F 9am-9pmm, Sa 9am-4pm, Su 1:30pm-5:30pm).

**Internet:** Wi-Fi, "WLAN," is free in the train station and around the city center for one hour; look for network Luzern. Register with a phone number. Many cafés, bars, and restaurants offer free Wi-Fi.

**BGLTQ+ Resources:** BGLTQ+ Helpline of Switzerland (Located in Bern, Monbijoustrasse 73; 080 013 31 33; hello@lgbt-helpline.ch; www.lgbt-helpline.ch/en); Queer Office hosts weekly meetings every Tuesday at Neubad to address issues affecting the BGLTQ+ community (hallo@queeroffice.ch, www.queeroffice.ch).

## EMERGENCY INFORMATION

**Emergency Numbers:** General (112); police (117); fire department (118); ambulance (144); Swiss Helicopter Rescue Service (1414).

**Police:** Station Hirschengraben 17a; 041 248 86 17; open daily 7am-7pm.

**US Embassy:** Nearest is US Consular Agency in Zürich. The US Embassy is in Bern.

**Rape Crisis Center:** Rape Crisis Network Europe in Switzerland, based in Geneva (3 des Charmilles; 022 345 20 20).

**Hospitals:** For most non-emergency problems, it is recommended that you set up an appointment at a Permanence with a doctor. There is one at Lucerne main station, open M-Th 7am-11pm, F 7am until Su 11pm nonstop (Medical Center Luzern AG; 041 211 14 44; www.permanence-luzern.ch).

- Hospital Kantonsspital Luzern (Spitalstrasse 16; 041 205 11 11; www.luks.ch; 24hr emergency services available).

**Pharmacies:** Pharmacies in German are called *apotheken.* The one with the longest opening hours is in Benu, in main train station.
- Benu Bahnof Luzern (M-Sa 7:30am-10pm, Su 10am-8pm; 041 220 13 13).

# ACCOMMODATIONS

### ⌂BELLPARK HOSTEL ($)
Luzernerstrasse 23; 413102515; www.
bellparkhostel.ch; reception open 7:45am-
10am and 4pm-11pm

Located in the small town of **Kriens**—mostly a stopping ground for people on their way back to Lucerne from **Mt. Pilatus**—Bellpark Hostel provides a relaxing and serene environment for the weary traveler. With its eggshell-white and sapphire-blue façade, this welcoming hostel looks as if it were transplanted directly from the rocky cliffs of Santorini. The ground floor houses the reception, lounge area, and dining room, where backpackers sit around long wooden tables and plan the best attack on their Alp of choice. A buffet-style breakfast is included in the nightly fare and so are bus rides for the duration of your stay, making Bellpark the complete package.

*i* Dorms from 27CHF, doubles from 80CHF; reservation recommended; max stay 14 days; BGLTQ+ friendly; no wheelchair accessibility; Wi-Fi; linens included; laundry facilities 8CHF

### BACKPACKERS HOSTEL ($$)
Alpenquai 42; 413600420; www.back-
packerslucerne.ch/index_en.php; reception
open 4:30am-10am and 4-11pm

A little off the beaten track, Backpackers Hostel is located on the southernmost tip of Lake Lucerne in a mostly suburban setting, amongst private residences and primary schools. With the nearest tram stop a five-minute walk away, it feels a bit secluded, but it is actually only a ten-minute tram ride away from the city center. The views from the en-suite balconies are serene, and if you visit during the summer, you'll be spending a good deal of your time outside, as the rooms lack air-conditioning. The hostel itself is very clean, has a friendly staff, and boasts a penthouse common room

with grand open spaces and a great view of the lake.

*i* Dorms 33CHF-39CHF, double 84CHF; reservation recommended; BGLTQ+ friendly; limited wheelchair accessibility; Wi-Fi; linens included; laundry 4.50CHF

# SIGHTS
## CULTURE

### ⌂LUCERNE RATHAUS
Kornmarkt 3; 412271717

Recently renovated and ornamented with the Swiss and Lucerne canton flags, the **Rathaus' maroon clock tower** is a prominent sublimity in the Reuss River skyline. Although not open to the public, the building, as the meeting place of the **Grand Council of the City,** buzzes with political energy. Every Saturday, the Rathaus hosts an open-air market, which, upon walking by, will envelop you with the smell of fresh herbs, farmer's cheese, warm bread, and ripe berries. The market, besides serving as a hub of cheap eats, is also a great place to meet locals. Stop by to experience the Rathaus' Renaissance architecture and emmentaler-style roof, fill your belly, and learn more about the people who make Lucerne the vibrant city that it is today.

*i* Free entry; market prices vary by stand

## LANDMARKS

### KAPELLBRÜCKE
Kapellbrücke; 412271717; www.luzern.
com/en/chapel-bridge

Kapellbrücke is the oldest surviving wooden bridge in Europe. During the summer time Kapellbrücke is particularly busy—the arrival of swans and honeybees brings with it the arrival of swarms of tourists, and with good reason. So beautiful that an ekphrasis of it would read like one taken from a Homeric epic, Chapel Bridge has become an emblem of the city with paintings along the bridge depicting its complex history. Sadly, a fire in 1993 destroyed most of these paintings, but the bridge itself stands strong today. The looming **Wasserturm,** or water tower next to the bridge was a dungeon

back in the day, but is no longer accessible to visitors.

*i* Free; wheelchair accessible

### LÖWENDENKMAL

Denkmalstrasse 4; 412271717; www.luzern.com/en/lion-monument; open daily 24hr

Mark Twain considered Löwendenkmal "the most mournful and moving piece of stone in the world," and we agree... with half of that statement. While the monument—an image of a dying lion chiseled out of a massive slab of marble—is quite moving, it's not as mournful as the horde of aggressive tourists trying to snap photos of it. This sculpture commemorates the death of the Swiss mercenaries that served under **King Louis XVI,** and has since become a symbol of both Lucerne and of the larger Swiss resistance. A keen eye might notice the outline of a pig encompassing the lion—a sly jab by the artist to the city that didn't pay him for his work.

*i* Free; wheelchair accessible

### MUSEGGMAUER

Schirmertorweg; 793566979; www.museggmauer.ch; open Apr 1-Nov 2 8am-7pm

Standing the test of time, Museggmauer consists of the remnants of the city's exterior fortifications dating back to the fifteenth century. With nine intact towers connected along the defense line, four of which are accessible to visitors, Museggmauer provides a breathtaking view of the city of Lucerne, the lake, and the mountains in the background. Make sure to climb up **Zeitturm** tower to see the large pendulum clock that

strikes a minute before the hour and **Männliturm** tower, which is topped with an iron soldier.

*i* Free; no wheelchair accessibility

## MUSEUMS

### ◪SWISS MUSEUM OF TRANSPORT

Lidostrasse 5; 413704444; www.verkehrshaus.ch/en; open daily 10am-6pm

Disneyland meets high-end car dealership. Swapping furry caricatures for flashy machines, the Swiss Museum of Transport is teeming with kids of all ages who usually come on organized outings and is the most popular museum in all of Switzerland. For a hefty price, you can gain access to an in-depth description the development of transportation and communication systems in Switzerland from the building of the **Gotthard railway** to the latest race cars and airplane models. With interactive models, railway simulations, and some expansive grounds, the museum is great for families seeking to keep children entertained for hours on end. It also includes a planetarium, film theatre, and "Swiss chocolate adventure" (for an additional cost).

*i* Admission 30CHF, student 26CHF, child 15CHF, 65CHF family planetarium and Swiss chocolate adventure additional 15CHF; last entry to complex 2hr. before closing; last entry to museum 15 min. before closing; limited wheelchair accessibility

### GLETSCHER GARTEN

Denkmalstrasse 4; 414104340; www.gletschergarten.ch/en; summer daily 9am-6pm, winter daily 10am-5pm

Located right next to the **Lion Monument,** the Gletscher Garten (Glacier Garden) tends to be overlooked. Entrance passes to this garden include access to the museum and a mirror maze, with convoluted and treacherous paths. Although the Gletscher Garten in itself is not extremely entertaining as it consists simply of the rock formation left by glaciers, the observation tower towards the back is worth the trek and provides a stunning view of Lucerne. The museum covers the life and work of **Joseph Wilhelm Amrein-Troller,** one of the garden's discoverers, and includes interactive exhibits demonstrating the geological timeline of the land where Lucerne currently stands.

*i Admission 15CHF, 12CHF student; last entry 30min. before closing, 45min. before closing adult price drops to 10CHF and 30min. before closing it drops to 7.50CHF; limited wheelchair accessibility; private tours by reservation only*

## FOOD

### ALPINEUM KAFFEHAUS BAR ($$$)

Denkmalstrasse 11; 774249098; open M-F 8am-12:30am, Sa 9am-12:30am, Su 12pm-6pm

We loved this place so much that we momentarily thought about excluding it from the book and keeping it our little secret. Despite being within walking distance of several major monuments and museums, Alpineum Kaffeehaus has yet to be overrun by tourists. Upon arriving on the premises—which are beautiful, might we add—it was clear that this was a more authentic local restaurant and bar than some of those we'd visited and we weren't sure how we would be received. Upon walking inside, however, we were welcomed warmly and handed a drink menu that (presumably) used to be a book about alpine skiing. Standouts include the classic cappuccino and the Sama Sama, a shot of house-made ginger liquor. During the weekdays, Alpineum offers a set menu (vegetarian 18.50CHF, meat 19.50CHF), the contents of which are subject to the whims of the chef. During the weekend, Alpineum hosts themed "food events" such as Big Bang Burger Sunday.

*i Entrées 18-20CHF; vegetarian options available; limited wheelchair accessibility*

### BISTRO DOGANS ($$)

Tribschenstrasse 66; 413616429; open daily 8am-12:30am

Ever heard of kebab calzones? Well, now you have. And after visiting Bistro Dogans, you'll never be able to eat just a kabob or just a calzone ever again. The kebab calzones (13.50CHF) and pizzas (12-16CHF) are large enough to feed two people, and the cheese is gooey enough for you and your boo to recreate the iconic scene from *Lady and the Tramp*. Dogans' interior, though small, is comfortable—at least during off-hours. During high time, a line stretches out the door and a cacophony of order-shouting, burger-flipping, and "More Life" pours through the shop's windows.

*i Entrées 10-16CHF; vegetarian options available; wheelchair accessible*

### TANDOORI ($$)

Löwengraben 4; 414106303; www.tandooriluzern.ch; open M-Sa 11:30am-9:30pm

Bejeweled from floor to ceiling in glass tiles and traditional Indian décor, Tandoori serves up excellent home-style food at an affordable price. For 10CHF, choose from a variety of plates that include meat, rice, vegetables, and paneer. We enjoyed the bitter-sweet **Chicken Makhani,** which consists of organic chicken sautéed in butter, lemon juice, ginger-garlic paste, garam malasa, chili powder, cumin, and bay leaf and topped with a scrumptious, spicy tomato sauce.

*i Entrées 10-15CHF; vegetarian options available; no wheelchair accessibility*

### DEAN AND DAVID ($$)

Morgartenstrasse 4; 412200222; www.deananddavid.de; open M-F 11am-9pm, Sa 11am-8pm, Su closed

Clean, fresh, eco-friendly. This Munich-based company provides healthy alternatives for travelers hoping to ditch the carbs and get their daily dose of greens. According to Dean and David's website, the menu was inspired by the cookshops of southeast Asia, juice bars of Australia, and salad culture of New York—a combination more apparent in the restaurant's leafy décor than the food itself. Create your own salad (small 9.90CHF, classic 11.50CHF), wrap (6.50CHF), or pressed juice, and tack on a tasty desert to complete a meal that will leave your tired, aching body feeling full and refreshed.

*i* Entrées 12-16CHF; vegetarian options available; limited wheelchair accessibility

## NIGHTLIFE

### BAR59
Industriestrasse 5; 413605200; www.bar59.ch; open W-Sa 8pm-4am

The street name says it all. An underground bar-club combo located in Lucerne's industrial district, Bar59 is known for its affordable drinks and grungy charm. If you manage to make it past the bouncer, you'll be greeted by poster-plastered walls, old-school sofas, and hundreds of sweaty twenty-somethings trying to catch a breath before venturing into Bar59's back room. When you're ready, follow them through the large black door at the rear

of the bar to experience what very well may be your best night in Lucerne.

*i* Beer 5-8CHF, pitcher of beer 19CHF, shots 5CHF, drinks 13CHF; BGLTQ+ friendly

### FRANKY BAR LOUNGE
Frankenstrasse 6; 412101073; bar open M-Th 5pm-12:30am, F-Sa 5pm-4am; club open Th-Sa 10pm-4am

Dim light cast by artisanal bulbs reflects off of the glass bottles stacked from floor to ceiling on the rear wall; the low *thump, thump, thump* of R&B fills the lulls in conversation between patrons; bartenders donning all-black attire run sprints behind the large wooden bar. Welcome to Franky's, one of the coolest lounges in Lucerne. Located a mere five minutes from the main train station, FBL's got a little for everyone: a lively upstairs bar area conducive to mingling, an underground club conducive to raging, and an outdoor patio conducive to chilling. The drinks aren't exactly cheap, but what you lose in drunkenness you make up for in suavity.

*i* No cover, shots 5CHF, beer 5CHF, drinks 14CHF; BGLTQ+ friendly

# ZURICH

Coverage by **Alejandro Lampell**

What do you get when you combine the financial prowess of New York with the rich cultural history of a European city at a crossroads and set it against the scintillating backdrop of the Swiss Alps? Zürich. Founded as a customs post by the Romans in 58 BCE, Zürich is now the largest populated city in Switzerland and one of the most significant financial and industrial centers in the world. Furthermore, as the birthplace of the Swiss Protestant Reformation and the Da Da movement, it also retains significant cultural importance as the home to over 50 museums and some of the largest music festivals in Europe. Zurich is a manageable size and has an impressive public transport system—most sights, restaurants, and clubs close to the city center are accessible by foot. With clean air, pristine water, and breathtaking views, it's no wonder Zürich is considered by many as one of the best places on Earth to live. While it's true that trips to Zürich (like the rest of Switzerland) do get pricey, don't worry fearless traveler–with our help, you can go in and get out with money left in your pocket.

## ORIENTATION

Zürich is located on the northwest tip of **Lake Zürich** in the central region of Switzerland. Southwest of the city, hugging the boundaries of the suburbs, lie the **Albis Mountains.** (Mt. Uetliberg, the best-known mountain in the range, provides a stunning view of the city.) The city consists of 12 different districts, which are colloquially referred to as neighborhoods. Zürich's **Old Town** is split in two by the **River Limmat,** which flows into Lake Zürich. The eastern part of the Old Town, **Niederdorf,** is a winding network of medieval streets and tight alleyways. The western part of the Old Town, on the other hand, is relatively commercial. Linden-lined **Bahnhofstrasse,** one of the most famous shopping streets in the world, constantly buzzes with tourists. This street leads straight to **Paradeplatz,** the financial district, housing major banks such as UBS and Credit Suisse. The major neighborhoods follow the river as it comes down from the northwest and winds along the northern portion of Lake Zürich. Just north of the old city is **Hauptbahnhof,** the main train station. **Zürich West** and **Langstrasse,** both located in the northwestern part of the city, are home to numerous entertainment venues and bars, and are frequented mostly by students and locals.

# ESSENTIALS

## GETTING THERE

The Zürich International Airport is easily accessible from almost anywhere, with connections to over 150 destinations. It is located 10km away from the city center and you need only take a one-way, 10-minute tram ride to Haubsthanof (single ticket 6.80CHF), the main railway station in the center of Zürich. When you land in the airport, exit the arrival area and go across to a building which houses a big shopping center. The train station is on the lower floor of this center; just follow the instructions and try not to confuse it with the tram system, which is located on the upper floor. Haubsthanof is the largest railway station in Switzerland, and it connects Zürich to many other Swiss cities and major European cities such as Paris, Milan, Hamburg, and others. Carparkplatz Sihlquai is the main bus station that connects Zürich to other European cities. Both the railway station and the bus station are located in the center of the city, a couple minutes south of Old Town.

## GETTING AROUND

The Zürich Transport Network (ZVV) controls all the transportation in the canton of Zürich, which includes tram, bus, boat, and train. The three former options are used to get around the city and Lake Zürich, and run from 5am–12:30am. On Friday and Saturday, the night network (Nachtnetze) runs from 1am–5am and requires two tickets, a normal transport ticket, and a night supplement ticket (one for 5CHF, or six for 27CHF, discounts and ZurichCARD not applicable).

Text "NZ" to (988) to purchase the supplement. Buy tickets at blue machines located at every stop (most take credit cards or coins only, no bills). For all purchased tickets, you must validate them once at a blue machine.

The public transport network is divided into zones. Zürich is zone 110, which includes the old city and most of the sights. Short-distance tickets (2.60CHF) are valid for 30min. in zones 110 (Zürich) and 120 (Winterthur), but usually span only five or six stops, so check the listing on the ticket machine at purchase. A day pass for zone 110 is 8.60CHF (river boat included), while a one hour pass is 4.30CHF. It costs an additional 2CHF per zone to travel through multiple zones. Travelers under 25 get a reduced price for multi-day passes, multiple-journey tickets, and group tickets. Carry ID in case of inspection.

Save money with the ZurichCARD (24CHF for 24hr, 4CHF for 72hr), which provides access to public transport for zone 110 and to and from the airport, as well as discounts or free entrance to many museums and clubs, and free sides or desserts at participating restaurants with purchases of an entrée. These are sold at most ticket machines and the tourist office in the main train station, where you can pick up a pamphlet for a complete list of benefits. Before using, validate once at a blue ticket machine or orange validator on one of the platforms.

Taxis are clean and safe but expensive (initial fee 6-8CHF, then 3.8-5CHF/km or 80CHF/hour). Taxis around the train station are especially exorbitant. Uber is cheaper.

Bicycle rentals are free, but require ID and a 20CHF deposit. Stations are located just outside train station, near tracks 3 (M-F 8am-9:30pm) and 18 (M-F 9am-7:30pm). More information available at www.zuerirollt.ch.

## PRACTICAL INFORMATION

**Tourist Offices:** Zürich Tourist Information, located in the main train station. Book city tours, purchase ZurichCARD and tickets for public transport or museums, make hotel reservations, pick up free pamphlets and guides, buy souvenirs.
• Hauptbahnhof Zürich (Main Train Station; 044 215 40 00; summer (May 1-October 31) M-Sa 8am-8:30pm, Su 8:30am-6:30pm; winter (Nov 1-Apr 31) M-Sa 8:30am-7pm, Su 9am-6pm).

**Banks/ATMs/Currency Exchange:** ATMs available at banks (UBS is ubiquitous). Banking hours M-F 8:30am-4:30pm; closed on major holidays. You can exchange money at any Swiss bank, the airport, the main railway station, and major hostels. Exchange houses are less common and usually do not have great rates, especially the ones in the airport. Usually the best option is to withdraw money from an ATM.

**Post Offices:** Central post office is Sihlpost (Kasernestrasse 97 (Sihlpost tram stop); 084 888 88 88; M-F 6:30am-10:30pm, Sa 6:30am-8pm, Su 10am-10:30pm).

**Internet:** The first hour of Wi-Fi is free in the train station (and all Swiss train stations), but you'll need to register the first time with a phone number. The Zürich airport offers two hours of free Wi-F; however, you must register using your phone number. At the tourist office, you can rent a Wi-Fi router, which provides unlimited 4G/LTE Internet (40CHF for three days, 65CHF for seven days, 83CHF for ten days, 130CHF for 15 days).

**Water:** Tap water is potable and fountains around town are drinkable. To save money, avoid purchasing bottled water at restaurants.

**Public Toilets:** There are free public toilets throughout the city, but you must pay 1CHF at major tram stops (Apr-Oct 6:30am –9:45pm, Nov-Mar 6:30am-8:45pm).

**BGLTQ+ Resources:** BGLTQ+ Helpline of Switzerland (Located in Bern;

Monbijoustrasse 73; 080 013 31 33; hello@lgbt-helpline.ch; www.lgbt-helpline.ch/en/).

## EMERGENCY INFORMATION

**Emergency Numbers:** General (112); police (117); fire department (118); ambulance (144); Swiss Helicopter Rescue Service (1414)

**Police:** The Cantonal Police Zürich takes responsibility for the canton of Zürich (Kasernenstrasse 29; 044 247 22 11). The Zürich City Police (Bahnhofquai 3; 044 411 71 17). In an emergency always call 117.

**US Embassy:** Consular Agency in Zürich (Dufourstrasse 101 third f Floor; M-F 10am-1pm (by appointment only), closed on US and Swiss/Local holidays; 043 499 29 60).

**Rape Crisis Center:** Zürich Frauzentrale (women's center) (Schanzengraben 29; 044 206 30 20).

**Hospitals:** For most non-emergency problems, it is recommended that you set up an appointment at a Permanence with a doctor. There is one at Zürich main station, open all year from 7am-10pm (Bahnhofplatz 15; 044 215 44 44; www.permanence.ch).
• Universitätsspital (Rämistrasse 100; 044 255 11 11; open daily 24hr).
• Stadtspital Triemli (Birmensdorfer-strasse 497, 044 466 11 11; open daily 24hr).
• Stadtspital Waid (Tièchestrasse 99, 044 366 20, 55; open daily 24hr).

**Pharmacies:** On Sundays, the only shops permitted to open are located in railway stops and petrol stations. Some groceries with pharmacies inside are open until 11pm. The large Coop supermarket next to the main railway station is open M-Sa 7am-10pm.
• Bahnhof Apotheke im Hauptbahn-hof (044 225 42 42).
• Bellevue Apotheke (044 266 62 22)
• Apotheke-Drogerie Bahnhof Enge (044 201 21 41).

# ACCOMMODATIONS

### ▓YOUTH HOSTEL ZÜRICH ($$)
Mutschellenstrasse 114; 433997800; www.youthhostel.ch/zurich; reception open 24hr, door locks at 11pm
Tired of the rapid pace of the city? Take a 15-minute tram ride to the

more relaxed suburbs where you'll find this friendly, well-equipped hostel. The clientele ranges from young children to older couples; the diversity makes for some fun and engaging conversations. The lobby, outfitted with air hockey and ping pong tables, seems like an attempt of a "teen section" for a cruise, but who are we kidding, we all love those sections. With linens included, lockers provided, and en-suite sinks, Youth Hostel Zürich is a good bargain. If you are looking to be in the main hustle of the city and truly be immersed in the backpacking culture, then this might not be the place for you.

*i* Dorms starting at 50CHF; reservation recommended; BGLTQ+ friendly; wheelchair accessible; Wi-Fi; linens included; laundry facilities

### CITY BACKPACKER – HOTEL BIBER ($)
Niederdorfstrasse 5; 442519015; www. city-backpacker.ch; reception open 8am-noon and 3pm-10pm

Follow the cartoon beaver—hidden in an alley of the **Old Town**—up four flights of stairs to the reception of this centrally-located and popular hostel. As its name suggests, City Backpacker is frequented mostly by backpackers and students who are attracted by the low prices in comparison to Zürich's exorbitant ones. The building is old and quite cramped, but the rooms are clean—some with kitchens—and there is a great rooftop upstairs where most travelers hang around. The hostel has a lot of information for budget travelers and the staff is eager to dish out recommendations.

*i* Dorms 37CHF, single 77CHF, double 118CHF, triple 159CHF; reservation recommended; max seven nights; BGLTQ+ friendly; no wheelchair accessibility; Wi-Fi; linens 3CHF; laundry facilities 10 CHF

### HOSTEL OTTER OLD TOWN ($$)
Oberdorfstrasse 7; 442512207; www. oldtownzurich.com/; reception open 7:30am-10pm

Tucked in among boutiques and restaurants in the heart of the **Old Town,** Hostel Otter Old Town is frequented by a wide variety of people due to its prime location and excellent prices. Located above the brightly colored **Wuste Bar,** the hostel has

several different stories with rooms ranging from dorms to themed private suites. A five-minute walk from main attractions **Grossmünster** and **Fraumünster,** Hostel Otter Old Town is also equipped with common rooms that are conducive to mingling.

*i* Dorms from 40CHF-49CHF, double 140CHF; reservation recommended; max stay 7 nights; BGLTQ+ friendly; wheelchair accessible; linens included; laundry facilities 10 CHF; dorms include budget breakfast, private rooms include continental breakfast (7CHF for dorms to upgrade)

## SIGHTS
### CULTURE
........................................

### LOWENBRAUKUNST
Oberdorfstrasse 2; 443077900; www. lowenbraukunst.ch; museums open T, W, F 11am-6pm, Th 11am-8pm

If you enjoy wandering through large empty spaces, staring at piercingly-white walls, and finding meaning in absurd combinations of mundane objects, consider Lowenbraukunst an essential stop during your tour of Zürich. A brewery-turned-arts-complex, it's home to two of the most important contemporary art museums in Switzerland, **Migros** and **Kunsthalle Zürich,** and contains many small galleries for local artists. Lowenbraukunst is the kind of place where it's difficult to differentiate between what is and what isn't art—we learned the hard way and recommend refraining from sitting on anything, no matter how heavy your pack may feel. Galleries are dispersed throughout the complex and open to the public; some are "working galleries," meaning you can watch the artists in live-time as they refine their masterpieces. Both museums display the work of a wide variety of artists and construct exhibitions around important universal issues and themes.

*i* Free entry to complex, single museum 12CHF, reduced 8CHF, both museums 20CHF, reduced 12CHF, free on Th 5pm-8pm; tours given twice a month, check online for details; last entry 15 min. before closing; wheelchair accessible

## SCHIFFBAU

Schiffbaustrasse 6; 442655858; www.schauspielhaus.ch/de; open M-F 11am-7pm, Sa 2pm-7pm

Reuse, reduce, recycle. Switzerland's eco-friendly approach to reusing old buildings has led to the creation of trendy new cultural centers. One such center, Schiffbau, was transformed from a derelict shipbuilding edifice to an expansive complex that houses a three-theater stage, restaurant LaSalle, and Moods Jazz Club. Tickets for the theater start at 10CHF, and shows, which range from classics to regionally specific originals, are performed almost exclusively in German. The complex is also used for different events throughout the year. Right behind the former shipbuilding yard is **turbinenplatz**, a large concrete garden where you can sit on a wooden bench and watch it light up at night.

*i* Free entrance to complex, theatre tickets half-priced on M; wheelchair accessible

## LANDMARKS
..................................................

### OLD TOWN
Open daily 24hr

Follow the beautiful church steeples through narrow cobblestone roads and you'll always find yourself in the heart of Zürich, the Old Town. Start off on **Lindenhof Hill,** a former Roman fort which provides an amazing view of the city center and the **River Limmat** passing through it. A walk around the winding streets is a treat for a history buff, as it offers views of the medieval churches Grossmünster, Fraumünster, and St. Peter, as well as Lenin's apartment during his exile. For those more interested in the present, Old Town provides some of the best shopping along **Bahnhofstrasse** (best for looking, unless you are into small, unknown brands like Gucci or

Channel) and a vibrant nightlife, with a bit less of the flare that Langstrasse and Zürich West possess.

*i* Free; free city tour every day at 11am, meets next to UBS at Paradeplatz

### FRAUMÜNSTER

Münsterhof 2; 442212063; www.fraumuenster.ch; open daily Jan 1-Feb 29 10am-5pm, Mar 1-Oct 31 10am-6pm, Nov 1-Dec 31 6am-4pm

With a long, poignant, turquoise church tower and a Romanesque golden clock, the Fraumünster is the belle of the **Old Town.** Fraumünster is often lumped in with the other Reformed Evangelical Churches of the Canton of Zürich, but stands out due to its colorful stained glass and massive organ. A mesmerizing anachronist piece, the glass window of Chagalls at the nave of the church steals the show, even against the massive gothic architectural details surrounding it.

*i* Admission 5CHF (includes audio guide or brochure + Crypt Museum), with reservations 3CHF, free for children (up to 16 years) and students with ID; last entry 45min. before closing; wheelchair accessible

## GROSSMÜNSTER

Grossmünsterplatz; 442513860; www.
grossmuenster.ch; open daily summer
10am-6pm, winter 10am-5pm; Karls-
turm open summer M-Sa 10am-5pm, Su
12:30am-5:30pm, winter M-Sa 10am-
4:30pm, Su 12:30am-4:30pm

Two stunning church towers with
views overlooking a city and the
surrounding mountain range—*yawn*.
Typical for a European city. However,
Grossmünster is no typical church.
It is the birthplace of Switzerland's
Protestant Reformation, when in
the sixteenth century **Huldrych
Zwingli** served as the parishioner.
Grossmünster's history is deeply
intertwined with local folklore, as
Grossmünsterplatz is the plot upon
which Felix and Regula, the patron
saints of Zürich, decided to carry their
severed heads and die. *Walking Dead*
much? The church is an emblem of
the city, and, if you're up to the task,
we recommend taking the 187 narrow
stairs up to the top of one of the towers
(**Karlstrum**) for a sweeping panorama
of Zürich.

*i* Free entrance to church, Karlstrum
adult 4CHF, 2CHF student, 3CHF per person
in group of 10; tours 180CHF; tours without guide run on M, W-F with reservation

## MUSEUMS
..................................................

### ▧LANDESMUSEUM ZÜRICH (SWISS NATIONAL MUSEUM)

Museumstrasse 2; 442186511; www.na-
tionalmuseum.ch; open Tu-Su 10am-5pm,
Th 10am-7pm

History buff? Want to learn about
the rise and fall of a combination of
European cantons? Look no further,
young Herodotus, and head over to
the Swiss National Museum, located
adjacent to the main train station in a
chateau of a building. For a reasonable
price, it provides a very extensive
and encompassing display of Swiss
history from the time of the settlers
to the present. We loved the exhibits
describing the influx of Greco-Roman
culture and Germanic tribes. With
entertaining exhibitions such as
miniature replicas of major battles and

rotating displays, history has never
been so tantalizing.

*i* Admission 10CHF, 8CHF student, free
child (up to 16) free; last entry 15min.
before closing; guided tours available;
wheelchair accessible

### FIFA WORLD MUSEUM

Seestrasse 27; 433882500; www.fifam-
useum.com; open Tu-Sa 10am-7pm, Su
9am-6pm

Recent corruption scandals have
left the name "FIFA" branded with
labels such as fraudulent, corporate,
and strictly money-driven. However,
the sport it represents—soccer—is
still associated with beauty, grace,
athleticism, and passionate fandoms.
The FIFA World Museum, although a
little pricey, is the Mecca of any avid
soccer fan and, even if you don't know
the difference between the EPL or La
Liga it's still entertaining for those who
prefer slam dunks, home runs, and
touchdowns. The lower level contains
soccer memorabilia and the complete
history of the World Cups, while the
upper level is decked-out with all
kinds of interactive games, foosball,
and **Fifa** video games—essentially the
dread of weary parents who have to
literally drag their kids out of there as
the museum closes. Don't go for the
money-driven conglomerate, go for the
sport it represents.

*i* Admission 24CHF, free children (0-6)
free, 14CHF children (7-15) 14CHF, 18 CHF
students; last entry 30min. before closing;
wheelchair accessible; free audio guide by
downloading app

### KUNSTHAUS

Heimplatz1; 442538497; www.kunsthaus.
ch; open Tu 10am-6pm, W-Th 10am-8pm,
F-Su 10am-6pm, closed major holidays

From the outside, Kunsthaus is
nothing special. It's big, rectangular,
and to be honest, pretty bland. Don't
let its unassuming exterior fool you
though. Housed within its walls are
some of the world's most prized pieces
of two-dimensional art—works by
**Monet, Picasso, Chagall, Pollock,**
and the like. The museum is organized
in ascending order; as you rise from
floor to floor, you travel through a
timeline spanning from the Medieval
Ages to contemporary art. Temporary
exhibitions are usually located near the

entrance along with free audio guides, for those of us who like to have the interpretation done for us.

*i* Admission 11CHF,16 and under free; public guided tours Sa 3pm, Su 11am, and W 6pm (in German), groups must register in advance; last entry 15min. before closing; wheelchair accessible

## OUTDOORS

### UETLIBURG MOUNTAIN

8143 Uetliberg; 444576666; www.uetliberg.ch; open daily 24 hr (restaurant open M-Sa 9am-11pm, Su 9am-6pm)

The Uetilberg is a mountain in the Swiss plateau, part of the **Albis chain,** that offers stunning views of the entire city of Zürich and a prime opportunity to fulfill your yodeling dreams. We recommend skipping the train and hiking to **Uto Kulm** (the summit); the trails are well-marked, but isolated enough for you to reenact a Ricola commercial without being heard. At the top, you'll find a viewing tower (2CHF) and a restaurant that overlooks the mountain range. Although its prices are on the higher end of the spectrum, consider stopping by to grab a drink. Considering all the yodeling you've been doing, you're probably parched.

*i* Free, train 50CHF, children under 16 25CHF; trains run every 30min. and take approximately 20min.

## FOOD

### ◪ÄSS BAR ($)

Stüssihofstatt 6; 435480544; aess-bar.ch; open M-Sa 9am-6:30pm

Go ahead, laugh a little. No, Äss Bar is not bacon-themed, nor are the bartenders voluptuous. The word "äss" translates to "eatable," and ties into the idea of sustainability. Not what you expected? Neither did we. Rather than discard excess pastries, this small bakery sells them at a discounted price (half-off!). Grab a hazelnut croissant (1.50CHF) and a sandwich (3CHF) to-go and head towards the river, where you'll be greeted with a shockingly-impressive view of **Uetilberg.**

*i* Pastries 1.50-3 CHF; cash only; vegetarian options available; no wheelchair accessibility

### ◪WURST AND MORITZ ($$)

Hardstrasse 318; 435404147; www.wurstundmoritz-zuerich.ch; open M-W 11am-10pm, Th-Sa 11am-11:45pm, Su 11am-10pm

While in the German-speaking region of Switzerland, you might find yourself wondering, "To wurst or not to wurst?" The answer, might we tell you, is *always* "to wurst," and there's no better place to do so in Zürich than Wurst and Moritz. Frequented mostly by locals and students, W&M's combo meals (16CHF) include your choice of sausage, toppings, dressing, a pile of lightly-salted fries, and a frothy pint of beer. Take a seat inside at one of the high tables or outside on the expansive street-side patio and relish in the greasy goodness in front of you. You deserve it.

*i* Entrées 12-16 CHF; vegetarian and vegan options available; limited wheelchair accessibility

### ◪YUME RAMEN ($$$)

Reitergasse 6; 442717273; www.yume-ramen.ch; open M-F 11:30am-1:30pm, 6pm-9:30pm, Sa noon-9:30pm

If you're a college student, the word "ramen" might send shivers down your spine reminding you of late nights, unfinished assignments, and cups of salty noodles. Yume Ramen, a lively Japanese restaurant decorated with oversized characters, wooden tables, and red lights, will erase your preconceptions and replace them with positive memories. Ramen dishes (22CHF) are made to order and are, in our humble opinion, a must-try. They're big enough to share and delicious enough to not want to, but if you still don't feel satisfied (highly doubtful), order an additional helping of noodles, a bento box, or a *donburi* bowl, warm rice topped with your choice of chicken, beef, or salmon.

*i* Ramen 20-22CHF, sake and whiskey 10CHF; vegetarian options available; no wheelchair accessibility

### RACLETTE FACTORY ($$)

Rindermarkt 1; 2610410; www.raclette-fac-tory.ch; open Su-Th 11am-10pm, F-Sa 11am-11pm

As you've already probably discovered, Swiss cuisine, like the rest of the country, is expensive. Enter the hero, Raclette Factory—a restaurant known for its supremely Swiss décor, fresh bread, melted cheese, and expansive wine collection, and your window into the Swiss culinary experience. We recommend skipping over the half-platter (80g) and going straight to the full-platter (160g); you'll receive much more bang for your buck.

*i* *Platters 12-16CHF; vegetarian options available; no wheelchair accessibility*

# NIGHTLIFE

### ⬛BQM

Leonhardstrasse 34; 446327503; www.bqm-bar.ch; open term time M-Th 11:45am-11pm, open during final exams M-F 11:45am-10pm

Being back on a college campus will inevitably bring back a flood of emotions, including a profound nostalgia for cheap alcohol (just us? Okay then). BQM, located under the same roof as the **University of Zürich's** cafeteria, is one of your best bets for meeting similarly-aged individuals and securing a liter and a half of beer for less than 20CHF. Inside you'll find wooden tables, lounging couches, and a small platform where DJs and live bands perform weekly. Outside you'll find a beautiful panorama of **Old Town,** with **Fraumunster, St. Peter's,** and **Grossmunster** in direct view. Because campus policy requires bars to shut down by 11pm during term time, BQM is best as a first stop.

*i* *No cover, shots 5-7CHF, 1.5L beer 18CHF*

### ⬛CABARET VOLTAIRE

Spiegelgasse 1; 432685720; www.cab-aretvoltaire.ch; open Tu-Th 6pm-12am, F 6pm-2am, Sa 4pm-2am, Su 4pm-12am

*"Switzerland is a birdcage, surrounded by roaring lions." – Hugo Ball*

Disgusted by WWI, Ball donned his construction-paper dunce cap and cape, chanted "blago bung blago bung," and the bizzare anti-artform known as **Dada** was born in this deliciously quirky nightclub. The ground floor houses a bookstore and art gallery, as well as a restroom full of performers and their eccentric props. On the upper level, share a beer (4-7CHF) with old poet types staring blankly into the ether and ask yourself, as does the black-and-white wall print, "to be da-da or not DaDa?" On certain nights, unintelligible, but fascinating live performances ensue in the back room, which is ever-permeated by the synthetic smell of the in-house fog machine.

*i* *Beer 6-7CHF, drinks 13CHF; minimum card charge; BGLTQ+ friendly*

### ZÜRI BAR ($)

Niederdorfstrasse 24; 442618874; open M-Th 4pm-12am, F 4pm-1am, Sa 12pm-1am

For a 70-year-old, Züri keeps things tight. It's famed as one of the oldest bars in Zurich's **Old Town,** and attracts its clientele accordingly. Find yourself conversing with a local who's been around longer than the bar itself or enjoying a scotch solo in a small, cushy booth. The friendly staff and reasonably-priced alcohol have caused the pool of regulars as well as the hoard of tourists that frequents the establishment, to grow steadily over the years.

*i* *Drinks 14.50CHF, beer 5-8CHF*

### NELSON'S PUB

Beatengasse 11; 442126016; www.nelsonpubzurich.ch; open M-Th 11:30am-2am, F 11:30am-4:30am, Sa 2pm-4:30am

Simply put, Nelson's Pub is where 30-year-old Zürchers go to get sloshed. This nautical-themed bar is the perfect place to spend the wee hours of the morning broadcasting your sorrows; the bartenders, like the diverse clientele, are eager to help talk things through, and. by the time you've resolved your issues, Nelson's will have filled up enough for you to not look like a total whacko when you start passionately lip syncing Taylor Swift's "We Are Never Ever Getting Back Together" in the middle of the dance floor.

*i* *Beer 6-8CHF, hard liquor 15CHF*

# SWITZERLAND ESSENTIALS

## CALLING

Switzerland's country code is +41.

## ELECTRICITY

The standard voltage in Switzerland is 220V and the power sockets used are of type J, particular to only Switzerland, Liechtenstein, and Rwanda. Type C plugs that are used throughout most of Europe fit into the type J socket, but double check to make sure the adapter you are taking works.

## MONEY

**Tipping:** Do not feel obligated to tip in Switzerland, as a federal law replaced tips with an all-inclusive bill back in the '70s. If you are very happy with your service, you can round your bill up to the nearest five or ten francs. However, waiters do not expect this tip, so don't feel bad if you're spending on backpackers' budget and cannot afford to tip at every single establishment.

## CITY TRAVEL

Intra-city travel operates on an honor system, where you are expected to have the proper ticket with you when riding public transportation. From time to time authorities will hop aboard to check tickets. If you are caught without a valid ticket, you will incur a hefty fine (90CHF).

## ALCOHOL

In Switzerland, the legal drinking age for beer and wine is 16 years old and 18 years old for all other drinks. Public drinking is legal for everybody of age, except in certain public spaces, which are determined by cantons.

## WATER

In Switzerland, almost all tap water is potable. If you are not 100% sure, look for signs in German that read "Trinkwasser "or "eau potable" in French.

# INDEX

# ACKNOWLEDGMENTS

First and foremost, we'd like to thank our team of Researcher-Writers whose voices fill the 672 pages of this book: Adrian for your constant support and motivating emails; Alejandro for your undying love of Irish pubs and kebabs; Antonia for your bravery while showering in rural Hungary; Emily for your cheeky humor and Parisian flair; Emma for your enthusiastic attitude and wine expertise; Eric for your stories about fermented shark and scuba diving; Gavin for your unashamed sporting of a wetsuit and time management skills; Joseph for your gelato addiction and hatred of Florence tourists; Julia for your extended metaphors and pleasant FaceTime calls; Mia for bringing us along on your adventure of *Mia Learns What Good Alcohol Tastes Like*; and Nicholas for keeping the office entertained through your notes from clubbing in Berlin. Collectively, you wrote thousands of pages of copy and you should be proud of each and every one of them. We are so grateful for your dedication and excited to share your experiences with our readers.

Thank you to Emily and Ethan at Placepass for playing a big role in our expansion this summer and for giving our Researcher-Writers priceless opportunities through your database of tours. Without you, we wouldn't have been able to implement the changes apparent in this book.

Thank you to our extremely helpful *Let's Go* alumni. To Nathaniel and Michael, for introducing Kristine to the impossible task of the Bookplan. To Sara and Michael, for working with Austin tirelessly to optimize our typesetting process. To all three of you, for hosting much-needed game nights over the summer, serving as a sounding board for our book production problems, and for imparting your *Let's Go* expertise onto us. You've taught us so much and we hope to pass that knowledge on to the next Bookteam.

We'd like to thank our families who talked to us constantly and checked in time and time again when things in the office looked bleak. Thank you for providing us with love, guidance, and support throughout this process. And, of course, we can't forget to thank our pseudo-family: our blockmates who came to the office throughout the summer bearing gifts of food and good company. Thank you to Mariah, Akshita, Karen, and Pablo for becoming a part of our extended *Let's Go* family.

Thank you to Dev for creating Sandbox. The program has truly made a difference in how we worked and flowed content into the book this year and you have made our lives easier with your tireless effort. Thank you for every meeting, technical change, and reboot—each one of them made a difference.

Thank you to the entire team of managers at HSA for your guidance and support. To Angelina and Ali, for supporting and supplying us with food. To Jim, for your extensive knowledge of *Let's Go* and your sage advice. To Max and Casey, for editing the Researcher Writer's photos. To Alejandra and Anthony, for buying us Insomnia cookies. And, finally, to all the managers who were constantly supportive throughout this process.

**PUBLISHING DIRECTOR,** Kathleen Cronin
**EDITOR IN CHIEF,** Kristine Guillaume
**CREATIVE DIRECTOR AND ASSOCIATE EDITOR,** Austin Eder
**MARKETING MANAGER,** Nicholas Nava

**PRESIDENT, HARVARD STUDENT AGENCIES,** Angelina Massa
**GENERAL MANAGER, HARVARD STUDENT AGENCIES,** Jim McKellar

# ABOUT US

## THE STUDENT TRAVEL GUIDE

*Let's Go* publishes travel guides written by its team of Researcher-Writers, who are all students at Harvard College. Armed with pens, notebooks, and laptops (hopefully, with chargers), our student researchers travel across Europe on pre-planned itineraries, hopping from city to city to seek out invaluable travel experiences for our readers. Because we are a completely student-run company, we have a unique perspective on how students travel, where they want to go, and what they're looking for when they get there. Whether you want to venture into the crater of Mount Etna, kayak in Lagos, or museum-hop in London, our guides have got you covered. We write for readers on a budget who know that there's more to travel than tour buses.

## FIFTY-EIGHT YEARS OF WISDOM

*Let's Go* has been on the road for 58 years and counting. We started in 1960 with a small, 20-page pamphlet that included travel tips and food, accommodation, and activity recommendations for Europe's major cities. Over the last five decades, however, our Researcher-Writers have written guides covering almost every corner of the planet. Europe? Check. Australia? You betcha. India? Been there, done that. And despite the growth, our witty, candid guides are still researched and written entirely by Harvard students on shoestring budgets who know how to deal with everything from debit card fraud to stolen phones to bad cuttlefish. This year, *Let's Go* has undergone an exciting design revamp, bringing you our first full-color guide: *Let's Go Europe 2018.* The guide also features a new and improved content architecture that allows readers to easily pinpoint reviews of hostels, sights, restaurants, and food in any given city. And, of course, like all other *Let's Go* guides, the one in your hand still features the same witty and irreverent voice that has been carried by *Let's Go* teams for decades.

## THE *LET'S GO* COMMUNITY

More than just a travel guide company, *Let's Go* is a community that reaches from our headquarters in Cambridge, MA all across the globe. Our small staff of dedicated student editors, designers, writers, and tech nerds is united by a shared passion for travel and desire to help other travelers get the most out of their experiences. We love it when our readers become part of the *Let's Go* community as well—when you travel, drop us a postcard (67 Mt. Auburn St., Cambridge, MA 02138, USA), send us an email (webmaster@letsgo.com), or sign up on our website (www.letsgo.com) to tell us about your adventures and discoveries.

**GET INVOLVED!** If you want to share your discoveries, suggestions, or corrections, please drop us a line. We appreciate every piece of correspondence, whether a postcard, a 10-page email, or a coconut. Visit *Let's Go* at **www.letsgo.com** or send an email to **webmaster@letsgo.com**, subject: Let's Go Europe 2018."

Address mail to:

**Let's Go**
**67 Mount Auburn St.**
**Cambridge, MA 02138, USA**

In addition to the invaluable travel advice our readers share with us, many are kind enough to offer their services as researchers or editors. Unfortunately, our charter enables us to employ only currently enrolled Harvard students.

Maps © Let's Go and **Avalon Travel**

Distributed by **Publishers Group West.**
Printed in Canada by **Friesens Corp.**

ISBN-13: 978-1-61237-052-1
Fifty-eighth edition
10 9 8 7 6 5 4 3 2 1

*Let's Go Europe* is written by Let's Go Publications, 67 Mt. Auburn St., Cambridge, MA 02138, USA.

# QUICK REFERENCE

## EMERGENCY PHONE NUMBERS (POLICE)

| Country | Number | Country | Number |
|---|---|---|---|
| Austria | 133 | Ireland | 999 |
| Belgium | 101 | Italy | 113 |
| Croatia | 192 | The Netherlands | 911 |
| Czech Republic | 158 | Norway | 112 |
| Denmark | 114 | Poland | 997 |
| France | 17 | Portugal | 112 |
| Germany | 110 | Slovenia | 133 |
| Great Britain | 999 | Spain | 092 |
| Greece | 100 | Sweden | 112 |
| Hungary | 107 | General Emergency (Europe) | 112 |

## USEFUL PHRASES

| ENGLISH | FRENCH | GERMAN | ITALIAN | SPANISH |
|---|---|---|---|---|
| Hello/Hi | Bonjour/Salut | Hallo/Tag | Ciao | Hola |
| Goodbye/Bye | Au revoir | Auf Wiedersehen/ Tschüss | Arrivederci/Ciao | Adiós/Chau |
| Yes | Oui | Ja | Sì | Sí |
| No | Non | Nein | No | No |
| Excuse me! | Pardon! | Entschuldigen Sie! | Scusa! | ¡Perdón! |
| Thank you | Merci | Danke | Grazie | Gracias |
| Go away! | Va t'en! | Geh weg! | Vattene via! | ¡Vete! |
| Help! | Au secours! | Hilfe! | Aiuto! | ¡Ayuda! |
| Call the police! | Appelez la police! | Ruf die Polizei! | Chiamare la polizia! | ¡Llame a la policía! |
| Get a doctor! | Cherchez un médecin! | Hol einen Arzt! | Chiamare un medico! | ¡Llame a un médico! |
| I don't understand | Je ne comprends pas | Ich verstehe nicht | Non capisco | No comprendo |
| Do you speak English? | Parlez-vous anglais? | Sprechen Sie Englisch? | Lei parla inglese? | ¿Habla inglés? |
| Where is...? | Où est...? | Wo ist...? | Dov' è...? | ¿Dónde está...? |

## TEMPERATURE CONVERSIONS

| °CELSIUS | -5 | 0 | 5 | 10 | 15 | 20 | 25 | 30 | 35 | 40 |
|---|---|---|---|---|---|---|---|---|---|---|
| °FAHRENHEIT | 23 | 32 | 41 | 50 | 59 | 68 | 77 | 86 | 95 | 104 |

## MEASUREMENT CONVERSIONS

| | |
|---|---|
| 1 inch (in.) = 25.4mm | 1 millimeter (mm) = 0.039 in. |
| 1 foot (ft.) = 0.305m | 1 meter (m) = 3.28 ft. |
| 1 mile (mi.) = 1.609km | 1 kilometer (km) = 0.621 mi. |
| 1 pound (lb.) = 0.454kg | 1 kilogram (kg) = 2.205 lb. |
| 1 gallon (gal.) = 3.785L | 1 liter (L) = 0.264 gal. |

FEB 1 4 2018